"I have long thought that what we need is to be able to place the Gospels much more precisely within the wide spectrum of ancient biographies. Keener has mastered the literature, primary and secondary—as one would expect."

— RICHARD BAUCKHAM, Ridley Hall, Cambridge

"This is a welcome guide to some of the best recent scholarship on the biographical purpose and composition of the Gospels, taking due account of the impact of memory in their composition. Prof. Keener sensibly concludes that living memory played a meaningful and consolidating role in the formation of these rhetorically constructed but essentially historical narratives about Jesus. A thorough and reliable introduction to this vital yet complex subject!"

— MARKUS BOCKMUEHL, University of Oxford

"Craig Keener's sophisticated knowledge of the classical world is in evidence in his impressive *Christobiography*. He not only knows the sources; he asks of them the proper questions, such as what first-century readers expected of biographies. Keener rightly focuses on the biographies of the early Roman Empire. He also rightly takes into account the important fact that the New Testament Gospels were composed within living memory of their subject and that this tradition arose from the disciples of Jesus, who by definition were committed to learning their master's teaching and recalling his deeds. Keener's book makes a much-needed contribution to a very important topic."

— CRAIG A. EVANS, Houston Baptist University

"Another vintage book by Craig Keener! Comprehensive information showing the relation of New Testament Gospels to early Roman Empire biography, embedded in argumentation for historical reliability of most information in the New Testament Gospels."

— VERNON K. ROBBINS, Emory University

"This work displays extensive knowledge of the major classical texts from around the New Testament period. Keener uses these judiciously and critically, as an ancient historian would do for any primary source, showing awareness of genre and bias and using modern studies of memory and its impact on historiography. Thus he provides an integrated and convincing historical picture."

— ALANNA NOBBS, Macquarie University

"Keener's ability to read both widely and deeply through an expansive swath of primary literature of the Greco-Roman world, to detect telling evidence and articulate those insights that transform conventional wisdom and reconfigure the terms of the debate, is, quite frankly, without parallel. Through new appropriations of 'memory studies,' biographical history in the early empire, and an illuminating taxonomy of both Greek and Jewish biography, Keener makes an exceptional case that the narration of the story of Jesus in the four Gospels is a thoroughly mixed hybrid of biographical and historiographical concerns such that a new subset of literature emerges, the *Christobiography*. Keener's opus now forms a new watershed in Gospels genre studies."

— DAVID P. MOESSNER, Texas Christian University

"Craig Keener argues convincingly that ancient readers of Greek and Latin biographies from the period of the early Roman Empire (e.g., Cornelius Nepos, Plutarch, Suetonius, and Tacitus) had the same expectation as those who read the Gospels, expecting them to preserve the gist of what their subjects had actually said and done. Along the way, Keener provides an up-to-date summary of modern memory studies. In the early Christian community, the eyewitnesses who provided data for inclusion in the Gospels were also disciples who were highly motivated to preserve the legacy of Jesus. Basically, this is a book that sheds light on the epistemology of historical Jesus research. Anyone seriously interested in the historical Jesus will find this book both rich and rewarding."

— DAVID AUNE, University of Notre Dame

"*Christobiography* is addressed to both scholars and students interested in Gospels and historical Jesus research and is, to say the least, a very impressive study. The Synoptic Gospels compare well with other ancient biographies as to the reliability of the information they provide. They told the same stories, but often without concern for details extraneous to their point. Not least of interest is the striking summary of the overlap between John and the Synoptics, showing that John is still a historical biography. There is a very helpful chapter on memory and the reliability of oral tradition in the context of Jesus's ministry and his followers, given that it was understood as teaching. The strong and justified conclusion is that Jesus's disciples would have learned and transmitted his teaching no less carefully than most other disciples the wisdom of their teachers. In short, the Gospels compare well with the other biographies of the time as to their historicity, and there is a strong historical probability that the Gospel memoirs have preserved the content and character of Jesus's ministry and teaching. I cannot commend this careful and thorough study too highly."

— JAMES D. G. DUNN, Durham University

Christobiography

Memory, History,
and the Reliability of the Gospels

Craig S. Keener

WILLIAM B. EERDMANS PUBLISHING COMPANY
GRAND RAPIDS, MICHIGAN

Wm. B. Eerdmans Publishing Co.
4035 Park East Court SE, Grand Rapids, Michigan 49546
www.eerdmans.com

25 24 23 22 21 20 19   1 2 3 4 5 6 7

ISBN 978-0-8028-7675-1

Library of Congress Cataloging-in-Publication Data

A catalog record for this book is available from the Library of Congress.

To Richard Burridge, Charles Talbert,
Vernon Robbins, David Aune: pioneers

Contents

Acknowledgments

I am grateful to my ever-persistent and fast-acting acquisitions editor at Eerdmans, my friend Michael Thomson. When, because of unforeseen logistical circumstances (not matters of content), this book (finished originally for a different publisher's deadline of December 1, 2017) needed a new publisher, Michael embraced it immediately. (The same weekend, I had suggested it to an editor at yet another publisher in correspondence; although that editor replied graciously and punctually, by then Michael had already fully convinced me to do it with Eerdmans.) I am grateful also to development editor Trevor Thompson, copyeditor Craig Noll (who was stuck with the tedious task of anglicizing and spelling out my ancient references), and others at Eerdmans who have worked on this book.

I am also grateful to my various conversation partners (in person) at various stages in this book's development. Michael Licona and I were discussing these matters together before either of us embarked on our respective books on this subject. Other valuable conversation partners have included Richard Burridge, Helen Bond, Vernon Robbins, Neil Elliott, and my esteemed colleagues and PhD students at Asbury Theological Seminary; as well as members of the Memory, Narrative, and Christology in the Synoptic Gospels Seminar of the Society for New Testament Studies (with additional conversations there, including with Roland Deines, Michal Beth Dinkler, Sandra Hubenthal, David Moessner, Armand Puig i Tàrrech, Jens Schröter, and Arie Zwiep). Of course my conversation partners hold a range of views, and I remain responsible for views or arguments in this book with which any readers may wish to take issue.

Abbreviations

AARTRSS	American Academy of Religion Teaching Religious Studies Series
AB	Anchor Bible
ABD	*Anchor Bible Dictionary*
ABIG	Arbeiten zur Bibel und ihrer Geschichte
ABR	*Australian Biblical Review*
ABRL	Anchor Bible Reference Library
AbrN	*Abr-Nahrain*
ACNT	Augsburg Commentary on the New Testament
AJP	*American Journal of Philology*
AJPS	*Asian Journal of Pentecostal Studies*
AJPSS	Asian Journal of Pentecostal Studies Series
AJSR	*Association for Jewish Studies Review*
AJT	*Asia Journal of Theology*
ALGHJ	Arbeiten zur Literatur und Geschichte des Hellenistischen Judentums
AmJT	*American Journal of Theology*
ANRW	*Aufstieg und Niedergang der Römischen Welt*
ANTC	Abingdon New Testament Commentaries
AnthCons	*Anthropology of Consciousness*
AnthHum	*Anthropology and Humanism*
Anton	*Antonianum*
ARAnth	*Annual Review of Anthropology*
AsJT	*Asia Journal of Theology*
ASNU	Acta Seminarii Neotestamentici Upsaliensis
ASOR	American Schools of Oriental Research
AUSS	*Andrews University Seminary Studies*
BA	*Biblical Archaeologist*
BAGB	*Bulletin de l'Association Guillaume Budé*

BangTF	*Bangalore Theological Forum*
BAR	*Biblical Archaeology Review*
BASOR	*Bulletin of the American Schools of Oriental Research*
BBR	*Bulletin of Biblical Research*
BCAW	Blackwell Companions to the Ancient World
BDF	Blass, F., A. Debrunner, and R. A. Funk. *A Greek Grammar of the New Testament and Other Early Christian Literature.* Chicago: University of Chicago Press, 1961.
BegC	*The Beginnings of Christianity.* Ed. F. J. Foakes-Jackson and K. Lake. 5 vols. London: Macmillan, 1922. Repr., Grand Rapids: Baker, 1977.
BeO	*Bibbia e Oriente*
BETL	Bibliotheca Ephemeridum Theologicarum Lovaniensium
Bib	*Biblica*
BiBh	*Bible Bhashyam (Biblebhashyam)*
BibInt	*Biblical Interpretation*
BibSem	The Biblical Seminar
BibT	*The Bible Today*
BIS	Biblical Interpretation Series
BJRL	*Bulletin of the John Rylands University Library of Manchester*
BJS	Brown Judaic Studies
BK	*Bibel und Kirche*
BN	*Biblische Notizen*
BNP	*Brill's New Pauly: Encyclopaedia of the Ancient World*
BNTC	Black's New Testament Commentaries
BPC	Biblical Performance Criticism
BR	*Biblical Research*
BRev	*Bible Review*
BrillPauly	*Brill's New Pauly, Encyclopaedia of the Ancient World: Antiquity.* Ed. Hubert Cancik, Helmuth Schneider, and Christine F. Salazar. Leiden: Brill, 2002–11.
BZ	*Biblische Zeitschrift*
BZAW	Beihefte zur Zeitschrift für die alttestamentliche Wissenschaft
BZNWK	Beihefte zur Zeitschrift für die neutestamentliche Wissenschaft und die Kunde der älteren Kirche
CaE	Cahiers Évangiles
CathW	*Catholic World*
CBC	Cambridge Bible Commentary
CBQ	*Catholic Biblical Quarterly*

CBQMS	Catholic Biblical Quarterly Monograph Series
CBull	*Classical Bulletin*
CCRMS	Cross-Cultural Research and Methodology Series
CH	*Church History*
Chm	*Churchman*
CIG	*Corpus Inscriptionum Graecarum*, ed. Boeckh
CIJ	*Corpus Inscriptionum Iudaicarum*, ed. Frey
CJ	*Classical Journal*
ClAnt	*Classical Antiquity*
ClQ	*Classical Quarterly*
CNS	*Cristianesimo nella storia*
CNT	Commentaire du Nouveau Testament
ColT	*Collectanea Theologica*
ConBNT	Coniectanea biblica: New Testament Series
Cont	*Continuum*
CP	*Classical Philology*
CRBR	*Critical Review of Books in Religion*
CSPhilRel	Cornell Studies in the Study of Religion
CurBR	*Currents in Biblical Research*
CW	*Classical World*
DBAM	*The Dictionary of the Bible and Ancient Media*. Ed. Tom Thatcher, Chris Keith, Raymond F. Person Jr., and Elsie R. Stern. New York: Bloomsbury T&T Clark, 2017.
DCLY	Deuterocanonical and Cognate Literature Yearbook
Did	*Didaskalia*
DJG	*Dictionary of Jesus and the Gospels*. Ed. Joel B. Green, Scot McKnight, and I. Howard Marshall. Downers Grove, IL: InterVarsity, 1992. 2nd ed., 2013. Ed. Joel Green, Jeannine K. Brown, and Nicholas Perrin.
DNTB	*Dictionary of New Testament Background*. Ed. Craig A. Evans and Stanley E. Porter. Downers Grove, IL: InterVarsity, 2000.
DTT	*Dansk Teologisk Tidsskrift*
ECL	Early Christianity and Its Literature
EJL	Early Judaism and Its Literature
EKKNT	Evangelisch-Katholischer Kommentar zum Neuen Testament
ESEC	Emory Studies in Early Christianity
EstBib	*Estudios Bíblicos*

ETL	*Ephemerides Theologicae Lovanienses*
EurH	Europäische Hochschulschriften
EvQ	*Evangelical Quarterly*
EvT	*Evangelische Theologie*
ExpT	*Expository Times*
FAT	Forschungen zum Alten Testament
FGrH	*Die Fragmente der griechischen Historiker.* Ed. Felix Jacoby. Leiden: Brill, 1954–64.
FoiVie	*Foi et Vie*
FourR	*The Fourth R*
FPhil	*Faith and Philosophy*
FRLANT	Forschungen zur Religion und Literatur des Alten und Neuen Testaments
FSCS	Faith and Scholarship Colloquies
GNS	Good News Studies
GR	*Greece & Rome*
GRBS	*Greek, Roman, and Byzantine Studies*
HDR	Harvard Dissertations in Religion
Hen	*Henoch*
Herm	*Hermathena*
Hok	*Hokhma*
HR	*History of Religions*
HThKNT	Herders theologischen Kommentar zum Neuen Testament
HTR	*Harvard Theological Review*
HTS/TS	*HTS Teologiese Studies/Theological Studies*
HUCA	*Hebrew Union College Annual*
ICC	International Critical Commentaries
IDS	*In die Skriflig / In Luce Verbi*
IntRevMiss	*International Review of Missions*
JAAR	*Journal of the American Academy of Religion*
JAM	*Journal of Asian Mission*
JANESCU	*Journal of the Ancient Near Eastern Society of Columbia University*
JAnthRes	*Journal of Anthropological Research*
JBL	*Journal of Biblical Literature*
JExpPsyc	*Journal of Experimental Psychology*
JGRCJ	*Journal of Greco-Roman Christianity and Judaism*
JHS	*Journal of Hellenic Studies*
JITC	*Journal of the Interdenominational Theological Center*

JJS	*Journal of Jewish Studies*
JNSL	*Journal of Northwest Semitic Languages*
JPFC	*The Jewish People in the First Century: Historical Geography, Political History, Social, Cultural, and Religious Life and Institutions.* 2 vols. Ed. S. Safrai and M. Stern, with D. Flusser and W. C. van Unnik. Section 1 of *Compendia Rerum Iudaicarum ad Novum Testamentum.* Vol. 1: Assen: Van Gorcum, 1974; vol. 2: Philadelphia: Fortress, 1976.
JPT	*Journal of Pentecostal Theology*
JQR	*Jewish Quarterly Review*
JR	*Journal of Religion*
JRASup	Journal of Roman Archaeology Supplementary Series
JRH	*Journal of Religious History*
JRS	*Journal of Roman Studies*
JSHJ	*Journal for the Study of the Historical Jesus*
JSJ	*Journal for the Study of Judaism in the Persian, Hellenistic, and Roman Periods*
JSNT	*Journal for the Study of the New Testament*
JSNTSup	Journal for the Study of the New Testament Supplement Series
JSOT	*Journal for the Study of the Old Testament*
JSOTSup	Journal for the Study of the Old Testament Supplement Series
JSP	*Journal for the Study of the Pseudepigrapha*
JSPSup	Journal for the Study of the Pseudepigrapha Supplement Series
JSQ	*Jewish Studies Quarterly*
JSSR	*Journal for the Scientific Study of Religion*
JTS	*Journal of Theological Studies*
KEKNT	Kritisch-exegetischer Kommentar über das Neue Testament
Laur	*Laurentianum*
LCL	Loeb Classical Library
LD	Lectio Divina
LEC	Library of Early Christianity
LNTS	Library of New Testament Studies
LPSt	Library of Pauline Studies
LS	*Louvain Studies*
LTP	*Laval théologique et philosophique*
LW	*Living Word: Journal of Philosophy and Theology*

MBPS	Mellen Biblical Press Series
MissSt	*Mission Studies*
Mnemosyne	*Mnemosyne: A Journal of Classical Studies*
NAC	New American Commentary
NBf	*New Blackfriars*
NCamBC	New Cambridge Bible Commentary
NCBC	New Century Bible Commentary
NedTT	*Nederlands Theologisch Tijdschrift*
Neot	*Neotestamentica*
NFTL	New Foundations Theological Library
NIB	*The New Interpreter's Bible.* Ed. Leander E. Keck. 12 vols. Nashville: Abingdon, 1994–2004.
NICNT	New International Commentary on the New Testament
NIDB	*New Interpreter's Dictionary of the Bible*
NIGTC	New International Greek Testament Commentary
NIVAC	NIV Application Commentary
NovT	*Novum Testamentum*
NovTSup	Supplements to Novum Testamentum
NSPR	New Studies in the Philosophy of Religion
NTG	New Testament Guides
NTM	New Testament Message
NTS	*New Testament Studies*
NTTS	New Testament Tools and Studies
OCD³	*The Oxford Classical Dictionary: The Ultimate Reference Work on the Classical World.* 3rd rev. ed. Ed. Simon Hornblower and Antony Spawforth. Oxford: Oxford University Press, 2003.
OJRS	*Ohio Journal of Religious Studies*
OrChrAn	Orientalia Christiana Analecta
OTP	*The Old Testament Pseudepigrapha.* Ed. James H. Charlesworth. 2 vols. Garden City, NY: Doubleday, 1983–85.
PAAJR	*Proceedings of the American Academy for Jewish Research*
PAST	Pauline Studies
PCNT	Paideia: Commentaries on the New Testament
PEQ	*Palestine Exploration Quarterly*
Phil	*Philologus*
PhilChr	*Philosophia Christi*
PhilSt	*Philosophical Studies*

PNTC	Pillar New Testament Commentary
PrRR	Princeton Readings in Religion
PRSt	*Perspectives in Religious Studies*
PSB	*Princeton Seminary Bulletin*
PsycTRPT	*Psychotherapy: Theory, Research, Practice, Training*
PTMS	Pittsburgh Theological Monograph Series
PzB	*Protokolle zur Bibel*
R&T	*Religion & Theology*
RB	*Revue Biblique*
RBL	*Review of Biblical Literature*
RC	*Religion Compass*
RCT	*Revista catalana de teología*
RefR	*Reformed Review*
REJ	*Revue des études juives*
ResQ	*Restoration Quarterly*
RevQ	*Revue de Qumran*
RevScRel	*Revue des Sciences Religieuses*
RHPR	*Revue d'histoire et de philosophie religieuses*
RMPhil	Rheinisches Museum für Philologie
RSLR	*Rivista di storia e letteratura religiosa*
RSR	*Recherches de Science Religieuse*
RStMiss	Regnum Studies in Mission
Salm	*Salmanticensis*
SANt	Studia Aarhusiana Neotestamentica
SBET	*Scottish Bulletin of Evangelical Theology*
SBFLA	*Studii Biblici Franciscani Liber Annuus*
SBL	Society of Biblical Literature
SBLAcBib	Society of Biblical Literature Academia Biblica
SBLBMI	Society of Biblical Literature Bible and Its Modern Interpreters Series
SBLBSNA	SBL Biblical Scholarship in North America
SBLCP	SBL Centennial Publications
SBLDS	Society of Biblical Literature Dissertation Series
SBLMS	Society of Biblical Literature Monograph Series
SBLSBS	Society of Biblical Literature Sources for Biblical Study/SBL Resources for Biblical Study
SBLSP	Society of Biblical Literature Seminar Papers
SBLSymS	Society of Biblical Literature Symposium Series
SBLTT	Society of Biblical Literature Texts and Translations

SBLWGRW	Society of Biblical Literature Writings from the Greco-Roman World
SBT	Studies in Biblical Theology
SCI	*Scripta Classica Israelica*
Sef	*Sefarad*
Sem	*Semitica*
SemeiaSt	Semeia Studies
SHBC	Smyth & Helwys Bible Commentary
SHCM	Studies in the History of Christian Mission
SIDIC	*Journal of the Service Internationale de Documentation Judeo-chrétienne*
SJFWJ	Studia Judaica: Forschungen zur Wissenschaft des Judentums
SJLA	Studies in Judaism in Late Antiquity
SJOT	*Scandinavian Journal of the Old Testament*
SJSJ	Supplements to the Journal for the Study of Judaism
SMedJ	*Southern Medical Journal*
SNTSMS	Society for New Testament Studies Monograph Series
SNTW	Studies of the New Testament and Its World
SP	Sacra Pagina
SPhiloA	*Studia Philonica Annual* (*Studia Philonica*)
SPhiloMon	Studia Philonica Monographs
SSAMD	Sage Series on African Modernization and Development
SSEJC	Studies in Scripture in Early Judaism and Christianity
StPB	Studia Post-Biblica
Su	*Studia Theologica Varsaviensia*
SUNT	Studien zur Umwelt des Neuen Testament
SVTP	Studia in Veteris Testamenti Pseudepigrapha
SWJT	*Southwestern Journal of Theology*
SymS	Symposium Series
TANZ	Texte und Arbeiten zum neutestamentlichen Zeitalter
TAPA	*Transactions of the American Philological Society*
TBei	*Theologische Beiträge*
TENTS	Texts and Editions for New Testament Study
TGST	Tesi Gregoriana, Serie Teologia
ThTo	*Theology Today*
TLZ	*Theologische Literaturzeitung*
TNTC	Tyndale New Testament Commentaries
TS	*Theological Studies*
TSAJ	Texte und Studien zum antiken Judentum

TTKi	*Tidsskrift for Teologi og Kirke*
TynBul	*Tyndale Bulletin*
TZ	*Theologische Zeitschrift*
UJT	Understanding Jesus Today
UNDCSJCA	University of Notre Dame Center for the Study of Judaism and Christianity in Antiquity
UTB	Uni-Taschenbücher
VC	*Vigiliae Christianae*
VT	*Vetus Testamentum*
WBC	Word Biblical Commentary
WGRWSup	Writings from the Greco-Roman World Supplement Series
WMQ	*William and Mary Quarterly*
WUNT	Wissenschaftliche Untersuchungen zum Neuen Testament
WW	*Word and World*
YCS	Yale Classical Studies
ZAW	*Zeitschrift für die Alttestamentliche Wissenschaft*
ZDPV	*Zeitschrift des Deutschen Palästina-Vereins*
ZKW	*Zeitschrift für Kunstwissenschaft*
ZNT	*Zeitschrift für Neues Testament*
ZNW	*Zeitschrift für die Neutestamentliche Wissenschaft*
ZPE	*Zeitschrift für Papyrologie und Epigraphik*
Zyg	*Zygon: Journal of Religion and Science*

Chapter 1

Introduction

Publishers get to name books or adapt authors' titles, so before explaining the main title, let me qualify this book's adapted subtitle. This book is not about the historical reliability of the details of the Gospels, although it should contribute to challenging frequent assumptions of their overall unreliability. Instead, more precisely, I explore here the degree of historical intention in comparable works from the era of the Gospels, as well as the sort of prior information to which the Gospel writers could possibly have had access. It is thus a prolegomenon to using the Gospels as historical sources, rather than an examination of the Gospels themselves.

I did, however, propose the main title, because it points to what I believe this prolegomenon suggests. That is, it suggests what ancient analogies lead us to expect in the Gospels: depending on and shaping earlier material, they proclaim the story of Christ. Preaching of Christ's passion and resurrection in light of the Scriptures, often in at least partly narrativized form, had been a central feature of the gospel message from the beginning (1 Cor 15:3–7; cf. 11:23–26; Acts 10:37–42). Not everyone has interest in exploring historical experiences recalled in such early Christian proclamation, but those who do will find it helpful to consider partial ancient analogies to gospel genre and memory.

Christobiography draws attention to an old and yet sometimes neglected insight for historical-Jesus research: in terms of recognizable ancient genres, the Gospels are like ancient biographies. That is, the type of literary work from the Gospels' era that they most closely resemble is the *bios*, or "life," of a subject—what we call (and this book regularly titles) ancient biography.

Although a majority of Gospels scholars today recognize that the Gospels are more like ancient biographies than like anything else, only a minority of Gospels scholars have actually *examined* other ancient biographies in order to understand what implications this shared basic genre might have for the Gospels. What does ancient biography tell us about the way the Gospels communicated their message about Jesus?

Examining other ancient biographies, however, entails a problem. Many have defined ancient biography so broadly that this wide genre appears to offer little of value in the way of specific comparison. Yet some forms of what they call biography are more relevant than others. The genre of biography developed over time, and naturally biographers typically had better sources for events within living memory than for subjects who lived many centuries earlier. ("Living memory" means that some people who knew the subject were still alive when the biographer wrote.)

Most relevant for comparison with the Gospels, then, are biographies from the early empire, especially biographies of real figures who lived within roughly a half century of the writers. They should also be full-length narrative biographies, not the less comparable "lives" that were sometimes just a few paragraphs. At the risk of marring suspense, producing synoptic charts of such biographies similar to those used for the Synoptic Gospels suggests that the sort of adaptations found in the Gospels were standard expectations for this kind of writing.

This conclusion is not particularly surprising, but it is, again, one that is sometimes neglected in historical-Jesus research. Establishing that somewhat analogous biographers drew on historical sources suggests implications for how we should approach the Evangelists' treatment of preexisting information. An ancient audience would have *expected* the features of both reliance on prior material and adaptation that we find in critical study of the Gospels today.

1.1. Jesus in Ancient Historians

Christianity recognizes Jesus as its founder, and Islam deems him a major prophet.[1] Together these religions encompass four billion adherents, more than half of the world's population. For this reason, if for no others, Jesus is a figure meriting significant attention among historians of antiquity, regardless of the historian's own religious horizons.[2]

---

1. Jesus is more complicated for some contemporary Jewish thinkers, for whom he may have been a great Jewish sage executed by the Romans but who was also appropriated out of his Jewish context by later gentile Christianity (see, e.g., discussions in Lapide, *Hebrew*; Lapide and Luz, *Jezus*; Heschel, *Geiger*; Klassen, *Contribution*; Levine, *Misunderstood Jew*). Many Christians and most historical-Jesus scholars today would share this recognition.

2. Some readers today express personal disinterest in historical questions. While I readily recognize that there are other subjects also worthy of interest, those who find historical questions uninteresting may wish to read a different book than this one, since this book addresses

Yet it has not always been so. The primary interest of Roman historians in the early empire was Rome and incidents that directly impacted Rome, such as revolts in the provinces, wars on the borders, or the moral antics of emperors that often dominated political gossip.[3] One crucified sage or rebel in a minor Asian province invited little attention until, a few decades later, his followers became public news in the Roman capital itself.

On a popular level, some writers dismiss all evidence for Jesus as inconsequential and view him as a pure creation of his followers. Even apart from the dismissal of many lines of evidence, this skeptical approach, if followed consistently for other topics, would make much of history unknowable.[4] As in the case of other new movements, whether from disciples of Socrates, Muhammad, Buddha, or Joseph Smith, the life of the founder was initially of little interest beyond the circle of his own followers. The Dead Sea Scrolls revere the founder of their community, the Teacher of Righteousness, yet he appears nowhere outside their own literature.

Likewise, the first-century Jewish historian Josephus claims to have been a Pharisee, yet he nowhere mentions the Pharisaic sage Hillel, whom most subsequent Pharisaic traditions name as one of their central figures.[5] Meanwhile, the Judean king Agrippa I, whom Josephus depicts as prominent even in Rome, merits only the barest passing mention in a Roman historian covering the period.[6] Another major Roman historian devotes little space even to Herod the Great.[7]

---

historical interests. For discussion of the value of historical questions (alongside others), see Keener, *Acts*, 1:16–28, esp. 26–28.

3. Cf., e.g., Laistner, *Historians*, 131.

4. Against this approach, see, e.g., Ehrman, *Did Jesus Exist?* Detractors cannot complain (as those who wish to avoid ad hominem arguments should not, in any case) that Ehrman, an agnostic, is motivated in this argument by religious bias. See also Casey, *Evidence* (from a non-Christian perspective; although sometimes polarizing and attributing more than appropriate to individuals' psychological backgrounds, he is probably right to observe that British academia tend to show a greater commitment to fairness than do some polarized US contexts); Elliott, "Pseudo-Scholarship" (focusing on T. Freke and P. Gandy and, on p. 10, noting "factual errors, misstatements, and methodological misunderstandings on nearly every page").

5. See the comments by Israeli historian Flusser, *Sage*, 1; Flusser, "Ancestry," 154, which compares the case of the Jesus movement with the followers of Simon Kimbangu or Joseph Smith. The analogies are of course inexact: for example, unlike Smith, Jesus left no written record; and unlike Jesus, Kimbangu did not train disciples (in the ancient Mediterranean sense). But the examples are sufficient for Flusser's point. For Socrates see Kennedy, "Source Criticism," 130; for the principle that it is those who care about a figure who preserve his or her memories, see Schwartz, "Smoke," 11.

6. Tacitus, *Annals* 12.23.

7. Dio Cassius, *Roman History* 49.22.6; 54.9.3.

By the same criterion of relevance, the earlier Greek historian Herodotus neglected not only Judea but Rome.[8] And Josephus himself, despite his prominent role in the Judean war and as an interpreter of Judea for the gentile Greco-Roman world, merits no interest in later rabbis (who in fact show greater interest in Jesus).

This is not to imply that non-Christian reports about Jesus are altogether absent. Most scholars today recognize that the first-century Judean writer Josephus, who wrote about John the Baptist and Jesus's brother James, also wrote about Jesus himself.[9] Josephus treats Jesus as a sage and wonder-worker executed by the governor, probably with the complicity of some of Jerusalem's elite.[10] Many scholars argue that an early Arabic version also confirms the key points about Jesus that scholars have reconstructed as original (before scribal tampering) in Josephus's account.[11] Possibly as early as forty-five years after Jesus's crucifixion, a Syrian philosopher named Mara bar Sarapion speaks of Jews executing their wise king, bringing judgment on Judea. (He probably heard this report from Syrian Christians.)[12]

By the early second century, one historian includes a report, from just two decades after the crucifixion, about Jewish debates in Rome, apparently concerning the Christ.[13] Another, reporting the slaughter of vast numbers of Jesus followers in Rome roughly thirty-four years after the crucifixion, mentions that Jesus himself was earlier crucified under Pontius Pilate.[14] Rome itself had finally taken notice, because subsequent events had made Jesus's movement a matter of local significance. In fact, the movement had become more significant in Rome than was the governor who executed Jesus. Although Jewish sources and an inscription mention Pilate,[15] this passage marks his only appearance in surviving Roman literature.

8. Josephus, *Against Apion* 1.60–66, esp. 66.

9. On Josephus's genuine mention of Jesus, see Meier, "Jesus in Josephus"; Meier, "Testimonium"; Whealey, "Josephus"; Whealey, "Testimonium"; Gramaglia, "*Testimonium*"; Paget, "Observations"; Vermes, *Jesus the Jew*, 79; Charlesworth, *Jesus within Judaism*, 90–98; Charlesworth, "Jesus, Literature, and Archaeology," 189–92; Dubarle, "Témoignage"; Ehrman, *Prophet*, 59–62; Theissen and Merz, *Guide*, 64–74; Van Voorst, *Jesus*, 81–104; Niemand, "Testimonium."

10. Josephus, *Jewish Antiquities* 18.63–64.

11. See Agapius in Charlesworth, *Jesus within Judaism*, 95–96; Puig i Tàrrech, *Jesus*, 48; Alfeyev, *Beginning*, 11 (noting Pines, *Version*, 16); but see Whealey, "Testimonium," esp. 587–88.

12. Theissen and Merz, *Guide*, 76–80.

13. Suetonius, *Claudius* 25.4; see Keener, *Acts*, 3:2697–2711, esp. 2708–11; Keener, "Edict."

14. Tacitus, *Annals* 15.44. Second-century authors also lampoon or criticize the Christian movement and its founder; see, e.g., Lucian, *Peregrinus* 11; cf. Celsus in Origen, *Against Celsus*.

15. See, e.g., Philo, *Embassy* 299, 304; Josephus, *Jewish Antiquities* 18.35, 55–64, 87–89, 177; *Jewish War* 2.169–75.

Most important and most early, we have considerable information about Jesus in Paul's letters to his congregations, beginning perhaps eighteen to twenty years after Jesus's execution. Paul was certainly a Christian, but by his own admission he began his involvement with the sect as one of its persecutors rather than as one of its friends. While focusing on Jesus's crucifixion and resurrection, Paul also mentions other information about Jesus, including the Twelve, Jesus's brothers, Jesus's being mocked and abused, his burial, his teaching about divorce, his words at the Last Supper, and so forth. Paul also attests what seems to be a widespread early Christian consensus about Jesus's role as Christ and exalted Lord. Nevertheless, Paul's situation-occasioned letters do not supply anything like a biography of Jesus or even narrate any episodes from his life before the passion.

1.2. What Can Be Known about Jesus?

Popular ideas have created a groundswell of skepticism that has begun to produce its own literature, so far largely nonacademic but eventually undoubtedly producing some work that will merit an academic response.[16] Some writers even question Jesus's historic existence, in some cases potentially fueled by religiously motivated bias,[17] although this concern is inconsistently not applied to other past religious figures such as Muhammad, the rise of whose movement is rightly recognized as implausible without him.

Yet in contrast to some popular ideas that circulate on the internet, specialists in the study of Jesus, almost without exception, agree that Jesus historically existed.[18] His movement had no reason to invent him, and certainly not his execution for treason as a "king"; following someone so executed was itself deemed treasonous, so inventing such a narrative would be suicidal. Certainly Jesus's execution by crucifixion is consistent with Pilate and/or members of the local elite viewing Jesus as a rebel king.

16. One scholar of English literature produced a highly speculative, weakly documented work (Helms, *Fictions*) that was mailed to many biblical studies scholars. One or more sophisticated arguments, however, are reportedly in the works. I say "reportedly" because internet broadsides, which are not peer-reviewed, do not typically merit academic responses, and academic works, by virtue of their own genre, are not typically expected to respond to such broadsides. Nevertheless, see again helpful responses in Ehrman, *Did Jesus Exist?*; Casey, *Evidence*; Elliott, "Pseudo-Scholarship."

17. Cf. esp. the ideological agendas of Nazi German and atheistic Soviet campaigns noted in Alfeyev, *Beginning*, 3–4.

18. See again Ehrman, *Did Jesus Exist?*

Imagine that we had documents today from multiple recent writers about someone who founded a movement a few decades ago. Further imagine that this movement revolved around that founder. Naturally, we would expect most writings from within the movement to take very positive views of the founder, but very rarely would we consider doubting that founder's existence. Yet this is precisely what we have in the case of Jesus; Paul's letters attest such a movement's devotion to its founder within twenty years of his death. Denying Jesus's historical existence hardly makes sense of the data available to us.

Furthermore, almost all scholars concur on some basic features of the gospel story. They agree that Jesus was a Galilean Jew from Nazareth, a popular sage and prophet whose disciples began a distinctive Jewish movement. Jesus was influenced by the (likely eschatological) baptizing prophet John, announced the approach of God's kingdom on earth, and taught in parables and often riddles.

Most scholars also agree that Jesus's contemporaries experienced him as a healer and exorcist, offering divine help to the vulnerable.[19] He viewed his healings and exorcisms as signs of the promised kingdom.[20] He embraced for the kingdom many people whose status was marginal and/or normally overlooked by their society, including those deemed marginal morally or (in the case of tax collectors) nationalistically. He appealed to the poor, the disenfranchised, the disabled, and the ill, and he encountered conflict with various elites.

This conflict climaxed in Jerusalem, probably at Passover, when Jesus and other Galileans made pilgrimage. Virtually indisputably, he died by Roman crucifixion, decreed by the governor, Pontius Pilate. Within days, his disciples were claiming that God had raised him from the dead and they had seen him, a message that may have become quickly coordinated with Jesus's teachings about the kingdom and with God's favor for the weak and the oppressed.[21] Distinctively, Jesus's movement claimed the restoration of the prophetic Spirit (in a fuller sense than in even the Dead Sea Scrolls), spread to major cities of the empire within a few decades, and in the Diaspora began converting gentiles, sometimes without requiring circumcision.

Besides the more direct sources, general information based on Jesus's environment allows us to screen out the plausibility of some approaches. Indis-

---

19. For this summary of consensus, see also, e.g., Brown, *Death*, 143–44; Meier, *Marginal Jew*, 2:617–45, 678–772; Eve, *Miracles*, 16–17; Dunn, *Remembered*, 670; Twelftree, "Message," 2518–19; discussion in *Christobiography*, ch. 12.

20. Matt 11:5//Luke 7:22 with Isa 35:5–6; 61:1; Matt 12:28//Luke 11:20.

21. Cf., e.g., 1 Cor 1:18–25; 2 Cor 13:4; 1 Thess 2:12.

putably, Jesus was Jewish, so we may dismiss reconstructions of Jesus that do not take this feature into account (from some thinkers' Aryan Jesus in Nazi-era Germany to today's populist mythicists in the United States). Recent decades' "Third Quest" for Jesus (e.g., as exemplified in the works of E. P. Sanders, one of my own professors; also Geza Vermes, James Charlesworth, and Amy-Jill Levine) has thus rightly focused on Jesus in his Jewish setting. Indeed, these Gospels, though all written in Greek for probably Diaspora audiences, reflect many Judean/Galilean traditions in a way that later alleged gospel works (such as Gospel of Peter) do not.[22]

On the basic outline of events, then, a wide consensus exists among scholars.[23] (I will not survey here the evidence that supports such a consensus, since I have treated that evidence elsewhere,[24] and these basic facts about Jesus are not the focus of this book.)

Beyond such an outline, however, even scholars disagree considerably on the details. That is partly because we differ in how we estimate the reliability of the primary sources that supply our fullest first-century information about Jesus—namely, the Gospels. Almost no scholars claim that the Gospels offer Jesus's words verbatim; such a claim would contradict the differing wording among the Gospels themselves.[25] (Any reader who assumes that the wording must be verbatim may disabuse themselves of such an idea by simply comparing enough parallel accounts; a reader who has never done this has no business pontificating about what "must" be the case.) Nor, as we shall see, did ancient audiences expect verbatim reporting. Nevertheless, most scholars accept the Gospels' reports of more teachings of Jesus and events in his life than the few mentioned above.

But which ones? And what do we mean by "accept"? Most of us would likely agree that the absolute minimum of virtually indisputable information that everyone with the slightest historical understanding should accept may be summarized fairly concisely (something like the survey above). Most of us also agree that a considerable amount of material in the Gospels is plau-

---

22. I enumerate a few examples in Keener, "Suggestions"; Keener, "Assumptions," 49–52. The Gospel of Peter reflects some Johannine tradition (cf. Kirk, *Memory*, 233–43) and might derive from Jewish Christian circles (Marcus, "Gospel of Peter"), but few today follow Crossan in dating parts of the Gospel of Peter to the first century; see Porter, "Reconstructing," 53.

23. So also Ehrman, *Before the Gospels*, 144, although beyond that outline our approaches often diverge.

24. Keener, *Historical Jesus*, 163–329, 339–44 passim.

25. For a quick, conspicuous example, see John 13:10–11; in the Evangelists' Bible, see, e.g., Gen 18:12–13; 39:17–19; Exod 6:12, 30; 1 Sam 15:3, 18; or Ezra 1:1–4; 5:13–15; 6:3–5.

sible and at least possible. Whether we argue for the maximum of possible information or the minimum of indisputable information depends on our objective (e.g., debunking unwarranted skepticism or populist naïveté). Most historians, however, are interested not only in what is absolutely certain or in what is potentially plausible but in what is most *probable*. And it is here that our consensus breaks down, again partly because scholars differ in how we estimate the reliability of our primary sources—the Gospels.

Noting contradictions in matters of detail, some scholars approach the substance of the gospel narratives with a priori suspicion. (Scholarship associated with the Jesus Seminar, for example, often exemplifies this tendency, although rarely with the absolute suspicion of the populist "Jesus mythers.") Conversely, some conservative scholars start with a default acceptance of the narratives' accuracy even down to most details of chronology. Probably the majority of Gospels scholars today fall in the range between these positions, leaving the burden of proof with whoever makes an argument for a particular event or saying.

In the range of Jesus scholarship today, scholars such as Sanders, Gerd Theissen, John Meier, and Mark Allan Powell represent a fairly centrist position, despite differences among themselves. Scholars such as John Dominic Crossan or, to a lesser extent, Marcus Borg (sadly, now deceased) would be to the left of this center; scholars such as myself or N. T. Wright would be to the right (no pun intended) of this center (though not, for example, assuming the narratives' chronology). We are all on the same map, but methodological differences and different assumptions about how to weigh the ancient evidence lead to different conclusions.

The dearth of surviving evidence means that filling the gaps requires some guesswork, so presuppositions cannot but affect where on this continuum particular interpretations fall.[26] Scholars often attempt to circumvent the limits of available information with speculative reconstructions.[27] Speculation should not be confused with information, though because educated guesses are correct more frequently than are uneducated ones, they may help insofar as we recognize varying degrees of probability.[28] Broader knowledge of the tradents' and Evangelists' environment may plug some gaps in our knowledge.

One's goal similarly affects one's final product; again, some tasks require a minimalist approach to establish the most certain evidence, and others a

---

26. Eve, *Behind Gospels*, 177–78, 184–85; Downing, "Researches." For such inferences in oral tradition, see Rubin, *Memory*, 36.

27. Vansina, *Oral Tradition*, 173, correctly chastises this habit.

28. Cf. comments in Keener, review of Malina.

maximalist approach to establish all possible evidence. Most of us are most interested in the most probable evidence rather than exclusively minimalist or maximalist approaches, but again, probability is a continuum, and various factors influence the levels of probability assessed for various passages.

Neither minimalist nor maximalist approaches prove their most eccentric claims in the public sphere; it is typically their presupposed methodology, rather than a shift in the evidence itself, that produces their conclusions.[29] Usually their adherents simply take for granted their method, and some members of other groups either ignore or use ad hominem arguments against those who differ.[30] That is, they take their assumptions as epistemic axioms not requiring proof. Each group often thus preaches to their own choirs, instead of engaging in fair dialogue with their methodological detractors.

As Barry Schwartz, noted social memory theorist and Abraham Lincoln scholar, warns, whereas some scholars accept as true about Jesus anything that might be, others exclude anything that might not be.[31] Some set "the bar of admissibility so high that it becomes impossible to accept less than perfect evidence. To assume that evidence is wrong until proven right" for the purpose of screening out all possible distortions would leave us with no knowledge of Lincoln's early years at all.[32] The usual goal is determining what is most probable.

One complication, too massive today to address in this book, is the question of the proper approach of historiography in general. Postmodernism has rightly discredited naive realism, leaving many properly chastened critical realists in its wake.[33] A number of other historians, however, have taken matters further, treating all historical narratives not only as rhetorical constructions, but as if they were almost *exclusively* rhetorical constructions without historical interest. Narratives *are* rhetorical constructions, but ancient historical narratives, like modern ones, normally use what they view as historical

---

29. Cf. Bauckham, *Eyewitnesses*, 613: "In good historical work it is no more an epistemic virtue to be sceptical than it is to be credulous." Bauckham's Cambridge PhD is in history.

30. Thus, e.g., those who take a more conservative approach than a critic prefers are "apologists"—as if only those who are more conservative defend a given thesis—or their views are reduced to their particular religious or philosophic commitments as if they could not have come to such commitments honestly. Others dismiss the arguments of those who take a more skeptical approach because they are "skeptics." Both are cases of ad hominem arguments, finding a priori excuses to avoid needing to address actual arguments.

31. Schwartz, "Origins," 53.

32. Schwartz, "Origins," 52.

33. Although not identifying himself as a critical realist (Le Donne, *Historiographical Jesus*, 11) and warning that critical realists often underestimate subconscious scripts, Le Donne values the corrective of critical realism against naive realism and deconstruction (9).

information as important building blocks in their constructions, despite the historian's role as architect. Shaping and even developing information differ from pure invention of stories. As some scholars have warned, recognizing or dismissing the reality of particular historical events, for example, Nazi murders of Jews, Roma people, gays, and others will produce significant ethical and moral consequences.[34]

Despite this tendency among some readers of histories, most historians do accept the possibility of highly probable historical information in ordinary historical writing, even while acknowledging the limitations of narratives in which they are embedded. This book cannot address at any length the minority of historians who reject historical claims in general; normally they are more consistent than to apply the skepticism only to the Gospels. The nature of historical discourse, however, is a question to be waged among philosophers of history themselves. This book addresses those who believe that some significant historical information appears in and can be outlined from many historical sources, whatever their weaknesses. Whatever one's approaches to the Gospels as historical sources, they should be consistent with one's approach to other biographies from the same period, except where differences in the works themselves invite different treatments.

1.3. Why Historical-Jesus Research Needs the Gospels

As already noted, non-Christian sources tell us something about Jesus, but not a great deal. Analogously, most of what is most valuable about Socrates is

---

34. Not all scholars need to focus on investigating historic events themselves; studying how material is framed for communication (rhetoric) and the development of perspectives on events or traditions (social memory) are valid and useful enterprises in themselves. Events are not self-interpreting but allow a (finite) range of interpretations. Nevertheless, the reality of some real events, however framed, is necessary for matters of justice and (more controversially today) the truths that must undergird it; some interpretations of the past are more morally satisfactory than others (cf. Kirk, "Social and Cultural Memory," 14–15). Emphasizing the importance of some real facts in history, Roland Deines (in discussion in the SNTS memory seminar in Athens, August 10, 2018) offered the following examples: some Palestinians' denial of the Nazi holocaust, and some Israelis' denial of early Israeli atrocities against Palestinians; "alternative facts" in recent US politics; and how long it has taken for the stories of some sex abuse survivors to surface. For other examples of disputed social memory where actual facts matter, one could add long delays before (or continued resistance to) acknowledgment of, e.g., the Armenian genocide, the rape of Nanjing (Chang, *Rape*), and the sexual abuse and often murder of Korean women in the Second World War (see Park, *Conflict*, 12–15).

known to us not from disinterested contemporaries but from his adherents. The situation is considerably worse for a Greek sage such as Demonax, whom Lucian knew and whom his fellow Athenians allegedly revered—but who, outside Lucian, is virtually unattested in contemporary sources.[35]

For any even partly full picture of Jesus, the Gospels are our best available source. Most historical-Jesus scholars thus focus on the first-century Gospels, especially the Synoptics, the first three Gospels, which follow the basic pattern of Mark.

This observation is not a "canonical bias." At one time other first-century sources about Jesus existed (Luke 1:1), and the vast majority of scholars, including myself, would eagerly engage them if we could. Unfortunately, they do not appear to exist, apart from hypothetical reconstructions, by far the most probable of which is "Q."[36] Against those who rely on purely hypothetical sources attested only later, Princeton's Dale Allison is right to point out that the only consensus documents about Jesus from the first roughly four decades are Paul, Q and Mark, all of which are readily available to us in our New Testament.[37]

The church preserved these works because they respected them. While many of us wish that someone had preserved some other works as well, we obviously cannot use such unpreserved works. Most of these other works, however, probably did not diverge too significantly from the overall portrait that remains available to us in the first-century Gospels. Whereas ancient writers sometimes did denigrate the inadequate knowledge of their predecessors,[38] Luke's mention of predecessors (Luke 1:1) is far more restrained.[39] He

---

35. See Beck, "Demonax," 82.

36. "Q" is a putative source shared by Matthew and Luke in addition to Mark. Although a majority of scholars, including myself, do infer Q, a substantial and growing minority of capable scholars demur; see, e.g., Goodacre, *Case*; Goodacre, *Synoptic Problem*. Discrepancies in the infancy narratives and incidents such as Judas's death convince me to a fair degree of probability that Luke and Matthew share common tradition and source(s) (or at most a very early version of Matthew's discourse material) rather than one depending on the other. For the purposes of this book I take for granted the Q hypothesis, but a different configuration of sources would yield similar results.

37. Allison, *Jesus of Nazareth*, 17. Some now date Mark shortly after 70, but the difference of a year or two does not affect the point under discussion.

38. Aristotle, *Heavens* 3.7–8, 305a33–307b24; 4.2, 308a34–b3; *Rhetoric to Alexander*, pref. opening, lines 1–12; Longinus, *On the Sublime* 1.1; Artemidorus, *Interpretation of Dreams* 1.pref.; 3.pref.; in historical works, see Polybius, *Histories* 3.32.4–5; Dio Cassius, *Roman History* 1.1.1–2; cf. Justus in Josephus, *Life* 357–59.

39. For gentle ways of distinguishing one's work from that of one's predecessors, or without criticizing the information they include, see, e.g., Diodorus Siculus, *Library of History*

may offer a more orderly account based on his thorough acquaintance with his movement, but he does not directly challenge most of the traditions about Jesus circulating in his day. In fact, he claims to confirm the reports about Jesus and his early movement that Theophilus has already heard (Luke 1:3–4).

Since the Gospels are the fullest sources we have to work with, we should examine carefully their genre and its implications for historical tradition.

1.4. Default Expectations and the Gospels

This book will not resolve all those questions, but it should help fill a gap that often exists in the historical study of Jesus. Most scholars who seek to use historical methods to learn more about Jesus do focus on the Gospels, our main sources for information about Jesus. Yet if the postmodern turn has taught us anything that nearly all of us agree on, it is that we all come to history with some perspectives and default expectations.

As noted above, at most only a handful of scholars expect frequent verbatim material from Jesus in the Gospels. (Even here, "verbatim" must be severely qualified, when sayings have been translated from Aramaic, which Jesus probably spoke most often in Galilee, into Greek, the language of the Gospels.) More often, scholars expect to find relatively few near-verbatim sayings but a significant historical core in the Gospels' reports. Some other scholars begin with a more default skepticism, expecting few of the specific accounts of Jesus's ministry or teachings to resemble actual events from Jesus's life or themes from his teaching.

Yet only a small minority of scholars have engaged the default setting that the shape of the primary sources, the Gospels, leads us to expect. Although the cumulative intersection of my own approaches (some beyond the subject of this book) anticipates more of a historical core than I will argue for in this book, I focus in this book more narrowly on the direction toward which the Gospels' genre points.

Like myself, some scholars will find reasons that the Gospels are more reliable than the argument of this book alone would sustain; others will find reasons for more unreliability than the argument of this book might lead them to expect. But the approach advanced here provides a supplemental, shared

---

1.3.1; Vitruvius, *Architecture* 7.pref.10–18; Valerius Maximus, *Memorable Doings and Sayings* 1.pref.; Pliny, *Natural History* 3.1.1–2; Quintilian, *Orator's Education* 1.pref.1–2, 4; 3.1.22; Aulus Gellius, *Attic Nights* pref.11–12.

minimum to which most scholars cognizant of ancient biography should basically agree. In this book I appeal to scholars across the spectrum to embrace the logical corollaries of the genre convictions that most of us already hold. The first-century Gospels are ancient biographies and are—pardon the tautology—from the first century.[40]

Those who deny that biographic genre implies much about the Gospels' dependence on historical tradition[41] tend to cite a range of ancient "lives" to argue that the line between ancient biographies and novels was sometimes thin.[42] Even if one stretches the definition of "biography" as far as they do (a matter discussed in the next chapter),[43] the legendary and fictitious "lives" they cite are not very analogous to the kind of biography we find in the Gospels. They involve characters of the remote or distant rather than the recent past. Even in more historical biographies about figures of the distant past, fictitious incidents often tell us more about the sources available to the biographer in these cases than anything about the genre itself.[44]

The research that led to Richard Burridge's widely acclaimed 1992 Cambridge monograph confirmed,[45] contrary to his prior expectations, the conclusions of some previous studies that affirmed that the Gospels are biographies.[46] His study swiftly and successfully shifted the consensus of scholarship about the Gospels.[47] I will not repeat his history of scholarship or major arguments, but his case seems fairly self-evident for the Gospels. After all, the Gospels are works recounting the activity of a single historical figure—which by definition

40. Although some scholars date some of the Gospels, most often Luke or John, in the second century, they rarely date them late in the second century, and the first-century date remains the majority view for all the four Gospels addressed here. I do not repeat here my discussion of these issues elsewhere, esp. Keener, *John*, 1:140–42; Keener, *Acts*, 1:383–401.

41. See, e.g., Crossan, "Necessary," 27.

42. See, e.g., *Life of Aesop* in Wills, "Aesop Tradition," 225.

43. E.g., largely novelistic works such as Xenophon's *Cyropedia* and Ps.-Callisthenes's *Alexander Romance*. Classification can be to some extent a matter of semantics, but most ancient narratives do diverge into distinct fundamental categories in terms of basic historical content and usually even their degree of historical referentiality.

44. Thus, for example, where legendary elements appear in Suetonius, they ordinarily reflect his sources, appearing particularly in his depictions of characters who lived some 150 years earlier; see Hägg, *Biography*, 218.

45. Burridge, *Comparison*.

46. See, e.g., Talbert, *Gospel*, throughout; Kennedy, "Source Criticism," 128–34; Aune, *Environment*, 46–76; Stanton, *Preaching*, 117–36; Robbins, *Teacher*, 10.

47. See, e.g., Burridge, *Gospels*, 105–251; Burridge, "People," 121–22; Burridge, "Biography"; Burridge, "Biography, Ancient"; Burridge, "Genre"; Frickenschmidt, *Evangelium*; Walton, "Burridge's Impact"; see the fuller listing in ch. 2.

was what ancient biographies were. That the Gospels concern a recent figure and depend on prior information narrows them further to historical biographies (as opposed to person-centered novels).

The dependence of the Synoptics on prior information is indisputable for at least two Gospels. The strong majority of scholars today believe that Matthew and Luke depend on Mark. (A much smaller minority believe that Matthew wrote first, but all recognize that at least two and possibly all three Gospels must depend on some prior information.)[48] I take for granted in this book the two-source hypothesis,[49] but on the question at hand here—namely, the relevance of the historical substance of ancient biographies—other approaches would yield the same overall results. These two Evangelists treat Mark as a reliable source of information,[50] which they were likely in a position to know.[51] The character of John is somewhat different (see ch. 13), but it claims to depend even more directly on the testimony of the beloved disciple.

Only recently, however, have some scholars begun to explore the implications that this consensus might have for how we approach the Gospels for historical information about Jesus. What should be a historian's default expectations for an ancient biography written within a generation or two of its subject? At the risk of ruining suspense, this study's conclusion will favor the median approach for public scholarship: as a matter of probability, we should expect a significant historical core in the average reports in the first-century Gospels except where evidence specifically points in a different direction. That is, neither the expectation of verbatim material nor a presupposed skepticism

48. For diverse approaches, see Porter and Dyer, *Synoptic Problem*; others support still other positions, e.g., Derico, *Tradition* (more orality); Burkett, *Case* (proto-Mark).

49. The disputed, but still the majority, approach. For argumentation, see, e.g., Derrenbacker, *Practices*. An author such as Josephus harmonizes discrepancies in his sources' details (Derrenbacker, *Practices*, 95), but some divergences in Luke's and Matthew's infancy narratives and accounts of Judas's death suggest to me that neither Evangelist knew the other's completed work. The putative Gospel of Judas is much later (Evans, "Gospel of Judas").

50. This is not to claim that they always shared Mark's perspectives (cf., e.g., the omission in Matt 15 of Mark 7:19b), but as Eusebius cited Papias on tradition where it suited him, so Matthew rehashes Mark—on many estimates, up to 90 percent of Mark. Critical thinkers can differ vehemently on some points without thereby rejecting all perspectives, and certainly all information, in another source. Matthew certainly values Mark as a source of information.

51. Although some scholars have argued plausibly that Matthew could precede AD 70 (e.g., Gundry, *Matthew*, 599–608; Robinson, *Redating*; Hagner, *Matthew*, 1:lxxiv; 2:712), the contents of the book suggest to more of us a post-70 first century date (e.g., Ellis, *Matthew*, 5; Senior, *Matthew*, 13–14; Davies and Allison, *Matthew*, 127–38). By the early second century, Matthew was mainstream Christians' favorite Gospel.

toward the historical core of the bulk of the material is warranted. This conclusion is consistent with what a majority of historical critics conclude based on other lines of evidence.

This conclusion does not obviate the value of traditional historical-critical methods, although some of those methods (esp. the criterion of dissimilarity) have been widely questioned for other reasons.[52] (Historians of antiquity have also had to challenge that criterion's abuse in their discipline.)[53]

I do not explore the particularities of gospel traditions here, not because such a quest is not important but because that would be a very different book, one that has, on other grounds, been written and will be written countless times. This is neither a synopsis of the Gospels (which all new students of the Gospels should engage) nor a historical reconstruction of Jesus. Rather, it is a relatively fresh consideration that scholars should take into account when reconstructing historical information about Jesus from the Gospels.

Research shows that ancient biographers depended heavily on prior information in composing biographies, a characteristic we would not expect in, for example, ancient novels. Moreover, other factors being equal, testimony about a figure from within living memory can in fact prove quite substantial.

In many cases, this consideration should adjust our default expectations. By this I mean that we should start with a more positive predisposition toward the material than is the case among those who reject any material that they cannot "prove." Claims of texts from within living memory of the subject are *themselves* historical evidence, even though historians must weigh such claims, like other evidence, as carefully as possible.

Granting a significant a priori degree of probability in general does not obviate the importance of other considerations in various individual cases. The Fourth Gospel makes no effort to disguise the Johannine style of its discourses; most Johannine scholars see these discourses as including homiletic elaboration on Jesus's teaching, interpretation that the author would undoubtedly claim was guided by the promised Spirit of truth. Similarly, the infancy narratives extend a generation earlier than the bulk of material in the Synoptic Gospels. We find parallels for both sorts of cases in ancient biographies.

---

52. An increasing number of scholars challenge the criteria generally, e.g., Allison, "Criteria"; Bernier, *Quest* (but cf. Keener, "Review of Bernier"); Keith, *Scribal Elite*, 78–81 (on "the demise of the criteria approach"); much of Keith and Le Donne, *Criteria*; most harshly, Crook, "Memory Theory" (1: "bankrupt"; but cf. Eck, "Memory"). In defense of retaining many of the criteria, see, e.g., Licona, "Sky Falling."

53. See, e.g., Beck, "Demonax," 81; others, however, maintain it (see, e.g., Power, "Poetry," 217).

But Mark and, on the majority view, the putative source Q stem from the period of the likely lifetime of some of Jesus's first followers. (Scholars typically date Mark to roughly four decades after Jesus's crucifixion, and often Q even earlier.)[54] When we lack compelling evidence to either embrace or reject particular Gospel reports about Jesus, therefore, our default expectation toward the material should be more positive than negative.[55]

1.5. We Know More about Jesus Than We Think: Ancient Biography

Scholars have classified different sorts of works under the rubric of ancient biographies, but the heart of the genre in the early empire (the period of the Gospels) is what ancient writers called "lives." Although these lives often focused on the subject's public career, and in cases of martyrs on their deaths, they usually include narrative episodes of the subject's life. As we shall see, readers in the early empire expected such works to be based on actual events of the past, although the facts chosen and emphasized could be used to offer various moral, political, or other lessons. Readers expected the same approach not only for biography but for ancient historiography in general.

Our earliest surviving, full examples of the fully developed genre come from the Roman biographer Cornelius Nepos in the first century BCE (BC). Our optimal examples come from Plutarch (in Greek) and from Suetonius and Tacitus (in Latin) in the early second century CE (AD). We also possess first-century Jewish examples, from Philo (his life of Moses) and, as an autobiography, from Josephus. Overall, these sources provide a range of accuracy on which one might plot the various Gospels. All of them, however, belong to a genre that generally developed prior information rather than displayed unrestrained creativity. They also adapted details to provide a coherent narrative rather than simply providing a jumbled assortment of unrelated information.

From Nepos to Suetonius, typical, full biographies from the period of the early empire reveal this period's preferred shape and substance for such works:

---

54. For dates for Mark around 65–70, see, e.g., Ehrman, *Introduction*, 82; Collins, *Mark*, 11–14; Spivey, Smith, and Black, *Anatomy*, 60–61; before Peter's martyrdom, Papias, frag. 21.1–2 (that it could be composed without his initial knowledge in 21.2 seems strange, but cf. Quintilian, *Orator's Education* 1.pref.7), with, e.g., Bock, *Mark*, 9; Schnabel, *Mark*, 17; for Q being even earlier, see, e.g., Theissen, *Gospels*, 220–21, 230–32. Some date even Mark as early as the 40s (see esp. Crossley, *Date*; cf. Casey, *Sources*).

55. This language of "default setting" also appears in Dunn, *Tradition*, esp. ch. 2 (pp. 41–79); similarly, see McIver, *Memory*, 186–87, speaking of the "burden of proof."

a full volume (usually in the length range of the Gospels) based on much information, to the extent that much information was available. This is the ideal in the early empire, and the ideal to which the Evangelists surely would have aspired.

The genre cues us to the authors' ideal historical intention, but how effectively could they execute this intention? How much *information* would they have *available*? The answer varies, depending on the biographers and their biographees. Public archives might provide material about political figures, but archives were not relevant for biographies of sages, including the Gospels' accounts about Jesus. Biographies of many ancient intellectual figures were often thus more limited, because of limited information or because the biographers wrote in eras before the fuller development of historical biography. Within their schools, however, disciples often preserved and transmitted important information about the founders.

Beyond archival material, biographies about figures within living memory, whether recent emperors (such as post-Julio-Claudian emperors in Suetonius) or recent teachers (such as some of those in Philostratus's *Lives of the Sophists*), could depend on substantial collective memory. While biographers writing too long after a biographee's death had to depend on sources that could no longer be verified by living witnesses, those writing during the biographee's lifetime were often thought to succumb to biases (esp. when the biographee held power) and to lack historical perspective. Those writing after the biographee's decease yet within living memory avoided both of these perceived dangers (see ch. 9). Here my final chapters (chs. 14–16) are more relevant: writers composing within living memory of their subjects normally have more detailed information available.

Some biographies from the early empire thus warrant more respect as historical sources than do others. In general, we should approach most respectfully those composed within or close to living memory of the person. This expectation is relevant for the canonical Gospels, and obviously for Mark. Such an expectation fits observations offered by other scholars on the basis of different evidence. The Synoptics, at least, are the "same yet different"[56]—they tell the same essential story (and many of the same essential substories) yet with variation in how they tell them. Of course, the same is true for history in a much more general way: "The narrative of a history can always be told and retold (at least, slightly) differently: it is thus the same yet is always different."[57]

---

56. The phrase is especially that of James D. G. Dunn (see, e.g., Dunn, *Tradition*, 5, 124, 164–65, 200, 214, 220, 230–31, 239, 243–47, 251, 256–57, 291–93, 305–6, following Dodd, *Founder*, 21–22), though the idea is much more pervasive.

57. Nikulin, "Introduction," 18.

Some Jesus followers were probably writing accounts about Jesus even earlier than our surviving Gospels, though they may have lacked literary pretensions (Luke 1:1). In the first generation, many might not have considered such reports necessary; it is often when the generation of eyewitnesses begins to die out that memoirs begin to be written.[58] From an ancient vantage point, however, this was often precisely the ideal time for writing, as noted above: it offered some historical perspective on which events proved most significant, and it avoided pressure from (often powerful) participants.[59]

So we actually may know quite a lot about Jesus in terms of the gist of episodes in his ministry. In cases where we lack other evidence to support or question an episode, the biographic genre and chronological proximity suggest that the report is likelier than not to reflect some early memory of an actual incident in Jesus's ministry, although by this point often filtered through collective as well as individual memory.

1.6. We Know Less about Jesus Than We Want: What History Remembers

Only a small portion of what we do in our lives is remembered by ourselves, much less by others. (Try to recall, for example, the specific fare for each of your meals over the past three years, assuming that you are not on a highly restricted diet.) Over the course of an average lifetime, one has thousands of conversations, but we recall few of these (perhaps none of them verbatim) and can document even fewer. Historiography is about what we can document or at least reasonably surmise.

That does not mean that we or someone close to us could not write a summary of some events in our lives that we or they consider to be significant. It does mean that what becomes "history" leaves out most events that actually happened.[60] It also means that our records of history inevitably reflect a process of selection in terms of what the sources consider to be *key* or significant events. History is always written from particular perspectives; without some perspectives, we would be left with simply a mass of unsorted data without much narrative cohesiveness, maybe something like *kajc*h8 wdap-d2v %ss-sa5h*. (And those are identifiable symbols only because I am using a Latin font.)

---

58. See Keith, "Prolegomena," 170–71, 179–80.

59. See, e.g., Josephus, *Jewish Antiquities* 20.154.

60. As Tucker, *Knowledge*, 240, observes, we cannot recover most events or motives in the past by historical means.

If the stories that we might report about our own lives are limited, what we could then verify of those stories externally would be much more limited still. This does not mean that such verifiable instances constitute the only incidents that ever happened. When I was working on my 831-page *Historical Jesus of the Gospels*, I emphasized the elements of Jesus's ministry that I believed I could support from multiple sources. That is a useful approach to historical investigation, but it should not a priori exclude the possible veracity of much testimony that one cannot verify externally, as I quickly learned.

At the height of that project, I became so accustomed to seeking secondary corroboration for any claim that when my wife would mention something, I would respond out of habit, "Can you provide evidence for that assertion?" My wife graciously but firmly made clear to me a point that people more prudent than myself ordinarily take for granted: namely, that the testimony of a reliable witness is itself evidence. (My wife's PhD dissertation was in history, but in this case she was also speaking from a more generic sort of everyday realism.)

The nature of historiography precludes the sort of certainty available in, for example, chemistry or mathematics. Most historians, however, do not abandon the historical quest in favor of epistemic nihilism. Even by fairly strict historical standards, we have considerable information. In contrast to many other world religions and traditions birthed before the printing press, the Christian religion has narrative biographies of its founder from within living memory of his ministry. Whatever one makes of their religious value, such narratives have rich historical value.

A generally positive default expectation does not by itself entail the belief that every story or idea in the Gospels was transmitted accurately. Still less would it dispose us to view the reports of Jesus's sayings to be verbatim, since, with a few exceptions such as aphorisms, memory normally preserves the conceptual gist rather than the precise wording. But a generally positive expectation would mean that, in general, the picture we have of Jesus in the Gospels—or at least those elements that we deem to be most reliable—reflects the essential character of the ministry of Jesus as understood by his first followers.

That may be as far as historical method can take us, but it certainly takes us much further than many detractors on a popular level (most conspicuously, the "Jesus mythers") suppose, and probably further than some scholars who accept only the likelihood of multiply attested information suppose.

1.7. My Procedure

Critics often complain about what a book does not treat even when the author(s) clearly delineates the contours of a book's approach. Nevertheless, I reiterate here that this is not a book about the historical Jesus himself, nor a survey of the evidence in the Gospels.[61] It is the latter that ultimately must decide *where* on the spectrum of biographies and where on the spectrum of memories of Jesus the Gospels lie. Examination of the evidence in the Gospels, however, is a well-worn path trodden by Gospels scholars and (usually) beginning students alike.[62]

My objective in this book is not to construct a portrait of the historical Jesus, thereby adding to a surfeit of publications on that subject (including my own), but to contribute to the epistemology of historical-Jesus research. Here I believe that I can contribute some fresh and useful insights on matters in which fewer Gospels scholars are trained. Newer contributions are always nuanced by subsequent scholarship, and I expect that the same will be the case here. Nevertheless, I trust that this work will provide useful foundations for its successors to nuance, just as I have profited from the work of my predecessors (including Richard Burridge and this volume's other dedicatees).

This book addresses both scholars and students interested in Gospels and historical-Jesus research. For the sake of readability, I shall thus remain more concise than in some of my other works. Although my notes cite many sources, the interested reader will often find fuller documentation in my previous works on which this book is partly based.

I began commenting on these subjects in the 1990s,[63] and the studies on which I draw include my articles on this and related subjects,[64] as well as my 800-page *Historical Jesus of the Gospels* (nearly half of which consists of end matter). In more updated form I further draw on some of this material in the 638-page introduction to my four-volume Acts commentary; that commentary cites roughly 45,000 extrabiblical ancient references, as well as more than

---

61. Cf., e.g., Porter, *Criteria*, 17–18, delimiting the aims of his study and excluding a reconstruction of the historical Jesus from his purview.

62. I carefully worked through Aland's synopsis of the Gospels well before entering a doctoral program, but I have few *distinctive* insights to offer in this sphere.

63. Keener, "Gospels as Historically Reliable Biography" (1993); the first edition of Keener, *Matthew* (1999).

64. "Biographies of a Sage"; esp. "Assumptions"; "Otho 1"; "Luke-Acts and Historical Jesus"; "Ancient Biography and Gospels"; "Otho 2"; "Before Biographies"; "Ehrman vs. McIver"; "Weeden's Critique."

10,000 secondary sources (albeit not by any means all related to this subject). Although I repeat some material from both works here, readers will find fuller treatment on those subjects there.

A number of my doctoral students have also been evaluating the historiographic approach of specific ancient biographies.[65] In chapter 11 I will often follow the insights of Michael R. Licona's recent Oxford University Press monograph.[66] At the time of my writing, Helen Bond, at the University of Edinburgh, is elucidating more fully the literary implications of Mark as biography, an approach that may prove more important for literary-theological questions (which I also prioritize in some other contexts) than the historical questions I am asking here.[67] In contrast to an earlier phase of scholarship, many or most scholars now recognize that literary and historical questions are not incompatible,[68] and I happily express in advance my appreciation for Bond's important work.

Most scholars will find this study's most *fundamental* conclusions informative but not earth-shattering: the sort of substance and variation we see in the Gospels is well within the bounds expected in ancient narratives about actual persons and events. Again, where precisely each Gospel lies within those bounds is beyond the limits of this prolegomenon, although at points my own inclinations (based on other factors that this book cannot address) inevitably surface. We scholars sometimes preach to our own choirs, whether addressing more conservative (as sometimes in my case) or more radical audiences. In this book I am trying to address a wider mainstream that welcomes both sorts of audiences in order to establish some features of the ancient evidence that I believe scholars across the range of approaches will find useful. Accordingly, there are some more contentious issues less relevant to my main point that I either leave aside or (as in the case of the "we" material in Acts) treat only cursorily. The larger case does not rest on these omitted or briefly treated issues.

I should add here two notes about language in this book. First, the English language employs the terms "history" and "historical" in multiple ways. These terms can apply to what "actually" happened, to ancient historical reports of what happened, to modern historical reports of what happened, and the like. Since English lacks simple nomenclature to distinguish these concepts

---

65. See Keener and Wright, *Biographies and Jesus.*

66. Licona, *Differences* (2017).

67. See Bond, *Mark*; cf. Bond, "Paragon"; Bond, "Fitting End."

68. See, e.g., McKnight and Malbon, "Introduction," 18; Donahue, "Redaction Criticism," 45–48; Byrskog, "History," 258–59, 283.

(although anything can be rendered more precisely if one is ready to employ cumbersome locutions), I shall normally simply trust my readers' intelligence to distinguish which senses are meant. I believe that context will normally clarify the distinctions sufficiently.[69]

Second, I am committed to inclusive language with reference to modern writers. I usually use masculine pronouns for ancient biographers and biographees only because all extant ancient biographers with whose works I am familiar, and the vast majority of personal subjects in full ancient biographies, were male. Happily, in most parts of the world that cultural situation has changed for the better.[70] But the ancient world did not always share our values.

Third, rather than repeatedly specifying "extant first-century Gospels" on each occasion, I follow the convention of capitalizing these works as "Gospels" to distinguish them from later apocryphal and gnostic works called gospels. Although the extant first-century Gospels coincide with our canonical Gospels, it is their date within living memory (and distinctively biographic genre), rather than their much wider acceptance by second-century Christians, that matters for historiographic purposes. The categories' coinciding is more than coincidence, since later criteria for canonicity required proximity to Jesus and his first apostles. Canonicity, however, is a later question irrelevant to the argument of the book, although some might challenge that point regarding the Fourth Gospel.

Finally, by terms such as "antiquity," Greek, Roman, and Jewish, I usually refer to Mediterranean antiquity and these groups in antiquity, not to antiquity elsewhere or to modern Greeks, Jews, or residents of Rome. Similarly, I refer to *bioi* (βίοι) as ancient biographies, in most contexts using "biography" with reference to ancient, rather than modern, biographic conventions. There are undoubtedly other caveats of nomenclature that will arise over time, but I depend on readers' good sense and familiarity with the conventional language of early twenty-first-century writing in NT studies to judge these.

1.8. Conclusion

For various historical reasons, scholarship in the United States is sometimes more polarized than in European, Australian, and some other contexts.[71] Some scholars, despite claims of liberal open-mindedness or of conservative assur-

---

69. Cf. discussion in Wright, "Response," 246; Le Donne, *Historiographical Jesus*, 33–34.
70. I address the usual ancient situation in Keener, *Acts*, 1:597–638, here esp. 629–37.
71. Cf. the observations of Horsley, "Patterns," 57.

ance of knowledge, refuse to even read or acknowledge the work of those with whom they disagree. More often, more skeptical and more traditional scholars often argue back and forth regarding which side bears the burden of proof.[72] Each side fulfills an important role by raising some challenges that the other should take into account. Both inside and outside the United States, however, most biblical scholars contend that, as a general rule of debate, *whichever* side offers an argument must bear the burden of proof for its argument.[73]

Most academic arguments today involve particular themes, incidents, or sayings. Yet sources themselves can also be deemed generally more or less reliable, so the nature of our sources may itself provide an argument. As British NT scholar Richard Bauckham points out, once we have estimated a particular range of reliability for sources, we should employ them accordingly. In normal historiography, "The whole point of testimony is that it tells us things to which we do not have independent access. We cannot verify, point by point, everything the witness says." It is not gullible to often depend on testimony of sources found to be reliable; critical historians must do so often.[74] Despite difficulties, testimony must play an essential role in historical reconstruction.[75]

We evaluate those sources partly based on how they compare with other available sources. All scholars recognize both a degree of consistency and a degree of flexibility when comparing many Gospel accounts, sometimes more of one or the other depending on the account. To the extent that we find a solid core that is trustworthy where we can test it, it makes sense to expect a similar level of trustworthiness in the core of the material that we cannot test in the source. After all, the writer did not know which pieces of his material would remain available for later examination.

Another factor that should be taken into account, however, is what sort of works the Evangelists were composing. If their goal was pure fiction (a view that scholars rarely suggest, but that is sometimes argued on a popular level),

72. Funk, Hoover, and Jesus Seminar, *Five Gospels*, 5, place the burden of proof on authenticity in any given case, an approach challenged by Rodríguez, "Authenticating Criteria," 154–55. More positively, see Goetz and Blomberg, "Burden of Proof." Most scholars start with a picture of Jesus and then accept only what seems consistent with it, but some reject the subjectivity of this approach (Rodríguez, "Authenticating Criteria," 160–62, 166–68, citing more favorably Allison, *Jesus of Nazareth*, 33, 44–45).

73. See esp. Winter, "Burden of Proof."

74. Bauckham, "Response," 238, esp. following Ricoeur, *Memory*; similarly, see Bauckham, *Eyewitnesses*, 608–13. Bauckham's original training at Cambridge as a historian (Gathercole, "Foreword," xvi) may have spared him some of the eccentricities of some of our sometimes more ingrown NT studies.

75. Nikulin, "Introduction," 23, regarding "collective traumatic memory."

the overlap among their accounts seems difficult to explain. If they wrote mainstream ancient biography, this basic genre has implications, I will argue, for the expected range of both historical information and flexibility in presenting that information. Moreover, their composition within living memory of Jesus suggests that they probably still had significant information available when they wrote.

As we shall see, biographies in the early empire sought to preserve significant information about their subjects. At least with regard to characters from the hundred years or so preceding them, evidence suggests that they generally still had trustworthy sources available for much of their narrative. At the same time, biographers also wrote from various perspectives, with consequently varied emphases, and often exercised the flexibility that they felt they needed to tell coherent stories. Those familiar with Gospel synopses will recognize that the ranges of consistency and flexibility in other biographies from the period resemble the ranges also characteristic of the Gospels.

If we frame expectations for the Gospels according to the conventions of biographies in the early empire, the Synoptics meet these expectations. Their range of variation on points of comparison is neither surprising nor (for those wanting to learn about the historical Jesus) disconcerting, since, as in most parallel passages in the Synoptics (and, in my view, probably also John), ancient biographers sought to use the substance of their sources while feeling free to adapt details. Although approaching the Gospels in this way does not resolve all questions about details, it should offer an opportunity for more rapprochement among scholars of different epistemic persuasions.

Part 1

Biographies about Jesus

It requires little acquaintance with the Gospels to recognize that they are works about Jesus. It also requires little acquaintance with ancient biography to recognize that its most conspicuous feature is that it nearly always focused on its personal subjects. It therefore comes as no surprise that most Gospels scholars today have embraced the view that the Gospels are ancient biographies.

But what does this identification mean, and what, if any, implications does it have for the Gospels as sources for studying the Jesus of history? First (ch. 2), ancient biographies are not novels, although, depending on how one defines "biography," some specimens on the fringe of the genre may overlap. This does not mean that biographies lacked any literary techniques also used by novels; it simply means that biographers writing about recent historical figures were constrained by prior material in a way that very few novelists were. The Gospels are not novels, nor are they the kind of biography that we find in the lives of the poets, for which the more historically oriented writers often had only a few paragraphs of material to work with. (As to whether the Gospels, written within living memory of Jesus, would likely have sufficient information to work with, see chs. 14–16.)

Second (ch. 3), tracing the historical development of biographies in Greek and Greco-Roman antiquity shows that the genre developed in a more historiographic direction by the time of the early Roman Empire. First-century Jewish models in Philo and Josephus, for all their flaws, confirm this direction. Ancient audiences would therefore generally expect significant veridicality, or at least significant dependence on prior reports, in first-century biographic works such as the Gospels.[1]

Third (ch. 4), scholars debate how to classify various ancient biographies and where to assign the Gospels in any such classification scheme. Such pro-

---

1. Because "significant" is a relative term, I explore the ranges of dependence and variation in ancient biographies in parts 2 and 3 of this book.

posed divisions are somewhat subjective, and classification schemes often overlap; different arrangements may be valid for different objectives. Insofar as our interests are historical, however, it is relevant to emphasize that the Gospels are biographies of a recent figure, composed in the early empire, and, like most other full biographies from this period, on the historiographic end of the genre broadly defined (even if on a more popular level than elite historiography).

Fourth (ch. 5), first-century audiences expected adaptations in biographies, lessons suitable for moral instruction, and an emphasis on the character of the biographees. They did not expect anecdotes to appear in actual chronological sequence, apart from (often) the subject's early development and (usually) the events surrounding his death. We should therefore expect ancient biographies to blend, to varying degrees, fidelity to their sources with flexibility in their presentation.

Chapter 2

Not a Novel Proposal

Most Gospels scholars today view the Gospels as belonging to the genre of ancient biography.[1] Both supporters and detractors now recognize this general consensus.[2] As one classicist notes, understanding the Gospels as biographies was "always the obvious reading."[3]

This designation makes good sense: biographies and one kind of historical monograph were the only kinds of works focused on a real, individual historical figure other than a historical novel—and historical novels were rarely

1. See, e.g., Talbert, *Gospel*, throughout; Kennedy, "Source Criticism," 128–34; Cancik, "Gattung"; Dormeyer and Frankemölle, "Evangelium"; Aune, *Environment*, 46–76; Aune, "Biography or Theology"; Aune, *Dictionary*, 204; Stanton, *Preaching*, 117–36; Stanton, *New People*, 63–64; Stanton, *Gospel Truth?*, 137 (reversing his earlier skepticism in Stanton, *Gospels*, 19; Stanton, "Reflection," 544–49); Robbins, *Teacher*, 10; Chance, "Fiction," 128–31; Burridge, *Gospels*, 105–251; Burridge, "People," 121–22; Burridge, "Biography, Ancient"; Burridge, "Genre"; Burridge, "Reading"; Fitzgerald, "Lives"; Dormeyer, "Ewangelie Marka"; Dunn, *Remembered*, 184–85; Dunn, "The Tradition," 173–74; Perkins, *Introduction to Gospels*, 2–11; Powell, *Introduction*, 7–9; Frickenschmidt, *Evangelium*, 351–510; Frickenschmidt, "Evangelium"; Culpepper, *Gospel and Letters*, 65–69, 86; Zuntz, "Heide"; Cross, "Genres," 402–4; Wright, *People*, 384, 390–91, 418; Tuckett, "Jesus and the Gospels"; Witherington, *Mark*, 1–9; Pelling, "Biography, Greek," 242; Balch, "Gospels: Forms," 948; Ehrman, *Introduction*, 62–65; Plümacher, *Geschichte*, 13–14; Allison, *Studies*, 142–47; Jáger, "Evanjelium"; Keener, *Matthew*, 16–24; Keener, *John*, 11–37; Keener, *Historical Jesus*, 73–84; Ytterbrink, *Biography*, 9–10; Smith, "Genre"; Freyne, "Gospel," 65; Bauckham, *Eyewitnesses*, 511; Bauckham, *World*, 96; Aletti, *Birth*; Rogers, "Baptism"; Pitre, *Case*, 67–83, 100–101; Schnabel, *Jesus in Jerusalem*, 4–5; Holladay, "Matthew"; Niebuhr, "Idea," 1; cf. Berschin, "Biography," 653; Crossan, "Necessary," 27. Kee, *Origins*, 144–47, argues that Luke combined Mark with Greco-Roman biography. Note also the response in Burridge, "Review," to the otherwise generally helpful work of Hägg, *Biography*.

2. Fitzgerald, "Lives," 211; Smith, "Genre," 184; Smith, βίος, 20; Burridge, *Gospels*, 253, 271; Walton, "Burridge's Impact"; Black, "Kennedy," 65; Walton, "Gospels," 48, 52–57 (esp. 52–54); Kwon, "Charting," 59, 65; Goh, "Galba," 173; Henderson, "Comparison," 263; Licona, "Viewing," 323; Bird, *Gospel*, 239; Adams, *Genre*, 58; Aletti, *Birth*, 25; Deines, "Jesus and Torah," 4. See now the extensive engagement with the secondary literature in Burridge, "Gospels and Biography."

3. Moles, "Influence," 99.

if ever written about *recent* figures.[4] Biographies normally introduced their main character directly within the first few words of the work (cf. Matt. 1:1; Mark 1:1; John 1:1; more conventionally historiographic in Luke 1:1). Biography is the closest available analogy for how the first audiences would initially approach the narrative, first-century Gospels. Because biographies, like letters, were among antiquity's most common genres, it is not surprising that they represent much of the earliest surviving Christian literature.[5]

That biography offers the closest analogy or genre for the Gospels does not mean that the Evangelists added nothing distinctive to the traditional, wider genre. There is little doubt, in fact, that they did.[6] Like other Jewish biographers with a Diaspora audience, they inhabit a world in continuity with ancient Israel's biblical heritage.[7] Their key protagonist is a mostly rural Middle Eastern figure, and they address a biblically literate subculture. Most distinctive of all, they proclaim no ordinary sage or king but one whom they deem the central figure of history.

Moreover, as subsequent chapters will show, biographies were not all the same; ancient writers often used literary conventions from one genre in another, producing what would appear, in any "purist" classification, an overlap in genres. The most common overlap between biography and another genre in the early empire was with the wider genre to which biography in this period normally belonged, namely historiography (see ch. 6). Even apart from overlap in genres, there are a range of biographic techniques, sometimes even in works by a single author (e.g., Plutarch). Given the distinctive elements of the Gospels and the range of differences in ancient biography, it is important to note at the outset that we cannot use ancient biography to predict or explain everything that we find in the Gospels. Given the fluidity of genre, analogies with works that are similar in many respects need not prove that they are similar in all respects.

Nevertheless, the significant points of analogy do suggest the strong probability that ancient hearers would have approached the Gospels with the expectations with which they approached other contemporary biographies.

---

4. Cf., e.g., Aletti, *Birth*, 9. Against Lucian's *Demonax* as a possible fiction (Clay, "Lucian," 3425–26; cf. De Temmerman, "Formalities," 11), a view based on extreme minimalism, see Beck, "Demonax."

5. Robbins, *Teacher*, 2–3.

6. See helpfully, e.g., Pennington, *Reading Wisely*, 25–35; Shim, "Suggestion," esp. 70–75; cf. Freyne, "Imagination," 10; Freyne, "Gospel," 72; Ytterbrink, *Gospel*, 16, 117, 224–29. The contrasts in Bruggen, *Narratives*, 75, involve *modern* biography.

7. See also, e.g., Dormeyer, "Ewangelie Marka"; cf. Aune, "Biography or Theology"; Aune, "Hellenistic Biography," 9; Telford, *Mark*, 100; Edwards, "Genre," 59.

The Gospels' use of prior material does correlate significantly with that found in the dominant form of biography that flourished in precisely their period, especially in those biographies that, like the Gospels, addressed public figures within living memory (see chs. 9–10). The dominant form of biography from the early empire thus should help us to better understand some of what the Evangelists and their first audiences would have taken for granted.

2.1. Coming Full Circle

By the mid-second century, Christians understood the Gospels as "memoirs of the apostles,"[8] a feature apparently more significant to many Christians of that period than individual attributions of the works' authorship.[9] Thus Justin speaks of "the memoirs communicated by his apostles and organized by those who were involved with them."[10] Although this title "memoirs" (ἀπομνημονεύματα, *apomnēmoneumata*) was used more widely,[11] including for biographic works,[12] some suggest that it recalls Xenophon's *Memoirs* about Socrates,[13] a work that contains some information that we would not consider historical but that most readers in the Evangelists' era presumably did. The title indicates the Christian belief, probably widespread among Christians within living memory of the last first-century Gospel, that the Gospels had biographic interest.[14]

Unfortunately, if used technically, "memoirs" may well underestimate the literary cohesiveness of the finished Gospels. (The technical designation would probably be more relevant to a document such as Q.) Second-century Chris-

---

8. Bockmuehl, *Seeing*, 185, cites Justin, *Dialogue with Trypho* 100.4; 101.3; 102.5; 103.6, 8; 104.1; 105.1, 5, 6; 106.1, 3h, 4; 107.1; *1 Apology* 33.5; 66.3; 67.3; see also Stanton, *New People*, 62–63; Abramowski, "Memoirs"; Edwards, "Genre," 54 (although not viewing this form as biographic).

9. Ehrman may make too much of the lack of early explicit names of Gospel authors, but he is correct that most of the earliest sources except Papias pay little attention to this (Ehrman, *Before Gospels*, 118–24). Most lay Christians today, however, also cite "Jesus" or "the Gospels" rather than a particular Gospel, esp. when their source is one of the Synoptics.

10. Justin, *Dialogue with Trypho* 103.8 (my rough translation).

11. See, e.g., Aragione, "Justin"; Moeser, *Anecdote*, 65–66, citing Theon, *Progymnasmata* 3.5–6, 15–18; Hermogenes, *Progymnasmata* 6.15–17; P.Oxy. 85.

12. Note Plutarch, *Brutus* 13.3, in Moeser, *Anecdote*, 65.

13. Cf. here, e.g., Votaw, "Biographies," 217; Robbins, *Teacher*, 66–67; Edwards, "Genre," 54; Freyne, "Gospel," 65–66.

14. Robbins, *Teacher*, 62–67; Stanton, *New People*, 62–63. See earlier Kennedy, "Source Criticism," 128–30 (cf. 136–41; although in discussion allowing flexible contours for genre; note Fuller, "Classics," 189).

tians often mined the Gospels for information about Jesus without paying as much attention to their more holistic form.[15] Apologetic harmonization dominated many ancient approaches to the Gospels.[16] If ancient Christian commentators often sought to harmonize the Gospels more than respecting the characteristic agendas of each Evangelist, the early twentieth-century emphasis on sources behind the Gospels often obscured their individuality no less.[17]

Still, through most of history, and as late as 1915, readers generally engaged the Gospels as if they were biographies of Jesus. Early twentieth-century scholars such as Johannes Weiss and Claude Votaw viewed the Gospels specifically in light of ancient biography.[18] But as Adela Yarbro Collins points out, Johann Gottfried Herder's proto-Romantic classification of the Gospels as unsophisticated folk literature strongly influenced most form critics, who treated the Gospels as a unique, "new Christian genre."[19]

Rudolf Bultmann further treated the Gospels as nonliterary products of uncontrolled oral transmission, rendering superfluous much interest in literary analogies.[20] One thing they were not, he was confident, was Hellenistic biographies, though he allowed comparison to collections of anecdotes such as the lives of Ahiqar, Aesop, or Apollonius.[21] Lack of biographical interest is why the Gospels "have nothing to say about Jesus' human personality, his appearance and character, his origin, education and development, quite apart from" their lack of literary sophistication.[22]

This dismissal seems premature, since not all biographies contained all these features. Jesus might not have been "educated" at an advanced level, but two of the Gospels do speak at some length about his origin. Early Christians' interest in recalling the ministry of Jesus, including his words and actions, is in fact one of the basic "accepted findings" of an international symposium on relations among the Gospels.[23] Moreover, even if tradents passed on the Gos-

---

15. Frickenschmidt, *Evangelium*, 501, in summarizing his history of research on 3–76.

16. Frickenschmidt, *Evangelium*, 501; note Wiles, *Gospel*, 14 (cf. 16–19).

17. See Frickenschmidt, *Evangelium*, 3–5, 16, 21, 501.

18. See Weiss, *Evangelium*, 11, 15 (comparing Plutarch; as cited in Collins, *Mark*, 22, 24); Votaw, "Biographies."

19. Collins, *Mark*, 19. See Schmidt, "Stellung"; followed also by Kümmel, *Introduction*, 37; discussion in Burridge, *Gospels*, 7–16. Some circles also perverted Romanticist interest in the Volk in sinister ways; see Heschel, *Aryan Jesus*, 29, 31. Frickenschmidt, *Evangelium*, 508, attributes this loss of focus on historical matters to theological agendas on a prenarrative kerygma.

20. Note criticisms in Byrskog, "Century," 5; Kwon, "Charting," 63–64.

21. Bultmann, *Tradition*, 371–72.

22. Bultmann, *Tradition*, 372.

23. Wansbrough, "Introduction," 12.

pels' oral sources in such a folk milieu (see discussion in chs. 15–16), forced categories such as literary and nonliterary prove unhelpful for genre criticism of the Gospels: they ignore the continuum between "folk literature" and the more stylish rhetoric and texts that strongly influenced them,[24] as well as differences among the Gospels themselves. (Luke writes on a much more sophisticated Greek level than Mark.)[25] "Biographies" in the general sense actually appear throughout the continuum.[26]

Because the Gospels differ significantly from modern biographies, scholars for much of the twentieth century denied that the Gospels were biographies at all.[27] Yet the features that form critics deemed necessary for true biographies are lacking not only in Mark but in Lucian's *Demonax*, which is specifically titled a *bios* and is a full work like the Gospels.[28]

The understandable form-critical focus on smaller narrative units inadvertently distracted attention from questions of the genre of the larger works. Critics were correct to notice that the Gospels are not modern biographies; they erred only in concluding that this meant that they were not ancient ones. In more recent decades scholars have been returning to the consensus that the Gospels represent biographies in the ancient sense of the term.

In 1977 Charles Talbert was one of the first scholars to challenge the mid-twentieth-century approach and to point to parallels with ancient biographies.[29] Although his approach has been somewhat justly evaluated as too rigid,[30] it broke essential ground for the works that followed.[31] Philip Shuler's 1982 work[32] displayed some more significant weaknesses,[33] but it was still a step toward proper comparison of the Gospels with other ancient biographies.

After an extensive survey of biographic works, Klaus Berger concluded in 1984 that the Gospels were biographies, related to the genre of enco-

24. Downing, "Literature"; Aune, *Environment*, 12, 63; Burridge, *Gospels*, 11, 153. Rhetorical principles influenced narrative techniques; see, e.g., Dowden, "Apuleius."

25. Koester, *Introduction*, 1:108; Kodell, *Luke*, 23; cf. Perry, *Sources*, 7. This estimation becomes even clearer in view of Luke's architectonic patterns (for which, see Goulder, *Type*; Talbert, *Patterns*; Talbert, *Luke*; Tannehill, *Luke*; Tannehill, *Acts*).

26. E.g., contrast the popular "Life of Aesop" with the more literary *Agricola*.

27. See Talbert, *Gospel*, 2–3; Stanton, *Gospels*, 15–17.

28. Burridge, *Gospels*, 93, following Cancik, "Bios."

29. Talbert, *Gospel*.

30. Aune, "Problem"; Burridge, *Gospels*, 81–82.

31. Burridge, *Gospels*, 81, credits him "for the paradigm shift away from form-critical notions of the gospels' uniqueness."

32. Shuler, *Genre*.

33. See Burridge, *Gospels*, 83–86.

mium.[34] Berger's student Dirk Frickenschmidt later developed his approach further, documenting extensive literary resemblances between ancient biographies and the Gospels[35] and ultimately making a case similar to Richard Burridge's conclusions about Gospel genre.[36]

Some of Frickenschmidt's points of contact include the following, although not all these features are limited to biography or appear in all biographies:[37]

- The three-part structure of full biographies
- Comparison (*synkrisis*) of figures within the narratives
- The importance of the subject's first significant public appearance, signaling the transition from the beginning to the middle part of the biography
- The relatively high frequency of focus on the subject's death, with some recurring topics
- The frequent prefiguring of the final section in the middle section, including indications of the person's coming violent death
- The frequency of conflicts and intrigues against the subject
- Emphasis on the subject's final words
- The narrative's slowing down to depict in greater detail the subject's final days and hours.

Richard Burridge, working from a background in classics, was originally skeptical of the biography hypothesis for the genre of the Gospels, but his detailed research changed his mind.[38] It was his resulting forceful Cambridge monograph[39] that largely effected the paradigm shift in Gospels studies.[40] He shows how both the Synoptics and John fit this genre.[41]

---

34. Berger, "Gattungen," using a very wide definition of biography.

35. Note esp. Frickenschmidt, *Evangelium*, 504–5.

36. As Burridge, *Gospels*, 285–86, notes, citing Frickenschmidt, *Evangelium*, 65–68.

37. See esp. the summary on Frickenschmidt, *Evangelium*, 505–6. For independent lists of rubrics covered in many biographies, see Martin, "Topic Lists," 21–23; Sollenberger, "Lives of Peripatetics," esp. 3800 (discussion in Smith, βίος, 73–74).

38. Burridge, *Gospels*, 101, 283.

39. Burridge, *Comparison*; revised as *Gospels*. For criteria for genre, see Burridge, *Comparison*, 109–27 (*Gospels*, 105–23); for pre-Christian Greco-Roman biographies, 128–53 (*Gospels*, 124–49); for later ones, 154–90 (*Gospels*, 150–84). For further helpful nuancing of his work on genre in light of more recent studies, see Shively, "Recognizing"; Shively, "Penguins."

40. Although the soil had become somewhat ripe for this transition; see the survey of approaches in ch. 4.

41. Burridge, *Gospels*, 185–212 on the Synoptics, and 213–32 on John.

Graham Stanton of Cambridge thus came to regard as "surprisingly inaccurate" the skepticism of earlier decades about the Gospels being biographies.[42] Indeed, Burridge's argument has proven so compelling that one reviewer claims that it ought to end any further dissent about the matter.[43] Some of those who remain skeptical of the *bios* hypothesis focus on features of biographic material more generally rather than the *bios* genre specifically, significantly weakening the force of their critique.[44] Arguments concerning the biographical character of the Gospels have thus come full circle: the Gospels, long viewed as biographies of some sort until the early twentieth century, now are widely viewed as biographies again.

2.2. Implications for Historical Information

Although classicists approach ancient historical biographies critically, most of them do not handle them as dismissively as some of the more skeptical NT scholars have handled the information in the Gospels. Certainly they do not handle biographies about recent historical figures the way that Jesus-mythicists handle the Gospels. Although Tacitus denounces Tiberius whereas Velleius Paterculus adores him, no one doubts that both provide valuable information for us about Tiberius. Nor, because Tacitus eulogizes his father-in-law, Agricola, or Suetonius emphasizes moral lessons in his biographies, do we dismiss most of the evidence that they provide.[45]

The boundaries of genres are malleable, and scholars can classify ancient biographies in various ways. The broadest definitions of biography encompass all works about historical persons. Because my specified interest in this book is the historical dimension of biographies, my interest is primarily in information-based biographies. This was by far the dominant form of person-centered work in this period (see ch. 3). In the period in which the Gospels were written, mainstream biography was understood as a narrative about a real individual based on available information, and in cases of recent figures, the information available could be substantial.

---

42. Stanton, *New People*, 63; Stanton, *Gospel Truth?*, 137, reversing his own earlier skepticism in Stanton, *Gospels*, 19.

43. Talbert, "Review," 715; cf. also Stanton, *New People*, 64; Walton, "Burridge's Impact."

44. Burridge, *Gospels*, 265–66, challenging the argument.

45. I owe the insights in this paragraph to James R. Harrison, now research director at Sydney College of Divinity and an honorary associate of the Macquarie Ancient History Department, personal correspondence, May 26, 2011. See also Boterman, "Heidenapostel," 64, 73 (as cited in Schnabel, *Jesus in Jerusalem*, 4); Nobbs, "Historians."

Historical novels then, as today, exploited the form, frequently tongue-in-cheek, yet most such novels were much more for entertainment than for information about a past important person or that person's actual teachings.[46] Entertaining novels would make a poor vehicle for a movement such as the first-century Jesus movement, which was above all intensely interested in its founder, especially given his followers' repeatedly emphasized commitment to him as Lord and thus commitment to follow his teachings. (His role as teacher is among the least disputed features of the Jesus tradition today.) Moral instruction is far more characteristic of biographies of teachers than of novels (see ch. 5), though there are some rare exceptions. Within living memory, followers of Jesus still had access to information about him and would not need to resort to the sorts of expedients that later novelists and gnostics used to satisfy curiosity about Jesus (see chs. 14–16).

As noted in the introduction, surprisingly few scholars so far have worked to develop the implications of the Gospels' genre for the question of how we approach the Gospels for historical information about Jesus.[47] In fact, one of my own doctoral professors suggested in our opening class on Mark that ancient biographies were fictitious and therefore Mark should be approached accordingly. (When I cautiously challenged his assumption, since I had already begun studying some ancient biographies, the professor humbly acknowledged that he lacked firsthand knowledge about the subject and had simply read that view somewhere.)

The Gospels are literary works in their own right and may be approached as such; I have spent more years publishing commentaries than publishing on historical-Jesus research. I readily acknowledge that it is not necessary for everyone to be interested in historical questions. For those who do have such interest, however, the Gospels provide our best source for learning about the ministry of the historical Jesus. Biographies normally *are* meant to tell us something about their subject and not only about their author.

---

46. As noted in Pervo, "Introduction," 3; Pervo, "Losers," 129–35 (cf. Horsfall, "Ephemeris"), novelistic accounts of Dares and Dictys exploit traditional markers of historical narratives (though Pervo emphasizes their use in fiction), misleading subsequent readers (though not necessarily their contemporaries).

47. Indeed, several noted historical-Jesus scholars display fairly little awareness of Gospel scholars' research, even while mining the Gospels selectively for information supporting their a priori hypotheses.

2.3. What Were Ancient Biographies?

The term "genre" refers to a work's literary type. Genre provides a broader (though sometimes somewhat amorphous) category that allows comparison with other works that share a number of key characteristics. Particular genres are not universal; rather, they highlight the culturally conditioned, conventional expectations according to which a work's implied author could expect the work to be read.[48]

Genres are useful for classifying similar works; they are not templates to which writers must adhere. That is, they are descriptive rather than prescriptive, an observation that immediately limits the degree to which we can project our expectations onto a given work, including any of the Gospels.

Nevertheless, ancient prose is not simply "mapless terrain";[49] the complication is just that the map's regions lack rigid boundaries, and scholars are thus sometimes understandably reticent to draw fixed maps. Just as we may infer likely reasons for ancient actions based on ancient customs or ideologies, we may infer as more probable some conscious or unconcious literary conventions when we observe in some similar works traits that tend to be characteristic of each.

Genre is by no means an exclusively modern conception. Not only did ancient readers recognize various genre categories;[50] they were, as classicist Christopher Pelling notes, "peculiarly sensitive to genre."[51] Indeed, ancient critics were sometimes *too* precise about such categories, detailing specific genres of letters and speeches more strictly than the empirical examples allow.[52] Still, others recognized that genres could develop, often through mixing,[53] and authors in prac-

---

48. Cf. Dubrow, *Genre*, 2–3, 31–34, 95; Shuler, *Genre*, 25–28; Hirsch, *Interpretation*, 68–126; Smith, "Genre," 215; Adams, *Genre*, 1; Konstan and Walsh, "Biography," 42; Kirk, "Collective Memory," 60.

49. Cf. Smith and Kostopoulos, "Biography," 397, 400, 410, using the language of Hägg, *Biography*, xi.

50. E.g., Theon, *Progymnasmata* 2.5–33 (Butts); Quintilian, *Orator's Education* 10.1.36; Maximus of Tyre, *Philosophical Orations* 26.4; 38.4; cf. Houston, "Evidence," 243 (noting flexibility on 244, 246); Race, "Introduction," 1. Of various models for genre criticism in antiquity (see Dubrow, *Genre*, 45–81; Adams, *Genre*, 26–57), Aristotle's (cf. Adams, *Genre*, 27–31) prevailed longest (Burridge, *Gospels*, 26–28).

51. Pelling, *Texts*, 2; see also Pelling, "Epilogue"; Pelling, "Bounds," 256.

52. See, e.g., examples in Malherbe, "Theorists"; Aune, *Dictionary*, 419.

53. Adams, *Genre*, 43, 53, citing, e.g., Horace.

tice often mixed them.[54] Genre categories are thus fluid and may overlap[55] (for biography and history, see esp. ch. 6).

Nevertheless, genres are not usually simply arbitrary.[56] Ancient writers could adapt them as needed, but genre conventions provided the social expectations that they could take for granted, tweak, or flaunt. So we may speak of works falling roughly into categories, or perhaps more organically, using genre prototypes heuristically, of some works resembling many other works in particular respects. Although there are a range of different sorts of prose works, more of them cluster in particular areas than others.

So what is the definition of ancient biography? The answer might be simple—if scholars could agree on it. In 1915 Clyde Votaw defined as biography "any writing which aims to make one acquainted with a historical person by giving some account of his deeds and words, sketchily chosen and arranged."[57] More recent and more frequently cited, Arnaldo Momigliano defined it as "an account of the life of a man from birth to death."[58] Others point to exceptions to Momigliano's definition[59] or complain that Momigliano's interest is biographic material or roots more generally rather than the specific, formal genre of biography as it developed by the early empire.[60] Talbert defines ancient biography as "prose narration about a person's life, presenting supposedly historical facts which are selected to reveal the character or essence of the individual, often with the purpose of affecting the behavior of the reader."[61] Geiger prefers a narrower definition, suggesting that "works belonging to associated literary genres, such as Isocrates' *Euagoras* and Xenophon's *Agesilaus*, as well as his *Cyropaedeia*," do not function as biographies per se.[62]

Frickenschmidt looks for persistent characteristics of biographies, such as the centrality of "authoritative people and decisive values," precharacterization of the biographee in the work's beginning, and full narrative treatment

54. Adams, *Genre*, 55–57, 67; Aune, *Dictionary*, 419; Shively, "Penguins"; Becker, *Birth*, 72, citing for literary innovation esp. Velleius Paterculus, *History* 2.9; Horace, *Epistle* 2.1.

55. With, e.g., Dubrow, *Genre*, 37, 106; Aune, *Environment*, 23; Smith, "Genre," 186–87; Smith, βίος, 28; Buster, "Genre," 153; Shively, "Penguins," 282, noting Frow, *Genre*; Newsom, "Spying."

56. Although genre categories cannot be applied rigidly, wholesale deconstructionist dismissals of their value are also misplaced; see Eddy and Boyd, *Legend*, 318–20.

57. Votaw, "Biographies," 49. Cf. focus on a person in Shively, "Penguins," 283.

58. Momigliano, *Development*, 11.

59. Adams, *Genre*, 70.

60. Geiger, *Nepos*, 14–15.

61. Talbert, *Gospel*, 17, helpfully; note his contrast between biography and historiography, on the one hand, and biography and novels, on the other (16–17).

62. Geiger, *Nepos*, 15.

with more attention to detail where relevant.[63] Like others, he distinguishes biography from historiography and encomium in some respects.[64] Biography was like the "mirror of history."[65]

One might consider biography more generally a narrative about a particular real person's life or phase in that person's life. As we shall see briefly in chapter 6 and at length in chapter 10, authors of full biographies in the early empire *did* have significant historical intention and, when addressing recent figures, normally had considerable information available. We should expect this pattern to hold true for the Gospels as well, since the Gospels and their sources circulated within living memory of Jesus's public ministry. Ancient biographers and historians viewed historical intention as fully compatible with edifying agendas.

2.4. A Unique Genre?

Before considering the implications of the biographic genre for the Gospels, however, we must examine other proposals for their genre. As noted earlier, the Gospels demonstrate special features that render them distinct in some ways from most other ancient biographies.[66] This observation limits the predictions that we can safely make on the basis of the wider genre classification, but it does not preclude estimations entirely, given the other features shared with ancient biography. Any subtype or variation of ancient biography (such as works about Jesus) might have features distinctive to that subtype.

Some scholars, however, focusing on the distinctive features, argue that the Gospels are simply "unique," or sui generis.[67] Once Gospels began to be written, they did constitute their own subgenre. The specific title "Gospel" is attested by the mid-second century[68] and probably earlier;[69] it echoes the LXX

---

63. Frickenschmidt, *Evangelium*, 211 (cf. 217, 224), 227, 238.

64. Frickenschmidt, *Evangelium*, 233–37, citing, e.g., Plutarch, *Alexander* 1; *Aemilius Paulus* 1; *Nicias* 1; *Cimon* 2.

65. Plutarch, *Aemilius Paulus* 1, in Frickenschmidt, *Evangelium*, 234.

66. Again, see, e.g., Pennington, *Reading Wisely*, 25–35.

67. E.g., Riesenfeld, *Tradition*, 2; Guelich, "Genre." For the distinctiveness of the Gospels more helpfully and less rigidly, see Pennington, *Reading Wisely*, 25–35.

68. Aune, *Environment*, 18, citing e.g., Justin, *Dialogue with Trypho* 10.2; 100.1; cf. *1 Apology* 66; see also, e.g., Papias, frag. 3.14; 6.2; 19.1; 20.1; 21.1; Irenaeus, *Against Heresies* 1.20.2; Diogn. 11.6; perhaps already Did. 8.2; 11.3; 15.3–4.

69. Bauckham, *Eyewitnesses*, 537–38, noting esp. Kelhoffer, "Book."

(see esp. Isa 52:7)[70] and might originate from Mark 1:1.[71] But with what larger category would their first audiences have classed them?

Since no one before Jesus's ministry had written stories about Jesus, or probably about anyone very much like him, the Gospels are unique in a sense. As one classicist puts it, "Mark could not have written a conventional life of such an unconventional figure as Jesus."[72] This difference, however, stems from the distinctiveness of the Gospels' chief character; as Maria Ytterbrink suggests, more likely than "a different kind of biography," a Gospel is "a biography about a different [kind of] character."[73]

Thus while the observation that the Gospels are unique is true in some sense, it is not very helpful for facilitating heuristic analogies. The main point of genre classification is finding a broader, culturally intelligible category that generates audience expectations concerning how to understand a given work.[74] For ancient audiences, a source-grounded work about a particular actual person—whether a ruler, a general, or a sage—remained a biography. As Ulrich Luz comments, an ancient reader encountering a scroll of Mark without prior knowledge would engage it as a *bios*.[75] Or as Eve-Marie Becker points out, the Gospels may be sui generis among other historical works, but they remain historical works.[76] Bart Ehrman rightly notes that the Gospels' shared, distinctive subgenre does not diminish the larger biographic genre in which a reader would naturally place them.[77]

2.5. Hysterical History or Knowledgeable Novels?

Among recognized ancient prose narrative genres, the only real alternatives to biography as a category for the Gospels would be historical monographs or

---

70. Stuhlmacher, "Theme," 19–25; Betz, "Gospel."

71. E.g., Kelber, *Story*, 15; Collins, *Mark*, 3. Some suggest Matthew (cf. Stanton, *New People*, 14–16), but cf. Marxsen, *Mark*, 25, 150n106, 205–6.

72. Edwards, "Genre," 60.

73. Ytterbrink, *Gospel*, 227.

74. Genres function as both cultural and cognitive schemas (with, e.g., Kirk, *Memory*, 219–20; cf. also 7, citing Zimmermann, "Gleichnisse," 108); an individual work's "uniqueness" precludes the comparative activity implied in discussion of genre with respect to whatever aspects are unique. For their role in tradition formation, see Zimmermann, "Gleichnisse," 109 (cited in Kirk, *Memory*, 64, 78, 220).

75. Luz, *Matthew*, 1:44–45.

76. Becker, *Birth*, 71.

77. Ehrman, *Introduction*, 64–65.

novels.[78] I defer discussion of historical monographs for chapter 6, since this proposal ultimately overlaps with biography and leads to similar conclusions about the Gospels' merit as historical sources.

Here, however, I address the question of the Gospels as novels. Of course, ancient novels are useful for literary comparisons with the Gospels, as many studies helpfully illustrate,[79] but we find these similarities because both biographies and novels reflect the larger genre of narrative. Similar narrative traits thus appear also in histories.[80] Identifying shared literary techniques, then, does not necessarily indicate a work's genre or the degree of historical information available in it.[81] (Nor, for the record, am I implying any hostility toward novels; if I had time, I would gladly write some. I am simply distinguishing genres.) The Gospels, especially Mark, are on a more popular level than elite historiography and in this respect are more like novels,[82] yet also again like many biographies.[83]

---

78. Cf. the polemical *Apocriticus* 2.12–15 (possibly from Porphyry); Mack, *Myth*, 11, 322–23; cf. the comparison in Tolbert, *Sowing*, 48–79; for the debate historically, see Cook, *Interpretation*, 14, 26–27, 336–37. One can speak of dramatic *modes* in a range of genres (Brant, "Drama," 87, 90), but the prose character of the Gospels rules out excessive analogies with ancient drama in the sense of plays (see Aristotle, *Poetics* 6.9, 1450a). Although intriguing, the wide net for parallels for Gospel narratives in Heever, "Tales" (including apocalyptic narratives [191], second-century cases of fraud [185], and a wide range of New Religious Movements [181]), requires qualification. Ron Hubbard was a science fiction writer before he inaugurated Scientology (181), a setting quite different from Jesus and his earliest movement. Moreover, why compare only *religious* figures, which could imply that stories from religious movements are invariably more fictionalized than political or literary or philosophic movements? And if one compares religious figures, why compare what most observers consider the deliberate fictionalizing of Hubbard and not, say, religious figures such as John Bunyan or Catherine Booth, about whom we have solid historical information? For ancient contexts, cf. Keener, "Parallel Figures."

79. As in, e.g., Fullmer, *Resurrection*, 15–26; Starner, *Kingdom*; for Acts, e.g., Chance, "Prognostications."

80. See Burridge, *Gospels*, 238–39; Aune, *Dictionary*, 285; Porter, "We Passages," 550–52; Marguerat, *Historian*, 29; Soards, "Review," 309; cf. Rothschild, *Rhetoric*, 291–92.

81. E.g., Roman historiography borrows some style details from Roman epics (Rebenich, "Prose," 312).

82. Cf. (regarding Acts) the remarks of Smith, "Understand," 49–50; Keener, *Acts*, 1:63, 65, 72, 89. The primary readership of novels, however, was people who were literate, leisured, and well-to-do enough to afford them (see Bowie, "Readership," 452–53; Stephens, "Who Read Novels?" 415).

83. Many of the biographies noted below are on roughly the same reading level as novels, though, like novels (see the note above) and unlike the Gospels, most of the surviving ones are written for the elite.

In distinguishing ancient biographies from novels, I am not contending that ancient biographies were written according to modern historical standards. Such a claim would be unreasonable, in effect evaluating ancient works by a standard that did not exist in their day. Even the best of ancient biographies by modern standards are more slanted and adaptive than historians today would formally permit (see chs. 7, 10, and 11). Nor do I claim that typical ancient biographies followed all the principles of the best (by our standards) ancient historians, though I will argue for a relationship between mainstream ancient biography and historiography.

But mainstream biographies were vastly more historical than their primary alternative. If we compare them with ancient novels, another genre from the Gospels' own milieu, they share narrative form but differ in their use of sources. On occasion a novel could recycle an earlier story line (compare, e.g., Apuleius's *Metamorphoses* with the story line also found in Lucian's *Lucius*). But the novelistic genre did not need to recount factual events, whereas the inclusion of factual events was part of what readers of biographies expected (or at least expected biographers to attempt), whatever the authors' adaptations. Both genres were meant to entertain or engage readers, but prior information was a mandatory element only in biography.

Occasionally a scholar does suggest that the Gospels are most like novels, although they usually must concede points at which they cannot fit.[84] But while scholars vary in their estimates of the degree of prior information in the Gospels, virtually all find more information there than is found in novels.[85] On the usual reconstruction of Gospel sources, Matthew and Luke clearly depend heavily on prior information (at least Mark and Q), and source-dependent Matthew and Luke, who undoubtedly knew the circumstances of Mark's writing better than we do, would use these sources for information only if they believed that these sources likewise depended on prior information.

---

84. Burridge, *Gospels*, 282–84, cites Vines, *Problem*, noting that Vines devotes only sixteen pages to Jewish novels, where he believes he finds the most significant genre parallels, and observing Vines's ultimate admission that the anecdotal, episodic approach of Mark does not fit the novels. Again, this complaint does not reduce the value of literary comparisons, and for more useful comparisons with Gospels in terms of their generally popular level, Burridge, *Gospels*, 92, cites Tolbert, *Sowing*, 59–79; Reiser, "Alexanderroman."

85. See my fuller discussion regarding Luke's work in *Acts*, 62–83.

2.5a. A Romantic Jesus?

Most ancient novels were not exclusively about a single individual; most frequently they were romances about two lovers,[86] which the Gospels' depictions of Jesus conspicuously are not. Moreover, novels usually focused on fictitious characters, which Jesus was not.[87] Even the later Christian apocryphal acts, which feature significantly earlier Christian figures, work to accommodate this romantic pattern (except within a framework of chastity),[88] but we see nothing of this interest in the earlier, canonical Gospels and Acts.

Romance novels appear at least as early as 100 BCE with the Ninus romance,[89] but many see Chariton's *Callirhoe* as the seminal romance that influenced its successors.[90] Although we know of *no* historical novels about *recent* historical figures, a minority of ancient novels did exist about figures of the distant past.[91] (Pure mythography normally addressed the even more remote past.)[92] Even these novels did not feel very constrained by actual historical information, and they did little research into the setting—particularly a setting as obscure and irrelevant to cosmopolitan audiences as rural Galilee.[93]

---

86. See, e.g., Fusillo, "Novel," 838–39; Konstan, "*Apollonius* and Novel," 173; Konstan, *Symmetry*; Konstan, "Subjectivity"; possibly Burrus, "Desiring." Cf. the German *Roman*, meaning "novel," albeit without "romantic" connotations.

87. Rather than expending space to defend this relatively noncontroversial point, I refer again to Ehrman, *Did Jesus Exist?* The questions that extreme skeptics raise about Jesus could be raised even more easily about many other ancient figures; see, e.g., De Temmerman, "Formalities," 11; esp. Beck, "Demonax," 80–82.

88. One may compare works such as the Acts of Paul and Thecla or Acts of John 53–64, 73–80, where elements of the romance story line are followed, except that the women become devotees of the male teacher in chastity, devoted not to sexual love but to God's word. See Hofmann, "Novels: Christian," 847–48; Eddy and Boyd, *Legend*, 338–39; cf. Aubin, "Reversing Romance," 260–62 (noting the subversion of conventional gender assumptions); Thomas, "Fluidity," 277. Later, see Gray, "Monk," 120, 127, citing Jerome *Vita Malchi* ch. 10.

89. Momigliano, *Development*, 55.

90. See Tilg, *Chariton*; but cf. Smith and Temmerman, "Ideal."

91. Besides the biographically shaped novels below, see also the Trojan accounts in Merkle, "True Story," 183–84; Schmeling, "Spectrum," 23; more extensively, Pervo, "Losers" (though noting that subsequent readers treated these stories as true). The degree of fictionalizing (or epicizing) of historic events such as we find in Lucan, *Civil War* (see, e.g., Chiu, "Importance"), is largely limited to poetry (cf. Fantuzzi, "Historical Epic").

92. Polybius, *Histories* 34.4.1–3 suggests that the *Odyssey* mixed history and myth; see ch. 9 for the contrast between history and myth.

93. See, e.g., Morgan, "Fiction," 554; Wiersma, "Novel"; Konstan, "Invention," 5–6; cf. also Tob 1:2–4; Jdt 1:1, 7; Droge, "Anonymously," 515.

2.5b. Novelistic Biographies or Historical Novels?

A range of different works, including the rare novels just noted, are sometimes classified today as biography.[94] Yet mainstream biographers from the Gospels' era claimed to, and presumably generally attempted to, report historically accurate information; they were not trying to fabricate fairy tales.[95]

In contrast to the dominant form of biographies in the early empire, some novels in antiquity did subvert the biographic genre for fiction. Unlike completely self-referential fiction, they do make note of at least some extratextual characters who existed, such as Aesop, Alexander, or Apollonius.[96] Whether we call them novelistic biographies or historical novels may be partly a semantic matter of preferred nomenclature, but they certainly differ significantly from mainstream biographies and histories.[97]

If we include some ancient historical novels in the genre of ancient biographies, then insofar as we wish to examine biographies as sources for historical reconstruction, we must divide biography into at least two subgenres: those that are novelistic in intent, and those primarily historical in intent. While one might find elements of history in the former and elements of fiction in the latter, most full-length works about individuals in our period fall comfortably into one category or the other, rather than in a supposedly heavily populated border between them. Works such as Ps.-Callisthenes's *Alexander Romance*, on the genre's margins, differ starkly from a Suetonius or Luke, who show extensive dependence on sources (see my chs. 7–8).

One competent NT scholar, writing before recent discussions of biography, suggested "four examples . . . which very clearly illustrate the prevalence of fiction in narrative accounts of historical subjects"[98]—but *all four* of his chief examples were novels: the Ninus romance, Xenophon's *Cyropaedia*, Phi-

---

94. See, e.g., Barr and Wentling, "Biography," 81–88; Pelling, "Biography: Greek," 241. Bowersock's examples of fictitionalized history (*Fiction*, 21) are also distinctly novelistic.

95. Pitre, *Case*, 77–78, cites Josephus, *Life* 336–39; Lucian, *Demonax* 1.

96. De Temmerman, "Formalities," 7–10. Pervo, "Losers," 135–36, is probably right to doubt that such authors (in his case, Dares and Dictys) intended to deceive, and is certainly right to note that many later readers were deceived; he suspects that they could have known that some would construe their stories literally, but rightly prescinds from certainty about their motives. Nevertheless, external tests show them fictitious (in contrast to, say, Acts; see Talbert, *Mediterranean Milieu*, 201–8; Keener, *Acts*, 1:166–57).

97. Kennedy, "Source Criticism," 139, cites Plutarch and Suetonius (both from the early empire) as the prime examples of biography; these are a far cry from *Life of Aesop* or Ps.-Callisthenes.

98. Chance, "Fiction," 136–41.

lostratus's *Life of Apollonius*, and Ps.-Callisthenes's *Alexander Romance*. None were written within living memory of their subjects. The scholar cites these examples to illustrate "just how unclear the line was between fact and fiction in narratives about historical persons."[99] I believe, however, that these very examples demonstrate the opposite conclusion. The line is so unclear, I would contend, only because it is drawn in the wrong place. Suetonius's lives exhibit historiographic intention in a way that Ps.-Callisthenes plainly does not.

Ancient historiography exercised some creative freedoms, but as Christopher Pelling notes, these were not the novelist's freedom "to make it all up."[100] For centuries before the period of the empire, historians had defined their activity as "getting the record straight" over against the claims of myth.[101] Likewise, while some biographers and historians were less accurate than others, this concession does not entail "that no distinctions were made between historians who used good sources and others who made their material up."[102] When biography involved deliberate falsification of events (as opposed to creative retelling of sources), it departed from the expected conventions of its genre (see ch. 6).

Of the three extant historical novels most often classified as biographies,[103] one is from long before the period of the canonical Gospels, and two are from long afterward, from the heyday of novels.[104] None derive from the period of the canonical Gospels, the early imperial period, when ancient biography was achieving its historiographic apex. In fact, because we know of no works that

99. Chance, "Fiction," 141. Cf. Almagor, "Narratives," 78 on the "very thin line between fictionality used to arrive at historical truth (used by historians) and fiction employed for its own sake."

100. Pelling, *Texts*, 9.

101. Fowler, "History," 196. Fowler acknowledges that this ancient distinction, while significant, can be overdrawn (196–97).

102. Bauckham, "Response," 247–48.

103. For some other ancient historical novels, see, e.g., Lindenberger, "Ahiqar"; and, not biographic but exploiting in conspicuous fiction the historiographic convention of eyewitnesses, Merkle, "True Story," 183–84; Schmeling, "Spectrum," 23; Ní-Mheallaigh, "Pseudo-Documentarism"; Ní-Mheallaigh, *Fiction*, xi. Earlier Jewish novels include Tobit (cf. Rost, *Judaism*, 63; Doran, "Narrative Literature," 296–99) and Judith (cf. Nickelsburg, *Literature*, 106; Baslez, "Polémique"; Gray, *Letters*, 11–12); closer to the model of Hellenistic romance (cf., e.g., West, "Joseph and Asenath"; Doran, "Narrative Literature," 290–91) is Joseph and Aseneth, though this work might include some motifs from Christian sources (cf. discussion in Keener, *Acts*, 2:1608).

104. Cf. Frickenschmidt, *Evangelium*, 188–90, classing together in one period *Alexander Romance*, Iamblichus's *Pythagorean Life*, and Philostratus's *Life of Apollonius*.

followed the model of Xenophon's *Cyropaedia* in this period, and because the *Cyropaedia* was anomalous in its day[105] (perhaps a protohistorical novel), one might even be tempted to argue that biographically shaped novels did not yet exist in the period of the Gospels. Since arguments from silence are precarious, and there may well be some specimens that have generated less attention, it might be safest to say that, in contrast to biographies, which were common in the early empire, biographic novels were at best unusual. It appears that such novels did not yet exist *as a genre*: novels and other fictitious works existed, and they could exploit historical features, but there does not yet seem to be a widespread fashion of producing novels about historical characters.

The three most prominent novelistic biographies, or historical novels, are Xenophon's *Cyropaedia*, Ps.-Callisthenes's *Alexander Romance*, and Philostratus's *Life of Apollonius*. Interestingly, the size of these works also distinguishes them from virtually all ancient extant ancient biographies,[106] though the size also differs from typical ancient novels. Probably the later ones, especially the *Alexander Romance*, are better classified as ancient historical novels (with the *Cyropaedia* as something like a forerunner of the genre).[107]

In contrast to the Gospels, all of the above-named historical novels were composed long after living memory of their subjects (i.e., long after anyone who knew the eyewitnesses had died). Moreover, scenes in these novels tend to be fleshed out with far more copious details than is possible in the anecdotes and often barer focus on events of many biographies (including the Synoptics). Mere use of historical characters is a far cry from historical research or the use of sources (such as the use, on the majority view, by Matthew and Luke of Mark and Q in their Gospels).

2.5c. *The* Cyropaedia, Life of Apollonius, *and* Alexander Romance

Some modern scholars treat Xenophon's *Cyropaedia* as a biography because it teaches virtues,[108] but Xenophon wrote before such genre distinctions were more clearly delineated. Unlike Xenophon's *Agesilaus* or *Memorabilia*, the *Cyropaedia* never became a typical model for biography in the later sense.

---

105. Smith and Kostopoulos, "Biography," 396, call it "impossible-to-classify," referring to Gera, *Cyropaedia*, 1.

106. Note the offhanded observations in Hägg, *Biography*, 7, 320–21, though Hägg classes them loosely as biographic; but cf. 197–98 for Nicolaus's *Augustus*, undoubtedly longer than usual.

107. Frickenschmidt, *Evangelium*, 112–13; Miller, "Introduction," viii.

108. Noted by Chance, "Fiction," 138.

Xenophon did have firsthand knowledge of Persia, but Xenophon's *Hellenica* shows that he knew how to write history, and that this is not it.

Cyrus died in 530 BCE, a century before Xenophon's birth (for the interval, one might compare the mid-second-century Gospel of Thomas, written probably well over a century after Jesus's crucifixion). This alone would not preclude his work from being biography or depending on substantial information (since later works, such as Arrian's treatment of Alexander, often depended on significantly earlier sources; see ch. 9).

Nevertheless, even ancient readers recognized that this work was meant to teach politics, not to recount Cyrus's actual life[109] (although a work could easily do both). The consensus seems clear that the work is a novel:

- Tomas Hägg notes that its "constant deviations from known history" suggest that in this particular work "Xenophon simply did not set out to write history," but rather to depict various ideals.[110]
- Arnaldo Momigliano calls it "a paedagogical novel" that "was not, and probably never claimed to be, a true account of the life of a real person. Like Ctesias before him, Xenophon took advantage of his oriental subject to disregard historical truth." Since Antisthenes had already written on Cyrus, Xenophon perhaps could expect his readers to take for granted "the fictitious character of his biography."[111]
- Mark Beck calls it "clearly . . . a fictional novelistic account," with "numerous historical distortions and lengthy conversations, of which there could be no surviving record in Xenophon's time . . . fiction in biographical dress."[112]

A measure of fiction featured in much of the historiography of Xenophon's day, so Xenophon probably felt a freer hand than did the generally more constrained biographers and historians of the early empire.[113]

---

109. Cicero, *Letter to Brother Quintus* 1.1.8.23. Chance, "Fiction," 138, adds Diogenes Laertius, *Lives* (*Plato* 3.34, though this is an inference from the less specific Plato, *Laws* 694). Cf. Socratic features (e.g., Xenophon, *Cyropaedia* 3.1.17) with Xenophon, *Memorabilia*, throughout. For the verdict of a modern commentator, see Hägg, *Biography*, 51–52.

110. Hägg, *Biography*, 65, following also Stadter, "Narrative," 467, and calling it a "utopian biography." (I would prefer "utopian novel," but Xenophon predates the later narrative categories.)

111. Momigliano, *Development*, 55, adding on 55–56 the subsequent popularity of "Xenophon" as a pseudonym for late antique novelists.

112. Beck, "Demonax," 81–82.

113. Momigliano, *Development*, 56–57, deeming fiction as even more common in that period's biography, given its popular level.

Of the two other works considered here, both later than the *Cyropaedia*, Flavius Philostratus (ca. 170–ca. 250 CE) is the more competent writer. His *Life of Apollonius*, commissioned by the empress, is the more biographic and clearly draws on some historiographic and biographic conventions. Nevertheless, it differs starkly from his genuine biographies of Greek sophists,[114] and its geography becomes demonstrably fictitious once it leaves the Roman world.[115] Although Philostratus's *Apollonius* includes some characteristics of biography, it defies many biographic conventions, including in length and structure.[116]

It borrows the trappings of biography to increase its effectiveness, something like the way that Dan Brown's *Da Vinci Code* subverts historical markers. It was novels that borrowed elements from history and other earlier genres, rather than the reverse.[117] (Even so, however, Philostratus's original title is not specifically biographic; in Greek it is not *Life of Apollonius of Tyana* but simply "Things about Apollonius of Tyana.")[118]

- Michael Licona deems it "a combination of history and fiction."[119]
- Noting its division into eight books, evoking the novels of Achilles Tatius and Chariton, Ewen Bowie sees it as only a novel.[120]
- Adela Yarbro Collins recognizes its "important similarities to the ancient novel."[121]

Unlike typical novelists, Philostratus does incorporate some genuine research. He used some "local oral traditions" from cities that Apollonius had reportedly visited,[122] although these traditions would now be considerably more than a

---

114. Also noted by Bowie, "Portrait," 143.

115. Jones, "Apollonius Passage," regarding it as a "travel romance." For complaints about ridiculous geography, see, e.g., Lucian, *How to Write History* 24. Although Capra, "Detour," blames a later copyist for a geographic anomaly in Xenophon, *Ephesiaca* 5.10.2, novelists were less committed to accurate geography.

116. Hägg, *Biography*, 321, though his exceptionally broad definition of biography includes it.

117. Aune, *Dictionary*, 321; Pitcher, "Story," 296–98; Ní-Mheallaigh, "Pseudo-Documentarism"; cf. Fowler, *Kinds of Literature*, 93. Ancient discussions of prose genre always begin with history (Adams, *Genre*, 51, citing, e.g., Quintilian, *Orator's Education* 10.1.73–5, 101–4).

118. Robiano, "*Apologia*," 97.

119. Licona, *Differences*, p. 6.

120. Bowie, "Apollonius," esp. 1664, as cited in Chance, "Fiction," 138–39; Bowie, "Portrait," 143.

121. Collins, *Mark*, 26n73.

122. Votaw, "Biographies," 63; Bowie, "Portrait," 142.

century old (hence beyond living memory).[123] More important, he was aware of the four-volume, second-century work of Moeragenes, another work that provided fodder regarding Apollonius's youth, as well as letters attributed to Apollonius, some already in the early second century.[124]

Still, Philostratus's alleged main source for Apollonius's life is the latter's former disciple Damis,[125] although Philostratus recognized that some of it was a "wonder-tale."[126] I tend to think that Philostratus would not have dared claim that the empress brought this source to his attention[127] unless he believed that she thought it to be authentically from Damis, however much Philostratus may have adapted it for literary purposes.[128] A clearly greater number of scholars, however, contend that even Damis is a fiction of either Philostratus[129] or (as I think somewhat more likely) an earlier pseudepigrapher.[130] If it is a fiction of Philostratus himself, even his appeal to this source would be subverting a biographic and historiographic authenticating device.

Philostratus discourages attention to Moeragenes[131] and otherwise mentions him only to corroborate Philostratus's main source.[132] Some think that Moeragenes depicted Apollonius as a philosopher,[133] others that he depicted him negatively as a magician,[134] and still others that he depicted him positively as a magus.[135] The negative view might be more likely; Moeragenes is cited by Origen[136] to show that even philosophers can be affected by magic.

123. In contrast to, say, Arrian's treatment of Epictetus or Xenophon's of Socrates; cf. Votaw, "Biographies," 55.

124. Bowie, "Portrait," 142.

125. Philostratus, *Life of Apollonius* 1.3, 19.

126. Votaw, "Biographies," 65.

127. Philostratus, *Life of Apollonius* 1.3.1. See Robiano, "*Apologia*," 100.

128. Cf. Conybeare, "Introduction," vii; Votaw, "Biographies," 61, 63–64; Derrenbacker, *Practices*, 71–74. That is, unless his relationship with the empress was such that she would enjoy being pulled into the fiction.

129. Jones, "Apollonius Passage"; Klauck, *Context*, 170; Edwards, "Damis"; Hägg, *Biography*, 325, 331–32 (citing Bowie, "Apollonius," 1663–64; Bowie, "Philostratus," 189; Gyselinck and Demoen, "Author," 99–101); Bowie, "Portrait," 142–43.

130. Though cf. Conybeare, "Introduction," vii.

131. Philostratus, *Life of Apollonius* 1.3.

132. Philostratus, *Life of Apollonius* 3.41.

133. Bowie, "Apollonius."

134. Bowie, "Apollonius," regards this as the usual view.

135. Raynor, "Moeragenes," noting Moeragenes's title *Memories of the Magus and Philosopher Apollonius of Tyana*, which he thinks evokes Xenophon's *Memorabilia*, and doubting that one would devote four volumes to one considered a charlatan.

136. Origen, *Against Celsus* 6.41.

Moeragenes also mentions an Epicurean philosopher who abandoned Philostratus, disillusioned after discovering him a charlatan. Philostratus may have discouraged attention to Moeragenes especially if this discoverer was Damis.[137]

In any case, Philostratus's own portrait suits a second- or third-century setting (i.e., his own) much better than a first-century setting (i.e., Apollonius's), in contrast with the many earlier Judean/Galilean features in the Gospels.[138] A number of his accounts of Apollonius even resemble reports from Christian gospels,[139] though most frequently of the apocryphal variety.[140] (Classifying the first-century Gospels by reference to Philostratus's *Life of Apollonius of Tyana*[141] is therefore highly anachronistic.) Given the relative dates, Christian stories would have been at least among the significant potential influences on his storytelling approach (offering literary fodder for miracle stories). The parts of the story most apt to be confirmed by Apollonius's letters[142] exhibit the least parallels with the Gospels.[143]

Whereas Philostratus was aware of at least some prior information about Apollonius, Ps.-Callisthenes was more interested in his own creative depiction of Alexander. Though some basic information about Alexander was widely known, this author is not writing anything close to mainstream biography.[144] Ps.-Callisthenes's *Alexander Romance* differs starkly from the biographic treatment of lives in the early empire, as expressed from Nepos to Suetonius and Plutarch. Ps.-Callisthenes freely mixes historical and fictitious sources, while adding his own fictions.[145]

---

137. Anderson, *Philostratus*, 299–300, here 300. Lucian, Dio Cassius, and Apollonius's letters also see him as a magician. The infancy material in Maximus of Aegae, used in *Life of Apollonius* 1.12, is probably later, like Christians' *Protevangelium of James*.

138. On which, see, e.g., sections 16.11–13 later in this book.

139. See Keener, *Miracles*, 1:53–56, esp. 55, and sources cited there.

140. Klauck, *Context*, 170. Admittedly, stories of Jesus as miracle worker are limited in extant apocryphal gospels (Achtemeier, *Miracle Tradition*, 177–78; cf. Remus, *Healer*, 92–95); but miracle stories are abundant in apocryphal acts (Achtemeier, *Miracle Tradition*, 179–88; cf. Remus, *Healer*, 102–3).

141. Cf. Moles, "Influence," 99.

142. Regardless of their authenticity (it may be doubtful), they predate Philostratus's story. The letters focus on Greek cities where Apollonius probably actually traveled (not Ethiopia, India, etc., where Philostratus's most fanciful tales transpire).

143. See further Keener, *Acts*, 1:330–33. Generic parallels (Votaw, "Biographies," 65) largely reflect the biographic format; differences in content (66) are substantial.

144. Talbert, "Monograph," 72.

145. E.g., *Alexander Romance* 1.23.

One leading expert opines that "the historical nucleus is small and unusable";[146] another rightly distinguishes this "popular fiction" from Alexander histories;[147] another speaks of it as "largely fictitious" and usually recognized as a romance;[148] and still others aver that it "in many respects seems as much a work of fiction as the anonymous *History of Apollonius King of Tyre*, usually regarded as a novel."[149] Ps.-Callisthenes wrote somewhere between 460 and 760 years after Alexander's death—i.e., likely over half a millennium later, centuries after living memory of Alexander and his associates had perished.[150]

2.5d. *The Fabled Aesop*

Another work frequently cited as a fictional biography is *Life of Aesop*. Unlike typical novels, it does rework considerable preexisting material, so some audiences may well have viewed this popular-level work as a biography. More likely, however, they viewed it as an entertaining folk tale.

Nevertheless, most scholars today consider it a novel, like the historical novels noted above.[151] Apart from Aesop possibly being a historical person and the work having a legendary nucleus, "almost everything else about this *Life* is fictive, and thought to be fiction."[152] The author creatively invests the story with motifs derived from other ancient stories,[153] expecting readers to understand that this story is fictitious rather than historically true.[154]

Even the prior legendary content represents a much longer period of oral tradition—probably over half a millennium—than is possibly relevant for the

---

146. Bosworth, "Pseudo-Callisthenes." On historical information dramatically transformed for narrative purposes, see Hägg, *Biography*, 126–27.

147. Zambrini, "Historians," 211; cf. Hägg, *Biography*, 4. Contrast Pervo's designation of it as a "history" (*Acts*, 15).

148. Hägg, *Biography*, 100.

149. Konstan and Walsh, "Biography," 27; see also 39n25.

150. Cf. Hägg, *Biography*, 99, for "some six hundred years or more." It must have been completed by the time of its Latin translation in the fourth century; cf. Fusillo, "Pseudo-Callisthenes."

151. Wojciechowski, "Tradition," 101–2 ("a Hellenistic novel with satirical elements"); Frickenschmidt, *Evangelium*, 180–81; Hägg, *Biography*, 100 (most scholars today deem it a romance), 310 (its "novelistic plot"); Karla, "*Life of Aesop*," 64. Cf. "forgery" in Momigliano, *Development*, 92.

152. Karla, "*Life of Aesop*," 47.

153. Karla, "*Life of Aesop*," 47–48 (Ahiqar, Hesiod, etc.).

154. Karla, "*Life of Aesop*," 48.

Gospels or the most typical biographies from the early empire.[155] Some literary traits, such as episodic structure and use of popular Koine, resemble the Gospels (esp. Mark),[156] but literary style and level differ from questions of genre. Episodic style fits many ancient biographies,[157] and structurally the Gospels' plots are closer to biographies.[158] The Gospels' premeditated literary arrangement also distinguishes them from purely folkloristic collections[159] such as *Life of Aesop*. Also, the sexual elements and motifs from Old Comedy[160] in *Life of Aesop* naturally do not feature in the Gospels.

2.5e. Entertaining Novel Hypotheses

Surviving manuscripts suggest that, throughout antiquity, history was far more valued and thus more pervasive than novels. For example, more copies of Herodotus and especially of Thucydides remain than copies of all ancient novels combined.[161] Discussions of prose genre began with history, turned to biography, and finally treated novels last of all, as least useful.[162] Ancient readers could almost always recognize the difference between information-based and novelistic works.[163]

Novels typically reflected the milieu of their readership more than that of their characters,[164] in contrast to the verisimilitude of histories and biographies that, despite embellishment, inference, and adaptation for their

---

155. Hägg, *Biography*, 99, suggests its present form dates to over six hundred years after Aesop.

156. Votaw, "Biographies," 45–46 (cf. 71, wrongly comparing Philostratus); Reiser, "Alexanderroman," 135–48 (comparing Ps.-Callisthenes), as cited in Chance, "Fiction," 132; Tolbert, discussed in Freyne, "Gospel," 68–70. Cf. traits in Karla, "*Life of Aesop*," 51–52.

157. Karla, "*Life of Aesop*," 51–52; cf. Aletti, *Birth*, 10.

158. Frickenschmidt, *Evangelium*, 181, noting esp. the biographies of Phocion in Nepos and Plutarch.

159. Cf. Byrskog, "Century," 24. Cf. folkloristic lives of Homer. Folklore in a general sense need not refer to long-term oral tradition, but that is what I envision here.

160. Karla, "*Life of Aesop*," 52–53.

161. Stephens, "Who Read Novels?" 415. For the longer survival of manuscripts that were highly prized and thus cared for, see Evans, "Longevity."

162. Adams, *Genre*, 51–52; cf. Becker, *Birth*, 60.

163. See, e.g., Lucian, *How to Write History* 12; Plutarch, *How the Young Man Should Study Poetry* 2, *Moralia* 16F; see Mosley, "Reporting," 26; Kany, "Bericht." Usually they could also distinguish specimens of these genres, at least if figures were recent.

164. See Wiersma, "Novel."

audiences, focused on historical content. Some novels contained some realism,[165] but many were inconsistent or uninterested in local color.[166] By contrast, local color pervades the Gospels so thoroughly (see some brief examples in ch. 16) that we sometimes wonder how well Diaspora audiences understood some of the details. (Who in the Diaspora, for example, had heard of Chorazin or Magdala?)

Could the Gospels be historical novels? Given the flexibility of genres, an author could create anything he wanted, but it nevertheless remains vastly improbable that the Gospels would look like biographies, use sources like mainstream biographies, and yet be novels. If they were novels, they would be the *only* ones we know about that treat a recent person. They would belong to a comparatively rare subgenre (historical novels) as opposed to a very common one (mainstream biography), though again, *no* extant examples in this subgenre involve recent persons. They would also be exceptional in being more for instruction (in the master's life and teaching) than for entertainment, making them much closer in purpose to a common sort of biographies than to typical novels.

In contrast to novels, Luke even includes a historical preface (see ch. 8);[167] and Luke uses Mark as if he expected that fairly recent work to be factual. Also in contrast to novels, the first-century Gospels do not present themselves as texts composed primarily for entertainment; rather, they present themselves as true accounts of Jesus's ministry, for their hearers' instruction (Luke 1:3–4).[168]

The engaging style of the Gospels cannot count against them being biographies. Historians and biographers wrote primarily to inform about historical truth but nevertheless wrote in an entertaining or engaging manner.[169] For

165. E.g., Longus is a countryman who knows the correct fauna of Lesbos, though much of his knowledge would apply to any eastern Mediterranean setting (and he apparently lacked firsthand acquaintance with trapping techniques; Arnott, "Realism," 211).

166. E.g., on cities (Saïd, "City," noting that some that were interested in cities used widely known information). On this point, Evans, *World*, 9–10, contrasts the first-century Gospels with later gnostic and apocryphal ones.

167. Though occasionally a novel could include a preface explaining how an author invented the story (as in Longus, *Daphnis and Chloe.* proem 1–2).

168. Cf. Becker, *Birth*, 92.

169. Dio Cassius, *Roman History* 1.1.1–2; Fornara, *Nature*, 120–33 (esp. 121, 133–34, citing Cicero, *Letters to Friends* 5.12.4); Palmer, "Monograph (1993)," 3, 29, citing, e.g., Cicero, *Letters to Friends* 5.12.5; Polybius, *Histories* 1.4.11; 3.31.13; Aune, *Environment*, 80; Aune, *Dictionary*, 285; cf. also Dionysius of Halicarnassus, *Demosthenes* 47; Tacitus, *Annals* 4.32–33; Maximus of Tyre, *Philosophical Orations* 22.5; Plümacher, "Fiktion"; Krasser, "Reading," 554 (though including Ps.-Callisthenes's *Alexander Romance* too readily in the history category); Burridge, *Gospels*, 146, 181–82, 237–38.

example, the author of 2 Maccabees claims that he writes historical narrative and that many sources were available, but he also emphasizes that readers would enjoy and easily remember his work.[170] Suetonius was happy to reveal character while also providing details of imperial sex lives that would titillate his audience.[171] Although only some biographers wrote primarily for entertainment, most biographers and most historians[172] expected their works to be enjoyed. A biography "could be entertaining as well as educational."[173] Through much of history, in fact, many authors have written essentially factual accounts in the entertaining style of fiction current in their day.[174]

Most ancient writers sought to entertain; the key genre question was whether they also sought to inform. Novelists wrote primarily to entertain rather to inform.[175] A few functioned as religious propaganda or suggested moral lessons as well as providing entertainment,[176] but historical instruction was not an interest. Readers would find moral lessons far more often in biographies, which offered role models for moral instruction (see ch. 6),[177] and in historiography (see ch. 7).

2.6. The Lives of the Poets

From the first century BCE through the second century CE, we have easily scores of extant, full biographies (even if we count only those of Nepos, Plutarch, and Suetonius). Again, probably none of the above-mentioned historical novels, probably excepting for one stage in the development of *Life of Aesop* if we so classify it, fit this period.

We do, however, have some sketchy and not very reliable lives of poets.[178] Whereas some novels exploited biographic conventions without genuine

---

170. 2 Macc 2:24–25.

171. Edwards, "Introduction," xii–xiii; cf. Hägg, *Biography*, 5.

172. See discussion in Maximus of Tyre, *Philosophical Orations* 22.5; 2 Macc 2:25; Tacitus, *Annals* 4.32–33; Fornara, *Nature*, 120–33.

173. Ytterbrink, *Gospel*, 116; Edwards, "Introduction," xiii.

174. For some examples, see Sterling, *Sisters*, 78; Hunt, *History*, 208, 239; Tomkins, *Wilberforce*, 15–17.

175. Talbert, *Gospel*, 17.

176. Most obviously, the late second-century Apuleius, *Metamorphoses*, though some view even this work's propagandistic element as satire.

177. E.g., Aune, *Environment*, 36.

178. Pelling, "Biography, Greek," 241–42, in *OCD*, 241; Frickenschmidt, *Evangelium*, 158–59.

biographic intention, lives of the poets could exhibit more biographic intention (thus we can call them "lives") but rarely had sufficient tradition to constitute the sort of full-length biographies that I treat elsewhere in this book. Some of them are only a few paragraphs long.

This observation, however, significantly reduces their value for comparison with the Gospels. The Gospels are all considerably more extensive than the tradition of the lives of the poets; the Gospels much more closely resemble the larger narrative works about public figures,[179] because the Gospels, like the latter sort of biographies, had much more information available about their subject than did ordinary biographers of poets.[180]

Because public history focused on politics and war, historians provided plenty of material for biographies of statesmen and generals, but little of poets.[181] Biographers composed such lives of poets, who left few traces about their lives, very differently than they composed lives of generals and kings, whose deeds were recorded by historians, or lives of philosophers, whose disciples preserved their memories.[182] Lives of poets thus "are traditionally considered more imaginative than their political counterparts."[183]

While most scholars recognize the differences between full biographies and the generally brief lives of poets, we can understand the rationale behind the formation of the latter. When publishers today lack contemporary images of NT figures or events, such as Jesus or Pentecost, they often employ on book covers scenes of these figures or events painted by medieval or Renaissance artists. Such images may be relevant to the history of interpretation, but no one supposes them to be authentic portraits.

In antiquity, when biographers wrote about figures of the distant past or very obscure figures, they would sometimes recount unlikely traditions because, like modern book cover designers, that was all they had. If the poet did not flourish within living memory, his or her biographer could not draw on historians or personal contacts as he could for political figures.

In the Hellenistic period, desire to fill this void led to vastly improbable speculations (we might compare some extreme speculations in the history of biblical interpretation). Greek writers in the Hellenistic period did focus

---

179. See Frickenschmidt, *Evangelium*, 504.

180. The Gospels date to within living memory and come from a discipleship movement, the sort of movement that normally valued information about the lives of their teachers. For Jesus's public influence, see also Josephus, *Jewish Antiquities* 18.63–64.

181. Geiger, *Nepos*, 115.

182. Momigliano, *Development*, 88.

183. De Temmerman, "Formalities," 4–5, following Pelling, *Plutarch and History*, 147–48.

especially on intellectual biography, often concerning poets.[184] Many writers inferred information about the poets' personal lives from their writings.[185] Since Mary Lefkowitz argued this case,[186] the consensus has been that the lives of poets, based on such inferences, are unreliable historically.[187] Still, even here historical information sometimes surfaces; poets could, after all, influence their own reception.[188]

Some, especially from before (but also some after) the heyday of historical biography, were purely fictitious. For example, Ps.-Herodotus's *Life of Homer* and other lives of the poets are meant primarily to entertain, not to give historical details.[189] Later, Ps.-Plutarch's[190] *Life of Homer* "bears a strong resemblance to a fairy tale."[191] But even Plutarch himself (not the genuine author of *Life of Homer*) had to work with more limited kinds of sources when he wrote about the distant past, poets or not, as his work about Theseus confirms; such work differs qualitatively from what he wrote about figures within living memory, namely, Galba and Otho (see ch. 10).

If writing about poets, especially much earlier ones, generally required more creativity than writing about better-documented figures, especially more recent ones, the difference between the two forms of lives grew more stark as the latter model prevailed in the early centuries of the empire. "Sober biographers like Nepos, Plutarch and Tacitus,"[192] who wrote historically oriented biographies, were quite different from entertainment-focused, more fictional-

184. Adams, *Genre*, 87; Frickenschmidt, *Evangelium*, 158–59. Cf. also the biographies *On Illustrious Men* in Adams, *Genre*, 94–101.

185. Geiger, *Nepos*, 115; Momigliano, *Development*, 70; Power, "Poetry," 217, 221, 236. This was presumably not unlike the sort of hypothetical guesswork involved in Judean and Babylonian midrashic haggadah.

186. Lefkowitz, *Lives*, ix, 70, 128, 177; also Lefkowitz, "Poet."

187. Adams, *Genre*, 87; Irwin, "Biographies," 13. Trepanier, "Review," warns that Chitwood's explanations of philosophers' deaths via their writings, using Lefkowitz's model from lives of poets (Chitwood, *Death*), is highly speculative.

188. Irwin, "Biographies," 14.

189. Adams, *Genre*, 2. Ps.-Herodotus *Life* is less than a third the length of Mark or a sixth that of Matthew or Luke. Still, among lives of the poets it is one of the *most* comparable in form; it has biographic structure and, like the *Life of Aesop*, surely draws on existing traditions. It may even date to the second or third century CE, although it might depend on a pseudepigraphically Herodotean source (cf. ¶ 1).

190. So see Keaney and Lamberton, *Essay*. There were also many other lives of Homer in antiquity—see Pitcher, "Story," 293, 295.

191. Konstan and Walsh, "Biography," 27. Nevertheless, the author claims only to recount traditions, some from named sources (e.g., 1.2–4; 2.2–3) and others anonymous (1.5; again, 2.2–3).

192. Frickenschmidt, *Evangelium*, 159.

izing lives of the poets.[193] From at least as early as Nepos onward, biographies of public figures contained historiographic elements no less than encomiastic ones.[194] Not surprisingly, then, Suetonius's political biographies differ significantly from his literary ones.[195]

Nevertheless, even regarding lives of the poets, standards of the early empire reveal an increased measure of historical sensitivity. Even in his generally brief lives of poets, Suetonius seems to do his best to offer historical information. Sometimes he does work from inference,[196] but sometimes he cites general knowledge or belief;[197] periodically he names his sources.[198] He sometimes indicates his acquaintance with a range of sources, even though, as in his imperial biographies, he names them only selectively.[199] Besides authors, he cites preserved speeches,[200] epigrams about the person,[201] letters,[202] and the authors themselves where they refer to themselves.[203] Sometimes he personally recalls oral reports spoken by witnesses.[204] At other times he lists no sources yet provides the same sort of details we find in his lives of emperors.[205] Sometimes he supplies historical context.[206] Sometimes his information is paralleled or somewhat paralleled elsewhere.[207]

193. Frickenschmidt, *Evangelium*, 161; Power, "Poetry," 236.

194. Frickenschmidt, *Evangelium*, 504. Likewise, encomiastic elements in some histories (Fornara, *Nature*, 36) did not make the histories fictitious (64–65).

195. Power, "Poetry," 237.

196. As in Suetonius, *Vergil* 9.

197. "It is believed," or "it is said" or "some say" (Suetonius, *Horace* 1, 4; *Grammarians* 5; 7; 13; 16; 23; *Rhetoricians* 3; an absurd claim in 4); "common talk" (*Grammarians* 23, probably not credited); "some" vs. "the general opinion" (*Vergil* 1); "common report" (*Vergil* 9) possibly countered by a named source (*Vergil* 10). In Eusebius, Dillon, "Interpretation," 157, regards such language as appropriate for oral tradition distinct from documents. In Philo, however, it can reflect a written source or inferences from it (Hidalgo, "Study," 278–80, on *Moses* 1.3.9; 1.4.13–14; 1.21.24, 135; 1.29.165–66).

198. Suetonius, *Terence* 3; *Vergil* 29, 34, 42, 46; *Grammarians* 4, 7–8, 11, 16.

199. E.g., Suetonius, *Terence* 5; cf. *Grammarians* 11: "According to some writers," but the biographee "himself . . . declares."

200. Suetonius, *Rhetoricians* 2; 5 (this one = Cicero, *Philippics* 2.17.42–43).

201. Suetonius, *Horace* 1; *Tibullus*; *Grammarians* 18; 22.

202. A number by Augustus (Suetonius, *Horace* 2–3; *Vergil* 31), to which he had access also in his *Augustus*; three by Cicero (*Grammarians* 14, citing Cicero, *Letters to Friends* 9.10; *Letters to Atticus* 12.26; Suetonius, *Rhetoricians* 2, citing one not today extant); and by others (*Grammarians* 10).

203. Suetonius, *Horace* 3; *Grammarians* 5.

204. Suetonius, *Grammarians* 4.

205. E.g., Suetonius, *Lucan*; esp. *Aulus Persius Flaccus*.

206. E.g., Suetonius, *Grammarians* 1; *Rhetoricians* 1.

207. E.g., Suetonius, *Grammarians* 9 (cf. Macrobius); *Grammarians* 16 (cf. Suetonius's own *Augustus* 66).

When Suetonius knows that his sources may be fictitious, he frames his claims cautiously here, as he does in the *Caesars*.[208] He is sometimes critical, rejecting some sources as spurious or contrary to better information,[209] or citing variant versions.[210] He often identifies "gossip" as such.[211]

Because he has limited material available for lives of the poets, he is forced to use what he has to express his subject's character.[212] Nevertheless, he is unwilling to do so at the expense of "his credibility as a factual source."[213] He is limited by his sources; thus, for many figures he can offer only a few paragraphs or, quite often, just a single one.[214] Sometimes he does so even when much more information must have been available.[215] Like historians filling out details lacking in reports of speeches, Suetonius stays as close to verisimilitude as possible, but some of his sources allow greater certainty or plausibility than others. Suetonius avoids the inventions "found in earlier literary biography."[216]

Suetonius's *Lives of the Caesars* may have been longer than his lives of poets for the same reason that he had more material for some Caesars than for others: for some he had more source material.[217] The ideal, as exemplified in most biographies of public figures from this period, was a full volume on a person, and this is the ideal to which the Evangelists would have aspired and

208. Power, "Poetry," 236–38.

209. Suetonius, *Horace* 4; *Vergil* 9–10; *Terence* 3–4.

210. Suetonius, *Life of Pliny the Elder*. Suetonius's first version accords with (though he does not cite) Pliny, *Letters* 6.16.19 (written to Tacitus for use in his history). He offers the different accounts of Terence's death (naming the one source that differed from most) in *Terence* 5 (discussed in a different connection in Davis, "Terence Interrupted").

211. "Common gossip" (Suetonius, *Terence* 3), which he counters with a named source (*Terence* 4).

212. Power, "Poetry," 237, 239.

213. Power, "Poetry," 237.

214. See *Tibullus*; *Passienus Crispus*. In *Grammarians*: Saevius Nicanor (*Grammarians* 5), Aurelius Opilius (6), Marcus Antonius Gnipho (7), Marcus Pompilius Andronicus (8), Horace and Domitius Marsus (9), Cornelius Epicadus (12), Staberius Eros (13), Lenaeus (15), Quintus Caecilius Epirota (16), Marcus Verrius Flaccus (17), Lucius Crassicus (18), Scribonius Aphrodisius (19, *very* short), Gaius Julius Hyginus (20), Gaius Melissus (21), Marcus Pomponius Marcellus (22). So also *Rhetoricians* 2–5.

215. E.g., for Pliny the Elder.

216. Power, "Poetry," 238. Aletti, *Birth*, 22, contends that Suetonius's interest is recounting whatever is true about his subjects, "the good and the bad, so that the portrait is consistent with reality." Cf. now "gist" in Licona, "Reliable."

217. See Votaw, "Biographies," 53; for source material determining length, cf. Geiger, *Nepos*, 27.

the form that the Gospels take.[218] Overall, the Gospels are far more like biographies of public figures, as in Nepos and Plutarch, than they are like lives of poets.[219] Again, this may be partly because of the nature of their sources: the Gospels are from within living memory of Jesus's ministry, potentially dependent on reports that go back to Jesus's disciples, who were also the movement's leaders (see Gal 2:9).

Unlike poets, whose initial appeal was solely their writings, or even some philosophers or other teachers, in whom only a few immediate followers were interested, Jesus was a public figure. The Gospels affirm that he drew crowds (Mark 2:4, 13 and throughout), and he was a figure significant enough to warrant public execution and comment in Josephus (*Jewish Antiquities* 18.63–64). Most important, his movement mushroomed to "public" proportions while his disciples remained leaders in the movement, sufficiently so that the movement soon drew attention even in Rome (Tacitus, *Annals* 15.44, for some three decades after Jesus's ministry; cf. Suetonius, *Claudius* 25.4, in the second decade). Jesus remained by far the central figure in this movement.[220] This means that in a fairly early phase of the movement, widespread interest in him flourished, quite in contrast with the lives of typical poets.

2.7. Errant Aretalogies?

Some scholars suggest that religious aretalogies helped generate the new genre of novel,[221] although religious propaganda does not seem to be the primary function of most ancient novels. Defining aretalogies as narratives celebrating marvelous deeds of heroes, some have compared the Gospels with such aretalogies,[222] or view their genre as aretalogical biography or novel.[223]

---

218. Cf. Frickenschmidt, *Evangelium*, 208–9, and the three-part, more complete biographic form characteristic of fuller biographies, as opposed to brief lives of poets (210–350).

219. Frickenschmidt, *Evangelium*, 169.

220. See, e.g., Mark 1:1; 1 Cor 15:3–11; Col 1:15–20; 1 Thess 1:10; Rev 1:17–18; 1 Clem. 7.4; 24.1; 36.1. Although Paul writes in the Diaspora before the Jesus tradition was as widely disseminated, he also assumes some knowledge of Jesus's ministry and character (e.g., 1 Cor 9:14; 2 Cor 10:1).

221. Merkelbach, "Novel and Aretalogy," 290.

222. Cf. Hadas and Smith, *Heroes*.

223. See Wills, *Quest*; Burridge, *Gospels*, 92, also compares Tolbert, *Sowing*, 59–79; Reiser, "Alexanderroman."

There is, however, no single ancient genre of aretalogy,[224] especially of early Hellenistic aretalogy with any predictable form.[225] Classicist Patricia Cox complains that scholars who treat aretalogies as a prototype for collections of gospel miracle stories exploit works much later than the Gospels, such as Philostratus's *Life of Apollonius of Tyana* and Porphyry's and Iamblichus's *Pythagorean Life*, to suggest pre-Gospel aretalogies, of which we lack extant examples.[226] In so doing, she warns, NT scholars have distorted even the point of these later works![227]

Technically, in antiquity an "aretalogy" was simply "a list of titles and prerogatives pertaining to a god,"[228] or "recitations of the virtuous and miraculous deeds of a divinity."[229] These were always of deities, never a way of divinizing mortals, and they do not provide a unified pattern for the post-Gospel works about divine men.[230] Another classicist complains that "anyone who cites Philostratus' life of Apollonius" as an example of miracle-heavy aretalogies "should be forced to read every one of its laboured speeches," where miracles are played down more often than highlighted.[231]

In contrast to such brief narrations or lists of divine acts, biographies that contain fuller episodes about their characters offer better analogies for the Gospels as whole works.[232] Even regarding miracle stories, the episodic Elijah and Elisha narratives in the OT offer a much more obvious background for works such as the Gospels, which conspicuously ground Jesus's ministry in the monotheistic heritage of Israel.[233]

Some others have gone so far as to use the later apocryphal gospels as analogies for the canonical Gospels.[234] This comparison, however, is not merely

---

224. Burridge, *Gospels*, 281–82; cf. in greater detail Kee, "Aretalogy"; Kee, *Aretalogies*.

225. Cox, *Biography*, 46, noting the designation's origin in 1885 based on a dream interpreter inscription.

226. Cox, *Biography*, 3–4. This is not to deny their use of earlier legends; cf. Aune, "Prolegomena," 92.

227. Cox, *Biography*, 4.

228. Edwards, "Genre," 59.

229. Cox, *Biography*, 47.

230. Cox, *Biography*, 47; she argues against Hadas on 47–48 and Morton Smith on 48.

231. Edwards, "Genre," 59.

232. Shuler, *Genre*, 15–20; cf. Talbert, *Gospel*, 12–13; Klauck, *Context*, 167–68.

233. Edwards, "Genre," 59; cf. Frickenschmidt, *Evangelium*, 127–28; Collins, *Mark*, 29; Ytterbrink, *Gospel*, 39, 227–28.

234. Thus, for example, one knowledgeable scholar seriously proposes that while comparing the Gospels to biographies, I should have taken "into account ancient works like the *Protevangelium of James* and other apocryphal gospels that closely resemble the canonical

mildly anachronistic but particularly conspicuously anachronistic, since apoc-ryphal gospels are a later and, more important, derivative genre.[235] We should no more read these developments into first-century Gospels, composed within living memory of Jesus, than we should read Paul's first-century letters in light of the theology of Origen, Tertullian, or Cyprian from that later period.

Most apocryphal gospels also stem from the heyday of ancient novels, the late second and early third centuries.[236] Because of their date and novelistic features,[237] these later Gospels are recognized by the majority of scholars as novels, not biographies.[238] There is moreover in them (as opposed to Matthew, Mark, Luke, and John) little indication of Judean or Galilean elements or other signs of earlier tradition.

Gospels in genre but obviously did invent material wholesale" (Powell, *Figure*, 260, summariz-ing the suggestion of Levine, "Christian Faith," 103). I know of no mainstream historical-Jesus scholars (such as E. P. Sanders, John Meier, or Gerd Theissen) who appeal to such documents, whereas, by contrast, a biographic genre for the first-century Gospels is currently and histor-ically the dominant position in Gospels scholarship.

235. Overlap with material in the canonical Gospels may reflect direct knowledge of them (likely by their period) but often via secondary orality; see Labahn, "Secondary Orality," and the sources he cites on 363.

236. See Bowie, "Readership," 443; Stephens, "Who Read Novels?," 414; Aune, *Dictionary*, 322.

237. For novelistic features in the apocryphal gospels and acts, see Aune, *Environment*, 151–52; Lalleman, "Apocryphal Acts," 67; Rebenich, "Prose," 307–8; Bauckham, "Acts of Paul"; Keylock, "Distinctness," 210; Krasser, "Reading," 554; Hofmann, "Novels: Christian," 846–48; Pervo, "Fabula"; Perkins, "World."

238. See Aune, *Dictionary*, 199–204; Bauckham and Porter, "Apocryphal Gospels"; Charlesworth and Evans, "Agrapha." Cf. also apocryphal acts as novels, Aune, *Environment*, 151–52; Lalleman, "Apocryphal Acts," 67; Rebenich, "Prose," 307–8; Bauckham, "Acts of Paul"; Keylock, "Distinctness," 210; Krasser, "Reading," 554; Hofmann, "Novels: Christian," 846–48; Perkins, "World." They do at least share a narrative framework (cf. Rodríguez, "Narrative Gospels," 240, noting P.Egerton 2; P.Köln 255; P.Oxy. 840), unlike most gnostic gospels (cf. Mournet, "Sayings Gospels," 349). The gnostic gospels develop the social memory of Je-sus in their era (cf. Schröter, "Contribution") but reflect a different, mostly nonnarrative genre, probably with knowledge of the earlier Gospels (Tuckett, *Nag Hammadi*, 149, 155, 158–59); even Thomas may be largely derivative (see Tuckett, "Thomas"; Tuckett, "Gospel of Thomas"; Tuckett, "Sources," 130; Heyer, *Jesus Matters*, 102–5; Charlesworth and Evans, "Agrapha," 496–503; cf. possibly Perrin, "Overlooked Evidence"; Perrin, *Thomas and Tatian*; but contrast DeConick, *Recovering*). Canonical sources (Paul, Q, and Mark) are our earliest extant sources (Allison, *Jesus of Nazareth*, 17); Mark is a biography, but Q's genre is much more debated beyond the predominance of sayings there (Kirk, "Elements"; cf. Rodríguez, "Narrative Gospels," 241).

2.8. Fictionalized Elements in Historical Biographies

Some scholars suggest that the "borderline between historicity and fictionality is profoundly blurred in many ancient biographies," so that we dare not "use these texts unproblematically as historical sources."[239]

While most scholars recognize that neither the Gospels nor ancient biographies in general are novels, the question of "fictionalization" is a different one. Fiction is a playful genre, not meant to be believed; fictiveness, by contrast, is merely something that is not historically accurate.[240]

Some definitions of "fictionalization" are so broad that not even modern historical studies can evade the charge at points; other definitions are narrower. Defining terms is thus important here. While ancient (and even modern) biographies may include considerable fictionalization by some definitions current in modern literary criticism, we should beware of anachronistically imposing these definitions on ancient authors, who probably would not have agreed with them.[241]

Most scholars find at least some fictionalization in ancient biography. Thus Richard Burridge quotes approvingly here another specialist in ancient biography, Christopher Pelling: "While Plutarch did not allow himself wholesale fabrication (as happened in encomium or invective), he does have an element of imaginative 'creative reconstruction' of the truth as he saw it, in order to illustrate the way 'it must have been.'"[242] (In other spheres we might speak of storyteller's license, poetic license, or preacher's license.)[243]

Postmodern perspectives rightly help us to recognize that everyone (including postmodernists) has perspectives. In the wake of postmodernism, however, it has become fashionable in some circles to define fictionalizing so broadly as to obscure the difference between interpreted information and free imagination, between substantially information-grounded works and pure fantasy. Most scholars, however, do not take matters so far and often explicitly qualify their claims. Thus, for example, one scholar observes that "poststructuralist historiography" recognizes that "language, rather than providing a transparent window onto the past, instead plays a constitutive role in creating the past." This much is true, but when she goes on to note that "the practice

239. De Temmerman and Demoen, "Preface," xi.
240. De Temmerman, "Formalities," 5–6.
241. See esp. De Pourcq and Roskam, "Virtues," 180.
242. Burridge, *Gospels*, 169–70, citing Pelling, "Truth"; Pelling, *Antony*, 33–36. See esp. helpfully Hodkinson, "Features."
243. "Storytelling" applies to any account concerning "a place and time different from" its narration (Person, "Storytelling," 385).

of writing historical narratives is identical to the practice of writing fiction," she rightly qualifies this claim with the caveat, "insofar as historians represent past events through emplotting them in narrative form."[244] She explains that this approach does not deny that past events happened, but simply that our recounting of the past includes interpretive structuring; the "fictive" element (the narrator's selection and adaptation of information) is inevitable.[245]

Insofar as one employs the language of fictionalization with such limitations understood, few would disagree, although many would still prefer to avoid the language of fictionalization to avoid obscuring distinctions between fully fictitious works and those narrativizing substantial information. Most scholars do allow for distinctions, but not always with the same nomenclature,[246] so it is important to clarify what different disciplines and scholars mean by "fictionalizing."

Postmodern critic Hayden White argues that all narrative, including narrative history, includes fictionality; its very narrativity transcends mere data, providing temporal structure, and thus fictionalizes.[247] In the absence of a controlling metanarrative, the arrangement of data into a collected plot thus constitutes fictionalization, mixed freely with fact.[248] To be consistent, one would need to apply this designation to any work that focuses on a particular theme and explores connections and causes—such as most of the best historical research today.[249]

Humans narrativize even personal-event memories;[250] such narrativization organizes memory, and may do so from the start, even from the first participants in the events.[251] Some thus describe all memory as "fictional to

244. Matthews, "Teaching Fiction," 214.

245. Matthews, "Teaching Fiction," 214n6.

246. E.g., already a generation ago, Caird, *Language*, 201–2, distinguished the actuality of an event from the language that signifies it. Although historical works and novels are both narratives, not every subgenre within narrative is fictitious in a narrower sense.

247. White, *Tropics*, as summarized by De Temmerman, "Formalities," 14; cf. also Becker, *Birth*, 89. As Licona, *Resurrection*, 79–89, notes, most historians and philosophers today reject the radical postmodern approach that treats even the Holocaust or Apartheid as fictions (although allowing for individual facts behind them). Still, narrativization is an important step in preserving memory (see Zimmermann, "Memory," 132).

248. Becker, *Birth*, 90.

249. See, e.g., Schnabel, *Jesus in Jerusalem*, 4. For examples of good modern historiography, which follow a particular issue in light of the remembered significance of its outcome, see, e.g., Tuttle, *Riot*; Foner, *Reconstruction*; Branch, *Parting*; Luijk, *Children*.

250. Elder, "Narrativity," 242.

251. Le Donne, *Historiographical Jesus*, 52–59, 63.

a certain extent," not because it never depicts historical events but because "it involves selectivity, rearranging, redescription, simplification, etc."[252] If we use such a broad definition, of course, no one will object that any narration, no matter how connected with past events, includes fictional elements. Clarity is important, however, since this is not how everyone uses the term. (Others of us simply prefer "narrativization," which includes both deliberate fiction and works seeking to represent actual persons and events.)[253]

When some scholars speak of "fictionalizing" in biographies, sometimes they refer to the historical novels or lives of the poets that we have mentioned.[254] This is a matter of semantics regarding the label "biography"; they are using a definition of biography that includes such works that all of us agree are largely fictionalized. If we subdivide such "biographies" in terms of where they stand on a continuum of apparent historical intention, virtually everyone will classify Philostratus's *Life of Apollonius* or Ps.-Callisthenes's *Alexander Romance* quite differently from the hasty but historically based lives of generals in Cornelius Nepos. Simply surveying a synopsis of the Gospels shows how strongly information-based Matthew and Luke are, and how information-based they expected Mark to be. As such, they fall much closer to Nepos than to the novels in terms of dependence on prior information.

Sometimes scholars count as fictionalization any encomiastic summaries of characteristics rather than recounting specific deeds; the latter serve a more deliberative purpose, offering greater rhetorical attention to moral lessons.[255] In other cases, however, they refer to the kinds of adjustments to which I refer more fully in chapters 5 and 11. I would define these as literary or rhetorical adjustments rather than as fictionalizing. The latter label risks anachronism, since ancient authors and audiences accepted such adjustments as simply part of making a narrative coherent. Many scholars have adopted for such adjustments the language of fictionalizing, however, and to some degree the difference is a matter of semantics—in this case regarding fictionalization—and of approaching the narrative from different subdisciplines. Various scholars may recognize the same techniques while assigning them differing nomenclature based on the sorts of comparisons being made.

252. Byrskog, "Hermeneutic," 4.
253. See Le Donne, *Historiographical Jesus*, 63.
254. Cf. De Temmerman, "Formalities," 4–5.
255. See Polybius's distinction between treating an individual encomiastically or historically (with moralistic application); cf. Farrington, "Action." For some fiction in ancient biography, see Chance, "Fiction."

Nomenclature aside, however, these adaptations were part and parcel of ancient biography and of historiography more generally[256] and not entirely absent in those genres' modern progenies. There is no question that some of these features appear also in the Gospels and Acts. Some of these features, such as perspective and agendas, are inherent in human communication in general; I believe that defining all such features as "fictionalizing" sunders objectivity and subjectivity more strictly than communication will bear.

Whatever one's preferred nomenclature, it is clear that such adjustments do not identify a work's genre. Literary devices such as characterization, which some treat as fictionalization,[257] are not limited to novels but appear in other narratives, including biographies and histories that tell their stories well.[258]

Keying figures to earlier paradigms is also sometimes treated as fictionalization.[259] Authors often conform scenes to earlier scenes.[260] On this approach, making allusions to an earlier work implies a work as literature and thus fictionalized.[261] For example, in late antiquity Sulpicius Severus keys his story of Martin to the Bible, filling in his accounts of Martin with biblical allusions.[262] Borrowings and parody in ancient works often took for granted that the works' ideal ancient audiences would catch the allusions.[263]

Nevertheless, scholars who consider such keying itself fictitious recognize that it appears in nonfictitious narratives such as historiography;[264] such historiography surely includes Israelite historiography that the Evangelists would have viewed as authentically historical.[265] Early biographers of Washington viewed him as "the American Moses" and compared him with the Roman

---

256. Cf. Dunn, *Tradition*, 200, responding to Holmberg, "Questions," who finds fictionalizing in all historiography. For some examples, with differences from novels, see Keener, *Acts*, 1:74–77.

257. De Temmerman, "Formalities," 21.

258. See Fornara, *Nature*, 185; Ash, Mossman, and Titchener, *Fame*.

259. Regarded in De Temmerman, "Formalities," 21, as fictionalizing.

260. De Temmerman, "Formalities," 23–25; Kirk, "Collective Memory," 61; for an example in late antique philosophic biography, see Tieleman, "Orality," 34.

261. Robiano, "*Apologia*," 104–5, following Genette, *Palimpsestes*, 12 = Genette, *Palimpsestes* (1997), 5.

262. Praet, "Cloak," 138, 143–57, esp. 143–48.

263. E.g., Pelling, *Texts*, 142–43.

264. De Temmerman, "Formalities," 21. For example, whether deliberate or, more likely, unplanned, the similarity of an event such as Josephus, *Jewish War* 6.316 to Ps 74 (LXX 73):3–4, 7 does not lead us to suppose that the event did not occur.

265. See, e.g., Hays, *Echoes*, 101; Cotter, "Miracle," 102; Levine, "Twice"; Keener, *Acts*, 1:573–74; in a contrasting manner, cf. 2 Chr 18:33; 35:23.

Cincinnatus and other figures, but they did not in so doing create Washington's story from whole cloth.[266] By reading Jesus within the context of Israel's history (cf. "according to the Scriptures" already in 1 Cor. 15:3–4), early Christian interpreters did not see themselves as changing his story.[267]

Skilled authors often developed or highlighted such parallelisms from interpretive observations of similar incidents in their sources rather than wholesale creation.[268] Keying is not deemed fictitious if the biographee modeled *himself* after someone, such as Lucian's Demonax after Socrates or, we might argue, John or Jesus after Elijah.[269]

Framing a death scene to evoke an earlier death scene could be an author's invention,[270] but sometimes it might require only slight adjustments to the narrative or tradition to imply such a connection. At other times deaths lent themselves to similar framing because some deaths happened in similar circumstances[271] or because the persons dying orchestrated their deaths in a way to evoke heroes of the past, as when Seneca dies like Socrates.[272] Earlier models of greatness could set expectations for subsequent ones.[273] Certainly Luke offers many implicit comparisons among figures and substantial patterning.[274]

One may define bias as a fictionalizing tendency, but it does not make biographies into novels; otherwise there would not *be* ancient biographies or histories, since in literature unbiased works do not exist. We take bias into account when we read works of ancient biography or history, yet at the same time we depend heavily on these sources to understand the persons about whom

---

266. Schwartz, "Jesus in Memory," 259–60.

267. See Schwartz, "Jesus in Memory," 251, 254.

268. E.g., Plutarch, *Sertorius* 1.1–4; *Cimon* 3.1–3; see further ch. 8; Keener, *Acts*, 1:550–74.

269. Beck, "Demonax," 95; De Temmerman, "Formalities," 21; on Socrates as a common model, see 22–23; also, e.g., Musonius Rufus 10, p. 78.12–14; 18B, p. 118.16–18 (all references to Musonius reflect the Lutz edition); Seneca, *Dialogues* 1.3.12–13; 2.18.5; 4.7.1; 7.25.4; *On Benefits* 5.4.3; 5.6.2–7; 5.7.5; 7.8.2; Epictetus, *Discourses* 1.12.23; 1.25.31; 1.29.65–66; 2.26.6; 3.1.19–23; 3.5.14–19; 3.23.32; 3.24.60; 4.1.159–60; 4.5.2–4; 4.5.33; 4.8.22–23; 4.9.6; 4.11.19; Plutarch, *How the Young Man Should Study Poetry* 2, *Moralia* 16C; Diogenes, *Letters* 28; Dio Chrysostom, *Orations* 3.1, 29; Pelling, "Socrates"; Keener, *Acts*, 3:2605–6.

270. Cf. the contrast between 2 Chr 18:33 and 35:23.

271. E.g., assassins could find inspiration and models from previous assassinations; see Ash, "Assassinating Emperors," 202. Likewise, some biographees may have been genuinely wise, provoked opposition, etc. (Chance, "Fiction," 136).

272. Ash, "Assassinating Emperors," 200, citing Tacitus, *Annals* 15.60–64. Cf. Cox, *Biography*, 30.

273. Chance, "Fiction," 133.

274. See, e.g., Ytterbrink, *Gospel*, 227–28; Keener, *Acts*, 1:556–74.

they wrote (on their often substantial information, see ch. 10). If this is true for other figures of antiquity, why should it be any less true of Jesus? (And if some of us assume that it must be less true of Jesus, because he posthumously became a famous religious figure, what must that say about our own biases?)

I address some such points later as features of historical biography, but suffice it to say that, while these techniques affect detail and perspective, in mainstream biographies (vs. historical novels), they normally need not entail the biographer's creation of events.[275] Novels, including historical ones, were not written about a real person from within living memory, whereas biographies did seek to convey prior information, sometimes about such recent figures; novels did not need to stick close to their material the way Matthew and Luke do, or the way that Matthew and Luke presumably believed that Mark did when they used his material in this way.

Constructive techniques do not necessarily constitute an entire narrative as fictional; ancient historians' constructions of speeches in character, in the context of more accurate narrative information, are a case in point.[276] More encomiastic early biographies such as Xenophon's *Agesilaus* often focused only on the subject's good features, offering a historically distorted perspective.[277] Such an exclusively positive approach contrasts with willingness to highlight negative features in later biographies.[278] Even Xenophon's imbalanced perspective, however, need not require us to discount the information that Xenophon does supply. (I discuss Xenophon's *Agesilaus* further in the next chapter.)

Affecting even modern biography, fictionalization is said to include "conjecture, interpretation and reconstruction of actions, private moments, motivations and attitudes."[279] By the wider definition, any biography that considers the subject's own thinking "goes beyond the mere compilation of vital facts" and so is involved in some fictionalization.[280] Certainly ancient biographies were much more prone to inferring characters' thoughts, thus

275. One can argue that verisimilitude is merely imitation of historical information (cf. Ash, "Assassinating Emperors," 214–15), but often where we can test it, it reflects the biographer's (correct or incorrect) sources or inferences from them.

276. De Temmerman, "Formalities," 14.

277. De Temmerman, "Formalities," 4, noting further Pernot, *Rhétorique*; Hägg, *Biography*, 41–51, 97; and, for discussions by ancient biographers, Gyselinck and Demoen, "Author"; Hägg, *Biography*, 197–204.

278. Kwon, "Reimagining," 288, after charting the use of compositional devices in Xenophon on the one hand and later biographers of Galba and Otho on the other.

279. De Temmerman, "Formalities," 4.

280. De Temmerman, "Formalities," 4, citing Cohn, *Distinction*, 18–37, esp. 26; Cohn, "Lives," 9–10.

creating a more engaging narrative, but such details can appear also in ancient historiography.[281] They may predominate in more popular-level works, but this predominance reflects the social level of the ideal audience more than whether the work's author has interest in the past or some prior information. What we might deem fictionalization, ancient historical writers could deem historical reconstruction—not always of what they knew happened, but at least of their best guess of what happened. That is, such characteristics do not collapse biography or historiography into novels; by themselves they do not identify traits specific to particular ancient genres.

Because "what if" questions ("what *might have happened*" under different circumstances) are counterfactual, some treat them as fictionalization.[282] Both Plutarch and the historian Livy explore such questions.[283] One should note, however, that they appear both in ancient historiography and regularly in modern historiography.[284] Nor are edifying concerns, characteristic of ancient biography, entirely absent from its modern descendant.[285] That is, if one defines fictionalizing in such a broad way, we should also recognize its presence in works designed especially to communicate information.

2.9. Conclusion

The Gospels are premeditated foundation documents. Scholars have proposed various genre forms for the Gospels; some proposals, such as novels, are wide of the mark; some others, such as "unique," are not very helpful. Still others, like "memoirs," are on the right track. Clearly the Gospels are not mythography, novels, or pure drama (which required poetic form). As works focused on a single, historical character, drawing on significant amounts of historical tradition, the Gospels are most readily recognized as ancient biography.

Although ancient biography differed from its modern heir and namesake, it was supposed to deal in historical information rather than the fanciful cre-

---

281. E.g., Tacitus, *Histories* 2.74; *Annals* 4.38–39; 12.4.

282. Almagor, "Narratives," 65–66. Pace Almagor ("Narratives," 66, 69), however, Aristotle *Poetics* 1451b1–8 probably refers to epic poetry, not to hypothetical speculation in historiography.

283. Almagor, "Narratives," 67–68; cf. Plutarch's use of this approach to add new twists to old stories, 78–79.

284. Pelling, *Texts*, 79, 81; Almagor, "Narratives," 66 (though the latter finds it more in biography, 69–70); esp. Sheppard, *Craft*, 172–78.

285. See Dillon, "Interpretation," 164.

ation of events. Some biographies were more true to historical information than were others (typically, those about recent generations were much more reliable than those about the distant past). But most full-length biographies clustered around historical intention, certainly where they narrated about an individual based on prior sources. Even if one Gospel substantially adapted such central expectations for full-length biographies about recent figures, one would hardly expect all four to do so independently. If some scholars today argue for such adaptation, it must be on grounds other than ancient expectations.

Ancient writers, whatever their human biases, were normally in a better historical position to evaluate matters of their day than we are today.[286] Luke was able to investigate or at least be aware of the information passed on to him. Roughly the same critical tools were available to him as are available to us, and much more information was available to him than is otherwise available to us. While we may recognize the Evangelists' emphases and question them on matters of detail, we ultimately have little to work with for alternative reconstructions if we dismiss the Gospels' materials.

---

286. With, e.g., Sumney, *Opponents*, 86.

Chapter 3

Examples and Development of Ancient Biography

One reason that Philipp Vielhauer in the 1970s rejected the biographic character of the Gospels is that he considered ancient biographies later than Mark, because his basis for comparison was Lucian's second-century *Peregrinus* and the still later *Life of Apollonius* and *Alexander Romance*.[1] But Vielhauer's basis for comparison was too limited. Partly biographic treatments of Greek sages, many now preserved only in fragments, predate the Gospels by a number of centuries,[2] and surviving, full-scale biographies predate them by at least a century.

This chapter surveys some examples of ancient biography, noting some general patterns in their development. The period of the early empire, fortuitously for NT scholars, is both the period of the Gospels and also the "best-documented period"[3] of ancient biography. From earlier times we have only fragments and titles,[4] but as Momigliano notes, the major Greek or Roman biographers we typically envision, such as Plutarch, Suetonius, or Diogenes Laertius, "all belong to the Imperial Age."[5]

3.1. Protobiography and Early Greek Biography

A number of generic predecessors with various degrees of biographic focus came before what we are apt to call full biographies. These works usually dif-

---

1. See Collins, *Mark*, 20, regarding Vielhauer, *Geschichte*, 350.

2. Hägg, *Biography*, 187; biographic interest appears among Peripatetics in the fourth century BCE (Laistner, *Historians*, 18). For Greek works showing biographic interest from the fifth century BCE onward, see (although including forms other than what we in this work designate as biographies) Hägg, *Biography*, 10–98 passim (note esp. Xenophon's memoirs on Socrates, 23–30; on Agesilaus, 41–51; on Aristoxenus, 69–77; memoirs of Antigonus, 89–93).

3. De Temmerman and Demoen, "Preface," xii, on "the first centuries CE."

4. Momigliano, *Development*, 9; Frickenschmidt, *Evangelium*, 153.

5. Momigliano, *Development*, 9.

fer considerably, not least in the matter of interest in and commitment to historical accuracy, from biographies of the early imperial period. Although authors composed many monographs about kings in the Hellenistic period, only samples—mostly fragments and titles—remain.[6] Because little from this period survives, comments are limited especially to the extant material, which differs considerably from most material from the early empire.

Possibly under Persian influence,[7] as perhaps in the case of Nehemiah[8] and Xenophon, Greeks developed a form of biographic writing in the fifth century BCE.[9] The works of this period probably focused on mythical heroes, past notable poets whose works generated public interest, and outstanding contemporaries, some perhaps autobiographic in character.[10] Such works are technically not biographies per se, but they did influence the development of biographies.[11]

The increased interest in great persons caused something prefiguring later biography to flourish more as a genre in fourth-century Greece.[12] For the fourth century, the key surviving samples are the *Euagoras* and *Agesilaus*, "which describe themselves as encomia, and . . . a philosophical novel, Xenophon's *Cyropaedia*"; from the third century we have little more than "a fragment of Satyrus' life of Euripides."[13]

Exemplified by the orator Isocrates, the fourth century generated the prose encomium, which valued praise of an individual above balanced, critical evaluation.[14] It was thus like a eulogy, but in incipient biographic material of Isocrates's *Euagoras* and Xenophon's *Agesilaus,* it was of a contemporary figure.[15] Encomiastic form, like that of a funeral oration, does not mean that all the contents must be fictitious, but one should certainly not expect a bal-

---

6. Momigliano, *Development*, 8–9. See further Frickenschmidt, *Evangelium*, 153–62.

7. Momigliano, *Development*, 102; Burridge, *Gospels*, 67; Adams, *Genre*, 73. For possible earlier Egyptian and Hittite precedents, see Mayes, "Biography," 1–2.

8. Burridge, *Gospels*, 67. Many compare Nehemiah with Late Period Egyptian funerary memoirs; see Von Rad, "Nehemia-Denkschrift"; Van Seters, *Search*, 129, 183–87; Mayes, "Biography," 2; Rüpke, *Religion*, 36; also highlighting differences, Blenkinsopp, *Judaism*, 94–97.

9. Momigliano, *Development*, 12; see further discussion on 23–42; cf. also Frickenschmidt, *Evangelium*, 93–114; Burridge, *Gospels*, 68.

10. Momigliano, *Development*, 102.

11. Geiger, *Nepos*, 14–15.

12. Momigliano, *Development*, 43, 45; see further discussion in 43–64.

13. Momigliano, *Development*, 8.

14. Momigliano, *Development*, 102.

15. Momigliano, *Development*, 50.

anced or always truthful picture.[16] Socrates's followers, most notably Plato and Xenophon, experimented with what are often considered biographically interested treatments of Socrates, yet with only limited interest in historical precision.[17] That is, most scholars contend that in this period the historical aspect of biography had not yet developed much beyond Isocrates.[18]

3.1a. Isocrates's Euagoras

Isocrates's *Euagoras* claims to recount truth, in contrast to the accounts of epic poetry,[19] the point of which was not historical education. Isocrates's stated purpose is, however, preserving forever the memory of Euagoras's virtues and inviting others to imitate him.[20] Euagoras's virtues include such later "cardinal" virtues[21] as "manly courage, wisdom and justice."[22] Isocrates narrates events such as his flight to Cilicia and his getting the throne,[23] but Isocrates dwells on his character.[24] Isocrates achieves this effect partly by comparing Euagoras with many other figures,[25] a practice that becomes common in many ancient biographies.[26]

Isocrates recounts Euagoras's virtues, but only his treatment of others' reactions to his achievements is arranged chronologically;[27] unlike later biographies, he does not narrate episodes.[28] Isocrates also had written biographic sketches, notably about Alcibiades, but he viewed his *Euagoras* as "the first

---

16. Chance, "Fiction," 133: not "necessarily . . . fabrication, but it did result in making the encomiast's subject conform to preconceived notions of greatness—to fit a mold, so to speak."

17. Momigliano, *Development*, 46; De Temmerman, "Formalities," 4. As Collins notes (*Mark*, 25), Votaw compares the Gospels with these sources (Votaw, *Gospels*, 33–34, 58–59), but Plato's dialogues are certainly not biographic in genre.

18. Momigliano, *Development*, 102.

19. Ytterbrink, *Gospel*, 76, cites *Euagoras* 10, 21, 36; see further Ytterbrink, *Gospel*, 76–80.

20. Ytterbrink, *Gospel*, 76, citing *Euagoras* 4, 76, 80–81. For the pedagogical function, see also Frickenschmidt, *Evangelium*, 108–9.

21. For some Stoic uses of the cardinal Aristotelian virtues, see Musonius Rufus 4, p. 44.10–22; p. 48.1, 4, 8, 13; 6, p. 52.15, 17, 19, 21; 8, pp. 60.22–64.9; 8, p. 66.7–8; 17, p. 108.9–10; Arius Didymus, *Epitome* 2.7.5a, p. 10.7–9; 2.7.5b1, p. 12.13–22; 2.7.5b2, p. 14.1–4; 2.7.5b5, p. 18.21–35.

22. Ytterbrink, *Gospel*, 77, citing *Euagoras* 23.

23. Ytterbrink, *Gospel*, 77, citing *Euagoras* 27–28, 32, 66.

24. Ytterbrink, *Gospel*, 79–80.

25. Ytterbrink, *Gospel*, 78, 84.

26. See, e.g., Frickenschmidt, *Evangelium*, 228, 505; Duff, *Lives*, 243, 257, 268.

27. Momigliano, *Development*, 49.

28. Momigliano, *Development*, 49–50.

attempt at a prose encomium by a contemporary."[29] Nevertheless, even this work probably had predecessors.[30]

Because these early biographic works were so closely related to encomium, encomiastic motifs surface frequently in the genre's later iterations.[31] But historiography as well as encomium fed into these early biographies.[32] In addition to his biographic experiments, Xenophon was one of the leading historical writers of his generation,[33] although not at the level of Thucydides.[34] Many histories had biographic sections,[35] and Polybius, a historian, also wrote an encomium, albeit explicitly with much less balance than his historiography.[36] Whereas historians focused on individuals primarily in relation to larger matters of the state, however, antiquarians wrote about a range of matters, including personal concerns such as those more prominent in biographies.[37]

Isocrates's *Euagoras* and Xenophon's *Agesilaus* and (still more) his *Cyropaedia* are not biographies in the fuller sense in which biographies appear in the imperial period.[38] For the purpose of distinguishing them from the form as it developed in succeeding centuries, it might be more helpful to designate them, with some scholars, as "protobiographies."[39]

Although Isocrates's *Euagoras* is encomiastic prose rather than a full biography, it remains relevant to the discussion because of its influence on subsequent biographies.[40]

3.1b. Xenophon's Agesilaus

Isocrates's biographic interest influenced some contemporary historians[41] and served as a model for Xenophon's *Agesilaus* soon afterward,[42] although Xeno-

---

29. Momigliano, *Development*, 47–49; see also Frickenschmidt, *Evangelium*, 110.

30. So Aristotle, *Rhetoric* 1368a17, in Momigliano, *Development*, 49.

31. Beck, "Demonax," 93n34, citing, e.g., Dihle, *Studien*, 20–29; Burridge, *Gospels*, 62–67.

32. With, e.g., Adams, *Genre*, 73.

33. Votaw, "Biographies," 225.

34. See Rhodes, "Documents," 60; cf. Dewald, "Construction," 95–96.

35. See Frickenschmidt, *Evangelium*, 136–42, on Herodotus.

36. See, e.g., Frickenschmidt, *Evangelium*, 142–43.

37. Cox, *Biography*, 5–6.

38. Momigliano, *Development*, 50; Geiger, *Nepos*, 15.

39. Konstan and Walsh, "Biography," 29.

40. Adams, *Genre*, 74.

41. Momigliano, *Development*, 48.

42. Momigliano, *Development*, 50. Perhaps also his *Memorabilia* (Votaw, "Biographies," 50).

phon had also shown earlier interest in individuals in his historical work.[43] Xenophon's various biographical experiments in turn became models for later biographies.[44]

Xenophon wants to honor and defend Agesilaus, as well as use him as a model for others to follow.[45] Xenophon divided *Agesilaus* into (1) chronological treatment, as in Isocrates, but also (2) "a nonchronological, systematic review of Agesilaus' virtues."[46] He arranged these virtues in a traditional way also followed by other contemporaries.[47] But Xenophon, whose other works demonstrate clearly his (often accurate)[48] historical predilections,[49] holds greater interest in Agesilaus's deeds than did Isocrates in those of Euagoras.[50]

Xenophon wrote more encomiastically about Agesilaus in his work of that name than he did in his *Hellenica*, which included Agesilaus but focused on public events rather than Agesilaus's character.[51] But in Xenophon's first section on Agesilaus, where he treats his actions chronologically before turning to his virtues, there is considerable overlap with what Xenophon treats earlier in his *Hellenica*.[52] The overlap shows Xenophon's strong historical interests; the divergences largely emphasize his greater concern for making Agesilaus look good.[53]

Xenophon also appeals directly to wide public knowledge available in his day; he avoids naming most individual witnesses not because they are

43. Momigliano, *Development*, 51–52 (in his *Anabasis*). For other possible models for Xenophon, see Momigliano, *Development*, 47.

44. Momigliano, *Development*, 47. For Xenophon's versatility in various forms of writing, see also Smith and Kostopoulos, "Biography," 396.

45. Woldemariam, "Comparison," 227, cites, for honoring him, e.g., *Agesilaus* 1.36; 2.24, 27–28, 37; 5.3–4; 8.4–6; as his "hero," 3.1; 5.7; 11.1; for defending him, 2.21; 4.4; 5.6; and as a model, 10.2.

46. Momigliano, *Development*, 50; Ytterbrink, *Gospel*, 82; Adams, *Genre*, 75.

47. Momigliano, *Development*, 51; Ytterbrink, *Gospel*, 82.

48. Despite some biased omissions. See Brownson, "Introduction to Hellenica," ix–xi; Brown, *Historians*, 93–94, 97. Like Thucydides, Xenophon largely avoids myth in his *Hellenica* (Fowler, "History," 198).

49. See, e.g., Ytterbrink, *Gospel*, 82n87, following Frickenschmidt, *Evangelium*, 111–12. Later Roman historians apparently sometimes evoked Xenophon's historical models; see Rood, "Cato."

50. Ytterbrink, *Gospel*, 82–83, 86, noting esp. *Agesilaus* 1.6; contrast Cox, *Biography*, 9.

51. Momigliano, *Development*, 50.

52. *Hellenica* 3.3.1–5.1.3; I owe this observation to the comparisons charted in the dissertations of my PhD students Youngju Kwon and T. Wright (see Kwon, "Reimagining," 144–219, esp. 158, 169; the chart on 159–60; adaptations using conventional compositional techniques, noted on 169–70). Plutarch, *Agesilaus* 8, also draws, directly or indirectly, on Xenophon, *Hellenica* 3 (Woldemariam, "Comparison," 219–20).

53. Wright, "Reliability," ch. 2.

too few but because they are too many.[54] Encomiastic though the protobiography may be, it reflects Xenophon's direct acquaintance with Agesilaus and thus significant historical information, more than is found in Isocrates's *Euagoras*.[55]

Besides his greater encomiastic focus, Xenophon's protobiography differs from most later biographies in some other respects. He quotes Agesilaus less often than one would expect from later biographies.[56] Despite Agesilaus's allegedly divine, Heraclid lineage, Xenophon also shows no interest in his birth or childhood.[57]

How does it compare historiographically? Resources for concrete evaluation are somewhat limited. The vast majority of Xenophon's material about Agesilaus is singly attested and can neither be verified nor dismissed a priori. The evidence, however, is compelling that he knew Agesilaus personally, which both strengthens and weakens his depiction: Xenophon knew much about Agesilaus, but he also was strongly partisan in his favor and probably dependent on his benefactions. Many others in antiquity (particularly Agesilaus's political enemies) construed Agesilaus's actions less favorably.

While perspectives do not require the fabrication of information, Xenophon's encomiastic approach probably did distort information at times. Comparing Xenophon's epideictic (i.e., encomiastic, praise-oriented) *Agesilaus* with his more sober *Hellenica* (as well as some other early sources such as the *Hellenica Oxyrhynchia*)[58] suggests that Xenophon's protobiography significantly changes some accounts about Agesilaus.

At the same time, the comparison shows that more often, where we can test him, the biography agrees on events with other extant sources.[59] Such protobiography was encomiastic, but its reports of events appear to be based on actual happenings more often than not. This does not mean that he does not invent material to supply narrative transitions where needed, for example,

---

54. Woldemariam, "Comparison," 218, noting esp. *Agesilaus* 3.1; 5.7; for the public character of information about Agesilaus, cf. also Wright, "Exploration," 240.

55. Burridge, *Gospels*, 126.

56. Ytterbrink, *Gospel*, 85.

57. Ytterbrink, *Gospel*, 83, 87, pace Cox, *Biography*, 9; cf. Cornelius Nepos, *On Great Generals* 17 (Agesilaus), 1.2.

58. This fragmentary work, possibly by Cratippus, is pieced together from several papyri; Diodorus Siculus followed but adapted the original.

59. I follow here the discussion and documentation in Wright, "Reliability," ch. 2, who compares also all other reports about Agesilaus through the early third century CE and teases out, where possible, any independent sources on which they may have depended.

the path taken to a battle; the battle, however, appears to reflect authentic information about an event.[60]

3.1c. Xenophon's "Memoirs" about Socrates

Xenophon, too creative a writer to be limited by artificial genre boundaries, experimented with a range of person-centered forms, from an early novel about a historical person (the *Cyropaedia*) to a protobiography (the *Agesilaus*, a biographic encomium) to something in between (his apologetic *Apomnemoneumata*,[61] today usually called *Memorabilia*, about Socrates).[62] Here Xenophon writes apologetically, defending Socrates's character against posthumous criticisms.[63] This approach does not invite a chronological structure.[64]

Xenophon recognized that traditional history did not recount noteworthy sayings,[65] in contrast to a more focused work on a person. This is not to say that no one collected sayings of sages before; these were apparently circulating already in the previous century,[66] and aphorisms are more often preserved in oral traditions than are other forms.[67] (Aphorisms or maxims are short, succinct statements that are easily recalled, such as, "Whoever is not against us is for us," Mark 9:40.[68] These appear in some form in most cultures.)[69]

Xenophon's *Memorabilia* probably recalls some noteworthy sayings of and surely themes and teachings of Socrates,[70] and sometimes his style.[71] Dialogue

60. Again following Wright.

61. See Xenophon, *Memorabilia* 1.3.1.

62. Frickenschmidt, *Evangelium*, 111–14, esp. 111; Momigliano, *Development*, 52.

63. Momigliano, *Development*, 52–53. Cf. Xenophon's *Apology*.

64. Adams, *Genre*, 75.

65. Momigliano, *Development*, 50, citing Xenophon, *Hellenica* 2.3.56.

66. Momigliano, *Development*, 53, citing esp. Herodotus, *Histories* 1.27; 2.134; Aristophanes, *Wasps* 1446. Earlier, cf., e.g., Proverbs; Ptah-hotep.

67. See chs. 14–15.

68. Even this brief saying in Mark might appear in a slightly different version in Q (Matt 12:30//Luke 11:23), though it is no less plausible that both versions reflect a wider sentiment in the Jesus tradition.

69. E.g., "If you merely chase away a spider into another room, you will find new cobwebs created there" (Kerala, South India; noted by George, *Philippians*, at Phil 1:12–26), or, "Wisdom is better than wealth" (Kenya; noted by Mburu, *Hermeneutics*, forthcoming); sayings of Confucius (China), Publilius Syrus (Rome), and the like.

70. For shared ideas between Xenophon and Plato, see Votaw, "Biographies," 222, 233–45; esp. Marchant, "Introduction," ix–xv.

71. See here Xenophon, *Apology* 1.

also was, as Plato and Xenophon together recognize, inherent in Socrates's pedagogy. Nevertheless, Xenophon's and the early Plato's depiction of Socrates's dialogues is a more apt portrayal of his pedagogic style than of any detailed content of actual specific conversations.[72]

The characters and probably even many occasions of dialogues were authentic, but we no more dare take them as a transcript of actual conversations[73] than we do the poetic account of Job and his comforters (Job 3–41). Dialogues continued to be an accepted, transparently fictional literary form for conveying an author's ideas.[74] Ancient critics could thus recognize that Plato's reports of Socrates's speeches were fictitious.[75] Later writers collecting biographic material about Socrates likewise felt freer to draw on Xenophon's or Plato's general information about Socrates than on their dialogical content.[76]

In 1915 Clyde Votaw observed that "Plato and Xenophon give us a portrait rather than a photograph of Socrates," shaping him to fit "their didactic and apologetic purpose." But once we take into account "the nature of their compositions, we can with considerable success extricate the biographical data, and so come to know the real Socrates."[77] Even though Votaw's confidence in historical reconstruction appears exaggerated (a feature more characteristic of his era than of ours), he rightly recognized that Xenophon drew on genuine information about Socrates.

3.1d. Aristotelians and Aristoxenus

Xenophon was not the only Socratic with biographic interests. Plato's former pupil Aristotle used many biographic anecdotes,[78] and his followers found anecdotes useful for illustrating vices and virtues.[79] This sort of historical exploration of individuals offered a more inductive approach to virtues than

---

72. Momigliano, *Development*, 53–54.

73. Votaw, "Biographies," 229, supposes that Diogenes Laertius takes this approach.

74. See Schenkeveld, "Prose," 213–30; Cicero, *Letters to Atticus* 12.12; cf. Lucian, *Nigrinus* 1–12, 38.

75. Dionysius of Halicarnassus, *Demosthenes* 23.

76. See Diogenes Laertius, *Lives* 2.18–47, esp. (for Plato) 18, 28–30, 38–39, 45 (though cf. 40); (for Xenophon) 20, 29, 31–32, 45; for the claim that Xenophon took notes, see 2.48.

77. Votaw, "Biographies," 247 (with greater confidence in Plato's earlier dialogues and Xenophon's *Memorabilia* bk. 1).

78. Momigliano, *Development*, 68–69; Burridge, *Gospels*, 69.

79. Momigliano, *Development*, 69; Chance, "Fiction," 135.

mere extrapolation from accepted norms.[80] Anecdotes would soon become a major feature of the biographic genre.

Although various Aristotelians displayed biographic interest,[81] scholars usually attribute the first actual Aristotelian (Peripatetic) biographies to Aristoxenus.[82] Despite Aristoxenus's Peripatetic associations, however, he was one-sided in his criticism of Socrates and praise of Pythagoras, omitting elements that did not fit his portrait.[83] Aristoxenus may have initiated the Hellenistic period of biographic depiction, with its mixture of "erudition, scholarly zeal, realism of details, and gossip";[84] the primary interest in this period seems to have been to entertain and satisfy curiosity.[85]

3.1e. The Hellenistic Era

Only in the Hellenistic era did biographic writing achieve the title of *bios*, or "life."[86] Greek biographic literature in this period often speculated about the lives of poets, often making inferences from their poems.[87] Other biographic literature focused on sages.[88] Some scholars go too far, however, acknowledging only such intellectual biographies and denying that political biography existed in this period.[89] Later citations belie that claim, at least if we define biography broadly; the early Alexander histories, drawn on by extant writers in the imperial period, blended elements of historical monograph, encomium, and biography.[90] Biographies of public figures, for whom biographers had access to more information than they did for lives of poets, display stronger historical interests.[91]

Little biographic material is extant from the second century BCE.[92] One fragmentary piece is Satyrus's life of Euripides. The later writer Athenaeus

80. Cf. Momigliano, *Development*, 103.
81. Momigliano, *Development*, 73.
82. Momigliano, *Development*, 74, 76, 79; Frickenschmidt, *Evangelium*, 154–55.
83. Cox, *Biography*, 10–11; Pelling, "Biography, Greek," 241–42.
84. Momigliano, *Development*, 103; cf. Chance, "Fiction," 135.
85. Momigliano, *Development*, 84.
86. Momigliano, *Development*, 12, noting that *biographia* is first attested in the late fifth century CE.
87. See Lefkowitz, *Lives*, ix, 70, 128, 177.
88. Adams, *Genre*, 87–88.
89. Geiger, *Nepos*, 65, 66 (cf. 116; the fuller treatment is in 30–65).
90. Frickenschmidt, *Evangelium*, 143–44.
91. See, e.g., Frickenschmidt, *Evangelium*, 161.
92. Momigliano, *Development*, 84–85.

associates Satyrus with the Peripatetic school, noted above; his biography of Euripides fits observations about lives of the poets already offered.[93]

Nevertheless, later surviving sources suggest that Antigonus of Carystus's *Lives of Philosophers* established a new standard for accuracy in depicting the philosophers of his era.[94] Providing biographic introductions for authors' works, Alexandrian scholars in this period delineated, without respect to chronology beyond the subject's birth and death, the subject's works, lifestyle, students, and friends.[95]

3.2. Nearly Nepotism: Cornelius Nepos

Not all the earlier biographic materials shared the same historiographic commitments, but such commitments clearly dominated by the era of the Gospels.

Extant biographies in the fullest sense begin with Cornelius Nepos (ca. 100–ca. 24 BCE), who wrote in the final generation of the Roman Republic.[96] Before this period, remains are too fragmentary to try to classify them or reconstruct the usual contours of the genre.[97] With Nepos, however, begins the flowering of ancient biography,[98] at least with regard to extant treatment of public figures.[99] At least one of his biographies was of a person then living, probably one of the first of its kind in his era.[100]

Varro's biographic work (including his autobiography) significantly influenced Nepos,[101] who had already worked in various relevant genres.[102] Late in his career, Nepos began writing lives of Roman and foreign generals,[103] in the process paving the way for later comparisons of Greek and Roman figures such as those best known in Plutarch.[104] His approach varies from one biography to

93. Note here also Frickenschmidt, *Evangelium*, 158–59.

94. Pelling, "Biography, Greek," 242; Walbank and Stewart, "Antigonus."

95. Pelling, "Biography, Greek," 242.

96. Momigliano, *Development*, 9.

97. Cf. Pryzwansky, "Nepos"; Adams, *Genre*, 79, noting esp. Swain, "Biography."

98. For this depiction of the period from Nepos forward, see Frickenschmidt, *Evangelium*, 161, 163–91.

99. See Frickenschmidt, *Evangelium*, 163–66. He may have additionally composed some lives of literary figures (Geiger, *Nepos*, 91).

100. Geiger, *Nepos*, 95; cf. Hägg, *Biography*, 188–97, esp. 189–90.

101. Momigliano, *Development*, 96–97; others in Jenkinson, "Nepos."

102. Geiger, *Nepos*, 116.

103. Geiger, *Nepos*, 88, 103–4, 116.

104. Momigliano, *Development*, 98; Stadter, "Biography," 533.

another; sometimes his arrangement is more topical, whereas at other times it is more chronological.[105]

Of the minority of surviving biographies by Nepos, "some are openly laudatory, a few vituperative, the rest more historically balanced."[106] Nepos does make historical errors in his biographies, but these are most evident in the sources most distant from his sphere of cultural and historical knowledge. Tomas Hägg observes that Nepos "has been singularly unlucky regarding what happened to survive of his main work: among the famous men he chose to depict, the non-Roman military commanders were no doubt the figures farthest from his competence." He lacks the context "necessary to assess and recreate their historical particularity," and he was less "versed in Greek culture, or fluent in Greek."[107] By contrast, his work on Atticus is strong,[108] fitting our expectations for a subject closer to the author's own period.[109]

Like his predecessors, Nepos treated a subject's manner of life as appropriate to biography in a way that it was not appropriate to historiography more generally.[110] Nevertheless, his works provide a standard of accuracy missing in what we know of Hellenistic biography.[111] Nepos was sometimes careless,[112] but he offers our first extant examples of full biographies, and like the biographers who follow in the imperial era, he was clearly interested in using historical information.[113] The historical interest in biographies has reached the range found in the early empire, while also assuming the basic three-part treatment of lives that differed from the continous flow in standard historical works.[114]

---

105. Burridge, *Gospels*, 73.

106. Hägg, *Biography*, 189. The verb tenses in Cornelius Nepos, *On Great Generals* 25 (Atticus), chs. 13–18, might suggest that these chapters are revisions for Nepos's second edition. Historians and biographers often revised their works; see, e.g., Dionysius of Halicarnassus, *Thucydides* 24. (Other writers also revised their works; see, e.g., Dionysius of Halicarnassus, *On Literary Composition* 9; Ovid, *Amores* prol.; Suetonius, *Vergil* 22–23, 33; Pliny, *Letters* 5.8.6–7; Aulus Gellius, *Attic Nights* 6.20.)

107. Hägg, *Biography*, 196.

108. Hägg, *Biography*, 197; Wright, "Reliability," ch. 3 (far stronger than Xenophon).

109. In this case, he knew Atticus personally; see Hägg, *Biography*, 189–90.

110. See Nepos, *On Great Generals* 16 (Pelopidas), 1, cited in Momigliano, *Development*, 99n40.

111. Frickenschmidt, *Evangelium*, 159.

112. For a survey of scholarly emphasis on his errors, see Pryzwansky, "Nepos," 97–100, cited by Christian, "Themistocles," 104; more favorable, Stem, *Biographies* (from T. Wright).

113. Frickenschmidt, *Evangelium*, 159; Alfred, "Valuation," 82–84 (in greater detail, see his "Source Valuation"); Christian, "Themistocles," 105–39; also (noted by Christian) Titchener, "Nepos," 90; Musnick, "Historical Commentary."

114. Frickenschmidt, *Evangelium*, 190, 504.

Biography served a useful public purpose by offering moral examples, yet it differed from nonhistorical genres by using historical information to do so. Nepos exemplifies both historical and encomiastic interests, as in the Gospels.[115]

Some have argued that in the first century BCE some historical writers stopped emphasizing utility as their purpose and emphasized instead that they simply would write a "true account of something."[116] Given our relatively few extant sources, however, it seems premature to play these purposes off against one another; in the second century CE, Lucian embraces both functions.[117] It is true, however, that historiography now emphasized greater attention to historical truth.

3.3. Biographies in the Empire

By the period of the empire "a new atmosphere" prevails.[118] Imperial-era biographies retain interest in gossip and irrelevant detail, but like the biographies of Nepos, most of them depend fairly heavily on prior information.

Nicolaus of Damascus wrote in Greek in the same part of the empire in which Jesus's movement later started.[119] His historical work comprised 144 books, nearly all now lost,[120] but it does reveal his strong interest in the remembered past. His fragmentary *bios* of Augustus is more encomiastic than some other early imperial biographies, harking back to Hellenistic models.[121] Nevertheless, Nicolaus occasionally reports his hero's early weaknesses, though trying to interpret them positively,[122] and is probably interpreting material from Augustus's own autobiography.[123] Some biographies

---

115. Frickenschmidt, *Evangelium*, 166; on virtues, see Beneker, "Method," esp. 112–15.

116. Callan, "Preface and Historiography," 579–80.

117. Usefulness in Lucian, *How to Write History* 53, but this comes from truth alone in §9.

118. Momigliano, *Development*, 104.

119. Nicolaus was involved even with Herod the Great and provided a key source for Josephus; see *Jewish Antiquities* 1.94, 108, 159; 7.101; 12.126–27; 13.250, 347; 14.9, 68, 104; 16.29–30, 58, 183, 299, 333, 335, 337–39, 342, 370; 17.54, 99, 106, 127, 219, 225, 240, 248, 315–16; *Jewish War* 1.574, 629, 637; 2.14, 21, 34, 37, 92.

120. Develin, "Introduction," 7.

121. See, e.g., Nicolaus, *Augustus* 1 (*FGrH* 125); 18 (*FGrH* 130).

122. Nicolaus, *Augustus* 9 (*FGrH* 127); 16 (*FGrH* 130).

123. Cf. Momigliano, *Development*, 86; Frickenschmidt, *Evangelium*, 166–67; Alfred, "Valuation," 84 (who notes on his sources Bellemore, *Nicolaus*, xxiv–xxvi); on Nicolaus, see further Hägg, *Biography*, 197–204.

of Nero that have not survived stem from roughly the same time as Mark's Gospel, though Josephus complains about their bias.[124] Other biographies from this period remain, however, biographies that we can evaluate more directly and fully.

3.3a. Philo's Life of Moses

Before the Gospels, the widely known[125] Jewish author Philo composed some works that exploit Greco-Roman biographic conventions. Some regard Philo's *Flaccus* and *Embassy to Gaius* as something like detailed biographies of figures in recent memory.[126] Although he is particularly adept at writing philosophic treatises, Philo can follow the conventions of biographic and historical genres when he uses them.[127]

Some of Philo's Pentateuchal "lives"[128] do not conform as well to mainstream Greco-Roman expectations for *bioi*.[129] Granted, his purpose there is partly encomiastic, to praise the honorable ancestors, and partly to make them models for imitation.[130] But most of Philo's essays on biblical personalities, though reflecting some Greek biographic influence, are more philosophic.[131] In these cases, his philosophic penchant for allegorizing Pentateuchal narratives somewhat limits the analogy for mainstream biographies.[132]

---

124. Josephus, *Jewish Antiquities* 20.154.

125. See Josephus, *Jewish Antiquities* 18.259-60.

126. So Borgen, *John*, ch. 13. *Flaccus* may fall closer to the genre of an apologetic historical monograph (Meiser, "Gattung").

127. Smallwood, "Historians," contends that Philo is even more accurate than Josephus when reporting the same historical events.

128. See Philo, *Joseph* 1; cf. *Abraham* 4.

129. Some more closely resemble allegorical exposition in the style of Alexandrian philosophic commentary; cf. Sandnes, "Markus."

130. Ytterbrink, *Gospel*, 100–101, correctly noting Philo, *Abraham* 4–5, 217; for praise, cf. also *Abraham* 247, 255; *Moses* 2.191; *Allegorical Interpretation* 2.67. On panegyrics in *Moses*, see, e.g., Feldman, *Portrayal*, 20.

131. Canevet, "Remarques." Philo adjusts figures to suit his idealizations of virtue (cf. Petit, "Traversée exemplaire"). For similarities between Philonic biography and Plutarch, see Niehoff, "Philo."

132. Although one might consider some mildly allegorical literary techniques in John, e.g., 1:5; 13:30. Philo's focus on characters of the distant past also allows him more freedoms than biographers writing about more recent figures.

More relevant in terms of genre is his *Life of Moses*, clearly called a "life,"[133] and with fewer allegorical features than many of his other works.[134] Although Philo is influenced by elite Hellenistic philosophy far more than are any of our Gospels, he offers a specifically Jewish biography that is not (unlike Josephus's *Life*) an autobiography. Philo's *Life of Moses* has generated considerable attention.[135]

Like Xenophon and some others, Philo combines both chronological and topical arrangements concerning his subject.[136] In book 1, Philo follows Moses's story from the accounts in Exodus 1:1–17:15 and then Numbers 13, 20–25, 31–32, with rare topical digressions.[137] In book 2, Philo's treatment is primarily topical, except for Moses's death;[138] Philo includes much more allegory here (e.g., on details of the tabernacle) than in book 1, which follows the more common Greco-Roman biographic tradition.[139] Even in the more chronological section, he sometimes displaces material chronologically.[140]

---

133. Philo, *Moses* 1.1–4; 2.66; see also McGing, "Adaptation," 118. Cf. *Decalogue* 1. Further on this work, see, e.g., Ytterbrink, *Gospel*, 94–100. For insightful comparisons and contrasts between Philo's *Life of Moses* and one of the Gospels, see recently Holladay, "Matthew"; contrasts include Philo's greater narrative symbolism and his far more explicit and abundant encomiastic asides (Holladay, "Matthew," 17–18).

134. Burridge, *Gospels*, 128. On biography and philosophy in Philo, cf. Termini, "Part." For comparison of this work with a Gospel, deeming both "encomiastic biography," see Shuler, "Moses."

135. E.g., Goodenough, "Exposition"; Robbins, *Study*; Granata, "Introduzione"; Feldman, *Portrayal*; for cosmological theology here, see Steyn, "Elemente"; for mediation in this work, see Parker, "Swiftly Runs the Word." On other particulars, see, e.g., McKnight, "Lion Proselytes"; Riaud, "Réflexions"; Berchmann, "Arcana Mundi." Damgaard, *Recasting Moses*, places this life in the larger framework of accounts of Moses from the LXX to later Christian works; on patristic use of this work, see, e.g., Geljon, *Exegesis*; cf. Malherbe and Ferguson, *Gregory of Nyssa*.

136. Ytterbrink, *Gospel*, 103; McGing, "Adaptation," 119. Burridge, "Review," 477, suggests, probably rightly, that *Moses* is modeled on Xenophon's *Agesilaus*; unlike the more typical single-volume biographies, these two works each present their protagonist as king and then elaborate his virtues.

137. McGing, "Adaptation," 119 (noting the digression in 1.148–62); Hidalgo, "Study," 281–86, esp. 286.

138. McGing, "Adaptation," 119; Feldman, *Portrayal*, 361.

139. Adams, *Negotiating Genre*, ch. 8. Adams views *Life of Moses* as straddling the (potentially overlapping) categories of rewritten Scripture and biography. He also sees Philo's *Abraham* as part of a collected biography (the essays on Isaac and Jacob being lost), albeit with more spiritual exposition than in *Moses* and in typical biographies. *Joseph* also adapts biographic conventions, with less allegory than *Abraham*.

140. McGing, "Adaptation," 125–26, noting esp. 1.33, 40–47.

Like the Gospels, Philo certainly shapes his material to communicate his message, for example, presenting Moses as a philosopher-king[141] and a military leader,[142] or contrasting Moses and Balaam.[143] Especially in his topical section, Philo presents Moses as a philosopher-king and corrects outsiders' misunderstanding of Moses as divine.[144]

Philo's *Life of Moses*, which we can compare with his OT source, follows the same literary techniques observed in Plutarch and the Gospels (see ch. 11). He follows quite closely the outline of the text. A majority of his expositional changes can be explained as inferences.[145] He omits episodes and abridges,[146] expands narratives with explanatory, apologetic, or dramatic details,[147] and occasionally expands them allegorically—though very rarely in contrast to his expository, nonbiographic works.[148] Often he follows the biblical narrative closely,[149] and his expansions generally do not change "the essence of the" biblical picture.[150]

He selects and omits elements according to what suits his purposes.[151] Not unlike traditional Jewish haggadic expansions, though here not to the same degree, Philo enhances his image of Moses by elaborations.[152] Con-

---

141. Fitting Greek expectations; Feldman, "Birth"; Feldman, *Portrayal*; earlier, Meeks, *Prophet-King*, 115; for Moses as philosopher-sage, see Clifford, "Moses"; as prophet, Meeks, *Prophet-King*, 125–29; as prophet-king, Meeks, *Prophet-King*, 107–17; as a wise political leader (vs. the rabble), cf. Feldman, "Korah." Moses is never king in Josephus (Meeks, *Prophet-King*, 134–36; not surprising, given his apologetic).

142. On Moses as a military leader, see also Canevet, "Remarques"; Feldman, "Spies." Josephus also depicts him as a commander (Meeks, *Prophet-King*, 133–34).

143. Remus, "Thaumaturges" (emphasizing the distinguishing of Moses from magic). Balaam is contrasted with Moses not only in Philo (Feldman, "Balaam," on *Moses* 1.263–99) but in some later Jewish sources; see, e.g., Sipre Deut. 357.18.1–2; b. B. Bat. 15b; Exod. Rab. 32:3; Num. Rab. 14:20; Eccl. Rab. 2:15, §2; see further discussion in Bowman, "Prophets," 108–14.

144. Feldman, *Portrayal*; cf. Scott, "Divine Man" (agreeing with Carl Holladay). Still, for connection with divinity, cf. Philo, *Moses* 1.157–58.

145. See Hidalgo, "Study" (esp. 278–86), frequently following Feldman, *Portrayal* (cf., e.g., 62).

146. McGing, "Adaptation," 120, 123–25.

147. McGing, "Adaptation," 127–30, 133. For apologetic in *Moses*, see further, e.g., Feldman, *Portrayal*, 12.

148. McGing, "Adaptation," 130–31.

149. McGing, "Adaptation," 121–23, giving the example of Num 23:7–10 in *Moses* 1.278–79.

150. McGing, "Adaptation," 128, on his treatment of Exod 7:14–12:36 in *Moses* 1.96–139.

151. See, e.g., Feldman, "Calf"; Feldman, "Interpretation of Joshua."

152. See, e.g., Begg, "Moves"; cf. expansion in Begg, "Rephidim Episode"; expansion in Philo but more omissions in Josephus, in Begg, "Retelling." For additional details about, e.g., the thornbush, see Josephus, *Jewish Antiquities* 2.266; Philo, *Moses* 1.65–66. On regular hag-

sciously or not, he might also read his own background into Moses's life.[153] Philo sometimes downplays other characters in order to highlight Moses's role more fully.[154] Some of Philo's adaptations of biblical narrative, however, such as Moses's education,[155] may also adapt prior traditions.[156] Thus scholars find both distinctive features and overlap with other early Jewish retellings.[157]

Philo thus tells the story in his own way but depends heavily on his sources for the material.

3.3b. Josephus's Historiography

Like Philo, Josephus is of special interest as a Jewish author writing for the Diaspora. Later in the first century than Philo, Josephus writes historiography, apologetic, and an autobiography, his *Life*. Although Josephus may be a freer historian than many,[158] his historiography provides our main source for postexilic Jewish history.[159] Like other historians whose writings we possess, Josephus affirms his intention to write truth, in contrast to those historians he thinks are unconcerned for it.[160] This claim recalls the standard that historians demanded but does not resolve the extent to which Josephus fulfills it.[161]

---

gadic and other early Jewish elaboration, see sources and discussion in Keener, *John*, 1:27–28; Keener, *Acts*, 1:145. Rabbis developed biblical stories more expansively than Philo or Josephus; see, e.g., Shinan, "Wyhlm."

153. Cf. Bloch, "Alexandria."

154. See, e.g., Feldman, "Interpretation of Joshua"; Feldman, "General" (on the same Num 31 ch. as Feldman, "General," cf. Begg, "Retelling").

155. Cf. Feldman, "Birth"; Petitfils, "Tale," 162–63; Philo, *Moses* 1.20–23; Josephus, *Jewish Antiquities* 2.232–37; Acts 7:22. For Philo and Greek education, see Piccione, "Παιδεία"; cf. McGing, "Adaptation," 134.

156. Cf., e.g., Ezekiel the Tragedian's *Exagoge* as a source in Lanfranchi, "Reminiscences."

157. E.g., Begg, "Marah Incident"; Begg, "Retelling." Josephus may have known this work of Philo; see Robertson, "Account," ch. 2.

158. E.g., Josephus uses conventional forms in his suicide accounts (Newell, "Forms"), though historians could employ conventional forms for authentic events, and suicide was common enough (cf. Keener, *Acts*, 3:2498–2507). In any case, Josephus does use tragic pathos like other rhetorical historians. Given his own experience, it is not surprising that he digresses to lament (e.g., *Jewish War* 5.19), though quickly returning to the subject with the notice that the rules of history prohibit such lamentation (5.20).

159. Hengel, *Acts and History*, 7; cf. Vermes, *Jesus and Judaism*, 139.

160. Josephus, *Jewish Antiquities* 20.156–57, 260, 262, 266. He condemns a rival historian for lack of accuracy (*Life* 336) and even compares him to a forger of contracts (337–39).

161. Though reporting various perspectives as a rhetorical technique, ancient critics rarely

How does Josephus *usually* fare in his reports of the postbiblical period? Scholars on Josephus range from skepticism to appreciation, generally depending on the aspects of his historiography on which they focus their attention. On a number of points he fails to impress, for example, in his speeches,[162] a point at which ancient historiographic convention diverges significantly from modern practice.[163]

Most historians today also argue that Josephus's population estimates are unreliable and that he is sometimes mistaken on distances.[164] Since it is unlikely that Josephus personally counted people or measured distances, such matters need not otherwise affect the substance of what he reports about events. Josephus occasionally makes mistakes on even his most public information,[165] but this appears to be the exception rather than the rule.[166] He is probably more accurate about specific events than in his summaries; he does not fabricate events, but he elaborates them and puts his slant on them. Indeed, his overarching summaries sometimes conflict with the information he himself reports.[167]

Josephus's biases are difficult to miss. Even many of his adaptations of biblical accounts emphasize points pleasing to his Roman sponsors and Gentile audience.[168] Some of his work favors Pharisees, a group to which he had

---

reckoned with the multivalence of perspectives the way we would today. Josephus sometimes legitimates his own historical work (vis-à-vis that of other historians) by citing tradition (Gillet-Didier, "*Paradosis*").

162. Josephus, like Herodotus, fared much better on narrative than speeches by our standards (cf. Mosley, "Reporting," 11–22); he is heavily influenced by rhetoric (see Botha, "Rhetoric and Josephus"). See Keener, *Acts*, 1:301–4.

163. See discussion in Keener, *Acts*, 1:258–319.

164. Safrai, "Description in Works," esp. 320–21. On population estimates, see further Keener, "Plausibility."

165. Cf., e.g., Josephus, *Jewish Antiquities* 18.206, which, at least, in the text as we have it, misconstrues Germanicus's relationship to Tiberius.

166. Sometimes there is considerable debate, e.g., surrounding Felix's full name; against Josephus, see tentatively Hemer, "Name of Felix," 47–48; in favor, Bruce, "Name of Felix"; Kokkinos, "*Gentilicium*"; Keener, *Acts*, 3:3329–31.

167. For proposed problems in Josephus's summaries, see, e.g., McLaren, "Josephus' Summary Statements"; for problematic summary statements by others, see, e.g., Justin, *Epitome of the "Philippic History" of Pompeius Trogus* [henceforth *Epitome*] 3.2.3.

168. Cf., e.g., Begg, "Amaziah," "Nahum," and "Uzziah"; Feldman, "Asa," "Joseph," "Manasseh," "Pharaohs," and "Ezra"; cf. also the transformation of Ahasuerus into a fully positive character in Josephus, *Jewish Antiquities* 11 (Feldman, "Ahasuerus"). Begg, "Gedaliah," suggests that some of Josephus's reports may also reflect influence from his experience.

allegedly belonged.[169] His apologetic *Tendenz* conspicuously dominates his history and autobiography;[170] he may also exaggerate Jewish privileges in the empire (albeit based on genuine precedents) to further his apologetic on their behalf; and he presented Jewish sects in terms of Greek philosophic ideals.[171]

He defends both Rome to his people and his people to Rome.[172] He presents the Judean-Roman war as virtually an accident in which incompetent governors and a few Jewish "bandits" forced Judea into unwilling conflict with Rome;[173] J. D. Crossan wryly but insightfully remarks of Josephus's *War*, "Nobody from the highest aristocracy on either side is guilty of anything."[174] (Josephus's own perspective, of course, is that of an aristocrat, favoring Jewish aristocrats.)[175]

Josephus's biases do not, however, usually significantly hamper our use of his work for historical reconstruction. As one historian notes: "These biases are to be expected" and are usually easy enough to recognize; "with proper allowance made for his special interests and recognition that he was sometimes misinformed, the reader will find Josephus on the whole reliable."[176]

If we leave aside examples of bias (including in summaries), speeches, and difficult estimates, however, Josephus proves generally accurate on matters of historical events. This probably suggests that most nonspeech events in his narrative reflect information that he believes to be correct. Inscriptions sometimes confirm his accuracy on disputed Judean details, sometimes against

---

169. Although some think that he emphasizes the Pharisaic connection because of the changed political landscape. Williams, "Josephus on Pharisees," attributes to Josephus the full force of his anti-Pharisaic passages (by denying them to Nicolaus of Damascus); he may have followed much of Pharisaism without having officially joined (Mason, "Pharisee").

170. See, e.g., Harrington, "Bible," 245; Sanders, *Judaism*, 6; on the autobiography, Mason, *Josephus and New Testament*, 41–42, 73–76. The narrower autobiographic genre of confessions, of baring one's soul and revealing significant personal weaknesses, might not predate Augustine.

171. With, e.g., Ferguson, *Backgrounds*, 387.

172. As widely noted, e.g., Neusner, *Politics to Piety*, 2; Crossan, *Jesus*, 93.

173. Nearly three centuries before this time an Italian city used the same excuse of being forced by a few troublemakers (in that case, their leaders) and escaped punishment (Livy, *History* 24.47.6). My experiences and observations in northern Nigeria have given me more respect for the possibility of a few extremists ultimately provoking wider conflict.

174. Crossan, *Historical Jesus*, 93. Sometimes Romans apparently accepted the excuse that a small band had forced others to resist Rome—but Judea's revolt was massive.

175. Cf., e.g., Pastor, "Strata." Although Josephus exaggerated his own prominence, it is less clear that (with Krieger, "Verwandter") he did not belong to the priestly aristocracy.

176. Ferguson, *Backgrounds*, 387.

other historians.[177] Archaeology allows us to test him regarding physical data; although it challenges some of his claims,[178] it has vindicated him on many points of even minor detail where his accuracy could not be accidental.[179]

Apart from distance estimates, Josephus proves generally reliable on geographic matters,[180] and archaeology confirms most of his observations about Jerusalem, which he knew well: here, despite some errors, he is often accurate in even some precise measurements.[181] With some exceptions, excavations confirm his descriptions of Caesarea.[182] Israeli archaeologist Yigael Yadin concluded that, despite Josephus's prejudices, excavations confirm him for both his own period and previous ones.[183]

Despite reservations, therefore, scholars normally accept Josephus's main outline of events as accurate.[184] As Mosley points out,[185] he not only claims accuracy[186] (itself no guarantee of it), but he presented copies to Vespasian, Titus, Herod of Chalchis, and Agrippa—so he dared not have seriously misrepresented the events also known to them.[187] While Josephus was not striving for modern standards of historical accuracy, E. P. Sanders concludes that "wherever he can be tested, he can be seen to have been a pretty fair historian."[188]

---

177. Cf. probably Kokkinos, "*Gentilicium.*"

178. Fischer and Stein, "Marble."

179. See, e.g., Syon, "Gamla"; Cotton and Geiger, "Yyn"; Mazar, "Josephus and Excavations"; Safrai, "Education," 995; Feldman, "Introduction," 45–46; Thackeray, *Josephus*, 49; Riesner, "Gate"; Pixner, "Gate"; Pixner, Chen, and Margalit, "Zion."

180. Safrai, "Description in Works," esp. 320–21.

181. Feldman, "Introduction," 45–46; Mazar, "Josephus and Excavations," 325–29; McRay, *Archaeology*, 117–18; Charlesworth, *Jesus within Judaism*, 118–19.

182. McRay, *Archaeology*, 140, 144.

183. Y. Yadin in Shanks, "BAR Interviews Yadin," 19.

184. Thackeray, *Josephus*, 49; Mosley, "Reporting," 23–24.

185. Mosley, "Reporting," 23–24, noting that Josephus composed speeches freely, but he has many firsthand sources (e.g., *Jewish Antiquities* 14.144–45, 189, 219, 224, 228).

186. In *Jewish Antiquities* 1.17; 20.154–57, 260–62; *Jewish War* pref.9–12, 30; 7.454–55; *Against Apion* 1.47; *Life*, 65.

187. Josephus, *Against Apion* 1.50–51. Just as, we may note, Luke could not have easily gotten away with fabricating new events contradicting those known to Theophilus (Luke 1:4); cf. also Xenophon, *Agesilaus* 3.1 in Woldemariam, "Comparison," 218. On appeals to common knowledge, see, e.g., Xenophon, *Agesilaus* 3.1; Dionysius of Halicarnassus, *On Literary Composition* 22; Cicero, *Against Verres* 2.3.30.71; Josephus, *Against Apion* 2.107; Keener, *Acts*, 4:3497–98, 3542; this one is a higher order appeal than some, since it encompasses a range of data.

188. Sanders, *Judaism*, 6. Many claims against his reliability are overstated; see, e.g., Rajak, *Josephus*, 9–10.

3.3c. Josephus's Autobiography

Although Josephus's historiography is generally relevant to the matter at hand, our primary interest here is his autobiography. Although some have tried to strictly distinguish autobiography from other sorts of biographic writing,[189] it was indeed a type of biography, certainly by this period.[190] Autobiographic writing appears in some form even as early as Pharaonic Egypt.[191] It developed further from journals and other personal memoirs,[192] such as Xenophon's eyewitness experience in the *Anabasis*.[193]

Autobiographic writing is known in the first century BCE, with one autobiography even by Emperor Augustus.[194] More than a century after Augustus's autobiography, Hadrian also produced autobiographic material, albeit pseudepigraphically and perhaps playfully attributed to some of his freedmen.[195] Nevertheless, scholars often identify Josephus's late first-century *Life* as the first surviving work that is a full autobiography.[196]

Rather than expounding evenly all of Josephus's life journey, his *Life* focuses on the crucial period of his involvement in the Judean-Roman war,[197] a period in his life that had drawn fire from his critics. Its clear connection with the *Jewish Antiquities* communicates the expectation that its texture will be historiographic, illustrating the compatibility of biography and history.[198]

How accurate was autobiography? It was considered sufficiently accurate to provide an acceptable source for subsequent biographies.[199] Because of cultural disdain for unjustifiable boasting,[200] autobiography was less free to be

---

189. Cohn, *Distinction*, 30–37 (cited in De Temmerman, "Formalities," 4n4). Geiger, *Nepos*, 79–80, allows for Greek memoirs but not autobiographies.

190. Geiger, *Nepos*, 79; Momigliano, *Development*, 14, 95; Stadter, "Biography," 530.

191. Simpson, *Literature*, 401–27.

192. Momigliano, *Development*, 14–15, 18, 62, 89–90.

193. Momigliano, *Development*, 57.

194. See Laistner, *Historians*, 35–37; Momigliano, *Development*, 86.

195. Burgersdijk, "Implications," 255 (*Historia Augusta* 16.1).

196. Rodgers, "Justice," 169.

197. Rodgers, "Justice," 169–70, noting Josephus, *Life* 28–413.

198. See Smith and Kostopoulos, "Biography," 404–5, noting esp. Josephus, *Jewish Antiquities* 20.266; *Life* 430; Eusebius, *Ecclesiastical History* 3.10.8.

199. Momigliano, *Development*, 86.

200. See, e.g., Prov 27:2; Aristotle, *Nicomachean Ethics* 4.3.36, 1125a; Thucydides, *History* 3.61.1; Dionysius of Halicarnassus, *Roman Antiquities* 1.1.1; Publilius Syrus, *Sentences* 597; Cicero, *In Defense of Caecina* 11.36; *Letters to Friends* 5.12.8; Quintilian, *Orator's Education*

directly encomiastic than were biographies of other persons.[201] As we shall see, however, Josephus's autobiography takes liberties, though these may be akin to the liberties in his other historical work.

Comparisons with Josephus's accounts in his *Antiquities*, a historical work, show some significant differences.[202] Perhaps most significantly, Josephus must now address Justus,[203] whom he previously ignored, because Justus had now composed his own account of the events.[204] A later writer familiar with both authors prefers Josephus's account to Justus's,[205] but in Josephus's day Justus offered serious potential competition. As Josephus also wrote an apologetic history of the Jewish people (the *Antiquities*), Justus reportedly wrote a record of Jewish rulers from Moses to Agrippa II.[206] More important, Justus worked for Agrippa and so was ready to challenge Josephus's inconsistencies and especially any apparent criticisms of Agrippa.[207] Josephus has to defend his reputation in Rome "as the literary spokeman of his people" and as loyal to the honored Agrippa.[208]

Still, Josephus is at least a firsthand source for what he claims. He condemns those who wrote about events without any firsthand knowledge, contrasting them with his own knowledge of the Judean-Roman war.[209] Not only was he an eyewitness of much that he claims,[210] he claims to have even taken notes,[211] receiving reports also from deserters from Jerusalem.[212]

11.1.15–19, 22; Josephus, *Against Apion* 2.135–36; Dio Chrysostom, *Orations* 45.2; 57.3–9; Pliny, *Letters* 1.8.4–6, 13; 7.4.10; 9.15; Plutarch, *Cicero* 24.1; *Marcus Cato* 14.2; 19.5; *Praising Oneself Inoffensively Moralia* 539A–547F (esp. 15, *Moralia* 544D; 19, *Moralia* 546F); Symmachus, *Letters* 1.1.6; 1.16.2; Forbes, "Self-Praise"; Marshall, *Enmity*, 353–57; Watson, "Boasting," 78–81; Aune, *Dictionary*, 81–84; Wojciechowski, "Boasting"; though cf. Cicero, *Against Piso* 1.2; Fronto, *To Antoninus* 1.2.9; Judge, *First Christians*, 66–70; Smit, "Practice," 347–52.

201. Momigliano, *Development*, 15; cf. Lyons, *Autobiography*, 53–59.

202. Rodgers, "Justice," 170; Mason, *Life*, 213–22; Henderson, "*Life* and *War*"; Henderson, "Comparison."

203. Rodgers, "Justice," 170, 175, noting *Life* 41; cf. 36, 65, 88, 175–78, 186, 346, 390–93, 410.

204. Cf. Rodgers, "Justice," 182, noting *Life* 40, 338; cf. 336, 340, 367.

205. Photius, *Bibliotheca* 33. The preference may stem partly from apologetic interests; see Henderson, "Comparison," 264.

206. Rodgers, "Justice," 183, citing Photius.

207. Rodgers, "Justice," 185, citing *Jewish Antiquities* 20.189–91, 145–46, 211–12, 214, 216–18.

208. Rodgers, "Justice," 185.

209. *Against Apion* 1.45–49.

210. E.g., *Against Apion* 1.48–49.

211. *Against Apion* 1.49. On ancient note-taking, see comment in ch. 15.

212. *Against Apion* 1.50. Josephus probably functioned as a translator and would be used to interrogate and interpret for fugitives concerning conditions inside the city.

Josephus's autobiography thus constitutes a useful source, when approached critically. But beyond testing with archaeological sources, we can test Josephus's redaction of his material by comparing his treatment of the LXX (in his *Antiquities*) and his elaboration of the same events in different works. Josephus makes all the sorts of adaptations noted in chapter 11.[213] Beyond speeches, however, he normally "does not create events or incidents, either out of his head or by midrashic exposition."[214] In this respect he resembles Plutarch,[215] addressed below.

While we see that Josephus tells essentially the same story as his source material, he also takes literary freedoms that modern academic biographers would not allow, but with which ancient audiences were apparently more comfortable. The greatest differences far exceed the typical differences between John and the Synoptics. See the discussion in chapter 10.

3.3d. *Tacitus's* Agricola

Tacitus is a highly respected historian of the early empire.[216] Like other historians of his era, he believed that history provided many illustrations relevant for moral instruction,[217] yet he insisted that historical writing be based on accurate information.[218]

Ancient genres were flexible, and Tacitus's *Agricola* mixes genres by bringing his other strengths to bear. Although Publius Cornelius Tacitus (58–120 CE) writes primarily in honor of his deceased father-in-law, Gnaeus Julius

213. See Downing, "Redaction Criticism 1," 49–55.

214. Downing, "Redaction Criticism 1," 55–56 (finding no new events in the section studied); Downing, "Redaction Criticism 2," 33.

215. On Plutarch, see De Pourcq and Roskam, "Virtues," 177, following Pelling, *Plutarch and History*, 143–70; on Josephus reflecting wider convention, see Downing, "Redaction Criticism 2," 30.

216. See, e.g., Laistner, *Historians*, 121, 129; Mosley, "Reporting," 20–22; Hadas, "Introduction," xviii; Syme, "Tacitus"; Pelling, "Historiography," 716; cf. Marincola, "Tacitus' Prefaces." Modern readers often trust historical works that summarize information rather than those that elaborate rhetorically, such as Tacitus (Woodman, *Rhetoric*, 204, preferring Velleius Paterculus on this point); yet comparing Tacitus with other extant sources suggests that he followed the story line of his sources for recent history, or at least that his contemporaries who might have drawn on him believed that he did (see Keener, "Otho").

217. Moore, "Introduction," xiii; Hadas, "Introduction," xvii–xix; Laistner, *Historians*, 113–14; see, e.g., Tacitus, *Agricola* 1; *Annals* 3.65.

218. Tacitus, *Annals* 4.11.

Agricola (40–93 CE), he also weaves in a massive amount of material related to the other genres in which he worked elsewhere: ethnography (such as his *Germania*) and historical content (such as his *Histories* and *Annals*).[219] Given the long tradition of geographic excurses in biographies (and histories), however, and the overlap between history and biography (see ch. 6), we may still read the *Agricola* as significantly biographic.

Tacitus naturally respected his father-in-law, so encomiastic elements are not surprising.[220] Such praise does not mean that he resorts to inventing fictitious episodes. Without distorting his historical core, Tacitus employs stock epideictic stereotypes to expand the account; archaeology confirms many of his reports.[221]

3.3e. Plutarch's Lives

Plutarch (45–50 to 120–125 CE) wrote in Greek roughly one and a half centuries after Nepos's Latin biographies, and he wrote at a much more sophisticated literary level.[222] Plutarch writes mostly about public figures; even some of the intellectual figures about whom he wrote, such as the orator Demosthenes or Dion, a disciple of Plato,[223] were also public leaders. Many of his reportedly 227 works have survived, including more than forty lives attributed to him.[224] His biographies include a collection of twenty-four parallel Greek and Roman lives; biographies of Caesars, of which only those of Galba and Otho have survived; and biographies about other persons of interest, including some poets, heroes, leaders, and a philosopher.[225]

Like Nepos's earlier biographies, those of Plutarch draw on historical sources that he believed to be historical, in contrast to some traditional biographies of poets.[226] He probably had available some of Nepos's own sources for his Roman biographies and may have followed Nepos's model for comparing

---

219. Whitmarsh, "Book," 307; cf. Frickenschmidt, *Evangelium*, 171–73; Collins, *Mark*, 26n73; Wright, "Reliability," ch. 4.

220. Whitmarsh, "Book," 309, citing esp. Tacitus, *Agricola* 2.1; 3.3; 42.5; 46.2.

221. Hägg, *Biography*, 204–14, esp. 213 (following esp. Martin, "Tacitus on Agricola," 12; Hanson, "Agricola").

222. Geiger, *Nepos*, 117.

223. Plutarch, *Dion* 1.1.

224. Frickenschmidt, *Evangelium*, 168.

225. Frickenschmidt, *Evangelium*, 168; cf. Geiger, *Nepos*, 93.

226. Frickenschmidt, *Evangelium*, 169, highlighting their comparability with the Gospels.

Greek and Roman lives, but his Greek lives reflect fuller information.[227] Despite the frequent adaptations I will note in chapter. 11,[228] so far as we can tell, Plutarch normally avoided inventing stories or falsifying matters he considered historically important, even when gaps in his information, such as in subjects' childhood, seemed to invite this practice.[229]

Despite chronological displacements and often random arrangement of anecdotes, Plutarch follows a more chronological organization than a topical one.[230] (His chronology is a narrative one, not necessarily corresponding to the sequence in which events happened, but it appears more historiographic-like.)[231] As the apex of Greco-Roman historical biography (by modern literary and historiographic standards), Plutarch's works will prove important in the chapters that follow.

3.3f. *Suetonius's* Lives of the Caesars

As Matthew and Luke developed Mark, Gaius Suetonius Tranquillus (ca. 69 CE to ca. 130–140 CE) may have developed the models of his older contemporaries Tacitus and Plutarch.[232] Suetonius began the *Lives of the Caesars* early in Hadrian's reign (117–138 CE).

Suetonius had much more material available for writing about the earlier emperors. He wrote more concisely on emperors for whom he had less information,[233] and considerably less in his separate works on poets and others for whom his sources were most slender. Although imperial biography was inseparable from the history of the period, Suetonius's lives value anecdotes or gossip about the emperors' private lives that would have been much more out of place in ordinary histories.[234] But while Suetonius includes much gos-

---

227. Geiger, *Nepos*, 118–19.

228. In greater detail, see Licona, *Differences*, 23–111. Although we cannot always be certain, many of Plutarch's adaptations appear to be deliberate; see, e.g., Pelling, *Plutarch and History*, 52, 77, 80, 87, 107, 155.

229. De Pourcq and Roskam, "Virtues," 177; Hägg, *Biography*, 254, both following Pelling, *Plutarch and History*, 143–70, 301–38.

230. With, e.g., Ytterbrink, *Gospel*, 108.

231. See, e.g., Pelling, "Adaptation," 128–29; Licona, *Differences*, 47, 50–51, 67, 72, 108, 110; Licona, "Viewing," 326.

232. For one bibliography, see Benediktson, "Survey."

233. Cf. Geiger, *Nepos*, 27.

234. Frickenschmidt, *Evangelium*, 171.

sip,[235] he does not always agree with it.[236] One study used inscriptions to test many of Suetonius's claims, showing that such evidence usually supports and sometimes explains what Suetonius wrote.[237]

Still, as Adela Yarbro Collins notes, Suetonius's approach to "collecting, ordering, and presenting material is that of the learned grammarian and antiquarian," but "he moved beyond the scholarly type [of biographic writing] into the historical type."[238] In comparison with many historians and biographers, Suetonius is less committed to filling out a consistent portrait but demonstrates a greater degree of objectivity than in some other biographies.[239] Like Plutarch, Suetonius will appear prominently in subsequent chapters, especially chapter 10.

3.3g. Lucian's Demonax

Although Pilate executed Jesus as a public, political figure, Jesus was certainly also a sage. Thus Lucian's *Demonax*, one of the few surviving biographies of a sage from the early empire,[240] merits some extended comment here. Some consider Lucian's critiques of Alexander and Peregrinus and his dialogues of Nigrinus biographic in the larger sense,[241] but we can be much more certain that Lucian intended *Demonax* as a life.[242]

Lucian writes both to honor Demonax's memory and to provide a contemporary model for imitation.[243] In this case, Lucian (120–after 180 CE) has little reason to depend on secondary sources. He writes about a recent figure, with whom, he claims, he personally spent a significant amount of time, apparently as a disciple.[244] Lucian, like Xenophon in the *Agesilaus*,

---

235. Cary and Haarhoff, *Life*, 272.

236. See, e.g., Suetonius, *Augustus* 68.

237. Nelson, "Value," brought to my attention in a student paper by Christopher Chandler. The explanations fit a historical argument from "undesigned coincidence."

238. Collins, *Mark*, 33.

239. Cf. Benediktson, "Survey," 388, brought to my attention by Christopher Chandler. Suetonius patterns his biographies, but flexibly, given the material he had to cover (cf. Hurley, "Rubric Sandwich").

240. Cf. Adams, *Genre*, 89.

241. Clay, "Lucian"; Adams, *Genre*, 89. For Peregrinus manipulating biographic and autobiographic expectations, see König, "Lives," 227, who contrasts (237) the motivation of Peregrinus and Demonax.

242. See Beck, "Demonax," 80.

243. Lucian, *Demonax* 2.1–8 (with Moeser, *Anecdote*, 247).

244. See Lucian, *Demonax* 1.

personally knows his subject.[245] Like Jesus, however, Demonax made much less of an impression on other contemporary sources not authored by his followers.[246]

Following a now-familiar biographic pattern, Lucian includes separate sections for encomium and anecdotes. Just as Xenophon's *Agesilaus* praised the king's achievements in a general way before providing anecdotes illustrating his virtues, so Lucian offers both.[247] First he eulogizes Demonax in 3–11, employing familiar biographic topics, before turning to anecdotes about him in 12–62 and then finally a eulogizing treatment of his death and burial in 63–67.[248] The many brief anecdotes in the long anecdote section seem to reflect no particular sequence, and Lucian uses them not to provide a comprehensive survey of the philosopher's career but rather to illustrate his character.[249] The emphasis on anecdotal scenes and the minor importance of chronology in the middle section resemble the Gospels.[250]

Whereas biographies of rulers and generals stress their deeds in those arenas, Lucian's anecdotes about his philosophic mentor stress his quick and often insulting wit.[251] In contrast to Jesus's detractors, however, more of Demonax's hearers seem to have taken his jibes in good humor;[252] Demonax sometimes did not take himself too seriously either.[253] Like any playful and familiar public figure, over time he became well-loved.[254] Lucian, for whom such quick wit epitomized rhetorical and literary skill, naturally highlighted this aspect of Demonax's memory more than did others,[255] though Lucian's own wit tends to be more biting than playful.

---

245. Beck, "Demonax," 93, 95–96. Some of his other autobiographical claims might reflect Old Comedy (Humble and Sidwell, "Dreams," 214) or be questionable (Sidwell, "Dreams," 222), but *Demonax* 1 exudes admiration rather than satire.

246. See Beck, "Demonax," 82.

247. Beck, "Demonax," 92–93; he cites as Xenophon's illustrations *Agesilaus* 4.6, 5.5, 7.5, 7.6, 8.3.

248. Widely recognized, e.g., Ytterbrink, *Gospel*, 110; Beck, "Demonax," 83.

249. Moeser, *Anecdote*, 247–48; Beck, "Demonax," 84, citing *Demonax* 67 and Branham, *Eloquence*, 58.

250. Frickenschmidt, *Evangelium*, 182, following Cancik.

251. With Beck, "Demonax," 87.

252. Lucian, *Demonax* 6–7, 11. Cf. more hostile responses in 12–13, 16. This was also a favored feature in much of the philosophic biography tradition; see Long, "Introduction," xxiii; Romm, "Humor," 567; Branham, "Cynicism," 602–3; Long, "Zeno," 609–10.

253. Lucian, *Demonax* 35, 66.

254. Lucian, *Demonax* 63, 67.

255. Beck, "Demonax," 89–91.

Philosophically eclectic,[256] Demonax resembled the engaging Socrates in some ways[257] and the frank Diogenes the Cynic in others.[258] As with most ancient biographies,[259] the character is flat and consistent rather than complex,[260] though Lucian's anecdotes paint a lively personality.[261]

3.3h. Philostratus's Lives of the Sophists

Although I addressed Philostratus's novelistic, literary biography of Apollonius in the previous chapter, Philostratus, like Xenophon, who wrote about Agesilaus as well as Cyrus, was capable of writing more historically oriented biographic material as well. Like the later biographer Eunapius, Philostratus (ca. 170–172 to 247–250 CE) collected lives of oratorical teachers in his *Lives of the Sophists*.

Not unlike Suetonius, Philostratus is ready to include significant "gossip and scandal."[262] Unlike the later Diogenes Laertius, Philostratus cites sources fairly rarely, apparently depending most often on his own reminiscences of what he heard from his teachers.[263] Although most individual lives are short, they seem much better informed than Hellenistic lives of the poets.

3.3i. Diogenes Laertius's Lives of the Eminent Philosophers

Although fragments, including those in Diogenes Laertius, demonstrate that Greeks had been writing lives of sages for centuries, it is Diogenes Laertius whose (probably) early third-century compendium survives as a whole.[264]

---

256. See Lucian, *Demonax* 62.

257. Lucian, *Demonax* 5; cf. Beck, "Demonax," 86, 95.

258. Lucian, *Demonax* 5.

259. Cf., e.g., Edwards, "Introduction," xvi.

260. Beck, "Demonax," 86, 89–90. Epics often worked hard to depict round characters (cf., e.g., Grillo, "Reflections"; Homer, *Odyssey* 18.119–56, 412–21; though contrast Lucan), though of course some biographees could be round as well.

261. Cf. Beck, "Demonax," 91.

262. Adams, *Genre*, 100, highlighing esp. *Lives of the Sophists* 516–17, 610.

263. Adams, *Genre*, 100; cf. 101, citing Eunapius, *Lives* 482, 485, 493–94, 500, 502.

264. Diogenes's failure to address Neoplatonism or anyone born in the third century leads a majority of scholars to date his work to the early third century (Miller, "Introduction [Diogenes]," x).

Diogenes probably overlaps with Philostratus chronologically,[265] and these works highlight third-century interest in intellectual biography,[266] as well as the increasing prominence of philosophers in the intellectual milieu. Relevant for comparison with the Gospels, Diogenes incorporates sages' teachings as well as their lives.[267]

Diogenes Laertius's collection includes ten books, each organized by a founder of a philosophic school, then his life, teachings, works, successors, and so forth.[268] Anecdotes dominate Diogenes's work;[269] both these anecdotes and sayings seem to be arranged almost randomly.[270] Perhaps because he treats many figures briefly, his lives, like many earlier lives of poets, lack the three-part structure characteristic of Nepos, Plutarch, and the Gospels.[271] This might be partly because these earlier full biographies focus on public figures more than private teachers,[272] although some of Diogenes's biographees were well-known publicly. Certainly one could write fuller biographies of sages; sages could be well-known publicly, and Lucian's *Demonax* shows a three-part structure.[273] Although Diogenes's sources, often from centuries after their subjects, vary greatly in their reliability, Diogenes's work is far more antiquarian or historical than novelistic, as conspicuously demonstrated by how tightly he is bound to the work of his predecessors. I address Diogenes Laertius somewhat further in chapter 4, with reference to biographies of sages.

3.4. Later Biographies and Hagiography

The *Historia Augusta*, probably from the late fourth to early fifth centuries, again differs from the acme of historical biography encountered in the early empire. It contains thirty lives (occasionally grouping some emperors together in a life), and most scholars today (as opposed to the past) attribute it to a single

265. Long and Sharples, "Diogenes Laertius," 475.

266. Cf. Burridge, *Gospels*, 75.

267. Votaw, "Biographies," 53; Fitzgerald, "Lives," 215.

268. Adams, *Genre*, 105.

269. Frickenschmidt, *Evangelium*, 183; Long, "Introduction," xxiii; Miller, "Introduction (Diogenes)," xiii–xiv.

270. Ytterbrink, *Gospel*, 112.

271. Frickenschmidt, *Evangelium*, 184.

272. Frickenschmidt, *Evangelium*, 504.

273. See also Frickenschmidt, *Evangelium*, 182.

author.[274] Comparison with other evidence shows that the author takes a very free hand with historical information, incorporating far more deliberate fiction than we find in biographers from the early empire.[275] The fictive elements in the *Historia Augusta* were probably meant to be recognized as such.[276]

The most notable development of biography in late antiquity, however, was its embrace of hagiography. Rooted in the element of encomium that had always remained part of ancient biography, such sacred idealization of the subject became a major force. After Constantine, therefore, biography changed significantly. "Pagan philosophers and sophists and Christian saints and martyrs," Momigliano notes, became "the main subjects of late Roman biography."[277] Whereas Christian martyr stories traditionally followed the Gospels' model of a suffering hero, by the fourth century CE emphasis shifted to the moral triumphs of the saints, more like civic biographies.[278] Eventually, Burridge notes, "philosophical biography seems to have given way to hagiography."[279]

Hagiography conflates the character concern of biography with the fictional and plot concerns of novel[280] to a degree possibly found in Xenophon's *Cyropaedia* but missing in our representatives of biographies of public figures in the early empire. A novelistic plot line in this sense[281] contrasts with biographies' emphasis on anecdotes, still found in other works of this period[282] (although medieval hagiography can include some of both).[283] It would be rash to assert, given the limited evidence, that no similar works intervened between Xenophon and late antiquity, but clearly what was once a marginal characteristic came to flourish as a dominant one in late antiquity.

Even in late antiquity, however, not all biographies were hagiographic. Patricia Cox, an expert on late antique, hagiographic biography, regards such works as largely imaginative caricatures of their subjects, involving "exaggerating, typ-

274. Burgersdijk, "Implications," 244.

275. Burgersdijk, "Implications," 254.

276. Burgersdijk, "Implications," 242, 254. Some suggest deliberate, playful parody (Knoppers, "Problem," 26).

277. Momigliano, *Development*, 9; cf. 10.

278. Konstan and Walsh, "Biography," 41.

279. Burridge, *Gospels*, 76, albeit referring to a still later period.

280. Gray, "Monk," 117; cf. Chance, "Fiction," 135.

281. Later hagiography often even recycles the plot lines of earlier hagiography (Gray, "Monk," 131–32).

282. Cf. Dillon, "Interpretation," 159–60.

283. Sulpicius Severus's *Life of Martin* plainly includes many anecdotes, though Praet, "Cloak," 137–39, 159, regards it as early Western hagiography.

ifying, stylizing, idealizing, and so on," expressing the "play between fact and fantasy."[284] Such biographies often evoke earlier figures,[285] a feature that had long been part of history and biography. She includes in this category lives by Philostratus (regarding the *Life of Apollonius*), Porphyry, Eusebius, and Iamblichus.[286]

Moreover, as philosophers in late antiquity increasingly came to be depicted as holy men reflecting the divine,[287] their biographies naturally moved to accommodate such notions.[288] (Cox distinguishes here between biographies that depicted philosophers as divinities or offspring of divinities on the one hand and, on the other, those that were merely godlike.)[289] This new tendency of biography to emphasize thinkers' holiness or nearness to the divine reflects "the heated religious conflicts between pagans and Christians in the third and fourth centuries."[290] Moreover, although the line between human and divine had always been somewhat thin for Greeks,[291] the increasing dominance of Platonism naturally exacerbated this tendency.[292] Although miracles were still not characteristic of late antique biography in the way that they became in later periods,[293] miracles begin to appear in some late antique pagan biographies to counter the frequency of miracles in Christian biographies.[294]

Others, however, have criticized aspects of Cox's approach.[295] In particular, John Dillon, an expert in Neoplatonism, deems her book as "rather annoying" and as following broader critical tendencies in modern literary philosophy rather than careful analysis of the texts. In his view, she blurs too much the distinction between *bios* and hagiography. Far from creating merely idealized figures, historical biographies continue to exist alongside hagiography and mixtures of the two. Eusebius's *Life of Origen* and Porphyry's *Life of Plotinus* are intended as more conventional biography, whereas Philostratus's *Life of Apollonius*, the lives of Pythagoras, and Athanasius's *Anthony* are more hagiographic.[296]

---

284. Cox, *Biography*, xi, xii; see further 65, 134.

285. Cox, *Biography*, xiii.

286. Cox, *Biography*, 19.

287. Cox, *Biography*, 17, 65.

288. Cox, *Biography*, 17–19; cf. Frickenschmidt, *Evangelium*, 263–66.

289. Cox, *Biography*, 21, 34–36, 134, comparing, e.g., Philostratus, *Life of Apollonius* 1.5–6; Porphyry, *Life of Pythagoras* 1–2; *Life of Plotinus* 23.

290. Cox, *Biography*, 65; see further 139, 142.

291. See fuller discussion in Keener, *Acts*, 1782–86, 1962–64.

292. See fuller discussion in Keener, *Mind*, 128–30.

293. Cox, *Biography*, 48; cf. Edwards, "Genre," 59.

294. Cox, *Biography*, 142. Consider, e.g., Athanasius's hagiographic portrait of Anthony.

295. Cf. Ytterbrink, *Gospel*, 83n89, 87.

296. Dillon, "Interpretation," 155–56.

Eunapius insists on distinguishing "between securely-attested fact and piety-driven rumour," even if we believe that he sometimes gets particular stories in the wrong category.[297] Eusebius likewise distinguishes between documents, such as Origen's letters, and oral reports from those who knew Origen.[298] Although revering Plotinus, Porphyry is "yet simply concerned to give as much accurate information about him as he can, in an effort to throw light on his character."[299] He does not invent early-life incidents that he has not heard and is particularly trustworthy for Plotinus's later life, with which he was personally acquainted. He includes faults as well as strengths.[300]

By contrast, Dillon acknowledges that Marinus's work on Proclus is essentially hagiographic, though including factual information. Likewise, most lives of the saints, such as Antony, are hagiographic. Damascius's *Life of Isidore* is encomiastic biography rather than hagiography, although it tends in the direction of the latter.[301] Ultimately, then, Dillon argues that a range of works exists in late antiquity, and he faults Cox not for affirming that hagiography was growing in this later period, but only for lack of nuance.

Some have linked the Gospels with such later lives of holy men,[302] but this comparison risks significant anachronism. Certainly Jewish biographies, such as Philo's *Life of Moses*, include the religious element much earlier, no less for the life of a sage-king,[303] with whose story the Gospels may thus be compared. Later sources draw, as we have seen, on the earlier Gospels, on civic biographies, on encomium, and on themes popular in novels.

3.5. *Lives of the Prophets*

Because the *Lives of the Prophets* is Jewish, it may prove relevant in many respects for study of the Gospels, but probably not so much in genre: the form is completely different. This *Lives* probably originated in Greek and evolved as

---

297. Dillon, "Interpretation," 157, on Eunapius, *Lives* 457–61 (esp. 459–60).

298. Dillon, "Interpretation," 157–58, esp. 157, citing Eusebius, *Ecclesiastical History* 6.2.1; for oral reports, see 6.1.1; 6.2.11; 6.3.12.

299. Dillon, "Interpretation," 158, noting Porphyry, *Life of Plotinus* 1.

300. Dillon, "Interpretation," 158–59.

301. Dillon, "Interpretation," 160–65.

302. E.g., Chance, "Fiction," 136; Moles, "Influence," 99.

303. Cf. McGing, "Adaptation," 119, who does use the religious element to link this work with later biographies.

a collection over time.[304] The work's different recensions might even suggest that it was collected more than once, when stories were in different stages of development.[305]

Some date the oldest recensions of the *Lives of the Prophets* to the first century, allowing them to stand as Jewish, possibly even Jerusalemite, examples of biography from the period of Philo's *Life of Moses*.[306] Unfortunately, this dating is probably too early. Robert A. Kraft, early Judaism expert and Berg Professor of Religious Studies Emeritus at the University of Pennsylvania, cautions that their current form may be from the Byzantine period, possibly in the fifth or sixth century.[307] This work shares aspects of the character of hagiography from this period.[308] Reconstructing its earliest phases thus becomes difficult.

Granted, the *Lives of the Prophets* may attest to the format followed in many earlier lives of the poets having persisted or having been revived, or at least at some point also being employed in a Jewish context. It not only appears similar in format to lives of poets,[309] but it also appears to have often grown in an analogous manner, collecting various traditions and making midrashic inferences about the lives of the prophets from their writings.

Despite the subject matter, however, the format of the *Lives* is much less comparable to the Gospels than what we find in early imperial biographies of public figures. Following the paragraph formatting in the standard English translation of the Pseudepigrapha, edited by James H. Charlesworth, one life (Ezekiel) is five paragraphs, and another (Daniel) is four; the one on Jeremiah is three. Most, however, are two paragraphs or one,[310] sometimes quite short, even as few as just two or three sentences.[311]

---

304. Hare, "Introduction," 380.

305. Cf. Robert Kraft, personal correspondence, August 30, 2017.

306. Hare, "Introduction," 381; Frickenschmidt, *Evangelium*, 173–76, esp. 173. On 175–76 Frickenschmidt notes their development from a more basic form to conform to the wider three-part biography with a more detailed middle section.

307. Robert Kraft, personal correspondence, August 30, 2017; see also Satran, *Prophets*, e.g., 6–7, 33, 73, 75, 79, 91, 118.

308. Cf. Satran, *Prophets*, 100, 105, 110–11.

309. Also Aune, *Environment*, 41–42.

310. Four prophets have two paragraphs (Isaiah, Habakkuk, Elijah, and Elisha); sixteen prophets have only one (Hosea, Micah, Amos, Joel, Obadiah, Jonah, Nahum, Zephaniah, Haggai, Zechariah, Malachi, Nathan, Ahijah, Joad, Azariah, and Zechariah son of Jehoida).

311. Two sentences are for Haggai and Azariah; three for Zephaniah and Joad.

3.6. Other Early Jewish Sources for the Biographic Form?

Earlier Jewish biographic material probably contributes to the Gospels more in terms of character models than in literary form. Various cycles of OT stories focus on particular figures,[312] some of them (such as the Moses[313] or Elijah/Elisha[314] narratives) very influential in the content of the Gospels. Nothing in earlier Jewish tradition opposed biographic interest, but little before Nehemiah would count as freestanding biography (i.e., it is otherwise embedded in larger works), and the conventional three-part biography of public figures rarely appears before the Roman period.

Such embedded biographic material continues in early Jewish historiography, including Ps.-Philo's *Biblical Antiquities*[315] and, closer to the Hellenistic biographic genre, Josephus.[316] Already in the Hellenistic period, Artapanus arranged biographically his history of the Jewish people, focusing first on the Jews as a whole, then Abraham, and especially on Moses. Still, Jewish haggadic expansions of Pentateuchal characters[317] are not close;[318] they sometimes resemble mythography because they treat the distant past.[319]

Although extant first-century Gospels reflect abundant Judean/Galilean material, they cannot be compared as easily with non-Hellenistic ancient Jewish biographies, since there are not very many.[320] It is well-known that later rabbis lacked interest in composing biographies.[321] In form, rabbinic anecdotes parallel the Gospels (as they do many Greek sage biographies),[322] but rabbinic literature lacks any overall genre analogous to biography,[323] because

---

312. See Frickenschmidt, *Evangelium*, 118–35. For the relevance of OT historiography for the Gospels, see also Collins, *Mark*, 29–30, 33, 41 (citing further Zahn, "Geschichtsschreiber"); Marcus, *Mark*, 1:65–66; esp. extensively now Rouvinez, "Mark."

313. Frickenschmidt, *Evangelium*, 120–22.

314. Frickenschmidt, *Evangelium*, 127–28; Collins, *Mark*, 29; Ytterbrink, *Gospel*, 39, 227–28; Edwards, "Genre," 59.

315. Frickenschmidt, *Evangelium*, 148–51, 178–79.

316. Frickenschmidt, *Evangelium*, 146–48.

317. On which cf., e.g., Fisk, "Bible"; Harrington, "Bible."

318. Cf. Keener, *Acts*, 1:146.

319. See ch. 9; also Keener, *Acts*, 1:145.

320. See much fuller discussion in Keener, *John*, 25–29.

321. With, e.g., Neusner, *Legend*, 8; Neusner, "Idea of History."

322. Burridge, *Gospels*, 301, following Alexander, "Rabbinic Biography," 42. Neusner, *Biography*, is skeptical even of the attributed sayings in rabbinic sources.

323. Burridge, *Gospels*, 301–2, following Alexander, "Rabbinic Biography," 40; Neusner, *Gospels*, 33–38; Neusner, *Incarnation*, 213; Goshen Gottstein, "Jesus and Hillel," 34–35.

their interest, unlike that of the Evangelists, was in the Torah rather than in specific teachers.[324]

Closer and more accessible to Gospel readers are the biblical stories of Ruth, Judith, Jonah, Esther, Daniel, and Tobit, particularly accessible in the LXX. At least some of these accounts were perceived as true accounts in this period, apparently including by some or all of the Evangelists.[325] Yet even here, events rather than the public lives of leading characters often dominate.[326] Except for Daniel, these works also are unified narratives, missing the apparent compilations of prior anecdotes that appear in most early imperial biographies, including the Gospels. Although not a compilation of anecdotes, Nehemiah offers a better example, as an autobiographic work that may involve the same literary stream that also came to influence Greek biographies.

The Gospel writers certainly did draw on the biographic content of biblical history (with which they were more likely familiar than individual Greek biographies); they probably also viewed some of these as containing substantial biographic material.[327] The most conventionally Jewish of the Gospels, namely Matthew and John, may have also incorporated some midrashic techniques, at least to a minor degree.[328] Like other Jews, the earliest Christians understood the OT as historically factual,[329] though they would presumably allow themselves some of the same narrative flexibility they found in the OT itself.[330]

Surely the OT and the experience of Jesus offer the primary theological backdrop for the Gospels,[331] but this observation does not negate the Evange-

324. Burridge, *Gospels*, 303, following Neusner, *Gospels*, 52–53; Alexander, "Rabbinic Biography," 41.

325. Cf. Matt 12:40–41//Luke 11:30–32; Matt 1:5; 24:15; perhaps Mark 4:11//Matt 13:11//Luke 8:10 (evoking Dan 2:28–30, 44, 47); Mark 6:23 (evoking Esth 5:3, 6; 7:2); Mark 13:14 (evoking Dan 9:27; 11:31; 12:11); and, evoking Dan 7:13–14, Mark 2:10; 13:26; 14:62; Matt 28:18.

326. Stanton, *Preaching*, 126; Aune, *Environment*, 37. The suggestion that ancient Near Eastern models provided the later Greek emphasis on individual characters (cf. Dihle, "Biography," 366–67) seems overstated.

327. Some do see OT and rabbinic biographic material as primary background for the Gospels; see, e.g., Baum, "Biographien." For focus on OT background, Hägg, *Biography*, 155n28, cites Hartman, "Reflections"; Reiser, *Sprache*, 102–5 (distinctively regarding Jeremiah as a chief model, pp. 17–20).

328. These may appear to a small extent already in the OT; e.g., cf. 2 Kgs 9:27 with 2 Chr 22:9, discussed in Keener, *Hermeneutics*, 196–97.

329. With Allison, *Constructing Jesus*, 444; cf., e.g., Philo, *Creation* 1–2; Rosner, "Biblical History," 81.

330. Cf. here Knoppers, "Problem."

331. At least some of the Gospel writers apparently saw themselves as continuing the earlier biblical salvation history; see Smith, "Gospels."

lists' use of a contemporary genre where the life or public life of an individual dominates a cohesive narrative. The Gospels exhibit a specifically Jewish and largely Judean-Galilean content, but as in the case of Philo's *Life of Moses* or most of Josephus's work, the form is a primarily Diaspora form as it was previously developed in the Greek and Roman world.[332] We might thus speak of OT historiography continued in contemporary form, a form that other Diaspora Jewish writers had already developed.

Nevertheless, Diaspora Jewish audiences in the first century—our closest available analogy for most of the circles that first received the Gospels—expected some biographic conventions inherited from the Greek world even in their own stories. And if this is so, one should not expect fewer biographic conventions from biographic works for Diaspora Christian audiences (with mixed Jewish and Gentile memberships) in the same period.

Scholars often argue that biographic treatments in Josephus's Jewish history, where he retains but adapts stories in ways more intelligible and amenable to a Hellenistic audience,[333] reflect Greek literary, often biographic, conventions.[334] Other Hellenistic Jewish historians probably used these conventions as well.[335]

Josephus and Philo wrote for more elite and very different sorts of audiences than any of our first Gospels; we may learn relevant points from their adaptations, while recognizing that the Gospel writers, especially Mark, probably wrote from their own monotheistic, biblical matrix with less self-conscious appeal than Philo or Josephus to audiences different from themselves.

3.7. Conclusion

Tracing examples of Greek and Roman biography chronologically reveals the development in their historiographic sensitivity. Expectations for reliable his-

---

332. Fitzgerald, "Lives," 211 (following Aune, "Hellenistic Biography," 9); Baum, "Biographien," noted and qualified by Aletti, *Birth*, 28–30, 108.

333. See, e.g., Begg, "Elisha's Deeds"; Begg, "Jotham"; and Begg's sample sources in the bibliography.

334. See, e.g., Van Veldhuizen, "Moses," 215–24; Höffken, "Hiskija"; Feldman, "*Aqedah*"; Feldman, "Jacob"; and the multiple articles by Feldman and Begg sampled in the bibliography; cf. Keener, *John*, 2:1262, 1298–99; Keener, *Acts*, 4:3807–8, 3866–67. Some particular adaptations are debated (e.g., Roncace, "Portraits"; Feldman, "Roncace's Portraits"; Roncace, "Samson").

335. Cf. Rajak, "Justus of Tiberias," 92; Cohen, *Maccabees*, 194; cf. in general Attridge, "Historiography," 326; cf. Eisman, "Dio and Josephus."

torical content seem to have been highest in roughly the period from the first century BCE to the early third century CE, perhaps peaking in the early second century. From the first century, we have two Jewish biographies and opportunities (developed somewhat further in chs. 10–11) to evaluate how they handle their sources. While literary techniques differ among ancient biographers and among the Evangelists themselves, biographies from the early empire offer the best model for exploring the expectations of the Gospels' contemporaries for historiographic content in ancient biography.

Chapter 4

What Sort of Biographies Are the Gospels?

Initial expectations for "reliability" or "flexibility" must match a work's apparent genre. By definition, genre includes the sets of culturally conditioned expectations with which an audience in a work's milieu would normally approach such a work. No one, for example, expects ordinary parables or (still less) psalms to be *historically* reliable; their genres do not imply historical claims.

Although modern biography and history evolved from their ancient namesakes, there are differences between the modern and ancient genres. What range of expectations could ancient biographic authors take for granted? Answering this question requires considering ancient expectations for reliability and flexibility, rather than anachronistic modern appeals to genre conventions that did not yet exist.

Although ancient biographies influenced their modern namesakes,[1] they also differed from them. What level of historical accuracy did audiences in the period of the early empire expect from biographies? Treating the Gospels as ancient biography has little bearing on their historical reliability if we do not know what sort of historical reliability ancient audiences expected. Would the Evangelists have even had an interest in what the Jesus of history did?[2]

As the previous chapter suggested, comparing generally biographic material in the widest sense offers little guidance, but a more targeted approach can be more productive. Which biographic works are most analogous to the Gospels? For purposes of historical information, the most helpful comparisons should be with other full, discrete narrative works from the early empire that treat figures within living memory (samples of which I explore in greater detail in ch. 10).

1. See, e.g., Mossman, "Plutarch and Biography"; for classical influence more generally on English literature, see esp. Copeland, *History*.
2. Bultmann, *Jesus and Word*, 13–14, wondered whether much about Jesus was preserved by their time; in *Tradition*, 372, he doubts "historical-biographical interest in the Gospels."

4.1. Kinds of Biographies

Most relevant for studying the Gospels would be other first-century biographies of Jesus (which we would then likely classify as Gospels themselves); unfortunately, we do not have any. Comparing the four extant ones to each other is a basic exercise, readers' familiarity with which I take for granted here. Since we lack other first-century biographies about Jesus, we have to fill in gaps as best we can, though in some cases that might feel like filling missing DNA sequences from cognate species. But which species are the closest cognates?

Scholars have proposed various typologies for biographies.[3] Most of those that follow are modern subjective ways of dividing biographies, based on our particular interests. In most cases, therefore, it is not that some ways of classifying are right and others wrong, although some allow for readier and more consistent classification than others. Some typologies may be complementary.[4]

Two particularly useful schemes for dividing ancient biographies are, first of all, by subject. Biographies often addressed political figures, military figures, poets, orators, or sages. Jesus's character overlaps between the public figure and sage dimensions of ancient biography. For the latter, some formal and literary considerations such as anecdotes about teaching, rhetorical encounters, and the like are therefore appropriate to them. I revisit this topic further below. The second classification scheme is particularly relevant to *Christobiography*'s focus on the potential value of the Gospels for historical reconstruction: the likelihood of substantial information.

Although additional criteria for exploring authors' historiographic approach are important (esp. how they employ their sources), I address two of them here as more formal, a priori ways to classify biographies.[5] First, as we noted in chapter 3, biographies from the early empire tend to reflect higher historiographic standards than their often more encomiastic precursors and their usually more hagiographic successors in late antiquity. Second, biographies within living memory of their subjects tend to have better sources available than those written about figures of the distant past.

First, however, I must survey some other classification schemes.

---

3. For surveys, see, e.g., Smith, "Genre," 193–203; Smith, βίος, 28–38.

4. With also Smith, "Genre," 212.

5. Formal features by themselves are not always sufficient to classify works in terms of historical interest; cf. Adams, *Genre*, 75.

4.1a. Leo's Lineage for Biographies: Chronological versus Topical

Scholars usually begin recounting modern attempts to classify ancient biographies with a 1901 work by F. Leo.[6] Leo divided biography into two major forms: a Peripatetic form, structured chronologically, that reaches its apex in Plutarch, versus an Alexandrian, topical form that reaches its apex with Suetonius. Both approaches remained acceptable for encomia in the first century.[7]

As is often the case with any early work in a new area of study, Leo's conjectures in this matter have required subsequent revision.[8] Leo himself recognized that not every biography fit readily in these two categories.[9] Others have pointed out that Peripatetics did not invent biography,[10] and the topical form existed before the Alexandrian era.[11] The differences may simply reveal that it is more economical to treat chronologically public figures whose exploits appear in historical sources, whereas it is simpler to treat more topically the sort of literary figures that also interested Alexandrian scholars.[12]

Yet even this division may be artificial.[13] The earliest extant Roman biographer, Cornelius Nepos, follows chronology in some biographies and a topical approach in others.[14] Moreover, some biographies include both chronological and topical sections.[15] The large, chronological middle section of a subject's life usually includes many anecdotes arranged randomly.

---

6. Leo, *Biographie*.

7. See Quintilian, *Orator's Education* 3.5.15, also noted in Bird, *Gospel*, 236, but there cited as 3.7.17.

8. See critiques in Geiger, *Nepos*, 13, 25–26; Momigliano, *Development*, 19; Smith, "Genre," 194–96; Smith, βίος, 30–31.

9. Noted by Smith, "Genre," 193; Collins, *Mark*, 22n40.

10. Momigliano, *Development*, 20.

11. Burridge, *Gospels*, 71. It continued throughout the Hellenistic period (Momigliano, *Development*, 86–87).

12. Burridge, *Gospels*, 71–72.

13. Momigliano, *Development*, 87.

14. Burridge, *Gospels*, 73.

15. Smith, "Genre," 195 (and Smith, βίος, 30), following, e.g., Aune, "Biography," 108; cf. already Isocrates, *Euagoras*; Xenophon, *Agesilaus*.

4.1b. Talbert's Types, Burridge on Biographies: Functions and Purposes

Looking for patterns in ancient biographies, Charles Talbert (1977) divides them into didactic and nondidactic types. He then breaks the larger didactic category, referring to sages, into five smaller categories:[16]

1. Type A: these "function simply to provide . . . a pattern" to imitate (e.g., Lucian's *Demonax*).[17]
2. Type B: these seek to supplant a false picture of the teacher, as well as providing a model (e.g., Xenophon's *Memorabilia*, Philodemus's *Life of Epicurus*, Philostratus's *Life of Apollonius*, Porphyry's *Life of Pythagoras*).[18]
3. Type C: these are exposés to discredit a harmful teacher (Lucian's *Peregrinus* and *Alexander*).[19]
4. Type D: these describe a teacher and his successors,[20] a category Talbert develops in the link between Luke and Acts.[21]
5. Type E: these focus on teachers' lives confirming or explaining their teachings (e.g., *Secundus*; Porphyry's *Plotinus*).[22]

Talbert's categories are not mutually exclusive,[23] but they do provide analogies for these functions from both before and after the Gospels.[24]

In a more advanced and nuanced way, Richard Burridge (1992) divides ancient biography according to its "many possible purposes" but readily acknowledges that "several intentions may be combined in one particular work."[25]

---

16. He parallels four of these categories in lives of rulers (Talbert, *Gospel*, 96–97).

17. Talbert, *Gospel*, 94.

18. Talbert, *Gospel*, 94–95.

19. Talbert, *Gospel*, 95. One might think even of Aristoxenus's opposition to Socrates.

20. Talbert, *Gospel*, 95–96. For collected biographies, see further Adams, *Genre*, 92–109 (noting among three general types "those that trace a succession, whether philosophers or kings" [92]).

21. See esp. Talbert, *Patterns*, 125–40. Beyond a simple list of successors, the pattern is not very common (Chance, "Perspectives," 200 [more fully, 181–201]; Aune, *Environment*, 78–79; Pervo, *Acts*, 16; Balch, "Genre," 6), but it does exist (Talbert, "Chance," 233–34; cf. Talbert, *Acts*, xix–xx, xxiii; Talbert, *Mediterranean Milieu*, 19–50). But see esp. Sterling, *Historiography*, 319–20.

22. Talbert, *Gospel*, 96. He assigns Philo's *Moses* to this category but among rulers (97).

23. Many critique the rigidity of Talbert's types; see Aune, "Problem"; Smith, "Genre," 200; Smith, βίος, 35.

24. Talbert, *Gospel*, 98.

25. Burridge, *Gospels*, 145.

That is, he rightly recognizes the danger of attempting a universal classification of mutually exclusive options; purposes overlap.

He distinguishes purposes as follows:[26]

1. Encomiastic (Isocrates; Xenophon, *Agesilaus*; Tacitus, *Agricola*)[27]
2. Exemplary (Isocrates; Xenophon, *Agesilaus*; Philo, *Life of Moses*; Plutarch, *Cato the Younger* 24.1; 37.5; *Pericles* 1; *Aemilius Paullus* 1; *Phocion* 3.3–5; Lucian, *Demonax* 2)
3. Informative (Satyrus; Philo; Nepos; Suetonius, *Caesars*; Philostratus, *Life of Apollonius* 1.2–3), because people were curious about famous lives
4. Entertainment value (Satyrus; Lucian, *Demonax*; Philostratus, *Life of Apollonius*; Suetonius, *Caesars*; Tacitus, *Agricola*)
5. To preserve memory (Isocrates; Tacitus, *Agricola* 46.3; Lucian, *Demonax* 2; maybe also Xenophon; Nepos)
6. Didactic (Philo; Plutarch, *Cato the Younger* 44.7–8 and throughout; Lucian, *Demonax* 67)
7. Apologetic and polemic (Xenophon and perhaps Philo defend their protagonists; Plutarch refutes accusations against some characters; Philostratus, *Life of Apollonius*).

Burridge finds little encomium in the Synoptics, but they are certainly exemplary, informative, and didactic; also, they include some apologetic and polemic and (at least from an aesthetic perspective), in Luke's literary parallelisms, some entertainment.[28] "As with other βίοι, it is clearly difficult, if not impossible, to restrict the synoptic gospels to just one purpose."[29] Any of these may include historical interest, although perhaps particularly in the informative and commemorative purposes.

Another way to divide biographies is between an emphasis on character models, evaluated by moral norms, and an emphasis on the subject's distinctive personality, evoking empathy (as in tragedy).[30] This approach, like some others, addresses characteristics of many biographies, yet one wonders whether how organic this classification is, since many biographies did both.

26. Burridge, *Gospels*, 145–47, 180–82.
27. Shuler, *Genre*, regards his subject (Matthew) as primarily laudatory biography; but such a specific genre probably did not exist (Burridge, *Gospels*, 85–86), since encomiastic elements were common in many biographies.
28. Burridge, *Gospels*, 208–10.
29. Burridge, *Gospels*, 210.
30. Gill, "Distinction," esp. 2–3, followed by Beck, "Demonax," 84–85.

4.1c. Typologies with Historical Concerns

Another approach, relevant to the historical focus of the present book, is classification by purpose or function. Thus Klaus Berger (1984) classifies biographies in four types: (1) encomium; (2) peripatetic/chronological, depicting character through deeds; (3) novelistic (e.g., *Life of Aesop*); and (4) Alexandrian/topical.[31] Although some overlap among these categories is inevitable, this classification is more organic than many others. With reference to historical interest, the second and fourth categories are most helpful, but Tacitus's genre-busting *Agricola*, which Berger places in the first category, shows that historical information can be substantive in that category as well.

In 1915 Votaw distinguished biographies in two ways. First, he distinguished historical biographies, which could also have additional agendas yet provided clear chronological and other historical details, from popular biographies, which emphasized the didactic at the expense of historical information. (Votaw did admit substantial overlap.)[32] As the previous chapter should illustrate, this way of dividing material obscures too much overlap. Many biographies (e.g., Suetonius's *Caesars*) used anecdotes without chronological setting not because they were popular level but because they neither needed nor wanted to *invent* such information. Votaw also divided biographies by subject: those about political and military leaders on the one hand and those of intellectuals (such as philosophers) on the other.[33]

Justin Smith (2007) divides ancient biographies along two axes, the first by reference to chronological proximity to their subject, and the second by reference to the nature of the audience. He thus arrives at the following typology:[34]

1. "Ancient-definite": addressing figures of the past, for a distinguishable audience
2. "Ancient-indefinite": figures of the past, for a general audience
3. "Contemporary-definite": contemporary figures for distinct audience
4. "Contemporary-indefinite": contemporary figures for general audience.

31. Berger, "Gattungen," 1236; summarized in Smith, "Genre," 195; Smith, βίος, 30; earlier, cf. Talbert, *Gospel*, 92–93.

32. Votaw, "Biographies," 51; among popular biographies of sorts he includes Xenophon's *Memorabilia* and Philostratus's *Life of Apollonius* (55).

33. Votaw, "Biographies," 52.

34. Smith, "Genre," 212; Smith, βίος, 55–61, 230.

The nature of the audience, while relevant for other concerns, is of less interest for the purpose of this book, but chronological proximity will prove to be of great interest (see ch. 9). Writers of contemporary biographies address figures within living memory, so that "the author had access to firsthand/ eyewitness accounts."[35] These include works such as Isocrates's *Euagoras*, Xenophon's *Agesilaus*, Porphyry's *Plotinus*, and Nepos's *Atticus*.[36] Biographers writing about "ancient" figures, by contrast, are less able to verify "eyewitness accounts," and these biographies "tend to be less 'historically' reliable."[37] Smith includes here Philo's *Life of Moses* and Arrian's *Alexander*.

More explicit in its interest in historiographic matters is Adela Yarbro Collins's typology, which further adjusts some of the earlier classifications. Collins ultimately regards Mark as a historical monograph (see ch. 6), but she provides a typology that recognizes a relationship between historical biographies and historical monographs about a person.[38] She offers the following categories:

1. Encomiastic, usually about rulers (Isocrates's *Euagoras* as a prototype; Xenophon's *Agesilaus*; Polybius's encomium on Philopoimen)
2. Scholarly, usually about writers and philosophers, "although Suetonius used it also for Roman emperors" (Satyrus; Diogenes Laertius)
3. Didactic, often "about the way of life" the figure "founded" (Philo's *Life of Moses*; Iamblichus's *Pythagorean Life*)
4. Ethical, offering ethical models (Plutarch)
5. Entertaining, with a focus on the well-told story (lives of Homer, Aesop, and Secundus)
6. Historical (Plutarch's *Caesar*; Tacitus's *Agricola*; Suetonius's *Caesars*).

Biographies in the final category "have the same aims as historiography: to give an account of an important series of events and to explain the events in terms of their causes."[39] Although the heavy didactic content of the Gospels

---

35. Smith, "Genre," 212n128; see also 216. Regarding contemporary biography, on the analogy of contemporary historiography, see Smith, βίος, 55–57.

36. Smith, "Genre," 212; Smith, βίος, 60–61. On the border would be Nepos's *On Great Generals* 24 (Cato) and Suetonius's *Caligula, Claudius*, and *Nero* ("Genre," 212n129). Those with "definite" audiences often seek to use eyewitness accounts to counter charges against their subject (213, citing Isocrates, *Euagoras* 4–6; Xenophon, *Agesilaus* 3.1; 10.3; Tacitus, *Agricola* 4.3; 24.3; 44.5).

37. Smith, "Genre," 213. They frequently depended on "written sources, both fictional and historical" (216).

38. Collins, *Mark*, 30–33.

39. Collins, *Mark*, 32.

suggests a strong affinity for didactic *bioi*,[40] "the historical type of biography is the one that is most similar to the Gospels."[41]

Although in practice many of the above categories overlap considerably—one's interest was rarely exclusively historical information or moral models, for example—historical interest is clear in the final category, as in many biographies from Nepos through Suetonius. Collins sees Mark as a historical monograph, but in terms of historical information this genre is close to her sixth category of biography here (see discussion in ch. 6). Both proposals correctly identify the historical interest present in the Gospels.

4.2. Biographies of Sages

Because Jesus was virtually indisputably a sage, one available biographic analogy for Jesus is biographies of sages, who were usually (in the gentile world) philosophers.[42]

It is common to divide subgenres by subject matter.[43] One recently proposed approach divides biographies in terms of their subjects' social power dynamics. These dynamics certainly vary, from kings to outsiders;[44] by these standards, early accounts about Socrates and Jesus function as "subversive biography."[45]

More commonly, scholars classify different sorts of biographies based on their subjects' careers or spheres of activity, for instance, distinguishing subjects such as political figures, military figures, poets, and sages (or more narrowly, Gospels as biographies specifically about Jesus). Classification by types of figures offers an organic and natural scheme.[46] Among these categories, works about sages were quite common.[47]

---

40. Collins, *Mark*, 31, 33.

41. Collins, *Mark*, 33.

42. See, e.g., Culpepper, *Gospel and Letters*, 64–66. For the interest of cultural memory in origins and founders, cf. Galinsky, "Introduction," 23.

43. Fowler, *Kinds of Literature*, 112.

44. Konstan and Walsh, "Biography," 43, find two types of biography, but the division seems more one of biographic subjects. Even here, some compare the Gospels in different respects to some imperial figures (e.g., Cancik, "Gattung," 104–10, on Suetonius, *Nero* 49.1–4; though the motif in question has also been simply labeled tragicomic, as in Via, *Kerygma*, 15, 56, 99–101).

45. Konstan and Walsh, "Biography," 39–42, esp. 39 (their treatment of Ps.-Callisthenes is less convincing).

46. See, e.g., Votaw, "Biographies," 52; Geiger, *Nepos*, 25–26; Wehrli, "Gnome," 193 (in Smith, "Genre," 194–95; Smith, βίος, 218).

47. Succinctly, note the many philosophers in the chart in Adams, *Genre*, 112–13.

Differences among such types of biographies tend to reflect their different subjects; for example, witty aphorisms and retorts dominate more in biographies of sages than in biographies of generals. Overall, of course, a person's acts remain important in most ancient biographies.[48] Nevertheless, most sages (and here Jesus is among the exceptions) led relatively uneventful lives, so their biographies tend to focus on their words more than on their actions.[49] Biographies of sages also tend to provide more information about the subjects' education, where available, and about publications.[50]

Though many extant examples of biographies about sages postdate the period of the Gospels, fragments reveal that some forms of biographic works about them began flourishing long before the Gospels.[51] One writer reportedly contributed 120 books on those distinguished in various fields of learning.[52] Peripatetics displayed special interest in philosophers' biography as early as the fourth century BCE.[53] "Of the lost late Hellenistic authors," Hägg notes, "most wrote varieties of philosophical biography," fragments of which surface later in Diogenes Laertius and in Pythagorean lives.[54]

Such lives honored the founders of philosophic schools, recounted their teachings, and often employed anecdotes about them to illustrate their moral teaching. As Loveday Alexander emphasizes, "The Hellenistic school tradition" often includes "isolated anecdotes about famous teachers."[55] Followers of ancient teachers were often deeply interested in their lives from soon after their death, writing about them whether or not in biographic form.[56]

48. E.g., Cox, *Biography*, 57; Ytterbrink, *Gospel*, 76, 85, 101; Burridge, *Gospel*, 71; Adams, *Genre*, 92; Edwards, "Introduction," xii; Beck, "Demonax," 93; Freyne, "Gospel," 66. Frickenschmidt, *Evangelium*, 505, finds this action emphasis esp. in Roman and Jewish biographies, but it might reflect the greater number of public figures in their extant samples.

49. Votaw, "Biographies," 52; Adams, *Genre*, 91–92.

50. Adams, *Genre*, 92.

51. Pelling, "Biography, Greek," 241–42; Adams, *Genre*, 79, 86–88, 102–4. Cf. also some of Josephus's biographic material (see Van Veldhuizen, "Moses," 215–24).

52. Adams, *Genre*, 95, citing *Suda* K 227.

53. Laistner, *Historians*, 18.

54. Hägg, *Biography*, 187; Tieleman, "Orality," 30; cf. also fragments of lives from the early empire (Hägg, *Biography*, 283).

55. Alexander, "Biography," 56; cf. Alexander, *Context*, 43–68. On philosophic biography, see briefly Stadter, "Biography," 529–30.

56. See Kennedy, "Source Criticism," 134 (noting that Plato began writing about Socrates within a decade of Socrates's death); cf. Tieleman, "Orality," 30, 35. Plato exercised great freedoms, although the likely anachronism in *Alcibiades II* 141D is from a later work not genuinely by Plato.

Could biographies of sages show historical interest? As early as 240 BCE, Antigonus of Carystus raised the standard of "accuracy in describing contemporary philosophers."[57] We have noted the historiographic interests of biographers in the early empire. Surviving works from the chief biographers of the early empire focus especially on political and military figures, but their works were not originally limited to these subjects. In addition to his works on statesmen, Plutarch wrote about several poets and philosophers, although these are no longer extant.[58] In addition to his *Lives of the Caesars*, Suetonius composed series of lives of poets, orators, historians, philosophers, and finally grammarians and rhetoricians, although only the last group has survived.[59] Although somewhat later, Lucian's *Demonax* seems to continue this tradition and probably resembles other biographies of sages in the early empire.[60]

Such interest continues in the later, more widely attested lives of sophists and philosophers. In contrast to Philostratus's *Life of Apollonius*, his *Lives of the Sophists* (βίοι σοφιστῶν, *bioi sophistōn*) is a series of fifty-nine biographies, including those of eight philosophers whose rhetorical effectiveness allowed them to be classed with sophists.[61] He depended on publications by his biographees and on what he heard directly from sophists regarding themselves and their predecessors.[62] Although some have questioned his reliability,[63] Ewen Bowie notes that "controls often support his version, and *Lives of the Sophists* is an invaluable, albeit tendentious, Greek cultural history of the period."[64]

The individual biographies in *Lives of the Sophists* tend to be brief, but the well-documented public lives of Polemo and Herodes are exceptions.[65] In general, intellectual biographies (attested in series by Philostratus and Diogenes Laertius) are shorter than those of political figures,[66] but this is because

57. Pelling, "Biography, Greek," 242; cf. Walbank and Stewart, "Antigonus."

58. Frickenschmidt, *Evangelium*, 168.

59. Frickenschmidt, *Evangelium*, 170–71.

60. Adams, *Genre*, 89, also treats Lucian's *Nigrinus* as a positive biography and *Alexander* and *Peregrinus* as negative ones, though these designations define biography rather broadly.

61. Bowie, "Portrait," 143, noting Philostratus, *Lives of the Sophists* 1.1–8.

62. Bowie, "Portrait," 143.

63. Bowie, "Portrait," 143, cites Jones, "Reliability."

64. Bowie, "Portrait," 143, noting for the controls Swain, "Reliability."

65. Bowie, "Portrait," 143, noting *Lives of the Sophists* 1.25; 2.1.

66. Geiger, *Nepos*, 28.

material about such thinkers was less available except in schools themselves, where teachings (as in Arrian's treatment of Epictetus) could fill volumes. (Nevertheless, even Philostratus's sketches of somewhat recent figures involve less guesswork than the often even briefer lives of poets addressed in ch. 2.) A disciple, by contrast, might provide a more substantial work, such as (again) Lucian's treatment of Demonax.

Many naturally find biographies of sages the nearest available analogy for the Gospels, especially when these reflect recent memory.[67] The Gospels present Jesus as more than a sage, but certainly not as less than one. So long as we allow for each of the Gospels' distinctiveness and recognize the limited character of each analogy, such comparisons can be fruitful.

This analogy too may have implications for the information available to the Evangelists in the first century. Would members of a movement have access to much information about a teacher within living memory? Disciples had published memoirs about their teachers (or about others) centuries before this time.[68] Greek disciples often took copious notes from their masters' teachings,[69] sometimes for use in such biographies.[70] This practice continued in and after the NT period. Just a generation after John's Gospel, Arrian's notes of Epictetus's teaching, in contrast to Arrian's own writing in *Alexander* or *Encheiridion*, reflect even much of the teacher's own rambling style.[71] (Whether any of Jesus's disciples would have taken notes is more open to debate; see discussion in ch. 15.)

Some scholars find unusual the possibly single-year focus of Mark's Gospel,[72] but biographies often focused on public careers, and Jesus's was not long. Many sage biographies focus on the period of the sage's teaching, with at most the barest introduction to the sage's background (see ch. 6).[73]

Talbert has compared Luke-Acts with the succession narratives of sages in

67. E.g., Votaw, "Biographies," 54, 217–49; Culpepper, *Gospel and Letters*, 64–66.

68. Cf. Xenophon, *Memorabilia*; Polybius, *Histories* 12.25e.1; Kennedy, "Source Criticism," 129–37; Laistner, *Historians*, 33–37. Some later examples of this form may borrow the gospel form (see Dillon and Hershbell, "Introduction," 25).

69. E.g., Quintilian, *Orator's Education* 11.2.2, 25; Seneca, *To Lucilius* 108.6; Epictetus, *Discourses* pref.2; for further discussion, see ch. 15.

70. Cf. Arrian's *Life of Epictetus*, no longer extant (Votaw, "Biographies," 56).

71. Epictetus, *Discourses* pref.2–3.

72. Hägg, *Biography*, 163.

73. Burridge, "Review," 476–77, notes the frequency of disproportionate attention to highlighted periods in other biographies (cf. Hägg's own comments in, e.g., *Biography*, 208, 293).

Diogenes Laertius;[74] others have criticized the comparison.[75] The comparison remains useful, however, so long as we view Diogenes Laertius as providing some elements of what sage biographies could include rather than as a complete analogy.[76]

4.3. The Reliability of Diogenes Laertius's Biographies

Diogenes Laertius's information is not always reliable, but this unreliability stems not from lack of dependence on sources but from dependence on often unreliable ones from outside the circle and living memory of his subjects. Unlike some other ancient scholars, Diogenes regularly names his sources, which include nearly 1,200 references, more than 200 authors, and more than 350 anonymous sources.[77] That amounts to roughly three references per page in the standard edition.[78] In 9.1.1–17 alone, on Heraclitus, he cites at least eighteen sources.[79] When he depends on sources cited in other sources, he sometimes cites the entire chain of sources, implicitly yet transparently admitting his distance from the earliest possible witnesses.[80]

Diogenes draws on a range of earlier compilations, and instead of following a single source for a significant time, he regularly switches sources.[81] Somewhat like Matthew's (sometimes) editorial redaction of Mark or Q, however, Diogenes himself seems more a compiler than a composer.[82] Indeed, where he

74. Talbert, *Patterns*, 125–40; see also Schneider, "Zweck."

75. E.g., Smith, "Genre," 198–200; Smith, *βίος*, 34–35; Chance, "Perspectives," 200; Aune, *Environment*, 78–79; Balch, "Genre," 6; Sterling, *Historiography*, 319–20.

76. Talbert, *Mediterranean Milieu*, 50–55, esp. 52; cf. Talbert, *Acts*, xix–xx; Keener, *Acts*, 1:712–13.

77. Fitzgerald, "Lives," 215 (following Hope, *Book*, 59–60); Long and Sharples, "Diogenes Laertius," 475; cf. Frickenschmidt, *Evangelium*, 182–83. For a list of about seventy biographic works that Diogenes cites, see Adams, *Genre*, 261–63; for an extensive list of biographic literature (defined generally), see Berger, "Gattungen," 1232–36; in summary form, Smith, *βίος*, 216–17; for those from the fourth century BCE through the third century CE, distinguishing full from fragmentary and contemporary from noncontemporary biographies, see Kwon, "Reimagining," 145–50.

78. Long, "Introduction," xix.

79. Southerland, "Valuation," 5, finds awareness of twenty-three sources here. In the seventy-one sections that Southerland sampled, Diogenes cites sources at least 127 times.

80. Southerland, "Valuation," 7–8.

81. Long and Sharples, "Diogenes Laertius," 475.

82. Diogenes's interest in collecting material fits trends of his era, exemplified also in the Mishnah and contemporary Christian sources (Grafton, "Inspiration," 554).

can be compared with an earlier extant work dependent on the same source, he sometimes appears to follow the common source more carefully than does his predecessor.[83] He depends heavily on hellenistic biographers.[84]

Although many of Diogenes's sources for earlier periods were sound, some were weaker, especially his main source on Aristotle, which may be more Stoic than Aristotelian.[85] His knowledge of Plato's thought (in bk. 3) proves deficient,[86] reflecting a Stoicized, "largely Antiochan form of Platonism."[87] Apart from his reliance on Plato's *Timaeus*, Diogenes turns to intermediate sources, drawing selectively from earlier doxographers.[88] Diogenes displays abundant information on some thinkers and little information on others; thus, for example, all or most of books 3, 7, and 10 are devoted to Plato, Zeno, and Epicurus, respectively.[89] Nevertheless, he seems ready to overlook material undoubtedly available in his sources when it does not interest him.[90]

The diversity in size among his lives suggests two factors: first, he felt the need to include something about all the sages; and second, more information was available to him about some than about others.[91] That is, he was compiling tradition, not freely filling in accounts from his imagination simply to produce literary symmetry. Sometimes accused of simply compiling his sources slavishly, Diogenes Laertius cannot easily fit a model of ancient biography that emphasizes fictionalization over dependence on prior information.

Diogenes also reveals diverse opinions about his subjects.[92] Kevin Southerland, one of my PhD students, is currently working on Diogenes Laertius.

83. Janácek, "Diogenes Laertius," on Diogenes Laertius, *Lives* 9.11.97–99, and Sextus Empiricus, *Against the Mathematicians* 9.207–17; Janácek, "Diogenes Laertius IX," on Diogenes Laertius, *Lives* 9.101, and Sextus Empiricus, *Against the Mathematicians* 9.69–75, both as cited in Southerland, "Valuation," 17. His internal cross-references are mostly accurate (Long, "Introduction," xviii), and he is "basically honest," though uncritical (xxiii).

84. Tieleman, "Orality," 30.

85. Fitzgerald, "Lives," 216, 219; Long and Sharples, "Diogenes Laertius," 475; Long, "Introduction," xxii.

86. Dillon, "Doctrines"; Long, "Introduction," xvii.

87. Dillon, "Doctrines," 594; cf. 597.

88. Dillon, "Doctrines," 597. For a brief history of reception of Cynicism from Plutarch and esp. Lucian to Diogenes Laertius, see Branham, "Cynicism," 601–2.

89. Adams, *Genre*, 106.

90. See Schofield, "Philosophers," 570–71.

91. Adams, *Genre*, 106–7.

92. Ytterbrink, *Gospel*, 112, citing, e.g., Diogenes Laertius, *Lives* 2.44. Note also the interest in varied perspectives in Plutarch (De Pourcq and Roskam, "Virtues," 170) and Suetonius (Edwards, "Introduction," xxv).

His initial survey of most sections of Diogenes's ninth book highlights its vast number of sources. Here Diogenes is so committed to recording all sides that he expressly dismisses a source only once.[93] Some suggest a bias toward Skeptics and Epicureans, as revealed in his first-person usage in books 9–10,[94] but if he has such a bias, it does not prevent him from compiling whatever information he found available. Most doubt that we can be certain of the school to which Diogenes adhered, if any; this conclusion could reflect his interest in traditions about philosophers' lives at the expense of details about their philosophies.[95]

As James Miller notes, Diogenes includes plenty of "odd and amusing anecdotes," but he "almost never praises or criticizes directly the characters he describes, nor does he venture any unambiguous opinion of his own" about philosophy.[96] If some earlier biographies were much more directly epideictic, Diogenes's interest reflects more the antiquarian fascination with scintillating tidbits to provoke and satisfy readers' curiosity. One of Diogenes's principles of selection is also the street value of his narration; sexual scandals invite repetition, even when his sources are surely unreliable.[97]

Diogenes compiles material without much evaluation, which is sometimes attributed to carelessness; certainly he drew from poor sources as well as strong ones, and usually secondary or tertiary collections rather than works of the philosophers themselves.[98] Another factor could be the oft-proposed idea that we have only Diogenes's unfinished notes, published posthumously.[99] Nevertheless, some of his reticence to evaluate might additionally reflect at least partly his inability to offer firm conclusions.[100] Biographers often remained neutral about sources more than a century before their time, since historical

---

93. Sotion in Diogenes Laertius, *Lives* 9.2.20 (Southerland, "Valuation," 18).

94. Southerland, "Valuation," 16, noting Diogenes Laertius, *Lives* 9.11.70; 10.3–12. He notes Diogenes's generally extreme approaches to sources on Pyrrho, yet his relatively neutral framing of these. On Diogenes's treatment of the Skeptic Pyrrho and of Epicurus, see respectively Allen, "Skeptics," 613–14, and "Epicurus."

95. Long, "Introduction," xvii–xviii; Laks, "Diogenes Laertius," 590. His only passionate passage is a defense of Epicurus at 10.3–12 (Long, "Introduction," xviii).

96. Miller, "Introduction (Diogenes)," ix. He may reveal his opinions more in his (poetically inferior) epigrams (Gutzwiller, "Epigrams," 561).

97. Romm, "Humor," 569–70.

98. Long, "Introduction," xxiv. (Diogenes in turn became a source for later compilers; cf. Dorandi, "Diogenes Laertius," 583–84.) Still, sometimes he does seem aware of, and distinguishes between, authentic and inauthentic works (Cambiano, "Diogenes Laertius," 576).

99. So, e.g., Most, "Diogenes Laertius and Nietzsche," 622.

100. Southerland, "Valuation," 20.

distance severely impairs their ability to evaluate those sources' reliability.[101] Some sources that Diogenes treats in this book are more than *seven* centuries before his time.

Diogenes's impartiality and sometimes irreverence toward various philosophers differ starkly from the Evangelists' commitment to their subject,[102] but they do reflect the influence on Diogenes of certain ancient historiographic principles. Although Diogenes's focus and conventional topics fit biography, his work is heavily influenced by contemporary historiography.[103]

How would the Gospels as sage biographies differ historiographically from those of Diogenes Laertius? Diogenes wrote at a more elite level and named far more sources, but he also wrote long after most of his biographees. Flourishing in the early third century CE, Diogenes Laertius collected chreiai regarding the Cynic Diogenes, who was from the fourth century BCE.[104] These chreiai employ material that had accumulated over the course of more than half a millennium. In historical terms, the trustworthiness of his material thus should differ appreciably from the accounts in the first-century Gospels, most of which depict events only some forty to sixty-five years before they were written.

4.4. More than a Sage

Naturally, biographies had to be adjusted to their subject matter, and the lives of kings and generals provided different material than did the lives of poets or philosophers.[105] In the case of Jesus, the subject matter requires further adjustment of other conventional paradigms, for Jesus appears as a healer, prophet, teacher, and, perhaps, as a threat to the political establishment.

Yet biographies of a divine man,[106] while resembling the *subject* matter of the Gospels, seem to begin appearing around the early third century CE, hence by normal standards of historiography should be judged to have been influenced by, rather than to have influenced, the content of the gospel tradi-

---

101. Southerland, "Valuation," 19, following and applying Alfred, "Valuation," 78.

102. Collins, *Mark*, 31; Fitzgerald, "Lives," 220–21. For his irreverence, see, e.g., Romm, "Humor."

103. Adams, *Genre*, 251. Mejer, "Diogenes Laertius," as cited in Adams, *Genre*, 107, does view it as biography more than a history of philosophy.

104. Cf. Hägg, *Biography*, 312. Still, he tends to favor the earliest sources.

105. Momigliano, *Development*, 88.

106. Cf. Chitwood, *Death*, 20–23, 47, 114–15, 182.

tion. The earlier Christian models were widely circulated and known by the third century.

Jesus was not a military or traditional political figure, but nearly all scholars concur that, whatever else he was, he was a teacher or sage. At the same time, he was a public figure as well as a sage, like Socrates, Crates, Demonax, and other figures who became publicly known in their communities.[107] His public execution, like that of Socrates, further reinforces his role as a public figure.

Perhaps most strikingly, the messianic title attributed to him in our earliest sources and his execution as if he were a political threat suggest that he was a public figure, not one whose sole interest was private instruction of disciples. Some people thought of Jesus as a potential king;[108] it seems highly unlikely that Jesus adopted the perspective of himself as a king merely from Pilate's execution of him as such. The Gospels thus depict him as a somewhat "political" figure.

Their political perspective is, of course, distinctive: Mark's "kingdom" (1:15; cf. 9:1, 47; 11:10; 15:43) climaxes in the king's crucifixion (15:2, 9, 12, 18, 26, 32), a subversion of imperial (and, more generally, human) politics (cf. 4:11, 26–32; 10:14–15, 23–25; 14:24–25). The Gospels together do form a distinctive new subtype of biography, but one that would remain intelligible with Jesus as both a public figure and a sage.[109]

Although biographies of teachers remain a valuable analogy, both Jesus's public role and the limited number of full-length sage biographies from the early empire invite us to cast the net of comparison more broadly. The difference between biographies of sages and those of emperors is one of topic, not one of overall genre. The nature of some sources, of course, differs: public records such as archives could readily supply biographers with information regarding imperial building projects, senate decrees, and the like; we cannot expect to find such matters in our Gospels.

What *is* analogous for biographies of emperors, sages, and Jesus alike is the heavy presence of anecdotes, dependent on reports that, putatively, are

---

107. Of these, only the biography of Demonax stems from both living memory and the historiographic apex era of ancient biography.

108. See discussion in Sanders, *Jesus and Judaism*, 234, 307, 321–22 (cf. eschatological viceroy on 242); Chilton, "Announcement," 168; Brown, *Death*, 473–80.

109. Moses is king as well as prophet, priest, and lawgiver in Philo; see, e.g., *Moses* 1.60; 2.2, 66, 187, 292; for Moses as king, see also Deut 33:5; Josephus, *Jewish Antiquities* 4.327; LAB 9:16; 20:5; Meeks, *Prophet-King*, 107–17, 147–50, 177–79, 181–96, 236. Joseph is a statesman in Philo, *Joseph* 1; more than 40 percent of the term's instances in the Philonic corpus appear in *Joseph*.

ultimately dependent on witnesses. We do not accept all anecdotes uncritically, but we give preference to those stemming from within living memory of the biographee.

Dirk Frickenschmidt's extensive research compared the Gospels with varieties of ancient biographies. He was surprised to discover greater parallels in form with Nepos's and Plutarch's biographies of public figures than with typical biographies of philosophers.[110] This finding may be partly because it is more common to have entire books devoted to public figures, but it is also because Jesus was, inevitably, a public figure.

4.5. Conclusion

Although the Gospels fit readily in the broader category of biographies, demarcating subcategories is a more subjective, less precise exercise. In terms of their subject, the Gospels are biographies of a miracle-working sage, a fairly distinctive category in their period. That he was also a public figure who drew large crowds and was executed by the state provides further distinctive elements and often different analogies.

Still, because Jesus was a sage, aspects of the Gospels resemble biographies of sages. The community that revered him would have desired to transmit his teaching. Moreover, the Gospels are also full biographies, like those of public figures in contrast to the sketchier lives of poets surveyed in chapter 2.

Insofar as our objective is to read the Gospels for historical information, the time of their composition, relative both to other biographies and to their biographee, is significant. That they were composed during the early empire, the period of greatest historiographic sensitivity among ancient biographers, reinforces the likelihood that the Evangelists had significant interest in recounting genuine historical information about their biographee. That they speak about a figure within living memory suggests that they had substantial information available.

I turn to some other characteristics of biographies (ch. 5) before returning to primarily historiographic questions. Then I will explore the historical interests of biographies (ch. 6) and what historical interests meant for ancient authors (ch. 7).

110. Frickenschmidt, *Evangelium*, 169.

Chapter 5

What Did First-Century Audiences Expect of Biographies?

Although biographies had historical interests, this does not mean that their only concern was historical information, still less that they meant to present facts randomly without overarching themes. Biographers very much shaped the information available to them to communicate their perspectives.

In what follows, I will comment on ancient biographers' and historians' biases (their perspectives, or *Tendenz*), their commitment to providing morally useful examples, biographies' focus on their subjects' character, their variation regarding chronology, their frequent components, and the general structure of full biographies. At the same time, it should become evident that historians and biographers treated such characteristics generally as ways of framing, rather than as features inimical to, historical information.

5.1. Adaptations in Biographies

Mainstream biographies in the early empire depended on historical information (see esp. ch. 6); writers who lacked this interest had other suitable and far less confining genres in which to communicate their agendas. Nevertheless, ancient biographers and historians did not write the way their modern successors do.

A rhetorical handbook dated probably to the first century CE[1] advises students to "expand" or "condense" stories by elaborating or abbreviating speeches or descriptive details.[2] While an author may add details known from

---

1. Some even suggest that the formal pattern for elaborating chreiai seems restricted to rhetorical handbooks (Hester, "Blame," 302n1, citing chreia expert Edward O'Neil).

2. Theon, *Progymnasmata* 4.37–42, 80–82 (Butts), on fables. If editing fables demanded only minimal tampering with details, one would not expect more when editing historical stories.

other sources and add some description that is either implicit in the narrative or inherently probable in itself, his example for expanding an account does not substantially alter its essential sense.[3] In rhetorical exercises one can elaborate a narrative by offering an encomium on a character; then paraphrasing; then explaining; and so forth.[4]

Yet adaptations were not always so minor. Readers expected narrators, historically based or otherwise, to provide a cohesive narrative, not simply bare statements of events and inferences. Thus some historians did flesh out scenes[5] and conversations,[6] sometimes based on inference,[7] just as nearly all historians fleshed out speeches.[8] They might even reveal a character's thoughts.[9]

For one extreme example, Josephus expects his audience not to mind him depicting a scene such as the suicide speech to the Sicarii at Masada,[10] for which he lacks potential eyewitnesses,[11] though if challenged he might have protested that this represented a special scene rather than a consistent pattern. Similarly, Josephus embellishes Moses's military exploits, and Philo his intellectual ones,[12] though the nucleus of these postbiblical traditions predate them.[13] But excessive use of such amplification was deemed to violate the can-

---

3. Theon, *Progymnasmata* 3.224–40; cf. 2.115–23; also Longinus, *On the Sublime* 11.1; Hermogenes, *Invention* 2.7.120–21 (cf. 2.1.108–9; 2.7.120–24).

4. Hermogenes, *Progymnasmata* 3. On Chreia, 7; Aphthonius, *Progymnasmata* 3. On Chreia, 23S, 4R; 4. On Maxim, 9–10.

5. To the chagrin of stricter historians such as Polybius (see *Histories* 2.56.7, 10–11; 3.38.3; 15.34.1).

6. E.g., 1 Macc 6:10–13; 2 Macc 3:37–39; Josephus, *Jewish Antiquities* 19.38–45, 53–58, 78–83; for Tacitus, see Hadas, "Introduction," xx–xxi; for biographers, see Hägg, *Biography*, 3; for Plutarch specifically, see De Pourcq and Roskam, "Virtues," 167, noting on 178 that this practice in biography was little different from that of ancient historiography.

7. E.g., presumably Josephus, *Jewish War* 2.319; also Nepos's additions to his sources noted in Christian, "Themistocles," 114, 118, 130, 139; Philo's additions in Hidalgo, "Study," 287, 300.

8. See Keener, *Acts*, 1:258–82.

9. E.g., Tacitus, *Histories* 2.74; *Annals* 4.38–39; 12.4; cf. Mark 2:6, 8; 5:28; 6:20, 48, 52; 12:15; 14:11; Matt 12:25; 27:18; Luke 2:19, 51; 3:15; 6:8; 9:47; 11:17; 22:6; John 2:24; 5:6; 6:6, 64; 12:4; 13:3, 11; 18:4; 19:28; Arrian, *Alexander* 7.1.4; Dewald, "Construction," 97. De Temmerman, "Formalities," 17–18, defines such amplification as fictionalizing.

10. See discussions in, e.g., Ladouceur, "Masada"; Ladouceur, "Josephus"; Cohen, "Masada"; Cohen, "What Happened?"; Luz, "Masada"; Bauernfeind and Michel, "Beiden Eleazarreden"; Bünker, "Disposition der Eleazarreden."

11. The two women who survived presumably lacked rhetorical training.

12. Petitfils, "Tale," 159–63.

13. See sections 3.3a and 10.7a.

ons of historiography, and developing a mere fiction to entertain one's readers was judged "culpable," even by ancient historical standards.[14]

The Gospels provide little if any rhetorical elaboration and rarely flesh out scenes enough for even modern readers' dramatic tastes. Still, Synoptic comparisons show that Matthew and Luke plainly availed themselves of some literary liberties accepted in their era. Thus, for example, in Mark supplicants dig through a typical Galilean roof of mud and branches (Mark 2:4), whereas in Luke, adapting the image to be more relevant for a northern Aegean audience, the men removed terra cotta tiles (Luke 5:19).[15] (Matthew simply omits the roof part of the account.)

More often noted, in Luke 7:3–6, after a significant sermon by Jesus, local Judean elders and the centurion's friends intercede for and deliver messages for him; he does not come directly to Jesus. In Matthew 8:5–7, shortly after Jesus's parallel sermon, the centurion comes directly to Jesus, with no intermediaries. Likewise, Matthew 9:18 omits the messengers mentioned in Mark 5; whereas in Mark these messengers inform Jairus of his daughter's death after he has asked Jesus to heal her (Mark 5:23, 35). In Matthew this synagogue official simply announces his daughter's death to Jesus directly.

These are minor changes by the standards of their day and even of ordinary speech in our own; we know that our hearers do not want elaborate explanations of irrelevant details, and so we often omit some. I note these changes, though, because they are fairly obvious and rarely denied. Matthew's apparent prohibition of sandals (Matt 10:10) is only a minor verbal variation from Jesus's command in Mark 6:9, although it would feel much more significant for someone who had to walk barefoot on rugged trails.[16] Some might find more troublesome Luke's change of a centurion's acclamation of Jesus as God's Son (Mark 15:39) to "This man was innocent" or "righteous" (Luke 23:47), although for Luke (though not for Greek mythology) the latter could follow as a corollary from the former.

---

14. Fornara, *Nature*, 134–36.

15. See, e.g., Stein, *Luke*, 176; Blomberg, *Reliability*, 163; Liefeld and Pao, *Luke*, 121–22; Culy, Parsons, and Stigall, *Luke*, 167; Chen, *Luke*, 75; Wolter, *Luke*, 1:236–37; Levine and Witherington, *Luke*, 144; less politely toward Luke, Leaney, *Luke*, 124–25. Others object that even in Galilee the roof sometimes could have been tiled (Marshall, *Luke*, 213; Edwards, *Luke*, 165), or (correctly) that Luke's term for clay here need not imply tiles (Bock, *Luke*, 104–5n), though that is its usual sense in reference to roofs (see BDAG).

16. Matthew more clearly reapplies and thus adapts the mission for missionaries of his own day, including here material that stretches until the eschaton (Matt 10:23). The context in both cases is dependence on hospitality (Mark 6:8–10; Matt 10:9–10), so perhaps the point in Matthew involves extra sandals, but the wording in any case certainly differs from Mark.

More important here, these comparisons illustrate that such changes cannot merely reflect simple ignorance; Matthew and Luke knew their Markan source, and probably many of their hearers had heard Mark's account as well. They further illustrate that Matthew and Luke did not feel that they were risking their credibility, nor would one have reasons to do so for such adaptations, which probably do not even touch on matters of theology. They simply take for granted, and expect their hearers to take for granted, what we do in ordinary speech. They told the same stories, but often without concern for details extraneous to their main point.

5.2. Biographic Biases

Biographers had biases, and early examples of the genre often exercised little restraint in exhibiting it. In the early empire, however, historiographic valuation of greater objectivity helped restrain some biases. Biographers did not always evaluate characters in the same way (e.g., one might deem a character virtuous, and another deem him vicious), but they generally agreed that one should try to evaluate the characters fairly. The Evangelists, of course, adored Jesus, but we may presume that they believed their admiration to be based on his genuine character.

5.2a. Rhetoric and Personal Commitments

Scholars have noted the encomiastic element in biography,[17] but this obviously appears more in some biographies than in others, and it works against accurate historical representation more in some biographies than in others.[18] Rhetorical conventions were widespread, though more so in rhetorical biographers like Isocrates than others.[19]

Opinions about figures influenced and motivated biographic works, with the least restraints in the early period. Isocrates seeks to commemorate Eu-

17. Shuler, *Genre*; cf. Penner, *Praise*, 135 (in Jewish apologetic historiography, Penner, *Praise*, 229–35); deeds in ancient encomia are in Malina and Neyrey, *Portraits*, 28–33.

18. It also appears in encomiastic biographies of more recent centuries, which mix facts and fiction; see, e.g., McClymond, *Redemption*, 1:447–48, 451.

19. See Burridge, "Biography." But biographies were rarely as partisan as forensic speech, where a primary object was legal victory (e.g., Dionysius of Halicarnassus, *Lysias* 8).

agoras's virtues, using them to invite imitation.[20] Xenophon's works on Socrates and Agesilaus cite favorably only sources favorable to his subjects.[21] In time, however, historiographic concerns introduced increasing balance to biographic writing. Some scholars associate specifically political biography with historical facts in opposition to encomium,[22] but encomia on political figures such as Euagoras or Agesilaus may suggest otherwise.

It is probably more appropriate to emphasize the wider development of more historically oriented biography by the Roman period (see ch. 3). Certainly most biographers became more objective in how they evaluated their sources, even with a fairly encomiastic biography such as Tacitus's work on his father-in-law.[23]

Ancient biographers were typically less embarrassed by their commitment to their subjects than are their modern counterparts. Against some earlier scholars, however, the difference in various ancient biographers' critical acumen does not translate into different genres of ancient biography.[24] Even the more historically adept had biases; thus, although multiple motives are possible, Plutarch freely imputes them in the ways that best fit the portraits of characters that he is painting.[25] For example, Plutarch plays down a part of Tiberius Gracchus's character that does not fit his narrative.[26] Yet he normally avoids inventing stories to fit his predilections.[27]

The biographic historian Arrian likewise filters a mass of traditions down to what he feels best communicates his hero's character.[28] He is also ready to supplement eyewitness accounts with other material, not always as trustworthy but nevertheless "worth telling."[29] Still, this less critical approach appears primarily in the epideictic sections, separated from the narrative materials that precede.[30]

---

20. Ytterbrink, *Gospel*, 76, citing Isocrates, *Euagoras* 4, 76, 80–81. Philo does the same for Israel's ancestors; see Ytterbrink, *Gospel*, 100–101, citing Philo, *Abraham* 4–5, 217, although this is not strictly a biography in the way that his *Moses* probably is.

21. Alfred, "Valuation," 79–82.

22. Geiger, *Nepos*, 16.

23. Alfred, "Valuation," 79–80, 99–100.

24. Collins, *Mark*, 25.

25. De Pourcq and Roskam, "Virtues," 169, 177; cf. Cox, *Biography*, 13.

26. De Pourcq and Roskam, "Virtues," 177, comparing Appian, *Civil Wars* 1.17.

27. De Pourcq and Roskam, "Virtues," 177, following Pelling, *Plutarch and History*, 143–70.

28. Bosworth, *Arrian*, 16.

29. Derrenbacker, *Practices*, 57–58.

30. Derrenbacker, *Practices*, 57–59, esp. 59. Others also follow more detailed narratives about figures with sections of eulogistic postmortem epideictic, e.g., Justin, *Epitome* 25.5.3–6; 32.4.10–12.

Biographers also could write for apologetic and polemical reasons.[31] Certainly, Jewish writers about the past who engaged the wider Greco-Roman world as minority voices often apologetically played down incidents in their history that could appear embarrassing.[32] Despite his promise not to omit anything,[33] Josephus omits the golden calf;[34] Josephus omits and Philo explains Moses killing the Egyptian.[35] Josephus explains the destruction of Canaanites in a manner intelligible to Romans; Philo and Ps.-Philo omit that command.[36] Philo omits Aaron's role in the golden calf incident and may focus on Israel imitating an Egyptian bull deity.[37] Already, for primarily Judahite consumption, the Chronicler omitted sins of David[38] and Solomon.[39]

5.2b. Biases and Information

The effects of bias on biographers' deployment of their material varied. Certainly bias would influence one's praise of an emperor's virtues, even if one avoided telling any untruths.[40] But while ancients were well aware that their affection or respect for a person could bias their judgments, they also believed that such affection could be based on sound evaluations.[41] This is likely how Tacitus understood his encomiastic biography of his father-in-law, Agricola.

Naturally one might omit negative perspectives if one genuinely viewed the protagonist favorably (mostly the case in Tacitus's *Agricola*) or even as di-

31. Burridge, *Gospels*, 147, 183; for apologetic autobiography, cf., e.g., Josephus, *Life* 336–67; 2 Cor 11:8–33; Gal 1:11–24; Lamour, "Organisation." Autobiographic writing in some form appears as early as ancient Egypt (Simpson, *Literature*, 401–27); on the genre of autobiography, see further Lyons, *Autobiography*; Aune, *Dictionary*, 79–81.

32. E.g., Josephus may play down negative elements of the biblical picture of Israelites during the exodus (Cheon, "Plagues"), the horror of the raped concubine (Feldman, "Concubine"), and problematic elements in Gen 18:22–33 and Gen 22 (Niehoff, "Technique").

33. Josephus, *Jewish Antiquities* 1.17.

34. Josephus, *Jewish Antiquities* 3.79–99, esp. 95–99.

35. McGing, "Adaptation," 130, on Philo, *Moses* 1.40–46; Josephus, *Jewish Antiquities* 2.254.

36. See Feldman, "Command"; for Philo, see also Berthelot, "Conquest."

37. So Feldman, "Calf," on Philo, *Moses* 2.161–73 (esp. 2.165, 169), though Feldman may overplay this point.

38. Contrast 2 Sam 11:1–27; 12:9–10; 1 Kgs 15:5.

39. Cf., e.g., Williamson, *Chronicles*, 236.

40. E.g., Pliny, *Letters* 6.27.1–2. Pliny's *Panegyric*, however, is conspicuously sycophantic.

41. Polybius, *Histories* 10.21.8; Pliny, *Letters* 3.3.5. For Polybius's distinction between treating an individual encomiastically or historically, cf. Farrington, "Action."

vinely authoritative (the Gospels; later, Iamblichus's *Pythagorean Life*). These emphases and omissions are normally cases of perspective, however, rather than of deliberate distortion. Historians themselves recognized the need for selectivity;[42] while this concern sometimes reflects what we would call bias,[43] it can also reflect their need to focus on the narratives' primary concerns.[44] Honoring his protagonist and guarding his commitment to providing moral exemplarity, Plutarch omits or minimizes Caesar's affairs.[45] Arrian cannot omit Alexander's worst acts, but he avoids focusing on them.[46] Philo and Josephus highlight Moses's virtue and play down embarrassing elements that their Scriptures readily included.[47]

The same is true for focus on particular interests. Suetonius may indulge some of his own interests in focusing on imperial administration, given his own involvement there at some point in his career.[48] Justin observed that earlier "Greek historians approached their work as specialists, each following his own interests and omitting what did not serve his purpose."[49] Modern his-

---

42. Historians themselves sometimes deemed selectivity a major distinction between "history" and "chronicles" (Whittaker, "Introduction," li–lii, citing Lucian, *How to Write History* 4–6, 27). Good historians should not focus on points they considered minor (Dionysius of Halicarnassus, *Thucydides* 13).

43. Some accuse of bias, based on omissions, Xenophon (Brownson, "Introduction to *Anabasis*," ix–x; Brown, *Historians*, 95–97, though regarding Xenophon as otherwise mostly evenhanded, 93–94), Arrian (Baynham, "Quintus Curtius," 428), and Tacitus (Laistner, *Historians*, 132). For omissions, see, e.g., Josephus, *Life* 339; *Against Apion* 1.60–66; Dio Cassius, *Roman History* 1.1.1–2; for apologetic reasons, Josephus omits the golden calf (*Jewish Antiquities* 3.79–99).

44. Tacitus frankly admits that he does not treat all Senate business, but only that of moral value for his audience (*Annals* 3.65). Polybius complains that some writers focus too much of their narrative on irrelevant matters (*Histories* 15.36.10); he insists that he must omit some matters about Roman customs (6.11.4–6), pleading with his critics that they should attribute omissions to ignorance only when what is recounted contains errors (6.11.7–8). Historians did not regard it as a criticism when someone else testified to the accuracy of what they reported but offered to supply additional information (Josephus, *Life* 365–67); sometimes hints of information suggest that a historian who omitted it did not lack the information itself (Whittaker, "Introduction," xlviii–lii, on Herodian).

45. See Beneker, "Chaste Caesar." Cf. royal apologists and spin doctors in Philostratus, *Heroicus* 31.5; Long, "Samuel," 270; apologetic for Socrates in Xenophon and Plato. Josephus's autobiography is widely recognized as apologetic (with, e.g., Lamour, "Organisation").

46. See Bosworth, *Arrian*, 63–64.

47. See, e.g., McGing, "Adaptation," 129–30 (on Philo, *Moses* 1.40–46; Josephus, *Jewish Antiquities* 2.254–57), 133; Hidalgo, "Study," 287–88.

48. Edwards, "Introduction," xi.

49. Justin, *Epitome* pref.3.

torians also have particular interests, for example, military or political history, women's history, and the like.

Holly Carey notes that ancient biographers had their favorites and presented the best side of their most heroic protagonists.[50] Since the Evangelists regard Jesus as God's Son, their uniformly (or, on some approaches, their almost uniformly) positive depiction of Jesus is not surprising—although, as Carey notes,[51] elements that would strike outsiders as negative, such as Jesus's crucifixion on the charge of treason, are not minimized. Perhaps it is of particular interest that the leading apostolic witnesses, though ultimately viewed as a "foundation" for the church (Eph 2:20; Rev 21:14), never achieve a heroic status in the Gospels.

Outside of formal biographies, Judean haggadic materials[52] even attempt to whitewash heroes by adding to the story, although the stories' original tellers and listeners presumably understood these to be edifying elaborations.[53] Negative incidents could be toned down,[54] omitted,[55] or justified[56] in the character's favor. Nevertheless, these appear in works of a genre quite different from conventional biography, apart from being narratives about the past.

5.2c. Bragging or Ragging on Biographees: Balancing Biases

Polybius, a Hellenistic historian who also wrote encomia in other settings, allows for slanted praise and blame in encomia, but in historiography he requires these verdicts to be consistent with facts.[57] In historical writing, he maintains,

---

50. Carey, "Importance," esp. 320, on Philo, *Moses*.

51. Carey, "Importance," 320–21.

52. Haggadic adaptation appears in both midrash and folk literature (Wright, "Midrash," 129). See further discussion in ch. 11.

53. As noted, even the rabbis themselves probably recognized that midrashic additions were homiletic, distinct from historical reconstructions (Milikowsky, "Midrash"), though one generation's traditions may have filled another's historical curiosity. Haggadic elaboration resembles techniques in Greek mythography more than historiography; cf. Maclean and Aitken, *Heroikos*, li–lii.

54. LAB 12:2–3. T. Job 39:12–13 (OTP) / 39:9–10 (Kraft) and 40:3/4 seem concerned to soften God letting Job's children die for his test.

55. Jub. 13:17–18; 14:21–16:22; 29:13; T. Zeb. 1:5–7. In Jubilees, see Wintermute, "Introduction," 35–36; in Josephus, cf. Aune, *Environment*, 108; in Greco-Roman literature, see Shuler, *Genre*, 50 (following Cicero, *Oratorical Partitions* 22).

56. CD 4.20–5.3 (also 11QT 56.18); Jub. 19:15–16; 27:6–7; 28:6–7; 30:2–17; 41; 1Qap Gen ar 20.10–11; Jos. Asen. 23; T. Jud. 8–12 (cf. Tg. Neof. 1 on Gen 38:25; Tg. Ps.-Jon. on Gen. 38:25–26); T. Iss. 3:1 (cf. Gen 49:15); Tg. Ps.-Jon. on Gen. 49:28.

57. Polybius, *Histories* 3.4.1; 8.8.3–6; 10.21.8; cf. Hägg, *Biography*, 96–97. Polybius's contrast

the appropriate place to praise or blame people's character was only while recounting their actual behavior.[58] Some of his successors embraced more rhetoric in their histories, but they also were not simply composing encomia.

Although partisanship was rife, biographies from the early empire, in contrast to earlier encomia, were generally not uncritical glorifications of their subjects. Honoring one's subject might influence selection of material, but it did not need to distort the information in that material.[59] Roman-period biographers often continued to take sides when evaluating behavior, but this practice differs from inventing behavior not in their sources. Even the oft-criticized Cornelius Nepos usually balances information and agendas.[60]

Most biographies mixed some measure of praise and blame.[61] (For that matter, even epics included flawed heroes.)[62] Biographers thus felt free to record negative as well as positive features of their protagonists, when appropriate.[63] Thus, for example:

- Plutarch at times criticizes figures that he greatly respects, such as Marcus Cato, Cicero, or Lucullus.[64]
- Some of Plutarch's reports are morally ambiguous rather than clear-cut.[65]
- Suetonius adores Augustus[66] but nevertheless includes some of his negative deeds.[67]
- Suetonius reports Nero's good deeds first to get them out of the way before

---

in 10.21.8 involves not biography per se but encomium (with Burridge, *Gospels*, 61). Polybius denounces Timaeus for presenting others too well (12.7.1) or too poorly (12.15.12).

58. Polybius, *Histories* 10.26.9.

59. Fornara, *Nature*, 64–65.

60. Hägg, *Biography*, 189; Ytterbrink, *Gospel*, 89–90.

61. E.g., Plutarch, *Cimon* 2.4–5; Cornelius Nepos, *On Great Generals* 11 (Iphicrates), 3.2; Suetonius, *Nero* 7, 9; *Domitian* 3.2.

62. The plot of the *Iliad* turns partly on the heroically magnified pride of Achilles and Agamemnon; the character of Odysseus in the sequel is flawed in different respects.

63. E.g., Arrian, *Alexander* 4.7.4; 4.8.1–4.9.6; Plutarch, *Cimon* 2.4–5; Cornelius Nepos, *On Great Generals* 11 (Iphicrates), 3.2; more fully, see Ytterbrink, *Gospel*, 90, 92, 116; Keener, *John*, 16 (cf. Keener, *Matthew*, 51n157).

64. See, e.g., Plutarch, *Marcus Cato* 5.1, 5; 12.4; Hägg, *Biography*, 260, 265; Lavery, "Lucullus." Cf. Dionysius of Halicarnassus, *Thucydides* 1, criticizing the style of a historian he respects. For his moral purposes, Plutarch may employ stock character traits from comedy to critique his protagonists; see Xenophontos, "Comedy."

65. See Duff, "Ambiguity."

66. Probably at least partly influenced by Augustus's autobiography and most sources permitted to survive; see Alfred, "Valuation," 97, 101.

67. E.g., Suetonius, *Augustus* 69.1.

turning to "his shameful and criminal deeds," which consume the rest of his account.[68]

- While Suetonius's Vespasian is mostly adulatory (contrast his biographies of Caligula, Nero, or Domitian), he reports this emperor's love of money.[69]
- Diogenes Laertius respects Aristotle but cites his critics as well as his supporters.[70]
- Philostratus reports an unflattering account about his own teacher, whom he respected.[71]
- Eunapius reports an unflattering account about Iamblichus, despite considering him supernatural.[72]

Biographers' differing treatment of different persons displays not indiscriminate praise but an attempt to assign praise and blame according to what the writers viewed as the preponderance of positive and negative actions—that is, based on an interpretation of, rather than free creation of, information. All memory, whether personal or collective, is interpretive; we lack any literary access to an uninterpreted past.[73]

Arrian's biographic history[74] avoids focus on Alexander's worst deeds but cannot avoid reporting them.[75] In his epideictic sections, Arrian follows any sources that support his praise of Alexander's heroism; in his main narratives, however, he follows only the sources he most respects historically.[76] Arrian exhibits clearly pro-Alexander bias,[77] but it can be overstated;[78] he was not fabricating new stories about Alexander.

---

68. Suetonius, *Nero* 19.3 (LCL 2:115). For him listing first the worst emperor's positive acts, see also Edwards, "Introduction," xii.

69. Likewise, Suetonius, *Julius* 52 (like much of the work) is full of scandal about Julius, but there is also praise (53). After recounting his noble deeds (e.g., 73–75), Suetonius concludes that his negative actions "so turn the scale, that it is thought that he abused his power and was justly slain" (76.1 [LCL 1:99]).

70. Fitzgerald, "Lives," 218.

71. Philostratus, *Lives of the Sophists* 2.21.602–3.

72. Eunapius, *Lives* 461; cf. 459–61.

73. See Le Donne, *Historiographical Jesus*, 38–39.

74. He identifies it as a history; cf., e.g., Arrian, *Indica* 17, 19, 21, 23, 26, 40, 43.

75. E.g., Arrian, *Alexander* 4.7.4; 4.8.1–4.9.6; see also Bosworth, *Arrian*, 63–64, citing 4.9.1; 4.12.6.

76. Derrenbacker, *Practices*, 57–59, following esp. Stadter.

77. Bosworth, "Pursuit," 447; Baynham, "Quintus Curtius," 428.

78. Bosworth, "Pursuit," 452–53.

5.2d. The Gospels Honor Jesus

Different biographers often differed considerably in their assessments of their subjects' virtues,[79] yet ordinarily they did not for this reason invent new incidents. Indeed, they usually draw interpretively on the same pool of information. They simply emphasized the particular incidents, and the particular aspects of those incidents, on which their own assessments rested.

Because biographers had freedom to report both good and harmful actions, those who depicted past figures favorably normally did so based on genuine respect. Isocrates and Xenophon composed their encomiastic protobiographies because they respected the characters about whom they wrote, though clearly not everyone shared their assessments. In the early empire, Tacitus praised his father-in-law, Agricola, and Lucian his mentor Demonax because they respected these figures.

Adherents deemed some teachers exceptional, hence meriting unmixed praise; for example, Xenophon has only good to report about Socrates.[80] Likewise, it comes as no surprise that the Gospels uniformly honor Jesus;[81] we would not expect early Christians to dishonor or find flaws in one whom they esteemed as their exalted Lord. Even so, the Gospels offer little direct encomium;[82] although they praise Jesus, they do so by reporting his words and deeds rather than by listing his virtues abstractly. When followers disagreed with teachers, they normally said so.[83] But sincere worshipers usually try to adjust their views to fit those of the one they worship.[84]

---

79. See, e.g., Davis, "Evaluations"; Ytterbrink, *Gospel*, 89, 91; Champlin, "Tiberius."

80. See, e.g., Xenophon, *Memorabilia* 4.8.11.

81. Cf., e.g., Ytterbrink, *Gospel*, 227.

82. Pace Shuler, *Genre*; see Burridge, *Gospels*, 208; Collins, *Mark*, 30.

83. See, e.g., Valerius Maximus, *Memorable Doings and Sayings* 8.15.ext.1; Seneca, *To Lucilius* 108.17, 20, 22; 110.14, 20; Musonius Rufus 1, 36.6–7; Philostratus, *Life of Apollonius* 7.22.

84. Notwithstanding the aberration of segments of Western Christendom and other expressions of cultural religion. Common Judaism, despite its diversity, remained Torah-centered; see Josephus, *Against Apion* 1.60; 2.282–84; m. 'Abot. 1:13; 6:5; Qidd. 4:14; t. Ḥag. 1:2; Sipre Deut. 41.6.1; Moore, *Judaism*, 1:235–50; Goodenough, *Symbols*, 2:6, 22; Neusner, *Beginning*, 13; Safrai, "Education," 945.

5.3. More Morals, Not Less Lessons

Like other kinds of historical writers, biographers frequently sought to teach moral lessons from their stories.[85] Biographic information was meant to be used to instruct learners in virtue through the process of imitation.[86] Some ancient biographers emphasize moral lessons in their stories more than do others; some writers, such as Plutarch, vary in their moralizing even from one biography to the next.[87] Suetonius is forthright in evaluating characters' morals,[88] but he differs from earlier encomiasts. He cites whatever material is available but is cautious about committing himself, guarding "his credibility as a factual source."[89]

In an earlier period, ancients permitted more freedom for encomiastic focus on a persons's virtues, for the sake of honor, teaching virtue, and inviting emulation, than was appropriate for academic history.[90] Biographers could dwell on the virtues of their subject in ways that historians did not; also, they intended their work for less technical audiences.[91]

Yet the emphasis on moral examples was a feature of historiography as well as biography; the historian Tacitus, for example, is hardly neutral about Nero or Domitian. Ancient historians used history to shed light on their own times, as do many historians today.[92] Although Plutarch exploits biography for moral lessons more clearly than do many others,[93] his focus on this function is not an innovation; it had long been a practice of historians (see ch. 7),[94] as well

---

85. Pelling, "Adaptation," 135; Burridge, *Gospels*, 145–46, 181; Hägg, *Biography*, 239–81, esp. 274; cf. Dihle, "Biography," 367–74.

86. Plutarch, *Aratus* 1.4; on encomia, cf. Proclus, *Poetics* 5, K58.6–14. Cf. Kurz, "Models," 182–83, on biography and narrative models for imitation.

87. Burridge, *Gospels*, 66.

88. See, e.g., Luke, "Ideology"; Wardle, "Augustus."

89. Power, "Poetry," 237. Aletti, *Birth*, 22, finds Suetonius less interested in moral instruction than in presenting both good and bad features of his subjects, "consistent with reality."

90. So Polybius, *Histories* 10.21.8 again.

91. Cornelius Nepos, *On Great Generals* 16 (Pelopidas), 1.1; cf. Pelling, "Biography, Greek," 242.

92. Aune, *Environment*, 62, cites esp. Isocrates, *To Nicocles* 35; *To Demonicus* 34; Polybius, *Histories* 1.1.2; Livy, *History* 1.pref.10–11; Plutarch, *Aemilius Paulus* 1.1; Lucian, *Demonax* 2.

93. E.g., Beneker, *Statesman*, on leaders' mastery of passion (see, e.g., 8, 16, 70–73, 105, 113, 122–27, 133, 139, 152, 160, 195–206); Duff, *Lives*, 13–72; Nikolaidis, "Introduction," xiii–xiv (and more generally, Nikolaidis, *Unity*); Adams, *Genre*, 83. For his possible use of patterns from comic invective, see Xenophontos, "Comedy."

94. See, e.g., Polybius, *Histories* 1.1.1; Dionysius of Halicarnassus, *Roman Antiquities* 1.2.1;

as biographic writers,[95] and biographers such as Nepos and Plutarch probably derived this emphasis especially from historiography.[96]

Plutarch expressly notes that his interest in moral lessons fits historiographic practice.[97] His interests may be particularly moral, but he claims concern for historical verity and "the historical correctness of his sources."[98] His asides often articulate his perspectives;[99] yet asides also appear in histories as well as romance.[100] Plutarch selects what he feels will benefit his readers,[101] but selection is not free invention. Thus, for example, when he needs to pad his life of Coriolanus with more information, he turns to knowable cultural matters only indirectly related to his narrative.[102] Plutarch does not typically invent special deaths for his heroes simply for moral purposes.[103] Despite exceptions, many of Plutarch's themes are those of earlier eras rather than his own; he may simply highlight those that he viewed as relevant for all eras.[104]

5.4. Interpretations and Information

For biographies to be prescriptive does not mean that they were not also descriptive.[105] Interest in values is not limited to ancient biography; modern biographies, too, seek to edify as well as inform.[106] New Testament scholars have our own biases and naturally focus more on positive traits of characters whom we perceive as generally positive figures. All historians, ancient and modern, write from some systems of values and perspectives, as is often noted.[107]

1.6.3–5; Valerius Maximus, *Memorable Doings and Sayings* 2.pref.; Tacitus, *Agricola* 1; *Annals* 3.65; Josephus, *Against Apion* 2.204.

95. See Momigliano, *Development*, 69; Adams, *Genre*, 93–94.

96. With Geiger, *Nepos*, 115.

97. Plutarch, *Aemilius Paulus* 1.1–2, emphasizes the role of morals in bio (*bios*), as he does in history (*historia*), 1.3.

98. De Pourcq and Roskam, "Virtues," 175, citing, e.g., Plutarch, *Solon* 27.1.

99. Hillman, "Statements."

100. See Sheeley, *Asides*, 41–78.

101. See De Pourcq and Roskam, "Virtues," 166–67, on Plutarch, *Aemilius Paulus* 1.2; *Alexander* 1.2.

102. Alfred, "Valuation," 91.

103. Pelling, "Bounds," 269.

104. Pelling, *Texts*, 58.

105. The overstatement in Praet, "Cloak," 134, may be more applicable to hagiography.

106. Votaw, "Biographies," 51; see esp. Dillon, "Interpretation," 164.

107. E.g., Marincola, "Introduction," 3; Ehrman, *Introduction*, 133; Enns, *Problem*, 66.

Agendas are not intrinsically incompatible with historical information; as modern journalists and other authors recognize, a writer or editor may slant a story by how one tells it rather than by inventing information.[108] Indeed, as Geza Vermes has argued, "a theological interest is no more incompatible with a concern for history than is a political or philosophical conviction," and we can allow for these in interpretation.[109]

The influence of perspectives is inevitable at every stage of historical tradition. Human brains are hardwired to seek explanations for events, so identifying patterns and learning what to predict, avoid, and embrace.[110] Although our knowledge of science is far greater than that of our ancestors, they were no less prone than we to think in terms of cause and effect. For this reason they too arranged their limited data in frameworks intelligible to them.[111] Interpretive grids begin even with our initial encoding of memories.[112]

Yet perspectives do not by themselves make a work fictitious.[113] "No fact," Pelling warns, "is wholly interpretation-free"; even announcing that Athens executed Socrates assumes that this particular incident in 399 BCE warrants our attention more than do others. Yet not all facts are *equally* "interpretation-laden"; "it is a dereliction of historical duty to assume that every version is as true and every interpretation is as good as any other."[114]

5.5. Characteristic Care for Character

Ancient biographers' emphasis on moral models is inseparable from their focus on their subjects' character.[115] Whereas encomia could list conventional virtues and exaggerate character, historical biography was supposed to be more

---

108. See De Temmerman, "Formalities," 13, citing, e.g., Pelling, "Truth," regarding Plutarch's usual refusal to create "lengthy new stories to fill gaps in source material." This is not to deny that slanted selection and narration can seriously affect understanding; I find, for example, the BBC more neutral regarding US politics than are many US sources.

109. Vermes, *Jesus and Judaism*, 19; cf. Levinskaya, *Setting*, 2; Hemer, *Acts*, 79–90.

110. Barber and Barber, *Severed*, 13–14; cf. also Berger, *Canopy*, 22 (oft-cited, e.g., Turner, *Regulating Bodies*, 83; Hamilton, *Sociology*, 165; Wuthnow et al., *Analysis*, 26; Dann, "Conclusion," 67n65; Day, *Believing*, 8; Back and Bennett, *Sociology*, 136; Brack, *Historiography*, xiii).

111. Barber and Barber, *Severed*, 13.

112. Barber and Barber, *Severed*, 33; Bauckham, *Eyewitnesses*, 330, 334–38, 350.

113. De Pourcq and Roskam, "Virtues," 164.

114. Pelling, *Texts*, 7.

115. Pelling, "Adaptation," 135; Burridge, *Gospels*, 65, 171.

evenhanded (despite the many biases noted above). Character was, however, a major or even the key focus.[116]

Plutarch wants to supplement historians' focus with greater insight into their characters,[117] though often inferring these insights from historical sources.[118] For him, offhand gestures or comments might reveal more about character than major events.[119] Often more than Plutarch, Suetonius focuses on minor personal details that reveal character but were of little interest to historians.[120] Such details provided entertainment, but Suetonius was especially interested in revealing *character*, which from a Roman perspective is important for evaluating the emperor. Suetonius's work is not for mere "idle curiosity."[121] Lucian offers merely sample anecdotes about Demonax, yet enough to reveal "the sort of man he was."[122] Interests in a subject's character are not incompatible with historical information, especially when the biographer praising the person knew them personally.[123]

Although ancient biography was less fond of characterization than are modern biographies or novels,[124] characterization does appear. Some works provide direct characterization more than others.[125] Because history was usually less focused on a single person, it generally displayed less emphasis on characterization than did biography.[126] Characterization does appear in histories,[127] but Greek historians usually expected their audiences to learn lessons

---

116. Cox, *Biography*, 12; Frickenschmidt, *Evangelium*, 277, 289–94; Ytterbrink, *Gospel*, 79–80; Licona, *Differences*, 5; for characterization in biography, see further Hägg, *Biography*, 5–6, 11–15, 23, 27–30, 45, 89; for examples, note Cornelius Nepos, *On Great Generals* 4 (Pausanias), 1.1; Feldman, "Jehoram."

117. Pelling, *Texts*, 45–46 (citing Plutarch, *Nicias* 1.5).

118. Pelling, *Texts*, 48, 53 (citing Thucydides, *History* 6.13.1; 6.18.6; 6.24.3).

119. Burridge, *Gospels*, 171, citing Plutarch, *Cato the Younger* 24.1; 37.5; *Phocion* 5.4; Licona, *Differences*, 4–5, citing Plutarch, *Alexander* 1.2–3.

120. Edwards, "Introduction," xiii, comparing Suetonius, *Julius* 45–75 with Plutarch's *Julius Caesar*.

121. Edwards, "Introduction," xiii.

122. Beck, "Demonax," 84, quoting *Demonax* 67; and citing Branham, *Eloquence*, 58.

123. See Beck, "Demonax," 95, on Xenophon's *Agesilaus* and Lucian's *Demonax*.

124. Direct, individualistic characterization is of course more common in modern biography (Burridge, "Review," 478).

125. Becker, *Birth*, 73.

126. See Fornara, *Nature*, 185. Laistner, *Historians*, 56, views Sallust's characters as too stark.

127. Pitcher, "Characterization," esp. 103–4, 106, 117. See, e.g., Marcius as the greatest general of his era, yet with fatal character flaws (Dionysius of Halicarnassus, *Roman Antiquities* 8.60.1–2; 8.61.1–3).

especially indirectly,[128] through characters' actions and words.[129] Biographers likewise could display a subject's character through his behavior;[130] but often they also comment on it directly.[131] Often the responses of other characters in a narrative emphasize the hero's character,[132] an observation no doubt of importance also for the interpretation of the Gospels (e.g., Mark 1:22; John 7:15, 43).[133]

Some scholars see biographers emphasizing moral *types*[134] in biographies, including Plutarch and Suetonius.[135] They do not expect to find character development in the modern sense; ancient readers were not interested in personality as conveyed through psychological complexity.[136] In many cases, then, the subject's character remained the same throughout their life, with childhood anecdotes morally prefiguring the character's later activity.[137] Biographers such as Suetonius were normally not interested in *why* their characters acted the ways that they did.[138] Even what sometimes appears to be character development (e.g., in Flaccus)[139] might be just his true negative nature coming out.[140]

Nevertheless, character change does appear in some biographies.[141] Readers of ancient biographies can sometimes recognize how early traumas affected

128. Pitcher, "Characterization," 105, 107–10.

129. Pitcher, "Characterization," 110–12; Marincola, "Speeches," 119 (speeches); Pelling, *Texts*, 8.

130. Stanton, *Preaching*, 125; Stanton, *Gospel Truth?*, 139; Burridge, *Gospels*, 139, 178–79; in the Gospels, see esp. Burridge, *Gospels*, 205, 227.

131. Cornelius Nepos, *On Great Generals* 4 (Pausanias), 1.1; Suetonius, *Caligula* 44; cf. Matt 21:5; Mark 6:34; Luke 1:32; 7:13; John 3:16; 11:5; 13:1; Ytterbrink, *Gospel*, 118 (on 228 noting the unusual lack of this in Luke). Many elite biographers were rhetoricians, who could describe a person's character directly (*Rhetorica ad Herennium* 4.50.63).

132. Frickenschmidt, *Evangelium*, 286–89; Ytterbrink, *Gospel*, 84; Pitcher, "Characterization," 107–8; De Pourcq and Roskam, "Virtues," 168–69 (citing, e.g., Plutarch, *Agis* 8.6; 10.2; 14.3; *Cleomenes* 13.3; 18.2; 26.5; *Caius Gracchus* 6.3); cf. Pelling, *Texts*, 53.

133. See Keith and Hurtado, *Friends and Enemies*.

134. For extensive and usually entertaining examples of such types, see Theophrastus, *Characters*.

135. Momigliano, *Development*, 13; Cox, *Biography*, 13.

136. Beck, "Demonax," 89 (following Pelling, *Plutarch and History*, 316). Oral tradition normally flattens characters as memorably "monumental" rather than round (Rosenberg, "Complexity," 87).

137. Edwards, "Introduction," xvi; cf. again Pelling, *Plutarch and History*, 316.

138. Edwards, "Introduction," xvi.

139. Philo, *Flaccus* 8–11.

140. Philo, *Flaccus* 1–2.

141. E.g., youth could differ from adult life (e.g., Plutarch, *Themistocles* 2.5). Note also Burridge, *Gospels*, 178–79, citing esp. Plutarch, *Aratus* 51.4; 54.2; *Sertorius* 10.2–5.

characters' development.[142] Indeed, characterization does appear even in histories,[143] though sometimes indirectly.[144] Likewise, character *development* appears not only in novels[145] but also in histories.[146] Moreover, while some viewed character as inborn and not changing,[147] others demurred.[148] Even a single biographer such as Plutarch could hold both static and developmental approaches to character simultaneously.[149]

More important to the present point, rarely are characters pure embodiments of virtue or vice.[150] Biographees were not flat characters simply invented to play moral roles;[151] indeed, other characters within the narratives often offer a range of perspectives on the central biographees, as noted earlier.[152]

One scholar argues that though the Gospels are "lives," they differ from Greek lives because they cannot trace moral development in one they regard as God incarnate.[153] Whether the Gospels include no character development might be debated (cf. Mark 14:32–42), but that is admittedly not their focus.[154]

142. See, e.g., Tiberius's loss of his first wife and his son and Herod's early experiences of violence.

143. Pitcher, "Characterization," esp. 103–4, 106, 115–17; see also, e.g., Velleius Paterculus, *History* 2.18.5; 2.25.3; 2.28.2; Tacitus, *Annals* 4.54; 6.51; cf. Hadas, "Introduction," xiv–xv. See now esp. Ash, Mossman, and Titchener, *Fame*.

144. Pitcher, "Characterization," 105, 107–10; it may be through actions and words (110–12; speeches in Marincola, "Speeches," 119) or other characters' observations (Pitcher, "Characterization," 107–8).

145. For one attempt to trace character development in Callirhoe, see De Temmerman, "Beauty."

146. E.g., Pitcher, "Characterization," 115–17; see also, e.g., Tacitus, *Annals* 6.51; cf. Tacitus's clarity on characters in Hadas, "Introduction," xiv–xv; e.g., Agrippina, in Tacitus, *Annals* 4.54; character changes in Velleius Paterculus, *History* 2.18.5; 2.25.3; 2.28.2.

147. Euripides, frag. 1068, from Stobaeus, *Anthology* 4.30.3; 1113, from Stobaeus 4.29.35; *Phoenix* frag. 810; *Dictys* frag. 333, from Stobaeus 4.30.5; Pindar, *Olympian Odes* 11.19–20; 13.12; cf. Galen, *Grief* 60.

148. Valerius Maximus, *Memorable Doings and Sayings* 6.9.pref.–6.9.9; cf. 2 Chr 24:17–22.

149. See Duff, "Models," though attributing one to his philosophic and the other to his biographic approach.

150. Cf., e.g., Duff, "Ambiguity." Philo tells of even Flaccus's good works (*Flaccus* 2–5, 8) before turning to his evil ones, claiming that mentioning these highlights that Flaccus acted not from ignorance of right and wrong but, less excusably, from malice (7).

151. De Pourcq and Roskam, "Virtues," 164–65; Burridge, *Gospels*, 178–79; Keener, *Acts*, 1:151.

152. See Edwards, "Introduction," xxv; cf., e.g., Nicolaus, *Augustus* 20–21, 23, 25, 27, 29 (*FGrH* 130).

153. Dihle, "Biography," 379.

154. Strauss, *Life*, 1:282, rightly contrasts Jesus and most other central biblical figures on this point.

Yet as we have noted, many biographies did not emphasize character development. As for Jesus's exalted status, later biographers and hagiographers, admittedly probably influenced by Christian models, did find biography a suitable format for speaking of divinely influenced humans.

5.6. Chronic Chronology? Ancient Biographies Were Not All Chronological

Momigliano rightly warns that "ancient biographies did not necessarily follow a chronological order; nor is chronological order a necessary feature even of modern biographies."[155] This disinterest contrasts with the more chronological practice of historians,[156] although, in contrast to Thucydides, even most historians tended to follow events to their conclusion and not simply follow a strict chronology.[157]

Many biographies included a basic chronology of background, life, and death,[158] but the large middle section about the life often consisted of anecdotes arranged randomly.[159] Thus Plutarch, for example, accidentally repeats material about Alexander.[160] Elsewhere he notes that he has anticipated a later event to keep together material on the same topic.[161] This freedom to arrange material without respect for chronology was especially true in typical biographies about sages, where the more chronologically ordered histories did not provide significant information.[162] Xenophon's seminal work *Memorabilia* does not try to trace Socrates's life more broadly, and chronology is not significant there.[163]

---

155. Momigliano, *Development*, 13–14; cf. Thorburn, "Tiberius."

156. E.g., Thucydides, *History* 2.1.1; 5.26.1.

157. E.g., Polybius, *Histories* 2.14; Diodorus Siculus, *Library of History* 16.1.1–2; Dionysius of Halicarnassus, *Thucydides* 9; *Letter to Gnaeus Pompeius* 3; cf. Trogus in Develin, "Introduction," 9–10; the alternating blocks of focus in Herodotus noted in Longenecker, *Rhetoric*, 27. A moralist could note that an event should occur at a certain point in his narrative (4 Macc 12:7) yet choose to recount it later.

158. See esp. Plutarch (e.g., Ytterbrink, *Gospel*, 108; Konstan and Walsh, "Biography," 32). Cf. the lives of Aesop, Homer, Secundus, and Herakles in Aune, *Environment*, 63–64.

159. E.g., Demonax anecdotes (cf. Cancik, "Gattung," 94–95; Beck, "Demonax," 82–83, 95) and anecdotes in Diogenes Laertius (Cambiano, "Diogenes Laertius," 574). The middle section could mix chronology and thematic treatments and could dislocate chronology; Frickenschmidt, *Evangelium*, 278, 505.

160. Plutarch, *Alexander* 37.4; 56.1.

161. Plutarch, *Cato the Younger* 25.5.

162. Cf. Momigliano, *Development*, 87–88, on literary figures; Konstan and Walsh, "Biography," 33.

163. Adams, *Genre*, 75.

Some other biographies freely arranged most of their content topically, often around virtues to imitate or vices to avoid.[164] This pattern is particularly conspicuous in Suetonius,[165] where it proves helpful in highlighting the character of his subjects.[166] When interested in chronology, Suetonius cites not biographers but historians.[167]

Both the chronological and topical forms existed long before the Gospels.[168] Apart from birth and death, chronology was of little importance to Hellenistic scholars in Alexandria.[169] But as noted earlier, biographic arrangement by chronology or theme does not easily divide biographies into two types, since there was overlap between these concerns, often even in the same biography.[170] Even Xenophon's protobiography *Agesilaus* has chronological (chs. 1–2) and topical (chs. 3–11) elements.[171] Some of Nepos's biographies are arranged chronologically, whereas others are topical or anecdotal.[172] After summarizing some key events of Augustus's early life, Suetonius turns to a topical treatment in explicit contrast to a chronological one.[173]

Sometimes elements of chronology were artificial to begin with, a mere literary construct for cohesiveness, even in ancient historiography.[174] Subsequent users of earlier works did not always feel constrained by their predecessors' chronology. Nepos and other biographers also feel free to rearrange the chronology of their sources.[175] Arrian's biographic historical monograph on Alexander likewise rearranges his sources.[176] Plutarch arranges his own

---

164. Cf. also topical arrangement of anecdotes in Valerius Maximus (Rüpke, "Knowledge," 89, 93). Even sayings could be arranged topically (e.g., Epictetus, *Encheiridion*).

165. E.g., Suetonius, *Augustus* 9; *Caligula* 22.1; *Nero* 19.3; Pelling, "Biography, Roman," 243; Görgemanns, "Biography"; Burridge, *Gospels*, 74; Konstan and Walsh, "Biography," 32.

166. Beck, "Demonax," 94, following Pelling, *Plutarch and History*, 288.

167. Suetonius, *Caligula* 8.3.

168. Momigliano, *Development*, 86.

169. Pelling, "Biography, Greek," 242.

170. Stanton, *Preaching*, 119–21; Aune, "Biography," 108; Aune, *Environment*, 34; Burridge, *Gospels*, 71–73; Ytterbrink, *Gospel*, 103 (on Philo, *Moses*); Smith, "Genre," 193–96; Smith, βίος, 30.

171. Cf. Beck, "Demonax," 93.

172. Burridge, *Gospels*, 73.

173. Suetonius, *Augustus* 9; with Edwards, "Introduction," ix (on xv she suggests this emphasis is partly to distinguish his treatment from that of Tacitus).

174. See Licona, *Differences*, 185–89, citing esp. helpfully Lucian, *How to Write History* 55; Mellor, *Historians*, 93; cf. Develin, "Introduction," 9–10.

175. Ytterbrink, *Gospel*, 94; Zadorojnyi, "Lords," 352 (though Zadorojnyi's citation of Aurelius Victor, *The Caesars* 11.5, is from the fourth century).

176. Bosworth, *Arrian*, 60.

material differently in different biographies, often to simplify and omit items irrelevant in a different life.[177] Late antique biographies were usually topical.[178]

Like many biographies, the Synoptic Gospels do not provide a clear chronological structure for their anecdotes. Mark's Gospel follows a logical progression, but his chronology is generally loose;[179] Luke usually follows Mark's sequence,[180] whereas Matthew arranges much discourse material topically.[181] The Synoptic Evangelists, and most commonly Matthew, freely rearrange some material.[182]

Thus, for example, Matthew appropriates almost verbatim some material from Jesus's eschatological discourse in Mark 13:9, 11–13 for his mission discourse in Matthew 10:17, 19–22, though he retains a summary of this paragraph again later in Matthew 24:9. Like any modern preacher, Matthew understands much of Jesus's teaching as relevant for more than one kind of situation. Matthew does omit the explicit point of Mark 13:10 (the good news being preached among all nations) until Matthew 24:14, because the setting of the mission discourse is explicitly limited to Galilee (10:5–6), though even here he retains hints of gentile mission (10:18). Matthew's account of the mission discourse extends until Jesus's return (10:23),[183] because Matthew, like any good preacher, wants his audience to understand that the mission Jesus gave his disciples on that day provides a spiritual model for the church's continuing mission (Matt 24:14; 28:19–20), a point not elaborated in Mark's more concise mission discourse (Mark 6:9–11).

---

177. Licona, *Differences*, 47 (on *Pompey* 47.3–48.3; *Caesar* 14.1–6; *Cato the Younger* 31.4–32.3).

178. Cox, *Biography*, 57.

179. Cancik, "Gattung," 94–95.

180. Though for Luke's disinterest in precise chronology, see also Licona, *Differences*, 136.

181. Compare, e.g., Matt 10:25 and 12:24. Topical arrangement was one of the forms of memorable organization (Vatri, "Writing," 764, citing Plutarch, *Advice to Bride and Groom* 138c4–6).

182. Licona, *Differences*, 185–96, esp. 191–96. Granted that it is likely that Jesus used some material on more than one occasion, a completely independent recounting of Jesus's ministry and teaching would probably include much less overlap among incidents and teachings than in the Synoptics (cf. John 21:25); Matthew overlaps with the vast majority of Mark's pericopes (some estimate 90 percent; see Hagner, *Matthew*, xlvii).

183. For the fleeing from any given city in Matt 10:23, cf. flight from Jerusalem under judgment (Mark 13:14–16; Matt 24:15–18). It is ironic that Schweitzer would earlier build his eschatology so fully on this singly attested verse (*Quest*, 360–61); see the criticism in Heyer, *Jesus Matters*, 48.

Such rearrangement can appear even within a pericope, as may be observed from the following simple but conspicuous example:

MARK 11:12–25	MATTHEW 21:12–13, 18–22
1. Jesus curses the fruitless fig tree (11:14)	2. Jesus challenges the temple (21:12–13)
2. Jesus challenges the temple (11:15–17)	1. Jesus curses the fruitless fig tree (21:19)
3. The next day, the disciples find the fig tree withered (11:20)	3. The fig tree withers at once (21:19)
4. The disciples are surprised (11:21)	4. The disciples are surprised (21:20)
5. Jesus gives a lesson on faith (11:23–25)	5. Jesus gives a lesson on faith (21:21–22)

Did Jesus curse *two* fig trees over the course of two days, though each Evangelist mentions only one, with one withering at once and the other withering later but the disciples needing precisely the same lesson on faith, in very similar words, each time?

Is is not more respectful to the text as it stands to allow the writers their different adaptations? Mark frames the evaluation of the temple with the fate of a fruitless tree, pointing to the temple's impending demise (cf. 13:2). By contrast, Matthew, who fairly consistently prefers order, prefers to keep the event of the fig tree together in his narrative, just as he sometimes distinguishes judgments that may be blended together in his sources (contrast Matt 24:3 with the presumably earlier Mark 13:4).

Ancient readers did not expect precise chronologies in ordinary biographies, so they would not demand them from the Gospels.[184] Augustine suggested the Evangelists wrote their Gospels as God recalled the accounts to

---

184. Subsuming chronological differences under the label "contradictions" (Ehrman, *Interrupted*, 7) thus anachronistically imposes modern historiographic expectations on documents written before such expectations existed, using norms quite different from those of the authors and their first audiences. That is not to imply that no one would have treated differences as contradictions if they found this approach polemically valuable; discrepancies concerning chronology could be used to discredit opposing arguments (cf., e.g., Dionysius of Halicarnassus, *Lysias* 15; Acts 24:11; Cicero, *Cross-Examination of Vatinius* 1.3).

their memory.[185] Much earlier, just a generation after the final first-century Gospel,[186] Papias claimed that Mark wrote what he heard from Jesus's disciple Peter, but that Peter did not narrate it (hence Mark did not write it) in order.[187] Technically, Papias may refer simply to rhetorically proper biographical order,[188] but the random character probably also suggests that Peter did not recount events in chronological sequence.[189] The earliest traditions were oral, and oral performance can vary the sequence of events.[190]

Modern readers sometimes hold the Evangelist to standards that not only deviate from ancient expectations but that modern readers do not follow in ordinary life. One professor puts it to his undergraduates this way: "When you go home for vacation and your parents ask what did you do this semester, nobody gets out their date book and says, I did this on September 1," and the like. Someone who demands that anecdotes be recalled chronologically might appear "anal retentive."[191]

5.7. Anecdotes and Chreiai

When we read the Synoptic Gospels, we are accustomed to a narrative enlivened with various anecdotes and sayings, followed by an extended account of the protagonist's end. Ancient hearers familiar with biographies would have recognized such characteristics as familiar from that genre.[192] Anecdotes and

185. Augustine, *Harmony of the Gospels* 21.51. Cf. Luther in Kolb, *Word*, 87–88.

186. A date for Papias of 130 remains plausible, but against such later dates once given (sometimes based on unlikely fifth-century evidence), many now date his work to within the first couple decades of the second century, sometimes as early as 110 CE (Shanks, *Papias*, 92–93) or even "the first decade of the second century" (Crossley, *Date*, 13; Bauckham, *World*, 143n2, 147), often based partly on the placement of his treatment in Eusebius (*Ecclesiastical History* 3.34–39). Papias is early by classical standards (cf. the Lamprias Catalogue).

187. Papias, frag. 3.15 (Holmes) in Eusebius, *Ecclesiastical History* 3.39. Black, "Kennedy," 65–66, notes the influence of a renowned classicist on revival of attention to Papias.

188. Moessner, "Voice," 490–91; see esp. Moessner, "Papian Fragments." Watson suggests that Papias evaluated Mark by Matthean standards; see Watson, "Survive," 15.

189. Recollection was easier if in random order (Seneca the Elder, *Controversiae* 1.pref.4), an observation characterizing memories generally (see, e.g., Larsen, Thompson, and Hansen, "Time," esp. 153–54; Wagenaar, "Memory," 187; Thatcher, *Why John Wrote*, 113–15; Bauckham, *Eyewitnesses*, 326, 333, 344).

190. Eddy and Boyd, *Legend*, 433–35; Vansina, *Oral Tradition*, 24, 122, 173–88, esp. 176; Barber and Barber, *Severed*, 115–17.

191. Terence Paige of Houghton College, November 9, 2017.

192. Burridge, *Gospels*, 196–98.

witty sayings were to biography, as Geiger says, "the raisins that are necessary to render the cake tasty."[193]

Anecdotes are widespread in Greco-Roman literature.[194] The form by itself was too pervasive to indicate genre; it is certainly consistent, however, with biography. Thus one particularly massive collection of anecdotes from antiquity includes examples from fables, histories, and the Gospels. The genre most often represented, however, is easily non-Christian biography, including biographies by Nepos, Suetonius, Plutarch (many), Lucian, and Diogenes Laertius.[195]

Any author who could have composed even the shortest Gospel, Mark, would easily be competent to recount anecdotes. Already at the most elementary level, students memorized the sayings of famous people; the next level taught paraphrase and composition of *chreiai* (Latin *chriai*; short narratives); the highest, rhetorical level taught narrative composition.[196] In the first-century Eastern empire, one sort of chreia was an anecdote.[197]

Biographers found anecdotes useful for depicting character,[198] and anecdotes often dominate biographies of philosophers.[199] Such an episodic format also appears in more fictitious biographic traditions such as the *Life of Aesop*,[200] but normally not in novels composed from whole cloth.[201]

Although not as episodic as Mark's Gospel,[202] Xenophon's *Memorabilia* was a thematic "collection of anecdotes or conversations featuring Socrates."[203] Although such anecdotes are more needed in stories of teachers than major political or military leaders, several appear even in Xenophon's more cohesive encomium on Agesilaus.[204] Although many people collected anecdotes even before Aristotle,[205] Peripatetics were particularly invested in collecting

193. Geiger, *Nepos*, 27.

194. See Moeser, *Anecdote*, 51–106.

195. Robbins, *Quotes*.

196. Moeser, *Anecdote*, 54, noting Quintilian, *Orator's Education* 1.2–3; 1.9.2–4; 2.4–6. Despite Seneca's disapproval, even adults sometimes still memorized chreiai (Aune, "Prolegomena," 95, citing Seneca, *To Lucilius* 33.7).

197. Moeser, *Anecdote*, 69–70, following Theon; for other terms for anecdotes in antiquity, see 66–68; in modern secondary literature, 57–62.

198. De Temmerman, "Formalities," 19.

199. Frickenschmidt, *Evangelium*, 504 (cf. 283–86); Ytterbrink, *Gospel*, 117.

200. Karla, "*Life of Aesop*," 56.

201. See Burridge, *Gospels*, 283, arguing against Michael Vines.

202. Freyne, "Gospel," 66.

203. Konstan and Walsh, "Biography," 32; cf. Votaw, "Biographies," 230.

204. Beck, "Demonax," 92–93, citing Xenophon, *Agesilaus* 4.6; 5.5; 7.5, 6; 8.3.

205. Momigliano, *Development*, 72.

anecdotes about philosophers, often for interschool polemic.[206] Later than our period, vivid anecdotes feature heavily in Diogenes Laertius's lives of philosophers.[207] They continue to appear in later hagiography.[208] Anecdotes also appear commonly in third-century rabbinic literature, although they are not chreiai and they primarily support interpretations of Torah rather than exalting individual rabbis.[209]

Scholars have commented extensively on the numerous anecdotes in Lucian's second-century *Life of Demonax*, which, as we have noted, is a full-length biography of a sage.[210] After a preface and an encomium for Demonax,[211] Lucian turns to fifty, mostly brief anecdotes about Demonax,[212] with two more in the story of Demonax's death.[213] These anecdotes, usually sayings with brief contexts, average roughly fifty words each,[214] and all but two of them fit ancient definitions of chreiai.[215] Lucian intends them not to provide a comprehensive survey of all that is known of Demonax, but as a sample that elucidates for readers Demonax's essential character.[216]

The anecdotes are loosely structured;[217] while an eye or imagination keener than mine might identify more connections, they appear to be arranged mostly randomly. Many of these anecdotes are quite brief; their climactic point is, as in the Gospels' pronouncement stories,[218] normally Demonax's quick and witty quip.[219] Because Lucian studied with Demonax, and because memorizing sayings and anecdotes was part of ancient education, Lucian may well have provided these accounts from memory, supplemented with others' analogous

206. Momigliano, *Development*, 71; cf. 76; Chance, "Fiction," 135; Burridge, *Gospels*, 69.

207. Frickenschmidt, *Evangelium*, 183.

208. Cox, *Biography*, 57.

209. See Moeser, *Anecdote*, 107–49, esp. 148–49 (also 248).

210. See, e.g., Momigliano, *Development*, 73; Moeser, *Anecdote*, 92–105; Beck, "Demonax."

211. Lucian, *Demonax* 1–2 and 3–11, respectively.

212. Lucian, *Demonax* 12–62. Cf. Beck, "Demonax," 84; Ytterbrink, *Gospel*, 110.

213. Moeser, *Anecdote*, 92–93, citing *Demonax* 64.1–5; 66.1–7.

214. Burridge, *Gospels*, 168.

215. The exceptions are dialogues (*Demonax* 13.1–8; 19.4–20.7; Moeser, *Anecdote*, 95–96, 105).

216. Moeser, *Anecdote*, 105–6, 247–48; Beck, "Demonax," 84, on *Demonax* 67.

217. Burridge, "Reading," 41.

218. On which, see Alsup, "Function"; Greenspoon, "Pronouncement Story"; Porton, "Pronouncement Story"; Poulos, "Pronouncement Story"; Robbins, "Pronouncement Stories"; VanderKam, "Pronouncement Stories"; concisely Aune, *Dictionary*, 378–79.

219. See Beck, "Demonax," 87; Ytterbrink, *Gospel*, 110. Anecdotes about Demonax outside Lucian are usually less original or humorous moralizing aphorisms; Lucian's favorites naturally fit his own personality (Beck, "Demonax," 91).

accounts.[220] Both chreiai and the maxims they contained were ideally brief and easy to remember.[221]

The Gospels recount anecdotes about their subject just as biographies of other sages do,[222] although those in the Gospels are often longer.[223] Nevertheless, their treatment is somewhat distinctive because they view their protagonist as distinctive. Thus whereas anecdotes about Demonax reveal his wit and humility about his impending death, like some anecdotes about Jesus, anecdotes about Demonax offer nothing comparable to Jesus forgiving sins or claiming to be Lord of the sabbath (see, e.g., Mark 2:10, 28).[224]

5.8. Structural Issues

Gospel anecdotes often participate in a larger narrative than those in the rabbis or *Demonax*.[225] The Gospels also follow a more structured plot than Lucian's anecdotes about Demonax[226] or in Diogenes's lives of philosophers.[227] That is, however, a macrostructural, literary observation rather than one that distances the Gospels from biographies of teachers.[228]

Still, this macrostructural pattern in the Gospels as a whole brings them closer to conventional biographies of public figures in Nepos or Plutarch rather than to biographies of sages primarily known to their own schools.[229] Jesus was a public figure as well as founder of a school, so it is not surprising to find elements comparable with biographies of multiple sorts of figures. For that matter, ancient historians, like others interested in producing literary works, sought to produce cohesive narratives, as noted below.

220. Moeser, *Anecdote*, 93.

221. Vatri, "Writing," 758, noting esp. Aelius Aristides, *Orations* 2.442, on Plato, *Gorgias* 527C3–4.

222. Moles, "Influence," 99, compares Cynic lives in Lucian's *Demonax*; Diogenes Laertius, *Lives* bk. 6.

223. Moeser, *Anecdote*, 245.

224. Cf. Ytterbrink, *Gospel*, 117, as well as miracles in the Gospels and Philostratus.

225. Moeser, *Anecdote*, 246.

226. Burridge, "Reading," 41.

227. Frickenschmidt, *Evangelium*, 183–84.

228. A community history may include something like a plot (see Le Donne, *Historiographical Jesus*, 55), as may any account of events retrospectively focused on a theme in light of an outcome. Ideally, plots should be of such length as to make recall easier (Vatri, "Writing," 756, citing Aristotle, *Poetics* 1451a3–6).

229. Frickenschmidt, *Evangelium*, 184, 504.

Scholars such as Burridge and especially Frickenschmidt emphasize that most biographies, or at least those of public figures, were self-
contained stories with beginning, middle, and end, like the Gospels.[230]
Such a structure is of course a typical narrative structure, hardly limited
to biographies;[231] but this structure reinforces the point that the Gospels
are cohesive wholes, like well-designed biographies of public figures about
whom more was known, rather than the often sketchy lives of poets or
lesser-known teachers.

Even lives of teachers can follow a three-part structure when the author
knows enough to provide a full biography. Despite its random arrangement
of anecdotes in the large middle section, Lucian's *Demonax* (a teacher about
whom Lucian knows a great deal) does boast a tripartite structure.[232] Biographies also often include a narrative transition explaining the subject's
passage into their career or public life, a feature that also appears in some
Gospels.[233]

In many respects, however, the structures of biographies vary. When
Plutarch composes parallel lives, the second component typically offers a complex variation of the first.[234] The specific arrangement of elements in Suetonius's biographies—addressing the subject's virtues, appearance, habits and so
forth—varies among his lives.[235]

Digressions are common in ancient biographies.[236] Some of these are
digressions on geography or local customs (cf. Mark 7:3–4).[237] Isocrates's *Euagoras*, for example, digresses on the history of Cyprus[238] and Xenophon's
Agesilaus digresses about Sparta.[239] Philo's *Moses* treats Egypt's climate, and
Tacitus's *Agricola* deals extensively with Britannia;[240] Plutarch sometimes di-

---

230. Frickenschmidt, *Evangelium*, 184, 192–350 (esp. 281). A three-part structure is evident
already in Isocrates's *Euagoras* (Frickenschmidt, *Evangelium*, 108–10; Ytterbrink, *Gospel*, 76);
cf. also Xenophon's *Agesilaus* (Beck, "Demonax," 92–93).

231. See, e.g., the episodes in *Life of Aesop* (Karla, "Life of Aesop," 56).

232. Beck, "Demonax," 85.

233. See Rogers, "Baptism," on Matthew.

234. Pelling, *Texts*, 58.

235. Edwards, "Introduction," x.

236. See, e.g., Cornelius Nepos, *On Great Generals* 16 (Pelopidas), 3.1; Josephus, *Life*
336–67; Plutarch, *Alexander* 35.8.

237. Ytterbrink, *Gospel*, 227, finds none in Luke.

238. *Euagoras* 19–20 (Ytterbrink, *Gospel*, 76, also noting *Euagoras* 66).

239. Ytterbrink, *Gospel*, 83; cf. 89, 91. Cf. the Spartan custom digression in Plutarch,
Lysander 1.2.

240. Ytterbrink, *Gospel*, 116; cf. Whitmarsh, "Book," 307.

gresses to explain customs.[241] Arrian's biographic historical monograph on Alexander also includes geographic digressions.[242]

Digressions are not, of course, limited to biography, appearing in rhetoric, narratives, and other genres.[243] For our purposes, it is relevant to note that historians also commonly employed them.[244] For example, Diodorus largely follows one source at a time, except for digressions.[245] Livy digresses to discuss what would have happened had Alexander battled Rome.[246]

5.9. Plot

Some features of the Gospels are more unusual among ancient biographies. Full-scale ancient biographies sometimes have plots, although this may be usually limited to the three-part structure just noted. Some scholars understand all emplotment of narrative, even historical narrative, as intrinsically fictional.[247] Less bound to prior information, novels do have greater freedom to develop plots.[248] But while narrative structuring of prior material reflects an author's interpretive selection, such interpretive selections can be interpretive without making the narrative as a whole fictitious (see the discussion of

241. E.g., Plutarch, *Pompey* 4.4.

242. Atkinson, "Introduction," xxix. For a different digression in Arrian, see Bosworth, *Arrian*, 63–64.

243. See, e.g., Dionysius of Halicarnassus, *Lysias* 13; Cicero, *On the Ends of Good and Evil* 2.32.104; *Letters to Atticus* 7.2; *Orator ad M. Brutum* 40.137–38; 43.148; *Brutus* 93.322; Pliny, *Natural History* 28.1.1; Quintilian, *Orator's Education* 4.3.1–17; Musonius Rufus 1, p. 34.34; Dio Chrysostom, *Orations* 12.38; 36.1–6; Josephus, *Against Apion* 1.57.

244. E.g., Xenophon, *Hellenica* 7.4.1; Thucydides, *History* 1.24.1ff. (digressing from 1.23.6); Polybius, *Histories* 1.41.6–1.42.7; 3.2.7; 3.9.6; 3.39.1; 3.59.9; 5.21.7–9; 6.1.2; 6.50.1; 31.30.4; Sallust, *Catiline's War* 5.9–13.5; Justin, *Epitome* 3.7.16–4.1.18; 17.3.1–22; 18.3.1–18.4.1; 41.1.1–41.3.10; 42.2.7–42.3.9; Livy, *History* 9.17.1–9.19.17; Valerius Maximus, *Memorable Doings and Sayings* 4.8.1 (with 4.7.ext.2b); Velleius Paterculus, *History* 1.14.1; 2.38.1–2.40.1; esp. 2.59.1; Josephus, *Jewish Antiquities* 20.224–251; Tacitus, *Histories* 2.2; Arrian, *Indica* 6.1; cf. also Eigler, "Excursus"; Aune, *Environment*, 102 (citing Josh 5:4–7; 1 Sam 9:9; 2 Kgs 7:6–7; 14:6–7; 17:23–41; 1 Macc 8:1–16); Develin, "Introduction," 7 (noting Trogus's ethnographic digressions); Broggiato, "Artemon" (including Artemon's geographic interests).

245. Bosworth, *Arrian*, 9–10.

246. Almagor, "Narratives," 67, citing Livy, *History* 9.17–19.

247. De Temmerman, "Formalities," 14, summarizing Hayden White; Becker, *Birth*, 89–90.

248. Thus some later hagiographic composites of biography and fiction, as in Gray, "Monk," 117.

the meaning of "fictionalization" in ch. 2). Mark's literary observations may be one characteristic closer to novels than to many biographies, though the anecdotes that he organizes in this manner characterize biographies more than novels.

Plots of a sort do appear even in history and biography. Thus, for example, one could envision a sort of plot in Taylor Branch's massive and thoroughly researched *Parting the Waters*,[249] but this is because Branch helpfully follows a particular issue in light of the remembered significance of its outcome. All remembering,[250] whether individual or collective, involves "narrative emplotment," or framing.[251] This is true of ancient historiography as well.[252]

The Gospels each follow more developed, coherent plots, which distinguishes them from most ancient biographies. Granted, there are likely developed plots in some other ancient biographies; scholars have combed through the Gospels far more thoroughly than through most other ancient works. Nor can one accuse Plutarch of inattention to literary design.[253] Plutarch offers biographies of paired Greek and Roman figures, specifically selected because their stories proved comparable in some ways (e.g., the rhetor Demosthenes with Cicero or the conqueror Alexander with Caesar).[254] He claims that he looked hard for the right people to compare with each other.[255]

But like Lucian's *Demonax*, biographies of sages often arrange anecdotes without forming them into coherent plots.[256] Historical works on public figures have more chronology and thus something more like a plot when, for example, matters build toward martyrdom, as in the Gospels.[257]

---

249. Branch, *Parting*.

250. Referring here to the conscious act, not to fragments of memories surfacing in isolation.

251. Brack, *Historiography*, 6, noting among other sources Ricoeur, *Time*; Phillips et al., *Memory*.

252. See, e.g., Dupont, "Question du plan"; Betori, "Strutturazione"; cf. Witherington, *Acts*, 59, citing Mellor, *Tacitus*, 70. For the importance of literary cohesiveness in historiography, see, e.g., Diodorus Siculus, *Library of History* 20.1.1, 5. On "rhetorical unity" in Plutarch's biographies, see Stadter, "Biography," 537. Suetonius arranges Tiberius's biography meaningfully (Thorburn, "Tiberius").

253. At least not usually; sometimes Plutarch did confuse material (see, e.g., Hammond, *Sources*, 126–27).

254. See, e.g., Plutarch, *Theseus* 1.2.

255. Plutarch, *Cimon* 3.1–3.

256. Ytterbrink, *Gospel*, 112, on Diogenes Laertius. Note also Dillon, "Interpretation," 159–60, on Porphyry's *Plotinus* and other biographies of that period.

257. Cf. Frickenschmidt, *Evangelium*, 232; Ytterbrink, *Gospel*, 117.

But even Suetonius's imperial *Lives* does not contain cohesive stories; each is simply "a summation of the life,"[258] especially in terms of what is relevant for moral instruction. They usually begin with the subject's background (including family and birth), then his career, and sometimes an outline for the following topics.[259] What follows, however, usually gives little regard to chronology.[260] By and large the Gospels seem to exhibit greater literary coherence than do even otherwise more sophisticated works by more elite biographers.[261] Narrative critics have rightly highlighted how large narrative works like the Gospels strive for largely consistent internal worlds.[262]

Then again, an Evangelist did not compose his Gospel as a biography on simply one individual among many about whom he hoped to write. Plutarch was composing a series of biographies and had to master an extraordinary amount of information about a range of figures. By contrast, each of the Gospels as foundation documents invited a significant and exclusive investment of attention, and probably a longer process of oral feedback before publication in their final forms.[263] Foundation documents may be shaped more by foundational events and less by contemporary events than are more contemporary-oriented works such as letters.[264] Whereas foundation stories about the distant, legendary past were inevitably mythical, schools could also preserve information about more recent founders, a more appropriate comparison for first-century Gospels about the recent sage Jesus.

5.10. Conclusion

In contrast to a theoretically objective approach, ancient biographers were also concerned with their subjects' character and value as positive, negative, or mixed moral examples. Their own perspectives shaped how they composed their works. At the same time, responsible biographers shaped information or traditions that came to them, rather than freely inventing new stories.

258. Edwards, "Introduction," x (without denying something of a plan; see ix).

259. Edwards, "Introduction," ix, cites *Julius* 44; cf. Luke 9:51; Acts 19:21; on advance outlines, see the discussion in Keener, *Acts*, 1:708–9.

260. Edwards, "Introduction," ix.

261. Ytterbrink, *Gospel*, 117–18, 228–29. I am also grateful to Vernon Robbins and Fred Long for dialogue on these points on October 4, 2017.

262. See Stibbe, *Gospel*, 32–34.

263. On publication, see Keener, *Acts*, 1:43–50.

264. Talbert, "Chance," 230.

The genre of *bios* evolved from a more encomiastic form rooted in historical information to a form more influenced by historiography in the early empire and finally, in late antiquity, sometimes into hagiography. The period from Cornelius Nepos at the end of the Roman Republic and through the late second and sometimes early third century constituted the historiographic high point of ancient biography. Even here, we find a range in terms of historiographic and literary capabilities and in the quality of sources available for various works. Nevertheless, this survey of some ancient biography suggests that the Gospels come from a period when biographers in general were interested in providing historical information.

Part 2

Biographies and History

As previous chapters have noted (esp. ch. 5) and some subsequent chapters (esp. chs. 10–11) will elaborate, ancient audiences recognized that biographers would exercise some flexibility in how they recounted their stories. For full biographies in the early empire, however, this flexibility did not normally extend to creating events.

Authors of full biographies in the early empire used this genre in particular rather than, say, a nonbiographic moral essay, because they sought to learn and teach from the past. Although their purpose was often to collect moral illustrations, poetry and imagination could also supply these. Biography specifically drew its moral illustrations from the lives of figures of the past. Indeed, the historiographic side of ancient biography and the biographic side of ancient historiography overlapped considerably, especially in the early empire. Sometimes it even appears debatable to which of these two genres a work belongs, or whether the authors of such borderline works even considered such a distinction (see ch. 6).

Historical interests did not mean that ancient authors followed modern historiographic rules. Ancient readers expected their historians to tell a good story, to reconstruct and recount scenes the way they might have (or most likely) happened. Most principles of modern historiography, however, do have ancient precedent, and ancient historiography, for all its frequent rhetorical pretensions, was expected to deal in actual events (ch. 7). Many scholars assign Luke-Acts to the genre of ancient historical writing (ch. 8).

Biographers and historians admitted that material from centuries earlier could contain legends, but they expressed much greater confidence in reports of more recent events, especially those within living memory. This is the subject of chapter 9.

Chapter 6

Biographies and Historical Information

The previous chapter surveys some frequent characteristics of ancient biographies but touches only sporadically on the questions of historical interest and veridical correspondence to actual events. This chapter focuses on these questions, as well as treating some related biographic characteristics not addressed in the previous chapter.

In the wake of postmodern insights about subjectivity and social location,[1] we naturally are inclined to emphasize how historians and biographers have shaped their material to communicate a point. These observations are important, but they do not require us to forgo the more strictly and traditionally historical question about what sort of material they believed they were shaping.[2] As Pelling points out, "Some things really happened back then, some ways of describing them are better than others, and we can do something to find out which."[3]

Particularly in the period from Cornelius Nepos through Diogenes Laertius, when biographers of public figures recounted an event without qualification, I suspect that they normally believed that it happened. These authors lie between the excessive earlier emphasis on encomium and the excessive later emphasis on hagiography; despite some remaining elements of encomium, their interest in figures of the real past invited heavy influence from historiography.

By the standards of Mediterranean antiquity, the early empire appears to be the apex of historical reliability in biographies. Plutarch believes that some writers in earlier times invented some details about Alexander's manner of

---

1. Modernist positivism introduced the dichotomy between proclamation and historical information to begin with; the two differ, but they are not inherently and necessarily incompatible.

2. For most historiography's appropriation and correction of the initial proposals of postmodernism, see esp. Sheppard, *Craft*, 164–69.

3. Pelling, *Texts*, viii.

death, designing tragic scenes suited for the topic.[4] Although tragedy still colored narrative composition in his own time, historical standards in biography had matured, as exemplified by himself, Suetonius, Tacitus, eventually Arrian (writing biographic history), and others.

6.1. Default Expectations

What should be our default expectation of a biographic source's likely relation to history? It depends on the source, but the criteria that Ben Meyer lists for historical works are noteworthy: "If the intention of the writer can be defined to include factuality and if the writer is plausibly knowledgeable on the matter and free of the suspicion of fraud, historicity may be inferred"[5] to a high degree of probability. If, as evidence strongly suggests, the Gospels seek to depict a story grounded in factual information,[6] and if they draw on recollections from within living memory, we should accept them as genuinely informative about historical events rather than as purely imaginative constructions.[7]

The general reliability of a writer, and not merely that of an individual pericope, is helpful background information in shaping what we expect from a historical work. As Richard Bauckham also notes, it makes the most sense historiographically to evaluate "the general reliability and character of a testimonial source and, if it is judged trustworthy, trusting it"[8] to the extent that the evidence for that source warrants.

The dependence of Luke and Matthew on information in Mark suggests two things:

1. their own commitment to information, rather than pure invention;
2. their recognition that Mark provided such information.

It is surely no denigration of modern scholarly ingenuity to suggest that Luke and Matthew, writing in the decades immediately following Mark, were in a

---

4. Plutarch, *Alexander* 70.3.

5. Meyer, *Aims of Jesus*, 85, quoted in Bernier, *Quest*, 44. Meyer offers further comments about inferring historicity in *Aims of Jesus*, 83–87. The context of this way of framing historical investigation may be designed to challenge Bultmann's inference of nonhistoricity (see 196).

6. See here, e.g., Bernier, *Quest*, 48–54, reconstructing the aims of the individual Gospels as telling a story related to facts.

7. Bernier, *Quest*, 50–51, regarding this as the conclusion that follows.

8. Bauckham, "Response," 229.

better position than are we (and were even second-century writers such as Papias) to know who Mark was and what the genre of his Gospel was.[9] Ancient historians felt free to draw on biographies as well as annals and memoirs when writing sober history,[10] and the Evangelists would have felt the same freedom.

That Matthew and Luke heavily employed Mark suggests their respect for Mark as a biographic/historical source, despite Luke's[11] and, more frequently, Matthew's, rearrangement of Mark's material.[12] Papias complains about Mark's order, his τάξις (*taxis*); David Moessner understands Papias's complaint to be about Mark's arrangement, a frequent rhetorical concern with narratives. Nevertheless, Papias accepts Mark as a legitimate link in tradition while apparently preferring the superior rhetorical arrangement of Mark's Evangelist successors.[13]

6.2. Biography as a Form of Historical Writing

In some circles ancient biography has "a bad press"[14] for a concern for historical accuracy that is supposedly inferior to that found in ancient historiography. This has often been based on Plutarch's distinction between biography and historiography.[15] More recent research, however, reveals the extent to which this approach misunderstands Plutarch.[16] In context, his claim that he is writing

---

9. Cf. Keener, "Luke-Acts," 622; Bernier, *Quest*, 53.

10. Hadas, "Introduction," xviii. Cicero already regarded history as arranging annals so as to teach public morals (Galinsky, "Introduction," 4, citing Cicero, *On the Orator* 2.52).

11. See Luke 1:3, καθεξῆς (*kathexēs*).

12. Writers often conspicuously imitated earlier (though normally *much* earlier) works but were expected to develop them and reappropriate them in new ways; see Knoppers, "Problem," 16, 32. The imitation was also normally conspicuous enough as to avoid ready confusion; cf. criticisms of the ingenious work of MacDonald (*Epics*; *Imitate Homer*) in Mitchell, "Homer"; Johnson, "Imitate"; Sandnes, "Imitatio," esp. 725; Sandnes, *Challenge*, 249-50; Snyder, "Review," 3.

13. See Papias, frag. 3.15 (Holmes), as articulated in Moessner, "Voice," and esp. Moessner, "Papian Fragments" (also noting that, by ancient standards, Mark fails roughly half of Theon's criteria for a good plot). Papias may have viewed himself as a historian (Aune, "Prolegomena," 81; Bauckham, *World*, 143-64).

14. De Pourcq and Roskam, "Virtues," 163.

15. Plutarch, *Alexander* 1.1.

16. Beneker, "Method," 117-18; De Pourcq and Roskam, "Virtues," 164, citing Duff, *Lives*, 14-22; Pelling, *Plutarch and History*, 143-70; Pelling, "Bounds," 266.

lives rather than histories "is in the first place an excuse for summarizing or omitting historically important facts in the cases of Alexander and Caesar (in reality, mostly the former), to focus instead on character-revealing incidents."[17]

Plutarch is not "drawing a sharp line between history and biography (as it is often supposed to mean when quoted in isolation) or stating what is generally suitable or admissible for each of these literary genres."[18] Plutarch does not even strictly follow this general division between history and biography in the pair of biographies that this announcement introduces![19]

Likewise, Plutarch's biographic emphasis on "signs of the soul"[20] refers in context to features such as the character's "sayings and jokes"[21] and "throw-away remarks."[22] The contrast is thus not about reporting genuine events but about one's literary focus; as Hägg points out, "Both historiography and biography may have a didactic purpose, but while historians convey political lessons, the biographer professes to teach ethics."[23] In other passages in his Lives, Plutarch even defines "his approach as historiography."[24]

6.2a. Biography and Historiography

Most critics since the sixteenth century have recognized biography as a form of historical writing.[25] Although ancient biographies of public figures selected, arranged and recounted their material in a manner different from history, the subject matter was mostly the same.[26] Nor is it fair to speak of different truth standards for the two genres.[27]

---

17. Hägg, *Biography*, 269; followed also by Smith and Kostopoulos, "Biography," 399. As noted in ch. 11, condensing and simplifying material was a common practice, not limited to biography.

18. Hägg, *Biography*, 269; cf. Edwards, "Introduction," xiv; Pitre, *Case*, 75.

19. Pelling, "Bounds," 266–67.

20. Plutarch, *Alexander* 1.3.

21. Hägg, *Biography*, 271. For the valuing of humor and wit, see, e.g., Rabbie, "Wit" (though it involved a different tone than dignified speech; Hall, "Delivery," 221).

22. Licona, *Differences*, 4–5; cf. Ehrman, *Introduction*, 63; Edwards, "Introduction," xiv.

23. Hägg, *Biography*, 273.

24. De Pourcq and Roskam, "Virtues," 164, citing Plutarch, *Aemilius Paulus* 1.1, and *Tiberius Gracchus* 1.1; cf. also Frickenschmidt, *Evangelium*, 234; Smith and Kostopoulos, "Biography," 400.

25. Momigliano, *Development*, 2; cf. 6.

26. Geiger, *Nepos*, 25.

27. Pelling, *Texts*, 259n2; Pelling, "Truth."

Biography shares with historiography an interest in exploiting the genuine past for useful examples, creating substantial overlap between these genres.[28] As David Aune observes, though biographies often underlined praise and blame more than did histories, biography "was still firmly rooted in historical fact rather than literary fiction."[29]

We may thus speak of biography as a subtype of historiography, provided we use the broader sense of the latter term.[30] Thus, for example, classics scholar George Kennedy classifies biography "as a subdivision of history."[31] Philip Stadter, another classics scholar, regards the boundaries between these two genres as quite "fluid."[32]

As noted above, ancient biographers intended their works to be more historical than novelistic,[33] despite their wide range of potential functions.[34] This observation is true especially for the character of biography in this era, from the first century BCE through at least the second century CE (encompassing writers such as Nepos, Plutarch, Suetonius, and Tacitus).

The genre of history significantly influenced the development of biography both in the Hellenistic period and afterward.[35] Even Isocrates's rhetorical encomium claims to support truth, at least in contrast to epic poetry,[36] a contrast frequent in ancient sources.[37] Explaining why he digressed to recount the life of an individual, the historian Polybius rejected too rigid a separation of biography and history.[38] Historiography likewise significantly influenced early Roman biography; Atticus, an associate and major source for Nepos, saw himself as a historian.[39] Likewise, history itself sometimes could be "encomiastic," magnifying its heroes.[40]

---

28. E.g., Bravo, "Antiquarianism," 516. Burridge, *Gospels*, 63–67, also notes the substantial overlap between the genres of ancient biography and history (as well as other genres).

29. Aune, "Biography," 125.

30. Becker, *Birth*, 69–70.

31. Kennedy, "Source Criticism," 136.

32. Stadter, "Biography," 528; see also Burridge, *Gospels*, 63–67.

33. For substantial overlap between the biography and history (as well as other) genres in antiquity, see Burridge, *Gospels*, 63–67.

34. Burridge, *Gospels*, 145–47, 180–83. For the divergence, see further Barr and Wentling, "Biography and Genre," 81–88, although I would not regard all their examples as biographies.

35. Adams, *Genre*, 114, 251.

36. Ytterbrink, *Gospel*, 76, citing Isocrates, *Euagorus* 10, 21, 36.

37. Aristotle, *Poetics* 9.2, 1451b; cf. Pliny, *Letters* 9.33.1; Lucian, *How to Write History* 8; Menander Rhetor, *Epideictic Treatises* 1.1.333.31–1.1.334.5; see discussion in ch. 7.

38. Becker, *Birth*, 67, on Polybius, *Histories* 10.21ff.

39. Geiger, *Nepos*, 99.

40. Fornara, *Nature*, 36. Such encomium could but did not always introduce distortion (64–65).

The character of the times made this influence even more pronounced during the empire. Caesar was so prominent that historical treatment of his period now required biographic focus on Caesar. History in turn amply supplied the material for biography, not least with Caesar's own writing as a major source.[41] History and biography thus overlapped significantly in the early empire.[42] Even later historians such as Dio Cassius, when discussing the period, incorporate both biographic and historical material when discussing the early empire.[43]

6.2b. A Range of Flexibility

To what extent does biographic genre tether biographies from the early empire to facts about the past? Such works were not perfect. At the end of the republic, Nepos inadvertently confuses information, especially in his Greek lives.[44] Plutarch takes liberties with some of his material, despite his accuracy elsewhere.[45] Plutarch and especially Suetonius make mistakes with numbers,[46] as does Josephus.[47] Sometimes mythical elements appear in Plutarch and Suetonius, particularly when writing about the distant past, as when Plutarch addresses Theseus.

Nevertheless, even nonbiographic historians differed among themselves regarding the degree of creative flexibility they exercised in "shaping detail,"[48] and Plutarch's biographic work frequently is close to historiography.[49] To create cohesive scenes Plutarch often had to reconstruct details creatively, but he did not simply invent events,[50] and where he supplements his sources by

---

41. Pelling, "Bounds," 255.

42. See Fornara, *Nature*, 34–36, 116, 185; Hose, "Historiography: Rome," 423.

43. Pelling, "Bounds," 257–58.

44. Geiger, *Nepos*, 110–11. So also historians, e.g., Justin, *Epitome* 3.6.12; 5.8.10; 12.4.11–12; 14.6.2; 42.4.1.

45. Cf. Pelling, "Method"; Kaesser, "Tweaking."

46. For Suetonius, see Kennedy, "Source Criticism," 141; for Plutarch, see Licona, *Differences*, 57, 104, 110, comparing, e.g., *Caesar* 22.3 with *Cato the Younger* 51.1; and *Caesar* 25.1 and *Pompey* 52.3, with *Cato the Younger* 45.3.

47. See ch. 11; cf. Henderson, "Comparison," 269. Historians were of course not the only scholars to make mistakes (see, e.g., Pliny, *Natural History* 4.5.18; Pliny the Younger, *Letters* 10.58.5; 10.81.6).

48. Pelling, *Texts*, 44.

49. Pelling, *Plutarch and History*, 143–70, as summarized in De Pourcq and Roskam, "Virtues," 164.

50. In contrast to epideictic rhetoric; see Pelling, "Truth," and *Antony*, 33–36, cited in Burridge, *Gospels*, 169–70.

describing observers' responses, he often does so based on what he feels that he can infer from material already in his sources.[51] Despite historians' creativity, they did not feel "the same creative freedoms as the novelist to make it all up."[52]

Although Plutarch often works from memory, his notes draw on a wide range of sources and are usually even arranged fairly chronologically.[53] Plutarch seems well aware of a significant range of sources[54] and evaluates them, often based on consistency with what else is known of the subject's character (though this approach is sometimes prone to bias).[55] He rejects claims in his sources that he believes are motivated by enmity;[56] he acknowledges when some readers may deem some accounts incredible[57] and urges in such cases both caution and open-mindedness.[58]

Suetonius proves less critically discerning about his material than Plutarch,[59] but he includes various and sometimes varying accounts and hesitates "to impose his own judgments," making it less difficult for modern scholars to evaluate his sources.[60] Historiographic convention heavily influenced Diogenes Laertius's work.[61] Even in the fourth century, when a source could not recall the substance of a speech, a biographer concerned with accuracy might not try to reproduce it.[62]

Often later biographers simply repeat what earlier biographers said.[63] I revisit the question of historical information in biographies of the early empire in greater detail in chapter 10, where I illustrate it more concretely with some case studies.

What implications do these observations have for the Gospels? Where a variety of genre options exist, authors typically select and adapt the basic

---

51. Pelling, *Texts*, 48.

52. Pelling, *Texts*, 9.

53. Kennedy, "Source Criticism," 139–41.

54. E.g., Plutarch, *Alexander* 2.5; 3.2; Burridge, *Gospels*, 169; Alfred, "Valuation," 86–92. The legendary and encomiastic texture of *Alexander* is shaped partly by the like character of Plutarch's sources.

55. See, e.g., Plutarch, *Solon* 27.1; *Themistocles* 2.6.

56. E.g., Plutarch, *Alcibiades* 3.1.

57. E.g., Plutarch, *Camillus* 5.5.

58. E.g., Plutarch, *Camillus* 6.3 (though most modern readers would reject the examples).

59. One of the standard criticisms of Suetonius, though criticism focused on what he omitted more than on errors of fact (Hägg, *Biography*, 230).

60. Kennedy, "Source Criticism," 141. Kennedy notes that the Gospels rely on simpler tradition, but he nevertheless deems useful this comparison with hard data.

61. Adams, *Genre*, 251.

62. Eunapius, *Lives* 484.

63. E.g., Dionysius of Halicarnassus, *Lysias* 1.

genres that they feel will best communicate their message to their audience.[64] As Aune notes, that "the Evangelists . . . chose to adapt Greco-Roman biographical conventions to tell the story of Jesus indicates that they were centrally concerned to communicate what they thought really happened."[65] The Evangelists could have chosen exclusively liturgical forms such as hymns to honor Jesus (as in Rev 5:9–13), but for the Gospels they chose to write especially in biographic form.[66]

Rather than borrowing popular myths, the Evangelists instead communicated stories genuinely rooted in earlier Galilean and Jerusalem contexts (for evidence, see ch. 16). Dunn concludes that the Gospels' "genre itself tells us at once that there was a considerable historical interest" in gathering material about the Jesus who lived in history.[67]

6.3. The Gospels as Historiography?

Because the Gospels include elements that connect them with historiography proper as well as with its biographic subtype,[68] some scholars have argued that the Gospels are history *rather than* biography.[69] After all, Origen called the Gospels ἱστορίαι (*historiai*),[70] though contending that some of their reports did not happen physically.[71] So are the Gospels history *instead of* biography?

---

64. Smith, βίος, 21; for their functional character, see 26–27.

65. Aune, "Biography," 125; cf. Aune, 64–65; Witherington, *Sage*, 339.

66. Polybius notes that even Timaeus recognizes that those who write falsehood should call their book something *other* than history (Polybius, *Histories* 12.11.7–8).

67. Dunn, *Remembered*, 185.

68. See Cancik, "Gattung"; Byrskog, *Story*, 45.

69. Dihle, "Biography," 381; Becker, *Birth*, 72. Eddy and Boyd, *Legend*, 324–30, point out elements of both biography and historiography. For historical features in John, see Bauckham, *Testimony*, 93–112 (on 95 noting also my observations in Keener, *John*, 11–37). Marcus, *Mark*, 65–66, points to historical characteristics in Mark's work (still something like a *bios*).

70. This term ("inquiries") can mean "histories," as in 2 Macc 2:24, 30, 32; perhaps 4 Macc 17:7; esp. Josephus, *Jewish Antiquities* 1.1, 3, 8, 13–14, 159; 6.346; 7.101; 8.56, 224; *Jewish War* 7.454; and often.

71. Collins, *Mark*, 16, citing Origen *Princ*. 4.3.1 = 4.1.16. For Origen's recognition of some adjustments of precision in the Gospels, Allison, *Constructing*, 445–46, cites also Origen *Comm. Jo.* 10.2, 4 (though he regarded most events as literally true; *Princ*. 4.3.4 on 446n35).

6.3a. History More than Biography?

Adela Yarbro Collins reasonably argues that Mark adapted biblical historiography in light of apocalyptic eschatology and Hellenistic historiography and biography.[72] After addressing arguments for Mark as biography[73] and allowing for some influence from ancient biography,[74] Collins argues for Mark being closer to historiography,[75] specifically in the form of an eschatological historical monograph.[76]

Much can be said for this proposal. Cicero felt that historical monographs were ideal for glorifying their subjects,[77] although this same goal is naturally also a key element in biography.[78] Some typical arguments against the historical monograph thesis are quite weak. For example, although most extant or partly extant histories were multivolume, the Gospels' length range does not count against them being historical monographs. One might contrast a half-book length biography by Plutarch with histories of Alexander running to seven or ten books long.[79] But while most universal histories were multivolume,[80] historical monographs allowed for more focused treatment on a particular subject,[81] often in a single volume.[82]

Likewise, if one contends that Mark's chronology is too imprecise for a historical monograph, one might charge the same for some of Sallust's monographs,[83] despite their deliberate imitation of Thucydides.[84] Yet, at least among writers whose works have survived, it is Sallust who pioneered the Roman composition of historical monographs.[85] Furthermore, many histories

---

72. Collins, *Mark*, 1.

73. Collins, *Mark*, 22–33.

74. Collins, *Mark*, 33.

75. Collins, *Mark*, 33–42.

76. Collins, *Mark*, 42–52.

77. Plümacher, *Geschichte*, 15–32; Plümacher, "Cicero und Lukas," 772–73, includes 2 Maccabees and a work of Cicero's as examples of monographs fulfilling this function.

78. Penner, *Praise*, 135.

79. Geiger, *Nepos*, 29.

80. As were some series of biographies.

81. Rebenich, "Prose," 311–12; see, e.g., war monographs (see Fornara, *Nature*, 29–32), though Polybius complained about the narrowness of the typical ones (Rood, "Development," 148–53).

82. Collins, *Mark*, 41, emphasizing the compatibility with Mark.

83. See Laistner, *Historians*, 58–59.

84. Hose, "Historiography: Rome," 423.

85. Pelling, "Historiography," 717. In contrast to his monographs, his lost *Histories* was annalistic (Levene, "Historiography," 282).

had biographic sections or approaches;[86] when Dionysius of Halicarnassus writes a substantial section on Tarquin,[87] it remains part of a larger history.[88] Biographic material does not make a work biography per se.[89]

The historical monograph proposal would also bring Mark into much closer alignment with the dominant perspective on the function of Acts, another early Christian work.[90] Then again, a historian could include a biographic volume in a larger history, as in the case of Diodorus Siculus's treatment of Alexander of Macedon.[91] Likewise, Dionysius of Halicarnassus chronicles numerous lives in his history;[92] the same could obviously be said for the ancient Israelite books of Samuel through Kings.[93] Luke's Gospel does belong to a two-volume history, but when taken by itself, it may be understood as biography. (Indeed, some leading exponents of the Gospels as biography find biographic elements also in Acts.)[94]

6.3b. Biography More than History?

Yet the rejection of biography as a genre based on elements missing in the Gospels would also be problematic. On the basis of some of Plutarch's works, some define all biography so rigidly that not even all of Plutarch's lives can fit their definition.[95] Some expect nearly all biographies to include most conven-

---

86. Although noting some typical distinctions between biography and history, Talbert, *Acts*, 251, helpfully notes that many histories contain biographic sections (citing Polybius, *Histories* 9.22; 10.2.2; Dionysius of Halicarnassus, *Roman Antiquities* 5.48.1; Diodorus Siculus, *Library of History* 17; Josephus, *Jewish Antiquities* bks. 14–17; Dio Cassius, *Roman History* 45–56; 73.11.2–4; Eusebius, *Ecclesiastical History* 6).

87. Dionysius of Halicarnassus, *Roman Antiquities* 4.41–85.

88. Balch, "ΜΕΤΑΒΟΛΗ ΠΟΛΙΤΕΙΩΝ," 143.

89. Stadter, "Biography," 528–29.

90. On which, see, e.g., Plümacher, *Geschichte*, 1–32; Plümacher, "Cicero und Lukas"; Plümacher, "Monographie"; Palmer, "Monograph" (1992); Palmer, "Monograph" (1993); Dormeyer, "Gattung," 457–59; Keener, *Acts*, 1:90–115, esp. 91–92.

91. Diodorus Siculus, *Library of History* 17; see Burridge, *Gospels*, 239; cf. Smith and Kostopoulos, "Biography," 401.

92. Smith and Kostopoulos, "Biography," 403, citing Dionysius of Halicarnassus, *Roman Antiquities* 2.58.2–2.76.6; 3.1.1–3.35.6; 3.36.1–3.45.2; 3.46.1–3.73.4; 4.1.1–4.40.7; 4.41.1–4.85.4.

93. With lengthy accounts concerning Saul, David, Solomon, Elijah, and Elisha, plus further accounts of many kings.

94. Talbert, *Patterns*, 125–40; Burridge, *Gospels*, 266–67; Adams, *Genre*, 116–71. Cf. discussion in Keener, *Acts*, 1:54–62.

95. Burridge, *Gospels*, 89–90. Burridge responds to Becker and others in "Gospels and

tional biographic motifs,[96] but, as discussed below, the variation in motifs is actually much wider than conventional lists might reveal.

Granted, some features often distinguish biography from other sorts of historical works. These include a concerted focus on the biographee and consequently various conventional biographic topics, such as ancestors, birth, education, appearance, character, friends, death, and burial.[97] The Gospels entirely neglect Jesus's appearance, and Mark (unlike Matthew and Luke) neglects his birth.[98] Yet it is not the only biography to neglect such points. (See discussion below, section 4.)

Burridge, who views the Gospels as *bioi*, acknowledges that some historical works with individual-focused sections are not *bioi*.[99] Yet Burridge responds that even if the Evangelists had only a basic Greek education,[100] they would know how to compose biography more readily than a historical monograph. Historical composition was part of education,[101] but biographic materials such as encomia appear even earlier in the curriculum.[102] Nepos is explicit that biography is intended for a more popular level than history.[103] Similarly, Witherington notes the overlap in genres but counters that "the more specific telltale signs of an historical monograph," such as synchronisms or "historical causality," are missing. Mark focuses not on events but on a person.[104]

Mark does not write on the elite literary level of the biographer Plutarch, and his framework is not only more eschatological but also in various other ways more specifically Jewish than the work of any gentile biographer. The same differences, however, could be leveled against the classification of Mark

---

Biography," 27–30; he also recognizes biography and historiography as related genres that can share many features (65).

96. Becker, *Birth*, 75.

97. Adams, *Genre*, 251. These topics overlap with the personal attributes noted in Cicero, *On the Composition of Arguments* 1.25.36 (Becker, *Birth*, 75).

98. Collins, *Mark*, 25.

99. Burridge, *Gospels*, 262–63.

100. It is quite unlikely that an author such as Luke had only a basic Greek education, even if he dictated the work; Mark's level of education might be more open to debate.

101. Becker, *Birth*, 43, citing Cicero, *On the Orator* 1.158; Quintilian, *Orator's Education* 10.1.34; 12.4.1–2.

102. Burridge, *Gospels*, 262–63. *Progymnasmata* included encomia that followed the common structure of biographies (Aletti, *Birth*, 11).

103. Cornelius Nepos, *On Great Generals* 16 (Pelopidas), 1.1. Still, history-writing became quite popular; see Lucian, *How to Write History* 2.

104. Witherington, *Mark*, 3. Given the disciples' role as foils in Mark, Witherington also counters the notion that Mark functions as the "biography of a movement" (*Mark*, 3n11).

as history, novel, or other genres; in the Diaspora these contrasts reflect social, cultural, and ethnic differences rather than a difference of basic genre.

Biographies were less exhaustive than histories, focusing more on the models of character they provided.[105] Histories also elaborated speeches in a way that biographies did not.[106] Whereas Tacitus composes speeches for his history, the biographer "Suetonius quotes the actual words of his subjects, cataloguing, for instance, the idiosyncrasies of Augustus' Latin."[107]

The most conspicuous difference between biographies and histories, however, was their focus. Ancient biographies, like their modern descendants, focused on a single person.[108] (Collected biographies, such as Philostratus's later *Lives of the Sophists* or Diogenes Laertius's lives of philosophers, could focus on multiple persons in succession.)[109] By contrast, history included a broader range of characters and events, especially large-scale ones.[110]

Granted, as noted above, first-century historiography often focused on notable individuals.[111] Structured by the reigns of emperors, Roman historiography included increasing elements of "imperial autobiography" by the end of the first century.[112] The question that arises here is what we would call an entire historical monograph *focused on a single individual*. Occasionally, as in the case of Arrian's multivolume treatment of Alexander, most see such a work as a historical monograph. In the vast majority of cases, however, ancient readers would engage a single-volume, person-focused work as a biography.

Mark's Greek education, and his knowledge of both Greco-Roman bioi and historiography, may have been limited, but he does know that he is writing about a person. Still, genre boundaries are far more fluid at this point than the boundaries between full biographies in the early empire and novels. To some degree, the distinction may be in many respects semantic.

---

105. Plutarch, *Alexander* 1.1–3; see discussion in ch. 5.

106. See Keener, *Acts*, 1:271–304. Hägg, *Biography*, 209, notes that Tacitus's inclusion of speeches in the *Agricola* resembles historiography.

107. Edwards, "Introduction," xxviii, noting that here Suetonius follows the technical, antiquarian tradition rather than historiography proper.

108. Lucian, *How to Write History* 7.

109. See Adams, *Genre*, 92–113, 252–53.

110. Lucian, *How to Write History* 7, 20, 28, 32; also Witherington, *Sage*, 339, citing Plutarch, *Alexander* 1.1–2.

111. Fornara, *Nature*, 34–36, 116.

112. Hose, "Historiography: Rome," 423, noting that the boundaries between these genres were fading; cf. Suetonius in Rolfe, "Introduction," xvii.

6.3c. An Overlap More Significant than the Difference

Most observations of those scholars who view Mark as a historical monograph are valid; I would simply suggest that they do not ultimately detract from treating Mark as biography. More important, whether one treats the Gospels as biographies or as historical monographs makes fairly little difference regarding their value as sources for historical reconstruction today. The concerns of historiography and biography significantly overlapped, as supporters of both theses note.

Thus, for example, in Collins's typology of biographies, she assigns Suetonius's *Caesars*, Plutarch's *Caesar*, and Tacitus's *Agricola* to the type "historical biography." "Lives of this type," she explains, "have the same aims as historiography: to give an account of an important series of events and to explain the events in terms of their causes." This is also the type "that is most similar to the Gospels." "The historical type of biography," she continues, "is very close to the historical monograph, which focuses on a single person."[113] "Since the history narrated by Mark coincides in large part with the life of Jesus, it is similar to the historical type of biography."[114] Dihle, who views the Gospels as historical monographs,[115] also points out that Roman biographies fall closer to history.[116]

Likewise, most of those who regard the Gospels as biographies, including myself, agree that they include historiographic elements.[117] Burridge notes that near genres such as biography and historical monograph "share many features in common, . . . where the subject of the former is a person's life and character, while the latter is more focussed on a single topic, often involving many people."[118] "There is bound to be a continuum between these genres, which is why it is important to remember the flexible nature of genre."[119] Pelling shows the proximity of biography and history as genres, although suggesting ways to distinguish them.[120]

---

113. Collins, *Mark*, 32–33.

114. Collins, *Mark*, 43.

115. Dihle, "Biography," 381.

116. Dihle, "Biography," 383–84, although his attribution of the connection to Suetonius fails to explain the similar mixture already in Tacitus's *Agricola* and even somewhat in Nepos.

117. Byrskog, *Story*, 45, noting esp. Cancik, "Gattung." Some argue this same point also for the Fourth Gospel; see esp. Bauckham, *Testimony*, 19–21, 93–112; Bauckham, "Historiographical Characteristics."

118. Burridge, *Gospels*, 263.

119. Burridge, *Gospels*, 264.

120. Pelling, "History," cited and followed by Burridge, *Gospels*, 267.

As noted earlier, any rigid boundary between biography and history would be artificial.[121] Andrew Pitts, following David Balch and others, notes that there is no "hard and fast distinction between history and biography."[122] Even Plutarch, who distinguishes history from biography in one widely cited passage,[123] elsewhere views his biographic work as "history."[124] Like Plutarch, the historians Appian and Dio Cassius also pressed the boundaries of these genres.[125] Despite his topical arrangements, Suetonius also straddled both genres.[126] Likewise, despite the carelessness of the first-century BCE biographer Cornelius Nepos, his intentions appear to be historical. Some writers blurred the difference even further, titling their works "Life" yet narrating the history of a people.[127]

Many features of biography naturally overlap with historiography more generally. Historians depended on sources,[128] but so did biographers (see discussion below).[129] A historical work could treat specifically the deaths of prominent people, a familiar subgenre and also a fitting biographic subject[130] (note biographic examples later in this chapter). Mark's style is much more episodic than Plutarch's *Caesar*,[131] but episodic style characterized many biographies.[132] Travel anecdotes do not differentiate biographies from person-centered histories.[133] Commentary asides appear in biographies[134] but also in both histories and novels.[135]

121. Adams, *Genre*, 69.

122. Pitts, "Citation," 377–78.

123. Plutarch, *Alexander* 1.1.

124. Plutarch, *Comparison of Theseus and Romulus* 1.2, noted by Balch, "ΜΕΤΑΒΟΛΗ ΠΟΛΙΤΕΙΩΝ," 143–44.

125. Burridge, *Gospels*, 268, citing Pelling, "Epilogue."

126. Rolfe, "Introduction," xvii.

127. Sheppard, *Craft*, 112 (also noted in Licona, *Differences*, 5), cites Dicaearchus (fourth century BCE) and Varro (second century BCE).

128. Becker, *Birth*, 92.

129. See, e.g., Kennedy, "Source Criticism," 141; Burridge, *Gospels*, 168–70; Edwards, "Introduction," xxii, xxvii–xxviii; and esp., already for Nepos, Geiger, *Nepos*, 108–14; Becker, *Birth*, 66.

130. Becker, *Birth*, 70, citing Pliny, *Letters* 5.5.3; 8.12.4–5.

131. Collins, *Mark*, 43.

132. See, e.g., Lucian, *Demonax* 12–62 (also noted in Collins, *Mark*, 43); Burridge, *Gospels*, 73; Frickenschmidt, *Evangelium*, 161, 208; De Temmerman, "Formalities," 19; further discussion on anecdotes in ch. 5.

133. Mossman, "Travel Writing," 281.

134. Such as Plutarch's on Caesar (Collins, *Mark*, 43); see Sheeley, *Asides*, 78–94, 179, finding fewer explanatory asides in the chosen samples.

135. For romances, see Sheeley, *Asides*, 41–56; for histories, 56–78.

History focused more on deeds[136] than on anecdotes that reveal one's character.[137] Influenced by the Roman emphasis on models, first-century Greeks and Romans "extended the definition of history by adding the life and character of famous men to speeches and deeds as the proper subject of history."[138] Some distinguish this approach from pure biography in terms of their distinct purposes.[139] Yet deeds are a key feature in many biographies.[140] (The Gospels include both deeds and anecdotes;[141] for anecdotes in ancient biography and the Gospels, see ch. 5.) Historical features are so pervasive in historical biographies that eliminating those with historiographic characteristics would virtually eliminate the genre.

As already noted, the *usual* primary distinction between biographies and other historical works is not biographic focus (which can appear in histories) but whether the work is limited to a single character. A particular single-volume historical work that actually focuses on a particular individual would not be easy to distinguish from a "life" (*bios*). Even here, however, the distinction is not rigid, even aside from Arrian's work on Alexander. By the third century CE some philosophic "biographies" included information on lives of a philosopher's disciples, as well as the philosopher himself;[142]

---

136. Becker, *Birth*, 65–66, on Nepos, *On Great Generals* 16 (Pelopidas), 1.1; cf. Becker, *Birth*, 3, 69, 73, 76, 121; Fornara, *Nature*, 29–46. Becker also associates sayings with historiography (Becker, *Birth*, 75–76), but (in contrast to set speeches) they are more characteristic of biography (Momigliano, *Development*, 50 [noting Xenophon, *Hellenica* 2.3.56], 73; Geiger, *Nepos*, 27; Chance, "Fiction," 135; Frickenschmidt, *Evangelium*, 182; Adams, *Genre*, 91–92; cf. Lucian, *Demonax* 12; Burridge, *Gospels*, 69, 94, 168, 171; Moeser, *Anecdote*, 66–68, 93, 148; Ytterbrink, *Gospel*, 112; Edwards, "Introduction," xxviii; Konstan and Walsh, "Biography," 28, 33).

137. While Jesus's mission dominates the Gospels more than his character traits, the character traits do shine through; see, e.g., Alfeyev, *Beginning*, 505–32, esp. 508–25.

138. Fornara, *Nature*, 116.

139. Fornara, *Nature*, 185, distinguishes primarily by noting that biography used only the features of history relevant to expounding character, whereas "characterizing anecdotes . . .were unsuitable to history." Biography became more like history in early second-century works like Tacitus's *Agricola* and Suetonius's *Lives* (Fornara, *Nature*, 186).

140. Momigliano, *Development*, 50; Cox, *Biography*, 9; Burridge, *Gospels*, 71–72; Frickenschmidt, *Evangelium*, 281–83, 286, 505; Ytterbrink, *Gospel*, 76, 82, 86, 101; Freyne, "Gospel," 66; Edwards, "Introduction," xii; Adams, *Genre*, 92, 171, 251, 258; Beck, "Demonax," 93.

141. Roman biographers preferred to report all significant public acts, whereas Greek biography (more directly relevant to the Gospels, written in Greek) had traditionally limited itself more to key actions that revealed character (Hägg, *Biography*, 192, 234; in the Gospels, see, e.g., Mark 6:34; 8:2; John 11:35–36).

142. Some contend that this pattern may have followed Christian models such as Luke-Acts; see Dillon and Hershbell, "Introduction," 25–26. But cf. earlier biographic series.

multiple lives already appear in some earlier collections, regarding poets and others. Valerius Maximus collects anecdotes topically that include biographic information.

With reference to a work's correspondence to historical events, the difference between historical monograph and historical biography is slight. One expects more set speeches in the former and more emphasis on character in the latter, but both genres depend heavily on prior information. Confusing the two genres might cause one to miss nuances, but one's understanding still "would not be too far off."[143] Whether we view a work as a biographic historical monograph or as a historical biography, the commitment to historical information remains clear. With regard to historical intention and literary adaptation, the line between early imperial-period biographies and histories is thin.

6.4. "Biographic Features" Missing in the Gospels?

Some reject the biographic genre for Mark because this early Gospel says little about Jesus's background, birth, or education, standard topics in biographies.[144] Some other features favored by some biographers, such as the subject's typical dress or diet, are of little interest to the Evangelists; others, such as "love affairs (especially if scandalous),"[145] are not relevant. But while such features are common in ancient biographies, (and background and birth appear in Matthew and Luke), such features are not mandatory.

6.4a. Applying Appearance

Ancient biographies commonly provided descriptions of their heroes,[146] especially physically magnificent ones.[147] Praise of physical beauty was naturally a common aspect of Greek epideictic.[148] Suetonius even uses physiognomy

---

143. Adams, *Genre*, 2.

144. Collins, *Mark*, 21, summarizing P. Vielhauer's objection.

145. Long, "Introduction," xxii.

146. E.g., Suetonius, *Julius* 45.1; *Tiberius* 68.1–2; *Nero* 51; Tacitus, *Agricola* 44; Plutarch, *Marcus Cato* 1.3; *Sulla* 2.1.

147. E.g., Plutarch, *Alexander* 60.6; cf. 1 Sam 9:2; 16:12; 25:3. Such comment may be more abundant in mythography and fiction (e.g., Apollonius Rhodius, *Argonautica* 1.307–11; 3.443–44; Philostratus, *Heroicus* 10.1–4, esp. 10.3; 26.4, 13; 29.2; 33.39–40; 48.1; 49.3).

148. E.g., Menander Rhetor, *Epideictic Treatises* 2.5, 398.14–18; Dio Cassius, *Roman History*

at times to discern personality or the future.[149] Indeed, while admitting that Augustus actually was short, he supplies the testimony of an aide of Augustus regarding Augustus's grander stature for those who might prefer that tradition![150] Nevertheless, even heroes could have physical quirks; one thinks of historical memories of Socrates's snub nose.[151]

Physical descriptions, however, were far from mandatory in biographies, and they were uncommon in histories. Whereas Aristotle stresses physical description, Xenophon mentions it rarely; Plutarch and Diogenes Laertius include it in only some of their biographies; Tacitus's *Agricola* provides it only briefly.[152] Philosophically minded reporters felt that describing a teacher's soul was far more important than describing his body.[153]

6.4b. Background, Birth, and Upbringing

Greeks and Romans expected great leaders' births to be heralded by unusual events;[154] dreams were frequent. Sometimes such an event could include a flame shining around the boy's head.[155] Later rhetoricians advised noting any

---

57.18.6; see further Anderson, *Glossary*, 125 (citing *Rhetorica ad Herennium* 4.63; for ridicule, Cicero, *On the Orator* 2.266).

149. E.g., Suetonius, *Titus* 2. See further Cox, *Biography*, 14–15; Edwards, "Introduction," xvi, contrasting Suetonius, *Augustus* 79 and *Caligula* 50. Descriptions appear at different points in different biographies; see Hurley, "Rubric Sandwich," 31–32.

150. Alfred, "Valuation," 97, on Suetonius, *Augustus* 79.2. Suetonius is otherwise praising his grand appearance, albeit diminished in his old age. We should note, however, that even here Suetonius does not create the report from nothing, but from an eyewitness, though one that he deems unreliable on this point.

151. See, e.g., Maximus of Tyre, *Philosophical Orations* 1.9; cf. other unpleasant physical characteristics in *Life of Aesop* 1; Philostratus, *Heroicus* 34.5–6.

152. Stanton, *Preaching*, 124.

153. Maximus of Tyre, *Philosophical Orations* 1.10.

154. E.g., Valerius Maximus, *Memorable Doings and Sayings* 1.8.ext.5; see further Shuler, *Genre*, 94. For announcement by a dream, cf., e.g., Plutarch, *Alexander* 2.1–3.2 (Boring, Berger, and Colpe, *Commentary*, 37–38); for miraculous omens, cf., e.g., Suetonius, *Augustus* 94 (Boring, Berger, and Colpe, *Commentary*, 43–44); Aulus Gellius, *Attic Nights* 6.1.2–4. For supernatural births of famous philosophers, Diodorus Siculus, *Library of History* 4.9.1–10; Diogenes Laertius, *Lives* 3.1–2, 45; Iamblichus, *Pythagorean Life* 2.3–5 (Boring, Berger, and Colpe, *Commentary*, 33–35).

155. Valerius Maximus, *Memorable Doings and Sayings* 1.6.1. In this case the boy, Servus Tullius, was then adopted into the royal family; a flame around a general's head later portended victory (1.6.2).

supernatural phenomena attending a person's birth.[156] Thus orators would praise a king's noble birth, looking for any phenomena that happened at the time that could be interpreted as favorable portents;[157] if these were not available, one could invent them,[158] and invent them obviously and extravagantly.[159] This could include one shining at one's birth; thus the deity Apollo shone and lit up all the cosmos.[160] Speeches were not, of course, biographies, but it seems safe to presume that some fictitious accounts that originated for speeches eventually were assumed to be ancient and thus worked themselves into biographic traditions.

Ancient biographies often depict the subject's background and youth.[161] Suetonius always includes such features (readily available for emperors), and Plutarch usually does so. In various genres, from veridical accounts to pure fiction, stories of child prodigies warranted special attention.[162] Biographers often liked to use reports of youthful actions to presage the virtues or vices depicted more fully later in life.[163]

Biographic novels expanded on material available about various famous figures' youth,[164] but many mainstream biographers were also happy to expand on stories of youth when these were available. Storytellers expanded, for example, on the details of Moses's childhood and young adulthood.[165] Philo

---

156. Hermogenes, *Progymnasmata* 7. On Encomion, 15–16.

157. Menander Rhetor, *Epideictic Treatises* 2.1–2, 371.5–6.

158. Menander Rhetor, *Epideictic Treatises* 2.1–2, 371.11–12.

159. E.g., Menander Rhetor, *Epideictic Treatises* 2.1–2, 371.15–17. The rhetorical principle naturally also applied to praising deities by describing marvelous births (e.g., Menander Rhetor, 2.17, 438.30–439.24).

160. Menander Rhetor, *Epideictic Treatises* 2.17, 439.18–19.

161. E.g., Nicolaus, *Augustus* 2 (*FGrH* 126); Frickenschmidt, *Evangelium*, 253, 260–61; Adams, *Genre*, 257–60; Beck, "Demonax," 93, on Xenophon, *Agesilaus* 1–2 (though cf. Ytterbrink, *Gospel*, 83). Sometimes also historians, e.g., supernatural accounts in Justin, *Epitome* 12.16.2–6; 15.4.2–6; 37.2.1–3; 43.2.3–7.

162. Cf. Sus 45, 50; Josephus, *Jewish Antiquities* 10.50; Cicero, *Philippics* 14.10.28; Justin, *Epitome* 12.16.7–8; Valerius Maximus, *Memorable Doings and Sayings* 3.1.1; 3.1.2ab; Pliny, *Natural History* 7.16.72; Philostratus, *Life of Apollonius* 1.7–8, 11; Iamblichus, *Pythagorean Life* 2.10–11; cf. Wis 8:10; Fronto, *To Marcus Caesar* 4.1; the Latin funerary inscription of Quintus Sulpicius Maximus and lines 1–2 of the Greek epigram (in Wright, "Inscription," 54–55, 57, 59).

163. E.g., Nicolaus, *Augustus* 3 (*FGrH* 127); Edwards, "Introduction," xvi, cites Suetonius, *Tiberius* 57; *Caligula* 11; *Nero* 26; and *Domitian* 1, with Otho being an exception; Ytterbrink, *Gospel*, 106–7, cites Plutarch, *Themistocles* 2.1; *Alcibiades* 12.1; *Alexander* 4.4–5; see also Burridge, *Gospels*, 207.

164. E.g., Ps.-Callisthenes, *Alexander Romance* 1.13–19; Infancy Gospel of Thomas.

165. See esp. Josephus, *Jewish Antiquities* 2.233–36; Philo, *Moses* 1.21–31.

elaborates on Moses's youthful character and education,[166] portending the lawgiver's later role as philosopher-king.[167] Despite his elaboration, however, Philo seems aware of at least some prior tradition about Moses's education.[168] Furthermore, Moses was particularly intelligent and beautiful as an infant.[169] As a child he portentously cast Pharaoh's crown down.[170] As already noted, great adults were often assumed to have been child prodigies;[171] thus, for example, Cyrus revealed his royal character by his authoritativeness already at age ten.[172] On the historical level, Fronto attributes such advanced maturity to Marcus Aurelius.[173] Josephus also presents himself as a prodigy.[174]

Some of these stories may be fictionalized by the extant biographers who report them,[175] but others might be inherited from previous sources; biographers might draw on earlier fictions, but they do not appear to have usually invented their own. Nepos, for example, has to omit the early life of his favorite character.[176]

Likewise, despite Plutarch's obvious interest in establishing character toward the beginning of a life,[177] he does not create infancy stories the way we find in novels. Thus he covers "Agis' childhood and early youth in one brief

166. Philo, *Moses* 1.5, 20–24; cf. 2.1; Petitfils, "Tale," 163.

167. Jews who believed that gentiles had appropriated their wisdom from Jews to begin with might find his gentile education less offensive; cf. Artapanus, frag. 3 (Eusebius, *Preparation for the Gospel* 9.27.4); Josephus, *Jewish Antiquities* 1.168.

168. See Ezekiel the Tragedian, *Exagoge* 36–38; Josephus, *Jewish Antiquities* 2.236; Koskenniemi, "Moses." Although Jewish authors varied in their expectations of how much Egyptian culture influenced Moses (Römer, "Vie de Moïse"; cf. Jub. 47:9), most ancient hearers would assume some education for a prince raised in a royal court.

169. Josephus, *Jewish Antiquities* 2.230–31; cf. Exod 2:2.

170. Josephus, *Jewish Antiquities* 2.233–34. In a much later source, Moses even placed it on his own head (Exod. Rab. 1:26).

171. E.g., Josephus, *Jewish Antiquities* 10.50; Valerius Maximus, *Memorable Doings and Sayings* 3.1.1; 3.1.2ab; Eunapius, *Lives* 468; see further examples in Bultmann, *Tradition*, 300–301. For growing in size, cf., e.g., Philostratus, *Heroicus* 45.5; for Moses, Josephus, *Jewish Antiquities* 2.230; cf. Luke 1:80; 2:52.

172. Herodotus, *Histories* 1.113–15. On Cyrus's precocity, see also Xenophon, *Cyropaedia* 1.4.3.

173. Fronto, *To Marcus Caesar* 4.1. Not all child prodigies, however, remained advanced (Quintilian, *Orator's Education* 1.3.3–5) or pleased their elders (y. Soṭah 3:4, §12).

174. Josephus, *Life* 9; cf. *Life* 80; Rajak, *Josephus*, 27–29.

175. So De Temmerman, "Formalities," 18; cf. Pelling, *Plutarch and History*, 308–9; expansion in Russell, "Coriolanus," 22–23 (as cited in Kwon, "Charting," 74). Suetonius apparently augments traditions about Augustus's birth in *Augustus* 94.6 (Lorsch, "Conception").

176. See Alfred, "Valuation," 99, noting Nepos, *On Great Generals* 8 (Thrasybulus), 1.1–5.

177. De Pourcq and Roskam, "Virtues," 168.

participial phrase";[178] "Plutarch's manipulation of the truth never appears to develop into unbridled imagination."[179] When reports about a figure's birth or childhood vary, Plutarch does not mind saying so.[180] He does not even fill in a Roman citizen's *tria nomina* when one element of the name is unknown.[181]

Lucian briefly mentions that Demonax hailed from a wealthy and influential Cyprian family, and, a few sentences later, that he yearned for philosophy even as a child.[182] But he offers no specific examples—perhaps because he lacks them.[183] Lucian knew Demonax only as an adult. Immediately Lucian moves beyond Demonax's background to declare that he surmounted it.[184] Although panegyric often praises a person's honorable background,[185] it could also praise a person overcoming a disadvantaged background.[186] That is, even rhetoricians could make one's description praiseworthy without necessarily or invariably fabricating the description.

By omitting Jesus's birth, Mark may seem less like a typical Greco-Roman biography than Matthew or Luke, despite sufficient other features to indicate its biographic genre.[187] Yet important as a figure's background (ancestry, birth, nurture, and education) were to epideictic speeches or biographies when these proved both available and useful,[188] birth and infancy stories were not central to or necessary for a work to fit the biographic genre.[189] Early biographic encomia stressed ancestral lineages, but such interests appear to have diminished by the early empire.[190] Thus biographies sometimes began in their subject's

---

178. De Pourcq and Roskam, "Virtues," 177, citing Plutarch, *Agis* 4.1; also *Cleomenes* 1.4–5 and *Tiberius Gracchus* 1.7–3.1.

179. De Pourcq and Roskam, "Virtues," 177.

180. Plutarch, *Aristides* 1.1; *Lycurgus* 1; cf. Diogenes Laertius, *Lives* 1.4.74; 1.5.82.

181. Plutarch, *Caius Marius* 1.1.

182. Lucian, *Demonax* 3.

183. Beck, "Demonax," 85.

184. Still, see Lucian, *Demonax* 3. He continues with his adult life in 3–67.

185. E.g., *Rhetoric to Alexander* 35, 1440b.23–1441a.5, esp. 1440b.29–32; Menander Rhetor, *Epideictic Treatises* 2.1–2, 370.9–28; Gorgias, *Encomium of Helen* 3; in history, Velleius Paterculus, *History* 2.59.2; in biography, Xenophon, *Agesilaus* 1.2; Cornelius Nepos, *On Great Generals* 2 (Themistocles), 1.2; 7 (Alcibiades), 1.2; Suetonius, *Augustus* 1–2; *Tiberius* 1.1–2.4; 3.1; Tacitus, *Agricola* 4; Eunapius, *Lives* 498.

186. E.g., *Rhetoric to Alexander* 35, 1441a.5–13; Philostratus, *Lives of the Sophists* 1.22.521–22.

187. Aletti, *Birth*, 25–26. Cf. Matthew in Aletti, *Birth*, 49–52, and Luke, 68–70.

188. E.g., Menander Rhetor, *Epideictic Treatises* 2.1–2, 370.28–372.2; for virtues and deeds from youth, see 372.5–9. Nurture was the subject after birth (Hermogenes, *Progymnasmata* 7. On Encomion, 16).

189. See Frickenschmidt, *Evangelium*, 505; Ytterbrink, *Gospel*, 117.

190. Ytterbrink, *Gospel*, 116–17.

adulthood, starting with the biographee's public career.[191] When included, birth or childhood narratives were sometimes extremely brief, at times no more than a mention,[192] or discussion of parentage is deferred until after an introductory section[193] (cf. Mark 6:3). The background can be a single line, as in, "Solon, the son of Execestides, was born at Salamis,"[194] or, "Chilon, son of Damagetas, was a Lacedaemonian."[195]

Such omission or brevity probably at least sometimes reflected simply lack of substantial information. Because Plotinus mentioned only a few childhood incidents and could not be persuaded to recount more, Porphyry's biography addresses his childhood far more sparsely than the adult Plotinus that Porphyry knew. He does not invent stories to fill in the gap.[196] Still, an author sometimes does know more about the background yet simply deems it less important to the matter at hand; Josephus, for example, summarizes the first thirty years of his life in about 4 percent of his autobiography.[197]

Mark begins Jesus's public ministry where his best information and early Christian preaching may have often begun,[198] and where Luke begins Peter's summary of Jesus's mission in Acts 10:37.[199]

191. E.g., Philo, *Abraham* (Ytterbrink, *Gospel*, 103); the *Life of Aesop* (Drury, *Design*, 29); Plutarch, *Timoleon* 1 (Pitre, *Case*, 71); *Caesar* 1.1–4; also in *Camillus*; *Galba* (though cf. 3.2); *Nicias* (clearly a *life*, paired with Crassus); *Otho*; *Publicola*; *Titus Flaminius* (though mentioning his youth, 1.4, and his success as a young man). Defining biography broadly, Borgen, *John*, 259, includes *Flaccum* and (starting with a cosmic-level introduction, as in John 1) *Legatio ad Gaium*.

192. E.g., Plutarch, *Caius Gracchus* 1.2; *Crassus* 1.1; *Eumenes* 1.1; *Marcellus* 2.2; Porphyry, *Life of Plotinus* 2–3.

193. As in Plutarch, *Caius Marius* 3.1 (then only briefly); *Pelopidas* 3.1; *Pericles* 3.1; *Phocion* 4.1; *Sertorius* 2.1; *Theseus* 3.1; *Timoleon* 3.2; mention of Pompey's youth (but not ancestry) in *Pompey* 2.1; 3.1; 4.2.

194. Diogenes Laertius, *Lives* 1.2.45, then turning to his public career (1.2.45–67).

195. Diogenes Laertius, *Lives* 1.3.68, then turning to his career (1.3.68–73). Cf. similarly Thales (1.1.22; his career in 1.1.22–44); Pittacus (1.4.74; his career in 1.4.74–81); Bias (1.5.82; his career in 1.5.82–88); Zeno (7.1.1; his career in 7.1.1–35; after recounting Zeno's death, however, he does recount a brief anecdote about Zeno as a boy from another source in 7.1.31).

196. Dillon, "Interpretation," 158.

197. Josephus, *Life* 1–16. Citing Josephus's use of information, Downing, "Redaction Criticism 2," 34, suggests that Luke may have created much "incidental matter" in his infancy narrative but not the basic story. Unfortunately, I cannot properly address the special cases of Matthew's or Luke's infancy narratives within the main argument of *Christobiography*, since they narrate accounts placed a generation further from the Evangelists than is most of the gospel tradition.

198. Cf. Robinson, *Problem*, 69.

199. This observation is consistent with the tradition of Mark as a Petrine gospel, if Luke knows that Peter or the early apostolic church often started with Jesus's public ministry.

6.5. Can a Biography Take the Form of an Extended Passion Narrative?

How does the cliché that Mark is "a passion narrative with an extended introduction" fit the possibility of Mark being a biography (or, for that matter, a history)? Mark probably draws his passion narrative itself from earlier material,[200] and Jesus's death left an indelible mark on Christian accounts within living memory of that traumatic experience.[201] Nevertheless, there is no intrinsic reason to find his focus on Jesus's death inappropriate for biographies.[202] Granted, Xenophon's early account of Agesilaus seems to deliberately sidestep his death, but other accounts about Agesilaus do report it,[203] and death scenes become common in biographies by the time of the early empire.

The vast majority of ancient biographies conclude with the subject's death, tomb, epitaph, will, and related events.[204] Plutarch devotes 17.3 percent of the *Cato Minor* to his subject's last days.[205] This is comparable to Mark's 19.1 percent, Matthew's 15.1 percent, and Luke's 15.6 percent.[206] Some biographies foreshadow the subject's death, as in the Gospels;[207] often they narrate conflicts, portents, final words, and other events leading to or surrounding the biographee's end.[208] Some Romans even composed books built entirely around the deaths of famous persons—"passion narratives," so to speak.[209] As Michael Bird points out, "The element of the Gospels thought to be most unique, their focus on Jesus' passion, turns out to be not so unique after all."[210]

---

200. See, e.g., Theissen, *Gospels*, 166–99; Brown, *Death*, 53–55, 77–80; Soards, "Passion Narrative"; cf. Dibelius, *Tradition*, 178–217; Dewey, "Curse," 102–3; Flusser, *Judaism*, 575–87.

201. Cf., e.g., Kirk, "Memory of Violence"; Kelber, "Works," 244.

202. Pace, e.g., Dodd, *Founder*, 33.

203. See Wright, "Exploration," 240–43.

204. See, e.g., Lucian, *Demonax* 63–67; further, Burridge, *Gospels*, 133, 136, 142, 174–75; Adams, *Genre*, 260. For burial, see, e.g., Frickenschmidt, *Evangelium*, 341–42.

205. Burridge, *Gospels*, 160. Note also 15 percent in a biography of Nepos and 26 percent for Philostratus's *Life of Apollonius* (192).

206. Burridge, *Gospels*, 192.

207. Burridge, *Gospels*, 193, 202.

208. Frickenschmidt, *Evangelium*, 312–50, 505–6 ("die relativ große Häufigkeit von Passionsgeschichten"). For final words, Frickenschmidt cites (331–33) e.g., Nepos, *On Great Generals* 25 (Atticus), 22; Philo, *Moses* 2.288–91; Plutarch, *Pompey* 79; Suetonius, *Augustus* 99; Diogenes Laertius, *Lives* 2.42. Ascension and accompanying divinization (Talbert, "Concept"; Talbert, "Myth"; though cf. Aune, "Problem," 47–48; Zwiep, *Ascension*, 194–95) are much rarer, as are encounters with the deceased; see Frickenschmidt, *Evangelium*, 342–45; Keener, *Acts*, 1:663, 720–21.

209. Edwards, "Introduction," xvii, rightly citing Pliny, *Letters* 5.5.3; 8.12; Becker, *Birth*, 70. Lucian may parody this form in *Peregrinus* (see König, "Lives," 227).

210. Bird, *Gospel*, 228. Admittedly, given the significance of Jesus's death for early Chris-

Where possible, biographers emphasized the gentler deaths of noble protagonists (obviously not possible in Jesus's case).[211] Even though an easy death could constitute a basis for praise,[212] death merited greater treatment when it was central to the person's achievements.[213] Thus biographies, like other works, were all the more likely to devote extensive space to a death that was particularly notable, such as that of a martyr.[214] In particular, Jewish tradition devoted extensive attention to their martyrs.[215] Likewise, Plutarch comments more extensively on Cato's death because of its distinctive features.[216] Much of what survives of Nicolaus's biography of Augustus focuses on the assassination plot against Julius Caesar and its aftermath.[217]

Biographers frequently slow their narration to treat a person's final days in greater detail.[218] No longer content with topically arranged, isolated anecdotes, "Suetonius shifts into a narrative mode" when depicting emperors' deaths,[219] since such scenes had long warranted dramatic elaboration (both in epic and

tians, it seems difficult to imagine a biography of Jesus without attention to this feature whether or not it belonged to typical biographies; then again, Mark manages to surprise us by not narrating resurrection appearances (a fixture of subsequent extant Gospels).

211. E.g., Ytterbrink, *Gospel*, 109 (citing Plutarch, *Pericles* 38; *Numa* 22.1–2); Wardle, "Send-off" (citing Suetonius, *Augustus* 99). Cf. Demonax's public funeral (Lucian, *Demonax* 67), which fits known practice (Jones, *Lucian*, 97, cited in Wright, "Exploration," 256). At least some depictions were truer to the subject's perceived character than to historical experience; as Bond, "Fitting End," notes, following Christopher Gill, Socrates's calm final demeanor does not cohere with the known physiological effects of hemlock poisoning (though this death eventually became proverbial; Seneca, *Dialogues* 1.3.12; Maximus of Tyre, *Philosophical Orations* 25.7).

212. Theon, *Progymnasmata* 9.19.

213. Key features of a person's activity consumed more space; Burridge, *Gospels*, 193, compares one battle in Tacitus's *Agricola* (26 percent) and Agesilaus's Persian campaign in Plutarch (37 percent).

214. Epameinondas 2 in Plutarch, *Sayings of Kings, Moralia* 192C; *Sayings of Spartan Women, Moralia* 240C; Diogenes Laertius, *Lives* 7.5.176; accounts of Socrates's brave end (e.g., Xenophon, *Apology* 1).

215. E.g., 2 Macc 6–7; Wis 2:12–20. For some differences from the Gospels, see Boring, Berger, and Colpe, *Commentary*, 152, 156; on the diversity of Jewish martyr stories, see van Henten, "Prolegomena."

216. Burridge, *Gospels*, 74, 161, 202.

217. See Nicolaus, *Augustus* 16–30 (*FGrH* 130).

218. Frickenschmidt, *Evangelium*, 334–39. Biography in general is more concerned to narrate at length points that reveal character rather than much longer episodes (De Pourcq and Roskam, "Virtues," 166–67, citing also Beck, "Plutarch," 397–98).

219. Edwards, "Introduction," xvii–xviii, citing esp. Suetonius, *Julius* 81–82; *Nero* 40–49; *Domitian* 15–17. Not so, however, in some other lives where he lacks much data; e.g., Suetonius, *Terence* 5.

in tragedy). Scholars often find considerable attention to literary design or moral message in these death scenes.[220] How they died could confirm or contrast with how they lived or taught;[221] some accounts may also play ironically on their doctrines.[222] For example, Mark may depict Jesus's death contrasting starkly with the good-death tradition, yet in a manner consistent with his teaching and other foreshadowing in his life.[223]

When details were historically inaccessible,[224] biographers probably used the best available models to fill in their narration with some verisimilitude.[225] They also provided key connections among figures, sometimes probably filling in minor details to create cohesiveness.[226]

Still, even in some of these cases, actual events may lie behind parallels.[227] Memory, whether personal or social, naturally structures events according to cultural scripts.[228] People were certainly interested in death scenes,[229] but this could contribute to people recalling genuine reports about events as well as to

220. See, e.g., Wardle, "Send-off"; Power, "Taunt"; cf. Benediktson, "Structure."

221. Edwards, *Death*, 142; Gutzwiller, "Epigrams," 564–65. For great interest in death scenes, see, e.g., Hurley, "Rhetorics," 146–47. I owe most of the references in this note to a paper by my student Christopher Chandler.

222. Cambiano, "Diogenes Laertius," 575 (e.g., Thales dying from thirst in 1.39). Early Christians could scarcely avoid dealing apologetically with Jesus's execution, given the scandal involved (Sumney, *Steward*, 167; cf. 1 Cor. 1:23).

223. See Bond, "Fitting End." Bond also observes that Luke has different ideas about what sort of end was fitting, and how Mark elaborates at length on Jesus's death in the longest crucifixion account from antiquity. Cf. the rhetorical practice of "dwelling on the point"; cf. Hermogenes, *Method in Forceful Speaking* 5.417–18; Anderson, *Glossary*, 48–49 and esp. 53.

224. As in the murky, secretive background of assassinations; Ash, "Assassinating Emperors," 201.

225. Biographers could follow Plato's model of Socrates's death (De Temmerman, "Formalities," 19, 23), the sages' teachings about facing death (De Temmerman, "Formalities," 23; Kechagia, "Philosophers," 182), the biographers' accounts of earlier deaths, providing parallelism (De Temmerman, "Formalities," 24–25) or earlier literary models (cf. Power, "Taunt," comparing Suetonius, *Galba* 20.2, with Homer, *Iliad* 5.254; *Odyssey* 21.426).

226. Cf., e.g., the repetition of omens in Power, "Ending," 62 (citing Suetonius, *Galba* 1; *Vitellius* 9, 18). Cf. Josephus's use of a bird omen for narrative cohesion in his account of Agrippa I (*Jewish Antiquities* 18.195; 19.346; Keener, *Acts*, 2:1966).

227. See discussion in Keener, *Acts*, 1:566; cf. further Trompf, *Recurrence*. Hornblower, "Thucydides," 636, recognizes Thucydides's literary, Homeric-like "comparisons" across the span of his history "by using similar phrasing." Note also patterns in Appian, *Civil Wars* 1 (Bucher, "Evaluation," 458–59). Suetonius cannot fit all his material into neat outlines (Hurley, "Rubric Sandwich," 37).

228. With, e.g., Le Donne, *Historiographical Jesus*, 58.

229. Note Pliny, *Letters* 5.5.3; 8.12.4–5, in Becker, *Birth*, 70.

their free invention. Memories of such events would likely be vivid, given what is known of flashbulb memories about significant public events (cf. ch. 14).[230] Fiction may include verisimilitude because it imitates reality, but historical narration can include verisimilitude because the author has access to information.

Suetonius, for example, often presents the various possibilities surrounding an emperor's private death without offering a firm opinion of his own; he does not simply invent a conclusion.[231] Although many of Diogenes Laertius's sources, which do not come from living memory, may be suspect, Diogenes himself usually takes death material from his sources.[232] (In Diogenes's case, this sometimes meant multiple versions of a philosopher's death because various versions circulated by his time.)[233] To reject the historical core behind a death scene because a philosopher died consistent with his teaching[234] risks the same minimalist assumption for which the negative use of the criterion of dissimilarity has been criticized.[235] Some teachers were of course inconsistent with their teaching, but surely this was not always the case.[236] Biographers could depict characters' deaths "in close proximity to reality."[237]

Some teachers may have even arranged their deaths to follow earlier models; Seneca's suicide, for example, might follow the model of Plato's *Phaedo*,[238]

---

230. Brought to my attention in this connection by Christopher Chandler. Chandler notes that while Suetonius may add details to his sources at these points, his interest could also be like that of Plutarch, who deliberately sought out new information not included by his predecessors. Flashbulb details are, however, often inaccurate.

231. Alfred, "Valuation," 96, cites Suetonius, *Julius* 78.1; *Tiberius* 78.2; *Claudius* 1.4; 44.2, 3; *Galba* 3.1; *Vitellius* 1.2–2.1; *Vespasian* 1.2.

232. Kechagia, "Philosophers," 181.

233. Miller, "Introduction (Diogenes)," xi, noting four versions of Pythagoras's demise from three of Diogenes's sources.

234. Cf. Kechagia, "Philosophers," 182 (concluding skeptically on 199), who cites Lefkowitz on the lives of poets. Schools of disciples, however, would presumably preserve veridical anecdotes about their teachers more often than would readers about poets.

235. For criticism of this criterion, see, e.g., Borg, *Conflict*, 20–23; Sanders, *Jesus and Judaism*, 16, 145; Meier, *Marginal Jew*, 1:173; Brown, *Death*, 19; Stanton, *Gospel Truth?*, 143; Tuckett, "Sources and Methods," 133; Theissen and Merz, *Guide*, 11, 115–16; Levine, "Introduction," 10–11; Holmén, *Covenant Thinking*, 20–31 (esp. 29–30); Dunn, *New Perspective*, 57–60; Bird, "Quest."

236. Cf. various discussions in Pliny, *Letters* 3.11.5–6; Aulus Gellius, *Attic Nights* 19.1.4–6, 11–21; Lucian, *Peregrinus* 42–44; Diogenes Laertius, *Lives* 2.71; Iamblichus, *Pythagorean Life* 32.220; the model of Socrates in Xenophon, *Memorabilia* 1.2.1; Maximus of Tyre, *Philosophical Orations* 3.7; Keener, *Acts*, 4:3627–29.

237. Ytterbrink, *Gospel*, 117.

238. Ash, "Assassinating Emperors," 200, citing Tacitus, *Annals* 15.60–64; Griffin, "Philosophy," 66.

and Peregrinus's may imitate that of Brahmans.[239] Assassins might also "take meaningful inspiration from literary accounts of previous killings."[240]

While Mark's emphasis on Jesus's death fits biographies of martyrs, it is unusual in another respect. Whereas biographers normally wrote about famous and respected people, Mark does not record Jesus's public vindication; his Gospel climaxes with Jesus's disciples abandoning him, the leaders condemning him and crowds rejecting him, and the women who do learn of his resurrection keeping silent.[241] Mark may have reshaped some typical elements of the genre for theological reasons;[242] nevertheless, his focus on words and deeds of a single historical figure maintains the work's status as biography, perhaps thereby drawing all the more attention to his work's less typical aspects.

6.6. Use of Sources

The use of sources in ancient biography mirrors fairly closely their use in ancient historiography (treated in 7.9 below); biographers developed preexisting material that they expected to usually contain genuine information. Biographers depend heavily on prior reports, which underlines their interest in the remembered past rather than sheer literary creativity; the line between biography and novel was normally not so thin as that between biography and history.

In the Roman period, biographers usually chose their sources for what they deemed their information value rather than displaying a consistent bias for or against given authors apart from this consideration.[243] Nepos often

239. König, "Lives," 235, noting Tertullian's *To the Martyrs* 4.

240. Ash, "Assassinating Emperors," 202. Today we may think of copycat crimes, made even simpler by media saturation.

241. Note the discussion in Aletti, *Birth*, 30–31, on the importance of final recognition in biography; 31–33, on the absence of this feature in Mark (apart from the isolated recognition of the centurion). Aletti cites as Mark's model the psalms of the righteous sufferer (33–38); Mark's opposition to triumphalism accounts for both this feature and the absence of praise of Jesus's origins or education (38–39). In contrast to qualities favored by typical Greco-Roman biographies, the Synoptics focus on his "messianic and filial identity," and "his religious and salvific role" (109).

242. I believe that a key factor behind this feature (including his omission of reports of resurrection appearances, despite their proliferation in the church—1 Cor 15:5–8, esp. 15:6) may be that Mark addresses most directly an audience facing persecution; I currently plan to address this subject in fuller detail in my ICC commentary on Mark, currently in process.

243. See Alfred, "Valuation."

rewrites earlier accounts, perhaps helping to account for his speed of production.[244] He prefers to depend on major histories from which he could compose a short life with minimal trouble.[245] Because his *Themistocles* overlaps significantly with Herodotus and Thucydides, and it sometimes cites Thucydides,[246] we can explore connections with these possible sources; a recent study finds more than eighty significant points of contact in this one biography.[247] (Ephorus, on whom Nepos may depend for other material, is unfortunately no longer extant.) Nepos usually follows these sources quite closely, omitting some material but generally adding relatively little.[248]

Writing about foreign generals, where Nepos lacks fuller background knowledge, sometimes strains his competence,[249] but for Roman lives he follows the best sources, sometimes including figures' personal letters[250] but probably especially dependent on his friend, the careful scholar Atticus.[251] Like historians, Nepos employed autopsy,[252] documents,[253] and earlier historians.[254] He does not appear to depend on such documents when writing about Greek generals,[255] but neither does he invent spurious sources to compensate for his lack of access to real ones. He sometimes cites divergent sources without personally deciding among them.[256]

Plutarch made use of Thucydides in his lives of Pericles and Nicias, using accepted contemporary historiographic conventions.[257] A recent thesis

244. Becker, *Birth*, 66. In his recent dissertation, Youngju Kwon illustrates where Nepos adapts Xenophon.

245. Geiger, *Nepos*, 108.

246. Christian, "Themistocles," 105, notes Thucydides, *History* 1.137.4; 1.138.3–6 in Nepos, *On Great Generals* 2 (Themistocles), 1.4; 9.1–2; 10.4–5 (also citing him in 7 [Alcibiades], 11.1, and 4 [Pausanias], 2.2).

247. See Christian, "Themistocles," 106–38.

248. Christian, "Themistocles," 139; notable exceptions are inferences and reducing Herodotus's inflated numbers.

249. Geiger, *Nepos*, 110; though cf. Christian, "Themistocles," for his close dependence on good sources for Themistocles.

250. Geiger, *Nepos*, 108, citing Cicero, *Letters to Atticus* 16.3–4.

251. Geiger, *Nepos*, 108–9, citing Nepos, *On Great Generals* 23 (Hannibal), 31.1; 25 (Atticus) 18.6.

252. Geiger, *Nepos*, 109.

253. Geiger, *Nepos*, 110.

254. Geiger, *Nepos*, 110–11, 114; Christian, "Themistocles," 105 (citing many).

255. Geiger, *Nepos*, 109.

256. Alfred, "Valuation," 83, noting Nepos, *On Great Generals* 7 (Alcibiades), 10.4; 23 (Hannibal), 8.2; 11.1.

257. See esp. Bishop, "Historiography," 80–157.

at Durham contends that Plutarch's additions to and divergences from Thucydides often reflect educated guesses based on his source material, just as historians today often must offer (albeit normally more explicitly). Plutarch made mistakes and his perspectives were fallible, but in the final analysis "we can agree with Pelling that Plutarch did try to get it right."[258]

Tacitus could write about his father-in-law, Agricola, from direct knowledge, from oral reports from the family, from Agricola's notes and letters and from public documents, as well as, for his geographic digressions, other writings.[259] Plutarch's extant works, meanwhile, cite 150 earlier historians, and he uses an estimated twenty-five specified sources even for just his seven biographees from the late Republic.[260] When possible, he uses authentic letters from his subjects[261] and other writings from the periods he describes.[262] As noted above, he also often critically evaluates his sources.[263]

Suetonius draws on his notes from official "libraries and archives," which he then arranged topically.[264] His *Caesars* draw on thirty-seven named authors plus inscriptions, a plethora of unattributed citations, and other sources.[265] He seems to know of histories that he does not explicitly cite,[266] and he often refers to material that he does not specify by name.[267] Suetonius also welcomes a range of sources, allowing differing accounts to stand in tension.[268]

258. Bishop, "Historiography," 160.

259. Burridge, *Gospels*, 168.

260. Burridge, *Gospels*, 169, citing Hamilton, *Plutarch*, xlix; Jones, *Plutarch and Rome*, 81–87; Pelling, "Method," 83–90. Likewise, he cites more than thirty-six writers in his *Theseus* and *Romulus* alone (Alfred, "Valuation," 86–89), about twenty in his *Alcibiades* and *Coriolanus* (Alfred, "Valuation," 89–92), and about thirteen authors (about twenty-two citations) in his *Agesilaus* (Woldemariam, "Comparison," 219n13, 231–34). Hägg, *Biography*, 243 (noting esp. Badian, "Skill") comments on Plutarch's interest in sources and evaluation of explanations, though Plutarch is far more creative in form (Hägg, *Biography*, 281) and far more given to moralizing comments than is Suetonius.

261. See, e.g., Plutarch, *Demosthenes* 26.2; *Cicero* 24.4, 6–7; 37.2–3; 45.2; *Brutus* 2.3–5; 53.5; Moles, "Letters," 159–60; cf. Plutarch, *Agesilaus* 13.4; 21.5; *Demosthenes* 20.5.

262. E.g., Plutarch, *Cicero* 41.3–4. For Plutarch's range of sources, see Rhodes, "Documents," 65–66; Hägg, *Biography*, 256–58, 264; for his creative use of them, see Badian, "Skill."

263. See, e.g., Plutarch, *Solon* 27.1; *Alcibiades* 3.1; *Themistocles* 2.6; *Camillus* 5.5; 6.3.

264. Kennedy, "Source Criticism," 141; cf. Townend, "Date," 285–93 (in Goh, "Galba," 194).

265. Alfred, "Valuation," 93–99, esp. 93–95, 99. Cf., e.g., Power, "Priscus."

266. See Suetonius, *Galba* 3.3.

267. E.g., Suetonius, *Galba* 3.2; 4.2, noted in Goh, "Galba," 196.

268. Edwards, "Introduction," xxii, citing, e.g., *Claudius* 44 vs. *Nero* 33 (the former passage, however, may involve spotlighting); Alfred, "Valuation," 96, on *Julius* 46.1; 49.1–2.

He depends on his subjects' own writings, such as poetry, letters, or autobiographies.[269] He also shares many of the same sources employed by Tacitus[270] and sometimes assumes his readers' prior knowledge of relevant matters.[271]

He is attentive to information even when he does not name sources; for example, he notes that he investigated thoroughly a claim by "some" and found no corroborating evidence in its favor.[272] He distinguishes between rumors and established sources such as an autobiography.[273] Granted that he focuses on the most interesting anecdotes, he may do so because he takes for granted that his literate Roman audience already knows the key historical details.[274] That he writes at significantly greater length about earlier emperors than more recent ones may reflect his sources; more written sources were available concerning the earlier reigns, whereas the more recent required him to depend more on oral history and direct knowledge.[275] I examine a test case for Suetonius's use of prior information in chapter 10.

Because Arrian's historical monograph on Alexander also has a person-centered focus, it offers another relevant example. Because Arrian had available far more material about Alexander than he needed, he notes that he selected, arranged, and reworked it in ways that would best honor his hero.[276] He depends especially on the two eyewitness sources that he deems most accurate,[277] weaving in other sources only if he deems them plausible and interesting enough to merit mention.[278] Although he changes the sequence and emphasis of the material, creating a new product, he does not appear to have invented events or to have significantly modified their content.[279]

---

269. Edwards, "Introduction," xxvii–xxviii, citing, e.g., *Tiberius* 61; *Nero* 23, 52, though some contend that Suetonius lost access to palace archives after completing his first installments (see xxviii; Jones and Milns, *Commentary*, 5). Cf. also Power, "Poetry," 239; Alfred, "Valuation," 95; Becker, *Birth*, 151, citing *Augustus* 5; *Caligula* 19.3.

270. Edwards, "Introduction," xxvii, citing, e.g., the work of Cluvius Rufus. Wallace-Hadrill, *Suetonius*, 9, sees Suetonius as supplementing Tacitus, but contrast Power, "Suetonius' Tacitus" (I owe this observation to Asbury PhD student John Wright).

271. Goh, "Galba," 196.

272. Suetonius, *Vespasian* 1.4; see Alfred, "Valuation," 98.

273. Power, "Poetry," 223; cf. 237 on *Julius* 49.1–4.

274. Becker, *Birth*, 150.

275. Becker, *Birth*, 151, citing *Nero* 57.2; *Domitian* 12.2.

276. Bosworth, *Arrian*, 16, 38.

277. Bosworth, *Arrian*, 39, 61, noting Ptolemy and Aristobulus. Aristobulus may have written first (Hammond, *Sources*, 36).

278. Bosworth, *Arrian*, 39, 61.

279. Bosworth, *Arrian*, 60.

In the early third century, Diogenes Laertius is a particularly industrious compiler and is much more committed to documenting his sources than was Suetonius. Recounting the lives of earlier philosophers, he cites 1,186 references, 250 different authors, and over 350 anonymous references.[280]

Although Luke does not name his sources,[281] not unlike Suetonius's usual practice, he acknowledges the existence of circulated accounts (Luke 1:1–3). Because he writes *recent* history (see ch. 9) dependent on a collective apostolic memory, he may not know of any wide divergence of opinion on the substance of what actually happened, and thus may have less reason to identify varying viewpoints. Those who wrote about events from living memory often did not name many of their sources.[282]

6.7. Conclusion

For the most part, biographers of the early empire, like historians, were bound to their sources, at least with regard to events (major incidents and occurrences). They could reshape them rhetorically, but the genre in which they chose to write meant a focus on shaping the remembered past, not on unrestrained literary creativity.

So long as we recognize the differences between ancient genres and their modern successors, it is fair to describe ancient biographies as works based in historical information. Ancient biographers had their agendas, but in contrast to writers in some other genres, they normally achieved such agendas by using historical information so far as it was available. Biography was, as David Aune points out, "firmly rooted in historical fact rather than literary fiction."[283] Accordingly, and without contradiction to their proclamatory function, we might expect the Gospels to preserve substantial genuine information about Jesus as well.

---

280. Fitzgerald, "Lives," 215, following Hope, *Book*, 59–60.
281. Cf. Ytterbrink, *Gospel*, 226.
282. See Alfred, "Valuation," 85 (noting Nicolaus's *Augustus*; Tacitus's *Agricola*), 92–93. Even the respected historian Thucydides usually does not name his sources, many of which were undoubtedly oral (see Aune, "Prolegomena," 78).
283. Aune, "Biography," 125; cf. 64–65; Witherington, *Sage*, 339.

Chapter 7

What Historical Interests Meant in Antiquity

As noted in chapter 6, ancient biography was closely related to ancient historiography. But while modern historiography and biography developed from their ancient namesakes, the ancient conventions were not quite the same as their successors, and it is anachronistic to judge ancient works by criteria that did not yet exist. Still, ancient thinkers were not as uncritical as some readers today suppose.

Knowing that ancient biographies used historical information is of only limited help for us to evaluate their value as historical sources unless we have a sense of how historical writers in antiquity handled information. What did ancient readers expect in historiographic works? How much did historians adapt and fill in the material that they inherited? After addressing this question with respect to the Gospels as ancient biographies, I will briefly explore the particular example of Luke-Acts, which was composed as a work of ancient historiography (see ch. 8).[1]

7.1. Concerns for Rhetorical Presentation

Biography was a form of historical writing (ch. 6), and history-writing was a form of literature.[2] As literature, history could include valuable literary techniques such as suspensefully or surprisingly holding back information until the appropriate moment.[3] Most surviving histories from the ancient Mediter-

---

1. I refer to Greco-Roman historiography. For discussions of earlier Israelite and ancient Near Eastern historiography, see Van Seters, *Search*; Frahm, Jansen-Winkeln, and Wiesehöfer, "Historiography"; Millard, Hoffmeier, and Baker, *Historiography*; for some possible parallels with Greek historiography, cf. Van Seters, "Historiography."

2. Becker, *Birth*, 59–60, 63.

3. Pelling, *Texts*, 69, 89; Keener, *Acts*, 1:63. Novelists of course deliberately create suspense; cf., e.g., Doulamis, "Storytelling."

ranean world rework still earlier narratives to provide a new "literary presentation of a known tradition."[4] Competent writers were expected to distinguish their work from those of predecessors partly by placing their own twist on their material. During the period of the empire, rhetoric heavily shaped Roman literature.[5]

Some estimate that barely 2 percent of Greek histories have survived, apart from fragments and summaries.[6] The most elite and rhetorically sophisticated authors are disproportionately represented, since their work most appealed to those most able to pay for its reproduction. This factor may help explain why ancient historiography was more reader-driven (better, hearer-driven) than its typical modern academic analogue.

Not surprisingly, therefore, rhetorical artistry pervades most extant historical writing from antiquity.[7] Some writers emphasized rhetoric more than others; these include Dionysius of Halicarnassus[8] and Josephus[9] (in biographic works, e.g., Isocrates).[10] Sallust regularly displays rhetorical tropes in his historical writing.[11] In the early empire, elite historians were often also orators.[12] Historians were interested not only in accuracy but also in plausibility and probability, as in rhetoric more generally.[13] They might claim to prefer truth over style, but so did orators; such claims merely show that they dealt with information as well as style.[14] Certain features became conventional in depict-

4. Bosworth, *Arrian*, v. Note, e.g., Philostratus's probable reworking of Damis (*Life of Apollonius* 1.3.1, in Robiano, "*Apologia*," 100).

5. Winterbottom, "Rhetoric"; cf. Penner, *Praise*, 129.

6. Schepens, "History," 54, citing Strasburger, "Umblick."

7. See Laistner, *Historians*, 3, 8–9, 30–31, 44; Meister, "Historiography: Greece," 421; Rebenich, "Prose"; Byrskog, *Story*, 203–13; Rothschild, *Rhetoric* (esp. 65–66, 291). Matijasik, *Canons*, should be useful, but was published too recently for me to engage personally here.

8. See Fox, "Dionysius."

9. Cf. Botha, "Rhetoric and Josephus." Even his *War* might contain Greek tragic allusions (see Forte, "Echoes Revisited"), e.g., in maternal cannibalism during the siege of Jerusalem (see Chapman, "Cannibalism," 422–24, on *War* 6.199–219). As we have noted, tragedy did influence the writing of history (for discussion of the complex relationship, see esp. Rutherford, "Tragedy"), as it influenced many genres (Rutherford, "Tragedy," 513).

10. See Burridge, "Biography." But biographies were rarely as partisan as genuine forensic speech, where a primary object was legal victory (e.g., Dionysius of Halicarnassus, *Lysias* 8).

11. Fronto, *To Antoninus* 2.6.1–2. A history written in a style between the normal historical and discursive styles could sell well among the rhetorically trained elite (Pliny, *Letters* 5.5.3).

12. See Pliny, *Letters* 1.16.4; 2.11.17.

13. Rothschild, *Rhetoric*, 62–64; cf. Penner, *Praise*, 217.

14. Rothschild, *Rhetoric*, 69. One should observe, however, that there is a difference in degree, as we have noted (see, e.g., Pliny, *Letters* 7.17.3; 8.4.1).

ing certain sorts of scenes, but then, many such details would be expected to recur in such circumstances.[15]

Although rhetorical styles varied,[16] elite readers expected historians to compose in the style considered appropriate to historiography.[17] Perhaps in contrast to some first-century thinkers,[18] later elite hearers, shaped by the Second Sophistic, preferred history in the "grand" (*splendide*) style.[19] Already in the first-century BCE, some writers, including the historian Dionysius, already advocated the literary use of old Attic Greek rather than the common language.[20]

The respective measures of historical information and rhetorical presentation varied from one historian to another, but historians in general both appealed to the historical research tradition and sought to represent the past persuasively.[21] Although a renowned orator, Tacitus[22] recounts considerable, solid historical information.[23] Likewise, Suetonius, despite his interest in rhetoric,[24] avoids embellishment and would not easily be classed a "rhetorical" historian.[25] Even the earlier, populist historian Theopompus did genuine research.[26]

Ancient readers expected historians to provide cohesive narratives rather than merely disjointed or even loosely organized information, which some-

15. E.g., although battle scenes are rhetorically similar in most ancient historians, battles naturally had similar characteristics (Laistner, *Historians*, 57, 95), and the more militarily knowledgeable historians could get even military details quite accurate (Laistner, *Historians*, 58).

16. See Rothschild, *Rhetoric*, 75n58; de Jonge, "Syntax," 458.

17. Cadbury, Foakes Jackson, and Lake, "Writing History," 13.

18. Cf. Quintilian, *Orator's Education* 10.2.73, 102; 12.10.59.

19. Fronto, *To Verus* 2.1.14. On this style, see, e.g., Dionysius of Halicarnassus, *Demosthenes* 15; Cicero, *Orator ad M. Brutum* 5.20–6.21; Pliny, *Letters* 3.13.4; 6.33.7–8; 7.12.4; 9.26.1; 9.26.10; Aulus Gellius, *Attic Nights* 6.14; Longinus, *On the Sublime*. In Latin, use of the grand style for historiography continues as late as Ammianus Marcellinus (Kelly, "Forge Tongues," 474).

20. See, e.g., Kennedy, "Survey," 18; Rowe, "Style," 156.

21. Rothschild, *Rhetoric*, 69–70, 93, 95; cf. similarly Nicolai, "Place," 21.

22. On Tacitus's rhetorical prowess, see Moore, "Introduction," ix (citing Pliny, *Letters* 2.1.6; 2.11.17); cf. Tacitus's *Dialogue on Oratory*; for embellished scenes, see Hadas, "Introduction," xvi–xvii.

23. See, e.g., Laistner, *Historians*, 129; Mosley, "Reporting," 20–22; Hadas, "Introduction," xviii; Syme, "Tacitus"; cf. Marincola, "Tacitus' Prefaces."

24. See, e.g., Suetonius, *Rhetoricians*, throughout.

25. Rolfe, "Introduction," xix.

26. Meister, "Theopompus"; Laistner, *Historians*, 4–5; but cf. Brown, *Historians*, 115.

times required authors to fill in gaps in their information. Chronology and outcomes provided some cohesiveness, but some details could make sense only in light of other ones. Thus historians would make inferences based on information they had and then provide their best guesses as to what the scene should have looked like. Both ancient and modern historians offer inferences from probability; what differs are the ways that we narrate those inferences and the particular assumptions (based on differing perspectives) that inform those inferences. Modern historians (and NT scholars) speculate regularly, but in ancient writing the speculation filled out details in depictions of events. Ancients narrativized their history, recounting it in story form.[27]

Still, interest in rhetorical framing did not correspond to lack of interest in historical truth.[28] One ancient critic emphasizes that, for all their commonalities, history and oratory are different disciplines: rhetoric focuses on trivial narratives, and history on famous deeds;[29] style, vocabulary, rhythm, and subject matter all differ.[30] In a later period, another historian emphasizes that he has sought to provide both tasteful literary style and historical accuracy in his history.[31] Because historians developed a factual "core" when they narrativized history,[32] we cannot easily separate history's story/narrative from its extratextual, factual past.[33] Ancient historiography allowed for flexibility in recounting the information, but mainstream historians envisioned their genre as based on facts.

This interest shows up in the ancient equivalent of scholarly peer review. Historians could criticize other historians whom they deemed more interested in showing off rhetorical skill than in historical truth.[34] Lucian expresses this concern in a particularly emphatic manner, lambasting authors who exces-

27. See Byrskog, *Story*, 199–253.

28. Byrskog, *Story*, 213, 223; Rothschild, Rhetoric, 88–91; Nicolai, "Place," 21.

29. Pliny, *Letters* 5.8.9.

30. Pliny, *Letters* 5.8.10–11. On the distinction between rhetoric and history in Cicero, see Nicolai, "Place," 21. Pure rhetoric, not bound by historical or other truth-telling conventions, can employ fabrications (Gorgias, *Encomium of Helen* 11, 13).

31. Dio Cassius, *Roman History* 1.1.1–2.

32. Byrskog, *Story*, 223. Byrskog means "core" in a much fuller sense than A. J. Woodman (see Byrskog, *Story*, 184), believing that ancient historians cared about facts (Byrskog, *Story*, 179–84). Cf. similarly Eddy and Boyd, *Legend*, 330–34.

33. Byrskog, *Story*, 253. The criticisms of Matthews, "Review," involve not so much Byrskog's analysis of ancient historiography (which I cite here) but his application of this category to the Gospels. As already noted, however, most scholars do believe that Luke was writing ancient historiography.

34. E.g., Josephus, *Against Apion* 1.24–25.

sively embellished histories.[35] One should produce narrative continuity[36] but avoid lavish and irrelevant description.[37]

7.2. Speaking of Rhetoric . . .

Inferential historical reconstruction applied above all to speeches. Compositional handbooks taught writers how to imaginatively reconstruct speeches, providing reconstructions as true to the occasion and extant sources as possible.[38] Historians followed this practice of composing speeches, though again usually as plausibly as possible in light of what was known, and usually even using the gist of a speech when it was known.[39] Even inscriptions of edicts were "not exact copies," and historians had even less reason to "aim at slavish imitation."[40]

Some historians, such as the rhetorical critic Dionysius of Halicarnassus, composed speeches more freely than others, such as Diodorus Siculus.[41] Philo makes up speeches for Moses in contexts where he otherwise follows the LXX or Jewish tradition fairly closely;[42] Josephus clearly takes significant liberties in speeches.[43]

Nevertheless, historians often instead followed (and adapted) speeches in their sources, whatever the origin of those sources.[44] The historian Pompeius Trogus critiques Livy for embellishing speeches too much.[45] Yet Livy, though

35. Lucian, *How to Write History* 7, 11, 15, 17, 22–23, 43–45.

36. Lucian, *How to Write History* 50, 55.

37. Lucian, *How to Write History* 19–20, 44, 57.

38. Licona, *Differences*, 11, 18; cf. Quintilian, *Orator's Education* 3.5.54.

39. See Keener, *Acts*, 1:258–319; Fornara, *Nature*, 143–68; Hammond, "Speeches"; Gempf, "Speaking" (esp. 264, 272, 283–84); Marincola, "Speeches," 121–27; Porciani, "Enigma," 333–34; cf. also Polybius, *Histories* 12.25a.4–5; 12.25b.1, 4; Cadbury, *Making*, 186–87; Laistner, *Historians*, 129; Walbank, *Speeches*, 1, 19; Hadas, "Introduction," xvi–xvii; Kennedy, *Classical Rhetoric*, 110; Horsley, "Speeches," 609; Padilla, *Acts*, 124–38; Padilla, *Speeches*; Becker, *Birth*, 98; also discussions on Thucydides, *History* 1.22.1 (e.g., Porter, "Thucydidean View?").

40. Aune, *Environment*, 82, comparing Tacitus, *Annals* 11.23–25, with an inscription; and Josephus, *Jewish Antiquities* 12.417–18, with 1 Macc 8:23–32.

41. Bosworth, *Arrian*, 94–96, noting Diodorus Siculus, *Library of History* 20.1–2.2 (see esp. 20.1.2; 20.2.1).

42. McGing, "Adaptation," 124, 128.

43. Downing, "Redaction Criticism 1," 62.

44. See, e.g., Gempf, "Speaking," 283–84; Forsythe, "Quadrigarius," 396; Marincola, "Speeches," 129.

45. Develin, "Introduction," 9, noting Justin, *Epitome* 38.3.11 (trans. p. 238): Trogus used

rhetorically adept, reproduces the essential gist of speeches in Polybius, while changing the wording and some details.[46] Comparing speeches shows that historians' speeches for Alexander often reflect a conventional core,[47] whatever that core's origins.[48]

Ancient authors and audiences alike expected this practice in histories. The pre-Christian historian Diodorus Siculus affirms historians composing speeches, provided they remain appropriate to the speakers within the narrative.[49] The pre-Christian rhetorical historian Dionysius comments on a speech "which Herodotus puts into the mouth of Xerxes."[50] The varying versions of Alexander's speech at Opis show that historians did not expect their audiences to read these orations as verbatim renditions of speeches delivered on the narrated occasion.[51] In the early second century CE, Pliny, whose standards for historical accuracy are normally high, praises an orator-historian who provides his characters speeches as excellent as his own, though more concisely.[52] Tacitus confesses that he does not need to reproduce Seneca's words exactly.[53] Other historians, too, sometimes explicitly disavowed verbatim reports.[54]

Composing speeches in histories differs from collecting anecdotes about and sayings of sages, such as we find in sage-related biographies and the Gospels, but the practice does remind us that ancient historical expectations for speech dif-

---

"indirect discourse, since he was critical of Livy and Sallust for having transgressed the proper bounds of history by inserting into their work speeches in direct discourse, but composed in their style." (Justin's version of the speech appears in Livy, *History* 38.4.1–38.7.10.) A sampling of Justin's epitome of Trogus's treatment of Jewish history (Justin, *Epitome* 36.2.1–36.3.9), however, suggests that at least one of these authors integrated by memory Jewish and anti-Jewish material fairly carelessly.

46. Fornara, *Nature*, 160–61; more generally, see 154–68. Livy probably works partly from memory and certainly does not copy Polybius slavishly (cf. here Mattila, "Question," 214).

47. Atkinson, "Introduction," xxix.

48. Atkinson, "Introduction," xxxiii, rightly suspects them of being "more free composition than authentic transcripts."

49. Diodorus Siculus, *Library of History* 20.1.1–4.

50. Dionysius of Halicarnassus, *Demosthenes* 41 (LCL). On Thucydides and Polybius being stricter regarding speeches than was Herodotus, see Aune, *Dictionary*, 448.

51. Atkinson, "Introduction," xxix, contrasting Arrian, *Alexander* 7.9–10, and Curtius Rufus 10.2.15–29.

52. Pliny, *Letters* 1.16.4.

53. Tacitus, *Annals* 15.63; see Talbert, *Mediterranean Milieu*, 210; Laistner, *Historians*, 128.

54. Marincola, "Speeches," 120, citing, e.g., Polybius, *Histories* 18.11; Sallust, *Catiline's War* 50.5; Livy, *History* 37.45.11; Arrian, *Alexander* 5.27.1; Tacitus, *Histories* 1.15–16; *Agricola* 29.4, and noting that emphasis on verbatim quotes were rare and dealt with short lines (e.g., Tacitus, *Annals* 14.59.4; 15.67.4).

fered from modern ones.[55] That the Gospels rearrange Jesus's sayings in speeches, often where they do not easily fit with one another, illustrates the extent to which the Gospels sought to draw on Jesus's sayings, as biographers (especially of teachers) normally drew on the sayings of those about whom they wrote.

7.3. Balancing Readers' Enjoyment and Truth

"Pleasure and beauty" remained valued purposes for any work,[56] and readers were supposed to be able to enjoy well-written histories.[57] Even generally reliable rhetorical historians could infuse scenes with tragic pathos when the events that they reported allowed it.[58] Seeking to communicate the *spirit* of the times as well as the specific events, one military historian complains, "No one has even been able to deplore the fortunes of this whole period with such tears as the theme deserves."[59] They simply sought to communicate the feeling that surely (one could infer) accompanied the events.

Nevertheless, some historians were stricter, at least in principle. One warns against a historian trying to thrill readers with exaggeration or reconstructing "the probable utterances of his characters."[60] Whereas tragic poets could settle for verisimilitude, he insists, a historian must stick with facts.[61]

Lucian insists that history's proper purpose is not to give pleasure but only to be useful; "and that comes from truth alone."[62] Usefulness and pleasure were not mutually exclusive objectives, and Lucian does not reject history's pleasure value altogether,[63] but he emphasizes instead history's edifying value (i.e., its moral lessons), which flows from truth.[64]

---

55. With, e.g., Fornara, *Nature*, 142.

56. Dionysius of Halicarnassus, *Demosthenes* 47 (LCL 1:418–19); cf. Let. Aris. 322.

57. Maximus of Tyre, *Philosophical Orations* 22.5; Justin, *Epitome* pref.4; 2 Macc 2:25; cf. Tacitus's apology in *Annals* 4.32–33; further discussion in Fornara, *Nature*, 120–33, esp. 121, 133–34, citing Cicero, *Letters to Friends* 5.12.4.

58. E.g., Tacitus, *Annals* 3.1; 4.62–63; 5.9; 16.30–32.

59. Velleius Paterculus, *History* 2.67.1.

60. Polybius, *Histories* 2.56.10. Of course, Polybius's own speeches are not verbatim recollections.

61. Polybius, *Histories* 2.56.11. See Keener, *Acts*, 1:126; Becker, *Birth*, 66–67. Poetic treatments of historical events (e.g., Silius Italicus; Lucan) enjoyed more freedom of expression (cf. Pliny, *Letters* 8.4.1).

62. Lucian, *How to Write History* 9 (LCL 6:15); cf. Polybius, *Histories* 9.2.6.

63. Cf. Lucian, *How to Write History* 9, 16, 43.

64. E.g., Lucian, *How to Write History* 59.

For most historians, rhetorical interest did not eradicate the goal of historical truth.[65] History was still written quite differently "from poetry, drama, oratory, and forensic argument."[66] Even the most rhetorically oriented historians recognized that historical inquiry required not merely rhetorical skill but research.[67] Despite sensational elements, Hellenistic and Roman historians retained the critical ideal.[68] Information is not inherently incompatible with persuasion or enjoyment.[69]

7.4. Buying into Bias?

Ancient historians, like modern ones, had their favorites and biases. Still, in general, fairness and honesty remained the goal in history and part of the genre's implicit "contract between author and reader."[70] It may overstate the case to claim that "tendentiousness . . . probably threatened the integrity of historiography no more than in present times,"[71] but the public ideal remained fairness.

Ancient historians recognized the danger of biases (typically *others'* biases) distorting the historical enterprise. Thus, for example, Josephus complains about the bias of other historians, whom he contrasts, not quite fairly, with his own accuracy.[72] Lucian does not rule out evaluating historical figures morally, but he does insist that "eulogy and censure" must be "free from slander, supported by evidence, cursory" and without forensic-style exaggerations.[73] Unlike encomia, true history must not include any lies.[74] Good

---

65. See Byrskog, *Story*, 213; Rothschild, *Rhetoric*, 88–91; Nicolai, "Place," 21.

66. Rothschild, *Rhetoric*, 81.

67. Dionysius of Halicarnassus, *Roman Antiquities* 1.1.2–4; 1.4.2.

68. Rothschild, "Irony," 291.

69. Cf. Bhatt's complaint about those who exaggerate the difference between ancient literary histories and modern "scientific" histories (Bhatt, "Rhetoric," 181–82).

70. Fornara, *Nature*, 72, 100.

71. Fornara, *Nature*, 104. If a history was too biased, it was probably the weakness of the particular historian (Fornara, *Nature*, 91).

72. Josephus, *Jewish Antiquities* 20.154–57. He challenges a source's bias in *Antiquities* 16.183–84.

73. Lucian, *How to Write History* 59 (LCL). The rhetorical historian Theopompus, by contrast, "impeached nearly everybody in a quarrelsome spirit." Writers such as Pompeius Trogus, often apparently reliable, seem to adopt their sources' encomiastic exaggeration at times (for one conspicuous example, see Justin, *Epitome* 12.9.7–8).

74. Lucian, *How to Write History* 7; cf. 11.

historians such as Xenophon or Thucydides may have had their private prejudices, but they tried to publicly evaluate characters fairly, not sparing their favorites.[75]

Modern critics try to take into account ancient authors' biases. Nevertheless, they sometimes differ regarding what those biases were, for example, the degree of Sallust's bias.[76] Xenophon was mostly evenhanded in his history,[77] except for failing to fully credit his enemy Epaminondas.[78] One modern critic identifies Tacitus's biases[79] yet commends his "candor" for often including information contrary to his own biases.[80] Sometimes historians who favored figures provided panegyric for them separate from—and sometimes in opposition to—their more honest narration of deeds.[81] Historians today can sometimes offset ancient writers' biases by comparing multiple sources.[82]

The pre-Christian historian Polybius recognized history's epideictic function: historians must evaluate whether figures merit "praise or blame."[83] But while one could exaggerate someone's achievements in a pure encomium, history must assign "praise and blame impartially," following strict truth and explaining why the person merits this verdict.[84] Not even Polybius was invariably "objective," but he sought to be fairer in history than in eulogies. When reading ancient historians, modern historians normally take epideictic factors into account, rather than simply discounting the value of their evidence.[85]

---

75. Lucian, *How to Write History* 39; cf. 41.

76. Emphasizing it, e.g., Laistner, *Historians*, 45–48, 55–56, 63; contrast Fornara, *Nature*, 72.

77. Brown, *Historians*, 93–94.

78. Brown, *Historians*, 97.

79. Laistner, *Historians*, 131–39.

80. Laistner, *Historians*, 132–34.

81. Bosworth, *Arrian*, 135, 153–56, on Tacitus and Arrian.

82. E.g., Laistner, *Historians*, 131.

83. Polybius, *Histories* 3.4.1 (LCL).

84. Polybius, *Histories* 10.21.8 (LCL). Historians often praised or presented views of both sides in a war, thereby amplifying pathos (e.g., Dionysius of Halicarnassus, *Roman Antiquities* bk. 3; 9.39.1–6; Livy, *History* 21.1.3) and the credit due the victor.

85. For Josephus, see, e.g., Curran, "War"; for nineteenth-century historiography, see, e.g., Tomkins, *Wilberforce*, 15–17.

7.5. Inferring Motives

Often biographers inferred what matters they could beyond what was explicit in their sources,[86] especially regarding motivations.[87] Plutarch could depict different motives for the same character at the same time in different lives.[88] Of course, a person can have multiple motivations, and various explanations for actions are possible, but Plutarch's inferences fit his respective narratives.[89] If inferring motives and uncovering thoughts was a biographic interest, it was not foreign to some forms of historiography more broadly; the rhetorical historian Dionysius of Halicarnassus praises the earlier rhetorical historian Theopompus for doing just that.[90]

Assigning motives to characters was a common practice.[91] Thus, for example, biography and other history-writing regularly lists envy as a motive for hostility,[92] sometimes even as a statement of general political life.[93] We need not suppose that they were always wrong about the assumption; envy was common in the agonistic, honor/shame society of ancient Mediterranean cities.[94] Sometimes, however, historians demurred from speculation about protagonists' plans apart from what could be inferred from their character.[95]

86. Cf. Licona, *Differences*, 78.

87. E.g., Hägg, *Biography*, 3. So also in historians, such as Thucydides; see Pelling, *Texts*, 77–81, esp. 77; cf. also, e.g., Justin, *Epitome* 6.1.1; 8.6.6; 35.2.3; 36.4.8; 38.9.10; Caesar's *Gallic War* (Grillo, "Scribam"). A historian could, however, admit ignorance of motives (e.g., Tacitus, *Annals* 15.36).

88. Licona, *Differences*, 52, 83, 99, 109.

89. De Pourcq and Roskam, "Virtues," 169.

90. Smith and Kostopoulos, "Biography," 402–3, citing Dionysius of Halicarnassus, *Letter to Gnaeus Pompeius* 6.

91. Note Pelling, *Texts*, 77–81, esp. 77.

92. E.g., Nepos, *On Great Generals* 5 (Cimon), 3.1; 8 (Thrasybulus), 4.1–2; 12 (Chabrias), 3.3; 14 (Datames), 5.2; 15 (Epaminondas), 7.1; 18 (Eumenes), 7.2; 10.2; 23 (Hannibal), 1.2; Velleius Paterculus, *History* 2.47.2; Josephus, *Life* 204, 423, 425; Tacitus, *Annals* 16.18; Plutarch, *Coriolanus* 39.1; Philostratus, *Lives of the Sophists* 1.21.515; Diogenes Laertius, *Lives* 5.76–77; Herodian, *History* 3.2.3. Pervo, *Acts*, 141n9, associates inference of motives too narrowly with popular and fictitious works.

93. Cornelius Nepos, *On Great Generals* 8 (Thrasybulus), 4.1–2; 12 (Chabrias), 3.3; Velleius Paterculus, *History* 2.40.4.

94. See, e.g., *Rhetoric to Alexander* 36, 1445a.12; Plutarch, *How to Profit by One's Enemies* 10, *Moralia* 91E.

95. Arrian, *Alexander* 7.14.

7.6. History and Agendas

Historians usually have interests in their subject matter, probably beyond merely achieving tenure.[96] Even today, historians select the events they will report based on what they find to be of greatest interest or of greatest relevance to their focus.[97] Historiography is constructive, involving social memory;[98] history-writing involves an "interplay between event and narration," between an event and its interpretation.[99]

Yet, even more overtly than today, ancient historians wrote from moral, political, and/or religious perspectives.[100] Ancient historians themselves, including the critical Polybius, recognized that they had interpretive grids.[101] Even writers intending to write the most accurate history often "enhanced" their narratives somewhat for literary, moralistic, and political purposes.[102]

7.6a. Political and National Agendas

Historians recognized the value of historical discourse for politics.[103] Historians usually displayed, in varying measures, national or ethnic biases, such as a pro-Roman *Tendenz*,[104] an anti-Aetolian bias,[105] a pro-Athenian bias,[106] or a pro-Judean apologetic.[107] Historians whose information was largely factual

96. I follow here my work in *Acts*, 1:148–65.

97. E.g., military history, women's history, church history; cf. Greek historians' comparable range of interest in Justin, *Epitome* pref.3.

98. Schröter, *Jesus to New Testament*, 50, 116.

99. Schröter, *Jesus to New Testament*, 47; cf. 37–40.

100. See at length, e.g., Hemer, *Acts*, 79–85; Byrskog, *Story*, 256–65; Penner, *Praise*, 129, 179; Mason, *Josephus and New Testament*, 63; Grant, "Introduction," 10, 13.

101. Byrskog, *Story*, 186–90.

102. See esp. Lyons, *Autobiography*, 29–32 (though he is not advising rejecting such texts' historical value wholesale; 66). Cf. Rodríguez, "Jesus Tradition," 195: an Evangelist could use "resources already latent within the tradition to bring the tradition to bear on a new situation in innovative ways."

103. E.g., Polybius, *Histories* 1.1.2; Fornara, *Nature*, 113; see also Penner, "Discourse," 73–77.

104. E.g., Polybius, *Histories* 36.9.1–17 (cf. Momigliano, *Historiography*, 71–73); Livy, *History* 1.pref.10.

105. Laistner, *Historians*, 6, 95; for discussion and nuancing, see Champion, "Aetolia," esp. 357–62.

106. E.g., Justin, *Epitome* 5.1.10–11; 9.3.10 and throughout.

107. E.g., Mason, *Josephus and New Testament*, 60–71, 77–81; cf. 196–98.

might also include stories that first circulated as imperial propaganda,[108] and they clearly included perspectives influenced by their political milieu.[109]

Historians often tried to evaluate character impartially.[110] Thus, despite Thucydides's biases as a participant in the Peloponnesian War, he proves surprisingly impartial.[111] Despite Polybius's pro-Roman *Tendenz*, he notes that he often praises both Romans and Carthaginians, though only so he can set before statesmen proper models for conduct.[112]

Although history is not always written by victors,[113] victory typically does affect its long-term preservation.[114] Nevertheless, historians often report sympathetically both sides of a conflict.[115] Lucian criticizes historians who praise their own leaders, while slandering the other side, as engaging merely in panegyric.[116] Herodotus, one of the earliest historians, criticizes Greek failings, praises Egyptians, and honors both Spartan and Athenian virtues.[117]

Nor were characters always simply stereotypes. Biographers included both "flat" and "round" characters.[118] A historian who focuses only on what is negative about a character can be accused of malice, unless this approach is necessary for the telling of the story.[119] Conversely, Callisthenes, though an eye-

---

108. See, e.g., Velleius Paterculus, *History* 2.80.3, on a putative event some sixty-six years earlier. The propaganda in 2.89.4–5 reflects the earliest sources (e.g., *Res Gestae* 6.35).

109. E.g., Velleius Paterculus, *History* 2.89.3.

110. See, e.g., Herodotus, *Histories* 2.4, 32, 50, 58, 77, 82 (and remarks in Meister, "Herodotus," 268); Dionysius of Halicarnassus, *Roman Antiquities* bk. 3; 9.39.1–6; Livy, *History* 21.1.3; Velleius Paterculus, *History* 2.18.1; cf. Marincola, "Speeches," 119.

111. On whose biases, cf. Wade-Gery, "Thucydides," 1519, adding, "Perhaps no good historian is impartial." Dionysius of Halicarnassus, *Letter to Gnaeus Pompeius* 3, thinks Thucydides more biased (in his case, against Athens, which had exiled him) than Herodotus was; but Dionysius accuses him of focusing on Athens' failings, not of inventing them.

112. Polybius, *Histories* 9.9.9–10.

113. Note, e.g., Josephus's *Jewish War*; Manetho's *Aegyptiaca*; Xenophon's *Anabasis*; Athenian writers after the Peloponnesian War; cf. Pompeians in Melchior, "Pompey" (not all voices in the early empire were positive even about Augustus; see Davis, "Evaluations").

114. For history "written by the winners" among Roman historians, see, e.g., Feldherr, "Translation," 390.

115. E.g., Dionysius of Halicarnassus, *Roman Antiquities* bk. 3 (Albans); 9.39.1–6; Livy, *History* 21.1.3; Velleius Paterculus, *History* 2.18.1; cf. also the speeches noted in Marincola, "Speeches," 119.

116. Lucian, *How to Write History* 7.

117. Meister, "Herodotus," 268. This approach did not commend him to everyone (cf., e.g., Plutarch, *Malice of Herodotus*).

118. Burridge, *Gospels*, 177–79.

119. Plutarch, *Malice of Herodotus* 3, *Moralia* 855C.

witness, reported only Alexander's heroism, hence was dismissed by posterity as a flatterer,[120] since the other side of Alexander was already well-known.

Partisan agendas were not limited to politics, also appearing among schools of thought.[121] Biographers also wrote at times for apologetic and polemical purposes.[122] Likewise, historians, and particularly historians belonging to subjugated or despised peoples, composed apologetic historiography.[123]

7.6b. Historians' Moral Agendas

Those who distinguish ancient biography from ancient historiography on the assumption that only the former offered moral lessons display their lack of knowledge about ancient historiography. Historians may have tended to highlight political interests more whereas biographers tended to highlight ethical interests more,[124] but such interests inevitably overlapped.

The moral agenda constituted a paramount element of ancient historiography; one taught history not simply to memorialize the past but to draw lessons from it.[125] Although moral agendas were common to many genres,[126] they characterized ancient historiography far more often than they characterized novels.[127] Some historians, such as Thucydides, were more interested in raising moral questions than in answering them.[128] Most historians, however, sought to communicate some moral lessons through their historical accounts.[129]

120. Brown, *Historians*, 125.

121. Cf., e.g., Eshleman, "Sophists," on biographies of sophists.

122. Burridge, *Gospels*, 147, 183; for apologetic autobiography, cf., e.g., Josephus, *Life* 336–67; 2 Cor 11:8–33; Gal 1:11–24; discussion in Lyons, *Autobiography*.

123. Sterling, *Historiography*, 103–310; see also Sterling, "Appropriation," 234–38; Wandrey, "Literature," 696; cf. Meiser, "Gattung."

124. Hägg, *Biography*, 273.

125. See Fornara, *Nature*, 115–16; Lang, *Kunst*, 7–13, 97–167 (esp. note problem-solving strategies in Sallust and Tacitus, 108–37). For moralizing elements in ancient historiography, Marguerat, *Histoire*, 28–29, cites examples from Dionysius, Livy, Sallust, and Plutarch. See, e.g., Livy's use of the legendary Romulus as an example (Stem, "Lessons").

126. See extended treatment in Keener, *Acts*, 1:152–53.

127. They were rare in novels except those modeled on historical figures; for those, see Karla, "*Life of Aesop*," 58–59; Chance, "Fiction," 138–39; Beck, "Demonax," 81.

128. Pelling, *Texts*, 100.

129. Cf., e.g., Chaplin, "Conversations"; Bosworth, *Arrian*, 155; McInerney, "Arrian and Romance"; Galinsky, "Introduction," 4, 21; Gowing, "Memory," 43–48, esp. 46–47 (on Livy, *History* pref.9–10, and Tacitus, *Agricola* 46.3–4); Becker, *Birth*, 23. Note Kelhoffer, "Maccabees at Prayer," on application-driven differences between 1 and 2 Maccabees.

History, ancients opined, preserves the memory of honorable or shameful acts for posterity and moral instruction.[130] As Edwin Judge observes, "The ancient historians . . . took it for granted that remembering the good and evil deeds of others was morally instructive."[131] Or as Jörg Rüpke emphasizes, "Exemplarity is by no means necessarily opposed to history"; it simply finds lessons in the past with values considered consistent with "continuing normativity."[132]

No less a careful ancient historian than Polybius begins his multivolume history by observing its utilitarian value: people "have no more ready corrective of conduct than knowledge of the past."[133] History alone can prepare us for crises without us having to experience them firsthand, he notes;[134] it provides strategies, warnings and other instruction.[135] Sometimes Polybius explicitly digresses to give lessons related to the events narrated.[136] He "treasured history as a sound inferential basis for present and future political activity."[137]

Likewise, Tacitus, one of our most reliable historical sources for the early empire, viewed exposing vice and praising virtue as his historical obligation.[138] He emphasizes that the study of honorable persons promotes virtue;[139] he omits material not of value to history's moral objective[140] and freely editorializes when he thinks it appropriate.[141] Lucian, a stickler for historical accuracy, nevertheless values moral lessons in historiography, provided they flow from truth.[142]

The same can be said for other writers about the past, for example:

130. E.g., Herodotus, *Histories* 1.1.pref.; Polybius, *Histories* 7.12; Diodorus Siculus, *Library of History* 10.3.1; 11.11.2, 6; 11.38.6; 15.1.1; 17.38.4; Justin, *Epitome* pref.4. History also records what is unusual; see, e.g., Thucydides, *History* 1.23.1–3; Polybius, *Histories* 1.1; 1.37; Diodorus Siculus, *Library of History* 11.11.2; 11.59.1; 11.61.7; 12.38.1; cf. 11.89.8; 12.17.3.

131. Judge, *First Christians*, 249; see also 250–51.

132. Rüpke, "Knowledge," 93–94, here esp. 94.

133. Polybius, *Histories* 1.1.1 (LCL).

134. Polybius, *Histories* 1.1; 1.35.

135. Polybius, *Histories* 1.57.

136. Polybius, *Histories* 1.35.1–10.

137. Fornara, *Nature*, 113, noting (115–16) that Romans emphasized this benefit even more.

138. Moore, "Introduction," xiii; Hadas, "Introduction," xvii–xix (noting the popular model of Livy); Laistner, *Historians*, 113–14 (citing *Annals* 2.65.1; 4.33.2), 123, 131–39 (criticizing his tendentiousness); Williams, "Germanicus" (addressing Tacitus's perspective in one work).

139. Tacitus, *Agricola* 1.

140. Tacitus, *Annals* 3.65.

141. Tacitus, *Annals* 4.33. In other cases, the ways he reports the accounts reveal his opinions as well as explicit asides would have (e.g., *Annals* 5.1–2; 14.39).

142. E.g., Lucian, *How to Write History* 59.

- The pre-Christian historian Dionysius of Halicarnassus felt that historians should choose a noble subject so their work would contribute to good moral character as well as to providing information[143]
- Valerius Maximus, a first-century collector of historical anecdotes, notes that history helps instruct "modern manners"[144]
- Writing in the first century, Velleius Paterculus even uses "an 'abstract catalogue of virtues and values'" to depict Tiberius's reign[145]
- The second-century intellectual orator Maximus of Tyre opines that history, by preserving memories of humanity, "guards its virtues"[146]

Historians frequently included even moralizing narrative asides to interpret history's meaning more directly for their readers, to illustrate the fulfillment of prophetic utterances, or to provide the author's perspective.[147] Jewish historiography was certainly no less interpretive.[148]

7.6c. The Value of Moral Examples

Historians felt that history provided moral instruction because the behavior of historical persons offered positive or negative moral examples. Roman emphasis on honor extended to posthumous memory, elevating further the importance of history as a means of preserving and perpetuating memory. Part of the point of history-writing, no less than that of biography, was honoring those who merit it, thus motivating meritorious acts.[149]

143. E.g., Dionysius of Halicarnassus, *Roman Antiquities* 1.2.1.

144. Valerius Maximus, *Memorable Doings and Sayings* 2.pref. (LCL); see further Rüpke, "Knowledge," 89.

145. Becker, *Birth*, 126, citing Velleius Paterculus, *History* 2.126.2–4.

146. Maximus of Tyre, *Philosophical Orations* 22.5 (trans. Trapp).

147. E.g., Polybius, *Histories* 1.35.1–10; Diodorus Siculus, *Library of History* 31.10.2; Dionysius of Halicarnassus, *Roman Antiquities* 7.65.2; Justin, *Epitome* 3.2.6; 12.3.12; 12.4.1; Velleius Paterculus, *History* 2.75.2; Cornelius Nepos, *On Great Generals* 16 (Pelopidas), 3.1; Tacitus, *Annals* 16.15; Arrian, *Alexander* 4.10.8; Dio Cassius, *Roman History* 1.5.4; characterizing asides throughout Velleius Paterculus (e.g., *History* 2.41.1–2; 2.66.3–5; 2.72.1–2; 2.91.2–3; 2.98.2–3). For narrative asides in histories and biographies, see Sheeley, *Asides*, 56–93; for Herodotus's judgments (e.g., *Histories* 1.34; 2.123.3; 4.205; 9.120), see Dewald, "Construction," 95; for Xenophon's, see Dewald, "Construction," 98; for Tacitus's, see Laistner, *Historians*, 139 (unhappily).

148. See, e.g., von Dobbeler, "Geschichte"; van der Kooij, "Death of Josiah"; Reinmuth, "Investitur"; Bergren, "Nehemiah"; Borgen, "Reviewing"; Derrenbacker, *Practices*, 93.

149. Pliny, *Letters* 5.8.1–2.

Historians, both Greek and Roman, thus considered whether characters merited praise or blame.[150] Some historians might criticize other historians for getting the mixture wrong,[151] but no one questioned whether history provided moral illustrations. Thus Polybius does not devalue praise and blame but insists that it be applied to the appropriate persons,[152] and only when recounting their behavior.[153] Even Lucian permitted it within careful bounds.[154] Historians' interest in these matters reflects the broader value assigned to imitating moral examples in antiquity.[155]

Historians generally believed that if one understood why events happened,[156] not merely historians but also statesmen[157] and orators[158] (both of which some of them were) could use these events and actions as precedents and guides for future decisions.[159]

Dionysius of Halicarnassus expressly lists three purposes for writing history: first, that the courageous will gain "immortal glory" that outlives them; second, that their descendants will recognize their own roots and seek to emulate their virtue; and finally, that he might show proper goodwill and gratitude toward those who provided him training and information.[160]

Similarly, Jewish interpreters in Greek understood biblical narratives as providing moral lessons: the writers recorded examples of virtue and vice for

150. See, e.g., Trompf, *Historiography*, 51; cf. Plümacher, *Geschichte*, 15–32; Plümacher, "Cicero und Lukas," 772–73.

151. Polybius, *Histories* 8.8.3–6, 8–9.

152. Polybius, *Histories* 3.4.1; 8.8.7. See also e.g., Dio Cassius, *Roman History* 1.1.1–2; Pliny, *Letters* 5.8.9–11; Lucian, *How to Write History* 8–9, 39–40; comments about Suetonius in Rolfe, "Introduction," xix.

153. Polybius, *Histories* 10.26.9.

154. Lucian, *How to Write History* 9.

155. Lysias, *Orations* 2.61, §196; Aeschines, *Embassy* 75–76. Thus some objected to (Dio Chrysostom, *Orations* 7.119; Philostratus, *Life of Apollonius* 4.2) or even censored (Valerius Maximus, *Memorable Doings and Sayings* 2.6.7b) immoral mimes that could teach wrong values by imitation; in fact, most mimes were vulgar (Friedländer, *Life*, 2:92).

156. See, e.g., Polybius, *Histories* 2.56.13; 3.32.2. Ancient historians did not, as some contend, ignore lines of cause and effect (Rajak, *Josephus*, 102).

157. Dionysius of Halicarnassus, *Roman Antiquities* 5.56.1; Polybius, *Histories* 3.31.11–13.

158. See, e.g., Dionysius of Halicarnassus, *Roman Antiquities* 6.80.1; *Rhetoric to Alexander* 8.1429a.21–1430a.13; Cicero, *On Defense of Sestius* 48.102; cf. also Kennedy, "Survey," 21.

159. On such historical "paradigms," see also Diodorus Siculus, *Library of History* 37.4.1; Herodian, *History* 3.13.3; on both past and present paradigms, cf. Velleius Paterculus, *History* 2.92.5.

160. Dionysius of Halicarnassus, *Roman Antiquities* 1.6.3–5; cf. Diodorus Siculus, *Library of History* 15.1.1; 37.4.1. Cf. Roman *exempla* in Petitfils, "Tale," 154–58; Gunderson, "Augustus."

their successors to emulate or avoid.[161] They could also employ postbiblical models for virtues.[162] Because Josephus repeats so much of the biblical narrative in the *Antiquities*, one can frequently observe the way he adapts biblical characters to accentuate their value as moral models.[163]

7.6d. Historians' "Theology"

Many historians displayed theological perspectives. Contrary to some modern interpretations of ancient historiography, some ancient historians did think in terms of cause and effect, though not all of these causes were divine.[164] Historians' moral illustrations, social commentary in speeches, and political interests often reveal their distinctive philosophic and theological perspectives.[165]

It is particularly important for understanding the Gospels that most ancient historians also sought to interpret the divine will in some patterns in history.[166] Oracles and omens were said to reveal Rome's divine destiny,[167] and oracles could function as plot-moving devices.[168] Escapes could be attributed to deities,[169] and history's lessons include the need for piety toward the gods.[170] Elsewhere historians often emphasize deities punishing violations of temples, for example.[171]

161. Philo, *Abraham* 4; Josephus, *Against Apion* 2.204; 1 Cor 10:11. On Abraham as *exemplum* in Philo and Josephus, cf. Reed, "Construction" (contrasting Testament of Abraham).

162. E.g., 4 Macc 1:7–8.

163. See extended documentation in Keener, *Acts*, 1:154–55, esp. nn. 50–63.

164. E.g., Polybius, *Histories* 2.56.13; 3.6.1–3.7.3; 3.31.11–13; 3.32.2. For many events, multiple complementary causes are possible (Pelling, *Texts*, 88).

165. Cf. causation by Fortune or deities in Nicolaus, *Augustus* 23 (*FGrH* 130); Tacitus in *Annals* 3.18; Hadas, "Introduction," xvi; Fortune in Polybius in Walbank, "Fortune"; see also Becker, *Birth*, 128, citing Polybius, *Histories* 1.4; Tacitus, *Annals* 6.22.1.

166. See, e.g., Justin, *Epitome* 24.3.10; Appian, *Roman History* 7.8.53; esp. Squires, *Plan*; Squires, "Plan"; Shauf, *Divine*. Of course, they did so less than priests and prophets; cf. Balentine, "Future," 146–51.

167. E.g., the interpretation of a head found beneath Rome (Dionysius of Halicarnassus, *Roman Antiquities* 4.59.2; 4.61.2; Plutarch, *Camillus* 31.4; Dio Cassius, frag., in Zonaras, *Extracts of History* 7.11).

168. E.g., Apollodorus, *Epitome* 5.10; Ps.-Callisthenes, *Alexander Romance* 1.30, 33; Xenophon, *Ephesiaca* 1.6–7; *Apollonius King of Tyre* 48; Bonz, *Past as Legacy*, 192; in historiography, e.g., Justin, *Epitome* 6.2.4–5; 7.1.7–8; 7.6.1–2; 12.2.3; 20.3.2–3; Velleius Paterculus, *History* 2.24.3; 2.57.2; Suetonius, *Julius* 81; Squires, *Plan*, 121–29; Walbank, "Fortune," 350–54.

169. Xenophon, *Anabasis* 5.2.24.

170. Dionysius of Halicarnassus, *Roman Antiquities* 8.56.1.

171. E.g., Polybius, *Histories* 31.9.1–4; 32.15.14; Diodorus Siculus, *Library of History* 14.63.1;

Strange as it seems to many readers today, through much of the past people believed that recognizable patterns existed in history.[172] Hellenistic historians perceived providence in history,[173] as did Josephus.[174] Luke's understanding of God's providential guidance of the early Christian movement closely fits the programmatic role of providence found in some other Hellenistic historians.[175]

Early Christians expected to learn theology not so much from abstractions as from history, since they inherited Jewish Scripture (Rom 15:4; 1 Cor 10:6, 11).[176] Even most Hellenistic Jewish intellectuals viewed most of Scripture as both historically and theologically true.[177] Apart from Apuleius's second-century *Metamorphoses*, few novels shared the religious propagandistic function found in much Jewish historiography, perhaps simply because a polytheistic environment could take polytheism for granted.[178] Interest in history distinguished most Jews and first-century Christians from circles such as mystery cults.[179]

14.69.4; 14.76.3; 16.58.6; 27.4.3; Cornelius Nepos, *On Great Generals* 17 (Agesilaus), 4.8; Justin, *Epitome* 2.12.8–10; 24.6.4–5, 8–16; 28.3.5–8; Valerius Maximus, *Memorable Doings and Sayings* 1.1.18–21; 1.1.ext.3 (posthumously); 1.ext.5; Livy, *History* 42.28.12; Pliny, *Natural History* 33.24.83; Appian, *Roman History* 3.12.1–2; Babrius, *Fables* 78; Phaedrus, *Fables* 4.11.1–13; Lucian, *Zeus Rants* 24, 32; Pausanias, *Description of Greece* 3.23.5; 9.33.6; 9.39.12; Quintilian, *Declamations* 323 intro; Athenaeus, *The Learned Banqueters* 12.523ab; cf. Cicero, *Against Verres* 2.5.72.184–89; 2 Macc 3:25–26; Josephus, *Jewish Antiquities* 12.358–59.

172. Frei, "Apologetics," 56, notes that this view was also influential in eighteenth-century England.

173. Squires, "Plan," 38; Squires, *Plan*, 15–17, 38–46; Balch, "Genre," 10–11; Marguerat, *Histoire*, 36–37; cf. Downing, "Theism"; Downing, "Common Ground"; sometimes Polybius (Walbank, "Fortune"); pace Pervo, *Profit*, 83, 123, 129. Hellenistic historiographers of Rome did seem less emphatic about the divine plan for Rome's destiny (e.g., Justin, *Epitome* 43.2.5) than were some Romans (Pelling, "Historians of Rome," 257–58).

174. Squires, *Plan*, 18–20, 46–51; Derrenbacker, *Practices*, 93.

175. Squires, *Plan*, 20–36, 52–77; Brawley, *Centering*, 86–106; Marguerat, *Histoire*, 59–61.

176. Some argue that the Christian theology of history provided the first serious *philosophy* of (and teleology for) historiography (Nicolai, "Place," 17–18).

177. E.g., Philo, *Creation* 1–2.

178. Some question the religious propagandistic function even of Apuleius, noting his satirical emphasis (Hofmann, "Novels: Latin," 844; Murgatroyd, "Ending"; Libby, "Moons"). I am not denying religious *content* in such novels; that was part of the cultural landscape, and sometimes also necessary for the climactic *deus ex machina*.

179. Metzger, "Considerations," 15, 19–20; cf. Martin, "Mithraism"; Blomberg, "Mithras," 79.

7.7. Editorial Perspectives and "True" History

Ancient biographers and historians could present the same information from the standpoint of strikingly different evaluations.[180] Because of the authors' different emphases, for example, pictures of Alexander's character diverge starkly in surviving sources, in ways far beyond the more moderately different portraits of Jesus's essential character in the Gospels.[181]

A range of interpretive variation, however, is not surprising. Even today, different biographers frequently offer divergent perspectives on their subjects in their selective narrations.[182] Dunn points to the varying estimates of Winston Churchill and Margaret Thatcher today as examples,[183] or varied attempts to "explain" the evil of Adolf Hitler.[184] Laistner points to how it took perhaps a century for British and US historians to be "fair to both sides" regarding "the American Revolution."[185] Biographers exercised even greater editorial and compositional freedom in earlier eras.[186] Even today, no historian can escape subjective bias; but a perspective concerning events does not discount the information about the events that historians include.[187]

Similarly, even news outlets in different countries (and sometimes in the same country) select and "spin" news in very different ways,[188] but the vast majority of free media still use genuine data. Authors write from particular perspectives, and readers evaluate their perspectives (e.g., theodicy for the gods, capitalism, or globalism) from our own perspectives (e.g., Enlighten-

---

180. See, e.g., Ytterbrink, *Gospel*, 89.

181. See Lee, "Source Criticism," 209–10, contrasting the primarily virtuous and primarily drunken portraits of Alexander.

182. Postmodern historians rightly note that while historians may correctly include facts, their selection and framing of material reflect particular perspectives. For one discussion of the strengths and weaknesses of postmodern historiography, favoring critical realism in approaching the Gospels, see Licona, *Resurrection*, 71–89. Before the postmodern turn, Caird already distinguished between events' actuality and their significance, noting that "no historical statement is purely referential" (Caird, *Language*, 201–2).

183. Dunn, *Acts*, xvi.

184. Dunn, *Remembered*, 185.

185. Laistner, *Historians*, 95. For varied applications of Francis Asbury (some quite one-sided), see Wigger, *Saint*, 405–18.

186. See Tomkins, *Wilberforce*, 15–16, on editorial shaping, and 16–17, on the genuineness of included recollections.

187. Marshall, *Historian*, 47, critiquing Perrin for his outdated understanding of historiography. Judge, "Sources," 280–81, even challenges the disengaged, depersonalizing preference of much modern (as opposed to ancient) historiography as unrealistic.

188. See my complaint in "Did Not Know."

ment rationalism, Marxism, or nationalism). Recognizing writers' perspectives does not, however, require us to assume that they falsified their data. In Luke-Acts, for example, when Stephen (Acts 7:2–50) or Paul (Acts 13:17–37) preach from biblical history, their retellings are selective but substantially correct rehearsals of the tradition that they narrate.

Ancient historians communicated moral, political, or theological points on the basis of stories that they believed to be true (or at least time-honored). One could produce an abstract or epideictic treatise without composing it in the historical genre, though even such treatises often used historical examples.[189] As Geza Vermes points out, "A theological interest is no more incompatible with a concern for history than is a political or philosophical conviction," and we can allow for these interests in interpretation.[190]

The same is true for apologetic interests.[191] Various Near Eastern peoples, especially priests guarding their sacred traditions, felt a need to respond to Hellenism's cultural imperialism,[192] frequently doing so by means of apologetic historiography.[193] Hellenistic Jewish historians thus reshaped their traditions in more Hellenistic forms to stress Judaism's greatness and antiquity.[194] Philo's *Flaccus* is probably a short example of Jewish apologetic historiography.[195]

The fullest example is Josephus's *Jewish Antiquities*, emphasizing God's providence in Israel's history.[196] He seeks to vindicate the Jewish God vis-à-vis Roman gods or Fortune, showing after the loss of 70 CE that the defeat belonged to God's plan.[197] For example, Josephus's story about Moses may challenge Alexandrian anti-Jewish propaganda influential in Rome.[198]

189. 4 Maccabees blends stories from 2 Maccabees with moral instruction.

190. Vermes, *Jesus and Judaism*, 19–20; cf. Levinskaya, *Setting*, 2; Hemer, *Acts*, 79–90.

191. As with Josephus; see Sterling, *Historiography*, 103–310.

192. E.g., Berossus (cf. Kuhrt, "Mesopotamia," 62–63; Dillery, "Historians," 222–25) and Manetho (Dillery, "Historians," 225–28); see further Sterling, "Historians," 502.

193. Sterling, *Historiography*, 103–36 (though cf. Dillery, "Historians," 228–30).

194. Sterling, *Historiography*, 137–225; see also Sterling, "Appropriation," 234–38; Harrington, "Bible," 245; Wandrey, "Literature," 696.

195. See Meiser, "Gattung." Its discourses help support this conclusion.

196. Sterling, *Historiography*, 226–310. More generally, others also emphasize Josephus's apologetic objectives (e.g., Feldman, "Apologist"; in defending himself, Vogel, "Vita"; Lamour, "Organisation").

197. See, e.g., Kelley, "Perspective."

198. See Hata, "Moses."

7.8. Concerns for Historical Information

Although historians adapted material, filled in speeches and sought to instill morals, they did not normally invent events in their sources. Even those that accused others of extensive embellishment rarely accused them of inventing battles and the like.

7.8a. Historians' Concern for Accuracy?

Contrary to what some have argued, ancient historians generally did care about accuracy regarding events and evaluated fellow historians accordingly.[199] They did not deem factual and rhetorical goals incompatible so long as rhetoric was kept within appropriate bounds.[200] Of course, not all historians agreed as to how much was appropriate, nor were all of them equally careful. Tacitus,[201] Herodotus, and Thucydides followed their material more carefully than, for example, Strabo or Plutarch.[202] But even Caesar, plainly writing from his own, honor-hungry perspective, did not likely deliberately falsify evidence.[203]

Ancient historians and their audiences expected the following features of history-writing, notwithstanding rhetorical embellishments:

- History was supposed to be truthful.[204]
- The historian must provide unmixed truth.[205]
- Historians therefore harshly criticized other historians whom they ac-

---

199. See, e.g., Mosley, "Reporting," 26; Fornara, *Nature*, 61; Hemer, *Acts*, 63–70; Byrskog, *Story*, 179–84; see, e.g., Josephus, *Jewish Antiquities* 20.156–57; cf. *Life* 336–39. On how history was written, see also Keener, *John*, 17–25; Keener, *Acts*, 1:116–65, much of which I have also incorporated into the larger discussion here.

200. See Byrskog, *Story*, 213, 223; esp. Rothschild, *Rhetoric*, throughout.

201. Laistner, *Historians*, 121; Mosley, "Reporting," 20–22; Pelling, "Historiography," 716; Hadas, "Introduction," xviii.

202. Mosley, "Reporting," 12–14, 16; for Greek historians in general, see 11–18.

203. Laistner, *Historians*, 36–38. Historians drew on earlier historians critically, but usually with the expectation that they reported historical facts, this being their understanding of their genre (Lendon, "Historians," 54).

204. E.g., Josephus, *Against Apion* 1.26; *Jewish Antiquities* 20.156–57; Dionysius of Halicarnassus, *Thucydides* 8.

205. Josephus, *Jewish Antiquities* 8.56.

cused of promoting falsehood, especially when they believed that they exhibited self-serving agendas.[206]

- To a lesser extent, they critiqued those who unknowingly got their facts wrong.[207]
- More damagingly, a writer who consistently presented the least favorable interpretation, ignoring the diverse views of his sources, could be accused of malice.[208]
- The goal of history, unlike myth, is purely truth.[209]
- Even a particularly rhetorically focused, pre-Christian historian, writing essays on earlier historians' rhetoric, might emphasize the importance of truth-telling,[210] insisting that a careful historian's literary skill "does not excuse history from such exaggeration"[211] and that history involves truth rather than legends, and that one should pursue facts, "neither adding to nor subtracting from" them.[212]
- In the early empire, Tacitus warns against comparing his sober history with implausible rumors and fictions.[213]

Some suppose that historians' claims to pursue accuracy were merely a literary convention of historians. Yet, while some writers parodied this convention and some earlier historians embellished freely[214] and even some his-

---

206. Josephus, *Life* 336–39; Diodorus Siculus, *Library of History* 21.17.1; Lucian, *How to Write History* 24–25; see esp. discussion of Polybius below. Those who claimed the superiority of their own works, however, could risk the charge of impudence from detractors (Josephus, *Life* 359); the charge of falsehood served polemical agendas well.

207. Diodorus Siculus, *Library of History* 1.37.4, 6.

208. So Plutarch, *Malice of Herodotus* 3–7, *Moralia* 855C–856B (though see rightly here Penner, *Praise*, 169); cf. Dionysius of Halicarnassus, *Letter to Gnaeus Pompeius* 3, on Thucydides's grudge against Athens.

209. Polybius, *Histories* 34.4.2–3. Saïd, "Myth," 85, notes Polybius's refusal to recount myth (see, e.g., Polybius, *Histories* 2.16.13–15; 4.40.2; 9.2.1; 12.24.5), though he reports critically some local legends connected with myth (4.43.6) and accepts some historical basis behind legends (34.2.4, 9–11). For further discussion of Polybius's high ideal standards, see Keener, *Acts*, 1:124–26.

210. Dionysius of Halicarnassus, *Thucydides* 55; cf. Josephus, *Jewish Antiquities* 8.56; 20.156–57.

211. Dionysius of Halicarnassus, *Thucydides* 19 (LCL 1:512–13); see Thucydides, *History* 1.1.1–2; 1.21.2; 1.23.1–2. For some other cases of hyperbole in historical writing, see Thucydides 8.96.1 (cf. 2.94.1); Polybius, *Histories* 1.4.5; Tacitus, *Histories* 1.2.

212. Dionysius of Halicarnassus, *Thucydides* 8 (LCL 1:478–79); this is an ideal, not the writer's exceptionless practice.

213. Tacitus, *Annals* 4.11.

214. Lucian's proto–science fiction/fantasy *True Story* remains humorous today, but ev-

torians in the early empire failed to live up to the aspirations expressed in such claims, historians were not alone in this demand for correct information in historiography.[215]

- The geographer Pausanias explicitly distinguishes historical research from childhood knowledge of choruses and tragedies.[216]
- Aristotle distinguishes "history" and "poetry" not by their literary style, since one could put Herodotus into verse if one wished; but history recounts what actually happened, whereas poetry (i.e., epic poetry and drama) recounts what might happen.[217]
- Thus, for Aristotle, poetry is more philosophical, conveying general truths, whereas history conveys specific facts.[218]
- In the first century BCE, Cicero recognized the standard expectation for historians to avoid falsehood and partiality.[219]
- The first-century CE rhetorician Quintilian divides narrative into (1) epic poetry and tragedy, which differs from current reality;[220] (2) com-

---

eryone would have recognized it as parody on works more fantastic than the Gospels or the mainstream biographies addressed here (cf. discussion in Keener, *Acts*, 1:76–77); cf. discussion in Tamiolaki, "Satire." Lucian plays even with the pseudonyms of those he critiques (such as Ctesias), if he does not invent them entirely; cf. Ní-Mheallaigh, *Fiction*, 150n27. But while Ctesias seems fanciful about India and Assyria, some of even his ingenuity might come from Persian tales, and Ephorus may have more substance than one would gather from Polybius (Schepens, "History," 50–51).

215. Thucydides (a careful historian by our standards) remained a primary model (see Marincola, "Speeches," 123–27; Croke, "Historiography," 567–68; for rhetorical reasons, cf. Kennedy, "Source Criticism," 145–46).

216. Pausanias, *Description of Greece* 1.3.3 (LCL 1:15, 17).

217. Aristotle, *Poetics* 9.2, 1451b; cf. Thucydides, *History* 1.21.1; Pliny, *Letters* 9.33.1; Lucian, *How to Write History* 8, 22; Menander Rhetor, *Epideictic Treatises* 1.1.333.31–1.1.334.5; Becker, *Birth*, 91 (cf. 121); Adams, *Genre*, 47; even Isocrates, *Euagoras* 10, 21, 36, in Ytterbrink, *Gospel*, 76. For history recounted in epic poetic form, as in Ennius's *Annales*, see Cicero, *On the Laws* 1.2.5 (Galinsky, "Introduction," 5). Herodotus does evoke some "epic conventions from Homer" (Knoppers, "Problem," 17, following Bratt, "Monarchs"); Homer offered the dominant narrative model of his era.

218. Aristotle, *Poetics* 9.3, 1451b. See also Momigliano, *Development*, 66, citing *Poetics* 9, 23. Historical discourse differed from others (e.g., forensic rhetoric or philosophy; see, e.g., [Philostratus] *Epistles of Apollonius* 19).

219. Laistner, *Historians*, 33–35, citing Cicero, *Letters to Friends* 5.12; *Letters to Atticus* 2.1.2; Fornara, *Nature*, 138–39, citing Cicero, *On the Orator* 2.15.62–63. When Cicero requests a eulogy of himself, he recognizes that this does not follow the historiographic convention of impartiality.

220. Most epic poetry and tragedy addressed the distant mythological or legendary past.

edy, which plays on realism; and (3) history, "which is an exposition of something done."[221]

- Likewise, Quintilian suggests being ready to provide illustrations both from history and from the fictional genre of poetry;[222] historians provide genuine facts.[223]
- The second-century satirist Lucian is particularly emphatic:
  - History employs rules "different from poetry and poems," which can blame their excesses on inspiration.[224]
  - True history must not include the slightest lies;[225] its utility comes from truth alone.[226]
  - Only bad historians invent data.[227]
  - The historian must recount only what happened, sacrificing to no deity except Truth.[228]
  - Truth "is the one thing peculiar to history," he noted; one writing history must ignore all other concerns.[229]
  - The historian must be faithful to truth, not flattery.[230]

The perspectives of Pliny the Younger (61–113 CE) are instructive. He was not a historian himself, hence was not simply following polite literary convention, the idea that some use to dismiss historians' claims about their own work. Ideal subjects for history offer original and interesting material, he opines, but only so long as the material is based on genuine facts.[231] History's primary goal, he recognizes, is truth and accuracy rather than rhetorical display.[232]

Of course, ancient historical standards demonstrate only that others would evaluate historians by this ideal, not that they always lived up to it.[233] Historians who should have known what happened sometimes gave quite dif-

221. Quintilian, *Orator's Education* 2.4.2, in Collins, *Mark*, 35.

222. Quintilian, *Orator's Education* 12.4.1 in Becker, *Birth*, 62.

223. Quintilian, *Orator's Education* 10.1.34 in Becker, *Birth*, 62.

224. Lucian, *How to Write History* 8 (trans. LCL 6:13).

225. Lucian, *How to Write History* 7.

226. Lucian, *How to Write History* 9.

227. E.g., Lucian, *How to Write History* 24–25.

228. Lucian, *How to Write History* 39.

229. Lucian, *How to Write History* 40 (LCL 6:55).

230. Lucian, *How to Write History* 62.

231. Pliny, *Letters* 8.4.1. For the emphasis on facts in ancient historiography, see also Byrskog, *Story*, 179–84.

232. Pliny, *Letters* 7.17.3. Accuracy was praiseworthy (5.5.3; 5.8.5; cf. 9.19.5).

233. Rightly, Eve, *Behind Gospels*, 141.

ferent reports.[234] Still, historical objectives contrast starkly with the lack of any such objectives in fictional works. Their interpretive biases and other frailties do not prevent our use of the significant information they actually contain.[235]

Because their works were public, historical standards did limit gratuitous errors. Major deviations without good reason from what was already known would undermine an author's claims.[236] Those thought guilty of inadequate research or lack of firsthand acquaintance with their reports were likely to be doubted.[237] Historians criticized other historians when they appeared to fail such tests.[238]

Hellenistic Jewish historians also valued historical information. Beyond speeches, even Josephus "does not create events or incidents, either out of his head or by midrashic exposition."[239] Even much-maligned 2 Maccabees[240] includes much historical information; as a condensation of Jason of Cyrene's work, the author is probably not inventing many new scenes, even if his Jason or earlier storytellers had added some. Second Maccabees may be independent from 1 Maccabees yet shows some major points of agreement with it.[241] Although we must allow for some hyperbole in Maccabean literature[242] as well as some likely errors or adaptations,[243] external evidence confirms some of the claims in 2 Maccabees.[244]

234. See, e.g., Almagor, "Narratives," 70, citing Plutarch, *Artaxerxes* 1.4; 6.9; 19.2–6 on his sources.

235. See esp. Grant, *Historians*; Schröter, *Jesus to New Testament*, 56–60, citing Ricoeur to qualify Johannes Fried (treated on 53–55).

236. Eve, *Behind Gospels*, 142.

237. Thucydides, *History* 1.20.3; Arrian, *Indica* 7.1.

238. E.g., Dio Cassius, *Roman History* 1.1.1–2; Herodian, *History* 1.1.1–2.

239. Downing, "Redaction Criticism 1," 55–56 (cf. also 60), quoted also in Derrenbacker, *Practices*, 93. Occasionally Josephus seems to have had access to archives, though many were destroyed (*Jewish War* 2.427; Yamauchi, "Archives," 80).

240. Penner, *Praise*, 136–37, notes that while everyone acknowledges 1 Maccabees as history, the measure of history and fiction in 2 Maccabees is debated. (By contrast, 3 Maccabees is universally agreed to be a novel; see, e.g., Johnson, "Fictions"; Hacham, "Polemic"; Mélèze-Modrzejewski, "Loi.")

241. See Reynolds, "Difference." Some scholars view it as refuting 1 Macc; it might, however, simply offer a Diaspora perspective on the same period (see Simkovich, "Influence"). Some scholars today reject even much of 1 Maccabees as fiction, but sometimes by unnecessarily treating religious narrative and historical information as incompatible.

242. See Hilbert, "Enemies"; arguments for exaggerations by the epitomizer in 2 Maccabees in Morrison, "Composition."

243. Cf. Rappaport, "Heliodoros," finding a core but also changes in 2 Macc 3.

244. Gera, "Olympiodoros"; cf. Jones, "Inscription"; Shanks, "Inscription."

History was supposed to be truthful, which does not tell us the extent to which it, and especially to which a given historian, was constrained by prior information. We can test the degree of fixity and flexibility in some historians, however, by comparing them with their sources where those remain extant, as with some Gospels. For concretely mapping information content and flexibility, see chapters 10–11 below.

7.8b. Investigation[245]

Although Greek historians had their weaknesses, primary research was one of their strengths.[246] Even the Greek term often used for research or investigation, ἱστορία (*historia*), indicates what many from an early period regarded as historiography's central characteristic: questioning those with firsthand knowledge before weaving their responses into a cohesive narrative.[247] Greek historians often traveled to the locations of events and consulted those whom they considered reliable oral sources.[248]

Herodotus, who traveled widely, initiated this emphasis on research;[249] Thucydides, who cross-examined his sources, assumes this approach as the standard.[250] Diodorus Siculus claims to have consulted records[251] and to have visited many of the relevant sites.[252] Although most of the subjects for Phi-

---

245. I take material here from Keener, *Acts*, 1:183–88.

246. Meister, "Historiography: Greece," 421.

247. Fornara, *Nature*, 47. See also Aune, *Environment*, 81–82, noting the interviewing of eyewitnesses (Polybius, *Histories* 4.2.2); other sources, when traveling to the scenes in question (Herodotus, *Histories* 2.52; Polybius, *Histories* 3.48.12; 4.38.11; 10.11.4) and reading accounts of eyewitnesses (Polybius, *Histories* 28.4.8; 38.4.8). The practice weighs more than the terminology; Schepens, "History," 39–40, notes this concept of *historia* (see also 47), but on 41–42 notes modern disagreements about it.

248. Aune, *Environment*, 81, citing Herodotus, *Histories* 2.52; Polybius, *Histories* 3.48.12; 4.38.11; 10.11.4; see also Plutarch, *Demosthenes* 2.1–2; Appian, *Roman History* pref.12. Even for the distant past, ancients sometimes found local oral sources that purported to have survived over the centuries (e.g., Pausanias, *Description of Greece* 1.23.2), though their reliability is much more in question (Pretzler, "Pausanias and Tradition"); for tenacious preservation of *local* traditions, Aune, "Prolegomena," 93, cites, e.g., Pausanias, *Description of Greece* 8.26.6; 8.29.1; 8.38.2; 8.42.1–2.

249. Herodotus, *Histories* 1.1.

250. Thucydides, *History* 1.22.2; 5.26. Fornara, *Nature*, 47–48; Schepens, "History," 47–48.

251. Diodorus Siculus, *Library of History* 1.4.4–5.

252. Diodorus Siculus, *Library of History* 1.4.1 (though for Mesopotamia, see Oldfather, "Introduction to Diodorus," xiii).

lostratus's sophistic biographies were long deceased, he interviewed some who remained alive, even on multiple occasions.[253]

Polybius most fully articulates the strictest criteria for evaluating other historians. For him, investigation is "the *most* important part" of writing history.[254] This investigation consists especially of interviewing people, critically evaluating reports, and accepting what prove to be the most reliable sources.[255] He disparages those who depend only on written sources[256] instead of traveling to sites and interviewing witnesses.[257] Condemning writers who sought to make guesses sound plausible, Polybius also notes that in his research he had also come across documentary evidence.[258]

In practice, not all historians in this period traveled.[259] Because of senatorial records, Roman historians often had sufficient information for their interests without the need for field research,[260] and because Romans' interest was more in providing examples than history for its own sake, Roman historians sometimes appear less careful with facts than Greeks.[261] But in any case, the Greek practice dominated the eastern Mediterranean, from which the Gospels, written in Greek, hail.

---

253. Philostratus, *Lives of the Sophists* 2.23.606. On other occasions his research came up empty, but he incidentally confirms that he had done some (2.5.576).

254. Polybius, *Histories* 12.4c.3 (LCL 4:316–17). Polybius's emphasis on investigation appears throughout 12.4c.1–5.

255. Polybius, *Histories* 12.4c.4–5.

256. Cf. Polybius, *Histories* 12.25e.7; 12.25i.2.

257. Polybius, *Histories* 12.9.2; 12.25e.1. He thinks Timaeus mistaken, even when he did travel and consult witnesses (*Histories* 12.4d.1–2). This was also the research standard for forensic rhetoric, at least in principle (e.g., Lysias, *Orations* 23.2–8, §§166–67).

258. Polybius, *Histories* 3.33.17–18 (citing here a bronze tablet of Hannibal).

259. Consulting distant records would be even more difficult (cf. Ben Zeev, "Capitol").

260. Fornara, *Nature*, 56. Second-century sources (Aulus Gellius, *Attic Nights* 11.17; 13.20.1; Fronto, *To Marcus Caesar* 4.5) might suggest that in libraries slaves brought books to the scholars (Houston, "Library"). Apart from Athens (Aulus Gellius, 7.17.1–2), Rome, (later) Ephesus, and (earlier) Alexandria (e.g., Aulus Gellius 7.17.3), however, the majority of libraries were private ones (Aune, *Dictionary*, 273–75).

261. So Cary and Haarhoff, *Life*, 263. They sometimes focused more on "trends" than details (Fornara, *Nature*, 88–89). But even among Romans, dishonesty "was a gross evasion of the rules of historical responsibility" (Fornara, *Nature*, 135; cf. also Laistner, *Historians*, 16).

7.8c. Peer Review: Developing Consensus Standards

Peer review from fellow historical writers made getting one's facts right a matter of honor.[262] Inventing events (rather than merely embellishing relevant details) risked refutation and serious denunciation, making most guilty works unlikely to survive their patrons' prestige interests. Historians criticized other historians for being just five years off on a figure's age.[263] Some historians especially criticized predecessors who valued rhetorical framing above accurate information;[264] more gently, some claimed that their predecessors embellished or omitted some key matters only because they lacked sufficient information.[265] Less easy to avoid were charges of distorted perspectives,[266] since the accusers, of course, had perspectives of their own.

The ancient paragon of critical historiographic method is Polybius. Polybius denounces authors who sensationalize their story too much to make it more graphic and provide cohesiveness.[267] He condemns those who include hearsay about distant lands that cannot be verified.[268] He complains about one historian's often contradictory accounts and "careless statements."[269]

Polybius's invective against the rhetorical historian Timaeus[270] is unfairly harsh.[271] Nevertheless, it illustrates the demands for accuracy to which ancient historians could expect to be subjected by their severest peers. Polybius complains that Timaeus's work reveals that he was unacquainted with the location

262. See fuller discussion in Keener, *Acts*, 1:123–26; cf. Thucydides, *History* 1.20.3; Arrian, *Indica* 7.1; Lucian, *How to Write History* 10; many sources in Becker, *Birth*, 117. For ancient striving for honor, see, e.g., Williams, *Shame*; Barton, *Honor* (esp. 29–130); Barton, "Moment"; Jewett, "Shame," 551–57; in Jewish contexts, see deSilva, "Honor"; deSilva, "Wisdom."

263. Velleius Paterculus, *History* 2.53.4.

264. Dio Cassius, *Roman History* 1.1.1–2; Herodian, *History* 1.1.1–2.

265. Diodorus Siculus, *Library of History* 1.37.4, 6; Tacitus, *Agricola* 10.

266. E.g., Josephus, *Jewish War* 1.7.

267. Polybius, *Histories* 2.56.7, 10; 15.34.1. Polybius himself reports graphic bloodshed (15.33), but he claims that he avoids amplifying it (15.34). Contrast the criticism of Dionysius of Halicarnassus, *Thucydides* 15, that Thucydides sometimes fails to evoke the full horror of war.

268. Polybius, *Histories* 3.38.3.

269. Polybius, *Histories* 2.56.1–3. Penner, *Praise*, 153–55, rightly challenges Polybius's ethnic plausibility criterion.

270. Polybius, *Histories* 12.3.1–12.15.12.

271. Polybius impugns Timaeus's motives (*Histories* 12.7.6), critiques his biases (12.7.1; 12.15.12), and justifies Polybius's own harshness (12.4a.1). See further Penner, *Praise*, 118; Fornara, *Nature*, 48; Schepens, "History," 51–54; Vattuone, "Historiography," 196–99; cf. Marincola, "Speeches," 124–26; Brown, *Historians*, 151, 164.

about which he writes,[272] failed to investigate adequately,[273] and mixed up his facts even when he did investigate properly.[274] Even though most ancient writers mentioned sources only sparingly, Polybius accuses Timaeus of inventing any sources that he fails to identify.[275]

Yet the most important standards are wider historiographic standards that Timaeus himself shares in principle. He admits that falsehood is the worst vice in writing history and that those who write falsehood should find a different name for their book than history.[276] Both historians agree that it is not a work's form, but the truth of its content, that makes it history.[277] In the early empire historians continued to insist on such standards, at least for others.[278]

Hellenistic historians may have rarely met Polybius's standard (probably often including Polybius himself),[279] but most of our surviving examples remain rooted in genuine events. Moreover, Thucydides (also a careful historian by our standards) remained a primary model,[280] sometimes even for more rhetorically oriented historians.[281]

7.9. Historians Used Sources

Although many scholars rightly underscore the rhetorical side of ancient historiography, it is unfortunate that some who do so also count this form of presentation against its historical value. On the basis of that emphasis, some knowledgeable scholars write as if the line between history and fiction is fairly thin.[282]

---

272. Polybius, *Histories* 12.3.1–2.

273. Polybius, *Histories* 12.4c.2–5.

274. Polybius, *Histories* 12.4d.1–2.

275. Polybius, *Histories* 12.9.1–12.11.7.

276. Polybius, *Histories* 12.11.7–8. For Timaeus's own invective against his predecessors, see Marincola, *Authority*, 228–29.

277. Polybius, *Histories* 12.12.1–3.

278. Tacitus, *Histories* 1.1; cf. similarly Josephus, *Jewish Antiquities* 20.154, criticizing some of his contemporaries.

279. See Penner, *Praise*, 145, 157, and esp. 118; see my comments in *Acts*, 1:124n69.

280. See Marincola, "Speeches," 123–27; Croke, "Historiography," 567–68; Lucian, *How to Write History* 2, 18–19, 39, 42 (also noting Herodotus and Xenophon, 2, 18, 23, 39).

281. Josephus, *Jewish Antiquities*, in bks. 17–19 (Kennedy, "Source Criticism," 145–46), though he esp. imitates the rhetorical historian Dionysius of Halicarnassus (145, noting twenty books in each; Downing, "Redaction Criticism 1," 47). For Herodotean echoes in Arrian, see in Bosworth, "Pursuit," 447.

282. See, e.g., Penner, "Discourse," 72–73; Penner, *Praise*, 175 (cf. 6).

Yet neither perspectives nor rhetorical strategies precluded ancient historians from using primarily historical information.[283] Although they exercised freedom to select, adapt, and often embellish their material, ancient writers made explicit claims to the effect that their material itself should be factual.[284] This practice differs starkly from typical ancient novels.

7.9a. Examples of Source-Usage

Good historians expected other good historians to consult sources when possible,[285] a practice mandatory only in information-based writing. Historians usually had multiple sources.[286]

Herodotus and Thucydides were perhaps the two most widely read historians in antiquity,[287] and both wrote especially based on the information available to them. Ancient readers recognized that Herodotus wrote more for his audience's pleasure than Thucydides did;[288] his charm consisted especially in making his readers feel that they were reading stories rather than history.[289] Thucydides, however, had superior access to the events that he recorded, and he acquired a reputation for notably accurate history-writing.[290]

That Herodotus depends on prior information does not mean that all of that information is correct, nor does it mean that he correctly interpreted all of it. Herodotus sometimes misunderstood his oral sources in his travels, and

283. For the right balance, see, e.g., Rothschild, *Rhetoric*, throughout; Tucker, *Knowledge*, 254–62; Dewald, "Construction," 90–91, 101; Porciani, "Enigma," 333.

284. E.g., Aristotle, *Poetics* 9.2–3, 1451b; Dionysius of Halicarnassus, *Roman Antiquities* 1.1.2–4; 1.4.2; *Thucydides* 8; Pliny, *Letters*. 7.17.3; 8.4.1; 9.33.1; Tacitus, *Annals* 4.11; Lucian, *How to Write History* 12, 24–25; Josephus, *Against Apion* 1.26. Pliny the Younger knew both Suetonius and Tacitus and even tried to stage a guest appearance in the latter's history (*Letters* 7.33).

285. Polybius, *Histories* 12.25d.1 (though documents [as in Rhodes, "Documents," 64–65] mattered less than visiting locations and reviewing historical context; 12.25e.1, 25i.2).

286. See, e.g., Évrard, "Polybe."

287. At least insofar as we may infer from the number of copies preserved in Egypt; see Stephens, "Who Read Novels?," 411, 415–16. Josephus was sufficiently familiar with Thucydides to imitate him in *Jewish Antiquities* bks. 17–19 (Kennedy, "Source Criticism," 145–46). For Thucydides, see Lucian, *How to Write History* 2, 18–19, 39, 42; for Herodotus, see Lucian, *How to Write History* 2, 18, 42; for Xenophon, see Lucian, *How to Write History* 2, 23, 39.

288. See, e.g., Cueva, "Longus."

289. Dio Chrysostom, *Orations* 18.10.

290. Josephus, *Against Apion* 1.18.

he could not read other nations' written ones.[291] Yet even Herodotus, who mostly pioneered[292] the sort of ethnographic research he undertook, genuinely depended on prior information. His depiction of the eastern Mediterranean coastal regions fits what other sources reveal of these regions.[293] Against some more radical critics, Herodotus's vast array of citations scattered throughout his work demonstrates his genuine travels and research.[294] Herodotus also displays far less Hellenic bias than we might expect.[295]

Even the rhetorically focused, pre-Christian historian Dionysius of Halicarnassus emphasizes that historical inquiry requires not merely rhetorical skill but research.[296] By virtue of their trade, ancient historians depended on sources, whether oral interviews or earlier texts.[297] When their sources were written, they usually adapted or at least paraphrased them to make them their own.[298]

Where ancient historians and biographers do not cite their sources, modern scholars debate about what sources they may have used, including many that are now fragmentary or no longer extant.[299] Nepos's biography of Themistocles closely follows some sources that happen to remain extant even today, even though he cites them only rarely.[300] Sometimes even some later historians had access to information that some of their predecessors lacked or omitted.[301]

---

291. On his method, see, e.g., Meister, "Herodotus," 267 (cf. 2.28.1; 4.76.6; 8.65.6; 125.6); West, "Rhampsinitos," 327; Brown, *Historians*, 40.

292. See Cicero, *On the Laws* 1.1.5; Meister, "Herodotus," 269. Some compare Herodotus with the Pentateuch (Van Seters, "Primeval Histories"; cf. Van Seters, *Search*), despite considerable differences (Blenkinsopp, *Pentateuch*, 39–42).

293. Rainey, "Herodotus' Description." Archaeology has often surprisingly confirmed Herodotus's claims regarding Scythians and Persians (Yamauchi, *Persia*, 77–78, 96, 100, 141, 153, 160–61, 190).

294. Herodotus generally does not evaluate his sources, but neither does he invent them; see Meister, "Herodotus," 267–68; cf. Rhodes, "Documents," 57–58. For the interpretive level of Herodotus's discourse, see Darbo-Peschanski, "Origin," 30 (contrasting Thucydides, *History* 32); but for his anchoring in data as accurately as possible, see Schepens, "History," 42; for his pursuit of the most original sources, see Schepens, "History," 43–47; on his many oral sources, cf. Aune, "Prolegomena," 77–78.

295. See fully Meister, "Herodotus," 268–69.

296. Dionysius of Halicarnassus, *Roman Antiquities* 1.1.2–4; 1.4.2.

297. Derrenbacker, *Practices*, 52; Becker, *Birth*, 92.

298. Derrenbacker, *Practices*, 44–46; on 44, note esp. Dionysius of Halicarnassus, *Letter to Gnaeus Pompeius* 6.

299. See, e.g., Muntz, "Sources"; Muntz, "Diodorus Siculus"; Martin, "Tacitus," 1470; Rondholz, "Rubicon"; in ancient biography, Buszard, "Parallel."

300. Christian, "Themistocles."

301. Cf., e.g., Dionysius of Halicarnassus, *Roman Antiquities* 1.6.1, 3; in the rabbis, see,

Although, for reasons of style, historians did not acknowledge all their sources,[302] elite authors often felt constrained to indicate some of them,[303] especially if their elite readers might recognize them anyway. A historical writer who omitted information available to some of his predecessors might explain that he had read almost everything but did not judge it all suitable for inclusion.[304]

The Gospels do not identify specific sources for the gospel tradition, but any Gospel synopsis reveals that at least some Gospels used some sources. The Evangelists' reticence to name sources might follow some Jewish conventions on this point; in some such works we can identify the sources only because they are extant.[305] The more popular audience anticipated might be a more important factor, since popular works of various genres were less likely to cite sources.[306] Earlier exaggerated contrasts between elite and popular literature aside,[307] the Gospels do not reflect an elite audience.[308]

Perhaps most important, they may fail to specify their sources because the shared tradition had not yet diverged widely regarding these events of a recent generation. Moreover, ancient historians most often mentioned their sources only when they conflicted[309] or the author disagreed or was unsure

---

e.g., Keener, *John*, 189–90. The vast majority of ancient histories (on which extant ancient historians could have also depended) have since perished (cf. Laistner, *Historians*, 5–6; Brown, *Historians*, 107).

302. Laistner, *Historians*, 51, 86; cf. Derrenbacker, *Practices*, 53.

303. Dionysius of Halicarnassus, *Roman Antiquities* 1.1.1; 1.6.1; Arrian, *Alexander* 6.2.4; Plutarch, *Alexander* 30.7; 31.2–3; 38.4; cf. further Keener, *John*, 22–23; Marguerat, *Histoire*, 30. Cf. Cook, "Use," for a suggested stylistic source indicator in Plutarch; for Plutarch's range of sources, see Rhodes, "Documents," 65–66. For biblical and early Jewish source citations, cf., e.g., Num 21:14; Josh 10:13; 2 Sam 1:18; 1 Kgs 14:19, 29; 15:7, 23, 31; 1 Chr 27:24; 29:29; 2 Chr 16:11; 20:34; 24:27; 2 Macc 2:24–25; one discussion in Holland, "Written."

304. Dio Cassius, *Roman History* 1.1.1–2.

305. E.g., 1 Esdras blends Chronicles, Ezra, and Nehemiah with some midrash (if the latter designation is not too anachronistic). Josephus does not state most of his extrabiblical sources (Nicolaus of Damascus being an important exception). Even Livy can mention that there are many sources while citing only one (*History* 42.11.1).

306. Even most elite authors do not always cite their sources; see Laistner, *Historians*, 51, 86.

307. Schmidt, "Stellung"; Kümmel, *Introduction*, 37; see discussion in, e.g., Keener, *Matthew*, 17. "High" literature influenced "low" literature, creating an overlap of style (Burridge, *Gospels*, 11, 143; Aune, *Environment*, 12, 63; Downing, "Literature").

308. Luke's may be higher than Mark's, but the dedicatee's status need not imply that of the ideal audience (Keener, *Acts*, 1:656–57).

309. See, e.g., Valerius Maximus, *Memorable Doings and Sayings* 5.7.ext.1; 6.8.3; Tacitus,

about their reliability.[310] Although writers often cited eyewitnesses when this might add authority to their claims,[311] recent eyewitness or oral sources did not always require documentation.[312] Writers of contemporary history often lacked "variant versions."[313] A historian might also more generally refer readers interested in more detail to "other historians,"[314] not unlike Luke's oblique reference to other authors in Luke 1:1 (cf. 1 Cor 15:6).

The limited extant first-century sources available today should not be used to judge what sources ancient writers typically had available.[315] Ancient authors obviously had access to many sources that are no longer extant.[316] For example, Pliny the Elder, while explaining that he could not survey everything,[317] notes that he surveyed about two thousand volumes and supplemented them with other data. He complains that many of these sources plagiarized others without crediting them.[318] Other cases were not plagiarism but deliberate literary referents to classic works, for those ingenious enough to catch them.[319] Seneca's secretaries recorded the philosopher's dying words, which Tacitus decides not to report because, he claims, they remained too well-known in his day to merit repetition in his work.[320] Tacitus normally follows annals and earlier histories (sometimes specified only when they be-

---

Annals 2.73, 88; 4.57; 13.20; Philostratus, *Lives of the Sophists* 2.4.570; note further examples above. Livy cites many sources (Laistner, *Historians*, 84) and cites a major source, Quadrigarius, esp. where his account varies from Livy's (Forsythe, "Quadrigarius," 391), hence may follow him at other times without citing him.

310. See Hemer, *Acts*, 65; cf. Laistner, *Historians*, 120, 127.

311. One could establish one's point better by naming various earlier sources supporting it (e.g., Suetonius, *Julius* 9.3).

312. Note fewer citations in, e.g., Tacitus, *Agricola*.

313. Marincola, *Authority*, 262. Judith Odor drew this reference to my attention.

314. E.g., Velleius Paterculus, *History* 2.48.5.

315. This section is borrowed and adapted from Keener, *Acts*, 1:170–73.

316. Cf. the many contemporary histories of Nero noted in Josephus, *Jewish Antiquities* 20.154; the forty-four volumes of Pompeius Trogus extant only in epitomized form (see Justin, *Epitome* pref.4). Cf. 700 volumes of Chrysippus (Suetonius, *Life of Aulus Persius Flaccus* 7).

317. Pliny, *Natural History* pref.18.

318. Pliny, *Natural History* pref.17.

319. Cf. Knoppers, "Problem," 27–30; the discussion of literary, often playful, intertextuality in Bing and Höschele, "Introduction," xxvi–xxxiv. Novels might also play on historical works; cf. Trzaskoma, "Echoes"; Trzaskoma, "Miletus."

320. Tacitus, *Annals* 15.63. For Tacitus using sources (and using them fairly critically), see Laistner, *Historians*, 121; for historians' use of documents (legal documents, inscriptions, and the like), see Rhodes, "Documents" (though they did not always cite them; Laistner, *Historians*, 51).

came notorious),[321] but also consulted personal memoirs from perhaps half a century earlier.[322]

7.9b. Critical Use of Historical Sources[323]

Historians not only had sources, but they were sometimes critical of them. Although accuracy of one's sources was not important in all genres, it was important for historians,[324] who often sought to confirm their information.[325] Likewise, Philostratus, in his biographies of sophists, complains that his research provided no definitive resolution of which of two divergent sources was more accurate;[326] his concern in wanting to resolve this question was thus historical accuracy.

Sources did diverge, especially though not exclusively regarding the distant past. Ancient authors often cite varying accounts, even when preferring one above another.[327] Arrian prefers above other sources his two earliest ones, which often agree, and he chooses between them when they diverge;[328] when sources diverge too much he frankly complains that the exact truth is unrecoverable.[329] At one point Plutarch names five sources for a "majority" position and nine for a minority one,[330] plus an extant letter attributed to the person about whom he writes. He then reminds his audience that the minor diver-

---

321. E.g., Tacitus, *Annals* 4.34–35.

322. Tacitus, *Annals* 4.53. Cf. also oral sources in Syme, "Tacitus."

323. Adapted from Keener, *Acts*, 1:122–24.

324. Pliny, *Letters* 9.33.1.

325. E.g., Suetonius, *Vespasian* 1.4. Herodian, *History* 1.1.3 claims, probably with exaggeration, that he never depended on unconfirmed information (he did not strive for chronological precision; see Whittaker, "Introduction," xxxix–xl).

326. Philostratus, *Lives of the Sophists* 2.5.576.

327. E.g., Dionysius of Halicarnassus, *Roman Antiquities* 1.87.4; 3.35.1–4; 8.79.1; Livy, *History* 9.44.6; 23.19.17; 25.17.1–6; Nicolaus, *Augustus* 19, 21 (*FGrH* 130); Appian, *Roman History* 11.9.56; 12.1.1; Plutarch, *Alexander* 31.3; 38.4; *Demosthenes* 5.5; 29.4–30.4; *Themistocles* 25.1–2; 27.1; 32.3–4; Apollodorus, *Library* 1.4.3; 1.5.2; 1.9.15, 19; 2.3.1; 2.5.11; Ovid, *Fasti* 6.1–2, 97–100; Philostratus, *Lives of the Sophists* 2.4.570; Pausanias, *Description of Greece* 2.5.5; 2.26.3–7; Arrian, *Alexander* 4.9.2–3; 4.14.1–4; 5.3.1; 5.14.4; 7.14.2; 7.27.1–3; Herodian, *History* 7.9.4, 9; Cornelius Nepos, *On Great Generals* 7 (Alcibiades), 11.1; 9 (Conon), 5.4; y. Soṭah 9:13, §2; see further E. T. Sage and A. C. Schlesinger in Livy, *History* (LCL 12:320n2).

328. Arrian, *Alexander* 1.pref.1–2.

329. Arrian, *Alexander* 3.3.6.

330. Thereby implying for the majority position far more than the five sources he has named. On the multiplicity of first-generation Alexander accounts, now lost, see Zambrini, "Historians."

gence does not affect what he considers more significant, namely, our view of his hero's character.[331]

Although there were plenty of cases of historical credulity,[332] and ancient historians were less critical of their sources than are their modern successors,[333] the more critical writers tried to distinguish or even explain, when possible, which sources tended to be more accurate.[334] They evaluated them based on:

- inscriptions;[335]
- material remains;[336]
- a criterion of coherency with other external evidence[337] such as
  - known customs of a report's day[338]
  - other historical context[339] (including chronological data)[340]
  - coherence with documentary sources[341]
  - consistency of reported behavior with a person's other known behavior (something like form critics' criterion of coherence);[342]
- internal consistency;[343]
- historical plausibility;[344]

---

331. Plutarch, *Alexander* 46.1–2.

332. E.g., Valerius Maximus, *Memorable Doings and Sayings* 1.8.7. Some cases of supposed credulity fail to recognize that historians sometimes simply recounted sources without intending to approve them (Schepens, "History," 46).

333. See, e.g., Meister, "Historiography: Greece," 421.

334. See, e.g., Polybius, *Histories* 2.56.1–3.

335. Plutarch, *Aristides* 19.5–6, challenging Herodotus, *Histories* 9.85.

336. As noted above, Thucydides, *History* 1.10.1–2, evaluating the *Iliad*.

337. Polybius, *Histories* 3.32.4.

338. Dionysius of Halicarnassus, *Roman Antiquities* 9.22.1–5.

339. Polybius, *Histories* 3.8.1–11; 3.20.1–5; 3.32.5. Polybius insisted on providing the longest-range historical context possible, both early (3.6.1–3.7.3, e.g., 3.6.10) and subsequent (9.2.5).

340. Plutarch, *Themistocles* 27.1, though admitting uncertainty; cf. Thucydides, *History* 1.3.2–3; Tacitus, *Dialogue on Oratory* 16.

341. Polybius, *Histories* 3.33.18; Plutarch, *Alexander* 46.2; *Demosthenes* 5.5; Philostratus, *Lives of the Sophists* 2.1.562–63.

342. Arrian, *Alexander* 7.14.4–6; Dio Cassius, *Roman History* 62.11.3–4; cf. Athenaeus, *The Learned Banqueters* 5.215–16, 219ab. The same criterion could apply, however, in fictitious composition or historical reconstruction based on plausibility (cf. Aristotle, *Poetics* 15.4–5, 1454a; Theon, *Progymnasmata* 1.46–52; 2.79–81; 8.2–3), whereas real persons do not always sound consistent (cf. Allison, *Constructing Jesus*, 91–92, 103–4).

343. Polybius, *Histories* 2.56.1–3, esp. 3.

344. Josephus, *Jewish Antiquities* 19.68, 106–7; Lucian, *How to Write History* 25; Aulus

- reason;[345]
- removing what they took to be some sources' bias;[346]
- comparison with earlier sources;[347]
- consistency with the person's character;[348]
- and sometimes even stylistic criteria for authenticity.[349]

Following the probability argument standard in the law courts,[350] the rhetorical historian Dionysius of Halicarnassus challenges an event recounted in earlier histories because of intrinsic improbabilities in their accounts.[351] Arrian often evaluates various reports by comparing them (as I do in ch. 10); he notes that one story too prominent to ignore is not reported by any of the eyewitness writers, hence it is likely unreliable.[352] When not offering their own evaluation, some authors simply urged readers to use discretion.[353]

Gellius, *Attic Nights* 10.12.8–10; cf. cautions in Sallust, *Catiline's War* 3.2; Plutarch, *Camillus* 6.4; Arrian, *Alexander* 5.2.7; cf. Derrenbacker, *Practices*, 75.

345. Thucydides, *History* 1.10.1–2; Plutarch, *Themistocles* 25.1–2; Suetonius, *Nero* 6; Pausanias, *Description of Greece* 1.3.3; Philostratus, *Lives of the Sophists* 1.21.516; cf. Alfred, "Valuation," 101. Thus Tacitus recounts the views of the majority and most reliable historians but then mentions another view (*Annals* 4.10), which he goes on to refute logically (4.11), despite its utility for his perspective.

346. Christian, "Themistocles," 139, noting that Nepos regularly "ignores" Herodotus's "bias against Thucydides."

347. Thucydides, *History* 1.3.3; Plutarch, *Alexander* 20.4–5; Velleius Paterculus, *History* 1.3.2–3; cf. Theopompus in Rhodes, "Documents," 62; Plutarch, *Alcibiades* 32.2–3, in Alfred, "Valuation," 91; Suetonius, *Caligula* 19.3, in Alfred, "Valuation," 96; Dionysius of Halicarnassus, *Dinarchus* 11; Tacitus, *Annals* 4.43.

348. Alfred, "Valuation," 96, on Suetonius, *Vespasian* 16.3.

349. Dionysius of Halicarnassus, *Lysias* 11; cf. *Demosthenes* 57. For critically evaluating authorship claims, see also Suetonius, *Caesar* 55–56.

350. See, e.g., Isaeus, *Cleonymus* 12.36; 22.37; Demosthenes, *False Embassy* 120; *Against Pantaenetus* 23; Aristotle, *Rhetoric* 1.15.17, 1376a; *Rhetoric to Alexander* 7, 1428a.19–23; Dionysius of Halicarnassus, *Roman Antiquities* 11.34.1–6; Hermogenes, *Invention* 3.5.142; see further discussion in Keener, *Acts*, 4:3393–95, 3503–4.

351. Dionysius of Halicarnassus, *Roman Antiquities* 4.6.1. Cf. also Tacitus, *Annals* 15.53; 16.6; Pausanias, *Description of Greece* 9.31.7; Plutarch, *Isis and Osiris* 8, *Moralia* 353F; and Theon's reasons for thinking the account of Medea murdering her children implausible (*Progymnasmata* 5.487–501; cf. 3.241–76, 4.112–16, 126–34).

352. Arrian, *Alexander* 6.28.2; cf. Arrian, *Indica* 15.7. Arrian does exhibit pro-Alexander bias (Bosworth, "Pursuit," 447; Baynham, "Quintus Curtius," 428), though it can be overstated (Bosworth, "Pursuit," 452–53).

353. E.g., Livy, *History* 4.29.5–6; 23.47.8; cf. Josephus, *Jewish Antiquities* 19.61, 108; Meister, "Herodotus," 268, on Herodotus, *Histories* 7.152; (more skeptically) Lucian, *How to Write History* 60.

Rather than simply rejecting given writers without reason, biographers usually did not consistently accept or reject any particular writer's account unless they found it consistently coherent with or contrary to available facts.[354] Still more conspicuously, they regularly cited sources where they felt that citations were needed.[355]

7.9c. Historians and Critical Thinking

Thucydides sometimes had to evaluate conflicting claims of eyewitnesses;[356] Livy was sometimes quite critical,[357] even if not consistently so.[358] Likewise, Arrian critically evaluated even his best sources;[359] some modern historians think that he evaluated some of them too strictly.[360] Biographers, too, might evaluate sources' or witnesses' biases or motives.[361]

When a distinction between accurate and inaccurate sources proved impossible, writers often simply presented several different current opinions on what had happened.[362] A writer might simply admit honestly that he did not know how something happened.[363] Josephus sometimes leaves final decisions about causation to the reader's discretion.[364] They could openly note that specific figures they took over from earlier annals could be exaggerated, yet they

354. See again Alfred, "Valuation." In historiography, cf., e.g., Polybius, *Histories* 3.9.1–5: Fabius may be right sometimes, but one must always critically evaluate his claims.

355. Alfred, "Valuation."

356. Thucydides, *History* 1.22.2–3. Thucydides, however, usually omits interpretations divergent from his own (Brown, *Historians*, 49).

357. Laistner, *Historians*, 85–87, citing, e.g., Livy, *History* 8.40.4; 37.48.7.

358. See Fornara, *Nature*, 116–19. Even when he is uncritical, he is sometimes our best—because our only available—source (Foster, "Introduction," xxxi), a virtue of necessity also attending some other historical narratives (e.g., Develin, "Introduction," 1).

359. Bosworth, *Arrian*, 38–39.

360. Bosworth, *Arrian*, 91–92.

361. E.g., Plutarch, *Alcibiades* 3.1; Alfred, "Valuation," 96, citing Suetonius, *Vitellius* 1.1.

362. E.g., Diogenes Laertius, *Lives* 1.23: "But according to others"; 6.1.13; 8.2.67–72; Velleius Paterculus, *History* 2.4.6; 2.27.5; 2.48.4; Plutarch, *Lycurgus* 1.1; Tacitus, *Annals* 2.67; 3.16, 18; 4.10; 14.51 (though happy to report negative views of Nero), 58–59; 15.38, 54; 16.3, 6 (though expressing his view); Philostratus, *Lives of the Sophists* 1.21.516; 2.5.576; y. Soṭah 9:13, §2.

363. E.g., Sallust, *Jugurthine War* 67.3; Tacitus, *Annals* 4.57. Although Tacitus knew Agricola, he admits when he cannot verify some information (Alfred, "Valuation," 85, citing *Agricola* 40); so Suetonius in *Galba* 3.1 (Alfred, "Valuation," 98). Quintilian, *Orator's Education* 2.4.19 (LCL), recognizes Livy's uncertainty about "what actually occurred."

364. Josephus, *Jewish Antiquities* 19.60–61, 108.

emphasize that the exaggeration did not affect the point that the slaughter was in any case great.[365]

Even Herodotus, who reports a range of sources without evaluating their accuracy, does not assume their full accuracy; he expressly expects his audience to understand that they are responsible to decide for themselves.[366] One could report a myth in one's source without commiting oneself to accept it.[367]

Biographers also shared this interest. In contrast to the earlier writer Xenophon, most biographers from the late Republic and early empire tried to assess their sources critically so they could discover genuine information about their subjects.[368]

7.10. Conclusion

Historians were concerned for rhetorical presentation, even to the extent of reconstructing some speech events with the most plausible guesswork possible. They inferred motives at times. They wanted readers to enjoy their narratives, yet they regularly insisted on maintaining truth about the events. Bias was inevitable, but the ideal in principle was objectivity, and this ideal often limited the most unfair effects of biases.

Ancient writers had their agendas, whether political, moral, or theological, often more overtly than their modern successors. Nevertheless, both historians and others repeatedly affirmed the ideal for accurate information in historical and biographic works. The eastern Mediterranean historical practice relevant to the Gospels included investigation, such as interviewing surviving sources that had been close to the events narrated.

Such consensus standards imposed some unofficial constraints on respectable historians' embellishments. Rather than historians making up events, they used sources, and often used them critically. In contrast to some modern assumptions about ancient historiography, the latter did value the preservation of historical memory.

---

365. Livy, *History* 3.8.10. For historical sources' exaggerated numbers or discussion of them, see further, e.g., Xenophon, *Hiero* 2.16; Thucydides, *History* 5.68.2; Polybius, *Histories* 12.17.1–12.22.7; Tacitus, *Histories* 3.61; Lucian, *How to Write History* 20; Keener, *Acts*, 1:995–96.

366. See Meister, "Herodotus," 268; Fowler, "History," 201–2; cf. Schepens, "History," 46; Rhodes, "Documents," 56 (citing 3.115.2; 3.123.1; 4.195.2; 7.152.3).

367. Lucian, *How to Write History* 60.

368. Alfred, "Valuation," 77.

Chapter 8

Luke-Acts as Biohistory

Most scholars see Luke's first volume as biography; most scholars see his second volume as a historical monograph; and most scholars see the two volumes as intimately connected. To many observers, these three mostly consensus views do not fit well together, and they therefore demur on one or more points.

Yet, in spite of elaborate classifications, mixed genres were common in the early imperial period.[1] As noted in chapters 6 and especially 7, the genres of biography and historiography (or the subgenre of biography with the rest of historiography) overlapped considerably in the early empire.[2] Among the Gospels, it is with Luke's Gospel that the line between biography and historiography most fully blurs.[3]

8.1. A Special Case: Is Luke's Gospel Historical Monograph or Historical Biography?

Although I have been approaching the Gospels generally as biographies, one Gospel invites a somewhat different approach, an approach that illustrates the often fine line between biography and history. Luke's Gospel is indeed biographic, but it belongs to a two-volume work (Luke-Acts) that when taken as a whole is more easily defined as historiography more generally. As part of Luke's two-volume work the Gospel becomes a biographic component in a larger history. Ancient auditors would not find such a combination difficult to

---

1. See Aune, "Problem," 10–11, 48; Aune, *Dictionary*, 307; Burridge, *Comparison*, 33–34, 56–61; Smith and Kostopoulos, "Biography," 394; cf. Selden, "Genre," 39–40; Fuller, "Classics," 189 (summarizing G. Kennedy). On the possibility of mixed genres for Luke and/or Acts, cf. Spencer, *Acts*, 13–14; Barrett, *Acts*, lxxviii–lxxix; Smith and Kostopoulos, "Biography."

2. See esp. Pelling, "History."

3. I adapt material here from Keener, *Acts*, 1:54–62; Keener, *Historical Jesus*, 85–94; and Keener, "Luke-Acts."

comprehend; authors of multivolume histories could devote an entire volume or section to a particularly prominent character.[4] Josephus's autobiography apparently originally was part of his historical work, the *Jewish Antiquities*.[5]

8.1a. *The Mixture*

Although majority positions change from time to time, the majority of current scholars view the Gospels and Acts as belonging to the genres of ancient biography and history, respectively, with the Gospel of Luke possibly straddling both.[6] Just as most scholars today recognize the Gospels as biographies, the dominant view concerning Acts today, earlier argued by Lukan scholars such as Martin Dibelius and Henry Cadbury,[7] is that it is a work of ancient historiography.[8] Writing in the *Anchor Bible Dictionary*, Luke Timothy

---

4. Burridge, *Gospels*, 239 (citing Diodorus Siculus, *Library of History* 17); Balch, "ΜΕΤΑΒΟΛΗ ΠΟΛΙΤΕΙΩΝ," 143 (citing Dionysius of Halicarnassus, *Roman Antiquities* 4.41–85). Talbert, *Acts*, 251, helpfully cites Polybius, *Histories* 9.22; 10.2.2; Dionysius of Halicarnassus, *Roman Antiquities* 5.48.1; Diodorus Siculus, *Library of History* 17; Josephus, *Jewish Antiquities* bks. 14–17; Dio Cassius, *Roman History* 45–56; 73.11.2–4; Eusebius, *Ecclesiastical History* 6.

5. Smith and Kostopoulos, "Biography," 404–5.

6. Cf., e.g., Keener, "Luke-Acts"; Barrett, *Acts*, 2:lxxviii–lxxix; Verheyden, "Unity," 47; Marshall, "Treatise," 180; Hemer, *Acts*, 33–43, 63–100; Dormeyer and Galindo, *Apostelgeschichte*, 19; on the possibility of mixed genres, cf. Spencer, *Acts*, 13–14; Barrett, *Acts*, 2:lxxviii–lxxix; for mixed genres being common in the early imperial period, see Aune, "Problem," 10–11, 48; Aune, *Dictionary*, 307; Burridge, *Comparison*, 33–34, 56–61.

7. Dibelius, *Studies*, 123–37; Cadbury, *Acts in History*, throughout.

8. For the latter, see several works by Plümacher ("Cicero und Lukas," 772–73; *Geschichte*, 1–32; "Historiker"; *Lukas*, 33–38 [comparing mission speeches], 137–39; "Luke as Historian," 398; "Monographie"); also Palmer, "Monograph" (1992); Palmer, "Monograph" (1993); Schmidt, "Influences," 59; Fuller, "Classics," 189 (regarding G. Kennedy's comments); Stagg, *Acts*, 17; Petersen, "Genre"; Bovon, *Theologian*, 5; Johnson, *Acts*, 3–7; Johnson, "Luke-Acts," 406; Fitzmyer, *Acts*, 127; Barnett, *Birth*, 195–96; Cross, "Genres," 404–6; Tuckett, *Luke*, 29; Ehrman, *Introduction*, 133–35; deSilva, *Introduction*, 349–51; Balch, "ΜΕΤΑΒΟΛΗ ΠΟΛΙΤΕΙΩΝ," 141–42, 149–54; Balch, "Genre," throughout, esp. 11–19; Balch, "Gospels (forms)," 948–49; Marguerat, *Histoire*, 49 (although noting overlap with biography); Marguerat, "Pionnier"; Eckey, *Apostelgeschichte*, 20–31; Jervell, *Apostelgeschichte*, 77–78; Flichy, *Oeuvre*; Flichy, "État," 28–32 (reviewing recent research); Litwak, *Echoes*, 36; Kisau, "Acts," 1297; Rothschild, *Rhetoric*, 296; Guijarro Oporto, "Articulación literaria"; Riesner, "Zuverlässigkeit," 39; Sterling, *Historiography*, 318n39, lists also as supporters Conzelmann, *Acts*, xl; Hengel, *Acts and History*, 14, 36–37; Schneider, *Apostelgeschichte*, 1:122; Pesch, *Apostelgeschichte*, 1:23; see also now Uytanlet, *Historiography*; Odor, "Families"; Schnabel, *Jesus, Paul, and Church*, 290. See further discussion in Keener, *Acts*, 1:90–115.

Johnson notes that most scholars today accept this assignment of genre for Luke-Acts as a whole.[9] Indeed, Hengel and Schwemer contend that those who deny Luke-Acts as acceptable first-century historiography need to read more ancient historiography.[10]

The complication is that, as Chris Forbes puts it, "Whatever Acts is, it is the sequel to Luke's Gospel."[11] Granted, Luke and Acts need not belong to the same genre,[12] although it is virtually certain that they were meant to be read together.[13] Some scholars identify biographic elements in Acts,[14] although, as noted in chapters 6–7, history could be written with a biographic focus.[15] In the case of Luke-Acts, many scholars retain Luke as biography[16] but speak of a biographic-historiographic double work,[17] in which the first volume is biography but the larger work is historiographic.[18] This would not be the only case of individual volumes in a larger series fulfilling somewhat different genre functions than the series.[19] Overlapping biographies appear in Plutarch's *Galba* and *Otho*, or in the biography of Crates extended to elaborate on two of his disciples.[20] Others point to the indisputable pervasiveness of biographies in

9. Johnson, "Luke-Acts," 406. Penner, *Praise*, 4, likewise summarizes that most scholars hold "the most obvious generic identification for" Acts, namely "ancient historiographical writing." Even in 1985, Callan could write that "It has long been almost taken for granted that Luke-Acts is a historical work" ("Preface," 576, noting that Talbert's biography proposal had reopened the question).

10. Hengel and Schwemer, *Damascus*, 11.

11. Forbes, "Acts as Source," 11, in the context of genre.

12. Cf. Palmer, "Monograph" (1993), 3; Parsons, "Unity," esp. 45–48; Pervo, "Same Genre?"; Parsons and Pervo, *Rethinking*, 20–44 (though overstating the case).

13. See Acts 1:1; and, e.g., Goulder, *Type*; Talbert, *Patterns*; Tannehill, *Luke*; Tannehill, *Acts*; Verheyden, "Unity"; Verheyden, *Unity*; Verheyden, "Unity of Luke-Acts"; Bergholz, *Aufbau*.

14. Taylor, "Acts as Biography," esp. 84; Alexander, "Biography," 56; cf. Alexander, *Context*, 43–68; see esp. Adams, *Genre*, 116–71; also discussion in Keener, *Acts*, 1:54–62.

15. Cf. Fornara, *Nature*, 29–46 (esp. 34–36), 116, 185; for Luke-Acts, see, e.g., Dormeyer, "Gattung," 461–65, 475; Barrett, *Acts*, 2:xxxv; Keener, *Acts*, 1:111–13. For complications with assigning Acts to the biographic genre, see, e.g., Plümacher, *Geschichte*, 1–4; Aune, *Environment*, 77; Keener, *Acts*, 1:59–60. Biographic material does not make a work biography per se (Stadter, "Biography," 528–29).

16. Frickenschmidt, *Evangelium*, 478–97.

17. Frickenschmidt, *Evangelium*, 498–500.

18. Frickenschmidt, *Evangelium*, 500.

19. In ch. 8 of *Negotiating Genre*, Sean Adams notes biographic components (*Abraham* and *Joseph*) in Philo's larger *Exposition*, thus drawing on biographic conventions while also providing philosophic textual commentary.

20. Frickenschmidt, *Evangelium*, 500.

collections[21] or more narrowly to parallel biographies[22] and OT succession narratives.[23]

Luke's claim to investigate or have close acquaintance with his information (Luke 1:3) is consistent with claims in historical works,[24] and many scholars contend that his other occasional uses of the first person (e.g., Acts 16:10) could fit the involvement considered ideal for a good Hellenistic historian.[25] Unlike histories, biographies were not constrained by chronological sequence.[26] That Luke usually follows Mark's sequence need not require, but supports, the contention that Luke views his biography of Jesus as part of his larger project of writing a history.

Other aspects of Luke-Acts fit the historical genre. Luke's extensive use of public monologues in Acts fits the conventions of ancient histories better than those of biographies or novels.[27] (Indeed, in Acts they may cumulatively consume a larger proportion of the work than in Thucydides or Sallust, though Luke's speeches are individually typically shorter than in the multivolume histories.)[28] Some other historiographic features include or are more specific to the Gospel.

8.1b. Luke's Preface

The preface to a two-volume work could cover both volumes,[29] which is probably the case for Luke 1:1–4.[30] In contrast to novels,[31] Luke includes a preface very

---

21. Adams, *Genre*, 92–109; for Acts, 116–71.

22. On which, see, e.g., Keener, *Acts*, 1:568, 571–73.

23. On which, see, e.g., Keener, *Acts*, 1:712–13. See Small, "Review," esp. with interest in the cohesive Deuteronomistic History.

24. Thucydides, *History* 1.22.2; see ch. 7.

25. See esp. Plümacher, "Luke as Historian," 398; see ch. 7; further discussion in Keener, *Acts*, 3:2353–55.

26. See ch. 5.

27. See Plümacher, "Mission Speeches," 251–66; as in Plümacher, "Missionsreden"; Plümacher, "Luke as Historian," 398; Horsley, "Speeches," 613.

28. See discussions in, e.g., Horsley, "Speeches"; Soards, *Speeches*, 183; Aune, *Environment*, 124–25.

29. E.g., Philostratus, *Lives of the Sophists* pref.479.

30. A secondary preface, as in Acts 1:1, could be briefer (see, e.g., Josephus, *Against Apion* 2.1; with Johnson, *Acts*, 28; Witherington, *Acts*, 105). My remarks about Luke's preface draw from Keener, *Acts*, 1:93–96, 174–76, 658–60 (and more generally 649–60).

31. Though occasionally a novel could include a preface explaining how an author invented the story (as in Longus, *Daphnis and Chloe*, proem 1–2).

similar to those in histories.[32] Although some features may resemble features in prefaces of ancient scientific treatises,[33] no one contends that this is the genre of either volume of Luke-Acts.[34] Rather, these features may suggest that Luke's history comes closer to the scholarly rather than the more rhetorical mode of writing.[35] Genuine technical treatises did seek to deal in information, not fiction.[36]

A good introduction should summarize what is to follow;[37] and Luke's summary of what will follow is explicitly historical: "an orderly narrative of the things fulfilled among us" (Luke 1:1, 3). Likewise, his explicit purpose is to confirm what Theophilus has learned about such events (1:4). "Given this statement of the question," Terrance Callan notes, "it is almost obvious that the preface of Luke-Acts most resembles the prefaces of histories."[38] Luke focuses on "a narrative of events."[39] That Luke's purpose is explicitly to confirm truth (Luke 1:4) fits expectations for historiography.[40] That Luke also sees his work as useful (Luke 1:4) would not conflict with this goal.[41]

Luke's language also fits known historical prefaces in other respects, such as close correspondences of vocabulary, as numerous scholars point

32. On Luke's prologue as fitting for historical works, see, e.g., Callan, "Preface"; van Unnik, "Once More Prologue"; Johnson, "Luke-Acts," 406, 407; Schmidt, "Influences"; Moessner, "Arrangement," 158–63; Moessner, "Synergy"; Porter, "We Narratives," 550; Aune, *Environment*, 80, 121 (cf. 89–90, 120–21); Aune, *"Prooimion"*; Penner, *Praise*, 219–22; Rothschild, *Rhetoric*, 93–94. For historiographic prefaces, see also Earl, "Prologue-form." For comparison of biographic and historiographic prefaces, see Smith, *βίος*, 231.

33. Alexander, *Preface*, 42–101 (though cf. 147); Alexander, "Preface." But cf. Callan, "Preface," 577; Aune, *Dictionary*, 371, and Aune, *"Prooimion"*; Adams, "Preface," 181–83.

34. Aune, *Dictionary*, 370. Alexander, *Context*, 12–13, clarifies that she never denied that Luke intended his work as "history" and suggests (17–18) that the preface might suggest the *kind* of history Luke intends.

35. Alexander, *Context*, 16, 41–42, suggesting also that Luke's "preface shows a strong interest both in 'reliability' and in the preservation of authentic tradition," despite some fictionalization (12–13).

36. Cf. Alexander, "Formal Elements," 23–24.

37. This is a conventional expectation; see Quintilian, *Orator's Education* 4.1.34; also *Rhetoric to Alexander* 29, 1436a, lines 33–39; Polybius, *Histories* 3.1.3–3.5.9 (esp. 3.1.7); 11.1.1–5; Dionysius of Halicarnassus, *Lysias* 24; *Thucydides* 19; Cicero, *Orator ad M. Brutum* 40.137; Virgil, *Aeneid* 1.1–6; Seneca the Elder, *Controversiae* 1.pref.21; Dio Chrysostom, *Orations* 38.8; Aulus Gellius, *Attic Nights* pref.25; Soranus, *Gynecology* 1.intro.2; 1.1.3; Philostratus, *Life of Apollonius* 7.1; 8.1.

38. Callan, "Preface," 577; cf. similarly Hemer, "Alexandria Troas," 98.

39. Callan, "Preface," 577, citing Herodotus, *Histories* 1.1; Lucian, *How to Write History* 7–14 (also 39–40).

40. Callan, "Preface," 578; cf. Aune, *Environment*, 136; Adams, "Preface," 186.

41. See Lucian, *How to Write History* 9, 53. For multiple objectives, see, e.g., Josephus, *Jewish Antiquities* 1.4; for both pleasure and benefit, see 2 Macc 2:24–25.

out.[42] Where we can check Luke against extrinsic data, he fits expectations for histories, not for novels about historical figures.[43] Some even suggest that Luke imitates not only the Septuagint but also the style of eastern Mediterranean historians from Polybius forward.[44]

Comparison with OT historiography also points to historical intention.[45] Some scholars even argue that Luke sought to write salvation history as he knew it from the Old Testament,[46] although, like contemporary Jewish historians, he combined this approach with Hellenistic conventions.[47] Luke's first volume includes Jesus's deeds and teachings (Acts 1:1; cf. Luke 24:19), which is both a biographic and a historical interest.[48]

8.1c. Luke's Claim of "Thorough Familiarity" (Luke 1:3)

Luke's claim of "thorough familiarity" (Luke 1:3) probably implies his participation in Jesus's movement or even in some events that Luke narrates. Translations often render παρακολουθέω (*parakoloutheō*) in 1:3 as "investigate,"[49] but it may refer, even more relevantly, to "participation." This verb indicates *thorough* acquaintance[50] or "informed familiarity."[51] Because the sort of familiarity expressed by the semantic domain often comes partly "through personal

---

42. Downing, "Redaction Criticism 2," 30–31; Moessner, "Arrangement," 158; Rothschild, *Rhetoric*, 67–69; Penner, *Praise*, 219–21; Becker, *Birth*, 103–4.

43. See, e.g., Talbert, *Mediterranean Milieu*, 203–8; Hemer, *Acts*, 108–220 (see esp. 108–58); Campbell, "Journeys"; Harnack, *Acts*, 264–74. I treat the question much more thoroughly than here in Keener, *Acts*, 1:62–83, 166–257.

44. See Mealand, "Historians." Although Luke shares some LXX verbs, the stylistic level of his verbs falls between a high level of Koine and Dionysius's atticizing (Mealand, "Verbs").

45. Rosner, "Biblical History," 81, after noting the common features on 65–81; cf. further Uytanlet, *Historiography*.

46. Jervell, "Future," 110–11; Johnson, *Acts*, 12; Smith, "Gospels," 8–14; Litwak, *Echoes*, 32, 206. Some earlier Greek historians (such as Thucydides and Xenophon) also envisioned their narratives as picking up where their predecessors left off (Darbo-Peschanski, "Origin," 33–34; Brown, *Historians*, 91–92).

47. Jewish historical writing by this period employed Hellenistic conventions (Cohen, *Maccabees*, 194; cf. in general Attridge, "Historiography," 326; Eisman, "Dio and Josephus").

48. For history, see Polybius, *Histories* 2.56.11; deeds in Aristotle, *Rhetoric* 1.1360 a.35; Valerius Maximus, *Memorable Doings and Sayings* 1.pref.; Quintilian, *Orator's Education* 2.4.2; Fornara, *Nature of History*, 1–2, 116, 185.

49. Cf. Becker, *Birth*, 105, on Luke "as the investigator of traditions."

50. See Alexander, *Preface*, 128–30.

51. Moessner, *Historian*, 68–107 (prior knowledge vs. investigation).

involvement," David Moessner concludes that it refers to Luke's involvement in the movement and prior knowledge of the tradition, possibly even anticipating Luke's "we" passages.[52]

Scholars offer various interpretations of Luke's "we" material.[53] Some view the "we" as a fictitious literary device, but this device is not attested in ancient historiography[54] or biography.[55] I have elsewhere presented my own conviction and case that if Luke's "we" (Acts 16:10–28:16) had appeared in virtually any other ancient historical work, we would take for granted that the author was present. A majority of scholars do hold that the "we" represents genuine eyewitness material;[56] at least a slight majority of Acts scholars also hold that Luke himself authored the "we" source.[57] If, as we would assume in another

52. Moessner, *Historian*, 106–7, 328; cf. Moessner, "Tradent." An informed participant in a movement will normally know it better than even an outsider doing research for a year, although the kinds of knowledge may also be different. This principle can be amply illustrated in publications about Pentecostals, Mormons, Ahmadiyya Muslims, etc.

53. For my fuller discussion, see Keener, *Acts*, 3:2350–74.

54. See Nock, *Essays*, 828; Porter, *Paul in Acts*, 24–27; Keener, "Claims"; cf., e.g., Herodotus, *Histories* 1.20; 1.51.3–4; 1.92.2; 1.105.3; 2.29; 2.99.1; 2.104.1; 2.127.1–2; 2.147.1; 2.148.1; 3.55.2; 4.81.2; 4.195.2; 5.59; 6.47.1; 7.114.2; Polybius, *Histories* 1.1.1–1.5.5; 36.11.1–4; 39.8.1; Diodorus Siculus, *Library of History* 17.52.6; Dionysius of Halicarnassus, *Roman Antiquities* 1.7.3; Ezra 8:15–32; 9:3–5. Polybius uses first-person claims when he was an observer (e.g., 29.21.8) but prefers third-person when he is an active participant in the narrative (31.23.1–31.24.12; 38.19.1; 38.21.1; 38.22.3; cf. 39.2.2). This is esp. frequent at the narratorial level: e.g., Herodotus, *Histories* 1.5.3; 1.15; 1.18.2; 1.22.2; 1.57.1; 1.75.1, 3, 6; 1.92.1; 1.95.1; 1.106.2; 1.130.3; 1.131.1; 1.137.1; 1.140.1–3; 1.169.2; 1.170.1; 1.171.2; 2.18.1; 4.197.2; 5.4.1; 5.9.1, 3; 5.22.1; 5.35.3; 5.36.4; 5.54.1; 5.62.1; 5.65.5; 5.66.1; 5.86.3; 6.19.2–3; 6.39.1; 6.43.3; 6.53.1–2; 6.55; 9.95; 9.101.1; Dionysius of Halicarnassus, *Roman Antiquities* 1.1; 1.5.1; 1.6.5; 1.7.1; 1.8.1; 1.90.2; 2.47.3; 9.60.1; 9.71.4; Josephus, *Jewish War* 2.114; Tacitus, *Histories* 1.51, 59; 2.8, 17, 27; 5.2, 10, 19. For other factually oriented works, see, e.g., Aulus Gellius, *Attic Nights* 1.4, 11, 13, 15, 18, 21–23, 26; 2.2, 6–7, 12–13, 15–16, 19–21; 8.sum.10; 14.sum.2; 15.sum.25.

55. See, e.g., Josephus, *Life* 1–3, 5–6, 8–17, 19–21, 27, 30–31, 41, 62–65, 68–70, 322, 329, 393; Suetonius, *Augustus* 7; *Caligula* 19.3; *Nero* 57.2; *Otho* 10.1; *Vespasian* 1; *Domitian* 12.2; Philostratus, *Lives of the Sophists* 2.21.602–4; Neh 1:1–6, 11; 2:17–20, and throughout; Baum, "Wir- und Er-Stellungen"; see discussion of historians' first- and third-person narration in Keener, *John*, 918. Fictional stories of course use a fictitious first person (see, e.g., Pervo, "Losers," 130; Sigmon, "Brothers"), but this usage is not relevant to historical works such as Acts, which, like other historical works, corresponds to external information far more often than not (see Talbert, *Mediterranean Milieu*, 201–8; Keener, *Acts*, 1:166–250 [esp. 203–6, 237–50]; Hemer, *Acts*).

56. E.g., Cadbury, "We"; Dibelius, *Studies*, 135–37; Dupont, *Sources*, 164–65; Packer, *Acts*, 3; Munck, *Acts*, xliii; Hanson, *Acts*, 21–24; Neil, *Acts*, 22–23; Dunn, *Acts*, x; Spencer, *Acts*, 12–13; Fitzmyer, *Acts*, 103; Pixner, *Paths*, 423–31; Wolter, *Luke*, 1:8–10.

57. E.g., Abbott, *Acts*, 131–4; Ramsay, *Luke the Physician*, 26; Rackham, *Acts*, xvi; C. Williams, *Acts*, 22–30; Spencer, *Acts*, 12–13; Dunn, *Acts*, x; Fitzmyer, *Acts*, 50; Le Cornu, *Acts*, xxvii–

historical work, the first-person reference includes the author, then the author of Luke-Acts spent up to two years in Judea, within three decades of most of the events described in Luke's Gospel (Acts 24:27 with 21:15; 27:1).[58]

First-person narration in Acts is consistent with authorial involvement. "We" appears only sporadically in Acts, whereas the fictitious "we" normally pervaded the ancient novels that use one. Without comment (as if the audience knows the identity of the narrator), the first person appears incidentally in Troas, leaves off in Philippi (Acts 16:10–16), and resumes years later, again in Philippi (20:6–21:18; 27:1–28:16). It does not appear at more theologically pregnant points where it would be most useful (say in Acts 1–2, 10, or 15, or in the Gospel).[59] Far from the author depicting himself as a Peter or Paul, he narrates his own participation as minimally as any participant could. As one might expect for eyewitness material, the "we" sections tend to be among Luke's most detailed material.[60] (Detractors often cite differences from Paul;[61] at least some of the more significant of these, however, may reflect a traditional Protestant misunderstanding of Paul.)[62]

By ἄνωθεν (anōthen, "from the top, from the beginning"), Luke also claims that his acquaintance began much earlier than the time of his writing.[63] Luke's claim to "accuracy" (ἀκριβῶς [akribōs], Luke 1:3) appears in historiography and usually designates contemporary history-writing, dependent on direct experience, as opposed to writing about the past.[64] Josephus thus employs the term and its cognates sparingly in his *Antiquities* but more consistently in his *War*.[65]

---

xxviii; Chance, *Acts*, 4; Parsons, *Luke*, 8; Fusco, "Sezioni-noi"; Botermann, "Heidenapostel"; Riesner, "Zuverlässigkeit," 38–39; Jervell, *Apostelgeschichte*, 66, 82; Wolter, *Luke*, 1:8–10. Many detractors nevertheless are significant (e.g., Barrett, "Acts and Corpus").

58. On the value of participation in ancient historiography, see, e.g., Byrskog, *Story*, 58–64, 153–57.

59. See, e.g., Dibelius, *Studies*, 136; Fitzmyer, *Theologian*, 11–16; Kurz, *Reading Luke-Acts*, 112–13.

60. With, e.g., Hengel and Schwemer, *Damascus*, 7; Neil, *Acts*, 22–23.

61. See esp. Vielhauer, "Paulinism" (note esp. his older approach to Paul and the law).

62. See critiques in Borgen, "Paul to Luke"; Donfried, *Thessalonica*, 90–96; Porter, *Paul in Acts*, 189–206; Thompson, "Paul in Acts."

63. See Bauckham, *Eyewitnesses*, 119–23.

64. Becker, *Birth*, 103–4, citing esp. Thucydides, *History* 1.22; Dionysius of Halicarnassus, *Roman Antiquities* 3.18.1; 7.66.1–5; 11.1.

65. Becker, *Birth*, 104, citing *Jewish War* 1.9, 17, 22, 26; 7.454 (and cf. 3.138); *Life* 412, though acknowledging also the less pervasive use in *Jewish Antiquities* 1.214; 9.208; 14.3; 19.15; 20.147, 260–62.

Whether or not one agrees with this briefly summarized argument for the eyewitness character of the "we" material, Luke's wording, in view of other ancient prologues using the same language, at least suggests thorough familiarity with reports and his belief that he is able to evaluate their accuracy.[66] One would use such language to display one's "impeccable credentials" for writing reliably.[67]

8.1d. Luke's Predecessors

Luke believes that his firsthand acquaintance is sufficient for him to be able to evaluate and confirm many of the oral traditions circulating (Luke 1:2), traditions already known to his audience (1:4). Presumably this confirmation would have at least included interviewing some Judean followers of Jesus who could confirm and augment the stories circulating among Diaspora Christians.[68] Luke's appeal to "eyewitnesses" (αὐτόπται, *autoptai*; Luke 1:2) fits the widespread convention of appeal to eyewitness sources,[69] emphasized by both Greek[70] and Roman[71] historians.

Like modern scholars, ancient prefaces treated their predecessors in different ways: some berated them,[72] whereas others, more charitably, simply

66. Moessner, "Poetics," 85–97. Cf. also Hemer, *Acts*, 322 (noting that Cadbury thought this wording involved even participation, a reasonable surmise only in Acts and not the Gospel).

67. Moessner, "Poetics," 97; Moessner, "Prologues," 413; cf. Josephus, *Against Apion* 1.54, 213ff.

68. As Bruggen, *Narratives*, 65–66, notes, it does not require Luke to have been an eyewitness for the events of the Gospel. On my view of the "we" material, Luke had ample opportunity in Judea in Acts 21:17; 24:27; 27:1.

69. Alexander, *Preface*, 34–36.

70. Byrskog, *Story*, 49–53, addresses Heraclitus and others; 53–57, Herodotus, 58–59, Thucydides; 59–62, Polybius (note esp. *Histories* 4.2.1–2 on p. 60); 62–63, Josephus (noting *Against Apion* 1.47).

71. Byrskog, *Story*, 63, noting Livy as the exception, most following the Greek preference. He notes (63) that Dionysius of Halicarnassus, *Roman Antiquities* 1.6.2, "praises Fabius Pictor and Cincius Alimentus . . . for relating with great exactness only the events at which they themselves had been present."

72. E.g., *Rhetoric to Alexander*, pref., opening, lines 1–12; Artemidorus, *Interpretation of Dreams* 1.pref.; 3.pref.; Longinus, *On the Sublime* 1.1; among historians, see Anaximenes and Theopompus (according to Dionysius of Halicarnassus, *Roman Antiquities* 1.1.1); Polybius, *Histories* 3.32.4–5; Josephus, *Jewish War* 1.1–2, 7 (cf. *Jewish Antiquities* 20.154–57); Justus (according to Josephus, *Life* 357–59); Dio Cassius, *Roman History* 1.1.1–2; Herodian, *History* 1.1.1–2;

distinguished their respective spheres of activity.[73] The former approach could be deemed rude, and some writers therefore specifically disavow this intention.[74] Luke's only stated cause of dissatisfaction with his predecessors' work is a matter of rhetorical arrangement (Luke 1:3), not of information; he has already expressed appreciation for "their eyewitness sources."[75]

As Moessner notes, Luke's "mention of *eyewitness* tradents and attendants and organizers who are responsible for the content and resulting forms of the traditions" (1:2–4) "makes it clear that, as a historian, Luke is treating matters he believes are more or less factual—affairs that have happened."[76] The ideal for ancient historians was to have seen events themselves;[77] since such direct experience of events is not always possible, whether for ancient historians or even modern journalists, historical authors often had to depend on oral sources.[78] Historians from Polybius through first-century authors often defended their work by underlining their reliance on oral sources and eyewitnesses.[79] When on occasion ancient historians use the precise term αὐτοψία (*autopsia*), cognate to Luke's term for eyewitnesses in 1:2, they generally refer to "those with personal/first-hand experience: those who know the facts at first hand."[80] Luke emphasizes eyewitness attestation not only in his preface but commonly enough to reinforce the preface's claim.[81]

Biographers of public figures often filled out biographic material from multiple sources,[82] so it is not surprising that Matthew and Luke fill out Mark's outline with other information. On the dominant hypothesis of gospel for-

---

implicitly Arrian, *Alexander* 1. pref.3. Wardle, *Valerius Maximus*, 67, cites Livy, *History* pref.2; Sallust, *Histories* frag. 3, 7; Tacitus, *Histories* 1.1.2–3; *Annals* 1.1.2.

73. Diodorus Siculus, *Library of History* 1.3.1–2; Vitruvius, *Architecture* 7.pref.10–18; Quintilian, *Orator's Education* 1.pref.1–2, 4–5; Aelius Aristides, *Panathenaic Oration* 4, 152D.

74. Valerius Maximus, *Memorable Doings and Sayings* 1.pref.; cf. Pliny, *Natural History* 3.1.1–2; Quintilian, *Orator's Education* 3.1.22.

75. Moessner, *Historian*, 109–23, here esp. 122.

76. Moessner, *Historian*, 317. The witnesses and servants in Luke 1:2 probably are the same group (with, e.g., Green, *Luke*, 41; Culy, Parsons, and Stigall, *Luke*, 3; Ytterbrink, *Gospel*, 123).

77. Byrskog, *Story*, 93–94.

78. Byrskog, *Story*, 94–99, esp. 94 (cf. also 149–53). See further ch. 9.

79. Byrskog, *Story*, 122 (excepting Livy); on Tacitus, see 63–64. For apologetic use of autopsy (as in Josephus), see Byrskog, *Story*, 214–22.

80. Alexander, *Preface*, 120. Historians considered firsthand experience the best evidence (Aune, *Environment*, 81, citing Herodotus, *Histories* 2.99; Polybius, *Histories* 12.27.1–6; 20.12.8; Lucian, *How to Write History* 47).

81. Most extensively, see Rothschild, *Rhetoric*, 213–90, noting this authenticating technique; see further comments above.

82. Frickenschmidt, *Evangelium*, 208–9.

mation, this information includes the shared material that we call Q; Luke, however, has a further body of tradition available, as we see, for example, from the distinctly Lukan parables.[83] We would expect Luke to follow roughly the same method where we cannot test him as where we can.

8.1e. Confirmation (Luke 1:4)

Luke's primary stated purpose is to confirm already-circulating knowledge (1:4),[84] which suggests that he ultimately arrives at conclusions reasonably consistent with his sources. Thus many stories that Luke includes in his Gospel were probably widely disseminated among many churches. Such dissemination is all the likelier on the recognition that early churches throughout the empire were already informally networked long before Luke wrote. In Mediterranean antiquity in general, travelers regularly carried news from one location to another;[85] whenever one learned of someone traveling near a place where one had friends, one might prepare and send a letter.[86]

Clearly already in the third decade of the Christian movement, many churches knew what was happening with churches in other cities (Rom 1:8; 1 Cor 11:16; 14:33; 1 Thess 1:7–9), and even shared letters (Col 4:16).[87] Missionaries could speak about some churches to others (Rom 15:26; 2 Cor 8:1–5; 9:2–4; Phil 4:16; 1 Thess 2:14–16) and send personal news by other workers (Eph 6:21–22; Col 4:7–9). Some urban Christians traveled (1 Cor 16:10, 12, 17; Phil 2:30; 4:18), carrying letters (Rom 16:1–2; Phil 2:25). They also relocated to other places (Rom 16:3, 5; perhaps 16:6–15 passim) and sent greetings to other churches (Rom 16:21–23; 1 Cor 16:19; Phil 4:22; Col 4:10–15). While different locations had their own struggles or theological emphases, the idea that the early, geographically distinct Christian communities were theologically and socially isolated from one another[88] is simply a fiction created by modern scholarship.

---

83. Cf. Tan-Gatue, "Coherence"; though for the possibility that some of this material was in Q, cf. Sloan, "Similitudes."

84. With, e.g., Maddox, *Purpose*, 21, 186.

85. E.g., Euripides, *Electra* 361–62; Demosthenes, *Letter* 5.1; Cicero, *Letters to Atticus* 2.11; Seneca, *To Lucilius* 47.1; P.Oxy. 32; Apuleius, *Metamorphoses* 1.26.

86. E.g., Cicero, *Letters to Atticus* 1.10, 13; 4.1; 8.14.

87. I draw here from Keener, *Acts*, 1:187–88; note also Willis, "Networking."

88. Perhaps most idiosyncratically, a distinct Q community with a nonmessianic, Cynic Jesus.

The reading of these earlier texts probably standardized the forms of many of the accounts; communal reading (or reading to the communities) was common in synagogues, churches, and the wider culture.[89] While such a "quality control"[90] may not have been relevant in the composition of Mark, it would likely be relevant to his successors, such as Matthew and Luke, who made use of Mark.

8.2. Luke's History and Rhetoric

Luke arranges his material in a manner pleasing to his ideal audience, especially drawing parallels among figures in his narratives. He also has apologetic and other agendas. These observations do not, however, undercut ancient expectations for Luke's work as historiography. Such features also appear in other ancient histories and are not necessarily incompatible with historical information.

8.2a. Luke's Rhetorical Level?

Although Luke demonstrates literary skill far beyond that of the average urban resident, he does not produce a work amenable to society's elite. Granted, Luke is more sophisticated than Mark,[91] and rhetorical conventions influenced Luke's literary techniques (cf. his emphasis on an "orderly" account, Luke 1:3).[92] Nevertheless, the literary level of Luke-Acts is far below that of elite Hellenistic histories.[93] Luke was no rhetorical historian like Theopompus; he was certainly not even as rhetorically trained as Tacitus or Suetonius. Although Luke provides excellent Greek where he needs to (e.g., Luke 1:1–4),[94] not even the

89. See Wright, *Reading*, esp. the extensive treatment of non-Christian sources in 61–115 (cf. also 211–30).

90. I borrow the term from Wright, *Reading*, e.g., 8, 169, 207–9.

91. See, e.g., Dibelius, *Tradition*, 161; Witherington, "Editing," 326, 328; Burridge, "Gospels and Acts," 526–27; Kilpatrick, "Style"; he includes even a few classical references (see Renehan, "Quotations," 22–23).

92. Satterthwaite, "Acts," 337; Penner, *Praise*, 220; cf. Moessner, "Poetics," 97–112. Cf. also the positive evaluation in Bultmann, *Tradition*, 366; Parsons, *Acts*, 9 (on Luke's speeches).

93. Pervo, *Profit*, 6, citing Julian, *Letter* 36.423d; on the NT generally, Townsend, "Education," 148–49.

94. See Blass, Debrunner, and Funk, *Grammar*, §464; Aune, *Dictionary*, 347.

speeches in Acts are extraordinarily sophisticated.[95] Although there were no "professional historians" in his day,[96] Luke writes for a more popular audience than did most elite historians.[97]

In contrast to more rhetorical historians, Luke declines to elaborate scenes rhetorically. One goal in rhetoric was to make hearers feel as if they witnessed events with their very eyes,[98] and historians often sought to achieve this goal.[99] Second Sophistic orators appreciated earlier rhetorical historians like Sallust painting a vivid picture of details and feelings,[100] and they thought that historians ought to describe the countryside.[101] The technique of ekphrasis, involving detailed descriptions, does appear in narrative works,[102] including in historical biographies such as those of Suetonius.[103] Rhetors demanded more graphic scenes providing visual horror;[104] but some historians protested if narration of such scenes exceeded necessary details of history.[105]

Luke, however, never comes close to such detailed elaboration, even in his "we" material. Luke lacks even the briefest sort of example of ekphrasis (such as Homer's Thersites being "bandy-legged, lame in one foot").[106] He avoids gore even in recounting martyrdoms. I thus differ from the scholars who see Acts as "dramatic" history in terms of such elaborations.[107] Aune offers a balanced

95. Cf. more rhetorical strategies in the later speeches, e.g., in Keener, "Rhetorical Techniques."

96. Rebenich, "Prose," 289.

97. Cf. similarly Barrett, *Acts*, xxxv (with Plümacher).

98. See, e.g., Aristotle, *Rhetoric* 2.8.14, 1386a; 3.11.1–2, 1411b; *Rhetorica ad Herennium* 4.55.68; Cicero, *Orator ad M. Brutum* 40.139; Quintilian, *Orator's Education* 9.2.40; Theon, *Progymnasmata* 7.53–55; Longinus, *On the Sublime* 15.2; further sources in Keener, *Galatians* (Cambridge), 120; Keener, *Galatians* (Baker), 212–13; Keener, *Acts*, 1:135.

99. E.g., Dionysius of Halicarnassus, *On Literary Composition* 18; Velleius Paterculus, *History* 2.89.5–6.

100. Fronto, *To Antoninus* 2.6.4–15.

101. Fronto, *To Antoninus* 2.6.6.

102. Rusten, "*Ekphrasis*"; Bowie, "Second Sophistic," 1377.

103. Edwards, "Introduction," xxvii, suggesting the sort of technique noted in Quintilian, *Orator's Education* 4.2.123.

104. Dionysius of Halicarnassus, *On Literary Composition* 18. Dionysius of Halicarnassus, *Thucydides* 15, complains that Thucydides often portrays successfully the abject cruelty and sufferings involved in war but at other times fails to evoke the appropriate horror involved. In art, cf., e.g., Martial, *Epigrams* 3.35.

105. Polybius, *Histories* 15.34.1.

106. In Hermogenes, *Progymnasmata* 10. On Ekphrasis 22 (trans. Kennedy, 86). See fuller discussion in Keener, *Acts*, 1:135–37.

107. This is not to deny any kind of dramatic elements; see Plümacher, *Lukas*, 80–136. They are a matter of degree even in the third century BCE (Laistner, *Historians*, 14–16); later,

conclusion: "Luke-Acts is a popular 'general history' written by an amateur Hellenistic historian with credentials in Greek rhetoric."[108]

8.2b. Parallelism

Whereas Matthew's organization can fit modern hierarchical outlines fairly well, Luke prefers to demonstrate his skill in arrangement more by comparing parallel figures. Luke introduces this strategy already in his opening scenes, providing multiple parallels between Zechariah and Mary (Luke 1:5–25, 26–38).[109] Note the careful structuring:

1:11: an angel (Gabriel, 1:19) appears	1:26: the angel Gabriel appears
1:12: the vision's recipient troubled	1:29: the vision's recipient troubled
1:13: do not be afraid	1:30: do not be afraid
1:13: reason for miracle	1:30: reason for miracle
1:13: child's name (John)	1:31: child's name (Jesus)
1:15: child will be great	1:32: child will be great
1:15: filled with the Holy Spirit from the womb	1:35: conceived through the Holy Spirit[110]
1:16–17: mission	1:32–33: mission
1:18: question	1:34: question
1:19–20: proof or explanation	1:35–37: proof or explanation
1:20: Zechariah muted for unbelief	1:38, 45: Mary praised for faith
1:80: child grows	2:40, 52: child grows[111]

Livy is the supreme extant example of the rhetorically lavish historian (Byrskog, *Story*, 207; cf. Quintilian, *Orator's Education* 10.1.32).

108. Aune, *Environment*, 77 (though I would doubt that Luke's "credentials" included tertiary training in rhetoric). Advanced education focused on rhetoric rather than history, as he goes on to note, which does not imply that historians would not learn techniques from reading other historians. For Acts as a "popular" history, see also Barrett, *Acts*, xxxv; Verheyden, "Unity," 55 (citing also Barrett, "First Testament," 101; *Acts*, 2:li); Pervo, *Acts*, 18 (though defining history loosely).

109. See Keener, *Acts*, 1:556–57; Edwards, *Luke*, 30, 41.

110. For the contrasting role of the Spirit in John's and Jesus's prenatal experience, see Tatum, "Epoch," 188–89.

111. I have omitted less obvious parallels such as circumcision (Luke 1:59; implicit in 2:21)

Luke's two volumes frequently parallel figures, as literary critics have lavishly demonstrated.[112] Although some scholars view as fictionalization such internal parallelisms in ancient sources, for example Plutarch's biography of Artaxerxes,[113] ancient biographers often treated such devices as simply rhetorical arrangement to present information in a more pleasing way. Writers sometimes reuse earlier plots and motifs to fill details in scenes where they lack information.[114]

Although this practice of drawing parallels necessarily involved interpretation, and some stories that historians found useful for this purpose may have been inauthentic, such parallel construction did not require historians to invent new material.[115] Indeed, factual writers today can evoke earlier accounts without inventing their material.[116] It seemed natural, and thus was common, for ancient authors to compare newer figures with earlier ones, for example, various emperors with Romulus,[117] others with Alexander,[118] or some later emperors with predecessors,[119] and so forth.[120] Some figures directly compared themselves with or even impersonated others.[121] The Greek historian Polybius compared the Roman general Scipio with the Spartan lawgiver Ly-

---

and "favor" for both Elizabeth (1:25) and Mary (1:30). Flender, *Theologian*, 29, helpfully views the contrast between Mary and Zechariah in light of a series of contrasts, often between religious insiders and others, in the Gospel (Luke 7:36–50; 10:29–37; 14:15–24; 15:24–32; 18:9–14; 20:45–21:4).

112. See, e.g., Goulder, *Type*; Talbert, *Patterns*; Tannehill, *Luke*; Tannehill, *Acts*; Edwards, "Parallels"; Keener, *Acts*, 1:550–74.

113. Almagor, "Narratives," 70–78. Repetition of key themes in various parts of a work was good rhetoric (see, e.g., *Rhetoric to Alexander* 22, 1434b.5–8; 36, 1444b.23; Menander Rhetor, *Epideictic Treatises* 2.3, 384.25–27).

114. De Temmerman, "Formalities," 24; Becker, *Birth*, 90.

115. See further Keener, *Acts*, 1:562–66.

116. Allison, *Constructing Jesus*, 389; Gray, *Letters*, 34; examples in Keener, *Acts*, 1:566; one could even use for examples (cf. 1:563) incidents in Keener and Keener, *Impossible Love*, e.g., 73–74, 207.

117. Velleius Paterculus, *History* 2.60.1; Suetonius, *Augustus* 7.2; *Caligula* 16.4; cf. Livy, *History* 5.49.7; Plutarch, *Camillus* 1.1; Haley, "Hadrian."

118. Menander Rhetor, *Epideictic Treatises* 2.14, 426.23–24. Cf. the comparison of Caesar with Alexander in Velleius Paterculus, *History* 2.41.1; Appian, *Civil Wars* 2.21.149.

119. Pliny, *Letters* 1.5.1; Suetonius, *Titus* 7.

120. Cicero, *Against Piso* 17.39; Lucan, *Civil War* 9.15–18; 1 Cor 15:45; Rev 17:11.

121. E.g., impostors claiming the mantles of Alexander (Lucian, *Book Collector* 20), Philip (Polybius, *Histories* 36.10.1–7; Velleius Paterculus, *History* 1.11.1; Lucian, *Book Collector* 20), or Nero (Tacitus, *Histories* 1.2; 2.8–9; Suetonius, *Nero* 57.2; Lucian, *Book Collector* 20; Dio Cassius, *Roman History* 66.19.3; cf. Dio Chrysostom, *Orations* 21.9–10; Sib. Or. 4.137–39; 5.33–34, 137–54, 361–85; 8.68–72, 139–50).

curgus, as a means of articulating Scipio's character more clearly.[122] Historians continued to parallel figures in late antiquity.[123]

Some works did admittedly bend stories to conform them to each other. Cicero permitted historians to choose (though not to fabricate) traditions according to which ones best fit the parallels they sought to articulate.[124] Ps.-Plutarch's work *Greek and Roman Parallel Stories* presents paired stories so similar that they must be either doublets of the same tradition or be deliberately assimilated by the writer.[125] Plutarch complains that some writers added details missing elsewhere, for example, composing a proper tragic finale for Alexander's life.[126]

But Plutarch himself, who provides our strongest extant examples of the subgenre, generally was more careful (though more flexible than modern historiography). One scholar who suggests that Plutarch sometimes depended on his imagination for details notes that what can be proven is that he rearranges chronology, selects and omits some material for the sake of parallels, and sometimes even transfers actions to different characters.[127]

While this much is true, Plutarch claims that he looked hard for the right people to compare with each other.[128] For those who valued selectivity,[129]

122. Polybius, *Histories* 10.2.8–13. He also compares with each other the final leaders of Greece and Carthage, who brought their nations to ruin before Rome (Polybius, *Histories* 38.8.14–15).

123. See, e.g., Ramelli, "Origen and Hypatia"; Pervo, "Introduction," 3–4. Paralleling figures would be natural for any biographers who had learned *synkrisis*, or comparison, in the basic *progymnasmata* (Aletti, *Birth*, 20).

124. For example, the account of Themistocles's death that best fit the author's intended parallel to Coriolanus, regardless of other criteria for evaluating the most likely end for Themistocles (Cicero, *Brutus* 11.42).

125. *Moralia* 305A–316B. As a rhetorical exercise, this method may have accelerated the transfer of traditions about one person to another (e.g., Philostratus, *Lives of the Sophists* 1.485, with LCL note; Alexander, "IPSE DIXIT," 121).

126. Plutarch, *Alexander* 70.3. His own romantic description of Darius's death (Plutarch, *Alexander* 43.2) is missing in Arrian (*Alexander* 3.21–23) but was evidently not his own invention (in the LCL note, 7:352n1, P. A. Brunt cites Quintus Curtius Rufus, *History* 5.13, 28; Diod. 17.73).

127. Clark, *Parallel Lives*, 92–93; see further discussion of Plutarch's methods in ch. 11 and Pelling, "Method." Analogous transfer appears in midrash.

128. Plutarch, *Cimon* 3.1–3.

129. E.g., Polybius, *Histories* 2.56.4; Plutarch, *Alexander* 1.1, 3; Aulus Gellius, *Attic Nights* pref.11–12; Menander Rhetor, *Epideictic Treatises* 2.4, 393.25–30; cf. 2 Macc 2:24–25; on conciseness, see, e.g., Dionysius of Halicarnassus, *Demosthenes* 18, 20, 46; *On Literary Composition* 11; Valerius Maximus, *Memorable Doings and Sayings* 1. pref.; 2.7.5; 3.7.ext.5; 3.8.ext.1; Velleius

available parallels with another notable character could simply provide a criterion for selecting relevant points to record. One does not need to invent parallels to discover them; reading backward, one can easily find some "parallels" among various characters in history (or among two persons conversing and looking for common ground). Modern readers might consider these parallels contrived, cherry-picked among many events; they are in the eyes of the beholder. Nevertheless, the writer noting the parallels need only select, not fabricate, the events.

Plutarch thus opines that nature itself supplies sufficient events for observers to find parallels if only the observers are sufficiently attentive. On a naturalistic view, he contends, potential elements for comparison are infinite, whereas on a providential view, the same agents would repeat patterns often.[130] Other writers even collected such accounts of accidents that appeared designed,[131] to which Plutarch added another: the most crafty, skillful. and warlike generals "have been one-eyed men,—Philip, Antigonus, Hannibal, and . . . Sertorius."[132] Plutarch himself believed that the similarities he was able to find were due to the *divine* power making people alike in many respects.[133]

Yet when his historical material required it, Plutarch sometimes highlighted a contrast (a sort of antithetic parallel) rather than conforming the subjects to each other.[134] Even when he says that two people are so much alike that it is difficult to discern the differences between them,[135] he goes on to point out differences.[136] (Naturally, the lives of statesmen will provide some parallels and contrasts with other statesmen, and even modern readers would understand such comparable features as part of the nature of social reality, though not necessarily finding as many parallels as Plutarch.)

Moreover, although we usually lack means to evaluate the sources of Luke's second volume, when we have them we can sometimes show that Luke finds parallels among figures in clearly preexisting material—such as the Septuagint

---

Paterculus, *History* 2.29.2; 2.46.1; 2.89.1, 5–6; Josephus, *Against Apion* 1.251; Tacitus, *Dialogue on Oratory* 23, 31; Philostratus, *Lives of the Sophists* 2.17.597; Keener, *Acts*, 4:3367–69.

130. Plutarch, *Sertorius* 1.1.

131. Plutarch, *Sertorius* 1.2.

132. Plutarch, *Sertorius* 1.4.

133. Plutarch, *Demosthenes* 3.2. Even Polybius believed that his task as a historian was merely to report how Fortune had designed history, observing the causal connections that were her marks (cf. *Histories* 1.4.1–3).

134. *Comparison of Lysander and Sulla* 5.5; *Comparison of Alcibiades and Coriolanus* 3.1.

135. *Comparison of Aristides with Marcus Cato* 1.1.

136. *Comparison of Aristides with Marcus Cato* 5.1, 3–4; 6.1.

(see Acts 7:9, 25, 35, 37).[137] That is, patterning can reflect interpretive structuring of information and not simply its fabrication.[138] In social memory, sacred texts frequently become a lens for contemporary events, and vice versa.[139] In fact, Luke may sometimes adopt interpretative structures already latent or blatant in his sources, which themselves structured their own material. In their current literary form, the Genesis-Exodus narratives themselves include some rather conspicuous parallels and contrasts among figures.[140] Many doublets once viewed as source indicators are now often viewed as deliberate patterning to invite reading one scene "in light of the other."[141] For example, the Jordan crossing in Josephus deliberately echoes the sea crossing at the exodus,[142] and the prophets' picture of a new exodus evoked its prototype.[143] Later Jewish historians and storytellers also recounted their narratives along patterns from earlier salvation history, believing that God had objectively authored these patterns in history.[144] Jewish eschatological literature even uses the Urzeit as a prototype for the Endzeit (especially Eden).[145]

8.3. Apologetic Historiography

Luke, like other writers, had agendas. Most scholars concur that one of the primary functions of Luke-Acts is apologetic (i.e., defending the faith) and many argue that the work fits the actual genre of apologetic historiography.[146] This purpose fits quite well into a well-known line of ancient historiography.

137. See discussion in Keener, *Acts*, 1:573–74; see further Hays, *Echoes*, 101; Kugel and Greer, *Interpretation*, 46–47; Satterthwaite, "Acts," 363.

138. Against simply presuming a dichotomy between history and typology, as an older generation of modern interpreters did; see, e.g., Le Donne, *Historiographical Jesus*, 2–5.

139. See Le Donne, *Historiographical Jesus*, 58.

140. See discussion in Keener, *Acts*, 2:1363–64.

141. Satterthwaite, "Acts," 363. On such patterns, see, e.g., Keener, *Acts*, 1:557–58, 573–74; 2:1363–64.

142. Hays, *Echoes*, 101. Cf. also, e.g., parallels between Elijah and Elisha, naturally between the teacher-model and his successor.

143. E.g., Isa 12:2; 40:3; Jer 31:32–33; Hos 2:15; 11:1, 5, 11; Kugel and Greer, *Interpretation*, 46–47.

144. Jacobson, "Visions."

145. Kugel and Greer, *Interpretation*, 47; cf. 4 Ezra 8:52–54; 9:5–6; Rev 22:1–3; T. Levi 18:10–12; T. Dan 5:12; 2 En. 8:3; m. 'Abot 5:20; Keener, *Acts*, 2:1111–12.

146. See esp. Sterling, *Historiography*, 311–89; cf. also, e.g., Mason, *Josephus and New Testament*, 196–97; Kee, *Every Nation*, 11–12; Johnson, *Acts*, xii; discussion in Keener, *Acts*, 1:161–66, 441–57.

Although the apologetic element is not always dominant, all extant ancient Jewish historiography to some degree emphasized the antiquity and superiority of Israel's religion.[147] The most complete example of Jewish apologetic historiography is Josephus's twenty-volume retelling of sacred Jewish history in his *Jewish Antiquities.* There Josephus emphasizes God's special providence in Israel's history.[148]

8.4. Conclusion

Along with other characteristics, Luke's preface suggests that he envisions his work as a work of history. He claims thorough familiarity with his subject, and perhaps even some participation in it. He also claims that he has corroborated material that he has taken over from his predecessors, material that he believes goes back to the original eyewitnesses. Luke did for history what no one at a subsequent remove could: he consulted and engaged what was still in his day living memory.

Although Luke does not elaborate like more rhetorical historians, he does arrange his material more suitably for his audience. This arrangement includes drawing parallels among figures, a common practice among ancient historians. This practice did not necessarily require historians to invent stories; Luke found such parallels even in clearly preexisting Scripture. Nevertheless, Luke develops these narrative patterns in his material, especially in his opening chapters. Luke also has apologetic and other agendas. Like historical writers addressed in the previous chapter, Luke tells an old story in a fresh way.

Martin Hengel rightly noted that Luke's adaptations and use of information both fit what we expect of ancient historiography. "His account always remains within the limits of what was considered reliable by the standards of antiquity."[149]

---

147. Wandrey, "Literature," 696; cf. Ferguson, *Backgrounds,* 349; for Philo's *Flaccus,* cf. Meiser, "Gattung."

148. Sterling, *Historiography,* 226–310. For Josephus's apologetic objectives, see also, e.g., Feldman, "Apologist"; in defending himself, see Vogel, "Vita"; Lamour, "Organisation."

149. Hengel, *Acts and History,* 61.

Chapter 9

Sources Close to the Events

Conventional biographic models imposed some limitations on conventional biographers. Biographers could not invent their chief characters or make up simply any traits or events they wished; in contrast to novelists, they were bound to the material they inherited.[1] But how accurate was their material? Historians were not supposed to invent historical events, even for ancient history, but hypothetical rhetorical exercises sometimes did so.[2] Over time, such inventions probably worked their way into memories as if they were true details. This is one reason that the temporal distance between an event and its earliest records matters.

The Gospels may reflect a more popular level of writing than more elite biographies,[3] but it is significant that they are also closer in time to their subject than are most ancient biographies.[4] As Momigliano notes in a different connection, "To write about men who lived long ago was not the same thing as writing about contemporaries." In contrast to "poets of the past," who left little information about themselves, "Philosophers had left behind disciples whose opinions had to be taken into account."[5] So, we should remember, did Jesus.

---

1. Noted even in De Temmerman, "Formalities," 9, who emphasizes a degree of fictionalization.

2. See, e.g., Hermogenes, *Invention* 2.1.108–9; 2.4.115.

3. Cf. Aletti, *Birth*, 12–13, 28, drawing on Baum, "Biographien," though Aletti concludes that their interest is more historiographic than in popular biography (24).

4. Cf. Fitzgerald, "Lives," 220.

5. Momigliano, *Development*, 88.

Some material in this chapter is adapted from Keener, *Acts*, 1:127–31.

9.1. Legends Rising Early, Retiring Late

Historical distance multiplies the potential for gratuitous errors.[6] In contrast to typical biographers and historians of the early empire, some earlier orators fabricated significant information surrounding history that lay beyond living memory.[7] Once told, such stories became part of the collective memory on which later writers might draw, knowingly or unknowingly. Over the span of centuries, adaptations by less conservative tradents and writers would accumulate significantly.

This could happen even with accounts less than two centuries old. Thus for example Suetonius's account of Caesar crossing the Rubicon adds an epiphany missing in Caesar's own account.[8] While some historians added such features for rhetorical purposes,[9] Suetonius could also draw on a legend from before his time.[10] Yet Suetonius recounts this event over a century and a half (from 49 BCE to the early second century CE) after its putative occurrence. By way of comparison, this period could be more than four times the length of the period between Jesus's public ministry and the composition of Mark. In ca. 30 CE, closer to the edge of living memory, an earlier historian, Velleius Paterculus, also mentions crossing the Rubicon, yet without this dramatic sign.[11]

Over longer periods, even more legends could arise. Scholars today are thus much more cautious about empire-period depictions of the early republic than they are about early empire-period depictions of early imperial history.[12] Reports from "within two generations" or at most a century are normally the most reliable.[13]

---

6. E.g., one in 4 Macc 4:15.

7. Pelling, *Texts*, 67, on a fourth-century BCE politician, although the politician also could have had an additional (presumably much less reliable) source. Cf. similarly Justin, *Epitome* 38.4.5, 15, suggesting greater flexibility with the past in speeches than in the epitome's narratives.

8. See Penner, *Praise*, 137.

9. See, e.g., the ominous bird in Josephus, *Jewish Antiquities* 18.195; 19.346.

10. Plutarch, *Caesar* 32.9, notes that before crossing the Rubicon, Caesar had an unusual dream; if this information was early, it may have been developed in later tellings.

11. Velleius Paterculus, *History* 2.49.4; for discussion of possibly the earliest version, see Rondholz, "Rubicon."

12. Scholars have usually found more plausible T. P. Wiseman's skepticism about the early Republic than A. J. Woodman's skepticism toward "authors of contemporary or near-contemporary history" (Damon, "Rhetoric," 439). At times, Woodman himself recognizes that likelihood increases with proximity; see, e.g., Woodman, *Rhetoric*, 204.

13. Downing, *Cynics and Churches*, 52.

9.2. Distrusting the Distant Past?

Ancient writers often noted that material from centuries earlier could be obscure, yet they expected a much higher standard of accuracy for reports closer to their own period.[14] Thus, for example, when Arrian writes about Alexander of Macedon half a millennium after Alexander's death, he complains about the widely divergent views circulating by his day.[15] Plutarch recognizes the major difference between his early historical sources regarding a still earlier king.[16]

This issue becomes even more acute when writing about the most distant past, perhaps a millennium before the writer. Most recognized that this earliest period was generally shrouded in myth,[17] even if they sometimes found the myths' basic outline acceptable.[18] Although universal historians often included in their works the period of ancient heroes, many distinguished the mythical period from the more realistic "historical" period.[19] Some writers considered the earlier period qualitatively different because of divine involvement;[20] by contrast, others mistrusted its reports precisely because of such unusual events.[21]

14. E.g., Thucydides, *History* 1.21.1; Livy, *History* 6.1.2–3; 7.6.6; Diodorus Siculus, *Library of History* 1.6.2; 1.9.2; 4.1.1; 4.8.3–5; Dionysius of Halicarnassus, *Roman Antiquities* 1.12.3; *Thucydides* 5; Pausanias, *Description of Greece* 9.31.7; Josephus, *Against Apion* 1.15, 24–25, 58; cf. Bowersock, *Fiction*, 1–2.

15. Arrian, *Alexander* 1.pref.1–2; Justin, *Epitome* 12.13.10, notes different versions but is overconfident in his knowledge as to which was correct—though as noted below, some divergences came from writers *too* close to Alexander's time. For disagreements among historians, see also Quintilian, *Orator's Education* 2.4.19; for various versions of Alcibiades's death, see, e.g., Nepos, *On Great Generals* 7 (Alcibiades), 10; Diodorus Siculus, *Library of History* 14.11; Justin, *Epitome* 5.8.14; Valerius Maximus, *Memorable Doings and Sayings* 1.7.ext.9; Plutarch, *Alcibiades* 38–39.

16. Almagor, "Narratives," 70–71, noting Plutarch, *Artaxerxes* 1.4; 6.9; 9.4; 10–11; 19.2–6.

17. Dionysius of Halicarnassus, *Thucydides* 5–7; Plutarch, *Theseus* 1.1; Justin, *Epitome* 2.6.7; 11.3.11 (with less recognition, cf. 42.2.10–42.3.9; 44.4.12); Keener, *John*, 20. See further Kennedy, "Source Criticism," 139, citing Quintilian, *Orator's Education* 2.4.18–19, and Livy's repeated qualifications in his first ten books.

18. E.g., Thucydides, *History* 1.21.1 (complaining in 1.21.2 that people make ancient events greater than they were). For his inconsistency, see Marincola, *Authority*, 96.

19. Fornara, *Nature*, 4–12, esp. 9–10. Becker, *Birth*, 121, parallels the genre distinction between Gen 1–11 and later OT historiography.

20. Hesiod, *Works and Days* 158–60, 165; Arrian, *Alexander* 5.1.2. For Rome, some early public records existed (Lintott, *Romans*, 15).

21. Thucydides, *History* 1.23.3. On smaller-scale supernatural reports, however, see ch. 12.

When writing about characters of the distant past, historians had to sort through legendary as well as actual historical data,[22] and they might well have difficulty ascertaining which was which.[23] When depending on historically remote sources, therefore, ancient historiography sometimes had to settle for mere verisimilitude.[24] Sometimes they sought to "demythologize" back to a probable historical core behind such stories,[25] but Plutarch, who sought such a core,[26] rightly recognized that most of his sources were unconfirmable.[27] Sometimes historical writers simply repeated apparently incredible information while warning readers to use discretion;[28] sometimes they deemed them too implausible even for that expedient.[29]

Their criteria for distinguishing what was credible from what was not were often inadequate, but they do at least illustrate ancient intellectuals' recognition of the problem and their critical intentions. In chapter 7 I noted various criteria that ancient historians sometimes adopted, including coherency with other evidence. One additional and particularly important concern was how close sources were to the events that they reported.

9.3. Wits about Witnesses

Historical writers' often cautious approach to early sources contrasts with their greater trust in more recent ones.[30] The next best source to witnesses, on which

22. Cf. Livy, *History* 1.1.1. Still, archaeology occasionally confirms even some information behind etiological explanations once deemed mythical; see, e.g., Egelhaaf-Gaiser, "Sites," 212.

23. Historians might recognize exaggerations in an account, while averring that genuine historical tradition stood behind it (Livy, *History* 3.8.10), or might regard an account as too implausible altogether (Aulus Gellius, *Attic Nights* 10.12.8–10). Some sources, like the *Life of Aesop*, may simply string together all available popular traditions into a narrative; these traditions had grown over six centuries (see Drury, *Design*, 28–29).

24. See Dio Cassius, *Roman History* 62.11.3–4; Aune, *Environment*, 83; Fornara, *Nature*, 134–36.

25. See, e.g., Thucydides, *History* 1.21.1–2; Dionysius of Halicarnassus, *Roman Antiquities* 1.39.1; 1.41.1 (cf. 1.84.4); *Thucydides* 6; Justin, *Epitome* 4.1.13, 16–17 (cf. 44.4.16); Livy, *History* 3.8.10; Arrian, *Alexander* 2.16.6; Philostratus, *Lives of the Sophists* 2.1.554. See also examples in Saïd, "Myth," 81–88; briefly, Fowler, "History," 204.

26. Plutarch, *Theseus* 1.3.

27. Alfred, "Valuation," 87.

28. E.g., Livy, *History* 4.29.5–6; 23.47.8; cf. (more skeptically) Lucian, *How to Write History* 60.

29. Aulus Gellius, *Attic Nights* 10.12.8–10.

30. For the greater confidence in historians recording recent events, see Marincola, *Authority*, 262. Too recent to engage fully, see esp. now Peters, "Historiography."

we depend today for knowledge of the distant past, is literary memory that may depend on eyewitnesses.[31] But while historians often used records to write about the distant past, the historiographic ideal was firsthand investigation and consulting witnesses.

Eyewitnesses are not a perfect source, of course; an individual witness's vantage point is limited, and he or she will not remember every detail. Whether because of bias,[32] memory lapse,[33] or sometimes even incompetence,[34] even eyewitnesses did not always agree on details, requiring some weighing of individual testimony.[35] Merely four decades after Galba's death, for example, sources offered no unanimity regarding who assassinated him.[36]

The second best source after the author being an eyewitness was the author's use of other eyewitnesses;[37] biographers were happy to use recent oral tradition from eyewitnesses.[38] Historians today are apt to trust eyewitness knowledge even in otherwise more questionable ancient historians.[39] Although some earlier modern historians treated personal involvement as permitting bias,[40] today's oral historiography allows greater appreciation for participation.[41]

31. Cf. Becker, *Birth*, 28.

32. Byrskog, *Story*, 176–79, notes that ancient historians were aware that eyewitnesses could be biased and tried to take this into account (sometimes through the grid of their own biases).

33. For gist generally being reliable in memory even where details are not, see Bauckham, *Eyewitnesses*, 333–34. Historians themselves often quoted their sources from memory, hence could get correct the gist while being confused on some details (Marincola, "Introduction," 2).

34. For failure to learn accurately from purported travels, see Strabo, *Geography* 2.5.10; Hengel, "Geography," 31; for suspected dishonesty, see Lucian, *How to Write History* 25, 29.

35. Thucydides, *History* 1.22.3; Arrian, *Alexander* 4.14.3. Cf. Becker, *Birth*, 27, regarding disputes about eyewitness testimony.

36. Ash, "Assassinating Emperors," 202, citing Tacitus, *Histories* 1.41.3. For discussion of Caligula's assassin in Josephus, cf. Kavanagh, "Identity."

37. Plutarch, *Lycurgus* 1 (Woldemariam, "Comparison," 219); Lucian, *How to Write History* 47; Jervell, "Future," 118; Derrenbacker, *Practices*, 73, 75; Pitcher, "Story," 296–97 (noting, e.g., Sallust, *Catiline's War* 48; Livy, *History* 21.38.3–5; Plutarch, *Marc Antony* 28.7).

38. E.g., Xenophon, *Apology* 2; *Agesilaus* 3.1; Dionysius of Halicarnassus, *Thucydides* 6–7; Cornelius Nepos, *On Great Generals* 23 (Hannibal), 13.3; 25 (Atticus), 13.7; 17.1; Plutarch, *Demosthenes* 11.1; *Otho* 14.1; Suetonius, *Otho* 10.1; *Vespasian* 1.4; Arrian, *Alexander* 1, pref.2–3; 6.11.8.

39. E.g., Brown, *Historians*, 142, 146; in more recent history, see, e.g., Wigger, *Saint*, 363.

40. Byrskog, *Story*, 19–22; less today, cf. 23–26.

41. Byrskog, *Story*, 153; for its wider use today, see, e.g., Moniot, "Profile," 50. For discussions of participant observation in anthropology, see, e.g., Tedlock, "Observation"; DeWalt and DeWalt, *Observation*; Jorgensen, "Observation"; Spradley, *Observation*.

Even better still than consulting witnesses was the historian's personal experience.[42] Historians and biographers who were eyewitnesses usually were happy to mention this fact.[43] Josephus condemns Greek historians willing to write about events where they were neither present nor dependent on those with firsthand knowledge.[44] Some, he complained, wrote about the war without having been there, which was inadequate research for appropriate histories.[45] By contrast, Josephus lived through the events he narrated.[46]

Best of all would be witnesses writing while other authoritative witnesses remained alive. Josephus emphasizes that he composed his account while witnesses remained alive who could verify or falsify his claims,[47] and he complains that Justus, one of his rivals, waited twenty years to publish, till after the eyewitnesses were dead.[48] Josephus contends that Justus should be less believable than himself, since the eyewitnesses knew Josephus's work and they never protested its claims.[49] In contrast to Josephus, Justus was not present during key events, and anyone who could have supplied Justus with such information perished in the siege of Jerusalem.[50] These claims also suggest that if Josephus's details included any embellishments (as they surely did), the eyewitnesses

42. See, e.g., Lucian, *How to Write History* 47; Josephus, *Life* 357; *Against Apion* 1.45–49, 56; *Jewish War* 1.2–3; Pitcher, "Story," 297 (citing Thucydides, *History* 2.48.3; Tacitus, *Agricola* 24); Aune, *Environment*, 81 (citing Herodotus, *Histories* 2.99; Polybius, *Histories* 3.4.13; 12.25g.1; 12.27.1–6; 12.28.1–5; 20.12.8; Lucian, *How to Write History* 47); Byrskog, *Story*, 153–57, 188; Meister, "Historiography: Greece," 421; cf. Alexander, *Preface*, 34; Keener, "Claims."

43. E.g., Xenophon, *Symposium* 1.1; Polybius, *Histories* 29.21.8; Cornelius Nepos, *On Great Generals* 25 (Atticus), 13.7; 17.1; Josephus, *Against Apion* 1.45–47; Philostratus, *Lives of the Sophists* 2.21.602–4; Keener, *Acts*, 3:2353, 2362. Some preferred to include their presence in the third person, as in Xenophon, *Anabasis* 2.5.41; 3.1.4–6; Thucydides, *History* 1.1.1; 2.103.2; 5.26.1; Polybius, *Histories* 31.23.1–31.24.12; 38.19.1; 38.21.1; 38.22.3; Caesar, *Civil War*, throughout, e.g., 1.1; *Gallic Wars*, throughout, 1.7; 2.1; 3.28; 4.13; 5.9; 6.4; 7.17 (despite phrases like "our own" and "our men," 2.9); Eunapius, *Lives* 494; first-person (when present, not at all important junctures) in Velleius Paterculus, *History* 2.101.2–3; 2.104.3; 2.106.1; 2.111.3–4; 2.114.1–3; 2.115.5; 2.121.3; 124.4.

44. Josephus, *Against Apion* 1.45.

45. Josephus, *Against Apion* 1.46. Naturally, Josephus would be happy to enforce a criterion that excluded his competitors but not himself. Yet Josephus hardly invented this criterion, useful as it proved in his case (for his *Jewish War* and *Life* more than his *Jewish Antiquities*).

46. Josephus, *Against Apion* 1.47; cf. 1.49, 56.

47. Josephus, *Jewish Antiquities* 20.266.

48. Josephus, *Life* 359–60.

49. Josephus, *Life* 361–66.

50. Josephus, *Life* 357. Nevertheless, Josephus is happy to depict a scene, such as the suicide of the Sicarii at Masada, where he lacks potential eyewitnesses.

did not complain, recognizing such embellishments of comparatively minor details as an accepted part of the genre.[51]

Many ancient historians and biographers besides Josephus had direct access to their subjects. Thus, for example, a noted fifth-century BCE historian claims to report what he has learned by inquiry and what he saw directly.[52] Likewise Xenophon, as a member of Agesilaus's staff, knew this king directly and could depend on his own experience for his account.[53] Against detractors, Xenophon also probably knew Socrates personally.[54] Key Alexander historians Ptolemy and Aristobulus knew Alexander personally; although their works have not survived, they are heavily mined by later writers such as Arrian, who valued their proximity to their subject.[55] Likewise, Eratosthenes wrote about a figure based on "personal knowledge."[56]

Closer to our period of primary interest, Atticus was Nepos's close friend; Nepos's biography of Atticus is longer than his other biographies precisely because Nepos had much more information available about Atticus.[57] (Where we can test this biography against external sources, it does fare well on most points.)[58] Nepos may have also written about Antony while he was alive[59] and probably wrote his multivolume work on Cicero within a few years of Cicero's death.[60] Nepos did not always understand his sources about foreign generals, valuable as those sources were, but his Roman lives are quite different. For some of these, he was himself a witness and had access to many other witnesses.[61]

Tacitus's fairly intimate knowledge of his father-in-law, Agricola, renders that life of special value, outweighing the risks of his bias.[62] Plutarch, who wrote biographies about Galba and Otho, was already alive when they reigned. Lucian's biography of the sage Demonax also commemorates someone that

---

51. Undoubtedly the portrayal was also not to their detriment; Josephus was careful to praise surviving political figures like Agrippa and any member of the Flavian dynasty.

52. Herodotus, *Histories* 2.99.1.

53. Ytterbrink, *Gospel*, 85; Beck, "Demonax," 93 (noting esp. Cartledge, *Agesilaus*).

54. Votaw, "Biographies," 55, 224 (on 56, comparing Arrian on Epictetus and contrasting Philostratus on Apollonius).

55. Derrenbacker, *Practices*, 54–55, noting Arrian, *Alexander* 1.pref.

56. Momigliano, *Development*, 84.

57. Geiger, *Nepos*, 28; cf. Hägg, *Biography*, 188–97, esp. 189–90.

58. Wright, "Exploration," 246–49, esp. 249, regarding his death.

59. Geiger, *Nepos*, 95.

60. Geiger, *Nepos*, 101.

61. Geiger, *Nepos*, 109.

62. See Alfred, "Valuation," 85.

he claims to have known and admired,[63] helping to explain the work's "emotional closeness."[64] Likewise, Porphyry personally knew his teacher Plotinus and focuses on the part of Plotinus's life that he knew directly.[65] We respect Thucydides and Polybius and (in the first century) Josephus as contemporaries of much of what they report.

9.4. Reasoning about Recent History

Unlike biographers just mentioned, most biographers wrote after their subjects had died. Still, many wrote about recent figures, and after firsthand sources, historical writers valued most highly those closest in date to the events reported.[66] Some biographers wrote about subjects soon after the subject's decease.[67] We depend heavily on imperfect but valuable writers of the early empire like Tacitus and Suetonius, who report relatively recent events.

Because oral traditions were most reliable in the generation they recounted, the ideal was for each generation of Greek historians to "establish the record of their own time."[68] The historian Polybius, for example, wrote within living memory of Scipio and had access to Scipio's own relatives and acquaintances.[69] A historian might mention even an account that he could not confirm if he received it from the previous generation.[70]

Many biographers likewise sought to offer a legacy based on "living memory," that is, composed at a time when they had "access to firsthand/eyewitness accounts."[71] Many of these biographers wrote as the subject's "students,

63. Lucian, *Demonax* 1; Beck, "Demonax," 80, 95; cf. Eunapius, *Lives* 454; Humble and Sidwell, "Dreams," 213, noting also his claims to have experienced Alexander the False Prophet (*Alexander* 53–57) and Peregrinus's suicide scene (*Peregrinus* 2.43–45).

64. Beck, "Demonax," 96.

65. Dillon, "Interpretation," 158.

66. E.g., Livy, *History* 7.6.6; 25.11.20; Tacitus, *Annals* 15.73; Plutarch, *Malice of Herodotus* 20, *Moralia* 859B.

67. Smith, "Genre," 212, cites Nepos's *On Great Generals* 24 (Cato) and Suetonius's *Caligula, Claudius,* and *Nero*; cf. Smith, βίος, 59–60.

68. Fornara, *Nature*, 48.

69. Bauckham, *Eyewitnesses*, 517. Even Pompeius Trogus, who aspired to a more universal history, was happy to note his direct family connections with recent events (Justin, *Epitome* 43.5.11–12).

70. Tacitus, *Annals* 3.16.

71. Smith, "Genre," 212n128; cf. also 213–16; Smith, βίος, 57n174, 60. On living memory, see ch. 16. For greater reliability for recent history, see esp. Peters, "Historiography," esp. chs. 4–6 (pp. 47–184).

disciples or friends"[72] (or, in some cases, enemies),[73] or had access to such acquaintances' direct accounts. Apologetic biographic works often use eyewitness accounts to counter slanders against their biographees.[74]

Not all "living memory" literary analogies are equally relevant, because not all appear in the same literary genre. Roughly half a century transpired between Socrates's most public activity and the extant writings about him. As some note, this span is roughly comparable to the usually accepted interval between Jesus and the Synoptic Gospels.[75] Although this analogy is valuable, however, it has some limitations. Plato and Xenophon knew Socrates personally, but they wrote in a formative period of what we have occasionally called protobiography. Moreover, readers recognized a fictional element of dialogues, which were not characteristic of typical early-empire biographies.

No one claims that all the Evangelists witnessed Jesus's ministry personally, but the Evangelists wrote at the apex of historical biography, hence, at least in the case of the Synoptics, would be less apt to fill out dialogues with abundant interpretive addenda. For this reason, in chapter 10 I compare them especially with some biographies from their own period that, also like the reports about Socrates, stem from roughly half a century after the events.

Among the Gospels, Luke apparently claims a level of participation; the Fourth Gospel recounts testimony from an eyewitness disciple (see ch. 13), and early tradition claims that Mark knew Peter (and that at least something related to Matthew, a literate disciple, circulated).

9.5. Narrowing the Gap for Earlier Figures

Did works ever contain accurate information even if, unlike the Gospels, their material was passed on for centuries? Beyond living memory, written sources were crucial. By its nature, historical writing about earlier (rather than more recent) events necessarily depended on earlier historians.[76] Authors often deferred to written sources as particularly authoritative in any case;[77] even an

---

72. Smith, "Genre," 216; cf. Smith, βίος, 61.

73. Cf. Aristoxenus's critique of Socrates; more strident if less biographic, Lucian's *Alexander* and *Peregrinus*.

74. Smith, "Genre," 213 (and Smith, βίος, 60), citing Isocrates, *Euagoras* 4–6; Xenophon, *Agesilaus* 3.1; 10.3; Tacitus, *Agricola* 4.3; 24.3; 44.5.

75. Votaw, "Biographies," 223, 246.

76. Pliny, *Letters* 5.8.12.

77. Eunapius, *Lives* 460. Suetonius depends more heavily on older written records than

eyewitness might cite another eyewitness source published before his own work.[78] Many understood that whereas oral tradition could be modified over time, written sources were fixed.[79]

At least occasionally, even evidence grounded in the most slender and distant connections to witnesses proves correct. Thus, for example, many historians doubted Sima Qian's sequential list of rulers from the Shang Dynasty, because he wrote in the early first century BCE, over a millennium after that second-millennium BCE dynasty. While many aspects of his account of the distant past are either unverifiable or legendary, however, the majority of the Shang rulers' names have now been confirmed by excavations at the final Shang capital.[80]

More often, even vastly earlier sources can prove valuable when we can be confident that they reflect sources close to the time of the events they report. Because of authors' agendas, later writers occasionally might even interpret earlier sources' information more accurately than the authors of those earlier sources,[81] although we should not expect this superior interpretation in the majority of cases.

Our earliest extant, fairly full biography of Aristotle comes from Diogenes Laertius, more than half a millennium after the philosopher's death. That Diogenes Laertius employed much earlier sources, however, somewhat narrows this gap.[82] In the case of Agesilaus, Plutarch's biography contains some information supplemental to that of Xenophon, probably reflecting some other very early sources no longer extant.[83]

---

interviews of more recent persons (Rolfe, "Introduction," xviii). The Greek method preferred interviews, but even Romans could write about contemporary figures (e.g., Pliny, *Letters* 9.19.5); even some Greek writers like Ephorus and Timaeus critically emphasized written sources, though Polybius appreciated the former and attacked the latter (Schepens, "History," 50–51).

78. Xenophon, *Hellenica* 3.1.2; those who attribute the Gospel of Matthew to one of the Twelve yet accept its dependence on Mark (e.g., Gundry, *Matthew*, 609–22) could adduce that case as a further example.

79. Eunapius, *Lives* 453; for anthropological observations consistent with this practice, see Lord, *Singer*, 138. Nevertheless, oral material can become fixed, and scribes can adapt written material (Niditch, "Hebrew Bible," 5, following Nagy, *Questions*, 68–69, who offers medieval examples of the latter).

80. Brought to my attention by David Marshall through his then-forthcoming book, *Jesus Is No Myth*, 72.

81. Pelling, *Texts*, 54.

82. Fitzgerald, "Lives," 214–15, 220. Even Hermippus, however, wrote roughly a century after Aristotle's death (216).

83. See, e.g., Theopompus in Plutarch, *Agesilaus* 10.5; 31.3; 32.8; 33.1; Spartan records in 19.6; with Woldemariam, "Comparison," 219.

All full works about Alexander that survive date to "three centuries or more after Alexander's death."[84] Scholars have commented particularly extensively on the date and sources for Arrian's account, generally considered the best extant account. Arrian had plenty of practice writing before turning to his monumental treatment of Alexander: he had already taken copious notes from the teaching of his mentor Epictetus and published biographies of political figures.[85]

Yet Arrian himself was quite aware that he wrote long after Alexander—close to half a millennium after him. Noting the contradictory sources, Arrian complains that everyone has been passing on falsehoods for centuries. He proposes to remedy this situation by noting the core of essential facts, on which there was unanimity, and by preferring the eyewitnesses' published testimony to that of others.[86] Arrian was critical, even if not all scholars today agree with some of his choices.

To supply anecdotes for his biography, Plutarch cites Alexander's chamberlain and his official (propagandistic) historian, but Arrian, writing military history, draws especially on the military sources.[87] Although allowing other sources for his more encomiastic praise of Alexander,[88] Arrian's historical narrative draws especially on Alexander's officer Ptolemy and his engineer Aristobulus.[89] Secondarily, he also draws on other sources that he deems authentic, including Nearchus, commander of Alexander's fleet, and the so-called Royal Journals.[90] Although other Alexander biographies drew heavily on Cleitarchus, who provided the most popular account about Alexander in Arrian's day, Arrian mistrusted this source, perhaps not entirely fairly.[91]

He reports some traditions that he finds in earlier historians, yet about which he personally expresses suspicion,[92] such as about the Amazons[93] or a

84. Lee, "Source Criticism," 208.

85. Atkinson, "Introduction," xiv, xvii.

86. Arrian, *Alexander* 6.11.2–3, 8.

87. Atkinson, "Introduction," xxx.

88. See discussion in Derrenbacker, *Practices*, 54–59.

89. Atkinson, "Introduction," xxvii.

90. Atkinson, "Introduction," xxxi. On these Ephemerides, see Hammond, *Sources*, 158, 162, 203, 331–32; Bosworth, *Arrian*, 157–84, esp. 183–84.

91. Atkinson, "Introduction," xxxii–xxxiii, contrasting the approach of Diodorus Siculus, *Library of History* bk. 17; Quintus Curtius Rufus; Trogus's *Philippica* bks. 11–12; and Plutarch; cf. Bosworth, *Arrian*, 7, 9.

92. Atkinson, "Introduction," xxix, citing, e.g., Arrian, *Alexander* 2.12.8.

93. Arrian, *Alexander* 7.13.2–6 (cf. 4.15.4); Atkinson, "Introduction," xxix; Bosworth, *Arrian*, 66; further discussion in Keener, *Acts*, 2:1557–60, 1576.

Roman embassy to Alexander.[94] He frequently omits details in his sources that he does not think worth recording,[95] but he apparently expects his readers to be familiar with some of his predecessors' accounts in any case.[96]

Despite his critical efforts, however, the half a millennium between Alexander and Arrian created difficulties. Arrian sometimes includes contradictory accounts,[97] unable to harmonize even his best sources.[98] Where even Ptolemy and Aristobulus differ, he has to choose between them.[99] In a matter as critical as how Alexander died, the reports available in Arrian's time diverged widely.[100] (Admittedly, both views could stem from the first generation; he may have died from fever that some others, seeking someone to blame, attributed to poison. For that matter, some poisons can produce fevers.)

Wherever possible, Arrian depends on sources from living memory of Alexander, from the period of those who knew him. Unfortunately, these direct sources were also writing in a period when biographic treatments were not as rigorously historical (by modern definitions) as (comparatively speaking) in Arrian's own time. Scholars, however, often differ regarding the authenticity of some of Arrian's centuries-older sources, a matter that Arrian could no longer evaluate directly in his own day, since none of his sources were from the lifetimes of anyone living in his own day.

If our only extant sources about Jesus were from as long after Jesus as Arrian is after Alexander, we would be depending on sources from the late fifth century, more than a generation after the death of Augustine or John Cassian. One can imagine what historical skeptics would say about Jesus if the first extant historical reports about him came from Paulus Orosius's *History against the Pagans*, from Socrates Scholasticus's *Ecclesiastical History*, or (more analogous chronologically though not in content) from still later sources such as the *Tome* of Pope Leo the Great.[101]

94. Bosworth, *Arrian*, 91; Atkinson, "Introduction," xxix, citing Arrian, *Alexander* 7.15.5–6. Bosworth, *Arrian*, 92–93, suggests that Cleitarchus rightly reported such an embassy, simply not considered important enough in immediately subsequent generations to be recorded by others.

95. See Arrian, *Alexander* 2.24.6.

96. Arrian, *Alexander* 7.3.6.

97. Atkinson, "Introduction," xxx.

98. Sometimes he cites potential solutions, e.g., Arrian, *Indica* 5.13.

99. "What I feel to be more likely and also better worth narrating" (*Alexander* 1.pref.; LCL); cf. Derrenbacker, *Practices*, 54.

100. For the different views of Alexander's death, see Lee, "Source Criticism," 209–14.

101. Orosius apparently died after 418 CE; Socrates of Constantinople, ca. 450 CE; and Leo in 461.

By contrast, the Gospels themselves stem from living memory of Jesus and come from a period when expectations for biographic treatments included greater historical care. The Gospels prove much more consistent on key points such as Jesus's death by crucifixion.[102] The span between Jesus's public ministry and the publication of Mark's Gospel may be just one-tenth the period after Jesus's ministry as Arrian's work was after Alexander's death, so one may question why many NT scholars are significantly more skeptical of the Gospels than are other historians of Arrian.[103]

9.6. Valuing Some Historical Distance for Contemporary History

Although sources within living memory are generally most reliable, ancient historians thought that some sources could be *too* close to the events to be reliable. Strictly speaking, this is not a matter of memory (for which the earliest sources are usually the best) but of bias, social and political pressure, and (more relevant for the Gospels) historical perspective.[104]

Self-praise in autobiographies or inscriptions[105] could distort the telling of current history. An often greater threat came from contemporary political exigencies.[106] Pleasing powerful potential readers was a significant temptation, and avoiding their wrath sometimes a necessity. The advantage of writing about ancient history, one orator noted, was that one could simply collect what earlier historians said, whereas writing about recent matters might lead to trouble![107] Given the political climate of the early empire, Nicolaus of Damascus was prudent to praise Augustus[108] and Herod the Great.[109] More strikingly, the historian Velleius Paterculus is far less reserved than later historians in his praise of

---

102. Lee, "Source Criticism," 214, notes also Josephus, *Jewish Antiquities* 18.63–64; Lucian, *Peregrinus* 11; and the implications of Tacitus, *Annals* 15.44.

103. Emphasized by Lee, "Source Criticism," 208–9, 214–15.

104. Cf. Velleius Paterculus, *History* 2.92.5; 2.126.1. Biographies of living persons may prove too encomiastic, though they also provide invaluable information once we take into account their perspectives (Laistner, *Historians*, 34–35). Cf. Marincola, *Authority*, 166.

105. Livy did not always trust written records, including recent inscriptions; too often they were designed for boasting by those who commissioned them (Small, *Wax Tablets*, 59).

106. Cf. also Momigliano, *Development*, 99–100; Becker, *Birth*, 152–53.

107. Pliny, *Letters* 5.8.12–13 (considering earlier times more praiseworthy); Tacitus, *Annals* 4.33; cf. also Becker, *Birth*, 149–50.

108. Becker, *Birth*, 150, citing *FGrH* 90, F 125–30 (though Augustus remained popular afterward as well).

109. Josephus, *Jewish Antiquities* 16.184.

Tiberius,[110] which probably has something to do with Tiberius being emperor while the historian was writing.[111] His praise of the praetorian prefect Sejanus Aelius[112] would have been inconceivable after Sejanus's shameful execution.[113] Velleius's bias was not wholesale,[114] but some topics would have been off-limits even if he privately entertained views unsafe for public expression. Extant early second-century historians do not complain much about constraints—though neither do they write much about contemporary emperors.[115] In the third century, political pressures apparently did affect the historian Dio Cassius.[116]

Life-and-death political pressures were not the only danger of contemporary history; friendship offered a different sort of peril.[117] Eager to appear in Tacitus's history, the orator Pliny the Younger reminds the historian that Pliny prosecuted a corrupt governor.[118] Since history must report only truth, Pliny readily concedes, Tacitus will not go beyond the facts.[119] To the extent, however, that Tacitus's sort of history focuses on major events, Pliny's deed hardly qualifies. Whether Tacitus included the account we cannot say (some of his work has not survived), but I am tempted to ask what hope there is for poor, beleaguered authors with too many friends? Pliny's family knew the risks of accusations of biased historiography. Pliny's uncle and namesake produced and confirmed a history of an elite family but withheld its publication during his life lest he be accused of writing it from ambition.[120]

The ideal, of course, was avoiding agendas pro or con. One historian declares that history should cater to leaders neither by flattering nor by attacking

110. Velleius Paterculus, *History*, throughout, e.g., 2.94.2–3; 2.129.1–2.130.5. See further Gowing, "Republic," 412–17.

111. E.g., Velleius Paterculus, *History* 2.94.3.

112. E.g., Velleius Paterculus, *History* 2.127.3; 2.128.4.

113. For history's later verdicts, see, e.g., Philo, *Flaccus* 1; *Embassy* 37, 159–60; Josephus, *Jewish Antiquities* 18.181–82, 250; Tacitus, *Annals* 1.69; 3.16; 3.29; 4.10–5.9; Suetonius, *Tiberius* 48, 55, 65; Juvenal, *Satires* 10.66, 76, 89–90, 104; Phaedrus, *Fables* 3, prol. 41–44.

114. Velleius fairly consistently unveils tragic weaknesses, errors, or misdeeds in otherwise strong characters (*History* 2.1.1–3; 2.3.1–2; 2.4.4; 2.6.1–2; 2.7.1; 2.33.2, 4; 2.46.2; 2.88.2; 2.91.2; cf. 2.98.2–3) and often positive traits in weak characters (2.24.2, 5); or characters changing (2.18.5; 2.25.3; 2.28.2).

115. Tacitus apparently never carried through his plans to write about his own time; see Marincola, *Authority*, 167.

116. Hose, "Cassius Dio," 462–63.

117. One might be thought biased when writing about close friends (Philostratus, *Lives of the Sophists* 2.33.628).

118. Pliny, *Letters* 7.33.1–9; cf. 6.16, 20.

119. Pliny, *Letters* 7.33.10.

120. Pliny, *Natural History* pref.

them.[121] More extensively, Lucian complains that writers who praise their rulers and generals while slandering the other side merely engage in panegyric.[122] Flatterers work for the present; historians must preserve truth for the future.[123] As particular models of good historians, Lucian offers Xenophon and Thucydides (both contemporaries of the events they report), who would not let personal bias make them change facts. "Public interest" and truth must take priority over personal enmity or friendship.[124] Likewise, good biographers avoid flattery that falsifies events.[125] Achieving the ideal, however, was usually easier after the demise of the corrupting influences.

Conspicuous flattery often disgusted readers,[126] who often contrasted it with honorable frankness[127] and viewed flattery as a form of servility.[128] Thus, for example, Aristobulus, wanting to please Alexander, allegedly inserted into the first draft of his history a false story of single combat between Alexander and the Indian king Porus. Alexander responded by discarding the fiction angrily and trusted Aristobulus less than before.[129] Callisthenes, Alexander's embedded historian, composed excessively encomiastic tributes of Alexander, which posterity condemned as flattery.[130] Such propaganda, Arrian recognized, could help create legend.[131] One reason that Arrian preferred Ptolemy

121. Tacitus, *Histories* 1.1.

122. Lucian, *How to Write History* 7.

123. Lucian, *How to Write History* 40. One must, he emphasized, tell the truth, no matter how offensive to one's own contemporaries; thus one would win praise in future generations (61–62)—assuming, of course, one's work survived. On writing for the future, for posterity, see also 42.

124. Lucian, *How to Write History* 39.

125. Lucian, *How to Write History* 12. Against flattery corrupting historiography, see further Lucian, *How to Write History* 13, 17, 38–41, 61–62.

126. See, e.g., Isocrates, *To Nicocles* 28; Seneca, *Dialogues* 10.15.2; Plutarch, *How to Tell a Flatterer from a Friend* 17–37, *Moralia* 59A–74E; cf. 1 Thess 2:5; Plutarch, *On the Education of Children* 17, *Moralia* 13B.

127. Dionysius of Halicarnassus, *Roman Antiquities* 11.9.1; Tacitus, *Histories* 1.15; Plutarch, *Aemilius Paulus* 11.3; *How to Tell a Flatterer from a Friend* 1–37, *Moralia* 48E–74E; *How to Profit by One's Enemies* 6, *Moralia* 89B; Dio Chrysostom, *Orations* 4.15; Lucian, *Nigrinus* 15; *Demonax* 3; cf. Kemp, "Flattery."

128. E.g., Velleius Paterculus, *History* 2.83.1; Musonius Rufus 7, p. 58.3; Dio Chrysostom, *Orations* 51.1; 66.13–14; Aelius Aristides, *Defense of Oratory* 309, §100D; Iamblichus, *Pythagorean Life* 32.226; Marshall, *Enmity*, 73–90, 256–57.

129. Lucian, *How to Write History* 12, commending Alexander. The story itself might be a fiction.

130. Brown, *Historians*, 125. His tributes, distinct from Ps.-Callisthenes's *Alexander Romance*, have not survived.

131. Arrian, *Alexander* 4.28.1–2.

and Aristobulus was that, because Alexander was dead when they wrote their histories, their works could not be motivated by flattery.[132]

Some biographies of Nero that have not survived stem from roughly the same time as the Synoptic Gospels.[133] The writers had directly benefitted from Nero's favors or suffered his repression. Nero died in 68, so these "many" (πολλοί, *polloi*; cf. Luke 1:1) writers, obviously varying in perspective, composed their works at the latest within two decades after Nero's death. Yet Josephus denounces many of these contemporary accounts (a genre he labels as ἱστορία, *historia*) as tendentious and including falsehoods, partly because they were too close to the events to write impartially.[134] Apart from documentation, Suetonius is ready to question some versions of an emperor's lineage if they might be attributed to partiality or hostility.[135]

Usually more relevant for the Gospels than concern for flattery or political pressure is the question of historical distance. Historians often need at least some space after events to discern which events will lead to significant effects in the long run.[136] Oxford's Markus Bockmuehl points out that the 1940 edition of *Encyclopaedia Britannica* devotes only a half column to Adolf Hitler, offering there more information about his "vegetarian diet and lack of respect for the Treaty of Versailles than about his ideological views on Greater Germany or the Jews." Likewise, its much longer article on Winston Churchill focuses on his military failures in the First World War and dismisses his current relevance as "a political has-been."[137] These two figures bear roles of entirely different significance when viewed from a vantage point several years later.

The ideal setting for historical writing is distant enough to avoid myopia yet within the period of living memory.[138]

132. Arrian, *Alexander* 1.pref.2. Atkinson, "Introduction," xxxi, suggests, however, that Aristobulus wrote almost *too* long after Alexander's death.

133. Josephus, *Jewish Antiquities* 20.154.

134. Despite the relatively short gap between the events in and writing of his *Life*.

135. Suetonius, *Vitellius* 1.

136. Noted already by Polybius, *Histories* 9.2.5; cf. 3.31.11–13.

137. Bockmuehl, *Seeing*, 167.

138. Bockmuehl, *Seeing*, 168. The same is true even in our personal lives; for example, long-range outcomes sift for me what in my old journal entries is ultimately "significant." It may also correspond with what some call "impact" (e.g., in the subtitle of Belmonte, *Joy*).

9.7. The Gospels and Recent Information

How much would Diaspora Christians have known about Jesus? Before the writing of the first Gospel, their knowledge may have been limited. Paul cites the Jesus tradition only intermittently (e.g., 1 Cor 9:14), although he also seems to assume at times his audience's familiarity with some of it, perhaps from his prior teaching (1 Cor 9:5; 11:23–26; 15:3–7; cf. Acts 18:11). But once it became more widely available, the Jesus tradition undoubtedly circulated quickly in the Diaspora as well as in Judea.

Most, though not all, scholars agree that Luke wrote in the first century, most often suggesting a date between 70 and 90.[139] That Luke can assume that he is merely confirming the matters that Theophilus had been taught (Luke 1:4) shows that by the time Luke wrote, the bulk of his accounts about Jesus had already been circulating widely in the Diaspora. This probably suggests that many memoirs about Jesus (cf. 1:1–2) were already being read in many of the communities.

By Theophilus's day, some of the narratives to which Luke refers (1:1), which claim to depend on the earliest witnesses (1:2),[140] were standard and respected sources, including almost certainly Mark and probably (on the majority view) Q. Luke seeks to improve the rhetorical order of the sources (perhaps esp. Mark)[141] but does not complain about their content. Rather, he affirms that his own acquaintance with the sources[142] confirms what The-

---

139. See the extensive survey of views in Pervo, *Dating Acts*, 359–63, although Pervo himself supported an early second-century date (*Dating Acts*, throughout; Pervo, "Dating Acts"); Tyson, *Marcion*, ix, also acknowledges that the second-century view, which he defends, is a minority. The later date requires a significant temporal gap between Luke and Acts, but most scholars affirm the work's unity (see, e.g., Pesch, *Apostelgeschichte*, 1:24–25; Schneider, "Zweck"; Marguerat, *Histoire*, 65–92; Marguerat, "Unité"; Marguerat, *Actes*, 17–18; Hemer, *Acts*, 3–33; Marshall, "Theme"; Marshall, "Reading"; Mekkattukunnel, "Proof"; Pate et al., *Story*, 177–87; Jervell, *Apostelgeschichte*, 91; Verheyden, *Unity*; Rothschild, *Rhetoric*, 115–16; Borgman, *Way*; Keener, *Acts*, 1:550–62, esp. 551; p⁴ (P.Paris 1120) offers fragments of Luke's Gospel from perhaps already the first half of the second century (Barnett, *Finding*, 35); cf. *1 Clem.* 2.1; 13.1; 18.1; 46.7; *Magn.* 5.1; *Smyrn.* 3.3; Polycarp 1.2. With a majority of scholars (see, e.g., Jervell, *Apostelgeschichte*, 86; Fitzmyer, *Acts*, 54–55; Sterling, *Historiography*, 329–30; Zwiep, *Ascension*, 168; Powell, *Acts*, 37), I have argued for a first-century date, in my case finding 70–80 somewhat more probable than the alternatives (Keener, *Acts*, 1:383–401; Keener, "Apologetic"). For a somewhat more recent survey, and supporting an earlier (pre-70) date, see Armstrong, "Plea," 98–108.

140. For discussion of the meaning of these verses, see Keener, *Acts*, 1:658–60.

141. Cf. possibly Papias, fragment, 3.15, depending on how he means τάξις, *taxis* ("order").

142. See Moessner, "Poetics," 85–97; Moessner, *Historian*, 68–107.

ophilus has learned, information that ultimately goes back to the tradition's originators (1:2). The Q material probably circulated while some of the original eyewitnesses remained in positions of leadership in the church (cf. Gal 2:9). (Theissen even contends for a date for Q in the 40s.)[143]

Clearly, the first-century Gospels depend on living memory. They are far enough from the initial events to have historical distance, witnessing some of their developments. At the same time, they are chronologically as close to the events as Suetonius was to Otho or Plutarch was to Galba. As Plutarch and Suetonius belonged to elites that had experienced the times they described, drawing especially on oral history and sources dependent on it, so the Evangelists belonged to a movement that had experienced the times they described, drawing again on oral history and sources dependent on it. Indeed, the Evangelists' movement had far more interest in the memory of Jesus than did Plutarch or Suetonius in those of Galba or Otho. The following chapter will explore more fully this analogous example of early second-century knowledge about Otho.

9.8. Conclusion

Ancient writers admitted that biographies about the distant past often had to work with legends; modern historians have shown that collective memory generally remains most reliable within living memory of the person—that is, within the lifetime of some who personally knew the eyewitnesses. (For discussion of memory within this time frame, see ch. 16.)

Conversely, ancient historians often considered contemporary accounts too prone to bias, primarily because of political pressure (not relevant to the Gospels). Moreover, it often takes time for the dust to settle and people to decide, retroactively, what sort of details matter for subsequent memory (thus the difficulty even today of writing contemporary "history"). In other words, the generation likeliest to supply the most useful memory of a person, by ancient standards, might be the generation just after the person's death.

Students of the Gospels should not forget that the Gospels depict events within living memory (see esp. discussion in chs. 14–16). What can we say about biographies from the early empire written within living memory of their subjects?

---

143. Theissen, *Gospels*, 220–21, 230–32.

Part 3

Testing the Range of Deviation

So far, we have observed that the Gospels fit the genre of ancient biography. Granted, the Gospels differ among themselves: for example, Mark's level is more popular, and Luke's interest is more historiographic (ch. 8), than the others. Each of the Gospels, however, falls within the range of biographic works (for the Fourth Gospel, see ch. 13). We have further observed (esp. in chs. 6–7) that biographies in the early empire overlapped considerably with historical monographs, and that they normally depended on substantial historical information. We have also noted that such biographies recounted their historical material in flexible ways (chs. 7 and esp. 5). Some took more liberties than others with filling in details, but any could fit anecdotes into their framework without concern for precise chronology.

We have not, however, explored specific case studies at greater length. In this section, therefore, I turn to some case studies that show the significant dependence on prior information of early imperial-era biographies about recent characters (ch. 10). I also note some specific literary techniques identified by other scholars that help quantify some of the sorts of liberties that biographers regularly took (ch. 11).

Such observations help us to recognize the sorts of expectations that ancient audiences would have brought to the Gospels. They would expect the essential story to be true or, if they regarded the Evangelists as charlatans, would at least expect that they were claiming the story to be true. "True" meant that they were recounting true events and fairly depicting the various characters involved (although human biases being what they are, various observers define fairness in different ways). "True" did not mean that audiences would expect chronological precision, verbatim recall, or precision on minor points.

Biographers differed among themselves in how much flexibility they displayed, and this factor must be determined on a case-by-case basis. Nevertheless, studying biographies of then-recent figures from the early empire provides us with a default expectation for the range of variations ancient audiences would ordinarily expect. Significantly, the quantity of historical substance encountered in these case studies of ancient biographies proves to be considerably greater than what more skeptical approaches to the Gospels would lead us to expect, as well as greater than what we might expect for protobiographies or for biographies composed centuries after their subjects.

Chapter 10

Case Studies: Biographies of Recent Characters Use Prior Information

Those of us who teach the Synoptic Gospels often ask even beginning students to chart differences and especially patterns of differences. Because it is such a basic exercise, I will not reproduce examples from a Gospel synopsis here; I take for granted that most readers have made some such comparisons and contrasts themselves, or are at least aware of them, and can therefore grasp the relevance of this chapter's analogies, without me adding superfluous pages to this book.

One unsurprising conclusion in the study of ancient biography is that the sort of differences evident in the Gospels are not unusual in ancient biography. My interest here is to show that the textual phenomena with which we are *already* familiar in the Gospels (parallels and variation) fall within the range of textual phenomena expected in analogous works of the era, hence should not be deemed idiosyncratic or (for those with theological concerns) problematic so long as we do not read the Gospels with anachronistic expectations.

In this chapter I focus at some length on one set of analogies, namely, how authors half a century after one figure, here the briefly reigning emperor Otho, overlapped in their reports about him. Like the Gospels, several accounts of Otho stem from the early empire and from within living memory of their subject. The comparison will display significant dependence on prior information. I then turn more briefly to some other potential analogies (with special attention to the first-century Jewish examples of Philo and Josephus) that suggest that this pattern of biographies depending on prior information obtains more widely.

10.1. Minimizing Minimalism?

While in many cases we cannot prove or disprove a biographer's or historian's claims,[1] only a minimalist methodological skepticism deems all claims

---

1. E.g., Humble and Sidwell, "Dreams," 222; König, "Lives," 248.

plainly false until proven true. Naturally, all history—indeed, any narration of memory—involves interpretation and selection based on perspectives. This question is not at issue here, so my focus will not be on what is omitted in one or another source, relevant as that is to the question of interpretation. (See below section 10.5b, "Omitting Omissions.") My interest here is the question: How much of the information that *is* included does the author have reason to believe is accurate?

Minimalism is heuristically useful if asking the question: What is the minimum of information about which we can be *certain*? Maximalism offers the analogously useful function of asking about the maximum information that could be *possible*.[2] Yet in most historical reconstruction our greater interest is what is *probable*.

To evaluate the historical probability of reports by minimalist standards even when their information that we can test proves generally reliable is to adopt an approach that we would often not imagine for analogous situations today. Though other memoirs might provide better examples, I take an example I can evaluate firsthand. My wife and I cowrote her refugee experience and our romance based especially on our journals and correspondence.[3] Eyewitnesses can also confirm many details, and interviews about the book have circulated. But if only the book survived, a minimalist critic several centuries from now might accept only some basic events, such as the fact that nearly everyone from her city that survived did so at least temporarily as a fugitive. By disregarding any of our testimony not identical with what they already knew, they would be dismissing firsthand evidence.[4]

Identifying the genre of our work as autobiographic would not resolve all problems. We could, for example, be mistaken in some details, and we certainly were selective and have biases (not least in the romance material). We write in light of the outcome; that some of my initial assumptions within the narrative prove wrong nuances my reliability as a narrator earlier in the book. It certainly is not an academic textbook. But given the book's genre as popular, inspirational autobiography, one expects that we reported only events

2. Since quite a range exists between "certain" and "possible," in a court of law minimalists and maximalists could debate what we *should* mean by "beyond *reasonable* doubt" in a criminal case. Civil cases require only a preponderance of evidence, closer to *probable* reconstructions.

3. Keener and Keener, *Impossible Love*.

4. I use this analogy as a sort of reductio ad absurdum to illustrate the vulnerability of extreme minimalism, not to suggest a direct analogy with the Gospels per se; no one claims that the Gospels rest on anyone's daily journal accounts.

that happened, even if a few memories are conflated and speakers' words are not verbatim. A twenty-fifth-century critic who misidentified the book's genre as a novel would get the book wrong and the motives of the authors wrong. If I composed a novel, it certainly would not look like this!

With some genres, such as ancient novels, we do not look for genuine historical information, although they inform us about ideas and customs. With some other genres, we expect some or much genuine historical information. What about ancient biography? Ancient "biography" in the most *general* sense offers only limited help in framing our historiographic expectations for these works as historical sources, especially for those who lump lives of poets and novels about historical figures with mainstream biographies of public figures. How do we evaluate which sorts of biographies (as a sort of subgenre within a genre) tend to be more reliable as historical sources? Some observations should already be obvious from previous chapters.

First, the brief "lives" of poets differ substantially from full "lives" of public figures, and we can expect much more historical substance from the latter. Second, the level of concern with historical facticity was greater in the early empire than either in the Hellenistic period or in late antique hagiography. Third, lives of figures from within living memory typically had available the most reliable oral sources. Such observations suggest that, as far as ancient biographies go, we should expect the Gospels to be among the more historically valuable sources, not among the less historically valuable ones.

10.2. How to Evaluate Particular Biographies

Nevertheless, even biographers of recent public figures from circa 100 BCE to circa 200 CE wrote differently from their modern successors, with a range of flexibility among themselves concerning details. To speak of biographic genre, or even of biography of recent figures in the early empire, does not resolve the degree of flexibility in any given work. Virtually all writers made decisions what to include, omit, and emphasize, and most also approached their subjects with a degree of appreciation or disdain that was subjective. All had to interpret their data in reconstructing events, and most also exercised some flexibility in how they presented the details.

How can we evaluate where on the spectrum of reliability, or at least the author's intention of reliability, a particular biography lies? To do so, we need to give further attention to how particular writers engaged their sources. Often we lack sources that allow us to test them. (For a New Testament example, consider, on the usual view of Synoptic relations, Mark.)[5] In other cases, though, we find sufficient material in other sources to help us answer the question.

Of course, the original source(s) on which other works depend could be deeply flawed or even fictitious; but we can offer at least two observations based on such comparisons. First, we can evaluate what the other works *did* with the original source, and second, we may conclude that, as source-based historical works, the authors of these works also *believed* that the original source did supply legitimate information on the points followed. If they write within living memory of the source or even the events, their belief about the soundness of their source is probably usually sounder than our guesses centuries or millennia later.

If, where we can test them, particular biographers use sources and handle them carefully, the probability in any given case should be that they also do so where we cannot test them, at least in the same document. That is, we expect that in this document they usually communicate what they believe to be true, and that the incidents that they report usually derive from their sources. For a New Testament example, if Matthew and Luke extensively use Mark and other shared material, they are clearly not simply composing freely from whole cloth.

10.3. Other Comparisons

Scholars often compare documents to ascertain the writer's methods and emphases. In Gospels research, we call this redaction criticism,[6] but its usefulness is not limited to the Gospels alone.[7] Scholars often evaluate historical traditions by comparing other works, as I do below with works about Otho. Mark Beck tests Lucian's depiction of Demonax with independent snippets about Demonax preserved elsewhere.[8] Christopher Pelling uses the historian

---

5. Except where we can identify overlap with other early tradition, using the criterion of coherence (e.g., showing that Jesus preached about God's kingdom or told parables).

6. Surveying, accepting, and challenging aspects of redaction criticism, see, e.g., Perrin, *Redaction Criticism*; Duling and Perrin, *New Testament*, 20–23; Spivey, Smith, and Black, *Anatomy*, 57–58; Güttgemanns, *Questions*, 399–400; Carson, Moo, and Morris, *Introduction*, 38–45; Osborne, "Redaction Criticism"; Goodacre, "Redaction Criticism." Ancient historians did not believe that editing for style or ideological emphasis ipso facto undermined the accuracy of their information (Dio Cassius, *Roman History* 1.1.1–2).

7. For comparing multiple ancient historians, see, e.g., Laistner, *Historians*, 131.

8. Beck, "Demonax," 82, although Beck is seeking simply to establish the historical existence of the sage Demonax.

Thucydides and the orator Andocides as independent sources against which to study their respective tendencies,[9] and then examines Apollodorus's redaction of Thucydides to evaluate his oratorical departures from his source.[10]

Variations are common in parallel acccounts. For example, in Xenophon's encomium on Agesilaus, the state selects Agesilaus as a better king than his rival; in Nepos, Lysander makes him king; in Plutarch, Agesilaus and Lysander together make Agesilaus king, and the people are unhappy about the result.[11] Plutarch apparently supplies a speech for Agesilaus unavailable in prior sources and depicts him as more "quick-witted" than in other surviving sources.[12] Still, Plutarch appears to have some very early sources about Agesilaus no longer available to us today.[13] Later, in the fifth century CE, Orosius can be seen "condensing, expanding and changing verbal expressions" in his source, Justin's epitome of Pompeius Trogus.[14] We may speculate on the reasons for the differences, but the differences are plainly there.

Then again, similarities are also common. Robert Derrenbacker charts similarities and differences among Diodorus Siculus, Strabo, and Arrian, examining how they adapt their shared sources. He observes how they often follow even the same sequence in treating particular topics.[15] Likewise, where comparison is possible, Diodorus abridges Ephorus by omitting episodes but follows fairly closely what he includes.[16] (One example of adaptation there is changing an adjective to prepare for a later portrayal.)[17] Similar differences and similarities obtain in parallel materials both in the OT[18] and in its ancient Near Eastern setting, so the OT itself provides models for understanding Synoptic parallels and variation.[19]

---

9. Pelling, *Texts*, 21.

10. Pelling, *Texts*, 62–67.

11. Ytterbrink, *Gospel*, 93, noting Xenophon, *Agesilaus* 1.5; Plutarch, *Agesilaus* 3.3–4.1 and 30.1.

12. Ytterbrink, *Gospel*, 93, also contrasting Xenophon, *Agesilaus* 1.4, 17, and Plutarch, *Agesilaus* 9.2, with Nepos, *On Great Generals* 17 (Agesilaus), 3.1, 5.

13. Wright, "Reliability," ch. 2, on Xenophon's *Agesilaus*.

14. Develin, "Introduction," 6, noting esp. Steele, "Trogus," 27.

15. Derrenbacker, *Practices*, 78–89.

16. Derrenbacker, *Practices*, 90–92.

17. Derrenbacker, *Practices*, 92.

18. Knoppers, "Problem," 12, notes, e.g., Samuel-Kings and Chronicles; 2Kgs 18–20//Isa 37–38; 2 Kgs 25//Jer 51–52; Ps 18:1–51//2 Sam 22:1–51; Ezra 1:1–4//5:13–15//6:3–5//2 Chr 36:22–23; and 1 Chr 16:8–36 with Ps 105:1–15; 96:1b–13; 106:1, 47–48.

19. See Knoppers, "Problem," helpfully drawing on Greek and Roman discussions of *mimēsis*, or *imitatio*.

10.4. The Most Useful Analogies?

As emphasized in chapter 9, ancients themselves often recognized that legendary and speculative elements increased with chronological distance from eyewitness material, especially after the living memory of eyewitnesses had passed.[20] Most scholars date Mark to within roughly forty years (about a generation) after Jesus's crucifixion; among the fairly small number of extant biographies from the early empire written within living memory of their subjects are Nicolaus's fragmentary *Augustus*, Josephus's autobiography (his *Life*), Tacitus's *Agricola*, and Lucian's *Demonax*. Each of these works preserves a substantial quantity of reliable information, though all these writers idolized their subjects, and Nicolaus in particular proved unduly encomiastic.

The Gospels derive from the period of ancient biographies' strongest historical content, and they are written within living memory of their subjects. We may still learn much from some analogies that do not fit these constraints, but our closest and most useful analogies will fit these criteria, which also narrow the biographies to be explored to more workable proportions.[21] Just as the Evangelists looked back to the central event of Jesus roughly half a century earlier,[22] so early second-century historians often recalled the traumatic time the Roman aristocracy suffered under Nero roughly half a century before them, followed by a civil war of imperial succession that involved some of their own relatives.

Here I focus first and most extensively on the treatment of Otho in biographers and historians (Suetonius, Plutarch, and Tacitus) roughly half a century after his death;[23] more briefly, noting treatment of some other figures such as

---

20. See, e.g., Thucydides, *History* 1.21.1; Livy, *History* 6.1.2–3; 7.6.6; 25.11.20; Diodorus Siculus, *Library of History* 1.6.2; 1.9.2; 4.1.1; 4.8.3–5; Dionysius of Halicarnassus, *Roman Antiquities* 1.12.3; *Thucydides* 5; Pausanias, *Description of Greece* 9.31.7; Josephus, *Against Apion* 1.15, 24–25, 58; further Kennedy, "Source Criticism," 139.

21. Of course even these works differ among themselves. The Gospels (esp. Mark) address more popular audiences (where popular storytelling techniques may matter more than elite rhetoric) and a more distinctively Jewish subculture. The lack of extant "popular" biographies for recent characters, however, leaves these biographies of recent public figures as particularly close analogies.

22. Votaw, "Biographies," 246, compares Plato's and Xenophon's accounts of Socrates after a comparable span of time. As noted, however, biography had not yet achieved the form identifiable during the empire.

23. I adapt my discussion of Otho from Keener, "Otho 1" and "Otho 2"; with permission from *BBR*.

Galba[24] or works by some other biographers such as Nepos; and finally some Jewish works, examining especially how Josephus (less strictly) treats the same events in his *Jewish War* and his *Life*.[25]

10.5. Lives of Otho

Accounts about Otho in Suetonius, Plutarch, and the historian Tacitus correspond with one another in ways analogous to correspondences among the Synoptics.[26] This observation is significant because Suetonius and Plutarch are the key extant examples of biographers from the early empire.[27] This brief comparison of elements in Suetonius's biography of a recent figure with his contemporaries' treatment of the same figure illustrates that biographers drew on and, like historians, adapted a repository of historical information available to them.

As already noted, experts regarding ancient biography often classify it as related to or even as a subtype of history.[28] If this observation is true for ancient full biographies in general, it is even more relevant for full biographies of then-recent figures in the early empire.

10.5a. Objectives and Methods

Here I compare a biography of Suetonius with a historical writing of Tacitus and biographies of Plutarch, concerning a figure who lived roughly forty to fifty years before they wrote.[29] Otho lived circa 32–69, with most of the relevant events taking place in his final decade. Writing about him a generation

24. Drawing on the work of Goh, "Galba."
25. Drawing esp. on Henderson, "*Life* and *War*"; Henderson, "Comparison."
26. For my own argument concerning the Gospels' relation to their sources, see *Historical Jesus*, 126–61.
27. Kennedy, "Source Criticism," 139. Others also offer comparisons with them, e.g., Theissen and Merz, *Historical Jesus*, 114.
28. Kennedy, "Source Criticism," 136; Aune, "Biography," 125; Burridge, *Comparison*, 63–67; Stadter, "Biography," 528; Hose, "Historiography: Rome," 6:422–26; Bravo, "Antiquarianism," 516; Pitts, "Citation," 377–78.
29. As Pliny, a contemporary of Suetonius and Tacitus, wrote, the days of Nero seemed near history, even though none of the consuls from that period, normally older men, remained alive (*Letters* 3.7.11). Some younger people from that period probably did remain alive.

later, Suetonius (ca. 70–130 CE) composed his imperial biographies before 121. Tacitus (ca. 56–at least 118 CE) may have composed his *Histories* circa 109–10.[30] Plutarch (before 50 CE–after 120) seems to have become most prolific in the last two decades of his life.[31]

For the sake of simplicity, I start here with Suetonius rather than Plutarch. Plutarch's information that is parallel regarding Otho appears in two biographies, his *Galba* and his *Otho*. Suetonius treats Otho in twelve chapters of about twenty-eight paragraphs altogether. That Suetonius, Tacitus, and Plutarch, though contemporaries and all members of the elite, do not share all the same perspectives on every historical figure also strengthens the value of their independent attestation of some elements of historical information.

Unlike pure novelists, biographers constructed the events they narrate largely from the raw materials of available tradition. Nevertheless, they had some freedom in how they constructed their portraits from this raw material, so I will also offer a few comparisons on the extent to which they employed that freedom. Here my observations must be more limited because of the limited nature of the evidence; my focus therefore remains on establishing that they mostly edited and adapted historical information rather than inventing new stories.

10.5b. Omitting Omissions

In comparing data, I will focus on points of overlap rather than on points included by only one source. When a biography of a recent figure by Suetonius or Plutarch offers information that is not corroborated elsewhere, we should not for that reason alone simply dismiss its claims (although we may question them if we have specific reason to do so). Negative arguments from omissions in a different source constitute arguments from silence, arguments that are particularly precarious, given the severely limited nature of extant evidence.[32] As mentioned, Suetonius's biography of Otho is very brief, for

---

30. Bradley, "Suetonius," 1451; Martin, "Tacitus," 1469.

31. Russell, "Plutarch," 1200; for Plutarch's firsthand knowledge about Galba and Otho, see Alfred, "Valuation," 92–93. Chronologically, it is possible that Plutarch could have written before Tacitus and Suetonius, but he is not likely their (esp. Tacitus's) direct source; many other writers no longer extant flourished in antiquity (as noted further in the book introduction).

32. Cf. Brown, *Death*, 7–8: "The evangelists certainly knew more of the Christian tradition about Jesus than they chose to convey in their Gospels; John 21:25 affirms that. Therefore we

which reason it could not have accommodated all the details found in Plutarch or (especially) Tacitus. This work in particular lacks much information about Otho's conflict with Vitellius (whether for textual reasons or for reasons of Suetonius's interest).

Omissions discard data but technically do not falsify the information that remains;[33] even if we view them as distorting the overall picture, they are not errors of fact per se. Such omissions are common in individual memory,[34] in ancient biographies,[35] and in ancient historiography.[36] Information-based writers must select from their information the elements most relevant to their genre, story, and agenda.[37] When Dionysius of Halicarnassus notes that, unlike historians satisfied merely to report facts, he wants to investigate the *causes* of events as well,[38] he is not discounting all the facts they report.

Again, the principle of relevant selectivity should make sense to us. Even in a court, when one promises to tell "the whole truth," an attorney would not likely allow a witness to take two hours on the stand, attempting to provide every conceivable detail about an incident that one might recall, whether directly related to the immediate questions or not.[39]

For recent figures for whom information abounded, different writers naturally select different information, to some extent even where one was copying much information from another or both copied the same common source. Nevertheless, if the writer draws on genuine preexisting information where we can check him, it is reasonable to infer that, writing for an era where readers could have checked him on many other issues, the writer would have

---

should maintain a certain distrust of negative arguments from silence, as if the failure to write meant the failure to know." Also McGrew, "Argument," 598: assumptions that a writer's failure to mention something means that he was ignorant of it or rejected it, frequent as they are in NT scholarship, cannot stand up in proper historiography.

33. Vansina, *Oral Tradition*, 172; cf. 188.

34. McIver, *Memory*, 48.

35. Ytterbrink, *Gospel*, 94; McGing, "Adaptation," 120, 131–33; Licona, *Differences*, 2, 20, 51, 56, 72, 75, 77, 95, 109; see further chs. 5, 11.

36. See Polybius, *Histories* 6.11.7–8; Bosworth, *Arrian*, 91, 211; Derrenbacker, *Practices*, 91, 93; Pelling, *Texts*, 100–101, 119; Keener, *Acts*, 194–96 (including Josephus, *Life* 339; *Against Apion* 1.60–66; Dio Cassius, *Roman History* 1.1.1–2); cf. Stanley, *Language*, 323.

37. See, e.g., Polybius, *Histories* 15.36.10; Tacitus, *Annals* 3.65; Plutarch, *Aemilius Paulus* 1.2; *Alexander* 1.2; Justin, *Epitome* pref.4; cf. Votaw, "Biographies," 231; De Pourcq and Roskam, "Virtues," 166–67, 176.

38. Dionysius of Halicarnassus, *Roman Antiquities* 5.56.1.

39. I owe this illustration to Terence Paige, November 9, 2017.

drawn on preexisting information in many more cases than where the information happens to remain extant today. Extant correspondences with other surviving sources, therefore, are undoubtedly merely a sample of correspondences that many works had with their real sources. Often reports of different historians may be complementary, allowing us to see what the other writer omitted because of bias or interest.[40] Both for the Gospels and for other ancient biographies, multiple attestation is helpful, but we need not approach even unique accounts (such as, e.g., distinctly Lukan parables)[41] with dismissive skepticism.[42]

10.5c. Listing Parallels and Some Differences

The parallels among authors addressed below exhibit the same sorts of variations one finds in the gospel tradition (although the elite authors naturally include less verbatim reproduction than appears in the Synoptics).[43] To discuss each of the following parallels and differences in the way commentators discuss variations in the Gospels would prove prohibitively long; that length would also prove superfluous at many points in view of my primary objective. The most concise and visually effective way to note areas of overlap among Suetonius, Tacitus, and Plutarch here is to simply list them.[44]

The abundance of shared information should lay to rest any suggestion that a biographer such as Suetonius was engaging primarily in free composition without regard for the reliability of his information.

---

40. Laistner, *Historians*, 131.

41. Despite their distinctive Lukan forms and emphases; cf., more skeptically on this point, Meier, *Marginal Jew*, 5:210.

42. For this logic, see Allison, *Constructing Jesus*, 454: a writer may add information to one of his major sources if he has other sources available.

43. See Aune, *Environment*, 125; Downing, "Redaction Criticism 2," 33. Deliberately rewording an account does, however, increase the danger of inadvertently changing its meaning (see observations on differences in our sources below).

44. Illustrating the range in ancient biography, Plutarch is far more moralistic than Suetonius in these accounts yet, like Suetonius, preserves substantial information. For Plutarch's emphasis on ethics in his parallel lives, see, e.g., Hägg, *Biography*, 239–81.

10.5d. Samples of Differences

SUETONIUS, *OTHO*	TACITUS, *HISTORIES*	PLUTARCH, *GALBA* AND *OTHO*
Otho's parentage and ancestry (1.1–3).	Otho's parentage and ancestry (2.50).	Otho had an honorable lineage (*Galba* 19.2).
Otho's birth (2.1).	—	—
Otho's wasteful, dissolute youth (2.1).	Otho's wasteful, dissolute youth (1.13).	Otho's luxury-corrupted youth (*Galba* 19.2).
Otho used an affair with an imperial freedwoman to gain access to Nero's court (2.2).	—	—
Otho gained friendship with Nero through their shared vices (2.2).	Otho gained friendship with Nero through their shared vices (1.13; cf. *Annals* 13.12, 45).	Their shared vices endeared Otho to Nero (*Galba* 19.3).
Nero took Poppaea Sabina from her husband and entrusted her in marriage to Otho (3.1).[45]	Nero entrusted his own mistress, Poppaea Sabina, to Otho for the present (1.13); in *Annals* 13.45, Otho seduced her from her first husband (his friendship with Nero enhancing his influence) and only afterward (*Annals* 13.46) did she begin an affair with Nero.[46]	Otho seduced Poppaea from her husband with promises of Nero's favor, obtaining her as his wife (*Galba* 19.4).

45. Suetonius, *Otho* 3.1, initially presents the marriage as a sham, but this reflects Suetonius's moral perspective rather than a legal one, as becomes clear in 3.2 (as well as in Tacitus, *Annals* 13.45).

46. Given Tacitus's cynical style, the instance in *Histories* 1.13 might imply only that she was going to be Nero's mistress and that his power aided Otho's objective of securing her; or the perspective may simply differ from that of the source followed in *Histories*, Suetonius, and Plutarch.

SUETONIUS, *OTHO*	TACITUS, *HISTORIES*	PLUTARCH, *GALBA* AND *OTHO*
Nero himself was already having affairs with Poppaea Sabina, and Otho's rivalry (3.1–2) led to his removal as general to Lusitania (3.2).	Nero himself was already having affairs with Poppaea Sabina, and Otho's rivalry led to his removal as general to Lusitania (1.13; cf. *Annals* 13.46).	Poppaea played on the rivalry between Otho and Nero, but she wanted Nero only as a lover (*Galba* 19.4–5); Nero thus wanted Otho dead (19.5), but Seneca arranged for him to be spared and sent to Lusitania (20.1).
Otho governed Lusitania well for ten years (3.2).	Otho governed Lusitania nobly, in contrast to the behavior of his youth (not in *Histories*, but cf. *Annals* 13.46).	Otho governed Lusitania well (*Galba* 20.1).
Once Galba revolted, Otho supported him (4.1).	Otho was Galba's chief supporter (1.13).	Otho was the first governor to support Galba (*Galba* 20.2).
An astrologer named Seleucus predicted that Otho would survive Nero and become emperor (4.1; cf. 6.1).	An astrologer named Ptolemy predicted that Otho would survive Nero and become emperor (1.22).	An astrologer named Ptolemy predicted that Otho would survive Nero and become emperor (*Galba* 23.4).
Galba thus pursued his ambition by flattering nobles and obligating his soldiers (4.2), and later bribing soldiers to share his plot (5.2).	Most of the soldiers favored Otho (1.13); he had long curried their favor (1.23), including with bribes (1.24–25).	Otho helped and curried favor with the soldiers (*Galba* 20.3–4), and they favored especially Otho for Galba's successor (*Galba* 21.2). Otho's friends had been corrupting the soldiers for him even before the conspiracy, but in the midst of the conspiracy corrupted them further with money and promises (*Galba* 24.1).

SUETONIUS, *OTHO*	TACITUS, *HISTORIES*	PLUTARCH, *GALBA* AND *OTHO*
Otho eagerly hoped to be adopted by Galba; Galba adopted Piso instead, incurring Otho's resentment (5.1).	Otho eagerly hoped to be adopted by Galba (1.13); Galba adopted Piso instead (1.14–15), incurring Otho's anger toward Galba and envy toward Piso (1.21).	Galba failed to adopt Otho because of the latter's fiscal irresponsibility (*Galba* 21.1–2); for the adoption of Piso, see *Galba* 23.1; for Otho's anger toward both Galba and Piso, see *Galba* 23.4.
Thus Otho realized that only by seizing the empire could he hope to pay his debts (5.1); he extorted a million sesterces from an imperial slave to finance his goal (5.2).	Once he realized that war might turn against Galba, Otho considered switching sides (1.14); one consideration for betraying Galba was Otho's massive debts (1.21).	Plutarch reports that Otho had debts of five million sesterces (*Galba* 21.2); Galba, by contrast, was independently wealthy (*Galba* 3.1; 29.1).
Galba's adoption speech is mentioned (though not recounted) in 18.3.[47]	Galba's adoption speech (1.15–16).	Galba's adoption speech is mentioned (though not recounted) in *Galba* 23.2.
A delay of several days (6.1)	Five days (1.29) before the assassination: January 10 (1.18) to the fifteenth (1.27).	Galba was assassinated on January 15, on the sixth day after the adoption (*Galba* 24.1).
Otho was with Galba at a sacrifice and heard the diviner's predictions (6.2).[48]	Otho was with Galba at a sacrifice in the temple of Apollo when the seer Umbricius declared unfavorable omens (1.27).	Otho was present at the sacrifice when the divining priest Umbricius declared unfavorable omens (*Galba* 24.2; 25.4).

47. Naturally, there certainly was a speech on this occasion, whether or not Tacitus composed his version from scratch.

48. Suetonius (*Galba* 19.1) has already indicated that a diviner's predictions involved assassins seeking Galba's life.

SUETONIUS, *OTHO*	TACITUS, *HISTORIES*	PLUTARCH, *GALBA* AND *OTHO*
A freedman announcing that the architects had arrived served as Otho's prearranged excuse to leave Galba, to go inspect a house for sale; Suetonius also offers an alternative report (6.2).	His freedman Onomastus announcing that his architect and contractors awaited him served as Otho's prearranged excuse to leave Galba, to go examine properties he was buying (1.27).	His freedman Onomastus arrived at this point with the prearranged excuse, namely that the builders had come and were waiting at the old house Otho had bought, where he wanted to negotiate down the price (*Galba* 24.3–4).[49]
Otho's coconspirators awaited at the golden mile marker in the Forum, right by the temple of Saturn (*aede Saturni*, 6.2).	Otho's coconspirators (23 members of the bodyguard) awaited at the golden mile marker, right by the temple of Saturn (*aedem Saturni*, 1.27).	Otho was first hailed (*Galba* 25.1) at this golden column in the Forum where the roads of Italy met (24.4).
Otho exited a palace door (6.2).[50]	Otho walked through the palace to leave (1.27).	Otho walked through the house of Tiberius on his way to the forum (*Galba* 24.4).
Soldiers took Otho on their shoulders, hailing him as emperor, and others who met them joined in (6.3).	Otho feared because initially just 23 members of the bodyguard hailed him as emperor; they drew other support and acquiescence more slowly and often reluctantly (1.27–28).	Otho feared because initially only 23 hailed him as emperor (*Galba* 25.1), but others quickly joined and hailed him (25.2).

49. Even before this scene, Plutarch (*Galba* 24.1) agrees that Otho's freedman was named Onomastus and that he was involved in Otho's conspiracy.

50. If they were at the Temple of Apollo rather than in the palace for a sacrifice (Tacitus, *Histories* 1.27), Suetonius has condensed something or depends on a source that has done so.

SUETONIUS, *OTHO*	TACITUS, *HISTORIES*	PLUTARCH, *GALBA* AND *OTHO*
—	Martialis, tribune in charge of the camp that day, was not part of the conspiracy but, fearing death, fell in with Otho's conspiracy (1.28).[51]	Martialis, tribune in charge of the camp that day, was not part of the conspiracy but, fearing death, fell in with Otho's conspiracy (*Galba* 25.3).
—	Piso's speech (1.29–30).	—
Otho dispatched agents to kill Galba and Piso (6.3).	The conflict is depicted in much greater detail (1.31–49); the soldiers in the camp favored Otho, who welcomed them (1.36); Galba (1.41) and Piso (1.43) were killed.[52]	Plutarch is more detailed here than Suetonius, but less than Tacitus (*Galba* 26.1–27.6); he also recounts the assassinations of Galba and Piso.
—	Atilius Vergilio, the standard-bearer for the cohort with Galba, cast Galba's portrait on the ground (1.41).	Atilius Vergilio cast down an "image" (LCL too readily translates "statue") of Galba (*Galba* 26.4).
—	Galba had assigned the centurion Sempronius Densus to guard Piso, and Densus defended him bravely (1.43).	The centurion Sempronius Densus bravely defended Galba himself (*Galba* 26.5).[53]

51. Martialis was later wounded in Otho's service (Tacitus, *Histories* 1.82).

52. Tacitus, *Histories* 1.41, offers varying versions of Galba's last words (Plutarch, *Galba* 27.1, choosing only the most positive of these), but Tacitus rightly observes that the assassins, who alone could have lived to report his words, would not have cared to report them.

53. Here Plutarch clearly diverges from Tacitus. If Plutarch is working from memory, the confusion is understandable, though one might have hoped that Plutarch would have been more careful about one he so valorizes.

SUETONIUS, OTHO	TACITUS, HISTORIES	PLUTARCH, GALBA AND OTHO
—	Sulpicius Florus and Statius Murcus dragged Piso (who was wounded) outside the temple of Vesta and killed him at the entrance (1.43).	Murcus killed the wounded Piso at the temple of Vesta (Galba 27.4).
Otho promised the soldiers that he would have only whatever they left for him (6.3).	Otho's speech to the soldiers (1.37–38), including promises of money (1.37); out of traditional control, the soldiers ruled themselves (1.46).	Otho's agents had been giving soldiers money and promises (Galba 24.1).
Otho told the Senate that the people had forced this role on him (7.1).	Once Otho prevailed, the Senate switched allegiance to him (1.45) and honored him (1.47).	The Senate immediately convened and switched allegiance to Otho (Galba 28.1).
Otho honored Nero's memory, again setting up his statues, and did not refuse acclaim as his successor (7.1).	Otho honored Nero's memory, allowing people to set up statues of Nero, and did not refuse acclaim as his successor (1.78).	Otho honored Nero's memory, allowing people to set up statues of Nero, and did not refuse acclaim as his successor (Otho 3.1; cf. 3.2).
Galba had depended on Titus Vinius and Icelus Marcianius (Galba 14.2; 22; cf. Nero 49.4; Vitellius 7.1).	Titus Vinius ran (corruptly) Galba's affairs (1.6), and Otho's agents killed him (1.42; cf. 1.48); Otho had Marcianus Icelus executed (1.46).	Galba had depended on Icelus (Galba 20.4) and especially Vinius (e.g., Galba 4.4; 17.1–2; 20.3; 21.1–2; 25.4; 26.1; 27.4; 29.4).
—	Tacitus allows that Vinius's protest that his execution was against Otho's orders may have simply been trying to prolong his life but suspects that he was part of the conspiracy (1.42).	Plutarch opines that Vinius's protest that his execution was against Otho's orders identifies him as part of the conspiracy (Galba 27.4; but contrast 25.4).

SUETONIUS, *OTHO*	TACITUS, *HISTORIES*	PLUTARCH, *GALBA* AND *OTHO*
Galba was influenced by Laco, as well as by Vinius and Icelus Marcianus; he was Galba's praetorian prefect but proud and incompetent (*Galba* 14.2).	Galba had relied on Laco as well as Vinius (1.6, 14); he was Galba's praetorian prefect (1.26), loyal but proud, corrupt, and incompetent (1.6, 26); after being banished to an island, he was assassinated (1.46).	Galba appointed Laco the praetorian prefect (*Galba* 13.1); Laco remained loyal to him (*Galba* 26.1) but was corrupt (*Galba* 29.4) and was killed by Otho's followers.[54]
—	Otho spared consul-elect Marius Celsus, despite his fidelity to Galba (1.45, 71), and Celsus became one of his generals (1.71, 87).	Otho spared Marius Celsus, despite his fidelity to Galba (*Otho* 1.1), and Celsus became one of his generals (*Otho* 5.3).
—	To the people's pleasure, Otho ordered Tigellinus's death; at Sinuessa (the famous baths there), Tigellinus cut his own throat with a razor (1.72).	To the people's pleasure, Otho ordered Tigellinus's death (*Otho* 2.1–3);[55] at his estate at Sinuessa, Tigellinus cut his own throat with a razor (*Otho* 2.3).
Galba disliked Dolabella; *Galba* 12.2.	Otho banished Dolabella to Aquinum, without harm (1.88).	Otho banished Dolabella to Aquinum, without harm (*Otho* 5.1).
A dream of Galba's avenging shade tormented Otho (7.2).	Galba's death disturbed the imagination of Otho's mind (44.1; "gloomy visions," LCL).	—

54. Apparently quickly, but Plutarch is summarizing (*Galba* 27.5).
55. According to Plutarch, *Galba* 17.4–5, Vinius had previously prevented this popular decision.

SUETONIUS, *OTHO*	TACITUS, *HISTORIES*	PLUTARCH, *GALBA* AND *OTHO*
Vitellius planned to revolt (8.1).	Vitellius planned to revolt (1.50–70).	Plutarch elaborates on how disaffected soldiers in Germany sought Vitellius (*Galba* 22.5–6), and he agreed (*Galba* 22.7–23.1; *Otho* 4.1).
Otho offered Vitellius a share in the empire and a marriage union between the families (8.1).	Otho offered Vitellius money and favor if he would accept peace, and Vitellius made the same offers to Otho (1.74).	Otho offered Vitellius great wealth and a city of his own (*Otho* 4.2).
—	After offers failed, Otho and Vitellius each reproached the other—both speaking truth (1.74).	After offers failed, Otho and Vitellius each reproached the other—both speaking truth (*Otho* 4.3).
—	Otho treated Vitellius's brother Lucius Vitellius graciously as a friend (1.88).	Otho treated Vitellius's brother Lucius Vitellius graciously, as a friend (*Otho* 5.2).
When some weapons were being moved near dusk, a mob of soldiers, suspecting treachery, hurried to the palace, demanding the death of the senators in honor of Otho (8.1–2, emphasizing Otho's lack of solid control over the revolution).[56]	When the 17th Cohort was being brought from Ostia to Rome, Crispinus was moving some weapons in the camp near dusk, to equip this cohort. The soldiers, however, suspected the senators' slaves of opposing Otho (1.80), and Otho tried to disperse them to protect the senate (1.81).	When Crispinus at night was having some weapons loaded in the camp because of his errand to bring back the 17th Legion from Ostia, some soldiers claimed that the Senate was arming itself against Otho (*Otho* 3.3). They wanted to kill the senators dining with Otho (*Otho* 3.4); Otho dismissed his guests (3.6).

56. Details among the accounts vary, as noted in Rolfe's LCL note in Suetonius (LCL 2:238–39 n.d.): "The same story is told by Tacitus (*Hist.* 1.80) and Plutarch (*Otho*, 3), but the three

SUETONIUS, *OTHO*	TACITUS, *HISTORIES*	PLUTARCH, *GALBA* AND *OTHO*
The soldiers burst into Otho's banquet hall (wounding and killing some who tried to stop them), demanding to see Otho. before they were quieted (8.2).[57]	The soldiers burst into Otho's banquet hall (wounding some who tried to stop them), demanding to see Otho, who had to stand on the couch to quiet them (1.82).	The soldiers burst into Otho's banquet hall, forcing their way past the guards, and Otho had to quiet them, standing on his couch to do so (*Otho* 3.6–7).
—	Otho's speech to the army, demanding that a few be punished for the army's actions (1.83–84).	Otho demanded that a few be punished for the army's actions (*Otho* 3.8, while not offering a full speech).
Flavius Sabinus holds an important role in Rome (*Vitellius* 15.2–3; *Vespasian* 1.3; *Domitian* 1.2).	Otho left Rome in charge of his brother Salvius Titianus (1.90);[58] yet Otho quickly brought Titianus (2.23) to help with the war (2.33). The soldiers requested and received Vespasian's brother Flavius Sabinus as Rome's prefect (1.46), which he remained for a time (2.55, 63; 3.64).[59]	Otho left Rome in charge of Vespasian's brother Flavius Sabinus (*Otho* 5.2); yet Plutarch also knows that Titianus held significant rank on Otho's side (*Otho* 8.1; 13.3) and that he was Otho's brother (*Otho* 7.4).

accounts seem to vary. According to Suetonius the arms were sent from the praetorian camp to Ostia, to fit out the (seventeenth) cohort, and the riot started in the praetorian camp; the account of Tacitus seems to imply that it was the soldiers from Ostia (joined by the praetorians) that burst into Otho's dining room. . . . The arms in question would seem to be a part of those belonging to the cohort." Suetonius might suppose that the arms were being sent to the cohort in Ostia before bringing them to Rome. Laistner, *Historians*, 129, notes that Suetonius's information makes Tacitus's account intelligible. (Earlier Gospels studies emphasized such interlocking, "undesigned coincidences" in the Gospels, an approach recently revived esp. in McGrew, *Hidden*.)

57. Some think that Suetonius's brevity here is because something is missing in the text.

58. Titianus had earlier been consul (*Annals* 12.52) but was now connected to Otho's reign (*Histories* 1.75) and was consul with Otho (1.77). Like Proculus, Titianus was less than competent (2.39–40).

59. Flavius Sabinus appears also in this prominent role in Tacitus, *Histories* 2.99; 3.59,

SUETONIUS, *OTHO*	TACITUS, *HISTORIES*	PLUTARCH, *GALBA* AND *OTHO*
Rather than going to the front himself, Otho retired to Brixellum (9.1).	Rather than going to the front himself, Otho retired to Brixellum (2.33; cf. 2.39); this decision disheartened the soldiers (2.33).	Rather than going to the front himself, Otho retired to Brixellum (*Otho* 5.3; 10.1); this decision disheartened his soldiers (*Otho* 10.1).
Otho won the first three battles (in the Alps, near Placentia, and at Castor's place), though these were not decisive (9.2).	The war started well for Otho (2.11–12, 14, 25–28, and mostly 2.15), which included battles at Placentia (2.17–23) and Castor's place (2.24).	The war started well for Otho (*Otho* 6–7), including his soldiers holding Placentia (*Otho* 6.1–7.1).
—	Proculus became a praetorian prefect (1.46, 82, 87; 2.33), and Otho depended especially on him (1.87).[60]	Plutarch notes that Proculus was Otho's praetorian prefect and that he held far more power than Titianus (*Otho* 7.4), Celsus, and Paulinus (*Otho* 7.5).[61]
—	Suetonius Paulinus was one of Otho's generals (1.87, 90; 2.25–26, 32; cf. *Annals* 14.31–39).	Suetonius Paulinus was one of Otho's generals (*Otho* 5.3; 7.3–5; 8.2–3; 13.1).
—	Marius Celsus was one of Otho's generals (1.71, 87; 2.60).	Celsus was one of Otho's generals (*Otho* 5.3; 13.4–5).
—	Fabius Valens was one of Vitellius's generals against Otho (e.g., 1.74; 2.24, 27–31, 55).	Fabius Valens was one of Vitellius's generals against Otho (e.g., *Galba* 22.6; *Otho* 5.1; 6.4; 11.4).

65, 69–70, 73–75. He should not be confused with T. Flavius Sabinus, consul suffect for two months in 69 CE (1.77; 2.36, 51).

60. Otho's dependence on the advice of his praetorian prefect Proculus spells his doom according to Tacitus, *Histories* 2.33.

61. Proculus appears as a general also in Plutarch, *Otho* 13.1.

SUETONIUS, *OTHO*	TACITUS, *HISTORIES*	PLUTARCH, *GALBA* AND *OTHO*
—	Caecina was one of Vitellius's generals (e.g., 1.90; 2.21–27).	Caecina was one of Vitellius's generals (e.g., *Otho* 5.1; 6.3, 5; 7.1; 10.3; 13.5–6).
Most advised Otho to prolong the war, but he insisted on deciding it quickly (9.1).	The best advisers (Paulinus—2.32; Celsus and Gallus—2.33) urged Otho to prolong the war (2.32–33; cf. 2.37), but following the inexperienced advice of Titianus and Proculus, he insisted on fighting quickly (2.33).[62]	The general Paulinus urged Otho to delay battle (*Otho* 8.2–3), and Celsus agreed (8.4), but Proculus and Titianus urged him to fight quickly (*Otho* 8.1); Otho chose to fight quickly (*Otho* 8.4–9.3).
—	The Vitellians began building a bridge at the Po, which the Othonians were trying to set ablaze (2.34); Otho's gladiators, trying to reach an island in the river, were beaten by Vitellius's Germans (2.35).	The Vitellians began building a bridge at the Po, which the Othonians were trying to set ablaze (*Otho* 10.2), to the Othonians' disadvantage (10.2–3); Vitellius's Germans beat Otho's gladiators at an island in the river (10.3).
The Vitellians prevailed near Betriacum (9.2).	The Vitellians prevailed (2.42–45) near Bedriacum (2.44–45; cf. 2.50, 57).[63]	Otho's army's camp settled near Betriacum (*Otho* 8.1; 9.1), where the Vitellians won (*Otho* 13.5; *Vitellius* 10.1; 15.2).

62. Unlike the biographers, Tacitus provides Paulinus with a full speech (*Histories* 2.32).

63. Both spellings (Bedriacum and Betriacum) appear in Salmon and Potter, "Bedriacum."

Suetonius, *Otho*	Tacitus, *Histories*	Plutarch, *Galba and Otho*
The Vitellians prevailed especially because they attacked when Otho's soldiers were expecting terms of peace (9.2).	Otho's army wrongly thought that the Vitellians had deserted; it was unprepared for the Vitellian onslaught (2.42); Vitellius granted terms to the vanquished, though delay caused confusion (2.45).	A rumor claimed that the Vitellians were surrendering, so the Othonian vanguard greeted Vitellius's men in a friendly way as fellow soldiers, but the Vitellians responded with hostility, making other Othonians suspect their own vanguard of treachery (*Otho* 12.1).
Otho's soldiers were not ready to give up the war (9.3) and initially refused to believe the report that they had experienced a defeat (10.1).	Otho's soldiers were not ready to give up the war (2.46).	The soldiers with Otho pledged their continuing loyalty (*Otho* 15.1–3).
Otho wanted to spare his followers further suffering on his behalf (9.3; 10.1; cf. 10.2–11.1).	Otho wanted to spare his followers further suffering on his behalf (2.47).	Otho wanted to spare his followers further suffering on his behalf (*Otho* 15.3–6).
Otho's final instructions, summarized (10.2).	Otho's final speeches and instructions (2.47–48).	Otho's final speech and instructions (*Otho* 15.3–17.2).
Otho gave final instructions for the safety of several people whom he addressed, including his nephew (10.2).	Otho consoled his nephew Salvius Cocceianus, noting that Otho had spared Vitellius's family, hence mercy should be expected, and warning him to remember neither too much nor too little that Otho had been his uncle (2.48).	Otho consoled his nephew Cocceianus, noting that Otho had spared Vitellius's family, hence mercy should be expected, and warning him to remember neither too much nor too little that Otho had been his uncle (*Otho* 16.2).

SUETONIUS, *OTHO*	TACITUS, *HISTORIES*	PLUTARCH, *GALBA* AND *OTHO*
Otho destroyed any letters that could incriminate his friends to Vitellius (10.2).	Otho destroyed any letters that could incriminate his friends to Vitellius (2.48).	—
Otho distributed money to his servants (11.1).	Otho distributed money, though frugally (2.48).	Otho distributed money to his servants, but carefully rather than lavishly (*Otho* 17.1).
Those beginning to leave the camp were being detained as deserters, but Otho prohibited harming them and met with friends until late (11.1).	Otho urged his friends to depart and provided means (2.48); the soldiers tried to prevent those departing, requiring his harsh intervention, and he met with those departing until late (2.49).	Otho persuaded his friends, especially those of rank, to depart (*Otho* 16.1–2) and provided means for their departure (17.2); the soldiers threatened to kill them unless they remained, forcing Otho to intervene harshly (16.3).
At a late hour Otho quenched his thirst with cold water (*gelidae aquae*, 11.2).	Near evening Otho quenched his thirst with cold water (*gelidae aquae*, 2.49).	That evening, Otho quenched his thirst with some water (*Otho* 17.1).
Otho chose the sharper of two daggers to place under his pillow (11.2).	Otho chose the sharper of two daggers to place under his head (2.49).	Otho chose the sharper of two daggers to place under his head (*Otho* 17.1).
Otho then slept soundly one more night (11.2).	Otho then spent a quiet night, reportedly even sleeping some (2.49).	Otho then slept so deeply for the rest of the night that his attendants heard his breathing (*Otho* 17.1).
At dawn Otho stabbed himself to death (11.2).	At dawn Otho fell on his weapon (2.49).	Just before dawn Otho fell on his sword (*Otho* 17.3).

SUETONIUS, *OTHO*	TACITUS, *HISTORIES*	PLUTARCH, *GALBA* AND *OTHO*
People rushed in when he groaned, as Otho was dying from a single wound (11.2).	People rushed in when he groaned, as Otho was dying from a single wound (2.49).	Hearing Otho's groan, the servants hurried in (*Otho* 17.3, leaving the implication that the single blow was sufficient to end his life).
Otho was quickly buried at his request (11.2).	Otho was quickly buried at his request, to prevent disfigurement by his enemies (2.49).	Plutarch implies that Otho was buried quickly (*Otho* 17.3–4).
Many soldiers killed themselves in mourning by Otho's bier (12.2).	Some soldiers killed themselves in mourning by Otho's bier (2.49).	Some soldiers killed themselves at Otho's funeral pyre (*Otho* 17.4).
Otho died in his thirty-eighth year (11.2).[64]	Otho died in his 37th year (2.49).	Otho lived 37 years (*Otho* 18.2).

One could add some other comparisons, but this list should be sufficient for our purposes. Before summarizing positive comparisons, I shall note some sample areas of difference and some possible reasons for them. These differences are important in helping to establish a potential range of accepted variation among contemporary biographies, which can help readers not to evaluate variations in the Gospels anachronistically.[65]

For example, the sequence of information in our sources sometimes differs, sometimes in a manner that affects how we understand the events. Thus, did Otho urge quick engagement before[66] or after[67] his initial victories? In the

---

64. Differences between Suetonius and the others here could reflect differences between inclusive and exclusive means of reckoning years. On inclusive reckoning, see Koester, *Introduction*, 2:102.

65. Differences in ancient historical reports are not uncommon; see, e.g., divergent approaches to crossing the Rubicon in sources in Beneker, "Crossing"; cf. Rondholz, "Rubicon." Still, even in recounting Nero's death, where Suetonius may take a particularly free hand, the parallels in Dio Cassius, *Roman History* 63.27.3–63.29.2, might suggest a common source, perhaps even Nero's secretary (Hägg, *Biography*, 226–27).

66. Suetonius, *Otho* 9.1–2.

67. Tacitus, *Histories* 2.11–33.

former case, events seemed to initially vindicate his choice; in the latter, his victories spurred on false hopes that his rashness quickly dashed. Since both writers consider his choice rash in retrospect,[68] one might argue that Tacitus rearranged the events to reinforce this point; but given Tacitus's enormous detail and sequencing of the material, and the fact that Suetonius merely summarizes various points here, Tacitus surely preserves the original sequence.[69]

Some differences in sequence probably reflect lack of knowledge or concern for sequence rather than deliberate changes.[70] Sometimes, however, similar events may have happened more than once, so that different sources may occasionally involve different occasions. Thus Plutarch recounts that Otho was not only in Brixillum earlier,[71] but that he returned to it[72] after visiting the camp at Bedricum.[73] Sometimes details appear garbled through Suetonius condensing the story.[74] Suetonius sometimes may condense in this way because his elite readers already knew the basic stories to which he was alluding.[75]

Our sources contradict each other in designating the name of the astrologer who spurred on Otho's ambitions. Suetonius designates him as Seleucus,[76] whereas Tacitus and Plutarch designate him Ptolemy.[77] In this case one might conjecture that Suetonius, working from memory, simply remembered the name as the same as that of one of Alexander's successors (which included both a Seleucus and a Ptolemy). Much more likely (or perhaps partly for the same reason), he apparently confused Ptolemy with Vespasian's court astrologer.[78] In any case, even elite biographers sometimes confused some details; this seems a case of simple confusion, rather than following some ideological agenda.

Likewise, Plutarch contradicts Tacitus in having the centurion Sempronius Densus bravely defend Galba himself,[79] whereas Tacitus has him defend-

---

68. Cf. Suetonius, *Otho* 8.3–9.1.

69. As noted in ch. 5, biography was typically less concerned with chronology than history was (e.g., Görgemanns, "Biography: Greek"; Stanton, *Preaching*, 119–21); for history as sequential, see, e.g., Pliny, *Letters* 1.1.1.

70. For chronological displacement, see chs. 6, 11.

71. Plutarch, *Otho* 5.3.

72. Plutarch, *Otho* 10.1.

73. Plutarch, *Otho* 8.1.

74. Suetonius, *Otho* 6.2; 8.2–3.

75. Cf., e.g., Tacitus, *Annals* 15.63.

76. Suetonius, *Otho* 4.1.

77. Tacitus, *Histories* 1.22; Plutarch, *Galba* 23.4.

78. Tacitus, *Histories* 2.78.

79. Plutarch, *Galba* 26.5.

ing Galba's adoptive son Piso.[80] This difference likely reflects an oversight of Plutarch's, the sort of detail that writers could easily confuse even in the first generation unless they had substantial feedback from audiences familiar with their stories.[81] We should note, however, the significant overlap in facts and the essential story in both of these accounts, despite the confusion of some secondary details.

In some cases differences may be somewhat semantic, such as who was left in charge of Rome. Tacitus claims that Otho left his brother Titianus in charge of Rome;[82] but while Titianus undoubtedly wielded great influence, it is clear even from Tacitus that Titianus did not remain in Rome,[83] whereas other sources seem clear that Flavius Sabinus did.[84] One might therefore incline to favor Plutarch's view that Otho left Flavius Sabinus in charge in Rome,[85] whatever Titianus's official designation may have been. Tacitus himself observes that Flavius Sabinus was Rome's prefect.[86]

Only Suetonius reports the dream in *Otho* 7.2, though the wording included in Tacitus's *Histories* 1.44.1 could possibly imply that Tacitus knows of it. Dreams are an interest of Suetonius, who also recounts a terrifying and ominous dream to Galba shortly before his own death.[87] Yet Tacitus also could include predictive dreams among his lists of omens[88] and divine signs.[89] Like other omens, they are common in historical works,[90] though we cannot be certain at what point they entered the traditions or texts that report them.[91] Generals often depended on dreams before battles and in other situations, probably both in reality and in their postbattle propaganda, as well as in later embellish-

---

80. Tacitus, *Histories* 1.43.

81. Feedback did occur in various genres during oral recitation; see, e.g., Suetonius, *Vergil* 33; see also Winterbottom, "*Recitatio*," 1296 (citing Pliny, *Letters* 5.12.1–2).

82. Tacitus, *Histories* 1.90.

83. Tacitus, *Histories* 2.33.

84. Suetonius, *Vitellius* 15.2–3; *Vespasian* 1.3; *Domitian* 1.2. Among the Gospels, cf. Matthew's special interest in dreams (1:20; 2:12–13, 19, 22; 27:19).

85. Plutarch, *Otho* 5.2.

86. Tacitus, *Histories* 1.46.

87. Suetonius, *Galba* 18.2. Elsewhere in Suetonius, Augustus took dreams seriously (*Augustus* 91), and Vespasian dreamed positively before becoming emperor (*Vespasian* 5.5).

88. Note the favorable one in Tacitus, *Annals* 2.14.

89. Tacitus, *Histories* 4.83.

90. See, e.g., Meister, "Herodotus," 269.

91. Josephus adds a *false* dream claim to the biblical narrative in *Jewish Antiquities* 5.193. Imperial historians regularly included portents presaging an emperor's death; see the massive work of Vigourt, *Présages*.

ments about them.[92] None of this is surprising, since people do often dream, and ancient readers usually believed that dreams portended the future.[93]

Even where the accounts clearly depict the same events, they vary on matters of detail, for example, the soldiers who came close to killing senators after some weapons were moved. In this case, comparing all three of our sources allows us to better reconstruct the larger context that makes sense of some details, though minor conflicts remain. As noted in chapter 7, in the absence of sufficient information ancient historians sometimes did elaborate details or speeches to flesh out scenes for the sake of a cohesive narrative, and ancient readers apparently expected this practice.

As noted below, Josephus does not mind anyone noticing his rhetorical adaptations of biblical narratives in much of his *Jewish Antiquities*. Tacitus develops dramatic scenes and dialogues[94] and infuses scenes with pathos where the events narrated invite this approach.[95] Various writers report private conversations in direct discourse.[96]

Nevertheless, differences need not all be explained in these terms. For example, multiple sources may have diverged on some such details by this point, or (very likely) some writers or their sources misconstrued some of their information. Sometimes more genuine information remains in accounts than we might suspect, simply because we lack the additional information that would reconcile more of the details.[97]

---

92. E.g., Alexander (Quintus Curtius, *History* 4.2.17; Plutarch, *Alexander* 24.3; 41.3–4; 49.3; Arrian, *Alexander* 2.18.1; Ps.-Callisthenes, *Alexander Romance* 1.35; cf. Hermogenes, *Issues* 33), P. Scipio (Polybius, *Histories* 10.4.5–10.5.5), Hannibal (Valerius Maximus, *Memorable Doings and Sayings* 1.7.ext.1; Silius Italicus, *Punica* 3.168–71), Sulla (Plutarch, *Sulla* 9.4; 28.6), Pompey (Plutarch, *Caesar* 42.1), Caesar (Valerius Maximus, *Memorable Doings and Sayings* 1.7.1), and others (Valerius Maximus, *Memorable Doings and Sayings* 1.7.3).

93. E.g., Valerius Maximus, *Memorable Doings and Sayings* 1.7.1–8; 1.7.ext.1–10; Velleius Paterculus, *History* 2.70.1; Plutarch, *Caesar* 42.1; 69.5; *Cicero* 44.2; *Sulla* 37.2. Note, e.g., Calpurnia's dream for her husband, Julius Caesar (Valerius Maximus, *Memorable Doings and Sayings* 1.7.2; Velleius Paterculus, *History* 2.57.2; Suetonius, *Julius* 81; Plutarch, *Caesar* 63.5; 64.3; cf. 68.2). Cf. brief discussion in Keener, *Miracles*, 2:870–84; Keener, *Acts*, 1:911–16; 3:2347–49.

94. See Hadas, "Introduction," xx–xxi.

95. E.g., Tacitus, *Annals* 3.1; 4.62–63; 5.9; 16.30–32.

96. Josephus, *Jewish Antiquities* 19.78–83; cf. Acts 25:14–22; Tacitus, *Annals* 12.65. For scenes behind closed doors: De Temmerman, "Formalities," 16, thinks that even Suetonius in his *Caesars* sometimes makes claims of sources to compensate for actual lack of sources. Such an approach renders verification or falsification difficult; given Suetonius's sometimes cited weakness in critical acumen, how do we know that the inaccessible details were not simply in his source?

97. See also, e.g., Eddy and Boyd, *Legend*, 424. My journal for events of April 23, 2001, seemed to contradict my wife's journal for the same time; information in her journal of April

In these works, we find both variation in detail and continuity of the substance most relevant to the larger story. The variations among the Gospel accounts appear well within the range of acceptable variation in ancient biographies from roughly the same period; they need not discourage readers from finding substantial historical information about Jesus there.

10.5e. Differences because of Genre

As noted in chapter 6, ancient histories contained many biographic elements,[98] but biographies more specifically tended to focus more on a single person and to emphasize characterization more.[99] Difference in genre sometimes explains why one source includes elements missing in another.

Elite historiography normally expected, not merely brief summaries of speech points or statements about the historian's inferences, but speeches *like* those the speaker might have given. Thus, not surprisingly, Tacitus includes set speeches that Suetonius, writing a short biography, lacks.[100] Even when Suetonius is aware of Otho offering instructions, he is far less interested in fleshing them out for his readers.[101] Tacitus and Plutarch offer different versions of Otho's final speech (despite agreements in narrative).[102] Even on occasions when speeches were surely offered, providing speeches for readers remains Tacitus's interest, not that of Suetonius.[103]

19, 2001, however, reconciled the contradiction. We discovered that a French translation variant explained the differences between my wife's journal and (three years later) her oral account regarding a detail of June 14, 1997. Different accounts also included additional details that others omitted without expressly contradicting each other (e.g., phone interview with Emmanuel Moussounga, February 20, 2010; my wife's journal from March 13, 1999; note Keener and Keener, *Impossible Love*, 236). Only a minority of the divergences remained after careful examination.

98. Fornara, *Nature*, 34–36, 116.

99. See Fornara, *Nature*, 185. Still, fleshing out character traits appears widely, e.g., in drama (e.g., tragedians expanding on Homeric characters), practice orations (e.g., Dio Chrysostom, *Orations* 61, on Chryseïs), and histories (Pitcher, "Characterization"; Ash, Mossman, and Titchener, *Fame*).

100. See, e.g., Tacitus, *Histories* 1.15–16, 29–30. Still, Plutarch (*Galba* 22.4–5; *Otho* 15.3–6) also provides a few speeches here.

101. Cf., respectively, Suetonius, *Otho* 6.3 and 10.2, vs. Tacitus, *Histories* 1.37–38 and 2.47–48.

102. Talbert, *Mediterranean Milieu*, 211, cites Plutarch, *Otho* 15, and Tacitus, *Histories* 2.47.

103. See Tacitus, *Histories* 1.83–84. Still, biographers could create conversations; see Hägg, *Biography*, 3.

Sometimes Tacitus's speeches here probably adapt his sources.[104] Nevertheless, Tacitus's works include many speeches for which we cannot expect exact words to have been preserved,[105] including private conversations.[106] Indirect speech also appears at events where we cannot be certain that scribes would have kept records.[107]

Speeches do not represent the only area of difference based on genre. Tacitus specifies more names of collaborators in the plot against Galba,[108] perhaps again reflecting the difference in genre expectations. Tacitus (and Plutarch) name generals; Suetonius summarizes the war and simplifies by omitting the names of generals, even where he includes their role.[109] Writing a simpler, one-volume biography of Otho rather than (like Tacitus's work) a more technical multivolume history, Plutarch also condenses, omitting some names, though less than does Suetonius.[110]

By contrast, Tacitus, being less biographically focused, recounts some of Otho's background only at the end of his life. By contrast, Tacitus the historian elaborates in far greater detail aspects both of Otho's plot[111] and of the military operations.[112]

Sometimes Suetonius may forgo details about other figures in the *Otho* because he says more about these figures elsewhere in his other imperial biographies, which would be read as a series.[113]

---

104. Tacitus elaborates speeches where Suetonius and Plutarch omit them (*Histories* 1.29–30) or merely mention them (1.15–16 with Suetonius, *Galba* 18.3; Plutarch, *Galba* 23.2), but sometimes he includes material that also appears in their summary (*Histories* 1.83–84 with Plutarch, *Otho* 3.8; Tacitus, *Histories* 2.47–48, with Suetonius, *Otho* 10.2; Plutarch, *Otho* 15.3–17.2; cf. Tacitus, *Histories* 1.37–38, with Suetonius, *Otho* 6.3).

105. E.g., Tacitus, *Annals* 2.71–72, 76–77; 6.48; 11.7; 12.48; 13.21; 16.22.

106. Tacitus, *Annals* 4.7, 52, 54, 68–69; 12.65.

107. E.g., Tacitus, *Annals* 12.2; 14.53–56; 15.51.

108. Tacitus, *Histories* 1.24–25.

109. E.g., those advising Otho, Suetonius, *Otho* 9.1.

110. E.g., Plutarch, *Galba* 27.4; Tacitus, *Histories* 1.43.

111. E.g., Tacitus, *Histories* 1.24–26.

112. Tacitus, *Histories* 2.11–45.

113. Thus Tacitus elaborates Galba's demise in far more detail than Suetonius does in his *Otho*, but Suetonius had a separate biography for Galba (though he treats the matter briefly there as well; *Galba* 19–20). Tacitus elaborates Vitellius's revolt, which Suetonius treats in *Vitellius*, and Vespasian (*Histories* 2.1–7), which Suetonius reserves for that biography. Because Plutarch wished to avoid duplication, much of his information about Otho appears only in his *Galba*.

10.5f. Points of Contact

While there are a few points at which the writers conflict and many points on which one is silent (not all of the latter are included in my list), the points of contact listed above are too numerous to entertain the possibility of random coincidence. The line between novelistic composition based on imagination and biographic or historical composition that constructs narratives with heavy reliance on preexisting information is not nearly so thin as some scholars have suggested. Even if the line appears thin in some kinds of sources, it is not at all thin in early imperial biographies concerning then-recent figures.

Which elements one counts makes the exact count subjective, but speaking roughly, in Suetonius's brief biography, I found thirty-one points with close correspondence to Tacitus and eighteen additional points of significant correspondence. I found thirty points of close contact between Suetonius and Plutarch, with eighteen further points of significant correspondence; besides these, I found twenty-eight further points of close correspondence between Plutarch and Tacitus.

Keep in mind again that Suetonius's biography of Otho is brief, the equivalent of roughly only twenty-eight paragraphs, with a total of less than two thousand words. This biography is less than one-fifth the length of Mark's Gospel, so if we extrapolated to suggest a comparable amount of information in Mark, we would be thinking of perhaps 250 points of significant correspondence with external reality, averaging some 15 to 16 points of significant correspondence per chapter. Moreover, this projection rests only on the points in Suetonius's *Otho* that may be confirmed externally. In Suetonius's own day, when much more information remained extant and some eyewitnesses could be consulted, the figure was undoubtedly much higher. (Regarding the frequent presence of sources even when they are not named—as they are not in the Gospels and usually are not even in Suetonius's *Otho*, though see below—see our earlier discussion at 7.9 above.)

One would not expect anything like this level of correspondence in a novel of comparable length, even in the most historical of novels (esp. Philostratus's *Apollonius*), where some correspondences are possible. The genre difference between such biographies and novels should, then, be plainly evident. At least two of our three sources, and probably all three of them, are closely bound to their own sources. Such an observation need not surprise us; ancient historians and biographers do sometimes name their sources.[114] They were particu-

---

114. For historians: e.g., Dionysius of Halicarnassus, *Roman Antiquities* 1.1.1; 1.6.1; Jose-

larly apt to identify their sources when alternate stories came to circulate over time.[115] What our comparison of some sample sources indicates is just how closely bound to their sources they could be. This appears particularly evident for Otho's final hours; as in the Gospel passion narratives, the chief character's end was a matter of interest inviting detailed comment.

10.5g. Use of Sources

Suetonius, then, follows sources, even though he does not usually name them. Some of the material regarding Otho's conspiracy and death corresponds so closely as to require the supposition of some common source or sources. If Suetonius drew on Tacitus, so that their works were not independent,[116] this dependence would still illustrate our primary point about Suetonius the biographer: he developed sources rather than engaging in purely free composition. (Chronology makes it less likely that Tacitus drew on Suetonius. Had he done so, however, the historian would have been accepting Suetonius's biographies as a legitimate historical source.)[117] Such dependence would also not oblige us to suppose that this was the only source available to him. Nevertheless, these authors agree so closely, even in sequence, only at particular points,

---

phus, *Jewish Antiquities* 1.94, 159; 1 Kgs 14:19, 29; 15:7, 23, 31; for biographers: Arrian, *Alexander* 6.2.4; Plutarch, *Alexander* 30.7; 31.2–3; 38.4.

115. For historians: Dionysius of Halicarnassus, *Roman Antiquities* 1.87.4; 3.35.1–4; 8.79.1; Livy, *History* 9.44.6; 23.19.17; 25.17.1–6; Valerius Maximus, *Memorable Doings and Sayings* 5.7.ext.1; 6.8.3; Herodian, *History* 7.9.4, 9; Appian, *Roman History* 11.9.56; 12.1.1; for biographers: Cornelius Nepos, *On Great Generals* 7 (Alcibiades), 11.1; 9 (Conon), 5.4; Arrian, *Alexander* 1.pref.1–2; 4.9.2–3; 4.14.1–4; 5.3.1; 5.14.4; 7.14.2; 7.27.1–3; Plutarch, *Alexander* 31.3; 38.4; 46.1–2; *Demosthenes* 5.5; 29.4–30.4; *Themistocles* 25.1–2; 27.1; 32.3–4; Philostratus, *Lives of the Sophists* 2.4.570; 2.5.576.

116. Plausible (cf. Wallace-Hadrill, *Suetonius*, 2, 9), but they may have simply drawn on common sources (Power, "Suetonius' Tacitus," 205). Dependence is more easily demonstrated in some cases than in others. Some argue, for example, that Arrian drew on Plutarch (Buszard, "Parallel"); others demur. Hägg, *Biography*, 240–41, suggests (I believe implausibly, given biographies of leaders in Nepos) that Suetonius and Plutarch, who organize their works quite differently, may have even invented imperial biographies independently.

117. Because Tacitus would have known contemporary expectations for ancient biographies far better than we could, his verdict would likewise reinforce our point about the historical texture of ancient biography (cf. Keener, *Historical Jesus*, 96–105). Similarly, Matthew and Luke, who knew much more about Mark than we do, regarded Mark as a reliable source for their biographies.

which might suggest that Suetonius drew not on Tacitus here but on a source or sources that Tacitus used.[118]

One source that they sometimes shared might be the no-longer-extant work of Fabius Rusticus.[119] Many other scholars prefer a lost work by Pliny the Elder.[120] Whatever their source or sources, their dependence on them indicates that even some of those writing within a generation of events (such as Mark) could conceivably depend on even earlier sources written by those who lived during the events in question and knew some of the participants.[121]

Tacitus elsewhere cites "historians of that era"[122] as sources for events a century before his time.[123] Tacitus knows of various earlier historians, sometimes naming them only when they themselves become subjects of history[124] and often mentioning both the verdict of "the majority" of historians from the earlier era noted and dissenters from that consensus.[125] Tacitus normally follows annals and earlier histories, but he also consulted personal memoirs from perhaps half a century earlier.[126]

The biographers likewise reveal some of their sources. Plutarch consulted witnesses, including an officer who described to him what he saw while Plutarch was touring the site with him.[127] Suetonius apparently made some

118. In his recent dissertation, Youngju Kwon cites in support of a common source Syme, *Tacitus*, 674–76; Fuhrmann, "Vierkaiserjahr," 264–69; Sage, "Works," 893–94; Damon, *Tacitus: Histories*, 291–302; Williams, "Embassies," 213. Many Gospels scholars analogously infer the existence of Q based on differences between Matthew and Luke that suggest neither's knowledge of the other's full work (esp. the infancy narratives and Judas's death).

119. Cf. Tacitus, *Annals* 13.20.2; 14.2; 15.61; cf. Martin, "Tacitus," 1470.

120. Kwon cites Georgiadou, "Lives," 254–55.

121. Observe, e.g., the many contemporary histories of Nero noted already in Josephus, *Jewish Antiquities* 20.154, though Josephus did not like the ones with whose perspectives he disagreed. Josephus published the *Antiquities* perhaps twenty-seven years after Nero's death.

122. Tacitus, *Annals* 5.9.

123. Historians could also refer readers more generally to "other historians" (Velleius Paterculus, *History* 2.48.5); cf. Luke 1:1. Earlier, Polybius readily critiqued historians who failed to consult earlier historians (*Histories* 12.25d.1); later, Dio Cassius had to defend his omission of some material by explaining that he had in fact read almost everything but did not judge it all suitable for inclusion (*Roman History* 1.1.1–2).

124. E.g., Tacitus, *Annals* 4.34; his books survived, 4.35.

125. E.g., Tacitus, *Annals* 4.57. Tacitus recounts the views of the majority and most reliable historians, but then he mentions another view (4.10), which he goes on to refute logically (4.11) despite its utility for his perspective.

126. Tacitus, *Annals* 4.53.

127. Plutarch, *Otho* 14.1–2. Plutarch (*Otho* 18.1) also visited Otho's tomb at Brixillum.

local inquiries for his work as well[128] and sometimes could establish his point by naming various earlier sources supporting it.[129] Suetonius's sources more generally include notes that he took from official archives and libraries and archives (see ch. 6).

One of Suetonius's sources in this biography about recent history is clear: his own father, Suetonius Laetus, was a tribune serving under Otho and shared with him information about Otho's character and actions.[130] In terms of major public events, a generation is, after all, not a very long time, for it remains within living memory of eyewitnesses and participants who would naturally be consulted.

That writers used sources does not prove that the sources are always correct. Even eyewitnesses have biases, and gossip and speculation were surely rife in the setting that Suetonius depicts.[131] Nevertheless, it appears that biographers writing within the first generation or two often had considerable historical information on which to depend.

On the most common reconstruction of the Gospels' relationship, Matthew and Luke depended heavily on their sources, and they treat Mark as a valid biographic source for reliable information rather than as a work of fiction. Matthew and Luke wrote at a time when the identity and qualifications of Mark were likely known. Whatever the exact actual sequence of the Gospels' publication, the Evangelists write like source-based biographers, hence expecting their audiences to assume that they depend on information.

Some NT scholars nitpick at the Gospels in a way that no one would have thought to do with other ancient biographies, for example, complaining that one Gospel reports the heavenly voice saying, "You are my son," and another, "This is my son."[132] Such minor differences pervade not only the Gospels, but ancient biography and historiography generally; dismissing the essential

---

128. Suetonius, *Vespasian* 1.4.

129. Suetonius, *Julius* 9.3.

130. Suetonius, *Otho* 10.1. Not to be confused with Suetonius Paulinus, a prominent general of the time.

131. Ancients themselves noted the speed and effectiveness of rumor (e.g., Nicolaus, *Augustus* 16, 20, 30, FGrH 130), e.g., rumors of conspiracy (Tacitus, *Annals* 14.58); of catastrophic losses in Germany (Tacitus, *Histories* 4.12); of mass exile (Tacitus, *Annals* 4.46); rumors exaggerating enemy numbers (4.23); a false rumor of a leader's death (4.34) or survival (Josephus, *Jewish Antiquities* 19.134; Tacitus, *Annals* 2.82–83) or that the enemy had fled (*Histories* 2.42); or even deliberately false rumors (disinformation; *Histories* 4.38, 54; *Annals* 4.24). Conflicting reports also emerged this way (e.g., *Histories* 1.51). Of course, even rumor was not always wrong (Tacitus, *Agricola* 9).

132. Ehrman, *Before Gospels*, 212–13; Ehrman, *Interrupted*, 39–40.

accuracy of ancient sources that exercise at least this much flexibility would probably leave us without credible historical sources from antiquity. As will be evident in our chapter on memory, such stringent standards judge ancient works by standards that were not possible or expected before modern recordings, and that are rarely expected in ordinary conversation even today.

10.5h. Conclusions regarding Otho Material

While the degree of adaptation in Suetonius is debatable, his heavy dependence on source material is not. In a work of perhaps twenty-eight paragraphs, we found nearly fifty correspondences with each of the other two works (a history and another biography) with which we compared it. Suetonius's understanding of biography involved not free composition but dependence on prior information; where we can test him, this biographer mostly edited and adapted historical information rather than inventing new stories. Given its chronological proximity to eyewitness sources, a large amount of Suetonius's information about events (if not always the participants' motives) is likely correct.

These features of Suetonian biography also support our expectations based on the Gospels: Matthew and Luke plainly depend on prior information. On this or any other configuration of Synoptic sources, the Synoptics do employ prior reports. On the majority view, Matthew and Luke presumably made use of Mark for their biographic projects because they believed that Mark likewise conveyed accurate information, whether from earlier published sources (cf. possibly Luke 1:1) or oral information from eyewitnesses (as Papias suggests; cf. Luke 1:2). Fictional accounts were not typically interested in prior information, nor were they written about recent historical figures.

Because Mark wrote his biography within a generation of Jesus (closer to his time, in fact, than Suetonius is in relation to Otho), we may expect that he also depends on substantial preexisting information, whatever his (or Suetonius's) literary adaptations for their respective sorts of audiences. If his approach is anything like that of Suetonius, he probably narrates prior information in every pericope of his work. In any case, Matthew and Luke, who probably wrote biographies within two decades of Mark, considered him a reliable source and were in a much better position to know circumstances surrounding his work than are we.

10.6. Comparing Other Greek and Roman Biographies

Although I reproduce in this chapter at length only some parallel treatments of Otho, the results would be relatively the same for biographies of Galba, another emperor from the same period.[133] Comparing Suetonius's approximately thirty-five paragraphs (about 3,000 words) with Plutarch's approximately thirty-nine longer paragraphs (about 6,500 words), Benson Goh found variation on some details that do not significantly affect the story or suggest the biographers' deliberate fabrication.[134]

At the same time, he also found "about 98 points of contact, 63 of which bear very close resemblance to each other by using nearly identical wording."[135] Likewise, he found roughly "76 points of contact between Suetonius and Tacitus, with 53 of them (approximately 70%) being very similar; and 131 between Plutarch and Tacitus, with 80 of them (approximately 61%) being significant."[136] Clearly, Suetonius reports events existing in his sources and neither fabricates them nor sees fabrication as his appropriate role as a biographer.[137] Most scholars view Tacitus as a fairly reliable historian for the period; we should therefore view the biographic work of Suetonius and Plutarch similarly.[138] Similarly, although their sources may differ, Suetonius and Josephus overlap in depicting some portents before Caligula's death; the obvious and significant differences between the accounts invite investigation rather than the wholesale dismissal of either writer's work.[139]

Many other potential test cases are obvious. We may learn about the acceptable range of variation in biographies also by comparing how different biographers treated the same figure, for example, how Nepos and Plutarch diverge from the earlier, eyewitness writer Xenophon in their portraits of Agesilaus.[140] Although both later writers often omit what Xenophon includes,[141]

133. Goh, "Galba," esp. the chart in 175–89.

134. Goh, "Galba," 197–99. Nathan Brasfield found only slightly fewer in a study with me in 2011.

135. Goh, "Galba," 190, estimating two and a half to three points of contact per Suetonian paragraph.

136. Goh, "Galba," 190.

137. Goh, "Galba," 190–92.

138. Goh, "Galba," 190.

139. Cf. Woods, "Robe," brought to my attention by my doctoral student Kevin Burr.

140. See Woldemariam, "Comparison"; cf. also Ytterbrink, *Gospel*, 93.

141. Woldemariam, "Comparison," 224. Plutarch also includes additional information, but his named sources include also some other contemporary (as well as somewhat later) sources; see 219.

the people[142] and places[143] named overlap considerably, especially between Xenophon and Plutarch. Discrepancies appear, though most are fairly easily explained; they may stem from "different sources or minor creative variations by one of the later writers."[144]

Similarly, one of Nepos's biographies closely follows the corresponding material in Herodotus and Thucydides, omitting many details but making minimal changes to the elements that Nepos includes (I draw here from a thirty-two-page chart of comparisons).[145] Apart from style and detail, he conflicts significantly with these sources just three times each, in some cases because of long-range perspective or memory,[146] whereas he follows them repeatedly.[147]

10.7. Comparing Diaspora Jewish Works

Another case is Philo's first-century, biographic adaptation of the OT. Although he sometimes allegorizes wildly, his *Life of Moses* stays closer to expectations for Greco-Roman biography. Philo conforms Moses to fit philosophical ideals for sages, at points ignoring the biblical portrait to do so.[148] Nevertheless, he normally follows the biblical story closely,[149] though he offers explanatory elaboration and rhetorically rearranges material.[150] All his episodes depend on the Pentateuch.[151] We should therefore not expect him to imaginatively invent entire events that he finds neither in Scripture nor in tradition. By contrast, he does expand and invent some speeches,[152] as readers would expect in ancient historiography.

142. See the chart in Woldemariam, "Comparison," 222–23.

143. See the chart in Woldemariam, "Comparison," 225–26.

144. Woldemariam, "Comparison," 227–29 (quotation from 229); cf. 224.

145. Christian, "Themistocles," esp. 139, and the chart on 106–38.

146. Christian, "Themistocles," 139–40, on Nepos, *On Great Generals* 2 (Themistocles), 2.5; 3.2; 5.2; 7.2; 8.3, 4.

147. Again, note Christian's chart ("Themistocles," 106–38).

148. Petit, "Traversée exemplaire" (on Philo's *Hypothetica*, and comparing similar practices in Artapanus, Josephus, and Ezekiel the Tragedian); Van Veldhuizen, "Moses" (emphasizing Stoic *apatheia*). Cf. also Philo's portrait of Moses as commander-in-chief (Canevet, "Remarques").

149. McGing, "Adaptation," 121–23, 128; Hidalgo, "Study," esp. 278–86, following esp. Feldman, *Portrayal*. Although Hidalgo acknowledges his use of Feldman's detailed work, their agreement is significant, since Hidalgo first charted the material in *Life of Moses* 1 inductively.

150. McGing, "Adaptation," 128.

151. Hidalgo, "Study," 300.

152. Hidalgo, "Study," 294–300.

Synopses of the Synoptic Gospels suggest, at least where we can test Matthew's and Luke's adaptations of Mark (including occasional use of verbatim material), that they normally treat their sources more conservatively than Philo treats the biblical life of Moses (i.e., more like Suetonius than like Philo). This conservatism may reflect the less rhetorical expectations of their less elite audiences. Nevertheless, both the Evangelists and Philo reflect similar constraints and freedoms: they retain the substance of the story while flexibly reframing it in contextually relevant forms. Granted, Matthew's and Luke's rearrangement of sayings and shorter discourses into speeches seems modest by comparison. Philo's occasional addition of full speeches,[153] as in Josephus's Hellenistic Jewish historiography,[154] exceeds what we can clearly demonstrate in the Synoptic tradition, but some might find it comparable to Johannine discourses.[155]

Although 2 Maccabees is not a biography, its adaptations of earlier material reveal Diaspora Jewish use of Hellenistic historiographic conventions long before Philo's time. This book condenses a five-volume work by Jason of Cyrene, but comparison with 1 Maccabees, from which it appears literarily independent, shows numerous correspondences where the scope of the two stories overlaps.[156] Besides normal compositional devices and variation in minor details,[157] some contradictions appear, for example, in troop estimates.[158] Nevertheless, such variation does not undermine the key features of the events that both documents address.[159]

10.7a. Josephus versus the Septuagint

Sometimes we lack means to test Josephus's sources,[160] but at other points we have access to them. We can test Josephus most clearly where his *Jewish Antiquities* uses

153. Hidalgo, "Study," 291–300, esp. the four added discourses on 297–300.

154. On Josephus and speeches, see sources in Keener, *Acts*, 1:301–4. Some Judean haggadic works also supplied interpretive speeches (cf. Endres, *Interpretation*, 198–99).

155. Cf. Bauckham, "Historiographical Characteristics." For Johannine discourse, cf. also helpfully Parsenios, "Rhetoric."

156. Reynolds, "Difference," 304–8.

157. See Reynolds, "Difference," 309–13.

158. Reynolds, "Difference," 315, noting that 2 Maccabees has the lower and likelier figure here.

159. Reynolds, "Difference," 315.

160. E.g., his account of Caligula's killing apparently lacks a common source with Suetonius's very different account (Scherberich, "Sueton und Josephus"). Note similarities and differences in the portents preceding that assassination in Woods, "Robe."

the Septuagint. Comparing Josephus's *Antiquities* with his source in the Septuagint reveals the degree of his rhetorical adaptation. While usually maintaining the biblical story line, he occasionally augments it with subsequent traditions and often reshapes it for apologetic purposes. See also discussion in chapter 3.

Josephus's claim not to have added anything may be simply conventional:[161] he does add some features, even if he personally deems them minimal. He also interprets his sources for his Hellenistic audience in various ways.[162] After promising to add nothing to Moses's laws,[163] he manages somehow to find among them a specific prohibition against theft from pagan temples, the requirement of seven judges per city, and a prohibition against receiving women's testimony.[164] Josephus seems to have viewed his "translation" task as including interpretation and adaptation for his audience; Plato, Cicero, and others understood the "translation" task similarly.[165]

Josephus follows but apparently modifies some literary sources;[166] he is not always correct, but neither does he normally appear to deliberately misrepresent his sources.[167] Like some other Jewish writers,[168] Josephus dramatizes, adds speeches,[169] omits what appears counterproductive, and inserts his own apologetic slant.[170] Sometimes Josephus apparently "corrects" or adjusts biblical accounts based on other biblical passages.[171] The pictures of Moses in Josephus and Artapanus also include imaginative features to conform to Hellenistic conventions.[172]

---

161. Feldman, "Abraham," 133, citing Dionysius of Halicarnassus, *Thucydides* 5, 8; Lucian, *How to Write History* 47.

162. Clearly not all changes stem from a desire to please Rome: it is unlikely that Josephus avoids Nineveh's repentance because of Roman antiproselytism views (Feldman, "Jonah"), given his reports of many conversions elsewhere, and still less likely are some parallels drawn between the Jonah story and the Argonautica (Hamel, "Argo").

163. Josephus, *Jewish Antiquities* 4.196; cf. 1.17.

164. Josephus, *Jewish Antiquities* 4.207, 214, 219.

165. Inowlocki, "Adding."

166. See Pucci Ben Zeev, "Reliability."

167. Pucci Ben Zeev, "Ambiguities."

168. Sometimes LAB dramatically rewrites an account (e.g., Begg, "Ceremonies"), but it usually depends on the biblical text for events. Feldman, "*Antiquities*," 76, argues that in narrative style LAB is closer to Luke-Acts than to Josephus.

169. E.g., Josephus, *Jewish Antiquities* 1.46; 4.25–34, 134–38; cf. Cohen, "What Happened?"; see Josephus's adaptation of speeches in 1 Macc (Gafni, "Josephus and Maccabees," esp. 126–27).

170. See, e.g., Penner, *Praise*, 113.

171. See Höffken, "Reichsteilung."

172. Silver, "Moses and Birds" (on Josephus, *Jewish Antiquities* 2.243–53; Artapanus in Eusebius's *Preparation for the Gospel* 9.27).

This practice may not represent his method everywhere; he may strive for greater rhetorical sophistication in his magnum opus, the *Jewish Antiquities* (where he overlaps most with Scripture), than in his earlier, more historiographically sophisticated *Jewish War*.[173] Even in the *Antiquities*, Josephus may exercise more freedom and stylize more in his first five books than afterward (in bks. 6–20).[174] More relevant for the present discussion, even in the *Antiquities*, Josephus tends to adapt events in his sources, rather than to create them.[175] While adding details and perspectives, he retains even the stories of David's sin with Bathsheba[176] and Uriah's murder,[177] although—perhaps with an eye toward anti-Judaic polemic such as Apion's sources—he omits the episode of Moses and the golden calf.[178]

Even when Josephus adds extrabiblical events to biblical accounts (such as Moses's exploits as an Egyptian prince),[179] our sources sometimes confirm that he is following earlier extrabiblical traditions, rather than composing from his imagination.[180] Thus, for example, Josephus's Moses wins Ethiopia (Nubia) peacefully as in Artapanus,[181] although Josephus may well adjust his material for apologetic purposes.[182] Josephus calls Pharaoh's daughter Thermuthis, which differs from Artapanus's name for her.[183] It

173. Cf., e.g., Attridge, *Interpretation*, 44–50; followed by Newell, "Forms," 285. Even in the *Jewish War* Josephus may write for Rome's elite, who might recognize Greek tragic allusions in bk. 1 (so Forte, "Echoes Revisited").

174. Cohen, "Josephus and Scripture."

175. See Downing, "Redaction Criticism 2," 33. For sample analyses of many of his accounts, often resembling gentile biographers' adaptations, see the many works by L. Feldman and C. Begg on this subject in the bibliography.

176. Josephus, *Jewish Antiquities* 7.130–31.

177. Josephus, *Jewish Antiquities* 7.131–46.

178. Josephus, *Jewish Antiquities* 3.95–99.

179. E.g., Petitfils, "Tale," 160–62 (though noting the probably earlier plotline in 161n31).

180. Note Moses's peaceful victory in Nubia; compare Artapanus, *Concerning the Jews* frag. 3 (Eusebius, *Preparation for the Gospel* 9.27.10); Josephus, *Jewish Antiquities* 2.238–57. For Josephus's historiographic conventions and apologetic adaptation here, see Rajak, "Moses in Ethiopia"; Runnalls, "Ethiopian Campaign."

181. Josephus, *Jewish Antiquities* 2.238–57, esp. 252–53; Artapanus, *Concerning the Jews* frag. 3 (Eusebius, *Preparation for the Gospel* 9.27.10). Similar stories are told of Alexander's diplomacy (Ps.-Callisthenes, *Alexander Romance* 1.23). The narrative follows conventions for Hellenistic historiography; see Rajak, "Moses in Ethiopia" (thinking Josephus's source and Artapanus shared a common source).

182. See Josephus, *Jewish Antiquities* 2.238–57; Runnalls, "Ethiopian Campaign" (thinking that Josephus subtly challenged Artapanus's account).

183. Josephus, *Jewish Antiquities* 2.224–36; Artapanus, *Concerning the Jews* frag. 3.

corresponds, however, to a second-century-BCE Judean source that calls her Tharmuth.[184]

Josephus also clearly depends on sources for postbiblical as well as biblical events,[185] such as the work of Nicolaus of Damascus,[186] although he critiques what he sees as Nicolaus's bias.[187] Josephus may have used Roman military commentaries for some of his accurate information about the Judean-Roman War.[188]

Numerous studies have traced Josephus's adaptation of biblical accounts, but whereas the degree of adaptation varies from one narrative to another, it remains balanced by his general fidelity to the basic biblical account.[189] As a rule, except for speeches, Josephus "does not create events or incidents, either out of his head or by midrashic exposition,"[190] with little if any room for free invention of incidents.[191] He freely chooses which material to include, rearranges it, and adapts the wording, but he does not invent material.[192] As others have noted, Matthew and Luke paraphrase Jesus's sacred words in their sources more conservatively than Josephus paraphrases Scripture.[193]

10.7b. Josephus versus Josephus

Comparing Josephus with the Septuagint is fruitful in exploring the range of liberties that Josephus felt free to take with his sources, even those he considered sacred. In Josephus's case, however, we may also compare Josephus

---

184. Jub. 47:5. Much later, rabbis called her Bithiah (Pesiq. Rab Kah. 7:6/9; Pesiq. Rab. 17:5; Exod. Rab. 18:3).

185. Bellemore, "Josephus, Pompey, and the Jews," suggests that Josephus depended on more Roman sources and fewer Jewish sources in the later *Jewish Antiquities* than in the *Jewish War*. He may employ genuinely Iranian material (whether originally accurate or not) in *Antiquities* 18.314–70 (cf. Herman, "Motifs").

186. E.g., Josephus, *Jewish Antiquities* 12.127. Probably Josephus depends on Nicolaus as his main source from Antiochus IV through Herod I (Stern, *Authors*, 1:229).

187. Josephus, *Jewish Antiquities* 14.9; 16.183–84. Josephus also writes from a Jewish perspective that differs from Nicolaus's Greco-Syrian one (Wacholder, "Nicolaus"). Josephus sounds less favorable to Herod in *Antiquities* than in *War*.

188. Broshi, "Credibility"; see esp. Josephus, *Life* 348, 352; *Against Apion* 56, on p. 381.

189. See esp. Cohen, *Josephus*. For specific examples of Josephus's adaptations, see, e.g., Begg, "Jotham"; "Fall"; "Putsch"; "Jehoahaz" (improving the character); Feldman, "Elijah"; see other articles by Feldman in the bibliography; Gafni, "Josephus and Maccabees," 126–27.

190. Downing, "Redaction Criticism 1," 55–56, quoted in Derrenbacker, *Practices*, 93.

191. Downing, "Redaction Criticism 1," 60, contends, "probably none."

192. Derrenbacker, *Practices*, 94, following Downing, "Redaction Criticism 1," 56.

193. Evans, "Foreword," x.

with himself—comparing his autobiographic *Life* with parallel events in the *War* and part of the *Antiquities*. Josephus seems to have followed his own *War* at points in his later magnum opus, the *Antiquities*.[194] Yet, whether because of conflicting sources,[195] careless composition, or neglecting to explain information that would resolve some of the tensions, Josephus sometimes contradicts himself, even in some of his most rhetorically refined material and closest to his own lifetime.[196] Josephus sometimes forgets to include promised information.[197]

Given how often Josephus contradicts himself on various points concerning events of his own time, one suspects that Josephus and some of his audience are more familiar with, or more concerned with the fixity of, the regularly retold biblical story than with his own. That Josephus did not expect his audence to mind such variation suggests a considerable degree of potential literary flexibility in at least some (and perhaps more) first-century autobiographic or historical writing. As Henderson notes, Josephus's discrepancies offer a "*possible outer range of variation that might have been acceptable*" in his milieu.[198]

Information in Josephus's autobiography differs from that in his history of his people regarding chronology, Josephus's mission to Galilee, and his relation to John of Gischala.[199] New circumstances dictate Josephus's most striking difference: whereas he omitted mention of Justus before, he now adds him as a rival, harmful to his people.[200] After Josephus had written about the war, Justus published his own account, which apparently depicted Josephus in an unflattering manner,[201] inviting Josephus's apologetic response. Josephus had greater *personal* apologetic incentive than the average biographer would have. Even so, his different accounts of the same events suggests, not that the events never happened, but that he presents them from different perspectives.[202]

---

194. Krieger, "Hauptquelle."

195. But cf. Mason, "Contradiction."

196. See Mason, *Life*, 213–22; Henderson, "*Life* and *War*"; Henderson, "Comparison." Cf. different views on who inherited the right to replace high priests (Josephus, *Jewish Antiquities* 20.16; cf. 20.103, 179, 196, 203). Granted, some apparent mistakes might instead betray deliberate literary connections (see the argument in Sievers, "Name").

197. Josephus, *Jewish Antiquities* 20.53 (though cf. 20.101).

198. Henderson, "Comparison," 275.

199. Rodgers, "Justice," 170; Henderson, "Comparison," 269–74.

200. Cf. Rodgers, "Justice," 170, 175, 182, noting Josephus, *Life* 40–41, 338; cf. 336, 340, 367; Henderson, "Comparison," 269.

201. Rodgers, "Justice," 182, citing esp. Josephus, *Life* 40, 338.

202. Wright, *People*, 378, also comparing Luke 24:51 and Acts 1:3. Cf. also the divergent details in Josephus and Philo on the same events (Theissen, *Gospels*, 149).

10.8. Conclusion

I have focused on biographers' treatment of Otho and secondarily on their treatment of Galba and on Josephus's adaptation of his sources. Other comparisons could also be marshaled to support those noted here. Comparisons of some ancient biographies with more contemporary accounts of figures (e.g., their letters) further suggest a general range of variation on details.[203] Such examples establish an approximate range for what first-century hearers might expect in the Gospels, probably with Matthew or Luke, for example, on the more conservative side of the genre (at least in how they handle Mark) and John on the more flexible side.

The evidence examined above suggests that biographers in the early empire built on information for their events and often for details. While Suetonius or even Tacitus might gladly report any widely known, hostile rumor that had circulated about Caligula, Nero, or Domitian, they did not likely invent these rumors. If their events are fictitious, therefore, it is likely because of fabricated material in their sources.

In the case of the Gospels, I believe that the authoritative status of the witnesses in the Jesus movement's formative period and the distance of the Diaspora movement from early Galilean populist rumors would probably suggest fewer, rather than more, errors in transmission. Transmission through disciples was one of ancient memory's most careful forms of transmission, especially regarding a teacher's message. I must, however, reserve further questions regarding pre-Gospel transmission for the closing chapters of the book, which address memories before memoirs. The point to note here is that, to the extent that they resembled normal biographies of their time, the Gospels would employ literary flexibility in shaping the stories they inherited, yet would not invent new stories, that is, incidents not in their sources.

203. See Hillard, Nobbs, and Winter, "Corpus."

Chapter 11

Flex Room: Literary Techniques in Ancient Biographies

Although ancient biographies influenced their modern namesakes,[1] they also differed from them. Although, as we have shown, biographers normally ideally did their best to use significant historical information and thus differed from novelists, they addressed audiences with expectations very different from those of most readers of modern biographies. The conventions of ancient biography permitted considerable freedom in how biographers recounted their information. Some Evangelists and some biographers exploited this literary flexibility more than did others.

Understanding the range of flexibility various ancient biographers exercised helps us understand better both the information content that ancient audiences would expect in the Gospels and the rhetorical and literary flexibility they would expect the gospel traditions and Evangelists to exercise.

Here I survey some ancient literary techniques evident in biographers' works, techniques that bear on the expectations with which we should approach the Gospels. I engage especially Michael R. Licona's valuable work that has recently applied to the Gospels literary techniques culled from Plutarch's works.[2] These techniques extend well beyond Plutarch to many other ancient biographers.

---

1. See, e.g., Mossman, "Plutarch and Biography"; for classical influence more generally on English literature, see esp. Copeland, *History*.

2. I believe that some of Licona's more conservative critics have prematurely treated potentially complementary approaches as contradictory, and that some more skeptical critics fixate on his theological background (Baldwin, "Review," provides context for why Licona articulates his arguments in the precise way that he does) more than on his arguments. Licona's data and approaches come from classicists with no stake in the debates in NT scholarship. To a priori dismiss another scholar's case based primarily on their background is to mount an ad hominem argument and—in principle, among the less courteous—to invite the same treatment in kind.

11.1. Flexibility in Ancient Biography

Both historians and biographers varied among themselves in historiographic quality, and even the most careful writers were expected to tell a good story.[3] The essential historical substance should remain, but the reason that writers composed *new* works, after all, was to provide their own literary interpretation or construction of events. Thus one expert on Arrian points out that this author "does not seem to have altered the data of his sources, but the original order and emphasis are altered. . . . He may be dependent on his sources for material, but he rises above them and creates a literary work that is wholly his own."[4]

What sort of freedoms did writers in factual genres take? Paraphrase was a conventional rhetorical exercise,[5] but flexibility extended much further than the use of paraphrase. Some historians were careless about details; most did not care about minor variations.[6] Thus, for example, two ancient historians report that a son died, and another reports the death as that of a daughter; many historians would have deemed such differences as minutiae irrelevant to their point.[7] Likewise, in his separate works, Josephus has Antipas banished to different distant locations.[8] More than likely, simple lapse of memory (sometimes based on how sources were envisioned) is often responsible for the variation, and the matters seemed too minor to warrant revision or concern.[9]

At other times, authors alter or add explanatory details to events.[10] Given the importance of vividness for rhetorical style,[11] it is not surprising that some

---

3. See also here Sanders, *Paul*, 98, recognizing that ancient historians distinguished truth from fiction but also composed in ways to make their stories flow well; cf. also Bauckham, *Eyewitnesses*, 595.

4. Bosworth, *Arrian*, 60.

5. See, e.g., Theon, *Progymnasmata* 1.93–171 (Butts); Hermogenes, *Method in Forceful Speaking* 24.440; Libanius, *Anecdote* 1.4; 2.3; *Maxim* 1.2–5; 2.3; 3.2; cf. Fronto, *On Eloquence* 3.5; Hock, "Paul and Education," 202–3; Licona, *Differences*, 10–13; in Plutarch, see Licona, *Differences*, 34, 56, 100, 109; in Josephus, see Derrenbacker, *Practices*, 94–95, 116, following Downing ("Redaction Criticism 1," 56, 62).

6. E.g., Licona, *Differences*, 32–33, 79–80. Likewise, the majority of variations in the Synoptic tradition are relatively minor (Allison, *Constructing*, 454).

7. Massey, "Disagreement," 54–55.

8. Josephus, *Jewish Antiquities* 18.252 (probably more accurate); *Jewish War* 2.183 (probably working from memory).

9. See, e.g., my comments in ch. 10 regarding Plutarch, *Galba* 26.5; Suetonius, *Otho* 4.1.

10. Aune, *Environment*, 82; Small, *Wax Tablets*, 195, 199.

11. E.g., Cicero, *On the Orator* 2.45.189; Dionysius of Halicarnassus, *Lysias* 7.

writers add details for dramatic effect.[12] After all, given the limitations of human memory (see ch. 14), they would not expect all details in their sources to be authentic in any case. Orally oriented cultures are less troubled by variations than are some modern Western critics.[13] (Still, it should be noted that the Gospels do not offer the sort of extensive detail found in more rhetorically sophisticated works.)[14]

Still, some authors complained when some of their peers went too far. Plutarch complains that some earlier writers added incidents missing elsewhere, for example, composing a proper tragic finale for Alexander's life.[15] Lucian objects to historical writers amplifying and omitting merely for literary or encomiastic purposes (i.e., to make the character look better).[16] Other writers voiced similar criticisms.[17]

How much flexibility was accepted in ancient biographies? That depended on individual biographers and on the sources available to them; variation was ordinarily much greater about figures of the distant past, for whom existing competing traditions were more often available. By contrast, comparison of biographies of a figure such as Otho, composed half a century after the events described, reveals substantial overlap of information, similar to what we witness in a synopsis of the Gospels (see ch. 10).

11.2. Flexibility in the Gospels

Simply because some biographers adapted their sources in particular ways does not mean that all biographers did so in the same ways. Nevertheless, that ancient biographers could exercise at least some flexibility will not surprise any attentive reader of the Gospels who has taken time to compare parallel

---

12. See again the complaint in Plutarch, *Alexander* 70.3.

13. Dunn, *Perspective*, 112; Eddy and Boyd, *Legend*, 429–30.

14. For even Luke, see Keener, *Acts*, 1:136. Probable examples of added details do appear; for a minor one, cf. δεξιός (*dexios*) in Luke 6:6 versus simply χείρ (*cheir*) in Mark 3:1, 3, 5.

15. Plutarch, *Alexander* 70.3. His own romantic description of Darius's death (Plutarch, *Alexander* 43.2) is missing in Arrian (*Alexander* 3.21–23), but it was evidently not his own invention (B. Perrin's LCL note, 7:352n1, cites Quintus Curtius Rufus, *History* 5.13, 28; Diodorus Siculus, *Library of History* 17.73).

16. Shuler, *Genre*, 11–12; cf. Bowersock, *Fiction*, 1–27. See esp. Lucian, *How to Write History* 7–13; in his *True Story* 1.4, he complains that novelizers fail to recognize how obvious their "lies" were.

17. E.g., Herodian, *History* 1.1.1–2, despite his own rhetorical adjustments (cf. Whittaker, "Introduction," xxxviii–xxxix)!

accounts. To repeat some particularly conspicuous but simple examples, did Jesus speak regularly of the kingdom of God, as in Mark and Luke, or of the kingdom of heaven, as usually in Matthew? Did the centurion cry out, "Truly, this was God's son!" (Mark 15:39), or (what Mark's version would necessarily entail), "Certainly, this man was righteous/innocent!" (Luke 23:47)?

Although some modern readers find these differences in wording troubling, such differences rarely bothered ancient audiences. Whether one agrees with Papias or not, his early second-century report about Mark's Gospel lets us know what he believed about it:

> Mark, having become Peter's interpreter, wrote down accurately everything he [Mark] remembered, though not in order, of the things either said or done by Christ. For he [Mark] neither heard the Lord nor followed him, but afterward, as I said, followed Peter, who adapted his teachings as needed[18] but had no intention of giving an ordered account of the Lord's sayings. Consequently Mark did nothing wrong in writing down some things as he remembered them, for he made it his one concern not to omit anything that he heard or to make any false statement in them.[19]

Papias apparently deemed neither sequence nor precise wording essential. Indeed, Papias seems to expect that Peter himself adapted Jesus's teachings, perhaps meaning that Peter contextualized the message homiletically or at least chose what to emphasize based on the needs of his hearers. Such flexibility appears so frequently in ancient factual accounts, including biographies, that it seems inherent in them and expected by audiences.

---

18. Papias's term *chreia* here could refer to rhetorical adaptation (see ch. 5), though that is not its common meaning outside rhetorical contexts (cf. Did. 1.5; 11.5).

19. Papias, frag. 3.15 (Holmes). Many interpreters think that Papias prefers the Johannine chronological sequence to Mark's here, but "order" (*taxis*) might refer instead to rhetorical arrangement, in which Mark's plot was deemed deficient (see Moessner, "Voice"). Likewise, Papias (according to Eusebius, *Ecclesiastical History* 2.15.2) reports that Peter's listeners "begged Mark (whose gospel is extant), since he was Peter's follower, to leave behind a written record of the teaching given to them verbally, and did not quit until they had persuaded the man" (Papias, frag. 21.1, Holmes). He seems to believe that Mark wrote before Peter's death and that Peter subsequently approved the work (21.2); this scenario could fit one commonly proposed date, i.e., during the Neronian persecution. Irenaeus, writing ca. 180 CE, believes that Mark wrote after Peter's death (*Against Heresies* 3.1.1), but Eusebius, though writing later, seems to depend here on Papias's own text.

11.3. Acceptable Differences: Philo, Josephus, Plutarch

It is sometimes blatantly obvious that biographers did not mind variation in details. A biographer can vary in such details even in his own works that cover the same events or can diverge from widely known sources. Sometimes such differences appear even in lives that a single biographer wrote at roughly the same time.[20] Sometimes this incongruity might reflect a difference in preferred source material,[21] but usually it probably simply reflects how the writer adapts his material for a particular life.[22]

11.3a. Adjustments in Philo

Philo's *Life of Moses*, which we can compare with his OT source, follows the same techniques observed below in Plutarch and the Gospels. Philo omits some OT episodes[23] and OT rhetorical repetitions;[24] he often abridges,[25] sometimes by conflating material.[26]

Nevertheless, although he cuts sections, "when he does follow the story he is more likely to elaborate than to abridge."[27] Like most commentators today, Philo usually expands narratives with explanatory detail; like storytellers, he also adds dramatic detail.[28] Occasionally, he must do so to justify Moses,[29] but usually his expansions do not change "the essence of the" biblical picture.[30] Sometimes he displaces material chronologically;[31] he even rearranges

---

20. Pelling, *Texts*, 49; Pelling, "Method"; Licona, *Differences*, 67 (cf. 22).

21. Cf. perhaps Edwards, "Introduction," xxii, contrasting Suetonius, *Claudius* 44 and *Nero* 33. Plutarch sometimes had to contend with differing source accounts (Almagor, "Narratives," 70–71).

22. Pelling, *Texts*, 51.

23. McGing, "Adaptation," 120; Hidalgo, "Study," 287; Feldman, "Calf."

24. McGing, "Adaptation," 125, on Philo, *Moses* 1.85–147.

25. McGing, "Adaptation," 123–25, noting Num 13–14 in Philo, *Moses* 1.220–38; Exod 17:1–7 in *Moses* 1.210–11; and Exod 3:7–4:17 in *Moses* 1.71–84.

26. McGing, "Adaptation," 124–25 (to deemphasize Moses's weakness), 128 (streamlining).

27. McGing, "Adaptation," 125; for elaboration, see also, e.g., Begg, "Moves"; Begg, "Rephidim Episode."

28. McGing, "Adaptation," 127–30, 133, noting, e.g., Exod 2:15–22 in *Moses* 1.51–59 (cf. Josephus, *Jewish Antiquities* 2.258–63).

29. McGing, "Adaptation," 129–30.

30. McGing, "Adaptation," 128, on his treatment of Exod 7:14–12:36 in *Moses* 1.96–139.

31. McGing, "Adaptation," 125–26.

the plagues to fit his contextualized explanation.[32] Philo sometimes downplays other characters in order to spotlight Moses more clearly,[33] a common biographic technique noted further below.

Yet he often follows the biblical text closely.[34] Some features identified in Plutarch are less frequent here; thus, for example, Philo only rarely transfers a matter to a different character.[35]

11.3b. Adjustments in Josephus

The first-century Jewish historian Josephus exercises considerable flexibility, yet he claims to add nothing to his account.[36] As Gerald Downing notes, comparing Josephus with his source suggests what Josephus can take for granted that his audience may expect: "what 'counts as' an accurate reproduction of a sacred text, what interpretation is so clearly legitimate as to need no defense, but also what limits are that he seems to feel bound to observe."[37]

Downing shows how Josephus uses his biblical sources.[38] Rather than following his sources' sequence, he rearranges material for coherence or narrative flow.[39] He selectively omits source material that repeats itself or conflicts with other passages; not to do so would make his narrative less cohesive and would make it harder to make his apologetic case for his wider audience.[40] Likewise, he adds some material for narrative flow, to clarify and to make moral, theological, or apologetic points.[41] His changes add "new colour,"[42] though most changes simply seem to function as avoidance of cribbing the

32. McGing, "Adaptation," 128, noting esp. *Moses* 1.96–97.

33. See, e.g., Feldman, "Interpretation of Joshua"; Feldman, "General."

34. McGing, "Adaptation," 121–23, giving the example of Num 23:7–10 in *Moses* 1.278–79; see further Hidalgo, "Study."

35. McGing, "Adaptation," 126–27, noting transfer to the Egyptians generally in 1.105, 112.

36. Josephus, *Against Apion* 1.42; *Jewish Antiquities* 1.17; 14.1; 20.261, noted in Downing, "Redaction Criticism 1," 47.

37. Downing, "Redaction Criticism 1," 48.

38. See Downing, "Redaction Criticism 1"; "Redaction Criticism 2."

39. Downing, "Redaction Criticism 1," 56. This rearrangement can conflate related accounts.

40. Downing, "Redaction Criticism 1," 50–51.

41. Downing, "Redaction Criticism 1," 51–54, noting esp. explanatory and sometimes interpretive additions but also some heightened rhetorical pathos.

42. Downing, "Redaction Criticism 1," 55.

biblical text verbatim.[43] Apart from speeches, however, Josephus does not invent new incidents;[44] even when he adapts material most freely rather than paraphrasing, he produces a "version" of his source accounts rather than a completely new story.[45] Josephus rearranges, paraphrases, conflates, and harmonizes his material, but he follows his sources rather than making up new stories; like other elite historians, he is freer in reworking speech and dialogue for dramatic, narrative purposes.[46] More recent work by Robert Derrenbacker confirms and develops further Downing's observations.[47]

John Jordan Henderson compares Josephus's apologetic autobiography with parallel (and sometimes contrasting) information in Josephus's historiographic corpus. In this case, the differences belong to the same author writing in two genres, suggesting some flexibility (or sometimes carelessness or tendentiousness) in how Josephus tells the same story. For various reasons, Josephus takes significant latitude,[48] producing some demonstrable contradictions between the works in matters of detail and even tension between the portrayals of the character of Josephus's Galilean mission.[49] That Josephus does not feel a need to qualify or defend such differences may suggest that he expects his Diaspora audience to appreciate a measure of flexibility in the biographic genre, certainly more than readers of modern biographies anticipate.

To a significant extent, the differences between the verdicts regarding Josephus are matters of emphasis, depending on the foil to which we compare them. Josephus's practice is certainly more flexible than modern historiography, but neither is it comparable to ancient novels. Josephus rewrites details rather than inventing incidents (at least normally). He is naturally more bound to a well-known and prior text in his *Antiquities* than in his autobiography, with differences also relating to the difference between writing sacred history and writing an autobiography that defends his own honor. The Gospels are biographies with undoubtedly apologetic elements, yet they also recount a sacred story, one that by Luke's day, at least, was already to some degree known (Luke 1:4).

---

43. Downing, "Redaction Criticism 1," 49, following Pelletier, *Josèphe*, esp. 29, 222, on Josephus's adaptations of the Letter of Ps.-Aristeas (cf. also Downing, "Redaction Criticism 2," 33).

44. Downing, "Redaction Criticism 1," 55–56, 60. The significant extrabiblical addition to the Moses story is pre-Josephan tradition attested in Artapanus (Downing, "Redaction Criticism 1," 55, citing Eusebius, *Preparation for the Gospel* 9.27.432a).

45. Downing, "Redaction Criticism 1," 64.

46. Downing, "Redaction Criticism 1," 62.

47. Derrenbacker, *Practices*, 92–116, expanding beyond Downing, esp. on 110–16.

48. Henderson, "*Life* and *War*"; Henderson, "Comparison."

49. See Henderson, "Comparison," 270.

11.3c. Adjustments in Plutarch

Nearly all writers adjusted their sources rather than reproduced them whole-sale. Even writers who follow their sources closely redact them, even in the case of sacred cultural texts.[50] Many differences were admittedly quite minor, such as one account "reporting minor information not included in the other"[51] or a slight variation in wording.[52]

Scholars have especially studied how Plutarch adapts his sources. Plutarch's flexibility was limited: "While Plutarch felt free to invent an occasional scene, he did not invent entire episodes"; he did not perpetrate "deliberate falsehood."[53] Yet Plutarch follows various literary techniques for fleshing out or simplifying his narrations. Analogous to how Josephus conflates his sources, such as Samuel-Kings and the Chronicler, Plutarch conflates Dionysius of Halicarnassus and Livy.[54]

Consistent with the probability that his sources have done so before him, he emphasizes or adjusts features of a story to depict a biographee as "more or less favorable" or "to create irony." Plutarch believes that he is communicating something true about the figure's character.[55]

Plutarch can mention any reports of events so long as they precede his time. He is willing to include prior but debatable material if it illustrates moral truth "about his subject."[56] He is ready to consider a story if it is "famous," "well-attested, and, what is more to the point, . . . it comports so well with the character" of the figure known from other sources.[57]

Although in different genres, preachers and some of us professors will sometimes speak similarly, using even an explicitly fictitious or legendary illustration to reinforce a point. (For example, I sometimes will cite, albeit explicitly as probably apocryphal, Augustus's alleged remark about Herod: "Better to be Herod's pig than his son.")[58]

---

50. E.g., Cicero, *On the Nature of the Gods* 3.16.42 (for Homer, *Odyssey* 11.600ff.); Diogenes Laertius, *Lives* 1.48 (for Homer, *Iliad* 2.557).

51. Licona, *Differences*, 31.

52. Licona, *Differences*, 32–33, 43, 79–80, 83.

53. Licona, *Differences*, 18, following Pelling, *Plutarch and History*, 156, 161; Edwards, *Plutarch*, 3; Jones, *Plutarch and Rome*, 85.

54. Downing, "Conventions"; Derrenbacker, *Practices*, 97.

55. Licona, *Differences*, 109.

56. Power, "Poetry," 238, following Pelling, *Plutarch and History*, 152–56; Duff, "Childhood," 92–93; Duff, "How *Lives* Begin," 201–2; Stadter, "Anecdotes," 293; Moles, "Letters," 144–45, 161; cf. Licona, *Differences*, 17.

57. Plutarch, *Solon* 27.1 (trans. B. Perrin, LCL).

58. Macrobius, *Saturnalia* 2.4.11 (cf., e.g., in Van der Horst, "Macrobius," 222; Reinhold, *Dias-*

Building on recent research in classics, especially insights from Oxford's Christopher Pelling, Michael Licona highlights a number of common literary techniques in Plutarch's biographies. He recognizes that various other factors account for some differences, such as "a slip of memory, the use of different sources, the elasticity of oral tradition."[59] But he also notes that some adaptations follow literary conventions already articulated in basic first-century textbooks.[60] One could, for example, convert a statement into a question, a command, or dialogue,[61] perhaps accounting for such differences in the Gospels as Matthew 8:7//Luke 7:6a.[62]

Some compositional techniques appear throughout ancient historiography, despite diverse designations assigned to them.[63] The devices that Licona lists include the following, although some of these (such as simplification) may encompass others or are closely related to one another:[64]

1. transferal of information about one figure to another;
2. displacement of an event from one context to another (Plutarch sometimes even *mentions* that he does this);[65]
3. conflation of material to simplify it;
4. compression of time sequences to maintain dramatic continuity;
5. spotlighting to keep the focus on a single character, despite knowledge that others were involved;[66]
6. simplification that removes or changes details to prevent the narrative from being cluttered;
7. filling in plausible details where they were unknown to maintain the narrative's realism;
8. paraphrase.

---

pora, 100), probably reflects tradition springing from the Gospel itself (Smallwood, *Jews*, 104n156), although it may follow a standard style of rhetorical insult (Diogenes Laertius, *Lives* 6.2.41).

59. Licona, *Differences*, 2.

60. Licona, *Differences*, 10–11, on Theon.

61. Licona, *Differences*, 12–13, noting Theon, *Progymnasmata* 87–90 (36–38).

62. The emphatic pronoun in Matt 8:7 may suggest a question (with, e.g., Jeremias, *Promise*, 30; Martin, "Pericope," 15; France, "Exegesis," 257; Carson, "Matthew," 201; Talbert, *Matthew*, 113; Evans, *Matthew*, 187).

63. Licona, *Differences*, 19.

64. Licona, *Differences*, 20. For the relevance of Pelling's "compositional devices" for the Gospels, cf. also Bauckham, *Eyewitnesses*, 595–96.

65. Licona, *Differences*, 20, cites here *Cato the Younger* 25.5. Cf. ch. 5.

66. This is an optimal example of the "law of biographical relevance" treated in Licona, *Differences*, 21.

Licona illustrates these devices by comparing thirty parallel pericopes within nine of Plutarch's lives.[67]

Many of the techniques observable in Plutarch also appear in other, earlier writers, for example, in how different biographers about Agesilaus edit their material.[68] Various writers offer the same forms of adaptation in biographic material about Galba and Otho.[69] Attentive listeners today will likely find themselves or others employing some of these same devices when we narrate events; without some simplification, narrations become impossible to follow in ordinary conversation.

In addition to these techniques, biographers also often use rhetorical *synkrisis*, paralleling characters in such a way as to invite readers to compare them.[70] For example, one could highlight a biographee's virtue by contrasting the vices of his detractors.[71] Similarly, although Plutarch's closing *synkrisis* sometimes contradicts the biographies themselves, offering a different angle from which to consider moral lessons, it often emphasizes the differences between figures analogous to how his prologues had highlighted their similarities.[72] Suetonius contrasts Vespasian with the profligate Nero[73] and may use Augustus as a standard for subsequent emperors.[74]

11.4. Surveying Some Literary Techniques

As already noted, paraphrase was a standard practice in rhetoric and composition,[75] and it was therefore also standard in adapting prior material in

---

67. Licona, *Differences*, 23–111; cf. Licona, "Viewing."

68. See Kwon, "Reimagining," 144–219, 297–303, esp. 211–19, 299; these include (212–13) paraphrase (28 times), compression (13–17 times), simplification (13 times), spotlighting (8 times), expansion of narrative details (8 times), transferal (8 times), conflation (6 times), and displacement (3 times). The techniques focus on the protagonist the strong majority of the time (299).

69. See Kwon, "Reimagining," 220–88; for charts of the devices, see esp. 255, 286–87; for totals and their functions, 299, 303; see earlier Keener, "Otho"; Goh, "Galba."

70. See Duff, *Lives*, e.g., 243, 268.

71. Cf. Ytterbrink, *Gospel*, 84, noting esp. Xenophon, *Agesilaus* 8.6.

72. Duff, *Lives*, 257; for contradictions, see also 278.

73. Luke, "Ideology."

74. Edwards, "Introduction," xix. Cf. the function of David in, e.g., 1 Kgs 3:14; 11:33, 38; 15:3, 11; 2 Kgs 14:3; 2 Chr 21:12; 34:2; or, negatively, Jeroboam I, in 1 Kgs 15:34; 16:2, 19, 26; 22:52; 2 Kgs 13:6, 11; 17:22.

75. See, e.g., Theon, *Progymnasmata* 1.93–171 (Butts); Hermogenes, *Method in Forceful*

biographies and histories.[76] In fact, literary works normally paraphrase much more freely than do Matthew or Luke; their verbal similarities to Mark are extraordinary by ancient standards.[77] To take over material without paraphrasing it could function as a deliberate allusion, but otherwise it was ordinarily considered simply literarily inept. Phaedrus feels free to adapt Aesop for aesthetic reasons, meanwhile seeking to keep to the *spirit* of Aesop.[78] One might also present events from a different rhetorical angle to stir emotion.[79]

Compression streamlines narratives, maintaining focus on the main character;[80] sometimes it simply eliminates or reduces the span of time between events, but sometimes it also requires conflating them.[81] For example, Plutarch condenses what are three sessions in one of his works into a single session in another.[82] Other authors similarly vary their elaboration of time spans concerning the same events within their own works, depending on factors such as

---

Speaking 24.440; Libanius, *Anecdote* 1.4; 2.3; *Maxim* 1.2–5; 2.3; 3.2; cf. Fronto, *Eloquence* 3.5; Hock, "Paul and Education," 202–3.

76. E.g., Licona, *Differences*, 10–13; in Nepos, see Christian, "Themistocles," 139; in Plutarch, see Pelling, "Adaptation," 127; Licona, *Differences*, 34, 56, 100, 109; Kwon, "Charting," 71–72; in Philo, Hidalgo, "Study," 290, 300; in Josephus, Derrenbacker, *Practices*, 94–95, 116, following Downing, "Redaction Criticism 1," 56, 62.

77. Downing, "Redaction Criticism 2," 33; Aune, *Environment*, 125; Downing, "Redaction Criticism 2," 33; Kirk, "Ehrman, Bauckham, and Bird," 105–6, and other works cited there. For ancient views of plagiarism, see Seneca the Elder, *Controversiae* 1.pref.19; *Suasoriae* 2.19; 3.7; McGill, "Seneca on Plagiarizing," 337–46; Knoppers, "Problem," 27–30. The Evangelists either shared popular lack of concern for some elite standards (cf. the complaint in Pliny, *Natural History* pref.17) or viewed the sacred tradition as community property.

78. Phaedrus, *Fables* 2, prol. 8.

79. See, e.g., Quintilian, *Orator's Education* 4.2.113.

80. Pelling, "Adaptation," 127–28; Licona, *Differences*, 20, 36, 39, 72, 98; Kwon, "Charting," 73. Thus, e.g., Nepos condenses material from his sources (Christian, "Themistocles," 139). See also Satterthwaite, "Acts," 345, citing esp. Lucian, *How to Write History* 56–57; cf. also 27–28; Cicero, *On the Orator* 3.27.104–5; 53.202–3; Quintilian, *Orator's Education* 8.4; Longinus, *On the Sublime* 11–12. The concise summary in Libanius, *Narration* 27, conspicuously connects events that in mythical legend spanned over a decade. Laistner, *Historians*, 58–59, notes that Sallust telescoped events in his historical monographs, where space was at a premium; cf. also, e.g., Matt 8:5–6 with Luke 7:3–5; Matt 9:18 with Mark 5:23, 35; on possible telescoping due to compression in Acts 7:15–16, see, e.g., Bruce, *Acts: Greek*, 165–66; Johnson, *Acts*, 119; cf. Keener, *Acts*, 2:1371–72; in Luke 24:1, 13, 28, 36, 50, see Keener, *Acts*, 1:648–49; on Acts 26:16, Keener, *Acts*, 4:3518.

81. Licona, *Differences*, 52, 108.

82. Small, *Wax Tablets*, 194, suggesting a memory lapse, though here deliberate abridgement is likelier.

the space allotted: in one account a death or ascension may appear immediate, and in another, after a number of days.[83]

Conflation was a common way to simplify material, both in shorter quotations from memory[84] and in following larger blocks of material.[85] Some instances of such blending may stem from memory lapses,[86] but conflation appears even in different accounts by the same author.[87] Josephus conflates related events in biblical history when narrating them together simplifies his narrative, avoiding needless repetition;[88] he also does so to harmonize varying material when possible.[89] Some earlier Jewish[90] and subsequent Christian[91] scribal sources might provide examples of microconflation that suggest particularly close attention to their texts, an attention some find also in the Gospels.[92] Even at the oral stage, traditions and varying versions of a single tradition can influence one another.[93]

In the most extreme form of conflation, ancient writers often tried to harmonize sources that they believed to be generally reliable.[94] Sometimes they produced two similarly named figures to harmonize divergent traditions.[95] Although harmonization is sometimes implausible,[96] at other times it rightly

---

83. Compare, e.g., Justin, *Epitome* 6.8.1 with 6.8.13; or Luke 24:36–51 with Acts 1:3; cf. also Acts 12:23 with Josephus, *Jewish Antiquities* 19.350.

84. For Greek and Roman writers, see, e.g., Stanley, *Language*, 290–91; Hill, "Words," 271; Pelling, *Texts*, 45; for many Jewish writers, see Stanley, *Language*, 322–23.

85. Burridge, *Gospels*, 169; Derrenbacker, *Practices*, 94–95, 110–13, 115–16.

86. See Small, *Wax Tablets*, 193.

87. See Pelling, *Texts*, 45; Licona, *Differences*, 20, 48, 52, 56, 67, 91, 95, 108.

88. Downing, "Redaction Criticism 1," 56.

89. Downing, "Redaction Criticism 1," 61–62; cf. 57–58.

90. Barker, "Reassessment," 113–15 (cf. still earlier in 112n11).

91. Barker, "Reassessment," 115–17.

92. Barker, "Reassessment," 114, 117–19, rightly noting also Kloppenborg, "Variation," 74.

93. Vansina, *Oral Tradition*, 153; cf. Small, *Wax Tablets*, 200.

94. E.g., Diodorus Siculus, *Library of History* 4.4.1–5; see also Josephus (Derrenbacker, *Practices*, 93, 95); the Diatessaron (Barker, "Reassessment," 116). Cf. also scribes with textual variants (Barker, "Reassessment," 112; cf. 115). Sometimes they probably have smoothed out contradictions in their sources in their own rewriting; Damon, "Source," suggests this approach with respect to Livy, *History* 34.54.4–8, and Tacitus, *Annals* bks. 1, 14.

95. As in Diodorus Siculus, *Library of History* 4.4.1–5; Arrian, *Alexander* 2.16.1–3; 4.28.2; *Indica* 5.13.

96. E.g., to harmonize accounts Origen suggested "three separate occasions of the anointing of Jesus by a woman at dinner" (Origen, *Commentary on Matthew* 77; noted in Wiles, *Gospel*, 16).

values what survives of our sources above what we think we know based on our lack of surviving information.[97] Thus, for example, scholars at one point noted two "contradictory" oral accounts of an 1881 lynching: in one, the men hang "from a railroad crossing," in the other, they hang from a pine tree. Subsequently, however, historians found "old photographs that showed the bodies hanging *at different times from both places*"; after being lynched in one place, they were hanged again in another.[98] Rather than assuming error at the outset, it seems best methodologically to begin by seeking to explain our sources as they are and attribute error to them only as a last resort after other plausible options have been exhausted.[99]

Biographers regularly simplified story lines by omitting irrelevant details, even when this practice required some adjustments to their narratives.[100] Examples are available in Philo, Josephus,[101] and Plutarch.[102]

Biographers often omit details to focus on their primary biographee at the time,[103] sometimes even writing from that character's vantage point.[104] In Mark, we might think of the focus on Peter as a representative disciple, though often as a foil to Jesus (cf. Mark 8:29–33; 9:5; 10:28; 11:21; 14:29–31, 37, 54, 66–72; 16:7).[105] To maintain focus on a main character or to simplify and streamline an account, biographers often "spotlighted" a particular character,[106] some-

---

97. Licona, *Differences*, 91, notes that some differences among ancient historians can be explained more plausibly than others.

98. Eddy and Boyd, *Legend*, 424 (citing Bogart and Montell, *Memory*, 77, a work on method in oral historiography).

99. See Brown, *Death*, 8; so also historian of antiquity Alanna Nobbs, personal correspondence, August 20, 2018. Cf. Dillon and Finamore, "Introduction," 4; after offering various solutions to a problem on which they comment, they write, "Another possibility, of course, is that Eunapius is profoundly confused, but that conclusion seems to be a counsel of despair." Writers can make mistakes, but plugging all holes with this explanation resembles appeal to God-of-the-gaps in scientific inquiry; it short-circuits a prior search for other plausible explanations. In everyday life we typically harmonize limited yet trusted resources.

100. See Licona, *Differences*, 20.

101. McGing, "Adaptation," 131–33, noting esp. Josephus, *Jewish Antiquities* 2.176; 11.68; Downing, "Redaction Criticism 1," 57.

102. See De Pourcq and Roskam, "Virtues," 176; Licona, *Differences*, 47–48, 77, 83, 109.

103. In Plutarch, see Licona, *Differences*, 42, 46, 48, 50–52, 56, 72, 75, 77, 80, 83, 95, 97, 100, 108.

104. In Plutarch, see Licona, *Differences*, 21, 39.

105. On others as foils to Jesus, see, e.g., Wrede, *Messianic Secret*, 106; Tolbert, *Sowing*, 222; Malbon, *Company*, 91–93; Horsley, *Hearing*, 91; Bond, "Paragon," 29; though not qualifications in Henderson, *Christology*, 13–14, 194.

106. Cf. focalization in De Pourcq and Roskam, "Virtues," 168.

times even omitting other characters who were present. This technique is quite common in Plutarch.[107] For example, he

- mentions only Brutus's wounds in his biography of Brutus, although he elsewhere displays knowledge of others who were wounded at the same time;[108]
- omits Cicero's role when highlighting Antony's;[109]
- takes for granted in his life of Cicero his readers' knowledge of the civil war and Caesar's assassination and addresses these details only when Cicero has a role.[110]

Nor is this practice limited to Plutarch. Thus, for example, Josephus once mentions four bodyguards staying with him and waking him, whereas in another, perhaps more dramatized version, he has only one.[111] Similarly, in his biography of Claudius, Suetonius focuses on Agrippina's role in Claudius's death, whereas his biography of Nero presents Nero as involved along with her.[112] In the Gospels, we may think of Matthew streamlining his narrative by omitting messengers in Mark and probably Q (Matt 8:5; 9:18; Mark 5:35; Luke 7:3–5).[113]

As noted earlier, biographies were not committed to strict chronology, and biographers often lacked knowledge of any sequence for anecdotes about their characters.[114] Even when unaware of an anecdote's original setting, biographers still had to place it somewhere in their narratives,[115] and they sought to do so in ways that provided the narrative cohesiveness that readers expected.[116] Chronological displacement of scenes and sayings was thus fairly

---

107. See, e.g., Licona, *Differences*, 20, 36, 39, 48, 61, 67, 69, 75, 103, 108–10.

108. Licona, *Differences*, 97, on Plutarch, *Brutus* 17.4.

109. Licona, *Differences*, 95.

110. Hägg, *Biography*, 261.

111. Josephus, *Jewish War* 2.600–601; *Life* 137 (Henderson, "Comparison," 270). The more dramatic version also urges suicide rather than flight.

112. Edwards, "Introduction," xxii, noting Suetonius, *Claudius* 44; *Nero* 33.

113. Cf. observations in, e.g., Ehrman, *Interrupted*, 41 (though perhaps anachronistically treating them as contradictions, since this was not how most ancient authors treated such differences except when writing polemic); taking into account ancient writing patterns, Keener, *Matthew*, 264n14, 302 (already in the 1999 edition). However they explain it, all careful readers will notice the differences, which the Evangelists themselves did not seek to conceal.

114. For possible examples of rearranging "free-floating" material, see Licona, *Differences*, 28, 32–33, 47–48, 89, 91.

115. See Licona, *Differences*, 89, 91.

116. See Licona, *Differences*, 89–90, on Quintilian, *Orator's Education* 9.5.129; Lucian, *How*

common,[117] sometimes even when an author clearly knew that an event had taken place at a different time.[118] Plutarch thus sometimes differs among his own biographies in narrative sequence.[119]

Numerical contradictions, even among a writer's own works, are common.[120] Some stem from erroneous memory, others from rounding or transcriptional errors,[121] but some may reflect deliberate changes. (Historical reports also often exaggerate numbers,[122] as their critics recognized.[123] Even the most careful usually had only approximations, as they often recognized.)[124]

Compositional handbooks, as well as biographers' practice, show that narrators could freely change an action's subject from one person to more or from multiple persons to one.[125] Thus, for example, Plutarch in one life depicts the reaction of Cato's sisters, but in another, the same reaction of his (singular) sister.[126] This practice may account for Mark omitting a second figure known to Matthew

---

to *Write History* 55 (cf. 50); see more extensively Longenecker, *Rhetoric*, 4–5, 10–18, 21–23, 34–37, 41, 46, 62–66 (on "chain-link interlock"); also Brack, *Historiography*, 8–14.

117. E.g., Pelling, "Adaptation," 128–29; McGing, "Adaptation," 125–26; Kwon, "Charting," 74; Henderson, "Comparison," 269, 272; Licona, *Differences*, 67, 72, 108; Licona, "Reliable," on Sallust; it leads to conflation in 91, 108. In 2 Macc, see Reynolds, "Difference," 309.

118. Licona, *Differences*, 20 (citing the explicit Plutarch, *Cato the Younger* 25.5).

119. Licona, *Differences*, 47, 50–51, 110; Licona, "Viewing," 326.

120. Clear Josephan examples in Henderson, "Comparison," 269 (following Cohen, *Josephus*, 7); Plutarchean examples in Licona, *Differences*, 57, 73, 104, 110. Cf. spelling or name differences in Henderson, "Comparison," 268, 271–72; Licona, *Differences*, 75, 109–10. Matthew and Luke tend to follow Mark more closely (e.g., Mark 6:44; Matt 14:21; Luke 9:14; cf. John 6:10).

121. For the latter, cf. blame on the scribe in Polybius, *Histories* 12.4.4–6; discussion of Josephus, *Jewish War* 2.261–63; *Jewish Antiquities* 20.169–72 in Lake and Cadbury, *Commentary*, 277; Conzelmann, *Acts*, 184; H. Aldrich in Lardner, *Works*, 1:436. Cf. also Livy, *History* 3.3.9, in B. O. Foster, LCL 2:251n1.

122. See Xenophon, *Hiero* 2.16; Livy, *History* 3.8.10; Tacitus, *Histories* 3.61. Josephus inflates numbers even in the biblical text (cf. *Jewish Antiquities* 6.203 with 1 Sam 18:27 MT; contrast the LXX).

123. Thucydides, *History* 5.68.2; Polybius, *Histories* 3.33.17–18; 12.17.1–12.22.7; Pliny, *Letters* 9.16.1; Lucian, *How to Write History* 20. Sometimes, however, great numbers appear in careful sources (e.g., Polybius, *Histories* 1.63.6; 3.117.4).

124. Rubincam, "Numbers"; cf. the warning in Quintus Curtius Rufus, *History* 4.16.26. The exception would be census records, as in, e.g., Dionysius of Halicarnassus, *Roman Antiquities* 5.20.1; 5.75.3; 6.96.4; 9.15.2; 9.36.3. Even here, reports are not always reliable (cf. Suetonius, *Julius* 41, with Plutarch, *Caesar* 55.3; note also Josephus, *Jewish War* 6.423–25; t. Pesaḥ. 4:15; cf. Byatt, "Numbers").

125. Licona, *Differences*, 11.

126. Licona, *Differences*, 43, comparing Plutarch, *Cato the Younger* 30.3–4 and *Pompey* 44.3. See also 109, comparing *Pompey* 67.3–4 and *Caesar* 41.1–2.

(Mark 5:2//Matt 8:28; Mark 10:46–52//Matt 9:27–31; 20:29–34), or, I think perhaps more likely, Matthew doubling a Markan figure to concisely compensate for omitting similarly delivered or healed figures elsewhere (Mark 1:23–26; 8:22–26).[127]

Transferring material about one person to another is more common in midrash than in biography, but it appears in the latter, whether deliberately or through confusion of memory.[128] Especially after living memory, tradents sometimes transfer proverbs from one teacher to another or attribute them to multiple teachers.[129] (On other occasions, however, the famous speaker himself may recycle sayings from others.)[130] This particular problem is not likely in the Gospels, however. One would hardly expect the early Jesus movement to confuse others' sayings with Jesus's, since they deemed him their unique teacher and accorded him a unique authority.[131] Our surviving evidence suggests that Jesus connected disciples to his own teaching the way rabbis at least formally connected students to the Torah.[132]

Omissions are common,[133] although as mentioned in chapter 10, they are always within a narrator's rights;[134] they appear regularly when authors abridge their material (see discussion below). Thus, for example, the historian Polybius

127. Cf. Goulder, *Midrash*, 44–45; Gundry, *Matthew*, 158; Holtzmann as cited in Bruce, "Matthew," 145. For Matthean style here, cf. Meier, *Matthew*, 230; possibly Mark 11:2//Matt 21:2; Mark 14:57//Matt 26:60.

128. For Philo's *Moses*, see McGing, "Adaptation," 126–27 (possibly and rarely); for Plutarch, see Licona, *Differences*, 20, 34, 50, 61, 67, 72, 98, 108; Licona, "Viewing," 325.

129. See here, e.g., Diogenes Laertius, *Lives* 2.60; Ariston 1 in Plutarch, *Sayings of Spartans*, *Moralia* 218A; Themistocles 2 in Plutarch, *Sayings of Kings and Commanders*, *Moralia* 185A, and Alexander in Dio Chrysostom, *Orations* 2; Alcibiades 1 in Plutarch, *Sayings of Kings and Commanders*, *Moralia* 186D, and a Spartan in *Moralia* 234E; Plutarch, *Marcus Cato* 2.4; the story in Philostratus, *Lives of the Sophists* 1.485; Athenaeus, *The Learned Banqueters* 550; and Diogenes Laertius, *Lives* 4.37 (W. C. Wright in Philostratus, *Lives of the Sophists*, LCL 14–15n2); note also Musonius Rufus, frag. 51, p. 144.3–7, 10–19; Philostratus, *Lives of the Sophists* 1.485 (with note in LCL 14–15n2); discussion in Alexander, "IPSE DIXIT," 121, with some specific limitations. For conflation of early namesakes in oral tradition, see Barber and Barber, *Severed*, 115.

130. Thus many of M. Cato's maxims were translated from Greek (Plutarch, *Marcus Cato* 2.4). A saying attributed to both Musonius and Cato (Musonius Rufus, frag. 51, p. 144.3–19) could be misattributed, or it could have been recycled (perhaps more than once).

131. See fully Byrskog, *Teacher*, 237–308, 350–68, and esp. 307–10; see also Yieh, *One Teacher*; Licona, *Differences*, 183; cf. Riesner, *Lehrer*, 259–64. One expects such confusion to be fairly rare in any case this early in the tradition process (see Keener, *Historical Jesus*, 142–44).

132. See Riesner, *Lehrer*, 417. Cf. Matt 7:24–27 with 'Abot R. Nat. 24A; see Jeremias, *Parables*, 194; Keener, *Matthew*, 254–56.

133. E.g., where we can test Nepos or Philo against their sources (Christian, "Themistocles," 139; Hidalgo, "Study," 287, 289).

134. Cf. here Pelling, *Texts*, 119.

recommends omitting material already too well known or not helpful for the reader.[135] Tacitus notes that he freely omitted material not of value to history's primary, moral objective.[136] Writers rarely include all possible information; ancient writers did not intend to do so.[137] Various early Jewish, including Judean, works often omit troublesome episodes.[138]

Some writers cover traits or episodes that others avoided.[139] Needing to be selective, biographers focused on points most relevant to their purpose,[140] slowing down to treat in greater detail the most relevant material but accelerating at less relevant points.[141] Still, as in redaction criticism of the Gospels, sometimes we can do no more than speculate concerning the reasons for omissions,[142] except where fairly consistent patterns emerge.

11.5. Expanding and Abridging

Contrary to early form-critical studies of the Gospels, which supposed that the tradition's tendency was always expansive, subsequent research demonstrated that it is impossible to predict whether the passage of time would lengthen or shorten an account.[143] Ancient authors sometimes expanded and at other times abridged their sources.

Many changes that writers made in their sources were simply matters of arrangement, which was of great importance to those trained in rhetoric.[144] Both

---

135. Polybius, *Histories* 15.36.10; cf. Tacitus, *Annals* 15.63.

136. Tacitus, *Annals* 3.65.

137. Still, criticism of Suetonius focused on what he omitted more than on errors of fact (Hägg, *Biography*, 230).

138. E.g., Jub. 13:17–18; 29:13; T. Zeb. 1:5–7; earlier, see, e.g., Williamson, *Chronicles*, 236.

139. For example, among biographers, both Plutarch (*Agesilaus* 2.1; 14.1) and Nepos (*On Great Generals* 17 [Agesilaus], 8.1) mention Agesilaus's lameness; his friend Xenophon does not. Nepos and Plutarch likewise cover Agesilaus's death, but Xenophon does not (Ytterbrink, *Gospel*, 94). Elsewhere in biography, see McGing, "Adaptation," 120, 131–33; Licona, *Differences*, 2, 20, 51, 56, 72, 75, 77, 95, 109; see further ch. 10.

140. De Pourcq and Roskam, "Virtues," 166–67 (noting esp. Plutarch, *Aemilius Paulus* 1.2), 176; McGing, "Adaptation," 131–33; cf. Votaw, "Biographies," 231. For histories, cf. Dionysius of Halicarnassus, *Thuc.* 13–17; Laistner, *Historians*, 132.

141. De Pourcq and Roskam, "Virtues," 167.

142. Pelling, *Texts*, 101.

143. See evidence in Sanders, *Tendencies*, esp. 19, 46–87, 88–189, 272; cf. Stein, "Criteria," 238–40.

144. Cf., e.g., Dionysius of Halicarnassus, *On Literary Composition* 2–4. For the impor-

poets and prose writers sometimes added clauses nonessential to the meaning or removed essential ones simply to make the arrangement sound better.[145] A first-century rhetorical handbook shows that elaboration and abridgement were fairly elementary exercises.[146] Ancient composers considered it a matter of arrangement, not of fabrication, to move sayings into different, preexisting narrative settings.[147] One matter reminding the narrator of another, for example, was a common rhetorical technique for transition.[148]

Ancient writers freely expanded or abridged accounts without any thought that their contemporaries might find this practice objectionable. Plutarch often expands material by filling in detail.[149] Biographers were more apt to create "fill" material when they lacked other sources, especially for ancient poets[150] or for a hero's childhood character.[151] To expand their material, they sometimes work by inference from the material available; such speculation increases verisimilitude at the expense of being able to be certain about the original details.[152]

Expanding a historical or biographic work did not, however, always require extensive inferences and did not normally entail a deliberate change in meaning. The basic rhetorical exercises of one handbook (probably from the first century) include the practice of "expanding" and "condensing" stories such as fables.[153] The writer also, however, deals with more realistic kinds of

tance of arrangement in rhetoric, see, e.g., *Rhetorica ad Herennium* 1.1.1–3; Cicero, *On the Composition of Arguments* 1.6.8; Menander Rhetor, *Epideictic Treatises* 2.4, 392.14; Aune, *Dictionary*, 62–64; Wuellner, "Arrangement," 51–87. For one clear example of rearrangement in the Gospels, cf. Matt 21:12–13, 19–22; Mark 11:13–25. For stylistic as well as halakic and ideological editing in the compilation of the Mishnah, see Kulp, "Patterns."

145. Dionysius of Halicarnassus, *On Literary Composition* 9.

146. See Licona, *Differences*, 13–14, on Theon.

147. Theon, *Progymnasmata* 4.73–79, on adding narrative to a fable or the reverse (although the narrative is added as a parallel, not as a setting, for the fable). Maxims could be added to narratives (5.388–425) or preexisting narratives combined to relate two or more of them at once (5.427–41).

148. Quintilian, *Orator's Education* 9.2.60–61. Cf. the discussion of catchwords in Gerhardsson, *Memory*, 145–49, 153; in the Gospels, cf. Bultmann, *Tradition*, 325–26.

149. Pelling, "Adaptation," 129–31; Russell, "Coriolanus," 21–28; Small, *Wax Tablets*, 199 (following Pelling, "Adaptation"); Kwon, "Charting," 73–74; Licona, *Differences*, 20.

150. Power, "Poetry," 237. Some would compare the speeches early in Acts (e.g., Johnson, *Acts*, 10).

151. Beck, "Demonax," 85, regarding Plutarch (following Pelling, *Plutarch and History*, 308–9) but not Lucian.

152. See, e.g., Christian, "Themistocles," 114, 118, 130, 139; Hidalgo, "Study," 287, 291, 300.

153. Theon, *Progymnasmata* 4.37–42 (Butts). Expansion involved matters such as length-

narrative, sometimes by simply adding details known from other sources or adding some description that is either implicit in the narrative or inherently probable in itself.[154] (Some historians, however, did take such descriptive elaboration too far.)[155]

Rhetorical exercises could develop sample narratives by rewording without fabrication.[156] Another writer describes amplification as adding more and more phrases to bring home the point increasingly forcefully.[157] In rhetorical exercises one can elaborate a chreia by offering an encomium on a character; then paraphrasing; then explaining; and so forth.[158]

Diaspora Jewish writers handled their material similarly. Philo often expands narratives with explanatory and dramatic detail.[159] Hellenizing Moses, Philo makes Moses a king and high priest; he emphasizes his "education and adolescence."[160] Josephus often follows accurately the sequence and substance of the biblical account, while expanding on some biblical narratives,[161] even though the addition would appear conspicuous to many Jewish readers.

Few stylistic critics would have complained about abridgements. Greco-Roman writers and rhetoricians appreciated conciseness in a narrative, provided that it did not impair clarity or plausibility.[162] Perhaps more impor-

---

ening speeches or describing terrain (4.80–82). Even oracles, which were considered divine utterances, could be expanded; see Aune, *Prophecy*, 58.

154. Theon, *Progymnasmata* 3.224–40. In 2.115–23 Theon compares elaborations in earlier historical sources. Elaboration (ἐργασίας, *ergasias*) was especially useful for rebuttal (1.172–75).

155. See the complaint of Lucian, *How to Write History* 19, 57.

156. The typical examples in Hermogenes, *Invention* 2.7.120–21; for development more fully, see 2.1.108–9; 2.7.120–24. Hypothetical declamations could invent new situations in history (e.g., Hermogenes, *Invention* 2.4.115), but the Gospels and their sources do not involve hypothetical rhetorical exercises.

157. Longinus, *On the Sublime* 11.1; cf. Menander Rhetor, *Epideictic Treatises* 2.3, 379.2–4. For a more detailed discussion of amplification, see Anderson, *Glossary*, 26–29 (with full reference to the sources).

158. Hermogenes, *Progymnasmata* 3. On Chreia, 7; Aphthonius, *Progymnasmata* 3. On Chreia, 23S, 4R; 4. On Maxim, 9–10.

159. McGing, "Adaptation," 127–30, 133, noting, e.g., Exod 2:15–22 in Philo, *Moses* 1.51–59 (cf. Josephus, *Jewish Antiquities* 2.258–63).

160. McGing, "Adaptation," 134, citing Philo, *Moses* 1.20–33, 148–62.

161. E.g., Begg, "Blanks," on Josephus, *Jewish Antiquities* 9.29–43, and 2 Kgs 3:4–27.

162. Theon, *Progymnasmata* 5.39–43, 52–53; Lucian, *How to Write History* 56; Phaedrus, *Fables* 2, prol. 12–13; 3, epil. 8–9; 4, epil. 7–9; Philostratus, *Heroicus* 29.6; in speeches, e.g., Diogenes Laertius, *Lives* 7.1.20; Dionysius of Halicarnassus, *Thucydides* 55; *Demosthenes* 18, 20, 24; *Lysias* 5; Philostratus, *Lives of the Sophists* 2.4.569. One could, however, be too brief at times (Dionysius of Halicarnassus, 2 *Letter to Ammaeus* 2; Lucian, *How to Write History* 30).

tant for many readers, longer works were not only more expansive but also more expensive. Plutarch sometimes abbreviates material;[163] so do historians such as Thucydides[164] and Diodorus Siculus.[165] Jewish writers quoting earlier material also freely omitted and grammatically adjusted points;[166] Philo[167] and Josephus[168] sometimes condense material, and all of 2 Maccabees is an abridgement of a larger work.[169] Most Synoptic scholars likewise recognize that Matthew (and less frequently Luke) abridges Markan accounts.[170]

Judean haggadah permitted greater amplification than did Hellenistic historiography,[171] but haggadah appears more comparable to Greek mythography than to Jewish biography.[172] (A significant element of the perceived difference between historical and mythical accounts was often the difference between recent historical figures and remote characters of the mythical or legendary past.)[173] The process was probably often incremental, preserving earlier legendary accretions and speculations.[174]

Although not writing biography, later rabbis illustrate the potential for long-term accretion of details through inference. They understood their amplification to have been implicit in the Sinai Torah from the very beginning.[175] Some suggest that the rabbis themselves at least initially recognized that midrashic additions were homiletic, distinct from historical reconstructions.[176] Jewish writers used amplification to answer questions posed by a narrative,[177]

---

163. Licona, *Differences*, 98, 100, 108.

164. Pelling, *Texts*, 119.

165. Derrenbacker, *Practices*, 91–92; for historical writers generally, 76.

166. Stanley, *Language*, 323. For abridged documents, cf. also Small, *Wax Tablets*, 177.

167. McGing, "Adaptation," 123–25; Hidalgo, "Study," 292–93.

168. Derrenbacker, *Practices*, 115.

169. 2 Macc 2:23, 26, 28, apparently following standard abridgement practices.

170. I believe that Mark may have also abridged for his preface material that he knew from Q (Keener, *Spirit*, 60–61, 94–95).

171. Cf. Penner, *Praise*, 247–60. Such haggadic adaptation appears in both midrash and folk literature (Wright, "Midrash," 129); rabbis also sometimes created stories using earlier rabbis for tongue-in-cheek homiletic purposes.

172. Cf. Greek elaboration of sacred stories in Maclean and Aitken, *Heroikos*, li–lii.

173. See discussion in ch. 9.

174. Some argue that even scribes adapted texts they copied, considering the needs of their audience with an oral mentality (Person, "Scribe," noting 1QIsaᵃ).

175. Sifre Deut. 313.2.4; cf. Urbach, *Sages*, 1:305, 376.

176. Milikowsky, "Midrash."

177. E.g., Demetrius the Chronographer (third century BCE), frag. 5 (Eusebius, *Preparation for the Gospel* 9.29.16); Jub. 4:1, 9; 12:14; 13:11; 27:1, 4–5 (Esau and Jacob vs. Isaac and Jacob); y. Ketub. 12:4, §8 (fanciful midrash).

to heighten the praise of God or the protagonist[178] (sometimes by fanciful midrash),[179] or to improve the story.[180] Sometimes they added names,[181] sometimes arrived at midrashically or for symbolic value.[182] One could emphasize a theme already present in one's source by reiterating it where it appeared and occasionally adding it elsewhere.[183] Similarly, as noted in chapter 5, negative incidents could be toned down, omitted, or justified in the character's favor. But while such traditional techniques may have influenced some sources used by Jewish historians, they did not characterize these writers' own historiographic method per se.

11.6. Composition Practices

Composition practices of ancient historical writers in general may help explain how some of the Evangelists worked. A biographer might compose a basic draft and subsequently arrange it more topically, adding relevant materials and otherwise revising it based on feedback from hearers.[184] A writer could also recycle parts of his work (or someone else's) when composing a new work.[185]

---

178. 2 Macc 2:1–8 (expanding Jeremiah's mission); Jub. 29:14–20 (rhetorically contrasts Jacob's respect for his parents with Esau's disrespect); T. Job 9–15 (see OTP 1:832); T. Jos. 3:1; cf. Josephus, *Jewish Antiquities* 6.203; LAB 31 (Burnette-Bletsch, "Jael").

179. Pesiq. Rab Kah. 4:3 ("the rabbis" on Solomon); Gen. Rab. 43:3; Exod. Rab. 10:4; Pesiq. Rab. 49:5; cf. Artapanus in Eusebius, *Preparation for the Gospel* 9.27.7 (cf. 1 Sam 18:17, 21–25).

180. Jub. 11:14–15, 13:18, 22; possibly 4Q160, frags. 3–5, 7; Tg. Ps.-Jon. on Gen. 50:26; Ps.-Jon. on Exod. 13:19.

181. Jub. 11:14–15; Liv. Pro. 19 (Joad) (§30 in Schermann's Greek text); Josephus, *Jewish Antiquities* 8.231; LAB 40:1 (in LAB in general, cf. Bauckham, "Liber antiquitatum," 67; in Jewish sources more generally, Pilch, "Naming"); cf. Plutarch, *Alexander* 20.4–5 (questioning Chares's report).

182. See Rook, "Names," on patriarchal wives in Jubilees. (Names are sometimes, however, the elements of tradition most resistant to change; cf., e.g., the observation of Bernal, *Athena*, 2:337.)

183. As LAB does in its polemic against idolatry (Murphy, "Idolatry").

184. Burridge, *Comparison*, 203; Aune, *Environment*, 82; see, e.g., Josephus, *Against Apion* 1.49–50; cf. Lucian, *How to Write History* 48; fuller detail in Small, *Wax Tablets*, 26–40; Derrenbacker, *Practices*, 39–44; Keener, *Acts*, 43–50. Proto-Gospels (cf. Streeter, *Gospels*, 199–222) may have thus existed—at least temporarily. Cf. perhaps Papias's Matthew as a proto-Matthew Q (cf. Filson, *History*, 83; Hill, *Matthew*, 23–27, 53) or a proto-Q (Knight, "Problem").

185. E.g., Josephus seems to have employed his *Jewish War* as his main source for the comparable portion of the *Jewish Antiquities* (Krieger, "Hauptquelle").

Given limited accessibility of sources, historians themselves often quoted excerpts or lines from memory, hence could recount the gist accurately while being confused at times on some details.[186] This practice of quoting from memory may also explain some textual variation and assimilation in patristic sources[187] as well as in NT quotations of the OT.[188] As Jocelyn Penny Small notes in her work regarding ancient memory practices, we often "hold ancient writers to a standard far higher than we ourselves could achieve." We generally do not recall what we wrote a few years ago; but whereas we can easily retrieve and check that work, such retrieval was typically far more difficult in antiquity.[189]

Source-dependent writers often followed their source material in blocks; apart from digressions, for example, Diodorus "followed a single source for chapters on end, transferring only when he came to the end of his subject-matter."[190] One observes the same pattern in Nepos's biography of Themistocles.[191] Because writing desks were not yet available,[192] it was difficult for a writer to directly follow more than one work at a time, although they often supplemented or adapted based on the memory of (or notes on) the other sources they had read.[193] On this model, Matthew and Luke inserted Q material, usually in blocks, into the narrative outline they had inherited from Mark.[194]

Still, it is also possible, as noted above, that some Jewish scribal sources may have worked with more than one source simultaneously, and this prac-

186. Marincola, "Introduction," 2; cf. Small, *Wax Tablets*, 193.

187. Cf. Riesner, *Lehrer*, 452; Hill, "Words."

188. Cf., e.g., Montanaro, "Use." In various ancient sources, cf. Stanley, *Language*, 304, 322, 334; for deliberate adaptation, see 290–91.

189. Small, *Wax Tablets*, 194; cf. 188–90.

190. Bosworth, *Arrian*, 9–10 (quotation from 9).

191. See Christian, "Themistocles," 139. Cf. Tatian in Mattila, "Question."

192. Small, *Wax Tablets*, 151, 155, 163–68, 176; Derrenbacker, *Practices*, 38.

193. Pelling, "Method," 91–92; Small, *Wax Tablets*, 151–55, 163–70, 176–81, 185–87 (citing also Luce, *Livy*, 144); Derrenbacker, *Practices*, 38–39. This factor remains likely, despite the usual practice of dictation (for which, see, e.g., Cicero, *Letters to Atticus* 14.21; Dio Chrysostom, *Orations* 18.18; Galen, *Grief* 83).

194. Aune, *Environment*, 65, 139; Burridge, *Comparison*, 204–5; esp. Downing, "Compositional Conventions"; Downing, "Actuality"; Small, *Wax Tablets*, 179–81; Derrenbacker, *Practices*, 38–39, 47–49. For Matthew's redaction of Q and dependence on memory at points, see now esp. Kirk, *Q in Matthew* (though cf. also considerations in Tuckett, "Matthew and Problem"); for limits in reconstructing Q, see esp. Weaks, "Problematizing."

tice may have also affected the final composition of the Gospels.[195] Like the Evangelists, such scribes had a limited "canon" of material from which they would be working.

11.7. The Degree of Adaptation in the Gospels

While biography was firmly rooted in historical information, it also potentially allowed significant flexibility in details. In general, human memory preserves primarily the gist, rather than all the details.[196] Ancient biographers and historians, then, felt it within their rights to adapt details in the ways most fitting to their accounts and audience needs.

This observation should inform the genre expectations that we bring to the Gospels. Both the similarities among the Gospels and their differences match the sorts of similarities and differences found when we compare ancient biographers of then-recent figures. Given such adaptability, it is not surprising that, for example, the gist of Peter's denial remains consistent among varying Gospel accounts, despite "variation in inessential detail."[197] Close readers in antiquity also recognized that the Gospels had differences on minor details.[198] As one fairly conservative modern exegete has noted, "Each Synoptic evangelist sometimes altered a narrative by omission or addition in order to fit it to his own scheme."[199]

Others likewise note that the sorts of variations in the Synoptics' treatment of shared material is no greater than the sorts of variations that appear more generally in other ancient works using sources.[200] In fact, John Kloppenborg rightly stresses that "Matthew and Luke used Q far more 'woodenly' than other writers employed their sources."[201] This is true even when another Jewish writer for a Diaspora audience is recounting divine speech from the LXX.[202] Greater wooden borrowing does appear in the scribal practices evidenced in Qumran texts,[203] but Matthew and Luke appear closer to Qumran

---

195. See Barker, "Reassessment," 113–19.

196. See, e.g., Bauckham, *Eyewitnesses*, 333–34; see discussion in ch. 14.

197. Bauckham, *Eyewitnesses*, 344–45.

198. Licona, *Differences*, 1, cites here John Chrysostom, *Homilies on Matthew* 1.6.

199. Ellis, "Making," 331.

200. Kloppenborg, "Variation," 63–74.

201. Kloppenborg, "Variation," 63.

202. Kloppenborg, "Variation," 67–70, noting Josephus, *Jewish Antiquities* 3.91; 6.368–73.

203. Kloppenborg, "Variation," 74–77; Barker, "Reassessment," 113–14.

texts "than they do to the practices of other historians or biographers, whose verbal indebtedness to their sources would rarely exceed 40% of their sources' words in any instance, and for whom generous paraphrase was a more common likely practice."[204]

If they believed that Peter's authority stood behind Mark's Gospel, Matthew and Luke possibly treated it as a semisacred text the way Qumran handled Scripture. Still, more study would be necessary to confirm such a suggestion; Matthew and Luke feel free to make adaptations. In any case, their adaptations are more conservative than those of many contemporaries; Josephus, writing for a Diaspora audience, does paraphrase Scripture more freely than we normally find at Qumran or in the Gospels.[205]

Licona's conclusions from Plutarch agree: Plutarch employs nothing "close to the near 'copy and paste' method that is very often employed by Matthew and Luke."[206] Indeed, after a detailed examination of the sources, Licona concludes that, as in the case of Plutarch, the vast majority of differences in the Gospels' parallel accounts are matters of secondary detail.[207] They no more call into question the basic events in the Gospels than they do in Plutarch.[208]

11.8. Conclusion

As any careful student of the Gospels recognizes, the Gospels vary in some details even when telling the same stories. Ancient audiences, both Jewish and gentile, expected such variation in the biographic genre, and those who were experienced in and alert to biographic conventions would even know where most often to anticipate them. Such differences in ancient biographies include chronological displacement and conflation of material, simplying narratives by, for example, omitting inessential characters and filling in details by inference when necessary to make sense of the story or, in some writers, to recount it in a more appealing way.

---

204. Kloppenborg, "Variation," 77. He compares the degree of verbal agreement with the activities of scribes (78–79).

205. For possible memorization variants in the Qumran sources, cf. Carr, *Writing*, 230; for one early evaluation of discussion on Qumran's possible scriptorium, see Culpepper, *School*, 156–68.

206. Licona, *Differences*, 20–21.

207. Licona, *Differences*, 200.

208. Licona, *Differences*, 201.

Nevertheless, ancient audiences expected historical authors to convey the essential story and what they believed to be the spirit of the material. In general, we should expect such variation to affect only details, not the essential events portrayed. Both the Gospels and other early-empire biographies of recent public figures provide substantial information about their subjects, as well as revealing the authors' agendas.

Part 4

Two Objections to Gospels as Historical Biographies

The evidence presented so far suggests both that the Gospels were ancient biographies and that ancient biographies from their period worked from prior information. Nevertheless, critics sometimes raise objections to counter the notion that the Gospels draw on historical information the way that other contemporary biographies of recent figures did. Two objections seem particularly frequent.

First, the Gospels report miracles, the subject of chapter 12. Can such reports truly reflect originally eyewitness testimony, or must they reflect lengthy legendary accretion or the Evangelists' (especially Mark's) creativity? Abundant information available today, however, both confirms that Jesus's contemporaries knew him for such activity and attests that many eyewitnesses do offer such claims. These observations do not require us to construe such claims as divine activity, but the observations themselves comport with the best historical evidence and together undercut the need to attribute such claims to legend or authorial imagination.

Second, John diverges so often from the story in the Synoptics that either he or they might be accused of greater flexibility than historical interests should have allowed (ch. 13). Yet John overlaps more often with the Synoptics than scholars sometimes recognize and probably depends on a genuine historical source that treats many occasions simply omitted in the Synoptics. John does appear to take some liberties, perhaps even conspicuously tweaking the traditional passion narrative with a hint toward its theological interpretation. Nevertheless, the liberties that John may take regarding details and especially discourse material appear well within the range of flexibility in both ancient biography and ancient historiography more generally.

Chapter 12

What about Miracles?

One objection that some scholars raise against the Gospels containing significant historical information is that the Gospels report miracles.[1] If multiple or recurrent attestation counts for anything, it seems significant that every layer of gospel tradition depicts Jesus as a healer and exorcist.

Surely this feature indicates widespread corruption in the gospel tradition? Yet all lines of evidence confirm that Jesus's contemporaries experienced him as a healer and exorcist. Moreover, evidence does not compel us to exclude such reports from dependence on originally eyewitness material. Although we may debate their causes, it is incontrovertible that eyewitnesses do report experiences of healings and exorcisms even today, sometimes even in dramatic ways and on a massive scale. This chapter will remain concise not because the issue is insignificant but because I have treated it extensively (in more than 1,300 pages) in other works, to which I refer the interested reader for further documentation.[2]

12.1. Paranormal Experiences in Ancient Sources

Although they have not survived and this model does not appear often again until late antiquity, even some earlier biographic works about Pythagorean holy men (some reports about Pythagoras and Empedocles) united magic

---

1. My focus here will be on healings and exorcisms. The modern definitions of miracles (on the often problematic character of which, see Horsley, *Magic*, 3–32; Johnson, *Miracles*, 21–43; a helpful alternative title for what is often intended could be "special divine action"; see, e.g., Gwynne, *Action*) often fail to correspond to biblical cases so classified, but I retain the conventional modern nomenclature for the sake of general intelligibility.

2. Keener, *Acts*, 1:320–82; "Comparisons"; "Miracle Reports and Argument"; "Miracle Reports: Perspectives"; *Miracles*; "Miracles (2017)"; "Possession"; "Raised"; "Reassessment"; "Spirits."

and philosophy.[3] It may be doubted that this was a biographic *type*, but both features were occasionally attributed to the same persons, just as OT narratives also spoke of some miracle-working prophets. Even in late antique biography, however, miracles were not an essential motif of the divine man[4] (important as they are in medieval Christian hagiography). The chief divine characteristic was wisdom,[5] also often revealed in asceticism.[6] Miracles came into play partly as pagan intellectuals sought "to neutralize Christian miracles" with miracles of their own.[7]

There is not space to digress at length here, but I must briefly treat objections against the Gospels being biographies based on their exalted views of Jesus[8] or, the focus here, because of their accounts of miracles and exorcisms.[9] Such objections usually start with the premise that the earliest witnesses would not have reported such elements, and then regard the gospel tradition as suspect because (or at least where) it includes such elements. Scholars sometimes dismiss the historical reliability of information behind miracle accounts or other anomalies without further consideration, lumping them all together as mythical or hagiographic. Some even appear to create a new, overarching and interpretive wonder-working category for the Gospels and much later sources potentially influenced by them.[10] Although some supernatural claims ultimately do merit dismissal, this a priori approach for information about anomalies behind all supernatural claims too readily assumes what it may hope to prove.

Most ancient historians did attribute some events to deities or to providence;[11] many reported prodigies or omens,[12] and even two historians gener-

---

3. Cox, *Biography*, 31–33.

4. Cox, *Biography*, 48; cf. Edwards, "Genre," 59.

5. Cox, *Biography*, 21–24.

6. Cox, *Biography*, 25–30.

7. Cox, *Biography*, 142; cf. also (cited by her) Dodds, *Pagan*, 109.

8. Answered somewhat in Keener, "Parallel Figures"; more fully, e.g., Hurtado, *Lord Jesus Christ*; Hays, *Reading Backwards*; Gathercole, *Son*; Tilling, *Christology*; Fletcher-Louis, *Christological Origins*; Loke, *Origin*.

9. Addressed more fully in Keener, "Comparisons"; *Miracles*; "Possession"; "Reassessment." Dismissal of Jesus's miracles and status has been a frequent basis for rejecting gospel accounts that claim them (noted, e.g., in Schnabel, *Jesus in Jerusalem*, 3).

10. See, e.g., De Temmerman, "Formalities," 17; Konstan and Walsh, "Biography," 28; cf. William Hansen in Becker, *Birth*, 120–21.

11. See esp. Squires, *Plan*, 15–20, 38–51; e.g., Josephus, *Jewish Antiquities* 1.209, 346; 2.174, 223, 236; 4.109; 17.353.

12. Tacitus, *Annals* 12.43, 64; 14.32; 15.22, 47; 16.13; Suetonius, *Julius* 81.3; Arrian, *Alexander*

ally reluctant to report signs mentioned the report of two healings connected with Vespasian.[13] Unlike the Evangelists, many ancient writers did avoid committing themselves either for or against supernatural explanations for some kinds of events that they found in their sources.[14] The Gospels are closer in this respect to Israelite historiography, which did not object to reporting divine action.[15]

Livy includes reports of many prodigies, or omens, for each year.[16] These are not Livy's creation; he has them from official reports, which go back to various popular claims.[17] Priests may have accepted many of these claims into their reports uncritically because they fit their role as not critical historians but as collectors and interpreters of omens. Some claims, such as lightning striking temples or the aurora borealis, were real phenomena but were gathered from anywhere in the whole of Italy.[18] This contrasts with reports in the Gospels, associated with a single figure whose chief witnesses were known to the entire movement (cf. chs. 14–16).

One may or may not accept some of the miracle accounts as reflecting traditions or reports about genuine experiences, but rejecting them simply because they are miracle accounts, a common recourse in the heyday of rationalism, is less universally appealing in a multicultural, twenty-first-century world.

In one venue where I presented an early version of this book's argument, an interlocutor replied that the Gospels are not comparable to other biographies, because the Gospels report miracles. Biographies of emperors relied on public information, he maintained, and biographies of sages relied on traditions within the sages' schools. But Jesus was a healer and an exorcist, and

---

4.15.7–8; Appian, *Civil Wars* 1.9.83; 2.5.36; 2.10.68; 4.1.4. See further Keener, *Acts*, 1:344–50; Keener, *Miracles*, 37, 80–82, 87–96; Squires, *Plan*, 78–84, 102; Edwards, "Introduction," xviii–xix; Becker, *Birth*, 112.

13. Tacitus, *Histories* 4.81; Suetonius, *Vespasian* 7.3. For "signs" in histories, cf. Plümacher, *Geschichte*, 33–84, though against his understanding of tragic-pathetic history, see Rutherford, "Tragedy," 513–14, following Walbank, "Tragedy" = *Papers*, 241.

14. See, e.g., Pliny, *Natural History* 28.5.29; Tacitus, *Histories* 2.50; Lucian, *How to Write History* 60; Aune, *Environment*, 134; McDonald, "Herodotus," 87; see further discussion in Keener, *Acts*, 1:344–48.

15. Cf. Dormeyer, "Historii."

16. E.g., Livy, *History* 21.62.1–5; 24.10.6–11; 24.44.8; 25.7.7–9; 26.23.4–5; 27.4.11–14; 27.11.2–5; 27.37.1–6; 29.14.2; 32.8.2; 33.26.7–8; 34.45.6–7; 35.9.2–4; 35.21.3–6; 36.37.2–3; 40.45.1–4; 41.13.1–2; 41.21.12–13; 42.2.4–5; 43.13.3–6; 45.16.5.

17. See Livy, *History* 21.62.1; 24.10.6; 27.37.2; 29.14.2.

18. See, e.g., Livy, *History* 21.62.5; 27.11.2–3; 27.37.1–4; 29.14.3; 32.1.10–12; 32.8.2–3; 35.9.2–4; Appian, *Civil Wars* 2.5.36; 2.10.68; 4.1.4; Orlin, "Religion," 60.

(he argued) we lack biographies of such figures. I would respond in part by pointing out that Jesus was of course a sage with disciples, and he had already conceded that schools normally preserved information about their founding sages. That, however, is a discussion reserved for a later chapter (ch. 15), so let me for the moment address his central problem with the analogy.

It is not true that we lack biographic-style accounts of miracle workers, but it is true that we lack extant biographic works about miracle workers before the time of Jesus. This is not, however, because the genre is different; biographies of emperors, of sages, and of miracle workers—or for that matter of generals or orators—differ not in overall genre (a work about a historic person) but in *subject* (the kind of person, which affects the sorts of accounts presented).

That is, we lack biographies of figures like Jesus not because the genre is different but because Jesus himself is different: we lack many comparable *figures* prior to Jesus, in terms of the combination of sages who were also known as miracle workers (i.e., what was once generalized as the "divine man" type).[19] Some viewed Pythagoras and Empedocles as both magicians and teachers,[20] but no biographic type united these characteristics, at least not outside Pythagoreanism, where it subsequently emerges with a narrative about Apollonius. Nor even centuries later were miracles a motif in hagiographies of "divine men."[21]

Biographies of sages were common enough, but not miracle-working sages. As classicist Mark Edwards points out, Mark "fills his book with miracles, more abundantly than any surviving pagan text."[22] There were alleged magicians and, in Jewish sources, figures more like Jesus such as Elijah, Elisha, and Onias (the rabbis' "Honi the Circle-Drawer").[23] Indisputably the Elijah and Elisha narratives strongly influenced Jesus, the gospel tradition, and the Gospels.[24] But Elijah and Elisha were not subjects of extant biographies, nor do most narratives about them stem from within living memory of them.

The issue is thus not one of genre—biography—but of the role that Jesus filled. As noted earlier, there are ways that the Gospels differ from other biographies (as also many other biographies differ from one another). Yet,

---

19. See, e.g., Tiede, *Figure*; Holladay, *Theios aner*; Gallagher, *Divine Man*; Pilgaard, "*Theios aner*"; Keener, "Parallel Figures."

20. Cox, *Biography*, 31–33.

21. Cox, *Biography*, 48.

22. Edwards, "Genre," 59.

23. See esp. the concerns of Eve, *Miracles*, 274–95; Theissen and Merz, *Guide*, 307–8.

24. See, e.g., Meier, *Marginal Jew*, 2:1044–45; Meier, "Project"; Frickenschmidt, *Evangelium*, 127–28; Collins, *Mark*, 29; Ytterbrink, *Gospel*, 39, 227–28; Edwards, "Genre," 59.

excluding literary analogies to the Gospels because Jesus's role is distinctive excludes a sort of evidence that is too relevant on other grounds to dismiss. Using Jesus's miracles to exclude the Gospels from the genre of biography contemporary in their period makes the Gospels' genre unique (with speedy new legends about Jesus's miracles) so that Jesus will not be. (And "If Jesus did nothing out of the ordinary," memory theorist Barry Schwartz points out, "why did his contemporaries remember him at all?")[25]

Granted, those who do not believe miracles possible, or at least not possible if associated with Jesus, may believe that they have other reasons to question such accounts. But the designation "miracles" involves a level of interpretation that different observers of the same sort of events or experiences describe as anomalies—and there is not much dispute as to whether anomalies occur. The strong majority of historical Jesus scholars affirm that, whatever the causes (e.g., psychosomatic or supernatural), Jesus was known as a wonder-worker. Because I have treated this subject extensively elsewhere, I survey it only briefly in this chapter here.[26]

12.2. The Early Christian Worldview

The earliest Christian sources never claim that healings and exorcisms were unique to Jesus. In fact, they report some non-Christian wonder-workers (e.g., Acts 8:9–11) and exorcists (e.g., Matt 12:27//Luke 11:19; Acts 19:13), as well as expectations of false prophetic or demon-inspired signs in the future (Mark 13:22; 2 Thess 2:9; Rev 13:13). They affirmed that some of Jesus's followers continued to perform such signs (e.g., Acts 4:30; 6:8; 14:3; 1 Cor 12:9–10, 28–29), some reported by eyewitnesses (e.g., Rom 15:19), and they even recalled them to other eyewitnesses (2 Cor 12:12).

Their belief in paranormal activity is consistent with the wider ancient Mediterranean culture. Contemporary reports of anomalies from their era

25. Schwartz, "Smoke," 30; on Schwartz's influence in contemporary memory studies, see, e.g., Thatcher, "Schwartz"; on Halbwach, Assmann and Schwartz, see Keith, "Social Memory Theory," 354–76. On Jesus's distinctive personality, which pervades the gospel tradition, scholars often cite Dodd, *Founder*, 21–22; see Dunn, *Tradition*, 200n3, 213n3; *Neither Jew nor Greek*, 213n12; "Remembering Jesus," 204n48; also McIver, *Memory*, 181; Bird, *Gospel*, 81n23. Noting the remark's subjectivity yet inclined to agree, see Allison, *Jesus of Nazareth*, 75n292; Allison, *Constructing Jesus*, 23.

26. Keener, *Acts*, 1:320–82; "Comparisons"; "Historicity of Nature Miracles"; "Miracle Reports and Argument"; "Miracle Reports: Perspectives"; *Miracles*; "Miracles (2015)"; "Miracles (2017)"; "Raised"; "Reassessment."

abound, though many of them are susceptible to varied explanations.[27] We weigh these reports one at a time rather than dismissing them outright, giving more credence to public reports (e.g., lightning striking a deity statue) than to random and unprovenanced, isolated reports (e.g., a lamb said to be born with a human head).[28] Biographies from the early empire do occasionally report healing experiences associated with recent public figures,[29] though these figures were not typically known for wonder-working.

Their beliefs and reports of experience are also consistent with most cultures through history and today.[30] However one chooses to explain them, anomalous experiences, often associated with cultic or spiritual activity, are widespread.[31] Many traditional religious contexts report healing, especially in ritual settings.[32] Some scholars thus compare Jesus with various other documented modern cases of shamans, folk healers, or other agents of numinous power reported, in historical documentation or anthropological field reports.[33]

The same may be said for the Gospel accounts of demonization and exorcism, although most Western readers today demur from the typical ancient understanding of such experiences.[34] Anthropologists have documented that

27. Celestial phenomena were public, but their interpretation was usually as subjective as it remains today (e.g., I write this a few hours after viewing an old friend's Facebook account on which she had posted a photograph of a cloud formation that she took to be an angel, a judgment that I do not share).

28. For such mismatched heads and the like, aside from some modern tabloids (or misconstruals of actual congenital cephalic malformations), see, e.g., Valerius Maximus, *Memorable Doings and Sayings* 1.6.5; Livy, *History* 32.8.3; Appian, *Civil Wars* 1.9.83; fictitiously, Phaedrus, *Fables* 3.3.4–5. Cf. even Livy's warnings in his *History* 21.62.1; 24.10.6.

29. Claims associated with Vespasian in Tacitus, *Histories* 4.81; Suetonius, *Vespasian* 7.2–3; later, Dio Cassius, *Roman History* 65.8.1.

30. See, e.g., comments in Pilch, *Visions*, 17; Pilch, *Dictionary*, 81–82. Emic explanations are no more biased than etic ones (cf. Vansina, *Oral Tradition*, 196–97); emic explanations are usually better informed about their local culture, whereas etic ones are informed about more cultures.

31. See, e.g., Cardeña, Lynn, and Krippner, *Varieties*; McClenon, *Events*; McClenon, *Healing*; McClenon, "Shamanic Healing"; McClenon and Nooney, "Experiences."

32. See, e.g., Barnes and Sered, *Religion and Healing*; Barnes and Talamantez, *Teaching Religion and Healing*; Turner, *Experiencing Ritual*; Turner, *Hands*; Turner, *Healers*, 39–50, 60–69, 76–82, 93–96, 96–100, 142–46; Scherberger, "Shaman," 59–64; and, though overlooked by a couple of critics who neglected to survey the table of contents, Keener, *Miracles*, 242–49. In Christian settings, see, e.g., Brown, *Healing*.

33. See, e.g., MacMullen, *Christianizing*, 7; Ashton, *Religion*, 32–40; Eve, *Miracles*, 357–59; Craffert, "Healer"; Craffert, *Life*; Klutz, *Exorcism Stories*, 196–97; McClymond, *Stranger*, 83; Pilch, "Usefulness," 100.

34. For ancient reports and conceptualizations, see esp. Ferguson, *Demonology*; Keener, *Miracles*, 769–87; Keener, *Acts*, 3:2429–41.

the strong majority of the world's cultures report experiences indigenously understood as possession by spirits.[35] For cultures that construe some such experiences negatively, some Western scholars find exorcism a culturally sensitive cure, whether or not they accept the indigenous belief in spirits.[36]

Likewise, some scholars have found here fertile bases for comparisons with NT accounts.[37] Indeed, already nineteenth-century critic David Friedrich Strauss, who viewed many miracle accounts in the Gospels as much later legends, explored, and materialistically reinterpreted, possession accounts in the German countryside to help him understand the accounts in the Gospels.[38] Insofar as we can compare any of the Gospels with their sources (here Matthew and Luke with Mark), the Evangelists do not seem to have transformed in significant ways the essential substance of the healing and exorcism accounts they received.[39] (To claim that Jesus was not deemed a miracle worker in his own day and that miracle stories simply "grew"[40] begs the question of what they grew from.)

12.3. Evidence for Jesus as a Healer

It would be difficult for scholars to dismiss the evidence that Jesus was experienced by his contemporaries as a healer. This evidence appears throughout the sources about Jesus and was acknowledged (though as sorcery) even by his earliest known detractors.

The earliest sources about Jesus unanimously depict him as a healer and exorcist, even though there was no tradition that required prophets to perform

35. See, e.g., Bourguignon, "Spirit Possession Belief," 18–21; Bourguignon, "Introduction," 17–19; see further Bourguignon, "Appendix"; Lewis, *Ecstatic Religion*; Zaretsky, *Bibliography*; Crapanzaro and Garrison, *Case Studies*; Ward, "Possession," 126; Boddy, "Spirit Possession," 428–34; Behrend and Luig, *Spirit Possession*; Keller, *Hammer*.

36. Martínez-Taboas, "Seizures"; Singleton, "Spirits," 478; Heinze, "Introduction," 14; Goodman, *Demons*, 125.

37. Borg, *Vision*, 62; Borg, *Jesus*, 149–50; Crossan, *Historical Jesus*, 315–17; Loubser, "Possession"; more extensively Davies, *Healer*, 22–42; Witmer, *Galilean Exorcist*, 22–60; Keener, "Possession"; Keener, *Miracles*, 788–856; esp. Keener, *Acts*, 3:2441–56; Tibbs, "Possession"; Crooks, "Psychology"; Keener, "Spirits"; Vaughn, "Possession."

38. See Fabisiak, *Side*, esp. 69–102, on his critique of miracles, and 103–39, on "the nocturnal side of nature." I am grateful to Prof. Juan Hernandez for bringing this work to my attention.

39. See McCasland, *Finger*, 51, 53; Williams, *Miracle Stories*, 53–54. Luke may add observers' reactions; Plutarch does the same, apparently with Thucydides (Pelling, *Texts*, 48).

40. Ehrman, *Before Gospels*, 221–22, conceding that his "is a minority position."

such actions. Although each of the other Gospels include some additional accounts, our earliest Gospel, Mark, expends the greatest proportion of space on Jesus as a healer and exorcist. Writing probably within four decades of Jesus's execution, Mark devotes some 40 percent of his narrative to these scenes.[41] Even some frequently skeptical scholars support the plausibility of Mark's "admission" that Jesus could not heal in one location where people refused to believe (Mark 6:5).[42]

Although Q does not include many narratives, it does include some summary statements by Jesus that confirm the sort of activity noted in Mark. In Q, Jesus presents his healings (Matt 11:5//Luke 7:22) and exorcisms (Matt 12:28//Luke 11:20) as signs of the kingdom. In a saying that surely stems from Galilee and probably from Jesus's public ministry,[43] Jesus expects God to judge Galilean villages that have not welcomed his miracles more fully (Matt 11:21//Luke 10:13). In all our traditions about Jesus, healing is as central to his activity as the kingdom is in his teaching.[44] The healing of the centurion's servant, placed at a similar location in the narratives of both Matthew (8:5–13) and Luke (7:1–10), also probably was in Q. Even if we had only our earliest sources devoted to Jesus's ministry or teaching, namely (on the predominant view), Mark and Q, Jesus's role as a miracle worker would remain paramount and include all the major forms of miracle stories in the Gospels.

So pervasive was the recollection of this dimension of Jesus's ministry that no ancient authors seek to deny it. Jesus's later detractors, including later rabbis and the hostile gentile writer Celsus, acknowledged Jesus's healings and exorcisms, though denying that they were divine acts (see already Mark 3:22).[45] (Later rabbis also associated Jesus's followers with healings,[46] as do the Book of Acts[47] and second-century Christian sources.)[48]

---

41. See, e.g., Placher, *Mark*, 76.

42. Cf. Funk and Jesus Seminar, *The Acts of Jesus*, 85.

43. Few outside Galilee knew Chorazin, and Bethsaida's consistent name in the Gospels was probably consistently its name only until roughly 30 CE (the likeliest date that it became the city Julias); see further Theissen, *Gospels*, 49–52; Charlesworth, "Sketch," 97; cf. Josephus, *Jewish Antiquities* 18.28; Adinolfi, "Lago"; Strickert, "Founding."

44. Betz, *Jesus*, 60; Theissen and Merz, *Guide*, 281 (see more fully 281–315).

45. See, e.g., Loos, *Miracles*, 156–67; Vermes, *Jesus the Jew*, 79.

46. See, e.g., Herford, *Christianity*, 103–17; Pritz, *Nazarene Christianity*, 96–97.

47. See discussion in Keener, *Acts*, 1:320–82.

48. See, e.g., Quadratus, *Apology* frag.; Keener, *Miracles*, 361–63, 543–44; the fuller surveys of ancient Christian healing in Woolley, *Exorcism*, 13–25; Frost, *Healing*, 61–110; Kelsey, *Healing*, 135–99; Young, "Miracles in History," 106–8; Kelhoffer, "Miracle Workers." The ascendancy of unbridled hagiography makes many Christian reports from the fourth century and following

More important (and more neutral), Josephus regards Jesus as a sage who "performed astonishing works," using the same expression that he uses elsewhere for Elisha's miracles.[49] A majority of scholars thus agree with the Jewish expert Geza Vermes, an Oxford professor renowned for his work on ancient Jewish sources and Jesus, that Josephus depicts Jesus as a miracle-working sage.[50]

Although they were offered in a milieu far more open to supernatural claims than our own, such claims were not invented to conform to any cultural expectations. No such claims were offered for other well-known prophetic figures such as John. Josephus mentions some figures soon after Jesus who promised public signs, but they failed to perform them, and their signs did not involve healing or exorcism.[51] All evidence also suggests that their movements, unlike that of Jesus, failed to outlive them.[52]

Because of such evidence, most scholars who research historical-Jesus questions agree that Jesus's contemporaries experienced him as a miracle worker.[53] To do otherwise would undermine all historical criteria used to evaluate other claims about Jesus. For example, E. P. Sanders considers it "almost indisputable,"[54] and Morton Smith, skeptical about much of the Jesus tradition, regards Jesus's miracles as the most certain memory about him.[55] This verdict remains the consensus, despite the wide divergence of opinion on the causes of such experiences.

---

less dependable, except where (as in Augustine's diocese; *City of God* 22.8) they were better documented. Whatever else might be debated in Knapp, *Dawn*, the centrality of miracle claims in early Christian expansion is clear.

49. Josephus, *Jewish Antiquities* 9.182; 18.63.

50. See esp. Vermes, "Notice"; Vermes, *Jesus the Jew*, 79; Meier, *Marginal Jew*, 2:621; Theissen and Merz, *Guide*, 74.

51. On the sign prophets, see, e.g., Barnett, "Sign Prophets"; Gray, *Prophetic Figures*, 112–44; Eve, *Miracles*, 296–325. For the contrast with Jesus, see, e.g., Theissen and Merz, *Guide*, 308–9.

52. Cf. also the distinctive continuing of OT-like claims among Jesus's followers regarding the prophetic experience of the divine Spirit and miracles; cf. discussion in Keener, *Acts*, 1:519–28, 537–49.

53. For this summary of consensus, see also Brown, *Death*, 143–44; Blackburn, "Miracles," 362; Eve, *Miracles*, 16–17; Welch, "Miracles," 360; Green, "Healing," 758; Dunn, *Remembered*, 670; Hultgren, "Stories," 134–35; Twelftree, "Message," 2518–19; Le Donne, *Historiographic Jesus*, 175–76.

54. Sanders, *Jesus and Judaism*, 11; cf. similarly Betz, *Jesus*, 58; see the detailed work of Meier, *Marginal Jew*, 2:617–45, 678–772.

55. Smith, *Magician*, 16.

12.4. A Nonbiographic Alternative?

Mythography was not biography, although it recycled tradition, and historians and biographers sometimes lacked other material to depend on for the legendary period many centuries earlier.[56] (Historians often noted this difference in the quality of such primeval materials.)[57] But such mythography addressed the distant past, not recent historical persons.

Whether one believes in supernatural activity or not, the Gospels' reports of healings and exorcisms differ starkly from the composite creatures and divine rapes that characterize so many myths in the engaging myth collections of Apollodorus or Ovid.[58] They appear comparable only through the lens of a modernist Western conflation of all supernatural claims, from all cultures and eras. The Gospels take for granted a theistic worldview, but this factor no more diminishes their character as ancient biography than the works of ancient polytheistic historians (sometimes replete with scenes understood as divine judgments)[59] exclude them from ancient historiography. Millions of people claim experiences today with what they consider miracles, but this does not make the *genre* of their claims, or even their collected claims, mythography.[60]

This observation is not meant to preclude the observation that legendary elements may grow in stories over time. Such elements may appear in infancy

56. Many spoke of "myths" (or particular myths) negatively for being untrue, e.g., Plato, *Republic* 2.377C–383C; Cicero, *On the Nature of the Gods* 2.28.70 (a Stoic); Valerius Maximus, *Memorable Doings and Sayings* 4.7.4; Lucian, *Amber* 3, 5–6; *Sacrifices* 5; Philostratus, *Lives of the Sophists* 2.1.554; *Heroicus* 34.4; 50.1–2; Iamblichus, *Pythagorean Life* 32.218; Libanius, *Anecdote* 3.27; Syncellus, *Chronography*, p. 73 (discussing Manetho, *Aegyptiaca* frag. 2.3). Others contended that myths communicated truth in pleasurable ways (Diodorus Siculus, *Library of History* 1.2.2; Maximus of Tyre, *Philosophical Orations* 4.5–6); cf. comments about poetry in ch. 7.

57. See, e.g., Diodorus Siculus, *Library of History* 1.6.2; Kennedy, "Source Criticism," 139, noting Quintilian, *Orator's Education* 2.4.18–19, and Livy's repeated warnings in the first ten books of his *History*.

58. Only later, and perhaps in response to the Gospels, do we see mythical figures treated individually in something like a biographic manner (perhaps in Philostratus's *Heroicus*).

59. See, e.g., Polybius, *Histories* 31.9.1–4; 32.15.3, 10–14; Diodorus Siculus, *Library of History* 14.63.1; 14.69.2; 27.4.3; Appian, *Roman History* 3.12.1–2; Josephus, *Jewish Antiquities* 12.358–59; cf. Pausanias, *Description of Greece* 3.23.3–5; 9.33.6; in biography, see Cornelius Nepos, *On Great Generals* 17 (Agesilaus), 4.8.

60. See "Spirit and Power: A 10–Country Survey of Pentecostals," Pew Forum Survey (October 2006), a 231-page report available at http://pewforum.org/surveys/pentecostal; Alexander, *Signs*, 17; Keener, *Miracles*, 237–39; cf. Woodward, "Miracles"; Währisch-Oblau, "Healthy," 92–93; Oblau, "Healing," 313; Tang, "Healers," 481.

narratives about key figures[61] or the apparition involved in Caesar's crossing of the Rubicon[62] (missing in Caesar's own account over a century and a half earlier). Yet I am aware of no instances of full-scale mythography in antiquity regarding figures within two generations; if exceptions exist, they are far from the norm.[63]

Although Jesus was distinctive in many respects, healing reports are not limited to him alone, as we have noted. Still, although we know of many sages and philosophic schools, we have few reports of itinerant individual healers. Most reports of healing in this period are connected instead with temples of Asclepius or the like. A more proximate model for Jesus, although not the subject of biographies per se, would be Elijah, who also provided the model for an eschatological prophet (cf. Mal 4:5; Sir 48:10).[64]

The closest Greek analogy is Apollonius, but our major account of Apollonius comes from the third century, in a period when the Gospels' accounts of Jesus were already influential and circulating widely.[65] Hero veneration led to hagiography in its late antique form, with a mythography in person-centered, biographic form less characteristic of earlier periods.[66] Reading this evolving genre back into first-century biographies, however, would be like viewing Jesus as a Hellenistic divine man—anachronistic and sometimes reversing the direction of influence.[67]

Some scholars also point out that only Jesus's miracles are explicitly associated with the kingdom[68] (at least if we exclude Josephus's subsequent proph-

---

61. Cf., e.g., Suetonius, *Augustus* 94.4; Aulus Gellius, *Attic Nights* 6.1.2–4; Philostratus, *Life of Apollonius* 1.4–5; Menander Rhetor, *Epideictic Treatises* 2.1–2, 371.5–6; Hermogenes, *Progymnasmata* 7.15; Shuler, *Genre*, 94; Klauck, *Context*, 300; Keener, *Matthew*, xxix, 84–85.

62. Suetonius, *Julius* 32; cf. discussions in Beneker, "Crossing"; Rondholz, "Rubicon." This apparition could have originated as political propaganda from Caesar's faction, but it does not appear even in Velleius Paterculus, *History* 2.49.4, composed ca. 30 CE, roughly eighty years after the crossing. Caesar's postmortem comet was a genuine astronomical event.

63. More generally, myths usually appear in other genres than in a work about a person in any case, but historians and biographers did treat mythical figures, albeit with the reservations noted in ch. 9.

64. For OT models, see Koskenniemi, *Miracle-Workers*.

65. See discussion in Keener, *Miracles*, 53–56; Keener, *Acts*, 1:330–33; cf. Klauck, *Context*, 170; Cangh, "Miracles," 224–26.

66. Thus contrast Philostratus, *Life of Apollonius* (on Apollonius) and *Heroicus* (on Protesilaos) with earlier works such as Apollodorus, *Library*, and Ovid, *Metamorphoses*. On Apollonius, see, e.g., Keener, *Acts*, 1:329–33.

67. See Tiede, *Figure*; Holladay, *Theios aner*; Gallagher, *Divine Man*; Pilgaard, "*Theios aner*"; Koskenniemi, "Background," 105–7; Lane, "Christology"; Blackburn, "ΘΕΙΟΙ ΑΝΔΡΕΣ."

68. Theissen and Merz, *Guide*, 290.

ets who failed to produce the promised signs) and that Jesus is a bearer, rather than just a petitioner, of numinous power.[69]

12.5. Miracle Reports Can Come from Eyewitnesses

Whereas the limited ancient analogies to Jesus's miracles help illustrate how Jesus's contemporaries understood him, modern analogies play a different role. By offering a sociological control, they challenge traditional hypotheses about how long it takes for miracle reports to develop.[70] That is, they undermine David Friedrich Strauss's nineteenth-century argument that miracle stories point up the Gospels' legendary character.[71] So far was Strauss captive to his philosophic assumptions that he failed to take adequate account of experiences about which he himself knew.[72] Modern memory theory also challenges Strauss's approach.[73] (Still, although his insistence on lengthy development for accounts of miracles is implausible, it is at least more plausible than that of some rationalists of the era who thought that Jesus used secret Essene medicines!)[74]

Far from being merely legendary, reports of what observers construe as miracles can stem even from eyewitnesses and can be reported even on the very day of the experience.[75] No one, of course, claims that the Gospels were composed immediately after the events they report, and virtually all scholars

---

69. See Eve, *Miracles*, 289, 295, 378.

70. Cf. Derico, *Tradition*, 249–50, for parallels in independent accounts of a miracle report from during the reporters' lifetimes; and see numerous accounts in Keener, *Miracles*.

71. Many form critics applied Strauss's approach regarding miracles to the larger Synoptic tradition (Collins, *Mark*, 34).

72. See Ising, *Blumhardt*, 92–94, 222–23. Strauss did, however, recognize possession experiences and the like, while interpreting them differently; see Fabisiak, *Side*. For theologians who honor Blumhardt's legacy, see Barth, *Letters*, 251; Heim, *Transformation*, 173–74; Moltmann, "Blessing," 149.

73. See Schwartz, "Smoke," 29–30.

74. As also noted in Dunn, "Quest," 304. For accounts of such eighteenth- and early nineteenth-century claims, see Schweitzer, *Quest*, 39–45. Aside from misrepresenting the Essenes, these critics grossly overestimated the capacities of ancient medicine (on which, see, e.g., Keener, *Acts*, 1:416–19).

75. E.g., my personal journal reports my eyewitness experience of a serious storm that stopped within seconds after a college student prayed for it to stop, November 6, 1993; an apparent resuscitation in John Wesley's journal for December 25, 1742 (cf. Kidd, "Healing," 159; Tomkins, *Wesley*, 106).

recognize that the Evangelists (and prior tradents) edited the traditions available to them. My point, however, is simply that their reports of healings and exorcisms need not be Markan or other inventions. Miracle stories can reflect imagination and legend, but especially in the first generation, they often reflect genuine recoveries.

Healing reports continue in various religious contexts, as already noted, including in Christian circles. When extrapolated in hard numbers, the results of a 2006 Pew Forum survey appear to suggest that hundreds of millions of Christians globally today claim to have directly witnessed divine healing.[76] While no one thinks that all these claims represent genuine anomalies, they do challenge the traditional argument against miracle claims—the argument that no respectable eyewitnesses offer such claims.[77]

Moreover, the Christian reports do not involve only people starting with Christian premises. Around the world, vast numbers of converts report socially costly abandonment of centuries of traditions to become Christians because of healings they or those near them witnessed;[78] presumably they considered such experiences different in kind from the natural recoveries with which they were familiar. Thus, for example, millions of conversions in China (not included in the above study) are attributed to what one official source deemed "faith healing experiences."[79] Large numbers of non-Christians in India report being healed through Christian prayer as well.[80] As Yale historian Ramsay MacMullen points out, exorcism and miracles also constituted the primary causes of conversion that Christians noted even in the fourth century.[81]

76. The United States was among the ten nations polled. The 231-page report, "Spirit and Power," includes not only percentages of Pentecostals and charismatics in the ten countries (the direct subject of the survey) who claim to have witnessed divine healing (totalling perhaps 200 million), but also an average of more than one-third of other Christians.

77. The argument of Hume (*Miracles*), which followed some earlier deists (Burns, *Debate*, 9–10, 70–95, 141). Although Hume retains philosophic defenders (see esp. Fogelin, *Defense*), a majority of philosophers today seem to reject Hume's argument; see, e.g., Swinburne, *Miracle*; Swinburne, "Evidence," 198; Ward, "Believing"; Evans, *Narrative*, 153–54; Parikh, "Argument" (cf. also discussion in Keener, *Miracles*, 107–70); esp. Houston, *Miracle*; Johnson, *Hume*; Earman, "Bayes"; Earman, *Failure*; Earman, "Hume."

78. See, e.g., Yung, "Integrity," 173–75; Bomann, *Faith*, 62; Knapstad, "Power," 78; Ma, "Encounter," 136; earlier, and particularly extensively, De Wet, "Signs."

79. Währisch-Oblau, "Healthy," 92–93, citing an estimate of half of all conversions; the estimate in Tang, "Healers," 481, is 90 percent.

80. Bergunder, *Movement*, 233; cf. Bergunder, "Miracle Healing," 298.

81. MacMullen, *Christianizing*, 61–62.

Scholars vary in their explanations for such recoveries. The placebo effect,[82] misdiagnosis[83] and misunderstanding likely account for many unexpected recoveries; some researchers also find connections between unusual cures and altered-state-of-consciousness experiences.[84] Some reports certainly involve fraud;[85] some involving an earlier period in one's life may involve memory distortions.[86] Drawing on medical anthropology and psychoimmunology, John Pilch, considering the Gospels, helpfully emphasizes the cultural framing of illnesses and how beliefs affect immune responses.[87] Psychiatrist Donald Capps also helpfully suggests that Jesus may have psychologically cured not only psychosomatic but also psychogenic disorders.[88]

Even such explanations, however, do not easily account for documented anomalous recoveries of infants or persons pronounced dead.[89] They also would presumably not account for most instant cures of blindness.[90] While Western prayer studies have remained inconclusive or even negative, some apparently organic prayer cures have been studied in their indigenous contexts with surprising results.[91] I or my wife personally know and trust many of the witnesses I have interviewed, including some relatives, for some of these extraordinary claims, although again this observation does not resolve the question of interpretation. So-called nature miracles are much more debated, being less frequent in both the Gospels and modern reports, although experiences that eyewitnesses interpret as such events are reported today.[92]

82. See Droege, *Faith Factor*, 15–33; Matthews and Clark, *Faith Factor*, 179–81; Benson, *Healing*, 34, 36–37, 45, 107–10, 117; Remus, *Healer*, 109–13; Davies, *Healer*, 77.

83. Cf. Remus, *Healer*, 109; Downing, *Death*, 61.

84. See the sources in McClenon, *Healing*, 67.

85. See, e.g., Frost, *Healing*, 183; Naswem, "Healing," 30–31.

86. Pekala and Cardeña, "Issues," 52–53; Slade, "Reports." On memory frailties and strengths, see ch. 14.

87. See, e.g., Pilch, *Healing*; cf. Craffert, *Life*, 260–80.

88. See Capps, *Village Psychiatrist*; cf. Davies, *Healer*, 70–72, 76; Gaztambide, "Psychoimmunology"; Gaztambide, "Role," esp. 303–6.

89. Cf. McNamara and Szent-Imrey, "Learn," 213.

90. For raising claims, see, e.g., Jenkins, *New Faces*, 114; Miller and Yamamori, *Pentecostalism*, 151–52; Ma, "Encounter," 137; Gaztambide, "Mission," 31; Sánchez Walsh, *Identity*, 43–44; Bomann, "Salve," 195–96; Chesnut, *Born Again in Brazil*, 86; reports and interviews in Keener, *Miracles*, 545–79; Keener, "Raised." For reports of healed blindness, see, e.g., Ramirez, "Faiths," 94–95; Ma, "Vanderbout," 130, 132; Ma, "Encounter," 137; Wiyono, "Timor Revival," 286; De Wet, "Signs," 103–4, 121–23; Castleberry, "Impact," 108, 112; Keener, *Miracles*, 512–22.

91. See, e.g., Brown et al., "Effects"; earlier, Gardner, "Miracles."

92. For various views, including my own, see Twelftree, *Nature Miracles*.

Global perspectives on "miracles," with some of which I am sympathetic, have also been much more open to supernatural explanations than are traditional modern Western approaches.[93] Philosophy of religion has also become more open to theistic explanations than it once was.[94] In any case, explanations may be treated separately from whether people had experiences such as those reported. Historians addressing religious cures may report them without passing judgment on their causes,[95] sometimes relegating that question to theologians or philosophers.[96]

12.6. Conclusion

Again, this chapter remains brief because I have treated the topics at length elsewhere. Nevertheless, the vast majority of historical-Jesus scholars affirm that many of Jesus's contemporaries experienced him as a healer and exorcist, however this is explained today. It is one of the most widely attested features of Jesus's ministry throughout the primary sources. Likewise, the evidence is overwhelming that eyewitnesses report dramatic healings and exorcisms today, however we explain them. If Jesus's contemporaries experienced him as a healer and exorcist, one would expect this element to feature in biographies of him, just as it does in modern biographies of modern healers. This focus thus does not count against the biographic character of the Gospels.

93. E.g., González, *Acts*, 84–85; Martell-Otero, "Satos," 31–32; Yung, *Quest*, 7.
94. Quentin Smith, himself not a theist, notes this change in "Metaphilosophy," 197. See further Quinn, "Epistemology" (noted in Deines, *Acts of God*, 9n20).
95. E.g., Porterfield, *Healing*; Opp, *Lord for Body*; discussion in Twelftree, "Historian."
96. MacMullen, *Christianizing*, 24.

Chapter 13

What about John?

If Mark is ancient biography and Luke is a sort of biographic volume in a popular two-volume history, what is John? The Fourth Gospel's apparent purpose statement (20:31) is consistent with the purpose of some ancient biographies, especially those of sages.[1] But is John the same kind of biography as the Synoptics? Like Matthew, John is influenced more by Judean/Galilean ways of thinking. But whereas Matthew seems ever the collector and arranger of Jesus's teachings, fitted (in its current form) around Mark's narrative, John develops a somewhat different side of Jesus the sage. The Jesus who often offers parables without public interpretations in Mark speaks in other sorts of riddles in John.[2]

In my *Historical Jesus of the Gospels*, I mostly ignored the Fourth Gospel because of the special questions surrounding it. Convicted by some pro-Johannine reviewers concerning my lapse, I have resolved to at least take John into account briefly here. Nevertheless, because I have written a 1,600-page commentary that treats John's material in much greater detail, I will survey the question of this Fourth Gospel only briefly here. Readers not persuaded by this chapter will have to settle for this book's arguments regarding the historically useful, biographic character of Mark and Luke.

13.1. John's Distinctiveness

If the Fourth Gospel is a biography from the late first century, how can it be so eccentric and we still suppose that biographies of recent characters are

---

1. See Burridge, *Gospels*, 229. Burridge treats John as ancient biography (Burridge, *Gospels*, 213–32).
2. Witherington, *Sage*, 336–38, calls this the esoteric side of the wisdom tradition. On Jesus as riddler in history and the Gospels, see esp. Thatcher, *Riddler*; on riddles in communication, see also Thatcher, "Riddles."

mostly reliable? As one careful scholar warns, if both Mark and John are factual, "the notion of historical fact is in mortal danger from the death of a thousand qualifications."[3] First, any possible adaptation of the biographic genre by John need not affect the argument for Mark's biographic approach, since John writes an estimated quarter century after Mark (slightly more on my own minority dating of Mark). Second, I have argued for what is probable for the Synoptics based on *most* comparable biographies, not that there were no exceptions. Again, mixing elements of genres was common, and John seems less constrained by the usual Greco-Roman biographic tradition of the early empire.[4]

But third, and the focus of this chapter: John's Gospel may be less eccentric than we first suppose. Insofar as ancient biographies were not bound to chronology, John is not required to follow the outline of Mark that is followed by Matthew and Luke. Indeed, intrinsic claims predicate this Gospel on eyewitness tradition more explicitly than they do Mark. As we shall note in a subsequent chapter, even eyewitnesses differ on details. This Gospel could therefore deliberately correct a tradition less interested in chronology than John was—though I prefer more theological, symbolic explanations for John's major narrative divergences.[5] Beyond chronologically, it is particularly the speeches that appear idiosyncratic in John (differing from often less cohesive collections of sayings or shorter interchanges in the Synoptics).

Suffice it to say that if Luke falls on the more historiographic end of biography, John seems to embrace the genre's flexibility more fully, perhaps more

---

3. Eve, *Behind Gospels*, 149; although the contrasts on which he focuses are mainly omissions (esp. the kingdom and exorcisms in John), they certainly emphasize different aspects of Jesus's ministry. Ehrman, *Interrupted*, 21–28, notes differences; I also note these, though sometimes explaining them differently, in my John commentary. Some in antiquity viewed John as deliberately supplementing the Synoptics (Eusebius, *Ecclesiastical History* 3.24.7–13; Smith, *John among Gospels*, 8).

4. Attridge, "Genre Bending," further developed in Attridge, "Genre Matters?"; I owe these references to Sean Adams, from his forthcoming work tentatively titled *Negotiating Genre*.

5. Some would compare the range of treatments in the Diaspora Jewish writer Philo: although the first volume of Philo's *Life of Moses* resembles Greco-Roman biography more generally, his lives of Abraham and Joseph revert to his penchant for allegorizing as edifying commentary in the Alexandrian philosophic tradition. For John and Philo, cf., e.g., Dodd, *Interpretation*, 54–73; Borgen, *John*; Attridge, "Philo and John"; Attridge, "Creation"; Attridge, "Name." Still, John's audience is far from the elite Hellenistic readership presupposed by Philo.

encomiastically.[6] (For the flexible end of biographic and historical writing, we may think of the different twist that Josephus places on the nature of his own Galilean mission in two of his works.)[7] John's messianic secret is far less subtle than in Mark, though the disciples are relatively equally clueless. Everything is expressed in Johannine idiom, even sayings paralleled in the Synoptics; almost all Johannine scholars, including the more conservative ones, recognize that John has framed everything in his own way.[8] We might speak of John's interpretive, homiletic development of his material.[9] Like a certain kind of ancient biography, John's focus highlights Jesus's character and mission.[10]

Yet the Fourth Gospel's discourses differ more starkly from the Synoptics than its narratives. Many of John's narratives are more Synoptic-like, that is, more episodic. D. Moody Smith, my dissertation mentor and a noted specialist in the relationship of John and the Synoptics,[11] has argued that where John's narrative departs from the Synoptics, such as in some details of Jesus's arrest and trial, John sometimes has an even better claim to what we should regard as reliable tradition than the Synoptics.[12]

Others note that Mark too may have imposed a grid on Jesus's story, so it should not a priori be used to exclude the reliability of John's approach.[13] Although they appear in different contexts, John includes some sayings that also appear in the Synoptics (e.g., 12:25, 48; 13:16, 20),[14] and if we broaden the

6. Cf. also Dunn, *Tradition*, 163, 195. Some compare John's Gospel to grand rhetoric; such rhetoric, however, tended to be far more lavish and pleonastic than John's simple prose, which was more suitable for normal historical discourse.

7. See Henderson, "Comparison," 270, 273–74. As Henderson notes, Josephus gives us a sense of how far some work could go in variations and still remain acceptable in a first-century context (275).

8. See, e.g., Lindars, *John*, 25; Bruce, *John*, 6, 16; Thompson, "Historical Jesus"; Dunn, "John and Tradition" (see esp. the essential conclusion on 377).

9. See again Bruce, *John*, 16.

10. Licona, *Differences*, 115, suggesting that John might focus on a "higher-level view" than on "the ground level of precise reporting."

11. See, e.g., Smith, "John and Synoptics"; Smith, *John among Gospels*.

12. Smith, "Historical Issues," 263–67.

13. Moloney, "Jesus of History."

14. Cf. Matt 10:24, 39; Mark 9:41; Luke 10:16; 17:33; perhaps John 14:13–14 with Matt 7:7//Luke 11:9; John 16:2 with Mark 13:9; John 15:26–27 (in the context of persecution) with Mark 13:11; John 16:24 with Matt 7:7//Luke 11:9; John 17:2 with Matt 11:27//Luke 10:22; see many further examples in Aland's synopsis. Cf. the much more extensive list of parallels in Howard, *Gospel*, 267–78; Anderson, *Quest*, 131–32. For aphorisms in John, see Anderson, *Quest*, 60–61.

discussion to coherence with Synoptic sayings, the net becomes still wider.[15] Even John's Christology in the discourses has earlier precedent.[16]

Philo's *Life of Moses* not only adapts and expands some speeches from the Pentateuch,[17] it adds four new ones, including three full ones for Moses, drawing inferences from the Pentateuch.[18] Even historians often used speeches to provide perspectives and interpretation on their material,[19] including in Josephus's Hellenistic Jewish historiography.[20] Xenophon's memoirs of Socrates offer John the potential precedent of even a firsthand witness who frames the master's teaching "not only in isolated sallies, but in colloquies with a single interlocutor, whose questions guide his tongue."[21] Although not a biography and reflecting an earlier literary milieu, Plato developed Socrates's teaching in a way he believed to accord with that teaching.[22]

But whereas good historians ideally were supposed to try to provide speeches that sounded like the speakers, everyone in this Gospel speaks in

---

15. Cf., e.g., Ensor, "John 4.35." Although I occasionally pointed these out in the commentary, I usually did not, since historical setting, rather than historicity of genre, was the commentary's primary focus.

16. See fuller discussion in Keener, *John*, 297–310. How much precedent is of course a matter of debate; in support of considerable precedent, see, e.g., Hurtado, *Lord Jesus Christ*; Hays, *Reading Backwards*; Gathercole, *Son*; Tilling, *Christology*; Loke, *Origins*; Bauckham, "Christology"; Capes, *Texts*; Capes, *Christ*; against it, see, e.g., Ehrman, *How Jesus Became God*; Kirk, *Man Attested by God*.

17. Expanded discourses include Philo, *Moses* 1.50.278–79, expanding Num 23:1–10; *Moses* 1.31.171–72, expanding Exod 14:11–12; *Moses* 1.31.173–75, expanding Exod 14:13–14; and esp. *Moses* 1.40.222–26, expanding Num 13:18–21; see Hidalgo, "Study," 293–97.

18. Hidalgo, "Study," 300, 291–300, esp. the four added discourses on 297–300 (Philo, *Moses* 1.16.92, developing Exod 7:11; *Moses* 1.10.54–56, developing Exod 2:17; *Moses* 1.44.244–46, developing Num 20:21; *Moses* 1.53.295–99, developing Num 25:1–3); cf. also Petitfils, "Tale," 163, on *Moses* 1.54–57.

19. Cadbury, *Making*, 185; Lindner, "Geschichtsauffassung"; Attridge, "Historiography," 326; Satterthwaite, "Acts," 355–56; Marincola, "Speeches," 119; with reference to John, Bauckham, "Historiographical Characteristics"; for adaptation, see also particularly helpfully Parsenios, "Rhetoric."

20. Josephus even composes speeches for the same occasion differently in his different works (*Jewish Antiquities* 15.127–46 vs. *Jewish War* 1.373–79; Talbert, *Mediterranean Milieu*, 211)! On Josephus and speeches, see sources in Keener, *Acts*, 1:301–4. Some Judean haggadic works also supplied interpretive speeches (cf. Endres, *Interpretation*, 198–99).

21. Edwards, "Genre," 55–56, here 55.

22. Kennedy, "Source Criticism," 129–30, 133 (noting W. K. C. Guthrie), comparing John as opposed to the Synoptics here, and noted appreciatively in Black, "Kennedy," 64–65. Cf. also Votaw, "Biographies," 249; Dodd, *Tradition*, 17; Keener, *John*, 50; esp. Parsenios, "Rhetoric." Questions from Socrates's sometimes-confused interlocutors help shape Plato's dialogues.

Johannine idiom.[23] (Still, Philo and Josephus can make Moses sound like a Greek orator appropriate for their audiences.) Elite biographers and historians paraphrased their sources much more than do the Synoptics;[24] at least John cannot be accused of cribbing material verbatim from his sources. That is, putting material in one's own words can be viewed as a literary virtue.[25]

13.2. John versus Mark

When forced to choose between John's and Mark's narratives on matters of detail, I have typically favored Mark (including in my John commentary) because of John's apparent interpretive freedom and later date of composition. Some prefer Johannine chronology to that of the Synoptics and the Johannine date of the Last Supper over that of Mark; they could be correct (some arguments are now stronger than I anticipated),[26] but I have normally tended more toward the Markan camp (along with Matthew and Luke).[27]

In my own exploration of the Fourth Gospel, I unexpectedly concluded that, mostly in the passion narrative, John deliberately tweaks, often in symbolically pregnant ways,[28] the more widely circulated passion narrative known to us from Mark (Mark 14–15) and, probably in very condensed form, in Paul (cf. 1 Cor 11:23–26; 15:3).[29] John is not the only Gospel (cf. Matt 27:34 with Mark

---

23. See, e.g., Burridge, "Gospels and Acts," 527.

24. E.g., for Philo's resistance to verbatim copying, see Hidalgo, "Study," 300.

25. Some people viewed use of preexisting lines as plagiarism (cf. Seneca the Elder, *Controversiae* 1.pref.19; *Suasoriae* 2.19; McGill, "Seneca on Plagiarizing"), others (when the incorporation was obvious) as flattering the source (*Suasoriae* 3.7); no consensus on the boundary existed (Knoppers, "Problem," 28–29, 33).

26. See Anderson, *Quest*, 158–66; briefly, Bernier, *Quest*, 82; earlier, e.g., Oesterley, *Liturgy*, 158–67; Grappe, "Essai"; Meier, *Marginal Jew*, 1:395–401; Brown, *Death*, 1351–73. But see now Pitre, *Last Supper*, 251–373.

27. Though it is not three against one, since Matthew and Luke may simply be following Mark; note Smith, "Criticism," 628–29.

28. Partly from apologetic concerns, church fathers often harmonized John with the Synoptics (something John conspicuously does *not* do); some, however, observed that John sometimes diverged to make a spiritual point (Origen, *Commentary on John* 10.2, 13–15; an approach, however, that I believe Origen often took too far). See Wiles, *Gospel*, 14–24.

29. Cf. here Allison, *Constructing Jesus*, 392–403; Eve, *Behind Gospels*, 163–67. Theissen, *Gospels*, 166–99, argues for a very early, continuous passion narrative; Soards, "Passion Narrative," contends both that Mark uses a source and that we probably cannot separate the tradition from the redaction (at least except where the agreement of other Gospels against Mark might

15:23; Luke 23:47 with Mark 15:39)[30] or ancient biography to tweak his sources, but the consistency of his tweaking in the passion narrative seems too conspicuous to be missed.[31] Like a bard surprising and engaging his audience by varying some expected features of a familiar story, John engages his audience by recounting a familiar story in a different way.

Jesus seems in greater control of the events, and the symbolism of particular acts (e.g., the Last Supper as a Passover meal) appears imported directly into the narrative. Thus, for example:

- In John, Jesus's crucifixion itself rather than the Last Supper appears to correspond to the Passover (cf. John 13:1; 18:28; 19:14).[32]
- John highlights the woman in Bethany anointing Jesus's feet (John 12:3; cf. Luke 7:38) rather than his head (as in Mark 14:3), so preparing for Jesus washing his disciples' feet in John 13:3–5 as an act of sacrificial servanthood that prefigures the cross.[33]
- John sounds as if Jesus rather than the disciples finds the donkey (Mark 11:2; John 12:14).
- In John, Jesus gives Judas the dipped piece of bread (John 13:26) rather than Judas himself dipping it (Mark 14:20).
- John emphasizes the Father being with Jesus (John 16:32) rather than him abandoning him (cf. Mark 15:34).
- John focuses on Jesus's prayer for his disciples (John 17:1–26) rather than a plaintive prayer in Gethsemane (Mark 14:36; but compare John 12:27–28 with Mark 14:34, 36; Heb 5:7).
- John emphasizes Jesus's commitment to drink the Father's cup (John 18:11) rather than his earlier plea for it to be removed (Mark 14:36; cf. 10:39).

---

suggest pre-Markan tradition, e.g., Mark 14:72; Dewey, "Curse," 102–3; cf., somewhat more daringly, Dunn, *Tradition*, 109–19; cf. further Soards, "Tradition").

30. Matthew may feel that he has already included the myrrh sufficiently in Matt 2:11; his use of "gall" recalls Ps 69:21. Jesus's "innocence," though an obvious corollary of being God's Son, fits Luke's apologetic.

31. For patterns of changes including redaction in ancient rhetoric, see Pelling, *Texts*, 65.

32. This conclusion results in an at least apparent changing of the day, though perhaps for more deliberate reasons than, e.g., the changing of the day in Mark 11:20 to Matt 21:19. Recounting here the range of scholarly explanations for the difference would digress at too great a length, but virtually everyone recognizes the difference between the accounts.

33. Admittedly, with Jesus being in a reclining position, Mary of Bethany could have easily anointed his feet with what remained from his head, with the better-known tradition focusing on the more prominent part. But whatever we suppose regarding this detail of the event itself, John has reason to emphasize the aspect that he emphasizes.

- In John alone, Jesus is both captured and crucified in a garden (John 18:1; 19:41, topographically framing the passion narrative).
- In John, Jesus asks whom his confronters seek (John 18:4, 7; cf. Mark 14:48) rather than Judas identifying him with a kiss (Mark 14:44–45).
- In John, Jesus rather than Simon carries Jesus's cross (Mark 15:21; John 19:17).
- John's final recorded cry sounds triumphant rather than pitiful (Mark 15:34; John 19:30).[34]
- In John, Jesus remains in control, laying down his own life (10:17–18).[35]

Not all these points are incompatible with the Markan line of tradition; writers can choose to emphasize different features of the same events, provided enough is remembered. The most basic understanding of communication recognizes that no one mentions every detail and that omitting some details is necessary for efficient and relevant communication. Moreover, some of these details likely do reflect authentic memories; prisoners, for example, typically carried their own crosses, and archaeology suggests gardens near the tomb.[36]

But John is conspicuously telling his own story, not following Mark's.[37] While this a simple matter of observation, scholars will differ as to the explanation proposed, but among the following possibilities I offer what I think the likeliest solution. On the one hand, different disciples probably remembered elements of the story differently, so John could either polemically challenge or simply supplement the earlier accounts. Though supplementation is a possible motive and is at least sometimes probably the case, if he *merely* supplements, one might expect him to show more frequently how his narrative fits with the others in cases where it appears most in tension, for example, where Jesus carries his

34. I speak here of a different emphasis, not claiming that John transmutes one saying into the other; if John's Gospel answers Mark 15:34, it is likelier in John 16:32 than in 19:30.

35. Cf. Keener, *John*, 1133–34; Keener, "Genre," 323. Note even the lack of stated mediation in John 6:11 (contrast Mark 6:41); while John is not denying such mediation, he certainly spotlights Jesus.

36. See Artemidorus, *Interpretation of Dreams* 2.56; Plutarch, *Delays of Divine Vengeance* 9, *Moralia* 554AB; Chariton, *Chaereas and Callirhoe* 4.2.7; 4.3.10; also Brown, *Death*, 913; Smith, "Historical Issues," 263–65. The nails of John 20:25 may be assumed in Col 2:14.

37. Cf. the conception of countermemory (in, e.g., Esler, "Memory," 156–57; Odor, "Countermemory," citing particularly relevantly Foucault, *Language*), though storytelling can also use variation for a purpose as mundane as surprise. I see the Fourth Gospel as independent in the sense that John was not following Mark; but I do believe that John must have known of Mark, and probably of other Gospels as well, given how widely networked the early church was (cf. Willis, "Networking"; Keener, *Acts*, 187–88).

cross. Signs of polemic are missing, but John could intend historical correction, though again one wonders why he does not more explicitly contrast the story lines of his predecessors (as biographers and historians sometimes did).[38]

On the other hand, the consistent direction of many of the above changes probably suggests that the differences are neither accidental nor corrections of mere historical detail. Rather, they appear to be deliberately rhetorical and especially theological. Good storytellers sometimes maintain audience suspense by slight variations in how they retell a familiar story.[39]

More important here, John highlights some theological points by these surprising variations (although, again, these features need not be incompatible with historical detail as well). That is, we find here not random accidents or mistakes but a consistent and therefore probably deliberate pattern of adaptation.[40] Such adaptation might continue in the resurrection narrative. As we have seen, ancient hearers would not consider such variations problematic, though (as most subsequent patristic comments illustrate) they would often seek to harmonize them.

Indeed, if some have summarized Mark's Gospel as "a passion narrative with an extended introduction,"[41] John may frame Jesus's ministry with the passion even more clearly by moving the temple cleansing, which Mark reports toward the beginning of the passion week (Mark 11:15–17), to the beginning of Jesus's public ministry (John 2:13–22). As we have noted, ancient biographies did not require chronological order, nor can episodic memory (as opposed to archives) usually provide such order. Nevertheless, John's rearrangement immediately cues any reader already familiar with Mark that John is going to tell the story his own way.

Critics in antiquity recognized that different historians would report events according to their respective emphases,[42] but they insisted, at least when criticizing others' work, that true works should not contradict one an-

---

38. E.g., Polybius, *Histories* 3.32.4–5; Josephus, *Jewish War* 1.1–2, 7.

39. Cf. Ong, *Orality*, 41; further comments are in sections 14.4a and 16.6 below. Keeping hearers alert, the Johannine Jesus even "contradicts" himself with deliberate paradoxes (Williams, *Trust*, 123–27).

40. Cf. a similar observation in Gundry, "Memories."

41. A phrase offered by Kähler (*Historical Jesus*, 80n11) but regularly repeated since then; see, e.g., Marxsen, *Mark*, 30; Best, *Mark*, 44; Bruce, "Date of Mark," 83. The label is, of course, hyperbolic: according to Burridge's estimate, Mark's passion narrative constitutes just 19.1 percent of his Gospel (Aletti, *Birth*, 26–27). Applying the title to John, see Collins, *Written*, 87–93. Hägg, *Biography*, 293, applies the title tongue-in-cheek to Lucian's passion-heavy *Passing of Peregrinus*.

42. Dionysius of Halicarnassus, *Roman Antiquities* 5.56.1.

other.[43] Still, they would understand that disciples often developed different aspects of their teachers' teachings.[44] Furthermore, when subjective individual or cultural memories diverge, we can often learn most by reading them in dialectical tension with one another, finding especially their shared core.[45] Different biographers also often highlighted different aspects of a teacher's teaching; thus Lucian emphasizes a side of Demonax largely missing in other traditions.[46]

13.3. John not-so-versus Mark

Nevertheless, focus on these adaptations, which I believe John intends to be fairly conspicuous, should not lead us to neglect the other side of the coin. John differs from the Markan outline of the Synoptics, but when compared with other ancient literature, even later Christian narratives about Jesus, John's kinship with the Synoptics becomes more obvious.

I agree with the significant strand of Johannine scholarship that finds in this Gospel the testimony of the beloved disciple (cf. John 19:35; 21:24; 1 John 1:1–3).[47] Papias depends on sayings of "John,"[48] or, on Eusebius's interpretation of Papias, two Johns;[49] the John whom Papias believed authored 1 John[50] is presumably closely connected with the Gospel's author.[51] (Again, I am not treating this question in greater depth here because I have treated it extensively elsewhere, where I include various views, objections, and more detailed arguments.)[52]

---

43. Josephus, *Against Apion* 1.15, 37–38. But as we have noted, Josephus sometimes contradicts himself.

44. Consider, e.g., Plato and Xenophon with respect to Socrates, albeit in an earlier period (cf. Votaw, "Biographies," 249; Dodd, *Tradition*, 17; Keener, *John*, 50; esp. Parsenios, "Rhetoric"), or the differing depictions of Musonius Rufus in the collections of Lucius and Pollio (Lutz, "Musonius," 12–13). John might also seek to play Deuteronomy to the Synoptics' Exodus (Keener, *John*, 51).

45. Bockmuehl, *Seeing*, 172.

46. Beck, "Demonax," 89–90.

47. E.g., varying solutions in Braun, *Jean*, 301–30; Ridderbos, *John*, 3, 680–82; Kysar, *John*, 12; O'Day, "John," 500; Hengel, *Question*; Dunn, "John," 299; Smith, *John* (1999), 400; Painter, *John*, 4; Bauckham, *Eyewitnesses*, 550–51; Wright, "Reliability," 206–21.

48. Though Papias, frag. 3.1 and 5.1 (Holmes) might mean indirect dependence; see frag. 3.4–5; 7.3.

49. Papias, frag. 3.5–6, attributing the Gospel to the apostle.

50. So Papias, frag. 3.17.

51. For second-century reception of the Johannine corpus, see esp. Hill, *Corpus*.

52. Keener, *John*, 1:81–115. Not addressed there, contrast Litwa, "Eyewitnesses" (somewhat

Moody Smith notes again that John, while distinctive among the Gospels, is more like the Synoptics than like any other documents.[53] John tells Jesus's story in a significantly different way from the Synoptics, yet recent studies of historical tradition in John[54] also show that this Gospel is a far cry from second- and third-century stories about Jesus that are typically far from Judean/Galilean roots. (Some genuine Jesus tradition does exist in the Gospel of Thomas, although it lacks the narrative form that characterizes biographies such as the first-century Gospels, and its current form clearly postdates living memory of Jesus.)[55]

John's topography reflects accurate knowledge of pre-70 greater Judea, often in narratives that do not appear in the Synoptics (e.g., 5:2; 9:7).[56] In keeping with ancient mnemonic practice,[57] this topography might also serve as memory prompts for the stories associated with it.[58] Some pre-70 Judean

---

too dismissive of the erudition of some with opposing perspectives). Despite Litwa's careful scholarship, I would not see Philostratus as quite so "contemporary"; possibly not even Antonius Diogenes (not necessarily before Lucian, cf. Morgan, "Histories and Wonders," but contrast Ní-Mheallaigh, *Fiction*, 71, 144, 150, 181; still, certainly before the third century: Sandy, "Introduction," 775). More important, although fictitious works sometimes parodied historical ones in using eyewitness claims, these were rarer than the form they parodied and often appear tongue-in-cheek, in contrast to the earnestness of John 21:24 (cf. 19:26–27; 20:2–4; 21:20–23).

53. See Smith, *John* (1999), 21–22; Schnelle, *Christology*, 229. Cf. Wright, *People*, 410–11.

54. See, e.g., Anderson, *Quest*; Anderson, "Project"; Anderson, Just, and Thatcher, *John, Jesus, and History* (3 vols.); Charlesworth, "Shift"; Charlesworth, *Mirrored in John* (esp. ch. 1); Charlesworth, *Symposium*. Earlier, see, e.g., Robinson, *Historical Character*; Hunter, "Trends"; Higgins, *Historicity*; Albright, "Discoveries," 170–71; Dodd, "Portrait"; Brown, *Essays*, 187–90; Robinson, *Priority*; most extensively, Dodd, *Tradition*, although his work is not persuasive on all points (note the caution also in Carson, "Tradition"). Also, for abundant parallels to the Synoptics despite Johannine idiom, and Judean/Galilean elements in John's Diaspora work, see Blomberg, *Reliability of John's Gospel*.

55. See discussion in Tuckett, "Thomas and Synoptics"; Tuckett, "Thomas: Evidence"; Tuckett, "Sources and Methods," 130; Charlesworth and Evans, "Agrapha," 498–502; Stanton, *Gospel Truth?*, 87; Wright, *People*, 437–43; Meier, *Marginal Jew*, 1:123–39; Perrin, *Thomas and Tatian*, 185–88; Gathercole, *Composition*; for putative, more apocalyptic earlier stages, DeConick, *Recovering*, 15–24; DeConick, "Reading." Puig i Tàrrech, *Jesus*, 31–32, finds just seven extracanonical authentic sayings of Jesus in Thomas.

56. See, e.g., Charlesworth and Aviam, "Galilee," esp. 122, 132–36; Burge, "Siloam"; Bauckham, "Historiographical Characteristics," 19–24; esp. and thoroughly, Wahlde, "Archaeology."

57. See Small, *Wax Tablets*, 95–101, 109–11; for other images, 111–16; Rubin, *Memory*, 46–47. Personal memory recalls locations better than chronology (some even used artificial locations as mnemonic devices; cf., e.g., Vatri, "Writing," 752).

58. Thatcher, "Shape," esp. 233–34. Geographic settings also appear in some 76.7 percent of Synoptic episodes (Ellis, "Making," 329).

customs also appear, despite their possible unfamiliarity to John's Diaspora audience in the 90s.[59] Literary analyses also show that John appears to presuppose his audience's knowledge of some of his information, including some information that does not appear in the Synoptics.[60]

13.3a. The Overlap

Moreover, no one would deny the significant overlap with incidents in the Synoptics, even though John arranges and words them in his own way. These appear especially in the passion narrative, since that narrative is material that all four narrative Gospels had to cover,[61] whereas a partly or fully independent tradition or witness might choose from a range of material to treat in the rest of the Gospel. For example:[62]

- Jesus comes from Nazareth in Galilee (Mark 1:9; John 1:45–46).
- Jesus is known as the son of Joseph (Matt 1:16; Luke 1:27; John 1:45), though Joseph, unlike Jesus's mother, appears nowhere during the narratives of Jesus's ministry.
- John's proclamation:[63]
  - John shows that he is not the Messiah (Luke 3:15–16; John 1:20).
  - John prepares the way for the Lord in the wilderness, in the language of Isaiah (Mark 1:3; John 1:23).[64]
  - John proclaims the one coming after him, the thong of whose sandals John is not worthy to release (Mark 1:7; John 1:26–27).
  - John baptizes merely in water, but that one will baptize in the Holy Spirit (Mark 1:8; John 1:26, 33; cf. Matt 3:11//Luke 3:16).
  - John recognizes that the Spirit descends on Jesus like a dove (Mark 1:10; John 1:32–33).
  - In different settings, a heavenly voice attests Jesus (Mark 1:11; John 12:28).
  - Jesus is thus shown to be God's Son (Mark 1:11; John 1:34).

---

59. See, e.g., Keener, *John*, 509–13, for John 2:6; Keener, *John*, 721–30, esp. 722–24, for 7:37–39.
60. See John 11:2; Culpepper, *Anatomy*, 222–23; Davies, *Rhetoric*, 255–59.
61. See, e.g., Smith, "Criticism," 626.
62. See more extensively Anderson, *Quest*, 128–45.
63. See in further detail Keener, "Baptizer."
64. The same text also used by a Judean wilderness sect to describe their identity; see 1QS 8.13–14; cf. 4Q176 frag. 1–2, 2i.7; 4Q259 3.4–5; cf. also Brownlee, "Comparison," 71; Brown, "Scrolls," 4.

- Key disciples taken for granted include Simon and Andrew (Mark 1:16; John 1:40),[65] Philip (Mark 3:18; John 1:43), Thomas (Mark 3:18; John 11:16), Judas Iscariot (Mark 3:19; John 6:71) and another Judas (Luke 6:16; Acts 1:13; John 14:22).
- Jesus names Simon, "Peter" (Mark 3:16; John 1:42).
- Jesus overturns tables in the temple and drives out money changers and sellers of doves (Mark 11:15–17; John 2:14–15).
- Jesus is reported as speaking of raising up the temple in three days after it is destroyed, albeit in ways interpreted quite differently by friend and foe (Mark 14:58; John 2:19).
- Jesus feeds the five thousand in the countryside.
  - There are just five loaves and two fish (Mark 6:38; John 6:9).
  - Jesus has the people sit down (Mark 6:39; John 6:10).
  - There are about five thousand people (Mark 6:44; John 6:10).
  - Jesus gives thanks, then distributes the food for all (Mark 6:41; John 6:11).
  - After the miracles they gathered twelve baskets of leftovers (Mark 6:43; John 6:13).
- Jesus comes to the disciples on the lake of Galilee.[66]
  - The disciples are crossing the lake to the west (to Bethsaida, Mark 6:45; to Capernaum, John 6:17).
  - The wind is stirring the lake and slowing their crossing (Mark 6:48; John 6:18).
  - Jesus comes to them, walking on the lake (Mark 6:48; John 6:19).
  - They are afraid (Mark 6:49–50; John 6:19).
  - Jesus assures them, "It is I," and tells them not to fear (Mark 6:50; John 6:20).
  - Jesus joins them in the boat (Mark 6:51; John 6:21).

- Peter confesses Jesus's identity as the Messiah (Mark 8:29) or the holy one of God (John 6:69).
- Annas and Caiaphas are among the high priests (Matt 26:3; Luke 3:2; John 18:13; and more precisely than in even Acts 4:6, Caiaphas is the *current* highest priest, hence perhaps John's "high priest that year," John 18:13).

65. They were also experienced in fishing (John 21:3), apparently along with the sons of Zebedee (21:2), though many critics still consider this chapter a post-Johannine appendix.

66. What outsiders called a "lake" retains its Galilean title as a "sea" in gospel tradition, which reflects the early perspective of that tradition (Theissen, *Gospels*, 105–8), just as do mentions of Bethsaida, Capernaum, and other villages not readily known to Diaspora audiences.

- Some leading aristocratic priests and others plot to arrest and kill Jesus, with a concern for public order (Mark 14:1–2; John 11:50, 53).[67]
- Jesus's final time in Jerusalem is for Passover (Mark 14:1; John 12:1).
- In the vicinity of Jerusalem, Jesus lodges at Bethany (Mark 11:11–12; John 12:1).
- Friends of Jesus include the sisters Martha and Mary (Luke 10:38–39; John 11:1).
- An anointing of Jesus early in the passion narrative:[68]
  - Jesus is dining in Bethany (Mark 14:3; John 12:2).
  - A woman anoints him with aromatic nard (Mark 14:3; John 12:3).
  - One or more bystanders complain that this ointment could have been sold for three hundred denarii and the money given to the poor (Mark 14:5; John 12:5).
  - Jesus defends her: "Let her alone . . . you always have the poor with you . . . but you do not always have me" (Mark 14:7; John 12:7–8).[69]
  - He associates the anointing with his burial (Mark 14:8; John 12:7).
- The triumphal entry:
  - Jesus obtains a colt (Mark 11:1–7; John 12:14).
  - Many throw branches on the road where Jesus is coming (Mark 11:8; John 12:13).
  - They shout a line from Ps 118 in the Passover Hallel: "Hosanna! Blessed is he who comes in the Lord's name!" (Mark 11:9; John 12:13).
- Jesus teaches about servanthood in the Last Supper context, with himself as the chief example (Luke 22:26–27;[70] John 13:4–5, 14).
- Jesus predicts the betrayal and also Peter's denials.
  - Jesus predicts the betrayal (Mark 14:18; John 13:21).
  - The disciples wonder whom he means (Mark 14:19; John 13:22).

---

67. For which John provides a plausible motive (along with a scene and theological irony; John 11:45–53); cf., e.g., Vermes, *Jesus the Jew*, 50; Vermes, *Jesus and Judaism*, 12; Keener, "Truth," 81; Keener, *John*, 851–52; cf. even Winter, *Trial*, 37.

68. John probably conflates with this anointing some details that appear in another anointing in the gospel tradition, including the hair and feet (Luke 7:38; John 12:3), thereby providing a model for Jesus washing his disciples' feet in John 13:4–5. Developing oral tradition can also conflate stories (Vansina, *Oral Tradition*, 153).

69. Although John does not include all of Mark's words and changes the wording about anointing with respect to burial, the words here are identical in both versions apart from one slight change in word order.

70. Parallels between Luke and John in the passion narrative might indicate John's knowledge of Luke's stories, but they could also indicate Luke's knowledge of stories from the tradition of the beloved disciple (cf. Luke 1:1–4; Anderson, *Quest*, 112–16; Matson, *Dialogue*, goes even further).

- Jesus predicts that his followers will abandon him and be scattered (Mark 14:27; John 16:32).
- Peter insists that he will follow no matter what (Mark 14:29, 31; John 13:37).
- Jesus predicts Peter's denials (Mark 14:30; John 13:38).
- Jesus and his disciples leave the place where they have dined for the countryside (Mark 14:26; John 18:1).
- Satan enters Judas Iscariot (Luke 22:3; John 13:27), who has pecuniary motives (Mark 14:11; John 12:6).
- Judas betrays Jesus (Mark 14:43; John 18:2–3).
  - One disciple strikes off the ear of the high priest's slave with a sword (Mark 14:47; John 18:10).
  - This action earns Jesus's reproof (Luke 22:51), even specifically, "Put your sword back in its place!" (Matt 26:52; John 18:11).
- Jesus must drink the Father's cup (Mark 14:36; John 18:11).
- Jesus before the high priest and his colleagues:
  - The high priest questions Jesus (Mark 14:60–61; John 18:19).
  - Jesus keeps silent or gives an evasive answer (Mark 14:61; John 18:20–21).
  - One way or the other, though, they know his claim to be God's Son (Matt 26:63//Luke 22:70; John 19:7; cf. 10:36).[71]
  - At least one Judean officer or servant strikes Jesus, apparently in the high priest's presence (Mark 14:65; John 18:22).
- Peter denies Jesus.
  - Peter follows Jesus from afar (Mark 14:54; John 18:15).
  - He enters the high priest's courtyard (Mark 14:54; John 18:15–16).[72]
  - Peter is warming himself in the high priest's courtyard (Mark 14:54, 67a; John 18:25).
  - Peter, confronted by a servant woman, denies Jesus (Mark 14:67–68; John 18:17).
  - Confronted by others, Peter denies Jesus a total of three times (Mark 14:69–71; John 18:25–27).

71. John does not report Jesus's response about his identity to the high priest (Mark 14:62), but Mark's "I am" might appear (or be paralleled?) instead in Jesus's "I am" response to those who came to arrest him in John 18:5–6.

72. Mark, who, like Josephus, often uses "high priest" in the plural, does not differentiate among high priestly figures; this is also a feature that storytelling might well condense, whereas the disciple in John 18:15 would know more (though whether this disciple is the beloved disciple is a matter of debate).

- The rooster crows during Peter's final denial (Mark 14:72; John 18:27; cf. Mark 14:30; John 13:38).[73]
- Members of the elite priesthood hand Jesus over to Pilate, apparently on the charge of sedition ("King of the Jews"; Mark 15:1; John 18:31, 33–35).
- Pilate, the governor, is not persuaded that Jesus is a threat (Mark 15:14; John 18:38).[74]
- Jesus answers Pilate somewhat ambivalently and then refuses to answer further (Mark 15:2, 5; John 18:36; 19:9).[75]
- Pilate offers to release Jesus, but the crowds choose Barabbas.
  - There is a local paschal amnesty practice (Mark 15:6, 8; John 18:39).
  - Pilate offers to release Jesus (Mark 15:9; John 18:39).
  - The elite priests request, or urge the crowd to request, Barabbas (Mark 15:7–15, esp. 11; John 18:40).
- Pilate has Jesus scourged (Mark 15:15; John 19:1).
- Gentile soldiers mock Jesus.
  - They place a crown of thorns on his head (Mark 15:17; John 19:2).
  - They drape a purple robe on him (Mark 15:17; John 19:2).
  - They offer a mock acclamation: "Hail, King of the Jews!" (Mark 15:18; John 19:3).
- The crucifixion:
  - Jesus is marched to Golgotha, "place of a skull" (Mark 15:22; John 19:17).
  - Jesus is crucified between two others (Mark 15:24, 27; John 19:18).
  - The titulus on Jesus's cross reads, "King of the Jews" (John 19:19; Mark 15:26).
  - The execution squad divides Jesus's garments (Mark 15:24; John 19:23).
  - A soldier raises a sponge of sour wine to Jesus's mouth (Mark 15:36; John 19:29).
  - Mary Magdalene, another Mary, and other women were at the cross (Mark 15:40, 47; John 19:25).
  - Jesus dies (Mark 15:37; John 19:30).
  - Jesus dies more quickly than was typical (Mark 15:44–45; John 19:33).
- Joseph of Arimathea:
  - Joseph requests Jesus's body from Pilate (Mark 15:43; John 19:38).

73. None of the other Gospels follow Mark's double crowing (Mark 14:30, 72); developing stories often progressively omit extraneous details.

74. I have argued that John's interpretation of Pilate's ambivalence offers a plausible approach to an enigma in Mark; see Keener, "Truth"; cf. Licona, *Differences*, 116. For Pilate finding no guilt in Jesus, compare Luke 23:4, 14, with John 18:38; 19:4, 6.

75. Though John provides more dialogue; see Keener, "Truth," cited above.

- Joseph then lays Jesus's body in a tomb (Mark 15:46; John 19:41–42).
- The anointing could not be completed because it was the preparation day before the Sabbath (Mark 15:42; 16:1; John 19:31, 42).[76]
- Followers experience the empty tomb and the risen Christ.
  - Mary Magdalene and others come to this tomb, in the vicinity of Jerusalem, early on/soon after the sabbath (Mark 16:1; Luke 24:1, 22; John 20:1–2).
  - At some point they see angels (Matt 28:5; Luke 24:4, 23; John 20:12), and they (Matt 28:9–10), or at least Mary (John 20:16), sees Jesus.
  - Mary or the women are sent with a message (Mark 16:7; Matt 28:7, 10; John 20:17) and/or report their experience (Luke 24:10, 23).
  - Peter runs and finds the tomb empty but does not yet see Jesus (Luke 24:12, 24; John 20:3–5).
- Jesus suddenly stands among the disciples and greets them with the peace blessing (Luke 24:36, most early MSS; John 20:19).
- Some do not believe (Matt 28:17; Luke 24:11, 37, 41; John 20:25, 27), but some (or the unbeliever, after seeing him) worship Jesus (Matt 28:17; Luke 24:52; John 20:28–29).
- Jesus invites the disciples to touch him, recognizing his hands (Luke 24:39; John 20:27).
- The disciples rejoice (Luke 24:41; John 20:20).
- Jesus's resurrection fulfills the Scriptures (Luke 24:44–46; 1 Cor 15:4; John 20:9).
- Jesus commissions disciples (Matt 28:18–20; Luke 24:48; John 20:22; cf. 15:27) in connection with the promise of the Spirit (Luke 24:49; Acts 1:8; John 15:26–27; 20:22; cf. Mark 13:11; Matt 28:20).
- Jesus will ultimately ascend (Luke 24:51; Rom 8:34; Heb 1:3; John 20:17).

13.3b. *The Differences*

In the same narratives we could catalog differences, probably no less extensively. Many of the variations in these accounts (such as sequencing, e.g., in the tomb encounters) fit the range of variation that appears in other ancient biographies.[77] For example, if John (or for that matter, Mark) has chrono-

---

76. Though Jesus had experienced a preburial anointing in Mark 14:8; cf. John 12:7.

77. The language of "nuanced range of variation" is also relevant for narrativizing of memories; see Kirk, *Memory*, 220, translating Welzer et al., "*Opa*," 12.

logically displaced Passover to make a point, this fits a practice observed in other ancient biographies, such as Plutarch shifting one story seven years to make a connection obvious.[78] John might develop some scenes from a core of information available to him (or depend on different memories), but in antiquity historians could develop scenes and dialogues in constructing cohesive narratives.[79]

A larger number of differences simply reflect omissions (common fare when witnesses, tradents, or authors select or condense material), sometimes (esp. in the final narratives) taking for granted that the audience already knew part of the story (e.g., John 11:1–2).[80] Oral tradition and storytelling tend to simplify narrative accounts, often omitting extraneous details,[81] and the same is true in ancient biography[82] and in memory itself.[83] John recognizes that he is offering only a sample of accounts about Jesus (20:30); he is not limited to the stories that the Synoptics chose.

Various other narrative incidents cohere in some respects with Synoptic incidents, such as:

- people demanding signs from Jesus, despite him having provided some (Mark 8:11; John 6:30; cf. 1 Cor 1:22);
- Sabbath controversies (Mark 2:24; 3:2; John 5:10, 16; 9:14, 16);
- Jesus healing someone unable to walk with a command to take up his mat (Mark 2:11–12; John 5:8–9);
- using spittle when healing (Mark 7:33), including for a blind person (Mark 8:23; John 9:6–7);

78. Licona, *Differences*, 163.

79. See Hadas, "Introduction," xx–xxi. For historians' inferences of events, including speaking, see Tacitus, *Annals* 14.57; 15.59; Quintus Curtius, *History* 3.2.11–16; 1 Macc 6:10–13; 2 Macc 3:37–39; Josephus, *Jewish War* 2.319; for reporting even internal thoughts, see, e.g., Tacitus, *Histories* 2.74; *Annals* 4.38–39; 12.4. These limited developments of information, however, differed starkly from novels, esp. the bulk of novels; see Fornara, *Nature*, 134–36; Marguerat, *Histoire*, 19–20, 25; Marguerat, *Historian*, 12–13; discussion in Keener, *Acts*, 72–77.

80. E.g., John leaves his audience hanging as to what if anything becomes of Judas (John 18:5), though our reports of Judas's death vary from Matthew to Luke to Papias, and Mark also omits Judas's fate. Similar assumptions of prior knowledge appear in other historical works, such as Xenophon's *Hellenica* (Brownson, "Introduction to *Hellenica*," x); cf. P.Mich. 202.3; Xenophon, *Cyropaedia* 7.2.15; Phaedrus, *Fables* 3.17; 5.10.10; Dio Chrysostom, *Orations* 34.3; Josephus, *Jewish Antiquities* 18.54; *Life* 412; 2 Thess 2:5.

81. Vansina, *Oral Tradition*, 172; Eve, *Behind Gospels*, 72, 97; Barber and Barber, *Severed*, 91.

82. Small, *Wax Tablets*, 194; Licona, *Differences*, 47–48, 77, 83, 109.

83. Kirk, "Nexus," 146.

- raising the dead (Matt 11:5//Luke 7:22; Mark 5:41–42; Luke 7:14–15; John 11:43–44);
- healing the member of a prominent petitioner's household at a distance (Matt 8:8–13//Luke 7:7–10; John 4:50–51);
- miraculously providing food (John 2:9; Mark 8:7–8; compare also John 21:3, 6 with Luke 5:4–7);
- having Samaritan encounters (John 4:4–42; Luke 9:52; 17:16), and so forth.

Many of the stories that John tells that are missing in the Synoptics also involve visits to Jerusalem for festivals and match details of Judean life known to us but not likely known to most of John's Diaspora audience in the 90s.[84]

One could argue that John's parallels with the Synoptics reflect his dependence on the Synoptics. This is a much-debated issue,[85] but let us for the present discussion grant such dependence, whether directly or simply (I think far more likely) from having heard them on some occasions. If this Gospel depends on or overlaps significantly with sources where we can test it, is it not reasonable to suppose that it might also depend on prior information elsewhere, not least the recollections of the beloved disciple (John 21:24)? John reworks information where we can test him, and he had no way to know what sources would survive to be tested, since there were apparently many available (Luke 1:1; John 21:25).[86] If John depends on historical tradition to such an extent, presumably he sees his work as bound somehow to information, rather than an opportunity for free invention.[87]

Comparison with Synoptic narratives suggests that such memories are imbued in this Gospel with fresh theological insights, but also that this Gospel tends to interpret memories and not mere fantasies.[88] John tells his story differently, but he is not writing a novel. He remains dependent on substantial information, much of it paralleled in the Synoptics and much of it probably in sources that we cannot now check. Indeed, due to what evidence remains

---

84. See Keener, *John*, on the relevant passages.

85. See esp. Smith, *John among Gospels*.

86. The sort of hyperbole in John 21:25 is common in ancient literature (esp. in epideictic declarations); see, e.g., Homer, *Odyssey* 3.113–17; Lysias, *Orations* 2.1, §190; Diodorus Siculus, *Library of History* 16.95.5; 1 Macc 9:22; Philo, *Abraham* 1; *Special Laws* 4.238; *Moses* 1.213; *Dreams* 2.63; Plutarch, *Malice of Herodotus* 1, *Moralia* 854F; Song Rab. 1:3, §1; Pesiq. Rab. 3:2.

87. His interest is especially in, to borrow the phrase from 1 John, the Jesus who "came in the flesh" (1 John 4:2; 2 John 7).

88. Cf., e.g., Keener, "Beheld," esp. 25.

extant, most material in most biographies written by those who knew a figure is singly attested, from Xenophon's *Agesilaus* to Nepos's *Atticus* and Tacitus's *Agricola*.[89]

13.4. Conclusion

John is a "maverick gospel";[90] he seems less interested in traditional biographic conventions than are his predecessors. Scholars are currently exploring the mysteries of John in fruitful ways that will likely produce greater understanding; for the purposes of this book, however, it seems sufficient to conclude this chapter with some brief comments.

If any extant first-century Gospel stretches the range of imperial-period biography beyond the contours traced in earlier chapters, it would be John. Some might even compare his flexibility with some earlier biographic models, such as that of Xenophon (though Xenophon may have gone further: we have less ground for certainty there).

At the same time, John is no Ps.-Callisthenes or author of the apocryphal gospels. By any standard that we have surveyed, his work remains much closer to biography than to a novel. Few if any novels would exhibit all the sorts of correspondences with other biographies noted above. Even if John falls in a different range of historical biography than, say, Luke, there is good reason to believe that this Gospel is no exception to the first-century Gospels falling in that wider category.

---

89. Multiple attestation for many accounts is below 5 percent; see Wright, "Reliability."
90. See Kysar, *Maverick Gospel*.

Part 5

Memories about Jesus:
Memories before Memoirs

Many ancient biographies depend on earlier biographies or on other written sources closer to the time of the events narrated. Apart from public annals, however, the earliest biographies inevitably depend on memories—those of the biographer, eyewitness interviewees, or those who had heard the stories. I believe that the foregoing research demonstrates that mainstream ancient biographers had historiographic intention. That is, they sought to follow ancient expectations for historiography: despite flexibility in telling their stories, they depended on information for events in ways that novels did not. I have not so far sought to address the question that is much more difficult to answer in the absence of extensive evidence—namely, how reliable were the first-generation memories?

Before memoirs, one must have memories, and the memoirs are only as valuable for historical reconstruction as the memories on which they rest.[1] Seeking to create cohesive accounts, ancient biographers sometimes imaginatively filled gaps in their information with plausible guesses, inferences, and the weakest of sources. The preference of mainstream biographers, however, was to adapt genuine information when they had it available. This context raises the question for the Gospels: would the Evangelists, writing decades after the events they narrate, have had access to much reliable information?

The focus of this book is on ancient biographies written within living memory of their subjects. Such biographies do not need to be written by eyewitnesses themselves, but they normally rested, at some remove, on memoirs or memories of those who were (see ch. 9). What might have happened to memories over the course of several decades?

---

1. Sections of the Memories chapters are adapted from Keener, "Before Biographies" (written with the present book in mind, a sort of prolegomenon to the prolegomenon). I use "memoir" in the general sense of an account based on personal knowledge or sources, not as one's autobiographic "memoirs."

Memory studies emphasize the frailty of human memory, but they also demonstrate that eyewitnesses are normally able to recount many significant episodes from the prime of their life decades after their experiences (ch. 14). Jesus was a teacher, which entails that he taught his disciples. For at least thirty years after Jesus taught them, these disciples remained in prominent roles in the church, respected even in the Diaspora.[2] While they did not formally "control" the tradition, they would be the most authoritative sources quoted by others for Jesus stories and would remain the go-to sources for evaluating what stories about Jesus were most reliable (ch. 15).

Could some of their stories, when retold secondhand or thirdhand, become garbled? We recognize even from everyday experience that such distortion happens at times, but granting the possibility of distortion, what measure of distortion should we anticipate? That is the subject of the final memory chapter (ch. 16), which addresses oral tradition and oral history. Studies of oral tradition suggest that over the course of generations collective memory condenses, conflates, and adapts its material, yet it ordinarily preserves the core of its stories. Evidence further suggests that, by the standards of such oral tradition, the time frame between Jesus's ministry and any of the first-century Gospels is quite brief.

That is, these chapters show that memory studies offer no reason to discount our earlier conclusions that the Gospels as ancient biography preserve substantial information about Jesus. Biographies from within living memory of their subject normally include stories from their subject's lives that go back to the earliest memories. In general, the core of any given story from within living memory is likelier than not to recount a genuine incident in the life of its subject. In the case of teachers, their message and the gist of even many of their sayings are likely to be correct.

By core, I mean something like the following. If disciples witnessed the raising of the widow of Nain's son (Luke 7:11–17), features they might well recall would include the locality (Nain)[3] and the raising of the widow's son

---

2. See 1 Cor 1:12; 3:22; 9:5; 15:5; Gal 1:17–19; 2:9; cf. Josephus, *Jewish Antiquities* 20.200.

3. A site that would be unknown in the Diaspora and barely known in Galilee; Josephus mentions a Nain apparently only in Idumea (Josephus, *Jewish War* 4.511, 517), although it attests the name in the region. Although Luke was not Galilean and cannot be expected to know the geography of his sources, commentators usually identify the Nain of this narrative with modern Nen or Nein (e.g., Leaney, *Luke*, 142; Marshall, *Luke*, 284), apparently near Shunem (Bovon, *Luke*, 1:268; Carroll, *Luke*, 164–65) or perhaps even abbreviating "Shunem" (Liefeld and Pao, "Luke," 144; but cf. LXX 2 Kgdms 4:8's Σουμαν [*Souman*] vs. Josh 19:18; 1 Sam 28:4; Josephus, *Jewish Antiquities* 6.327). These features would reinforce the allusions to the raising

in the midst of the burial procession. Luke would be within his rights as a historian to reconstruct Jesus's wording, to infer (based on his other knowledge) the crowds and Jesus's compassion, and to mention the gate (7:12), even if these features were not in his oral or written source (although they may have been).

Since Mark knows Jairus's name (in contrast to that of many other characters in his Gospel, e.g., in 1:40; 2:3; 3:1; 5:2), the ultimate source of the account may have been familiar with this locally prominent family (cf. 5:22). Jesus's immediate disciples (5:37) could well have remembered mourners' scorn (5:40), obviously the previously apparently dead girl responding to Jesus, walking and eating (5:41–43), and a feature as striking as Jesus touching someone presumed dead (5:41). While we normally do not expect the recollection of direct discourse, the preservation of the Aramaic command "Talitha kum!" (5:41) presumably reflects a reminiscence rather than Mark's elaboration, since Mark must translate it for his audience.[4] Details such as the witnesses' astonishment could well be in Mark's source, but neither would any of us likely begrudge him this inference.

Others will insist on a core larger or smaller for these examples, but the point is that the Evangelists normally derive the basic putative events from their sources; in the case of these illustrations, the genre leads me to expect that Luke and Mark did not invent the stories that Jesus raised this young man and woman. Nevertheless, as I have repeatedly noted, this approach does not settle all historical questions. Individual sources must still be weighed critically on their own terms, keeping in mind for example that Suetonius is happy to report any negative stories about Nero or Domitian available, and the Gospel writers adored Jesus. Some ancient stories are better attested than others; some appear to be distortions of other stories, albeit with a core shared between them.

Neither the Gospels' genre nor patterns of oral tradition offer certainty about particular passages. They do, however, offer a general default expectation to follow when other evidence does not point in a different direction, to the extent that particular Gospels cohere with their sources where we can test them. Even a general default setting provides a potentially significant way forward in what is sometimes the quagmire of historical-Jesus research.[5] In this case, I

---

at Shunem (2 Kgs 4:8, 34–36); Luke's failure to explain this point may suggest that he was unaware of this nuance already in his source.

4. Cf. Lane, *Mark*, 198; Garland, *Mark*, 223.

5. For one sober evaluation of the quagmire already a quarter century ago, see Crossan, *Historical Jesus*, xxviii.

believe that the default setting should be significantly more positive than the default skepticism embraced by some members of the guild (and far more than the popular Jesus mythers). That is, in full-length, first-century biographies within living memory of their subjects, we have more reason to trust than to reject the core of even singly attested incidents or themes in Jesus's message, where we lack other compelling arguments either way.

Chapter 14

Memory Studies

Nearly all scholars agree that Jesus was a teacher and therefore also recognize the likelihood that he had disciples. Not all scholars have been as cognizant of the implications of this role for how and what Jesus's disciples should have learned, based on the nearly universal practices of ancient pedagogy. But while ancient pedagogy will tell us what the disciples *should* have learned (ch. 15), questions still remain as to what they would have *remembered* about Jesus until elements of their testimony began being written in the sources we have extant today, or at least until it became standardized in community traditions.

14.1. Fixity and Fluidity

The question of what Jesus's disciples may have remembered invites us to explore some recent research on personal, psychological memory. (Such psychological memory differs from the longer process of oral tradition and cultural memory, namely, what happens after the memories are retold beyond the eyewitnesses, an issue addressed more fully in ch. 16.)[1]

While various scholars have offered opinions about how much Jesus's followers "could have" remembered, studies of psychological memory offer a useful control on such speculation. They suggest what we can expect of memory at its best—and at its worst. Because this area of research is continually developing, in a single chapter only introductory comments are possible; nevertheless, the research offers insights for historical reconstruction based on testimony.

One limitation of most psychological memory studies so far is that they focus on contemporary Western memories, which most scholars recognize as

---

1. One considering "eyewitnesses of Jesus" will deal with "cognitive and autobiographical approaches" (as Person and Keith, "Media Studies," 5), whereas subsequent reception and shaping of those memories turn to collective- and cultural-memory approaches.

generally less disciplined than ancient Mediterranean ones.[2] Those of us who have taught and evaluated students over multiple decades may recognize a shift in mnemonic skills even over the course of our own teaching careers. Ready access to disconnected bits of information in the wired West often deprives our memories of rigorous exercise in a manner analogous to how calculators permit our arithmetical skills to atrophy.

I will cite some examples of ancient Mediterranean memory and oral tradition in other cultures in chapters 15–16, but even the Western studies noted here offer some important insights regarding the character of recall. Although the scholars I cite here reflect a range of perspectives, they all agree on a central (and not very counterintuitive) point: memories include both fixity and fluidity.

Citing memory's frailties, some scholars dismiss as implausible the idea that the Gospels would preserve much reliable memory about Jesus. That side of the data accurately challenges our assumptions that tradents would preserve precise wording and details, matters generally of less concern in oral cultures in any case. Our long-term memory does not retain most of our experiences.

The other side of the data, though, suggests that the substance of most of what people do recall decades after the events still bears a strong resemblance to what actually happened. Despite many frailties of memory, it is not at all implausible that Jesus's disciples would have correctly remembered the core of a number of noteworthy incidents in Jesus's ministry and many of his more memorable teachings, certainly enough to fill some Gospels. The period between that ministry and the first written sources appears to be just a few decades.

Everyday assumptions about memory are usually sufficient for everyday purposes, but their precision is limited by suggestibility, susceptibility to bias, and chronological independence. Recall is rarely verbatim, except in the case of aphorisms. Still, memory is generally effective for personally significant and often multisensory events and for events frequently rehearsed. Memories significant enough to persist for five years may well persist for decades.

---

2. Cf. Galinsky, "Introduction," 17: "Ancient Rome was a memory culture par excellence"; Rhoads, "Events," 173. Cf. also the concessions in Redman, "Eyewitnesses," 179, 192–93.

14.2. Everyday Assumptions about Long-Term Memory

Most of us take for granted that, barring unusual circumstances such as amnesia, schizophrenia, or dementia,[3] we can recall key events within our own posttoddler lifetimes. We live our lives based on such assumptions.[4]

Like most other people, I normally live with such assumptions. Granted, at one time or another, I have experienced all the memory frailties mentioned in this chapter. Many memories that I have not used have faded over time; while I recall some close friends from forty years ago as if we were together in person yesterday, I have forgotten most acquaintances with whom I was not close. Having grown up with ADHD (attention deficit hyperactivity disorder), I also easily personify the stereotypical absent-minded professor.[5]

Yet I can also recall memorable incidents, information I learned, and some sermon illustrations I heard about four decades ago; I still reuse some of the jokes I heard at that time. On my fortieth-year high school reunion, a friend casually narrated to me a specific incident about me that she remembered clearly from when we were in third grade (I was age eight, about fifty years ago), and that, her husband added, she had also recounted to him. I had been humming the song to Gilligan's Island, whereupon the teacher demanded that if I was going to hum it loud enough for anyone to hear, I ought to sing it. I then sang it perfectly, she recounted. I confess that I also recall that incident (which I find embarrassing), though I have long forgotten the words to that song.[6]

As a deliberate albeit amateur memory experiment,[7] I recalled and listed more than twenty-five details from a family road trip from fifty years ago,

---

3. See, e.g., Larsen, Thompson, and Hansen, "Time," 153; Baddeley et al., "Delusions," 384, 423–24 (though cf. 427); Schacter, "Memory, Amnesia, and Dysfunction"; Koutstaal, Verfaellie, and Schacter, "Objects"; Simons et al., "Gist"; Pierce et al., "Effects"; Budson et al., "Memory."

4. Bockmuehl, *Seeing*, 170–71, observes that he has told his children stories about his great-grandmother's childhood before World War I.

5. Absent-minded professors may find encouragement from the observation that "absent-mindedness assists in preventing the memory capacity of an individual from being overwhelmed" (McIver, "Personal Memory," 54).

6. Cindy Johnson Meyerson, August 25, 2018. I had also forgotten in which elementary grade it happened. The other side of memory was also in evidence, however; most of us who traded stories there recalled details that other participants had forgotten or had forgotten details that others had remembered, and I mixed up memories of some persons with others.

7. Undertaken, even if somewhat tongue in cheek, in consideration of some oft-cited experiments by researchers on their own autobiographic memory, although theirs were far more carefully controlled than mine; see, e.g., Linton, "Memory"; Wagenaar, "My Memory" (cited in, among many others, McIver, *Memory*, 30–34).

when I was seven. I then consulted other surviving witnesses, whose testimony confirmed that a number of these memories had persisted independently over these five decades.[8] Whereas my memories from when I was seven are quite limited, my memories from when I was seventeen are abundant. For some periods in my life, I can confirm the accuracy of my recall regarding the substance of such experiences, including even conversations, because I have personal journals or letters from those periods.[9] Similarly, I carefully compared my oral interviews with my wife about her war experience with her journal.

Naturally, I recall my own memories best, but some secondhand accounts have stuck with me. Mentors at Duke University, such as Moody Smith, E. P. Sanders, and Dan Via, told us stories about their own teachers and other older scholars, a number of which I remember.[10]

I have also learned from others whose memories connected me back to a more distant past. I recall some of my grandparents' stories about the Great Depression. My dad explained to me about people and events in old photos, usually sure about their subjects. One photo was merely a generic-looking scene from a second-story window, so I wondered why anyone had ever snapped it. "That was where I yelled out that the war [World War II] had ended," he explained.[11]

Eager to learn more about a great uncle, I consulted a person in her eighties who filled me in on numerous concrete details from the 1940s, roughly

8. Esp. Gail Keener, interview, Massillon, Ohio, June 30, 2017. Naturally, we did not always recall the same details—as a child I was more prone to recall the sherbet in the freezer or my scary first experience with "hush puppies," for example—but our memories overlapped significantly and did not contradict.

9. When I do consult detailed written accounts, even decades later, they inevitably preserve details that I have forgotten; in the vast majority of cases, however, what I do recollect is fully consistent with the written accounts. Popular-level memoirs can illustrate dependence on memory in a way obviously irrelevant to pure novels. Much of the information in Keener and Keener, *Impossible Love*, comes from our journals. Under editorial constraints, I deleted roughly 45 percent of its original draft, retaining what seemed most useful to the basic thread of our stories that we chose to emphasize. On several occasions, cutting required conflation of similar scenes. The content, however, consists entirely of actual events; our source material constrained our telling in ways not necessary to a novel. Indeed, a well-written novel would be able to appeal to popular interest better than our true account by reducing the number of active characters and including far fewer toponyms and names unfamiliar to our audience.

10. I am not alone. In 2002, for example, scholars recounted their early experiences with Adolf Schlatter (d. 1938; Bockmuehl, *Seeing*, 170–71n13).

11. Exchange with John W. Keener, as he recounted many stories from his childhood (August 2–10, 2014).

seventy years ago.[12] Noting that even in the United States repeating family stories was once a common pastime, a neighbor in her nineties shared memories of family stories reaching back to the 1700s, some of which I was able to subsequently verify independently.[13] My wife, whose PhD is in women's history, has assigned students to interview seniors for oral history projects and obtain a sampling of what life was like a generation or two ago.

If Westerners, even absent-minded ones with attention deficits, remember many experiences, surely we should not expect less from individuals in cultures that value and frequently recount their reminiscences, even if those cultures often also value supplying more engaging narrative frameworks.

Simple, yes? Not quite.

14.3. Reconstructive Recollection

Everyday assumptions about memory are usually sufficient for everyday purposes, but they need to be qualified in light of memory's limitations. When we remember events, our mind reconstructs memory from various subsystems, sometimes filling in gaps with inferences, including mental elaborations and explanations fused to our memories.[14] This process can lead to errors, but overall they "are the price of having a constructive memory that can fill gaps with best guesses."[15] Like anecdotes in some ancient biographies noted earlier in the book, our piecemeal memories are linked topically rather than chronologically. Even ancient orators with phenomenal memories recognized the chronological randomness of normal recollection.[16]

To prevent our brains from overloading with useless stimuli, we forget more of the input into them than we remember. One can arrange and narrate recollections in different ways, but our brains maximize efficiency by arranging memories according to learned narrative scripts or patterns[17]

---

12. Mary Jane Bogg, phone interview, July 12, 2017.

13. She also recounted some of these stories in Gulick, *Windows*, 6–8. For passing on family tales in the modern Mediterranean world, see, e.g., Pizzuto-Pomaco, "Shame," 38, 42; Pizzuto-Pomaco, *Shame*, 35.

14. Barber and Barber, *Severed*, 33.

15. Cohen, "Overview," 389.

16. Seneca the Elder, *Controversiae* 1.pref.4.

17. Schemata can be "patterns of what usually happens in such cases" (so Bauckham, "Psychology of Memory" [3 in my preliminary version]). For the social dimension of schemata, see Eve, *Behind Gospels*, 91, 96; Schwartz, "Smoke," 24; Kirk, *Memory*, 193, 199–200,

that help us to frame and so make sense of the memories.[18] By economizing memory, such framing can be either a strength[19] or a weakness,[20] depending on the script. As memory theorist Barry Schwartz notes, "Some genres and scripts are based on more detailed and accurate information than others."[21] Often these conforming to scripts stem from the earliest memories or even direct emulation, hence not always a subsequent literary imposition on earlier tradition.[22]

Video-compression algorithms today may compress videos by reducing redundancy. Apparently less efficiently, memories include bits for which a framework is assumed rather than provided. Each time we reconstruct a memory, we form a new reconstruction of the memory that can affect subsequent recollections, a process that both fixes the recollection and may attach to it new associations.[23] No less than with the points I took for granted about everyday memory in the previous section, I find that my own experience comports with these observations as well.

In short, our memories are not videocameras. They are not straightforward, objective records of what happened, though they function well for normal, everyday purposes.[24] Instead, as we learn and exercise them in given ways, they grow and adapt organically to the frameworks we construct for them. If all this sounds academic, a concrete example may illustrate the problem.

218–19; for the interplay between memories and schemata, see, e.g., Schwartz, "Harvest," 322–23.

18. On such interpretive scripts and schemata, see, e.g., Rubin, *Memory*, 21–28, 63; Rubin, "Introduction," 4; Small, *Wax Tablets*, 196–97; Kirk, "Memory Theory," 824–26 (including information from Bonanno, "Remembering," 177); Kirk, "Nexus," 146 (noting neurological encoding into engrams); Eve, *Behind Gospels*, 89–91; Nikulin, "Introduction," 9, 27; Kesteren et al., "Schema and Novelty."

19. They can provide relevant context (e.g., in Larsen, Thompson, and Hansen, "Time," 153).

20. Since such schemata are fallible, they sometimes generate errors (Brewer, "Recollective Memory," 41, 44–45; Eve, *Behind Gospels*, 90).

21. Cf. Schwartz, "Harvest," 321. Older persons with poorer memory depend more on stereotypical frameworks than do younger persons (Mather, Johnson, De Leonardis, "Reliance").

22. Le Donne, *Historiographic Jesus*, 77.

23. Eve, *Behind Gospels*, 90–91; cf. Small, *Wax Tablets*, 199.

24. Against excessive pessimism, see, e.g., Schwartz, "Smoke," 31; Schwartz, "Harvest," 313.

14.3a. Nixing Dean's Faculties? A Neisser Reading

In a study published in 1981, Ulric Neisser compared taped conversations between John Dean and Richard Nixon with Dean's recollections of those conversations in sworn testimony.[25] Dean's biases surface in his testimony, as he inflates his own role and justifies himself where possible at Nixon's expense.[26] As we shall see below, Dean was not alone; bias commonly shapes memories.

More important, Dean's recollections blended elements of various conversations, recalling what was typical in his conversations with the president rather than specific topics covered on specific occasions.[27] As Bart Ehrman correctly observes, this fallibility is hardly surprising; very few of us would claim to remember past conversations verbatim.[28] Memory for conversations differs from episodic memory of life experiences,[29] or at least extraordinary life experiences. Dean's most frequent mistakes are timing errors; as McIver points out, Dean "reports things that did happen but that happened on occasions other than the one he is reporting."[30]

Although such observations might have surprised Dean, they would not surprise twenty-first-century psychologists. Time-slice errors that conflate occasions are among memory's most common frailties.[31] If this is true today, we might expect even more such conflations in antiquity, when even writers had to depend on their memories because they could not access multiple works simultaneously.[32] In antiquity, expectations for precision in detail thus differed from those of today.[33] Conflation of events to condense a story was a common and apparently accepted practice.[34]

---

25. Neisser, "Dean's Memory."

26. McIver, *Memory*, 19 (following Edwards and Potter, "Memory," 193); cf. Brewer, "Recollective Memory," 45.

27. Ehrman, *Before Gospels*, 144–48, esp. 146.

28. Ehrman, *Before Gospels*, 146–47.

29. Brewer, "Recollective Memory," 40–41 (challenging Neisser).

30. McIver, *Memory*, 19.

31. Rubin, "Introduction," 4; Brewer, "Recollective Memory," 41–42; McIver, *Memory*, 47, and sources cited there. Both McIver and Rubin, "Introduction," 4, note the study of time-slice errors in Brewer, "Memory for Events."

32. Pelling, "Method," 91–92; Small, *Wax Tablets*, 81, 151–53, 160–68, 176, 181–82, 185–87, 201; Derrenbacker, *Practices*, 38–39, 46–47, 54. Cf. Barker, "Reassessment," for possible contrast in early Jewish and Christian scribal practices.

33. Small, *Wax Tablets*, 4–7, 194–95, 223; for oral tradition, see Rosenberg, "Complexity," 78.

34. See, e.g., Derrenbacker, *Practices*, 94, 100–113 (albeit identifying alternating chunks

Even while pointing out such problems, however, Neisser concludes that Dean's testimony is "essentially correct, even though it is not literally faithful to any one occasion. He is not remembering the 'gist' of a single episode by itself, but the common characteristics of a whole series of events."[35] Nixon hoped that transcripts of the tapes would discredit Dean's testimony, but instead they confirmed it for what mattered: the basic substance of the testimony.[36]

There are of course significant differences between the kind of memory represented in Dean's testimony and that found in typical oral tradition.[37] The demands of legal testimony differ from those for ordinary recollection.[38] Yet Dean's chronological confusion is precisely what various lines of evidence lead us to expect for oral tradition, as well as for individual witnesses, as noted further below. Simplifying stories commonly leads to conflation in cultural memory,[39] sometimes conflating "distinct people and events into archetypal landmarks."[40]

14.3b. Memory Frailties

Some scholars cite modern Western psychological memory studies to address the variations in the gospel tradition, some of which could reflect variations in memory.[41] Frailties and variations should not, however, be inflated into massive distortion. Most memory research targets memory frailties rather than its more typical sufficiency, sometimes leaving lay interpreters of the material with a disproportionately negative perspective.[42]

Yet research commonly focuses on errors not because all memories are wrong but because, as memory researcher Gillian Cohen points out, "In ex-

---

of source material), following esp. Downing, "Redaction Criticism 1," 56; see also Licona, *Differences*, 20, 48, 52, 56, 67, 91, 95, 109.

35. McIver, *Memory*, 18, quoting Neisser, "Dean's Memory," 19–20. Compare also Bock, "Note," esp. 22, challenging as selective Ehrman's representation of Neisser.

36. Small, *Wax Tablets*, 193, quoting and concurring with Neisser.

37. See, e.g., Rubin, *Memory*, 23.

38. Bauckham, *Eyewitnesses*, 355–57.

39. Vansina, *Oral Tradition*, 171; Small, *Wax Tablets*, 200; Kirk, "Memory Theory," 825; Thatcher, *Why John Wrote*, 122; Barber and Barber, *Severed*, 115–18; Kloppenborg, "Memory," 289.

40. Thatcher, *Why John Wrote*, 118.

41. E.g., Ehrman, *Before Gospels*.

42. Schwartz, "Smoke," 22; Schwartz, "Harvest," 313; Cohen, "Overview," 389; Kirk, *Memory*, 212; Bauckham, "Psychology of Memory," citing Pillemer, *Momentous Events*, 55; cf. McIver, *Memory*, 22, and Kirk, *Memory*, 212, both citing Schacter, "Distortions," 25.

periments it is usually more informative to set task difficulty at a level where people make errors so that the nature of the errors and the conditions that provoke them can be identified."[43] William Brewer similarly points out that "laboratory studies of memory" are not always compatible with normal recollective memory.[44] This contrast also applies to longer collective memory.

Even in laboratory settings, differences in interpretation of data affect conclusions;[45] for example, as we have noted for ancient biographies (ch. 10), omissions are not actual errors.[46] David Rubin, chair of the psychology department at Duke University, likewise contrasts the stability of oral tradition with memory in laboratory contexts and even with "most everyday activity."[47]

Nevertheless, we should explore what these memory frailties are. In this section and at some other points in these closing chapters, I draw frequently, though by no means exclusively, on the extensive work of Robert McIver. Of the most common memory frailties identified in experimental settings, those most relevant for eyewitness memory are "transience, suggestibility, and bias."[48] Transience means that we forget most of what we encounter. This frailty is a survival strength, conveniently preventing normal brains from being overloaded—except when they belong to my students preparing for examinations. I address this first issue, that of transience, separately and more extensively later in this chapter. Here I turn to other memory frailties.

14.3c. Suggestibility

The second major memory frailty potentially relevant to the case is suggestibility. False memories may involve distortions "or, in extreme cases, involve

43. Cohen, "Overview," 389, adding that "the conditions of laboratory testing provoke errors and magnify their importance"; cf. Rubin, "Introduction," 4. Testing in everyday settings helps qualify and thus is complementary to experimental settings (Cohen, "Everyday Memory," 16–17).

44. Brewer, "Recollective Memory," 53–60. Cf. Goody, *Interface*, 253, for other limitations with some experimental settings.

45. Brewer, "Recollective Memory," 41.

46. Brewer, "Recollective Memory," 42.

47. Rubin, *Memory*, 7–8; cf. 28. The context of oral tradition thus contrasts, as he notes, with Bartlett's seminal laboratory studies (Rubin, *Memory*, 130–32, esp. 131; cf. also Horsley, "Patterns," 64–65; Derico, *Tradition*, 174–82; Kirk, *Memory*, 190). Even dictation of stories differs from their natural, indigenous performance contexts (Goody, *Interface*, 94–95, 172).

48. McIver, *Memory*, 21.

remembering events that never happened at all."[49] Because of suggestibility, a false memory can be injected into collective memory.[50]

Still, the events depicted normally remain authentic. Even in memory experiments, planted memories tend to lack "perceptual detail," are much more difficult to recall afterward, and are "more readily subject to correction or suppression in healthy adults."[51]

Because this frailty normally comes into play only when what is suggested seems plausible and coherent with existing memories,[52] most typical memory experiments for suggestibility, which deliberately seek to mislead on specific points, are of limited relevance for the gospel tradition.[53] Scholars offer even the example of an experiment in which memories were found as often false as true, a situation that in ordinary life would make memory so nonadaptive as to make its (and our) survival difficult to explain.[54]

Both cognitive scientists and experimental psychologists have criticized the abuse of distortion experiments as if such distortions represent the normal social settings for memory. In the words of Alan Kirk, "Experiments studying memory distortion contrive to *manufacture* it, making use of deception, lures and misleading questions . . . and the like."[55] Thus McIver asks, "What have doctored photos, misleading questions, and memorizing lists of words and all the other diverse ways that have been shown to generate false memories have in common? The answer is that they all are able to induce false memories because they share the same characteristic of plausibility."[56] For example, participants often recall the word "sleep" when given a list of words related

---

49. Schacter, "Neuropsychology," 193; cf. Spanos, *Multiple Identities*. Severe cases may involve brain damage, as in cases studied in Dab, Claes, Morais, and Shallice, "Confabulation"; Ward et al., "Recognition."

50. Cf. Redman, "Eyewitnesses," 185–88; Stock, Gajsar, and Güntürkün, "Neuroscience," 386–88; Kloppenborg, "Memory," 290, following, e.g., Schacter, "Sins," 192.

51. Bockmuehl, *Seeing*, 174, citing Loftus et al., "Manufacturing Memory"; Kensinger and Schacter, "Memories."

52. McIver, *Memory*, 60–61, 156; cf. Brewer, "Recollective Memory," 41.

53. McIver, *Memory*, 153–56.

54. Kirk, *Memory*, 212, citing the warning of Koriat, Goldsmith, and Pansky, "Psychology," 522: "If information retrieved were as likely to be correct as wrong, then memory would be totally useless."

55. Kirk, "Ehrman, Bauckham, and Bird," 91–92 (quotation from 92); Kirk, *Memory*, 211–16. Kirk cites Campbell, "Memory"; Harris, Paterson, and Kemp, "Recall"; Koriat, Goldsmith, and Pansky, "Psychology"; and Kirk's own fuller treatment of sources and the subject in Kirk, "Cognition."

56. McIver, *Memory*, 154–55.

to sleep. Such results challenge the potency of verbatim memory, but they fit expectations for gist memory. That is, we remember meaning better than wording.[57]

Memory errors often arise in the process of reconstructing a gist that is coherent.[58] Thus McIver contends that even any false collective memories that survived in the Jesus tradition may well have been consistent with the overall gist of Jesus's ministry.[59] As scholars regularly note, it is the gist and not verbatim recall that we normally should expect in any case. Gist recollection in the gospel tradition is likelier a more accurate representation of Jesus than many modern sermons about him. Given the union of both gist and adaptation in all our sources, some scholars suggest that the conventional scholarly approach of distinguishing "authentic" from "inauthentic" elements may not even reflect the best categories.[60]

Although entirely forged accounts do sometimes appear in collective memory, they seem to be very rare.[61] Today such forged accounts sometimes include unintentionally fabricated memories "recovered" in therapy,[62] but this phenomenon was not available to adjust memories in antiquity.[63]

Rather than inventing new stories, collective memory usually just shapes existing tradition to address present concerns. McIver thus concludes that any "nonauthentic Jesus tradition" in the early period would have likely

---

57. McIver, *Memory,* 60; McIver, "Personal Memory," 54; cf. already Rosenberg, "Complexity," 83.

58. McIver, *Memory,* 79. Memories often conform details to the broader gist of one's life story (Small, *Wax Tablets,* 192, citing Barclay, "Truth," 291).

59. McIver, *Memory,* 154–56. McIver, *Memory,* 181, quotes here Dodd, *Founder,* 33 (21–22 in my 1971 edition), regarding Jesus's "consistent" and "distinctive" character; see also Dunn, *Tradition,* 200, 213n3. Long-term oral tradition is not always concerned with internal consistency (Anderson, "Oral Tradition," 23).

60. Rodríguez, "Authenticating Criteria," 162–64, following Tonkin, *Narrating,* 6; cf. Rodríguez, *Structuring,* 51. The earliest Christians were in a much better position to understand what Jesus meant, in light of their early environment and the full context of the Jesus tradition, than are modern armchair scholars (see Rodríguez, "Authenticating Criteria," 164).

61. McIver, *Memory,* 157.

62. See Loftus, "Reality"; Belli and Loftus, "Pliability," esp. 172–76. See a clear case of fabrication in Wagenaar, "Memory."

63. For this reason, Bernier, *Quest,* 66, and Bauckham, "Psychology of Memory," criticize the relevance of Crook's use of tales of Satanic ritual abuse as an analogy for misremembering in the Jesus tradition (Crook, "Distortion," though Crook, unlike many more traditional Jesus scholars, is at least exploring questions of memory).

persisted only if it "had considerable congruence with what he actually did and said."[64] In a given case, it is far more probable that a memory depends on a real event.

While everyone recognizes that memory is limited, not every scholar who emphasizes that point limits memory to the same degree. For example, Dale Allison, who emphasizes memory's limitations,[65] nevertheless affirms memory for gist[66] and believes that a motivated tradent could have naturally recalled even a passage such as the Q version behind Luke 6:27–42.[67]

14.3d. Bias

The third major potentially relevant factor in memory distortion is bias. (This factor also applies to collective memory in ancient biography and history, as noted in chs. 5 and 7.) In both personal and corporate memory, "*People tend to select and pass down the view or version of events that puts themselves in the best light—and enemies in the worst light.*"[68] Personal constructed identity and bias do shape our storage, recall, and (along the way) reconstruction of memory,[69] a tendency that helps individuals to cope and adapt as their settings change,[70] but it can produce errors. Ideally, the value of fairness should restrain biased tendencies from producing deliberate distortion,[71] but even today, disputed grades, elections, and religious preferences suggest that subjectivity in interpretation is difficult to avoid. In ancient courts, the bias of loyalty distorted and sometimes falsified eyewitness testimony.[72]

---

64. McIver, *Memory*, 157, against Bultmann and Dibelius.

65. Allison, *Constructing Jesus*, 1–7; but cf. 8–9. Bauckham, "General," critiques Allison's limitations, and Allison responds in "Memory"; among other differences, they are working for different levels of certainty.

66. Allison, *Constructing Jesus*, 11–13, 28.

67. Allison, *Constructing Jesus*, 374.

68. Barber and Barber, *Severed*, 89; in social memory, see Barber and Barber, *Severed*, 89–95; Rodríguez, *Structuring*, 75–76.

69. McIver, *Memory*, 21; Barber and Barber, *Severed*, 89–95, esp. 89; note, e.g., the example of nostalgic distortion in Campbell, *Faithfulness*, 25–26; for personal constructed identity, see Bruner and Fleisher Feldman, "Narrative," 292. McIver, *Memory*, 71–75, focuses on hindsight bias (on which, see also Barber and Barber, *Severed*, 13).

70. McIver, *Memory*, 75.

71. Cf. Bernier, *Quest*, 29.

72. Pelling, *Texts*, 26. For deliberate cases, see *Rhetoric to Alexander* 15, 1432a.3–11; Dionysius of Halicarnassus, *Isaeus* 16; Keener, *Acts*, 2:1313–15.

Ideology also shapes memory.[73] While we typically do recall events that we regard as key, we remember them from our own perspectives.[74] Memory studies show that interpretive grids affect what is remembered and how it is remembered.[75] Interpretive structures are not necessarily signs of lateness, since they arise early in the recollection process; but this observation also means that no accounts, even those from eyewitnesses soon after the events, reach us in completely uninterpreted form.[76]

Thus, for example, adult siblings may confer about past events and supplement or even correct one another's memories on matters of detail, even when they recall the same events.[77] More conspicuously, a husband and wife will likely recall a recent argument from very different standpoints.[78] (They may both forget some less recent arguments.) Both may remember the argument (the event) and perhaps overlapping elements of the argument, but they may well also remember different elements and may perceive different motives or meanings behind what was said. They might even conflate what was said on this occasion with what was said on previous occasions, and certainly hear it in light of previous occasions.

Of course, if they talked matters through and came to an understanding, their perceptions may be very similar—even if their final perceptions reshape the original event into a less conflictual form than that in which it actually occurred. Conferring can reshape shared memories with fuller details and fuller standardization. Repeating the memories will standardize them further. Similarly, the dialogue with one another of first-century eyewitnesses surely influenced and adapted their memories of Jesus.

Hindsight bias reconstructs prior views in light of current information, as in, for example, "I knew that the candidate was crooked all along." Hindsight bias

73. Rodríguez, *Structuring*, 47–51. "Prejudices and stereotypes" can shape memories (Stock, Gajsar, and Güntürkün, "Neuroscience," 388).

74. Thus "events can be experienced in qualitatively different ways" (Robinson, "Perspective," 199).

75. Redman, "Eyewitnesses," 180–82; Corbin, Crawford, and Vavra, "Misremembering Emotion."

76. Bauckham, *Eyewitnesses*, 330, 334–38, 350; cf. Elder, "Narrativity," 242. Redman, "Eyewitnesses," though highly informative, seems to regard Bauckham as claiming more than he actually claims; see briefly Keener, *Acts*, 1:299n357, but esp. the balanced conclusions in McIver, "Eyewitnesses" (see esp. 535, 540–41, 545–46).

77. E.g., my wife's mother and siblings (July 16, 2008) and Aimé Moussounga (January 21, 2013) supplemented and confirmed my wife's accounts of their experiences in the Congolese war.

78. Cf., e.g., Baucom and Adams, "Communication," 170.

helps individuals adjust to new situations,[79] with cognition shaping memory, as well as the reverse. Interestingly, the Gospels do not credit the disciples with much postresurrection insight before the resurrection (e.g., Mark 8:32; 9:10; 10:37, 41; John 11:12, 16), except on occasion possibly the beloved disciple (cf. John 19:26; 20:8–9). But no one will doubt that the conviction of Jesus's exalted status stands behind the gospel tradition as we find it in the Gospels; the Evangelists believed in Jesus's resurrection, for example, before they began composing their works.

Bias is more likely to shape earlier tradition than to fabricate it.[80] Although such bias may affect which events ancient historians narrate, it does not usually mean that they fabricated the events themselves. They often tried to compensate for eyewitnesses' potential biases, though of course they had their own.[81] Thucydides complained about the partisan character of some recollections but still believed that he could provide a reasonably accurate account by building on common elements among these sources.[82]

Although we typically employ the term "bias" pejoratively, in its broader usage it simply means a perspective, which all interpreters have. By its very nature, memory has to be selective and perspectival. Even what we call memory "distortion" is thus not always negative, producing historical revisionism only in its more extreme form.[83]

14.3e. Time Zone Out: Chronological Conflations

Another memory frailty, highlighted above in the case of John Dean, is the lack of accurate chronological connection for memories. Individual memory usually preserves episodes, a familiar memory form for personal-event memories, piecemeal, organizing them interpretively rather than chronologically.[84] Although episodic memory may preserve location and other

79. McIver, *Memory*, 75; on hindsight bias more fully, see 71–75; Barber and Barber, *Severed*, 13.

80. McIver, *Memory*, 158–60. He cites here Schwartz, *Forge*, 293–312; Schwartz, *Post-heroic Era*, 219–68.

81. Byrskog, *Story*, 176–79. Against counting a problem already compensated for, see, e.g., Breggen, "Scale."

82. Thucydides, *History* 1.22.2–3.

83. Le Donne, *Historiographical Jesus*, 50–52 (preferring the more neutral label "refraction" to "distortions").

84. Thatcher, *Why John Wrote*, 113–15; Bauckham, *Eyewitnesses*, 326, 333, 344; cf. Brewer, "Recollective Memory," 52; Allison, *Constructing Jesus*, 5. For topical associations, semantic substitutions, schematization according to relevance, etc., see Kloppenborg, "Memory," 289

elements, the timing of events normally must be reconstructed from other memory cues rather than simply retrieved from memory.[85] Memory often thus conflates experiences that are similar.[86]

As I shall discuss in chapter 16, long-term cultural memory also usually collapses chronology.[87] Such lack of precise chronology and conflation of "related" events probably disturbs modern readers more than it did ancient ones. As noted in chapter 5, the gospel tradition's contemporaries did not expect chronological arrangement for the anecdotes in most biographies.[88]

Not surprisingly, the same pattern also appears to apply broadly to both the gospel tradents and the Evangelists. As is obvious to anyone who compares the Gospels in a synopsis, the Evangelists do not always follow a set sequence of episodes or retain Jesus's sayings in their received frameworks. (For example, to pick a few examples at random, one may compare the varying contexts of Matt 6:9–13// Luke 11:2–4; Matt 7:7//Luke 11:9; Matt 7:13–14//Luke 13:24; Matt 8:11//Luke 13:29.)[89]

Rearranging material, for example, by setting sayings in new contexts, can change their application,[90] but such a practice was not at all limited to the Gospels. Ancient composition practices presumed such rearrangement. Rhetorical handbooks demonstrate that writers inserted existing sayings freely into existing narratives as a matter of arrangement, not considering it a matter of fabrication.[91] Unlike annals and most material in histories, ancient biographies also often diverged from chronological sequence, especially when they had literary reasons to do so.[92] Indeed, their frequent dependence on episodic recollections made precise chronology neither possible nor expected.

(here following Schacter, Norman, and Koutstaal, "Neuroscience," 294; and Schacter and Addis, "Neuroscience," 778).

85. See Larsen, Thompson, and Hansen, "Time," esp. 153–54; Wagenaar, "Memory," 187.

86. Kirk, "Memory," 166; Kloppenborg, "Memory," 289.

87. E.g., in periods before the floating gap, Vansina, *Oral Tradition*, 24, 122, 173–88, esp. 176; Bailey, "Tradition" (*ExpT*), 365; Barber and Barber, *Severed*, 115–17.

88. E.g., Stanton, *Preaching*, 119–21; Aune, *Environment*, 31–34, 63–64; on the Gospels, cf. Augustine, *Harmony of the Gospels* 21.51.

89. Commentators rightly point out that Jesus probably reused the same sayings on multiple occasions (cf. Dunn, *Tradition*, 56, 281), but such explanations go only so far, in view of the limited range of material in the Synoptics.

90. With, e.g., Kloppenborg, "Memory," 304. Some sorts of teaching, however, including many proverbs, were meant to be applied in diverse settings.

91. See Theon, *Progymnasmata* 4.73–79; cf. 5.388–441.

92. See, e.g., Aune, *Environment*, 31–34, 63–64; Stanton, *Preaching*, 119–21; Thorburn, "Tiberius"; esp. the concrete cases in Licona, *Differences*, 32–33, 47, 50–51, 89–91, 110 (with reference to the Gospels on 136, 163, 185–96).

14.3f. What Such Limitations Mean

We remember within the framework of our own perspectives—whether individually or as communities—which suggests one of the limits of memory. This acknowledgment is not very controversial; no one, including those who attribute the Evangelist's perspectives to divine inspiration, doubts that the Evangelists (or their tradents) wrote from their own particular perspectives.

How we argue from here depends largely on our goal. If our goal is to show that memory is far less dependable than people commonly assume in daily life, we can appeal to many Western studies of psychological memory to demonstrate memory's limitations. If, conversely, we are trying to reconstruct from early collective memory a picture of historical events to the most probable extent possible, we will try to sift the evidence of memory for the sorts of matters people actually should have remembered.

The former goal is useful in Gospels studies when challenging assumptions of verbatim recall and the like, rare as those assumptions are among scholars (apart from the case of particular literary forms such as concise proverbs). The latter goal is useful when working for historical reconstruction and combatting extreme historical skepticism, which unfortunately does flourish in some academic circles. Most scholars fall on the continuum between these poles.

Although some doubt the value of multiple attestation for individual sayings, most accept the value of this criterion (in the form of "recurrent attestation") for major themes or events.[93] Historical-Jesus scholars widely agree on some basic facts about Jesus: for example, Jesus had twelve key disciples, probably related to his intentions for a kingdom renewal of God's people; he was executed by Romans on a cross after conflict with elites in Jerusalem; and many of his followers believed that they saw him alive from the dead a few days after his execution. (See further examples in ch. 1.)

That is, most of the basic emphases of the Gospels are not much in dispute; questions arise primarily concerning the details that fill out this picture. While the limitations of historical method do not allow scholars to assert such specific details with the same level of assurance as the overall picture, there is good historical reason to believe that even the picture of many particular events or themes goes back to Jesus and his immediate circle of disciples. Their memories would not need to be perfect to recall the substance of key events

---

93. See, e.g., Tuckett, "Sources and Methods," 134; Holmén, *Covenant Thinking*, 33–34; Allison, *Constructing Jesus*, 16–23; Allison, "Criteria," 22–26; Keener, "Epitome," 10–11.

and teachings that they began retelling soon after Jesus's departure, as the rest of Jesus's movement looked to them for leadership in his name.

14.4. Verbatim Is Verboten

Politicians are not the only people who sometimes misrepresent their detractors' positions. Hardly anyone, including the scholars most often accused of it, claims that the memories of Jesus's teachings in the Gospels are verbatim recollections.[94] As noted in chapter 11, it is obvious that the Evangelists themselves did not pretend to capture Jesus's words verbatim; one need only compare, for example, Matthew's fairly regular reference to "the kingdom of heaven" with Mark's regular "kingdom of God."[95] Or one may compare Luke's varied wording for words spoken in the scenes that Luke himself repeats.[96] Early Christians often paraphrase the Old Testament freely to communicate what they understand to be its message (cf., e.g., Joel 2:28 in Acts 2:17).[97] Why should we expect verbatim quotation of Jesus?

Of course, in the most technical sense, *none* of Jesus's words in the Gospels purport to be precisely his exact words, except for Mark's brief quotations of him in Aramaic.[98] Anyone who claims that the Gospels consistently offer Jesus's words verbatim (perhaps as an untested theological assumption) has simply never read them closely;[99] it is simply impossible for an honest person

94. See Luther (in Kolb, *Word*, 87); Bock, "Words," 75–77; Bock, "Note," 21 (arguing for *ipsissima vox*, summarizing, and allowing for variations); Bauckham, "Response," 229, 245; Eve, *Behind Gospels*, 38–39 (regarding Gerhardsson), 88–89 (regarding Bauckham), 115 (regarding Dunn); with respect to speeches in Acts, see, e.g., Bruce, *Speeches in Acts*, throughout; cf. Bruce, "Speeches Thirty Years After"; with respect to oral tradition generally, Finnegan, *Oral Poetry*, 139–40. Quotation marks are modern (Williams, *Trust*, 98, cites Houston, *Characters*, 197–200).

95. Cf. similar examples in other ancient biographies in ch. 11.

96. Compare Luke 24:47–49 with Acts 1:4–8; Acts 9:5–6 with 22:8, 10; 9:15–16 and 22:10 with 26:16–18; 10:4–6 with 31–32 and 11:13–14; 10:14 with 11:8; cf. also John 13:10–11.

97. Indeed, many Jewish contemporaries apparently *required* paraphrase of the Ten Commandments rather than reciting them verbatim (Josephus, *Jewish Antiquities* 3.90).

98. As in Mark 5:41; 7:34; 14:36. Nor can anyone with even a rudimentary understanding of translation between languages expect completely word-for-word translation; translation requires gist, whereas insistence on the original text often lends itself to verbatim recitation more than grasping the meaning, and insistence on equivalent words produces nonequivalent phrasing and obscures semantic units.

99. Agreeing with, e.g., Sanders, *Paul*, 211n22, and many others, e.g., Kelber, *Gospel*, 27, 67.

to read many parallel Gospel accounts side by side and conclude that they all are word-for-word the same. (It would not make much sense to have separate Gospels if they had to be identical.)

Parallel Gospel accounts may use different wording and sometimes vary in storytelling details precisely because ancient Christians understood, far better than do their sometimes inflexible textual descendants, that we usually neither have nor need Jesus's precise words. What matters more is the substance of his acts and teachings—the gist, the sense. And we have very good reason to believe that this is what the Gospels offer us, though some of the Evangelists (such as John) may develop their understanding of that gist more extensively than others.

14.4a. Verbatim Recall Is Very Rare

Not only in the Gospels or in ancient practice must we expect some flexibility. It characterizes human memory in general. Paraphrase, substitution of synonyms, as well as abbreviation and conformity to one's interpretive grid are far more common than verbatim recall, especially for narratives.[100] Wording is rarely preserved verbatim, especially in long-term memory, but central images and concepts are more stable.[101] Memory usually preserves the gist of events it includes,[102] which is all that ancient readers of biographies would ask.[103]

Different subsystems in the brain process different types of memory. Gist memory, encoding meaning, begins forming only a fraction of a second sooner than verbatim memory, but verbatim memory decays much faster.[104] Gist memory focuses on meaning more than on precise wording. Thus, for exam-

---

100. See here Kloppenborg, "Memory," 291, following helpfully DeConick, "Memory"; cf. Person and Keith, "Media Studies," 11, following Carr, *Formation*, 33. Cf. again Kloppenborg, "Memory," 318: "The Jesus tradition was [likely] condensed, schematized, paraphrased and occasionally elaborated in the course of transmission."

101. See Kloppenborg, "Memory," 291 (again summarizing DeConick, "Memory").

102. Bauckham, *Eyewitnesses*, 327, 333–34, 345; Allison, *Constructing Jesus*, 11–13; Kloppenborg, "Memory," 289, 293–94.

103. Vatri, "Writing," 770–71, shows that ancient writers could distinguish gist memory of texts, including the sequence of their topics, from verbatim memorization of their precise words (citing Aristophanes, *Knights* 346–50; Plato, *Menexenus* 236b7–c1; Alcidamas, *Sophists* 18–19; Cicero, *On the Orator* 2.359; Quintilian, *Orator's Education* 11.2.8).

104. McIver, *Memory*, 61–62, noting, e.g., Brainerd, "Theory," 220; McIver, "Gist Memory," 157.

ple, high comprehenders of material are no better than low comprehenders at verbatim memory, but they are better at gist memory.[105]

Although speeches are a special case, it is noteworthy that where their sources ended, ancient historians simply composed speeches with as much verisimilitude for the speaker and occasion as possible.[106] They did so partly because of the narrative demands of ancient historiography, but it is also relevant that ancient historians recognized that neither they nor their informants would remember speeches verbatim.[107] (Consider how many speeches *you* recall word for word after hearing them just once.)[108] Historians themselves sometimes were even explicit about disavowing verbatim reports.[109] Ancient writers also reported conversations or dialogue according to their gist rather than trying to capture exact wording.[110]

In contrast to historians' reconstructed speeches from the past, collections of teachings might be more careful to preserve a teacher's content and even style,[111] since the content of the teacher's message was normally the point of the collection. This latter observation is relevant for the Synoptic tradition, but teachings remain subject to the general limitations of verbatim memory.

In all ancient historical work, the primary interest was the gist more than precise wording.[112] Historians necessarily employed standards of accuracy appropriate to memory rather than to recordings.[113] Until the nineteenth century, most historians, including all ancient historians, were storytellers who wanted to engage their audiences by how they communicated their stories.[114]

---

105. Small, *Wax Tablets*, 195, following Baddely, *Memory*, 138–39.

106. With, e.g., Horsley, "Speeches," 609; Ehrman, *Introduction*, 133–34; Balch, "Ἀκριβῶς," 244; Small, *Wax Tablets*, 191–92, 206–9.

107. Thucydides, *History* 1.22.1–2; Walbank, *Speeches*, 4; in later philosophic lives, Eunapius, *Lives* 484. Alleged exceptions (Pliny, *Letters* 2.3.3) were rare.

108. Ancient audiences probably recalled more than we do, because speeches were themselves noteworthy events (Gempf, "Speaking," 261) and usually fit preexisting rhetorical frames.

109. Marincola, "Speeches," 120, citing, e.g., Polybius, *Histories* 18.11; Sallust, *Catiline's War* 50.5; Livy, *History* 37.45.11; Arrian, *Alexander* 5.27.1; Tacitus, *Histories* 1.15–16 (note "to this effect," LCL 1:27, 33); *Agricola* 29.4.

110. Small, *Wax Tablets*, 202–6.

111. See, e.g., Epictetus, *Discourses* 1.pref; contrast Epictetus's freer adaptation in *Encheiridion*. For recollections of a teacher's style, cf. also Porphyry, *Life of Plotinus* 3.

112. Small, *Wax Tablets*, 192, 195, 202, giving the example of Plato on 205; also 311n94, quoting Pelling, "Truth," 36.

113. Small, *Wax Tablets*, 223.

114. Bauckham, "Response," 247.

Arguing that the Evangelists and other ancient biographers or historians worked from information is thus not meant to suggest that they rigidly limited themselves to verbatim citations.

Ancient writers, who often had prior texts, had to decide whether to paraphrase their written sources or to repeat their material verbatim.[115] Yet beyond at most one written source open at a time, they normally could produce only the gist of their sources because limitations of manuscript retrieval meant that they needed to rely on memory.[116] Nor had their predecessors in the ancient Near East expected verbatim reproduction of texts; "The reproduction of the sense in the approximate wording was all they aimed at."[117] Variation also was often deliberate.[118] Thus, for example, Phaedrus feels free to adapt Aesopic fables for aesthetic reasons, meanwhile seeking to keep to the *spirit* of Aesop.[119] Short dialogues could be redacted to fit collections more neatly.[120]

14.4b. Except for Exceptions . . .

Without written texts, fully verbatim recall of any substantial body of material is nearly impossible, which naturally makes it quite rare[121] (though scholars note some exceptions).[122] It can occur and is attested in societies where literacy exists as a control,[123] sometimes even among persons who are them-

---

115. Derrenbacker, *Practices*, 44, 52 (noting Dionysius of Halicarnassus, *On Literary Composition* 6).

116. See Pelling, "Method," 92; Small, *Wax Tablets*, 81, 129, 151–55, 167–68, 176, 181–82, 185–87, 223; Derrenbacker, *Practices*, 38–39, 47, 96–97. For proposed exceptions in the Jewish scribal tradition, see Barker, "Reassessment"; cf. earlier Cadbury, Foakes-Jackson, and Lake, "Writing History."

117. Gordon, *Near East*, 107.

118. For historians' frequent preference for variation, see Aune, *Environment*, 125; stylistic preferences for variation in Aulus Gellius, *Attic Nights* 1.4; 2.5.1; Cicero, *On the Orator* 46.156–57; *Letters to Friends* 13.27.1; Nock, "Vocabulary," 137; Anderson, *Glossary*, 53–54, 114; examples in, e.g., Xenophon, *Anabasis* 5.1.8–10; *Cyropedia* 3.1.36, 41; Lee, "Translations: Greek," 776–77.

119. Phaedrus, *Fables* 2, prol. 8.

120. Cf., e.g., the redactional structure of m. 'Abot 2:9.

121. Finnegan, *Oral Poetry*, 140; Ong, *Orality*, 56–57; Goody, *Interface*, 86–91, 168, 180; Rubin, *Memory*, 7, 319; Small, *Wax Tablets*, 7, 192; McIver, *Memory*, 120; see further Hunter, "Recall."

122. See Finnegan, *Oral Poetry*, 73–86, 142; Finnegan, *Literacy*, 90, 158, 166–67, 172–73 (although she defines accuracy more generally than do her detractors); Ong, *Orality*, 61–63; Byrskog, *Teacher*, 323–24; Goody, *Interface*, 176; Anderson, "Oral Tradition," 40. On Ong, see, e.g., Lumpp, "Ong"; on Goody, see Person, "Goody"; on Finnegan, see Eve, "Finnegan."

123. Ong, *Orality*, 56–57; cf. Goody, *Interface*, 189.

selves illiterate.[124] Early Christianity did flourish in a culture that included writing.[125] Even such a context does not entail, however, that witnesses would preserve information verbatim.

Variations in the Gospels themselves, already noted, show that Jesus's followers did not insist on preserving all his teaching verbatim. Such a requirement could have been difficult even in a society with much wider literacy. Memory is very rarely verbatim. The disciples' role involved remembering more than memorization.[126]

There are, however, some exceptions to the lack of verbatim memory. Aphorisms (short, pithy sayings such as proverbs) are typically preserved in verbatim memory.[127] (In English, one might think of, for example, "Haste makes waste," "Silence is golden," or, "Crap, my screen just froze!") They also are fairly durable in long-term oral tradition; being memorable, proverbs can persist widely even far beyond the duration of living memory relevant to the first-century Gospels.[128] (Thus scholars often suggest that some extracanonical sayings attributed to Jesus in the second century may be authentic—though we rarely know which of the sayings qualify.)[129] Incidental written sources attest the oral preservation of some proverbs over a wide geographic area for more than one thousand years.[130] Likewise, in Middle Eastern culture even today, a number of Arabic works, inaccessible to most Western NT scholars, attest the current circulation of *thousands* of proverbs.[131] Preserving proverb-like sayings of Jesus within living memory should not have been a herculean task.

Aphorisms constitute the "literary form most frequently attributed to Je-

---

124. Cf. Lord, *Singer*, 137. For Greco-Roman antiquity, see Byrskog, *Teacher*, 324, and the sources noted there.

125. Byrskog, *Teacher*, 324. Byrskog recognizes Mark and at least parts of Q as written sources employed by Matthew (337–38).

126. Kelber, *Gospel*, 59, 197, highlighting Mark 8:18.

127. McIver, *Memory*, 176–80, here 176, 180; McIver, "Gist Memory," 157; more extensively, McIver and Carroll, "Experiments"; McIver and Carroll, "Characteristics."

128. Thus, e.g., Bauckham, *Eyewitnesses*, 284, citing Vansina, *Oral Tradition*, 51.

129. See, e.g., Jeremias, *Unknown Sayings*; Hofius, "Sayings," 336–60; cf. Charlesworth and Evans, "Agrapha," 483–91.

130. McIver, *Memory*, 176–77n12, citing Dundes, *Writ*, 9–10, on a proverb independently attested in fifth-century-BCE Egypt, an Arab manuscript from 1127 CE, "Serbia in 1885, in India in 1920, and in Kurdistan in 1937." On Dundes, cf. Mieder, "Dundes."

131. Bailey, "Tradition" (*Themelios*), 6–7; Bailey, "Tradition" (*ExpT*), 365; cf. Bailey, "Oral Tradition," 41. One work that he cites, collecting six thousand proverbs, is that of 'Isa 'Atallah, *Qalu fi al-Mathal: Mowsu'ah fi al-Amthal wa al-Hikam al-Sa'ira (The Proverb Says: Encyclopedia of Current Proverbs and Wisdom Sayings)* (Bethlehem, 1985).

sus."[132] Unless Jesus did not really teach very often, the Gospels' brevity suggests that Jesus's disciples even cumulatively did not recall all his aphorisms. Nevertheless, what we know about aphorisms suggests that the ones they did remember would likely have been remembered fairly accurately.[133]

To preserve material verbatim, one must deliberately rehearse material until it becomes part of long-term memory.[134] Yet, given the pervasive ancient practice of rote learning of such sayings (see ch. 9), Jesus's disciples would likely have been able to recall many of Jesus's aphorisms in forms close to those in which he gave them.[135] Aphorisms were a common rhetorical form used by Jewish sages, which supports the suggestion that some of Jesus's sayings would have been remembered and circulated in such a form.[136]

The Evangelists apparently understood the forms of material with which they were working and exercised freedom to adapt wording more with some kinds of material than with others. Thus when we compare, for example, the Evangelists' respective treatment of particular parables, we find gist relationships, as expected for stories.[137] The point usually remains stable, although the wording may vary.[138] Comparing the Gospels confirms that the Evangelists often preserved aphorisms in a form closer to verbatim than is the case with their other material, probably reflecting wider practice regarding aphorisms.[139]

14.5. Functional though Fallible

Our memories are fallible, but that does not mean that they are nonfunctional. A degree of fallibility no more necessarily equates to general unreliability than do the limitations of language underscored by deconstructionists make language inadequate for ordinary communication. This functionality often

---

132. Aune, "Aphorisms," 211, noting a similar observation already in Justin, *1 Apology* 14.5.

133. They are typically recalled "accurately or . . . *not at all*" (McIver, *Memory*, 176).

134. McIver, *Memory*, 167.

135. McIver, *Memory*, 180. For some material preserved in close form in antiquity, Byrskog, *Teacher*, 324, cites Gerhardsson, *Memory*, 123–30; Riesner, *Lehrer*, 441–43; Harris, *Literacy*, 30–33.

136. As in, e.g., Proverbs, Sirach, and Pirke Aboth; cf. Vermes, *Jesus the Jew*, 27.

137. McIver, *Memory*, 171–76 (esp. 171).

138. McIver, *Memory*, 174. Of course, for those lacking direct knowledge of the stories, arrangement can affect the point envisioned (contrast, e.g., Mark 4:21 with Matt 5:15; Mark 4:22 with Matt 10:26//Luke 12:2), though usually even floating logia carry the same general punch (compare Mark 9:43 with Matt 5:30; 18:8).

139. McIver, *Memory*, 177.

prevails beyond individuals; present needs shape collective memory, but that memory normally depends on genuine experience, not pure fabrication.[140]

14.5a. Memory Usually Refers to Something

Historical data can constrain many excesses of bias;[141] as Schwartz puts it, *"Reality counts more than bias in the remembering of most events most of the time."*[142] Thus memory in the real world is generally successful for ordinary tasks,[143] especially "considering how grossly it is overloaded."[144] Even in the modern West, most of our memories are substantially referential.

Some scholars contend that current research even renders superfluous older debates between proponents of careful memory in oral tradition and those who favor re-creation; "memorization using constraints and re-creation within constraints produce much more similar results."[145]

While our imaginations do affect how we reconstruct memories,[146] normal human memories do not usually confuse our own experiences with fictional ones. For example, I fairly regularly dream vividly and in color and often record these dreams in my journal,[147] yet I do not normally confuse them with incidents I have experienced in real life.

McIver contends that memory studies should lead us to expect inaccuracy in no more than "20 percent of the details" of eyewitness reports behind the gospel tradition, also that such errors would not negate substantial memory.[148] Moreover, even these details "are almost always consistent with the broader picture of what actually happened, even if, strictly speaking, they are errors of detail."[149] While the 20 percent estimate may be debated (depending largely

140. McIver, *Memory*, 158–60, esp. here 160, following Schwartz, *Forge*, 293–312; Schwartz, *Post-heroic Era*, 219–68.

141. Bosworth, *Arrian*, 63–64; Larsen, Thompson, and Hansen, "Time," 153.

142. Schwartz, "Smoke," 21, emphasis his.

143. Bauckham, "Psychology of Memory," citing Neisser and Libby, "Remembering Experiences," 318; Pillemer, *Momentous Events*, 55; Hoffman and Hoffman, "Memory Theory," 282.

144. Cohen, "Overview," 389, cited in Bauckham, "Psychology of Memory."

145. Rubin, *Memory*, 293, on ballads.

146. See the helpful survey of evidence in Ehrman, *Before Gospels*, 89–94.

147. Against Hume, imagination can sometimes appear more vivid than reality; see Brewer, "Recollective Memory," 27; cf. Rubin, "Introduction," 5.

148. McIver, "Eyewitnesses," 545. The 20 percent figure might be low, based on a single study.

149. McIver, "Eyewitnesses," 545–56.

on a single study), most scholars agree that, in general and for the purposes at hand, memory is more reliable than unreliable.[150]

Were memory not dependable at all, we could never trust the substance of memoirs. Already in the second century the Gospels were viewed as "memoirs" (ἀπομνημονεύματα, *apomnēmoneumata*) of the apostles.[151] We regularly learn from modern memoirs, despite their biases and imperfections; why should we dismiss ancient ones? As N. T. Wright puts it, Jesus impacted people's memories no less than do other significant figures: "Just as the friends of C. S. Lewis still bring out books of reminiscences about the great man forty or fifty years after his death, and people who worked with Winston Churchill during the war still dine out on their memories of his temper, his wit and his prodigious intake of alcohol."[152]

Of course, scholars debate how close the Gospels are to apostolic testimony, which adds a remove to the concept of "memoirs"—thus the need for chapter 15. But before memories can be passed on, they must be remembered to begin with. What sorts of memories do eyewitnesses usually preserve?

---

150. See Allison, *Constructing Jesus*, 8n46.

151. See, e.g., Justin, *1 Apology* 66; 67; *Dialogue with Trypho* 100–107, esp. 103.8; 106.3 (with Stanton, *New People*, 62–63; Abramowski, "Memoirs"; Kennedy, "Source Criticism," 136; Bockmuehl, *Seeing*, 185; Bird, *Gospel*, 250–53, 280; cf. discussion in Robbins, *Teacher*, 62–67). Cf. perhaps Papias, frag. 3.16 (Holmes; Eusebius, *Ecclesiastical History* 3.39.1), if Papias's "Matthew" is our Q (e.g., Filson, *History*, 83; Hill, *Matthew*, 23–27, 53; Bruce, *Documents*, 40; Trevijano Etcheverría, "Obra"; Edwards, "Genre," 55; cf. Hagner, *Matthew*, xliv, citing also Schleiermacher, T. W. Manson, and M. Black; rejected by, e.g., Jeremias, *Theology*, 38). Papias's *logia* could refer to something dominated by sayings (such as Q), fitting common usage (see, e.g., BDF), and explaining the contextual contrast with Mark if (and Eusebius's selectivity with Papias leaves this uncertain) his treatment of Matthew followed in the original (Papias, frag. 3.14–16; but cf. Kok, "Papias"); but the term may not be used so narrowly in Papias, frag. 3.1, 15; 5.1; 6.3; cf. Stanton, *New People*, 117n1. Such "memoirs" should not be confused with the later (esp. fifth- and sixth-century) genre of apostolic memoirs, fresh interpretations of the Jesus tradition; see, e.g. (from citations by Niklas, "Gospel of Peter," 4), Suciu, *Apocryphon*; Broek, *Apocryphon*.

152. Wright, *Faithfulness*, 649. Ancient historiographically oriented writers also consulted memoirs; see, e.g., Polybius, *Histories* 12.25e.1; Plutarch, *Demosthenes* 5.5; Laistner, *Historians*, 35; earlier, on Xenophon's memoirs of Socrates, despite their limitations, cf. Kennedy, "Source Criticism," 137; Hägg, *Biography*, 23–30. For Cicero's memoirs, see Cicero, *Letters to Atticus* 2.1. History today takes into account impacts and "history of effects," which can often be explained only through the events that initiate them (Le Donne, *Historiographic Jesus*, 75), an idea developed by Dunn (*Perspective*, 15-34, esp. 29; cf. Piovanelli, "Authority"; Wright, *Faithfulness*, 649; for limitations in this approach, cf. Schröter, "Begründer"); one cannot explain early Christianity without Jesus.

14.5b. Kinds of Memories Preserved

We generally recall memories that are memorable—that is, unusual and emotionally charged personal experiences that we have shared with others and that are matters of great interest to us.[153] People are not apt to recall everyday events such as conversations that lack evident long-range significance. Memory assimilates matters that happen regularly, focusing instead on experiences that are more distinctive.[154] We are thus more likely to remember important or unusual experiences.[155] I do not remember what I ate for lunch last Tuesday, but I remember that my Doktorvater, Moody Smith, and my physical father, John Keener, died within hours of each other.[156] I do not remember which pages I was typing a month ago, but I recall my unpleasant confrontation with a US consular official in Kinshasa in 2008. As Dale Allison observes, memory can be especially reliable when handling atypical events that one personally participated in, found mentally engaging, experienced as emotionally intense, and then later rehearsed.[157]

We are most apt to remember personally relevant and emotionally charged memories,[158] though emotion can distort recall of events as well as impress them in one's memory as significant.[159] Emotion helps imprint memories by

---

153. See here also Bauckham, *Eyewitnesses*, 330–35.

154. For the memorability of distinctive events, see Brewer, "Recollective Memory," 50; see also Conway, "Autobiographical Knowledge," 81, though his approach is highly constructivist (cf. 67, 76, 90), as the volume's editor observes (Rubin, "Introduction," 6). Constructiveness per se does not equate to distortion (see Kirk, *Memory*, 213).

155. Bauckham, *Eyewitnesses*, 331; cf. Redman, "Eyewitnesses," 182–83; Galinsky, "Introduction," 18. On the neuroscience of novelty in memory formation, cf. Kesteren et al., "Schema and Novelty"; Otmakhova et al., "Loop."

156. May 10, 2016.

157. Allison, *Constructing Jesus*, 9n46. Allison urges caution rather than "hyperskepticism"; he doubts that the disciples were "amnesiacs" (9n47).

158. For emotionally charged events, see Rubin, "Introduction," 3; Christianson and Safer, "Emotional Events," 219, 237–38; Pillemer et al., "Memories of College," 336; Bauckham, *Eyewitnesses*, 331–32, 492–505; Redman, "Eyewitnesses," 184; Kirk, *Memory*, 218–19; McIver, *Memory*, 33, citing Hulse et al., "Arousal," 73–90; Otani et al., "Memory," 23–42.

159. Eve, *Behind Gospels*, 155. Depression can focus recall on negative events (Williams, "Depression," 244), trauma may interfere with recall (Christianson and Safer, "Emotional Events," 219), even regarding details of unrelated events (Williams, "Depression," 245), and emotion can concentrate on a particular element of an event while detracting from recall of other details (Rubin, "Introduction," 3); cf., e.g., the distracting presence of a weapon in McIver, *Memory*, 11.

creating multiple associations;[160] ancient rhetoricians recognized and even played on this feature of memory.[161] (We recall emotional events themselves better than the emotions experienced during the events.)[162] The veridicality of "flashbulb memories," often connected with events learned secondhand through the media, has generated greater criticism,[163] but such experiences (esp. focused on the contexts in which one learned of a more public or other event) differ from typical personal experiences.[164]

Personal-event memories may even include a respected mentor's words that had a significant impact on one's life.[165] Memory theorist David Pillemer notes that memorable "personal life episodes are generally true to the original experience, although specific details may be omitted or misremembered and substantial distortions do occasionally occur."[166]

Because narrative and sensory memory represent distinct subsystems, experiences impressed on multiple senses (e.g., sight, sound, and smell) also are more memorable.[167] This multisensory reinforcement of memory is one reason that we are more apt to remember our own experiences than merely those we have heard about from others. We reconstruct memory based on

---

160. Stock, Gajsar, and Güntürkün, "Neuroscience," 379–80; cf. Harkins, *Reading*, 183–84, 187.

161. See *Rhetorica ad Herennium* 3.22; Galinsky, "Introduction," 17.

162. Christianson and Safer, "Emotional Events," 238.

163. See Allison, *Constructing Jesus*, 7n40; Redman, "Eyewitnesses," 184; Slade, "Reports"; though cf. Brewer, "Recollective Memory," 39–43, 47–51; Hirst et al., "Follow-Up"; Gandolphe and El Haj, "Memories" (citing negative emotion); recent work brought to my attention by Christopher Chandler, in Lanciano, Curci, and Semin, "Determinants"; Kraha and Boals, "Negative"; in cases of trauma, cf. Stock, Gajsar, and Güntürkün, "Neuroscience," 384. Rehearsal stimulated by emotional intensity may play a direct role in clear flashbulb memories (Tinti et al., "Processes").

164. Brewer, "Recollective Memory," 50; Tinti et al., "Processes."

165. McIver, *Memory*, 52. Cf. also, e.g., Pillemer et al., "Memories of College," 319.

166. Pillemer, *Momentous Events*, 59, quoted in Bauckham, "Psychology of Memory."

167. See Pillemer, *Momentous Events*, 53, 99, 100–102, 138, 147, 164, often considering traumatic experiences (though some distinguish traumatic from other emotional experiences; see discussion in Sotgiu and Rusconi, "Memories"); McIver, *Memory*, 49–50, following Pillemer, *Momentous Events*, 50–51; cf. Rubin, *Memory*, 46, 54–56; Rubin, "Introduction," 3; Small, *Wax Tablets*, 105–6, 119–22. With Pillemer's "momentous events" Bauckham, "Psychology of Memory," also compares Schmidt's "exceptional events" (Schmidt, *Memories*). Note discussions of visual imagery and sound, respectively, in Rubin, *Memory*, 39–64, and 65–89; imagery in Rubin, "Introduction," 3; Brewer, "Recollective Memory," 35–36. Multiple sensory stimuli impress the memory even in simulations and reenactments (Harkins, *Reading*, 189).

multiple memory subsystems[168] distributed in different parts of the brain.[169] This multiple-location distribution provides reinforcement for memories that the brain deems vital; when different subsystems preserve aspects of an experience, memories can prove particularly resilient.[170]

The Gospels do suggest that Jesus's closest followers would have had such stark, emotive experiences (e.g., Mark 4:38–41; 6:49–51; 8:17–21, 33; 9:32; 10:13–14, 24, 26, 32; 14:18, 22–25, 29–31, 37, 43–52, 72). Jesus's teachings also incorporate graphic, often vivid visual imagery that could impress itself through hearers' imagination in multiple subsystems (e.g., Matt 5:34–36, 39–41, 45; 6:2, 26–30; Mark 9:42–43; Luke 12:6–7). Morally salient information also invites "evaluative attention," hence reinforces retention;[171] evaluative attention is relevant to the consideration demanded by Jesus's ethical pronouncements and riddles.

For individuals, different memory systems produce different outcomes; personal-event/episodic memory, for example, differs from cognitive/semantic memory, and both differ from procedural memory.[172] Indeed, episodic personal memory may be processed in different regions of the brain than conceptual aspects of autobiographic memory.[173] Tradition tends to preserve more semantic elements of community memory than episodic details because of the process of consolidation to essential, meaningful points.[174] Both Jesus's disciples and the stories shaped in community retellings undoubtedly found many points meaningful, as patterns of meaning in the Gospel narratives suggest (e.g., faith in Matt 8:10//Luke 7:9; Mark 2:5; 4:40; 5:34, 36; 9:23; 10:52; 11:22–24; John 11:40).[175]

---

168. McIver, *Memory*, 60; see more fully 76–80.

169. McIver, *Memory*, 79.

170. Cf. McIver, *Memory*, 79; Barber and Barber, *Severed*, 11.

171. Kirk, *Memory*, 219, noting esp. DiMaggio, "Culture."

172. Eve, *Behind Gospels*, 88. Still, episodic and semantic memory are interdependent, with the former involving scripts and the latter generalizations (Williams, Conway, and Cohen, "Autobiographical Memory," 22; cf. also Cohen, "Memory for Knowledge," 207). Tulving viewed episodic memory as distinctively "self-knowing" (O'Connor, Moulin, and Cohen, "Memory and Consciousness," 343).

173. Williams, Conway, and Cohen, "Autobiographical Memory," 39.

174. Kirk, *Memory*, 227, 230.

175. The linkage of πιστ- (*pist-*) terms with σωζ- (*sōz-*) terms (Mark 5:34; 10:52; Luke 7:50; 17:19; Acts 14:9; James 5:15; possibly 1 Tim 2:15; cf. Josephus, *Jewish Antiquities* 10.167), though suitable for physical restoration, also suits some early Christian thought (Luke 8:12; Acts 15:11; 16:31; Rom 1:16; 10:9–10; 1 Cor 1:21; 15:2; Eph 2:8; 2 Thess 2:13; 2 Tim 3:15; 1 Pet

Interest in what is being learned also provides motivation.[176] Thus, as David Rubin notes, "the interest aroused by participating in an oral tradition," where meaning is valued, "far exceeds that aroused by participating in an experiment on the learning of lists of nonsense syllables" in typical laboratory settings.[177] Or as Kirk notes, "Subjects are more highly motivated to encode information that is *salient*—that matters—to them."[178]

Interest motivates memory in both literate[179] and illiterate persons. Swazi herdsmen, for example, with normal memories on other matters, could readily and nearly precisely recite verifiable details of cattle purchases that they had merely witnessed a year earlier.[180] Illiterate !Kung bushmen and doctoral-level ethnographers who interview them each may remember what the other finds impossible to recall; different cultures value and develop memory skills for different subjects.[181]

Apostles and tradents who staked their lives on the message of Jesus obviously had deep interest in it.[182] These long-term memories were not a mere matter of random recollections.[183] As Samuel Byrskog notes, "*Since Jesus was a qualitatively unique teacher, it must have been generally essential to transmit his words and deeds*" (emphasis his).[184] In chapter 15 I compare them to other ancient disciples, but ultimately they had more reason, not less reason, than disciples of other teachers to transmit carefully their master's words and deeds.[185]

1:5, 9; 1 Clem. 12.1; Ignatius, *Philadelphians* 5.2; cf. Jude 5; the terms do not appear together, e.g., in Epictetus).

176. Rubin, *Memory*, 129, 157; cf. 319.

177. Rubin, *Memory*, 122, 125, 129, 155; cf. 157; Schwartz, "Smoke," 24.

178. Kirk, *Memory*, 218; cf. 214. The terms "salient" and "salience" appear more than sixty times in Kirk's book.

179. Rubin, *Memory*, 319.

180. Rubin, *Memory*, 132, following Bartlett. Despite his patronizing attitudes, Lévy-Bruhl, *Natives*, 111–13 (noted by Jerry Breen in a doctoral paper for my Seminar on the Historical Jesus, May 2018), respected some mental feats in traditional societies, such as Australian indigenous people for being able to recognize each person's distinctive tracks.

181. Small, *Wax Tablets*, 4, citing Cole and Scribner, *Culture*, 138; cf. Rubin, *Memory*, 169, 317.

182. With Schwartz, "Smoke," 24–25; Byrskog, *Teacher*, 400.

183. Dunn, *Tradition*, 238.

184. Byrskog, *Teacher*, 307. Insofar as other Jews thought of a unique teacher, they would presumably think of Moses; see, e.g., Philo, *Cherubim* 49; *The Worse Attack the Better* 86; *Studies* 177; *Names* 42; *Moses* 2.205; *Special Laws* 1.319, 345; 2.88, 256; *Contemplative Life* 63; 'Abot R. Nat. 1A; Pesiq. Rab. 31:3.

185. Byrskog, *Teacher*, 308.

As noted earlier, perspectives are inevitable,[186] and in this case, far from their faith in Jesus as Lord invalidating their perspective, it shaped their perspective for the very reason that the disciples preserved and propagated his teaching widely to begin with, despite the enormous cost.[187] Even disciples of other teachers normally preserved their teachers' message; they did not, however, always stake their lives on its propagation, as most of Jesus's disciples ultimately seemed ready to do.

14.5c. Rehearsal

We are also most apt to recall events narrated to others, since this activity reinforces narrative memory.[188] (Even narrating memories to ourselves strengthens recall.)[189] Autobiographic memory usually quickly assumes narrative form from the start.[190] As noted in the following chapter (ch. 15), Jesus's disciples probably recounted Jesus's deeds and teachings from the start, even if initially only among themselves.

Frequent repetition or rehearsal helps memory.[191] Even we absent-minded professors often recall the substance of courses that we have taught repeatedly over the years. Rubin points out that memory research has recognized from the beginning that "*recitation*, the technical term for the mixing of test trials with study trials, aids learning."[192] Granted, repetition that consolidates memories can also contaminate them.[193] Frequent rehearsal can also fix in memory the form in which one is accustomed to telling a story rather than the story itself.[194] On the whole, however, the effect usually reinforces memory. Rehearsal for communication to others is a particularly common form

186. Cf. Bruner and Fleisher Feldman, "Narrative," 291: far from inhibiting the communication of information, "narrative patterning . . . provides a framework for both telling and understanding."

187. Cf. Dunn, *Tradition*, 270–71, regarding Jesus's impact.

188. McIver, *Memory*, 50–51; cf. Pillemer, *Momentous Events*, 48, 53–54, 99, 101; Rubin, "Introduction," 2.

189. Small, *Wax Tablets*, 118–20 (noting the emphasis on repeating aloud in both modern studies and in Quintilian, *Orator's Education* 11.2.33).

190. Rubin, "Introduction," 2; cf. Elder, "Narrativity," 242.

191. Bauckham, *Eyewitnesses*, 334; see Goody, *Interface*, 177; Rubin, *Memory*, 129.

192. Rubin, *Memory*, 129, citing Thompson, Wenger, and Bartling, "Recall."

193. Stock, Gajsar, and Güntürkün, "Neuroscience," 385.

194. Eve, *Behind Gospels*, 156, 180.

of rehearsal, and for positive (as opposed to negative) events correlates with reduced affective fading.[195]

Like others, I could illustrate the point from my own experience. For example, I often recount a condensed version of my own conversion story from atheism, highlighting the features that I or others have found most interesting during repeated retellings.[196] Retelling this form from habit is less vivid than reexperiencing more of the details. Nevertheless, this fixed form need not obliterate all other elements of the memory; after decades, I still recall other elements that I almost never have reason to recount (including the names of others present during my confrontation with the theists).

Even apart from the disciples' role as preachers about Jesus, the disciples' hearers surely would have invited them to recount their stories of Jesus again and again.[197] Such factors in personal memory would suggest that Jesus's disciples would have remembered many incidents from his ministry and many of his teachings. But for how long?

14.6. Transience and the Longevity of Memories

Can personal memories last long enough to become sources for the Gospels? Ancient thinkers, like modern ones, recognized that witnesses' memories were most complete and reliable when the events remained fairly fresh.[198] Jesus's primary followers presumably would not have remembered everything he said to them or did among them.[199]

In one study, even emotional memories faded quickly over the first year, but then the forgetting curve leveled off, so that what was still remembered tended to persist even after ten years.[200] Citing memory studies, McIver notes that after five years the witnesses might recall as many as half of "distinctive episodes" and particularly significant personal memories.[201] Memory studies also suggest that memories that remain after those five years typically remain

---

195. Walker et al., "Why People Rehearse."

196. See, e.g., Keener and Keener, *Impossible Love*, 17–20.

197. McIver, "Memory, Persistence," 223. For a more recent parallel in Middle Eastern practice, see Derico, *Tradition*, 208.

198. Lysias, *Orations* 20.22, §160.

199. McIver, *Memory*, 143–61, addresses memory frailties and the gospel traditions.

200. Hirst et al., "Follow-Up." This recall included inconsistencies, though engagement with others often corrected inaccuracies.

201. McIver, *Memory*, 144.

stable for at least the following quarter century.[202] Significant personal-event memories for the disciples would include their callings (Mark 1:16–20; 2:14) and extraordinary healings.[203]

What they did remember after a few years, however, should have easily filled more than a Gospel, rather than less.[204] Indeed, if we add up the time necessary for the occurrence of all episodes reported in all four Gospels, it would represent only a fraction of even a one-year ministry. Mark's 11,000 words are brief compared to Irish bards' tradition of about 100,000 words.[205] Some might in fact wonder how eyewitness testimony could be so brief, but biographers normally chose to present only samples that were valuable for their purpose,[206] even when they knew their subjects directly.[207]

Of forms of long-term memory, episodic memory is particularly vulnerable to blending of analogous events;[208] nevertheless, it can preserve significant information. Laboratory studies can most easily test short-term memory, but some studies have confirmed the tendency to recall memorable personal events for even six decades.[209] Thus, for example, researchers compared Danes who had experienced the time of the German invasion (April 9, 1940) and subsequent surrender (May 4, 1945) with others who had merely studied it in school. More than two-thirds of those who lived through the invasion cor-

202. McIver, "Memory, Persistence," 223; McIver, *Memory,* 23, 35–39, 144; cf. also 183; Rubin, *Memory,* 147; Brewer, "Recollective Memory," 49–50. McIver's sources include Bahrick, "Memory Content"; Bahrick, "Maintenance"; Bahrick, Bahrick, and Wittlinger, "Fifty Years"; Conway, Cohen, and Stanhope, "Retention." It is important to distinguish different forms of memory in these sources; episodic personal memory is more relevant than language learning (e.g., in Bahrick, "Memory Content"), name recognition, etc. The cases he notes in Offer et al., "Altering," 737, all reflect subjective judgments rather than information.

203. McIver, *Memory,* 146. For other lines of evidence regarding genuine historical memory in the call narratives, see Witherington, *Christology,* 129–30; Davies and Allison, *Matthew,* 2:393–94; Sanders, *Figure,* 119.

204. In a different context, Ehrman, *Before Gospels,* 116, calculates that it takes just "about two hours to read" through Mark.

205. Riesner, *Lehrer,* 451, citing Gaechter, *Gedächtniskultur,* 49–53. Crossan, *Birth,* 51–53, draws lessons for gospel tradition from Irish oral tradition; Derico, *Tradition,* 60–63, challenges the analogy for its distance from ancient Galilean culture (and on 129–42, Crossan's attempted analogy with modern Greek laments).

206. E.g., De Pourcq and Roskam, "Virtues," 167, on Plutarch.

207. Beck, "Demonax," 83–84, 87, noting esp. Lucian, *Demonax* 67.

208. Steussy, "Memory," 211; cf. Kirk, *Memory,* 217.

209. Many research studies have focused on the molecular neurochemistry of long-term memory; e.g., Bekinschtein et al., "BDNF"; Rossato et al., "Dopamine."

rectly remembered the weather during the invasion, as opposed to about one-twentieth of the control group. Roughly one-sixth of survivors could even recall the time of the German surrender within five minutes, a feat not replicated by any members of the control group (and hard for many of the rest of us to imagine). Those who did not recall the correct answer normally did not substitute an incorrect one.[210]

Similarly, more than four decades after the closure of Camp Erika, a Dutch prison camp, nearly all interviewed survivors recalled it vividly. Over half could recall even the precise date of their imprisonment; over half likewise remembered their registration number.[211] McIver concludes that memory does not preserve all details accurately, but that the gist of memories of key personal events normally persists for decades.[212]

The crucial period for the eyewitnesses' ability to remember what they recounted is thus "not the thirty to sixty years . . . before the writing of the Gospels" but "the first three to six years" after Jesus's execution.[213] Most of what the disciples remembered at that point would have remained through the following decades, especially when it was reinforced through retellings.

14.7. Conclusion

Everyday assumptions about memory are usually sufficient for everyday purposes, but they need to be qualified in light of memory's limitations. Our memories must reconstruct experiences, and as in the case of John Dean, that reconstruction is an approximation that is most helpful regarding the overall gist rather than sequence or verbatim wording. Typical memory frailties include suggestibility, susceptibility to bias, and chronological displacement and even conflation. Recall is rarely verbatim, except in the case of aphorisms.

Still, memory usually depends on actual experience or learning and is especially effective for personally significant and often multisensory events. Rehearsal embeds memories more thoroughly. Memories significant enough to persist for five years may well persist for decades. These factors should have been relevant to the experience of the disciples.

210. McIver, *Memory*, 54–55, noting the study of Bernsten and Thomsen, "Memories," esp. 245, 248–49.

211. McIver, *Memory*, 56, following Wagenaar and Groeneweg, "Memory," esp. 84.

212. McIver, *Memory*, 58 (distinguishing personal-event memories from some other kinds); cf. Schwartz, "Smoke," 21.

213. McIver, *Memory*, 144.

Chapter 15

Jesus Was a Teacher

Nearly all scholars agree that Jesus was a teacher with disciples. In light of ancient pedagogic practices, what implications should this consensus have for the gospel tradition? Various considerations support the probability that the disciples and those who heard them would have preserved and transmitted more than sufficient, reliable memories about Jesus to fill early sources such as Mark and Q, most likely with plenty left over. This observation does not mean that no one misremembered what he heard. But it does suggest that, in general, we should at least expect a fairly reliable overall picture of Jesus in the Gospels.

As suggested in chapter 14, telling the stories about Jesus over and over again would eventually produce patterns for recitation. The disciples would presumably omit less useful elements, focus on useful ones, and offer their interpretations. Such patterning, however, would not automatically render unreliable the pieces of information that such accounts contained. Emphasizing or possibly even adding some details for storytelling purposes should not have changed the core elements of those accounts.

Even though some echoes of Jesus's original figures of speech appear to show up in the Gospels, no one expected retellings to preserve wording verbatim. Variation appears in our Gospels, but as noted in chapter 12, paraphrase was a standard practice, even in elite rhetorical training.[1] What is significant in the Jesus tradition, however, is the preservation of much of its original substance, including persistent themes, stories, the substance of climactic key sayings, and the like.[2]

---

1. See, e.g., Theon, *Progymnasmata* 1.93–171; later, Hermogenes, *Method in Forceful Speaking* 24.440; Libanius, *Anecdote* 1.4; 2.3; *Maxim* 1.2–5; 2.3; 3.2.

2. See the varied discussions in Allison, *Constructing Jesus*; Bauckham, "Eyewitnesses"; Bauckham, *Eyewitnesses*, 325–41 (esp. on gist in 333–34); Redman, "Eyewitnesses"; McIver, "Eyewitnesses."

15.1. Eyewitnesses

Whom would someone consult if seeking to produce an authoritative work? Even if we ignore Jesus's own disciples holding key leadership positions in the church (Gal 1:18–19; 2:9; cf. 1 Cor 15:5–7), the plain preponderance of evidence from antiquity demonstrates that ancients did regularly prefer eyewitnesses. Failing the eyewitnesses themselves, they would appeal to material that they believed came from the eyewitnesses. They thus sought information from sources as close to the eyewitnesses as possible.

15.1a. Evangelists Would Heed Eyewitnesses

In antiquity someone seeking to produce an authoritative work, rather than simply to recount stories to a neighbor, would generally seek to consult the same sorts of sources we do, especially eyewitnesses.[3] This was the historical and biographic practice everywhere favored in antiquity.[4] Whenever possible, ancient historians and biographers drew on recent oral memory from eyewitnesses.[5] This historiographic practice appears at least as early as Herodotus,[6] and the Jewish historian Josephus shares the same ideal.[7] (See further ch. 9.)

One would not expect the Evangelists, who chose the biographic medium and obviously valued Jesus's example and teachings, to treat their material more cavalierly than their contemporaries treated less essential material. They must

---

3. Pace Kloppenborg, "Memory," 296.

4. See, e.g., Byrskog, *Story*, 153–57; Bauckham, "Response," 237; see ch. 9. If someone wishes to argue that nonextant popular historiography must have differed from extant evidence, they should admit that they are arguing from silence, rather than from the limited evidence that survives. Analogies work from *available* evidence.

5. E.g., Xenophon, *Apology* 2; *Agesilaus* 3.1; Dionysius of Halicarnassus, *Thucydides* 7; Plutarch, *Demosthenes* 11.1; Arrian, *Alexander* 1.pref.2–3; 6.11.8; Cornelius Nepos, *On Great Generals* 23 (Hannibal), 13.3; 25 (Atticus), 13.7; 17.1; cf. Xenophon, *Hellenica* 6.2.31 (refusing to believe a report until an eyewitness was available); Tacitus, *Annals* 3.16 (reporting an unlikely account, though not committed to it, because he received it from the previous generation). See also Aune, *Environment*, 81; Alexander, *Preface*, 34. Historians today are apt to trust eyewitness knowledge even in otherwise questionable ancient historians (e.g., Brown, *Historians*, 142, 146; in more recent history, see, e.g., Wigger, *Saint*, 363).

6. See Meister, "Herodotus," 267–68; Byrskog, "History," 279. Cf., e.g., Herodotus, *Histories* 3.55; Egyptian priests had earlier but not always accurate information in 2.99–101, 109, 111–13, 116, 118–24.

7. See Josephus, *Life* 357; *Against Apion* 1.45–49, 56; *Jewish War* 1.2–3.

have at least believed that their material cohered in basic substance and spirit with the testimony of the witnesses present at the events they depict. Indeed, Luke explicitly claims that his material goes back to eyewitnesses (Luke 1:2).[8]

The most authoritative voices in the church—leaders such as elders—presumably would have the greatest contact with the earliest and most prominent leaders, who had personally known Jesus (cf. Acts 6:6; 14:23; 15:6). Given the time frame, even some or most of the Evangelists may have had direct contacts with eyewitnesses.

There are reasons why second-century Christians viewed the Gospels as memoirs of the apostles.[9] Gospel tradition spread widely in the earliest church, but those with the most direct experience would typically have the fullest and generally clearest memories, and those in leadership, appointed by Jesus as his apostles and in some sense successors, would command the greatest respect. While many besides the eyewitnesses would be recounting stories about Jesus, the eyewitnesses' claims would surely be the authoritative standard and be deemed the most authoritative source for others.

15.1b. Apostolic Connections?

Most scholars today doubt that any eyewitnesses directly composed the Gospels; the minority of scholars who demur (including myself) admit at most one or two exceptions, and not always in the sense of full authorship. (Probably a majority of Johannine scholars, including myself, do view the beloved disciple, the main source behind the Fourth Gospel, as an eyewitness personally acquainted with Jesus.[10] This Gospel diverges from the Synoptics in numerous respects, but see ch. 13.) Yet, even church tradition does not attribute all the Gospels to eyewitnesses; in the late second and early third century, some Christians deemed Matthew and John's authority more persuasive than that of Mark or Luke because of the reputed apostolic authorship of the former two.[11]

Arguing for apostolic authorship of any of the Gospels would require a major study of its own, would not persuade most scholars, and is outside the

8. See discussion in, e.g., Keener, *Acts*, 1:185–87.

9. See, e.g., Justin, *Dialogue with Trypho* 103.8; 106.3; comment in ch. 14.

10. See, e.g., Kysar, *John*, 12; O'Day, "John," 500; Smith, *John* (1999), 400; Hengel, *Question*; Bauckham, *Testimony*; Bauckham, *Eyewitnesses*, 550–51 (listing examples); Keener, *John*, 1:81–139.

11. But cf. Tertullian. *Against Marcion* 4.2, 5; Origen in Eusebius, *Ecclesiastical History* 6.25.3–6.

scope and point of this book. To my knowledge, no one claims that Mark, widely regarded as the first of the Gospels, comes from an eyewitness. (A number of scholars do at least believe that Mark was from Judea.)[12]

What matters more here is whether the information on which the Evangelists depend ultimately goes back to eyewitnesses. Like other questions in ancient history, this one cannot be demonstrated with any mathematical sort of certainty. Historical inquiry looks for the preponderance of evidence. In this case, however, the evidence already surveyed supports the likelihood that works composed as soon after the events as the Gospels ordinarily would depend especially on material that the Evangelists believed went back to the eyewitnesses, and that they had good reason to believe that it did.

Writing in the early second century, Papias (admittedly an imperfect source) was probably beyond most living memory of Jesus's ministry, but he was within living memory of Mark's Gospel.[13] Papias claims that Mark got his information from Peter.[14] (Other ancient sources repeat this claim.)[15] Papias

---

12. Collins, *Mark*, 2–6; cf. Hengel, "Geography," 33n19. Diaspora Jews who settled in Jerusalem, which could include John Mark's relatives (cf. Acts 4:36; Col 4:10), would certainly know Greek (see, e.g., Keener, *Acts*, 2:1253–59; cf. the example of Paul); funerary inscriptions also show that many of Jerusalem's elite knew Greek well; most Judean works in Greek, such as Mark, were preserved in the Diaspora. But nothing in my argument depends on Mark being Judean in any case.

13. Although I cannot appeal to consensus or hope to persuade all readers here, I believe that, by standards of external attestation used for other ancient literature, extant reports about the Gospels from within living memory include Mark recording the memories of a leading eyewitness; Matthew recording his own eyewitness memories (though I take this original, Jewish sayings record to be more like Q than our completed Gospel of Matthew, which combined that material with Mark's narrative); and John's Gospel being from an eyewitness. I also believe that the current Gospels of Matthew and Luke depend on two of these eyewitness sources, with Luke possibly knowing some oral material later incorporated in the Fourth Gospel, and Luke having been a traveling companion of Paul. We can evade attributing the apostolic fathers' reports about the Gospels to living memory only by dating the Gospels much earlier than our consensus dating, or by dismissing the truthfulness of the early second-century sources, inasmuch as they do not fit our currently dominant scholarly schema.) Thus, on my reconstruction, our Gospels reflect at least three major, mostly independent *witnesses* of Jesus. So many surviving sources so close to the figure reported is very rare for ancient literature (although we have instances, such as with Socrates), as others also note (e.g., Puig i Tàrrech, *Jesus*, 2). I believe that NT scholars typically underestimate the wealth of early material genuinely available to them. (On points such as the passion and resurrection, we may add Paul; if James reflects early material, some of Jesus's sayings in Matthew also surface there.)

14. Cf. Bockmuehl, *Seeing*, 186; Thornton, "Justin und Markusevangelium"; Trevijano Etcheverría, "Obra"; discussion in Keener, "Ehrman vs. McIver," 300–301.

15. E.g., Irenaeus, *Against Heresies* 3.1.1; 3.10.5; Clement of Alexandria fragments (Euse-

concedes that Mark did not "closely follow" (παρακολουθέω, *parakoloutheō*) the Lord himself. Papias might frame this observation in contrast to Luke, who followed (*parakoloutheō*) matters from the first (Luke 1:3),[16] very possibly indicating some personal participation (see ch. 8). Instead, Mark "followed" Peter and learned his stories that had been shaped by presentation.[17] On this view, Mark accurately preserves Peter's living voice (Papias, frag. 7.3–4) but lacks suitable arrangement.

Given Peter's prominence in the 50s (1 Cor 1:12; 3:22; Gal 1:18; 2:9–14), his role as Jesus's follower (1 Cor 9:5; 15:5), and the usual dating of Mark, the belief that Mark knew and would have reported what he knew of Peter's teaching is not unreasonable.[18] Certainly Mark reports many memorable scenes to which Peter would have been privy (Mark 1:16, 29, 36; 3:16; 5:37; 8:29–33; 9:2, 5; 10:28; 11:21; 13:3; 14:29–31, 33–37, 54, 66–72).[19]

Had Papias wished to invent a fictitious connection with Peter, he could have simply attributed the Gospel of Mark directly to him,[20] since narrators who participated in narratives sometimes did depict themselves in the third person.[21] He did not do so, yet he identifies an author, which suggests that he believed the author of this Gospel to be already known. That au-

---

bius, *Ecclesiastical History* 2.15; 6.14; comments on 1 Peter in Cassiodorus). Some so construe also Justin, *Dialogue with Trypho* 106 (see Kruger, *Crossroads*, 215).

16. Cf. the clear allusion to Luke 1:2 in Eusebius, *Ecclesiastical History* 3.36.1, in a context also discussing Papias (frag., 3.36.2), but the language is Eusebius's (cf. 3.4.6).

17. Papias, frag., 3.15 (Holmes). Papias applies this verb elsewhere to those who "followed" the apostles (3.4–5). In 3.15 I take the subject of "adapted," the first "remembered," and perhaps the second "remembered" (a different term) to be Peter; the reference to memory could, however, be to Mark's (see Barnett, *Finding*, 79). Some find internal evidence for oral shaping in Mark; see, e.g., Dewey, "Methods" (brought to my attention by Elia Mesrico Abdi Kasih); Zwiep, "Orality." Papias's Mark apparently recalls Peter's ministry from natural performance settings, not dictation.

18. With Eve, *Behind Gospels*, 143.

19. Bauckham, *Eyewitnesses*, 509–49 (esp. 510–20), goes further, emphasizing Peter as the Gospel's first and last disciple named (Mark 1:16; 16:7) and comparing apparent implicit allusions to witnesses in other ancient works, a comparison that merits further exploration.

20. Cf. the later apocryphal Gospel of Peter (Origen, *Commentary on Matthew* 10:17; Eusebius, *Ecclesiastical History* 3.3, 25; 6.12), usually identified with the manuscript discovered in 1886 that has been given that title (see Gospel of Peter 14.60; cf. 7.26).

21. See, e.g., Xenophon, *Anabasis* 2.5.41; 3.1.4–6; Thucydides, *History* 1.1.1; 2.103.2; 5.26.1; Polybius, *Histories* 31.23.1–31.24.12; 38.19.1; 38.21.1; 38.22.3; Caesar, *Civil War*, throughout, e.g., 1.1; *Gallic Wars*, throughout, e.g., 1.7; 2.1; 3.28; 4.13; 5.9; 6.4; 7.17; Campbell, "Narrator"; Jackson, "Conventions"; Keener, *John*, 105; Keener, "Claims."

thor's dependence on Peter's testimony may also be known.[22] By contrast, Papias seems displeased with Mark's arrangement, so his temptation may otherwise have been to downplay rather than to emphasize apostolic associations.[23] If Mark did work with Peter (cf. perhaps 1 Pet 5:13), he probably heard Peter recount his favorite stories more than once as Peter addressed various gatherings.

Although Eric Eve notes that Petrine influence on Mark is not proven, he adds that "the preaching of such an authoritative figure who was known to have been an eyewitness to the earthly Jesus is likely to have been given considerable weight," which could also explain "the apparently ready acceptance of Mark's Gospel" by Matthew and Luke.[24]

Richard Bauckham has developed the thesis of eyewitnesses particularly extensively. Some of his detractors have misrepresented his thesis as claiming more than it does (Bauckham nowhere implied verbatim recall).[25] Others, such as Eric Eve, more reasonably point out that Bauckham has not *demonstrated* that everything in the Gospels derives from the eyewitnesses or that they must have recalled everything accurately.[26] Nevertheless, Eve concedes that Bauckham shows that what appears in the Gospels *could* derive from fairly accurate eyewitness testimony,[27] and that Bauckham has raised valuable questions: "It is completely fair to point out that the tradition was more likely to have been transmitted and controlled by certain individuals such as authorized teachers rather than simply passed round an anonymous collective, and it is entirely reasonable to suggest that recognized eyewitnesses

---

22. Papias seems to depend on information prior to himself from "the Elder"; see France, *Mark*, 7–8; Bauckham, *World*, 114–20, 153–64. Cf. 1 Pet 5:13.

23. Cf. Collins, *Mark*, 4.

24. Eve, *Behind Gospels*, 143.

25. E.g., Redman, "Eyewitnesses," although adding helpful insights. Ehrman, *Before Gospels*, 101, complains that few scholars "have found Bauckham's case persuasive," but this verdict depends on what one means by "persuasive" and to which *elements* of his case one refers. Fairly positive reviews include Anthony Harvey (in the *Times Literary Supplement*), James Carleton Paget of Cambridge (*Journal of Ecclesiastical History*), and Gary A. Anderson of Notre Dame (*First Things*). Like some others who largely have appreciated Bauckham's work (Dunn, "Eyewitnesses," 105; Keener, "Review of Bauckham," 132), Byrskog, "Eyewitnesses," was largely positive but found least convincing (158–59) Bauckham's argument that the gospel traditions sometimes specifically identify their witnesses (though cf. now Bauckham's response, with further evidence, in "Response," 226–28; Bauckham, *Eyewitnesses*, 510–36); for some initial respectful counterarguments, see Kirk, "Ehrman, Bauckham, and Bird," 104–6.

26. Eve, *Behind Gospels*, 156, 158.

27. Eve, *Behind Gospels*, 156.

were likely to have had a continuing role in this process for as long as they were around."[28]

Such possibilities do not render moot the question of social memory. Even if Mark has his material directly from Peter (a connection the likelihood of which some of my readers may find less plausible than I), Peter's retellings were shaped in, and at least in most of the passion narrative must have depended on, the larger community.[29] That is, whether the steps between eyewitnesses and the Evangelists were many or few, both questions about psychological (ch. 14) and social (ch. 16; also 15.2 below) memory remain relevant when considering the historical roots and subsequent shaping of the memory of Jesus in the early Christian movement.

15.1c. How Accurate Is Eyewitness Memory?

Does it even matter whether the gospel tradition depended on eyewitnesses? Eyewitness memory is not always accurate, and its accuracy varies depending on the kind of matters witnessed (see also ch. 14).

For example, on September 22, 1993, I confronted a burglar who had broken into my apartment; even immediately after the confrontation, however, I could not recall much about his face or what color clothes he was wearing. My

---

28. Eve, *Behind Gospels*, 158; cf. 180. As Eve notes, even Patterson, "Review," 197–98, recognizes the common sense in this approach for some of the gospel tradition, while demurring from Bauckham's fuller confidence. This is not to suggest, as many scholars do, that the Gospels were originally anonymous; their first recipients presumably knew the authors' identity (cf. Luke 1:3–4). Ancient works often omitted the author's name inside the document itself, taking for granted the readers' knowledge of the author; cf., e.g., historical prefaces that identify their authors only by speaking in the first person singular (Livy 1.pref.; Arrian, *Alexander* pref.; Tacitus, *Annals* 1.1; *Histories* 1.1; Herodian, *History* 1.1.1–6). The foreign wars attributed to Appian identifies him as the author (pref.15), but his *Civil Wars* does not; Tacitus, *Germania* 1 does not name the author, yet the first-person singular in, e.g., *Germania* 2, 46 implies that he is known. Josephus never names himself as author of the *Jewish Antiquities*, but his identification of himself there as author of the *Jewish War* (cf. Campbell, "Narrator," 400) confirms that Josephus's audience knew his identity. Among biographical prefaces, Diogenes Laertius does not name himself, nor does Tacitus, *Agricola* 1–3 (though his first-person singular usage in *Agricola* 1, 3, and mention of Agricola as his father-in-law in *Agricola* 2 are plain enough); Suetonius cites the testimony of his father, whom he names (*Otho* 10) in a biography that does not open by identifying himself (*Otho* 1). See now Gathercole, "Anonymity."

29. In empirical studies, commemorated community traditions become so familiar that they restructure individual memory (Kirk, *Memory*, 224, noting Harris, Paterson, and Kemp, "Recall").

attention was focused instead on the situation (and the self-evident fact that the burglar had broken into my apartment with his knife).[30] Still, if you ask me how he broke in, what he drank, what he left behind or various other details surrounding the incident, I can recount those details clearly and accurately today, though I have only rarely had occasion to recall or retell the story.[31]

Eyewitnesses are crucial yet fallible. Evidence suggests that "erroneous eyewitness testimony is the leading cause of wrongful conviction";[32] often witnesses are pressed to remember details that their memories never captured to begin with. Yet this standard differs from normal recall,[33] and even in such forensic contexts witnesses sometimes do better. In one study, eyewitnesses had a good gist memory of a crime and were also 80 percent correct on details—despite extraordinarily stringent measuring criteria: "height and age estimates had to be within plus or minus 2 (inches/years), weight within 5 pounds, and no leeway was given for the number of shots fired."[34]

I find this study astonishing, perhaps because I rarely can estimate such parameters so closely even when a person is in front of me. Even if we deem this study an outlier with unusually perceptive witnesses, it graphically illustrates that people often do remember the gist and at least some details of a striking incident. A more important qualification in the use of such studies, however, is that the difficult, quantitative forensic standard is not the norm for most memory, where salience is most relevant.[35]

Discerning which details in the minority of divergent testimony is correct usually requires weighing independent testimonies.[36] We cannot weigh the gospel traditions in quite this way today. (Multiple attestation in different independent sources, such as Mark and Q, is valuable, but discerning *independent*

---

30. Lack of recall of the face is not uncommon (Hanley and Cohen, "Memory for People," 108), and the presence of a weapon often distracts attention from the face (McIver, *Memory*, 11). I do recall the frightened expression on the burglar's face and the angry tone of my own voice, both the opposite of what one might expect. The duration of exposure to the incident also affects recall (Wright and Loftus, "Eyewitness Memory," 97).

31. My journal entry for that date can verify these memories.

32. Wright and Loftus, "Eyewitness Memory," 93.

33. Bauckham, *Eyewitnesses*, 355–57; Bauckham, "Psychology of Memory" (noting also that even here a case study may prove more optimistic than laboratory settings; he cites Yuille and Cutshall, "Case Study"); Kirk, *Memory*, 213–14.

34. McIver, *Memory*, 12–16, esp. 13–14; McIver, "Eyewitnesses," 535, 545. One could also cite examples from history; a recent example is archaeological confirmation of eyewitnesses' timing of an 1838 shipwreck (cf. Price, "Shipwreck").

35. Kirk, *Memory*, 214.

36. Confirming material that overlaps; cf. Robinson, "Perspective," 214.

oral traditions *before* them is next to impossible.)[37] Nevertheless, the early Christian communities may have already undertaken this process of evaluation in the lifetime of the first witnesses,[38] and in any case, the bulk of material would likely remain dependable. Some eyewitnesses probably remained alive at least into the later decades of the first century, though of course the larger number of survivors clustered earlier.[39] Those who outlive others often do increase in relative prominence.

Surely most of the Jesus movement recognized that Jesus's immediate disciples, who also led the church (see, e.g., 1 Cor 9:5; Gal 2:9), were more authoritative as sources than were others.[40] Paul's letters show that these disciples remained in leadership positions and remained respected in the churches of the Diaspora into the mid-50s.[41] Evidence from Josephus suggests that Jesus's brother James remained in prominent leadership in Jerusalem itself until roughly 60.[42] Luke-Acts offers no reason to doubt that these figures continued to command respect in the Diaspora, even after their decease, into Luke's own day (cf. also Rev 21:14). Those who, unlike myself, view Acts as a second-century synthesis of Pauline and Jerusalem strands should recognize that, on their view, the apostles retained respect into the second century.

15.2. The Collective Memory of Eyewitnesses

The eyewitnesses would not testify exclusively independently of one another; their memories, and especially those of Jesus's closest disciples, would interact and would be pooled in the community's shared memory alongside the continuing teaching of the surviving apostles.

---

37. Vansina, *Oral Tradition*, 159, rejects using the Synoptics themselves for multiple attestation because he views them as interdependent rather than independent. This approach may, however, raise the question of the first sources.

38. McIver, *Memory*, 16, 186.

39. Cf., e.g., Quadratus, frag. 2 (Holmes; Eusebius, *Ecclesiastical History* 4.3.2). Although estimates are debatable, for the likelihood of a number surviving late, Kirk, "Nexus," 144, cites Os, *Analyses*, 57, 83; see also Bockmuehl, *Seeing*, 178–79; for a fairly small number, see McIver, *Memory*, 189–209, esp. 208–9.

40. See also Schwartz, "Smoke," 17.

41. For the identity of Cephas as Peter, see, e.g., Allison, "Peter," with the strong majority of scholars; pace Ehrman, "Cephas."

42. Josephus, *Jewish Antiquities* 20.200.

15.2a. Experiments and Experiences

As noted in the previous chapter on memory studies, communal memory is susceptible to false memories from any strong-willed or persuasive member of the group. On the whole, however, it tends to be more stable than individual memory.[43]

While the core of spaced rehearsed learning and prominent personal experiences can persist in a student's or witness's psychological memory for years, what about word that is circulated secondhand? Although witnesses remained in key positions of leadership in the early Christian movement into the 50s of the first century (Gal 1:18–19; 2:9; cf. 1 Cor 1:12; 3:22; 9:5; 15:5), stories about Jesus ultimately circulated widely. Could wide circulation become wild circulation?

For quick testing, laboratory experiments often use a single chain of transmission, which of course quickly skews "traditions," since any fallible link can introduce significant change.[44] Yet cultural memory expert David Rubin notes that this setting differs starkly from the real life settings in which oral transmission occurs.[45] "The changes that occur when a passage is transmitted from person to person are much greater in psychology experiments than they are in oral tradition."[46] Oral tradition provides far more overlearning and spaced practice than is possible in typical experiments.[47] For example, "A favorite song can be sung hundreds of times."[48]

Oral tradition is specifically designed to counter the frailties of memory such as those suggested in laboratory studies.[49] Oral tradition typically depends on various cues as well as constraints such as rhythm.[50] Together,

---

43. Redman, "Eyewitnesses," 186–87.

44. See, e.g., Bartlett, *Remembering*, followed by Crossan, *Birth*, 79–83. But this laboratory research addresses primarily semantic memory, and more recent research highlights how the usual conditions of such earlier research differ from communal memory; see Schwartz, "Smoke," 24–25; Rubin, *Memory*, 130–32, 144; Kirk and Thatcher, "Tradition," 37; Kirk, "Memory Theory," 822–24. Bartlett's primary experiments were also with students for whom the material was culturally alien (Horsley, "Patterns," 64–65; Rosenberg, "Complexity," 85, noting why folklorists regularly qualify Bartlett's classic study).

45. Rubin, *Memory*, 7–8, 133–35.

46. Rubin, *Memory*, 122.

47. Rubin, *Memory*, 124, 144, 154–55, 228; on overlearning, see Rubin, *Memory*, 123–24; on spaced learning, 124–27.

48. Rubin, *Memory*, 155.

49. Rubin, *Memory*, 144.

50. Ong, *Orality*, 22; Rosenberg, "Complexity," 82–83; Rubin, *Memory*, 8, 63, 87, 146, 155, 306; Kirk, "Memory Theory," 829–30 (following, e.g., Rubin, *Memory*, 90, 101, 293); Kirk, *Memory*, 75,

meaning, imagery, and sound provide constraints "that cue recall and limit choices,"[51] providing stability in oral tradition.[52]

15.2b. A Telephone Game?

NT scholar Bart Ehrman has sometimes compared oral transmission with the so-called telephone game, which seeks to replicate in a very compressed time frame generations of chain transmission.[53] Yet the comparison is problematic for the gospel tradition, which involved net (group) rather than chain (a single line of) transmission.[54]

Communities, including groups of disciples, more often practice "net" transmission, because their memories belonged to the entire group to start with.[55] Ancient disciples sometimes joined together to compile memories of their teachers' teachings.[56] The collective memory of Jesus's disciples would not even need to await his departure; it would start already as the disciples conversed among themselves during Jesus's ministry.[57]

Moreover, Jesus's disciples presumably taught *publicly*, to *many* people, rather than entrusting their message only to isolated individuals or (like later gnostics) passing on alleged secret teachings. Those hearers who did misunderstand a story would surely correct it if they subsequently heard Jesus's disciples, who doubled as the community's leaders, or from those whom they in turn commissioned or recognized.[58]

87, 105, 195–99; Nikulin, "Introduction," 8–9 (though Goody, *Interface*, 98, associates some metrical forms with literate culture); on cuing more generally, see esp. Rubin, *Memory*, 161–67, 175, 304–5. Such features were noted in the Jesus tradition before modern oral tradition studies; see, e.g., Jeremias, *Theology*, throughout; Burney, *Poetry*; on cues, see discussion of Bultmann and Dibelius in Kirk, *Memory*, 198. Mark lacks rhythm but includes numerous formulas (Wire, "Mark," 53).

51. Rubin, *Memory*, 88.

52. Rubin, *Memory*, 90; see further 90–121. For the role of meaning-making in memory, cf. Zimmermann, "Memory," 135–36.

53. Ehrman, *Introduction*, 52–53; cf. Ehrman, *Before Gospels*, 190–91 on chain transmission. Ehrman's current work on memory is more sophisticated, and I address it in "Ehrman vs. McIver"; note also the stronger critique in Gundry, "Memories."

54. See Kirk, "Memory Theory," 823–24; Kirk, *Memory*, 189–91. Bockmuehl, *Seeing*, 180, 184–85, depends on chains of connection in a different sense.

55. Dunn, *Perspective*, 43, 114–15.

56. E.g., Philostratus, *Lives of the Sophists* 1.22.524.

57. Dunn, *Tradition*, 242; cf. Mark 8:16; 9:10, 34; Luke 24:15–17.

58. For at least some delegation in the early Christian community, see, e.g., Acts 6:6; 14:23; 2 Tim 2:2; Tit 1:5; James 5:14; cf. Gal 6:6; 1 Thess 5:12–13; 1 Pet 5:5; 3 John 9.

Several memory theorists have thus explicitly challenged Ehrman's "telephone game" approach to the gospel tradition. Barry Schwartz, for example, on whose expertise Ehrman elsewhere draws,[59] counters his telephone game illustration by appealing to the way reports can grow exponentially,[60] the probability of multiple original versions, and network theory.[61] Alan Kirk cites Ehrman's "telephone game" analogy as a major example of a flawed understanding of memory on the part of some outdated NT scholarship.[62] More generally, one introduction to Gospels research complains that the telephone game analogy "limps badly."[63]

Even regarding the reliability of chain (individual) transmission, cultures vary. Kenneth Bailey, a NT scholar with four decades of experience in the Middle East, recounts observing the telephone game played with Middle Eastern students, who, "to the amazement and dismay of the western guest," transmitted the story "almost intact."[64]

Content also matters; experiences of events significant to us differ from the typically trivial and less relevant material transmitted in the telephone game. Communities preserve their stories that relate to community identity in a manner starkly different from mere rumor transmission; it is rumor transmission that resembles the telephone game.[65]

59. Ehrman, *Before Gospels*, 5–8.

60. Ehrman himself does recognize such growth; see *Before Gospels*, 80–81.

61. Schwartz, "Smoke," 12. On multiple original versions, see also Dunn, *Tradition*, 56, 281; Aune, "Aphorisms," 225. No one regarded a speaker's reuse and adaptation of a basic saying in multiple contexts "as a secondhand version of the first" time he used it (Kelber, "Works," 236–37). Because verbatim preservation is not expected in oral memory, it is difficult to speak of an "original" version even of the same story (Anderson, "Oral Tradition," 29; cf. Mournet, "Original," 263).

62. Kirk, "Memory Theory," 822; Kirk, "Ehrman, Bauckham, and Bird," 89–101 (particularly devastating on this point, 94–98); Kirk, *Memory*, 50–51n8, 189.

63. Murphy, *Introduction*, 22 (fuller discussion on 22–23); brought to my attention by Blomberg, *Reliability*, 61; cf. Williams, *Trust*, 77–78.

64. Bailey, "Tradition" (*ExpT*), 366. In his traditional rural Middle Eastern setting, the main lines of a story can be transmitted intact, even through long chains (Bailey, "Tradition" [*Themelios*], 7–8).

65. Byrskog, *Teacher*, 308n2; Rubin, *Memory*, 130; Kirk, "Memory Theory," 822–23; Kirk, "Ehrman, Bauckham, and Bird," 93.

15.2c. Strengths and Weaknesses of Collective Memory

Individual memory and collective memory always interact.[66] Indeed, reminiscing, or sharing memories together, often acquires narrative patterns even within a family setting, as children and parents interact.[67] When a group of witnesses confers, a confident but erroneous witness can introduce error into the group's collective memory.[68] On the one hand, this means that interviewing witnesses as a group provides less information than interviewing them individually.[69] Pooling individual memories provides more than simply relying on the group.[70] On the other hand, however, the group still provides more information than an isolated individual would. The aggregate of information from all the individual witnesses far exceeds the information from simply a single witness.[71] For one example of this principle, I was able to confirm and supplement the story of my wife's war experience through interviews with her family members.[72]

When groups share important memories, these memories quickly assume a standardized story form. Thus, for example, within days after refugees fled the 1972 genocide in Burundi, their narrative world became increasingly formalized and didactic, their experiences being arranged into "moral ordering stories."[73]

---

66. Rodríguez, *Structuring*, 42–45, challenging (on 45) Halbwachs's apparently exclusive emphasis on the social dimension (cf. also Le Donne, *Historiographical Jesus*, 49). Through his enthusiasm for the social context of all memory, Halbwachs's work lent itself to the misinterpretation that he excluded any role for individual memory, but he simply emphasized the social context of individual memory (Person and Keith, "Media Studies," 9; Le Donne, "Presentism," 307; Hubenthal, "Social Memory"; cf. Kirk, "Collective Memory," 59; Kirk, "Social and Cultural Memory," 2). Halbwachs stressed the interpenetration of autobiographical memory and the memory of those who knew such accounts (Esler, "Memory," 156).

67. Fivush, Haden, and Reese, "Reminiscing," 341–42, 357–58.

68. See Ehrman, *Before Gospels*, 76. Still, the more common effect of "social contagion" is positive, by enabling individuals to *learn* by incorporating new details (McIver, *Memory*, 70). Wrong confidence can encourage false memories (Barclay, "Autobiographical Remembering," 121–22), though some argue that confidence correlates with accuracy more often than not (Brewer, "Recollective Memory," 46; but cf. 49).

69. Ehrman, *Before Gospels*, 75.

70. McIver, *Memory*, 70. Cf. Redman, "Eyewitnesses," 186–87.

71. Cf. Redman, "Eyewitnesses," 186–87.

72. Mentioned briefly in Keener and Keener, *Impossible Love*, 235–36.

73. Kirk, "Nexus," 148; Kirk, "Memory Theory," 835, and Kirk, *Memory*, 81, following Malkki, *Purity and Exile*, 56, 106, 244.

413

Communal memory is common in older Middle Eastern culture[74] and would have been relevant for Jesus's movement: Jesus did not normally instruct disciples one-on-one, but as a group (cf., e.g., Mark 3:14; 4:10), and he also taught large crowds (e.g., Mark 3:9; 4:1; and throughout).[75] According to our earliest NT writer, some key events included at least five hundred followers who were witnesses (1 Cor 15:6–7). The Twelve (1 Cor 15:5), of course, were among those closest to Jesus during his ministry and functioned as the most authoritative witnesses (Mark 3:14–16; Acts 1:21–22).[76]

As already noted, the collective memory of Jesus's disciples started already as the disciples conversed among themselves during Jesus's ministry.[77] Furthermore, if Jesus ever sent disciples to extend his mission during his ministry, "there must have been agreement between Jesus and these disciples on the message they should preach and the life-style they should follow."[78] Even afterward, important traditions were usually delivered or "performed" in group settings.[79]

Given the numbers in Jesus's early movement, probably at least a few had exceptional memories (though not likely on the extraordinary level of their contemporary Seneca the Elder, who claims that he could at one time repeat back in sequence 2,000 just-learned names). But even if none of them had exceptional memories, the sum total of all their memories together could fill gaps in individual memories.

Preserving a teacher's message is not simply a modern interest. Disciples of an ancient teacher sometimes would gather after the teacher's death and weave together their memories of his teachings.[80] Jesus's disciples discussed Jesus's words among themselves during Jesus's ministry (Mark 8:16; 9:10) and surely discussed them even more afterward.

---

74. Dunn, *Perspective*, 45–46.

75. Those skeptical of more specific textual evidence should consider that a teacher without popular influence would probably have posed little threat to the elite.

76. In 1 Cor 15 Paul speaks esp. of witnesses of the resurrection (15:15) because that is his subject and possibly his most controversial point. On the reliability of the tradition about the Twelve, see, e.g., Sanders, *Jesus and Judaism*, 11, 98–101; Meier, "Circle."

77. Dunn, *Tradition*, 242; cf. Mark 8:16; 9:10, 34; Luke 24:15–17.

78. Dunn, *Tradition*, 242; cf. Bauckham, *Eyewitnesses*, 284–85, citing Matt 10:40; Mark 9:37; Luke 10:16; John 13:20; and Schürmann, "Anfänge." On the likelihood of such missions (albeit condensed in the Gospels to one or two), see Bernier, *Quest*, 62. Teachers typically gave students practice (e.g., Pliny, *Letters* 2.3.5–6); wonder-working prophets also trained prophet disciples (1 Sam 3:1; 19:20–24; cf. 2 Kings 2:3–18; y. Ta'an. 3:8, §2; Pesiq. Rab. Kah. 24:18).

79. Horsley, "Patterns," 61–62.

80. Philostratus, *Lives of the Sophists* 1.22.524.

15.2d. Collective Memory and the Overall Portrait of Jesus

The memory frailties mentioned in the previous chapter are more relevant for details than for any overall thrust of Jesus's ministry, such as his teaching in parables, healing the sick, or the like. As noted, suggestibility mostly confuses memory when the suggestions are plausible, that is, when they are coherent with veridical memories. This observation suggests that even false collective memories among tradents are likely consistent with the overall gist of Jesus's ministry.[81]

McIver thus concurs with C. H. Dodd's observation of the "consistent . . . coherent, and . . . distinctive" character of the Synoptic tradition of Jesus's sayings, which reflect behind them "the thought of a single, unique teacher."[82]

In fact, it is highly improbable that the overall portrait of Jesus in the Gospels' narratives diverges significantly from the general character of Jesus experienced by the disciples, whatever the omissions and adaptations. Barry Schwartz points to collective memories sometimes providing a composite portrait that can outweigh the limitations of individual testimony. He offers examples of the slave narratives compiled in interviews seven decades after the Civil War[83] and Katsuichi Honda's 1999 interviews concerning the 1937–38 genocidal Rape of Nanjing.[84] Historiography cannot say much about the past apart from testimony.[85]

Although collective memory occasionally includes some completely forged accounts, such fabrications normally "are quite rare."[86] (Such forged accounts today, though not in antiquity,[87] sometimes include unintentionally fabricated accounts due to "recovered memories.")[88] More frequently, collective memories merely reshape existing tradition to fit present concerns. Thus, McIver suggests, "if there was nonauthentic Jesus tradition circulating in the collective memory of his early followers, then it must have had considerable

---

81. McIver, *Memory,* 154–56.

82. McIver, *Memory,* 181, quoting Dodd, *Founder,* 33 (21–22 in the 1971 edition); cf. Dodd, *Parables,* 1. Distinctive events are more memorable (Brewer, "Recollective Memory," 50).

83. For a few selections, see *Unchained Memories*; Taylor, *Born a Slave*; Bland, *Slave Narratives.*

84. Schwartz, "Smoke," 8.

85. See, e.g., Provan, Long, and Longman, *History,* 47–58, and Schnabel, *Jesus in Jerusalem,* 7, both following esp. Coady, *Testimony* (esp. 46–47).

86. McIver, *Memory,* 157; McIver, "Eyewitnesses," 545–46.

87. Cf. Bernier, *Quest,* 66. For different approaches to ancient forged accounts, see Ehrman, *Forgery*; Baum, "Content."

88. See Belli and Loftus, "Pliability," esp. 172–76.

congruence with what he actually did and said. . . . The process of wholesale fabrication of the Jesus traditions envisaged by Dibelius and Bultmann is highly unlikely."[89]

15.3. The Sage and His Disciples

Although such evidence merely encourages us to expect the preservation of events and the general tenor or themes of a figure's views, in Jesus's case there is also important reason to consider the preservation of more specific teachings.[90] Almost all scholars agree that whatever else Jesus was, he was a teacher with disciples.[91] But against the popular nineteenth-century Romanticist approach of a folk tradition without content, Jesus's role as a teacher implies that he did communicate content.[92]

This generally agreed datum adds a particularly relevant though usually neglected dimension to this discussion. Whereas the ancient Mediterranean value of memory cultivation suggests the possibility of mnemonic capabilities greater than average in the modern West (see ch. 16), it is the specific role of Jesus's disciples as disciples that invites us to expect that they passed on the gist or substance of what they learned from Jesus. With regard to the biographies of sages, observations about human memory in general are less relevant than the specific memory practices expected for disciples.

This point would have been obvious to ancient audiences: Jesus's disciples, *as* disciples, would be *expected* to learn and pass on his teaching. When the second-century critic Celsus challenges the Christian story, he does not deny that Jesus had disciples but seeks to discredit them by contending that they were disreputable sailors and tax collectors[93]—what today we call an *ad hominem* argument, which we ordinarily do not apply to other biographies of the period, whatever our religious dispositions.[94] Learning the teaching of a master is inher-

---

89. McIver, *Memory,* 157. Dibelius, *Tradition,* 62, was generally less radical than Bultmann; on Dibelius as a pioneer but lacking in nuance, cf. Thatcher, "Dibelius," esp. 83.

90. McIver, *Memory,* 163–82.

91. McIver, *Memory,* 163. Dunn, *Tradition,* 237, concedes developing this point inadequately in *Remembered.* The term for disciples can mean "followers" or "adherents" more generally, but the pervasive picture in the gospel tradition is of Jesus's pupils (see Wilkins, *Discipleship*; also Byrskog, *Teacher,* 221–28).

92. Riesner, "Teacher," 938.

93. Origen, *Against Celsus* 1.63, 65.

94. At this point some critics might circle back to miracle claims: Hume (*Miracles,* 27,

ent in the role of disciples. Continuity of message between Jesus and his movement was thus hard for ancient critics to challenge, although those who called Jesus a sorcerer had little incentive to treat his successors more charitably.[95]

Not only do virtually all scholars agree that Jesus was a teacher with disciples; virtually all scholars also agree that Paul wrote 1 Corinthians and Galatians. These undisputed letters in turn attest that some of Jesus's closest disciples remained in the most respected leadership roles in Jesus's continuing movement, along with Jesus's brothers. They still held these positions within just a few years of when Mark (and possibly others, see Luke 1:1) wrote their Gospels (Gal 1:17–19; 2:1–2, 7–10; cf. 1 Cor 1:12; 3:22; 9:5; 15:5–7). They were probably in leadership when Q was produced, possibly even under the supervision of one or more of them.

Ancient hearers, in contrast to most modern ones, would recognize that these facts have clear implications for the character of the gospel tradition: normally disciples in this period accurately represented the spirit of their teachers' message, as well as many of the teachers' anecdotes and teachings.

15.3a. Passing On Teachings

Confidence about teaching methods "is possible," McIver notes, "because both the content and pedagogical method showed remarkable uniformity over the entire period of the Roman Empire."[96] Disciples were normally adherents of a school[97] or, at the beginning, its founder; they passed on teachings.[98] Thus, for example, Theophrastus became a great philosopher by imitating his teacher Aristotle and passing on his life and teaching.[99] Likewise, as already mentioned, historians normally consulted eyewitnesses when they were available.

29, 32, 34, 38–39, 43, 52) essentially dismissed claimants of miracles as fools or liars, but this prejudice simply exposes Hume's hidden religious agenda (see Cramer, "Miracles," 136–37; cf. Weintraub, "Credibility," 371). His argument is widely recognized today as circular (see ch. 12; Houston, *Miracle*; Johnson, *Hume*; Earman, "Bayes"; Earman, *Failure*).

95. Cf. John 15:20; Origen, *Against Celsus* 1.68, 71; esp. Mark 3:22; Matt 10:25.

96. McIver, *Memory*, 164–65 (cf. also 167–68, 180), citing, e.g., Morgan, *Literate Education*, 3; Atherton, "Children," 217. I have addressed this elsewhere in further detail, e.g., in Keener, "Assumptions."

97. Cf. Wilkins, *Discipleship*.

98. Emphasis remained on the gist, passing on reminiscences, with both fixity and flexibility, as in Bailey's Middle East tradition approach; see Alexander, "Memory," 143.

99. See, e.g., Libanius, *Anecdote* 4.1. Likewise Isocrates's teaching multiplied his role (Libanius, *Anecdote* 3.2).

By definition, teachers passed on their teachings to others. At elementary levels, learning might be simply from the standard curriculum, but a sage expected his disciples to learn his teachings. One familiar term for this practice, παραδίδωμι (*paradidōmi*),[100] was also applicable to passing down a founder's teachings[101] or practices,[102] passing down traditional practices from ancestors,[103] and passing down information in a historian.[104] In the disciples' setting, the cognate noun applies explicitly to Pharisaic traditions that were believed to be passed on meticulously,[105] and ultimately the noun and verb apply also to the gospel tradition, beginning already in first-century sources.[106]

Indeed, as Loveday Alexander points out, in all schools "teaching was passed down from master to pupils, who in turn passed it on to their own pupils";[107] the founder's teachings often functioned as canonical for their communities.[108] Greek schools transmitted sayings attributed to their founders from one generation to the next.[109] Often the founders themselves encouraged this practice of transmission.[110] Teachers also often left it to their students to publish their teachings;[111] if followers were illiterate, of course, they could entrust this dimension of the activity to others. Yet the question of the disciples' literacy is a red herring in any case, since dictation was the dominant practice for both the well-to-do and the illiterate in any case.[112]

---

100. E.g., in Lucian, *Alexander* 61; Socratics, *Letters* 20; Philostratus, *Lives of the Sophists* 2.29.621; Iamblichus, *Pythagorean Life* 28.148–49; 32.226; cf. Seneca, *To Lucilius* 40.3. See further Eve, *Behind Gospels*, 179; Klauck, "Presence," 61–62; Alexander, "IPSE DIXIT," 120; van der Horst, "Cornutus," 168–69; Metzger, "Considerations," 17–18n84; BDAG.

101. Lucian, *Alexander* 61; Iamblichus, *Pythagorean Life* 28.148. Sometimes Jewish teachers cited only what they believed to be the tradition's original source (m. 'Ed. 8:7; 'Abot 1:1; cf. 1 Cor 11:23).

102. Iamblichus, *Pythagorean Life* 28.149.

103. Thucydides, *History* 1.85.1.

104. Dio Chrysostom, *Orations* 18.10.

105. See Matt 15:2; Mark 7:3, 5; Gal 1:14; Josephus, *Jewish Antiquities* 13.297, 408.

106. Luke 1:2; 1 Cor 11:23; 15:3; 2 Thess 2:15; cf. Acts 16:4; Papias, frag. 3.7–8, 11, 14; 20.1; 21.1; perhaps Diogn. 11.1, 6; 1 Clem. 7.2.

107. Alexander, "IPSE DIXIT," 112. For Epicureans, Riesner, *Lehrer*, 441–42, cites Cicero, *On the Ends of Good and Evil* 2.20; Diogenes Laertius, *Lives* 10.12, 139–54; Culpepper, *School*, 109.

108. Alexander, "IPSE DIXIT," 112–13; Sedley, "Debate," 149.

109. Culpepper, *School*, 193; Alexander, "Memory," 141; Aulus Gellius, *Attic Nights* 7.10.1; Socrates, *Letters* 20.

110. See Diogenes Laertius, *Lives* 10.1.12; Culpepper, *School*, 50.

111. Kennedy, "Source Criticism," 129.

112. See, e.g., Cicero, *Letters to Atticus* 14.21; Dio Chrysostom, *Orations* 18.18; Suetonius, *Vergil* 22; Galen, *Grief* 83; P.Tebt. 104.40; P.Lond. 1164h.30; P.Oxy. 269.17–18; 1636.45–46; cf.

One older approach[113] promoted suspicion of any alleged teachings of Jesus with which his followers agreed. Yet ancient (and modern) followers usually *did* agree with their teachers. And even if Jesus's disciples did disagree with him, would they have chosen to misrepresent his views? That is unlikely. A minority of ancient pupils did abandon their teachers' views, but when they did so, they were normally clear about their disagreements, rather than claiming that the teacher instead would have agreed with them.[114] If one argues that Jesus's disciples would not dare disagree with their former teacher publicly, given his exalted status, one should also recognize that genuine belief in his exalted status would ensure private respect for his teaching even more than would his status as teacher. The disciples surely believed that their representation of Jesus was consistent with what they experienced of him.

Like most disciples of other teachers, whether Jewish[115] or gentile,[116]

---

further Stambaugh and Balch, *Environment*, 40; Harvey, *Listening*, 54n129; Richards, *Letter Writing*, 64–80, 143.

113. Namely, the negative use of the criterion of dissimilarity; see critiques in, e.g., Borg, *Conflict*, 20–23; Sanders, *Jesus and Judaism*, 16, 145; Sanders, "Know," 60n12; Wright, *People*, 106; Meier, *Marginal Jew*, 1:173; Brown, *Death*, 19; Theissen and Merz, *Guide*, 11, 115; Theissen and Winter, *Quest* (drawing on Winter's dissertation on that criterion); Ehrman, *Prophet*, 92 (cautiously); Holmén, "Doubts"; Holmén, *Covenant Thinking*, 20–31 (esp. 29–30); Tuckett, "Sources and Methods," 133; Dunn, *Perspective*, 57–78, esp. 58; Levine, "Introduction," 10–11; Kazen, "Imagery," 87; Broadhead, "Priests," 125; Neufeld, *Recovering Jesus*, 46; Deines, *Acts of God*, 60; Puig i Tàrrech, *Jesus*, 58–59; Keith, *Scribal Elite*, 79. Stein, *Messiah*, 48, compares what would happen if we applied it to Luther, accepting only what differed from both "sixteenth-century Roman Catholicism and Lutheranism." Cf. also Wright, *Victory*, 339n88: "One might equally suggest that Martin Luther wrote the Letter to the Galatians."

114. See, e.g., Valerius Maximus, *Memorable Doings and Sayings* 8.15.ext.1; Seneca, *To Lucilius* 108.17, 20, 22; 110.14, 20; Musonius Rufus 1, 36.6–7; Philostratus, *Life of Apollonius* 7.22; for disagreeing with the dominant view of one's school, see, e.g., Seneca, *To Lucilius* 117.6; toward founders of a school, e.g., Reydams-Schils, "Authority." For respect for teachers, see, e.g., 'Abot R. Nathan 1A; 25A; Sipra Shemini Mekhilta deMiluim 99.5.6; Fronto, *To Verus* 2.3; Philostratus, *Life of Apollonius* 5.38. One pupil reportedly did omit *some* of his teacher's sayings, doing so because they were rhetorically inappropriate (Philostratus, *Lives of the Sophists* 2.29.621).

115. See, e.g., Josephus, *Life* 10; m. 'Abot 5:21; 'Abot R. Nat. 23A; Safrai, "Education," 953; discussion in Keener, *Acts*, 3:3210–12; cf. 2:1387, 1447–49.

116. Quintilian, *Orator's Education* 2.2.3; Lucian, *Career* 1; Philostratus, *Life of Apollonius* 1.7; Eunapius, *Lives* 493; Hock, "Paul and Education," 204; Hock, "Curriculum," 23; Heath, *Hermogenes*, 11–12; Stowers, *Letter Writing*, 32; Kaster, "Grammaticus"; Beck and Thomas, "Education," 508; Cicero in Stamps, "Children," 198; cf. Pliny, *Letters* 5.8.8; Marrou, *History*, 82–83; Cribiore, *Gymnastics*, 70; Keener, "Rhetoric," 337. Although some continued study long afterward (Seneca, *To Lucilius* 108.5; Porphyry, *Life of Plotinus* 3; Eunapius, *Lives* 461) or even commenced studies later (b. Pesaḥ 49b; satire in Lucian, *Hermotimus* 2, 13), advanced education most often began in the teens.

most of Jesus's disciples were probably in their teens, with a few possibly (like perhaps Peter, who was married)[117] in their early twenties. At least in modern Western studies, subsequent recollections are most complete concerning exactly this impressionable age range.[118] Schwartz even applies this information directly to Jesus's disciples, noting that "individuals are most likely to remember important events that occur in their late adolescence and early adulthood."[119]

As observed in the previous chapter, studies of personal memory demonstrate that personally significant events and emotional experiences reinforce memory.[120] These factors are obviously relevant for Jesus's disciples.[121]

15.3b. Extraordinary Memory in Antiquity

Feats of extraordinary ancient memory, some of which I survey here, are not intended as representative of ancient memories in general, but they graphically illustrate a culture that valued memory in ways rarely considered in the modern West. Ancient mnemonic skills often astonish readers in our less memory-centered modern Western culture.[122] Some reports of ancient memory seem exaggerated,[123] but ancient mnemonic practices make even some of the more astonishing feats plausible.[124] The elder Seneca complains that in his old age he can no longer perform the feats of his younger days, such as repeating back

117. Mark 1:30; later rabbis, at least, valued marrying around eighteen to twenty (m. 'Abot 5:21, 32).

118. Rubin, "Introduction," 13; Fitzgerald, "Meanings," 372–74; also McIver, *Memory*, 85–86, citing Schuman and Scott, "Generations." In the West, most of us experience more unique events in young adulthood, whereas until bereavement and decline in health, older life often follows more predictable patterns.

119. Schwartz, "Smoke," 17.

120. With, e.g., Rubin, "Introduction," 3; Christianson and Safer, "Emotional Events," 219, 237–38; Pillemer et al., "Memories of College," 336.

121. Bauckham, *Eyewitnesses*, 341–46; cf. Allison, *Constructing Jesus*, 9n46; Redman, "Eyewitnesses," 183–84; Elliott, *Feelings*, 44–45; though cf. limitations in Woodman, *Rhetoric*, 18–22; Allison, *Constructing Jesus*, 7n40.

122. Small, *Wax Tablets*, 126–31, cites examples from Vitruvius 7.intro.6–7; Seneca the Elder, *Controversiae* 1.pref.2; Pliny the Elder, *Natural History* 7.24.88; Quintilian, *Orator's Education* 11.2.51; Plutarch, *Themistocles* 5.4.

123. E.g., Valerius Maximus, *Memorable Doings and Sayings* 8.7.ext.16; Pliny the Elder, *Natural History* 7.24.88.

124. Kennedy, "Source Criticism," 143; Kennedy, *Art of Rhetoric*, 123–25; Small, "Memory," 204; more extensively, Blum, *Mnemoteknik*.

two thousand names in precise sequence after hearing them once.[125] (Even back then, however, repeating back just fifty names after hearing them was considered impressive.)[126] After lamenting the decline of his memory,[127] Seneca proceeds to recount from memory long sections of more than a hundred declamations that he heard in his youth![128]

Seneca is an extreme example, but he was not alone in significant mnemonic prowess; another man could repeat a poem on hearing it once; yet another, after attending an auction all day, repeated every item that was sold, the price for which it was sold, and the person to whom it was sold.[129] Such memory skills sometimes surface also in other cultures that value memory. Thus Pandita Ramabai, as a girl in nineteenth-century India, could recite from memory "for an hour or more," and eventually she "could recite eighteen thousand verses" of Hindu texts.[130]

One might dismiss all such stories, were not mnemonic feats of this magnitude recorded today. Thus, for example, modern analysts studied two mnemonists, one of whom reportedly memorized π (*pi*) to 31,811 digits and the other who, though slower, memorized it to 40,000 digits.[131] A British mathematician memorized it to a thousand decimal places, complaining that the undertaking would have been a waste of time had it not been so simple.[132] A chess master playing multiple simultaneous games must recall each of the various boards in detail, a feat that seems impossible to those focused on other disciplines.[133]

Jocelyn Penny Small cites examples from *The Guinness Book of World Records*, emphasizing its requirement for verification: In 1974 a resident of Myanmar "recited 16,000 pages of Buddhist canonical texts." A Chinese news

125. Seneca the Elder, *Controversiae* 1.pref.2. Was his current gist memory exaggerating the accuracy of his earlier verbatim memory?

126. Philostratus, *Lives of the Sophists* 1.11.495.

127. Lowering expectations was a standard rhetorical ploy; see, e.g., Isocrates, *Panathenaicus* 3; Lysias, *Orations* 2.1, §190; 12.3, §120; 19.1–2, §152; Isaeus, *Astyphilus* 35; *Aristarchus* 1; Cicero, *In Defense of Quinctius* 1.1–4; Dio Chrysostom, *Orations* 1.9; 12.16; 32.39; 46.7; 47.1, 8; Pliny, *Letters* 8.3.3; Tacitus, *Histories* 4.73; Josephus, *Against Apion* 1.27; see esp. Quintilian, *Orator's Education* 4.1.8–9, 11.

128. Seneca, *Controversiae*, throughout (presumably just the gist).

129. Seneca, *Controversiae* 1.pref.19. For exceptional memory, see also Suetonius, *Grammarians* 23.

130. Noll and Nystrom, *Clouds*, 127, 129. Further on Ramabai, cf. also Burgess, "Pandita Ramabai"; Arles, "Study"; Arles, "Appraisal"; Frykenberg, *Christianity in India*, 382–410.

131. Small, *Wax Tablets*, 110–12.

132. Small, *Wax Tablets*, 111; cf. 114.

133. Pointed out by Alfeyev, *Beginning*, 67.

agency reported that a resident "memorized more than 15,000 telephone numbers." In 1989 a resident of Texas "memorized a random sequence of thirty separate packs of cards (1,560) that had been all shuffled together on a single sighting with two errors."[134]

Comparing the last example to Seneca the Elder's feat with two thousand names, Small concludes that "memory training works and enables mnemonists to accomplish astounding stunts that lesser souls cannot." She judiciously adds, "The real question is whether you want to spend the time to learn how to memorize 1560 cards or 2000 names just to show off."[135] Even in antiquity, such skills were not typical, but they do illustrate the high value that ancient Mediterranean culture placed on mnemonic prowess, and how those who value memory most can often train memory for excellence.[136]

Rhetorical handbooks instructed their readers in "artificial" memory, which could exceed the skills of natural (untrained) memory.[137] Artificial memory involved techniques for recalling blocks of data astonishing to us modern, Google-dependent readers.[138] Special mnemonic practices appear among Greeks as early as the fifth century BCE,[139] and even earlier among Egyptians.[140] Less artificially, a first-century professor of Roman rhetoric advised that one could memorize a work one part at a time;[141] practice and then quiz oneself,[142] and rehearse the lines out loud.[143] Increasing literacy *increased*

134. Small, *Wax Tablets*, 128, citing McFarlin, *Book of Records*, 16.

135. Small, *Wax Tablets*, 129.

136. On the importance and nature of memory in antiquity, see also Byrskog, *Story*, 160–65; on ancient theories of memory, see, e.g., Farrell, "Phenomenology"; Bloch, *Aristotle on Memory*; Sorabji, *Aristotle on Memory*; Thatcher, "Theories"; Gibbons, "Plato"; for the wax tablet conception, see Brickle, "Wax Tablet."

137. *Rhetorica ad Herennium* 3.16.28–40.

138. Cf. Cicero, *On the Orator* 2.351 (and Olbricht, "Delivery and Memory," 163); *Rhetorica ad Herennium* 3.22.35; Byrskog, *Story*, 82–83, 110–11, 163–65; Walde, "Mnemonics"; Gaines, "Handbooks," 167; Galinsky, "Introduction," 17; see esp. Small, *Wax Tablets*, 81–94; Small, "Memory," 196.

139. Kennedy, "Source Criticism," 98; Kennedy, *Classical Rhetoric*, 98; Small, *Wax Tablets*, 82–86, citing Cicero, *On the Orator* 2.351–354; Quintilian, *Orator's Education* 11.2.16; Nikulin, "Memory," 36, 74. See also Hippias in Plato, *Lesser Hippias* 368d2–7; Xenophon, *Symposium* 4.62, both cited in Joyal, McDougall, and Yardley, *Education*, 66; cf. Marrou, *History*, 55.

140. Riesner, *Lehrer*, 195.

141. Quintilian, *Orator's Education* 11.2.27.

142. Quintilian, *Orator's Education* 11.2.34–35. On the value of spaced practice, see, e.g., Rubin, *Memory*, 124–27.

143. Quintilian, *Orator's Education* 11.2.33; as noted in Small, "Memory," 202–3. Cf. other sorts of mental exercises in Sorabji, *Emotion*, 211–27. On Quintilian's understanding of how children learn, cf. Bloomer, "Quintilian."

rather than decreased dependence on memory, because the literate lacked other adequate retrieval systems.[144]

Orators were supposed to memorize their own speeches[145]—even though these could run for two or three hours.[146] This practice was fundamental to their training.[147] Oratorical students could learn by reciting model speeches from memory.[148] Moreover, they were required to offer practice speeches "from memory."[149] Particularly impressive was a rhetorician so skillful that he could repeat verbatim even speeches that he had delivered extemporaneously.[150] Another orator reportedly could recall word for word every declamation he had ever delivered.[151] More commonly, rhetorically sensitive hearers could also recall elements of speeches that they heard, their memories valuably supplementing even written sources.[152]

None of this is meant to imply that any of Jesus's first disciples had formal training in rhetoric or mnemotechnics. It is simply to emphasize the extent to which memory can be and often is developed where it is valued, and that the ancient Mediterranean world was one such milieu. Jesus's disciples belonged to a world that prized memory in a way that is rare in our modern, information-glutted world.[153]

15.3c. Memory in Ancient Education

In discussing ancient pedagogy, I do not assume that Jesus's disciples had a standard education (though neither need one simply assume that all were

144. Small, *Wax Tablets*, 83.

145. Quintilian, *Orator's Education* 11.2.1–51; see further Kennedy, *Art of Rhetoric*, 403; Satterthwaite, "Acts," 344; cf. Aeschines, *Embassy* 48, 112; Olbricht, "Delivery," 159, 163.

146. E.g., Cicero, *Brutus* 93.324; Tacitus, *Dialogue on Oratory* 38.

147. On memorization in oratory, see also Marrou, *History*, 55, 199, 286; Nikulin, "Memory," 72–78; e.g., Aeschines, *Embassy* 48, 112; Eunapius, *Lives* 502. Memorizing speeches goes back as early as Gorgias (Riesner, *Lehrer*, 441, citing Aristotle, *Sophistical Refutations* 183b–184a; cf. also Vatri, "Writing," 770–71, following Heath, *Menander*, 266–67).

148. Dio Chrysostom, *Orations* 18.19.

149. Watson, "Education," 310.

150. Pliny, *Letters* 2.3.3 (meaning "verbatim" by ancient standards).

151. Seneca the Elder, *Controversiae* 1.pref.18.

152. Lucian, *Peregrinus* 3; Eunapius, *Lives* 494. Some apparently circulated orators' speeches without the orators' knowledge (Botha, "Publishing," 347, on Philostratus *Vit. soph.* 579–80).

153. On the centrality of memory in antiquity, see, e.g., Rhoads, "Events," 173; Rhoads, "Performance Criticism," 285; Boomershine, "Performance," 290; Galinsky, "Introduction," 17.

necessarily completely illiterate). My purpose is twofold: first, to continue to highlight the great emphasis on memory in ancient Mediterranean culture and, second, to point to the necessity for memory in all ancient learning, whether formal or informal, literate or illiterate, in Greek elementary schools or for disciples following an itinerant teacher.

Ancient pedagogy without a focus on memory did not exist.[154] Thus, for example, the first-century teacher Theon would teach a passage by reading it and having students "try to write it out from memory," then paraphrase and develop it.[155] An "oral component" pervaded "ancient learning."[156] The emphasis does not begin with Greeks; students in New Kingdom Egypt, for example, were reminded, "You should become a book container!"[157]

Widespread illiteracy and, even for the literate, the relatively rare possession of books brought memory to the fore in ancient pedagogy.[158] Because written materials were less accessible, the focus of ancient education was on recall of content, although such recollection was not verbatim memorization in the modern sense.[159] The point of ancient education was "mastery of content,"[160] without which it would be impossible to access historical and literary allusions.[161]

Thus a certain Nicoratus may have boasted that he learned all of Homer by heart, but he was hardly alone; more learned people complained that the "stupid" rhapsodes could all do the same, without understanding the true sense of what they were reciting.[162] Boys memorized various parts of the *Iliad*, though

154. For memory in ancient education, Riesner, *Lehrer*, 442–43, cites, e.g., *Rhetorica ad Herennium* 3.28–40, esp. 3.39; Quintilian, *Orator's Education* 11.2.1; 11.2.27–11.35.40; Cicero, *On the Orator* 1.157a; Epictetus, *Encheiridion* 49.3; Philostratus, *Lives of the Sophists* 523; Longinus, *De memoria* 202.21–203.3; 204.21–23; Plotinus, *Enneades* 4.6.3; cf. briefly Riesner, "Preacher," 203.

155. Kennedy, *Classical Rhetoric* (2), 27.

156. Cribiore, *Gymnastics*, 181.

157. Riesner, *Lehrer*, 452, citing Brunner, *Erziehung*, 179, and comparing also Longinus as "living library" (Eunapius, *Lives* 456). For oral tradition in the OT, see discussion in Rüger, "Tradition."

158. Small, *Wax Tablets*, 129; even for the highly literate, see 81, 188.

159. McIver, *Memory*, 165; Dunn, *Tradition*, 237. McIver notes that sources from greater Judea remain consistent with this picture (*Memory*, 166–67).

160. McIver, *Memory*, 165. For elites, such mastery of content had long been geared toward learning for oral performance (Carr, *Writing*, 27; cf. 278; Niditch, *World*).

161. Small, *Wax Tablets*, 129, 179–81; Derrenbacker, *Practices*, 46; McIver, *Memory*, 165.

162. Xenophon, *Symposium* 3.5–6. For Nicoratus in this passage, see also Riesner, *Lehrer*, 451; Small, *Wax Tablets*, 129–30; Joyal, McDougall, and Yardley, *Education*, 41–42.

apparently most successfully the first two books and the beginnings of other books.[163] Greeks deemed memorizing some of Homer quintessential to Greek culture,[164] and Homer continued to be memorized into the Middle Ages.[165]

An emphasis on rote memory pervaded the most basic educational level,[166] often tested with drilling.[167] The most valued learning skills in children were memory and imitating what was taught.[168] Even in a literate environment, oral memorization reinforced learning.[169]

Higher education, beginning in the mid-teens, did not focus on rote memory,[170] but memory remained important, for example, for memorizing model speeches.[171] Close attention to texts and reciting them simplified the process of memorizing them.[172] Students had to remain attentive not only with texts but also during lectures.[173] Those trained in rhetoric could adjust the accounts they remembered, but such adjustments at this stage were normally not supposed to add to or change content in any substantive manner.[174]

---

163. Cribiore, *Gymnastics*, 197; cf. Puig i Tàrrech, *Jesus*, 20. In contrast to poems that varied more flexibly, the *Iliad* persisted in a more consistent form because it functioned canonically for Greeks (see Finkelberg, "*Cypria*"). Various repetition devices aided memory (Harvey, *Listening*, 45, 56).

164. Cribiore, *Gymnastics*, 248.

165. Browning, "Homer," esp. 15–21 (noted in Joyal, McDougall, and Yardley, *Education*, 266). Cf. Browning, "Homer," 15: "always a schoolbook . . . from which generation after generation learned to read with understanding").

166. See, e.g., Quintilian, *Orator's Education* 2.4.15; Plutarch, *On the Education of Children* 13, *Moralia* 9E; Musonius Rufus, frag. 51, p. 144.3–7; Diogenes Laertius, *Lives* 6.2.31; Eunapius, *Lives* 481; Marrou, *History*, 154, 279; Cribiore, *Gymnastics*, 49, 138, 144, 191, 194; Watson, "Education," 310, 312; Heath, *Hermogenes*, 11; Moeser, *Anecdote*, 54; Aune, *Dictionary*, 143; Eve, *Behind Gospels*, 39; Keener, "Before Biographies," 338–41; Kwon, "Reimagining," 128–37, 293; Boomershine, "Performance," 290; Gorman, "Education," 112.

167. Joyal, McDougall, and Yardley, *Education*, 198.

168. Quintilian, *Orator's Education* 1.1.36; 1.3.1.

169. Carr, *Writing*, 111–73 (brought to my attention by Ehrensperger, *Paul*, 119); see esp. 72–73, 106, 128, 181; in a Jewish setting, 160.

170. See Morgan, *Literate Education*, 208; Epictetus, *Discourses* 2.19.6–7, in Joyal, McDougall, and Yardley, *Education*, 199; for the mid-teens, note 267; the sources in Keener, *Acts*, 3:3209–10; esp. Josephus, *Life* 10; Pliny, *Letters* 5.8.8; Watson, "Education," 312; Stamps, "Children," 198.

171. Quintilian, *Orator's Education* 11.2.1–51; Dio Chrysostom, *Orations* 18.19; cf. Cribiore, *Gymnastics*, 200, 231 (citing Theon, *Progymnasmata* 137.18–21); Morgan, *Literate Education*, 90.

172. Marrou, *History*, 166.

173. E.g., Aulus Gellius, *Attic Nights* 8.3; Philostratus, *Lives of the Sophists* 2.8.578.

174. Cited earlier, see Theon, *Progymnasmata* 3.224–40; cf. 2.115–23; also Longinus, *On the Sublime* 11.1; Hermogenes, *Invention* 2.7.120–21 (cf. 2.1.108–9; 2.7.120–24); Hermogenes, *Progymnasmata* 3. On Chreia, 7; on fables, cf. Theon, *Progymnasmata* 4.37–42, 80–82 (Butts).

Both attributed and unattributed maxims were memorized and passed on for centuries, even in elementary educational settings.[175] Students memorized and copied these maxims "letter by letter."[176] Such maxims did double duty: they not only provided grist for writing, reading, and memory, but they also offered moral principles believed to remain with students for life.[177] Like the broader Greco-Roman circulation of maxims, Judean oral training circulated various sorts of wise sayings (proverbs, parables, and the like), rhetorical forms also plainly used by Jesus.[178] One widely known pre-Christian sage speaks of those who study the law as preserving wise parables and searching out obscure proverbs or maxims.[179]

As noted in the previous chapter, such aphorisms, or concise and often witty statements, were normally memorable and initially remembered fairly accurately.[180] Like most sages, Jesus probably used some of his sayings in various settings;[181] nevertheless, this practice does not likely explain all the variations in context that we find. Such sayings circulated both in collections and independently and could be combined with stories about the teacher in question.[182] Sayings could circulate independently,[183] but sayings for which context was necessary, such as in brief narratives climaxing in the protagonist's quip,[184] were often transmitted with the gist of the basic story or context that

175. Cf. Musonius Rufus, frag. 51, p. 144.3–7; Hermogenes, *Progymnasmata* 4. On Maxim, 8–10; Moeser, *Anecdote*, 54–55. (By the strictest definition, "maxims" might be unattributed; cf. the later Nicolaus of Myra, *Progymnasmata* 5, On Maxim, 25.) On boys learning these and chreiai, see also Anderson, *Glossary*, 126–27 (citing Seneca, *To Lucilius* 33.7). Historians did not reproduce speeches verbatim, but they sometimes reproduced brief sayings thus (see Marincola, "Speeches," 120).

176. Cribiore, *Gymnastics*, 167; on learning the maxims, cf. also Morgan, *Literate Education*, 71; Moeser, *Anecdote*, 54; Joyal, McDougall, and Yardley, *Education*, 167, 170; in Egypt, cf. Doran, "Paideia," 136.

177. Quintilian, *Orator's Education* 1.1.35–36, in Joyal, McDougall, and Yardley, *Education*, 172; later, cf. Proclus, *Poetics* 5, K58.6–14.

178. Cf. Pirke Aboth; Vermes, *Jesus the Jew*, 27.

179. Sir 38:34; 39:2–3, 9.

180. McIver, *Memory*, 176; more extensively, McIver and Carroll, "Experiments"; McIver and Carroll, "Characteristics."

181. Frye, "Synoptic Problems," 291; Aune, "Aphorisms," 225; Dunn, *Tradition*, 281. The same may be noted for ancient speakers like Lucian, who gave orations in multiple locations (Harmon, "Introduction"); Dio Chrysostom also reused his own speeches (cf. H. L. Crosby, "Introduction to Discourse 66," LCL 5:86).

182. See, e.g., Theon, *Progymnasmata* 4.73–79; cf. 5.388–441.

183. E.g., Seneca, *To Lucilius* 94.27–28.

184. E.g., Diogenes Laertius, *Lives* 2.72, 6.2.51; Plutarch, *Agesilaus* 21.4–5.

fueled their sense;[185] biographers sometimes expressed confidence regarding the incidents in their subject's life in which a particular saying was given.[186] Thus we probably have some sayings of Jesus in the Gospels in their original essential contexts, though others (e.g., Matt 7:13–14//Luke 13:24; Matt 8:11// Luke 13:29) clearly appear in distinct contexts.

Some memories of sayings could be quite significant. Verbatim memory requires rehearsal of the material, but in nearly universal ancient pedagogical practice, students did regularly rehearse such sayings, so Jesus as a teacher presumably expected his disciples to do likewise.[187] This is not to imply that all of Jesus's aphorisms would be remembered, but rather to imply that those that were remembered were probably remembered quite accurately. Noting psychological studies, McIver emphasizes, "Once in long-term memory, aphorisms would usually be remembered accurately or—and this is the important point— *not at all.*"[188] Jesus's reported aphorisms tend to be memorable: concise and vivid.[189] Not surprisingly, then, the Evangelists tend to report aphorisms with something closer to verbatim agreement than found in parables.[190] Genre does make a difference here; historians' rare appeal to verbatim quotes generally consisted of short lines,[191] but teachings often appear in biographies of sages.[192]

Jesus's teachings in the tradition are predesigned "for easy remembering," as Dunn notes. "Prominent features are various kinds of parallelism, alliteration, assonance and paronomasia," as cataloged by a host of modern scholars.[193] Dunn notes the difference between this and random long-term recall of facts: "What is envisaged is not a casual recall across several decades of something once heard and little thought about since. . . . What is in view is a deliberate instruction intended to be retained for its value in discipleship."[194]

---

185. Cf. Hermogenes, *Progymnasmata* 3. On Chreia, 6–7; Aphthonius, *Progymnasmata,* 3. On Chreia, 23S, 4R; Nicolaus, *Progymnasmata* 4. On Chreia, 19–20; 5. On Maxim, 26.

186. Plutarch, *Themistocles* 11.2.

187. McIver, *Memory,* 167, 176, 180, 184.

188. McIver, *Memory,* 176.

189. McIver, *Memory,* 176.

190. McIver, *Memory,* 177.

191. Marincola, "Speeches," 120, citing Tacitus, *Annals* 14.59.4; 15.67.4.

192. See, e.g., Diogenes Laertius, *Lives,* throughout.

193. Dunn, *Tradition,* 238, citing esp. Burney, *Poetry*; Manson, *Teaching*; Black, *Aramaic Approach*; Jeremias, *Theology*; Riesner, *Lehrer,* 392–404; see also Riesner, "Preacher," 201–8, esp. 202–4.

194. Dunn, *Tradition,* 238. But he prefers to emphasize Jesus's personal impact on the disciples, which goes beyond anything like simply memorizing multiplication tables (240). Cf. Bird, *Gospel,* 42.

Prominent as sayings were in ancient education, students also carefully learned historical examples.[195] Although teachers often emphasized learning their teachings, students studied and emulated teachers' behavior as well.[196] Not surprisingly, then, they also transmitted it.[197] Both Greek[198] and Jewish[199] disciples sought to imitate their teachers, and later Jewish disciples even cited earlier rabbis' behavior as legal precedent.[200]

Teachers expected disciples to develop their memories to learn teachings. All schools of philosophy emphasized memory, though not all to an equal degree,[201] and they offered their various theories about it.[202] Some schools emphasized memorizing texts; others, the teacher's words.[203] Among Jesus's disciples, the teacher's words would necessarily be the focus (all the more if the disciples were illiterate, as some scholars contend).

This practice would have implications for a disciple's memoirs about a former teacher. Thus Lucian's *Demonax* contains fifty-two anecdotes about his teacher Demonax; one commentator observes that "Lucian may have written the series of anecdotes from memory, given the ancient practice of memorizing anecdotes and sayings."[204]

15.3d. Ancient Jewish Memory

All our sources indicate that Jewish families, of whatever social class, brought up their children with knowledge of Jewish law and customs.[205] Apologeti-

---

195. Theon, *Progymnasmata* 2.5–8.

196. See, e.g., Philostratus, *Life of Apollonius* 5.21; Liefeld, "Preacher," 223; Robbins, *Teacher*, 64; cf. Tieleman, "Orality," 23, 28.

197. E.g., Philostratus, *Lives of the Sophists* 1.22.524; Eunapius, *Lives* 458.

198. Xenophon, *Memorabilia* 1.2.3; Seneca, *To Lucilius* 108.4.

199. Josephus, *Life* 11.

200. E.g., t. Pesaḥ. 2:15–16; Sipre Deut. 221.1.1.

201. Alexander, "Memory," 133, 138.

202. For Platonists, see Nikulin, "Memory," 44–60; cf. Philo, *Immutable* 43; Maximus of Tyre, *Philosophical Orations* 10.6–9; Iamblichus, *Soul* 2.14, §609; for Peripatetics, Aristotle, *Memory*; Nikulin, "Memory," 60–69; for Stoics, more ambiguously, Nikulin, "Memory," 69–71; cf. Arius Didymus, *Epitome* 2.7.7b, p. 44.25–26; generally, Sorabji, *Emotion*, 231–33; Farrell, "Phenomenology."

203. Culpepper, *School*, 177. The textual focus dominates primarily in later times; see Blyth, "Cicero," 71–98.

204. Moeser, *Anecdote*, 92.

205. See, e.g., Deut 4:10; 6:7; 11:19; 26:5–10; Ps 78:5; Prov 6:20; Riesner, *Lehrer*, 115–17, 440. Though Riesner's passages on 117 may address esp. discipline, cf. Hogan, "*Musar*," esp. 82,

cally underlining Jewish virtue, Philo declares that Jews are trained from the beginning to carry in their very souls the images of the commandments.[206] Jewish sources teach much about disciples learning from their teachers well before the period of the rabbis.[207] But although rabbinic sources postdate the Gospels, they provide the fullest concrete examples of Jewish education, and these examples comport with virtually all the other ancient Mediterranean evidence.[208]

Some scholars[209] have underlined the rabbis' emphasis on the careful transmission of tradition.[210] It does not seem probable, prima facie, that the later rabbinic method simply arose *ex nihilo* after 70 CE.[211] Rabbis believed that they continued much earlier discipleship practices, a belief probably relevant at least for then-recent generations.[212]

Few scholars today would dispute that "elaborations" and "innovations" also occurred.[213] But while early studies sometimes drew criticism by overplaying the analogy between Jesus's disciples and those of later rabbis,[214] subsequent refinement has allowed scholars today to build on the early studies'

92–93, 98. LXX translators vary in their approaches to these latter passages, with only some Qumran texts developing a sense of *ysr* as education in the law; see Pouchelle, *Dieu éducateur*; Pouchelle, "*Kyropaideia*."

206. Philo, *Embassy* 210.

207. See Byrskog, *Teacher*, 35–75, 88, esp. Sir 51:23, 29 (Cairo Geniza B; though the OT evidence depends on significant OT scholarship, I do not deem all of it equally compelling); early tradition in m. 'Abot 1:4. Cf. also early interpretations of OT discipleship in CD 8.20–21; Mek. Pesaḥ. 1.150–53.

208. See comments above and esp. Riesner, *Lehrer*.

209. Initially, see esp. Gerhardsson, *Memory*, 122–70; Gerhardsson, *Origins*, 19–24; Gerhardsson, "Path"; Riesenfeld, *Tradition*, 14–17; more recently, and more sophisticated, Gerhardsson, *Gospel Tradition*. Some earlier German form critics had earlier drawn analogies between the gospel tradition and rabbinic tradition (Dibelius, *Tradition*, 39).

210. E.g., t. Yebam. 3:1; Mek. Pesaḥ. 1.135–36; Sipre Deut. 48.2.6.

211. See Hagner, *Matthew*, xlix.

212. Mek. Pesaḥ. 1.150–53. Cf. perhaps Prov 3:1; Sir 28:7; esp. Sir 51:23–25 (Riesner, *Lehrer*, 166–67).

213. Byrskog, *Teacher*, 160, 397; Alexander, "Orality," 182; Hezser, "Randomness," 50–51; see esp. Neusner, *Traditions*; Instone-Brewer, *Traditions*; cf. discussion and further sources in Keener, *John*, 1:185–94.

214. Gerhardsson, *Memory*, drew the characteristically harsh critique of Smith ("Comparison"). Byrskog, *Teacher*, 337, rejects Smith's response as an "old and polemical article," contradicted by more recent research, esp. Zimmermann, *Lehrer*. For respectful and helpful nuancing in light of more recent memory research, see Kirk, *Memory*, 93–113; noting that Gerhardsson has been caricatured, see 94.

central point.[215] Even some former critics of the early studies now find some value in the approach.[216] Although the earliest studies did compare Jesus's disciples too closely with more formal ancient schools,[217] it may be noteworthy that outsiders did compare churches, like synagogues,[218] with schools,[219] a comparison that became fairly common in the second century.[220]

For the purpose of argument, however, I set aside here rabbinic evidence, since some critics dispute any post-70 evidence even for post-70 Gospels. Well before 70, Pharisees were known for passing on their oral traditions.[221] More generally, Judeans and Galileans were known for instructing boys meticulously in the law,[222] probably especially orally and presumably therefore requiring the boys to develop skills in oral memory.[223] Many Jews as early as the period of 2 Maccabees apparently liked to memorize details of Jewish history.[224] Diaspora Jews valued memory practices; one Hellenistic Jewish tradition alle-

215. See esp. Riesner, *Lehrer*.

216. Kelber, "Work," 194, contends that Neusner's earlier critique, based on his literary focus, misunderstood Gerhardsson's oral one. Neusner has since recognized that Gerhardsson's work, though overstated, contains valuable elements (Neusner, "Foreword"). Gerhardsson's work, appreciated by many rabbinics scholars, did recognize both the "conservation" and "mobility" of tradition (Kelber, "Work," 191–92; more nuanced and appreciative than earlier in Kelber, *Gospel*, 8–15, 23, 28), though he underestimated the impingement of subsequent social reality on memory, just as earlier form critics overestimated it (Kirk and Thatcher, "Tradition," 35). Cf. appreciation for much of Gerhardsson's key thesis and foundational insights, with subsequent refinements, also in, e.g., Kelber, "Works," 232–34; Talmon, "Tradition," 123; Meyer, "Consequences," 440; Person and Keith, "Media Studies," 12; Kirk, "Collective Memory," 61; Kirk, *Memory*, 93–113; Byrskog, "Form Criticism," 144; Byrskog, "Gerhardsson."

217. Note the criticism in Smith, "Comparison," 174.

218. Cf. Alexander, "IPSE DIXIT," 105.

219. Judge, "Scholastic Community," 137; Wilken, "Christians," 107–10; Wilken, "Interpretation"; Aune, *Prophecy*, 229; Meeks, *Moral World*, 114; Stowers, "Resemble Philosophy?" 81–102.

220. Schmeller, "Gegenwelten"; Wilken, "Interpretation," 444–48; Wilken, "Collegia," 277; Alexander, "IPSE DIXIT," 107.

221. Mark 7:3, 8–9; Josephus, *Jewish Antiquities* 13.297, 408. Oral tradition might also inform some apocalyptic literature; cf. Henze, "Composition."

222. Josephus, *Jewish Antiquities* 4.211; *Against Apion* 1.60; 2.204; cf. *Life* 8; *Against Apion* 2.171–73; m. 'Abot 6:6. At Qumran, although this is a special case, cf. Carr, *Writing*, 228–30; suggesting nightly oral recitations there, cf. Horsley, "Mark," 146 (interpreting 1QS 6.5–8); later, perhaps most relevant to the intelligentsia, cf. m. 'Abot 5:21.

223. Everyone could learn orally in synagogue contexts (e.g., Josephus, *Against Apion* 2.173, 175; Philo, *Hypothetica* 7.12–13; Sanders, *Judaism*, 199; Gorman, "Education," 113); boys were also taught to recite Torah (cf. Josephus, *Jewish Antiquities* 20.264–65; *Life* 9–12; m. 'Abot 5:21; Riesner, "Éducation élémentaire"; Riesner, *Lehrer*).

224. 2 Macc 2:25.

gorically interpreted cud-chewing as memory rehearsal.[225] Teachers retained a central role in various pre-Christian Jewish circles.[226]

If one chooses to dismiss all such reports about Jewish memory as mere propaganda, one should be clear about what one is doing. One is discarding virtually all extant evidence and then complaining that no evidence supports the only position for which we have any substantial evidence at all—namely, that disciples in this period did normally seek to remember their teacher's message. Those who became teachers themselves and remained within the same school of thought were expected to pass on the teaching of their school. This was true whether the sages were philosophers or Jewish teachers of wisdom.

Although those who heard the disciples would not all be disciples themselves, they would likely value what they learned. Because weekly synagogue meetings included learning the Torah,[227] many gentiles viewed Jews as a "nation of philosophers."[228] Synagogue liturgy eventually included recitation;[229] while that full practice is debated for this period,[230] it is clear that Jewish people regularly recited the Decalogue, Shema,[231] and many psalms and hymns.[232]

Early Christians highlighted the teaching role, which suggests that they, like synagogue communities, also cared about propagating content.[233] This

225. Let. Aris. 154; Philo, *Special Laws* 4.107. For the early influence of Hellenistic pedagogical approaches on Judean education, see Clark, "Education"; Doran, "Paideia" (although also noting the reaction after Antiochus's desecration of the temple, 147–48); cf. Koskenniemi, "Moses." Even in Wisdom of Solomon, *paideia* is not restricted to Hellenistic education, though it might be included (see Zurawski, "Paideia").

226. See Sir 6:34–38; 8:8–9; 51:23 (cf. 50:27); in Sirach and some Qumran scrolls, see, e.g., Goff, "Gardens," 171–72. Cf. royal instructors in Ps 119:99; Prov 5:13.

227. Philo, *Hypothetica* 7.12–13; *Special Laws* 2.62–63; *Free* 81; Josephus, *Against Apion* 2.175; *Jewish Antiquities* 16.43; CIJ 2:333, §1404.

228. Stern, *Authors*, 1:8–11, 46–50; Gager, *Anti-Semitism*, 39; cf. Mayer, "Abrahambildes," 125–26; Satlow, "Philosophers"; Bosch-Veciana, "Filosofia."

229. Riesner, *Lehrer*, 139; cf. 440. For cantillation, see 141–42; this reflects a wider practice in old Egyptian, Greek, and Roman schools (Riesner, *Lehrer*, 196; cf. 448).

230. For evidence that does not suggest a common liturgy, cf. Levine, "Synagogue," 19–20; Cohen, "Evidence," 175; for evidence that could favor some common Jewish liturgy, cf. Schiffman, "Scrolls"; Maier, "Kult"; Goodman, *State*, 86. Qumran's early institutional prayer (1QS 9.26–10.3; 4Q504; 4Q507–9) appears unusual (Talmon, "Institutionalized Prayer," 273–74). See discussion in Keener, *Acts*, 2:1045–46.

231. Riesner, *Lehrer*, 139. See the second-century-BCE Nash papyrus (e.g., noted in Bright, *History*, 415; McNamara, *Targum*, 39).

232. Philo, *Special Laws* 2.145; Riesner, *Lehrer*, 140–41. In particular, Levites and priests learned certain songs thoroughly (Josephus, *Jewish Antiquities* 20.216–18).

233. Dunn, *Tradition*, 281, noting the prominence of both teaching (Acts 2:42; 13:1; Rom

interest persisted; Irenaeus in the late second century integrates faith with the classical Greco-Roman curriculum,[234] and in the fourth century Christians trained in the same schools as pagans.[235] According to the fourth-century rule of Pachomius, ideally everyone in the monastery should "know by heart at least the Psalter and the New Testament."[236] Memorizing the entire Psalter might take two or three years, "though gifted individuals could manage it in six months."[237] If a novice entering a monastery was illiterate, he had to listen "to the teacher reading aloud Biblical texts until he memorized them."[238] Presumably in view of the shortage of manuscripts, a later Coptic bishop required prospective deacons to memorize or transcribe at least one Gospel.[239]

Many medieval European thinkers likewise knew large sections of Scripture by heart.[240] In the twelfth century, for example, Hugh of St. Victor prescribed memorization of psalms—as well as of his seventy some folio pages of introduction to biblical history.[241] The skill of memorizing texts has persisted into living memory of our own times in the West.[242] Performance critics note how oral performers often memorize verbatim passages or books of the Bible.[243] These are texts rather than purely oral traditions (i.e., more like Mark than like whatever oral accounts that informed him), but these cases do illustrate possibilities for human memory that our generation does not always imagine.

12:7; 1 Cor 12:28–29; Gal 6:6; Jas 3:1) and tradition (Phil 4:9; Col 2:6–8; 1 Thess 4:1; 2 Thess 3:6). Cf. Manson, "Review of Jeremias": "The early Church remembered better than it understood"; cited in Gerhardsson, *Memory*, 129n2; Riesner, *Lehrer*, 453.

234. See Bingham, "Paideia," esp. 353.

235. Cribiore, "Compete," 359, 361–62, 369–72.

236. Marrou, *History*, 330–31, citing *Rule of Pachomius* 139–40; for clergy in the fifth through the seventh centuries knowing the psalms, see Marrou, *History*, 337; cf. Riesner, "Preacher," 206.

237. Carruthers, *Book of Memory*, 112.

238. Cribiore, *Gymnastics*, 177, though noting that most students learned to write before reading.

239. Deissmann, *Light*, 223; also noted in Riesner, *Lehrer*, 452, who cites additional examples.

240. Kelber, "History," 87; cf. Kelber, "Works," 224–25.

241. Carruthers, *Book of Memory*, 100.

242. E.g., Alanna Nobbs shares a punishment her mother endured in a 1920s English boarding school: "She had to learn" a hundred lines of Longfellow's "Hiawatha overnight and recite it to the teacher in the morning" (personal correspondence, August 22, 2018).

243. Boomershine, "Research Unit," 39; cf. Rhoads, "Events," 166; Boomershine, "Performance," 290.

15.3e. Re-re-re-repeating

Ancient thinkers widely recognized the value of repetition for hearers' memory.[244] Even advanced students often rehearsed what they had learned;[245] this practice could include repeatedly testing oneself.[246] Studies show that repetition establishes the main points both in personal memory[247] and in oral tradition,[248] while also condensing them and conforming them more to an overarching schema[249] and modifying the memory by its association with the new contexts.[250]

Lucian portrays a philosophic student as rehearsing each of the points of the previous day's lectures in his mind.[251] Pythagoreans, who also employed repetition to reinforce memorization,[252] offer a particularly vivid, though presumably extreme, illustration of learning a school's teachings.[253] Disciples reportedly could not get out of bed in the morning until they had recited the

244. Vatri, "Writing," 759–61, citing, e.g., Aristotle, *Rhetoric* 1414a4–7; 1419b10–13, 28–32; *Rhetorica ad Alexandrum* 21.2; 22.4; 32.6; 36.45; 37.7; Anonymous Seguerianus, *Art of Political Speech* 10.211–13. Cf. also Deut 6:7; Montefusco, "Exercitatio," 265.

245. See Diodorus Siculus, *Library of History* 10.5.1; Lucian, *Hermotimus* 1; Iamblichus, *Pythagorean Life* 29.164–65; 35.256; Philostratus, *Life of Apollonius* 1.14; 2.30; 3.16; Small, *Wax Tablets*, 118; cf. Sipre Deut. 48.1.1–4; Goodman, *State*, 79.

246. Small, *Wax Tablets*, 118, citing Quintilian, *Orator's Education* 11.2.34–35, 44.

247. E.g., Small, *Wax Tablets*, 117–21; Rubin, *Memory*, 129; Stock, Gajsar, and Güntürkün, "Neuroscience," 375, 385.

248. See, e.g., Assmann, *Cultural Memory*, 3–4, 81; Assmann, "Memory and Culture," 341; Finnegan, *Oral Poetry*, 78; Barber and Barber, *Severed*, 10; Kirk, "Memory Theory," 823; Eve, *Behind Gospels*, 92; Rubin, *Memory*, 72–75, 124–29, 144, 155, 170, 228; Byrskog, *Teacher*, 397; Mournet, *Oral Tradition*, 174–79, 190; Schwartz, "Smoke," 14.

249. Vansina, *Oral Tradition*, 171; Small, *Wax Tablets*, 200; Rubin, "Introduction," 4; Bauckham, *Eyewitnesses*, 346–47, 350; Redman, "Eyewitnesses," 189; Schwartz, "Smoke," 23; Eve, *Behind Gospels*, 156; Kirk, "Nexus," 148; Kirk, "Jesus Tradition"; Kirk, "Ehrman, Bauckham, and Bird," 92; Kirk, *Memory*, 191–93, 216–18; McIver, "Personal Memory," 54; earlier, cf. Mandler, *Stories*. For a personal example during the editing of this book (August 25, 2018), at a fortieth-year high school reunion an old friend described my sudden conversion, from an anti-Christian atheism and an unchurched background, in language borrowed from Paul's experience on the road to Damascus, though (as I explained) my admittedly abrupt experience was much less dramatic than Paul's.

250. Stock, Gajsar, and Güntürkün, "Neuroscience," 385.

251. Lucian, *Hermotimus* 1.

252. Iamblichus, *Pythagorean Life* 31.188.

253. E.g., Quintilian, *Orator's Education* 11.2.27; Iamblichus, *Pythagorean Life* 20.94; 29.164; 35.256; Philostratus, *Life of Apollonius* 1.14, 19; 2.30; 3.16. Although Iamblichus and Philostratus write after our period, Diodorus Siculus (below) writes in the first century BCE.

previous day's learning![254] The sources that have survived indicate that Jewish disciples also learned by repetition.[255]

This pervasive pedagogic pattern presumably would hold for Jesus's disciples as well, since, again, they were *disciples*.[256] Jesus may have supervised his disciples in disseminating his teachings at times even during his ministry;[257] in any case, they certainly propagated his message afterward. Presumably, adherents of Jesus's movement would call on them to recount stories about him over and over again. Communicating his acts and teachings over and over would have shaped and reinforced their memories of it.[258] (Even today, professors who teach a course repeatedly can often recount much of its content from memory.)

Studies show that spaced practice (with intervals for rest) significantly aids retention and recall,[259] with long-term effects demonstrated after even eight years.[260] That the disciples were with Jesus for an extended period of time (perhaps a year or more) naturally would have made them quite familiar with his character and teaching.

15.3f. Taking Note of Note-Taking

It is far from certain that any of Jesus's disciples took notes during his ministry, but ancient practice at least allows the possibility.[261] Note-taking as a memory aid[262] was common among those with sufficient literacy to employ it. In the northern Mediterranean sphere, some hearers of speeches took

254. Diodorus Siculus, *Library of History* 10.5.1; Iamblichus, *Pythagorean Life* 29.165.

255. See m. 'Abot 2:8; Sipre Deut. 48.1.1–4; 48.2.6; Goodman, *State*, 79; Byrskog, *Teacher*, 136–96, esp. 158–60 (esp. m. 'Abot 2:8; 'Ed. 1:3; Yad. 4:3; Neg. 9:3; t. Yebam. 3:4; cf. Zlotnick, "Memory," 229–41.

256. McIver, *Memory*, 184; Bauckham, *Eyewitnesses*, 341–46; cf. Allison, *Constructing Jesus*, 9n46.

257. See Bernier, *Quest*, 62; cf. Dunn, *Tradition*, 242. Such apprenticeship of disciples was not uncommon.

258. McIver, *Memory*, 130; see also 167, 176, 180, 184.

259. Small, *Wax Tablets*, 122; Rubin, *Memory*, 125–27, 144, 154.

260. Rubin, *Memory*, 127.

261. See, e.g., Kennedy, "Source Criticism," 136–37; noted appreciatively also by Black, "Kennedy," 65–66.

262. Cf. Montanari, "Hypomnema"; Small, *Wax Tablets*, 179; Wright, *Reading*, 119–20; Odor, "Enchiridion," 118; cf. Cicero, *On the Ends of Good and Evil* 3.3.10; 5.5.12; Aulus Gellius, *Attic Nights* pref.2, 22.

notes to capture the gist of the speeches,[263] sometimes even during school declamations.[264]

Disciples of advanced Greek teachers, both in philosophy and rhetoric, often took notes during their teachers' lectures.[265] As early as five centuries before the era of Jesus's disciples, such notes were sometimes published,[266] a practice that continued in the period in which the Gospels were published.[267]

Especially in urban academic settings, however, note-taking prevailed. These settings differ from Jesus's typically rural Galilean teaching venue. Moreover, some Jewish pedagogy highlighted orality more than did most Greek pedagogy.[268] Nevertheless, some contend that even some Jewish disciples took rudimentary notes for use as initial mnemonic devices to recall larger blocs of material.[269] Mnemonic devices appear earlier in Egypt and apparently in the OT and Dead Sea Scrolls.[270] The potential use of rudimentary notes is compatible with models of predominantly oral transmission.[271]

Some scholars suggest that at least one of Jesus's followers, a tax-collector (Mark 2:14), should have had the skills to take such notes,[272] at least if we may infer anything from ancient tax records.[273] This is not to assume that ordinary tax collectors could compose literary works such as our Gospels. But note-taking, like scrawling names on voting shards, was a far more elementary exercise than literary composition.[274]

263. Gempf, "Speaking," 299.

264. Seneca the Elder, *Suasoriae* 3.2.

265. Cf. Quintilian, *Orator's Education* 11.2.2, 25; Seneca, *To Lucilius* 108.6; Epictetus, *Discourses* pref.2; Arius Didymus, *Epitome* 2.7.11k, p. 80.36–82.1; Lucian, *Hermotimus* 2; see also Votaw, "Biographies," 53, 56; Lutz, "Musonius," 7, 10; Kennedy, "Source Criticism," 131; Gempf, "Speaking," 299; cf. Hippolytus, *Refutation of All Heresies* 1.15.

266. Kennedy, *Classical Rhetoric*, 19.

267. Quintilian, *Orator's Education* 1.pref.7–8; Epictetus, *Discourses* 1.pref. For the nature of ancient publication, cf. discussion in Keener, *Acts*, 1:43–50.

268. See, e.g., Hezser, *Literacy*, 98.

269. Cf. Gerhardsson, *Memory*, 160–62; Safrai, "Education," 966.

270. Riesner, *Lehrer*, 195–96, for the scrolls citing Slomovic, "Understanding"; cf. oral memory at Qumran in Talmon, "Tradition," 157–58.

271. Kelber, *Gospel*, 23.

272. E.g., Gundry, *Use*, xii; Eddy and Boyd, *Legend*, 250; cf. Papias, frag. 3.16, although the accuracy and meaning are much disputed.

273. See, e.g., Day and Keyes, *Documents*, 114; Harris, *Literacy*, 143; Bagnall, *Reading Papyri*, 16, 32–33; Cuvigny, "Finds of Papyri," 43, 48; Johnson and Goodrich, *Papyri* 3. Judea may have required less tax paperwork than Egypt, but what was done still required some writing (see Hezser, *Literacy*, 499–500).

274. For commercial literacy, which was insufficient for prose composition but adequate

Whether or not any disciples took notes when Jesus was teaching them, many ancient students who could take notes did so, which does reinforce my more general point that ancient pupils valued the preservation of their masters' teachings.

15.3g. So What about Jesus and His Disciples?

If Jesus was a sage with disciples, we might reasonably expect that his disciples paid attention to his teachings. If Jesus's disciples were not learning his teaching, why would we even envision them as disciples in the first place?[275] Indeed, given the pervasive practice of memory in learning everywhere else, Jesus might have had to explicitly warn his disciples *against* memorization if he expected his disciples *not* to learn his teachings![276] And if they inherited his role as leaders in his movement, what would they have been teaching his movement more than his teaching? This conclusion would be all the more true if they were, as some argue, uneducated apart from what they learned from Jesus.

Memory was crucial to every form of education we know in antiquity, including purely oral instruction. To suppose that Jesus would not have instructed disciples to remember his teachings, contrary to the basic role expected for disciples, is to make Jesus's pedagogy completely idiosyncratic in antiquity. It is also to reject virtually all the hard evidence available and to construct the opposite picture based on the silence that remains[277]—unfortunately a time-honored approach in some circles of NT scholarship.[278] To argue that Jesus's disciples were unlike other disciples from the period of the early empire is to dismiss our normal academic approach of understanding information in its historical context. Some may do so in an attempt to tame

---

for basic needs, see Thomas, "Writing," 25–28 (cf. also officials' literacy versus compositional literacy in 37–41). Other evidence suggests basic literacy without compositional literacy; see esp. Woolf, "Literacy"; Hurtado, "Fixation," 330–33, 339; Evans, "Graffiti," 161; Keith, "Literacy," 207; Longenecker, "Pompeii," 305; Rhoads, "Performance Criticism," 283; cf. Milnor, "Literacy"; Morgan, *Literate Education*, 260–61; illiterates' contact with literacy in Cribiore, *Gymnastics*, 163; ability to read *familiar* texts in Carr, *Writing*, 4–6.

275. On disciples' function of sharing Jesus's life and supporting his preaching, see Riesner, *Lehrer*, 426, 440; on his expectation of attention and obedience to his teaching, 427, 444–46 (citing, e.g., Matt 8:22//Luke 9:60; Luke 9:44; 11:1).

276. Cf. Riesner, *Lehrer*, 440.

277. McIver, *Memory*, 165.

278. Unfortunately, an argument used in some public responses to Keener, "Assumptions."

the Gospels' portraits of Jesus, but this recourse makes the disciples culturally idiosyncratic and unintelligible in an attempt to make Jesus less so.

Granted, Plato reshapes Socrates's dialogues, and John reshapes Jesus's discourses, but the norm in the early empire (which Plato preceded by more than three centuries) handled teachers' teachings more conservatively. This is especially the case with individual sayings (aphorisms) and stories, which, unlike lengthy dialogues, dominate the Synoptics.

While Jesus's disciples were like other disciples in many respects, however, the tradition does highlight a key feature that differentiates them from many kinds of disciples. Their adherence to Jesus was not to one teacher among many, as in the rabbinic movement or among many popular philosophers.[279] It is closer to that of disciples of a teacher founding a new school or movement, thus to disciples of Pythagoras or to followers of Qumran's teacher of righteousness. And whereas some of the teaching of the Qumran community's founder may have passed into community doctrine anonymously, the gospel tradition regularly credits Jesus and Jesus alone as the source of all authoritative teaching.[280]

15.4. What about the Witnesses' Illiteracy?

Some critics dismiss the relevance of all this evidence, contending that it derives mostly from the ranks of the elite. Since barely any nonelite textual evidence survives, however, this argument might be deployed to facilitate the dismissal of all textual evidence, so that critics can then offer arguments from the silence that remains.

Modern Western scholars sometimes assume an elitist posture toward those who lack the opportunities for literary education available to us. Learners can develop needed expertise in other areas. For example, when I have a toilet leak, the plumber's skills and mechanical knowledge readily trump my humanities PhD. Likewise, I have encountered greater biblical content literacy among many high school students in some parts of Africa than among some North American seminary graduates (I except here the studious ones, of course).

More to the point of illiteracy proper, some prominent examples of skill in oral composition are illiterate.[281] Although illiterate bards may fail in precise

---

279. See Byrskog, *Teacher*, throughout, esp. 307–8.

280. Byrskog, *Teacher*, 310. Against this factor providing incentive to invent teachings for Jesus, see our discussion of 1 Cor 7:10–12.

281. Bailey, "Tradition" (*Themelios*), 7.

verbatim recall, in many societies they can recite large selections of tradition.[282] In the third century BCE, Herodas's *Didaskalos* depicts a widowed grandmother as illiterate, yet "at least able to recite speeches from tragedy."[283] This description could reflect Herodas's comic poetic license, but the humor might reflect an incongruity of real life.[284]

A key objection raised to Jesus's disciples being the source of gospel tradition is that they were illiterate and low-class, hence they could not have taken notes.[285] Some scholars argue against much literacy in Judea and Galilee,[286] though others have been more optimistic.[287] Generalities about most Galileans being illiterate aside, few would argue that Jesus's disciples had "professional" training respected by the scribes; their teacher was Jesus, who did not belong to the elite (John 7:15; Acts 4:13).[288]

15.4a. Was Everyone in the Movement's First Generation Illiterate?

Regardless of general literacy, I noted above that tax collectors, relevant to at least one follower during Jesus's ministry (Mark 2:14), could take basic notes; Papias, writing in the early second century, thinks that the tax collector provided material followed by other disciples.[289] None of my arguments depend on note-taking or on disciples being literate, though I allow above for the possibility of at least some basic notes.

282. See, e.g., Lord, *Singer*; Eve, *Behind Gospels*, 5; in antiquity, e.g., Xenophon, *Symposium* 3.6.

283. Cribiore, *Gymnastics*, 163.

284. Cf. Marrou, *History*, 241, contending that in old Rome residents learned by heart the Twelve Tables (summarizing the rights and duties of Roman citizens); though note also Livy, *History* 3.34.2, on "reading" these.

285. Ehrman, *Before Gospels*, 197.

286. See esp. Hezser, *Literacy*.

287. Millard, *Reading*; Millard, "Literacy"; Head, "Note"; Evans, *World*, 63–88; cf. 1 Enoch 83:2; Porter, "Reconstructing," 45, citing important essays in Beard, *Literacy*. Cf. also possible implications of Wright, *Reading*.

288. See further Keith, *Scribal Elite*.

289. Papias, frag. 3.16, although this testimony is debated (and I myself doubt that it refers to our completed Gospel of Matthew). Only Matthew's Gospel informs us that the apostle Matthew was also this tax collector (Matt 9:9; 10:3; contrast Mark 2:14; 3:18); Papias, however, would assume Matt 9:9 correct in this identification. Given Jesus's reputation, presumably not invented by non-tax-collecting followers, it is likely that multiple tax collectors in fact followed Jesus, even if the calling of one proved particularly prominent (see Mark 2:15–16; Matt 11:19// Luke 7:34; cf. Matt 21:31; Luke 15:1).

More important, one might expect some in the rapidly growing Jerusalem church to be able to make notes even in the earliest years,[290] *if* such notes were a matter of interest. Literacy was more common in urban areas;[291] even in impoverished Egypt, most metropolites (citizens of Greek-speaking nome capitals), in contrast to typical rural agriculturalists, could read and write.[292] Some followers able to write, who heard the apostles recount Jesus's life and teachings, may well have taken notes. Even an average literacy as low as 3 percent would yield some literate persons, even if the Jesus movement included only several hundred persons.[293] Teachers often left the matter of publication to their followers.[294] If Jesus's immediate disciples could not write, some of *their* followers surely could.[295]

Indeed, we know of even an outsider to the movement in the first century—Josephus—who preserved *some* information about Jesus;[296] Paul did not write at the level of Josephus, but he was certainly literate and converted probably within at the most just a few years after Jesus's death (1 Cor 15:8),[297] and it is most improbable that he alone was literate.[298] Even if only 1 percent of the new apostolic movement in Judea was literate, that would have provided plenty of recorders had anyone wished to write accounts about Jesus at that time.[299]

290. With Bernier, *Quest*, 136–37.

291. Curchin, "Literacy"; cf. Dewey, "Event," 146–47. Social class may be a more specific determining factor; see Keith, "Urbanization."

292. Lewis, *Life*, 61–62.

293. A quite minimal estimate (1 Cor 15:6, although this figure probably represents primarily Galileans at the movement's beginning).

294. Kennedy, "Source Criticism," 129; Tieleman, "Orality," 28, 32; cf. Dio Chrysostom, *Oration* 54.3–4. Students were publishing notes of their teachers' lectures as early as five centuries before Jesus (Kennedy, *Classical Rhetoric*, 19), and the practice continued into the early empire (Quintilian, *Orator's Education* 1.pref.7–8; Epictetus, *Discourses* 1.pref.).

295. See Bernier, *Quest*, 136–37. As Eve observes, in principle early notes could have circumvented the need for four decades of oral transmission, but we cannot know whether there were such notes (*Behind Gospels*, 14).

296. Josephus, *Jewish Antiquities* 18.63–64; 20.200.

297. Jewett, *Chronology*, 99, suggests 34 CE; Riesner, *Early Period*, 64–74, for 31/32 CE.

298. Cf. Acts 4:36–37; 6:7, 9–10; 15:22–29; 16:37; 18:24 (see Keener, *Acts*, on these various passages); Rom 16:7, 22–23; 2 Cor 1:19; 1 Thess 1:1; Tit 3:13; 1 Pet 5:12.

299. Cf. Keener, "Plausibility."

15.4b. Did They Need to Be Literate to Pass On Information?

But the disciples' literacy is a moot point in any case. Apart from what rhetoricians called artificial memory, which uses elaborate mnemonic devices, memory practices noted among ancient disciples apply to disciples in general, not exclusively to the literate. Not all disciples of sages came from the ranks of the educated.[300] Lucian complains that not only many disciples but even their teachers were uneducated members of the working class.[301] Greek schools varied among themselves whether to emphasize oral memory or learning texts.[302] Literacy is not necessary to pass on the substance of what one learns orally. Nor do all the memory feats mentioned earlier, such as those of Seneca the Elder, require an intermediate step of writing (though Seneca was nothing if not literate).

Whether literate or illiterate, disciples by definition were supposed to learn their teachers' teachings, whether in writing or orally. Even later rabbis emphasized oral more than written transmission of their legal traditions,[303] although their emphasis on the Torah involved a relatively fixed text.[304] Perhaps most significantly, if one appeals to lack of literacy in Galilee to contend for the disciples' illiteracy, one should reckon with the corollary that follows from the same ancient evidence: Jewish disciples especially learned orally.[305] If Jesus's disciples learned orally, their literacy is strictly irrelevant.

Verbatim memory is stronger in societies where literacy exists, but gist memory, more relevant to most of the Jesus tradition, can flourish with or without literacy.[306] Even were we referring to verbatim memory, however, ancient Mediterranean society *was* a society where literacy existed. Orality and

---

300. Among Greeks, cf., e.g., uneducated farmers in Alciphron, *Letters of Farmers* 11 (Sitalces to Oenopion, his son), 3.14; 38 (Euthydicus to Philiscus), 3.40, ¶3; among Jewish people, cf. accounts concerning the backgrounds of Hillel and Akiba, e.g., b. Ned. 50a; Pesaḥ. 49b.

301. Lucian, *Runaways* 12, 14; *Philosophies for Sale* 11.

302. Culpepper, *School*, 177; for oral instruction, see, e.g., Hezser, *Literacy*, 99; cf. Carr, *Writing*, 28.

303. See, e.g., the purportedly late first-century traditions regarding oral law in Sipra Behuq. pq. 8.269.2.14; Sipre Deut. 306.25.1; 351.1.2–3; probably early material in Sipra Behuq. par. 2.264.1.1; Sipre Deut. 115.1.1–2; 161.1.3; 'Abot R. Nat. 15A; 29, §§61–62 B.

304. See Eve, *Behind Gospels*, 40; cf. Sipre Deut. 154.2.1.

305. This could help explain why, apart from Sirach, we have very few writings from Second Temple Jewish sages, compared to many Greek and Roman sources from teachers or their disciples. Most students of later rabbis could read Torah, though that was not their education's focus, and some may have been unable to write more than their name (Hezser, *Literacy*, 98).

306. See Kloppenborg, "Memory," 293–94.

literacy coexisted in much of the Mediterranean world.[307] The condition is for literacy to exist as a control, not necessarily for all tradents to be literate.[308]

But let us assume for a moment that all Jesus's disciples, even (astonishingly) the tax collector, were illiterate. In such a case, when they taught, they would need to rely all the more on what they had learned from Jesus. Of course, as already noted, since most authors of all social classes dictated their work orally, objections to the disciples' ability to write is a red herring anyway.[309]

15.4c. Memory among Nonelites: General Considerations

Not only elites but a significant proportion of people in some other oral societies can recall extensive amounts of shared tradition.[310] Illiterate and minimally literate people normally recall themes and gist, not exact wording; still, their cultural-memory specialists can recount epics that astound modern Westerners.[311]

Variation is standard fare in oral performance; just as a good preacher or professor today may take account of implicit audience feedback in presenting his or her sermon or lecture, so oral performers adapt their presentations for their audiences.[312] Oral performers typically display originality not by "making up new stories" but by contextualizing them for their current audience.[313]

---

307. See, e.g., Talbert, "Response"; Aune, *Dictionary*, 325; Gamble, "Literacy," 646; Byrskog, *Story*, 107–44; Goldhill, "Anecdote"; Habinek, "Literacy"; in most societies, see Goody, *Interface*, 78; Rosenberg, "Complexity," esp. 74, 88. Nearly all current media scholars reject the older Great Divide thesis between orality and literacy; see, e.g., Niditch, "Hebrew Bible," 6–7; Person and Keith, "Media Studies," 2, 8, 13; Rodríguez, "Great Divide"; Person, "Goody"; Person, "Havelock"; Eve, "Kelber"; and esp. Foley, *Theory*; Foley, "Plenitude"; cf. Kirk, *Memory*, 139–41.

308. Cf. Lord, *Singer*, 137; Byrskog, *Teacher*, 324.

309. See, e.g., Cicero, *Letters to Atticus* 14.21; Richards, *Letter Writing*, 64–80, 143.

310. Today, it is said that all "true" Dulong can remember their epics, even though recounting them all fully can take several days (Yamamori and Chan, *Witnesses*, 22).

311. Harvey, *Listening*, 41; Noll and Nystrom, *Clouds*, 129.

312. Bazin, "Past," 70–71; Rosenberg, "Complexity," 80, 85; cf. Goody, *Interface*, 81; Anderson, "Oral Tradition," 19–20.

313. Ong, *Orality*, 41; cf. the same point on 59, 157. Ong contrasts modern Western ideals of originality in terms of distinct works (23, 131). For audience contextualization in performances today, see Rhoads, "Events," 18–88. We might also think of how producers and screenwriters adapt stories for different audiences (say, the various versions of Ben Hur, such as the earlier, macho Ben Hur [1959] and the more sensitive recent version [2016]).

This usual practice of variation suggests that even the eyewitnesses of Jesus's ministry would have retold the same stories in varying ways; the Evangelists, therefore, had little reason to strive for verbatim reproduction. Not surprisingly, then, some scholars suggest that this practice in most renditions of oral tradition helps explain some of the range of differences in the Gospels, a variation that in specific traditions nevertheless leaves the essential gist.[314] Still, many of these variations may also reflect the ancient rhetorical practice of paraphrase[315] and literary use of gist memory in adapting sources.[316]

Yet most Synoptic accounts actually diverge from one another far less than one encounters in many oral traditions and in many cases of ancient literary dependence.[317] Their conspicuous similarity may reflect their respect for the authoritative status of their material, their lesser rhetorical interest in paraphrase, and most relevantly here, their brief chronological distance from their material. Again, the period of exclusively oral transmission between Jesus's execution and the first of the circulated Gospels cannot be more than about four decades, that is, well within living memory.

15.4d. Memory among Nonelites: Ancient Reports

Regarding ancient memory, however, we need not settle for generalized analogies regarding various cultures' oral traditions today. Naturally, most extant evidence from antiquity comes from elites, since elites circulated texts (other than business documents, graffiti, and occasional letters) most widely. Nevertheless, some concrete evidence also confirms that nonelites valued memory.

For example, probably allowing for some performance variation, many bards could recite from memory the entire *Iliad* and *Odyssey*, even though the educated often looked down on them as lacking critical skills.[318] (Songs

---

314. Dunn, *Perspective*, 110, 112, 118, 122; Dunn, *Tradition*, 301. For oral history in NT scholarship, see Byrskog, *Story*, 33–40; Eddy and Boyd, *Legend*, 239–68, esp. 252–59.

315. See, e.g., Theon, *Progymnasmata* 1.93–171.

316. Small, *Wax Tablets*, 192.

317. For the latter, see Derrenbacker, *Practices*, 95–96 (citing Downing, "Redaction Criticism 1," 62 and "Redaction Criticism 2," 42); Kloppenborg, "Variation"; Licona, *Differences*, 199 (citing further Downing, "Use," 529, 531).

318. Xenophon, *Symposium* 3.6; cf. West, "Rhapsodes"; Boomershine, "Research Unit," 39. Cf. how later rabbis looked down on Torah copyists (Hezser, "Scribes," 357–58). Poetry and song involved memorization (Apollodorus, *Library* 1.3.1; Seneca the Elder, *Controversiae* 1.pref.2, 19), which is easier than memorizing prose (Ong, *Orality*, 22, 57; Rubin, *Memory*, 8, 75–77, 87, 107–8, 155, 227–56; McIver, *Memory*, 167).

were used even for children's learning, but only the most highly educated used mnemotechnics.)[319] Some persons today who are illiterate in Arabic memorize the Qur'an,[320] which makes plausible even the ancient claim that one ancient people knew the *Iliad* from memory, even though they no longer spoke good Greek.[321]

Ordinary people in antiquity informally passed on stories and songs that they believed to be ancient.[322] Ancient researchers trusted local oral traditions sufficiently that they often depended on them, even when they were centuries old,[323] which illustrates the expectation that those interested in memories (such as localities to whom they mattered) preserved them. Dependence on such centuries-old cases was probably sometimes ill-advised,[324] but we must keep in mind that all the canonical Gospels, by contrast, were likely composed within a maximum of six and a half decades after the events they narrate.[325] Yet the Gospels, too, may be like islands in a wider sea of oral tradition.[326]

Jewish people also informally passed on various stories.[327] Most relevantly, Jewish boys necessarily developed memory skills; whether or not they could read and (still more rarely) write, Jewish boys learned to recite Torah.[328] Those who were not literate therefore learned Torah orally.[329] Ordinary Galileans who passed on stories with family or neighbors probably had memory skills more developed than those of their highly literate modern Western critics.[330] Like Jesus's disciples, ordinary Judean and Galilean boys lacked

319. Small, *Wax Tablets*, 123.

320. See section 16.7 below.

321. Dio Chrysostom, *Orations* 36.9. One need not suppose that all the people knew the entire *Iliad* by heart, but external sources confirm at least some of Dio's report (cf. *CIG* 2.2077 in the Loeb translator's note).

322. Cf., e.g., Xenophon, *Cyropaedia* 1.2.1, which he expects to sound plausible, although the *Cyropaedia* is largely fictitious. For widespread valuing and practice of memory skills in antiquity, not limited to the educated, Kwon, "Reimagining," 138–39, cites Shiner, "Technology," 150–56.

323. E.g., Pausanias, *Description of Greece* 1.23.2. Cf. Philostratus's possible access to century-old local stories about Apollonius (Bowie, "Portrait," 142).

324. Cf. Pretzler, "Pausanias and Tradition."

325. I have addressed elsewhere the dates of Matthew, John, and Luke-Acts, tentatively favoring the majority, median ranges of scholarly opinion, sometimes plus or minus a decade (Keener, *Matthew*, 42–44; Keener, *John*, 1:140–42; Keener, *Acts*, 1:383–401).

326. See McGrath, "Islands," emphasizing the material's complex potential relationships.

327. Charlesworth, *Pseudepigrapha*, 1–3; cf. Bailey, "Oral Tradition."

328. Cf. Riesner, "Education élémentaire"; Riesner, *Lehrer*.

329. Kirk, "Memory," 157–58.

330. Note, e.g., the concession in Redman, "Eyewitnesses," 192–93; cf. also 179.

any "professional" training, but they were brought up to know and obey their ancestral laws, which they would also teach to their own children.[331] Other illiterate persons would naturally learn stories about Jesus that they heard repeatedly.[332]

What sort of memories would predominate among eyewitnesses? Apart from teachings, eyewitnesses would remember special occasions they had experienced.

15.5. What Should Genuine Memories Look Like?

Science often tests hypotheses by making predictions based on them and observing the outcomes. After a thorough survey of the results of memory studies, Robert McIver offers some basic predictions of what form the gospel traditions would take "if they are derived from eyewitness memories."[333] Based on his earlier, detailed treatment of eyewitness memory, he concludes that any tradition originally promulgated by eyewitnesses should heavily reflect episodic memory.[334] As David Rubin also observes, autobiographic memory normally assumes a narrative form from the start.[335]

Although some elements of learning from Jesus presumably drew on semantic memory, which is the primary sort of memory tested in older research, the sort most relevant to Jesus's disciples would be personal-event memory. People are more apt to recall personal experiences than experiences that they have simply heard about.[336] Presumably the disciples would have remembered quite a number of these. (Personally, I would expect them to have paid some attention to particularly dramatic incidents such as putative restorations from blindness and death, at least until these sorts of experiences became too common to recall distinct incidents!)

I quote here McIver's list of predictions for tradition shaped by eyewitnesses:

331. Cf. Josephus, *Jewish Antiquities* 4.211; *Against Apion* 1.60; 2.178, 204, even allowing for some likely hyperbole; see Deut 6:7; 11:19; Ps 78 (LXX 77):4–8. Cf. also Freyne, *Galilee*, 208.

332. Dunn, *Perspective*, 119; cf. Byrskog, *Story*, 110. For learning by repeated hearing, Riesner, *Lehrer*, 441, cites Plato, *Parmenides* 126c.

333. McIver, *Memory*, 123. His exploration "Eyewitness Memory and the Gospel Traditions" appears in McIver, *Memory*, 123–61.

334. McIver, *Memory*, 123. He is not claiming that episodic narration is limited to eyewitness memory (see 124–25).

335. Rubin, "Introduction," 2; cf. Elder, "Narrativity," 242.

336. With, e.g., Small, *Wax Tablets*, 194–95, citing Neisser et al., "Earthquake."

1. It consists of narratives of events, places, and people.
2. These narratives are particularly vague with respect to time and often with respect to place.
3. The narratives usually lack further narrative context.
4. The narratives usually describe events that took place over a short time period.
5. The narratives can be full of sensory information and often contain irrelevant details.[337]

Long-term oral traditions are often linear rather than episodic,[338] but that is not the case for personal memories. Unlike some OT traditions, the Gospels stem from the period of oral history (living memory), rather than extended oral tradition. Episodic memory, therefore, is their appropriate form.

Although episodic form is certainly not limited to true stories,[339] as McIver acknowledges, it is appropriate to them. This form is not limited to and thus does not prove eyewitness foundations,[340] but it undercuts a traditional argument against them. McIver thus concludes that, contrary to the assumptions of many earlier form critics, the mostly episodic form of Synoptic passages (pericopes) outside the passion narrative is consistent with accounts deriving from witnesses.[341] Memory studies lead us to expect witnesses to remember extraordinary events surrounding Jesus, such as unusual miracles, more than precisely worded sayings.[342] Disciples might also recall some events in connection with special locations.[343]

---

337. McIver, *Memory*, 124, although he does not limit such features to eyewitness testimony. Cf. also Rubin, "Introduction," 3; Brewer, "Recollective Memory," 35–39.

338. E.g., Rubin, *Memory*, 317.

339. See, e.g., Karla, "*Life of Aesop*," 56.

340. Kirk ("Collective Memory," 62; Kirk, "Ehrman, Bauckham, and Bird," 106; Kirk, *Memory*, 54) regards McIver's results as quite limited, contrasting the results with more salient information preserved in community tradition. He notes that "an ad hoc personal account . . . has little cultural value" (*Memory*, 85; though communities often do value any memories of leading figures). Traditions restructure individual memory (Kirk, *Memory*, 224). For discussion of social memory, see esp. ch. 16.

341. McIver, *Memory*, 125; "Personal Memory," 55; "Flashbulb Memory," 135. Nineham's older assumptions about eyewitness tradition contradict current psychological knowledge (McIver, *Memory*, 126–27).

342. McIver, *Memory*, 131, noting esp. Winger, "Word and Deed," 683, 685.

343. See Brewer, "Recollective Memory," 52; Wagenaar, "Memory," 187; for mnemonic association with locations in longer-term tradition, see Rubin, *Memory*, 39, 47, 51; in Roman mnemonics, Small, *Wax Tablets*, 98–101, 109–11; Vatri, "Writing," 751 (noting *Rhetorica ad Herennium*

But would the eyewitnesses' episodic memory also be passed on in episodic format? Not necessarily, but on average, most episodes in living-memory biographies more likely reflect accounts of episodes than not: episodes *remain* episodes more easily than disconnected material or a longer story *becomes* episodes. Episodes can fit naturally into the ancient rhetorical form of chreiai. A chreia is a saying with a meaningful context. While chreiai could equally reflect either genuinely veridical experiences or fabricated ones, the overall description is certainly suitable for the sort of material that would be more readily remembered.[344] (The length and form of ancient chreiai did, however, vary considerably.)[345] Elementary students regularly copied, memorized, and eventually developed chreiai as part of their practice in reading and writing.[346]

According to one quite disputed understanding of Papias, Peter "used to give his teachings in the form of *chreiai*."[347] Whether or not Papias had this rhetorical sense in view, chreiai often appear in ancient biographic sources,[348] although those closest in time to the authors tend to be more reliable than earlier ones. The combination of such narratives with anecdotes, teaching material (esp. in accounts of sages), and an extended account of the protago-

---

3.28–37; Cicero, *On the Orator* 2.351–54; Marmor Parium 54.70; Quintilian, *Institutes* 11.2; earlier, *Dialexis*, frag. 9; Aristotle, *Topics* 163b28–32; *Soul* 427b18–20; *On Dreams* 458b20–22); Thatcher, "Memory Theatre"; for John's Gospel, Thatcher, "Shape," 232–34; cf. the "realms of memory" approach (for discussion, see, e.g., Le Donne, *Historiographical Jesus*, 43–45) in Jantsch, "Jerusalem" (developing the work of Pierre Nora); Nicklas, "Literature," 97; Nicklas, "Landscapes," 9–18; Gospel locations in Williams, *Trust*, 52–63. Some recent research suggests that temporal scaffolding may prove effective like spatial mnemonics (Bouffard et al., "Strategies"). "Time and locale" trigger memories associated with them (Kirk, "Social and Cultural Memory," 2); for recalling the setting in which one learned something, thereby incorporating it into episodic as well as semantic memory, see, e.g., Hugh of St. Victor in Carruthers, *Book of Memory*, 100.

344. McIver, *Memory*, 132. The form is primarily Hellenistic (Aune, "Aphorisms," 220), but recounters may have enlisted such forms early, given their compatibility with episodic memory. Some ancient historians recognized that self-contained episodes were easier to remember (Vatri, "Writing," 766, citing Diodorus Siculus, *Library of History* 16.1.1).

345. Cf. Theon, *Progymnasmata* 3.22–23, 27–28 (Butts); Robbins, "Chreia," 3; Mack and Robbins, *Patterns*, 196–97.

346. Marrou, *History*, 172–75; Cribiore, *Gymnastics*, 224.

347. Papias, frag. 3.15 (Eusebius, *Ecclesiastical History* 3.39.15; Holmes translates, "as needed"). McIver, *Memory*, 134n10, cites in support of the rhetorical interpretation Bauckham, *Eyewitnesses*, 203, 214–17. Cf. Byrskog, "Eyewitnesses," 162–65; Byrskog, "Church." But contrast now more fully Moessner, "Papian Fragments."

348. See ch. 5. Next to reading through ancient sources firsthand, by far the most useful resource for this study would be Robbins, *Quotes*.

nist's end was common in ancient biography in general.[349] It fits the episodic character of most Synoptic narratives.[350]

As noted in the previous chapter, the central eyewitnesses might well remember nearly half of their most significant experiences with Jesus for decades thereafter.[351] McIver reasons that we should not expect the disciples to remember all details precisely, but the gist of witnessed episodes that they did recall would be mostly accurate, and they would likely also accurately recall many random details.[352] That we cannot reconstruct every detail of the Jesus tradition in the Synoptics no more undermines its general portrait of Jesus than does the imperfection of language emphasized by deconstructionists render all communication useless.[353]

Eyewitness testimony is mostly reliable, especially in gist and more often than not even in the key details that it does preserve.[354] Our *default* approach, then, should be to assume, when we lack evidence to the contrary, that biographic anecdotes from living memory more *likely* represent real events, rather than that they do not.[355] This observation would normally hold true for biographies of then-recent figures from the early empire.

Of course, one could argue that the disciples deliberately falsified Jesus's teaching. But again, this would make them unlike nearly all other disciples from this period. This accusation would refer, not to the sort of "fictionalizing" or adaptation characteristic of ancient storytelling or biographies (chs. 2, 11), but to outright lying and conspiracy.[356]

But if their report was a conspiracy this widespread, we might expect persecutions[357] to produce some renunciations, and detractors to cite such recantations, for which any evidence is lacking. Nor, among apologetic problems of early Christians, do we find them needing to defend themselves against charges of witnesses' renunciations. Why would any critic assume something so out of

---

349. Burridge, *Comparison*, 203.

350. See discussion also in, e.g., Hezser, "Verwendung"; Byrskog, "Church"; Byrskog, "Teacher," 43–44.

351. McIver, *Memory*, 23, 35–39, 144.

352. McIver, *Memory*, 147, suggesting "up to 80 percent when measured by very stringent criteria." The qualification "up to," of course, is important, given variation in the studies.

353. On the latter point, cf. Vanhoozer, *Meaning*, 211–12; Keener, *Hermeneutics*, 86, 333nn50–51.

354. McIver, *Memory*, 160.

355. McIver, *Memory*, 186–87.

356. Cf. Schwartz, "Origins," 50, following Clifford Geertz: "Not everyone is a liar, and one need not know everything in order to know something."

357. E.g., 1 Cor 4:12; 15:9; 2 Cor 4:9; Gal 1:23; Phil 3:6; Tacitus, *Annals* 15.44.

the ordinary, specifically for *Jesus's* disciples and not for most others?[358] Perhaps one might feel compelling religious objections to Jesus more than to other ancient teachers, but such objections do not methodologically justify such an idiosyncratic view of his earliest followers. Other critics may simply be skeptical of all oral history; this approach is at least methodologically consistent, although I and many oral historians (see ch. 16) would demur from it.

15.6. Conclusion

Jesus's disciples would not have remembered everything that Jesus said, nor would they have recalled his teachings in a form close to verbatim, apart from many of his aphorisms or persistent figures of speech. Nevertheless, by any normal historiographic standards we should expect much of the substance of key teachings to remain.

Ancient Mediterranean culture valued and thus trained memory more than modern Western culture does. Ancient memories could be highly developed, as illustrated in oratory, storytelling, basic education, and advanced education. Most important, disciples, whether literate or not, normally preserved the substance of their masters' teachings and, where relevant, stories about their behavior.

In light of the foregoing discussion, the most appropriate starting assumption should be that Jesus's disciples would have learned and transmitted his teachings no less carefully than most other ancient disciples transmitted the wisdom of their mentors.[359]

To assume that Jesus's disciples acted completely unlike other disciples with regard to transmitting their teachers' ideas—despite the comparatively early publication of sources about Jesus—is to value one's skepticism about Jesus more highly than the concrete comparative evidence. Whereas some scholars may exhibit an unfair canonical bias, scholars who treat the gospel traditions as significantly less reliable than analogous traditions from antiquity reflect either an anticanonical bias or, perhaps more often, inadequate direct knowledge of the analogous ancient sources to make the comparisons.

Unless, of course, most of those who heard these disciples substantially distorted their message. I turn to this question in the next chapter.

358. See earlier comments in this chapter about miracles and the discussion, cited there, in Cramer, "Miracles," 136–37.
359. Cf. similarly Eddy and Boyd, *Legend*, 269–306.

Chapter 16

Oral Tradition, Oral History

Clearly, Jesus's disciples were eyewitnesses and remained in prominent positions in the Jerusalem church, probably until within a few years of the first Gospel's writing. But what difference would this fact make for our Gospels? What if the Evangelists drew on other, less reliable sources besides the eyewitnesses?

Since the disciples were highly prominent in the early church, these other sources might also be based on their testimony. But what might have happened to the testimony in the meantime? Should we expect it to have been radically transformed, as Rudolf Bultmann thought?

16.1. Critically Reforming Form Criticism?

More recent scholarship, however, has revisited Bultmann's radical approach. Bultmann's approach, no less than the opposite approach of total memorization, is largely inconsistent with "what is known of collective memory."[1] As Oxford scholar Eric Eve notes, "The study of oral tradition has moved on a long way since form criticism represented the cutting edge of New Testament scholarship."[2]

---

1. McIver, *Memory*, 120; cf. Byrskog, "Century," 12, 14, 19; Keith, *Scribal Elite*, 77 ("New Testament scholarship eventually abandoned the form criticism of Bultmann and others"); Kirk, *Memory*, 179, 187, 199.

2. Eve, *Behind Gospels*, xiii. Some complain that current memory studies are closer to form criticism than is the criteria approach (Eck, "Memory," esp. 1, 9). Many others suggest that, despite its advances, classic form criticism remained bound to a textual paradigm (Boomershine, "Research Unit," 37) and resists social-memory approaches (Kirk, "Social and Cultural Memory," 1; Kirk, "Ehrman, Bauckham, and Bird," 113–14; Kirk and Thatcher, "Tradition," 29–33; Horsley, "Patterns," 62–64; Kelber, "Works," 230–31). Kirk, "Ehrman, Bauckham, and Bird," 90; Kirk, *Memory*, 135–36, views Ehrman's "telephone game" as reflecting his text-critical framework.

Indeed, in many ways traditional form criticism is seriously outdated.[3] Thus, for example, Dibelius's model of folklore followed J. G. Herder's "romantic" view of orality, a mere ideal contradicted by subsequent empirical study.[4] Studies of memory and oral tradition in other disciplines are now roughly a century advanced beyond the concepts on which the early form critics drew.

Bultmann's more skeptical approach to Jesus tradition followed a model of form criticism based on OT traditions, which in turn followed a model used to explain centuries of transmission of European folk tales.[5] As even some of Bultmann's contemporaries noted, this approach ignored the much shorter time frame between Jesus and the Gospels.[6]

Most of the tendencies that Bultmann postulated (e.g., expansion, adding names) were later countered by E. P. Sanders, who demonstrated from ancient texts that tradition did not always follow the tendencies in Bultmann's hypotheses.[7] Indeed, as Cambridge scholar Richard Bauckham notes, "The kinds of differences we find between Plutarch and his sources are quite comparable to the differences between the Gospels, and *nothing in the least like form criticism is postulated by experts on Plutarch.*"[8]

Modern memory studies, the initial contributions to which were already being published in Bultmann's day,[9] illustrate further that Bultmann was far too skeptical about collective memory.[10] In this chapter I draw heavily on the undervalued work of Robert McIver and, to a somewhat lesser extent, Eric Eve, Alan Kirk, Tom Thatcher, and other NT scholars most familiar with memory studies and oral historiography.[11]

---

3. See already Güttgemanns, *Candid Questions*, e.g., 335–36.

4. Eve, *Behind Gospels*, 20–21, following Güttgemanns, *Questions*, 127, 184–93. Folklore studies today are more balanced and do not require predetermined assessments of historicity (Mournet, *Oral Tradition*, 166–72, noting and nuancing Dundes, *Writ*, 5, 10–11; cf. Park, "Folklore," 140).

5. See Bultmann, *Tradition*. My remarks here do not apply to all form criticism, such as the less sweeping approaches of, e.g., Taylor, *Formation*, or Jeremias, *Theology*.

6. E.g., Davies, *Invitation*, 116. Today, note, e.g., Bauckham, *World*, 91.

7. See Sanders, *Tendencies*. In fact, oral tradition tends to condense, conflate, and remove secondary characters (with, e.g., Rubin, *Memory*, 36; Small, *Wax Tablets*, 200), the opposite of Bultmann's assumptions. E.g., in Acts, Luke includes names of some centurions (Acts 10:1; 27:1) and a tribune (23:26), but he does not therefore invent a name to add to his tradition in Luke 7:2 (cf. Matt. 8:5); Matthew omits Jairus's name (Matt. 9:18; contrast Mark 5:22; Luke 8:41).

8. Bauckham, "Response," 237, following Pelling, "Adaptation"; Bauckham, *World*, 187.

9. Kirk, "Memory Theory," 809; Kirk, *Memory*, 179.

10. McIver, *Memory*, 120, 184, 186; Kirk, "Memory Theory," 809–15 (esp. 813), 833. Philosophically, meanwhile, radical skepticism on memory is logically self-defeating (Bernier, *Quest*, 65).

11. For oral transmission more generally, cf. also, e.g., Dunn, *Perspective*, 45–46, 110–22;

Some recent scholarship in oral history and tradition contends that trying to separate authentic and inauthentic elements of it in the modern, "objective" sense typically exceeds the tools available. For such scholars, modern studies of memory call into question some of the time-honored scholarly criteria of authenticity.[12] Having too often observed the periodic swing of the scholarly pendulum, I believe that dismissing the criteria rather than merely using them circumspectly is an overreaction. But while I affirm that most of those criteria can remain valuable (and have applied them in some earlier works), they are already too well-known for rehearsal in this book, and their application would prove more relevant for an actual reconstruction of the historical Jesus than for a prolegomenon of this sort. My focus here therefore remains on how oral tradition generally transmits information and shapes it in the process.

16.2. Oral Tradition: Connecting Past and Present

Some scholars examine oral traditions only in their own right; others try to use them for clues about the past.[13] Social-memory approaches are designed not to deal with historical reliability of narrated experiences but to examine how groups reappropriate memories for their own settings.[14] The focus of social-memory studies is more cultural than historiographic.[15] Nevertheless, those exploring historical questions today cannot ignore contemporary questions about individual and especially collective memory. Historical method

---

Bauckham, *Eyewitnesses*, 325–50; Keener, *Historical Jesus*, 139–61; Keener, "Assumptions," 39–53. Although Dunn's *Jesus Remembered* uses an approach different from social-memory theory, its model of tradition seems compatible (so Kirk and Thatcher, "Tradition," 39n4).

12. See, e.g., Rodríguez, "Authenticating Criteria"; Keith and Le Donne, *Criteria*; earlier, Porter, *Criteria*; questioning both approaches, Downing, "Researches."

13. Note the summary in Kelber, "Oral Tradition," 257.

14. See Keith, *Scribal Elite*, 83; Kirk, "Ehrman, Bauckham, and Bird," 100–101, 113–14; Kirk, *Memory*, 206 (on 207–8 distinguishing "implications for historiographical method" from facile claims of historicity). As Jens Schröter and Samuel Byrskog articulated in dialogue in the memory seminar at SNTS in Athens, August 10, 2018, the social-memory approach corrects naive historical positivism, recognizing that we always reconstruct the past from our own perspective (as even a chronological study of historical-Jesus scholarship will show).

15. Kirk, *Memory*, 226. Some scholars question the value of social-memory theory for historical-Jesus research; see, e.g., Foster, "Memory," 173–75, responding to its defense in Porter and Ong, "Memory," 147–54. For a survey of the state of the question as of 2015, see Keith, "Social Memory Theory."

cannot guarantee that any given memory or tradition goes back to Jesus, but because there is no unmediated access to the past, no uninterpreted memory on which we may draw,[16] contemporary historians cannot speak of historically authentic information about Jesus (or other figures) without acknowledging matters of memory. Because some scholars challenge the possibility of knowledge about the historical Jesus based on the fallibility of memory, those engaged in historical-Jesus research cannot avoid the issue. The limitations of memory limit our access to historical information, but those interested in historical information cannot neglect memories when they are our only access to the past.

Oral sources lack the fixity that written texts can offer, as ancient biographers also recognized.[17] Nevertheless, oral history can and often must be used to supplement written records.[18] Where written sources are limited, we sometimes possess only oral history—a source that often stands behind the best written research in any case. While spurious information, even if very old, cannot correctly fill lacunae in our historical knowledge (despite the sometimes contrary literary approach of ancient historians and biographers), oral history does often provide genuinely valuable information.[19]

Westerners' earlier neglect of such sources has sometimes reflected ethnocentric prejudices.[20] Memory is, of course, preserved from the community's perspective.[21] All memory, whether personal or collective, is colored by assumptions, biases, and so forth, yet such memory about persons and events also normally rests on genuine experiences.[22]

---

16. See, e.g., Le Donne, *Historiographical Jesus*, 13, 17, 38–39 (esp. 39: "The historian is never able to interpret an uninterpreted past"). Halbwachs was thus wrong to envision objective historiography as beginning where collective memory died out (Le Donne, *Historiographical Jesus*, 44–45).

17. Eunapius, *Lives* 453.

18. E.g., Aron-Schnapper and Hanet, "Archives orales"; Hoeree and Hoogbergen, "History."

19. Cf. Byrskog, *Story*, 26–40; for Africa, see, e.g., Horton, "Types," 14; Moniot, "Profile," 50. My wife, who is from Congo and has a French PhD in history, has confirmed this observation.

20. Chrétien, "Exchange," 77. Cf. Campbell, *Faithfulness*, 193–203, on the marginalization by some of Indigenous/Aboriginal perspectives.

21. Communal memory is not comprehensive but selects what it deems relevant (Kirk, "Memory," 168).

22. Cf., e.g., Thatcher, "Cold Memory," 58. For a survey of research in orality and Gospels studies to 2009, see Iverson, "Orality"; earlier, Byrskog, *Story*, 33–40; for a survey of literacy studies in classics, see Werner, "Studies."

Cultures are typically defined by a shared cultural identity rooted in a shared cultural memory.[23] Repetition of shared memories reinforces the shared culture, although these memories may be presented in a variety of fresh ways.[24] When communities deem some memories important to their group identity, they usually develop some more formal and deliberate ways of rehearsing these memories.[25]

Communities not only pass on but also reshape their stories. Because oral cultures use collective memory for identity formation,[26] they focus on features most relevant to their present needs.[27] Thus collective memories may embellish or exaggerate pleasing elements, omit inconvenient information, and prefer one causal nexus over another.[28] (Even individual speakers, both ancient and modern, tend to do the same.)[29]

Oral tradition often shapes stories in accordance with culturally designed expectations or scripts,[30] thus reading one story in light of another, as the Gospels regularly read Jesus's story in light of the OT.[31] Still, Goodacre, Allison, and others are correct to emphasize that biblical allusions need entail fiction in the Gospels no more than John Bunyan's shaping of his own conversion story in light of Paul's voids the information in the former.[32] We should also

---

23. See Assmann, *Cultural Memory*, 2–3. Contested cultural memories thus often produce partisan or sectarian polemic.

24. Assmann, *Cultural Memory*, 3–4.

25. Eve, *Behind Gospels*, 92 (offering rituals as an example; 92–93); Assmann, *Cultural Memory*, 40 (and for rituals, 41–44; cf. commemorative practices in, e.g., Kirk, *Memory*, 185–87, 221–22; ritual, in Keightley, "Memory," 144–47; the Lord's Supper, in Fernandez, "Memory").

26. McIver, *Memory*, 88.

27. McIver, *Memory*, 91, noting selective "structural amnesia"; cf. also 184; Vansina, *Oral Tradition*, 108, 118, 172–73.

28. McIver, *Memory*, 106, offering the example of differing Northern and Southern emphases on the causes of the US Civil War; cf. also Eve, *Behind Gospels*, 181. Bailey, "Tradition" (*Themelios*), 8, suggests that elements that can be most grossly exaggerated, such as jokes, news, and atrocity stories, normally do not persist in community tradition.

29. With Pelling, *Texts*, 6.

30. Cf. Schwartz, *Forge*, 231; Schwartz, "Harvest," 321; Rodríguez, *Structuring*, 57–63; Eve, *Behind Gospels*, 99.

31. For such "keying" (or "types"), see, e.g., Vansina, *Oral Tradition*, 107; Eve, *Behind Gospels*, 97, 106, 125, 175, 178; Schwartz, "Smoke," 15–16; Rodríguez, *Structuring*, 57; Rodríguez, "Suffering." Cf. similarly Lukan use of typology in Aletti, *Birth*, 89–106; Keener, *Acts*, 1:573–74; 2:1363–64.

32. Allison, *Constructing Jesus*, 389, offering as examples Matthew's interweaving such allusions in Mark, and Mark 15:40 employing the language of LXX Ps 37:12, although the presence of the women is rarely disputed historically. On Bunyan, see also Le Donne, *Historiographical Jesus*, 56.

keep in mind that Jesus himself may have offered some of these associations (cf., e.g., Mark 9:13) [33] and even very sober historians often followed earlier historical[34] and literary[35] models.

Individuals and groups reshape memories about the past to meet the needs of the present. Starting from the first witnesses and continuing in subsequent generations, interests shape the elements considered significant and thus sift what is worth preserving from what may be omitted.[36] Recounters of traditional stories also want to engage and please their audiences, an interest that affects which elements of a story are told. Community ideals thus shape the passing on of tradition.[37] For example, already the Fourth Gospel omits some key elements from the Synoptics such as individual exorcisms;[38] with similar selectivity, most church fathers also show far more interest in Jesus's teachings than in the accounts of his miracles.

Like individual memory (ch. 14), long-term cultural memory also usually collapses chronology. This is especially the case for its older memories, what oral historians consider the period before a culture's "floating gap."[39] (The floating gap is the period before which memories are blended together and for which no comparative chronology exists.) Characters of the past may be blended and idealized, or features of one character reattributed to another,[40] though this is less true of accounts from within living memory and "in historical accounts."[41]

33. Cf. Le Donne, *Historiographical Jesus*, 4–5.

34. See, e.g., Kennedy, "Source Criticism," 145–46; Bosworth, "Pursuit," 447; Croke, "Historiography," 567–68.

35. E.g., Pelling, *Texts*, 45.

36. Vansina, *Oral Tradition*, 118; Rubin, *Memory*, 36, 157.

37. Vansina, *Oral Tradition*, 108–14, esp. 108; cf. 190–92; Kirk, "Memory," 168. Stories may thus be recounted differently to outsiders, esp. when they are thought to hold different values or superior knowledge (Vansina, *Oral Tradition*, 111). Kirk, Memory, 80, notes that audiences may coax responses to fit local genres, and every retelling molds a story more into an acceptable narrative rather than just arbitrary data.

38. This is not meant to deny that John has a demonology of one sort; see John 6:70; 8:44; 13:2, 27; cf. 7:20; 8:48–49, 52; 10:20–21.

39. E.g., in periods before the floating gap, Vansina, *Oral Tradition*, 24, 122, 173–88, esp. 176; Bailey, "Tradition" (*ExpT*), 365; Barber and Barber, *Severed*, 115–17; Assmann, "Memory and Culture," 333–34.

40. Vansina, *Oral Tradition*, 105–6. This feature would be less prominent in Jesus tradition, since it contained only one central figure.

41. Vansina, *Oral Tradition*, 105.

16.3. But a Past Actually Happened

A community's reconstructive consolidation of memory does not, however, mean that communities typically simply fabricate the past.[42] The process of reading traditions in light of scripts rereads the present in light of the past, as well as the past in light of the present.[43] McIver, who addresses collective memory at significant length,[44] cites the warning of researchers on memory distortion: "It seems that by and large outright fabrication of collective memory is rare"; facts partly constrain the collective memory.[45] Even over extensive periods of time, "traditions about past events and figures generally correspond in important ways to what actually happened,"[46] and the most "essential elements of collective memories resist change."[47]

And whatever might be the case for centuries, living memory is, apart from deception or serious memory disorders, rarely wholesale creation. Although our access to it is mediated through interpretive structures, there was an "actual past."[48] Extreme "continuitists" read historical accounts as pure, uninterpreted data, and extreme "presentists" treat all memory as pure constructions for present interests, but the vast majority of social memory theorists today allow for both past and present connections.[49]

---

42. Eve, *Behind Gospels*, 93–95, citing sources that correct earlier misreadings of Halbwachs; cf. Vansina, *Oral Tradition*, 122; Rodríguez, *Structuring*, 45; for further treatment of Halbwachs, see, e.g., Assmann, *Cultural Memory*, 21–33; Le Donne, *Historiographical Jesus*, 41–45; Schwartz, "Halbwachs". Using a sort of positive criterion of dissimilarity, Vansina, *Oral Tradition*, 107, suggests that while we cannot certainly discount tradition where it conforms figures to ideal types, we can surely trust tradition behind accounts that run counter to such types.

43. Rodríguez, *Structuring*, 59, following, e.g., Schudson, "Present," 113; cf. also Kirk, "Memory Theory," 819–20; Kirk, "Nexus," 152 (regarding oral tradition); Le Donne, *Historiographic Jesus*, 58; Thatcher, "Cold Memory," 58. For individual memory, the influence of the past on the present is a major premise of psychotherapy.

44. McIver, *Memory*, 81–121. Cf. Dunn, *Perspective*, 43–46, 114–15.

45. McIver, *Memory*, 106, citing Baumeister and Hastings, "Distortions," 282.

46. McIver, *Memory*, 109. Distortion increases as narratives are reapplied to new frameworks, but "the initial interpretations of that event" constrain such distortion (Le Donne, *Historiographic Jesus*, 63). Continuity of memory allows one to link developed trajectories with their initiating contexts (73).

47. McIver, *Memory*, 184.

48. See Thatcher, "Actual Past"; cf. Pioske, "Retracing," cited in Person and Keith, "Media Studies," 11.

49. Le Donne, "Presentism," 307; Le Donne, "Traditionalism," 428; cf. Kirk, "Social and Cultural Memory," 14–15; Kirk, "Collective Memory," 61–62; Schwartz, "Origins," 53; Baker, "Identity," 189; Thatcher, "Actual Past." Schwartz, "Origins," 47–49, esp. 47, classifies Bultmann

As memory expert Barry Schwartz notes, "the past" is no mere "hallucination pressed to the service" of the present.[50] Both personal and corporate memory often omit inconvenient material,[51] but given the limits of memory, more material is always omitted than remembered in any case. While such omissions discard information, they do not fabricate the information that remains;[52] we may believe that they distort the larger picture, but omissions are not the same thing as mistaken information. As Schwartz notes, "Partial knowledge is not synonymous with faulty knowledge."[53] Ancient audiences would not expect otherwise; as we have noted, omissions were expected also in ancient literature.[54]

For example, Schwartz has documented how different groups in different periods have reshaped the cultural memory of Abraham Lincoln,[55] but Schwartz observes that most of these differences reflect interpretive standpoints rather than falsified information.[56] Thus he emphasizes that, "as these memories were passed on, they were modified, but the essence of the events to which they refer remained unchanged."[57] Nor must we dismiss as wholly inappropriate even all interpretive standpoints. Thus some have appropriated Lincoln as emancipator, others as preserver of the Union, others as a man of the frontier who achieved greatness, and

---

and his brand of form criticism as unrealistically "presentist" (cf. Schwartz, "Jesus in Memory," 258, for Bultmann as unduly constructionist).

50. Schwartz, "Smoke," 19, challenging Halbwachs's treatment of ancient Christian memory in *Collective Memory*, 35–235; cf. Nikulin, "Introduction," 16, 18, 24–27.

51. For omissions in individual memory, see, e.g., McIver, *Memory*, 48; in corporate memory, McIver, *Memory*, 91, 106; Vansina, *Oral Tradition*, 122.

52. Vansina, *Oral Tradition*, 172; cf. 122, 188, 190–92.

53. Schwartz, "Smoke," 18; in personal memory, see Brewer, "Recollective Memory," 42.

54. See ch. 10. In ancient biographies, see Bosworth, *Arrian*, 211; Licona, *Differences*, 2, 20, 51, 56, 72, 75, 77, 95, 109; in ancient historiography, see Polybius, *Histories* 6.11.7–8; Derrenbacker, *Practices*, 91, 93; Keener, *Acts*, 194–96 (including Josephus, *Life* 339; *Against Apion* 1.60–66; Dio Cassius, *Roman History* 1.1.1–2).

55. Ehrman, *Before Gospels*, 5–7. The vast majority of Ehrman's comparisons for reshaped tradition, though useful for understanding cultural memory, are from periods subsequent to the first century (see Keener, "Ehrman vs. McIver," 272–73, 293–97), and/or represent a process beyond living memory.

56. Addressing cultural memory, McIver also (*Memory*, 89–91) notes Barry Schwartz's study of Lincoln, commenting (160) that present needs largely reshape, rather than fabricate, memories of Lincoln, following Schwartz, *Forge*, 293–312; Schwartz, *Post-heroic Era*, 219–68.

57. Schwartz, "Smoke," 9; see further 7–9; cf. Schwartz, "Harvest," 322, 327–28; Schwartz, "Origins," 49.

so forth, but none of these portraits is necessarily wrong or incompatible with the others.[58]

And in any case, long-term, multigenerational cultural memory of Lincoln is better compared with long-term cultural memory of Jesus through subsequent multigenerational history[59] than with Mark's Gospel, composed within living memory of Jesus.

In 1889, almost a quarter century after Lincoln's assassination, his former law partner published a biography of Lincoln. His research included contacting 250 people who had known Lincoln, including many who had known him in the 1830s. "Because thirty-five to forty years had passed," Schwartz notes, "since these people last saw Lincoln (an interval equal to that separating Mark from the crucifixion of Jesus)," this biographer worked hard to exclude misinformation.[60]

Nearly three decades after Lincoln's death another biographer conducted similar interviews but produced a more positive characterization of Lincoln, reconfiguring the popular memory of the former president.[61] Schwartz compares this later biographer's different reading of Lincoln with John's reading of Jesus that differs from Mark.[62] Jesus's disciples did not vanish at his death; analogously, many who knew Lincoln's later years survived long afterward to recount their memories. "Each witness need not tell the same story in order for a fair estimate of the 'real Lincoln' to appear.... Not every valid story about the past has a single point of origin."[63]

Observations about George Washington might illustrate the requisite balance between a larger story's legendary additions and continuing information. Most historians deem fictitious the tale of Washington cutting down the cherry tree.[64] By contrast, no one doubts major elements of his military career (such as the disastrous Braddock expedition in 1755), that he com-

---

58. Schwartz, "Harvest," 327–28.
59. As in Rodríguez, "Suffering," 241.
60. Schwartz, "Smoke," 7.
61. Schwartz, "Smoke," 7–8.
62. Schwartz, "Smoke," 8. One difference in the analogy is that whereas Lincoln's first biographer knew him, it is the later, Fourth Gospel's beloved disciple who claims to have known Jesus. Schwartz, "Smoke," 8–9, compares the Gospels with the work of historical novelists like Sandburg on Lincoln, since they bring the character to life by dramatizing his "personality, motives, character, aims, and priorities." The Gospels, however, notoriously *fail* to do much of that (cf. Keener, *Acts*, 1:135–37), a "deficiency" (by modern literary standards) that various Jesus movies have struggled to compensate for in very diverse ways.
63. Schwartz, "Smoke," 13.
64. So Ehrman, *Introduction*, 53.

manded the colonial army, served as the first US president from 1789 to 1797, and so forth. As Schwartz points out, "The George Washington that we find in a biography written in 1800 . . . is easily recognizable in a book published in 2000, for expert custodians prevent the Washington biography from being unduly modified."[65]

Either-or assertions work best when premises are mutually exclusive; they are logically incoherent when premises may prove complementary. The most extreme postmodern interpreters may reduce all of history to rhetoric, but most historians affirm instead that history, however shaped by rhetoric, remains a valid discipline no less than rhetoric.[66] Reception history shows the development of tradition but does not negate the initial events.

Thus Alan Kirk compares denying any history behind witnesses' memory with "claiming that the Vietnam War Memorial in Washington D.C., because it is the product of politically charged commemorative debates of the 1980s, has no historical relationship to the Vietnam War."[67] Memory encoding efficiently condenses information to schemas, but this "amounts to abstracting from originating occurrences," not pure invention.[68] No one would claim that Holocaust survivors' vivid recollections of the Holocaust disprove events standing behind their recollections.[69] In the same way, interpretation in the gospel tradition does not negate genuine information that was being interpreted.

Schwartz declares that "interpretation is more often forced upon the observer of an event by its inherent quality than imposed by the observer's worldview and interests. Put another way, *reality counts more than bias in the remembering of most events most of the time.*"[70] "Significant distortions" occur but remain exceptional.[71]

---

65. Cf. Schwartz, "Harvest," 322.

66. Cf. Schwartz, "Smoke," 23, who also cites here Ricoeur, *Memory*, 21 (cf. 257, 278), against the radical constructivism of White, *Content.* (Ricoeur, *Memory*, 257–58, 556n34, also cites against White the critiques of numerous historians.) Reasoning from memory frailties to the illegitimacy of history tends to produce "a conceptual and procedural dead end" (Bernier, *Quest*, 67). Ironically, some (e.g., the controversial Sardar, *Postmodernism*) argue that such extreme postmodernism can become culturally insensitive.

67. Kirk, "Memory Theory," 837; Kirk, *Memory*, 202.

68. Kirk, *Memory*, 217; see also (cited there) Koriat, Goldsmith, and Pansky, "Psychology," 489. Kirk, *Memory*, 8n30, 69, elsewhere cites helpful observations of Ruben Zimmermann (Zimmermann, "Formen," 164; Zimmermann, "Gleichnisse," 113–14).

69. Cf. Bauckham, *Eyewitnesses*, 493–505.

70. Schwartz, "Smoke," 20–21, as also noted earlier.

71. Schwartz, "Smoke," 21.

16.4. Examples of Distorted Oral Tradition

In some cultures without literacy, even some central features of a myth may disappear in retellings in just two decades,[72] although such changes are far more common after a floating gap, often marked by major social changes that render aspects of the tradition less intelligible.[73]

Certainly significant divergences do accumulate in oral tradition over time.[74] While retaining a massacre, for example, the Song of Roland poetically transforms the extermination of Charlemagne's small rear guard by local shepherds three centuries earlier into a valiant stand against 100,000 Muslim fighters.[75]

In some cases, such as medieval hagiography[76] and tales about the Baal Shem Tov,[77] significant distortions can arise within a couple generations. Tales of the Baal Shem Tov were written fifty-four years after the Besht's death but most often refer to purported events many years prior to that death. Since the Synoptics address the final year or years before Jesus's execution, only the infancy narratives (Matt 1–2; Luke 1–2) would be of comparable distance

---

72. Ehrman, *Before Gospels,* 188.

73. On the floating gap, see Vansina, *Oral Tradition,* 23–24, 168–69, 226n10 (cf. also 122, 177); Assmann, *Cultural Memory,* 34–35 (aptly comparing ancient Greece's "dark ages," ca. 1100 to 800 BCE); King, *Kurdistan,* 94–96 (cf. also 66, 68, 187–88); King and Stone, "Lineal Masculinity," 328–29; Barber and Barber, *Severed,* 115–18, 139. On the original schema necessary for intelligibility, see, e.g., Schwartz, "Smoke," 23–24. On social changes inevitably requiring new understandings of religious movements (and often institutional interpreters or clergy) by the third to fourth century, Assmann, *Cultural Memory,* 49, cites Halbwachs. Even after the floating gap, some material that is no longer intelligible may be preserved verbatim if appropriate constraints exist (Ong, *Orality,* 62–63).

74. See, e.g., Kloppenborg, "Memory," 296–97 (noting limitations in Goody and Watt, "Consequences," 310; Goody, *Logic,* 9, but recognizing the balanced approach of Rodriguez, *Structuring,* 41–80); Harms, "Tradition"; Raphael, "Travail"; Iglesias, "Reflexoes"; Henige, "History," 103; though cf. Eddy and Boyd, *Legend,* 260–64. Goody's examples of wide variation are deliberately from purely oral cultures that he explicitly *distinguishes* from ancient Mediterranean culture even in the Homeric era (Goody, *Interface,* 78–79, 98, 107).

75. See Barber and Barber, *Severed,* 90.

76. For mostly Christian examples, most evolving over centuries but some arising more quickly, see Keener, *Miracles,* 857–66; e.g., Budge, *Takla Hâymânôt;* cf. Aune, "Aphorisms," 224 (following Thomas Becket's death).

77. See Ehrman, *Before Gospels,* 95–100. I earlier associated the pattern of tradition in the tales of the Baal Shem Tov with the contemporary hagiographic tradition (Keener, *Miracles,* 205n213); see now much more fully Keener, "Ehrman vs. McIver," 293–97. For some possible historical value in the traditions, see Etkes, "Besht," 300–301, cited in Kirk, "Ehrman, Bauckham, and Bird," 98n38); but esp. now the balance in Dynner, "Tale."

from the events. Experts note that fanciful tales were characteristic in general of the early Hasidism who revered the Baal Shem Tov.[78] As noted in my brief discussion of late antique hagiography and mythography, these patterns do not fit conventions dominant in first-century biography.

Probable influence of Christian models also renders anachronistic some other proposals, though they offer a degree of social analogy. In the seventeenth century a Jewish messianic movement followed Sabbatai Sevi.[79] Some of his followers failed to be deterred by his apostasy to Islam,[80] and some even by his death,[81] but English Christian millenarianism, Kabbalah, and Islam provided them a range of conceptual options that do not seem to have existed in the first century.[82]

Somewhat more analogously, some compare with Jesus's early movement that of Simon Kimbangu,[83] yet direct Christian influence is explicitly present in this case. Kimbangu himself, a Baptist, naturally had Jesus as a model. Like Jesus, he had a healing ministry that expanded his movement;[84] like Jesus, he also confronted repression by the colonial elite.[85] There were also some prior Congolese prophetic models[86] and a contemporary rise in highly effective African Christian prophets in this period.[87]

Unlike Jesus, however, Kimbangu was not so much of a sage, and their respective mnemonic cultures differed. Kimbangu did not train disciples by passing on easily memorizable sayings, disciples who then led the movement and cited his teachings. Indeed, many of Kimbangu's "closest disciples were also arrested,"[88] putting out of circulation many of the movement's key leaders.[89] Much more than is evident in our first-century sources about

---

78. Ben-Amos and Mintz, "Introduction," xxiii. Kirk, "Ehrman, Bauckham, and Bird," 98–99, instead counters the Besht analogy by noting that the Besht, unlike Jesus, lacked an immediate community of followers.

79. Price, *Shrinking*, 29.

80. Grayzel, *History*, 516; Bamberger, *Story*, 240.

81. Scholem, *Sabbatai Sevi*, 920; Greenstone, *Messiah*, 225–30.

82. Despite its (different) range of messianic options; see discussion in Keener, *Historical Jesus*, 153, 256–67; Keener, "Parallel Figures."

83. Price, *Shrinking*, 29.

84. Koschorke, Ludwig, and Delgado, *History*, 260.

85. See, e.g., McClenon, "Miracles," 188.

86. McClenon, "Miracles," 185–86; Hanciles, *Beyond Christendom*, 103.

87. See Hanciles, "Conversion," 169–70; Sanneh, *West African Christianity*, 123–25, 181–83; Yates, *Expansion*, 170, 172; Kalu, *African Pentecostalism*, 31, 36, 38–39.

88. Gray, "Christianity," 158.

89. Less directly, Kimbangu influenced Daniel Ndoundou, a leader in a revival move-

Jesus,[90] views about their movement's founder varied widely among Kimbangu's followers, especially after his son's death some forty years later.[91]

In contrast to Kimbanguism, Jesus's early Galilean Jewish followers lacked close models for rapid deification; his later Gentile followers in the Diaspora would hardly have invoked the category "Messiah."[92] Despite varying emphases, an exalted core Christology pervades even Paul's earliest letters, starting some two decades after Jesus's execution as a suspected royal claimant. Despite serious disagreements on other issues, Paul seems to presuppose shared agreement regarding Jesus's resurrection and exalted status (1 Cor 8:6; 15:1–8; Gal 2:7–9).

Even the somewhat short-term examples of distortion noted above are all far removed from Jesus's context. Even apart from the analogy's risk of anachronism, however, such stark distortions are outliers deviating from the norm in collective memory about community origins,[93] especially within living memory.

Granted, I can cite plenty of ancient examples of almost immediate rumors,[94] at least on occasion deliberate.[95] But having read through ancient sources rather than cherry-picked among them, I can also confirm that these differ from the usual core of information typically accepted in ancient biographies within living memory of their subjects. Short-term rumors are also often falsified by subsequent, better-informed reports.[96]

---

ment in Congo-Brazzaville (Keener, "Ndoundou") and a friend of my Congolese father-in-law (Keener, "Moussounga").

90. Some early Christian sources say little about matters emphasized in other sources, but this silence differs from widely conflicting views such as found among Kimbanguists. Those who speak of communities of Jesus-followers who denied his messiahship or resurrection always must argue from silence.

91. Gondola, "Kimbangu," 767; Kalu, *African Pentecostalism*, 70, 78–79. Keep in mind that the basic contours of earliest Christian theology already appear in Paul and Mark, within forty years of the beginning of the Jesus movement.

92. See Keener, "Parallel Figures."

93. See McIver, *Memory*, 109, 157.

94. E.g., rumors of conspiracy (Tacitus, *Annals* 14.58), battle outcomes (Plutarch, *Camillus* 24.1; Tacitus, *Histories* 4.12), and mass exile (*Annals* 4.46); rumors exaggerating enemy numbers (*Annals* 4.23); a false rumor of a leader's death (*Histories* 1.34; 4.34) or survival (Josephus, *Jewish Antiquities* 19.134; Tacitus, *Annals* 2.82–83) or that the enemy had fled (Tacitus, *Histories* 2.42); or even deliberately false rumors (disinformation; Justin, *Epitome* 31.1.7; Tacitus, *Histories* 4.38, 54; *Annals* 4.24). See further discussion in Keener, *Acts*, 3:2836.

95. I hope that those who borrow my citation, Lucian, *Peregrinus* 39–40 (see A. M. Harmon in LCL 5:45; also see König, "Lives," 241), will be fair enough to borrow my broader observation that this case does not reflect the norm.

96. Some rapidly propagated rumors, however, also proved true; see, e.g., Pindar, *Nemean Odes* 5.2–3; Justin, *Epitome* 2.14.8–9; 20.3.9; Cicero, *Letter to Brother Quintus* 1.1.1; Tacitus, *Agricola* 9.

In oral tradition generally, rumor transmission differs from the transmission of stories central to the community's identity.[97] Rumor experiments certainly differ starkly from the normal conditions of oral tradition.[98] The distorted oral traditions here are far from the norm within living memory; barring significant arguments to the contrary, we should prefer more mainstream analogies for the gospel tradition.

16.5. Examples of Tenacious Oral Tradition

If examples of distortions in oral tradition are possible, counterexamples are no less possible. Ethnic conflicts around the world today demonstrate that communities can remember for generations events that they consider significant. This was no less the case in antiquity. Seven centuries after conflicts between Megara and Athens, for example, Megarians continued to hate Athenians.[99]

One cannot easily speak of inflexible, universal laws of tradition.[100] Yet, contrary to an assumption of some hyperskeptics that memory frailties force complete agnosticism about stories transmitted orally from the past, many societies pass on key stories and wisdom for centuries, despite fluidity of language and details.[101] As Eric Eve points out, communities "generally devise more formal means of rehearsing the collective memories they deem important."[102]

Although we usually lack external means to evaluate how long traditions have continued, sometimes we do have such sources. Thus for example Guaraní Indians in Argentina orally preserved the tradition of the gospel they

---

97. See Byrskog, *Teacher*, 308n2; Rubin, *Memory*, 130; Kirk, "Memory Theory," 822–23; Kirk, "Ehrman, Bauckham, and Bird," 93. Experiences of atrocities spread quickly (Bailey, "Tradition" [*Themelios*], 8) but often lack an initially adequate narrative schema (cf. Barclay, "Autobiographical Remembering," 94). McGrath, "Islands," 8, compares rumor transmission but notes that such transmission disseminates most widely, far from wild elaboration, "the least common denominator, the basic outline."

98. See, e.g., Rubin, *Memory*, 130.

99. Philostratus, *Lives of the Sophists* 1.24.529; cf. the oft-cited earlier accounts in Aristophanes, *Acharnians* 530–40; Thucydides, *History* 1.139.

100. Eve, "Orality," 261; cf. Kelber, "Oral Tradition," 257, on Ruth Finnegan's warnings.

101. Cf. Lord, *Singer*, 138; Lewis, *History*, 43; Vansina, "Afterthoughts," 110; Yamauchi, "Historic Homer"; see, e.g., Eddy and Boyd, *Legend*, 260–64. Still, in some such cases, poetic or musical form aids retention (Redman, "Eyewitnesses," 191–92; cf. Kennedy, "Source Criticism," 143).

102. Eve, *Behind the Gospels*, 92.

had learned from the Jesuit mission before it was dispersed two centuries earlier, in the 1700s.[103] Information about cultural contacts suggests that some biblically based stories apparently entered local traditions in some African oral societies three centuries before their next attestation.[104] Because of incidental preservation in an old Ethiopian chronicle, we can confirm fairly accurate preservation of oral tradition about a Hadiya leader over the course of half a millennium.[105] Geology confirms the transmission over centuries of a New Guinea Highlands tradition about a volcanic eruption.[106]

Similarly, Vansina points out that the oral traditions of the Abenaki Indians "were not written down before 1869," but they "confirm both French and British accounts" of a 1759 conflict "and resolve at least one contradiction between the written versions."[107] Many Middle Eastern stories refer to events that investigators outside the communities can date five, ten, or even fifteen centuries earlier.[108]

Some scholars cite arguments for even far older traditions. Such arguments are not directly relevant for this book's thesis, but if any are correct, they illustrate more graphically the possibility of shorter periods of oral tradition. In 1865 outsiders reported a story from the Klamath people that described accurately a volcanic eruption in their neighborhood, one that formed Crater Lake. This particular tradition was apparently transmitted orally for millennia, albeit with the help of Crater Lake as a conspicuous, nearby visual aid: ice-dating demonstrates that the eruption occurred nearly 7,700 years ago.[109]

Some Hawaiian traditions similarly appear to be very ancient. Traditions there include genealogies supposedly going back ninety-five generations, as well as mythical battles of volcano goddesses that formed specific lava flows in specific generations at named locations. To the astonishment of the researcher, "The radiocarbon dates for these lava flows matched not only the relative order of the named chiefs in the genealogical record, but closely matched absolute dates as well if a 22-year period were used for the length of each chiefly gen-

---

103. Riesner, *Lehrer*, 451.

104. Vansina, *Oral Tradition*, 155. Cf. African traditions noted in Lewis, *History*, 43.

105. Vansina, *Oral Tradition*, 188.

106. Vansina, *Oral Tradition*, 188–89 (the transmission period is roughly 180 to 340 years).

107. Vansina, *Oral Tradition*, 189, noting from another example that sometimes an oral version is even superior to a written one.

108. See, e.g., Bailey, "Tradition" (*ExpT*), 365; Bailey, "Tradition" (*Themelios*), 6–8. For my more detailed engagement with Bailey and his critics, see again Keener, "Weeden's Critique."

109. Barber and Barber, *Severed*, 7–8, citing Zdanowicz, Zielinski, and Germani, "Eruption."

eration."[110] Still others recount information reportedly transmitted orally for up to ten thousand years.[111]

While unbroken tradition chains of such inordinate length are at best plainly exceptional,[112] they do suggest that sometimes traditions can be preserved orally for centuries. Even if we discount the possibility of exclusively oral transmission over the course of millennia, the possibility of significant transmission over the course of generations is clearly established. As noted below, transmission within living memory can be especially accurate.

Although traditions are rarely verbatim, on occasion the core can be quite close.[113] Ruth Finnegan, for example, notes the somewhat close (but not verbatim) correspondence of two recorded performances by the same griot.[114] More relevant for multigenerational transmission, she notes versions of the folk ballad *Barbara Allen* attested roughly two centuries apart, transmitted orally yet with striking similarities.[115] Walter Ong also notes some cases of "more exact verbatim memorization," even at times among exclusively "oral peoples,"[116] although these are, again, exceptional. Nevertheless, similarity in wording is usually far greater than a modern Western reader would guess from our own experience of memory.[117]

---

110. Masse, "Earth," 55, as quoted in Barber and Barber, *Severed*, 9. Less persuasively, Barber and Barber, *Severed*, 144, 217, also follow Masse ("Basis," 466–67) regarding a Hawaiian story that can be connected with tenth-century celestial phenomena.

111. Barber and Barber, *Severed*, 9, noting additionally a lengthy oral tradition in Australia in Dixon, *Searching*, 153–55, 295; cf. Lulu Morris, "7,000 Year Old Indigenous Story Proved True," *National Geographic*, May 1, 2017, http://www.nationalgeographic.com.au/australia/7000-year-old-indigenous-story-proved-true.aspx.

112. Barber and Barber, *Severed*, 9–10, emphasize the sort of factors necessary for long-term persistence of tradition.

113. Byrskog, *Teacher*, 324n2, cites here Finnegan, *Oral Poetry*, 73–86, 142; Finnegan, *Literacy*, 90, 158, 166–67, 172–73. Cf. cases of roughly 50 percent verbal correspondence in Derico, *Tradition*, 156, 170 (less in some other cases, e.g., 160), following and evaluating Baum, *Faktor* (Derico, *Tradition*, 142–71, engages Baum's extensive evidence from various cultures). For griots, cf. Goody, *Interface*, 101–3.

114. Finnegan, *Oral Poetry*, 76–78. She notes (78) that compositional variation is usually greater for extended epics than for shorter performances and then cites (79–80) cases of (non-verbatim) memorization in various cultures.

115. Finnegan, *Oral Poetry*, 136–37, though emphasizing that this is not the norm (139) and that the versions are not identical (140). See also examples in Rubin, *Memory*, 5–6; on folk ballads more fully, see 257–98.

116. Ong, *Orality*, 61.

117. Rubin, *Memory*, 37. See now also Finnegan, *Beyond*, 220 (as noted in Bauckham, *Eyewitnesses*, 597).

Factors that allow oral tradition to flourish, by keeping it memorable, include the following, most of them analogous to factors for memory in individual, psychological memory:

1. The information is significant to the community.[118]
2. The story includes vivid imagery that engages audiences' senses.[119]
3. The core is reinforced through redundancy and repetition.[120]
4. Stories are simplified, elements being conflated, to conserve room in the cultural memory.[121]

Oral traditions are also normally concrete rather than abstract.[122] Given ancient discipleship practices of rehearsal and the special role accorded Jesus in his movement, such factors were likely at work in the gospel tradition.

16.6. Just the Gist

Oral tradition generally features both stability and flexibility.[123] Eve's summary of general observations about memory is as difficult to dispute as it is common sense: "(1) oral tradition typically exhibits both stability and change; (2) collective memory reflects both the impact of the past and the needs of our present; and (3) individual memory (insofar as it can be distinguished from social aspects of memory) is both generally reliable and capable of being seriously misleading."[124]

Even purely oral cultures usually retain the gist,[125] but often only that. Oral tradition does not depend primarily on verbatim, rote memory, which

118. With, e.g., Vansina, *Oral Tradition*, 118; Barber and Barber, *Earth Severed*, 9; Bailey, "Tradition" (*ExpT*), 365.

119. With, e.g., Rubin, *Memory*, 11, 39–64, 305 (for antiquity, 39, 46); Barber and Barber, *Earth Severed*, 10–11, 156. Cf. the train wreck in Rubin, *Memory*, 282.

120. See, e.g., Assmann, *Cultural Memory*, 3–4, 81; Finnegan, *Oral Poetry*, 78; Barber and Barber, *Severed*, 10; Kirk, "Memory Theory," 823; Eve, *Behind Gospels*, 92; Rubin, *Memory*, 72–75, 124–29, 144, 155, 170, 228; Byrskog, *Teacher*, 397; Mournet, *Oral Tradition*, 174–79, 190; Schwartz, "Smoke," 14; for redundancy, see also Anderson, "Oral Tradition," 32.

121. Vansina, *Oral Tradition*, 171; Rubin, *Memory*, 36; Kirk, "Memory Theory," 825; Barber and Barber, *Severed*, 115–18; Kloppenborg, "Memory," 289. Sometimes minor characters are conflated into the central heroes (Barber and Barber, *Severed*, 115, 124).

122. Rubin, *Memory*, 60–61.

123. So, e.g., Mournet, *Oral Tradition*, 174–90, 292.

124. Eve, *Behind Gospels*, 178.

125. See Kloppenborg, "Memory," 293–94.

is not the process for which human memory is primarily adapted.[126] Gist is usually the best that ordinary memory can offer, but memory does usually preserve the gist of events that it retains.[127] Paraphrase and conformity to one's interpretive schema are far more common than verbatim recall, especially for narratives.[128] (Frequent exceptions such as proverbs are noted below.)

In oral cultures, reciters' insistence that their recall is verbatim really means only "verbatim to the best of unaided human memory." Balkan singers of epics may insist that their songs remain unchanged, but this claim proves true only for the gist; each performance recomposes some elements of an epic, especially some wording and inessential points.[129] In one study of such oral performances, just 60 percent of words were identical[130]—far higher than most of us in the West would achieve, but nevertheless hardly verbatim by modern standards.

And why would anyone in most cultures expect otherwise? Many of us adults in the West can repeat the story of Goldilocks and the Three Bears and may insist that we have told it correctly. We are not, however, reciting it verbatim from some hypothetical original.[131] We would not be likely to achieve anywhere close to 60 percent—even if we could agree on the "original" form to recount.

Moreover, not all traditions are equal; some are more relevant to community identity and thus more apt to be preserved with greater attentiveness and group concern.[132] Over time, the *core* of such traditions tends to assume a relatively fixed shape because all previous performances constrain each new

126. Ong, *Orality*, 22; Rosenberg, "Complexity," 82; Kirk, "Memory Theory," 829. Cf. Kirk, *Memory*, 111: although "oral genres frequently enable close replication," it is not verbatim, a skill associated more with written media.

127. See Bauckham, *Eyewitnesses*, 327, 333–34, 345; Allison, *Constructing Jesus*, 11–13; Eddy and Boyd, *Legend*, 275–85; Kloppenborg, "Memory," 289, 293–94.

128. See here Kloppenborg, "Memory," 291, following helpfully DeConick, "Memory." Cf. again Kloppenborg, "Memory," 318: "The Jesus tradition was" likely "condensed, schematized, paraphrased, and occasionally elaborated in the course of transmission."

129. Ong, *Orality*, 60, 64–65; Rubin, *Memory*, 7–8, 137–39; Small, *Wax Tablets*, 5–7; Kirk, "Memory Theory," 832; Ehrman, *Before Gospels*, 185–86, 192; cf. Kwon, "Reimagining," 137–38. Cf. similarly Allison, *Constructing Jesus*, 29: "Tradents are always introducing changes."

130. Ong, *Orality*, 60.

131. With Small, *Wax Tablets*, 4.

132. Those "who have a stake in a person's or event's memory being maintained . . . form the 'carrier groups'" (Schwartz, "Smoke," 11), a stake particularly relevant to sacred histories (11–12); cf. Bailey, "Tradition" (*Themelios*), 7. On some scripts being more accurate than others, see Schwartz, "Harvest," 323.

performance.[133] In many societies oral tradition even *limits* "the potential for innovation" concerning the *core* of the story; the tradition "only remains in the cultural memory if it gives expression to something familiar."[134] Any divergence from community tradition or perceived fabrication of the community's past will normally be rejected outright.[135] Likewise, various versions of a story may circulate and influence one another[136] and, in so doing, reinforce the core.[137]

Tradents may also remain more attentive when recounting stories that they believe to be true,[138] as would be the case with early stories about Jesus. They also seem more careful with respect to stories "sacred" to their communities.[139] In societies where honor and shame are paramount, public communal correction also serves as a deterrent against altering the story line,[140] though altering details has entertainment value.

Storytelling naturally takes liberties, and oral tradents often exhibit flexibility each time they tell a story. Flexibility allows for tradition to address the present community "in fresh ways" without inhibiting "the animating moral authority of the salient past."[141] Normally there are recognized limits, however, that require the core to remain stable, even as minor details are varied by telling the story in slightly different ways.[142] (Remember Goldilocks: had I told the story to my children, the porridge might have temporarily become highly nutritious broccoli soup, even though that is not what bears, though omniv-

133. Rodríguez, *Structuring*, 87.

134. Assmann, *Cultural Memory*, 81; see also Rubin, *Memory*, 135: "An audience knowledgeable in a tradition is a strong conservative force that keeps the singer within traditional bounds." Cf. similarly Dunn, *Tradition*, 54; regarding written sources, Eve, *Behind Gospels*, 142.

135. Le Donne, *Historiographical Jesus*, 58.

136. Vansina, *Oral Tradition*, 153; cf. 158–60.

137. Kirk, "Memory Theory," 823.

138. Cf. Rubin, *Memory*, 141.

139. Anderson, "Oral Tradition," 35, following Kiparsky, "Oral Poetry," but both noting that there are exceptions. Early generations, which have greater access to actual information, are also in many cases less apt to create fictitious folk stories about their protagonists; contrast Josephus's *Jewish War* with the Testaments of the Twelve Patriarchs.

140. Rubin, *Memory*, 135 (cf. 228); Bailey, "Tradition" (*Themelios*), 7; Bailey, "Tradition" (*ExpT*), 365–66; Bird, *Gospel*, 96, 110; David Instone-Brewer, personal correspondence, May 22, 2017; Arkan al-Amin, personal correspondence, July 4, 2017 (going beyond Bailey in noting the correction even of jokes).

141. Kirk, *Memory*, 199.

142. Bailey, "Tradition" (*Themelios*), 7–8; Arkan al-Amin, personal correspondence, July 4, 2017.

orous, generally cook.)[143] Traditional storytellers exercise creativity, "but not by trying to break the rules"; they follow the expected schema.[144] Schwartz finds this pattern of a solid core even in divergent versions of folk tales, noting documentation of "almost ten thousand popular tales representing stable oral traditions spanning many generations."[145]

Because stories central to community identity are retold countless times, good storytellers vary details during different tellings; but this "vividness must come in the noncentral details," because "one is not allowed to tamper with the key information."[146] Audiences may correct deviations, insofar as the story is already property of the community.[147] (Usually the result of the error is just shame, which is difficult enough to endure in many cultures. Among one people in Rwanda, however, the penalty was traditionally death,[148] certainly a serious incentive to get one's lesson right!)

Instead of increasing distortion, wider knowledge of stories may constrain their subsequent telling.[149] This constraint seems quite probable in the case of at least some of our Gospels. Luke not only affirms that his account about Jesus rests on information going back to the beginning of the movement (Luke 1:1–2) but also expects that Theophilus will find it consistent with what he has already learned (1:3–4). By the time that Luke writes, there were hundreds or perhaps thousands of Christians even in distant Rome.[150] The familiarity of Luke's audience with much of Jesus's story at the time that he wrote (Luke 1:4) presumably constrained his telling.

With respect to the gospel tradition, scholars normally insist only on the gist, which, given variation among the Gospels, seems to be also all that the Evangelists themselves expected. Nor would their initially anticipated audiences demur; as noted in chapter 15, the standard of accuracy for ancient memory was the gist.[151] As Licona observes after collecting various examples in Plutarch, "It is safe to assume that nearly every conversation narrated in the

---

143. Unlike traditional folklorists, I belong to the more freewheeling era of Disney and Shrek.

144. Rubin, *Memory*, 36.

145. Schwartz, "Smoke," 13–14.

146. Barber and Barber, *Severed*, 11; cf. 156.

147. As noted above, e.g., Rubin, *Memory*, 135; Rosenberg, "Complexity," 83, 85–86.

148. Assmann, *Cultural Memory*, 40, citing on the culture Borgeaud, "Approche," 13.

149. See Rodríguez, *Structuring*, 87.

150. See Tacitus, *Annals* 15.44; cf. Rom 1:8.

151. Small, "Artificial Memory"; Rhoads, "Performance Events," 175. For paraphrase, see, e.g., Theon, *Progymnasmata* 1.93–171.

ancient literature, if historical, is [only] a summary of content recalled by the author and/or his sources," usually as gist or paraphrase.[152]

16.7. Traditional Middle Eastern Memory

Societies that value memory and traditionally have lacked literary or electronic resources for recall are more likely to exhibit memory skills.[153] In the wake of modern technology, such skills are declining. In the West, a person who can recite the *Aeneid* or the Talmud by heart (already textually based skills) is much rarer today than in the past.[154] My wife, who is from Congo and has a French PhD in history, notes that electronic media have virtually displaced such skills and interests among younger-generation Africans. Even traditional Middle Eastern memory culture is quickly giving way to electronic media,[155] though at the moment traces of the stronger traditional emphasis on memory persist.

Kenneth Bailey offers a model of oral tradition positioned in the wide gap between Bultmannian skepticism and Gerhardsson's controlled tradition.[156] Arguing that the Synoptics are too much alike for mere fiction and too different for wooden transmission, Kenneth Bailey opts for the sort of oral transmission found in traditional Middle Eastern society.

Bailey's approach has been both hailed and vilified: British scholars Dunn and Wright have developed his model;[157] on my side of the Atlantic, Weeden and Ehrman have challenged it.[158] Some of Bailey's claims were inaccurate, but some of his critics have exaggerated the inaccuracies and caricaturized his position,

---

152. Licona, *Differences*, 117.

153. Cf. Thatcher, *Why John Wrote*, 132: "Historical documents . . . make it unnecessary for us to remember." Pace Byrskog, *Story as History*, 110–11, however, oral cultures are not superior in verbatim memorization, since they lack the resources necessary to test it; see Kloppenborg, "Memory," 293–94.

154. Small, *Wax Tablets*, 287n76, noting esp. Jousse, *Style*, 167, and referring also to Neusner, *Memorized Torah*.

155. Bailey, "Tradition" (*Themelios*), 9; Bailey, "Tradition" (*ExpT*) 363–64; cf. Hamilton, "Story-Tellers"; Hamilton, "Storytelling"; Davies, "Storytellers"; Dunn, "Theory," 46, 62; McIver, *Memory*, 115, 121.

156. Bailey, "Oral Tradition"; Bailey, "Tradition" (*Themelios*); Bailey, "Tradition" (*ExpT*). For such a centrist position, cf. also Chilton, *Study*, 21–50, noted in Chance, "Fiction," 126.

157. Wright, *Victory*, 133–37; Dunn, *Tradition*, 2, 52–53, 59, 205, 219, 239, 279, 320, 322; Mournet, *Oral Tradition*, 187–90, 292. Balanced evaluations include McIver, *Memory*, 115; Kloppenborg, "Memory," 300–303; Eve, *Behind Gospels*, 66–85.

158. Weeden, "Theory"; Ehrman, *Before Gospels*, 71.

which is, in the final analysis, fairly mainstream. The gap between Bultmann and Gerhardsson is hospitably spacious, and Bailey identifies his own position as close to that of the renowned British NT scholar C. H. Dodd.[159] (I address the strengths and weaknesses of Bailey's argument more fully in a separate, detailed article.)[160]

While Bailey was not always current in the secondary literature on NT scholarly opinions, he, unlike his critics, had decades of experience with Middle Eastern perspectives. Diane King, a University of Kentucky anthropology professor with expertise in traditional Middle Eastern oral tradition, observed to me that Bailey was at his best when describing what he saw around him. That is the approach that ethnographers use.[161] The usual period of fieldwork for ethnographers and anthropologists is one to three years;[162] although Bailey was not trained for ethnography and presumably was not taking ethnographic field notes, his four decades of experience deeply immersed in Middle Eastern culture and language should qualify him to offer sounder observations about that culture than any suggested by his most ardent critics so far.[163]

Although some of Bailey's illustrations prove unfortunate, his overall sense that the essential core of stories generally persists in Middle Eastern memory seems to hold true, certainly within living memory.[164] Besides his own experience, Bailey cites significant documentation, from a number of works, for the current circulation of thousands of proverbs in Middle Eastern culture,[165] perhaps neglected by some of his academic critics because they are comparatively illiterate in Arabic.[166]

159. Bailey, "Tradition" (*Themelios*), 5; Bailey, "Oral Tradition," 36–37; Bailey, "Tradition" (*ExpT*), 353–54. McIver, *Memory*, 120, straddles the same chasm.

160. See Keener, "Weeden's Critique." See also quite fully (though I discovered it too late for engagement in my own article), Derico, *Tradition*, 63–101, including his evaluation of Weeden's critique on 89–114.

161. Personal discussion with Diane King on this topic, Wilmore, Kentucky, March 14, 2017.

162. E.g., Bronisław Malinowski stayed two or three years with Trobriand Islanders.

163. Derico, *Tradition*, 79, notes Bailey's lack of formal field notes, but on 90 warns that Bailey's harshest critic "demands from him a level of descriptive precision that no professional ethnographer or folklorist ever attempts to meet." Turner, *Experiencing Ritual*, 4, complains about some fellow anthropologists ethnocentrically supposing that their training qualifies them to "understand aspects of a culture better than field subjects."

164. Again, argued at length in Keener, "Weeden's Critique." Professor King notes (again, our discussion, March 14, 2017) her own quarter century of experience with oral memory in Kurdistan.

165. Bailey, "Tradition" (*Themelios*), 6–7; Bailey, "Tradition" (*ExpT*), 365; cf. Bailey, "Oral Tradition," 41.

166. In an online lecture, Bailey dismisses those who write about "Mediterranean peasants" without having met any.

16.7a. Some Examples

Bailey also offers both Islamic and Christian examples of Middle Eastern memory practices that are either documented in Middle Eastern sources or have been standard practices easily observable, for example, in a Middle Eastern Orthodox seminary.[167]

Bailey is hardly alone. For example, T. M. Derico more formally interviewed three Middle Eastern leaders who had known a recent historical figure. Although each leader naturally had some accounts not mentioned by the others, they also included numerous parallel accounts based on their direct knowledge of the figure, but independent from one another. They had recited such stories repeatedly among the spiritual communities of which the figure was considered a founder.[168] The forms included travel narratives, miracle accounts, sayings, and the like.[169]

Likewise, Arkan al-Amin, a Lebanese minister trained in both psychology and Scripture, shared with me the core of a story that he heard just once at age twelve nearly thirty years earlier. He then located the full story for me, because it illustrates the value once placed on oral memory. I paraphrase here his translation of the Arabic poem:

> The story begins with a princess poet by the name of Da'd, who offers her hand in marriage to any poet better than she. Whoever married her would also receive a small kingdom ["emirate" in Arabic]. A poet from Tihama heard the news, composed an extraordinary poem, and then went off to see the princess. On his long journey, a man from Hijaz stayed with him and asked him why he was traveling. Trusting him, the poet naively recited his poem. The Hijazi man then killed the poet while he was sleeping, desiring the anticipated bride for himself. The Hijazi man proceeded to Princess Da'd and recited the poem from memory, until he reached the verse that declared, "If you go to Tihama, Tihama is my nation, and if you go to Najd, then my love will be in Najd." So the princess asked the Hijazi man where he was from. When he said Hijaz, she shouted, "Capture the killer of my husband!"

167. Bailey, "Tradition" (*Themelios*), 5–6; Bailey, "Oral Tradition," 39.

168. Derico, *Tradition*, 205–11; for the transcripts, 267–90; for their repeated recounting of the stories, see 208. I regret discovering this work too late for Keener, "Weeden's Critique"; I learned of it only through Zwiep, "Review of Derico."

169. Derico, *Tradition*, 207.

I have already noted that oral tradition often includes variations in details. Al-Amin had heard a variant version, which he also was able to locate, which specified that the Hijazi traveler's accent had given him away (not an implausible guess from this version as well). Both versions assume the ability to memorize a poem while hearing it. Noting this traditional emphasis on memory in Middle Eastern culture, al-Amin concluded, "This type of story doesn't phase us at all."[170]

Scholars often underscore memory's potential by noting Qur'an memorization, which is widely attested. Although memorizing the Qur'an follows an established text,[171] it illustrates the emphasis on memory, and one does not need to be literate, or even to understand Arabic, to memorize it.[172] Bailey cites a traditional Middle Eastern expectation for a *shaykh* to "memorize the entire Qur'an."[173] He notes even wider experience with Eastern Orthodox clergy who recite hours of liturgy representing "hundreds of pages"; he further illustrates his point by mentioning his then-recent encounter with a taxi driver he met who "had recently memorized the entire Psalter."[174] Such practices prevailed also in the nineteenth century,[175] and rote memorization remains part of education even in parts of the Middle East today.[176]

Such recitation differs, of course, from memory of community stories, since textually constrained memorization is usually closer to verbatim memory, whereas oral stories depend only on gist memory.[177] Oral tradition can

170. Arkan al-Amin, personal correspondence, July 4 and 26, 2017.

171. Traditionally established under Caliph Uthman, although some argue for earlier variants; see Wansbrough, *Quranic Studies*, 44; Cook, *Muhammad*, 67–69, 74; Koren and Nevo, "Approaches," 104–5; Peters, *Muhammad*, 257.

172. Cf. Wagner, *Literacy*, 47, 269 (noting recent decline, 48); Zubaida, *Law and Power*, 27–28; Touati, *Literacy*, 12; Goody, *Interface*, 194, 234–35 (to some extent); Rosenberg, "Complexity," 81 (following Clark and Clark, *Psycholinguistics*, 136); Anderson, "Oral Tradition," 34; Graham, *Beyond*, 79–80, 101–2, 105 (cf. 131 for illiterate Christians memorizing Scripture as a prerequisite for the monastery; cf. also 43, 124); Johnson and Musser, *Story*, 101; old Arabic poems in Janin, *Pursuit*, 49. For Qur'an memorization, see also Small, *Wax Tablets*, 287n76; Eickelman, *Middle East*, 41, 50, 63–65, 70 (fading in newer times, 171); Bailey, "Tradition" (*Themelios*), 5–6 (including personal acquaintance with such reciters); McIver, *Memory*, 115.

173. The estimate that it is two-thirds the length of the Hebrew Bible, however, is amiss; it apparently contains just over half the word count of the New Testament (and over three-quarters the number of verses) and roughly the same number of letters as the Torah.

174. Bailey, "Tradition" (*ExpT*), 364.

175. Hogg, *Master-Builder*, 156.

176. Arkan Al Amin, personal correspondence, July 4, 2017, also noting that until the mid-1800s storytellers had to provide most education for typical Lebanese village children.

177. Note the studies in McIver, *Memory*, 61–62; cf. also Bailey, "Tradition" (*ExpT*), 364; Kelber, *Gospel*, 9.

rely more simply on "a system of constraints and cues" rather than rote memorization.[178] It does illustrate, however, the value that a Middle Eastern context
has traditionally placed on memory of matters central to community identity.

It is not usually disputed that traditional Middle Eastern memory valued
and therefore transmitted sayings and stories orally better than do modern
Google-driven Westerners.[179] After the course of two millennia, the culture
has obviously changed, but on the whole, especially outside urban settings, it
likely remains much closer to Jesus's milieu than are the Western approaches
that many readers take for granted.

Some weaknesses in Bailey's methodology and illustrations notwithstanding, Eric Eve is probably correct to suggest that Bailey's work illustrates concretely the sort of "oral tradition" that others have articulated theoretically.[180]
Bailey's approach may be more helpful for Galilee than for Jerusalem, however;
most of the Diaspora church traced its origins to Antioch and especially to
Jerusalem, while the Twelve were in leadership there, not to Galilee.[181]

16.7b. The Role of Prominent Tradents

Societies normally highlight the more qualified agents of tradition. Bailey recounts how in one Middle Eastern community that he visited, "The ranking
patriarch was given the honour of telling the story to the newcomer" (i.e., to
Bailey).[182] Enlivening his teaching with anecdotes fits his Middle Eastern setting, but Bailey's anecdotal observation is not isolated. It is consistent not only
with Bailey's other illustrations where a more prominent person is present[183]

---

178. Kirk, *Memory*, 111, 196, 199.

179. See Redman, "Eyewitnesses," 192–93; Dunn, *Tradition*, 305; Dunn, *Perspective*, 45–46;
Mournet, *Oral Tradition*, 190; Eve, *Behind Gospels*, 84–85.

180. Eve, *Behind Gospels*, 83–84; cf. also Mournet, *Oral Tradition*, 187–90, 292; Dunn,
Tradition, 305.

181. Rom 15:19; Gal 1:17–19; 2:1–2 (and in light of these passages, 1 Cor 9:5; 15:5); cf. Acts
11:19 (although Manaen in Acts 13:1 may have *originated* in Galilee, as did the Twelve). For
what it is worth, Acts 9:2 suggests that this was true even in Damascus. Galilee's two minor
cities were "not large enough to attract substantial international trade" (Reed, *Archaeology*, 96).

182. Bailey, "Tradition" (*Themelios*), 6–7; Bailey, "Oral Tradition," 43. In antiquity, the
eldest member of a community usually knew the most about the people who had lived there
(Lysias, *Orations* 23.5, §167).

183. E.g., Bailey, "Tradition" (*Themelios*), 6, noting both formal settings (such as those
with teachers and disciples) and the informal settings on which he focuses; Bailey, "Tradition"
(*ExpT*), 364.

and elsewhere in Middle Eastern accounts,[184] but also in other societies valuing group tradition,[185] including in antiquity.[186] Some traditions are community property; some others are known or known best by elites.[187]

Many traditional societies even have special persons known as repositories of community tradition.[188] Even modern Western folk tradition sometimes highlights those with special expertise; many singers of traditional North Carolina ballads, for example, "learned orally from other singers."[189] As Rubin notes, the role of such select tradents in oral tradition differs from experiments involving "randomly selected people" transmitting to other "randomly selected people."[190]

In Middle Eastern and rural Mediterranean culture, deference to authority and tradition would reinforce the role of Jesus's designated apostles on both counts. They were both the chief eyewitnesses and the chief leaders of the Christian community in Jerusalem (cf. Gal 1:18–19; 2:7–9), to which even Diaspora Christians looked as the mother church (Rom 15:25–27; Gal 1:17–18; 2:1–2; cf. 1 Cor 16:3). (Where Jewish practice depended on widespread Jewish knowledge rather than special expertise, it was because it was in a matter in which all Jews were supposed to have mnemonic expertise.)[191]

As the leading eyewitnesses and also leaders of the early Christian movement, Jesus's chief associates would be accepted as leading authorities on what Jesus said and did. Theirs would be the standard version to which other members of their movement would wish to conform. Their direct influence would be less in many of the northern Mediterranean urban centers where Paul min-

---

184. See Derico, *Tradition*, 206. Unlike Bailey, Derico recorded and archived his information in forms accepted for ethnographic fieldwork.

185. On such social control of information, see Vansina, *Oral Tradition*, 96–97; Assmann, *Memory and Civilization*, 39. See here esp. Schwartz, "Smoke," 17, citing Katz and Lazarsfeld, *Influence*; for Brahmans alone reciting the Vedas, see Finnegan, *Oral Poetry*, 234, although variants show (Ong, *Orality*, 64–65) that the Vedas were transmitted less precisely than their tradents supposed, and some challenge the pure orality of their transmission (Goody, *Interface*, 110–22, esp. 122). Cf. Rosenberg, "Complexity," 81, who notes that Finnegan is more accurate when addressing Africa (the accuracy of Finnegan's work is respected in Africa; see, e.g., numerous references in Mburu, *Hermeneutics*).

186. Bockmuehl, *Seeing*, 176; for churches, cf. Byrskog, "Century," 21.

187. Anderson, "Oral Tradition," 37.

188. Vansina, *Oral Tradition*, 36–39; Assmann, *Cultural Memory*, 38–39 (for cultural, not communicative, memory); Dunn, *Tradition*, 55, 279–80, citing Havelock, *Muse*, 57–58.

189. Rubin, *Memory*, 265.

190. Rubin, *Memory*, 132.

191. See Assmann, "Memory and Culture," 341, noting (without the reference) Josephus, *Against Apion* 2.188–89.

istered, though even there Paul seems to have made his congregations aware of Cephas, the Twelve, other apostles, and the Lord's brothers (1 Cor 1:12; 3:22; 9:5; 15:5-7; Gal 1:18-19; 2:7-9; cf. Rom 15:26-27).

The Christian tradition subsequent to the Gospels also maintained an emphasis on connections to the authentic witnesses.[192] Thus, for example, Irenaeus emphasized that, as a young man, he saw Polycarp, and Polycarp had learned from the apostles and associated with those who had seen the Lord.[193] By the end of living memory, tracing traditions to named witnesses of Jesus had become important, evident already in Papias.[194] Such appeal to links to named, authoritative teachers of the past resembles appeals among rabbis, teachers in Greek philosophic schools, and for that matter some modern German scholarship. While it cannot guarantee that all memories or attributions are correct,[195] it does underline the high value placed on, and presumably desire for, memory.

16.7c. Ancient Mediterranean Memory

I survey here briefly some evidence for the character of ancient Mediterranean memory; I have provided fuller detail elsewhere[196] and have addressed ancient Mediterranean education in the previous chapter.

Writers who drew on multiple written sources had to depend heavily on memory, since even scribes could have open in front of them normally at most one source at a time.[197] At least for first drafts, they also normally composed and arranged in their heads before writing.[198]

Ancient teachers highly valued memory. For example, to an associate who had lost his notes, one philosopher reportedly replied, "You should have

---

192. See Bockmuehl, *Seeing*, 180-89, esp. on Papias (Eusebius, *Ecclesiastical History* 3.39.3-4; p. 186), and, on 184-85, Irenaeus, *Against Heresies* 3.1-5, and Irenaeus's memories of Polycarp in Eusebius, *Ecclesiastical History* 5.20.5-7 (the narrated elements presumably made a large impression because of their significance).

193. Irenaeus, *Against Heresies* 3.3.4 (I have rendered συναναστρέφω [*synanastrephō*] as "associate with").

194. See Bauckham, *Eyewitnesses*, 294-95. Papias may commit his material to writing because the oral tradition is fading (Nicklas, "Literature," 94).

195. See, e.g., Neusner, *Traditions*.

196. Keener, *Historical Jesus*, 139-64; Keener, "Assumptions"; Keener, "Biographies of a Sage." I draw especially here on my work in Keener, *Historical Jesus*.

197. Small, *Wax Tablets*, 151-55, 163-70, 176, 185-87, 189, 201.

198. Small, *Wax Tablets*, 180-87.

inscribed them . . . on your mind instead of on paper."[199] Exhortations to remember are frequent in ancient moralists.[200] Ancient Jewish[201] and early Christian[202] sources emphasize the same value.

In the early second century, even a literate Christian leader with access to written sources still preferred direct contact with oral memories about Jesus. Thus Papias insisted that he "did not suppose that matters written in books would benefit me as much as matters from a living and remaining voice" of eyewitnesses or those who heard them.[203] More generally, authors commonly used oral sources alongside written ones.[204] Certainly, far more traditions about Jesus circulated in the first century than those that survived (cf. Acts 20:35; John 20:30; 21:23).[205]

16.8. Living Memory

Given the brief period between Jesus's ministry and the first Gospels, and given what we know of ancient interest in and dependence on memory, the survival of significant testimony should normally be considered far more likely than not.

199. Diogenes Laertius, *Lives* 6.1.5 (LCL 2:7).

200. E.g., Epictetus, *Discourses* 4.13.23; Marcus Aurelius, *Meditations* 8.36; Porphyry, *Letter to Marcella* 8.139–41; 10.187–89; note also P.Mich. 202.3 in Hansen, *Abraham*, 28; see also Aune, *Environment*, 191.

201. Cf., e.g., Exod 12:14; 13:3, 9; Deut 7:18; 8:2; Jub. 36:6; 49:1; Let. Aris. 154; 2 Macc 2:25; 4 Macc 17:8; Philo, *Studies* 170; Josephus, *Jewish War* 5.377; 4 Ezra 2:8; 2 Bar. 20:3; 84:2.

202. See Mark 8:18; Luke 17:32; 22:19; John 14:26; 15:20; 16:4; 2 Thess 2:5; 2 Tim 2:8; Jude 5, 17; see here esp. Acts 20:35; Rom 15:15; 1 Cor 11:24–25; 15:1; 2 Pet 1:15; 3:2; Papias, frag. 3.3, 15 (cf. also 3.7, 9); 1 Clem. 53.1; 2 Clem. 17.3; Pol. *Phil.* 2.3.

203. Papias, frag. 3.4. Papias's "elders" in 3.4 seems to refer especially to apostles past and (for Aristion and John) still living into his own time (taking his knowledge of the "elders" in 3.3 as indirect; but "elders" applies to those who knew John in 14.1). Against most, I take the distinction between the two Johns in 3.5–6 as Eusebius's interpretation of Papias based on later tradition and Eusebius's negative view on Revelation. Plato's preference for oral instruction persisted into the early empire (cf. Alexander, "Voice"; Tieleman, "Orality," 35); cf. Plutarch's Middle Platonic adaptation in Zadorojnyi, "Ethico-Politics." Despite Papias's preference for orality, he may write traditions because he recognizes that the oral voice is fading (Nicklas, "Literature," 94) or because he seeks to be more comprehensive than Mark (Carlson, "Papias," 269).

204. Derrenbacker, *Practices*, 75. Against incompatibility, cf., e.g., Henderson, "*Didache*," 306.

205. Some eyewitnesses survived for many years; see Quadratus in Eusebius, *Ecclesiastical History* 4.3.1–2; Evans, *World*, 7–8. Kee, *Origins*, 134, notes invitations to "remember" Jesus's words in Acts 11:16; 20:35; 1 Clem. 13.1; 46.7; Pol. *Phil.* 2.3; cf. also Papias, frag. 3.3; 2 Clem. 17.3.

Scholars usually date the Gospel of Mark between 64 and 75 CE (some thirty-four to forty-five years after Jesus's ministry)[206] and thus well within the period of living memory. Other written sources, probably referred to in Luke 1:1, may have been circulating in the same period. Only a few surviving ancient biographies come from within roughly four decades of their chief character, as Mark likely does. (I date Q earlier than Mark, although I recognize that the date and even existence of Q continue to be a matter of debate.) If we can look to any ancient biographies to preserve reliable memory, surely this should include Mark.

Someone might protest, however, that no ancient biographies, even those close in time to their subjects, preserved accurate memories, at least if not written by eyewitnesses. Answering this criticism could require more than a single book, much less a single chapter, since literature regarding memory and oral history multiplies today at a phenomenal rate.[207] Nevertheless, the question warrants at least some discussion. I have responded to some related points in greater detail elsewhere.[208]

16.8a. Some Eighty Years of Living Memory

To what extent could ancient memory and oral tradition preserve the substance of events and ideas for such a span of time? Ancient historiography almost by definition included collecting oral reports; each generation's historians established the historical record for their own generation.[209] This procedure became problematic only when Romans tried to write ancient history for which they no longer had oral traditions,[210] but even Romans valued depending on oral tradition when it remained within living memory. Thus, for example, Suetonius reports what he heard from an earlier generation.[211]

---

206. For 65–70, see, e.g., Ehrman, *Introduction*, 82; Collins, *Mark*, 11–14; Spivey, Smith, and Black, *Anatomy*, 60–61; for shortly after 70, e.g., Marcus, "War," 460; for mid-60s (my own tentative view), cf. Lane, *Mark*, 17–18; Bock, *Mark*, 21; for earlier, while Peter remained alive, see France, *Mark*, 37–38.

207. On the use of, and methodologies for, oral history in historiography, see Byrskog, *Story*, 26–33; on its use in NT scholarship, see 33–40.

208. Keener, "Before Biographies"; "Ehrman vs. McIver," 273–93; and "Weeden's Critique."

209. Fornara, *Nature*, 48.

210. Fornara, *Nature*, 166–67.

211. Suetonius, *Vergil* 42; *Grammarians* 4. Such memories were often preserved even for debates in rhetorical schools (Suetonius, *Rhetoricians* 1).

Although I have argued that apostolic testimony would be the Evangelists' ideal source, I have not argued that the source was always direct. Let us say that many of the stories come not from the mouths of those who witnessed events forty years before, but from the mouths of those who heard the eyewitnesses, or other teachers who heard them, in the interim period, say, twenty years before. Even in the West, many people remember many stories they learned in childhood or in history classes and the like. Remembering the core in the form of episodes may point to more careful transmission from those who experienced the events, but in any case we are not speaking of a long period of time. This is all the more true for matters that are important to us. I still remember many of the eschatological rumors I heard as a new Christian convert from atheism in the late 1970s four decades ago, for example, because at the time they mattered deeply to me, though within a few years I discovered that they were almost entirely nonsense. How much more do we remember stories that we continue to value and retell as foundational for our activity?

The period within living memory—the period within the lifetime of some eyewitnesses or their hearers—is different in kind from subsequent tradition. This does not mean that stories are not reshaped for good storytelling or moral lessons. Obviously, the generation that inherits the witnesses' testimony also will not recall as much as the eyewitnesses who experienced events. They will have much less detail, far fewer episodes, and more need to focus on the gist. Studies show that apologetic and other interests may significantly reshape the moral perspectives of accounts already in the third generation.[212]

Nevertheless, the survival of original witnesses often serves as a control on memory. Today "living memory" can include memories such as survivors' testimonies of life before Nazi concentration camps[213] or apartheid-era forced relocations in South Africa.[214] Most scholars consider such recollections fairly stable and reliable within living memory.[215]

---

212. Bockmuehl, *Seeing*, 179–80, citing European examples, including "grandchildren of Nazi-era Germans"; Bird, *Gospel*, 53.

213. E.g., Schwartz, *Living Memory*; Jilovsky, *Remembering Holocaust*, 103. Such accounts began to proliferate esp. four decades after the Holocaust, as the generation began to disappear (Assmann, *Cultural Memory*, 36).

214. Field, *Communities*; Field, *Oral History*.

215. Vansina, *Oral Tradition*, 192–93, 197; cf. 158–59; Bockmuehl, *Seeing*, 161–88; Kirk, "Nexus," 144. Because we have written sources, our culture often neglects oral sources, but potential connections exist; e.g., I belonged to one African-American church in North Carolina where some people had known persons born in slavery (i.e., born before 1865), and I sometimes attended another that sang some spirituals passed down since the days of slavery.

Different disciplines sometimes speak of "memory" in different ways.[216] Modern social-memory research frequently distinguishes "collective" or "communicative memory" from "cultural memory."[217] Communicative memory occurs within a period in which direct communication is possible, often taken as three or "four generations or some eighty to a hundred years."[218] (In some more deliberate settings, including some ancient Mediterranean ones, some scholars suggest even 150 years.)[219]

In fact, in the period of living (i.e., communicative) memory, scholars usually speak not of "oral tradition" at all, but rather of "oral history," that is, the kind of information that one could in principle (and ideally should in practice) collect from witnesses.[220] Oral history depends on people's memories communicated orally; in virtually any kind of society it lasts no more than eighty to one hundred years.[221] "Tradition," Kirk explains, "is successor to memory; it appears when living memory is not extant."[222]

"Communicative memory" includes the individual in his or her social context, whereas "cultural memory" passes on the community's agreed un-

216. Nikulin, "Introduction," 4.

217. Assmann later changed the wording from "communicative" to "collective" memory (Hubenthal, "Communicative Memory," 65), but since the latter phrase in English can be confused with (and I sometimes use it interchangeably with) the "communal" memory, even among Jesus's hearers, I have retained the older expression. The German nomenclature currently lacks precise and standardized English equivalents (Hubenthal, "Cultural Memory," 70; Hubenthal, "Social Memory," 369). Cultural memory refers to "a community's canonized memory of the remote past" (Hubenthal, "Cultural Memory," 69).

218. Galinsky, "Introduction," 12. See Assmann, *Cultural Memory*, 6, 19, 35–38 (esp. 36); Assmann, *Religion and Memory*, 3–30; Assmann, "Memory and Culture," 331, 338; Keith, "Prolegomena," 170; Kirk, "Social and Cultural Memory," 5–6; Kirk, "Memory Theory," 840–41 (noting the ancient example in Thomas, *Oral Tradition*, 125–29); Kirk, *Memory*, 16; Dunn, *Tradition*, 236; Hubenthal, "Communicative Memory," 65. As early as 1936, cf. Raglan, *Hero*, 27–28.

219. Bockmuehl, *Seeing*, 169–72 (noting Murray, "Herodotus," 19, 21, for Herodotus and oral history); Kirk, "Nexus," 144. Citing Irenaeus, *Against Heresies* 3.3.4, and Eusebius, *Ecclesiastical History* 5.20.6, Bockmuehl, *Seeing*, 178, argues that Irenaeus knew people who knew the first apostles; cf. further connections on 180–89. Raglan, *Hero*, 13, allowed only 150 years for oral memory, but Barber and Barber, *Severed*, 244, note the resilience of oral tradition beyond this length of time.

220. See, e.g., Morrison, "Perspective," 2; Hamilton and Shopes, *Oral History*, xi; Field, "Dialogues," 269; Sheppard, "Historiography," 176. Even the history of medicine now often takes into account oral sources if they lie within living memory; see Winslow and Smith, "Challenges," 372. Some scholars, however, contend that oral history and tradition overlap, inviting greater consideration in the social context of the former (Byrskog, "Eyewitnesses," 159); cf. the nuanced position of Eve, *Behind Gospels*, 1.

221. Assmann, *Cultural Memory*, 37; and "Memory and Culture," 334, 338.

222. Kirk, *Memory*, 56.

derstanding.[223] Memory more recent than the floating gap (i.e., within living memory) may be biographic in character. Cultural memory about periods before the floating gap can include myths of origins preserved institutionally.[224] Cultural memory concerning the earlier period is what is remembered as history, but its correspondence to actual facts is usually not verifiable.[225]

Oral historian Jan Vansina notes that the major weaknesses of oral tradition are far less relevant "for data that are less than a few generations old."[226] Against some earlier generalizations about oral tradition, recent oral traditions include diverse information, with independent attestation, less reinterpretation, and sounder chronology.[227] Such "oral sources do not share the limitations of oral tradition," he observes, "and recent oral tradition—one or two generations beyond the eldest living members in a community—suffers only small damage."[228] Within the first two generations, it is difficult to isolate an event from its impact.[229]

16.8b. Mark Comes from the Period of Living Memory

By these standards, the period of transmission before the writing of the Gospels is relatively short;[230] rather than later oral tradition, they stem from the period of oral history.[231] (In this book I nevertheless retain the label "tradition," which remains standard in our discipline.) Against some scholars, "radical amnesia" in the span of merely several decades is highly improbable.[232] The skepticism of some early form-critics about accurate memories of Jesus reflected their treating the gospel traditions like European folk traditions that

223. Assmann, *Cultural Memory*, 6. For the political and power dimensions, see, e.g., Kirk, "Social and Cultural Memory," 11–14.

224. Assmann, *Cultural Memory*, 37, and "Memory and Culture," 338.

225. Assmann, *Cultural Memory*, 37–38, noting that even factual information becomes community myth. "Myth is the past condensed into foundational narrative" (61).

226. Vansina, *Oral Tradition*, 173.

227. Vansina, *Oral Tradition*, 192, 197.

228. Vansina, *Oral Tradition*, 192–93.

229. Le Donne, *Historiographical Jesus*, 61.

230. Thucydides complained about the potential bias and diversity of eyewitness reports of some events (*History* 1.22.2–3) but recognized that he could nevertheless provide a fairly reliable account by identifying shared features among these accounts.

231. Bauckham, *World*, 95, following also Byrskog, *Story*; Hengel, "Memory," 87.

232. For the idea, see already Taylor, *Formation*, 41; for "amnesia," see Witherington, *Christology*, 14; Keener, *Matthew*, 29; Bird, *Gospel*, 111, who adds Meier, *Marginal Jew*, 1:169–70.

developed over the course of centuries. Even in antiquity, ancient observers expected centuries of oral tradition to produce variations, even in poetry.[233] But the gospel tradition took decades, not centuries, to reach the Gospels. As W. D. Davies notes, probably only a single lifespan "separates Jesus from the last New Testament document,"[234] an observation a fortiori all the more applicable to Mark. Schwartz agrees, given the character of oral history; that is, the Gospels "refer to a real historical figure" and "were written shortly (a few decades) after his [Jesus's] death."[235]

In the case of the Gospels, the major upheavals for believers in greater Judea from 66 to 73 (leading to many survivors relocating to the Diaspora)[236] could constitute a transition for some elements of the tradition, since the original setting of the gospel traditions would make less sense to audiences born in the Diaspora.[237] Nevertheless, the major effect in oral tradition would mostly be felt after the death of nearly all of the last surviving Judean tradents, probably toward the end of the first century.[238] The distance of that past floating gap, before which all the past blends together, can vary depending on the culture, but it is, as noted, sometimes about eighty years.[239]

Before this time, communities often experience a crisis of tradition when the generation of eyewitnesses begins to die out, frequently starting about four decades after the foundational experiences. At this critical juncture, they often seek other forms to perpetuate their traditions.[240] (The Roman historian Tacitus thus makes special note of the death of the last known survivor from the period of the Roman Republic.)[241] Although ancients also recognized that

233. On Homer, see Josephus, *Against Apion* 1.12; Diogenes Laertius, *Lives* 9.12.113.

234. Davies, *Invitation*, 116; cf. similarly Benoit, *Gospel*, 33; Sanders, *Tendencies*, 28; Dunn, *Tradition*, 234–35, 314; Bauckham, *World*, 93.

235. Schwartz, "Smoke," 14.

236. See Josephus, *Jewish Antiquities* 20.256; Eusebius, *Ecclesiastical History* 3.5.3; cf. Pritz, *Nazarene Christianity*, 122–27; Aune, *Revelation*, 164; perhaps Smith, "Sarcophagus."

237. Note Luke's contextualization of Mark's Galilean roof (Mark 2:4; Luke 5:19).

238. This conclusion is consistent with the floating gap often following living memory of up to eighty years (Assmann, *Cultural Memory*, 37).

239. Vansina, *Oral Tradition*, 24, citing the example of the Tio tradition in Congo.

240. Assmann, *Cultural Memory*, 36; cf. 85, 187, 206; many cite the language of the earlier German version, Assmann, *Gedächtnis*, 11, 218–21; see Kirk, "Memory Theory," 824, 840–41; Dunn, *Tradition*, 236–37; Keith, "Prolegomena," 170–71; Schwartz, "Jesus in Memory," 249 (comparing early nineteenth-century US history-writing); Kelber, "Works," 244; Hubenthal, "Communicative Memory," 65; Kirk, "Traditionsbruch."

241. Assmann, *Cultural Memory*, 36, citing Tacitus, *Annals* 3.75, for the year 22, about half a century after the end of the Republic.

memory could fade in old age,[242] they also recognized cases of sharp memories even then,[243] noting that teachers with fading memories might be more diligent in passing on their instruction to a new generation.[244]

Jan Assmann observes that death ruptures the connection "between yesterday and today"; "posthumous commemoration" of an individual differs from one's own autobiographic memory.[245] Assmann suggests that memory of individuals may continue orally for three to four generations to roughly eighty years, but a crisis often happens midway, at around forty years.[246] This situation may help explain why authors began producing written accounts about Jesus within roughly this time frame (cf. Luke 1:1).[247]

The material that most scholars call Q is probably even earlier than Mark.[248] Even if Mark is the first finished story about Jesus, which we cannot know, it stems from within about forty years.[249] I have argued elsewhere that, as the majority of scholars hold, the other Gospels also stem from no later than about sixty-five years after Jesus's public ministry.[250]

242. E.g., Theophrastus, *Characters* 27.2; Cicero, *Letters to Atticus* 12.1; Iamblichus, *Pythagorean Life* 5.21; Philo, *Creation* 103; Jub. 23:11.

243. E.g., Xenophon, *Agesilaus* 2.28; 11.14–15; Polybius, *Histories* 36.16.1–5, 11; Diodorus Siculus, *Library of History* 32.16.1; Cicero, *Brutus* 20.80; 64.229; Livy, *History* 4.14.2; Valerius Maximus, *Memorable Doings and Sayings* 8.7.1; 8.7.ext.5, 8–13; 8.13.2–3; 8.13.ext.1; Plutarch, *Marcus Cato* 15.4; Philostratus, *Lives of the Sophists* 1.11.495; Eunapius, *Lives* 482.

244. Iamblichus, *Pythagorean Life* 5.21.

245. Assmann, *Cultural Memory*, 19; cf. *Traditionsbruch* also in Kirk, *Memory*, 204. On Assmann's influence, see Keith, "Assmann."

246. Assmann, *Cultural Memory*, 36. Kirk, *Memory*, 205. Hubenthal, "Communicative Memory," 65, defines the span more precisely as thirty to fifty years. Kirk, *Memory*, 205n141, notes how ancient Athenian family traditions fit the three- to four-generation model, citing Thomas, *Oral Tradition*, 125–29. Note that many writers speak of generations as reproductive eras (today often thirty to thirty-five years in the West; Assmann and others use twenty-year generations for the more common ancient pattern). The Greek term commonly translated "generation" in English Bible translations (e.g., Matt 23:36; 24:34), sometimes envisioning an adult lifespan (Num 32:13; Ps 95:10; cf. Philo, *Moses* 1.238), represents roughly forty years in biblical parlance.

247. See Keith, "Prolegomena," regarding Mark and citing patristic sources (esp. 174, 179–80); cf. Schwartz, "Smoke," 17; Kirk, "Traditionsbruch," 429.

248. Maybe as early as the 40s; see Theissen, *Gospels*, 220–21, 230–32. Others suggest the late 50s or early 60s for the majority of Q (as a possibility, Kloppenborg, *Excavating Q*, 87).

249. Even aside from the tradition in Papias, scholars date Mark this early (and sometimes earlier) partly because Matthew and Luke most likely depend on Mark, and Matthew, at least, must be sufficiently early for its widespread use in the earliest of the Apostolic Fathers.

250. A growing minority of scholars now date Acts to the second century; I cannot digress here, but I address this question more fully in Keener, *Acts*, 1:383–401; cf. 1:402–22; 3:2350–74.

This point is fundamental. The four Gospels and maybe some traditions preserved as late as the time of Papias might stem from within the period of living memory—in the case of Jesus's ministry, eighty to a hundred years—and this would take us to as late as 110 to 130 CE.[251] By comparison, most of what we know about a majority of other events in ancient history derives from surviving historical and biographic sources written far more than four to seven decades after the events that they narrate. This is also true of the noncanonical gospels, probably including Thomas; they are problematic for historians not because they are noncanonical but because they stem from a period after communicative memory.

That Mark's Gospel or Q originated within living memory cannot guarantee beyond all doubt that their accounts are true. Such guarantees in any case exceed the capabilities of historiographic epistemology.[252] Usual standards of historical probability, however, should weight the case strongly in favor of their usefulness as exceptionally valuable historical sources about Jesus.

If we count back from approximately 65–75 CE to Jesus's ministry, we are thinking of thirty-five to forty-five years. By the standards of oral history, this is a remarkably short time. For a comparable span of time in US history before the writing of this book, we could think of the era when Nixon, Carter, and Reagan were US presidents. We teachers in our fifties or older still know information we learned relevant to our disciplines during those years, and we can probably still recount many events and experiences of our own and from our environment from those years.

Some ancient evidence, which professes to be based on witnesses who knew the first-century apostles, supports this general picture. I have already mentioned the testimony of Papias, and, more important and less disputable, the confidence that Matthew and Luke, who likely knew the origins of Mark's Gospel, placed in that Gospel as a valuable source for their information-based works.

---

251. Whether or not Papias is correct, it appears noteworthy that he himself writes within living memory of the Gospels' composition.

252. In contrast to positivist historiography, historians today recognize the provisional and probabilistic character of historical reconstruction; see the thorough survey of recent thought in Schröter, *Jesus to New Testament*, 9–27.

16.9. Expect Variations

I do not deny that some diverse traditions about Jesus arose by the later decades of the first century. Even if we explain many Johannine divergences from the Synoptics as homiletical and theological extrapolations that ancient Christian auditors might recognize as such, particularly obvious divergences in our sources surface in the specifics of Judas's grisly death[253] or Jesus's genealogy (Matt 1:2–16; Luke 3:24–38).[254]

Nevertheless, and in contrast to such examples, the strong majority of gospel tradition reflected in our first-century sources appears remarkably stable. This is likely in part because our written sources derive from the period of living memory of Jesus.

What we expect of those who passed on the gospel tradition should be consistent with the expectations of their contemporaries. It is anachronistic to expect them to have written by historiographic standards that did not yet exist, as if those later genre expectations are the inspired canon by which all literary endeavors should be judged. As documented in chapters 5, 7, 10, and 11, ancient standards allow a degree of flexibility,[255] the sort of flexibility evident in the Gospels themselves. Early rabbis, for example, not only preserved but adapted prior tradition.[256] Sometimes they condensed teachings[257] or presented apparently similar sayings in different words.[258]

Greek traditions display similar flexibility.[259] As noted in chapter 11, basic

---

253. Matt 27:5; Acts 1:18; Papias, frag. 18.1–7 Holmes; cf. Mart. Pol. 6.2. See discussion in Keener, *Matthew*, 657–60, and *Acts*, 1:760–65, where parallels among the accounts are noted and preference on details (from the standpoint of modern historical method) is given in both cases to Luke's account.

254. See discussion in Keener, *Matthew*, 73, 75–77; Ehrman, *Introduction*, 94–95; Ehrman, *Interrupted*, 35–39, esp. 39.

255. E.g., whereas some Q pericopes exhibit more than 80 percent verbal correspondence, more than one-third exhibit "less than 40 percent" (Dunn, *Perspective*, 110). (Where close verbal correspondence exists, it probably typically suggests a written source, and even divergences can simply reflect memory rather than consultation of texts; see Kloppenborg, "Memory," 292, 304, following DeConick's research).

256. Davies, "Reflexions," 156.

257. Gerhardsson, *Memory*, 136–48, 173–74; Goulder, *Midrash*, 64–65. Everyone recognized that they and their sources could at best provide selections of what was said (Acts 2:40; Xenophon, *Apology* 22; Musonius Rufus 7, p. 58.29–30; Gen. Rab. 55:7; 93:8; Exod. Rab. 44:5; Van der Horst, "Parallels," 57; Kennedy, "Survey," 15).

258. E.g., m. Šabb. 9:1; 'Abod. Zar. 3:6.

259. Kennedy, "Source Criticism," 132–33.

rhetorical exercises included paraphrasing sayings,[260] and no one objected to recontextualizing or rhetorically improving sayings. Thus one biographer praises a speaker who not only accurately "received" disciple-instruction but "passed it on" more eloquently than he had received it.[261] Although writers could expand narratives without introducing new information, unless from another source,[262] writers sometimes added details for dramatic effect.[263] Philosophic schools could hand on their traditions with much variation "by altering and expanding" them.[264] The variation in wording of some of Jesus's sayings, from Matthew to Luke to the Didache, is therefore not surprising.[265]

For that matter, Greek and Roman writers quoting earlier texts in new contexts often substituted words, paraphrased, and sometimes even changed the sense by quoting lines out of context.[266] For example, they barely ever quote Herodotus verbatim.[267] Philo,[268] and Josephus,[269] and even Judean sources[270] paraphrase their sacred Scriptures. Any expectation that the Gospels would necessarily follow their sources verbatim is naive.

16.10. Reticence to Invent Jesus Tradition

As E. P. Sanders concludes, "The gospel writers . . . developed [their material], shaped it and directed it in the ways they wished," but they "did not wildly invent it."[271] Had the first Christian voices indulged in free invention among

---

260. Theon, *Progymnasmata* 1.93–171; cf. also Libanius, *Anecdote* 1.4; 2.3; *Maxim* 1.2–5; 2.3; 3.2; Hermogenes, *Method in Forceful Speaking* 24.440.

261. Philostratus, *Lives of the Sophists* 2.29.621.

262. On expanding material rhetorically, see Theon, *Progymnasmata* 3.224–40; 4.80–82; Longinus, *On the Sublime* 11.1; Hermogenes, *Invention* 2.7.120; cf. Theon, *Progymnasmata* 2.115–23; Hermogenes, *Progymnasmata* 3. On Chreia, 7; Menander Rhetor, *Epideictic Treatises* 2.3, 379.2–4; Aphthonius, *Progymnasmata* 3. On Chreia, 23S, 4R; 4. On Maxim, 9–10.

263. Plutarch, *Alexander* 70.3. Even such augmentation elicited some protests; see Lucian, *How to Write History* 7–13; Shuler, *Genre*, 11–12.

264. Riesner, "Preacher," 203, citing Seneca, *To Lucilius* 33.4.

265. See Draper, "Tradition." For possibly independent Jesus tradition in what he views as the original part of the Didache, see Rordorf, "Didache"; cf. also Janicki, *Way*, 9.

266. Stanley, *Language*, 267–91, esp. 290–91; Hill, "Words," 268–73, 280–81, noting also esp. Turner, *Greek Papyri*, 106–7.

267. Hill, "Words," 269, citing Lenfant, "Fragments," 119.

268. Stanley, *Language*, 334–36; Hill, "Words," 274–75.

269. Hill, "Words," 275–76, following esp. Inowlocki, "Adding."

270. Stanley, *Language*, 292–323, 336–37, esp. 304–6, 322–23.

271. Sanders, *Figure*, 193.

their different geographic communities, we would expect Gospels much more diverse than our Synoptics are—more like the later gnostic sources formed under such conditions.[272] Or as memory theorist Barry Schwartz emphasizes, it is reasonable to expect that "Jesus' followers were determined to get his message right."[273] This introduction brings us to the subject of the reticence of Jesus's early movement to invent Jesus tradition.

Almost all scholars today believe that Paul's letters represent the earliest documents in the NT. They sometimes attest early traditions about Jesus's life and teaching (e.g., 1 Cor 7:10–12; 9:14; 11:23; 15:3; 1 Thess 4:15), and in some of these cases Paul explicitly distinguishes his teaching from that of Jesus (1 Cor 7:10, 12, 25).[274]

Some question why Paul fails to cite the Jesus tradition more often than he does. Paul does appeal to his audience's prior knowledge of such tradition in 1 Corinthians 11:23; 15:1–3; and probably 7:10; 9:14; 1 Thessalonians 4:15.[275] Paul uses formal language for passing on preexisting tradition, tradition typically received from other agents.[276] There is good reason to find echoes of Jesus's teachings elsewhere as well.[277] Thus Paul did instruct his churches in some Jesus tradition.

But Paul probably did not instruct all churches equally. Even his appeal to Scripture is uneven in his letters, probably depending partly on the issues and partly on the biblical literacy of the respective congregations. In the same way, his appeal to Jesus tradition varies among churches. He invokes his audience's knowledge of Jesus tradition most frequently in Corinth, where he had stayed for a particularly extended period (cf. Acts 18:11; 1 Cor 2:3; 2 Cor 11:9).

Yet Paul probably knew the OT more thoroughly than he knew the Jesus tradition, partly because the former was textual, and partly because he was

272. Cf. Hill, *Prophecy*, 163, 172; Sanders, *Figure*, 193.

273. Schwartz, "Origins," 55.

274. On Paul and the Jesus tradition, see, e.g., Allison, "Parallels"; Allison, *Constructing Jesus*, 346–48; Wenham, *Rediscovery*; Wenham, "Story"; Richardson and Gooch, "Logia," 52; Sauer, "Erwägungen"; Holtz, "Paul and Tradition"; Dunn, "Jesus Tradition"; Dunn, *Theology of Paul*, 189–95; Taylor, "Quest"; Eddy and Boyd, *Legend*, 216–28; Kim, *New Perspective*, 259–90; Keener, *Historical Jesus*, 361–71; Blomberg, "Quotations"; Fee, *Jesus the Lord*, 64–73; Sumney, *Steward*, 4, 137–56; see esp. Dungan, *Sayings* (e.g., 83–131, on Jesus's divorce saying); Hiestermann, *Tradition* (noting the frequent Matthean form).

275. Also see 2 Thess 2:5, 15. See discussion in Keener, *Historical Jesus*, 361–71; likely also in Galatians, notably including Q material that was apparently already in circulation, at least orally: see Keener, *Galatians* (Baker), 538–39.

276. E.g., Josephus, *Jewish Antiquities* 13.297, 408; cf. Eve, *Behind Gospels*, 179.

277. See, e.g., Thompson, *Clothed*.

better trained in the former. The Gospels were not available when Paul wrote, and his own knowledge of the Jesus tradition was presumably less complete than that of the Twelve. And as suggested by 1 Corinthians 7:10–12, 25, mentioned above, Paul did not presume to invent teachings for Jesus where he did not have them.

Some have argued for early Christian prophecy generating elements of the Jesus tradition,[278] but others demur or at least find it very rare.[279] The Jesus tradition was likelier a source for the wording of prophecies than the reverse. Otherwise, with which prophecies would one start as authoritative, unless those of Jesus or his earliest disciples? If an average of two prophecies occurred in each of a hundred house churches in the empire each week in the generation before 70 CE (cf. 1 Cor 14:29–31), we should expect more than 400,000 prophecies during that period.[280] How would a particular prophecy gain the traction accorded to the historical-Jesus tradition?

The most explicit NT records of prophecies (Acts 11:28; 21:11; Rev 2–3)[281] are distinguished from words of Jesus during his ministry, apart from any prophecies uttered by the historical Jesus himself (cf., e.g., Matt 11:21–24//Luke 10:13–15; Mark 13:2). It would be especially prophecies by Jesus himself that would prove foundational in his movement,[282] and subsequent prophecies might often echo the language of the gospel tradition just as they echoed the OT.[283] The tradition was also used to evaluate prophecies.[284] I have addressed this matter elsewhere in more detail.[285]

Could someone, hearing secondhand about a word from Jesus, confuse a Christian prophecy with an earlier teaching from Jesus's ministry? It is pos-

278. Beare, "Sayings," 181; Bultmann, *Tradition*, 163; Boring, "Oracles," 501–2; Boring, *Sayings*; Miller, "Rejection."

279. See Aune, *Prophecy*; Hill, "Evidence"; Hill, *Prophecy*; Bauckham, "Parables"; Dunn, "Sayings"; Byrskog, *Teacher*, 350–68; occasionally but rarely, Sanders, *Figure*, 62–63.

280. I take 100 as a median figure, with the number fewer early and greater later in the period.

281. Our few clear examples of prophecies in the NT are always explicitly identified as such (cf., e.g., Hill, *Prophecy*, 160–70; Aune, *Prophecy*, 243–44; Stanton, *Gospel Truth?*, 97).

282. See Hill, *Prophecy*, 180–81; cf. even Boring, *Sayings*, 138–39. On eschatological prophets and Jesus as one, see, e.g., Barnett, "Sign Prophets"; Gray, *Prophetic Figures*; Sanders, *Jesus and Judaism*, 173, 238–39; Ehrman, *Prophet*; Keener, *Historical Jesus*, 238–55.

283. See, e.g., Rev 1:7 (with Matt 24:30); Rev 1:13 ("one like a son of man," probably evoking the regular title in the gospel tradition); Rev 2:7a and 13:9 (Mark 4:9, 23; cf. 8:18); Rev 3:3 and 16:15 (Matt 24:43//Luke 12:39); Rev 3:5 (Matt 10:32//Luke 12:8); Rev 13:13 (Mark 13:22); Rev 18:21 (Matt 18:6//Luke 17:2).

284. Dunn, *Tradition*, 323.

285. Keener, *Historical Jesus*, 364–65; *Matthew*, 57; and *Acts*, 2:1851–52.

sible. We lack evidence, however, that this confusion happened very often, whereas extant evidence suggests that the first Christians avoided doing so deliberately.[286]

16.11. Examples of Early Judean/Galilean Traits

Parallelomania in the popular sphere today, especially on the internet, often seeks to derive the plot of Jesus's story from every cultural expression possible (Greek myth, Persian myth, Egyptian myth, and maybe someday Elvis or Godzilla), apart from the ancient Jewish culture that Jesus's own location and era make most obvious.

The impetus for such approaches in the late nineteenth and early twentieth century was an anti-Semitic trend that climaxed with the syncretistic Aryan Jesus promoted by the pro-Nazi "German Christian" movement during the Nazi regime.[287] The quest to find non-Jewish backgrounds for Christianity fueled much of the so-called history of religions school:[288] "Jesus's religious teachings originated in Hellenism, Buddhism, Hinduism, or Iranian culture," Susannah Heschel laments; "anything but Judaism."[289] Seeking to distance Jesus from ethnic Jews, she notes, they argued that his region of Galilee was ethnically gentile,[290] a thesis that archaeological knowledge today renders absurd.[291]

By contrast, most voices in what is often called the Third Quest for the historical Jesus recognize that Jesus was a Galilean Jew, and they seek to un-

---

286. While probably not incorporating prophecies, John undoubtedly trusts the Spirit's inspiration as he expounds Jesus's message (John 14:26; 15:26; 16:7–15), perhaps not unlike Greek epic poets or Israelite prophet-historians (in this period, cf. Hall, "History," 13–46; Hall, *Histories*); but regular ancient historiographic speech-writing practices would also make such exposition uncontroversial, even without claims of inspiration; see further, e.g., Keener, *John*, 60–62; Bauckham, "Historiographical Characteristics," 30–36; cf. Keener, *Acts*, 258–319, esp. 271–82.

287. Heschel, *Aryan Jesus*, 8, 16, 19, 24, 26–66, 191, 285–86; cf. Head, "Nazi Quest"; Poewe, *Religions*; Theissen and Merz, *Guide*, 163. Earlier, even Schweitzer praised the unique "German temperament" (*Quest*, 1), yet without affirming an Aryan Jesus (a thesis that he rejects on 329).

288. Heschel, *Aryan Jesus*, 58–60, 202, 225, 227, 272.

289. Heschel, *Aryan Jesus*, 27; cf. 29–30, 33, 40–41, 64, 59–60. Pagan Germanic religious ideology drove some of the pressure (see Poewe, *Religions*, e.g., 5, 11–14, 112–13).

290. Heschel, *Aryan Jesus*, 32, 35, 60–63, 286. See esp. Grundmann, *Jesus der Galiläer*.

291. For the thoroughly Jewish character of most of Galilee, see, e.g., Chancey and Meyers, "Sepphoris"; Reed, *Archaeology*, 43–51; Reed, "Contributions," 53; Dunn, "Synagogue," 207–12; Chancey, *Galilee*; Chancey, "Jewish"; Deines, *Acts of God*, 53–93; Keener, *Acts*, 2:1697–1701.

derstand him in that setting.[292] The Gospels are written in Greek and contextualized for (at least mostly) Diaspora audiences, which only highlights all the more clearly the frequent non-Diaspora elements that remain. Note, for example, the preponderance of fishing and fishing images in the Gospels, in contrast to the rest of the New Testament.

More significantly, most names in the Gospels are not the names a later Diaspora writer would make up for characters; they are precisely the names that archaeology associates with their time and place, even though no reference works in antiquity collected this information. In general, the most common names in the Gospels were the most popular Judean/Galilean names in that period.[293] If later Diaspora Christians were to invent Judean names based on knowledge of Scripture, we would have names such as Ruth and Esther rather than Mary and Salome, names such as Moses and David rather than Simon and Judas. If the names originated in Judea, by contrast, then by default they likelier originate closer to the circles of the eyewitnesses.

Many scholars recognize Galilean traits in Q. Some explain these traits as the result of Galilean memories formulated after Jesus's resurrection; others contend that these reflect memories from Galilee before the resurrection.[294] Our earliest literary evidence shows the Galilean[295] disciples leading the church from Jerusalem (Gal 1:18–19; 2:1, 9), which would also be the main conduit through which the stories reached Diaspora Gospels. (Connections in the ancient Mediterranean world were largely urban, and Galilean stories

292. With Meier, *Marginal Jew*, 3:3; Charlesworth, "Theology"; Holmén, "Introduction," 4, 8; Tuckett, "Sources and Methods," 133; Bird, "Quest." See, e.g., Sanders, *Jesus and Judaism*; *Figure*; "Know," 57; Kee, "Century of Quests"; Meier, "Project"; Theissen and Merz, *Guide*, 240–80; Allison, "Eschatological Jesus"; Allison, *Jesus of Nazareth* (esp. 96–171); McKnight, *Vision*; Ehrman, *Prophet*, 125–39; Chilton, *Rabbi Jesus*; Charlesworth, *Jesus within Judaism*; Levine, *Misunderstood Jew*; Evans, "Context"; Tomson, "Jesus and Judaism," 25–40; Deines, *Acts of God*, 95–102.

293. See Williams, "Names"; Bauckham, *Eyewitnesses*, 39–92, using the database of 2,826 persons in Ilan, *Lexicon*; Bauckham, *World*, 97–98.

294. Dunn, *Perspective*, 27; Dunn, *Tradition*, 272, favoring the latter. Against a special Galilean "Q community," see, e.g., Taylor, "Q and Galilee?"; Pearson, "Community"; favoring a Galilean context for the earliest material in Q, see Kloppenborg, *Excavating Q*, 255–61. The movement's backwater Galilean origins were not quickly forgotten (cf., e.g., Epictetus, *Discourses* 4.7.6; later, for Julian the Apostate, see Judge, *Jerusalem and Athens*, 222; also Lucian's association of Christians with Palestine in *Peregrinus* 11, though he also recognizes their presence elsewhere, 13).

295. Because reconstructing the setting in which one first experienced something aids recall (Small, *Wax Tablets*, 121), the disciples' own Galilean background should have aided their memories of experiences with Jesus there.

would reach Diaspora cities mostly through the Judean cities of Jerusalem and, on the coast, Caesarea.)

While this information does not contradict the likelihood of a subsequently growing movement in Galilee (cf. Acts 9:31), it does cohere with the idea that Galilean features reflect genuine memories of Jesus, memories mediated to the Diaspora via the Jerusalem mother church. What we can say for certain is that such features are early and not from the Diaspora, and thus that they reflect the earliest memories of Jesus, from the time when eyewitnesses were the prominent leaders of the movement.

16.12. Memorable Forms

Although we cannot expect most preserved material to be preserved verbatim, some sorts of material can be preserved in a format closer to verbatim than others. Since memory often retains rhythm and structure, poetry and songs tend to be remembered in closer to verbatim form than prose narratives.[296] (In antiquity, songs and jingles were among the most elementary mnemonic practices.[297] Even in prose, rhythm was employed to support memory.)[298]

Although usually teaching in prose,[299] Greek and Roman teachers sometimes spoke in easily memorizable forms;[300] this practice was conventional among Jewish teachers, including Jesus.[301] While the Gospels are clearly prose narratives, the underlying Aramaic oral tradition behind many of Jesus's sayings frequently appears to display rhythmic features.[302] Although the Gospels

---

296. McIver, *Memory*, 167, following Rubin, *Memory*, 65–121; cf. meter in Ong, *Orality*, 22, 62; also (for Homer) epithets in Rubin, *Memory*, 199–200, 301; cf. Homer in Nikulin, "Introduction," 8–9; Nikulin, "Memory," 39–41; OT passages in Carr, *Writing*, 128, 152.

297. Small, *Wax Tablets*, 123. For poetry memorization in classical Athenian education, see Joyal, McDougall, and Yardley, *Education*, 31.

298. See Vatri, "Writing," 752–56, noting esp. Plato, *Phaedrus* 267a2–5; Aristotle, *Rhetoric* 1409a35–b8; Ps.-Scymnus, *Ad Nicomedem regem* 33–35; Ps.-Longinus, *Rh.* 310.20–25 (Spengel = *Concerning Memory* 122–26 Patillon-Brisson); Galen, *On Antidotes* 14.32.5–9 Kuhn; 14.89.10–17; 14.191.2–3; *De compositione medicamentorum per genera* 13.455.7–9. This was the only mnemonic device directly supporting *verbatim* memorization (Vatri, "Writing," 771).

299. Some used poetry to reinforce their teaching for rudimentary students (Seneca, *To Lucilius* 108.9–10).

300. Philostratus, *Lives of the Sophists* 1.22.523.

301. Allison, *Constructing Jesus*, 375–77; Keener, *Matthew*, 25–29.

302. See Jeremias, *Theology*, throughout; cf. also Dunn, *Tradition*, 238, citing further Burney, *Poetry*; Manson, *Teaching*; Black, *Aramaic Approach*; Riesner, *Lehrer*, 392–404.

are in Greek, Semitic figures of speech (most consistently, "Son of man") also remain. Such demonstrable (as opposed to some merely possible) Aramaisms and the like thus point to earliness and thus likely the preservation of the gist of Jesus's teachings. Granted, the earliest traditioning community spoke Aramaic no less than did Jesus,[303] but it is that earliest community that we would most expect to have preserved Jesus's sayings.

More generally, some stylistic features characteristic of oral tradition (and perhaps a teaching style designed to facilitate such transmission) appear to pervade Jesus's teachings recorded in the Gospels.[304] Whereas rural Middle Eastern oral tradition can transmit news and jokes more flexibly than parables or community narratives, it transmits proverbs and poems much more rigidly.[305] Most of Jesus's sayings, which were neither news nor jokes,[306] would thus be conveyed with significant continuity. Although no one sought verbatim memory of all a teacher's words, both Jewish[307] and Greek[308] sources sometimes preserved elements of a teacher's distinctive style.[309]

---

303. Meier, *Marginal Jew*, 1:178–80. Nor was linguistic influence unidirectional (see Stuckenbruck, "Influence," cited in Keith, *Scribal Elite*, 79; cf. Porter, *Criteria*); the author of Revelation, which probably stems from the end of the first century, may have felt at home in a Semitic linguistic milieu.

304. See, e.g., Dunn, *Perspective*, 115. Pryke, *Style*, looked for pre-Markan material on stylistic grounds; Zwiep, "Orality," offers an initial attempt to distinguish orality markers pointing to pre-Markan material (cf. also others, such as Hearon, "Mapping"). These attempts are useful but necessarily hypothetical, since similar markers may appear in both oral and written sources (Mournet, *Oral Tradition*, 153–54; cf. Rosenberg, "Complexity," 74; Wansbrough, "Introduction," 12; Tate, "Formulas," 147; Niditch, "Hebrew Bible," 6–7).

305. Bailey, "Oral Tradition" (cf. Bailey, "Tradition" [*Themelios*], 7; Bailey, "Oral Tradition," 42); also noted in Aune, *Dictionary*, 326; cf. Bauckham, *World*, 93. Weeden's critique ("Theory") of Bailey's argument does not undermine its essential insights about significant continuity (see Dunn, "Critiquing"), but it does undermine some of his key examples, which should illustrate rumor rather than controlled transmission (see also Kloppenborg, "Memory," 300–303); cf. Keener, "Weeden's Critique."

306. The Jesus tradition includes humor (e.g., Matt 7:3–5//Luke 6:41–42), sometimes at opponents' expense, as often in ancient debate (cf. Rabbie, "Wit," 207, 213), but not jokes for jokes' sake; so also news (cf. Luke 13:2, 4).

307. See Keener, *Historical Jesus*, 187–88; m. 'Ed. 1:3.

308. Xenophon, *Apology* 1; Epictetus, *Discourses* 1.pref.

309. Sayings may have often been transmitted with greater attention to preserving wording than were narratives (Witherington, *Christology*, 28–29; Theissen, *Gospels*, 60), as often in oral societies (Bauckham, *World*, 92).

16.13. Sayings Reflecting Jesus's Environment

Ancient novels usually reflect the environment of their authors far better than the environment in which the story is set. This tendency is true also of many later apocryphal gospels; for example, the Gospel of Peter's Jewish priests waiting in a burial plot makes no sense in Jesus's original environment.[310] The Gospel of Thomas's closing image of a woman being saved by becoming male[311] fits Philo's Platonic Alexandrian milieu far better than that of Jesus.[312]

By contrast, many of Jesus's reported sayings in the Synoptics[313] (and for that matter, some in John)[314] address a setting that fits Jesus's particular geographic or chronological milieu, even though these Gospels, too, are written for a later audience. Granted, Jesus's milieu is also the milieu of Jesus's disciples, but the important point is that most such sayings do reflect an early milieu. Jesus's disciples were the tradents with the most direct and complete memories of Jesus's ministry, and their memories are those most likely to be directly accurate. These features likely reflect an origin far earlier than Mark's, roughly four decades after Jesus was on the earth. Following are just a few examples to illustrate the point:[315]

- The Pharisees' question about divorce (Mark 10:2; Matt 19:3) reflects a debate that extant sources attribute to Pharisaic schools in Jesus's generation.[316]
- Jesus plays on current Pharisaic debates about purity regarding the inside or outside of cups (Matt 23:25–26//Luke 11:39–41).[317]
- Jesus's warning that it would be "measured" to one as one measured to others echoes a specifically Jewish tradition (Matt 7:2//Luke 6:38).[318]

---

310. Evans, *Fabricating Jesus*, 79–85, esp. 83 (citing Gos. Pet. 8.31; 10.38); cf. discussion in Brown, *Death*, 1317–49; Wright, "Apologetic." Still, a case can be made for a second-century Syrian Jewish Christian origin (see Marcus, "Gospel of Peter").

311. Gos. Thom. 114.2–3.

312. Cf., e.g., Baer, *Categories*, esp. 45–49, 55–64, 69; briefly, Meeks, "Androgyne," 176–77.

313. See Theissen, *Gospels*, 25–59.

314. E.g., John 7:37–38; see Keener, *John*, 722–30 and sources cited there.

315. I borrow these examples from somewhat fuller treatments in Keener, "Suggestions" and "Assumptions," 49–52. Cf. now more fully Williams, *Trust*, 51–86.

316. See m. Giṭ. 9:10; Sipre Deut. 269.1.1.

317. For various approaches, cf. Neusner, "Cleanse," 492–94; McNamara, *Judaism*, 197; Sanders, *Jesus to Mishnah*, 39. For an Aramaic wordplay or confusion behind the variation in Matthew and Luke, see Black, *Aramaic Approach*, 2; Burney, *Aramaic Origin*, 9.

318. Smith, *Parallels*, 135.

- Jewish teachers often employed the phrase "to what shall I/we compare?" (Matt 11:16//Luke 7:31), especially to introduce parables.[319]
- The first half of the so-called Lord's Prayer (Matt 6:9–10//Luke 11:2) corresponds closely to the language of some early Judean prayers.[320]
- Later Jewish teachers, not likely influenced by Jesus, could depict what was almost impossible as a large animal passing through a needle's eye (Mark 10:25).[321]
- In gospel tradition, Bethsaida always retains its pre-30 CE name (Matt 11:21//Luke 10:13; Mark 6:45; 8:22; John 1:44; 12:21), rather than its new civic name (Julias), which was common after 30.[322]

Many characteristic features of Jesus's style, such as story parables,[323] "Amen," and "Son of man" are also distinctively Jewish.[324] Meanwhile, more than in the settings of many later rabbinic parables,[325] the settings of the majority of Jesus's extant parables reflect an agrarian environment.[326] (Because later Christians did not take up their style, Jesus's parables are accepted as authentic more often than some other features of the Jesus tradition.)[327]

319. E.g., m. 'Abot 3:17; Sukkah 2:10; t. Ber. 1:11; 6:18; Sanh. 1:2; 8:9.

320. Vermes, *Jesus and Judaism*, 43. Liturgical repetition would also preserve memory of the Lord's Prayer; cf. Le Donne, *Historiographical Jesus*, 229.

321. Abrahams, *Studies*, 2:208; Dalman, *Jesus-Jeshua*, 230; Jeremias, *Parables*, 195.

322. Charlesworth, "Sketch," 97–98.

323. See, e.g., Johnston, "Observations," 355; Johnston, "Interpretations," esp. 43, 628–35; Abrahams, *Studies* 1:106; Young, *Parables*, 1, 317–18; Stewart, "Parable Form"; Cave, "Parables," 387; Barth, "Ethik"; Maisonneuve, "Parables"; Goulder, *Midrash*, 47–69; Scott, *Parable*, 14; D'Angelo, "Background"; Gerhardsson, "Illuminating"; compare Stern, *Parables in Midrash*. (Greeks did use other kinds of moral stories such as fables; see, e.g., Phaedrus and Babrius, *Fables*.) Before Jesus, see, e.g., 2 Sam 12:1–7; Isa 5:1–7; 1 En. 1:2–3; 37–71; 4Q302 f2ii.2–9; Sir 1:24; 3:29; 20:20; 39:2; 47:17.

324. Dunn, *Tradition*, 286.

325. Fields do figure prominently as settings in rabbinic parables, though their meaning is ad hoc rather than standard (Johnston, "Interpretations," 596). But whereas royal courts appear in only a few parables attributed to Jesus (Matt 18:23; 22:2; cf. Matt 25:34; Luke 14:31; 19:12), they are common in Tannaitic parables, where the king represents God: e.g., t. Ber. 6:18; Sukkah 2:6; Mek. Beshallah 6.8–9; Shirata 2.131ff; 3.30, 65; 4.54ff; Amalek 2.22–23; Bahodesh 5.2–3, 82–83; 6.114ff; 8.72ff; Sipra Shemini Mekhilta deMiluim 99.2.2, 5; Behuq. pq. 2.262.1.9; pq. 3.263.1.5; Sipre Num. 84.2.1; 86.1.1; Sipre Deut. 3.1.1; 8.1.2; 11.1.2; 28.1.1; 29.4.1; 36.4.5; 43.8.1; 43.16.1; 45.1.2; 48.1.3; 312.1.1; 313.1.1; 343.5.2.

326. Earlier biblical prophets had also depicted judgments, esp. those of the end time, in agricultural terms (Isa 32:13–17; 35:1–2; 44:3–4; Jer 31:28; 51:33; Joel 3:13; Amos 8:1–2; Riesenfeld, *Tradition*, 150).

327. E.g., Dodd, *Parables*, 1; Jeremias, *Parables*, 11; Stein, *Method*, 44–45; Vermes, *Religion*, 90–91; Snodgrass, *Stories*, 31; see more fully Payne, "Authenticity of Parables"; Payne, "Sower."

Moreover, even though the Synoptics apply Jesus's ministry and teaching to their audience settings (as rightly emphasized by redaction critics), neither they nor, presumably, their tradents invented new stories about Jesus to resolve even the most burning issues of their day. Otherwise they would surely have addressed circumcising Gentiles (cf. Gal 2:3–4, 12; 5:11).[328] When Mark addresses the issue of kosher foods (on the usual interpretation), he does so in an interpretive aside (Mark 7:14), and in his one story about a gentile supplicant, Jesus first insults her (7:27).[329] In this respect, the Gospels resemble biographies of Plutarch, who emphasized themes in his sources still relevant for his own day but rarely imposed his own era's issues into sources that lacked them.[330]

Although they cannot address every pericope, traditional historical-critical approaches often lend independent support to the antiquity of many traditions about Jesus beyond what I address specifically here.[331] I have treated other relevant observations in greater detail elsewhere.[332]

Aside from such arguments addressing specific pericopes, however, default starting assumptions do shape the standard of evidence that scholars require. What do these larger considerations suggest? Recognizing that individual and collective memories can persist for more than four decades should allow for greater respect for the evidence of the Gospels than we find in circles highly skeptical of preserved memories.[333] This does not mean, as Chris Keith warns, "*reconstruction* of the past" by means of "leftover parts"; rather, "the historian's task" is "*representation* of the past, an informed hypothesis about what it could have looked like in light of the sources that remain" and their environment.[334]

Contrast Meier, *Marginal Jew*, 5, whose rigorous but more limited criteria do not allow for these prima facie formal considerations. In Q, see, e.g., Matt 7:24–27//Luke 6:47–49. "Authenticity," of course, does not preclude adaptation (Jeremias, *Parables*, throughout; Johnston, "Interpretations," 621–24, 639).

328. Theissen and Merz, *Guide*, 105; Wright, *People*, 421; Stanton, *Gospel Truth?*, 60–61.

329. For one interpretation, see Cotter, *Miracle Stories*, 148–54. On dogs as an insult, see, e.g., Homer, *Iliad* 8.527; 11.362; 20.449; 22.345 (cf. 9.373; 21.394, 421); *Odyssey* 17.248; 22.35; Callimachus, *Hymn* 6 (to Demeter), 63; for its harshness when addressed to women, cf., e.g., Homer, *Odyssey* 11.424; 18.338; 19.91.

330. Pelling, *Texts*, 58.

331. See fuller recent discussions about historical-Jesus research in Porter and Holmén, *Handbook*; Charlesworth, Rhea, and Pokorný, *Jesus Research*.

332. Esp. in Keener, *Historical Jesus*, throughout.

333. Keener, "Assumptions."

334. Keith, *Scribal Elite*, 82.

Because all access to the past is mediated, a memory approach leads investigators back to the data supplied by the text.[335]

Or as Anthony Le Donne summarizes the thesis of his influential study *The Historiographical Jesus*:

> The historical Jesus is the memorable Jesus; he is the one who set refraction trajectories in motion and who set the initial parameters for how his memories were to be interpreted by his contemporaries. If this is so, then the historian does not "find" Jesus in spite of the refractions of the evangelists. Rather, the historian discerns his historical presence and impact on the basis of those refractions. It is because these refractions exist that we can confidently postulate the mnemonic sphere in which the memories of Jesus were located.[336]

16.14. Implications

Actually testing in any detail where any Gospel lies on the continuum of flexibility and stability would move beyond the specified limits of this book; I refer readers to my larger Matthew commentary for some of my own earlier (and admittedly less mature) redactional observations and to others' studies for other views.

Testing Mark, our first Gospel, is more difficult than testing Matthew or Luke because we lack Mark's sources. Nevertheless, some of Mark's information is attested independently. Because Paul, our earliest extant Christian source, was not an eyewitness of Jesus's ministry and wrote pastoral letters rather than biographies, he does not focus on episodes in Jesus's life as do the Gospels. Nevertheless, he does at times specify that he has passed along some Jesus traditions (1 Cor 11:23; 15:1–7), and where Paul and Mark independently address the same material (1 Cor 7:10–11; 11:23–26; Mark 10:9–12; 14:22–25), the gist remains the same in both, though they also (supporting their independence) include some different elements.[337]

The default setting that the genre and first-century date of the Gospels

---

335. Keith, *Scribal Elite*, 81, 83.

336. Le Donne, *Historiographical Jesus*, 268.

337. See, e.g., Eve, *Behind Gospels*, 166–67. He prefers Josephus over Mark on 169–75 (while acknowledging that both reflect their own interests), but most of the variations involve one's omissions of elements in the other, and Mark is earlier; cf. also observations in Meier, "John the Baptist"; Sumney, *Steward*, 137–56; Jensen, "Josephus."

offer supports the limited other evidence available: we *do* know a lot about Jesus's ministry and teaching. Biographies from within a generation or two of their subjects can be expected to have preserved at least the gist of most of the events they report, whatever details they may have omitted.

As noted before in this book, Luke's preface reveals quite a bit about what he thinks that he and his audience know. He believes that they share knowledge of narratives about Jesus and of oral sources going back to the original witnesses (Luke 1:1–2). Luke also believes that his own narrative confirms the basic overarching story and presumably many individual stories that at least some of his audience already know (1:3–4). Given that Luke wrote at a time when he had access to such information (Luke 1:2–3; cf. Acts 21:8, 17–18),[338] his claim should outweigh the speculations of his modern Western armchair critics (including myself). The dismissal of his claims too often rests on dismissing all the hard evidence we have and arguing the contrary based on the silence that remains, a too-common practice in some sectors of NT scholarship.

16.15. Conclusion

Oral tradition sometimes preserves core information accurately for centuries; preservation is most consistent, however, within the period of living memory. This is the period in which the Evangelists composed their Gospels, when eyewitnesses and those who had heard them could challenge their claims.

Many of Jesus's teachings are in the sort of readily memorizable forms in which sages often offered them to facilitate retention. Moreover, many of Jesus's sayings reflect their original context in his Galilean ministry far better than they reflect the situations of the churches for whom they were being presented afresh in the Gospels. The Gospels commemorate the collective memory of Jesus and his impact on the movement that he founded.

Furthermore, we must keep in mind the relatively short period between Jesus's public ministry and the first Gospels. We may compare that interval with what we can learn today about key events a comparable distance in our own circles' past, based on memories of even Western persons close to us. If we do so, I believe that we cannot escape the likelihood that the testimonies offered in the first Gospels do in fact offer a portrait of Jesus's character, message, and deeds that brings us into contact with many key features of what his first disciples experienced.

338. See Keener, *Acts*, 1:51–422; 3:2350–74.

Chapter 17

The Implications of This Study

Traditional skeptical and fundamentalist approaches to the Gospels have generally committed the same error: judging the Gospels by standards foreign to their original genre. In this book I have sought to support a more historically and culturally sensitive approach.

The many variables already noted preclude us from using the Gospels' genre to pronounce decisions on the historical authenticity of all their reports a priori; such an approach would run far beyond the evidence. Thus, none of the foregoing discussion by itself proves that any given pericope in the Gospels reports genuine historical information. Although historical and literary analogies may offer evidence, by their limited nature they fall short of proof. An exclusively historical epistemology is restricted to probabilities, genre is descriptive rather than prescriptive (suggesting but not controlling expectations), and analogies are always incomplete and imperfect. Historiography today can thus plot only degrees of probability.

This is one of the cases, however, where historical evidence does suggest a higher degree of prior probability for teaching themes and narrated events in the Gospels than some circles assume. The Gospels most likely serve a function at least in many ways similar to that of other biographies from the early empire about figures in living memory. This fairly self-evident analogy suggests a significant a priori probability in favor of at least a core of genuine historical information behind the average account in the Gospels. In contrast to the position of radical skeptics that the burden of proof rests on any claim in the Gospels, a more historically probable starting point is that these biographies written within living memory of Jesus do in fact succeed in preserving many of Jesus's acts and teachings, even for many events that are not independently attested in multiple sources.[1]

---

1. That is, the criterion of multiple attestation is more effective in supporting than in denying genuine tradition. I comment less here on the other extreme (that of expecting verbatim

Historical method is limited in what it can tell us about the past, and certainly about events two thousand years ago. In a real sense, however, the gap in our case is not two thousand years but three to seven decades, since we have accounts about Jesus from within living memory. If the earliest biographic sources available to us about Lincoln were from a comparable period after his death, we would have to deal with tendentious constructions of memory, but we would still have very substantial information about a real historical figure. Studies about the historical Jesus based on material in the Gospels present some additional complications, but in terms of chronological distance, the sources are not unlike the imaginary material about Lincoln offered here for the purpose of illustration.

If *any* ancient biographers have much historical information to teach us about the biographees, the Gospels are surely among them. Various factors support this recognition:

1. They are full biographies of a publicly known figure, rather than brief lives of poets.
2. They are from the most information-based period in the development of ancient biography, namely, the period of the early empire. Biographies in this period are generally developed beyond less historically minded earlier encomia, yet they also predate later hagiography. Comparing different biographies from this period about the same figure illustrates these biographies' anchoring in information.
3. The Gospels were composed within living memory of their subject, making substantive accurate information likely.
4. The most respected leaders in the traditioning community were eyewitnesses.
5. Not only were the most respected leaders in the traditioning community eyewitnesses; they were also *disciples*, who of all people would work hardest from the start to preserve their mentor's legacy and teaching.
6. Something not explored in this volume, but easily confirmed by perusing a synopsis of the Gospels, is the significant overlap of material in the Synoptics. This overlap confirms that these works are information-based rather than novelistic and that their authors regarded their own sources as sufficiently trustworthy for information-based composition.

---

quotations and strict chronological arrangement) because proponents of those views are not even paying attention to the Gospels themselves. I therefore do not flatter myself by supposing them likely to read this book anyway.

7. Information-based first-century Gospels that used sources cannot have been significantly (more than a few decades) later than those sources that they used, and they likely had good reason to assess the reliability of their sources the way that they did.

8. Logic suggests a further conclusion. More sources circulated in their day (Luke 1:1) than remain, and the Gospel authors could not know what information would remain extant in subsequent eras. Therefore, we should expect them to adapt their sources where we cannot test them in ways comparable to where we can. When Matthew and Luke (on the standard view) follow Mark so closely, sometimes nearly word for word, it seems incredible to suppose that they often simply invent entire stories from whole cloth wherever we cannot test them, any more than we would expect such invention from other ancient writers who follow their sources where we can test them.[2] In short: it is not fair to simply say, "For such-and-such a point, we have no evidence outside the Gospels, *and therefore we lack evidence.*" The Gospel narratives *are themselves evidence.*

Inevitably, presuppositions and objectives inform one's comparisons; one could thus emphasize, for example, more differences in biographies of Otho or Galba than I have, or emphasize more common features in different works by Josephus than I have. Less plausibly, one could undercut the value of any ancient comparisons by denying, for example, that Jesus's disciples were like typical disciples or that the Evangelists were like normal biographers of the period in terms of preserving information. But normal historical method requires more substantive evidence when one rejects contemporary analogies than when one accepts them.

In any case, I believe that my two most essential primary points are difficult to dispute: in the early empire, normal biographers writing full works about recent figures attempted to recount or reconstruct what they believed to be historical information (or perhaps in some cases, traditions that were at least possibly historical), normally for edifying purposes; and biographers could exercise a degree of flexibility in how they recounted that information.

More precisely, audiences from the Gospels' era did not expect biographers to freely invent events, but they did allow them to flesh out scenes and discourse for the purpose of what they considered narrative verisimilitude. Biographers were not supposed to invent a teacher's message, but they could

---

2. Cf. Downing, "Redaction Criticism 2," 47, on the bizarreness of an analogous sort of incongruity.

interpret and communicate it from their own perspectives. If biographies of recent figures in the early empire normally recount genuine historical events, then this expectation follows, to a reasonable degree of probability, for the Gospels. If biographers of recent figures in the early empire felt free to adapt wording, chronology, and so forth, then this expectation likewise follows, to a reasonable degree of probability, for the Gospels. That is, neither the similarities of the Gospels nor their differences should catch us by surprise.

To note this range of flexibility is not to claim a priori where on the continuum any given biography or a Gospel falls, but the observation does provide a probable range to expect and within which historians may search.

Biographers varied among one another, and sometimes in their own works, as to the degree of fidelity and flexibility with which they treated their sources. Where do the Gospels, or more specifically individual Gospels, fit on this continuum? For this question scholars can still resort to source-, redaction-, and narrative-critical analyses of the Gospels, an analysis that lies beyond the stated limitations of this study. Moreover, as scholars increasingly recognize, the limited nature of the evidence means that for many passages more specific conclusions will often continue to elude our best available historiographic methods, leaving scholars to argue on philosophic grounds or to confess our uncertainties.

Helpful further research would include, ideally, quantifying more precisely the range of variation in various *bioi* where we can identify and evaluate their material. How much is prior information? How much is redaction? Such quantification cannot be an exact science, given the uncertainties and the variables to consider, but it may at least suggest orders of magnitude to help scholars plot individual works, including individual Gospels, on the spectrum. (Although the possibility might be presumptuous to assume, it would be ideal if it could yield more consensus than the seemingly simpler matter of quantifying the proportion of Acts devoted to its speeches.) The approximate results can then be applied to each of the Gospels (or at least Matthew's and Luke's use of Mark, on the most common configuration) to estimate where each of them lies on the spectrum.

What can be concluded already is that the Synoptics, and probably all four Gospels, fit within the range of variation found in ancient historical sources in general. These sources reflect a significant core of prior information and a degree of flexibility in recounting it. Most ancient historical writing was, in other words, both history and literature, both information and its rhetorical shaping.

The conclusions of the study are thus consistent with what one might expect by working from a synopsis of the Gospels—except where faulty paradigms have sometimes prevented some circles from attending to what such synopses show us. Following Bultmann, some have assumed a long folk tradition and have doubted early Christians' interest in much reliable historical information about Jesus. Less commonly among scholars but not uncommonly on a popular level, some other circles have performed remarkable gymnastics to harmonize the Gospels' chronology and sometimes even their wording.

The majority of scholars today, despite our diversity on particulars, lie between these poles. This study should encourage historical-Jesus researchers to speculate less about what *might* have happened to the tradition and to focus more on the basic staples of what the Gospels themselves suggest to us *did* happen to it.

Bibliography of Secondary Sources Cited

Abbott, *Acts*.　Abbott, Lyman. *The Acts of the Apostles: With Notes, Comments, Maps, and Illustrations*. New York: A. S. Barnes, 1876.

Abrahams, *Studies* 1.　Abrahams, I. *Studies in Pharisaism and the Gospels*. 1st ser. Cambridge: Cambridge University Press, 1917. Repr., Library of Biblical Studies. New York: Ktav, 1967.

Abrahams, *Studies* 2.　Abrahams, I. *Studies in Pharisaism and the Gospels*. 2nd ser. Cambridge: Cambridge University Press, 1924.

Abramowski, "Memoirs."　Abramowski, Luise. "The 'Memoirs of the Apostles' in Justin." Pages 323–35 in *The Gospel and the Gospels*. Edited by Peter Stuhlmacher. Grand Rapids: Eerdmans, 1991.

Achtemeier, *Miracle Tradition*.　Achtemeier, Paul J. *Jesus and the Miracle Tradition*. Eugene, OR: Cascade, 2008.

Adams, *Genre*.　Adams, Sean A. *The Genre of Acts and Collected Biography*. SNTSMS 156. Cambridge: Cambridge University Press, 2013.

Adams, *Negotiating Genre*.　Adams, Sean A. *Negotiating Genre: Jewish Authors and Greek Literary Forms*. Waco, TX: Baylor University Press, Forthcoming.

Adams, "Preface."　Adams, Sean A. "Luke's Preface and Its Relationship to Greek Historiography: A Response to Loveday Alexander." *JGRCJ* 3 (2006): 177–91.

Adinolfi, "Lago."　Adinolfi, Marco. "Il lago di Tiberiade e le sue città nella letteratura greco-romana." *SBFLA* 44 (1994): 375–80.

Albright, "Discoveries."　Albright, William Foxwell. "Recent Discoveries in Palestine and the Gospel of St John." Pages 153–71 in *The Background of the New Testament and Its Eschatology: Essays in Honour of Charles Harold Dodd*. Edited by W. D. Davies and D. Daube. Cambridge: Cambridge University Press, 1964.

Aletti, *Birth*.　Aletti, Jean-Noël. *The Birth of the Gospels as Biographies: With Analyses of Two Challenging Pericopae*. Translated by Peggy Manning Meyer. Analecta Biblica Studia 10. Rome: Gregorian & Biblical Press, Pontificia Università Gregoriana, 2017.

Alexander, "Biography."　Alexander, Loveday C. A. "Acts and Ancient Intellectual Biography." Pages 31–63 in *The Book of Acts in Its Ancient Literary Setting*. Edited by Bruce W. Winter and Andrew D. Clarke. Vol. 1 of *The Book of Acts in Its First Century Setting*. Edited by Bruce W. Winter. Grand Rapids: Eerdmans, 1993.

Alexander, *Context*.   Alexander, Loveday C. A. *Acts in Its Ancient Literary Context: A Classicist Looks at the Acts of the Apostles*. Early Christianity in Context. LNTS 298. London: T&T Clark, 2005.

Alexander, "Formal Elements."   Alexander, Loveday C. A. "Formal Elements and Genre: Which Greco-Roman Prologues Most Closely Parallel the Lukan Prologues?" Pages 9–26 in *Jesus and the Heritage of Israel: Luke's Narrative Claim upon Israel's Legacy*. Edited by David P. Moessner. Luke the Interpreter of Israel 1. Harrisburg, PA: Trinity Press International, 1999.

Alexander, "IPSE DIXIT."   Alexander, Loveday C. A. "IPSE DIXIT: Citation of Authority in Paul and in the Jewish Hellenistic Schools." Pages 103–27 in *Paul beyond the Judaism/Hellenism Divide*. Edited by Troels Engberg-Pedersen. Louisville: Westminster John Knox, 2001.

Alexander, "Memory."   Alexander, Loveday. "Memory and Tradition in the Hellenistic Schools." Pages 113–53 in *Jesus in Memory: Traditions in Oral and Scribal Perspectives*. Edited by Werner H. Kelber and Samuel Byrskog. Waco, TX: Baylor University Press, 2009.

Alexander, "Orality."   Alexander, Philip S. "Orality in Pharisaic-Rabbinic Judaism at the Turn of the Eras." Pages 159–84 in *Jesus and the Oral Gospel Tradition*. Edited by Henry Wansbrough. JSNTSup 64. Sheffield: Sheffield Academic Press, 1991.

Alexander, *Preface*.   Alexander, Loveday C. A. *The Preface to Luke's Gospel: Literary Convention and Social Context in Luke 1.1–4 and Acts 1.1*. SNTSMS 78. Cambridge: Cambridge University Press, 1993.

Alexander, "Preface."   Alexander, Loveday C. A. "The Preface to Acts and the Historians." Pages 73–103 in *History, Literature, and Society in the Book of Acts*. Edited by Ben Witherington III. Cambridge: Cambridge University Press, 1996.

Alexander, "Rabbinic Biography."   Alexander, Philip S. "Rabbinic Biography and the Biography of Jesus: A Survey of the Evidence." Pages 19–50 in *Synoptic Studies: The Ampleforth Conferences of 1982 and 1983*. Edited by Christopher M. Tuckett. JSNTSup 7. Sheffield: JSOT, 1984.

Alexander, *Signs*.   Alexander, Paul. *Signs and Wonders: Why Pentecostalism Is the World's Fastest Growing Faith*. San Francisco: Jossey-Bass, 2009.

Alexander, "Voice."   Alexander, Loveday C. A. "The Living Voice: Scepticism towards the Written Word in Early Christian and in Graeco-Roman Texts." Pages 221–47 in *The Bible in Three Dimensions: Essays in Celebration of Forty Years of Biblical Studies in the University of Sheffield*. Edited by David J. A. Clines, Stephen E. Fowl, and Stanley E. Porter. JSOTSup 87. Sheffield: JSOT Press, 1990.

Alfeyev, *Beginning*.   Alfeyev, Metropolitan Hilarion. *The Beginning of the Gospel*. Vol. 1 of *Jesus Christ: His Life and Teaching*. 6 vols. Yonkers, NY: St. Vladimir's Seminary Press, 2017.

Alfred, "Source Valuation."   Alfred, Chris. "Source Valuation in Greek and Roman Biography." PhD diss., Asbury Theological Seminary, in process.

Alfred, "Valuation."   Alfred, Chris. "Source Valuation in Greek and Roman Biography:

From Xenophon to Suetonius." Pages 77–102 in Keener and Wright, *Biographies and Jesus*.

Allen, "Epicurus." Allen, James. "Epicurus in Diogenes Laertius." Pages 614–18 in *Diogenes Laertius "Lives of the Eminent Philosophers."* Edited by James Miller. Translated by Pamela Mensch. New York: Oxford University Press, 2018.

Allen, "Skeptics." Allen, James. "Skeptics in Diogenes Laertius." Pages 610–14 in *Diogenes Laertius "Lives of the Eminent Philosophers."* Edited by James Miller. Translated by Pamela Mensch. New York: Oxford University Press, 2018.

Allison, *Constructing Jesus.* Allison, Dale C., Jr. *Constructing Jesus: Memory, Imagination, and History.* Grand Rapids: Baker Academic, 2010.

Allison, "Criteria." Allison, Dale C., Jr. "How to Marginalize the Traditional Criteria of Authenticity." Pages 3–30 in *How to Study the Historical Jesus.* Vol. 1 of *Handbook for the Study of the Historical Jesus.* 4 vols. Edited by Tom Holmén and Stanley E. Porter. Leiden: Brill, 2011.

Allison, "Eschatological Jesus." Allison, Dale C. "The Eschatological Jesus: Did He Believe the End Was Near?" *BRev* 12 (5, 1996): 34–41, 54–55.

Allison, *Jesus of Nazareth.* Allison, Dale C. *Jesus of Nazareth: Millenarian Prophet.* Minneapolis: Fortress, 1998.

Allison, "Memory." Allison, Dale C. "Memory, Methodology, and the Historical Jesus: A Response to Richard Bauckham." *JSHJ* 14 (1, 2016): 13–27.

Allison, "Parallels." Allison, Dale C., Jr. "The Pauline Epistles and the Synoptic Gospels: The Pattern of the Parallels." *NTS* 28 (1, January 1982): 1–32.

Allison, "Peter." Allison, Dale C. "Peter and Cephas: One and the Same." *JBL* 111 (3, 1992): 489–95.

Allison, *Studies.* Allison, Dale C. *Studies in Matthew: Interpretation Past and Present.* Grand Rapids: Baker Academic, 2005.

Almagor, "Narratives." Almagor, Eran. "Parallel Narratives and Possible Worlds in Plutarch's *Life of Artaxerxes.*" Pages 65–79 in *Writing Biography in Greece and Rome: Narrative Technique and Fictionalization.* Edited by Koen De Temmerman and Kristoffel Demoen. Cambridge: Cambridge University Press, 2016.

Alsup, "Function." Alsup, John E. "Type, Placement, and Function of the Pronouncement Story in Plutarch's *Moralia.*" *Semeia* 20 (1981): 15–27.

Anderson, *Glossary.* Anderson, R. Dean, Jr. *Glossary of Greek Rhetorical Terms Connected to Methods of Argumentation, Figures, and Tropes from Anaximenes to Quintilian.* Leuven: Peeters, 2000.

Anderson, "Oral Tradition." Anderson, Øivind. "Oral Tradition." Pages 17–58 in *Jesus and the Oral Gospel Tradition.* Edited by Henry Wansbrough. JSNTSup 64. Sheffield: Sheffield Academic Press, 1991.

Anderson, *Philostratus.* Anderson, Graham. *Philostratus: Biography and Belles Lettres in the Third Century A.D.* Routledge Revivals. New York: Routledge, 2014.

Anderson, "Project." Anderson, Paul. "The John, Jesus, and History Project and a Fourth Quest for Jesus." Paper presented in the "Memory, Narrative, and Christology in the

Synoptic Gospels" Seminar at the Annual Meeting of the Society for New Testament Studies. Athens, Greece, August 10, 2018.

Anderson, *Quest.* Anderson, Paul N. *The Fourth Gospel and the Quest for Jesus: Modern Foundations Reconsidered.* LNTS 321. London: T&T Clark, 2006.

Anderson, Just, and Thatcher, *John, Jesus, and History.* Anderson, Paul N., Felix Just, and Tom Thatcher. *John, Jesus, and History.* 3 vols. SBLSymS 44. ECL 2.18. Atlanta: SBL Press, 2007–16.

Aragione, "Justin." Aragione, Gabriella. "Justin, 'philosophe' chrétien et les 'Mémoires des Apôtres qui sont appelés Évangiles.'" *Apocrypha (Turnhout)* 15 (2004): 41–56.

Arles, "Appraisal." Arles, Nalini. "Pandita Ramabai—an Appraisal from Feminist Perspective." *BangTF* 31 (1, July 1999): 64–86.

Arles, "Study." Arles, Nalini. "Pandita Ramabai and Amy Carmichael: A Study of Their Contributions toward Transforming the Position of Indian Women." MTh thesis, University of Aberdeen, 1985.

Armstrong, "Plea." Armstrong, Karl L. "A New Plea for an Early Date of Acts." *JGRCJ* 13 (2017): 79–110.

Arnott, "Realism." Arnott, W. Geoffrey. "Longus, Natural History, and Realism." Pages 199–215 in *The Search for the Ancient Novel.* Edited by James Tatum. Baltimore: Johns Hopkins University Press, 1994.

Aron-Schnapper and Hanet, "Archives orales." Aron-Schnapper, Dominique, and Daniele Hanet. "Archives orales et histoire des institutions sociales." *Revue française de sociologie* 19 (2, 1978): 261–75.

Ash, "Assassinating Emperors." Ash, Rhiannon. "Never Say Die! Assassinating Emperors in Suetonius' *Lives of the Caesars.*" Pages 200–216 in *Writing Biography in Greece and Rome: Narrative Technique and Fictionalization.* Edited by Koen De Temmerman and Kristoffel Demoen. Cambridge: Cambridge University Press, 2016.

Ash, Mossman, and Titchener, *Fame.* Ash, Rhiannon, Judith Mossman, and Frances B. Titchener, eds. *Fame and Infamy: Essays for Christopher Pelling on Characterization in Greek and Roman Biography and Historiography.* Oxford: Oxford University Press, 2015.

Ashton, *Religion.* Ashton, John. *The Religion of Paul the Apostle.* New Haven: Yale University Press, 2000.

Assmann, *Cultural Memory.* Assmann, Jan. *Cultural Memory and Early Civilization: Writing, Remembrance, and Political Imagination.* Cambridge: Cambridge University Press, 2011.

Assmann, *Gedächtnis.* Assmann, Jan. *Das kulturelle Gedächtnis: Schrift, Erinnerung und politische Identität in frühen Hochkulturen.* 6th ed. Munich: Beck, 1992.

Assmann, *Memory and Civilization.* Assmann, Aleida. *Cultural Memory and Western Civilization: Functions, Media, Archives.* New York: Cambridge University Press, 2013.

Assmann, "Memory and Culture." Assmann, Jan. "Memory and Culture." Pages 325–49 in *Memory: A History.* Edited by Dmitri V. Nikulin. New York: Oxford University Press, 2015.

Assmann, *Religion and Memory.* Assmann, Jan. *Religion and Cultural Memory: Ten Studies.* Translated by Rodney Livingstone. Stanford, CA: Stanford University Press, 2006.

Atherton, "Children." Atherton, Catherine. "Children, Animals, Slaves, and Grammar." Pages 214–44 in *Pedagogy and Power: Rhetorics of Classical Learning.* Edited by Yun Lee Too and Niall Livingstone. Cambridge: Cambridge University Press, 1998.

Atkinson, "Introduction." Atkinson, John. "Introduction." Pages xi–xxxix in *Arrian— Alexander the Great: The* Anabasis *and the* Indica. Translated by Martin Hammond. New York: Oxford University Press, 2013.

Attridge, "Creation." Attridge, Harold W. "Creation and Sacred Space: The Reuse of Key Pentateuchal Themes in Philo, the Fourth Evangelist, and the Epistle to the Hebrews." Pages 243–58 in *Pentateuchal Traditions in the Late Second Temple Period: Proceedings of the International Workshop in Tokyo, August 28–31, 2007.* Edited by Akio Moriya and Gohei Hata. SJSJ 158. Leiden: Brill, 2012.

Attridge, "Genre Bending." Attridge, Harold W. "Genre Bending in the Fourth Gospel." *JBL* 121 (2002): 3–21.

Attridge, "Genre Matters." Attridge, Harold W. "The Gospel of John: Genre Matters?" Pages 27–45 in *The Gospel of John as Genre Mosaic.* Edited by K. Bro Larsen. SANt 3. Göttingen: Vandenhoeck & Ruprecht, 2015.

Attridge, "Historiography." Attridge, Harold W. "Jewish Historiography." Pages 311–43 in *Early Judaism and Its Modern Interpreters.* Edited by Robert A. Kraft and George W. E. Nickelsburg. SBLBMI 2. Atlanta: Scholars Press, 1986.

Attridge, *Interpretation.* Attridge, Harold W. *The Interpretation of Biblical History in the* Antiquitates judaicae *of Flavius Josephus.* HDR 7. Missoula, MT: Scholars Press, 1976.

Attridge, "Name." Attridge, Harold W. "What's in a Name: Naming the Unnameable in Philo and John." Pages 85–94 in *Sybils, Scriptures, and Scrolls: John Collins at Seventy.* Edited by Joel Baden, Hindy Najman, and Eibert Tigchelaar. Leiden: Brill, 2016.

Attridge, "Philo and John." Attridge, Harold W. "Philo and John: Two Riffs on One Logos." *SPhiloA* 17 (2005): 103–17.

Aubin, "Reversing Romance." Aubin, Melissa. "Reversing Romance? The *Acts of Thecla* and the Ancient Novel." Pages 257–72 in *Ancient Fiction and Early Christian Narrative.* Edited by Ronald F. Hock, J. Bradley Chance, and Judith Perkins. SBLSymS 6. Atlanta: SBL, 1998.

Aune, "Aphorisms." Aune, David E. "Oral Tradition and the Aphorisms of Jesus." Pages 211–65 in *Jesus and the Oral Gospel Tradition.* Edited by Henry Wansbrough. JSNTSup 64. Sheffield: Sheffield Academic Press, 1991.

Aune, "Biography." Aune, David E. "Greco-Roman Biography." Pages 107–26 in *Greco-Roman Literature and the New Testament: Selected Forms and Genres.* Edited by David E. Aune. SBLSBS 21. Atlanta: Scholars Press, 1988.

Aune, "Biography or Theology." Aune, David E. "The Gospels: Biography or Theology?" *BRev* 6 (1, 1990): 14–21, 37.

Aune, *Dictionary.* Aune, David E. *The Westminster Dictionary of New Testament and Early Christian Literature and Rhetoric.* Louisville: Westminster John Knox, 2003.

Aune, *Environment*.   Aune, David E. *The New Testament in Its Literary Environment*. LEC 8. Philadelphia: Westminster, 1987.

Aune, "Hellenistic Biography."   Aune, David E. "The Gospels as Hellenistic Biography." *Mosaic* 20 (4, Fall 1987): 1–10.

Aune, "Problem."   Aune, David E. "The Problem of the Genre of the Gospels. A Critique of C. H. Talbert's *What Is a Gospel?*" Pages 9–60 in *Studies of History and Tradition in the Four Gospels*. Vol. 2 of *Gospel Perspectives*. Edited by R. T. France and David Wenham. Sheffield: JSOT Press, 1981.

Aune, "Prolegomena."   Aune, David E. "Prolegomena to the Study of Oral Tradition in the Hellenistic World." Pages 59–106 in *Jesus and the Oral Gospel Tradition*. Edited by Henry Wansbrough. JSNTSup 64. Sheffield: Sheffield Academic Press, 1991.

Aune, "*Prooimion*."   Aune, David E. "Luke 1.1–4: Historical or Scientific *prooimion?*" Pages 138–48 in *Paul, Luke, and the Graeco-Roman World*. Edited by Alf Christophersen et al. JSNTSup 217. Sheffield: Sheffield Academic, 2002; London: T&T Clark, 2003.

Aune, *Prophecy*.   Aune, David E. *Prophecy in Early Christianity and the Ancient Mediterranean World*. Grand Rapids: Eerdmans, 1983.

Aune, *Revelation*.   Aune, David E. *Revelation*. 3 vols. WBC 52, 52B, 52C. Dallas: Word, 1997.

Back and Bennett, *Sociology*.   Back, Les, and Andy Bennett. *Cultural Sociology: An Introduction*. New York: Wiley & Sons, 2012.

Baddeley, *Memory*.   Baddeley, Alan D. *Human Memory: Theory and Practice*. Boston: Allyn & Bacon, 1990.

Baddeley et al., "Delusions."   Baddeley, Alan, Andrew Thornton, Siew Eng Chua, and Peter McKenna, "Schizophrenic Delusions and the Construction of Autobiographical Memory." Pages 384–428 in *Remembering Our Past: Studies in Autobiographical Memory*. Edited by David C. Rubin. Cambridge: Cambridge University Press, 1996.

Badian, "Skill."   Badian, Ernst. "Plutarch's Unconfessed Skill: The Biographer as a Critical Historian." Pages 26–44 in *Laurea internationalis. Festschrift für Jochen Bleicken zum 75. Geburtstag*. Edited by Theodora Hantos. Stuttgart: Franz Steiner, 2003.

Baer, *Categories*.   Baer, Richard A., Jr. *Philo's Use of the Categories Male and Female*. ALGHJ 3. Leiden: Brill, 1970.

Bagnall, *Reading Papyri*.   Bagnall, Roger S. *Reading Papyri, Writing Ancient History*. New York: Routledge, 2003.

Bahrick, "Maintenance."   Bahrick, Harry P. "Long Term Maintenance of Knowledge." Pages 247–362 in *The Oxford Handbook of Memory*. Edited by Endel Tulving and Furgus I. M. Craik. Oxford: Oxford University Press, 2000.

Bahrick, "Memory Content."   Bahrick, Harry P. "Semantic Memory Content in Permastore: Fifty Years of Memory for Spanish Learned in School." *JExpPsyc: General* 113 (1984): 1–29.

Bahrick, Bahrick, and Wittlinger, "Fifty Years."   Bahrick, Harry P., P. O. Bahrick, and R. P. Wittlinger. "Fifty Years of Memory for Names and Faces: A Cross-Sectional Approach." *JExpPsyc: General* 104 (1975): 54–75.

Bailey, "Oral Tradition."   Bailey, Kenneth Ewing. "Informal Controlled Oral Tradition and the Synoptic Gospels." *AsJT* 5 (1, 1991): 34–54.

Bailey, "Tradition" (*ExpT*).   Bailey, Kenneth E. "Middle Eastern Oral Tradition and the Synoptic Gospels." *ExpT* 106 (1995): 363–67.

Bailey, "Tradition" (*Themelios*).   Bailey, Kenneth E. "Informal Controlled Oral Tradition and the Synoptic Gospels." *Themelios* 20 (2, January 1995): 4–11.

Baker, "Identity."   Baker, Coleman A. "Identity." *DBAM* 188–90.

Balch, "ἀκριβῶς."   Balch, David L. "Ἀκριβῶς . . . γράψαι (Luke 1:3): To Write the *Full History of God's Receiving All Nations.*" Pages 229–50 in *Jesus and the Heritage of Israel: Luke's Narrative Claim upon Israel's Legacy*. Edited by David P. Moessner. Luke the Interpreter of Israel 1. Harrisburg, PA: Trinity Press International, 1999.

Balch, "Genre."   Balch, David L. "The Genre of Luke-Acts: Individual Biography, Adventure Novel, or Political History?" *SWJT* 33 (1990): 5–19.

Balch, "Gospels: Forms."   Balch, David L. "Gospels (Literary Forms)." *BNP* 5:947–49.

Balch, "ΜΕΤΑΒΟΛΗ ΠΟΛΙΤΕΙΩΝ."   Balch, David L. "ΜΕΤΑΒΟΛΗ ΠΟΛΙΤΕΙΩΝ—Jesus as Founder of the Church in Luke-Acts: Form and Function." Pages 139–88 in *Contextualizing Acts: Lukan Narrative and Greco-Roman Discourse*. Edited by Todd Penner and Caroline Vander Stichele. SBLSymS 20. Atlanta: SBL, 2003.

Baldwin, "Review."   Baldwin, Matthew C. Review of *Why Are There Differences in the Gospels?*, by Michael R. Licona. *RBL*, May 17, 2018, 8 pages.

Balentine, "Future."   Balentine, Samuel. "The Future beyond the End: Lessons from History by Herodotus and Daniel." *PRSt* 43 (2, 2016): 145–59.

Bamberger, *Story*.   Bamberger, Bernard J. *The Story of Judaism*. New York: Union of American Hebrew Congregations, 1962.

Barber and Barber, *Severed*.   Barber, Elizabeth Wayland, and Paul T. Barber. *When They Severed Earth from Sky: How the Human Mind Shapes Myth*. Princeton: Princeton University Press, 2004.

Barclay, "Autobiographical Remembering."   Barclay, Craig R. "Autobiographical Remembering: Narrative Constraints on Objectified Selves." Pages 94–125 in *Remembering Our Past: Studies in Autobiographical Memory*. Edited by David C. Rubin. Cambridge: Cambridge University Press, 1996.

Barclay, "Truth."   Barclay, Craig R. "Truth and Accuracy in Autobiographical Memory." Pages 289–93 in *Practical Aspects of Memory*. Edited by M. M. Gruneberg, P. E. Morris, and R. N. Sykes. Chichester: Wiley, 1988.

Barker, "Reassessment."   Barker, James W. "Ancient Compositional Practices and the Gospels: A Reassessment." *JBL* 135 (1, 2016): 109–21.

Barnes and Sered, *Religion and Healing*.   Barnes, Linda L., and Susan S. Sered, eds. *Religion and Healing in America*. New York: Oxford University Press, 2005.

Barnes and Talamantez, *Teaching Religion and Healing*.   Barnes, Linda L., and Inés Talamantez. *Teaching Religion and Healing*. AARTRSS. Oxford: Oxford University Press, 2006.

Barnett, *Birth*.   Barnett, Paul W. *The Birth of Christianity: The First Twenty Years*. Grand Rapids: Eerdmans, 2005.

Barnett, *Finding.*   Barnett, Paul. *Finding the Historical Christ.* Grand Rapids: Eerdmans, 2009.

Barnett, "Sign Prophets."   Barnett, Paul W. "The Jewish Sign Prophets—A.D. 40–70—Their Intentions and Origin." *NTS* 27 (5, October 1981): 679–97.

Barr and Wentling, "Biography."   Barr, David L., and Judith L. Wentling. "The Conventions of Classical Biography and the Genre of Luke-Acts: A Preliminary Study." Pages 63–88 in *Luke-Acts: New Perspectives from the Society of Biblical Literature Seminar.* Edited by Charles H. Talbert. New York: Crossroad, 1984.

Barrett, *Acts.*   Barrett, C. K. *A Critical and Exegetical Commentary on the Acts of the Apostles.* 2 vols. ICC. Edinburgh: T&T Clark, 1994–98.

Barrett, "Acts and Corpus."   Barrett, C. K. "Acts and the Pauline Corpus." *ExpT* 88 (1, 1976): 2–5.

Barrett, "First Testament."   Barrett, C. K. "The First Testament?" *NovT* 38 (1996): 94–104.

Barth, "Ethik."   Barth, M. "Autonome statt messianische Ethik?" Review of *Die rabbinischen Gleichnisse und der Gleichniserzähler Jesus. 1. Teil,* by David Flusser. *Judaica* 37 (1981): 220–33.

Barth, *Letters.*   Barth, Karl. *Letters 1961–1968.* Translated and edited by Geoffrey W. Bromiley. Grand Rapids: Eerdmans, 1981.

Bartlett, *Remembering.*   Bartlett, Frederic C. *Remembering: A Study in Experimental Social Psychology.* Cambridge: Cambridge University Press, 2003. Orig., 1932.

Barton, *Honor.*   Barton, Carlin A. *Roman Honor: The Fire in the Bones.* Berkeley: University of California Press, 2001.

Barton, "Moment."   Barton, Carlin A. "The 'Moment of Truth' in Ancient Rome: Honor and Embodiment in a Contest Culture." *Stanford Humanities Review* 6 (2, 1998): 16–30.

Baslez, "Polémique."   Baslez, Marie-Françoise. "Polémique et histoire dans le Livre de Judith." *RB* 111 (3, 2004): 362–76.

Bauckham, "Acts of Paul."   Bauckham, Richard. "The Acts of Paul as a Sequel to Acts." Pages 105–52 in *The Book of Acts in Its Ancient Literary Setting.* Edited by Bruce W. Winter and Andrew D. Clark. Vol. 1 of *The Book of Acts in Its First Century Setting.* Edited by Bruce W. Winter. Grand Rapids: Eerdmans, 1993.

Bauckham, "Christology."   Bauckham, Richard. "Is 'High Human Christology' Sufficient? A Critical Response to J. R. Daniel Kirk's *A Man Attested by God.*" *BBR* 27 (4, 2017): 503–25.

Bauckham, *Eyewitnesses.*   Bauckham, Richard. *Jesus and the Eyewitnesses: The Gospels as Eyewitness Testimony.* 2nd ed. Grand Rapids: Eerdmans, 2017.

Bauckham, "Eyewitnesses."   Bauckham, Richard. "The Eyewitnesses and the Gospel Traditions." *JSHJ* 1 (1, 2003): 28–60.

Bauckham, "General."   Bauckham, Richard. "The General and the Particular in Memory: A Critique of Dale Allison's Approach to the Historical Jesus." *JSHJ* 14 (1, 2016): 28–51.

Bauckham, "Historiographical Characteristics."   Bauckham, Richard. "Historiographical Characteristics of the Gospel of John." *NTS* 53 (1, 2007): 17–36.

Bauckham, "Liber antiquitatum."   Bauckham, Richard. "The Liber antiquitatum biblicarum of Pseudo-Philo and the Gospels as 'Midrash.'" Pages 33–76 in *Studies in Midrash and Historiography*. Vol. 3 of *Gospel Perspectives*. Edited by R. T. France and David Wenham. Sheffield: JSOT Press, 1983.

Bauckham, "Parables." Bauckham, Richard. "Synoptic Parousia Parables and the Apocalypse." *NTS* 23 (1976/77): 162–76.

Bauckham, "Psychology of Memory." Bauckham, Richard. "The Psychology of Memory and the Study of the Gospels." *JSHJ* 16 (2018): 1–21.

Bauckham, "Response." Bauckham, Richard. "In Response to My Respondents: *Jesus and the Eyewitnesses* in Review." *JSHJ* 6 (2008): 225–53.

Bauckham, *Testimony*. Bauckham, Richard. *The Testimony of the Beloved Disciple: Narrative, History, and Theology in the Gospel of John*. Grand Rapids: Baker Academic, 2007.

Bauckham, *World*. Bauckham, Richard. *The Christian World around the New Testament: Collected Essays*. Vol. 2. WUNT 386. Tübingen: Mohr Siebeck, 2017.

Bauckham and Porter, "Apocryphal Gospels." Bauckham, Richard, and Stanley E. Porter. "Apocryphal Gospels." *DNTB* 71–79.

Baucom and Adams, "Communication." Baucom, Donald H., and Alexandra N. Adams. "Assessing Communication in Marital Interaction." In *Assessment of Marital Discord (Psychology Revivals): An Integration for Research and Clinical Practice*. Edited by K. Daniel O'Leary. New York: Routledge, 2013.

Bauernfeind and Michel, "Beiden Eleazarreden." Bauernfeind, Otto, and Otto Michel. "Die beiden Eleazarreden in Jos. bell. 7,323–336; 7,341–388." *ZNW* 58 (3–4, 1967): 267–72.

Baum, "Biographien." Baum, Armin D. "Biographien im alttestamentlich-rabbinischen Stil. Zur Gattung der neu-testamentlichen Evangelien." *Bib* 94 (4, 2013): 534–64.

Baum, "Content." Baum, Armin D. "Content and Form: Authorship Attribution and Pseudonymity in Ancient Speeches, Letters, Lectures, and Translations—A Rejoinder to Bart Ehrman." *JBL* 136 (2, 2017): 381–403.

Baum, *Faktor*. Baum, Armin D. *Der mündliche Faktor und seine Bedeutung für die synoptische Frage. Analogien aus der antiken Literatur, der Experimentalpsychologie, der Oral Poetry-Forschung und dem rabbinischen Traditionswesen*. Tübingen: Francke, 2008.

Baum, "Wir- und Er-Stellungen." Baum, Armin D. "Autobiografische Wir- und Er-Stellungen in den neutestamentlichen Geschichtsbüchern im Kontext der antiken Literaturgeschichte." *Bib* 88 (4, 2007): 473–95.

Baumeister and Hastings, "Distortions." Baumeister, Roy F., and Stephen Hastings. "Distortions of Collective Memory: How Groups Flatter and Deceive Themselves." Pages 277–93 in *Collective Memory of Political Events: Social Psychological Perspectives*. Edited by James W. Pennebaker, Dario Paez, and Bernand Rimé. Mahwah, NJ: Erlbaum, 1997.

Baynham, "Quintus Curtius." Baynham, Elizabeth J. "Quintus Curtius Rufus on the 'Good King': The Dioxippus Episode in Book 9.7.16–26." Pages 427–33 in *A Companion to Greek and Roman Historiography*. Edited by John Marincola. 2 vols. Oxford: Blackwell, 2007.

Bazin, "Past." Bazin, Jean. "The Past in the Present: Notes on Oral Archaeology." Pages 59–74 in *African Historiographies: What History for Which Africa?* Edited by Bogumil Jewsiewicki and David Newbury. SSAMD 12. London: Sage, 1986.

Beard, *Literacy.*   Beard, Mary, ed. *Literacy in the Roman World.* JRASup 3. Ann Arbor: University of Michigan, 1991.

Beare, "Sayings."   Beare, Francis Wright. "Sayings of the Risen Jesus in the Synoptic Tradition: An Inquiry into Their Origin and Significance." Pages 161–81 in *Christian History and Interpretation: Studies Presented to John Knox.* Edited by William R. Farmer, C. F. D. Moule, and R. R. Niebuhr. Cambridge: Cambridge University Press, 1967.

Beck, "Demonax."   Beck, Mark. "Lucian's *Life of Demonax*: The Socratic Paradigm, Individuality, and Personality." Pages 80–96 in *Writing Biography in Greece and Rome: Narrative Technique and Fictionalization.* Edited by Koen De Temmerman and Kristoffel Demoen. Cambridge: Cambridge University Press, 2016.

Beck, "Plutarch."   Beck, Mark. "Plutarch." Pages 397–411 in *Time in Ancient Greek Literature.* Edited by I. J. F. de Jong and R. Nünlist. Studies in Ancient Greek Narrative 2. Leiden: Brill, 2007.

Beck and Thomas, "Education."   Beck, Frederick Arthur George, and Rosalind Thomas. "Education, Greek." *OCD*[3] 506–10.

Becker, *Birth.*   Becker, Eve-Marie. *The Birth of Christian History: Memory and Time from Mark to Luke-Acts.* ABRL. New Haven: Yale University Press, 2017.

Begg, "Abigail."   Begg, Christopher T. "The Abigail Story (1 Samuel 25) according to Josephus." *EstBib* 54 (1, 1996): 5–34.

Begg, "Abimelech."   Begg, Christopher T. "Abimelech, King of Shechem according to Josephus." *ETL* 72 (1, 1996): 146–64.

Begg, "Ahab."   Begg, Christopher. "The Death of King Ahab according to Josephus." *Anton* 64 (2–3, 1989): 225–45.

Begg, "Amaziah."   Begg, Christopher T. "Amaziah of Judah according to Josephus (*Ant.* 9.186–204)." *Anton* 70 (1, 1995): 3–30.

Begg, "Blanks."   Begg, Christopher T. "Filling in the Blanks: Josephus' Version of the Campaign of the Three Kings, 2 Kings 3." *HUCA* 64 (1993): 89–109.

Begg, "Ceremonies."   Begg, Christopher T. "The Ceremonies at Gilgal/Ebal according to Pseudo-Philo: *LAB* 21,7–10." *ETL* 73 (1, 1997): 72–83.

Begg, "Deeds."   Begg, Christopher T. "Elisha's Great Deeds according to Josephus (*AJ* 9,47–94)." *Hen* 18 (1–2, 1996): 69–110.

Begg, "Disappearance."   Begg, Christopher T. "'Josephus's Portrayal of the Disappearances of Enoch, Elijah, and Moses': Some Observations." *JBL* 109 (4, 1990): 691–93.

Begg, "Doves."   Begg, Christopher. "Doves and Treaty-Making: Another Possible Reference." *BN* 48 (1989): 8–11.

Begg, "Elisha's Deeds."   Begg, Christopher T. "Elisha's Great Deeds according to Josephus (*AJ* 9,47–94)." *Hen* 18 (1–2, 1996): 69–110.

Begg, "Fall."   Begg, Christopher T. "Ahaziah's Fall (2 Kings 1): The Version of Josephus." *Sef* 55 (1, 1995): 25–40.

Begg, "Gedaliah."   Begg, Christopher T. "The Gedaliah Episode and Its Sequels in Josephus." *JSP* 12 (1994): 21–46.

Begg, "Illness." Begg, Christopher T. "Hezekiah's Illness and Visit according to Josephus." *EstBib* 53 (3, 1995): 365–85.

Begg, "Jehoahaz." Begg, Christopher T. "Jehoahaz, King of Israel, according to Josephus." *Sef* 55 (2, 1995): 227–37.

Begg, "Jehoshaphat" Begg, Christopher T. "Jehoshaphat at Mid-Career according to *AJ* 9,1–17." *RB* 102 (3, 1995): 379–402.

Begg, "Josiah." Begg, Christopher T. "The Death of Josiah: Josephus and the Bible." *ETL* 64 (1, 1988): 157–63.

Begg, "Jotham." Begg, Christopher T. "Jotham and Amon: Two Minor Kings of Judah according to Josephus." *BBR* 6 (1996): 1–13.

Begg, "Marah Incident." Begg, Christopher T. "The Marah Incident according to Josephus and Philo." *Laur* 49 (2–3, 2008): 321–33.

Begg, "Moves." Begg, Christopher T. "Moses' First Moves (Exod 2:11–22) as Retold by Josephus and Philo." *Polish Journal of Biblical Research* 9 (1–2, 2010): 67–93.

Begg, "Nahum." Begg, Christopher T. "Josephus and Nahum Revisited." *REJ* 154 (1–2, 1995): 5–22.

Begg, "Portrait." Begg, Christopher T. "Josephus' Portrait of Jehoshaphat Compared with the Biblical and Rabbinic Portrayals." *BN* 78 (1995): 39–48.

Begg, "Putsch." Begg, Christopher T. "Josephus's Version of Jehu's Putsch (2 Kgs 8,25–10,36)." *Anton* 68 (4, 1993): 450–84.

Begg, "Rape of Tamar." Begg, Christopher T. "The Rape of Tamar (2 Samuel 13) according to Josephus." *EstBib* 54 (4, 1996): 465–500.

Begg, "Rephidim Episode." Begg, Christopher T. "The Rephidim Episode according to Josephus and Philo." *ETL* 83 (4, 2007): 367–83.

Begg, "Retelling." Begg, Christopher T. "Josephus' and Philo's Retelling of Numbers 31 Compared." *ETL* 83 (1, 2007): 81–106.

Begg, "Sheep." Begg, Christopher T. "The Identity of the Three Building Sheep in 1 Enoch 89,72–73." *ETL* 64 (1, 1988): 152–56.

Begg, "Uzziah." Begg, Christopher T. "Uzziah (Azariah) of Judah according to Josephus." *EstBib* 53 (1, 1995): 5–24.

Begg, "Zedekiah." Begg, Christopher T. "Josephus's Zedekiah." *ETL* 65 (1, 1989): 96–104.

Behrend and Luig, *Spirit Possession.* Behrend, Heike, and Ute Luig. *Spirit Possession: Modernity and Power in Africa.* Madison: University of Wisconsin Press, 1999.

Bekinschtein et al., "BDNF." Bekinschtein, Pedro, et al. "BDNF Is Essential to Promote Persistence of Long-Term Memory Storage." *Proceedings of the Natural Academy of Sciences* 105 (7, February 19, 2008): 2711–16.

Bellemore, "Josephus, Pompey, and Jews." Bellemore, Jane. "Josephus, Pompey, and the Jews." *Historia* 48 (1, 1999): 94–118.

Bellemore, *Nicolaus.* Bellemore, Jane. *Nicolaus of Damascus "Life of Augustus."* Edited and translated by Jane Bellemore. Bristol, UK: Bristol Classical, 1984.

Belli and Loftus, "Pliability." Belli, Robert F., and Elizabeth F. Loftus. "The Pliability of Autobiographical Memory: Misinformation and the False Memory Problem." Pages

157–79 in *Remembering Our Past: Studies in Autobiographical Memory*. Edited by David C. Rubin. Cambridge: Cambridge University Press, 1996.

Belmonte, *Joy*. Belmont, Kevin. *Defiant Joy: The Remarkable Life and Impact of G. K. Chesterton*. Nashville: Thomas Nelson, 2011.

Ben-Amos and Mintz, "Introduction." Ben-Amos, Dan, and Jerome R. Mintz. "Introduction." Pages xi–xxx in *In Praise of the Baal Shem Tov [Shivhei ha-Besht]: The Earliest Collection of Legends about the Founder of Hasidism*. Edited and translated by Dan Ben-Amos and Jerome R. Mintz. New York: Schocken, 1984. Orig., Bloomington: Indiana University Press, 1970.

Benediktson, "Structure." Benediktson, D. Thomas. "Structure and Fate in Suetonius' Life of Galba." *CJ* 92 (2, 1997): 167–73.

Benediktson, "Survey." Benediktson, D. Thomas. "A Survey of Suetonius Scholarship, 1938–1987." *CW* 86 (5, May 1993): 377–447.

Beneker, "Chaste Caesar." Beneker, Jeffrey. "No Time for Love: Plutarch's Chaste Caesar." *GRBS* 43 (1, 2002–3): 13–29.

Beneker, "Crossing." Beneker, Jeffrey. "The Crossing of the Rubicon and the Outbreak of Civil War in Cicero, Lucan, Plutarch, and Suetonius." *Phoenix* 65 (1–2, 2011): 74–99.

Beneker, "Method." Beneker, Jeffrey. "Nepos' Biographical Method in the *Lives of Foreign Generals*." *CJ* 105 (2, 2009): 109–21.

Beneker, *Statesman*. Beneker, Jeffrey. *The Passionate Statesman: Eros and Politics in Plutarch's Lives*. New York: Oxford University Press, 2012.

Benoit, *Gospel*. Benoit, Pierre. *Jesus and the Gospel*. Translated by Benet Weatherhead. 2 vols. London: Darton, Longman & Todd, 1973–74.

Benson, *Healing*. Benson, Herbert, with Marg Stark. *Timeless Healing: The Power and Biology of Belief*. New York: Scribner, 1996.

Ben Zeev, "Ambiguities." Ben Zeev, Miriam Pucci. "Josephus' Ambiguities: His Comments on Cited Documents." *JJS* 57 (1, 2006): 1–10.

Ben Zeev, "Capitol." Ben Zeev, Miriam Pucci. "Polybius, Josephus, and the Capitol in Rome." *JSJ* 27 (1, 1996): 21–30.

Ben Zeev, "Reliability." Ben Zeev, Miriam Pucci. "The Reliability of Josephus Flavius: The Case of Hecataeus' and Manetho's Accounts of Jews and Judaism; Fifteen Years of Contemporary Research (1974–1990)." *JSJ* 24 (2, 1993): 215–34.

Berchmann, "Arcana Mundi." Berchmann, Robert M. "Arcana Mundi: Prophecy and Divination in the *Vita Mosis* of Philo of Alexandria." Pages 385–423 in *SBL Seminary Papers, 1988*. Edited by David J. Lull. SBLSP 27. Atlanta: SBL, 1988.

Berger, *Canopy*. Berger, Peter L. *The Sacred Canopy: Elements of a Sociological Theory of Religion*. Garden City, NY: Doubleday, 1967.

Berger, "Gattungen." Berger, Klaus. "Hellenistische Gattungen im Neuen Testament." *ANRW* 2.25.2 (1984): 1031–1432.

Bergholz, *Aufbau*. Bergholz, Thomas. *Der Aufbau des lukanischen Doppelwerkes. Untersuchungen zum formalliterarischen Charakter von Lukas-Evangelium und Apostelgeschichte*. EurH, Series 23, Theologie 545. Frankfurt: Peter Lang, 1995.

Bergren, "Nehemiah." Bergren, Theodore A. "Nehemiah in 2 Maccabees 1:10–2:18." *JSJ* 28 (3, 1997): 249–70.

Bergunder, "Miracle Healing." Bergunder, Michael. "Miracle Healing and Exorcism in South Indian Pentecostalism." Pages 287–305 in *Global Pentecostal and Charismatic Healing*. Edited by Candy Gunther Brown. Oxford: Oxford University Press, 2011.

Bergunder, *Movement.* Bergunder, Michael. *The South Indian Pentecostal Movement in the Twentieth Century.* SHCM. Grand Rapids: Eerdmans, 2008.

Bernal, *Athena.* Bernal, Martin. *Black Athena: The Afroasiatic Roots of Classical Civilization.* 3 vols. London: Free Association; New Brunswick, NJ: Rutgers University Press, 1987–2006.

Bernier, *Quest.* Bernier, Jonathan. *The Quest for the Historical Jesus after the Demise of Authenticity: Toward a Critical Realist Philosophy of History in Jesus Studies.* LNTS 540. New York: Bloomsbury, 2016.

Bernsten and Thomsen, "Memories." Bernsten, Dorthe, and Dorthe K. Thomsen. "Personal Memories for Remote Historical Events: Accuracy and Clarity of Flashbulb Memories Related to World War II." *JExpPsyc: General* 134 (2005): 242–57.

Berschin, "Biography." Berschin, Walter. "Biography: Late Antiquity." *BNP* 2:653–55.

Berthelot, "Conquest." Berthelot, Katell. "Philo of Alexandria and the Conquest of Canaan." *JSJ* 38 (1, 2007): 39–56.

Best, *Mark.* Best, Ernest. *Mark: The Gospel as Story.* SNTW. Edinburgh: T&T Clark, 1983.

Betori, "Strutturazione." Betori, Giuseppe. "Strutturazione degli Atti e storiografia antica." *CNS* 12 (2, 1991): 251–63.

Betz, "Gospel." Betz, Otto. "Jesus' Gospel of the Kingdom." Pages 53–74 in *The Gospel and the Gospels.* Edited by Peter Stuhlmacher. Grand Rapids: Eerdmans, 1991.

Betz, *Jesus.* Betz, Otto. *What Do We Know about Jesus?* Philadelphia: Westminster; London: SCM, 1968.

Bhatt, "Rhetoric." Bhatt, Shreyaa. "Rhetoric and Truth: Tacitus's Percennius and Democratic Historiography." *Helios* 43 (2, 2016): 163–89.

Bing and Höschele, "Introduction." Bing, Peter, and Regina Höschele. "Introduction." Pages xi–xxxvi in *Aristaenetus "Erotic Letters."* Translated by Peter Bing and Regina Höschele. SBLWGRW 32. Atlanta: Scholars Press, 2014.

Bingham, "Paideia." Bingham, D. Jeffrey. "Paideia and Polemic in Second-Century Lyons: Irenaeus on Education." Pages 323–57 in *Pedagogy in Ancient Judaism and Early Christianity.* Edited by Karina Martin Hogan, Matthew Goff, and Emma Wasserman. EJL 41. Atlanta: SBL Press, 2017.

Bird, *Gospel.* Bird, Michael F. *The Gospel of the Lord: How the Early Church Wrote the Story of Jesus.* Grand Rapids: Eerdmans, 2014.

Bird, "Quest." Bird, Michael F. "Is There Really a 'Third Quest' for the Historical Jesus?" *SBET* 24 (2, 2006): 195–219.

Bishop, "Historiography." Bishop, Paul Bernard. "Historiography in *Lives*: Plutarch's Use of Thucydides in the Lives of *Pericles* and *Nicias*." MA thesis, Department of Classics and Ancient History, University of Durham, 2015.

Black, *Aramaic Approach.*   Black, Matthew. *An Aramaic Approach to the Gospels and Acts.* Oxford: Clarendon, 1967.

Black, "Kennedy."   Black, C. Clifton. "Kennedy and the Gospels: An Ambiguous Legacy, A Promising Bequest." Pages 63–80 in *Words Well Spoken: George Kennedy's Rhetoric of the New Testament.* Edited by C. Clifton Black and Duane F. Watson. Waco, TX: Baylor University Press, 2008.

Blackburn, "Miracles."   Blackburn, Barry L. "The Miracles of Jesus." Pages 353–94 in *Studying the Historical Jesus: Evaluations of the State of Current Research.* Edited by Bruce Chilton and Craig A. Evans. NTTS 19. Leiden: Brill, 1994.

Blackburn, "ΘΕΙΟΙ ΑΝΔΡΕΣ."   Blackburn, Barry L. "'Miracle Working ΘΕΙΟΙ ΑΝΔΡΕΣ' in Hellenism (and Hellenistic Judaism)." Pages 185–218 in *The Miracles of Jesus.* Vol. 6 of *Gospel Perspectives.* Edited by David Wenham and Craig Blomberg. Sheffield: JSOT, 1986.

Bland, *Slave Narratives.*   Bland, Sterling Lecater. *African American Slave Narratives: An Anthology.* 3 vols. Westport, CT: Greenwood, 2001.

Blenkinsopp, *Judaism.*   Blenkinsopp, Joseph. *Judaism: The First Phase; The Place of Ezra and Nehemiah in the Origins of Judaism.* Grand Rapids: Eerdmans, 2009.

Blenkinsopp, *Pentateuch.*   Blenkinsopp, Joseph. *The Pentateuch: An Introduction to the First Five Books of the Bible.* ABRL. New York: Doubleday, 1992.

Bloch, "Alexandria."   Bloch, René. "Alexandria in Pharaonic Egypt: Projections in De Vita Mosis." *SPhiloA* 24 (2012): 69–84.

Bloch, *Aristotle on Memory.*   Bloch, David. *Aristotle on Memory and Recollection: Text, Translation, Interpretation, and Reception in Western Scholasticism.* Boston: Brill, 2007.

Blomberg, "Mithras."   Blomberg, Craig L. "Matthew, Mithras, and Midrash." Pages 76–92 in *Treasures New and Old: Essays in Honor of Donald A. Hagner.* Edited by Carl S. Sweatman and Clifford B. Kvidahl. GlossaHouse Festschrift Series 1. Wilmore, KY: GlossaHouse, 2017.

Blomberg, "Quotations."   Blomberg, Craig L. "Quotations, Allusions, and Echoes of Jesus in Paul." Pages 129–43 in *Studies in the Pauline Epistles: Essays in Honor of Douglas J. Moo.* Edited by Matthew S. Harmon and Jay E. Smith. Grand Rapids: Zondervan, 2014.

Blomberg, *Reliability.*   Blomberg, Craig L. *The Historical Reliability of the Gospels.* 2nd ed. Downers Grove, IL: InterVarsity, 2007.

Blomberg, *Reliability of John's Gospel.*   Blomberg, Craig L. *The Historical Reliability of John's Gospel: Issues and Commentary.* Downers Grove, IL: InterVarsity, 2001.

Bloomer, "Quintilian."   Bloomer, W. Martin. "Quintilian on the Child as a Learning Subject." *CW* 105 (1, 2011): 109–37.

Blum, *Mnemoteknik.*   Blum, Herwig. *Die antike Mnemoteknik.* Hildesheim: George Olms, 1969.

Blyth, "Cicero."   Blyth, Dougal. "Cicero and Philosophy as Text." *CJ* 106 (1, 2010): 71–98.

Bock, *Luke.*   Bock, Darrell L. *Luke.* IVP New Testament Commentary. Downers Grove, IL: InterVarsity, 1994.

Bock, *Mark.*   Bock, Darrell L. *Mark.* NCamBC. New York: Cambridge University Press, 2015.

Bock, "Note."   Bock, Darrell L. "A Note on the Gospels' Jesus Tradition, Memory, and Issues Raised by Bart Ehrman." *Journal of Gospels and Acts Research* 1 (September 2017): 18–22.

Bock, "Words."   Bock, Darrell L. "The Words of Jesus in the Gospels: Live, Jive, or Memorex?" Pages 73–99 in *Jesus under Fire*. Edited by Michael J. Wilkins and J. P. Moreland. Grand Rapids: Zondervan, 1995.

Bockmuehl, *Seeing.*   Bockmuehl, Markus. *Seeing the Word: Refocusing New Testament Study*. Grand Rapids: Baker Academic, 2006.

Boddy, "Spirit Possession."   Boddy, Janice. "Spirit Possession Revisited: Beyond Instrumentality." *ARAnth* 23 (1994): 407–34.

Bogart and Montell, *Memory.*   Bogart, Barbara Allen, and William Lynwood Montell. *From Memory to History: Using Oral Sources in Local History*. Nashville: American Association for State and Local History, 1981.

Bomann, *Faith.*   Bomann, Rebecca Pierce. *Faith in the Barrios: The Pentecostal Poor in Bogotá*. Boulder, CO: Lynn Rienner, 1999.

Bomann, "Salve."   Bomann, Rebecca Pierce. "The Salve of Divine Healing: Essential Rituals for Survival among Working-Class Pentecostals in Bogotá, Colombia." Pages 187–205 in *Global Pentecostal and Charismatic Healing*. Edited by Candy Gunther Brown. Oxford: Oxford University Press, 2011.

Bonanno, "Remembering."   Bonanno, George A. "Remembering and Psychotherapy." *Psychotherapy* 27 (1990): 175–86.

Bond, "Fitting End."   Bond, Helen K. "A Fitting End? Self-Denial and a Slave's Death in Mark's *Life of Jesus*." Paper presented in the "Memory, Narrative, and Christology in the Synoptic Gospels" Seminar at the Annual Meeting of the Society for New Testament Studies. Athens, Greece, August 8, 2018.

Bond, *Mark.*   Bond, Helen K. *Mark: The First Biography of Jesus*. Grand Rapids: Eerdmans, forthcoming.

Bond, "Paragon."   Bond, Helen K. "Paragon of Discipleship? Simon of Cyrene in the Markan Passion Narrative." Pages 18–35 in *Matthew and Mark across Perspectives: Essays in Honour of Stephen C. Barton and William R Telford*. Edited by Kristian A. Bendoraitis and Nijay K. Gupta. LNTS 538. London: Bloomsbury T&T Clark, 2016.

Bonz, *Past as Legacy.*   Bonz, Marianne Palmer. *The Past as Legacy: Luke-Acts and Ancient Epic*. Minneapolis: Fortress, 2000.

Boomershine, "Performance."   Boomershine, Thomas E. "Performance of the Gospels (in Antiquity)." *DBAM* 289–91.

Boomershine, "Research Unit."   Boomershine, Thomas E. "Bible in Ancient and Modern Media Research Unit (Society of Biblical Literature)." *DBAM* 36–40.

Borg, *Conflict.*   Borg, Marcus J. *Conflict, Holiness, and Politics in the Teachings of Jesus*. Studies in the Bible and Early Christianity 5. New York: Edwin Mellen, 1984.

Borg, *Jesus.*   Borg, Marcus J. *Jesus: Uncovering the Life, Teachings, and Relevance of a Religious Revolutionary*. New York: HarperOne, 2006.

Borg, *Vision.*   Borg, Marcus J. *Jesus, a New Vision: Spirit, Culture, and the Life of Discipleship*. San Francisco: Harper & Row, 1987.

Borgeaud, "Approche." Borgeaud, Philippe. "Pour une approche anthropologique de la mémoire religieuse." Pages 7–20 in *La mémoire des religions*. Edited by J. C. Basset et al. Geneva: Labor et Fides, 1988.

Borgen, *John*. Borgen, Peder. *The Gospel of John: More Light from Philo, Paul, and Archaeology*. NovTSup 154. Leiden: Brill, 2014.

Borgen, "Paul to Luke." Borgen, Peder. "From Paul to Luke: Observations toward Clarification of the Theology of Luke-Acts." *CBQ* 31 (1969): 168–82.

Borgen, "Reviewing." Borgen, Peder. "Philo of Alexandria: Reviewing and Rewriting Biblical Material." *SPhiloA* 9 (1997): 37–53.

Borgman, *Way*. Borgman, Paul. *The Way according to Luke: Hearing the Whole Story of Luke-Acts*. Grand Rapids: Eerdmans, 2006.

Boring, "Oracles." Boring, M. Eugene. "How May We Identify Oracles of Christian Prophets in the Synoptic Tradition? Mark 3:28–29 as a Test Case." *JBL* 91 (4, 1972): 501–21.

Boring, *Sayings*. Boring, M. Eugene. *Sayings of the Risen Jesus: Christian Prophecy in the Synoptic Tradition*. SNTSMS 46. Cambridge: Cambridge University Press, 1982.

Boring, Berger, and Colpe, *Commentary*. Boring, M. Eugene, Klaus Berger, and Carsten Colpe, eds. *Hellenistic Commentary to the New Testament*. Nashville: Abingdon, 1995.

Bosch-Veciana, "Filosofia." Bosch-Veciana, Antoni. "La 'filosofia' del judaisme alexandrí com a 'manera de viure.'" *RCT* 34 (2, 2009): 503–21.

Bosworth, *Arrian*. Bosworth, A. B. *From Arrian to Alexander: Studies in Historical Interpretation*. Oxford: Clarendon Press, 1988.

Bosworth, "Pseudo-Callisthenes." Bosworth, A. B. "Pseudo-Callisthenes." *OCD*³ 1270.

Bosworth, "Pursuit." Bosworth, A. B. "Arrian, Alexander, and the Pursuit of Glory." Pages 447–53 in *A Companion to Greek and Roman Historiography*. Edited by John Marincola. 2 vols. Oxford: Blackwell, 2007.

Botermann, "Heidenapostel." Botermann, Helga. "Der Heiden apostel und sein Historiker. Zur historischen Kritik der Apostelgeschichte." *TBei* 24 (2, 1993): 62–84.

Botha, "Publishing." Botha, Pieter J. J. "'Publishing' a Gospel: Notes on Historical Constraints to Gospel Criticism." Pages 335–52 in *The Interface of Orality and Writing: Speaking, Seeing, Writing in the Shaping of New Genres*. Edited by Annette Weissenrieder and Robert B. Coote. WUNT 260. Tübingen: Mohr Siebeck, 2010. Repr. in BPC 11. Eugene, OR: Wipf & Stock, 2015.

Botha, "Rhetoric and Josephus." Botha, Pieter J. J. "History, Rhetoric, and the Writings of Josephus." *Neot* 31 (1, 1997): 1–20.

Bouffard et al., "Strategies." Bouffard, Nichole, et al. "Temporal Encoding Strategies Result in Boosts to Final Free Recall Performance Comparable to Spatial Ones." *Memory and Cognition* 46 (1, January 2018): 17–31.

Bourguignon, "Appendix." Bourguignon, Erika. "Appendix." Pages 359–76 in *Religion, Altered States of Consciousness, and Social Change*. Edited by Erika Bourguignon. Columbus: Ohio State University Press, 1973.

Bourguignon, "Introduction." Bourguignon, Erika. "Introduction: A Framework for the Comparative Study of Altered States of Consciousness." Pages 3–35 in *Religion, Altered*

States of Consciousness, and Social Change. Edited by Erika Bourguignon. Columbus: Ohio State University Press, 1973.

Bourguignon, "Spirit Possession Belief." Bourguignon, Erika. "Spirit Possession Belief and Social Structure." Pages 17–26 in *The Realm of the Extra-Human: Ideas and Actions.* Edited by Agehananda Bharati. The Hague: Mouton, 1976.

Bovon, *Luke.* Bovon, François. *Luke 1: A Commentary on the Gospel of Luke 1:1–9:50.* Edited by Helmut Koester. Translated by Christine M. Thomas. Hermeneia. Minneapolis: Fortress, 2002.

Bovon, *Theologian.* Bovon, François. *Luke the Theologian: Thirty-Three Years of Research (1950–1983).* Translated by Ken McKinney. Allison Park, PA: Pickwick, 1987.

Bowersock, *Fiction.* Bowersock, G. W. *Fiction as History: Nero to Julian.* Berkeley: University of California Press, 1994.

Bowie, "Apollonius." Bowie, Ewen. "Apollonius of Tyana: Tradition and Reality." *ANRW* 2.16.2 (1978): 1652–99.

Bowie, "Philostratus." Bowie, Ewen Lyall. "Philostratus: Writer of Fiction." Pages 181–99 in *Greek Fiction: The Greek Novel in Context.* Edited by J. R. Morgan and Richard Stoneman. London: Routledge, 1994.

Bowie, "Portrait." Bowie, Ewen. "Portrait of the Sophist as a Young Man." Pages 141–53 in *The Limits of Ancient Biography.* Edited by Brian McGing and Judith Mossman. Swansea, Wales: Classical Press of Wales, 2006.

Bowie, "Readership." Bowie, Ewen L. "The Readership of Greek Novels in the Ancient World." Pages 435–59 in *The Search for the Ancient Novel.* Edited by James Tatum. Baltimore: Johns Hopkins University Press, 1994.

Bowie, "Second Sophistic." Bowie, Ewen L. "Second Sophistic." *OCD*³ 1377–78.

Bowman, "Prophets." Bowman, John. "Prophets and Prophecy in Talmud and Midrash." *EvQ* 22 (2, 1950): 107–14; (3, 1950): 205–20; (4, 1950): 255–75.

Brack, *Historiography.* Brack, David. *Luke's Legato Historiography: Remembering the Continuity of Salvation History through Rhetorical Transitions.* Eugene, OR: Pickwick, 2017.

Bradley, "Suetonius." Bradley, Keith R. "Suetonius (Gaius Suetonius Tranquillus)." *OCD*³ 1451–52.

Brainerd, "Theory." Brainerd, C. J. "Fuzzy-Trace Theory: Memory." Pages 219–38 in *Human Learning and Memory: Advances in Theory and Application.* Edited by Chizuko Izawa and Nobuo Ohta. Mahwah, NJ: Erlbaum, 2005.

Branch, *Parting.* Branch, Taylor. *Parting the Waters: America in the King Years, 1954–63.* New York: Simon & Schuster, 1988.

Branham, "Cynicism." Branham, R. Bracht. "Cynicism: Ancient and Modern." Pages 597–603 in *Diogenes Laertius "Lives of the Eminent Philosophers."* Edited by James Miller. Translated by Pamela Mensch. New York: Oxford University Press, 2018.

Branham, *Eloquence.* Branham, R. Bracht. *Unruly Eloquence: Lucian and the Comedy of Traditions.* Cambridge, MA: Harvard University Press, 1989.

Bratt, "Monarchs." Bratt, Kenneth L. "Herodotus' Oriental Monarchs and Their Counsellors: A Study in Typical Narration." PhD diss., Princeton University, 1985.

Braun, *Jean.*   Braun, François-M. *Jean le théologien et son Evangile dans l'Église ancienne.* Paris: Librairie Lecoffre, 1959.

Bravo, "Antiquarianism."   Bravo, Benedetto. "Antiquarianism and History." Pages 515–27 in *A Companion to Greek and Roman Historiography.* Edited by John Marincola. 2 vols. Oxford: Blackwell, 2007.

Brawley, *Centering.*   Brawley, Robert L. *Centering on God: Method and Message in Luke-Acts.* Louisville: Westminster John Knox, 1990.

Breggen, "Scale."   Breggen, Hendrik van der. "Hume's Scale: How Hume Counts a Miracle's Improbability Twice." *PhilChr* 4 (2, 2002): 443–53.

Brewer, "Memory for Events."   Brewer, William F. "Memory for Randomly Sampled Autobiographical Events." Pages 21–90 in *Remembering Reconsidered: Ecological and Traditional Approaches to the Study of Memory.* Edited by U. Neisser and E. Winograd. Cambridge: Cambridge University Press, 1988.

Brewer, "Recollective Memory."   Brewer, William F. "What Is Recollective Memory?" Pages 19–66 in *Remembering Our Past: Studies in Autobiographical Memory.* Edited by David C. Rubin; Cambridge: Cambridge University Press, 1996.

Brickle, "Wax Tablet."   Brickle, Jeffrey E. "Wax Tablet." *DBAM* 454.

Bright, *History.*   Bright, John. *A History of Israel.* 3rd ed. Philadelphia: Westminster, 1981.

Broadhead, "Priests."   Broadhead, Edwin K. "Jesus and the Priests of Israel." Pages 125–44 in *Jesus from Judaism to Christianity: Continuum Approaches to the Historical Jesus.* Edited by Tom Holmén. European Studies on Christian Origins. LNTS 352. London: T&T Clark, 2007.

Broek, *Apocryphon.*   Broek, R. van den. *Pseudo-Cyril of Jerusalem "On the Life and the Passion of Christ": A Coptic Apocryphon.* Supplements to Vigiliae Christianae 118. Leiden: Brill, 2013.

Broggiato, "Artemon."   Broggiato, Maria. "Artemon of Pergamum (*FGrH* 569): A Historian in Context." *ClQ* 61 (2, 2011): 545–52.

Broshi, "Credibility."   Broshi, Magen. "The Credibility of Josephus." *JJS* 33 (1–2, 1982): 379–84.

Brown, *Death.*   Brown, Raymond E. *The Death of the Messiah—from Gethsemane to Grave: A Commentary on the Passion Narratives in the Four Gospels.* 2 vols. New York: Doubleday, 1994.

Brown, *Essays.*   Brown, Raymond E. *New Testament Essays.* Garden City, NY: Doubleday, 1968.

Brown, *Healing.*   Brown, Candy Gunther. *Global Pentecostal and Charismatic Healing.* Oxford: Oxford University Press, 2011.

Brown, *Historians.*   Brown, Truesdell S. *The Greek Historians.* Lexington, MA: D. C. Heath, 1973.

Brown, "Scrolls."   Brown, Raymond E. "The Dead Sea Scrolls and the New Testament." Pages 1–8 in *John and Qumran.* Edited by James H. Charlesworth. London: Geoffrey Chapman, 1972.

Brown et al., "Effects."   Brown, Candy Gunther, Stephen C. Mory, Rebecca Williams, and

Michael J. McClymond. "Study of the Therapeutic Effects of Proximal Intercessory Prayer (STEPP) on Auditory and Visual Impairments in Rural Mozambique." *SMedJ* 103 (9, September 2010): 864–69.

Browning, "Homer." Browning, Robert. "Homer in Byzantium." *Viator* 6 (1975): 15–33.

Brownlee, "Comparison." Brownlee, William H. "A Comparison of the Covenanters of the Dead Sea Scrolls with Pre-Christian Jewish Sects." *BA* 13 (3, September 1950): 49–72.

Brownson, "Introduction to *Anabasis*." Brownson, Carleton L. Introduction to *Anabasis*. Pages 231–38 in vol. 2 of *Xenophon*. Translated by Carleton L. Brownson, O. J. Todd, and E. C. Marchant. 4 vols. LCL. New York: G. P. Putnam's Sons, 1918–23.

Brownson, "Introduction to *Hellenica*." Brownson, Carleton L. "Introduction to *Hellenica*." Pages vii–xi in vol. 1 of *Xenophon*. Translated by Carleton L. Brownson, O. J. Todd, and E. C. Marchant. 4 vols. LCL. New York: G. P. Putnam's Sons, 1918–23.

Bruce, *Acts*. Bruce, F. F. *The Acts of the Apostles: The Greek Text, with Introduction and Commentary*. Grand Rapids: Eerdmans, 1951.

Bruce, "Date of Mark." Bruce, F. F. "The Date and Character of Mark." Pages 69–89 in *Jesus and the Politics of His Day*. Edited by Ernst Bammel and C. F. D. Moule. Cambridge: Cambridge University Press, 1984.

Bruce, *Documents*. Bruce, F. F. *The New Testament Documents: Are They Reliable?* 5th ed. Grand Rapids: Eerdmans; Leicester, UK: Inter-Varsity, 1981.

Bruce, *John*. Bruce, F. F. *The Gospel of John: Introduction, Exposition, and Notes*. Grand Rapids: Eerdmans, 1983.

Bruce, "Matthew." Bruce, Alexander Balmain. "Matthew." Pages 61–340 in vol. 1 of *The Expositor's Greek Testament*. Edited by W. Robertson Nicoll. 5 vols. New York: Hodder & Stoughton, 1897–1910. Repr., Grand Rapids: Eerdmans, 1979.

Bruce, "Name of Felix." Bruce, F. F. "The Full Name of the Procurator Felix." *JSNT* 1 (1978): 33–36.

Bruce, *Speeches in Acts*. Bruce, F. F. *The Speeches in the Acts of the Apostles*. London: Tyndale, 1942.

Bruce, "Speeches Thirty Years After." Bruce, F. F. "The Speeches in Acts—Thirty Years After." Pages 53–68 in *Reconciliation and Hope*. Edited by Robert Banks. Grand Rapids: Eerdmans, 1974.

Bruggen, *Narratives*. Bruggen, Jakob van. *Christ on Earth: The Gospel Narratives as History*. Translated by Nancy Forest-Flier. Grand Rapids: Baker, 1998. Original Dutch ed., Kampen: J. H. Kok, 1987.

Bruner and Fleisher Feldman, "Narrative." Bruner, Jerome, and Carol Fleisher Feldman. "Group Narrative as a Cultural Context of Autobiography." Pages 291–317 in *Remembering Our Past: Studies in Autobiographical Memory*. Edited by David C. Rubin. Cambridge: Cambridge University Press, 1996.

Brunner, *Erziehung*. Brunner, Helmut. *Altägyptische Erziehung*. Wiesbaden: Harrassowitz, 1957.

Bucher, "Evaluation." Bucher, Gregory S. "Toward a Literary Evaluation of Appian's *Civil*

Wars, Book 1." Pages 454–60 in *A Companion to Greek and Roman Historiography*. Edited by John Marincola. 2 vols. Oxford: Blackwell, 2007.

Budge, *Takla Hâymânôt*.   Budge, E. A. Wallis. *The Life of Takla Hâymânôt in the Version of Dabra Lîbanôs; and, The Miracles of Takla Hâymânôt in the Version of Dabra Lîbânôs; and, The Book of the Riches of Kings: The Ethiopic Texts, from the British Museum Ms. Oriental 723, Edited with English Translations, to Which Is Added an English Translation of the Waldebbân Version*. London: privately printed for Lady Meux, 1906.

Budson et al., "Memory."   Budson, A. E., J. S. Simons, J. D. Waring, A. L. Sullivan, T. Hussoin, and D. L. Schacter. "Memory for the September 11, 2001, Terrorist Attacks One Year Later in Patients with Alzheimer's Disease, Patients with Mild Cognitive Impairment, and Healthy Older Adults." *Cortex* 43 (2007): 875–88.

Bultmann, *Jesus and Word*.   Bultmann, Rudolf. *Jesus and the Word*. Translated by Louise Pettibone Smith and Erminie Huntress Lantero. New York: Scribner's, 1958.

Bultmann, *Tradition*.   Bultmann, Rudolf. *The History of the Synoptic Tradition*. Translated by John Marsh. 2nd ed. Oxford: Blackwell, 1968.

Bünker, "Disposition der Eleazarreden."   Bünker, Michael. "Die rhetorische Disposition der Eleazarreden (Josephus, *Bell.* 7,323–388)." *Kairos* 23 (1–2, 1981): 100–107.

Burge, "Siloam."   Burge, Gary M. "Siloam, Bethesda, and the Johannine Water Motif." Pages 259–69 in *Glimpses of Jesus through the Johannine Lens*. Vol. 3 of *John, Jesus, and History*. Edited by Paul N. Anderson, Felix Just, and Tim Thatcher. SBLSymS 44. ECL 18. Atlanta: SBL Press, 2016.

Burgersdijk, "Implications."   Burgersdijk, Diederik. "*Qui vitas aliorum scribere orditur*: Narratological Implications of Fictional Authors in the *Historia Augusta*." Pages 240–56 in *Writing Biography in Greece and Rome: Narrative Technique and Fictionalization*. Edited by Koen De Temmerman and Kristoffel Demoen. Cambridge: Cambridge University Press, 2016.

Burgess, "Pandita Ramabai."   Burgess, Ruth Vassar. "Pandita Ramabai: A Woman for All Seasons; Pandita Ramabai Saraswati Mary Dongre Medhavi (1858–1922)." *AJPS* 9 (2, 2006): 183–98.

Burkett, *Case*.   Burkett, Delbert. *The Case for Proto-Mark: A Study in the Synoptic Problem*. WUNT 399. Tübingen: Mohr Siebeck, 2018.

Burnette-Bletsch, "Jael."   Burnette-Bletsch, Rhonda. "At the Hands of a Woman: Rewriting Jael in Pseudo-Philo." *JSP* 17 (1998): 53–64.

Burney, *Aramaic Origin*.   Burney, C. F. *The Aramaic Origin of the Fourth Gospel*. Oxford: Clarendon, 1922.

Burney, *Poetry*.   Burney, C. F. *The Poetry of Our Lord*. Oxford: Clarendon, 1925.

Burns, *Debate*.   Burns, Robert M. *The Great Debate on Miracles: From Joseph Glanvill to David Hume*. Lewisburg, PA: Bucknell University Press, 1981.

Burridge, "Biography."   Burridge, Richard A. "Biography." Pages 371–91 in *Handbook of Classical Rhetoric in the Hellenistic Period, 330 B.C.–A.D. 400*. Edited by Stanley E. Porter. Leiden: Brill, 1997.

Burridge, "Biography, Ancient."   Burridge, Richard A. "Biography, Ancient." *DNTB* 167–70.

Burridge, *Comparison.*   Burridge, Richard A. *What Are the Gospels? A Comparison with Graeco-Roman Biography.* SNTSMS 70. Cambridge: Cambridge University Press, 1992.

Burridge, "Genre."   Burridge, Richard A. "Biography as the Gospels' Literary Genre." *RCL* 38 (1, 2013): 9–30.

Burridge, "Genre of Acts."   Burridge, Richard A. "The Genre of Acts—Revisited." Pages 3–28 in *Reading Acts Today: Essays in Honour of Loveday C. A. Alexander.* Edited by Steve Walton et al. LNTS 427. London: T&T Clark, 2011.

Burridge, *Gospels.*   Burridge, Richard A. *What Are the Gospels? A Comparison with Graeco-Roman Biography.* 2nd ed. Grand Rapids: Eerdmans, 2004.

Burridge, "Gospels and Acts."   Burridge, Richard A. "The Gospels and Acts." Pages 507–32 in *Handbook of Classical Rhetoric in the Hellenistic Period, 330 B.C.–A.D. 400.* Edited by Stanley E. Porter. Leiden: Brill, 1997.

Burridge, "Gospels and Biography."   Burridge, Richard A. "Gospels and Biography, 2000–2018: A Critical Review and Implications for Future Research." Pages 1–113 in *What Are the Gospels? A Comparison with Graeco-Roman Biography.* 25th ann. ed. Waco, TX: Baylor University Press, 2018.

Burridge, "People."   Burridge, Richard A. "About People, by People, for People: Gospel Genre and Audiences." Pages 113–46 in *The Gospels for All Christians: Rethinking the Gospel Audiences.* Edited by Richard Bauckham. Grand Rapids: Eerdmans, 1998.

Burridge, "Reading."   Burridge, Richard A. "Reading the Gospels as Biography." Pages 31–49 in *The Limits of Ancient Biography.* Edited by Brian McGing and Judith Mossman. Swansea, Wales: Classical Press of Wales, 2006.

Burridge, "Review."   Burridge, Richard A. "*The Art of Biography in Antiquity*: A Review." *JSNT* 37 (4, June 2015): 474–79.

Burrus, "Desiring."   Burrus, Virginia. "Desiring Women: Xanthippe, Polyxena, Rebecca." Pages 9–27 in *Reading and Teaching Ancient Fiction: Jewish, Christian, and Greco-Roman Narratives.* Edited by Sara R. Johnson, Rubén R. Dupertuis, and Christine Shea. WGRWSup 11. Atlanta: SBL Press, 2018.

Buster, "Genre."   Buster, Aubrey E. "Genre." Pages 152–55 in *The Dictionary of the Bible and Ancient Media.* Edited by Tom Thatcher, Chris Keith, Raymond F. Person Jr., and Elsie R. Stern. New York: Bloomsbury T&T Clark, 2017.

Buszard, "Parallel."   Buszard, Bradley. "A Plutarchan Parallel to Arrian *Anabasis* 7.1." *GRBS* 50 (4, 2010): 565–85.

Byatt, "Numbers."   Byatt, Anthony. "Josephus and Population Numbers in First Century Palestine." *PEQ* 105 (1, 1973): 51–60.

Byrskog, "Century."   Byrskog, Samuel. "A Century with the *Sitz im Leben*: From Form-Critical Setting to Gospel Community and Beyond." *ZNW* 98 (2007): 1–27.

Byrskog, "Church."   Byrskog, Samuel. "The Early Church as a Narrative Fellowship: An Exploratory Study of the Performance of the *Chreia.*" *TTKi* 78 (3–4, 2007): 207–26.

Byrskog, "Eyewitnesses."   Byrskog, Samuel. "The Eyewitnesses as Interpreters of the Past: Reflections on Richard Bauckham's *Jesus and the Eyewitnesses.*" *JSNT* 6 (2008): 157–68.

Byrskog, "Form Criticism."   Byrskog, Samuel. "Form Criticism." *DBAM* 142–46.

Byrskog, "Gerhardsson." Byrskog, Samuel. "Gerhardsson, Birger." *DBAM* 155–56.

Byrskog, "Hermeneutics." Byrskog, Samuel. "Towards a Hermeneutics of Memory: Suggestions for Future Research." Paper presented to "Memory, Narrative, and Christology in the Synoptic Gospels" Seminar at the Annual Meeting of the Society for New Testament Studies. Athens, Greece, August 10, 2018.

Byrskog, "History." Byrskog, Samuel. "History or Story in Acts—a Middle Way? The "We" Passages, Historical Intertexture, and Oral History." Pages 257–83 in *Contextualizing Acts: Lukan Narrative and Greco-Roman Discourse*. Edited by Todd Penner and Caroline Vander Stichele. SBLSymS 20. Atlanta: SBL, 2003.

Byrskog, *Story*. Byrskog, Samuel. *Story as History, History as Story: The Gospel Tradition in the Context of Ancient Oral History*. Tübingen: Mohr Siebeck, 2000. Repr., Leiden: Brill, 2002.

Byrskog, *Teacher*. Byrskog, Samuel. *Jesus the Only Teacher: Didactic Authority and Transmission in Ancient Israel, Ancient Judaism, and the Matthean Community*. ConBNT 24. Stockholm: Almqvist & Wiksell International, 1994.

Byrskog, "Teacher." Byrskog, Samuel. "Jesus the Only Teacher: Further Thoughts." Pages 36–46 in *Treasures New and Old: Essays in Honor of Donald A. Hagner*. Edited by Carl S. Sweatman and Clifford B. Kvidahl. GlossaHouse Festschrift Series 1. Wilmore, KY: GlossaHouse, 2017.

Cadbury, *Acts in History*. Cadbury, Henry J. *The Book of Acts in History*. London: Adam & Charles Black, 1955.

Cadbury, *Making*. Cadbury, Henry J. *The Making of Luke-Acts*. London: SPCK, 1968.

Cadbury, "We." Cadbury, Henry J. "'We' and 'I' Passages in Luke-Acts." *NTS* 3 (2, 1957): 128–32.

Cadbury, Foakes-Jackson, and Lake, "Writing History." Cadbury, Henry J., F. J. Foakes-Jackson, and Kirsopp Lake. "The Greek and Jewish Traditions of Writing History." *BegC* 2:7–29.

Caird, *Language*. Caird, G. B. *The Language and Imagery of the Bible*. Philadelphia: Westminster, 1980.

Callan, "Preface." Callan, Terrance. "The Preface of Luke-Acts and Historiography." *NTS* 31 (4, 1985): 576–81.

Cambiano, "Diogenes Laertius." Cambiano, Giuseppe. "Diogenes Laertius and Philosophical Lives in Antiquity." Pages 574–77 in *Diogenes Laertius "Lives of the Eminent Philosophers."* Edited by James Miller. Translated by Pamela Mensch. New York: Oxford University Press, 2018.

Campbell, *Faithfulness*. Campbell, Sue. *Our Faithfulness to the Past: The Ethics and Politics of Memory*. Oxford: Oxford University Press, 2014.

Campbell, "Journeys." Campbell, Thomas H. "Paul's 'Missionary Journeys' as Reflected in His Letters." *JBL* 74 (2, 1955): 80–87.

Campbell, "Memory." Campbell, Sue. "Memory, Truth, and the Search for an Authentic Past." Pages 175–95 in *Memory Matters: Contexts for Understanding Sexual Abuse Recollections*. Edited by Janice Haaken and Paula Reavey. New York: Routledge, 2010.

Campbell, "Narrator." Campbell, William Sanger. "The Narrator as 'He,' 'Me,' and 'We': Grammatical Person in Ancient Histories and in the Acts of the Apostles." *JBL* 129 (2, 2010): 385–407.

Cancik, "Bios." Cancik, Hubert. "Bios und Logos. Formengeschichtliche Untersuchungen zu Lukians 'Leben des Demonax.'" Pages 115–30 in *Markus-Philologie. Historische, literargeschichtliche und stilistische Untersuchungen zum zweiten Evangelium*. Edited by H. Cancik. WUNT 33. Tübingen: Mohr Siebeck, 1984.

Cancik, "Gattung." Cancik, Hubert. "Die Gattung Evangelium. Das Evangelium Markus im Rahmen der antiken Historiographie." Pages 85–113 in *Markus-Philologie. Historische, literargeschichtliche und stilistische Untersuchungen zum zweiten Evangelium*. Edited by Hubert Cancik. WUNT 33. Tübingen: Mohr Siebeck, 1984.

Canevet, "Remarques." Canevet, Mariette. "Remarques sur l'utilisation du genre littéraire historique par Philon d'Alexandrie dans la *Vita Moysis*, ou Moïse général en chef-prophète." *RevScRel* 60 (3–4, 1986): 189–206.

Cangh, "Miracles." Cangh, Jean-Marie Van. "Miracles grecs, rabbiniques et évangéliques." Pages 213–36 in *Miracles and Imagery in Luke and John: Festschrift Ulrich Busse*. Edited by J. Verheyden, G. van Belle, and J. G. van der Watt. BETL 218. Leuven: Uitgeverij Peeters, 2008.

Capes, *Christ*. Capes, David B. *The Divine Christ: Paul, the Lord Jesus, and the Scriptures of Israel*. Grand Rapids: Baker Academic, 2018.

Capes, *Texts*. Capes, David B. *Old Testament Yahweh Texts in Paul's Christology*. WUNT 2.47. Tübingen: Mohr, 1992.

Capps, *Village Psychiatrist*. Capps, Donald. *Jesus the Village Psychiatrist*. Louisville: Westminster John Knox, 2008.

Capra, "Detour." Capra, Andrea. "Detour en Route in the Aegean Sea? Xenophon of Ephesus 5.10.2." *CP* 107 (1, 2012): 70–74.

Cardeña, Lynn, and Krippner, *Varieties*. Cardeña, Etzel, Steven Jay Lynn, and Stanley Krippner, eds. *Varieties of Anomalous Experience: Examining the Scientific Evidence*. Washington, DC: American Psychological Association, 2000.

Carey, "Importance." Carey, Holly J. "The Importance of the 'How' and 'Why' in Ancient Biographies." Pages 319–22 in Keener and Wright, *Biographies and Jesus*.

Carlson, "Papias." Carlson, Stephen C. "Papias (on Writing)." *DBAM* 269–70.

Carr, *Formation*. Carr, David M. *The Formation of the Hebrew Bible: A New Reconstruction*. New York: Oxford University Press, 2011.

Carr, *Writing*. Carr, David M. *Writing on the Tablet of the Heart: Origins of Scripture and Literature*. New York: Oxford, 2005.

Carroll, *Luke*. Carroll, John T. *Luke: A Commentary*. Louisville: Westminster John Knox, 2002.

Carruthers, *Book of Memory*. Carruthers, Mary J. *The Book of Memory: A Study of Memory in Medieval Culture*. 2nd ed. Cambridge: Cambridge University Press, 2008.

Carson, "Matthew." Carson, D. A. "Matthew." Pages 3–599 in vol. 8 of *The Expositor's Bible Commentary*. Edited by Frank Gaebelein. Grand Rapids: Zondervan, 1984.

Carson, "Tradition." Carson, D. A. "Historical Tradition in the Fourth Gospel: After Dodd, What?" Pages 83–145 in *Studies of History and Tradition in the Four Gospels*. Vol. 2 of *Gospel Perspectives*. Edited by R. T. France and David Wenham. Sheffield: JSOT Press, 1981.

Carson, Moo, and Morris, *Introduction*. Carson, D. A., Douglas J. Moo, and Leon Morris. *An Introduction to the New Testament*. Grand Rapids: Zondervan, 1992.

Cartledge, *Agesilaos*. Cartledge, Paul. *Agesilaos and the Crisis of Sparta*. London: Duckworth, 1987.

Cary and Haarhoff, *Life*. Cary, M., and T. J. Haarhoff. *Life and Thought in the Greek and Roman World*. 4th ed. London: Methuen, 1946.

Casey, *Evidence*. Casey, Maurice. *Jesus: Evidence and Arguments or Mythicist Myths?* London: A&C Black, 2014.

Casey, *Sources*. Casey, Maurice. *Aramaic Sources of Mark's Gospel*. SNTSMS 102. New York: Cambridge University Press, 1999.

Castleberry, "Impact." Castleberry, Joseph Lee. "It's Not Just for Ignorant People Anymore: The Future Impact of University Graduates on the Development of the Ecuadorian Assemblies of God." EdD diss., Teachers College, Columbia University, 1999.

Cave, "Parables." Cave, Cyril H. "The Parables and the Scriptures." *NTS* 11 (1965): 374–87.

Champion, "Aetolia." Champion, Craige B. "Polybius and Aetolia: A Historiographical Approach." Pages 356–62 in *A Companion to Greek and Roman Historiography*. Edited by John Marincola. 2 vols. Oxford: Blackwell, 2007.

Champlin, "Tiberius." Champlin, Edward. "Tiberius the Wise." *Historia* 57 (4, 2008): 408–25.

Chance, *Acts*. Chance, J. Bradley. *Acts*. SHBC. Macon, GA: Smyth & Helwys, 2007.

Chance, "Fiction." Chance, J. Bradley. "Fiction in Ancient Biography: An Approach to a Sensitive Issue in Gospel Interpretation." *PRSt* 18 (2, 1991): 125–42.

Chance, "Perspectives." Chance, J. Bradley. "Talbert's New Perspectives on Luke-Acts: The ABC's of Ancient Lives." Pages 181–201 in *Cadbury, Knox, and Talbert: American Contributions to the Study of Acts*. Edited by Mikeal C. Parsons and Joseph B. Tyson. SBLBSNA 18. SBLCP. Atlanta: Scholars Press, 1992.

Chance, "Prognostications." Chance, J. Bradley. "Divine Prognostications and the Movement of Story: An Intertextual Exploration of Xenophon's *Ephesian Tale* and the Acts of the Apostles." Pages 219–34 in *Ancient Fiction and Early Christian Narrative*. Edited by Ronald F. Hock, J. Bradley Chance, and Judith Perkins. SBLSymS 6. Atlanta: SBL, 1998.

Chancey, *Galilee*. Chancey, Mark. *Greco-Roman Culture and the Galilee of Jesus*. SNTSMS 134. New York: Cambridge University Press, 2006.

Chancey, "Jewish." Chancey, Mark A. "How Jewish Was Jesus' Galilee?" *BAR* 33 (4, 2007): 42–50, 76.

Chancey and Meyers, "Sepphoris." Chancey, Mark, and Eric M. Meyers, "How Jewish Was Sepphoris in Jesus' Time?" *BAR* 26 (4, 2000): 18–33, 61.

Chang, *Rape*. Chang, Iris. *The Rape of Nanking: The Forgotten Holocaust of World War II*. London: Hachette UK, 2014.

Chaplin, "Conversations." Chaplin, Jane D. "Conversations in History: Arrian and Herodotus, Parmenio and Alexander." *GRBS* 51 (4, 2011): 613–33.

Chapman, "Cannibalism." Chapman, Honora Howell. "Josephus and the Cannibalism of Mary (*BJ* 6.199–219)." Pages 419–26 in *A Companion to Greek and Roman Historiography*. Edited by John Marincola. 2 vols. Oxford: Blackwell, 2007.

Charlesworth, "Jesus, Literature, and Archaeology." Charlesworth, James H. "Jesus, Early Jewish Literature, and Archaeology." Pages 177–98 in *Jesus' Jewishness: Exploring the Place of Jesus within Early Judaism*. Edited by James H. Charlesworth. Philadelphia: American Interfaith Institute. New York: Crossroad, 1991.

Charlesworth, *Jesus within Judaism*. Charlesworth, James H. *Jesus within Judaism: New Light from Exciting Archaeological Discoveries*. ABRL. New York: Doubleday, 1988.

Charlesworth, *Mirrored in John*. Charlesworth, James H. *Jesus as Mirrored in John: The Genius in the New Testament*. New York: T&T Clark, 2018.

Charlesworth, *Pseudepigrapha*. Charlesworth, James H. *The Old Testament Pseudepigrapha and the New Testament: Prolegomena for the Study of Christian Origins*. SNTSMS 54. Cambridge: Cambridge University Press, 1985.

Charlesworth, "Shift." Charlesworth, James H. "The Historical Jesus in the Fourth Gospel: A Paradigm Shift?" *JSHJ* 8 (1, 2010): 3–46.

Charlesworth, "Sketch." Charlesworth, James H. "The Historical Jesus: Sources and a Sketch." Pages 84–128 in *Jesus Two Thousand Years Later*. Edited by James H. Charlesworth and Walter P. Weaver. FSCS. Harrisburg, PA: Trinity Press International, 2000.

Charlesworth, *Symposium*. Charlesworth, James H., with Jolyon G. R. Pruszinski, eds. *Jesus Research: The Gospel of John in Historical Inquiry; The Third Princeton-Prague Symposium on Jesus Research, Princeton 2016*. New York: Bloomsbury T&T Clark, forthcoming.

Charlesworth, "Theology." Charlesworth, James H. "The Historical Jesus and Exegetical Theology." *PSB* 22 (1, 2001): 45–63.

Charlesworth and Aviam, "Galilee." Charlesworth, James H., and Mordechai Aviam. "Reconstructing First-Century Galilee: Reflections on Ten Major Problems." Pages 103–37 in *Jesus Research: New Methodologies and Perceptions; The Second Princeton-Prague Symposium on Jesus Research*. Edited by James Charlesworth, with Brian Rhea and Petr Pokorný. Grand Rapids: Eerdmans, 2014.

Charlesworth and Evans, "Agrapha." Charlesworth, James H., and Craig A. Evans. "Jesus in the Agrapha and Apocryphal Gospels." Pages 479–533 in *Studying the Historical Jesus: Evaluations of the State of Current Research*. Edited by Bruce Chilton and Craig A. Evans. NTTS 19. Leiden: Brill, 1994.

Charlesworth, Rhea, and Pokorný, *Jesus Research*. Charlesworth, James H., Brian Rhea, and Petr Pokorný, eds. *Jesus Research: New Methodologies and Perceptions; The Second Princeton-Prague Symposium on Jesus Research*. Grand Rapids: Eerdmans, 2014.

Chen, *Luke*. Chen, Diane G. *Luke*. New Covenant Commentary. Eugene, OR: Cascade, 2017.

Cheon, "Plagues."   Cheon, Samuel. "Josephus and the Story of the Plagues: An Appraisal of a Moralising Interpretation." *AJT* 18 (1, 2004): 220–30.

Chesnut, *Born Again in Brazil.*   Chesnut, R. Andrew. *Born Again in Brazil: The Pentecostal Boom and the Pathogens of Poverty.* New Brunswick, NJ: Rutgers University Press, 1997.

Chilton, "Announcement."   Chilton, Bruce. "Announcement in Nazara: An Analysis of Luke 4:16–21." Pages 147–72 in *Studies of History and Tradition in the Four Gospels.* Vol. 2 of *Gospel Perspectives.* Edited by R. T. France and David Wenham. Sheffield: JSOT Press, 1981.

Chilton, *Rabbi Jesus.*   Chilton, Bruce. *Rabbi Jesus: An Intimate Biography.* New York: Doubleday, 2000.

Chilton, *Study.*   Chilton, Bruce. *Beginning New Testament Study.* Grand Rapids: Eerdmans, 1986.

Chitwood, *Death.*   Chitwood, Ava. *Death by Philosophy: The Biographical Tradition in the Life and Death of the Archaic Philosophers Empedocles, Heraclitus, and Democritus.* Ann Arbor: University of Michigan Press, 2004.

Chiu, "Importance."   Chiu, Angeline. "The Importance of Being Julia: Civil War, Historical Revision, and the Mutable Past in Lucan's Pharsalia." *CJ* 105 (4, 2010): 343–60.

Chrétien, "Exchange."   Chrétien, Jean-Pierre. "Confronting the Unequal Exchange of the Oral and the Written." Pages 75–90 in *African Historiographies: What History for Which Africa?* Edited by Bogumil Jewsiewicki and David Newbury. SSAMD 12. Beverly Hills, CA: Sage, 1986.

Christian, "Themistocles."   Christian, Timothy J. "Cornelius Nepos's *Themistocles*: A Targeted Comparison with the Histories of Herodotus and Thucydides, with Implications for the Historical Reliability of the Gospels." Pages 103–41 in Keener and Wright, *Biographies and Jesus.*

Christianson and Safer, "Emotional Events."   Christianson, Sven-Åke, and Martin A. Safer. "Emotional Events and Emotions in Autobiographical Memories." Pages 218–43 in *Remembering Our Past: Studies in Autobiographical Memory.* Edited by David C. Rubin. Cambridge: Cambridge University Press, 1996.

Clark, "Education."   Clark, Timothy. "Jewish Education in the Hellenistic Period and the Old Testament." *St. Vladimir's Theological Quarterly* 54 (3–4, 2010): 281–301.

Clark, *Parallel Lives.*   Clark, Andrew C. *Parallel Lives: The Relation of Paul to the Apostles in the Lucan Perspective.* Carlisle, UK: Paternoster, 2001.

Clark and Clark, *Psycholinguistics.*   Clark, Herbert H., and Eve V. Clark. *Psychology and Language: An Introduction to Psycholinguistics.* New York: Harcourt Brace Jovanovich, 1971.

Clay, "Lucian."   Clay, Diskin. "Lucian of Samosata: Four Philosophical Lives (Nigrinus, Demonax, Peregrinus, Alexander Pseudomantis)." *ANRW* 2.36.5 (1992): 3406–50.

Clifford, "Moses."   Clifford, Hywel. "Moses as Philosopher-Sage in Philo." Pages 151–67 in *Moses in Biblical and Extra-biblical Traditions.* Edited by Axel Graupner and Michael Wolter. BZAW 372. Berlin: de Gruyter, 2007.

Coady, *Testimony.* Coady, C. A. J. *Testimony: A Philosophical Study.* Oxford: Clarendon, 1992.

Cohen, "Everyday Memory." Cohen, Gillian. "Everyday Memory." Pages 1–20 in *Memory in the Real World.* Edited by Gillian Cohen and Martin A. Conway. Hove, East Sussex: Psychology Press, 2007.

Cohen, "Evidence." Cohen, Shaye J. D. "Pagan and Christian Evidence on the Ancient Synagogue." Pages 159–81 in *The Synagogue in Late Antiquity.* Edited by Lee I. Levine. Philadelphia: ASOR, 1986.

Cohen, *Josephus.* Cohen, Shaye J. D. *Josephus in Galilee and Rome: His Vita and Development as a Historian.* Edited by William V. Harris. Vol. 3. Columbia Studies in the Classical Tradition. Leiden: Brill, 1979.

Cohen, "Josephus and Scripture." Cohen, Naomi G. "Josephus and Scripture: Is Josephus' Treatment of the Scriptural Narrative Similar throughout the *Antiquities* I–XI?" *JQR* 54 (4, 1964): 311–32.

Cohen, *Maccabees.* Cohen, Shaye J. D. *From the Maccabees to the Mishnah.* LEC 7. Philadelphia: Westminster, 1987.

Cohen, "Masada." Cohen, Shaye J. D. "Masada: Literary Tradition, Archaeological Remains, and the Credibility of Josephus." *JJS* 33 (1982): 385–405.

Cohen, "Memory for Knowledge." Cohen, Gillian. "Memory for Knowledge: General Knowledge and Expert Knowledge." Pages 207–26 in *Memory in the Real World.* Edited by Gillian Cohen and Martin A. Conway. Hove, East Sussex: Psychology Press, 2007.

Cohen, "Overview." Cohen, Gillian. "Overview: Conclusions and Speculations." Pages 381–90 in *Memory in the Real World.* Edited by Gillian Cohen and Martin A. Conway. Hove, East Sussex: Psychology Press, 2007.

Cohen, "What Happened?" Cohen, Shaye J. D. "What Really Happened at Masada?" *Moment* 13 (5, 1988): 28–35.

Cohn, *Distinction.* Cohn, Dorrit. *The Distinction of Fiction.* Baltimore: Johns Hopkins University Press, 1999.

Cohn, "Lives." Cohn, Dorrit. "Fictional versus Historical Lives: Borderlines and Borderline Cases." *Journal of Narrative Technique* 19 (1, 1989): 3–24.

Cole and Scribner, *Culture.* Cole, Michael, and Sylvia Scribner, *Culture and Thought: A Psychological Introduction.* New York: Wiley & Sons, 1974.

Collins, *Mark.* Collins, Adela Yarbro. *Mark: A Commentary.* Minneapolis: Fortress, 2007.

Collins, *Written.* Collins, Raymond F. *These Things Have Been Written: Studies on the Fourth Gospel.* Louvain Theological and Pastoral Monographs 2. Louvain: Peeters, 1990.

Conway, "Autobiographical Knowledge." Conway, Martin A. "Autobiographical Knowledge and Autobiographical Memories." Pages 67–93 in *Remembering Our Past: Studies in Autobiographical Memory.* Edited by David C. Rubin. Cambridge: Cambridge University Press, 1996.

Conway, Cohen, and Stanhope, "Retention." Conway, Martin A., Gillian Cohen, and Nicola Stanhope. "On the Very Long-Term Retention of Knowledge Acquired through

Formal Education: Twelve Years of Cognitive Psychology." *JExpPscy: General* 120 (1991): 395–409.

Conybeare, "Introduction." Conybeare, F. C. "Introduction." Pages v–xv in vol. 1 of Philostratus, *The Life of Apollonius of Tyana*. Translated by F. C. Conybeare. 2 vols. LCL. Cambridge, MA: Harvard University Press, 1912.

Conzelmann, *Acts*. Conzelmann, Hans. *A Commentary on the Acts of the Apostles*. Edited by Eldon Jay Epp, with Christopher R. Matthews. Translated by James Limburg, A. Thomas Kraabel, and Donald H. Juel. Hermeneia. Philadelphia: Fortress, 1987.

Cook, *Interpretation*. Cook, John Granger. *The Interpretation of the New Testament in Greco-Roman Paganism*. Peabody, MA: Hendrickson, 2002. Orig., Tübingen: J. C. B. Mohr, 2000.

Cook, *Muhammad*. Cook, Michael. *Muhammad*. New York: Oxford University Press, 1983.

Cook, "Use." Cook, Brad L. "Plutarch's Use of *legetai*: Narrative Design and Source in *Alexander*." *GRBS* 42 (4, 2001): 329–60.

Copeland, *History*. Copeland, Rita, ed. *The Oxford History of Classical Reception*. Vol. 1: *800–1558*. Oxford: Oxford University Press, 2016.

Corbin, Crawford, and Vavra, "Misremembering Emotion." Corbin, Jonathan C., L. Elizabeth Crawford, and Dylan T. Vavra. "Misremembering Emotion: Inductive Category Effects for Complex Emotional Stimuli." *Memory and Cognition* 45 (5, July 2017): 691–98.

Cotter, "Miracle." Cotter, Wendy. "Miracle." *NIDB* 4:99–106.

Cotter, *Miracle Stories*. Cotter, Wendy J. *The Christ of the Miracle Stories: Portrait through Encounter*. Grand Rapids: Baker Academic, 2010.

Cotton and Geiger, "Yyn." Cotton, Hannah M., and Joseph Geiger. "Yyn lhwrdws hmlk." *Cathedra* 53 (1989): 3–12.

Cox, *Biography*. Cox, Patricia. *Biography in Late Antiquity: A Quest for the Holy Man*. Transformation of the Classical Heritage 5. Berkeley: University of California Press, 1983.

Craffert, "Healer." Craffert, Pieter F. "Crossan's Historical Jesus as Healer, Exorcist, and Miracle Worker." *R&T* 10 (3–4, 2003): 243–66.

Craffert, *Life*. Craffert, Pieter F. *The Life of a Galilean Shaman: Jesus of Nazareth in Anthropological-Historical Perspective*. Matrix: The Bible in Mediterranean Context. Eugene, OR: Cascade, 2008.

Cramer, "Miracles." Cramer, John A. "Miracles and David Hume." *Perspectives on Science and Christian Faith* 40 (3, September 1988): 129–37.

Crapanzaro and Garrison, *Case Studies*. Crapanzaro, Vincent, and Vivian Garrison. *Case Studies in Spirit Possession*. New York: Wiley & Sons, 1977.

Cribiore, *Gymnastics*. Cribiore, Raffaella. *Gymnastics of the Mind: Greek Education in Hellenistic and Roman Egypt*. Princeton: Princeton University Press, 2001.

Croke, "Historiography." Croke, Brian. "Late Antique Historiography, 250–650 CE." Pages 567–81 in *A Companion to Greek and Roman Historiography*. Edited by John Marincola. 2 vols. Oxford: Blackwell, 2007.

Crook, "Distortion." Crook, Zeba. "Collective Memory Distortion and the Quest for the Historical Jesus." *JSHJ* 11 (3, 2013): 53–76.

Crook, "Memory Theory." Crook, Zeba. "Matthew, Memory Theory, and the New No Quest." *HTS/TS* 70 (1, 2014), 11 pages.

Crooks, "Psychology." Crooks, Mark. "The Psychology of Demon Possession: The Occult Personality." *Journal of Mind and Behavior* 39 (4, Autumn 2018): 257–344.

Cross, "Genres." Cross, Anthony R. "Genres of the New Testament." *DNTB* 402–11.

Crossan, *Birth*. Crossan, John Dominic. *The Birth of Christianity: Discovering What Happened in the Years Immediately after the Execution of Jesus*. San Francisco: Harper, 1999.

Crossan, *Historical Jesus*. Crossan, John Dominic. *The Historical Jesus: The Life of a Mediterranean Jewish Peasant*. San Francisco: HarperSanFrancisco, 1991.

Crossan, "Necessary." Crossan, John Dominic. "Why Is Historical Jesus Research Necessary?" Pages 7–37 in *Jesus Two Thousand Years Later*. Edited by James H. Charlesworth and Walter P. Weaver. FSCS. Harrisburg, PA: Trinity Press International, 2000.

Crossley, *Date*. Crossley, James G. *The Date of Mark's Gospel: Insight from the Law in Earliest Christianity*. JSNTSup 266. New York: T&T Clark, 2004.

Cueva, "Longus." Cueva, Edmund P. "Longus and Thucydides: A New Interpretation." *GRBS* 39 (4, 1998): 429–40.

Culpepper, *Anatomy*. Culpepper, R. Alan. *Anatomy of the Fourth Gospel: A Study in Literary Design*. Philadelphia: Fortress, 1983.

Culpepper, *Gospel and Letters*. Culpepper, R. Alan. *The Gospel and Letters of John*. IBT. Nashville: Abingdon, 1998.

Culpepper, *School*. Culpepper, R. Alan. *The Johannine School: An Evaluation of the Johannine-School Hypothesis Based on an Investigation of the Nature of Ancient Schools*. SBLDS 26. Missoula, MT: Scholars Press, 1975.

Culy, Parsons, and Stigall, *Luke*. Culy, Martin M., Mikeal C. Parsons, and Joshua J. Stigall. *Luke: A Handbook on the Greek Text*. Waco, TX: Baylor University Press, 2010.

Curchin, "Literacy." Curchin, Leonard A. "Literacy in the Roman Provinces: Qualitative and Quantitative Data from Central Spain." *AJP* 116 (3, 1995): 461–76

Curran, "War." Curran, John R. "The Jewish War: Some Neglected Regional Factors." *CW* 101 (1, 2007): 75–91.

Cuvigny, "Finds of Papyri." Cuvigny, Hélène. "The Finds of Papyri: The Archaeology of Papyri." Pages 30–58 in *The Oxford Handbook of Papyrology*. Edited by Roger S. Bagnall. Oxford: Oxford University Press, 2011.

Dab, Claes, Morais, and Shallice, "Confabulation." Dab, Saskia, Thierry Claes, José Morais, and Tim Shallice. "Confabulation with a Selective Descriptor Process Impairment." *Cognitive Neuropsychology* 16 (3–5, 1999): 215–42.

Dalman, *Jesus-Jeshua*. Dalman, Gustaf. *Jesus-Jeshua: Studies in the Gospels*. New York: Macmillan, 1929.

Damgaard, *Recasting Moses*. Damgaard, Finn. *Recasting Moses: The Memory of Moses in Biographical and Autobiographical Narratives in Ancient Judaism and Fourth-Century Christianity*. Early Christianity in the Context of Antiquity 13. Frankfurt: Lang, 2013.

Damon, "Rhetoric." Damon, Cynthia. "Rhetoric and Historiography." Pages 439–50 in

A Companon to Roman Rhetoric. Edited by William Dominik and Jon Hall. BCAW. Oxford: Blackwell, 2007.

Damon, "Source." Damon, Cynthia. "From Source to *sermo*: Narrative Technique in Livy 34.54.4–8." *AJP* 118 (2, 1997): 251–66.

Damon, *Tacitus: Histories*. Damon, Cynthia. *Tacitus: Histories Book I*. Cambridge: Cambridge University Press, 2003.

D'Angelo, "Background." D'Angelo, Thomas P. "The Rabbinic Background of the Parables of Jesus." *CathW* 235 (1992): 63–67.

Dann, "Conclusion." Dann, G. Elijah. "Conclusion." Pages 27–76 in Richard Rorty. *An Ethics for Today: Finding Common Ground between Philosophy and Religion*. New York: Columbia University Press, 2011.

Darbo-Peschanski, "Origin." Darbo-Peschanski, Catherine. "The Origin of Greek Historiography." Pages 27–38 in *A Companion to Greek and Roman Historiography*. Edited by John Marincola. 2 vols. Oxford: Blackwell, 2007.

Daube, *New Testament and Judaism*. Daube, David. *The New Testament and Rabbinic Judaism*. London: University of London, Athlone Press, 1956. Repr., Peabody, MA: Hendrickson, 1996.

Davies, *Healer*. Davies, Stevan L. *Jesus the Healer: Possession, Trance, and the Origins of Christianity*. New York: Continuum, 1995.

Davies, *Invitation*. Davies, W. D. *Invitation to the New Testament: A Guide to Its Main Witnesses*. Garden City, NY: Doubleday, 1966.

Davies, "Reflexions." Davies, W. D. "Reflexions on Tradition: The Aboth Revisited." Pages 129–37 in *Christian History and Interpretation: Studies Presented to John Knox*. Edited by W. R. Farmer, C. F. D. Moule, and R. R. Niebuhr. Cambridge: Cambridge University Press, 1967.

Davies, *Rhetoric*. Davies, Margaret. *Rhetoric and Reference in the Fourth Gospel*. JSNTSup 69. Sheffield: JSOT Press, 1992.

Davies, "Storytellers." Davies, Rhiannon J. "The Middle East's Travelling Storytellers." BBC News, Nov. 20, 2018. http://www.bbc.com/travel/story/20181119-the-middle-easts -travelling-storytellers.

Davies and Allison, *Matthew*. Davies, W. D., and Dale C. Allison. *A Critical and Exegetical Commentary on the Gospel according to Saint Matthew*. 3 vols. ICC. Edinburgh: T&T Clark, 1988–97.

Davis, "Evaluations." Davis, Peter J. "'Since My Part Has Been Well Played': Conflicting Evaluations of Augustus." *Ramus* 28 (1, 1999): 1–15.

Davis, "Terence Interrupted." Davis, Josiah E. "Terence Interrupted: Literary Biography and the Reception of the Terentian Canon." *AJP* 135 (3, Sept. 2014): 387–409.

Day, *Believing*. Day, Abby. *Believing in Belonging: Belief and Social Identity in the Modern World*. Oxford: Oxford University Press, 2011.

Day and Keyes, *Documents*. Day, John, and Clinton Walker Keyes. *Tax Documents from Theadelphia: Papyri of the Second Century A.D.* New York: Columbia University Press, 1956.

DeConick, "Memory." DeConick, April D. "Human Memory and the Sayings of Jesus: Contemporary Exercises in the Transmission of Jesus Tradition." Pages 135–79 in *Jesus, the Voice, and the Text: Beyond the Oral and the Written Gospel.* Edited by Tom Thatcher. Waco, TX: Baylor University Press, 2008.

DeConick, "Reading." DeConick, April D. "Reading the *Gospel of Thomas* as a Repository of Early Christian Communal Memory." Pages 207–20 in *Memory, Tradition, and Text: Uses of the Past in Early Christianity.* Edited by A. Kirk and Tom Thatcher. Semeia 52. Atlanta: SBL, 2005.

DeConick, *Recovering.* DeConick, April D. *Recovering the Original Gospel of Thomas: A History of the Gospel and Its Growth.* LNTS 286. London: T&T Clark, 2005.

Deines, *Acts of God.* Deines, Roland. *Acts of God in History.* Edited by Christoph Ochs and Peter Watts. WUNT 317. Tübingen: Mohr Siebeck, 2013.

Deines, "Jesus and Torah." Deines, Roland. "Jesus and the Torah according to the Gospel of Matthew." Paper presented at the International Conference on the Gospel of Matthew in Its Historical and Theological Context. Moscow, September 28, 2018.

Deissmann, *Light.* Deissmann, G. Adolf. *Light from the Ancient East.* Grand Rapids: Baker, 1978.

De Pourcq and Roskam, "Virtues." De Pourcq, Maarten, and Geert Roskam. "Mirroring Virtues in Plutarch's Lives of Agis, Cleomenes, and the Gracchi." Pages 163–80 in *Writing Biography in Greece and Rome: Narrative Technique and Fictionalization.* Edited by Koen De Temmerman and Kristoffel Demoen. Cambridge: Cambridge University Press, 2016.

Derico, *Tradition.* Derico, Travis M. *Oral Tradition and Synoptic Verbal Agreement: Evaluating the Empirical Evidence for Literary Dependence.* Eugene, OR: Pickwick, 2016.

Derrenbacker, *Practices.* Derrenbacker, R. A., Jr. *Ancient Compositional Practices and the Synoptic Problem.* BETL 186. Leuven: Leuven University Press, 2005.

deSilva, "Honor." deSilva, David A. "Honor and Shame." Pages 431–36 in *Dictionary of the Old Testament: Pentateuch.* Edited by T. Desmond Alexander and David W. Baker. Downers Grove, IL: InterVarsity, 2003.

deSilva, *Introduction.* deSilva, David A. *An Introduction to the New Testament: Contexts, Methods, and Ministry Formation.* Downers Grove, IL: InterVarsity, 2004.

deSilva, "Wisdom." deSilva, David A. "The Wisdom of Ben Sira: Honor, Shame, and the Maintenance of the Values of a Minority Culture." *CBQ* 58 (3, 1996): 433–55.

De Temmerman, "Beauty." De Temmerman, Koen. "Blushing Beauty: Characterizing Blushes in Chariton's *Callirhoe.*" *Mnemosyne* 60 (2, 2007): 235–52.

De Temmerman, "Formalities." De Temmerman, Koen. "Ancient Biography and Formalities of Fiction." Pages 3–25 in *Writing Biography in Greece and Rome: Narrative Technique and Fictionalization.* Edited by Koen De Temmerman and Kristoffel Demoen. Cambridge: Cambridge University Press, 2016.

De Temmerman and Demoen, "Preface." De Temmerman, Koen, and Kristoffel Demoen. "Preface." Pages xi–xiii in *Writing Biography in Greece and Rome: Narrative Technique and Fictionalization.* Edited by Koen De Temmerman and Kristoffel Demoen. Cambridge: Cambridge University Press, 2016.

Develin, "Introduction." Develin, Robert. "Introduction." Pages 1–11 in *Justin: Epitome of the Philippic History of Pompeius Trogus*. Translated by J. C. Yardley. American Philological Association Classical Resources Series 3. Atlanta: Scholars Press, 1994.

Dewald, "Construction." Dewald, Carolyn. "The Construction of Meaning in the First Three Historians." Pages 89–101 in *A Companion to Greek and Roman Historiography*. Edited by John Marincola. 2 vols. Oxford: Blackwell, 2007.

DeWalt and DeWalt, *Observation*. DeWalt, Kathleen M., and Billie R. DeWalt. *Participant Observation: A Guide for Fieldworkers*. Lanham, MD: Rowman & Littlefield, 2011.

De Wet, "Signs." De Wet, Christiaan Rudolph. "Signs and Wonders in Church Growth." MA thesis, Fuller Theological Seminary, 1981.

Dewey, "Curse." Dewey, Kim E. "Peter's Curse and Cursed Peter (Mark 14:53–54, 66–72)." Pages 96–114 in *The Passion in Mark: Studies in Mark 14–16*. Edited by Werner H. Kelber. Philadelphia: Fortress Press, 1976.

Dewey, "Event." Dewey, Joanna. "The Gospel of Mark as an Oral-Aural Event: Implications for Interpretation." Pages 145–63 in *The New Literary Criticism and the New Testament*. Edited by Edgar V. McKnight and Elizabeth Struthers Malbon. Valley Forge, PA: Trinity Press International, 1994.

Dewey, "Methods." Dewey, Joanna. "Oral Methods of Structuring Narrative in Mark." *Interpretation* 43 (1, January 1989): 32–44.

Dibelius, *Studies*. Dibelius, Martin. *Studies in the Acts of the Apostles*. Edited by H. Greeven. Translated by M. Ling. New York: Scribner's, 1956.

Dibelius, *Tradition*. Dibelius, Martin. *From Tradition to Gospel*. Translated by Bertram Lee Woolf. Cambridge: James Clarke, 1971.

Dihle, "Biography." Dihle, Albrecht. "The Gospels and Greek Biography." Pages 361–86 in *The Gospel and the Gospels*. Edited by Peter Stuhlmacher. Grand Rapids: Eerdmans, 1991.

Dihle, *Studien*. Dihle, Albrecht. *Studien zur griechischen Biographie*. Göttingen: Vandenhoeck & Ruprecht, 1956.

Dillery, "Historians." Dillery, John. "Greek Historians of the Near East: Clio's 'Other' Sons." Pages 221–30 in *A Companion to Greek and Roman Historiography*. Edited by John Marincola. 2 vols. Oxford: Blackwell, 2007.

Dillon, "Doctrines." Dillon, John. "Plato's Doctrines in Diogenes Laertius." Pages 592–97 in *Diogenes Laertius "Lives of the Eminent Philosophers."* Edited by James Miller. Translated by Pamela Mensch. New York: Oxford University Press, 2018.

Dillon, "Interpretation." Dillon, John. "Holy and Not So Holy: On the Interpretation of Late Antique Biography." Pages 155–67 in *The Limits of Ancient Biography*. Edited by Brian McGing and Judith Mossman. Swansea, Wales: Classical Press of Wales, 2006.

Dillon and Finamore, "Introduction." Dillon, John M., and John F. Finamore, "Introduction." Pages 1–25 in John F. Finamore and John M. Dillon. *Iamblichus "De Anima": Text, Translation, and Commentary*. Philosophia Antiqua 42. Leiden: Brill, 2002. Repr., Atlanta: SBL, 2010.

Dillon and Hershbell, "Introduction." Dillon, John M., and Jackson Hershbell. "Introduction." Pages 1–29 in *Iamblichus "On the Pythagorean Way of Life": Text, Translation, and Notes.* Edited and translated by John M. Dillon and Jackson Hershbell. SBLTT 29. Graeco-Roman Religion Series 11. Atlanta: Scholars Press, 1991.

DiMaggio, "Culture." DiMaggio, Paul. "Culture and Cognition." *Annual Review of Sociology* 23 (1997): 263–87.

Dixon, *Searching.* Dixon, Robert M. W. *Searching for Aboriginal Languages: Memoirs of a Field Worker.* Chicago: University of Chicago Press, 1984.

Dobbeler, "Geschichte." Dobbeler, Stephanie von. "Geschichte und Geschichten. Der theologische Gehalt und die politische Problematik von 1 und 2 Makkabäer." *BK* 57 (2, 2002): 62–67.

Dodd, *Founder.* Dodd, C. H. *The Founder of Christianity.* London: Collins, 1971.

Dodd, *Interpretation.* Dodd, C. H. *The Interpretation of the Fourth Gospel.* Cambridge: Cambridge University Press, 1965.

Dodd, *Parables.* Dodd, C. H. *The Parables of the Kingdom.* London: Nisbet, 1936.

Dodd, "Portrait." Dodd, C. H. "The Portrait of Jesus in John and in the Synoptics." Pages 183–98 in *Christian History and Interpretation: Studies Presented to John Knox.* Edited by W. R. Farmer, C. F. D. Moule, and R. R. Niebuhr. Cambridge: Cambridge University Press, 1967.

Dodd, *Tradition.* Dodd, C. H. *Historical Tradition in the Fourth Gospel.* Cambridge: Cambridge University Press, 1965.

Dodds, *Pagan.* Dodds, E. R. *Pagan and Christian in an Age of Anxiety: Some Aspects of Religious Experience from Marcus Aurelius to Constantine.* Cambridge: Cambridge University Press, 1996.

Donahue, "Redaction Criticism." Donahue, John R. "Redaction Criticism: Has the *Hauptstrasse* Become a *Sackgasse?*" Pages 27–57 in *The New Literary Criticism and the New Testament.* Edited by Edgar V. McKnight and Elizabeth Struthers Malbon. Valley Forge, PA: Trinity Press International, 1994.

Donfried, *Thessalonica.* Donfried, Karl P. *Paul, Thessalonica, and Early Christianity.* Grand Rapids: Eerdmans, 2002.

Doran, "Narrative Literature." Doran, Robert. "Narrative Literature." Pages 287–310 in *Early Judaism and Its Modern Interpreters.* Edited by Robert A. Kraft and George W. E. Nickelsburg. SBLBMI 2. Atlanta: Scholars Press, 1986.

Doran, "Paideia." Doran, Robert. "Paideia and the Gymnasium." Pages 135–51 in *Pedagogy in Ancient Judaism and Early Christianity.* Edited by Karina Martin Hogan, Matthew Goff, and Emma Wasserman. EJL 41. Atlanta: SBL Press, 2017.

Dorandi, "Diogenes Laertius." Dorandi, Tiziano. "Diogenes Laertius in Byzantium." Pages 582–85 in *Diogenes Laertius "Lives of the Eminent Philosophers."* Edited by James Miller. Translated by Pamela Mensch. New York: Oxford University Press, 2018.

Dormeyer, "Ewangelie Marka." Dormeyer, Detlev. "Ewangelie Marka jako dawna biografia." *Su* 36 (1, 1998): 11–30.

Dormeyer, "Gattung." Dormeyer, Detlev. "Die Gattung der Apostelgeschichte." Pages 437–75 in *Die Apostelgeschichte im Kontext antiker und frühchristlicher Historiographie.*

Edited by Jörg Frey, Clare K. Rothschild, and Jens Schröter, with Bettina Rost. BZNW 162. Berlin: de Gruyter, 2009.

Dormeyer, "Historii." Dormeyer, Detlev. "Pragmatyczne i patetyczne pisanie historii w historiografii greckiej, we wczesnym judaizmie i w Nowym Testamencie." *ColT* 78 (2, 2008): 81–94.

Dormeyer, *Markus-Evangelium.* Dormeyer, Detlev. *Das Markus-Evangelium.* Darmstadt: Wissenschaftliche Buchgesellschaft, 2005.

Dormeyer and Frankemölle, "Evangelium." Dormeyer, Detlev, and Hubert Frankemölle. "Evangelium als literarische Gattung und als theologischer Begriff. Tendenzen und Aufgaben der Evangelienforschung im 20. Jahrhundert, mit einer Untersuchung des Markusevangeliums in seinem Verhältnis zur antiken Biographie." *ANRW* 2.25.2 (1984): 1543–1704.

Dormeyer and Galindo, *Apostelgeschichte.* Dormeyer, Detlev, and Florencio Galindo. *Die Apostelgeschichte. Ein Kommentar für die Praxis.* Stuttgart: Katholisches Bibelwerk, 2003.

Doulamis, "Storytelling." Doulamis, Konstantin. "All's Well That Ends Well: Storytelling, Predictive Signs, and the Voice of the Author in Chariton's Callirhoe." *Mnemosyne* 65 (1, 2012): 18–39.

Dowden, "Apuleius." Dowden, Ken. "Apuleius and the Art of Narration." *ClQ* 32 (2, 1982): 419–35.

Downing, "Actuality." Downing, F. Gerald. "Actuality versus Abstraction: The Synoptic Gospel Model." *Cont* 1 (3, 1991): 104–20.

Downing, "Common Ground." Downing, F. Gerald. "Common Ground with Paganism in Luke and in Josephus." *NTS* 28 (4, October 1982): 546–59.

Downing, "Conventions." Downing, F. Gerald. "Compositional Conventions and the Synoptic Problem." *JBL* 107 (1988): 69–85.

Downing, *Cynics.* Downing, F. Gerald. *Cynics, Paul, and the Pauline Churches: Cynics and Christian Origins II.* London: Routledge, 1998.

Downing, *Death.* Downing, Raymond. *Death and Life in America: Biblical Healing and Biomedicine.* Scottsdale, PA: Herald, 2008.

Downing, "Literature." Downing, F. Gerald. "A bas les aristos: The Relevance of Higher Literature for the Understanding of the Earliest Christian Writings." *NovT* 30 (3, 1988): 212–30.

Downing, "Redaction Criticism 1." Downing, F. Gerald. "Redaction Criticism: Josephus' *Antiquities* and the Synoptic Gospels (I)." *JSNT* 8 (1980): 46–65.

Downing, "Redaction Criticism 2." Downing, F. Gerald. "Redaction Criticism: Josephus' *Antiquities* and the Synoptic Gospels (II)." *JSNT* 9 (1980): 29–48.

Downing, "Researches." Downing, F. Gerald. "Feasible Researches in Historical Jesus Tradition: A Critical Response to Chris Keith." *JSNT* 40 (1, 2017): 51–61.

Downing, "Theism." Downing, F. Gerald. "Ethical Pagan Theism and the Speeches in Acts." *NTS* 27 (4, July 1981): 544–63.

Downing, "Use." Downing, F. Gerald. "Writers' Use or Abuse of Written Sources." Pages 523–45 in *New Studies in the Synoptic Problem: Oxford Conference, April 2008; Essays in*

Honour of Christopher M. Tuckett. Edited by P. Foster, A. Gregory, J. S. Kloppenborg, and J. Verheyden. BETS 239. Leuven: Peeters, 2011.

Draper, "Tradition." Draper, Jonathan. "The Jesus Tradition in the Didache." Pages 269–87 in *The Jesus Tradition outside the Gospels.* Vol. 5 of *Gospel Perspectives.* Edited by David Wenham. Sheffield: JSOT Press, 1984.

Droege, *Faith Factor.* Droege, Thomas A. *The Faith Factor in Healing.* Philadelphia: Trinity Press International, 1991.

Droge, "Anonymously." Droge, A. J. "Did 'Luke' Write Anonymously? Lingering at the Threshold." Pages 495–518 in *Die Apostelgeschichte im Kontext antiker und frühchristlicher Historiographie.* Edited by Jörg Frey, Clare K. Rothschild, and Jens Schröter, with Bettina Rost. BZNW 162. Berlin: de Gruyter, 2009.

Drury, *Design.* Drury, John. *Tradition and Design in Luke's Gospel: A Study in Early Christian Historiography.* London: Darton, Longman & Todd, 1976.

Dubarle, "Témoignage." Dubarle, André-Marie. "Le témoignage de Josèphe sur Jésus d'après la tradition indirecte." *RB* 80 (4, 1973): 481–513.

Dubrow, *Genre.* Dubrow, Heather. *Genre.* New York: Methuen, 1982.

Duff, "Ambiguity." Duff, Tim E. "Moral Ambiguity in Plutarch's *Lysander-Sulla.*" Pages 169–88 in *Plutarch and His Intellectual World: Essays on Plutarch.* Edited by Judith Mossman. London: Duckworth, with Classical Press of Wales, 1997.

Duff, "Childhood." Duff, Tim E. "Plutarch on the Childhood of Alkibiades (*Alk.* 2–3)." *Proceedings of the Cambridge Philological Society* 49 (2003): 89–117.

Duff, "How *Lives* Begin." Duff, Tim E. "How *Lives* Begin." Pages 187–207 in *The Unity of Plutarch's Work: "Moralia" Themes in the "Lives," Features of the "Lives" in the "Moralia."* Edited by Anastasios G. Nikolaidis. Millennium Studies in the Culture and History of the First Millennium C.E. 19. New York: de Gruyter, 2008.

Duff, *Lives.* Duff, Tim E. *Plutarch's Lives: Exploring Virtue and Vice.* Rev. ed. New York: Oxford University Press, 2002.

Duff, "Models." Duff, Timothy E. "Models of Education in Plutarch." *JHS* 128 (2008): 1–26.

Duling and Perrin, *New Testament.* Duling, Dennis C., and Norman Perrin. *The New Testament: Proclamation and Parenesis, Myth and History.* 3rd ed. Fort Worth, TX: Harcourt Brace College Publishers, 1994.

Dundes, *Writ.* Dundes, Alan. *Holy Writ as Oral Lit: The Bible as Folklore.* Lanham, MD: Rowman & Littlefield, 1999.

Dungan, *Sayings.* Dungan, David L. *The Sayings of Jesus in the Churches of Paul: The Use of the Synoptic Tradition in the Regulation of Early Church Life.* Philadelphia: Fortress, 1971.

Dunn, *Acts.* Dunn, James D. G. *The Acts of the Apostles.* Narrative Commentaries. Valley Forge, PA: Trinity Press International, 1996.

Dunn, "Eyewitnesses." Dunn, James D. G. "Eyewitnesses and the Oral Jesus Tradition." *JSHJ* 6 (2008): 85–105.

Dunn, "Jesus Tradition." Dunn, James D. G. "Jesus Tradition and Paul." Pages 155–78 in *Studying the Historical Jesus: Evaluations of the State of Current Research.* Edited by Bruce Chilton and Craig A. Evans. NTTS 19. Leiden: Brill, 1994.

Dunn, "John." Dunn, James D. G. "Let John Be John: A Gospel for Its Time." Pages 293–322 in *The Gospel and the Gospels*. Edited by Peter Stuhlmacher. Grand Rapids: Eerdmans, 1991.

Dunn, "John and Tradition." Dunn, James D. G. "John and the Oral Gospel Tradition." Pages 351–79 in *Jesus and the Oral Gospel Tradition*. Edited by Henry Wansbrough. JSNTSup 64. Sheffield: Sheffield Academic Press, 1991.

Dunn, *Neither Jew nor Greek*. Dunn, James D. G. *Neither Jew nor Greek*. Vol. 3 of *Christianity in the Making*. Grand Rapids: Eerdmans, 2015.

Dunn, *Perspective*. Dunn, James D. G. *A New Perspective on Jesus: What the Quest for the Historical Jesus Missed*. Grand Rapids: Baker, 2005.

Dunn, "Quest." Dunn, James D. G. "The Quest for the Historical Jesus and Its Implications for Biblical Interpretation." Pages 300–318 in *The Enlightenment through the Nineteenth Century*. Edited by Alan J. Hauser and Duane F. Watson. Vol. 3 of *A History of Biblical Interpretation*. Grand Rapids: Eerdmans, 2017.

Dunn, *Remembered*. Dunn, James D. G. *Jesus Remembered*. Vol. 1 of *Christianity in the Making*. Grand Rapids: Eerdmans, 2003.

Dunn, "Remembering Jesus." Dunn, James D. G. "Remembering Jesus." Pages 183–205 in *How to Study the Historical Jesus*. Vol. 1 of *Handbook for the Study of the Historical Jesus*. 4 vols. Edited by Tom Holmén and Stanley E. Porter. Leiden: Brill, 2011.

Dunn, "Sayings." Dunn, James D. G. "Prophetic 'I'-Sayings and the Jesus Tradition: The Importance of Testing Prophetic Utterances within Early Christianity." *NTS* 24 (1978): 175–98.

Dunn, "Synagogue." Dunn, James D. G. "Did Jesus Attend the Synagogue?" Pages 206–22 in *Jesus and Archaeology*. Edited by James H. Charlesworth. Grand Rapids: Eerdmans, 2006.

Dunn, *Theology of Paul*. Dunn, James D. G. *The Theology of Paul the Apostle*. Grand Rapids: Eerdmans, 1998.

Dunn, "Theory." Dunn, James D. G. "Kenneth Bailey's Theory of Oral Tradition: Critiquing Theodore Weeden's Critique." *JSHJ* 7 (1, 2009): 44–62.

Dunn, "The Tradition." Dunn, James D. G. "The Tradition." Pages 167–84 in *The Historical Jesus in Recent Research*. Edited by James D. G. Dunn and Scot McKnight. Winona Lake, IN: Eisenbrauns, 2005.

Dunn, *Tradition*. Dunn, James D. G. *The Oral Gospel Tradition*. Grand Rapids: Eerdmans, 2013.

Dupont, "Question du plan." Dupont, Jacques. "La question du plan des Actes des apôtres à la lumière d'un texte de Lucien de Samosate." *NovT* 21 (3, 1979): 220–31.

Dupont, *Sources*. Dupont, Jacques. *The Sources of the Acts: The Present Position*. Translated by Kathleen Pond. New York: Herder & Herder, 1964.

Dynner, "Tale." Dynner, Glenn. "The Hasidic Tale as a Historical Source: Historiography and Methodology." *RC* 3–4 (2009): 655–75.

Earl, "Prologue-Form." Earl, Donald. "Prologue-Form in Ancient Historiography." *ANRW* 1.2 (1972): 842–56.

Earman, "Bayes." Earman, John. "Bayes, Hume, and Miracles." *FPhil* 10 (3, 1993): 293–310.

Earman, *Failure*. Earman, John. *Hume's Abject Failure: The Argument against Miracles*. Oxford: Oxford University Press, 2000.

Earman, "Hume." Earman, John. "Bayes, Hume, Price, and Miracles." Pages 91–109 in *Bayes's Theorem*. Edited by Richard Swinburne. Oxford: Oxford University Press, 2005.

Eck, "Memory." Eck, Ernest Van. "Memory and Historical Jesus Studies: Formgeschichte in a New Dress?" *HTS/TS* 71(1, 2015), 10 pages.

Eckey, *Apostelgeschichte*. Eckey, Wilfried. *Die Apostelgeschichte. Der Weg des Evangeliums von Jerusalem nach Rom*. 2 vols. Neukirchen-Vluyn: Neukirchener Verlag, 2000.

Eddy and Boyd, *Legend*. Eddy, Paul Rhodes, and Gregory A. Boyd. *The Jesus Legend: A Case for the Historical Reliability of the Synoptic Jesus Tradition*. Grand Rapids: Baker Academic, 2007.

Edwards, "Damis." Edwards, M. J. "Damis the Epicurean." *ClQ* 41 (2, 1991): 563–66.

Edwards, *Death*. Edwards, Catharine. *Death in Ancient Rome*. New Haven: Yale University Press, 2007.

Edwards, "Genre." Edwards, Mark. "Gospel and Genre: Some Reservations." Pages 51–62 in *The Limits of Ancient Biography*. Edited by Brian McGing and Judith Mossman. Swansea, Wales: Classical Press of Wales, 2006.

Edwards, "Introduction." Edwards, Catharine. "Introduction." Pages vii–xxx in *Suetonius: Lives of the Caesars*. Translated by Catharine Edwards. New York: Oxford University Press, 2000.

Edwards, *Luke*. Edwards, James R. *The Gospel according to Luke*. PNTC. Grand Rapids: Eerdmans, 2015.

Edwards, "Parallels." Edwards, James R. "Parallels and Patterns between Luke and Acts." *BBR* 27 (4, 2017): 485–501.

Edwards, *Plutarch*. Edwards, Michael J. *Plutarch: The Lives of Pompey, Caesar, and Cicero*. London: Bristol Classical Press, 1991.

Edwards and Potter, "Memory." Edwards, Derek, and Jonathon Potter. "The Chancellor's Memory: Rhetoric and Truth in Discursive Remembering." *Applied Cognitive Psychology* 6 (1992): 187–215.

Egelhaaf-Gaiser, "Sites." Egelhaaf-Gaiser, Ulrike. "Roman Cult Sites: A Pragmatic Approach." Pages 205–21 in *A Companion to Roman Religion*. Edited by Jörg Rüpke. BCAW. Oxford: Blackwell, 2011.

Ehrensperger, *Dynamics*. Ehrensperger, Kathy. *Paul and the Dynamics of Power: Communication and Interaction in the Early Christ-Movement*. LNTS 325. New York: T&T Clark, 2007.

Ehrman, *Before Gospels*. Ehrman, Bart D. *Jesus before the Gospels: How the Earliest Christians Remembered, Changed, and Invented Their Stories of the Savior*. New York: HarperOne, 2016.

Ehrman, "Cephas." Ehrman, Bart D. "Cephas and Peter." *JBL* 109 (3, 1990): 463–74.

Ehrman, *Did Jesus Exist?* Ehrman, Bart D. *Did Jesus Exist? The Historical Argument for Jesus of Nazareth*. New York: HarperOne, 2012.

Ehrman, *Forgery*.   Ehrman, Bart D. *Forgery and Counterforgery: The Use of Literary Deceit in Early Christian Polemics*. Oxford: Oxford University Press, 2012.

Ehrman, *How Jesus Became God*.   Ehrman, Bart D. *How Jesus Became God: The Exaltation of a Jewish Preacher from Galilee*. New York: HarperOne, 2015.

Ehrman, *Interrupted*.   Ehrman, Bart D. *Jesus Interrupted: Revealing the Hidden Contradictions in the Bible (and Why We Don't Know about Them)*. New York: HarperCollins, 2009.

Ehrman, *Introduction*.   Ehrman, Bart D. *The New Testament: A Historical Introduction to the Early Christian Writings*. 3rd ed. New York: Oxford University Press, 2004.

Ehrman, *Prophet*.   Ehrman, Bart D. *Jesus: Apocalyptic Prophet of the New Millennium*. Oxford: Oxford University Press, 1999.

Eickelman, *Middle East*.   Eickelman, Dale F. *The Middle East: An Anthropological Approach*. 2nd ed. Englewood Cliffs, NJ: Prentice Hall, 1989.

Eigler, "Excursus."   Eigler, Ulrich. "Excursus." *BNP* 5:258–59.

Eisman, "Dio and Josephus."   Eisman, Michael M. "Dio and Josephus: Parallel Analyses." *Latomus* 36 (3, 1977): 657–73.

Elder, "Narrativity."   Elder, Nicholas A. "Narrativity." *DBAM* 242–43.

Elliott, *Feelings*.   Elliott, Matthew. *Faithful Feelings: Emotion in the New Testament*. Leicester, UK: Inter-Varsity, 2005.

Elliott, "Pseudo-Scholarship."   Elliott, Susan M. "Pseudo-Scholarship Illustrated: Was the 'Original Jesus' a Pagan God?" *FourR* 24 (3, 2011): 9–14.

Ellis, "Making."   Ellis, E. Earle. "The Making of Narratives in the Synoptic Gospels." Pages 310–33 in *Jesus and the Oral Gospel Tradition*. Edited by Henry Wansbrough. JSNTSup 64. Sheffield: Sheffield Academic Press, 1991.

Ellis, *Matthew*.   Ellis, Peter F. *Matthew: His Mind and His Message*. Collegeville, MN: Liturgical, 1974.

Endres, *Interpretation*.   Endres, John C. *Biblical Interpretation in the Book of Jubilees*. CBQMS 18. Washington, DC: Catholic Biblical Association of America, 1987.

Enns, *Problem*.   Enns, Peter. *Inspiration and Incarnation: Evangelicals and the Problem of the Old Testament*. Grand Rapids: Baker Academic, 2005.

Ensor, "John 4.35."   Ensor, Peter W. "The Authenticity of John 4.35." *EQ* 72 (1, 2000): 13–21.

Eshleman, "Sophists."   Eshleman, Kendra. "Defining the Circle of Sophists: Philostratus and the Construction of the Second Sophistic." *CP* 103 (4, 2008): 395–413.

Esler, "Memory."   Esler, Philip F. "Collective Memory and Hebrews 11: Outlining a New Investigative Framework." Pages 151–71 in *Memory, Tradition, and Text: Uses of the Past in Early Christianity*. Edited by A. Kirk and Tom Thatcher. SemeiaSt 52. Atlanta, SBL, 2005.

Etkes, "Besht."   Etkes, Immanuel. "The Historical Besht: Reconstruction or Deconstruction?" *Polin* 12 (1999): 297–306.

Evans, "Context."   Evans, Craig A. "Context, Family, and Formation." Pages 11–24 in *The Cambridge Companion to Jesus*. Edited by Markus Bockmuehl. Cambridge: Cambridge University, 2001.

Evans, *Fabricating Jesus.*   Evans, Craig A. *Fabricating Jesus: How Modern Scholars Distort the Gospels.* Downers Grove, IL: InterVarsity, 2006.

Evans, "Foreword."   Evans, Craig A. "Foreword." Pages ix–xi in Michael R. Licona. *Why Are There Differences in the Gospels? What We Can Learn from Ancient Biography.* New York: Oxford University Press, 2017.

Evans, "Gospel of Judas."   Evans, Craig A. "Understanding the Gospel of Judas." *BBR* 20 (4, 2010): 561–74.

Evans, "Graffiti."   Evans, Craig A. "Graffiti." *DBAM* 160–61.

Evans, "Longevity."   Evans, Craig A. "Longevity of Late Antique Autographs and First Copies: A Postscriptum." In *Scribes and Their Remains.* Edited by P. Arzt-Grabner, C. A. Evans, and J. J. Johnston. SSEJC 21. New York: Bloomsbury T&T Clark, forthcoming.

Evans, *Matthew.*   Evans, Craig A. *Matthew.* NCamBC. New York: Cambridge University Press, 2012.

Evans, *Narrative.*   Evans, C. Stephen. *The Historical Christ and the Jesus of Faith: The Incarnational Narrative as History.* Oxford: Clarendon, 1996.

Evans, *World.*   Evans, Craig A. *Jesus and His World: The Archaeological Evidence.* Louisville: Westminster John Knox, 2012.

Eve, *Behind Gospels.*   Eve, Eric. *Behind the Gospels: Understanding the Oral Tradition.* London: SPCK, 2013.

Eve, "Finnegan."   Eve, Eric. "Finnegan, Ruth." *DBAM* 134–35.

Eve, "Kelber."   Eve, Eric. "Kelber, Werner." *DBAM* 202.

Eve, *Miracles.*   Eve, Eric. *The Jewish Context of Jesus' Miracles.* JSNTSup 231. London: Sheffield Academic Press, 2002.

Eve, "Orality."   Eve, Eric. "Orality." *DBAM* 260–61.

Évrard, "Polybe."   Évrard, Étienne. "Polybe et Tite-Live, à propos d'Antiochus IV." *Latomus* 70 (4, 2011): 977–82.

Fabisiak, *Side.*   Fabisiak, Thomas. *The "Nocturnal Side of Science" in David Friedrich Strauss's* Life of Jesus Critically Examined. ESEC 17. Atlanta: SBL, 2015.

Fantuzzi, "Historical Epic."   Fantuzzi, Marco. "Historical Epic." *BNP* 6:409–11.

Farrell, "Phenomenology."   Farrell, Joseph. "The Phenomenology of Memory in Roman Culture." *CJ* 92 (4, 1997): 373–83.

Farrington, "Action."   Farrington, Scott. "Action and Reason: Polybius and the Gap between Encomium and History." *CP* 106 (4, 2011): 324–42.

Fee, *Jesus the Lord.*   Fee, Gordon D. *Jesus the Lord according to Paul the Apostle: A Concise Introduction.* Grand Rapids: Baker Academic, 2018.

Feldherr, "Translation."   Feldherr, Andrew. "The Translation of Catiline." Pages 385–90 in *A Companion to Greek and Roman Historiography.* Edited by John Marincola. 2 vols. Oxford: Blackwell, 2007.

Feldman, "Abraham."   Feldman, Louis H. "Hellenizations in Josephus' *Jewish Antiquities*: The Portrait of Abraham." Pages 133–53 in *Josephus, Judaism, and Christianity.* Edited by Louis H. Feldman and Gohei Hata. Detroit: Wayne State University Press, 1987.

Feldman, "Ahab." Feldman, Louis H. "Josephus' Portrait of Ahab." *ETL* 68 (4, 1992): 368–84.

Feldman, "Ahasuerus." Feldman, Louis H. "Josephus' Portrait of Ahasuerus." *ABR* 42 (1994): 17–38.

Feldman, "*Antiquities.*" Feldman, Louis H. "Josephus' *Jewish Antiquities* and Pseudo-Philo's *Biblical Antiquities.*" Pages 59–80 in *Josephus, the Bible, and History.* Edited by Louis H. Feldman and Gohei Hata. Detroit: Wayne State University Press, 1989.

Feldman, "Apologist." Feldman, Louis H. "Josephus as an Apologist of the Greco-Roman World: His Portrait of Solomon." Pages 69–98 in *Aspects of Religious Propaganda in Judaism and Early Christianity.* Edited by Elisabeth Schüssler Fiorenza. UNDCSJCA 2. Notre Dame, IN: University of Notre Dame Press, 1976.

Feldman, "Aqedah." Feldman, Louis H. "Josephus as a Biblical Interpreter: The '*Aqedah.*'" *JQR* 75 (3, 1985): 212–52.

Feldman, "Asa." Feldman, Louis H. "Josephus' Portrait of Asa." *BBR* 4 (1994): 41–59.

Feldman, "Balaam." Feldman, Louis H. "Philo's Version of Balaam." *Hen* 25 (3, 2003): 301–19.

Feldman, "Birth." Feldman, Louis H. "Philo's View of Moses' Birth and Upbringing." *CBQ* 64 (2, 2002): 258–81.

Feldman, "Calf." Feldman, Louis H. "Philo's Account of the Golden Calf Incident." *JJS* 56 (2, 2005): 245–64.

Feldman, "Command." Feldman, Louis H. "The Command, according to Philo, Pseudo-Philo, and Josephus, to Annihilate the Seven Nations of Canaan." *AUSS* 41 (1, 2003): 13–29.

Feldman, "Concubine." Feldman, Louis H. "Josephus' Portrayal (*Antiquities* 5.136–74) of the Benjaminite Affair of the Concubine and Its Repercussions (Judges 19–21)." *JQR* 90 (3–4, 2000): 255–92.

Feldman, "Daniel." Feldman, Louis H. "Josephus' Portrait of Daniel." *Hen* 14 (1–2, 1992): 37–96.

Feldman, "David." Feldman, Louis H. "Josephus' Portrait of David." *HUCA* 60 (1989): 129–74.

Feldman, "Elijah." Feldman, Louis H. "Josephus' Portrait of Elijah." *SJOT* 8 (1, 1994): 61–86.

Feldman, "Ezra." Feldman, Louis H. "Josephus' Portrait of Ezra." *VT* 43 (2, 1993): 190–214.

Feldman, "General." Feldman, Louis H. "Moses the General and the Battle against Midian in Philo." *JSQ* 14 (1, 2007): 1–17.

Feldman, "Hezekiah." Feldman, Louis H. "Josephus's Portrait of Hezekiah." *JBL* 111 (4, 1992): 597–610.

Feldman, "Interpretation of Joshua." Feldman, Louis H. "Philo's Interpretation of Joshua." *JSP* 12 (2, 2001): 165–78.

Feldman, "Introduction." Feldman, Louis H. "Introduction." Pages 17–49 in *Josephus, the Bible, and History.* Edited by Louis H. Feldman and Gohei Hata. Detroit: Wayne State University Press, 1989.

Feldman, "Isaac." Feldman, Louis H. "Josephus' Portrait of Isaac." *RSLR* 29 (1, 1993): 3–33.

Feldman, "Jacob." Feldman, Louis H. "Josephus' Portrait of Jacob." *JQR* 79 (2–3, 1988–89): 101–51.

Feldman, "Jehoram."   Feldman, Louis H. "Josephus's Portrait of Jehoram, King of Israel." *BJRL* 76 (1, 1994): 3–20.

Feldman, "Jehoshaphat."   Feldman, Louis H. "Josephus' Portrait of Jehoshaphat." *SCI* 12 (1993): 159–75.

Feldman, "Jeroboam."   Feldman, Louis H. "Josephus' Portrait of Jeroboam." *AUSS* 31 (1, 1993): 29–51.

Feldman, "Jonah."   Feldman, Louis H. "Josephus' Interpretation of Jonah." *AJSR* 17 (1, 1992): 1–29.

Feldman, "Joseph."   Feldman, Louis H. "Josephus' Portrait of Joseph." *RB* 99 (2, 1992): 397–417; (3, 1992): 504–28.

Feldman, "Joshua."   Feldman, Louis H. "Josephus's Portrait of Joshua." *HTR* 82 (4, 1989): 351–76.

Feldman, "Josiah."   Feldman, Louis H. "Josephus' Portrait of Josiah." *LS* 18 (2, 1993): 110–30.

Feldman, "Korah."   Feldman, Louis H. "Philo's Interpretation of Korah." *REJ* 162 (1–2, 2003): 1–15.

Feldman, "Manasseh."   Feldman, Louis H. "Josephus' Portrait of Manasseh." *JSP* 9 (1991): 3–20.

Feldman, "Moses."   Feldman, Louis H. "Josephus' Portrait of Moses." *JQR* 82 (3–4, 1992): 285–328; 83 (1–2, 1992): 7–50.

Feldman, "Nehemiah."   Feldman, Louis H. "Josephus' Portrait of Nehemiah." *JJS* 43 (2, 1992): 187–202.

Feldman, "Noah."   Feldman, Louis H. "Josephus' Portrait of Noah and Its Parallels in Philo, Pseudo-Philo's *Biblical Antiquities*, and Rabbinic Midrashim." *PAAJR* 55 (1988): 31–57.

Feldman, "Pharaohs."   Feldman, Louis H. "Josephus' Portraits of the Pharaohs." *Syllecta Classica* 4 (1993): 49–63.

Feldman, *Portrayal*.   Feldman, Louis H. *Philo's Portrayal of Moses in the Context of Ancient Judaism*. Christianity and Judaism in Antiquity 15. Notre Dame, IN: University of Notre Dame, 2007.

Feldman, "Roncace's Portraits."   Feldman, Louis H. "On Professor Mark Roncace's Portraits of Deborah and Gideon in Josephus." *JSJ* 32 (2, 2001): 193–220.

Feldman, "Samson."   Feldman, Louis H. "Josephus' Version of Samson." *JSJ* 19 (2, 1988): 171–214.

Feldman, "Samuel."   Feldman, Louis H. "Josephus' Portrait of Samuel." *AbrN* 30 (1992): 103–45.

Feldman, "Saul."   Feldman, Louis H. "Josephus' Portrait of Saul." *HUCA* 53 (1982): 45–99.

Feldman, "Solomon."   Feldman, Louis H. "Josephus as an Apologist of the Greco-Roman World: His Portrait of Solomon." Pages 69–98 in *Aspects of Religious Propaganda in Judaism and Early Christianity*. Edited by Elisabeth Schüssler Fiorenza. UNDCSJCA 2. Notre Dame, IN: University of Notre Dame Press, 1976.

Feldman, "Spies."   Feldman, Louis H. "Philo's Version of the Biblical Episode of the Spies." *HUCA* 73 (2002): 29–48.

Ferguson, *Backgrounds.* Ferguson, Everett. *Backgrounds of Early Christianity.* Grand Rapids: Eerdmans, 1987.

Ferguson, *Demonology.* Ferguson, Everett. *Demonology of the Early Christian World.* SymS 12. New York: Edwin Mellen, 1984.

Fernandez, "Memory." Fernandez, Cyprian E. "Memory and Its Social Vitality: A Biblical Understanding." *LW* 121 (1, 2015): 8–28.

Field, *Communities.* Field, Sean. *Lost Communities, Living Memories: Remembering Forced Removals in Capetown.* Center for Popular Memory, University of Capetown. Cape Town: David Philip, 2002.

Field, "Dialogues." Field, S. P. "Developing Dialogues: The Value of Oral History." Pages 268–78 in *World Civilizations and History of Human Development.* Edited by Robert Holton and William Richard Nasson. Encyclopedia of Life Support Systems. Ramsey, Isle of Man: Eolss Publishers, 2010.

Field, *Oral History.* Field, Sean. *Oral History, Community, and Displacement: Imagining Memories in Post-Apartheid South Africa.* New York: Palgrave Macmillan, 2012.

Filson, *History.* Filson, Floyd V. *A New Testament History.* Philadelphia: Westminster Press, 1964.

Finkelberg, "*Cypria.*" Finkelberg, Margalit. "The *Cypria,* the *Iliad,* and the Problem of Multiformity in Oral and Written Tradition." *CP* 95 (1, 2000): 1–11.

Finnegan, *Beyond.* Finnegan, Ruth H. *The Oral and Beyond: Doing Things with Words in Africa.* Chicago: University of Chicago Press, 2007.

Finnegan, *Literacy.* Finnegan, Ruth H. *Literacy and Orality.* Oxford: Oxford University Press, 1988.

Finnegan, *Oral Poetry.* Finnegan, Ruth H. *Oral Poetry: Its Nature, Significance, and Social Context.* Bloomington: Indiana University Press, 1992.

Fischer and Stein, "Marble." Fischer, Moshe L., and Alla Stein. "Josephus on the Use of Marble in Building Projects of Herod the Great." *JJS* 45 (1, 1994): 79–85.

Fisk, "Bible." Fisk, Bruce N. "Rewritten Bible in Pseudepigrapha and Qumran." *DNTB* 947–53.

Fitzgerald, "Lives." Fitzgerald, John. "The Ancient Lives of Aristotle and the Modern Debate about the Genre of the Gospels." *ResQ* 36 (4, 1994): 209–21.

Fitzgerald, "Meanings." Fitzgerald, Joseph M. "Intersecting Meanings of Reminiscence in Adult Development and Aging." Pages 360–83 in *Remembering Our Past: Studies in Autobiographical Memory.* Edited by David C. Rubin. Cambridge: Cambridge University Press, 1996.

Fitzmyer, *Acts.* Fitzmyer, Joseph A. *The Acts of the Apostles: A New Translation, with Introduction and Commentary.* AB 31. New York: Doubleday, 1998.

Fitzmyer, *Theologian.* Fitzmyer, Joseph A. *Luke the Theologian: Aspects of His Teaching.* New York: Paulist, 1989.

Fivush, Haden, and Reese, "Reminiscing." Fivush, Robyn, Catherine Haden, and Elaine Reese. "Remembering, Recounting, and Reminiscing: The Development of Autobiographical Memory in Social Context." Pages 341–59 in *Remembering Our Past: Studies in Autobiographical Memory*. Edited by David C. Rubin. Cambridge: Cambridge University Press, 1996.

Flender, *Theologian*.   Flender, Helmut. *St Luke: Theologian of Redemptive History*. Translated by Reginald H. Fuller and Ilse Fuller. London: SPCK, 1967.

Fletcher-Louis, *Origins*.   Fletcher-Louis, Crispin. *Christological Origins: The Emerging Consensus and Beyond*. Vol. 1 of *Jesus Monotheism*. Eugene, OR: Cascade, 2015.

Flichy, "État."   Flichy, Odile. "État des recherches actuelles sur les Actes des apôtres." Pages 13–42 in *Les Actes des apôtres—histoire, récit, théologie. XXe congrès de l'Association catholique française pour l'étude de la Bible (Angers, 2003)*. Edited by Michel Berder. LD 199. Paris: Cerf, 2005.

Flichy, *Oeuvre*.   Flichy, Odile. *L'oeuvre de Luc. L'Évangile et les Actes des apôtres*. CaE 114. Paris: Cerf, 2000.

Flusser, "Ancestry."   Flusser, David. "Jesus, His Ancestry, and the Commandment of Love." Pages 153–76 in *Jesus' Jewishness: Exploring the Place of Jesus within Early Judaism*. Edited by James H. Charlesworth. New York: American Interfaith Institute, Crossroad, 1991.

Flusser, *Judaism*.   Flusser, David. *Judaism and the Origins of Christianity*. Jerusalem: Magnes, 1988.

Flusser, *Sage*.   Flusser, David, with R. Steven Notley. *The Sage from Galilee: Rediscovering Jesus' Genius*. 4th ed. Grand Rapids: Eerdmans, 2007.

Fogelin, *Defense*.   Fogelin, Robert J. *A Defense of Hume on Miracles*. Princeton Monographs in Philosophy. Princeton: Princeton University Press, 2003.

Foley, "Plenitude."   Foley, John Miles. "Plenitude and Diversity: Interactions between Orality and Writing." Pages 103–18 in *The Interface of Orality and Writing: Speaking, Seeing, Writing in the Shaping of New Genres*. Edited by Annette Weissenrieder and Robert B. Coote. WUNT 260. Tübingen: Mohr Siebeck, 2010. Repr., BPC 11. Eugene, OR: Wipf & Stock, 2015.

Foley, *Theory*.   Foley, John Miles. *The Theory of Oral Composition: History and Methodology*. Bloomington: Indiana University Press, 1988.

Foner, *Reconstruction*.   Foner, Eric. *Reconstruction: America's Unfinished Revolution, 1863–1877*. New York: Harper & Row, 1988.

Forbes, "Acts."   Forbes, Christopher. "The Acts of the Apostles as a Source for Studying Early Christianity." Pages 5–36 in *Into All the World: Emergent Christianity in Its Jewish and Greco-Roman Context*. Edited by Mark Harding and Alanna Nobbs. Grand Rapids: Eerdmans, 2017.

Forbes, "Self-Praise."   Forbes, Christopher. "Comparison, Self-Praise, and Irony: Paul's Boasting and the Conventions of Hellenistic Rhetoric." *NTS* 32 (1, 1986): 1–30.

Fornara, *Nature*.   Fornara, C. W. *The Nature of History in Ancient Greece and Rome*. Berkeley: University of California Press, 1983.

Forsythe, "Quadrigarius."   Forsythe, Gary. "Claudius Quadrigarius and Livy's Second Pentad." Pages 391–96 in *A Companion to Greek and Roman Historiography*. Edited by John Marincola. 2 vols. Oxford: Blackwell, 2007.

Forte, "Echoes Revisited."   Forte, Anthony J. "Book I of Josephus' 'Bellum iudaicum': Sources and Classical Echoes Revisited." *Did* 36 (2, 2006): 31–52.

Foster, "Introduction."   Foster, B. O. "Introduction." Pages ix–xxxv in vol. 1 of Livy, *Ab urbe condita*. Translated by B. O. Foster et al. 14 vols. LCL. Cambridge, MA.: Harvard University Press, 1919–59.

Foster, "Memory."   Foster, Paul. "Memory, Orality, and the Fourth Gospel: An Ongoing Conversation with Stan Porter and Hughson T. Ong." *JSHJ* 12 (1–2, 2014): 165–83.

Foucault, *Language*.   Foucault, Michel. *Language, Counter-memory, Practice: Selected Essays and Interviews*. Edited by Donald F. Bouchard. Translated by Donald F. Bouchard and Sherry Simon. Ithaca, NY: Cornell University Press, 1977.

Fowler, "History."   Fowler, Robert. "History." Pages 195–209 in *The Oxford Handbook of Ancient Greek Religion*. Edited by Esther Eidinow and Julia Kindt. Oxford: Oxford University Press, 2015.

Fowler, *Kinds of Literature*.   Fowler, Alastair. *Kinds of Literature: An Introduction to the Theory of Genre and Modes*. Oxford: Clarendon, 1982.

Fox, "Dionysius."   Fox, Matthew. "Dionysius, Lucian, and the Prejudice against Rhetoric in History." *JRS* 91 (2001): 76–93.

Frahm, Jansen-Winkeln, and Wiesehöfer, "Historiography."   Frahm, Eckart, Karl Jansen-Winkeln, and Josef Wiesehöfer. "Historiography: Ancient Orient." *BNP* 6:415–18.

France, "Exegesis."   France, R. T. "Exegesis in Practice: Two Examples." Pages 252–81 in *New Testament Interpretation: Essays on Principles and Methods*. Edited by I. Howard Marshall. Grand Rapids: Eerdmans, 1977.

France, *Mark*.   France, R. T. *The Gospel of Mark: A Commentary on the Greek Text*. NIGTC. Grand Rapids: Eerdmans, 2002.

Frei, "Apologetics."   Frei, Hans. "Apologetics, Criticism, and the Loss of Narrative Interpretation." Pages 45–64 in *Why Narrative? Readings in Narrative Theology*. Edited by Stanley Hauerwas and L. Gregory Jones. Grand Rapids: Eerdmans, 1989.

Freyne, *Galilee*.   Freyne, Sean. *Galilee, Jesus, and the Gospels: Literary Approaches and Historical Investigations*. Philadelphia: Fortress, 1988.

Freyne, "Gospel."   Freyne, Sean. "Mark's Gospel and Ancient Biography." Pages 63–75 in *The Limits of Ancient Biography*. Edited by Brian McGing and Judith Mossman. Swansea, Wales: Classical Press of Wales, 2006.

Freyne, "Imagination."   Freyne, Sean. "Early Christian Imagination and the Gospels." Pages 2–12 in *The Earliest Gospels: The Origins and Transmission of the Earliest Christian Gospels*. Edited by Charles Horton. London: T&T Clark, 2010.

Frickenschmidt, *Evangelium*.   Frickenschmidt, Dirk. *Evangelium als Biographie. Die vier Evangelien im Rahmen antiker Erzählkunst*. TANZ 22. Tübingen: Francke, 1997.

Frickenschmidt, "Evangelium."   Frickenschmidt, Dirk. "Evangelium als antike Biographie." *ZNT* 1 (2, 1998): 29–39.

Friedländer, *Life*.   Friedländer, Ludwig. *Roman Life and Manners under the Early Empire*. Translated from the 7th rev. ed. by Leonard A. Magnus, J. H. Freese, and A. B. Gough. 4 vols. London: G. Routledge & Sons; New York: E. P. Dutton, 1908–13.

546

Frost, *Healing.*   Frost, Evelyn. *Christian Healing: A Consideration of the Place of Spiritual Healing in the Church of Today in the Light of the Doctrine and Practice of the Ante-Nicene Church.* London: A. R. Mowbray, 1940.

Frow, *Genre.*   Frow, John. *Genre.* 2nd ed. The New Critical Idiom. New York: Routledge, Taylor & Francis, 2015.

Frye, "Synoptic Problems."   Frye, Roland Mushat. "The Synoptic Problems and Analogies in Other Literatures." Pages 261–302 in *The Relationships among the Gospels: An Interdisciplinary Dialogue.* Edited by William O. Walker Jr. San Antonio: Trinity University Press, 1978.

Frykenberg, *Christianity in India.*   Frykenberg, Robert Eric. *Christianity in India: From Beginnings to the Present.* Oxford History of the Christian Church. New York: Oxford University Press, 2010.

Fuhrmann, "Vierkaiserjahr."   Fuhrmann, Manfred. "Das Vierkaiserjahr bei Tacitus. Über den Aufbau der Historien Buch I–III." *Phil* 104 (1960): 250–78.

Fuller, "Classics."   Fuller, Reginald H. "Classics and the Gospels: The Seminar." Pages 173–92 in *The Relationships among the Gospels: An Interdisciplinary Dialogue.* Edited by William O. Walker Jr. San Antonio: Trinity University Press, 1978.

Fullmer, *Resurrection.*   Fullmer, Paul M. *Resurrection in Mark's Literary-Historical Perspective.* LNTS 360. New York: T&T Clark, 2007.

Funk, Hoover, and Jesus Seminar, *Five Gospels.*   Funk, Robert, Roy Hoover, and the Jesus Seminar. *The Five Gospels: The Search for the Authentic Words of Jesus.* New York: Macmillan, 1993.

Funk and Jesus Seminar, *The Acts of Jesus.*   Funk, Robert W., and the Jesus Seminar. *The Acts of Jesus: The Search for the Authentic Deeds of Jesus.* San Francisco: HarperSanFrancisco, 1998.

Fusco, "Sezioni-noi."   Fusco, Vittorio. "Le sezioni-noi degli Atti nella discussione recente." *BeO* 25 (2, 1983): 73–86.

Fusillo, "Novel."   Fusillo, Massimo. "Novel: Greek." *BNP* 9:837–42.

Fusillo, "Pseudo-Callisthenes."   Fusillo, Massimo. "Pseudo-Callisthenes." *BNP* 12:114.

Gaechter, *Gedächtniskultur.*   Gaechter, Paul. *Die Gedächtniskultur in Irland.* Innsbruck: Innsbrucker Beiträge zur Sprachwissenschaft der Universität Innsbruck, 1970.

Gafni, "Josephus and Maccabees."   Gafni, Isaiah M. "Josephus and 1 Maccabees." Pages 116–31 in *Josephus, the Bible, and History.* Edited by Louis H. Feldman and Gohei Hata. Detroit: Wayne State University Press, 1989.

Gager, *Anti-Semitism.*   Gager, John G. *The Origins of Anti-Semitism: Attitudes toward Judaism in Pagan and Christian Antiquity.* New York: Oxford University Press, 1983.

Gaines, "Handbooks."   Gaines, Robert N. "Roman Rhetorical Handbooks." Pages 163–80 in *A Companion to Roman Rhetoric.* Edited by William Dominik and Jon Hall. Oxford: Blackwell, 2007.

Galinsky, "Introduction."   Galinsky, Karl. "Introduction." Pages 1–39 in *Memory in Ancient Rome and Early Christianity.* Edited by Karl Galinsky. Oxford: Oxford University Press, 2016.

Gallagher, *Divine Man.*   Gallagher, Eugene V. *Divine Man or Magician? Celsus and Origen on Jesus.* SBLDS 64. Chico, CA: Scholars Press, 1982.

Gamble, "Literacy."   Gamble, Harry. "Literacy and Book Culture." *DNTB* 644–48.

Gandolphe and El Haj, "Memories."   Gandolphe, Marie-Charlotte, and Mohamad El Haj. "Flashbulb Memories of the Paris Attacks." *Scandinavian Journal of Psychology* 58 (3, June 2017): 199–204.

Gardner, "Miracles."   Gardner, Rex. "Miracles of Healing in Anglo-Celtic Northumbria as Recorded by the Venerable Bede and His Contemporaries: A Reappraisal in the Light of Twentieth-Century Experience." *British Medical Journal* 287 (December 24–31, 1983): 1927–33.

Garland, *Mark.*   Garland, David E. *Mark.* NIVAC. Grand Rapids: Zondervan, 1996.

Gathercole, "Anonymity."   Gathercole, Simon. "The Alleged Anonymity of the Canonical Gospels." *JTS* 69 (2, 2018): 447–76.

Gathercole, *Composition.*   Gathercole, Simon J. *The Composition of the Gospel of Thomas: Original Language and Influences.* SNTSMS 151. New York: Cambridge University Press, 2014.

Gathercole, "Foreword."   Gathercole, Simon J. "Foreword." Pages xi–xvii in Richard Bauckham. *Jesus and the Eyewitnesses: The Gospels as Eyewitness Testimony.* Grand Rapids: Eerdmans, 2017.

Gathercole, *Son.*   Gathercole, Simon J. *The Pre-existent Son: Recovering the Christologies of Matthew, Mark, and Luke.* Grand Rapids: Eerdmans, 2006.

Gaztambide, "Psychoimmunology."   Gaztambide, Daniel J. "Psychoimmunology and Jesus' Healing Miracles." Pages 94–113 in *Medical and Therapeutic Events.* Vol. 2 of *Miracles: God, Science, and Psychology in the Paranormal.* Edited by J. Harold Ellens. Westport, CT: Praeger, 2008.

Gaztambide, "Role."   Gaztambide, Daniel J. "The Role of the Placebo Effect, Individual Psychology, and Immune Response in Regulating the Effects of Religion on Health." Pages 302–24 in *Psychodynamics.* Vol. 3 of *The Healing Power of Spirituality: How Faith Helps Humans Thrive.* Edited by J. Harold Ellens. Santa Barbara, CA: Praeger, 2010.

Geiger, *Nepos.*   Geiger, Joseph. *Cornelius Nepos and Ancient Political Biography.* Historia Einzelschriften 47. Stuttgart: Steiner Verlag Wiesbaden, 1985.

Geljon, *Exegesis.*   Geljon, Albert C. *Philonic Exegesis in Gregory of Nyssa's De vita Moysis.* BJS 333. SPhiloMon 5. Providence, RI: BJS, 2002.

Gempf, "Speaking."   Gempf, Conrad. "Public Speaking and Published Accounts." Pages 259–303 in *The Book of Acts in Its Ancient Literary Setting.* Edited by Bruce W. Winter and Andrew D. Clarke. Vol. 1 of *The Book of Acts in Its First Century Setting.* Edited by Bruce W. Winter. Grand Rapids: Eerdmans, 1993.

Genette, *Palimpsestes.*   Genette, Gérard. *Palimpsestes. La littérature au second degré.* Paris: Éd. du Seuil, 1982.

Genette, *Palimpsests* (1997).   Genette, Gérard. *Palimpsests: Literature in the Second Degree.* Translated by Channa Newman. Lincoln: University of Nebraska Press, 1997.

George, *Philippians.*   George, Roji T. *Philippians.* Carlisle, UK: Langham, 2019.

Georgiadou, "Lives." Georgiadou, Aristoula. "The Lives of the Caesars." Pages 249–66 in *A Companion to Plutarch*. Edited by Mark Beck. Malden, MA: Wiley-Blackwell, 2014.

Gera, *Cyropaedia*. Gera, Deborah Levine. *Xenophon's Cyropaedia: Style, Genre, and Literary Technique*. Oxford: Clarendon, 1993.

Gera, "Olympiodoros." Gera, Dov. "Olympiodoros, Heliodoros, and the Temples of Koile Syria and Phoinike." *ZPE* 169 (2009): 125–55.

Gerhardsson, "Illuminating." Gerhardsson, Birger. "Illuminating the Kingdom: Narrative Meshalim in the Synoptic Gospels." Pages 266–309 in *Jesus and the Oral Gospel Tradition*. Edited by Henry Wansbrough. JSNTSup 64. Sheffield: Sheffield Academic Press, 1991.

Gerhardsson, *Memory*. Gerhardsson, Birger. *Memory and Manuscript: Oral Tradition and Written Transmission in Rabbinic Judaism and Early Christianity*. ASNU 22. Uppsala: C. W. K. Gleerup, 1961.

Gerhardsson, *Origins*. Gerhardsson, Birger. *The Origins of the Gospel Traditions*. Philadelphia: Fortress, 1979.

Gerhardsson, "Path." Gerhardsson, Birger. "The Path of the Gospel Tradition." Pages 75–96 in *The Gospel and the Gospels*. Edited by Peter Stuhlmacher. Grand Rapids: Eerdmans, 1991.

Gerhardsson, *Reliability*. Gerhardsson, Birger. *The Reliability of the Gospel Tradition*. Grand Rapids: Baker Academic, 2001.

Gibbons, "Plato." Gibbons, Kathleen. "Plato (on Writing and Memory)." *DBAM* 297–98.

Gill, "Distinction." Gill, Christopher. "The Character-Personality Distinction." Pages 1–31 in *Characterization and Individuality in Greek Literature*. Edited by C. B. R. Pelling. Oxford: Clarendon, 1990.

Gillet-Didier, "*Paradosis*." Gillet-Didier, Veronique. "*Paradosis*: Flavius Josèphe et la fabrique de la tradition." *REJ* 158 (1–2, 1999): 7–49.

Goetz and Blomberg, "Burden of Proof." Goetz, Stewart C., and Craig L. Blomberg, "The Burden of Proof." *JSNT* 11 (1981): 39–63.

Goff, "Gardens." Goff, Matthew. "Gardens of Knowledge: Teachers in Ben Sira, 4QInstruction, and the Hodayot." Pages 171–93 in *Pedagogy in Ancient Judaism and Early Christianity*. Edited by Karina Martin Hogan, Matthew Goff, and Emma Wasserman. EJL 41. Atlanta: SBL Press, 2017.

Goh, "Galba." Goh, Benson. "Galba: A Comparison of Suetonius's and Plutarch's Biographies and Tacitus's *Histories*, with Implications for the Historical Reliability of the Gospels." Pages 173–200 in Keener and Wright, *Biographies and Jesus*.

Goldhill, "Anecdote." Goldhill, Simon. "The Anecdote: Exploring the Boundaries between Oral and Literate Performance in the Second Sophistic." Pages 96–113 in *Ancient Literacies: The Culture of Reading in Greece and Rome*. Edited by William A. Johnson and Holt N. Parker. New York: Oxford University Press, 2009.

Gondola, "Kimbangu." Gondola, Charles Didier. "Kimbangu, Simon, and Kimbanguism." Pages 766–67 in vol. 2 of *Encyclopedia of African History*. Edited by Kevin Shillington. 3 vols. New York: Fitzroy Dearborn, 2005.

González, *Acts.*   González, Justo L. *Acts: The Gospel of the Spirit.* Maryknoll, NY: Orbis Books, 2001.

Goodacre, *Case.*   Goodacre, Mark S. *The Case against Q: Studies in Markan Priority and the Synoptic Problem.* Harrisburg, PA: Trinity Press International, 2002.

Goodacre, "Redaction Criticism."   Goodacre, Mark S. "Redaction Criticism." *DJG*² 767–71.

Goodacre, *Synoptic Problem.*   Goodacre, Mark S. *The Synoptic Problem: A Way through the Maze.* New York: Sheffield Academic Press, 2001.

Goodenough, "Exposition."   Goodenough, E. R. "Philo's Exposition of the Law and His *De Vita Mosis.*" *HTR* 27 (2, April 1933): 109–25.

Goodenough, *Symbols.*   Goodenough, Erwin R. *Jewish Symbols in the Greco-Roman Period.* 13 vols. Bollingen Series 37. Vols. 1–12: New York: Pantheon, 1953–65. Vol. 13: Princeton: Princeton University Press, 1968.

Goodman, *Demons.*   Goodman, Felicitas D. *How about Demons? Possession and Exorcism in the Modern World.* Bloomington: Indiana University Press, 1988.

Goodman, *State.*   Goodman, Martin. *State and Society in Roman Galilee, A.D. 132–212.* Oxford Centre for Postgraduate Hebrew Studies. Totowa, NJ: Rowman & Allanheld, 1983.

Goody, *Interface.*   Goody, Jack. *The Interface between the Written and the Oral.* Cambridge: Cambridge University Press, 1987.

Goody, *Logic.*   Goody, Jack. *The Logic of Writing and the Organization of Society.* Studies in Literacy, Family, Culture, and the State. Cambridge: Cambridge University Press, 1986.

Goody and Watt, "Consequences."   Goody, Jack, and I. Watt. "The Consequences of Literacy." *Comparative Studies in Society and History* 5 (1963): 304–45.

Gordon, *Near East.*   Gordon, Cyrus H. *The Ancient Near East.* New York: W. W. Norton, 1965.

Görgemanns, "Biography."   Görgemanns, Herwig. "Biography: Greek." *BNP* 2:648–51.

Gorman, "Education."   Gorman, Heather. "Greco-Roman Education." *DBAM* 111–13.

Goshen Gottstein, "Jesus and Hillel."   Goshen Gottstein, A. "Jesus and Hillel: Are Comparisons Possible?" Pages 31–55 in *Hillel and Jesus: Comparative Studies of Two Major Religious Leaders.* Minneapolis: Fortress, 1997.

Goulder, *Midrash.*   Goulder, Michael D. *Midrash and Lection in Matthew.* Speaker's Lectures in Biblical Studies, 1969–71. London: SPCK, 1974.

Goulder, *Type and History.*   Goulder, Michael D. *Type and History in Acts.* London: SPCK, 1964.

Gowing, "Memory."   Gowing, Alain M. "Memory as Motive in Tacitus." Pages 43–64 in *Memory in Ancient Rome and Early Christianity.* Edited by Karl Galinsky. Oxford: Oxford University Press, 2016.

Gowing, "Republic."   Gowing, Alain M. "The Imperial Republic of Velleius Paterculus." Pages 411–18 in *A Companion to Greek and Roman Historiography.* Edited by John Marincola. 2 vols. Oxford: Blackwell, 2007.

Grafton, "Inspiration."   Grafton, Anthony. "Diogenes Laertius from Inspiration to Annoyance (and Back)." Pages 546–54 in *Diogenes Laertius "Lives of the Eminent Philosophers."*

Edited by James Miller. Translated by Pamela Mensch. New York: Oxford University Press, 2018.

Graham, *Beyond.* Graham, William Albert. *Beyond the Written Word: Oral Aspects of Scripture in the History of Religion.* Cambridge: Cambridge University Press, 1993.

Gramaglia, *"Testimonium."* Gramaglia, Pier Angelo. "Il *Testimonium Flavianum.* Analisi linguistica." *Hen* 20 (2, 1998): 153–77.

Granata, "Introduzione." Granata, Giovanna. "Introduzione allo studio del *De Vita Mosis* di Filone Alessandrino." PhD diss., Piso, 1995.

Grant, *Historians.* Grant, Michael. *Greek and Roman Historians: Information and Misinformation.* New York: Routledge, 1995.

Grant, "Introduction." Grant, Michael. "Introduction." Pages 7–26 in Tacitus, *The Annals of Imperial Rome.* Translated by Michael Grant. Rev. ed. Baltimore: Penguin, 1959.

Grappe, "Essai." Grappe, Christian. "Essai sur l'arrière-plan pascal des récits de la dernière nuit de Jésus." *RHPR* 65 (2, 1985): 105–25.

Gray, "Christianity." Gray, Richard. "Christianity." Pages 140–90 in *From 1905–1940.* Edited by A. D. Roberts. Vol. 7 of *The Cambridge History of Africa.* Edited by J. D. Fage and Roland Oliver. 8 vols. Cambridge: Cambridge University Press, 1986.

Gray, *Letters.* Gray, Patrick. *Opening Paul's Letters: A Reader's Guide to Genre and Interpretation.* Grand Rapids: Baker Academic, 2012.

Gray, "Monk." Gray, Christa. "The Emended Monk: The Greek Translation of Jerome's *Vita Malchi.*" Pages 117–32 in *Writing Biography in Greece and Rome: Narrative Technique and Fictionalization.* Edited by Koen De Temmerman and Kristoffel Demoen. Cambridge: Cambridge University Press, 2016.

Gray, *Prophetic Figures.* Gray, Rebecca. *Prophetic Figures in Late Second Temple Jewish Palestine: The Evidence from Josephus.* New York: Oxford University Press, 1993.

Grayzel, *History.* Grayzel, Solomon. *A History of the Jews.* Philadelphia: Jewish Publication Society of America, 1961.

Green, "Healing." Green, Joel B. "Healing." Pages 755–59 in vol. 2 of *The New Interpreter's Dictionary of the Bible.* 5 vols. Nashville: Abingdon, 2007.

Green, *Luke.* Green, Joel B. *The Gospel of Luke.* NICNT. Grand Rapids: Eerdmans, 1997.

Greenspoon, "Pronouncement Story." Greenspoon, Leonard. "The Pronouncement Story in Philo and Josephus." *Semeia* 20 (1981): 73–80.

Greenstone, *Messiah.* Greenstone, Julius H. *The Messiah Idea in Jewish History.* Philadelphia: Jewish Publication Society of America, 1906.

Griffin, "Philosophy." Griffin, Miriam. "Philosophy, Cato, and Roman Suicide I." *GR* 33 (1, 1986): 64–77.

Grillo, "Reflections." Grillo, Luca. "Leaving Troy and Creusa: Reflections on Aeneas' Flight." *CJ* 106 (1, October 2010): 43–68.

Grillo, "Scribam." Grillo, Luca. "Scribam ipse de me: The Personality of the Narrator in Caesar's Bellum Civile." *AJP* 132 (2, 2011): 243–71.

Grundmann, *Jesus der Galiläer.* Grundmann, Walter. *Jesus der Galiläer und das Judentum.* Leipzig: G. Wigand, 1941.

Guelich, "Genre." Guelich, Robert. "The Gospel Genre." Pages 173–208 in *The Gospel and the Gospels*. Edited by Peter Stuhlmacher. Grand Rapids: Eerdmans, 1991.

Guijarro Oporto, "Articulación literaria." Guijarro Oporto, Santiago. "La articulación literaria del libro de los Hechos." *EstBib* 62 (2, 2004): 185–204.

Gulick, *Windows*. Gulick, Anna. *Windows on a Different World*. Lexington, KY: Emeth, 2014.

Gunderson, "Augustus." Gunderson, Erik. "Augustus: *exemplum* in the *Augustus* and *Tiberius*." Pages 130–45 in *Suetonius the Biographer: Studies in Roman Lives*. Edited by Tristan Power and Roy K. Gibson. Oxford: Oxford University Press, 2013.

Gundry, *Matthew*. Gundry, Robert H. *Matthew: A Commentary on His Literary and Theological Art*. Grand Rapids: Eerdmans, 1982.

Gundry, "Memories." Gundry, Robert H. "Messed-Up Memories of Jesus?" *Books and Culture* 22 (4, November 2016): 14–16.

Gundry, *Use*. Gundry, Robert H. *The Use of the Old Testament in St. Matthew's Gospel, with Special Reference to the Messianic Hope*. NovTSup 18. Leiden: Brill, 1975.

Güttgemanns, *Questions*. Güttgemanns, Erhardt. *Candid Questions concerning Gospel Form Criticism: A Methodological Sketch of the Fundamental Problems of Form and Redaction Criticism*. PTMS 26. Pittsburgh: Pickwick, 1979.

Gutzwiller, "Epigrams." Gutzwiller, Kathryn. "Diogenes' Epigrams." Pages 561–67 in *Diogenes Laertius "Lives of the Eminent Philosophers."* Edited by James Miller. Translated by Pamela Mensch. New York: Oxford University Press, 2018.

Gwynne, *Action*. Gwynne, Paul. *Special Divine Action: Key Issues in the Contemporary Debate (1965–1995)*. TGST 12. Rome: Gregorian University Press, 1996.

Gyselinck and Demoen, "Author." Gyselinck, Wannes, and Kristoffel Demoen. "Author and Narrator: Fiction and Metafiction in Philostratus' *Vita Apollonii*." Pages 95–127 in *Theios Sophistes: Essays on Flavius Philostratus' Vita Apollonii*. Edited by Kristoffel Demoen and Danny Praet. Mnemosyne Supplements 305. Leiden: Brill, 2009.

Habinek, "Literacy." Habinek, Thomas. "Situating Literacy at Rome." Pages 114–40 in *Ancient Literacies: The Culture of Reading in Greece and Rome*. Edited by William A. Johnson and Holt N. Parker. New York: Oxford University Press, 2009.

Hacham, "Polemic." Hacham, Noah. "3 Maccabees: An Anti-Dionysian Polemic." Pages 167–83 in *Ancient Fiction: The Matrix of Early Christian and Jewish Narrative*. Edited by Jo-Ann A. Brant, Charles W. Hedrick, and Chris Shea. SBLSymS 32. Atlanta: SBL, 2005.

Hadas, "Introduction." Hadas, Moses. "Introduction." Pages ix–xxiii in *The Complete Works of Tacitus*. Edited by Moses Hadas. Translated by Alfred John Church and William Jackson Brodribb. New York: Random House, 1942.

Hadas and Smith, *Heroes*. Hadas, Moses, and Morton Smith. *Heroes and Gods: Spiritual Biographies in Antiquity*. Religious Perspectives 13. New York: Harper & Row, 1965.

Hägg, *Biography*. Hägg, Tomas. *The Art of Biography in Antiquity*. Cambridge: Cambridge University Press, 2012.

Hagner, *Matthew*. Hagner, Donald A. *Matthew*. 2 vols. WBC 33A, 33B. Dallas: Word, 1993–95.

Halbwachs, *Collective Memory.*   Halbwachs, Maurice. *On Collective Memory.* Edited and translated by Lewis A. Coser. Chicago: University of Chicago Press, 1992.

Haley, "Hadrian."   Haley, Evan. "Hadrian as Romulus; or, the Self-Representation of a Roman Emperor." *Latomus* 64 (4, 2005): 969–80.

Hall, "Delivery."   Hall, Jon. "Oratorical Delivery and the Emotions: Theory and Practice." Pages 218–34 in *A Companion to Roman Rhetoric.* Edited by William Dominik and Jon Hall. Oxford: Blackwell, 2007.

Hall, *Histories.*   Hall, Robert G. *Revealed Histories: Techniques from Ancient Jewish and Christian Historiography.* JSPSup 6. Sheffield: JSOT Press, 1991.

Hall, "History."   Hall, Robert Givin. "Revealed History: A Jewish and Christian Technique of Interpreting the Past." PhD diss., Duke University, 1986.

Hamel, "Argo."   Hamel, Gildas. "Taking the Argo to Nineveh: Jonah and Jason in a Mediterranean Context." *Judaism* 44 (3, 1995): 341–59.

Hamilton, *Plutarch.*   Hamilton, James R. *Plutarch: Alexander.* 2nd ed. Classical Commentaries on Latin and Greek Texts. London: Bristol Classical Press, 1999.

Hamilton, *Sociology.*   Hamilton, Malcolm B. *The Sociology of Religion: Theoretical and Comparative Perspectives.* London: Routledge, 2012.

Hamilton, "Story-Tellers."   Hamilton, Richard. "The Story-Tellers of Marrakesh." BBC News, February 19, 2007, http://news.bbc.co.uk/2/mobile/programmes/from_our_own_correspondent/6368057.stm.

Hamilton, "Storytelling."   Hamilton, Richard. "Can the Art of Storytelling Be Preserved?" BBC News, October 5, 2011, https://www.bbc.com/news/world-middle-east-15091860.

Hamilton and Shopes, *Oral History.*   Hamilton, Paula, and Linda Shopes, *Oral History and Public Memories.* Philadelphia: Temple University Press, 2009.

Hammond, *Sources.*   Hammond, N. G. L. *Sources for Alexander the Great: An Analysis of Plutarch's* Life *and Arrian's* Anabasis Alexandrou. New York: Cambridge University Press, 2007.

Hammond, "Speeches."   Hammond, Nigel G. L. "The Speeches in Arrian's *Indica* and *Anabasis.*" *ClQ* 49 (1, 1999): 238–53.

Hanciles, *Beyond Christendom.*   Hanciles, Jehu J. *Beyond Christendom: Globalization, African Migration, and the Transformation of the West.* Maryknoll, NY: Orbis Books, 2008.

Hanciles, "Conversion."   Hanciles, Jehu J. "Conversion and Social Change: A Review of the 'Unfinished Task' in West Africa." Pages 157–80 in *Christianity Reborn: The Global Expansion of Evangelicalism in the Twentieth Century.* Edited by Donald M. Lewis. SHCM. Grand Rapids: Eerdmans, 2004.

Hanley and Cohen, "Memory for People."   Hanley, Richard, and Gillian Cohen. "Memory for People: Faces, Names, and Voices." Pages 107–40 in *Memory in the Real World.* Edited by Gillian Cohen and Martin A. Conway. Hove, East Sussex: Psychology Press, 2007.

Hansen, *Abraham.*   Hansen, G. Walter. *Abraham in Galatians—Epistolary and Rhetorical Contexts.* JSNTSup 29. Sheffield: Sheffield Academic Press, 1989.

Hanson, *Acts.*   Hanson, R. P. C. *The Acts in the Revised Standard Version, with Introduction and Commentary.* Oxford: Clarendon, 1967.

Hanson, "Agricola." Hanson, William S. "Tacitus' 'Agricola': An Archaeological and Historical Study." *ANRW* 2.33.3 (1991):1741–84.

Hare, "Introduction." Hare, D. R. A. "The Lives of the Prophets: A New Translation and Introduction." *OTP* 2:379–84.

Harkins, *Reading*. Harkins, Angela Kim. *Reading with an "I" to the Heavens: Looking at the Qumran Hodayot through the Lens of Visionary Traditions*. Ekstasis: Religious Experience from Antiquity to the Middle Ages 3. Boston: de Gruyter, 2018.

Harmon, "Introduction." Harmon, A. M. "Introduction to *Charon*." Page 395 in vol. 2 of *Lucian*. Edited by A. M. Harmon, K. Kilburn, and M. D. Macleod. 8 vols. LCL. Cambridge, MA: Harvard University Press, 1913–67.

Harms, "Tradition." Harms, Robert. "Oral Tradition and Ethnicity." *Journal of Interdisciplinary History* 10 (1, summer 1979): 61–85.

Harnack, *Acts*. Harnack, Adolf von. *The Acts of the Apostles*. Translated by J. R. Wilkinson. New Testament Studies 3. London: Williams & Norgate, 1909.

Harrington, "Bible." Harrington, Daniel J. "The Bible Rewritten (Narratives)." Pages 239–47 in *Early Judaism and Its Modern Interpreters*. Edited by Robert A. Kraft and George W. E. Nickelsburg. SBLBMI 2. Atlanta: Scholars Press, 1986.

Harris, *Literacy*. Harris, William V. *Ancient Literacy*. Cambridge, MA: Harvard University Press, 2009.

Harris, Paterson, and Kemp, "Recall." Harris, Celia B., Helen M. Paterson, and Richard I. Kemp. "Collaborative Recall and Collective Memory: What Happens When We Remember Together?" *Memory* 16 (2008): 213–30.

Hartman, "Reflections." Hartman, Lars. "Some Reflections on the Problem of the Literary Genre of the Gospels." Pages 3–23 in Lars Hartman, *Text-Centered New Testament Studies*. Edited by David Hellholm. WUNT 102. Tübingen: Mohr Siebeck, 1997.

Harvey, *Listening*. Harvey, John D. *Listening to the Text: Oral Patterning in Paul's Letters*. Grand Rapids: Baker, 1998.

Hata, "Moses." Hata, Gohei. "The Story of Moses Interpreted within the Context of Anti-Semitism." Pages 180–97 in *Josephus, Judaism, and Christianity*. Edited by Louis H. Feldman and Gohei Hata. Detroit: Wayne State University Press, 1987.

Havelock, *Muse*. Havelock, Eric Alfred. *The Muse Learns to Write*. New Haven: Yale University Press, 1986.

Hays, *Echoes*. Hays, Richard B. *Echoes of Scripture in the Letters of Paul*. New Haven: Yale University Press, 1989.

Hays, *Reading Backwards*. Hays, Richard B. *Reading Backwards: Figural Christology and the Fourfold Gospel Witness*. Waco, TX: Baylor University Press, 2014.

Head, "Nazi Quest." Head, Peter M. "The Nazi Quest for an Aryan Jesus." *JSHJ* 2 (1, 2004): 55–89.

Head, "Note." Head, Peter M. "A Further Note on Reading and Writing in the Time of Jesus." *EQ* 75 (4, 2003): 343–45.

Hearon, "Mapping." Hearon, Holly. "Mapping Written and Spoken Word in the Gospel of Mark." Pages 379–92 in *The Interface of Orality and Writing: Speaking, Seeing, Writing in the Shaping of New Genres.* Edited by Annette Weissenrieder and Robert B. Coote. WUNT 260. Tübingen: Mohr Siebeck, 2010. Repr., BPC 11. Eugene, OR: Wipf & Stock, 2015.

Heath, *Hermogenes.* Heath, Malcolm, ed. and trans. *Hermogenes on Issues: Strategies of Argument in Later Greek Rhetoric.* Oxford: Clarendon, 1995.

Heath, *Menander.* Heath, Malcolm. *Menander: A Rhetor in Context.* New York: Oxford University Press, 2004.

Heever, "Tales." Heever, Gerhard van den. "Grotesque and Strange Tales of the Beyond: Truth, Fiction, and Social Discourse." Pages 179–95 in *Reading and Teaching Ancient Fiction: Jewish, Christian, and Greco-Roman Narratives.* Edited by Sara R. Johnson, Rubén R. Dupertuis, and Christine Shea. WGRWSup 11. Atlanta: SBL Press, 2018.

Heim, *Transformation.* Heim, Karl. *The Transformation of the Scientific World View.* New York: Harper & Brothers, 1953.

Heinze, "Introduction." Heinze, Ruth-Inge. "Introduction." Pages 1–18 in *Proceedings of the Fourth International Conference on the Study of Shamanism and Alternate Modes of Healing, Held at the St. Sabina Center, San Rafael, California, September 5–7, 1987.* Edited by Ruth-Inge Heinze. Madison, WI: A-R Editions, 1988.

Helms, *Fictions.* Helms, Randel. *Gospel Fictions.* Amherst, NY: Prometheus, 1988.

Hemer, *Acts.* Hemer, Colin J. *The Book of Acts in the Setting of Hellenistic History.* Edited by Conrad H. Gempf. WUNT 49. Tübingen: Mohr Siebeck, 1989.

Hemer, "Alexandria Troas." Hemer, Colin J. "Alexandria Troas." *TynBul* 26 (1975): 79–112.

Hemer, "Name of Felix." Hemer, Colin J. "The Name of Felix Again." *JSNT* 31 (1987): 45–49.

Henderson, *Christology.* Henderson, Suzanne Watts. *Christology and Discipleship in the Gospel of Mark.* SNTSMS 135. New York: Cambridge University Press, 2006.

Henderson, "Comparison." Henderson, Jordan. "A Comparison of Josephus' *Life* and *Jewish War*: An Attempt at Establishing the Acceptable Outer Limits of Biographies' Historical Reliability." Pages 261–75 in Keener and Wright, *Biographies and Jesus.*

Henderson, "*Didache.*" Henderson, Ian H. "*Didache* and Orality in Synoptic Comparison." *JBL* 111 (2, 1992): 283–306.

Henderson, "*Life* and *War.*" Henderson, Jordan. "Josephus's *Life* and *Jewish War* Compared to the Synoptic Gospels." *JGRCJ* 10 (2014): 113–31.

Hengel, *Acts and History.* Hengel, Martin. *Acts and the History of Earliest Christianity.* Translated by John Bowden. London: SCM, 1979; Philadelphia: Fortress, 1980.

Hengel, "Geography." Hengel, Martin. "The Geography of Palestine in Acts." Pages 27–78 in *The Book of Acts in Its Palestinian Setting.* Edited by Richard Bauckham. Vol. 4 of *The Book of Acts in Its First Century Setting.* Grand Rapids: Eerdmans, 1995.

Hengel, "Memory." Hengel, Martin. "Eye-Witness Memory and the Writing of the Gospels." Pages 70–96 in *The Written Gospel.* Edited by Markus Bockmuehl and Donald A. Hagner. Cambridge: Cambridge University Press, 2005.

Hengel, *Question.* Hengel, Martin. *The Johannine Question.* Translated by John Bowden. Philadelphia: Trinity Press International, 1989.

Hengel and Schwemer, *Damascus.* Hengel, Martin, and Anna Maria Schwemer. *Paul be-*

tween Damascus and Antioch: The Unknown Years. Translated by John Bowden. London: SCM, 1997.

Henige, "History." Henige, David. "African History and the Rule of Evidence: Is Declaring Victory Enough?" Pages 91–104 in *African Historiographies: What History for Which Africa?* Edited by Bogumil Jewsiewicki and David Newbury. SSAMD 12. Beverly Hills, CA: Sage, 1986.

Henze, "Composition." Henze, Matthias. "4 Ezra and 2 Baruch: Literary Composition and Oral Performance in First-Century Apocalyptic Literature." *JBL* 131 (1, 2012): 181–200.

Herford, *Christianity.* Herford, R. Travers. *Christianity in Talmud and Midrash.* London: Williams & Norgate, 1903.

Herman, "Motifs." Herman, Geoffrey. "Iranian Epic Motifs in Josephus' Antiquities (XVIII, 314–370)." *JJS* 57 (2, 2006): 245–68.

Heschel, *Aryan Jesus.* Heschel, Susannah. *The Aryan Jesus: Christian Theologians and the Bible in Nazi Germany.* Princeton: Princeton University Press, 2008.

Heschel, *Geiger.* Heschel, Susannah. *Abraham Geiger and the Jewish Jesus.* Chicago: University of Chicago Press, 1998.

Hester, "Blame." Hester, James D. "Placing the Blame: The Presence of Epideictic in Galatians 1 and 2." Pages 281–307 in *Persuasive Artistry: Studies in New Testament Rhetoric in Honor of George A. Kennedy.* Edited by Duane F. Watson. JSNTSup 50. Sheffield: Sheffield Academic Press, 1991.

Heyer, *Jesus Matters.* Heyer, C. J. den. *Jesus Matters: 150 Years of Research.* Valley Forge, PA: Trinity Press International, 1997.

Hezser, *Literacy.* Hezser, Catherine. *Jewish Literacy in Roman Palestine.* TSAJ 81. Tübingen: Mohr-Siebeck, 2001.

Hezser, "Randomness." Hezser, Catherine. "From Oral Conversation to Written Texts: Randomness in the Transmission of Rabbinic Traditions." Pages 36–51 in *Interface of Orality and Writing: Speaking, Seeing, Writing in the Shaping of New Genres.* Edited by Annette Weissenrieder and Robert B. Coote. BPC 11. Eugene, OR: Wipf & Stock, 2015.

Hezser, "Scribes." Hezser, Catherine. "Scribes/Scribality." *DBAM* 355–59.

Hezser, "Verwendung." Hezser, Catherine. "Die Verwendung der hellenistischen Gattung Chrie im frühen Christentum und Judentum." *JSJ* 27 (4, 1996): 371–439.

Hidalgo, "Study." Hidalgo, Esteban. "A Redaction-Critical Study on Philo's *On the Life of Moses,* Book One." Pages 277–300 in Keener and Wright, *Biographies and Jesus.*

Hiestermann, *Tradition.* Hiestermann, Heinz. *Paul and the Synoptic Jesus Tradition.* Arbeiten zur Bibel und ihrer Geschichte 58. Leipzig: Evangelische Verlagsanstalt, 2017.

Higgins, *Historicity.* Higgins, A. J. B. *The Historicity of the Fourth Gospel.* London: Lutterworth Press, 1960.

Hilbert, "Enemies." Hilbert, Benjamin D. H. "185,000 Slain Maccabean Enemies (Times Two): Hyperbole in the Books of Maccabees." *ZAW* 122 (1, 2010): 102–6.

Hill, *Corpus.* Hill, Charles E. *The Johannine Corpus in the Early Church.* Oxford: Oxford University Press, 2004.

Hill, "Evidence." Hill, David. "On the Evidence for the Creative Role of Christian Prophets." *NTS* 20 (1974): 262–74.

Hill, *Matthew.* Hill, David. *The Gospel of Matthew.* NCBC. Grand Rapids: Eerdmans, 1972.

Hill, *Prophecy.* Hill, David. *New Testament Prophecy.* NFTL. Atlanta: John Knox, 1979.

Hill, "Words." Hill, Charles E. " 'In These Very Words': Methods and Standards of Literary Borrowing in the Second Century." Pages 261–81 in *The Early Text of the New Testament.* Edited by Charles E. Hill and Michael J. Kruger. Oxford: Oxford University Press, 2012.

Hillard, Nobbs, and Winter, "Corpus." Hillard, T., A. Nobbs, and B. Winter. "Acts and the Pauline Corpus I: Ancient Literary Parallels." Pages 183–213 in *The Book of Acts in Its Ancient Literary Setting.* Edited by Bruce W. Winter and Andrew D. Clarke. Vol. 1 of *The Book of Acts in Its First Century Setting.* Edited by Bruce W. Winter. Grand Rapids: Eerdmans, 1993.

Hillman, "Statements." Hillman, Thomas P. "Authorial Statements, Narrative, and Character in Plutarch's Agesilaus-Pompeius." *GRBS* 35 (3, 1994): 255–80.

Hirsch, *Interpretation.* Hirsch, E. D. *Validity in Interpretation.* New Haven: Yale University Press, 1967.

Hirst et al., "Follow-Up." Hirst, W. "A Ten-Year Follow-Up of a Study of Memory for the Attack of September 11, 2001: Flashbulb Memories and Memories for Flashbulb Events." *JExpPscy: General* 144 (3, June 2015): 604–23.

Hock, "Curriculum." Hock, Ronald F. "The Educational Curriculum in Chariton's *Callirhoe.*" Pages 15–36 in *Ancient Fiction: The Matrix of Early Christian and Jewish Narrative.* Edited by Jo-Ann A. Brant, Charles W. Hedrick, and Chris Shea. SBLSymS 32. Atlanta: SBL, 2005.

Hock, "Paul and Education." Hock, Ronald F. "Paul and Greco-Roman Education." Pages 198–227 in *Paul in the Greco-Roman World: A Handbook.* Edited by J. Paul Sampley. Harrisburg, PA: Trinity Press International, 2003.

Hodkinson, "Features." Hodkinson, Owen. "Distinguishing Features of Deliberate Fictionality in Greek Biographical Narratives." *Phrasis* 51 (2010): 11–35.

Hoeree and Hoogbergen, "History." Hoeree, Joris, and Wim Hoogbergen. "Oral History and Archival Data Combined: The Removal of the Saramakan Granman Kofi Bosuman as an Epistemological Problem." *Communication and Cognition* 17 (2–3, 1984): 245–89.

Höffken, "Hiskija." Höffken, Peter. "Hiskija und Jesaja bei Josephus." *JSJ* 29 (1, 1998): 37–48.

Höffken, "Reichsteilung." Höffken, Peter. "Eine Reichsteilung bei Josephus Flavius. Beobachtungen zu seiner Auffassung von Daniel 5." *JSJ* 36 (2, 2005): 197–205.

Hoffman and Hoffman, "Memory Theory." Hoffman, Alice M., and Howard S. Hoffman. "Memory Theory: Personal and Social." Pages 275–96 in *Handbook of Oral History.* Edited by Thomas L. Charlton, Lois E. Myers, and Rebecca Sharpless; Lanham, MD: AltaMira Press, 2006.

Hofius, "Sayings." Hofius, Otfried. "Unknown Sayings of Jesus." Pages 336–60 in *The Gospel and the Gospels.* Edited by Peter Stuhlmacher. Grand Rapids: Eerdmans, 1991.

Hofmann, "Novels: Christian." Hofmann, Heinz. "Novels: Christian." *BNP* 9:846–49.

Hofmann, "Novels: Latin." Hofmann, Heinz. "Novels: Latin." *BNP* 9:843–46.

Hogan, "*Musar.*" Hogan, Karina Martin. "Would Philo Have Recognized Qumran *Musar* as Paideia?" Pages 81–98 in *Pedagogy in Ancient Judaism and Early Christianity*. Edited by Karina Martin Hogan, Matthew Goff, and Emma Wasserman. EJL 41. Atlanta: SBL Press, 2017.

Hogg, *Master-Builder.* Hogg, Rena L. *A Master-Builder on the Nile: Being a Record of the Life and Aims of John Hogg, Christian Missionary.* Pittsbugh: United Presbyterian Board of Education; New York: Fleming H. Revell, 1914.

Holladay, "Matthew." Holladay, Carl R. "The Gospel of Matthew within the Context of Second Temple Judaism." Paper presented at the International Conference on the Gospel of Matthew in Its Historical and Theological Context. Moscow, September 26, 2018.

Holladay, *Theios aner.* Holladay, Carl R. "*Theios aner*" in *Hellenistic Judaism: A Critique of the Use of This Category in New Testament Christology.* SBLDS 40. Missoula, MT: Scholars Press, 1977.

Holland, "Written." Holland, Drew S. "They Are Written Right There: An Investigation of Royal Chronicles as Sources in 1–2 Kings." PhD diss., Asbury Theological Seminary, 2018.

Holmberg, "Questions." Holmberg, Bengt. "Questions of Method in James Dunn's *Jesus Remembered.*" *JSNT* 26 (2004): 445–57.

Holmén, *Covenant Thinking.* Holmén, Tom. *Jesus and Jewish Covenant Thinking.* BIS 55. Leiden: Brill, 2001.

Holmén, "Doubts." Holmén, Tom. "Doubts about Double Dissimilarity: Restructuring the Main Criterion of Jesus-of-History Research." Pages 47–80 in *Authenticating the Words of Jesus.* Edited by Bruce Chilton and Craig A. Evans. NTTS 28.1. Leiden: Brill, 1999.

Holmén, "Introduction." Holmén, Tom. "An Introduction to the Continuum Approach." Pages 1–16 in *Jesus from Judaism to Christianity: Continuum Approaches to the Historical Jesus.* Edited by Tom Holmén. European Studies on Christian Origins. LNTS 352. London, New York: T&T Clark, 2007.

Holtz, "Paul and Tradition." Holtz, Traugott. "Paul and the Oral Gospel Tradition." Pages 380–93 in *Jesus and the Oral Gospel Tradition.* Edited by Henry Wansbrough. JSNTSup 64. Sheffield: Sheffield Academic Press, 1991.

Hope, *Book.* Hope, Richard. *The Book of Diogenes Laertius: Its Spirit and Its Method.* New York: Columbia University Press, 1930.

Hornblower, "Thucydides." Hornblower, Simon. "Thucydides." *BNP* 14:631–37.

Horsfall, "Ephemeris." Horsfall, Nicholas. "Dictys' Ephemeris and the Parody of Scholarship." *Illinois Classical Studies* 33–34 (2008–9): 41–63.

Horsley, *Hearing.* Horsley, Richard A. *Hearing the Whole Story: The Politics of Plot in Mark's Gospel.* Louisville: Westminster John Knox, 2001.

Horsley, *Magic.* Horsley, Richard A. *Jesus and Magic: Freeing the Gospel Stories from Modern Misconceptions.* Eugene, OR: Cascade, 2014.

Horsley, "Mark." Horsley, Richard A. "The Gospel of Mark in the Interface of Orality and Writing." Pages 144–65 in *The Interface of Orality and Writing: Speaking, Seeing, Writing in the Shaping of New Genres.* Edited by Annette Weissenrieder and Robert B.

Coote. WUNT 260. Tübingen: Mohr Siebeck, 2010. Repr., BPC 11. Eugene, OR: Wipf & Stock, 2015.

Horsley, "Patterns."   Horsley, Richard A. "Prominent Patterns in the Social Memory of Jesus and Friends." Pages 57–78 in *Memory, Tradition, and Text: Uses of the Past in Early Christianity*. Edited by A. Kirk and Tom Thatcher. Semeia 52. Atlanta: SBL, 2005.

Horsley, "Speeches."   Horsley, G. H. R. "Speeches and Dialogue in Acts." *NTS* 32 (4, 1986): 609–14.

Horton, "Types."   Horton, Robin. "Types of Spirit Possession in Kalabari Religion." Pages 14–49 in *Spirit Mediumship and Society in Africa*. Edited by John Beattie and John Middleton. New York: Africana, 1969.

Hose, "Cassius Dio."   Hose, Martin. "Cassius Dio: A Senator and Historian in the Age of Anxiety." Pages 461–67 in *A Companion to Greek and Roman Historiography*. Edited by John Marincola. 2 vols. Oxford: Blackwell, 2007.

Hose, "Historiography: Rome."   Hose, Martin. "Historiography: Rome." *BNP* 6:422–26.

Houston, *Characters*.   Houston, Keith. *Shady Characters: The Secret Life of Punctuation, Symbols and Other Typographical Marks*. London: Norton, 2013.

Houston, "Evidence."   Houston, George W. "Papyrological Evidence for Book Collections and Libraries in the Roman Empire." Pages 233–67 in *Ancient Literacies: The Culture of Reading in Greece and Rome*. Edited by William A. Johnson and Holt N. Parker. New York: Oxford University Press, 2009.

Houston, "Library."   Houston, George W. "How Did You Get Hold of a Book in a Roman Library? Three Second-Century Scenarios." *CBull* 80 (1, 2004): 5–13.

Houston, *Miracles*.   Houston, J. *Reported Miracles: A Critique of Hume*. Cambridge: Cambridge University Press, 1994.

Howard, *Gospel*.   Howard, Wilbert Francis. *The Fourth Gospel in Recent Criticism and Interpretation*. 3rd ed. London: Epworth Press, 1945.

Hubenthal, "Communicative Memory."   Hubenthal, Sandra. "Communicative Memory." *DBAM* 65–66.

Hubenthal, "Cultural Memory."   Hubenthal, Sandra. "Cultural Memory." *DBAM* 69–70.

Hubenthal, "Social Memory."   Hubenthal, Sandra. "Social Memory." *DBAM* 368–69.

Hulse et al., "Arousal."   Hulse, Lynn M., Kevin Allan, Amina Memon, and J. Don Read. "Emotional Arousal and Memory: A Test of the Poststimulus Processing Hypothesis." *American Journal of Psychology* 120 (2007): 73–90.

Hultgren, "Stories."   Hultgren, Arland J. "The Miracle Stories in the Gospels: The Continuing Challenge for Interpreters." *WW* 29 (2, Spring 2009): 129–35.

Humble and Sidwell, "Dreams."   Humble, Noreen, and Keith Sidwell, "Dreams of Glory: Lucian as Autobiographer." Pages 213–25 in *The Limits of Ancient Biography*. Edited by Brian McGing and Judith Mossman. Swansea, Wales: Classical Press of Wales, 2006.

Hume, *Miracles*.   Hume, David. *Of Miracles*. La Salle, IL: Open Court, 1985.

Hunt, *History*.   Hunt, Rosalie Hall. *Bless God and Take Courage: The Judson History and Legacy*. Valley Forge, PA: Judson, 2005.

Hunter, "Recall."   Hunter, Ian M. L. "Lengthy Verbatim Recall: The Role of Text." Pages

207–35 in *Progress in the Psychology of Language*. Edited by Andrew W. Ellis. London: Erlbaum, 1985.

Hunter, "Trends."   Hunter, Archibald M. "Recent Trends in Johannine Studies." *ExpT* 71 (6, March 1960): 164–67; (7, April 1960): 219–22.

Hurley, "Rhetorics."   Hurley, Donna W. "Rhetorics of Assassination: Ironic Reversal and the Emperor Gaius." Pages 146–58 in *Suetonius the Biographer: Studies in Roman Lives*. Edited by Tristan Power and Roy K. Gibson. Oxford: Oxford University Press, 2013.

Hurley, "Rubric Sandwich."   Hurley, Donna W. "Suetonius' Rubric Sandwich." Pages 21–37 in *Suetonius the Biographer: Studies in Roman Lives*. Edited by Tristan Power and Roy K. Gibson. Oxford: Oxford University Press, 2013.

Hurtado, "Fixation."   Hurtado, Larry W. "Oral Fixation and New Testament Studies? 'Orality,' 'Performance,' and Reading Texts in Early Christianity." *NTS* 60 (3, July 2014): 321–40.

Hurtado, *Lord Jesus Christ*.   Hurtado, Larry W. *Lord Jesus Christ: Devotion to Jesus in Earliest Christianity*. Grand Rapids: Eerdmans, 2003.

Iglesias, "Reflexoes."   Iglesias, Esther. "Reflexoes sobre o quefazer da historia oral no mundo rural." *Dados* 27 (1, 1984): 59–70.

Ilan, *Lexicon*.   Ilan, Tal. *Lexicon of Jewish Names in Late Antiquity. Part I: Palestine 330 BCE–200 CE*. TSAJ 91. Tübingen: Mohr Siebeck, 2002.

Inowlocki, "Adding."   Inowlocki, Sabrina. "'Neither Adding nor Omitting Anything': Josephus' Promise Not to Modify the Scriptures in Greek and Latin Context." *JJS* 56 (2005): 48–65.

Instone-Brewer, *Traditions*.   Instone-Brewer, David. *Traditions of the Rabbis from the Era of the New Testament*. Vol. 1. Grand Rapids: Eerdmans, 2004.

Irwin, "Biographies."   Irwin, Elizabeth. "The Biographies of Poets: The Case of Solon." Pages 13–30 in *The Limits of Ancient Biography*. Edited by Brian McGing and Judith Mossman. Swansea, Wales: Classical Press of Wales, 2006.

Ising, *Blumhardt*.   Ising, Dieter. *Johann Christoph Blumhardt, Life and Work: A New Biography*. Translated by Monty Ledford. Eugene, OR: Cascade, 2009. Translated from *Johann Christoph Blumhardt: Leben und Werk*. Göttingen: Vandenhoeck & Ruprecht, 2002.

Iverson, "Orality."   Iverson, Kelly R. "Orality and the Gospels: A Survey of Recent Research." *CurBR* 8 (1, 2009): 71–106.

Jackson, "Conventions."   Jackson, Howard M. "Ancient Self-Referential Conventions and Their Implications for the Authorship and Integrity of the Gospel of John." *JTS* 50 (1, 1999): 1–34.

Jacobson, "Visions."   Jacobson, Howard. "Visions of the Past: Jews and Greeks." *Judaism* 35 (4, 1986): 467–82.

Jáger, "Evanjelium."   Jáger, Róbert. "Evanjelium ako anticky bios. Definovanie literárneho zánru." *Studia Biblica Slovaca* 1 (2, 2009): 146–65.

Janácek, "Diogenes Laertius."   Janácek, Karel. "Diogenes Laertius and Sextus Empiricus (1959)." Pages 93–104 in *Studien zu Sextus Empiricus, Diogenes Laertius und zur pyr-*

rhonischen Skepsis. Edited by Filip Karfík and Jan Janda. Beiträge zur Altertumskunde 249. New York: de Gruyter, 2008.

Janáček, "Diogenes Laertius IX." Janáček, Karel. "Diogenes Laertius IX 101 and Sextus Empiricus M XI 69–75 (–78) (1962)." Pages 110–15 in *Studien zu Sextus Empiricus, Diogenes Laertius und zur pyrrhonischen Skepsis.* Edited by Filip Karfík and Jan Janda. Beiträge zur Altertumskunde 249. New York: de Gruyter, 2008.

Janicki, *Way.* Janicki, Toby. *The Way of Life: The Rediscovered Teachings of the Twelve Apostles to the Gentiles. Didache: A New Translation and Messianic Jewish Commentary.* Jerusalem: Vine of David, 2017.

Janin, *Pursuit.* Janin, Hunt. *The Pursuit of Learning in the Islamic World.* Jefferson, NC: McFarland, 2005.

Jantsch, "Jerusalem." Jantsch, Torsten. "Jerusalem as 'Realm of Memory' (lieu de mémoire) in the Gospel of Luke." Paper presented in the "Memory, Narrative, and Christology in the Synoptic Gospels" Seminar at the Annual Meeting of the Society for New Testament Studies. Athens, Greece, August 9, 2018.

Jenkins, *New Faces.* Jenkins, Philip. *The New Faces of Christianity: Believing the Bible in the Global South.* New York: Oxford University Press, 2006.

Jenkinson, "Nepos." Jenkinson, Edna. "Genus scripturae leve: Cornelius Nepos and the Early History of Biography at Rome." *ANRW* 1.3 (1973): 703–19.

Jensen, "Josephus." Jensen, Morten Hørning. "Josephus and Mark 6:6b–29: Herod Antipas's Execution of John the Baptist." Pages 92–99 in *Reading Mark in Context: Jesus and Second Temple Judaism.* Edited by Ben C. Blackwell, John K. Goodrich, and Jason Maston. Grand Rapids: Zondervan, 2018.

Jeremias, *Parables.* Jeremias, Joachim. *The Parables of Jesus.* 2nd rev. ed. New York: Scribner's, 1972.

Jeremias, *Promise.* Jeremias, Joachim. *Jesus' Promise to the Nations.* Translated by S. H. Hooke. SBT 24. London: SCM, 1958.

Jeremias, *Theology.* Jeremias, Joachim. *New Testament Theology.* New York: Scribner's, 1971.

Jeremias, *Unknown Sayings.* Jeremias, Joachim. *Unknown Sayings of Jesus.* Translated by Reginald H. Fuller. 2nd ed. London: SPCK, 1964.

Jervell, *Apostelgeschichte.* Jervell, Jacob. *Die Apostelgeschichte.* 17th ed. KEKNT 3. Göttingen: Vandenhoeck & Ruprecht, 1998.

Jervell, "Future." Jervell, Jacob. "The Future of the Past: Luke's Vision of Salvation History and Its Bearing on His Writing of History." Pages 104–26 in *History, Literature, and Society in the Book of Acts.* Edited by Ben Witherington III. Cambridge: Cambridge University Press, 1996.

Jewett, *Chronology.* Jewett, Robert. *A Chronology of Paul's Life.* Philadelphia: Fortress, 1979.

Jewett, "Shame." Jewett, Robert. "Paul, Shame, and Honor." Pages 551–74 in *Paul in the Greco-Roman World: A Handbook.* Edited by J. Paul Sampley. Harrisburg, PA: Trinity Press International, 2003.

Jilovsky, *Remembering Holocaust.*   Jilovsky, Esther. *Remembering the Holocaust: Generations, Witnessing, and Place.* New York: Bloomsbury, 2015.

Johnson, *Acts.*   Johnson, Luke Timothy. *The Acts of the Apostles.* SP 5. Collegeville, MN: Liturgical Press, 1992.

Johnson, "Fictions."   Johnson, Sara. "Third Maccabees: Historical Fictions and the Shaping of Jewish Identity in the Hellenistic Period." Pages 185–97 in *Ancient Fiction: The Matrix of Early Christian and Jewish Narrative.* Edited by Jo-Ann A. Brant, Charles W. Hedrick, and Chris Shea. SBLSymS 32. Atlanta: SBL, 2005.

Johnson, *Hume.*   Johnson, David. *Hume, Holism, and Miracles.* CSPhilRel. Ithaca, NY: Cornell University Press, 1999.

Johnson, "Imitate."   Johnson, Luke Timothy. "Does the New Testament Imitate Homer? Four Cases from the Acts of the Apostles." *TS* 66 (3, 2005): 489–90.

Johnson, "Luke-Acts."   Johnson, Luke Timothy. "Luke-Acts, Book of." *ABD* 4:403–20.

Johnson, *Miracles.*   Johnson, Luke Timothy. *Miracles: God's Presence and Power in Creation.* Louisville: Westminster John Knox, 2018.

Johnson and Goodrich, *Papyri* 3.   Johnson, Allan Chester, and Sidney Pullman Goodrich, eds. *Papyri in the Princeton University Collections.* Vol. 3: *Taxation in Egypt from Augustus to Hadrian.* Princeton: Princeton University Press, 2017.

Johnson and Musser, *Story.*   Johnson, Dennis, and Joe Musser. *Tell Me a Story: Orality; How the World Learns.* Colorado Springs, CO: David C. Cook, 2012.

Johnston, "Interpretations."   Johnston, Robert Morris. "Parabolic Interpretations Attributed to Tannaim." PhD diss., Hartford Seminary Foundation, 1977.

Johnston, "Observations."   Johnston, Robert Morris. "The Study of Rabbinic Parables: Some Preliminary Observations." Pages 337–57 in *SBL Seminar Papers, 1976.* Edited by George MacRae. SBLSP 1976. Missoula, MT: Scholars Press, 1976.

Jones, "Apollonius Passage."   Jones, C. P. "Apollonius of Tyana's Passage to India." *GRBS* 42 (2, 2001): 185–99.

Jones, "Inscription."   Jones, C. P. "The Inscription from Tel Maresha for Olympiodoros." *ZPE* 171 (2009): 100–104.

Jones, *Lucian.*   Jones, C. P. *Culture and Society in Lucian.* Cambridge, MA: Harvard University Press, 1986.

Jones, *Plutarch and Rome.*   Jones, C. P. *Plutarch and Rome.* Oxford: Oxford University Press, 1971.

Jones, "Reliability."   Jones, C. P. "The Reliability of Philostratus." Pages 11–16 in *Approaches to the Second Sophistic: Papers Presented to the American Philological Association.* Edited by Glen W. Bowersock. University Park, PA: American Philological Association, 1974.

Jones and Milns, *Commentary.*   Jones, Brian W., and Robert D. Milns. *Suetonius: The Flavian Emperors; A Historical Commentary.* Bristol: Bristol Classical Press, 2003.

Jonge, "Syntax."   Jonge, Casper C. de. "Dionysius of Halicarnassus on Thucydides' Syntax." In *Ancient Scholarship and Grammar: Archetypes, Concepts, and Contexts.* Edited by Stephanos Matthaios, Franco Montanari, and Antonios Rengakos. Berlin: de Gruyter, 2011.

Jorgensen, "Observation." Jorgensen, Danny L. "Participant Observation." Pages 1–15 in *Emerging Trends in the Social and Behavioral Sciences: An Interdisciplinary, Searchable and Linkable Resource*. New York: Wiley & Sons, 2015.

Jousse, *Style*. Jousse, Marcel. *The Oral Style*. Translated by Edgard Sienart and Richard Whitaker. New York: Garland, 1990.

Joyal, McDougall, and Yardley, *Education*. Joyal, Mark, Iain McDougall, and J. C. Yardley. *Greek and Roman Education: A Sourcebook*. New York: Routledge, 2009.

Judge, *First Christians*. Judge, Edwin A. *The First Christians in the Roman World: Augustan and New Testament Essays*. Edited by James R. Harrison. WUNT 229. Tübingen: Mohr Siebeck, 2008.

Judge, *Jerusalem and Athens*. Judge, Edwin A. *Jerusalem and Athens: Cultural Transformation in Late Antiquity*. Edited by Alanna Nobbs. Tübingen: Mohr Siebeck, 2010.

Judge, "Scholastic Community." Judge, Edwin A. "The Early Christians as a Scholastic Community." *JRH* 1 (1, 1960): 4–15; (3): 125–37. Reprinted in Judge, *First Christians*, 526–52.

Judge, "Sources." Judge, Edwin A. "Biblical Sources of Historical Method." Pages 276–81 in *Jerusalem and Athens: Cultural Transformation in Late Antiquity*. Edited by Alanna Nobbs. Tübingen: Mohr Siebeck, 2010.

Kaesser, "Tweaking." Kaesser, Christian. "Tweaking the Real: Art Theory and the Borderline between History and Morality in Plutarch's *Lives*." *GRBS* 44 (4, 2004): 361–74.

Kähler, *Historical Jesus*. Kähler, Martin. *The So-Called Historical Jesus and Historic, Biblical Christ*. Philadelphia: Fortress, 1964.

Kalu, *African Pentecostalism*. Kalu, Ogbu. *African Pentecostalism: An Introduction*. Oxford: Oxford University Press, 2008.

Kany, "Bericht." Kany, Roland. "Der lukanische Bericht von Tod und Auferstehung Jesu aus der Sicht eines hellenistichen Romanlesers." *NovT* 28 (1, 1986): 75–90.

Karla, "*Life of Aesop*." Karla, Grammatiki A. "*Life of Aesop*: Fictional Biography as Popular Literature?" Pages 47–64 in *Writing Biography in Greece and Rome: Narrative Technique and Fictionalization*. Edited by Koen De Temmerman and Kristoffel Demoen. Cambridge: Cambridge University Press, 2016.

Kaster, "*Grammaticus*." Kaster, Robert A. "*Grammaticus*." *OCD³* 646.

Katz and Lazarsfeld, *Influence*. Katz, Elihu, and Paul Lazarsfeld. *Personal Influence: The Part Played by People in the Flow of Mass Communications*. Glencoe, IL: Free Press, 1955.

Kavanagh, "Identity." Kavanagh, Bernard J. "The Identity and Fate of Caligula's Assassin, Aquila." *Latomus* 69 (4, 2010): 1007–17.

Kazen, "Imagery." Kazen, Thomas. "Son of Man as Kingdom Imagery: Jesus between Corporate Symbol and Individual Redeemer Figure." Pages 87–108 in *Jesus from Judaism to Christianity: Continuum Approaches to the Historical Jesus*. Edited by Tom Holmén. European Studies on Christian Origins. LNTS 352. London: T&T Clark, 2007.

Keaney and Lamberton, *Essay*. Keaney, John J., and Robert Lamberton. *Essay on the Life and Poetry of Homer*. American Classical Studies 40. Atlanta: Scholars Press, 1996.

Kechagia, "Philosophers." Kechagia, Eleni. "Dying Philosophers in Ancient Biography:

Zeno the Stoic and Epicurus." Pages 181–99 in *Writing Biography in Greece and Rome: Narrative Technique and Fictionalization.* Edited by Koen De Temmerman and Kristoffel Demoen. Cambridge: Cambridge University Press, 2016.

Kee, *Aretalogies.* Kee, Howard Clark. *Aretalogies, Hellenistic "Lives," and the Sources of Mark: Protocol of the Twelfth Colloquy, 8 December 1974.* Berkeley, CA: Center for Hermeneutical Studies in Hellenistic and Modern Culture, 1975.

Kee, "Aretalogy." Kee, Howard Clark. "Aretalogy and Gospel." *JBL* 92 (3, September 1973): 402–22.

Kee, "Century of Quests." Kee, Howard Clark. "A Century of Quests for the Culturally Compatible Jesus." *ThTo* 52 (1, 1995): 17–28.

Kee, *Every Nation.* Kee, Howard Clark. *To Every Nation under Heaven: The Acts of the Apostles.* Harrisburg, PA: Trinity Press International, 1997.

Kee, *Origins.* Kee, Howard Clark. *Christian Origins in Sociological Perspective: Methods and Resources.* Philadelphia: Westminster, 1980.

Keener, *Acts.* Keener, Craig S. *Acts: An Exegetical Commentary.* 4 vols. Grand Rapids: Baker Academic, 2012–15.

Keener, "Ancient Biography and Gospels." Keener, Craig S. "Ancient Biography and the Gospels: Introduction." Pages 1–45 in Keener and Wright, *Biographies and Jesus.*

Keener, "Apologetic." Keener, Craig S. "Paul and Sedition: Pauline Apologetic in Acts." *BBR* 22 (2, 2012): 201–24.

Keener, "Assumptions." Keener, Craig S. "Assumptions in Historical Jesus Research: Using Ancient Biographies and Disciples' Traditioning as a Control." *JSHJ* 9 (1, 2011): 26–58.

Keener, "Before Biographies." Keener, Craig S. "Appendix: Before Biographies; Memory and Oral Tradition." Pages 329–54 in Keener and Wright, *Biographies and Jesus.*

Keener, "Beheld." Keener, Craig S. "'We Beheld His Glory': John 1:14." Pages 15–25 in *Aspects of Historicity in the Fourth Gospel.* Edited by Paul N. Anderson, Felix Just, and Tom Thatcher. Vol. 2 of *John, Jesus, and History.* SBL Early Christianity and Its Literature 2. Atlanta: SBL, 2009.

Keener, "Biographies of a Sage." Keener, Craig S. "Reading the Gospels as Biographies of a Sage." *Buried History* 47 (2011): 59–66.

Keener, "Claims." Keener, Craig S. "First-Person Claims in Some Ancient Historians and Acts." *JGRCJ* 10 (2014): 9–23.

Keener, "Comparisons." Keener, Craig S. "Cultural Comparisons for Healing and Exorcism Narratives in Matthew's Gospel." *HTS/TS* 66 (1, 2010), art. 808, 7 pages.

Keener, *Corinthians.* Keener, Craig S. *1–2 Corinthians.* NCamBC. New York: Cambridge University Press, 2005.

Keener, "Did Not Know." Keener, Craig S. "We Cannot Say We Did Not Know." *Prism* 11 (2, March 2004): 14–15.

Keener, "Edict." Keener, Craig S. "Edict of Claudius." In *Brill Encyclopedia of Early Christianity.* Leiden: Brill, forthcoming.

Keener, "Ehrman vs. McIver." Keener, Craig S. "Bart Ehrman vs. Robert McIver on Oral Tradition." Pages 271–318 in *Treasures New and Old: Essays in Honor of Donald A. Hag-*

ner. Edited by Carl S. Sweatman and Clifford B. Kvidahl. GlossaHouse Festschrift Series 1. Wilmore, KY: GlossaHouse, 2017.

Keener, "Epitome." Keener, Craig S. "An Epitome of Matthean Themes: Matthew 28:18–20." Paper presented at the SNTS International Conference on the Gospel of Matthew in Its Historical and Theological Context. Moscow, September 28, 2018.

Keener, *Galatians* (Baker). Keener, Craig S. *Galatians*. Grand Rapids: Baker Academic, 2019.

Keener, *Galatians* (Cambridge). Keener, Craig S. *Galatians*. NCamBC. New York: Cambridge University Press, 2018.

Keener, "Genre." Keener, Craig S. "Genre, Sources, and History: Response to D. Moody Smith." Pages 321–23 in *What We Have Heard from the Beginning: The Past, Present, and Future of Johannine Studies*. Edited by Tom Thatcher. Waco, TX: Baylor University Press, 2007.

Keener, "Gospels as Historically Reliable Biography." Keener, Craig S. "The Gospels as Historically Reliable Biography." *The A.M.E. Zion Quarterly Review* 105 (4, October 1993): 12–23.

Keener, *Hermeneutics*. Keener, Craig S. *Spirit Hermeneutics: Reading Scripture in Light of Pentecost*. Grand Rapids: Eerdmans, 2016.

Keener, *Historical Jesus*. Keener, Craig S. *The Historical Jesus of the Gospels*. Grand Rapids: Eerdmans, 2009.

Keener, "Historical Tradition." Keener, Craig S. "Historical Tradition in the Fourth Gospel's Depiction of the Baptist." Paper presented at the Third Princeton-Prague Symposium on the Historical Jesus, Princeton, NJ, March 18, 2016. Pages 155–67 in *Jesus Research: The Gospel of John in Historical Inquiry*. Edited by James H. Charlesworth, with Jolyon G. R. Pruszinski. New York: Bloomsbury T&T Clark, 2019.

Keener, "Historicity of Nature Miracles." Keener, Craig S. "The Historicity of the Nature Miracles." Pages 41–65 in *The Nature Miracles of Jesus: Problems, Perspectives, and Prospects*. Edited by Graham Twelftree. Eugene, OR: Cascade, 2017.

Keener, *John*. Keener, Craig S. *The Gospel of John: A Commentary*. 2 vols. Peabody, MA: Hendrickson, 2003.

Keener, "Luke-Acts." Keener, Craig S. "Luke-Acts and the Historical Jesus." Pages 600–623 in *Jesus Research: New Methodologies and Perceptions; The Second Princeton-Prague Symposium on Jesus Research*. Edited by James Charlesworth, with Brian Rhea and Petr Pokorný. Grand Rapids: Eerdmans, 2014.

Keener, *Matthew*. Keener, Craig S. *The Gospel of Matthew: A Socio-rhetorical Commentary*. Grand Rapids: Eerdmans, 2009. Rev. version of *A Commentary on the Gospel of Matthew*. Grand Rapids: Eerdmans, 1999.

Keener, "Miracle Reports and Argument." Keener, Craig S. "Miracle Reports and the Argument from Analogy." *BBR* 25 (4, 2015): 475–95.

Keener, "Miracle Reports: Perspectives." Keener, Craig S. "Miracle Reports: Perspectives, Analogies, Explanations." Pages 53–65 in *Hermeneutik der frühchristlichen Wunder-*

erzählungen. Historiche, literarische und rezeptionsästhetische Aspekte. Edited by Bernd Kollmann and Ruben Zimmermann. WUNT 339. Tübingen: Mohr Siebeck, 2014.

Keener, *Miracles.*   Keener, Craig S. *Miracles: The Credibility of the New Testament Accounts.* Grand Rapids: Baker Academic, 2011.

Keener, "Miracles (2015)."   Keener, Craig S. "Miracles." Pages 101–7 in vol. 2 of *The Oxford Encyclopedia of Bible and Theology.* Edited by Samuel E. Balentine. 2 vols. New York: Oxford University Press, 2015.

Keener, "Miracles (2017)."   Keener, Craig S. "Miracles." Pages 443–49 in *Dictionary of Christianity and Science.* Edited by Paul Copan, Tremper Longman III, Christopher L. Reese, and Michael G. Strauss. Grand Rapids: Zondervan, 2017.

Keener, "Moussounga."   Keener, Médine Moussounga. "Jacques Moussounga." *DACB.* Online: https://dacb.org/stories/congo/moussounga-jacques/.

Keener, "Ndoundou."   Keener, Médine Moussounga. "Daniel Ndoundou." *DACB.* Online: https://dacb.org/stories/congo/ndoundou-daniel/.

Keener, "Otho 1."   Keener, Craig S. "Otho: A Targeted Comparison of Suetonius' Biography and Tacitus' History, with Implications for the Gospels' Historical Reliability." *BBR* 21 (3, 2011): 331–55.

Keener, "Otho 2."   Keener, Craig S. "Otho: A Targeted Comparison of Suetonius' Biography and Tacitus' History, with Implications for the Gospels' Historical Reliability." Pages 143–71 in Keener and Wright, *Biographies and Jesus.*

Keener, "Parallel Figures."   Keener, Craig S. "Jesus and Parallel Jewish and Greco-Roman Figures." Pages 85–111 in *Christian Origins and Greco-Roman Culture: Social and Literary Contexts for the New Testament.* Edited by Stanley Porter and Andrew W. Pitts. Vol. 1 of *Early Christianity in Its Hellenistic Context.* TENTS 9. Leiden: Brill, 2013.

Keener, "Plausibility."   Keener, Craig S. "The Plausibility of Luke's Growth Figures in Acts 2.41; 4.4; 21.20." *JGRCJ* 7 (2010): 140–63.

Keener, "Possession."   Keener, Craig S. "Spirit Possession as a Cross-Cultural Experience." *BBR* 20 (2, 2010): 215–36.

Keener, "Raised."   Keener, Craig S. "'The Dead Are Raised' (Matthew 11:5//Luke 7:22): Resuscitation Accounts in the Gospels and Eyewitness Testimony." *BBR* 25 (1, 2015): 55–79.

Keener, "Reassessment."   Keener, Craig S. "A Reassessment of Hume's Case against Miracles in Light of Testimony from the Majority World Today." *PRSt* 38 (3, Fall 2011): 289–310.

Keener, "Review of Bauckham."   Keener, Craig S. Review of *Jesus and the Eyewitnesses,* by Richard Bauckham. *BBR* 19 (2009): 130–32.

Keener, "Review of Bernier."   Keener, Craig S. Review of *The Quest for the Historical Jesus after the Demise of Authenticity,* by Jonathan Bernier. *BibInt* 26 (2018): 428–31.

Keener, "Review of Malina."   Keener, Craig S. Review of *Windows on the World of the New Testament,* by Bruce Malina. *CRBR* 7 (1994): 225–27.

Keener, "Rhetoric."   Keener, Craig S. "Rhetoric in Antiquity." *DBAM* 337–42.

Keener, "Rhetorical Techniques."   Keener, Craig S. "Some Rhetorical Techniques in Acts 24:2–21." Pages 221–51 in *Paul's World.* Edited by Stanley E. Porter. PAST 4. Leiden: Brill, 2008.

Keener, *Spirit.*   Keener, Craig S. *The Spirit in the Gospels and Acts: Divine Purity and Power.* Peabody, MA: Hendrickson, 1997. Repr., Grand Rapids: Baker Academic, 2010.

Keener, "Spirits."   Keener, Craig S. "Crooked Spirits and Spiritual Identity Theft: A Keener Response to Crooks?" *Journal of Mind and Behavior* 39 (2018): 345–71.

Keener, "Suggestions."   Keener, Craig S. "Suggestions for Future Study of Rhetoric and Matthew's Gospel." *HTS/TS* 66 (1, 2010), art. 812, 6 pages.

Keener, "Truth."   Keener, Craig S. "'What Is Truth?': Pilate's Perspective on Jesus in John 18:33–38." Pages 77–94 in *Glimpses of Jesus through the Johannine Lens*. Vol. 3 of *John, Jesus, and History*. Edited by Paul N. Anderson, Felix Just, and Tom Thatcher. SBL Early Christianity and Its Literature 18. Atlanta: Scholars Press, 2016.

Keener, "Weeden's Critique."   Keener, Craig S. "Weighing T. J. Weeden's Critique of Kenneth Bailey's Approach to Oral Tradition in the Gospels." *JGRCJ* 13 (2017): 41–78.

Keener and Keener, *Impossible Love.*   Keener, Craig S., and Médine Moussounga Keener. *Impossible Love: The True Story of an African Civil War, Miracles, and Hope against All Odds.* Grand Rapids: Chosen, 2016.

Keener and Wright, *Biographies and Jesus.*   Keener, Craig S., and Edward T. Wright, eds. *Biographies and Jesus: What Does It Mean for the Gospels to Be Biographies?* Lexington, KY: Emeth, 2016.

Keightley, "Memory."   Keightley, Georgia Masters. "Christian Collective Memory and Paul's Knowledge of Jesus." Pages 129–50 in *Memory, Tradition, and Text: Uses of the Past in Early Christianity*. Edited by A. Kirk and Tom Thatcher. Semeia 52. Atlanta: SBL, 2005.

Keith, "Assmann."   Keith, Chris. "Assmann, Jan." *DBAM* 26–27.

Keith, "Literacy."   Keith, Chris. "Literacy." *DBAM* 206–10.

Keith, "Prolegomena."   Keith, Chris. "Prolegomena on the Textualization of Mark's Gospel: Manuscript Culture, the Extended Situation, and the Emergence of the Written Gospel." Pages 161–86 in *Memory and Identity in Ancient Judaism and Early Christianity: A Conversation with Barry Schwartz*. Edited by Tom Thatcher. SemeiaSt 78. Atlanta: SBL, 2014.

Keith, *Scribal Elite.*   Keith, Chris. *Jesus against the Scribal Elite: The Origins of the Conflict.* Grand Rapids: Baker Academic, 2014.

Keith, "Social Memory Theory."   Keith, Chris. "Social Memory Theory and Gospels Research: The First Decade." *Early Christianity* 6 (3, 2015): 354–76 and (4, 2015): 517–42.

Keith, "Urbanization."   Keith, Chris. "Urbanization and Literate Status in Early Christian Rome: Hermas and Justin Martyr as Examples." Pages 187–204 in *The Urban World and the First Christians*. Edited by Steve Walton, Paul R. Trebilco, and David W. J. Gill. Grand Rapids: Eerdmans, 2017.

Keith and Hurtado, *Friends and Enemies.*   Keith, Chris, and Larry W. Hurtado, eds. *Jesus among Friends and Enemies: A Historical and Literary Introduction to Jesus in the Gospels.* Grand Rapids: Baker Academic, 2011.

Keith and Le Donne, *Criteria.*   Keith, Chris, and Anthony Le Donne. *Jesus, Criteria, and the Demise of Authenticity.* New York: T&T Clark, 2012.

Kelber, *Gospel.*   Kelber, Werner H. *The Oral and the Written Gospel: The Hermeneutics of*

Speaking and Writing in the Synoptic Tradition, Mark, Paul, and Q. Bloomington: Indiana University Press, 1997.

Kelber, "History." Kelber, Werner H. "The History of the Closure of Biblical Texts." Pages 71–99 in *The Interface of Orality and Writing: Speaking, Seeing, Writing in the Shaping of New Genres.* Edited by Annette Weissenrieder and Robert B. Coote. WUNT 260. Tübingen: Mohr Siebeck, 2010. Repr., BPC 11. Eugene, OR: Wipf & Stock, 2015.

Kelber, "Oral Tradition." Kelber, Werner H. "Oral Tradition, the Comparative Study of." *DBAM* 252–59.

Kelber, *Story.* Kelber, Werner H. *Mark's Story of Jesus.* Philadelphia: Fortress, 1979.

Kelber, "Work." Kelber, Werner H. "The Work of Birger Gerhardsson in Perspective." Pages 173–206 in *Jesus in Memory: Traditions in Oral and Scribal Perspectives.* Edited by Werner H. Kelber and Samuel Byrskog. Waco, TX: Baylor University Press, 2009.

Kelber, "Works." Kelber, Werner H. "The Works of Memory: Christian Origins as MnemoHistory—a Response." Pages 221–48 in *Memory, Tradition, and Text: Uses of the Past in Early Christianity.* Edited by A. Kirk and Tom Thatcher. Semeia 52. Atlanta: SBL, 2005.

Kelhoffer, "Book." Kelhoffer, James A. " 'How Soon a Book' Revisited: ΕΥΑΓΓΕΛΙΟΝ as a Reference to 'Gospel' Materials in the First Half of the Second Century." *ZNW* 95 (2004): 1–34.

Kelhoffer, "Maccabees at Prayer." Kelhoffer, James A. "The Maccabees at Prayer: Pro- and Anti-Hasmonean Tendencies in the Prayers of First and Second Maccabees." *Early Christianity* 2 (2, 2011): 198–218.

Kelhoffer, "Miracle Workers." Kelhoffer, James A. "Ordinary Christians as Miracle Workers in the New Testament and the Second and Third Century Christian Apologists." *BR* 44 (1999): 23–34.

Keller, *Hammer.* Keller, Mary. *The Hammer and the Flute: Women, Power, and Spirit Possession.* Baltimore: Johns Hopkins University Press, 2002.

Kelley, "Perspective." Kelley, Nicole. "The Cosmopolitan Expression of Josephus' Prophetic Perspective in the *Jewish War.*" *HTR* 97 (3, 2004): 257–74.

Kelly, "Forge Tongues." Kelly, Gavin. " 'To Forge Their Tongues to Grander Styles': Ammianus' Epilogue." Pages 474–80 in *A Companion to Greek and Roman Historiography.* Edited by John Marincola. 2 vols. Oxford: Blackwell, 2007.

Kelsey, *Healing.* Kelsey, Morton T. *Healing and Christianity in Ancient Thought and Modern Times.* New York: Harper & Row, 1973.

Kemp, "Flattery." Kemp, Jerome. "Flattery and Frankness in Horace and Philodemus." *GR* 57 (1, 2010): 65–76.

Kennedy, *Art of Rhetoric.* Kennedy, George A. *The Art of Rhetoric in the Roman World: 300 B.C.–A.D. 300.* Princeton: Princeton University Press, 1972.

Kennedy, *Classical Rhetoric.* Kennedy, George A. *Classical Rhetoric and Its Christian and Secular Tradition from Ancient to Modern Times.* Chapel Hill: University of North Carolina Press, 1980.

Kennedy, *Classical Rhetoric* (2). Kennedy, George A. *Classical Rhetoric and Its Christian and Secular Tradition from Ancient to Modern Times.* 2nd ed. Chapel Hill: University of North Carolina Press, 2003.

Kennedy, "Source Criticism." Kennedy, George A. "Classical and Christian Source Criticism." Pages 125–55 in *The Relationships among the Gospels: An Interdisciplinary Dialogue.* Edited by William O. Walker Jr. San Antonio: Trinity University Press, 1978.

Kennedy, "Survey." Kennedy, George A. "Historical Survey of Rhetoric." Pages 3–41 in *Handbook of Classical Rhetoric in the Hellenistic Period, 330 B.C.–A.D. 400.* Edited by Stanley E. Porter. Leiden: Brill, 1997.

Kensinger and Schacter, "Memories." Kensinger, E. A., and Daniel L. Schacter. "When True Memories Suppress False Memories: Effects of Ageing." *Cognitive Neuropsychology* 16 (1999): 399–415.

Kesteren et al., "Schema and Novelty." Kesteren, Marlieke T..R. van, et al. "How Schema and Novelty Augment Memory Formation." *Trends in Neurosciences* 35 (4, April 2012): 211–19.

Keylock, "Distinctness." Keylock, Leslie R. "Bultmann's Law of Increasing Distinctness." Pages 193–210 in *Current Issues in Biblical and Patristic Interpretation: Studies in Honor of Merrill C. Tenney Presented by His Former Students.* Edited by Gerald F. Hawthorne. Grand Rapids: Eerdmans, 1975.

Kidd, "Healing." Kidd, Thomas S. "The Healing of Mercy Wheeler: Illness and Miracles among Early American Evangelicals." *WMQ* 63 (1, January 2006): 149–70.

Kilpatrick, "Style." Kilpatrick, G. D. "Two Studies of Style and Text in the Greek New Testament." *JTS* 41 (1, 1990): 94–98.

Kim, *New Perspective.* Kim, Seyoon. *Paul and the New Perspective: Second Thoughts on the Origin of Paul's Gospel.* Grand Rapids: Eerdmans, 2002.

King, *Kurdistan.* King, Diane E. *Kurdistan on the Global Stage: Kinship, Land, and Community in Iraq.* New Brunswick, NJ: Rutgers University Press, 2014.

King and Stone, "Lineal Masculinity." King, Diane E., and Linda Stone. "Lineal Masculinity: Gendered Memory within Patriliny." *American Ethnologist* 37 (2, 2010): 323–36.

Kiparsky, "Oral Poetry." Kiparsky, Paul. "Oral Poetry: Some Linguistic and Typological Considerations." Pages 73–106 in *Oral Literature and the Formula.* Edited by Benjamin A. Stolz and Richard S. Shannon, III. Ann Arbor: Center for the Coordination of Ancient and Modern Studies, University of Michigan, 1976.

Kirk, "Cognition." Kirk, Alan. "Cognition, Commemoration, and Tradition: Memory and the Historiography of Jesus Research." *Early Christianity* 6 (3, Sept. 2015): 285–310.

Kirk, "Collective Memory." Kirk, Alan. "Collective Memory/Social Memory." *DBAM* 59–62.

Kirk, "Ehrman, Bauckham, and Bird." Kirk, Alan. "Ehrman, Bauckham, and Bird on Memory and the Jesus Tradition." *JSHJ* 15 (1, 2017): 88–114.

Kirk, "Elements." Kirk, Alan. "Bios Elements in the Q Tradition." Paper presented in the "Memory, Narrative, and Christology in the Synoptic Gospels" Seminar at the Annual Meeting of the Society for New Testament Studies. Athens, Greece, August 8, 2018.

Kirk, "Jesus Tradition." Kirk, Alan. "Jesus Tradition and Memory." *DBAM* 196–97.

Kirk, *Man Attested by God.* Kirk, J. R. Daniel. *A Man Attested by God: The Human Jesus of the Synoptic Gospels.* Grand Rapids: Eerdmans, 2016.

Kirk, *Memory.* Kirk, Alan. *Memory and the Jesus Tradition.* NewYork: Bloomsbury: T&T Clark, 2018.

Kirk, "Memory." Kirk, Alan. "Memory." Pages 155–72 in *Jesus in Memory: Traditions in Oral and Scribal Perspectives.* Edited by Werner H. Kelber and Samuel Byrskog. Waco, TX: Baylor University Press, 2009.

Kirk, "Memory of Violence." Kirk, Alan. "The Memory of Violence and the Death of Jesus in Q." Pages 191–206 in *Memory, Tradition, and Text: Uses of the Past in Early Christianity.* Edited by A. Kirk and Tom Thatcher. Semeia 52. Atlanta: SBL, 2005.

Kirk, "Memory Theory." Alan Kirk, "Memory Theory and Jesus Research." Pages 809–42 in *How to Study the Historical Jesus.* Vol. 1 of *Handbook for the Study of the Historical Jesus.* 4 vols. Edited by Tom Holmén and Stanley E. Porter. Leiden: Brill, 2011.

Kirk, "Nexus." Kirk, Alan. "The Memory-Tradition Nexus in the Synoptic Tradition: Memory, Media, and Symbolic Representation." Pages 131–59 in *Memory and Identity in Ancient Judaism and Early Christianity: A Conversation with Barry Schwartz.* Edited by Tom Thatcher. Semeia Studies 78. Atlanta: SBL, 2014.

Kirk, *Q in Matthew.* Kirk, Alan. *Q in Matthew: Ancient Media, Memory, and Early Scribal Transmission of the Jesus Tradition.* LNTS 564. New York: Bloomsbury, 2016.

Kirk, "Social and Cultural Memory." Kirk, Alan. "Social and Cultural Memory." Pages 1–24 in *Memory, Tradition, and Text: Uses of the Past in Early Christianity.* Edited by A. Kirk and Tom Thatcher. Semeia 52. Atlanta: SBL, 2005.

Kirk, "Traditionsbruch." Kirk, Alan. "Traditionsbruch." *DBAM* 429–30.

Kirk and Thatcher, "Tradition." Kirk, Alan, and Tom Thatcher. "Jesus Tradition as Social Memory." Pages 25–42 in *Memory, Tradition, and Text: Uses of the Past in Early Christianity.* Edited by A. Kirk and Tom Thatcher. Semeia 52. Atlanta: SBL, 2005.

Kisau, "Acts." Kisau, Paul Mumo. "Acts of the Apostles." Pages 1297–1348 in *Africa Bible Commentary.* Edited by Tokunboh Adeyemo. Grand Rapids: Zondervan; Nairobi: WordAlive, 2006.

Klassen, *Contribution.* Klassen, William. *The Contribution of Jewish Scholars to the Quest for the Historical Jesus.* Cambridge: Centre for Jewish-Christian Relations, 2000.

Klauck, *Context.* Klauck, Hans-Josef. *The Religious Context of Early Christianity: A Guide to Graeco-Roman Religions.* Translated by Brian McNeil. Minneapolis: Fortress, 2003.

Klauck, "Presence." Klauck, Hans-Josef. "Presence in the Lord's Supper: 1 Corinthians 11:23–26 in the Context of Hellenistic Religious History." Pages 57–74 in *One Loaf, One Cup—Ecumenical Studies of 1 Cor 11 and Other Eucharistic Texts: The Cambridge Conference on the Eucharist, August 1988.* Edited by Ben F. Meyer. New Gospel Studies 6. Macon, GA: Mercer University Press, 1993.

Kloppenborg, *Excavating Q.* Kloppenborg, John S. *Excavating Q: The History and Setting of the Sayings Gospel.* Minneapolis: Fortress, 2000.

Kloppenborg, "Memory." Kloppenborg, John S. "Memory, Performance, and the Sayings of Jesus." Pages 286–323 in *Memory in Ancient Rome and Early Christianity*. Edited by Karl Galinsky. Oxford: Oxford University Press, 2016.

Kloppenborg, "Variation." Kloppenborg, John S. "Variation in the Reproduction of the Double Tradition and an Oral Q?" *ETL* 83 (2007): 53–80.

Klutz, *Exorcism Stories*. Klutz, Todd. *The Exorcism Stories in Luke-Acts: A Sociostylistic Reading*. SNTSMS 129. Cambridge: Cambridge University Press, 2004.

Knapp, *Dawn*. Knapp, Robert. *The Dawn of Christianity: People and Gods in a Time of Magic and Miracles*. Cambridge, MA: Harvard University Press, 2017.

Knapstad, "Power." Knapstad, Bård Løkken. "Show Us the Power! A Study of the Influence of Miracles on the Conversion Process from Islam to Christianity in an Indonesian Context." ThM thesis, Norwegian Lutheran School of Theology, 2005.

Knight, "Problem." Knight, Christopher C. "The Synoptic Problem: Some Methodological Considerations and a New Hypothesis." *Heythrop Journal* 58 (2, 2017): 247–61.

Knoppers, "Problem." Knoppers, Gary N. "The Synoptic Problem? An Old Testament Perspective." *BBR* 19 (1, 2009): 11–34.

Kodell, *Luke*. Kodell, Jerome. *The Gospel according to Luke*. Collegeville Bible Commentary. Collegeville, MN: Liturgical Press, 1983.

Koester, *Introduction*. Koester, Helmut. *Introduction to the New Testament*. 2 vols. Philadelphia: Fortress, 1982.

Kok, "Papias." Kok, Michael J. "Did Papias of Hierapolis Use the Gospel according to the Hebrews as a Source?" *Journal of Early Christian Studies* 25 (1, Spring 2017): 29–53.

Kokkinos, "Gentilicium." Kokkinos, Nikos. "A Fresh Look at the *gentilicium* of Felix, Procurator of Judaea." *Latomus* 49 (1, 1990): 126–41.

Kolb, *Word*. Kolb, Robert. *Martin Luther and the Enduring Word of God: The Wittenberg School and Its Scripture-Centered Proclamation*. Grand Rapids: Baker Academic, 2016.

König, "Lives." König, Jason. "The Cynic and Christian Lives of Lucian's *Peregrinus*." Pages 227–54 in *The Limits of Ancient Biography*. Edited by Brian McGing and Judith Mossman. Swansea, Wales: Classical Press of Wales, 2006.

Konstan, "*Apollonius* and Novel." Konstan, David. "*Apollonius, King of Tyre*, and the Greek Novel." Pages 173–82 in *The Search for the Ancient Novel*. Edited by James Tatum. Baltimore: Johns Hopkins University Press, 1994.

Konstan, "Invention." Konstan, David. "The Invention of Fiction." Pages 3–17 in *Ancient Fiction and Early Christian Narrative*. Edited by Ronald F. Hock, J. Bradley Chance, and Judith Perkins. SBLSymS 6. Atlanta: SBL, 1998.

Konstan, "Subjectivity." Konstan, David. "A New Subjectivity? Teaching Ἔρως through the Greek Novel and Early Christian Texts." Pages 251–60 in *Reading and Teaching Ancient Fiction: Jewish, Christian, and Greco-Roman Narratives*. Edited by Sara R. Johnson, Rubén R. Dupertuis, and Christine Shea. WGRWSup 11. Atlanta: SBL Press, 2018.

Konstan, *Symmetry*. Konstan, David. *Sexual Symmetry: Love in the Ancient Novel and Related Genres*. Princeton: Princeton University Press, 1994.

Konstan and Walsh, "Biography." Konstan, David, and Robyn Walsh. "Civic and Subversive Biography in Antiquity." Pages 26–43 in *Writing Biography in Greece and Rome:*

Narrative Technique and Fictionalization. Edited by Koen De Temmerman and Kristoffel Demoen. Cambridge: Cambridge University Press, 2016.

Koren and Nevo, "Approaches." Koren, J., and Y. D. Nevo. "Methodological Approaches to Islamic Studies." *Der Islam* 68 (1991): 87–107.

Koriat, Goldsmith, and Pansky, "Psychology." Koriat, Asher, Morris Goldsmith, and Ainat Pansky. "Toward a Psychology of Memory Accuracy." *Annual Review of Psychology* 51 (2000): 481–537.

Koschorke, Ludwig, and Delgado, *History*. Koschorke, Klaus, Frieder Ludwig, and Mariano Delgado, eds., with Roland Spliesgart. *A History of Christianity in Asia, Africa, and Latin America, 1450–1990: A Documentary Sourcebook*. Grand Rapids: Eerdmans, 2007.

Koskenniemi, "Apollonius." Koskenniemi, Erkki. "Apollonius of Tyana: A Typical θεῖος ἀνήρ?" *JBL* 117 (3, 1998): 455–67.

Koskenniemi, "Background." Koskenniemi, Erkki. "The Religious-Historical Background of the New Testament Miracles." Pages 103–16 in *Religious and Spiritual Events*. Vol. 1 of *Miracles: God, Science, and Psychology in the Paranormal*. Edited by J. Harold Ellens. 3 vols. Westport, CT; London: Praeger, 2008.

Koskenniemi, *Miracle-Workers*. Koskenniemi, Erkki. *The Old Testament Miracle-Workers in Early Judaism*. WUNT 2.206. Tübingen: Mohr Siebeck, 2005.

Koskenniemi, "Moses." Koskenniemi, E. "Moses—a Well-Educated Man: A Look at the Educational Idea in Early Judaism." *JSP* 17 (4, 2008): 281–96.

Koutstaal, Verfaellie, and Schacter, "Objects." Koutstaal, W., M. Verfaellie, and D. L. Schacter. "Recognizing Identical vs. Similar Categorically Related Common Objects: Further Evidence for Degraded Gist-Representations in Amnesia." *Neuropsychology* 15 (2001): 268–89.

Kraha and Boals, "Negative." Kraha, Amanda, and Adriel Boals, "Why So Negative? Positive Flashbulb Memories for a Personal Event." *Memory* 22 (4, May 2014): 442–49.

Krasser, "Reading." Krasser, Helmut. "Light Reading." *BNP* 7:553–55.

Krieger, "Hauptquelle." Krieger, Klaus-Stefan. "Zur Frage nach der Hauptquelle über die Geschichte der Provinz Judäa in den Antiquitates judaicae des Flavius Josephus." *BN* 63 (1992): 37–41.

Krieger, "Verwandter." Krieger, Klaus-Stefan. "War Flavius Josephus ein Verwandter des hasmonäischen Königshauses?" *BN* 73 (1994): 58–65.

Kruger, *Crossroads*. Kruger, Michael J. *Christianity at the Crossroads: How the Second Century Shaped the Future of the Church*. Downers Grove, IL: IVP Academic, 2018.

Kugel and Greer, *Interpretation*. Kugel, James L., and Rowan A. Greer. *Early Biblical Interpretation*. LEC 3. Philadelphia: Westminster, 1986.

Kuhrt, "Mesopotamia." Kuhrt, Amélie. "Ancient Mesopotamia in Classical Greek and Hellenistic Thought." Pages 55–66 in vol. 1 of *Civilizations of the Ancient Near East*. Edited by Jack M. Sasson. 4 vols. New York: Scribner's, 1995.

Kulp, "Patterns." Kulp, Joshua. "Organisational Patterns in the Mishnah in Light of Their Toseftan Parallels." *JJS* 58 (1, 2007): 52–78.

Kümmel, *Introduction.* Kümmel, Werner George. *Introduction to the New Testament.* London: SCM, 1965.

Kurz, "Models." Kurz, William S. "Narrative Models for Imitation in Luke-Acts." Pages 171–89 in *Greeks, Romans, and Christians: Essays in Honor of Abraham J. Malherbe.* Edited by David L. Balch, Everett Ferguson, and Wayne A. Meeks. Minneapolis: Fortress, 1990.

Kurz, *Reading Luke-Acts.* Kurz, William S. *Reading Luke-Acts: Dynamics of Biblical Narrative.* Louisville: Westminster John Knox, 1993.

Kwon, "Charting." Kwon, Youngju. "Charting the (Un)charted: Gospels as Ancient Biographies and Their (Un)explored Implications." Pages 59–76 in Keener and Wright, *Biographies and Jesus.*

Kwon, "Reimagining." Kwon, Youngju. "Reimagining the Jesus Tradition: Orality, Memory, and Ancient Biography." PhD diss., Asbury Theological Seminary, 2018.

Kysar, *John.* Kysar, Robert. *John.* ACNT. Minneapolis: Augsburg Publishing House, 1986.

Kysar, *Maverick Gospel.* Kysar, Robert. *John, the Maverick Gospel.* Atlanta: John Knox Press, 1976.

Labahn, "Secondary Orality." Labahn, Michael. "Secondary Orality." *DBAM* 362–64.

Ladouceur, "Josephus and Masada." Ladouceur, David J. "Josephus and Masada." Pages 95–113 in *Josephus, Judaism, and Christianity.* Edited by Louis H. Feldman and Gohei Hata. Detroit: Wayne State University Press, 1987.

Ladouceur, "Masada: Consideration." Ladouceur, David J. "Masada: A Consideration of the Literary Evidence." *GRBS* 21 (3, 1980): 245–60.

Laistner, *Historians.* Laistner, M. L. W. *The Greater Roman Historians.* Berkeley: University of California Press, 1947.

Lake and Cadbury, *Commentary.* Lake, Kirsopp, and Henry J. Cadbury. *English Translation and Commentary.* Vol. 4 of *The Beginnings of Christianity: The Acts of the Apostles.* Edited by F. J. Foakes-Jackson and Kirsopp Lake. London: Macmillan, 1933. Repr., Grand Rapids: Baker Book House, 1979.

Laks, "Diogenes Laertius." Laks, André. "Diogenes Laertius and the Pre-Socratics." Pages 588–92 in *Diogenes Laertius "Lives of the Eminent Philosophers."* Edited by James Miller. Translated by Pamela Mensch. New York: Oxford University Press, 2018.

Lalleman, "Apocryphal Acts." Lalleman, Pieter J. "Apocryphal Acts and Epistles." *DNTB* 66–69.

Lamour, "Organisation." Lamour, Denis. "L'organisation du récit dans l'*Autobiographie* de Flavius Josèphe." *BAGB* 55 (2, 1996): 141–50.

Lanciano, Curci, and Semin, "Determinants." Lanciano, Tiziana, Antonietta Curci, and Gün R. Semin. "The Emotional and Reconstructive Determinants of Emotional Memories: An Experimental Approach to Flashbulb Memory Investigation." *Memory* 18 (5, 2010): 473–85.

Lane, "Christology." Lane, William L. "*Theios Anēr Ch*ristology and the Gospel of Mark." Pages 144–61 in *New Dimensions in New Testament Study.* Edited by Richard N. Longenecker and Merrill C. Tenney. Grand Rapids: Zondervan Publishing House, 1974.

Lane, *Mark*.   Lane, William L. *The Gospel of Mark*. NICNT. Grand Rapids: Eerdmans, 1974.

Lanfranchi, "Reminiscences."   Lanfranchi, Pierluigi. "Reminiscences of Ezekiel's *Exagoge* in Philo's *De Vita Mosis*." Pages 144–50 in *Moses in Biblical and Extra-biblical Traditions*. Edited by Axel Graupner and Michael Wolter. BZAW 372. Berlin: de Gruyter, 2007.

Lang, *Kunst*.   Lang, Manfred. *Die Kunst des christlichen Lebens. Rezeptionsästhetische Studien zum lukanischen Paulusbild*. ABIG 29. Leipzig: Evangelische Verlagsanstalt, 2008.

Lapide, *Hebrew*.   Lapide, Pinchas E. *Hebrew in the Church: The Foundations of Jewish-Christian Dialogue*. Translated by Erroll F. Rhodes. Grand Rapids: Eerdmans, 1984.

Lapide and Luz, *Jezus*.   Lapide, Pinchas, and Ulrich Luz. *A Zsidó Jézus. Zsidó tézisek, Kerensztény válaszok*. Budapest: Logos Kiado, 1994.

Lardner, *Works*.   Lardner, Nathaniel. *Works of Nathaniel Lardner, D.D., with a Life by Dr. Kippis*. 10 vols. London: William Ball, 1838. Orig. pub., 1788.

Larsen, Thompson, and Hansen, "Time."   Larsen, Steen F., Charles P. Thompson, and Tia Hansen. "Time in Autobiographical Memory." Pages 129–56 in *Remembering Our Past: Studies in Autobiographical Memory*. Edited by David C. Rubin. Cambridge: Cambridge University Press, 1996.

Lavery, "Lucullus."   Lavery, Gerald B. "Plutarch's Lucullus and the Living Bond of Biography." *CJ* 89 (3, 1994): 261–73.

Leaney, *Luke*.   Leaney, A. R. C. *A Commentary on the Gospel according to St. Luke*. BNTC. London: Black, 1958.

Le Cornu, *Acts*.   Le Cornu, Hilary, with Joseph Shulam. *A Commentary on the Jewish Roots of Acts*. 2 vols. Jerusalem: Academon, 2003.

Le Donne, *Historiographical Jesus*.   Le Donne, Anthony. *The Historiographical Jesus: Memory, Typology, and the Son of David*. Waco, TX: Baylor University Press, 2009.

Le Donne, "Presentism."   Le Donne, Anthony. "Presentism/Constructionism." *DBAM* 307–8.

Le Donne, "Traditionalism."   Le Donne, Anthony. "Traditionalism/Continuitism." *DBAM* 428–29.

Lee, "Source Criticism."   Lee, Soo Kwang. "Source Criticism of Accounts of Alexander's Life, with Implications for the Gospels' Historical Reliability." Pages 201–15 in Keener and Wright, *Biographies and Jesus*.

Lee, "Translations: Greek."   Lee, John A. L. "Translations of the Old Testament: I. Greek." Pages 775–83 in *Handbook of Classical Rhetoric in the Hellenistic Period, 330 B.C.–A.D. 400*. Edited by Stanley E. Porter. Leiden: Brill, 1997.

Lefkowitz, *Lives*.   Lefkowitz, Mary R. *Lives of the Greek Poets*. 2nd ed. Baltimore: Johns Hopkins University Press, 2012.

Lefkowitz, "Poet."   Lefkowitz, Mary R. "The Poet as Hero: Fifth-Century Autobiography and Subsequent Biographical Fiction." *ClQ* 28 (1978): 459–69.

Lendon, "Historians."   Lendon, J. E. "Historians without History: Against Roman Historiography." Pages 41–61 in *The Cambridge Companion to the Roman Historians*. Edited by Andrew Feldherr. Cambridge: Cambridge University Press, 2009.

Lenfant, "Fragments." Lenfant, Dominique. " 'Peut-on se fier aux 'fragments' d'historiens? L'Example des citations d'Hérodote." *Ktèma* 24 (1999): 103–21.

Leo, *Biographie.* Leo, Friedrich. *Die griechisch-römische Biographie nach ihrer literarischen Form.* Leipzig: Teubner, 1901.

Levene, "Historiography." Levene, D. S. "Roman Historiography in the Late Republic." Pages 275–89 in *A Companion to Greek and Roman Historiography.* Edited by John Marincola. 2 vols. Oxford: Blackwell, 2007.

Levine, "Christian Faith." Levine, Amy-Jill. "Christian Faith and the Study of the Historical Jesus: A Response to Bock, Keener, and Webb." *JSHJ* 9 (1, 2011): 96–106.

Levine, "Introduction." Levine, Amy-Jill. "Introduction." Pages 1–39 in *The Historical Jesus in Context.* Edited by Amy-Jill Levine, Dale C. Allison Jr., and John Dominic Crossan. PrRR. Princeton: Princeton University Press, 2006.

Levine, *Misunderstood Jew.* Levine, Amy-Jill. *The Misunderstood Jew: The Church and the Scandal of the Jewish Jesus.* San Francisco: HarperSanFrancisco, 2006.

Levine, "Synagogue." Levine, Lee I. "The Second Temple Synagogue: The Formative Years." Pages 7–31 in *The Synagogue in Late Antiquity.* Edited by Lee I. Levine. Philadelphia: ASOR, 1986.

Levine, "Twice." Levine, Nachman. "Twice as Much of Your Spirit: Pattern, Parallel, and Paronomasia in the Miracles of Elijah and Elisha." *JSOT* 85 (1999): 25–46.

Levine and Witherington, *Luke.* Levine, Amy-Jill, and Ben Witherington III. *The Gospel of Luke.* NCamBC. New York: Cambridge University Press, 2018.

Levinskaya, *Setting.* Levinskaya, Irina. *The Book of Acts in Its Diaspora Setting.* Vol. 5 of *The Book of Acts in Its First Century Setting.* Edited by Bruce W. Winter. Grand Rapids: Eerdmans, 1996.

Lévy-Bruhl, *Natives.* Lévy-Bruhl, Lucien. *How Natives Think.* Translated by Lilian A. Clare. London: Allen & Unwin, 1926.

Lewis, *Ecstatic Religion.* Lewis, I. M. *Ecstatic Religion: An Anthropological Study of Spirit Possession and Shamanism.* Pelican Anthropology Library. Middlesex: Penguin, 1971.

Lewis, *History.* Lewis, Bernard. *History Remembered, Recovered, Invented.* New York: Simon & Schuster, 1975.

Lewis, *Life.* Lewis, Naphtali. *Life in Egypt under Roman Rule.* Oxford: Clarendon, 1983.

Libby, "Moons." Libby, Brigitte B. "Moons, Smoke, and Mirrors in Apuleius' Portrayal of Isis." *AJP* 132 (2, 2011): 301–22.

Licona, *Differences.* Licona, Michael R. *Why Are There Differences in the Gospels? What We Can Learn from Ancient Biography.* New York: Oxford University Press, 2017.

Licona, "Reliable." Licona, Michael R. "Are the Gospels 'Historically Reliable'? A Focused Comparison of Suetonius's *Life of Augustus* and the Gospel of Mark." *Religions* 10 (3, 2019): 148.

Licona, *Resurrection.* Licona, Michael R. *The Resurrection of Jesus: A New Historiographical Approach.* Downers Grove, IL: InterVarsity, 2010.

Licona, "Sky Falling." Licona, Michael. "Is the Sky Falling in the World of Historical Jesus Research?" *BBR* 26 (3, 2016): 353–68.

Licona, "Viewing." Licona, Michael R. "Viewing the Gospels as Ancient Biographies Resolves Many Contradictions." Pages 323–28 in Keener and Wright, *Biographies and Jesus.*

Liefeld, "Preacher." Liefeld, Walter Lewis. "The Wandering Preacher as a Social Figure in the Roman Empire." PhD diss., Columbia University, 1967.

Liefeld and Pao, "Luke." Liefeld, Walter L., and David W. Pao. "Luke." Pages 19–355 in *The Expositor's Bible Commentary: Luke-Acts.* Vol. 10 of *The Expositor's Bible Commentary.* Rev. ed. Grand Rapids: Zondervan, 2007.

Lindars, *John.* Lindars, Barnabas. *John.* NTG. Sheffield: Sheffield Academic Press, 1990.

Lindenberger, "Ahiqar." Lindenberger, J. M. "Ahiqar: A New Translation and Introduction." *OTP* 2:479–93.

Lindner, "Geschichtsauffassung." Lindner, Helgo. "Die Geschichtsauffassung des Flavius Josephus im Bellum judaicum. Gleichzeitig ein Beitrag zur Quellenfrage, Diss., Tübingen 1970." *TLZ* 96 (12, 1971): 953–54.

Linton, "Memory." Linton, Marigold. "Memory for Real World Events." Pages 376–404 in *Explorations in Cognition.* Edited by Donald A. Norman and David E. Rumelhart. San Francisco: W. H. Freeman, 1975.

Lintott, *Romans.* Lintott, Andrew. *The Romans in the Age of Augustus.* Malden, MA: Wiley-Blackwell, 2010.

Litwa, "Eyewitnesses." Litwa, M. David. "Literary Eyewitnesses: The Appeal to an Eyewitness in John and Contemporaneous Literature." *NTS* 64 (3, July 2018): 343–61.

Litwak, *Echoes.* Litwak, Kenneth Duncan. *Echoes of Scripture in Luke-Acts: Telling the History of God's People Intertextually.* JSNTSup 282. London: T&T Clark, 2005.

Loftus, "Reality." Loftus, Elizabeth F. "The Reality of Repressed Memories." *American Psychologist* 48 (1993): 518–37.

Loftus et al., "Manufacturing Memory." Loftus, Elizabeth F., Mary Nucci, and Hunter G. Hoffman. "Manufacturing Memory." *American Journal of Forensic Psychology* 16 (1998): 63–76.

Loke, *Origin.* Loke, Andrew Ter Ern. *The Origin of Divine Christology.* SNTSMS 169. Cambridge: Cambridge University Press, 2017.

Long, "Introduction." Long, Herbert S. "Introduction." Pages xv–xxvi in *Diogenes Laertius "Lives of Eminent Philosophers."* Translated by R. D. Hicks. Rev. ed. 2 vols. LCL. Cambridge, MA: Harvard University Press, 1972.

Long, "Samuel." Long, V. Phillips. "1 Samuel." Pages 267–411 in vol. 2 of *Zondervan Illustrated Bible Backgrounds Commentary: Old Testament.* Edited by John Walton. 5 vols. Grand Rapids: Zondervan, 2009.

Long, "Zeno." Long, A. A. "Zeno of Citium: Cynic Founder of the Stoic Tradition." Pages 603–10 in *Diogenes Laertius "Lives of the Eminent Philosophers."* Edited by James Miller. Translated by Pamela Mensch. New York: Oxford University Press, 2018.

Long and Sharples, "Diogenes Laertius." Long, Herbert S., and Robert W. Sharples. "Diogenes Laertius." *OCD*[3] 474–75.

Longenecker, "Pompeii." Longenecker, Bruce W. "Pompeii (Writing/Literacy in)." *DBAM* 303–5.

Longenecker, *Rhetoric*.   Longenecker, Bruce W. *Rhetoric at the Boundaries: The Art and Theology of New Testament Chain-Link Transitions*. Waco, TX: Baylor University Press, 2005.

Loos, *Miracles*.   Loos, Hendrik van der. *The Miracles of Jesus*. NovTSup 9. Leiden: Brill, 1965.

Lord, *Singer*.   Lord, Albert B. *The Singer of Tales*. New York: Atheneum, 1965.

Lorsch, "Conception."   Lorsch, Robin S. "Augustus' Conception and the Heroic Tradition." *Latomus* 56 (4, 1997): 790–99.

Loubser, "Possession."   Loubser, J. A. "Possession and Sacrifice in the New Testament and African Traditional Religion: The Oral Forms and Conventions behind the Literary Genres." *Neot* 37 (2, 2003): 221–45.

Luce, *Livy*.   Luce, Torrey J. *Livy: The Composition of His History*. Princeton: Princeton University Press, 1977.

Luijk, *Children*.   Luijk, Ruben van. *Children of Lucifer: The Origins of Modern Religious Satanism*. New York: Oxford University Press, 2016.

Luke, "Ideology."   Luke, Trevor. "Ideology and Humor in Suetonius' *Life of Vespasian* 8." *CW* 103 (4, 2010): 511–27.

Lumpp, "Ong."   Lumpp, Randy F. "Ong, Walter J." *DBAM* 250–52.

Lutz, "Musonius."   Lutz, Cora E. "Musonius Rufus: The Roman Socrates." *YCS* 10 (1947): 3–147.

Luz, "Masada."   Luz, Menahem. "Eleazar's Second Speech on Masada and Its Literary Precedents." *RMPhil* 126 (1, 1983): 25–43.

Luz, *Matthew*.   Luz, Ulrich. *Matthew 1–7: A Commentary*. Translated by Wilhelm C. Linss. Minneapolis: Fortress, 1989.

Lyons, *Autobiography*.   Lyons, George. *Pauline Autobiography: Toward a New Understanding*. SBLDS 73. Atlanta: Scholars Press, 1985.

Ma, "Encounter."   Ma, Julie C. "'A Close Encounter with the Transcendental': Proclamation and Manifestation in Pentecostal Worship in Asian Context." Pages 127–45 in *Asian Church and God's Mission: Studies Presented in the International Symposium on Asian Mission in Manila, January 2002*. Edited by Wonsuk Ma and Julie C. Ma. Manila: OMF Literature; West Caldwell, NJ: Mountain World Mission, 2003.

Ma, "Mission."   Ma, Julie C. "Pentecostalism and Asian Mission." *Missiology* 35 (1, January 2007): 23–37.

Ma, "Vanderbout."   Ma, Julie C. "Elva Vanderbout: A Woman Pioneer of Pentecostal Mission among Igorots." *JAM* 3 (1, 2001): 121–40.

MacDonald, *Epics*.   MacDonald, Dennis R. *The Homeric Epics and the Gospel of Mark*. New Haven: Yale University Press, 2000.

MacDonald, *Imitate Homer*.   MacDonald, Dennis R. *Does the New Testament Imitate Homer? Four Cases from the Acts of the Apostles*. New Haven: Yale University Press, 2003.

Mack, *Myth*.   Mack, Burton L. *A Myth of Innocence: Mark and Christian Origins*. Philadelphia: Fortress, 1988.

Mack and Robbins, *Patterns.* Mack, Burton L., and Vernon K. Robbins. *Patterns of Persuasion in the Gospels.* Sonoma, CA: Polebridge, 1989.

Maclean and Aitken, *Heroikos.* Maclean, Jennifer K. Berenson, and Ellen Bradshaw Aitken, eds. and trans. *Flavius Philostratus: Heroikos.* SBLWGRW 1. Atlanta: SBL, 2001.

MacMullen, *Christianizing.* MacMullen, Ramsay. *Christianizing the Roman Empire.* New Haven: Yale University Press, 1984.

Maddox, *Purpose.* Maddox, Robert. *The Purpose of Luke-Acts.* SNTW. Edinburgh: T&T Clark, 1982. FRLANT. Göttingen: Vandenhoeck & Ruprecht, 1982.

Maier, "Kult." Maier, Johann. "Zu Kult und Liturgie der Qumrangemeinde." *RevQ* 14 (4, 1990): 543–86.

Maisonneuve, "Parables." Maisonneuve, Dominique de la. "The Parables of Jesus and the Rabbinic Parables." *SIDIC* 20 (1987): 8–15.

Malbon, *Company.* Malbon, Elizabeth Struthers. *In the Company of Jesus: Characters in Mark's Gospel.* Louiville: Westminster John Knox, 2000.

Malherbe, "Theorists." Malherbe, Abraham J. "Ancient Epistolary Theorists." *OJRS* 5 (2, 1977): 3–77.

Malherbe and Ferguson, *Gregory of Nyssa.* Malherbe, Abraham J., and Everett Ferguson. *Gregory of Nyssa "The Life of Moses."* New York: Paulist Press, 1978.

Malina and Neyrey, *Portraits.* Malina, Bruce J., and Jerome H. Neyrey. *Portraits of Paul: An Archaeology of Ancient Personality.* Louisville: Westminster John Knox, 1996.

Malkki, *Purity and Exile.* Malkki, Liisa H. *Purity and Exile: Violence, Memory, and National Cosmology among Hutu Refugees in Tanzania.* Chicago: University of Chicago Press, 1995.

Mandler, *Stories.* Mandler, Jean Matter. *Stories, Scripts, and Scenes: Aspects of Schema Theory.* John M. MacEachran Memorial Lecture Series, 1983. Hillsdale, NJ: L. Erlbaum Associates, 1984.

Manson, "Review of Jeremias." Manson, T. W. Review of *Die Gleichnisse Jesu*, by Joachim Jeremias. *NTS* 1 (1954–55): 58.

Manson, *Teaching.* Manson, T. W. *The Teaching of Jesus*, Cambridge: Cambridge University Press, 1931.

Marchant, "Introduction." Marchant, E. C. "Introduction to *Memorabilia* and *Oeconomicus.*" Pages vii–xxvii in vol. 4 of *Xenophon.* Translated by Carleton L. Brownson, O. J. Todd, and E. C. Marchant. 4 vols. LCL. New York: G. P. Putnam's Sons, 1918–23.

Marcus, "Gospel of Peter." Marcus, Joel. "The Gospel of Peter as a Jewish Christian Document." *NTS* 64 (4, October 2018): 473–94.

Marcus, *Mark.* Marcus, Joel. *Mark.* 2 vols. AB 27, 27A. New Haven: Yale University Press, 1999, 2009.

Marcus, "War." Marcus, Joel. "The Jewish War and the Sitz im Leben of Mark." *JBL* 111 (3, 1992): 441–62.

Marguerat, *Actes.* Marguerat, Daniel. *Les Actes des apôtres (1–12).* CNT, 2nd ser., 5A. Geneva: Labor et Fides, 2007.

Marguerat, *Histoire.*   Marguerat, Daniel. *La première histoire du christianisme (les Actes des apôtres).* LD 180. Paris: Cerf, 1999.

Marguerat, *Historian.*   Marguerat, Daniel. *The First Christian Historian: Writing the "Acts of the Apostles."* Translated by Ken McKinney, Gregory J. Laughery, and Richard Bauckham. SNTSMS 121. Cambridge: Cambridge University Press, 2002.

Marguerat, "Pionnier."   Marguerat, Daniel. "Luc, pionnier de l'historiographie chrétienne." *RSR* 92 (4, 2004): 513–38.

Marguerat, "Unité."   Marguerat, Daniel. "Luc-Actes. Une unité à construire." Pages 57–81 in *The Unity of Luke-Acts.* Edited by Joseph Verheyden. BETL 142. Leuven: Leuven University Press, 1999.

Marincola, *Authority.*   Marincola, John. *Authority and Tradition in Ancient Historiography.* Cambridge: Cambridge University Press, 1997.

Marincola, "Introduction."   Marincola, John. "Introduction." Pages 1–9 in *A Companion to Greek and Roman Historiography.* Edited by John Marincola. 2 vols. Oxford: Blackwell, 2007.

Marincola, "Speeches."   Marincola, John. "Speeches in Classical Historiography." Pages 118–32 in *A Companion to Greek and Roman Historiography.* Edited by John Marincola. 2 vols. Oxford: Blackwell, 2007.

Marincola, "Tacitus' Prefaces."   Marincola, John. "Tacitus' Prefaces and the Decline of Imperial Historiography." *Latomus* 58 (2, 1999): 391–404.

Marrou, *History.*   Marrou, H. I. *A History of Education in Antiquity.* Translated by George Lamb. Madison: University of Wisconsin Press, 1956.

Marshall, *Enmity.*   Marshall, Peter. *Enmity in Corinth: Social Conventions in Paul's Relations with the Corinthians.* WUNT 2.23. Tübingen: Mohr Siebeck, 1987.

Marshall, *Historian.*   Marshall, I. Howard. *Luke: Historian and Theologian.* Exeter, UK: Paternoster, 1970.

Marshall, *Luke.*   Marshall, I. Howard. *The Gospel of Luke: A Commentary on the Greek Text.* NIGTC. Grand Rapids: Eerdmans, 1978.

Marshall, *No Myth.*   Marshall, David. *Jesus Is No Myth: The Fingerprints of God on the Gospels.* Fall City, WA: Kuai Mu Press, 2016.

Marshall, "Reading."   Marshall, I. Howard. "Reading the Book, 7: Luke-Acts." *ExpT* 108 (7, 1997): 196–200.

Marshall, "Theme."   Marshall, I. Howard. "'Israel' and the Story of Salvation: One Theme in Two Parts." Pages 340–57 in *Jesus and the Heritage of Israel: Luke's Narrative Claim upon Israel's Legacy.* Edited by David P. Moessner. Luke the Interpreter of Israel 1. Harrisburg, PA: Trinity Press International, 1999.

Marshall, "Treatise."   Marshall, I. Howard. "Acts and the 'Former Treatise.'" Pages 163–82 in *The Book of Acts in Its Ancient Literary Setting.* Edited by Bruce W. Winter and Andrew D. Clarke. Vol. 1 of *The Book of Acts in Its First Century Setting.* Edited by Bruce W. Winter. Grand Rapids: Eerdmans, 1993.

Martell-Otero, "Satos."   Martell-Otero, Loida I. "Of Satos and Saints: Salvation from the

Periphery." Edited by Renata Furst-Lambert. *Perspectivas: Hispanic Theological Initiative Occasional Paper Series* 4 (Summer 2001): 7–33.

Martin, "Mithraism." Martin, Luther H. "Roman Mithraism and Christianity." *Numen* 36 (1, 1989): 2–15.

Martin, "Pericope." Martin, Ralph P. "The Pericope of the Healing of the Centurion's Servant/Son (Matt 8:5–13 par. Luke 7:1–10): Some Exegetical Notes." Pages 14–22 in *Unity and Diversity in New Testament Theology: Essays in Honor of George E. Ladd*. Edited by Robert A. Guelich. Grand Rapids: Eerdmans, 1978.

Martin, "Tacitus." Martin, Ronald Haithwaite. "Tacitus." *OCD³* 1469–71.

Martin, "Tacitus on Agricola." Martin, Ronald H. "Tacitus on Agricola: Truth and Stereotype." Pages 9–12 in *Form and Fabric: Studies in Rome's Material Past in Honour of B. R. Hartley*. Edited by Joanna Bird. Oxbow Monograph 80. Oxford: Oxbow, 1998.

Martin, "Topic Lists." Martin, Michael W. "Progymnastic Topic Lists: A Compositional Template for Luke and Other Bioi?" *NTS* 54 (1, 2008): 18–41.

Martínez-Taboas, "Seizures." Martínez-Taboas, Alfonso. "Psychogenic Seizures in an Espiritismo Context: The Role of Culturally Sensitive Psychotherapy." *PsycTRPT* 42 (1, Spring 2005): 6–13.

Marxsen, *Mark.* Marxsen, Willi. *Mark the Evangelist: Studies on the Redaction History of the Gospel.* Translated by James Boyce, Donald Juel, and William Poehlmann, with Roy A. Harrisville. Nashville: Abingdon, 1969.

Mason, "Contradiction." Mason, Steven. "Contradiction or Counterpoint? Josephus and Historical Method." *Review of Rabbinic Judaism* 6 (2–3, 2003): 145–88.

Mason, *Josephus and New Testament.* Mason, Steven. *Josephus and the New Testament.* Peabody, MA: Hendrickson, 1992.

Mason, *Life.* Mason, Steve, trans. *Life of Josephus.* Vol. 9 of *Flavius Josephus: Translation and Commentary.* Edited by Steve Mason. Leiden: Brill, 2001.

Mason, "Pharisee?" Mason, Steven. "Was Josephus a Pharisee? A Re-examination of Life 10–12." *JJS* 40 (1, 1989): 31–45.

Masse, "Basis." Masse, W. Bruce. "The Celestial Basis of Civilization." *Vistas in Astronomy* 39 (1995): 463–77.

Masse, "Earth." Masse, W. Bruce. "Earth, Air, Fire, and Water: The Archaeology of Bronze Age Cosmic Catastrophes." Pages 53–92 in *Natural Catastrophes during Bronze Age Civilisations.* Edited by Benny Peiser, Trevor Palmer, and Mark Bailey. BAR International Series S728. Oxford: Archaeopress, 1998.

Massey, "Disagreement." Massey, Preston T. "Disagreement in the Greco-Roman Literary Tradition and the Implications for Gospel Research." *BBR* 22 (1, 2012): 51–80.

Mather, Johnson, De Leonardis, "Reliance." Mather, Mara, Marcia K. Johnson, and Doreen M. De Leonardis. "Stereotype Reliance in Source Monitoring: Age Differences and Neuropsychological Test Correlates." *Cognitive Neuropsychology* 16 (3–5, 1999): 437–58.

Matijasik, *Canons.* Matijasik, Ivan. *Shaping the Canons of Ancient Greek Historiography: Imitation, Classicism, and Literary Criticism.* Beiträge zur Altertumskunde 359. Boston: de Gruyter, 2018.

Matson, *Dialogue.* Matson, Mark A. *In Dialogue with Another Gospel: The Influence of the Fourth Gospel on the Passion Narrative of the Gospel of Luke.* SBLDS 178. Atlanta: SBL, 2001.

Matthews, "Review." Matthews, Christopher R. Review of *Story as History—History as Story*, by Samuel Byrskog. *RBL*, July 17, 2001.

Matthews, "Teaching Fiction." Matthews, Shelly. "Teaching Fiction, Teaching Acts: Introducing the Linguistic Turn in the Biblical Studies Classroom." Pages 213–31 in *Reading and Teaching Ancient Fiction: Jewish, Christian, and Greco-Roman Narratives.* Edited by Sara R. Johnson, Rubén R. Dupertuis, and Christine Shea. WGRWSup 11. Atlanta: SBL Press, 2018.

Matthews and Clark, *Faith Factor.* Matthews, Dale A., with Connie Clark. *The Faith Factor: Proof of the Healing Power of Prayer.* New York: Viking Penguin, 1998.

Mattila, "Question." Mattila, Sharon Lea. "A Question Too Often Neglected." *NTS* 41 (1995): 199–217.

Mayer, "Abrahambildes." Mayer, Günter. "Aspekte des Abrahambildes in der hellenistisch-jüdischen Literatur." *EvT* 32 (2, 1972): 118–27.

Mayes, "Biography." Mayes, Andrew D. H. "Biography in the Ancient World: The Story of the Rise of David." Pages 1–12 in *The Limits of Ancient Biography.* Edited by Brian McGing and Judith Mossman. Swansea, Wales: Classical Press of Wales, 2006.

Mazar, "Josephus and Excavations." Mazar, Benjamin. "Josephus Flavius and the Archaeological Excavations in Jerusalem." Pages 325–29 in *Josephus, the Bible, and History.* Edited by Louis H. Feldman and Gohei Hata. Detroit: Wayne State University Press, 1989.

Mburu, *Hermeneutics.* Mburu, Elizabeth. *African Hermeneutics.* Carlisle, UK: Langham, Hippobooks, 2019.

McCasland, *Finger.* McCasland, S. Vernon. *By the Finger of God: Demon Possession and Exorcism in Early Christianity in the Light of Modern Views of Mental Illness.* New York: Macmillan, 1951.

McClenon, *Events.* McClenon, James. *Wondrous Events: Foundations of Religious Belief.* Philadelphia: University of Pennsylvania Press, 1994.

McClenon, *Healing.* McClenon, James. *Wondrous Healing: Shamanism, Human Evolution, and the Origin of Religion.* DeKalb, IL: Northern Illinois University Press, 2002.

McClenon, "Miracles." McClenon, James. "Miracles in Kongo Religious History: Evaluating the Ritual Healing Theory." Pages 176–97 in *Medical and Therapeutic Events.* Vol. 2 of *Miracles: God, Science, and Psychology in the Paranormal.* Edited by J. Harold Ellens. Westport, CT: Praeger, 2008.

McClenon, "Shamanic Healing." McClenon, James. "Shamanic Healing, Human Evolution, and the Origin of Religion." *JSSR* 36 (1997): 323–37.

McClenon and Nooney, "Experiences." McClenon, James, and Jennifer Nooney. "Anomalous Experiences Reported by Field Anthropologists: Evaluating Theories Regarding Religion." *AnthCons* 13 (2, 2002): 46–60.

McClymond, *Redemption.* McClymond, Michael J. *The Devil's Redemption: A New History and Interpretation of Christian Universalism*. 2 vols. Grand Rapids: Baker Academic, 2018.

McClymond, *Stranger*.   McClymond, Michael J. *Familiar Stranger: An Introduction to Jesus of Nazareth*. Grand Rapids: Eerdmans, 2004.

McDonald, "Herodotus."   McDonald, A. H. "Herodotus on the Miraculous." Pages 81–92 in *Miracles: Cambridge Studies in Their Philosophy and History*. Edited by C. F. D. Moule. London: Mowbray, 1965.

McFarlin, *Book of Records*.   McFarlin, Donald, ed. *The Guinness Book of Records 1991*. New York: Facts on File, 1991.

McGill, "Seneca on Plagiarizing."   McGill, Scott. "Seneca the Elder on Plagiarizing Cicero's *Verrines*." *Rhetorica* 23 (4, 2005): 337–46.

McGing, "Adaptation."   McGing, Brian. "Philo's Adaptation of the Bible in his *Life of Moses*." Pages 117–40 in *The Limits of Ancient Biography*. Edited by Brian McGing and Judith Mossman. Swansea, Wales: Classical Press of Wales, 2006.

McGrath, "Islands."   McGrath, James F. "Written Islands in an Oral Stream: Gospel and Oral Traditions." Pages 3–12 in *Jesus and Paul: Global Perspectives in Honor of James D. G. Dunn for His Seventieth Birthday*. Edited by B. J. Oropeza, C. K. Robertson, and Douglas C. Mohrmann. LNTS 414. New York: T&T Clark, 2009.

McGrew, "Argument."   McGrew, Timothy. "The Argument from Miracles: A Cumulative Case for the Resurrection of Jesus of Nazareth." Pages 593–662 in *The Blackwell Companion to Natural Theology*. Edited by J. P. Moreland and William Lane Craig. Malden, MA: Blackwell, 2009.

McGrew, *Hidden*.   McGrew, Lydia. *Hidden in Plain View: Undesigned Coincidence in the Gospels and Acts*. Chilicothe, OH: DeWard, 2017.

McInerney, "Arrian and Romance."   McInerney, Jeremy. "Arrian and the Greek Alexander Romance." *CW* 100 (4, 2007): 424–30.

McIver, "Eyewitnesses."   McIver, Robert K. "Eyewitnesses as Guarantors of the Accuracy of the Gospel Traditions in the Light of Psychological Research." *JBL* 131 (3, 2012): 529–46.

McIver, "Flashbulb Memory."   McIver, Robert K. "Flashbulb Memory." *DBAM* 135–36.

McIver, "Gist Memory."   McIver, Robert K. "Gist Memory." *DBAM* 156–57.

McIver, *Memory*.   McIver, Robert K. *Memory, Jesus, and the Synoptic Gospels*. SBLSBS 59. Atlanta: SBL, 2011.

McIver, "Memory, Persistence."   McIver, Robert K. "Memory, Persistence and Decay of." *DBAM* 222–24.

McIver, "Personal Memory."   McIver, Robert K. ""Cognitive/Personal Memory." *DBAM* 53–55.

McIver and Carroll, "Characteristics."   McIver, Robert K., and Marie Carroll, "Distinguishing Characteristics of Orally Transmitted Material Compared to Material Transmitted by Literary Means." *Applied Cognitive Psychology* 18 (2004): 1251–69.

McIver and Carroll, "Experiments."   McIver, Robert K., and Marie Carroll. "Experiments to Develop Criteria for Determining the Existence of Written Sources, and Their Potential Implications for the Synoptic Problem." *JBL* 121 (2002): 667–87.

McKnight, "Lion Proselytes." McKnight, Scot. "*De Vita Mosis* 1.147: Lion Proselytes in Philo?" *SPhiloA* 1 (1989): 58–62.

McKnight, *Vision.* McKnight, Scot. *A New Vision for Israel: The Teachings of Jesus in National Context.* Grand Rapids: Eerdmans, 1999.

McKnight and Malbon, "Introduction." McKnight, Edgar V., and Elizabeth Struthers Malbon. "Introduction." Pages 15–26 in *The New Literary Criticism and the New Testament.* Edited by Edgar V. McKnight and Elizabeth Struthers Malbon. Valley Forge, PA: Trinity Press International, 1994.

McLaren, "Josephus' Summary Statements." McLaren, James S. "Josephus' Summary Statements Regarding the Essenes, Pharisees, and Sadducees." *ABR* 48 (2000): 31–46.

McNamara, *Judaism.* McNamara, Martin. *Palestinian Judaism and the New Testament.* GNS 4. Wilmington, DE: Michael Glazier, 1983.

McNamara, *Targum.* McNamara, Martin. *Targum and Testament.* Grand Rapids: Eerdmans, 1972.

McNamara and Szent-Imrey, "Learn." McNamara, Patrick, and Reka Szent-Imrey. "What We Can Learn from Miraculous Healings and Cures." Pages 208–20 in *Religious and Spiritual Events.* Vol. 1 of *Miracles: God, Science, and Psychology in the Paranormal.* Edited by J. Harold Ellens. Westport, CT: Praeger, 2008.

McRay, *Archaeology.* McRay, John R. *Archaeology and the New Testament.* Grand Rapids: Baker, 1991.

Mealand, "Historians." Mealand, David L. "Hellenistic Historians and the Style of Acts." *ZNW* 82 (1–2, 1991): 42–66.

Mealand, "Verbs." Mealand, David L. "Luke-Acts and the Verbs of Dionysius of Halicarnassus." *JSNT* 63 (1996): 63–86.

Meeks, "Androgyne." Meeks, Wayne A. "The Image of the Androgyne: Some Uses of a Symbol in Earliest Christianity." *HR* 13 (3, 1974): 165–208.

Meeks, *Moral World.* Meeks, Wayne A. *The Moral World of the First Christians.* LEC 6. Philadelphia: Westminster, 1986.

Meeks, *Prophet-King.* Meeks, Wayne A. *The Prophet-King: Moses Traditions and the Johannine Christology.* NovTSup 14. Leiden: Brill, 1967.

Meier, "Circle." Meier, John P. "The Circle of the Twelve: Did It Exist during Jesus' Public Ministry?" *JBL* 116 (3, 1997): 635–72.

Meier, "Jesus in Josephus." Meier, John P. "Jesus in Josephus: A Modest Proposal." *CBQ* 52 (1, 1990): 76–103.

Meier, "John the Baptist." Meier, John P. "John the Baptist in Josephus: Philology and Exegesis." *JBL* 111 (2, 1992): 225–37.

Meier, *Marginal Jew.* Meier, John P. *A Marginal Jew: Rethinking the Historical Jesus.* 5 vols. ABRL. New York: Doubleday, 1991–2016.

Meier, *Matthew.* Meier, John P. *Matthew.* NTM 3. Wilmington, DE: Michael Glazier, 1980.

Meier, "Project." Meier, John P. "The Quest for the Historical Jesus as a Truly Historical Project." *Grail* 12 (3, 1996): 43–52.

Meier, "Testimonium." Meier, John P. "The Testimonium, Evidence for Jesus outside the Bible." *BRev* 7 (3, 1991): 20–25, 45.

Meiser, "Gattung." Meiser, Martin. "Gattung, Adressaten und Intention von Philos 'In Flaccum.'" *JSJ* 30 (4, 1999): 418–30.

Meister, "Herodotus." Meister, Klaus. "Herodotus." *BNP* 6:265–71.

Meister, "Historiography: Greece." Meister, Klaus. "Historiography: Greece." *BNP* 6:418–21.

Meister, "Theopompus." Meister, Klaus. "Theopompus." *OCD*³ 1505–6.

Mejer, "Biography." Mejer, Jørgen. "Biography and Doxography: Four Crucial Questions Raised by Diogenes Laertius." Pages 431–41 in *Die Griechische Biographie in hellenistischer Zeit. Akten des internationalen Kongresses vom 26.–29. Juli 2006 in Würzburg.* Edited by Michael Erler and Stefan Schorn. Berlin: de Gruyter, 2007.

Mekkattukunnel, "Proof." Mekkattukunnel, Andrews George. "Further Proof for the Unity of Luke-Acts." *BiBh* 29 (3, 2003): 221–29.

Melchior, "Pompey." Melchior, Aislinn. "What Would Pompey Do? *Exempla* and Pompeian Failure in the *Bellum Africum*." *CJ* 104 (3, 2009): 241–57.

Mélèze-Modrzejewski, "Loi." Mélèze-Modrzejewski, Joseph. "Loi du Seigneur et loi du roi. Le Troisième livre des Maccabées: un drame judiciaire judéo-alexandrin." *FoiVie* 107 (4, 2008): 47–62.

Mellor, *Historians*. Mellor, Ronald. *The Roman Historians*. London: Routledge, 1999.

Mellor, *Tacitus*. Mellor, Ronald. *Tacitus*. New York: Routledge, 1993.

Merkelbach, "Novel and Aretalogy." Merkelbach, Reinhold. "Novel and Aretalogy." Pages 283–95 in *The Search for the Ancient Novel*. Edited by James Tatum. Baltimore: Johns Hopkins University Press, 1994.

Merkle, "True Story." Merkle, Stefan. "Telling the True Story of the Trojan War: The Eyewitness Account of Dictys of Crete." Pages 183–96 in *The Search for the Ancient Novel*. Edited by James Tatum. Baltimore: Johns Hopkins University Press, 1994.

Metzger, "Considerations." Metzger, Bruce M. "Considerations of Methodology in the Study of the Mystery Religions and Early Christianity." *HTR* 48 (1, 1955): 1–20.

Meyer, *Aims of Jesus*. Meyer, Ben F. *The Aims of Jesus*. London: SCM, 1979.

Meyer, "Consequences." Meyer, Ben F. "Some Consequences of Birger Gerhardsson's Account of the Origins of the Gospel Tradition." Pages 424–40 in *Jesus and the Oral Gospel Tradition*. Edited by Henry Wansbrough. JSNTSup 64. Sheffield: Sheffield Academic Press, 1991.

Mieder, "Dundes." Mieder, Wolfgang. "Dundes, Alan." *DBAM* 90–91.

Milikowsky, "Midrash." Milikowsky, Chaim. "Midrash as Fiction and Midrash as History: What Did the Rabbis Mean?" Pages 117–27 in *Ancient Fiction: The Matrix of Early Christian and Jewish Narrative*. Edited by Jo-Ann A. Brant, Charles W. Hedrick, and Chris Shea. SBLSymS 32. Atlanta: SBL, 2005.

Millard, "Literacy." Millard, Alan. "Literacy in the Time of Jesus." *BAR* 29 (4, 2003): 36–45.

Millard, *Reading*. Millard, Alan. *Reading and Writing in the Time of Jesus*. BibSem 69. Sheffield: Sheffield Academic Press, 2000.

Millard, Hoffmeier, and Baker, *Historiography*. Millard, Alan, James K. Hoffmeier, and

David W. Baker, eds. *Faith, Tradition, and History: Old Testament Historiography in Its Near Eastern Context*. Winona Lake, IN: Eisenbrauns, 1994.

Miller, "Introduction." Miller, Walter. "Introduction." Pages vii–xiii in vol. 1 of *Xenophon "Cyropaedia."* Translated by Walter Miller. 2 vols. LCL. Cambridge, MA: Harvard University Press, 1914.

Miller, "Introduction (Diogenes)." Miller, James. "Introduction." Pages vii–xviii in *Diogenes Laertius "Lives of the Eminent Philosophers."* Edited by James Miller. Translated by Pamela Mensch. New York: Oxford University Press, 2018.

Miller, "Rejection." Miller, Robert J. "The Rejection of the Prophets in Q." *JBL* 107 (1988): 225–40.

Miller and Yamamori, *Pentecostalism*. Miller, Donald E., and Tetsunao Yamamori. *Global Pentecostalism: The New Face of Christian Social Engagement*. Berkeley: University of California Press, 2007.

Milnor, "Literacy." Milnor, Kristina. "Literary Literacy in Roman Pompeii: The Case of Vergil's *Aeneid*." Pages 288–319 in *Ancient Literacies: The Culture of Reading in Greece and Rome*. Edited by William A. Johnson and Holt N. Parker. New York: Oxford University Press, 2009.

Mitchell, "Homer." Mitchell, Margaret M. "Homer in the New Testament?" *JR* 83 (2, 2003): 244–60.

Moeser, *Anecdote*. Moeser, Marion C. *The Anecdote in Mark, the Classical World, and the Rabbis*. JSNTSup 227. Sheffield: Sheffield Academic Press, 2002.

Moessner, "Arrangement." Moessner, David P. "Dionysius's Narrative 'Arrangement' (οἰκονομία) as the Hermeneutical Key to Luke's Re-vision of the 'Many.'" Pages 149–64 in *Paul, Luke, and the Graeco-Roman World*. Edited by Alf Christophersen et al. JSNTSup 217. Sheffield: Sheffield Academic, 2002; London: T&T Clark, 2003.

Moessner, *Historian*. Moessner, David Paul. *Luke the Historian of Israel's Legacy, Theologian of Israel's 'Christ': A New Reading of the 'Gospel Acts' of Luke*. BZNW 182. Berlin: de Gruyter, 2016.

Moessner, "Papian Fragments." Moessner, David P. "The Papian Fragments." In *The Second Century*. Vol. 2 of *The Reception of Jesus in the First Three Centuries*. Edited by Jens Schröter, Helen Bond, et al. London: Bloomsbury T&T Clark, forthcoming.

Moessner, "Poetics." Moessner, David P. "The Appeal and Power of Poetics (Luke 1:1–4): Luke's Superior Credentials (παρηκολουθηκότι), Narrative Sequence (καθεξῆς), and Firmness of Understanding (ἡ ἀσφάλεια) for the Reader." Pages 84–123 in *Jesus and the Heritage of Israel: Luke's Narrative Claim upon Israel's Legacy*. Edited by David P. Moessner. Luke the Interpreter of Israel 1. Harrisburg, PA: Trinity Press International, 1999.

Moessner, "Prologues." Moessner, David P. "The Lukan Prologues in the Light of Ancient Narrative Hermeneutics: Παρηκολουθηκότι and the Credentialed Author." Pages 399–417 in *The Unity of Luke-Acts*. Edited by Joseph Verheyden. BETL 142. Leuven: Leuven University Press, 1999.

Moessner, "Synergy." Moessner, David P. "The Triadic Synergy of Hellenistic Poetics in the Narrative Epistemology of Dionysius of Halicarnassus and the Authorial Intent of the Evangelist Luke (Luke 1:1–4; Acts 1:1–8)." *Neot* 42 (2, 2008): 289–303.

Moessner, "Tradent." Moessner, David P. "Luke as Tradent and Hermeneut: 'As one who has a thoroughly informed familiarity with all the events from the top' (παρηκολουθηκότι ἄνωθεν πᾶσιν ἀκριβῶς, Luke 1:3)." *NovT* 58 (3, 2016): 259–300.

Moessner, "Voice." Moessner, David P. "'The Living and Enduring Voice': Papias as Guarantor of Early Apostolic Plotting of Incipient Synoptic Traditions." *Early Christianity* 9 (4, 2018): 484–519.

Moles, "Influence." Moles, John. "Cynic Influence upon First-Century Judaism and Early Christianity?" Pages 89–116 in *The Limits of Ancient Biography*. Edited by Brian McGing and Judith Mossman. Swansea, Wales: Classical Press of Wales, 2006.

Moles, "Letters." Moles, John. "Plutarch, Brutus, and Brutus' Greek and Latin Letters." Pages 141–68 in *Plutarch and His Intellectual World: Essays on Plutarch*. Edited by Judith Mossman. London: Duckworth, with Classical Press of Wales, 1997.

Moloney, "Jesus of History." Moloney, Francis J. "The Fourth Gospel and the Jesus of History." *NTS* 46 (1, 2000): 42–58.

Moltmann, "Blessing." Moltmann, Jürgen. "The Blessing of Hope: The Theology of Hope and the Full Gospel of Life." *JPT* 13 (2, 2005): 147–61.

Momigliano, *Development*. Momigliano, Arnaldo. *The Development of Greek Biography: Four Lectures*. Cambridge, MA: Harvard University Press, 1971.

Momigliano, *Historiography*. Momigliano, Arnaldo. *Essays in Ancient and Modern Historiography*. Middletown, CT: Wesleyan University Press, 1977.

Moniot, "Profile." Moniot, Henri. "Profile of a Historiography: Oral Tradition and Historical Research in Africa." Pages 50–58 in *African Historiographies: What History for Which Africa?* Edited by Bogumil Jewsiewicki and David Newbury. SSAMD 12. Beverly Hills, CA: Sage, 1986.

Montanari, "Hypomnema." Montanari, Franco. "Hypomnema." *BNP* 6:641–43.

Montanaro, "Use." Montanaro, Andrew. "The Use of Memory in the Old Testament Quotations in John's Gospel." *NovT* 59 (2, 2017): 147–70.

Montefusco, "Exercitatio." Montefusco, Lucia Calboli. "Exercitatio." *BNP* 5:265–66.

Moore, "Introduction." Moore, Clifford H. "Introduction: Life and Works of Tacitus." Pages vii–xiii in vol. 1 of *Tacitus*. Translated by Clifford H. Moore and John Jackson. 4 vols. LCL. Cambridge, MA: Harvard University Press, 1931–37.

Moore, *Judaism*. Moore, George Foot. *Judaism in the First Centuries of the Christian Era*. 3 vols. Cambridge, MA: Harvard University Press, 1927–30. Repr., 3 vols. in 2. New York: Schocken, 1971.

Morgan, "Fiction." Morgan, J. R. "Fiction and History: Historiography and the Novel." Pages 553–64 in *A Companion to Greek and Roman Historiography*. Edited by John Marincola. 2 vols. Oxford: Blackwell, 2007.

Morgan, "Histories and Wonders." Morgan, J. R. "Lucian's *True Histories* and the *Wonders beyond Thule* of Antonius Diogenes." *ClQ* 35 (2, December 1985): 475–90.

Morgan, *Literate Education.* Morgan, Teresa. *Literate Education in the Hellenistic and Roman World.* Cambridge: Cambridge University Press, 1998.

Morrison, "Composition." Morrison, Gary. "The Composition of II Maccabees: Insights Provided by a Literary *topos.*" *Bib* 90 (4, 2009): 564–72.

Morrison, "Perspective." Morrison, James H. "A Global Perspective of Oral History in Southeast Asia." Pages 1–16 in *Oral History in Southeast Asia: Theory and Method.* Edited by Patricia Pui Huen Lim, Chong Guan Kwa, and James H. Morrison. Singapore: Institute of Southeast Asian Studies, 1998.

Mosley, "Reporting." Mosley, A. W. "Historical Reporting in the Ancient World." *NTS* 12 (1, 1965): 10–26.

Mossman, "Plutarch and Biography." Mossman, Judith. "Plutarch and English Biography." *Herm* 183 (2007): 75–100.

Mossman, "Travel Writing." Mossman, Judith. "Travel Writing, History, and Biography." Pages 281–303 in *The Limits of Ancient Biography.* Edited by Brian McGing and Judith Mossman. Swansea, Wales: Classical Press of Wales, 2006.

Most, "Diogenes Laertius and Nietzsche." Most, Glenn W. "Diogenes Laertius and Nietzsche." Pages 619–22 in *Diogenes Laertius "Lives of the Eminent Philosophers."* Edited by James Miller. Translated by Pamela Mensch. New York: Oxford University Press, 2018.

Mournet, *Oral Tradition.* Mournet, Terence C. *Oral Tradition and Literary Dependency: Variability and Stability in the Synoptic Tradition and Q.* WUNT 2.195. Tübingen: Mohr Siebeck, 2005.

Mournet, "Original." Mournet, Terence C. "Original." *DBAM* 262–63.

Mournet, "Sayings Gospels." Mournet, Terence C. "Sayings and Dialogue Gospels." *DBAM* 348–50.

Munck, *Acts.* Munck, Johannes. *The Acts of the Apostles.* Revised by W. F. Albright and C. S. Mann. AB 31. Garden City, NY: Doubleday, 1967.

Muntz, "Diodorus Siculus." Muntz, Charles E. "Diodorus Siculus and Megasthenes: A Reappraisal." *CP* 107 (1, 2012): 21–37.

Muntz, "Sources." Muntz, Charles E. "The Sources of Diodorus Siculus, Book 1." *ClQ* 61 (2, 2011): 574–94.

Murgatroyd, "Ending." Murgatroyd, P. "The Ending of Apuleius' *Metamorphoses.*" *ClQ* 54 (1, 2004): 319–21.

Murphy, "Idolatry." Murphy, Frederick J. "Retelling the Bible: Idolatry in Pseudo-Philo." *JBL* 107 (2, 1988): 275–87.

Murphy, *Introduction.* Murphy, Frederick James. *An Introduction to Jesus and the Gospels.* Nashville: Abingdon, 2005.

Murray, "Herodotus." Murray, Oswyn. "Herodotus and Oral History." Pages 16–44 in *The Historian's Craft in the Age of Herodotus.* Edited by Nino Luraghi. Oxford: Oxford University Press, 2001.

Musnick, "Historical Commentary." Musnick, Larry Jason. "A Historical Commentary on Cornelius Nepos' *Life of Themistocles.*" MA diss., University of Cape Town, 2008.

Nagy, *Questions.*   Nagy, Gregory. *Homeric Questions.* Austin: University of Texas Press, 1996.

Naswem, "Healing."   Naswem, R. A. "Healing in Twentieth-Century Christian Churches: Gimmicks, Reality, or Abuses?" Pages 26–32 in *Religion, Medicine, and Healing.* Edited by Gbola Aderibigbe and Deji Ayegboyin. Lagos: Nigerian Association for the Study of Religions and Education, 1995.

Neil, *Acts.*   Neil, William. *The Acts of the Apostles.* NCBC. London: Marshall, Morgan & Scott, 1973.

Neisser, "Dean's Memory."   Neisser, Ulric. "John Dean's Memory: A Case Study." *Cognition* 9 (1981): 1–22.

Neisser et al., "Earthquake."   Neisser, Ulric, et al. "Remembering the Earthquake: Direct Experience vs. Hearing the News." *Memory* 4 (1996): 337–57.

Neisser and Libby, "Remembering Experiences."   Neisser, Ulric, and Lisa K. Libby. "Remembering Life Experiences." Pages 315–32 in *The Oxford Handbook of Memory.* Edited by Endel Tulving and Fergus I. M. Craik. Oxford: Oxford University Press, 2000.

Nelson, "Value."   Nelson, Narka. "The Value of Epigraphic Evidence in the Interpretation of Latin Historical Literature." *CJ* 37 (5, Februry 1942): 281–90.

Neufeld, *Recovering Jesus.*   Neufeld, Thomas R. Yoder. *Recovering Jesus: The Witness of the New Testament.* Grand Rapids: Brazos, 2007.

Neusner, *Beginning.*   Neusner, Jacob. *Judaism in the Beginning of Christianity.* Philadelphia: Fortress, 1984.

Neusner, *Biography.*   Neusner, Jacob. *In Search of Talmudic Biography: The Problem of the Attributed Saying.* BJS 70. Chico, CA: Scholars Press, 1984.

Neusner, "Cleanse."   Neusner, Jacob. "First Cleanse the Inside." *NTS* 22 (1976): 486–95.

Neusner, "Foreword."   Neusner, Jacob. "Foreword." Pages xxv–xlvi in Birger Gerhardsson, *Memory and Manuscript: Oral Tradition and Written Transmission in Rabbinic Judaism and Early Christianity; Tradition and Transmission in Early Christianity.* Grand Rapids: Eerdmans, 1998.

Neusner, *Gospels.*   Neusner, Jacob. *Why No Gospels in Talmudic Judaism?* BJS 135. Atlanta: Scholars Press, 1988.

Neusner, "Idea of History."   Neusner, Jacob. "The Idea of History in Rabbinic Judaism: What Kinds of Questions Did the Ancient Rabbis Answer?" *NBf* 90 (1027, 2009): 277–94.

Neusner, *Incarnation.*   Neusner, Jacob. *The Incarnation of God: The Character of Divinity in Formative Judaism.* Philadelphia: Fortress, 1988.

Neusner, *Legend.*   Neusner, Jacob. *Development of a Legend: Studies on the Traditions concerning Yohanan ben Zakkai.* StPB 16. Leiden: Brill, 1970.

Neusner, *Memorized Torah.*   Neusner, Jacob. *The Memorized Torah: The Mnemonic System of the Torah.* Chico, CA: Scholars Press, 1985.

Neusner, *Politics to Piety.*   Neusner, Jacob. *From Politics to Piety: The Emergence of Pharisaic Judaism.* 2nd ed. New York: Ktav, 1979.

Neusner, *Traditions.*   Neusner, Jacob. *The Rabbinic Traditions about the Pharisees before 70.* 3 vols. Leiden: Brill, 1971.

Newell, "Forms." Newell, Raymond R. "The Forms and Historical Value of Josephus' Suicide Accounts." Pages 278–94 in *Josephus, the Bible, and History*. Edited by Louis H. Feldman and Gohei Hata. Detroit: Wayne State University Press, 1989.

Newsom, "Spying." Newsom, Carol A. "Spying Out the Land: A Report from Genealogy." Pages 437–50 in *Seeking Out the Wisdom of the Ancients: Essays Offered to Honor Michael V. Fox on the Occasion of His Sixty-Fifth Birthday*. Edited by Ronald L. Troxel, Kelvin G. Friebel, and Dennis R. Magary. Winona Lake, IN: Eisenbrauns, 2005.

Nickelsburg, *Literature*. Nickelsburg, George W. E. *Jewish Literature between the Bible and the Mishnah*. Philadelphia: Fortress, 1981.

Nicklas, "Gospel of Peter." Nicklas, Tobias. "The Gospel of Peter between the Synoptics and Late Antique 'Apostolic Memoirs.'" Paper presented to "Memory, Narrative, and Christology in the Synoptic Gospels" Seminar at the Annual Meeting of the Society for New Testament Studies. Pretoria, South Africa, August 10, 2017.

Nicklas, "Landscapes." Nicklas, Tobias. "New Testament Canon and Ancient 'Landscapes of Memory.'" *Early Christianity* 7 (2016): 5–23.

Nicklas, "Literature." Nicklas, Tobias. "Early Christian Literature." *DBAM* 94–99.

Nicolai, "Place." Nicolai, Roberto. "The Place of History in the Ancient World." Pages 13–26 in *A Companion to Greek and Roman Historiography*. Edited by John Marincola. 2 vols. Oxford: Blackwell, 2007.

Niditch, "Hebrew Bible." Niditch, Susan. "Hebrew Bible and Oral Literature: Misconceptions and New Directions." Pages 3–18 in *The Interface of Orality and Writing: Speaking, Seeing, Writing in the Shaping of New Genres*. Edited by Annette Weissenrieder and Robert B. Coote. WUNT 260. Tübingen: Mohr Siebeck, 2010. Repr., BPC 11. Eugene, OR: Wipf & Stock, 2015.

Niditch, *World*. Niditch, Susan. *Oral World and Written Word: Ancient Israelite Literature*. Louisville: Westminster John Knox, 1996.

Niebuhr, "Idea." Niebuhr, Karl-Wilhelm. "Matthew's Idea of Being Human: God's Righteousness and Human Responsibilities according to the Gospel of Matthew." Paper presented at the International Conference on the Gospel of Matthew in Its Historical and Theological Context. Moscow, September 28, 2018.

Niehoff, "Technique." Niehoff, Maren R. "Two Examples of Josephus' Narrative Technique in His 'Rewritten Bible.'" *JSJ* 27 (1996): 31–45.

Niehoff, "Philo." Niehoff, Maren R. "Philo and Plutarch as Biographers: Parallel Responses to Roman Stoicism." *GRBS* 52 (3, 2012): 361–92.

Niemand, "Testimonium." Niemand, Christoph. "Das Testimonium Flavianum. Befunde, Diskussionsstand, Perspektiven." *PzB* 17 (1, 2008): 45–71.

Nikolaidis, "Introduction." Nikolaidis, Anastasios G. "Introduction." Pages xiii–xviii in *The Unity of Plutarch's Work: "Moralia" Themes in the "Lives," Features of the "Lives" in the "Moralia."* Edited by Anastasios G. Nikolaidis. Millennium Studies in the Culture and History of the First Millennium C.E., 19. New York: de Gruyter, 2008.

Nikolaidis, *Unity*. Nikolaidis, Anastasios G., ed. *The Unity of Plutarch's Work: "Moralia"*

Themes in the "Lives", Features of the "Lives" in the "Moralia." Millennium Studies in the Culture and History of the First Millennium C.E., 19. New York: de Gruyter, 2008.

Nikulin, "Introduction." Nikulin, Dmitri. "Introduction: Memory in Recollection of Itself." Pages 3–34 in *Memory: A History.* Edited by Dmitri V. Nikulin. New York: Oxford University Press, 2015.

Nikulin, "Memory." Nikulin, Dmitri. "Memory in Ancient Philosophy." Pages 35–84 in *Memory: A History.* Edited by Dmitri V. Nikulin. New York: Oxford University Press, 2015.

Ní-Mheallaigh, *Fiction.* Ní-Mheallaigh, Karen. *Reading Fiction with Lucian: Fakes, Freaks and Hyperreality.* Cambridge: Cambridge University Press, 2014.

Ní-Mheallaigh, "Pseudo-Documentarism." Ní-Mheallaigh, Karen. "Pseudo-Documentarism and the Limits of Ancient Fiction." *AJP* 129 (3, 2008): 403–31.

Nobbs, "Historians." Nobbs, Alanna. "What Do Ancient Historians Make of the New Testament?" *TynBul* 57 (2, 2006): 285–90.

Nock, *Essays.* Nock, Arthur Darby. *Essays on Religion and the Ancient World.* Edited by Zeph Stewart. 2 vols. Cambridge, MA: Harvard University Press, 1972.

Nock, "Vocabulary." Nock, Arthur Darby. "The Vocabulary of the New Testament." *JBL* 52 (2–3, 1933): 131–39.

Noll and Nystrom, *Clouds.* Noll, Mark A., and Carolyn Nystrom. *Clouds of Witnesses: Christian Voices from Africa and Asia.* Downers Grove, IL: InterVarsity, 2011.

Oblau, "Healing." Oblau, Gotthard. "Divine Healing and the Growth of Practical Christianity in China." Pages 307–27 in *Global Pentecostal and Charismatic Healing.* Edited by Candy Gunther Brown. Oxford: Oxford University Press, 2011.

O'Connor, Moulin, and Cohen, "Memory and Consciousness." O'Connor, Akira, Chris J. A. Moulin, and Gillian Cohen. "Memory and Consciousness." Pages 327–56 in *Memory in the Real World.* Edited by Gillian Cohen and Martin A. Conway. Hove, East Sussex: Psychology Press, 2007.

O'Day, "John." O'Day, Gail R. "The Gospel of John: Introduction, Commentary, and Reflections." Pages 491–865 in vol. 9 of *The New Interpreter's Bible.* Edited by Leander E. Keck. 12 vols. Nashville: Abingdon, 1995.

Odor, "Countermemory." Odor, Judith. "Countermemory." *DBAM* 67–68.

Odor, "Enchiridion." Odor, Judith. "Enchiridion." *DBAM* 117–18.

Odor, "Families." Odor, Judith. "Literary Families and Ancient Hermeneutics: Acts and Greco-Roman Contemporary Historiography." PhD diss., Asbury Theological Seminary, 2018.

Oesterley, *Liturgy.* Oesterley, William Oscar Emil. *The Jewish Background of the Christian Liturgy.* Oxford: Clarendon, 1925.

Offer et al., "Altering." Offer, Daniel, Marjorie Kaiz, Kenneth I. Howard, and Emily S. Bennett. "The Altering of Reported Experiences." *Journal of the American Academy of Child and Adolescent Psychiatry* 39 (2000): 735–42.

Olbricht, "Delivery." Olbricht, Thomas H. "Delivery and Memory." Pages 159–67 in *Hand-*

book of Classical Rhetoric in the Hellenistic Period, 330 B.C.–A.D. 400. Edited by Stanley E. Porter. Leiden: Brill, 1997.

Oldfather, "Introduction to Diodorus." Oldfather, C. H. "Introduction." Pages vii–xxvii in vol. 1 of *Diodorus Siculus.* Translated by C. H. Oldfather et al. 12 vols. LCL. Cambridge, MA: Harvard University Press, 1933–67.

Ong, *Orality.* Ong, Walter J. *Orality and Literacy: The Technologizing of the Word.* New York: Routledge, 1982.

Opp, *Lord for Body.* Opp, James. *The Lord for the Body: Religion, Medicine, and Protestant Faith Healing in Canada, 1880–1930.* Montreal: McGill-Queen's University Press, 2005.

Orlin, "Religion." Orlin, Eric. "Urban Religion in the Middle and Late Republic." Pages 58–70 in *A Companion to Roman Religion.* Edited by Jörg Rüpke. BCAW. Oxford: Blackwell, 2011.

Os, *Analyses.* Os, Bas van. *Psychological Analyses and the Historical Jesus: New Ways to Explore Christian Origins.* LNTS 432. London: T&T Clark, 2011.

Osborne, "Redaction Criticism." Osborne, Grant R. "Redaction Criticism." *DJG¹* 662–69.

Otani et al., "Memory." Otani, Hajime, Terry M. Libkuman, Robert L. Widner Jr., and Emily I. Graves. "Memory for Emotionally Arousing Stimuli: A Comparison of Younger and Older Adults." *Journal of General Psychology* 134 (2007): 23–42.

Otmakhova et al., "Loop." Otmakhova, Nonna, et al. "The Hippocampal-VTA Loop: The Role of Novelty and Motivation in Controlling the Entry of Information into Long-Term Memory." Pages 235–54 in *Intrinsically Motivated Learning in Natural and Artificial Systems.* Edited by Gianluca Baldassarre and Marco Mirolli. Berlin: Springer, 2013.

Packer, *Acts.* Packer, J. W. *Acts of the Apostles.* CBC. Cambridge: Cambridge University Press, 1966.

Padilla, *Acts.* Padilla, Osvaldo. *The Acts of the Apostles: Interpretation, History, and Theology.* Downers Grove, IL: IVP Academic, 2016.

Padilla, *Speeches.* Padilla, Osvaldo. *The Speeches of Outsiders in Acts: Poetics, Theology, and Historiography.* SNTSMS 144. Cambridge: Cambridge University Press, 2008.

Paget, "Observations." Paget, James Carleton. "Some Observations on Josephus and Christianity." *JTS* 52 (2, 2001): 539–624.

Painter, *John.* Painter, John. *John: Witness and Theologian.* London: SPCK, 1975.

Palmer, "Monograph (1992)." Palmer, Darryl W. "Acts and the Historical Monograph." *TynBul* 43 (2, 1992): 373–88.

Palmer, "Monograph (1993)." Palmer, Darryl W. "Acts and the Ancient Historical Monograph." Pages 1–29 in *The Book of Acts in Its Ancient Literary Setting.* Edited by Bruce W. Winter and Andrew D. Clarke. Vol. 1 of *The Book of Acts in Its First Century Setting.* Edited by Bruce W. Winter. Grand Rapids: Eerdmans, 1993.

Parikh, "Argument." Parikh, Joshua. "Is There a Defensible Argument from Contemporary Miracles in Natural Theology?" Master of studies in philosophical theology, Oxford University, 2018.

Park, *Conflict.* Park, Andrew Sung. *Racial Conflict and Healing: An Asian-American Theological Perspective.* Maryknoll, NY: Orbis Books, 1996.

Park, "Folklore." Park, Suzie. "Folklore/Folkloristics." *DBAM* 137–41.

Parker, "Swiftly Runs the Word." Parker, Emily. "Swiftly Runs the Word: Philo's Doctrine of Mediation in De Vita Mosis." MA thesis, Dalhousie University, 2010.

Parsenios, "Rhetoric." Parsenios, George. "How and in What Ways Does John's Rhetoric Reflect Jesus' Rhetoric?" Paper presented at the Third Princeton-Prague Symposium on the Historical Jesus, Princeton, NJ, March 18, 2016. Pages 85–95 in *Jesus Research: The Gospel of John in Historical Inquiry.* Edited by James H. Charlesworth, with Jolyon G. R. Pruszinski. New York: Bloomsbury T&T Clark, 2019.

Parsons, *Acts.* Parsons, Mikeal C. *Acts.* PCNT. Grand Rapids: Baker Academic, 2008.

Parsons, *Luke.* Parsons, Mikeal C. *Luke: Storyteller, Interpreter, Evangelist.* Peabody, MA: Hendrickson, 2007.

Parsons, "Unity: Rethinking." Parsons, Mikeal C. "The Unity of Luke-Acts: Rethinking the *opinio communis.*" Pages 29–53 in *With Steadfast Purpose: Essays on Acts in Honor of Henry Jackson Flanders Jr.* Edited by N. H. Keathley. Waco, TX: Baylor University Press, 1990.

Parsons and Pervo, *Rethinking.* Parsons, Mikeal C., and Richard I. Pervo. *Rethinking the Unity of Luke and Acts.* Minneapolis: Fortress, 1993.

Pastor, "Strata." Pastor, Jack. "Josephus and Social Strata: An Analysis of Social Attitudes." *Hen* 19 (3, 1997): 295–312.

Pate et al., *Story.* Pate, C. Marvin, et al. *The Story of Israel: A Biblical Theology.* Downers Grove, IL: InterVarsity, 2004.

Patterson, "Review." Patterson, Stephen J. "Can You Trust a Gospel? A Review of Richard Bauckham's *Jesus and the Eyewitnesses.*" *JSHJ* 6 (2008): 194–210.

Payne, "Authenticity of Parables." Payne, Philip Barton. "The Authenticity of the Parables of Jesus." Pages 329–44 in *Studies of History and Tradition in the Four Gospels.* Vol. 2 of *Gospel Perspectives.* Edited by R. T. France and David Wenham. Sheffield: JSOT Press, 1981.

Payne, "Sower." Payne, Philip Barton. "The Authenticity of the Parable of the Sower and Its Interpretation." Pages 163–207 in *Studies of History and Tradition in the Four Gospels.* Vol. 1 of *Gospel Perspectives.* Edited by R. T. France and David Wenham. Sheffield: JSOT Press, 1980.

Pearson, "Community." Pearson, Birger A. "A Q Community in Galilee?" *NTS* 50 (4, October 2004): 476–94.

Pekala and Cardeña, "Issues." Pekala, Ronald J., and Etzel Cardeña. "Methodological Issues in the Study of Altered States of Consciousness and Anomalous Experiences." Pages 47–82 in *Varieties of Anomalous Experience: Examining the Scientific Evidence.* Edited by Etzel Cardeña, Steven Jay Lynn, and Stanley Krippner. Washington, DC: American Psychological Association, 2000.

Pelletier, *Josèphe.* Pelletier, André. *Flavius Josèphe, adaptateur de la lettre d'Aristée. Une réaction atticisante contre la Koiné.* Études et commentaires 45. Paris: Klincksieck, Université de Paris, 1962.

Pelling, "Adaptation." Pelling, C. B. R. "Plutarch's Adaptation of His Source-Material." *JHS* 100 (1980): 127–40.

Pelling, *Antony*. Pelling, C. B. R. *Life of Antony*. New York: Cambridge University Press, 1988.

Pelling, "Biography, Greek." Pelling, C. B. R. "Biography, Greek." *OCD³* 241–42.

Pelling, "Biography, Roman." Pelling, C. B. R. "Biography, Roman." *OCD³* 242–43.

Pelling, "Bounds." Pelling, Christopher. "Breaking the Bounds: Writing about Julius Caesar." Pages 255–80 in *The Limits of Ancient Biography*. Edited by Brian McGing and Judith Mossman. Swansea, Wales: Classical Press of Wales, 2006.

Pelling, "Epilogue." C. B. R. Pelling, "Epilogue." Pages 325–60 in *The Limits of Historiography: Genre and Narrative in Ancient Historical Texts*. Edited by Christina Shuttleworth Kraus. Leiden: Brill, 1999.

Pelling, "Historians of Rome." Pelling, Christopher. "The Greek Historians of Rome." Pages 244–58 in *A Companion to Greek and Roman Historiography*. Edited by John Marincola. 2 vols. Oxford: Blackwell, 2007.

Pelling, "Historiography." Pelling, C. B. R. "Historiography, Roman." *OCD³* 716–17.

Pelling, "History." Pelling, C. B. R. "Biographical History? Cassius Dio on the Early Principate." Pages 117–44 in *Portraits: Biographical Representations in the Greek and Latin Literature of the Roman Empire*. Edited by M. J. Edwards and Simon Swain. Oxford: Clarendon, 1997.

Pelling, "Method." Pelling, C. B. R. "Plutarch's Method of Work in the Roman Lives." *JHS* 99 (1979): 74–96.

Pelling, *Plutarch and History*. Pelling, C. B. R. *Plutarch and History: Eighteen Studies*. Swansea, Wales: Classical Press of Wales, 2002.

Pelling, "Socrates." Pelling, C. B. R. "Plutarch's Socrates." *Herm* 179 (2005): 105–39.

Pelling, *Texts*. Pelling, Christopher. *Literary Texts and the Greek Historian*. New York: Routledge, 2000.

Pelling, "Truth." Pelling, C. B. R. "Truth and Fiction in Plutarch's *Lives*." Pages 19–52 in *Antonine Literature*. Edited by D. A. Russell. New York: Oxford, 1990.

Penner, "Discourse." Penner, Todd. "Civilizing Discourse: Acts, Declamation, and the Rhetoric of the *polis*." Pages 65–104 in *Contextualizing Acts: Lukan Narrative and Greco-Roman Discourse*. Edited by Todd Penner and Caroline Vander Stichele. SBLSymS 20. Atlanta: SBL, 2003.

Penner, *Praise*. Penner, Todd. *In Praise of Christian Origins: Stephen and the Hellenists in Lukan Apologetic Historiography*. New York: T&T Clark, 2004.

Pennington, *Reading Wisely*. Pennington, Jonathan T. *Reading the Gospels Wisely: A Narrative and Theological Introduction*. Grand Rapids: Baker Academic, 2012.

Perkins, *Introduction to Gospels*. Perkins, Pheme. *Introduction to the Synoptic Gospels*. Grand Rapids: Eerdmans, 2007.

Perkins, "World of *Acts of Peter*." Perkins, Judith. "The Social World of the *Acts of Peter*." Pages 296–307 in *The Search for the Ancient Novel*. Edited by James Tatum. Baltimore: Johns Hopkins University Press, 1994.

Pernot, *Rhétorique*.   Pernot, Laurent. *La rhétorique de l'éloge dans le monde gréco-romain.* Paris: Institut d'Études Augustiniennes, 1993.

Perrin, "Overlooked Evidence."   Perrin, Nicholas. "NHC II,2 and the Oxyrhynchus Fragments (P.Oxy 1, 654, 655): Overlooked Evidence for a Syriac *Gospel of Thomas.*" *VC* 58 (2004): 138–51.

Perrin, *Redaction Criticism*.   Perrin, Norman. *What Is Redaction Criticism?* Philadelphia: Fortress, 1984.

Perrin, *Thomas and Tatian*.   Perrin, Nicholas. *Thomas and Tatian: The Relationship between the* Gospel of Thomas *and the* Diatessaron. SBLAcBib 5. Atlanta: SBL, 2002.

Perry, *Sources*.   Perry, Alfred Morris. *The Sources of Luke's Passion Narrative.* Chicago: University of Chicago Press, 1920.

Person, "Goody."   Person, Raymond F. "Goody, Jack." *DBAM* 159–60.

Person, "Havelock."   Person, Raymond F. "Havelock, Eric Alfred." *DBAM* 170.

Person, "Scribe."   Person, Raymond F. "The Ancient Israelite Scribe as Performer." *JBL* 117 (4, 1998): 601–9.

Person, "Storytelling."   Person, Raymond F. "Storytelling." *DBAM* 385–88.

Person and Keith, "Media Studies."   Person, Raymond F., and Chris Keith. "Media Studies and Biblical Studies: An Introduction." *DBAM* 1–15.

Pervo, *Acts*.   Pervo, Richard I. *Acts: A Commentary.* Minneapolis: Fortress, 2009.

Pervo, *Dating Acts*.   Pervo, Richard I. *Dating Acts: Between the Evangelists and the Apologists.* Santa Rosa, CA: Polebridge, 2006.

Pervo, "Dating Acts."   Pervo, Richard I. "Dating Acts." *Forum* 5 (1, 2002): 53–72.

Pervo, "Fabula."   Pervo, Richard I. "A Nihilist Fabula: Introducing *The Life of Aesop.*" Pages 77–120 in *Ancient Fiction and Early Christian Narrative.* Edited by Ronald F. Hock, J. Bradley Chance, and Judith Perkins. SBLSymS 6. Atlanta: SBL, 1998.

Pervo, "Introduction."   Pervo, Richard I. "Introduction." Pages 1–6 in *Reading and Teaching Ancient Fiction: Jewish, Christian, and Greco-Roman Narratives.* Edited by Sara R. Johnson, Rubén R. Dupertuis, and Christine Shea. WGRWSup 11. Atlanta: SBL Press, 2018.

Pervo, "Losers."   Pervo, Richard I. "History Told by Losers: Dictys and Dares on the Trojan War." Pages 123–36 in *Reading and Teaching Ancient Fiction: Jewish, Christian, and Greco-Roman Narratives.* Edited by Sara R. Johnson, Rubén R. Dupertuis, and Christine Shea. WGRWSup 11. Atlanta: SBL Press, 2018.

Pervo, *Profit*.   Pervo, Richard I. *Profit with Delight: The Literary Genre of the Acts of the Apostles.* Philadelphia: Fortress, 1987.

Pervo, "Same Genre?"   Pervo, Richard I. "Must Luke and Acts Belong to the Same Genre?" Pages 309–16 in *SBL Seminar Papers, 1989.* Edited by D. J. Lull. SBLSP 28. Atlanta: Scholars Press, 1989.

Pesch, *Apostelgeschichte*.   Pesch, Rudolf. *Die Apostelgeschichte.* 2 vols. EKKNT 5. Zurich: Benziger, 1986.

Peters, "Historiography."   Peters, John J. "Ancient Historiography and Jesus Research: Reassessing Luke's Preface and Historical Narrative." PhD dissertation, Regent University, 2018.

Peters, *Muhammad.*   Peters, F. E. *Muhammad and the Origins of Islam.* Albany: State University of New York Press, 1994.

Petersen, "Genre."   Petersen, Norman R. "Can One Speak of a Gospel Genre?" *Neot* 28 (3, 1994): 137–58.

Petit, "Traversée exemplaire."   Petit, Madeleine. "À propos d'une traversée exemplaire du désert du Sinaï selon Philon (*Hypothetica* VI, 2–3.8). Texte biblique et apologétique concernant Moïse chez quelques écrivains juifs." *Sem* 26 (1976): 137–42.

Petitfils, "Tale."   Petitfils, James M. "A Tale of Two Moseses: Philo's *On the Life of Moses* and Josephus's *Jewish Antiquities* 2–4 in Light of the Roman Discourse of Exemplarity." Pages 153–64 in *Reading and Teaching Ancient Fiction: Jewish, Christian, and Greco-Roman Narratives.* Edited by Sara R. Johnson, Rubén R. Dupertuis, and Christine Shea. WGRWSup 11. Atlanta: SBL Press, 2018.

Phillips et al., *Memory.*   Phillips, Kendall R., et al., eds. *Framing Public Memory.* Tuscaloosa: University of Alabama Press, 2004.

Piccione, "Παιδεία."   Piccione, Rosa Maria. "De vita Mosis 1.60–62. Philon und die griechische παιδεία." Pages 345–57 in *Philo und das Neue Testament. Wechselseitige Wahrnehmungen. I. Internationales Symposium zum Corpus Judaeo-Hellenisticum (Eisenach/Jena, Mai 2003).* Edited by Roland Deines and Karl-Wilhelm Niebuhr. WUNT 172. Tübingen: Mohr Siebeck, 2004.

Pierce et al., "Effects."   Pierce, B. H., J. D. Waring, D. L. Schacter, and A. E. Budson. "Effects of Distinctive Encoding on Source-Based False Recognition: Further Examination of Recall-to-Reject Processing in Aging and Alzheimer's Disease." *Cognitive and Behavioral Neurology* 21 (2008): 179–86.

Pilch, *Dictionary.*   Pilch, John J. *The Cultural Dictionary of the Bible.* Collegeville, MN: Liturgical Press, 1999.

Pilch, *Healing.*   Pilch, John J. *Healing in the New Testament: Insights from Medical and Mediterranean Anthropology.* Minneapolis: Fortress, 2000.

Pilch, "Naming."   Pilch, John J. "Naming the Nameless in the Bible." *BibT* 44 (5, 2006): 315–20.

Pilch, "Usefulness."   Pilch, John J. "The Usefulness of the Meaning Response Concept for Interpreting Translations of Healing Accounts in Matthew's Gospel." Pages 97–108 in *The Social Sciences of Biblical Translation.* Edited by Dietmar Neufeld. SBLSymS 41. Atlanta: SBL, 2008.

Pilch, *Visions.*   Pilch, John J. *Visions and Healing in the Acts of the Apostles: How the Early Believers Experienced God.* Collegeville, MN: Liturgical Press, 2004.

Pilgaard, "*Theios aner.*"   Pilgaard, Aage. "The Hellenistic *theios aner*—a Model for Early Christian Christology?" Pages 101–22 in *The New Testament and Hellenistic Judaism.* Edited by Peder Borgen and Søren Giversen. Peabody, MA: Hendrickson, 1997.

Pillemer, *Momentous Events.*   Pillemer, David. *Momentous Events, Vivid Memories.* Cambridge, MA: Harvard University Press, 1998.

Pillemer et al., "Memories of College."   Pillemer, David B., Martha L. Picariello, Anneliesa Beebe Law, and Jill S. Reichman. "Memories of College: The Importance of Specific Educational Episodes." Pages 318–37 in *Remembering Our Past: Studies in Autobiographical Memory*. Edited by David C. Rubin. Cambridge: Cambridge University Press, 1996.

Pines, *Version*. Pines, Shlomo. *An Arabic Version of the Testimonium Flavianum and Its Implications*. Jerusalem: Israel Academy of Sciences and Humanities, 1971.

Pioske, "Retracing." Pioske, Daniel D. "Retracing a Remembered Past: Methodological Remarks on Memory, History, and the Hebrew Bible." *BibInt* 23 (2015): 291–315.

Piovanelli, "Authority." Piovanelli, Pierluigi. "Jesus' Charismatic Authority: On the Historical Applicability of a Sociological Model." *JAAR* 73 (2, 2005): 395–427.

Pitcher, "Characterization." Pitcher, L. V. "Characterization in Ancient Historiography." Pages 102–17 in *A Companion to Greek and Roman Historiography*. Edited by John Marincola. Malden, MA: Wiley-Blackwell, 2011.

Pitcher, "Story." Pitcher, Luke V. "A Shaggy Thigh Story: Kalasiris on the *Life of Homer*." Pages 293–305 in *Writing Biography in Greece and Rome: Narrative Technique and Fictionalization*. Edited by Koen De Temmerman and Kristoffel Demoen. Cambridge: Cambridge University Press, 2016.

Pitre, *Case*. Pitre, Brant, *The Case for Jesus: The Biblical and Historical Evidence for Christ*. New York: Image, 2016.

Pitre, *Last Supper*. Pitre, Brant. *Jesus and the Last Supper*. Grand Rapids: Eerdmans, 2015.

Pitts, "Citation." Pitts, Andrew W. "Source Citation in Greek Historiography and in Luke (-Acts)." Pages 349–88 in *Christian Origins and Greco-Roman Culture: Social and Literary Contexts for the New Testament*. Edited by Stanley Porter and Andrew W. Pitts. Vol. 1 of *Early Christianity in Its Hellenistic Context*. TENTS 9. Leiden: Brill, 2013.

Pixner, "Gate." Pixner, Bargil. "The History of the 'Essene Gate' Area." *ZDPV* 105 (1989): 96–104 and plates 8–16a.

Pixner, *Paths*. Pixner, Bargil. *Paths of the Messiah and Sites of the Early Church from Galilee to Jerusalem: Jesus and Jewish Christianity in Light of Archaeological Discoveries*. Edited by Rainer Riesner. Translated by Keith Myrick, Sam Randall, and Miriam Randall. San Francisco: Ignatius Press, 2010.

Pixner, Chen, and Margalit, "Zion." Pixner, Bargil, Doron Chen, and Shlomo Margalit. "Mount Zion: The 'Gate of the Essenes' Reexcavated." *ZDPV* 105 (1989): 85–95 and plates 8–16a.

Pizzuto-Pomaco, *Shame*. Pizzuto-Pomaco, Julia. *From Shame to Honour: Mediterranean Women in Romans 16*. Lexington, KY: Emeth, 2017.

Pizzuto-Pomaco, "Shame." Pizzuto-Pomaco, Julia. "From Shame to Honour: Mediterranean Women in Romans 16." PhD diss., University of St. Andrews, 2003.

Placher, *Mark*. Placher, William C. *Mark*. Louisville: Westminster John Knox, 2010.

Plümacher, "Cicero und Lukas." Plümacher, Eckhard. "Cicero und Lukas. Bemerkungen zu Stil und Zweck der historischen Monographie." Pages 759–75 in *The Unity of Luke-Acts*. Edited by Joseph Verheyden. BETL 142. Leuven: Leuven University Press, 1999.

Plümacher, "Fiktion." Plümacher, Eckhard. "ΤΕΡΑΤΕΙΑ. Fiktion und Wunder in der hellenistisch-römischen Geschichtsschreibung und in der Apostelgeschichte." *ZNW* 89 (1–2, 1998): 66–90.

Plümacher, *Geschichte.* Plümacher, Eckhard. *Geschichte und Geschichten. Aufsätze zur Apostelgeschichte und zu den Johannesakten.* Edited by Jens Schröter and Ralph Brucker. WUNT 170. Tübingen: Mohr Siebeck, 2004.

Plümacher, "Historiker." Plümacher, Eckhard. "Stichwort: Lukas, Historiker." *ZNT* 9 (18, 2006): 2–8.

Plümacher, *Lukas.* Plümacher, Eckhard. *Lukas als hellenisticher Schriftsteller. Studien zur Apostelgeschichte.* SUNT 9. Göttingen: Vandenhoeck & Ruprecht, 1972.

Plümacher, "Luke as Historian." Plümacher, Eckhard. "Luke as Historian." Translated by Dennis Martin. *ABD* 4:398–402.

Plümacher, "Mission Speeches." Plümacher, Eckhard. "The Mission Speeches in Acts and Dionysius of Halicarnassus." Pages 251–66 in *Jesus and the Heritage of Israel: Luke's Narrative Claim upon Israel's Legacy.* Edited by David P. Moessner. Luke the Interpreter of Israel 1. Harrisburg, PA: Trinity Press International, 1999.

Plümacher, "Missionsreden." Plümacher, Eckhard. "Die Missionsreden der Apostelgeschichte und Dionys von Halikarnass." *NTS* 39 (2, 1993): 161–77.

Plümacher, "Monographie." Plümacher, Eckhard. "Die Apostelgeschichte als historiche Monographie." Pages 457–66 in *Les Actes des apôtres. Traditions, rédaction, théologie.* Edited by Jacob Kremer. BETL 48. Gembloux, Belgium: J. Duculot, 1979.

Poewe, *Religions.* Poewe, Karla. *New Religions and the Nazis.* New York: Routledge, 2006.

Porciani, "Enigma." Porciani, Leone. "The Enigma of Discourse: A View of Thucydides." Pages 328–35 in *A Companion to Greek and Roman Historiography.* Edited by John Marincola. 2 vols. Oxford: Blackwell, 2007.

Porter, *Criteria.* Porter, Stanley E. *The Criteria for Authenticity in Historical-Jesus Research: Previous Discussion and New Proposals.* New York: T&T Clark, 2004.

Porter, *Paul in Acts.* Porter, Stanley E. *Paul in Acts.* LPSt. Peabody, MA: Hendrickson, 2001. Repr. of *The Paul of Acts: Essays in Literary Criticism, Rhetoric, and Theology.* WUNT 115. Tübingen: Mohr Siebeck, 1999.

Porter, "Reconstructing." Porter, Stanley E. "What Do We Know and How Do We Know It? Reconstructing Early Christianity from Its Manuscripts." Pages 41–70 in *Christian Origins and Greco-Roman Culture: Social and Literary Contexts for the New Testament.* Edited by Stanley Porter and Andrew W. Pitts. Vol. 1 of *Early Christianity in Its Hellenistic Context.* TENTS 9. Leiden: Brill, 2013.

Porter, "Thucydidean View?" Porter, Stanley E. "Thucydides 1.22.1 and Speeches in Acts: Is There a Thucydidean View?" *NovT* 32 (2, 1990): 121–42.

Porter, "We Passages." Porter, Stanley E. "Excursus: The 'We' Passages." Pages 545–74 in *The Book of Acts in Its Graeco-Roman Setting.* Edited by David W. J. Gill and Conrad Gempf. Vol. 2 of *The Book of Acts in Its First Century Setting.* Edited by Bruce W. Winter. Grand Rapids: Eerdmans, 1994.

Porter and Dyer, *Synoptic Problem.* Porter, Stanley E., and Bryan R. Dyer, eds. *The Synoptic Problem: Four Views.* Grand Rapids: Baker Academic, 2016.

Porter and Holmén, *Handbook.* Porter, Stanley E., and Tom Holmén, eds. *Handbook for the Study of the Historical Jesus.* 4 vols. Leiden: Brill, 2011.

Porter and Ong, "Memory." Porter, Stanley E., and Hughson T. Ong. "Memory, Orality, and the Fourth Gospel: A Response to Paul Foster, with Further Comments for Future Discussion." *JSHJ* 12 (1–2, 2014): 143–64.

Porterfield, *Healing.* Porterfield, Amanda. *Healing in the History of Christianity.* New York: Oxford University Press, 2005.

Porton, "Pronouncement Story." Porton, Gary G. "The Pronouncement Story in Tannaitic Literature: A Review of Bultmann's Theory." *Semeia* 20 (1981): 81–99.

Pouchelle, *Dieu éducateur.* Pouchelle, Patrick. *Dieu éducateur. Une nouvelle approche d'un concept de la théologie biblique entre Bible Hébraïque, Septante et littérature grecque classique.* FAT 2/77. Tübingen: Mohr Siebeck, 2015.

Pouchelle, "*Kyropaideia.*" Pouchelle, Patrick. "*Kyropaideia* versus *Paideia Kyriou*: The Semantic Transformation of Paideia and Cognates in the Translated Books of the Septuagint." Pages 101–34 in *Pedagogy in Ancient Judaism and Early Christianity.* Edited by Karina Martin Hogan, Matthew Goff, and Emma Wasserman. EJL 41. Atlanta: SBL Press, 2017.

Poulos, "Pronouncement Story." Poulos, Paula Nassen. "Form and Function of the Pronouncement Story in Diogenes Laertius' *Lives.*" *Semeia* 20 (1981): 53–63.

Powell, *Acts.* Powell, Mark Allan. *What Are They Saying about Acts?* New York: Paulist, 1991.

Powell, *Figure.* Powell, Mark Allan. *Jesus as a Figure in History: How Modern Historians View the Man from Galilee.* 2nd ed. Louisville: Westminster John Knox, 2013.

Powell, *Introduction.* Powell, Mark Allan. *Fortress Introduction to the Gospels.* Minneapolis: Fortress, 1998.

Power, "Ending." Power, Tristan. "The Endings of Suetonius' *Caesars.*" Pages 58–78 in *Suetonius the Biographer: Studies in Roman Lives.* Edited by Tristan Power and Roy K. Gibson. Oxford: Oxford University Press, 2013.

Power, "Poetry." Power, Tristan. "Poetry and Fiction in Suetonius's *Illustrious Men.*" Pages 217–39 in *Writing Biography in Greece and Rome: Narrative Technique and Fictionalization.* Edited by Koen De Temmerman and Kristoffel Demoen. Cambridge: Cambridge University Press, 2016.

Power, "Priscus." Power, Tristan J. "Helvidius Priscus in Suetonius *Domitian* 10.3." *CP* 109 (1, January 2014): 79–82.

Power, "Suetonius' Tacitus." Power, Tristan. "Suetonius' Tacitus." *JRS* 104 (2014): 205–25.

Power, "Taunt." Power, Tristan J. "The Servants' Taunt: Homer and Suetonius' Galba." *Historia* 58 (2, 2009): 242–45.

Praet, "Cloak." Praet, Danny. "The Divided Cloak as *redemptio militiae*: Biblical Stylization and Hagiographical Intertextuality in Sulpicius Severus' *Vita Martini.*" Pages 133–59 in *Writing Biography in Greece and Rome: Narrative Technique and Fictionalization.* Edited by Koen De Temmerman and Kristoffel Demoen. Cambridge: Cambridge University Press, 2016.

Pretzler, "Pausanias and Tradition." Pretzler, Maria. "Pausanias and Oral Tradition." *ClQ* 55 (1, 2005): 235–49.

Price, "Shipwreck." Price, Mark S. "Gold Watch Found at 1838 Shipwreck Stuns Recovery Experts." *Charlotte Observer,* June 17, 2018, https://www.charlotteobserver.com/news /local/article213337689.html.

Price, *Shrinking.* Price, Robert M. *The Incredible Shrinking Son of Man: How Reliable Is the Gospel Tradition?* Amherst, NY: Prometheus, 2003.

Pritz, *Nazarene Christianity.* Pritz, Ray A. *Nazarene Jewish Christianity: From the End of the New Testament Period until Its Disappearance in the Fourth Century.* StPB 37. Jerusalem: Magnes, 1988.

Provan, Long, and Longman, *History.* Provan, Iain, V. Philips Long, and Tremper Longman. *A Biblical History of Israel.* 2nd ed. Westminster John Knox, 2015.

Pryke, *Style.* Pryke, E. J. *Redactional Style in the Marcan Gospel: A Study of Syntax and Vocabulary as Guides to Redaction in Mark.* Cambridge: Cambridge University Press, 1978.

Pryzwansky, "Nepos." Pryzwansky, Molly M. "Cornelius Nepos: Key Issues and Critical Approaches. " *CJ* 105 (2009): 97–108.

Puig i Tàrrech, *Jesus.* Puig i Tàrrech, Armand. *Jesus: A Biography.* Waco, TX: Baylor University Press, 2011.

Quinn, "Epistemology." Quinn, Philip L. "Epistemology in Philosophy of Religion." Pages 513–38 in *The Oxford Handbook of Epistemology.* Edited by Paul K. Moser. Oxford: Oxford University Press, 2002.

Rabbie, "Wit." Rabbie, Edwin. "Wit and Humor in Roman Rhetoric." Pages 207–17 in *A Companion to Roman Rhetoric.* Edited by William Dominik and Jon Hall. Oxford: Blackwell, 2007.

Race, "Introduction." Race, William H. "Introduction." Pages 1–41 in vol. 1 of Pindar, *Odes.* Translated by William H. Race. 2 vols. LCL. Cambridge, MA: Harvard University Press, 1997.

Rackham, *Acts.* Rackham, Richard Belward. *The Acts of the Apostles.* 14th ed. London: Methuen, 1951. Repr., Grand Rapids: Baker, 1964.

Raglan, *Hero.* Raglan, FitzRoy Richard Somerset, Baron. *The Hero: A Study in Tradition, Myth, and Drama.* Mineola, NY: Dover, 2003. Orig., London: Methuen, 1936.

Rainey, "Herodotus' Description." Rainey, Anson F. "Herodotus' Description of the East Mediterranean Coast." *BASOR* 321 (February 2001): 57–63.

Rajak, *Josephus.* Rajak, Tessa. *Josephus: The Historian and His Society.* London: Gerald Duckworth, 1983; Philadelphia: Fortress, 1984.

Rajak, "Justus of Tiberias." Rajak, Tessa. "Josephus and Justus of Tiberias." Pages 81–94 in *Josephus, Judaism, and Christianity.* Edited by Louis H. Feldman and Gohei Hata. Detroit: Wayne State University Press, 1987.

Rajak, "Moses in Ethiopia." Rajak, Tessa. "Moses in Ethiopia: Legend and Literature." *JJS* 29 (2, 1978): 111–22.

Ramelli, "Origen and Hypatia." Ramelli, Ilaria. "Origen and Hypatia: Parallel Portraits of Platonist Educators." Pages 199–212 in *Reading and Teaching Ancient Fiction: Jewish, Christian, and Greco-Roman Narratives.* Edited by Sara R. Johnson, Rubén R. Dupertuis, and Christine Shea. WGRWSup 11. Atlanta: SBL Press, 2018.

Ramirez, "Faiths." Ramirez, Daniel. "Migrating Faiths: A Social and Cultural History of Pentecostalism in the U.S.-Mexico Borderlands." PhD diss., Duke University, 2005.

Ramsay, *Luke the Physician.* Ramsay, William M. *Luke the Physician and Other Studies in the History of Religion.* London: Hodder & Stoughton, 1908. Repr., Grand Rapids: Baker, 1979.

Raphael, "Travail." Raphael, Freddy. "Le travail de la memoire et les limites de l'histoire orale." *Annales* 35 (1, January 1980): 127–45.

Rappaport, "Heliodoros." Rappaport, Uriel. "Did Heliodoros Try to Rob the Treasures of the Jerusalem Temple? Date and Probability of the Story in II Maccabees, 3." *REJ* 170 (1–2, 2011): 3–19.

Raynor, "Moeragenes." Raynor, D. H. "Moeragenes and Philostratus: Two Views of Apollonius of Tyana." *ClQ* 34 (1, 1984): 222–26.

Rebenich, "Prose." Rebenich, Stefan. "Historical Prose." Pages 265–337 in *Handbook of Classical Rhetoric in the Hellenistic Period, 330 B.C.–A.D. 400.* Edited by Stanley E. Porter. Leiden: Brill, 1997.

Redman, "Eyewitnesses." Redman, Judith C. S. "How Accurate Are Eyewitnesses? Bauckham and the Eyewitnesses in the Light of Psychological Research." *JBL* 129 (1, 2010): 177–97.

Reed, *Archaeology.* Reed, Jonathan L. *Archaeology and the Galilean Jesus: A Re-examination of the Evidence.* Harrisburg, PA: Trinity Press International, 2000.

Reed, "Construction." Reed, Annette Yoshiko. "The Construction and Subversion of Patriarchal Perfection: Abraham and Exemplarity in Philo, Josephus, and the *Testament of Abraham.*" *JSJ* 40 (2, 2009): 185–212.

Reed, "Contributions." Reed, Jonathan L. "Archaeological Contributions to the Study of Jesus and the Gospels." Pages 40–54 in *The Historical Jesus in Context.* Edited by Amy-Jill Levine, Dale C. Allison Jr., and John Dominic Crossan. PrRR. Princeton: Princeton University Press, 2006.

Reinhold, *Diaspora.* Reinhold, Meyer. *Diaspora: The Jews among the Greeks and Romans.* Sarasota, FL: Samuel Stevens, 1983.

Reinmuth, "Investitur." Reinmuth, Eckart. "Zwischen Investitur und Testament. Beobachtungen zur Rezeption des Josuabuches im Liber antiquitatum biblicarum." *JSP* 16 (1, 2002): 24–43.

Reiser, "Alexanderroman." Reiser, Marius. "Der Alexanderroman und das Markusevangelium." Pages 131–63 in *Markus-Philologie. Historische, literargeschichtliche und stilistische Untersuchungen zum zweiten Evangelium.* Edited by H Cancik. WUNT 33. Tübingen: Mohr Siebeck, 1984.

Reiser, *Sprache.* Reiser, Marius. *Sprache und literarische Formen des Neuen Testaments. Eine Einführung.* UTB 2197. Paderborn: Schöningh, 2001.

Remus, *Healer.* Remus, Harold. *Jesus as Healer.* UJT. Cambridge: Cambridge University Press, 1997.

Remus, "Thaumaturges." Remus, Harold. "Moses and the Thaumaturges: Philo's De Vita Mosis as a Rescue Operation." *LTP* 52 (3, 1996): 665–80.

Renehan, "Quotations." Renehan, Robert. "Classical Greek Quotations in the New Testament." Pages 17–46 in *The Heritage of the Early Church: Essays in Honor of the Very Reverend Georges Vasilievich Florovsky*. OrChrAn 195. Rome: Pontificium Institutum Studiorum Orientalium, 1973.

Reydams-Schils, "Authority." Reydams-Schils, Gretchen. "Authority and Agency in Stoicism." *GRBS* 51 (2, 2011): 296–322.

Reynolds, "Difference." Reynolds, Adrian. "Comparing First and Second Maccabees: Do Their Differences Make Them Unreliable?" Pages 301–18 in Keener and Wright, *Biographies and Jesus*.

Rhoads, "Performance Criticism." Rhoads, David. "Performance Criticism (Biblical)." *DBAM* 281–89.

Rhoads, "Performance Events." Rhoads, David. "Performance Events in Early Christianity: New Testament Writings in an Oral Context." Pages 166–93 in *The Interface of Orality and Writing: Speaking, Seeing, Writing in the Shaping of New Genres*. Edited by Annette Weissenrieder and Robert B. Coote. WUNT 260. Tübingen: Mohr Siebeck, 2010. Repr., BPC 11. Eugene, OR: Wipf & Stock, 2015.

Rhodes, "Documents." Rhodes, P. J. "Documents and the Greek Historians." Pages 56–66 in *A Companion to Greek and Roman Historiography*. Edited by John Marincola. 2 vols. Oxford: Blackwell, 2007.

Riaud, "Réflexions." Riaud, J. "Quelques réflexions sur les Thérapeutes d'Alexandre à la lumière de *De vita Mosis* II, 67." Pages 184–91 in *Heirs of the Septuagint: Philo, Hellenistic Judaism, and Early Christianity; Festschrift for Earle Hilgert*. Edited by David T. Runia, David M. Hay, and David Winston. BJS 230. SPhiloA 3. Atlanta: Scholars Press, 1991.

Richards, *Letter Writing*. Richards, E. Randolph. *Paul and First-Century Letter Writing: Secretaries, Composition, and Collection*. Downers Grove, IL: InterVarsity, 2004.

Richardson and Gooch, "Logia." Richardson, Peter, and Peter Gooch, "Logia of Jesus in 1 Corinthians." Pages 39–62 in *The Jesus Tradition outside the Gospels*. Vol. 5 of *Gospel Perspectives*. Edited by David Wenham. Sheffield: JSOT Press, 1984.

Ricoeur, *Memory*. Ricoeur, Paul. *Memory, History, Forgetting*. Translated by Kathleen Blamey and David Pellauer. Chicago: University of Chicago Press, 2004.

Ricoeur, *Time*. Ricoeur, Paul. *Time and Narrative*. Translated by Kathleen Blamey and David Pellauer. Chicago: University of Chicago Press, 1990.

Ridderbos, *John*. Ridderbos, Herman N. *The Gospel according to John: A Theological Commentary*. Translated by John Vriend. Grand Rapids: Eerdmans, 1997.

Riesenfeld, *Tradition*. Riesenfeld, Harald. *The Gospel Tradition*. Philadelphia: Fortress, 1970.

Riesner, *Early Period*. Riesner, Rainer. *Paul's Early Period: Chronology, Mission Strategy, Theology*. Translated by Doug Stott. Grand Rapids: Eerdmans, 1998.

Riesner, "Education élémentaire." Riesner, Rainer. "Education élémentaire juive et tradition évangélique." *Hok* 21 (1982): 51–64.

Riesner, "Gate." Riesner, Rainer. "Josephus' 'Gate of the Essenes' in Modern Discussion." *ZDPV* 105 (1989): 105–9 and plates 8–16a.

Riesner, *Lehrer.*   Riesner, Rainer. *Jesus als Lehrer. Eine Untersuchung zum Ursprung der Evangelien-Überlieferung.* 2nd ed. WUNT 2.7. Tübingen: J. C. B. Mohr, 1984.

Riesner, "Preacher."   Riesner, Rainer. "Jesus as Preacher and Teacher." Pages 185–210 in *Jesus and the Oral Gospel Tradition.* Edited by Henry Wansbrough. JSNTSup 64. Sheffield: Sheffield Academic Press, 1991.

Riesner, "Teacher."   Riesner, Rainer. "Teacher." *DJG*² 934–39.

Riesner, "Zuverlässigkeit."   Riesner, Rainer. "Die historische Zuverlässigkeit der Apostelgeschichte." *ZNT* 9 (18, 2006): 38–43.

Robbins, "Chreia."   Robbins, Vernon K. "The Chreia." Pages 1–23 in *Greco-Roman Literature and the New Testament: Selected Forms and Genres.* Edited by David E. Aune. SBLSBS 21. Atlanta: Scholars Press, 1988.

Robbins, "Pronouncement Stories."   Robbins, Vernon K. "Classifying Pronouncement Stories in Plutarch's *Parallel Lives.*" *Semeia* 20 (1981): 29–52.

Robbins, *Quotes.*   Robbins, Vernon K. *Ancient Quotes and Anecdotes: From Crib to Crypt.* Sonoma, FL: Polebridge, 1989.

Robbins, *Study.*   Robbins, William Joseph. "A Study in Jewish and Hellenistic Legend, with Special Reference to Philo's *Life of Moses.*" PhD diss., Brown University, 1947.

Robbins, *Teacher.*   Robbins, Vernon K. *Jesus the Teacher: A Socio-rhetorical Interpretation of Mark.* Minneapolis: Augsburg Fortress, 1992.

Robertson, "Account."   Robertson, Stuart D. "The Account of the Ancient Israelite Tabernacle and First Priesthood in the 'Jewish Antiquities' of Flavius Josephus." PhD diss., Annenberg Research Institute, Philadelphia, 1991.

Robiano, "Apologia."   Robiano, Patrick. "The *Apologia* as a *mise-en-abyme* in Philostratus' *Life of Apollonius of Tyana.*" Pages 97–116 in *Writing Biography in Greece and Rome: Narrative Technique and Fictionalization.* Edited by Koen De Temmerman and Kristoffel Demoen. Cambridge: Cambridge University Press, 2016.

Robinson, *Historical Character.*   Robinson, J. Armitage. *The Historical Character of St John's Gospel.* 2nd ed. New York: Longmans, Green, 1929.

Robinson, "Perspective."   Robinson, John A. "Perspective, Meaning, and Remembering." Pages 199–217 in *Remembering Our Past: Studies in Autobiographical Memory.* Edited by David C. Rubin. Cambridge: Cambridge University Press, 1996.

Robinson, *Priority.*   Robinson, John A. T. *The Priority of John.* Edited by J. F. Coakley. London: SCM Press, 1985.

Robinson, *Problem.*   Robinson, James M. *The Problem of History in Mark and Other Marcan Studies.* Philadelphia: Fortress, 1982.

Robinson, *Redating.*   Robinson, John A. T. *Redating the New Testament.* Philadelphia: Westminster, 1976.

Rodgers, "Justice."   Rodgers, Zuleika. "Justice for Justus: A Re-examination of Justus of Tiberias' Role in Josephus' *Autobiography.*" Pages 169–92 in *The Limits of Ancient Biography.* Edited by Brian McGing and Judith Mossman. Swansea, Wales: Classical Press of Wales, 2006.

Rodríguez, "Authenticating Criteria." Rodríguez, Rafael. "Authenticating Criteria: The Use and Misuse of a Critical Method." *JSHJ* 7 (2009): 152–67.

Rodríguez, "Great Divide." Rodríguez, Rafael. "Great Divide." *DBAM* 163–64.

Rodríguez, "Jesus Tradition." Rodríguez, Rafael. "Jesus Tradition." *DBAM* 194–95.

Rodríguez, "Narrative Gospels." Rodríguez, Rafael. "Narrative Gospels." *DBAM* 240–42.

Rodríguez, *Structuring.* Rodríguez, Rafael. *Structuring Early Christian Memory: Jesus in Tradition, Performance, and Text.* LNTS 407. New York: T&T Clark, 2010.

Rodríguez, "Suffering." Rodríguez, Rafael. "'According to the Scriptures': Suffering and the Psalms in the Speeches in Acts." Pages 241–62 in *Memory and Identity in Ancient Judaism and Early Christianity: A Conversation with Barry Schwartz.* Edited by Tom Thatcher. Semeia Studies 78. Atlanta: SBL, 2014.

Rogers, "Baptism." Rogers, Trent A. "The Baptism and Temptation in Matthew: Transition Narratives in a Graeco-Roman Biography?" *Hen* 35 (2, 2013): 252–72.

Rolfe, "Introduction." Rolfe, J. C. "Introduction to *The Lives of the Caesars.*" Pages xvii–xxxi in vol. 1 of *Suetonius.* Translated by J. C. Rolfe. 2 vols. LCL. Cambridge, MA: Harvard University Press, 1914.

Römer, "Vie de Moïse." Römer, Thomas C. "La construction d'une 'vie de Moïse' dans la Bible hébraïque et chez quelques auteurs hellénistiques." *Transversalités* 85 (2003): 13–30.

Romez, "Report." Romez, Clarissa, David Zaritzky, and Joshua W. Brown. "Case Report of Gastroparesis Healing: 16 Years of a Chronic Syndrome Resolved After Proximal Intercessory Prayer." *Complementary Therapies in Medicine* 43 (2019): 289–94.

Romm, "Humor." Romm, James. "Corporeal Humor in Diogenes Laertius." Pages 567–70 in *Diogenes Laertius "Lives of the Eminent Philosophers."* Edited by James Miller. Translated by Pamela Mensch. New York: Oxford University Press, 2018.

Roncace, "Portraits." Roncace, Mark. "Josephus' (Real) Portraits of Deborah and Gideon: A Reading of *Antiquities* 5.198–232." *JSJ* 31 (3, 2000): 247–74.

Roncace, "Samson." Roncace, Mark. "Another Portrait of Josephus' Portrait of Samson." *JSJ* 35 (2, 2004): 185–207.

Rondholz, "Rubicon." Rondholz, Anke. "Crossing the Rubicon. A Historiographical Study." *Mnemosyne* 62 (3, 2009): 432–50.

Rood, "Cato." Rood, Tim. "Cato the Elder, Livy, and Xenophon's *Anabasis.*" *Mnemosyne* 70 (2017): 1–27.

Rood, "Development." Rood, Tim. "The Development of the War Monograph." Pages 147–58 in *A Companion to Greek and Roman Historiography.* Edited by John Marincola. 2 vols. Oxford: Blackwell, 2007.

Rook, "Names." Rook, John T. "The Names of the Wives from Adam to Abraham in the Book of *Jubilees.*" *JSP* 7 (1990): 105–17.

Rordorf, "Didache." Rordorf, Willy. "Does the Didache Contain Jesus Tradition Independently of the Synoptic Gospels?" Pages 394–423 in *Jesus and the Oral Gospel Tradition.* Edited by Henry Wansbrough. JSNTSup 64. Sheffield: Sheffield Academic Press, 1991.

Rosenberg, "Complexity." Rosenberg, Bruce A. "The Complexity of Oral Tradition." *Oral Tradition* 2 (1, 1987): 73–90.

Rosner, "Biblical History." Rosner, Brian S. "Acts and Biblical History." Pages 65–82 in *The Book of Acts in Its Ancient Literary Setting*. Edited by Bruce W. Winter and Andrew D. Clark. Vol. 1 of *The Book of Acts in Its First Century Setting*. Edited by Bruce W. Winter. Grand Rapids: Eerdmans, 1993.

Rossato et al., "Dopamine." Rossato, Janine I., et al. "Dopamine Controls Persistence of Long-Term Memory Storage." *Science* 325 (5943, August 21, 2009): 1017–20.

Rost, *Judaism*. Rost, Leonhard. *Judaism outside the Hebrew Canon: An Introduction to the Documents*. Translated by David E. Green. Nashville: Abingdon, 1976.

Rothschild, "Irony." Rothschild, Clare K. "Irony and Truth: The Value of *De Historia Conscribenda* for Understanding Hellenistic and Early Roman Period Historiographical Method." Pages 277–91 in *Die Apostelgeschichte im Kontext antiker und frühchristlicher Historiographie*. Edited by Jörg Frey, Clare K. Rothschild, and Jens Schröter, with Bettina Rost. BZNW 162. Berlin: de Gruyter, 2009.

Rothschild, *Rhetoric*. Rothschild, Clare K. *Luke-Acts and the Rhetoric of History: An Investigation of Early Christian Historiography*. WUNT 2.175. Tübingen: Mohr Siebeck, 2004.

Rouvinez, "Mark." Rouvinez, Francis Aldo. "The Gospel of Mark in the Context of Ancient Biography." PhD dissertation, University of St. Andrews, 2019.

Rowe, "Style." Rowe, Galen O. "Style." Pages 121–57 in *Handbook of Classical Rhetoric in the Hellenistic Period, 330 B.C.–A.D. 400*. Edited by Stanley E. Porter. Leiden: Brill, 1997.

Rubin, "Introduction." Rubin, David C. "Introduction." Pages 1–15 in *Remembering Our Past: Studies in Autobiographical Memory*. Edited by David C. Rubin. Cambridge: Cambridge University Press, 1996.

Rubin, *Memory*. Rubin, David. *Memory in Oral Traditions: The Cognitive Psychology of Epic, Ballads, and Counting-Out Rhymes*. New York: Oxford, 1995.

Rubincam, "Numbers." Rubincam, Catherine. "Numbers in Greek Poetry and Historiography: Quantifying Fehling." *ClQ* 53 (2, 2003): 448–63.

Rüger, "Tradition." Rüger, Hans-Peter. "Oral Tradition in the Old Testament." Pages 107–20 in *Jesus and the Oral Gospel Tradition*. Edited by Henry Wansbrough. JSNTSup 64. Sheffield: Sheffield Academic Press, 1991.

Runnalls, "Ethiopian Campaign." Runnalls, Donna. "Moses' Ethiopian Campaign." *JSJ* 14 (2, 1983): 135–56.

Rüpke, "Knowledge." Rüpke, Jörg. "Knowledge of Religion in Valerius Maximus' *Exempla*: Roman Historiography and Tiberian Memory Culture." Pages 89–111 in *Memory in Ancient Rome and Early Christianity*. Edited by Karl Galinsky. Oxford: Oxford University Press, 2016.

Rüpke, *Religion*. Rüpke, Jörg. *Religion: Antiquity and Its Legacy*. Ancients and Moderns. New York: Oxford University Press, 2013.

Russell, "Coriolanus." Russell, D. A. "Plutarch's Life of Coriolanus." *JRS* 53 (1963): 21–28.

Russell, "Plutarch." Russell, Donald A. F. M. "Plutarch." *OCD*[3] 1200–1201.

Rusten, "*Ekphrasis*." Rusten, Jeffrey Stuart. "*Ekphrasis*." *OCD*[3] 515.

Rutherford, "Tragedy." Rutherford, Richard. "Tragedy and History." Pages 504–14 in *A Companion to Greek and Roman Historiography*. Edited by John Marincola. 2 vols. Oxford: Blackwell, 2007.

Safrai, "Description in Works." Safrai, Zeev. "The Description of the Land of Israel in Josephus' Works." Pages 295–324 in *Josephus, the Bible, and History*. Edited by Louis H. Feldman and Gohei Hata. Detroit: Wayne State University Press, 1989.

Safrai, "Education." Safrai, Shemuel. "Education and the Study of the Torah." *JPFC* 945–70.

Sage, "Works." Sage, Michael M. "Tacitus' Historical Works: A Survey and Appraisal." *ANRW* 2.33.2 (1990): 851–1030.

Saïd, "City." Saïd, Suzanne. "The City in the Greek Novel." Pages 216–36 in *The Search for the Ancient Novel*. Edited by James Tatum. Baltimore: Johns Hopkins University Press, 1994.

Saïd, "Myth." Saïd, Suzanne. "Myth and Historiography." Pages 76–88 in *A Companion to Greek and Roman Historiography*. Edited by John Marincola. 2 vols. Oxford: Blackwell, 2007.

Salmon and Potter, "Bedriacum." Salmon, Edward T., and T. W. Potter. "Bedriacum (or Betriacum)." Page 237 in *OCD*.

Sánchez Walsh, *Identity*. Sánchez Walsh, Arlene M. *Latino Pentecostal Identity: Evangelical Faith, Self, and Society*. New York: Columbia University Press, 2003.

Sanders, *Figure*. Sanders, E. P. *The Historical Figure of Jesus*. New York: Penguin, 1993.

Sanders, *Jesus and Judaism*. Sanders, E. P. *Jesus and Judaism*. Philadelphia: Fortress, 1985.

Sanders, *Jesus to Mishnah*. Sanders, E. P. *Jewish Law from Jesus to the Mishnah: Five Studies*. London: SCM, 1990.

Sanders, *Judaism*. Sanders, E. P. *Judaism: Practice and Belief, 63 BCE–66 CE*. London: SCM, 1992.

Sanders, "Know." Sanders, E. P. "How Do We Know What We Know about Jesus?" Pages 38–61 in *Jesus Two Thousand Years Later*. Edited by James H. Charlesworth and Walter P. Weaver. FSCS. Harrisburg, PA: Trinity Press International, 2000.

Sanders, *Paul*. Sanders, E. P. *Paul: The Apostle's Life, Letters, and Thought*. Minneapolis: Fortress, 2015.

Sanders, *Paul and Judaism*. Sanders, E. P. *Paul and Palestinian Judaism: A Comparison of Patterns of Religion*. Philadelphia: Fortress, 1977.

Sanders, *Tendencies*. Sanders, E. P. *The Tendencies of the Synoptic Tradition*. SNTSMS 9. Cambridge: Cambridge University Press, 1969.

Sandnes, *Challenge*. Sandnes, Karl Olav. *The Challenge of Homer: School, Pagan Poets, and Early Christianity*. LNTS 400. New York: T&T Clark, 2009.

Sandnes, "Imitatio." Sandnes, Karl O. "*Imitatio Homeri*? An Appraisal of Dennis R. MacDonald's 'Mimesis Criticism.'" *JBL* 124 (4, 2005): 715–32.

Sandnes, "Markus." Sandnes, K. O. "Markus—en allegorisk biografi?" *DTT* 69 (4, 2006): 275–97.

Sandy, "Introduction." Sandy, Gerald N. "Introduction to Antonius Diogenes, *The Won-*

ders Beyond Thule." Pages 775–77 in *Collected Ancient Greek Novels*. Edited by B. P. Reardon. Berkeley: University of California Press, 1989.

Sanneh, *West African Christianity*.   Sanneh, Lamin. *West African Christianity: The Religious Impact*. Maryknoll, NY: Orbis Books, 1983.

Sardar, *Postmodernism*.   Sardar, Ziauddin. *Postmodernism and the Other: New Imperialism of Western Culture*. London: Pluto Press, 1998.

Satlow, "Philosophers."   Satlow, Michael L. "Theophrastus's Jewish Philosophers." *JJS* 59 (1, 2008): 1–20.

Satran, *Prophets*.   Satran, David. *Biblical Prophets in Byzantine Palestine: Reassessing the Lives of the Prophets*. SVTP 11. Leiden: Brill, 1995.

Satterthwaite, "Acts."   Satterthwaite, Philip E. "Acts against the Background of Classical Rhetoric." Pages 337–79 in *The Book of Acts in Its Ancient Literary Setting*. Edited by Bruce W. Winter and Andrew D. Clark. Vol. 1 of *The Book of Acts in Its First Century Setting*. Edited by Bruce W. Winter. Grand Rapids: Eerdmans, 1993.

Sauer, "Erwägungen."   Sauer, Jürgen. "Traditionsgeschichtliche Erwägungen zu den synoptischen und paulinischen Aussagen über Feindesliebe und Wiedervergeltungsverzicht." *ZNW* 76 (1–2, 1985): 1–28.

Schacter, "Distortions."   Schacter, Daniel L. "Memory Distortions: History and Current Status." Pages 1–43 in *Memory Distortion: How Minds, Brains, and Societies Reconstruct the Past*. Edited by Daniel L. Schacter. Cambridge, MA: Harvard University Press, 1995.

Schacter, "Memory, Amnesia, and Dysfunction."   Schacter, Daniel L. "Memory, Amnesia, and Frontal Lobe Dysfunction." *Psychobiology* 15 (1987): 21–36.

Schacter, "Neuropsychology."   Schacter, Daniel L. "The Cognitive Neuropsychology of False Memories: Introduction." *Cognitive Neuropsychology* 16 (3–5, 1999): 193–95.

Schacter, "Sins."   Schacter, Daniel L. "The Seven Sins of Memory: Insights from Psychology and Cognitive Neuroscience." *American Psychologist* 54 (1999): 182–203.

Schacter and Addis, "Neuroscience."   Schacter, Daniel L., and Donna Rose Addis. "The Cognitive Neuroscience of Constructive Memory: Remembering the Past and Imagining the Future." *Philosophical Transactions of the Royal Society* B362 (1481, May 29, 2007): 773–86.

Schacter, Norman, and Koutstaal, "Neuroscience."   Schacter, Daniel L., Kenneth A. Norman, and Wilma Koutstaal. "The Cognitive Neuroscience of Constructive Memory." *Annual Review of Psychology* 49 (1998): 289–318.

Schenkeveld, "Prose."   Schenkeveld, Dirk M. "Philosophical Prose." Pages 195–264 in *Handbook of Classical Rhetoric in the Hellenistic Period, 330 B.C.–A.D. 400*. Edited by Stanley E. Porter. Leiden: Brill, 1997.

Schepens, "History."   Schepens, Guido. "History and *Historia*: Inquiry in the Greek Historians." Pages 39–55 in *A Companion to Greek and Roman Historiography*. Edited by John Marincola. 2 vols. Oxford: Blackwell, 2007.

Scherberger, "Shaman."   Scherberger, Laura. "The Janus-Faced Shaman: The Role of Laughter in Sickness and Healing among the Makushi." *AnthHum* 30 (1, 2005): 55–69.

Scherberich, "Sueton und Josephus." Scherberich, Klaus. "Sueton und Josephus über die Ermorderung des Caligula." *RMPhil* 142 (1, 1999): 74–83.

Schiffman, "Scrolls." Schiffman, Lawrence H. "The Dead Sea Scrolls and the Early History of Jewish Liturgy." Pages 33–48 in *The Synagogue in Late Antiquity*. Edited by Lee I. Levine. Philadelphia: ASOR, 1986.

Schmeling, "Spectrum." Schmeling, Gareth. "The Spectrum of Narrative: Authority of the Author." Pages 19–29 in *Ancient Fiction and Early Christian Narrative*. Edited by Ronald F. Hock, J. Bradley Chance, and Judith Perkins. SBLSymS 6. Atlanta: SBL, 1998.

Schmeller, "Gegenwelten." Schmeller, Thomas. "Gegenwelten. Zum Vergleich zwischen paulinischen Gemeinden und nichtchristlichen Gruppen." *BZ* 47 (2, 2003): 167–85.

Schmidt, "Influences." Schmidt, Daryl D. "Rhetorical Influences and Genre: Luke's Preface and the Rhetoric of Hellenistic Historiography." Pages 27–60 in *Jesus and the Heritage of Israel: Luke's Narrative Claim upon Israel's Legacy*. Edited by David P. Moessner. Luke the Interpreter of Israel 1. Harrisburg, PA: Trinity Press International, 1999.

Schmidt, *Memories*. Schmidt, Stephen R. *Extraordinary Memories for Exceptional Events*. New York: Psychology Press, 2012.

Schmidt, "Stellung." Schmidt, K. L. "Die Stellung der Evangelien in der allgemeinen Literaturgeschichte." Pages 59–60 in vol. 1 of *ΕΥΧΑΡΙΣΤΗΡΙΟΝ. Studien zur Religion und Literatur des Alten und Neuen Testaments: Festschrift für Hermann Gunkel*. Edited by Hans Schmidt. 2 vols. in 1. FRLANT 19. Göttingen: Vandenhoeck & Ruprecht, 1923.

Schnabel, *Jesus in Jerusalem*. Schnabel, Eckhard J. *Jesus in Jerusalem in the Last Days*. Grand Rapids: Eerdmans, 2018.

Schnabel, *Jesus, Paul, and Church*. Schnabel, Eckhard J. *Jesus, Paul, and the Early Church: Missionary Realities in Historical Contexts*. WUNT 406. Tübingen: Mohr Siebeck, 2018.

Schnabel, *Mark*. Schnabel, Eckhard J. *Mark*. TNTC. Downers Grove, IL: IVP Academic, 2017.

Schneider, *Apostelgeschichte*. Schneider, Gerhard. *Die Apostelgeschichte*. HThKNT 5. Freiburg im Breisgau: Herder, 1980–82.

Schneider, "Zweck." Schneider, Gerhard. "Der Zweck des Lukanischen Doppelwerks." *BZ* 21 (1, 1977): 45–66.

Schnelle, *Christology*. Schnelle, Udo. *Antidocetic Christology in the Gospel of John: An Investigation of the Place of the Fourth Gospel in the Johannine School*. Translated by Linda M. Maloney. Minneapolis: Fortress Press, 1992.

Schofield, "Philosophers." Schofield, Malcolm. "Philosophers and Politics in Diogenes Laertius." Pages 570–73 in *Diogenes Laertius "Lives of the Eminent Philosophers."* Edited by James Miller. Translated by Pamela Mensch. New York: Oxford University Press, 2018.

Scholem, *Sabbatai Sevi*. Scholem, Gershom. *Sabbatai Sevi: The Mystical Messiah*. Princeton: Princeton University Press, 1973.

Schröter, "Begründer." Schröter, Jens. "Der erinnerte Jesus als Begründer des Christentums? Bemerkungen zu James D. G. Dunns Ansatz in der Jesusforschung." *ZNT* 10 (20, 2007): 47–53.

Schröter, "Contribution." Schröter, Jens. "The Contribution of Non-canonical Gospels to the Memory of Jesus: The Gospel of Thomas and the Gospel of Peter as Test Cases." *NTS* 64 (4, October 2018): 435–54.

Schröter, *Jesus to New Testament.* Schröter, Jens. *From Jesus to the New Testament: Early Christian Theology and the Origin of the New Testament Canon.* Translated by Wayne Coppins. Waco, TX: Baylor University Press, 2013.

Schudson, "Present." Schudson, Michael. "The Present in the Past versus the Past in the Present." *Communication* 11 (1989): 105–13.

Schuman and Scott, "Generations." Schuman, Howard, and Jacqueline Scott. "Generations and Collective Memories." *American Sociological Review* 54 (1989): 359–81.

Schürmann, "Anfänge." Schürmann, Heinz. "Die vorösterlichen Anfänge der Logientradition. Versuch eines formgeschichtlichen Zugangs zum Leben Jesu." Pages 342–70 in *Der Historische Jesus und der Kerygmatische Christus.* Edited by H. Ristow and K. Matthiae. Berlin: Evangelische, 1962.

Schwartz, *Forge.* Schwartz, Barry. *Abraham Lincoln and the Forge of National Memory.* Chicago: University of Chicago Press, 2000.

Schwartz, "Halbwachs." Schwartz, Barry. "Halbwachs, Maurice." *DBAM* 168–69.

Schwartz, "Harvest." Schwartz, Barry. "Harvest." Pages 313–37 in *Memory and Identity in Ancient Judaism and Early Christianity: A Conversation with Barry Schwartz.* Edited by Tom Thatcher. SemeiaSt 78. Atlanta: SBL, 2014.

Schwartz, "Jesus in Memory." Schwartz, Barry. "Jesus in First-Century Memory—a Response." Pages 249–61 in *Memory, Tradition, and Text: Uses of the Past in Early Christianity.* Edited by A. Kirk and Tom Thatcher. Semeia 52. Atlanta: SBL, 2005.

Schwartz, *Living Memory.* Schwartz, Andor. *Living Memory.* Melbourne, Vic.: Black, 2010.

Schwartz, "Origins." Schwartz, Barry. "Christian Origins: Historical Truth and Social Memory." Pages 43–56 in *Memory, Tradition, and Text: Uses of the Past in Early Christianity.* Edited by A. Kirk and Tom Thatcher. Semeia 52. Atlanta: SBL, 2005.

Schwartz, *Post-heroic Era.* Schwartz, Barry. *Abraham Lincoln in the Post-heroic Era: History and Memory in Late Twentieth-Century America.* Chicago: University of Chicago Press, 2008.

Schwartz, "Smoke." Schwartz, Barry. "Where There's Smoke, There's Fire: Memory and History." Pages 7–37 in *Memory and Identity in Ancient Judaism and Early Christianity: A Conversation with Barry Schwartz.* Edited by Tom Thatcher. SemeiaSt 78. Atlanta: SBL, 2014.

Schweitzer, *Quest.* Schweitzer, Albert. *The Quest of the Historical Jesus.* Translated by W. Montgomery. New York: Macmillan, 1968.

Scott, "Divine Man." Scott, Ian W. "Is Philo's Moses a Divine Man?" *SPhiloA* 14 (2002): 87–111.

Scott, *Parable.* Scott, Bernard Brandon. *Hear Then the Parable: A Commentary on the Parables of Jesus.* Minneapolis: Augsburg Fortress, 1989.

Sedley, "Debate." Sedley, David. "The Stoic-Platonist Debate on *kathêkonta*." Pages 128–52 in *Topics in Stoic Philosophy.* Edited by Katerina Ierodiakonou. Oxford: Oxford University Press, 1999.

Selden, "Genre." Selden, Daniel L. "Genre of Genre." Pages 39–64 in *The Search for the Ancient Novel*. Edited by James Tatum. Baltimore: Johns Hopkins University Press, 1994.

Senior, *Matthew*. Senior, Donald. *What Are They Saying about Matthew?* New York: Paulist, 1983.

Shanks, "*BAR* Interviews Yadin." Shanks, Hershel. "*BAR* Interviews Yigael Yadin." *BAR* 9 (1, 1983): 16–23.

Shanks, "Inscription." Shanks, Hershel. "Inscription Reveals Roots of Maccabean Revolt." *BAR* 34 (6, 2008): 56–59.

Shanks, *Papias*. Shanks, Monte A. *Papias and the New Testament*. Eugene, OR: Wipf & Stock, 2013.

Shauf, *Divine*. Shauf, Scott. *The Divine in Acts and in Ancient Historiography*. Minneapolis: Fortress, 2015.

Sheeley, *Asides*. Sheeley, Steven M. *Narrative Asides in Luke-Acts*. JSNTSup 72. Sheffield: Sheffield Academic, 1992.

Sheppard, *Craft*. Sheppard, Beth M. *The Craft of History and the Study of the New Testament*. SBLSBS 60. Atlanta: SBL, 2012.

Sheppard, "Historiography." Sheppard, Beth M. "Historiography, Ancient." *DBAM* 172–76.

Shim, "Suggestion." Shim, Ezra S. B. "A Suggestion about the Genre or Text-Type of Mark." *Scriptura* 50 (1994): 69–89.

Shinan, "Wyhlm." Shinan, Avigdor. "'Wyhlm ywsp hlwm' (brsyt lz 5). Hlwmwt ywsp bry hsprwt hyhwdyt hqdwmh." *Beit Mikra* 55 (1, 2010): 138–50 (NTA).

Shiner, "Technology." Shiner, Whitney. "Memory Technology and the Composition of Mark." Pages 147–65 in *Performing the Gospel: Orality, Memory, and Mark*. Edited by Richard A. Horsley, Jonathan A. Draper, and John Miles Foley. Minneapolis: Fortress, 2006.

Shively, "Penguins." Shively, Elizabeth. "Recognizing Penguins: Audience Expectation, Cognitive Genre Theory, and the Ending of Mark's Gospel." *CBQ* 80 (2018): 273–92.

Shively, "Recognizing." Shively, Elizabeth. "Recognizing Mark and Matthew: How to Extend Burridge's Contribution to the Gospels' Genre with a Cognitive Model." Paper presented in the Synoptic Gospels section, Society of Biblical Literature Annual Meeting, Denver, November. 17, 2018.

Shuler, *Genre*. Shuler, Philip L. *A Genre for the Gospels: The Biographical Character of Matthew*. Philadelphia: Fortress, 1982.

Shuler, "Moses." Shuler, Philip L. "Philo's Moses and Matthew's Jesus: A Comparative Study in Ancient Literature." *SPhiloA* 2 (1990): 86–103.

Sievers, "Name." Sievers, Joseph. "What's in a Name? Antiochus in Josephus' '*Bellum judaicum*.'" *JJS* 56 (1, 2005): 34–47.

Sigmon, "Brothers." Sigmon, Brian O. "According to the Brothers: First-Person Narration in the Testaments of the Twelve Patriarchs." Pages 137–52 in *Reading and Teaching Ancient Fiction: Jewish, Christian, and Greco-Roman Narratives*. Edited by Sara R. Johnson, Rubén R. Dupertuis, and Christine Shea. WGRWSup 11. Atlanta: SBL Press, 2018.

Silver, "Moses and Birds." Silver, Daniel J. "Moses and the Hungry Birds." *JQR* 64 (2, 1973): 123–53.

Simkovich, "Influence." Simkovich, Malka Zeiger. "Greek Influence on the Composition of 2 Maccabees." *JSJ* 42 (3, 2011): 293–310.

Simons et al., "Gist." Simons, J. S., A. C. H. Lee, K. S. Graham, M. Verfaellie, W. Koutstaal, J. R. Hodges, D. L. Schacter, and A. E. Budson. "Failing to Get the Gist: Reduced False Recognition of Semantic Associates in Semantic Dementia." *Neuropsychology* 19 (2005): 353–61.

Simpson, *Literature.* Simpson, William Kelly, ed. *The Literature of Ancient Egypt: An Anthology of Stories, Instructions, Stelae, Autobiographies, and Poetry.* 3rd ed. New Haven: Yale University Press, 2003.

Singleton, "Spirits." Singleton, Michael. "Spirits and 'Spiritual Direction': The Pastoral Counseling of the Possessed." Pages 471–78 in *Christianity in Independent Africa.* Edited by Edward Fasholé-Luke, Richard Gray, Adrian Hastings, and Godwin Tasie. Bloomington: Indiana University Press, 1978.

Slade, "Reports." Slade, Darren M. "Miracle Eyewitness Reports." *Encyclopedia of Psychology and Religion.* 3rd ed. Edited by David A. Leeming. Berlin: Springer, 2018. http://dx.doi.org/10.1007/978-3-642-27771-9_200227-1.

Sloan, "Similitudes." Sloan, David B. "The τίς ἐξ ὑμῶν Similitudes and the Extent of Q." *JSNT* 38 (3, 2016): 339–55.

Slomovic, "Understanding." Slomovic, Elieser. "Toward an Understanding of the Exegesis in the Dead Sea Scrolls." *RevQ* 7 (1969): 3–15.

Small, "Artificial Memory." Small, Jocelyn Penny. "Artificial Memory and the Writing Habits of the Literate." *Helios* 22 (2, 1995): 159–66.

Small, "Memory." Small, Jocelyn Penny. "Memory and the Roman Orator." Pages 195–206 in *A Companion to Roman Rhetoric.* Edited by William Dominik and Jon Hall. Oxford: Blackwell, 2007.

Small, "Review." Small, Brian C. Review of *The Genre of Acts and Collected Biography*, by Sean A. Adams. *RBL,* October 26, 2017, 6 pages, www.bookreviews.org/pdf/10406_11553.pdf.

Small, *Wax Tablets.* Small, Jocelyn Penny. *Wax Tablets of the Mind: Cognitive Studies of Memory and Literacy in Classical Antiquity.* London: Routledge, 1997.

Smallwood, "Historians." Smallwood, E. Mary. "Philo and Josephus as Historians of the Same Events." Pages 114–29 in *Josephus, Judaism, and Christianity.* Edited by Louis H. Feldman and Gohei Hata. Detroit: Wayne State University Press, 1987.

Smallwood, *Jews.* Smallwood, E. Mary. *The Jews under Roman Rule: From Pompey to Diocletian.* SJLA 20. Leiden: Brill, 1976.

Smit, "Practice." Smit, Peter-Ben. "Paul, Plutarch, and the Problematic Practice of Self-Praise (περιαυτολογία): The Case of Phil 3.2–21." *NTS* 60 (3, July 2014): 341–59.

Smith, *Βίος.* Smith, Justin Marc. *Why Βίος? On the Relationship between Gospel Genre and Implied Audience.* LNTS 518. New York: Bloomsbury, 2015.

Smith, "Comparison." Smith, Morton. "A Comparison of Early Christian and Early Rabbinic Tradition." *JBL* 82 (2, 1963): 169–76.

Smith, "Criticism." Smith, D. Moody. "Redaction Criticism, Genre, Narrative Criticism, and the Historical Jesus in the Gospel of John." Pages 624–33 in *Jesus Research: New Methodologies and Perceptions; The Second Princeton-Prague Symposium on Jesus Research*. Edited by James Charlesworth, with Brian Rhea and Petr Pokorný. Grand Rapids: Eerdmans, 2014.

Smith, "Genre." Smith, Justin M. "Genre, Sub-Genre, and Questions of Audience: A Proposed Typology for Greco-Roman Biography." *JGRCJ* 4 (2007): 184–216.

Smith, "Gospels." Smith, D. Moody. "When Did the Gospels Become Scripture?" *JBL* 119 (1, 2000): 3–20.

Smith, "Historical Issues." Smith, D. Moody. "Historical Issues and the Problem of John and the Synoptics." Pages 252–67 in *From Jesus to John: Essays on Jesus and NT Christology in Honour of Marinus de Jonge*. Edited by Martinus C. De Boer. JSNTSup 84. Sheffield: JSOT Press, 1993.

Smith, *John* (1999). Smith, D. Moody. *John*. ANTC. Nashville: Abingdon, 1999.

Smith, *John among Gospels*. Smith, D. Moody. *John among the Gospels*. 2nd ed. Columbia: University of South Carolina Press, 2001.

Smith, "John and Synoptics." Smith, D. Moody. "John and the Synoptics: Some Dimensions of the Problem." *NTS* 26 (4, July 1980): 425–44.

Smith, *Magician*. Smith, Morton. *Jesus the Magician*. San Francisco: Harper & Row, 1978.

Smith, "Metaphilosophy." Smith, Quentin. "The Metaphilosophy of Naturalism." *Philo* 4 (2, 2001): 195–215.

Smith, *Parallels*. Smith, Morton. *Tannaitic Parallels to the Gospels*. Philadelphia: SBL, 1951.

Smith, "Sarcophagus." Smith, Robert Houston. "A Sarcophagus from Pella: New Light on Earliest Christianity." *Archaeology* 26 (1973): 250–56.

Smith, "Understand." Smith, Abraham. "'Do You Understand What You Are Reading?': A Literary Critical Reading of the Ethiopian (Kushite) Episode (Acts 8:26–40)." *JITC* 22 (1, 1994): 48–70.

Smith and Kostopoulos, "Biography." Smith, Daniel Lynwood, and Zachary Lundin Kostopoulos. "Biography, History, and the Genre of Luke-Acts." *NTS* 63 (2017): 390–410.

Smith and Temmerman, "Ideal." Smith, S. D., and K. De Temmerman. "How Ideal Is the Oldest Greek Novel?" *Mnemosyne* 63 (3, 2010): 465–78.

Snodgrass, *Stories*. Snodgrass, Klyne R. *Stories with Intent: A Comprehensive Guide to the Parables of Jesus*. Grand Rapids: Eerdmans, 2008.

Snyder, "Review." Snyder, Glenn E. Review of *Mythologizing Jesus: From Jewish Teacher to Epic Hero*, by Dennis R. MacDonald. *RBL*, October 25, 2018, 3 pages.

Soards, "Passion Narrative." Soards, Marion L. "Appendix IX: The Question of a Premarcan Passion Narrative." Pages 1492–1524 in *The Death of the Messiah: From Gethsemane to Grave; A Commentary on the Passion Narratives in the Four Gospels*. 2 vols. New York: Doubleday, 1994.

Soards, "Review." Soards, Marion L. Review of *Profit with Delight*, by Richard Pervo. *JAAR* 58 (2, 1990): 307–10.

Soards, *Speeches.* Soards, Marion L. *The Speeches in Acts: Their Content, Context, and Concerns.* Louisville: Westminster John Knox, 1994.

Soards, "Tradition." Soards, Marion L. "Oral Tradition before, in, and outside the Canonical Passion Narrative." Pages 334–50 in *Jesus and the Oral Gospel Tradition.* Edited by Henry Wansbrough. JSNTSup 64. Sheffield: Sheffield Academic Press, 1991.

Sollenberger, "Lives of Peripatetics." Sollenberger, Michael G. "The Lives of the Peripatetics: The Analysis of the Contents and Structure of Diogenes Laertius' 'Vitae Philosophorum' Book 5." *ANRW* 2.36.6 (1992): 3793–879.

Sorabji, *Aristotle on Memory.* Sorabji, Richard. *Aristotle on Memory.* 2nd ed. Chicago: University of Chicago Press, 2006.

Sorabji, *Emotion.* Sorabji, Richard. *Emotion and Peace of Mind: From Stoic Agitation to Christian Temptation.* Gifford Lectures. New York: Oxford University Press, 2000.

Sotgiu and Rusconi, "Memories." Sotgiu, Igor, and Maria Luisa Rusconi. "Why Autobiographical Memories for Traumatic and Emotional Events Might Differ: Theoretical Arguments and Empirical Evidence." *Journal of Psychology: Interdisciplinary and Applied* 148 (5, September 2014): 523–47.

Southerland, "Valuation." Southerland, Kevin. "Source Valuation and Use in Book Nine of Diogenes Laertius's *Lives of Eminent Philosophers*." Research paper for the doctoral Seminar on the Historical Jesus, Asbury Theological Seminary, May 8, 2018.

Spanos, *Multiple Identities.* Spanos, Nicholas P. *Multiple Identities and False Memories.* Washington, DC: American Psychological Association, 1996.

Spencer, *Acts.* Spencer, F. Scott. *Acts.* Sheffield: Sheffield Academic, 1997.

Spivey, Smith, and Black, *Anatomy.* Spivey, Robert A., D. Moody Smith, and C. Clifton Black. *Anatomy of the New Testament.* 6th ed. Upper Saddle River, NJ: Pearson Prentice Hall, 2007.

Spradley, *Observation.* Spradley, James P. *Participant Observation.* Long Grove, IL: Waveland Press, 2016.

Squires, *Plan.* Squires, John T. *The Plan of God in Luke-Acts.* SNTSMS 76. Cambridge: Cambridge University Press, 1993.

Squires, "Plan." Squires, John T. "The Plan of God." Pages 19–39 in *Witness to the Gospel: The Theology of Acts.* Edited by I. Howard Marshall and David Peterson. Grand Rapids: Eerdmans, 1998.

Stadter, "Anecdotes." Stadter, Philip A. "Anecdotes and the Thematic Structure of Plutarchean Biography." Pages 291–303 in *Estudios sobre Plutarco. Aspectos formales.* Edited by J. A. Fernández Delgado, J. Antonio, and F. Pordomingo Pardo. Madrid: Ediciones Clásicas, 1996.

Stadter, "Biography." Stadter, Philip. "Biography and History." Pages 528–40 in *A Companion to Greek and Roman Historiography.* Edited by John Marincola. 2 vols. Oxford: Blackwell, 2007.

Stadter, "Narrative." Stadter, Philip A. "Fictional Narrative in the *Cyropaideia.*" *AJP* 112 (1991): 461–91.

Stagg, *Acts.* Stagg, Frank. *The Book of Acts: The Early Struggle for an Unhindered Gospel.* Nashville: Broadman, 1955.

Stambaugh and Balch, *Environment.* Stambaugh, John E., and David L. Balch. *The New Testament in Its Social Environment.* LEC 2. Philadelphia: Westminster, 1986.

Stamps, "Children." Stamps, D. L. "Children in Late Antiquity." *DNTB* 197–201.

Stanley, *Language.* Stanley, Christopher D. *Paul and the Language of Scripture: Citation Technique in the Pauline Epistles and Contemporary Literature.* SNTSMS 69. Cambridge: Cambridge University Press, 1992.

Stanton, *Gospels.* Stanton, Graham N. *The Gospels and Jesus.* Oxford Bible Series. Oxford: Oxford University Press, 1989.

Stanton, *Gospel Truth?* Stanton, Graham N. *Gospel Truth? New Light on Jesus and the Gospels.* Valley Forge, PA: Trinity Press International, 1995.

Stanton, *New People.* Stanton, Graham N. *A Gospel for a New People: Studies in Matthew.* Edinburgh: T&T Clark, 1992; Louisville: Westminster John Knox, 1993.

Stanton, *Preaching.* Stanton, Graham N. *Jesus of Nazareth in New Testament Preaching.* Cambridge: Cambridge University Press, 1974.

Stanton, "Reflection." Stanton, Graham N. "The Gospel Traditions and Early Christological Reflection." Pages 543–52 in *The Historical Jesus in Recent Research.* Edited by James D. G. Dunn and Scot McKnight. Winona Lake, IN: Eisenbrauns, 2005.

Starner, *Kingdom.* Starner, Rob. *Kingdom of Power, Power of Kingdom: The Opposing World Views of Mark and Chariton.* Eugene, OR: Pickwick, 2011.

Steele, "Trogus." Steele, R. B. "Pompeius Trogus and Justinus." *AJP* 38 (1, 1917): 19–41.

Stein, "Criteria." Stein, Robert H. "The 'Criteria' for Authenticity." Pages 225–63 in *Studies of History and Tradition in the Four Gospels.* Vol. 1 of *Gospel Perspectives.* Edited by R. T. France and David Wenham. Sheffield: JSOT Press, 1980.

Stein, *Luke.* Stein, Robert H. *Luke.* NAC 24. Nashville: Broadman, 1992.

Stein, *Messiah.* Stein, Robert H. *Jesus the Messiah: A Survey of the Life of Christ.* Downers Grove, IL: InterVarsity, 1996.

Stein, *Method.* Stein, Robert H. *The Method and Message of Jesus' Teachings.* Philadelphia: Westminster, 1978.

Stem, *Biographies.* Stem, Rex. *The Political Biographies of Cornelius Nepos.* Ann Arbor: University of Michigan, 2012.

Stem, "Lessons." Stem, Rex. "The Exemplary Lessons of Livy's Romulus." *TAPA* 137 (2007): 435–71.

Stephens, "Who Read Novels?" Stephens, Susan A. "Who Read Ancient Novels?" Pages 405–18 in *The Search for the Ancient Novel.* Edited by James Tatum. Baltimore: Johns Hopkins University Press, 1994.

Sterling, "Appropriation." Sterling, Gregory E. "The Jewish Appropriation of Hellenistic Historiography." Pages 231–43 in *A Companion to Greek and Roman Historiography.* Edited by John Marincola. 2 vols. Oxford: Blackwell, 2007.

Sterling, "Historians." Sterling, Gregory E. "Historians, Greco-Roman." *DNTB* 499–504.

Sterling, *Historiography.* Sterling, Gregory E. *Historiography and Self-Definition: Josephos, Luke-Acts, and Apologetic Historiography.* NovTSup 64. Leiden: Brill, 1992.

Sterling, *Sisters.* Sterling, Dorothy, ed. *We Are Your Sisters: Black Women in the Nineteenth Century.* New York: W. W. Norton, 1984.

Stern, *Authors.* Stern, Menahem, ed. *Greek and Latin Authors on Jews and Judaism.* 3 vols. Jerusalem: Israel Academy of Sciences and Humanities, 1974–84.

Stern, *Parables in Midrash.* Stern, David. *Parables in Midrash: Narrative and Exegesis in Rabbinic Literature.* Cambridge, MA: Harvard University Press, 1991.

Steussy, "Memory." Steussy, Marti J. "Long-Term/Short-Term Memory." *DBAM* 210–12.

Stewart, "Parable Form." Stewart, Roy A. "The Parable Form in the Old Testament and the Rabbinic Literature." *EvQ* 36 (1964): 133–47.

Steyn, "Elemente." Steyn, Gert J. "Elements of the Universe in Philo's *De Vita Mosis:* Cosmological Theology or Theological Cosmology?" *IDS* 47 (2, July 2013), 9 pages, https://www.indieskriflig.org.za/index.php/skriflig/article/view/699.

Stibbe, *Gospel.* Stibbe, Mark W. G. *John's Gospel.* New Testament Readings. London: Routledge, 1994.

Stock, Gajsar, and Güntürkün, " Neuroscience." Stock, Ann-Kathrin, Hannah Gajsar, and Onur Güntürkün. "The Neuroscience of Memory." Pages 369–91 in *Memory in Ancient Rome and Early Christianity.* Edited by Karl Galinsky. Oxford: Oxford University Press, 2016.

Stowers, *Letter Writing.* Stowers, Stanley K. *Letter Writing in Greco-Roman Antiquity.* LEC 5. Philadelphia: Westminster, 1986.

Stowers, "Resemble Philosophy?" Stowers, Stanley K. "Does Pauline Christianity Resemble a Hellenistic Philosophy?" Pages 81–102 in *Paul beyond the Judaism/Hellenism Divide.* Edited by Troels Engberg-Pedersen. Louisville: Westminster John Knox, 2001.

Strasburger, "Umblick." Strasburger, Hermann. "Umblick in Trümmerfeld der griechischen Geschichtsschreibung." Pages 3–52 in *Historiographia Antiqua. Commentationes Lovanienses editae in honorem W. Peremans septuagenarii.* Symbolae Facultatis litterarum et philosophiae Lovaniensis A6. Leuven: Leuven University Press, 1977.

Strauss, *Life.* Strauss, David Friedrich. *A New Life of Jesus.* 2 vols. London: Williams & Norgate, 1865.

Streeter, *Gospels.* Streeter, Burnett Hillman. *The Four Gospels: A Study of Origins, Treating of the Manuscript Tradition, Sources, Authorship, and Dates.* Rev. ed. London: Macmillan, 1930.

Strickert, "Founding." Strickert, Frederick. "The Founding of the City of Julias by the Tetrarch Philip in 30 CE." *JJS* 61 (2, 2010): 220–33.

Stuckenbruck, "Influence." Stuckenbruck, Loren T. " 'Semitic Influence on Greek': An Authenticating Criterion in Jesus Research?" Pages 73–94 in *Jesus, Criteria, and the Demise of Authenticity.* Edited by Chris Keith and Anthony Le Donne. London: T&T Clark, 2012.

Stuhlmacher, "Theme." Stuhlmacher, Peter. "The Theme: The Gospel and the Gospels."

Pages 1–25 in *The Gospel and the Gospels*. Edited by Peter Stuhlmacher. Grand Rapids: Eerdmans, 1991.

Suciu, *Apocryphon*.   Suciu, Alin. *The Berlin-Strasbourg Apocryphon: A Coptic Apostolic Memoir*. WUNT 370. Tübingen: Mohr Siebeck, 2017.

Sumney, *Opponents*.   Sumney, Jerry L. *Identifying Paul's Opponents: The Question of Method in 2 Corinthians*. JSNTSup 40. Sheffield: JSOT Press, 1990.

Sumney, *Steward*.   Sumney, Jerry L. *Steward of God's Mysteries: Paul and Early Church Tradition*. Grand Rapids: Eerdmans, 2017.

Swain, "Biography."   Swain, Simon. "Biography and Biographic in the Literature of the Roman Empire." Pages 1–37 in *Portraits: Biographical Representations in the Greek and Latin Literature of the Roman Empire*. Edited by M. J. Edwards and Simon Swain. Oxford: Clarendon, 1997.

Swain, "Reliability."   Swain, Simon C. R. "The Reliability of Philostratus' Lives of the Sophists." *ClAnt* 10 (1991): 148–63.

Swinburne, "Evidence."   Swinburne, Richard. "Evidence for the Resurrection." Pages 191–212 in *The Resurrection: An Interdisciplinary Symposium on the Resurrection of Jesus*. Edited by Stephen T. Davis, Daniel Kendall, and Gerald O'Collins. Oxford: Oxford University Press, 1997.

Swinburne, *Miracle*.   Swinburne, Richard. *The Concept of Miracle*. NSPR. London: Macmillan, 1970.

Syme, *Tacitus*.   Syme, Ronald. *Tacitus*. Oxford: Clarendon Press, 1958.

Syme, "Tacitus."   Syme, Ronald. "Tacitus: Some Sources of His Information." *The Journal of Roman Studies* 72 (Nov. 1982): 68–82.

Syon, "Gamla."   Syon, Danny. "Gamla: Portrait of a Rebellion." *BAR* 18 (1, 1992): 20–37, 72.

Talbert, *Acts*.   Talbert, Charles H. *Reading Acts: A Literary and Theological Commentary on the Acts of the Apostles*. Rev. ed. Macon, GA: Smyth & Helwys, 2005.

Talbert, "Chance."   Talbert, Charles H. "Reading Chance, Moessner, and Parsons." Pages 229–40 in *Cadbury, Knox, and Talbert: American Contributions to the Study of Acts*. Edited by Mikeal C. Parsons and Joseph B. Tyson. Atlanta: Scholars Press, 1992.

Talbert, "Concept."   Talbert, Charles H. "The Concept of Immortals in Mediterranean Antiquity." *JBL* 94 (3, 1975): 419–36.

Talbert, *Gospel*.   Talbert, Charles H. *What Is a Gospel? The Genre of the Canonical Gospels*. Philadelphia: Fortress, 1977.

Talbert, *Luke*.   Talbert, Charles H. *Reading Luke: A Literary and Theological Commentary on the Third Gospel*. New York: Crossroad, 1982.

Talbert, *Matthew*.   Talbert, Charles H. *Matthew*. PCNT. Grand Rapids: Baker Academic, 2010.

Talbert, *Mediterranean Milieu*.   Talbert, Charles H. *Reading Luke-Acts in Its Mediterranean Milieu*. NovTSup 107. Leiden: Brill, 2003.

Talbert, "Monograph."   Talbert, Charles H. "The Acts of the Apostles: Monograph or *bios*?" Pages 58–72 in *History, Literature, and Society in the Book of Acts*. Edited by Ben Witherington III. Cambridge: Cambridge University Press, 1996.

Talbert, "Myth." Talbert, Charles H. "The Myth of a Descending-Ascending Redeemer in Mediterranean Antiquity." *NTS* 22 (4, 1976): 418–40.

Talbert, *Patterns.* Talbert, Charles H. *Literary Patterns, Theological Themes, and the Genre of Luke-Acts.* SBLMS 20. Missoula, MT: Scholars Press, 1974.

Talbert, "Response." Talbert, Charles H. "Oral and Independent or Literary and Interdependent? A Response to Albert B. Lord." Pages 93–102 in *The Relationships among the Gospels: An Interdisciplinary Dialogue.* Edited by William O. Walker Jr. San Antonio: Trinity University Press, 1978.

Talbert, "Review." Talbert, Charles H. Review of *What Are the Gospels?* by Richard A. Burridge. *JBL* 112 (4, 1993): 714–15.

Talmon, "Institutionalized Prayer." Talmon, Shemaryahu. "The Emergence of Institutionalized Prayer in Israel in the Light of the Qumran Literature." Pages 265–84 in *Qumrân. Sa piété, sa théologie, et son milieu.* Edited by M. Delcor. BETL 46. Gembloux, Belgium: J. Duculot, 1978.

Talmon, "Tradition." Talmon, Shemaryahu. "Oral Tradition and Written Transmission; or, the Heard and the Seen Word in Judaism of the Second Temple Period." Pages 121–58 in *Jesus and the Oral Gospel Tradition.* Edited by Henry Wansbrough. JSNTSup 64. Sheffield: Sheffield Academic Press, 1991.

Tamiolaki, "Satire." Tamiolaki, Melina. "Satire and Historiography: The Reception of Classical Models and the Construction of the Author's Persona in Lucian's 'De historia conscribenda.'" *Mnemosyne* 68 (6, 2015): 917–36.

Tang, "Healers." Tang, Edmond. "'Yellers' and Healers—Pentecostalism and the Study of Grassroots Christianity in China." Pages 467–86 in *Asian and Pentecostal: The Charismatic Face of Christianity in Asia.* Edited by Allan Anderson and Edmond Tang. RStMiss, AJPSS 3. Oxford: Regnum; Baguio City, Philippines: APTS, 2005.

Tan-Gatue, "Coherence." Tan-Gatue, Peter. "The Coherence of Justification in Luke 18:9–14 with Authentic Jesus Tradition." PhD diss., Asbury Theological Seminary, 2019.

Tannehill, *Acts.* Tannehill, Robert C. *The Acts of the Apostles.* Vol. 2 of *The Narrative Unity of Luke-Acts: A Literary Interpretation.* Minneapolis: Fortress, 1990.

Tannehill, *Luke.* Tannehill, Robert C. *The Gospel according to Luke.* Vol. 1 of *The Narrative Unity of Luke-Acts: A Literary Interpretation.* Philadelphia: Fortress, 1986.

Tate, "Formulas." Tate, Aaron P. "Formulas." *DBAM* 146–48.

Tatum, "Epoch." Tatum, W. Barnes. "The Epoch of Israel: Luke I–II and the Theological Plan of Luke-Acts." *NTS* 13 (2, 1967): 184–95.

Taylor, "Acts as Biography." Taylor, Justin. "The Acts of the Apostles as Biography." Pages 77–88 in *The Limits of Ancient Biography.* Edited by Brian McGing and Judith Mossman. Swansea, Wales: Classical Press of Wales, 2006.

Taylor, *Born a Slave.* Taylor, Yuval. *I Was Born a Slave: An Anthology of Classic Slave Narratives.* 2 vols. Chicago: Lawrence Hill, 1999.

Taylor, *Formation.* Taylor, Vincent. *The Formation of the Gospel Tradition.* 2nd ed. London: Macmillan, 1935.

Taylor, "Q and Galilee?" Taylor, Nicholas H. "Q and Galilee?" *Neot* 37 (2, 2003): 283–311.

Taylor, "Quest." Taylor, Nicholas H. "Paul and the Historical Jesus Quest." *Neot* 37 (1, 2003): 105–26.

Tedlock, "Observation." Tedlock, Barbara. "From Participant Observation to the Observation of Participation: The Emergence of Narrative Ethnography." *JAnthRes* 47 (1991): 69–94.

Telford, *Mark*. Telford, William R. *Mark*. NTG. Sheffield: Sheffield Academic Press, 1995.

Termini, "Part." Termini, Cristina. "The Historical Part of the Pentateuch according to Philo of Alexandria: Biography, Genealogy, and the Philosophical Meaning of the Patriarchal Lives." Pages 265–95 in *History and Identity: How Israel's Later Authors Viewed Its Earlier History*. Edited by Núria Calduch-Benages and Jan Liesen. DCLY 2006. Berlin: de Gruyter, 2006.

Thackeray, *Josephus*. Thackeray, H. St. John. *Josephus: The Man and the Historian*. New York: Jewish Institute of Religion Press, 1929. Repr., New York: Ktav, 1967.

Thatcher, "Actual Past." Thatcher, Tom. "Actual Past." *DBAM* 18.

Thatcher, "Cold Memory." Thatcher, Tom. "Cold Memory/Hot Memory." *DBAM* 58–59.

Thatcher, "Dibelius." Thatcher, Tom. "Dibelius, Martin." *DBAM* 81–83.

Thatcher, "Memory Theatre." Thatcher, Tom. "Memory Theatre." *DBAM* 224–25.

Thatcher, *Riddler*. Thatcher, Tom. *Jesus the Riddler: The Power of Ambiguity in the Gospels*. Louisville: Westminster John Knox, 2006.

Thatcher, "Riddles." Thatcher, Tom. "Riddles." *DBAM* 342–44.

Thatcher, "Schwartz." Thatcher, Tom. "Schwartz, Barry." *DBAM* 351–52.

Thatcher, "Shape." Thatcher, Tom. "The Shape of John's Story: Memory-Mapping the Fourth Gospel." Pages 209–39 in *Memory and Identity in Ancient Judaism and Early Christianity: A Conversation with Barry Schwartz*. Edited by Tom Thatcher. SemeiaSt 78. Atlanta: SBL, 2014.

Thatcher, "Theories." Thatcher, Tom. "Memory, Greco-Roman Theories of." *DBAM* 220–22.

Thatcher, *Why John Wrote*. Thatcher, Tom. *Why John Wrote a Gospel: Jesus—Memory—History*. Louisville: Westminster John Knox, 2006.

Theissen, *Gospels*. Theissen, Gerd. *The Gospels in Context: Social and Political History in the Synoptic Tradition*. Translated by Linda M. Maloney. Minneapolis: Fortress, 1991.

Theissen and Merz, *Guide*. Theissen, Gerd, and Annette Merz. *The Historical Jesus: A Comprehensive Guide*. Translated by John Bowden. Minneapolis: Fortress, 1998.

Theissen and Winter, *Quest*. Theissen, Gerd, and Dagmar Winter. *The Quest for the Plausible Jesus: The Question of Criteria*. Translated by M. Eugene Boring. Louisville: Westminster John Knox, 2002.

Thomas, "Fluidity." Thomas, Christine M. "Stories without Texts and without Authors: The Problem of Fluidity in Ancient Novelistic Texts and Early Christian Literature." Pages 273–91 in *Ancient Fiction and Early Christian Narrative*. Edited by Ronald F. Hock, J. Bradley Chance, and Judith Perkins. SBLSymS 6. Atlanta: SBL, 1998.

Thomas, *Oral Tradition*. Thomas, Rosalind. *Oral Tradition and Written Record in Classical Athens*. Cambridge: Cambridge University Press, 1989.

Thomas, "Writing." Thomas, Rosalind. "Writing, Reading, Public and Private 'Literacies': Functional Literacy and Democratic Literacy in Greece." Pages 13–45 in *Ancient Literacies: The Culture of Reading in Greece and Rome*. Edited by William A. Johnson and Holt N. Parker. New York: Oxford University Press, 2009.

Thompson, *Clothed*. Thompson, Michael B. *Clothed with Christ: The Example and Teaching of Jesus in Romans 12.1–15.13*. JSNTSup 59. Sheffield: JSOT Press, 1991.

Thompson, "Historical Jesus." Thompson, Marianne Meye. "The Historical Jesus and the Johannine Christ." Pages 21–42 in *Exploring the Gospel of John: In Honor of D. Moody Smith*. Edited by R. Alan Culpepper and C. Clifton Black. Louisville: Westminster John Knox, 1996.

Thompson, "Paul in Acts." Thompson, Michael B. "Paul in the Book of Acts: Differences and Distance." *ExpT* 122 (9, June 2011): 425–36.

Thompson, Wenger, and Bartling, "Recall." Thompson, Charles P., Steven K. Wenger, and Carl A. Bartling. "How Recall Facilitates Subsequent Recall: A Reappraisal." *JExpPsyc* 4 (3, 1978): 210–21.

Thorburn, "Tiberius." Thorburn, John E. "Suetonius' Tiberius: A Proxemic Approach." *CP* 103 (4, 2008): 435–48.

Thornton, "Justin und Markusevangelium." Thornton, C.-J. "Justin und das Markusevangelium." *ZNW* 84 (1–2, 1993): 93–110.

Tibbs, "Possession." Tibbs, Clint. "Mediumistic Divine Possession among Early Christians: A Response to Craig S. Keener's 'Spirit Possession as a Cross-cultural Experience.'" *BBR* 26 (2016): 17–38.

Tiede, *Figure*. Tiede, David Lenz. *The Charismatic Figure as Miracle Worker*. SBLDS 1. Missoula, MT: SBL, 1972.

Tieleman, "Orality." Tieleman, Teun L. "Orality and Writing in Ancient Philosophy: Their Interrelationship and the Shaping of Literary Forms." Pages 19–35 in *Interface of Orality and Writing: Speaking, Seeing, Writing in the Shaping of New Genres*. Edited by Annette Weissenrieder and Robert B. Coote. BPC 11. Eugene, OR: Wipf & Stock, 2015.

Tilg, *Chariton*. Tilg, Stefan. *Chariton of Aphrodisias and the Invention of the Greek Love Novel*. New York: Oxford University Press, 2010.

Tilling, *Christology*. Tilling, Chris. *Paul's Divine Christology*. Tübingen: Mohr Siebeck, 2012. Repr., Grand Rapids: Eerdmans, 2015.

Tinti et al., "Processes." Tinti, Carla, et al. "Distinct Processes Shape Flashbulb and Event Memories." *Memory and Cognition* 42 (May 2014): 539–51.

Titchener, "Nepos." Titchener, Frances. "Cornelius Nepos and the Biographical Tradition." *GR* 50 (2003): 85–99.

Tolbert, *Sowing*. Tolbert, Mary Ann. *Sowing the Gospel: Mark's World in Literary-Historical Perspective*. Minneapolis: Fortress, 1996.

Tomkins, *Wesley*. Tomkins, Stephen. *John Wesley: A Biography*. Grand Rapids: Eerdmans, 2003.

Tomkins, *Wilberforce*. Tomkins, Stephen. *William Wilberforce: A Biography*. Grand Rapids: Eerdmans, 2007.

Tomson, "Jesus and Judaism." Tomson, Peter J. "Jesus and His Judaism." Pages 25–40 in *The Cambridge Companion to Jesus*. Edited by Markus Bockmuehl. Cambridge: Cambridge University Press, 2001.

Tonkin, *Narrating*. Tonkin, Elizabeth. *Narrating Our Pasts: The Social Construction of Oral History*. Cambridge: Cambridge University Press, 1992.

Touati, *Literacy*. Touati, Samia. *Literacy, Information, and Development in Morocco during the 1990s*. Lanham, MD: University Press of America, 2012.

Townend, "Date." Townend, Gavin B. "The Date of Composition of Suetonius' *Caesares*." *ClQ* 9 (2, 1959): 285–93.

Townsend, "Education." Townsend, John T. "Ancient Education in the Time of the Early Roman Empire." Pages 139–63 in *The Catacombs and the Colosseum: The Roman Empire as the Setting of Primitive Christianity*. Edited by Stephen Benko and John J. O'Rourke. Valley Forge, PA: Judson, 1971.

Trepanier, "Review." Trepanier, Simon. Review of *Death by Philosophy: The Biographical Tradition in the Life and Death of the Archaic Philosophers Empedocles, Heraclitus, and Democritus*, by Ava Chitwood. *Classical Review* 56 (2, 2006): 286–87.

Trevijano Etcheverría, "Obra." Trevijano Etcheverría, Ramón. "La obra de Papías y sus noticias sobre Mc y Mt." *Salm* 41 (2, 1994): 181–212.

Trompf, *Historiography*. Trompf, G. W. *Early Christian Historiography: Narratives of Retributive Justice*. London: Continuum, 2000.

Trompf, *Recurrence*. Trompf, G. W. *The Idea of Historical Recurrence in Western Thought*. Berkeley: University of California Press, 1979.

Trzaskoma, "Echoes." Trzaskoma, Stephen M. "Echoes of Thucydides' Sicilian Expedition in Three Greek Novels." *CP* 106 (1, 2011): 61–66.

Trzaskoma, "Miletus." Trzaskoma, Stephen M. "Why Miletus? Chariton's Choice of Setting and Xenophon's Anabasis." *Mnemosyne* 65 (2, 2012): 300–307.

Tucker, *Knowledge*. Tucker, Aviezer. *Our Knowledge of the Past: A Philosophy of Historiography*. Cambridge: Cambridge University Press, 2004.

Tuckett, "Jesus and the Gospels." Tuckett, Christopher M. "Jesus and the Gospels." Pages 71–86 in vol. 8 of *The New Interpreter's Bible*. Edited by Leander E. Keck. 12 vols. Nashville: Abingdon, 1995.

Tuckett, *Luke*. Tuckett, Christopher M. *Luke*. NTG. Sheffield: Sheffield Academic, 1996.

Tuckett, "Matthew and Problem." Tuckett, Christopher. "Matthew and the Synoptic Problem." Paper presented at the International Conference on the Gospel of Matthew in Its Historical and Theological Context. Moscow, September 25, 2018.

Tuckett, *Nag Hammadi*. Tuckett, Christopher M. *Nag Hammadi and the Gospel Tradition: Synoptic Tradition in the Nag Hammadi Library*. Edited by John Riches. Edinburgh: T&T Clark, 1986.

Tuckett, "Sources and Methods." Tuckett, Christopher. "Sources and Methods." Pages 121–37 in *The Cambridge Companion to Jesus*. Edited by Markus Bockmuehl. Cambridge: Cambridge University, 2001.

Tuckett, "Thomas and Synoptics." Tuckett, Christopher. "Thomas and the Synoptics." *NovT* 30 (2, 1988): 132–57.

Tuckett, "Thomas: Evidence." Tuckett, Christopher M. "The Gospel of Thomas: Evidence for Jesus?" *NedTT* 52 (1, 1998): 17–32.

Turner, *Experiencing Ritual.* Turner, Edith, with William Blodgett, Singleton Kahoma, and Fideli Benwa. *Experiencing Ritual: A New Interpretation of African Healing.* Series in Contemporary Ethnography. Philadelphia: University of Pennsylvania Press, 1992.

Turner, *Greek Papyri.* Turner, Eric G. *Greek Papyri: An Introduction.* Oxford: Oxford University Press, 1968, 1980.

Turner, *Hands.* Turner, Edith. *The Hands Feel It: Healing and Spirit Presence among a Northern Alaskan People.* DeKalb: Northern Illinois University Press, 1996.

Turner, *Healers.* Turner, Edith. *Among the Healers: Stories of Spiritual and Ritual Healing around the World.* Religion, Health, and Healing. Westport, CT: Praeger, 2006.

Turner, *Regulating Bodies.* Turner, Bryan S. *Regulating Bodies: Essays in Medical Sociology.* London: Routledge, 2002.

Tuttle, *Riot.* Tuttle, William M. *Race Riot: Chicago in the Red Summer of 1919.* New York: Atheneum, 1977.

Twelftree, "Historian." Twelftree, Graham H. "The Historian and the Miraculous." *BBR* 28 (2, 2018): 199–217.

Twelftree, "Message." Twelftree, Graham H. "The Message of Jesus I: Miracles, Continuing Controversies." Pages 2517–48 in *The Historical Jesus.* Vol. 3 of *Handbook for the Study of the Historical Jesus.* 4 vols. Edited by Tom Holmén and Stanley E. Porter. Leiden: Brill, 2010.

Twelftree, *Nature Miracles.* Twelftree, Graham H., ed. *Nature Miracles.* Eugene, OR: Cascade, 2017.

Tyson, *Marcion.* Tyson, Joseph B. *Marcion and Luke-Acts: A Defining Struggle.* Columbia: University of South Carolina Press, 2006.

Unchained Memories. *Unchained Memories: Readings from the Slave Narratives.* Boston: Bullfinch, 2002.

Urbach, *Sages.* Urbach, Ephraim E. *The Sages: Their Concepts and Beliefs.* Translated by Israel Abrahams. 2nd ed. 2 vols. Jerusalem: Magnes, 1979.

Uytanlet, *Historiography.* Uytanlet, Samson. *Luke-Acts and Jewish Historiography: A Study on the Theology, Literature, and Ideology of Luke-Acts.* WUNT 2.366. Tübingen: Mohr Ssiebeck, 2014.

Van der Horst, "Cornutus." Van der Horst, Pieter W. "Cornutus and the New Testament." *NovT* 23 (2, 1981): 165–72.

Van der Horst, "Macrobius." Van der Horst, Pieter W. "Macrobius and the New Testament: A Contribution to the Corpus hellenisticum." *NovT* 15 (3, 1973): 220–32.

Van der Horst, "Parallels." Van der Horst, Pieter W. "Hellenistic Parallels to the Acts of the Apostles." *JSNT* 8 (25, 1985): 49–60.

VanderKam, "Pronouncement Stories." VanderKam, James C. "Intertestamental Pronouncement Stories." *Semeia* 20 (1981): 65–72.

Van der Kooij, "Death of Josiah." Van der Kooij, Arie. "The Death of Josiah according to 1 Esdras." *Textus* 19 (1998): 97–109.

Van Henten, "Prolegomena." Van Henten, Jan Willem. "Einige Prolegomena zum Studien der jüdischen Martyrologie." *Bijdr* 46 (1985): 381–90.

Vanhoozer, *Meaning.* Vanhoozer, Kevin J. *Is There a Meaning in This Text? The Bible, the Reader, and the Morality of Literary Knowledge.* Grand Rapids: Zondervan, 1998.

Van Seters, "Historiography." Van Seters, John. "Is There Any Historiography in the Hebrew Bible? A Hebrew-Greek Comparison." *JNSL* 28 (2, 2002): 1–25.

Van Seters, "Primeval Histories." Van Seters, John. "The Primeval Histories of Greece and Israel Compared." *ZAW* 100 (1988): 1–22.

Van Seters, *Search.* Van Seters, John. *In Search of History: Historiography in the Ancient World and the Origins of Biblical History.* New Haven: Yale University Press, 1983.

Vansina, "Afterthoughts." Vansina, Jan. "Afterthoughts on the Historiography of Oral Tradition." Pages 105–10 in *African Historiographies: What History for Which Africa?* Edited by Bogumil Jewsiewicki and David Newbury. SSAMD 12. Beverly Hills, CA: Sage, 1986.

Vansina, *Oral Tradition.* Vansina, Jan. *Oral Tradition as History.* Madison: University of Wisconsin Press, 1985.

Van Unnik, "Once More Prologue." Van Unnik, W. C. "Once More St. Luke's Prologue." *Neot* 7 (1973): 7–26.

Van Veldhuizen, "Moses." Van Veldhuizen, Milo. "Moses: A Model of Hellenistic Philanthropia." *RefR* 38 (3, 1985): 215–24.

Vatri, "Writing." Vatri, Alessandro. "Ancient Greek Writing for Memory." *Mnemosyne* 68 (2015): 750–73.

Vattuone, "Historiography." Vattuone, Riccardo. "Western Greek Historiography." Pages 189–99 in *A Companion to Greek and Roman Historiography.* Edited by John Marincola. 2 vols. Oxford: Blackwell, 2007.

Vaughn, "Possession." Vaughn, Joy Ames. "Spirit Possession in Luke-Acts and Modern Eyewitnesses: An Analysis of Anthropological Accounts as Evidence for the Plausibility of the Lukan Accounts." PhD diss., Asbury Theological Seminary, in process.

Verheyden, *Unity.* Verheyden, Joseph. *The Unity of Luke-Acts.* BETL 142. Leuven: Leuven University Press, 1999.

Verheyden, "Unity." Verheyden, Joseph. "The Unity of Luke-Acts." *ETL* 74 (4, 1998): 516–26.

Verheyden, "Unity of Luke-Acts." Verheyden, Joseph. "The Unity of Luke-Acts." *HTS/TS* 55 (4, 1999): 964–79.

Vermes, *Jesus and Judaism.* Vermes, Geza. *Jesus and the World of Judaism.* London: SCM, 1983; Philadelphia: Fortress, 1984.

Vermes, *Jesus the Jew.* Vermes, Geza. *Jesus the Jew: A Historian's Reading of the Gospels.* Philadelphia: Fortress, 1973.

Vermes, "Notice." Vermes, Geza. "The Jesus Notice of Josephus Re-examined." *JJS* 38 (1, 1987): 1–10.

Vermes, *Religion.* Vermes, Geza. *The Religion of Jesus the Jew.* Minneapolis: Augsburg Fortress, 1993.

Van Voorst, *Jesus.* Van Voorst, Robert E. *Jesus outside the New Testament: An Introduction to the Ancient Evidence.* Grand Rapids: Eerdmans, 2000.

Via, *Kerygma.* Via, Dan O. *Kerygma and Comedy in the New Testament: A Structuralist Approach to Hermeneutic.* Philadelphia: Fortress, 1975.

Vielhauer, *Geschichte.* Vielhauer, Philipp. *Geschichte der urchristlichen Literatur.* New York: de Gruyter, 1975.

Vielhauer, "Paulinism." Vielhauer, Philipp. "On the 'Paulinism' of Acts." Pages 33–50 in *Studies in Luke-Acts: Essays in Honor of Paul Schubert.* Edited by Leander E. Keck and J. Louis Martyn. Nashville: Abingdon, 1966.

Vigourt, *Présages.* Vigourt, Annie. *Les présages impériaux d'Auguste à Domitien.* Études d'archéologie et d'histoire ancienne. Strasbourg: Université Marc Bloch, 2001; Paris: Éditions de Boccard, 2002.

Vines, *Problem.* Vines, Michael. *The Problem of Markan Genre: The Gospel of Mark and the Jewish Novel.* AcBib 3. Atlanta: SBL, 2002.

Vogel, "Vita." Vogel, Manuel. "Vita 64–69, das Bilderverbot, und die Galiläapolitik des Josephus." *JSJ* 30 (1, 1999): 65–79.

Von Rad, "Nehemia-Denkschrift." Von Rad, Gerhard. "Die Nehemia-Denkschrift." *ZAW* 76 (1964): 176–87.

Votaw, "Biographies." Votaw, Clyde Weber. "The Gospels and Contemporary Biographies." *AmJT* 19 (1, January 1915): 45–73; (2, April 1915): 217–49.

Wacholder, "Nicolaus." Wacholder, Ben Zion. "Josephus and Nicolaus of Damascus." Pages 147–72 in *Josephus, the Bible, and History.* Edited by Louis H. Feldman and Gohei Hata. Detroit: Wayne State University Press, 1989.

Wade-Gery, "Thucydides." Wade-Gery, Henry Theodore. "Thucydides." *OCD*³ 1516–19.

Wagenaar, "Memory." Wagenaar, Willem A. "Autobiographical Memory in Court." Pages 180–96 in *Remembering Our Past: Studies in Autobiographical Memory.* Edited by David C. Rubin. Cambridge: Cambridge University Press, 1996.

Wagenaar, "My Memory." Wagenaar, Willem A. "My Memory: A Study of Autobiographical Memory over Six Years." *Cognitive Psychology* 18 (2, April 1986): 225–52.

Wagenaar and Groeneweg, "Memory." Wagenaar, Willem A., and Jop Groeneweg, "The Memory of Concentration Camp Survivors." *Applied Cognitive Psychology* 4 (1990): 77–87.

Wagner, *Literacy.* Wagner, Daniel A. *Literacy, Culture, and Development: Becoming Literate in Morocco.* Cambridge: Cambridge University Press, 1993.

Wahlde, "Archaeology." Wahlde, Urban C. von. "Archaeology and John's Gospel." Pages 523–86 in *Jesus and Archaeology.* Edited by James H. Charlesworth. Grand Rapids: Eerdmans, 2006.

Währisch-Oblau, "Healthy." Währisch-Oblau, Claudia. "God Can Make Us Healthy Through and Through: On Prayers for the Sick and the Interpretation of Healing Experiences in Christian Churches in China and African Immigrant Congregations in Germany." *IntRevMiss* 90 (356–57, 2001): 87–102.

Walbank, "Fortune." Walbank, Frank W. "Fortune (*tychē*) in Polybius." Pages 349–55 in *A Companion to Greek and Roman Historiography*. Edited by John Marincola. 2 vols. Oxford: Blackwell, 2007.

Walbank, *Papers*. Walbank, Frank W. *Selected Papers: Studies in Greek and Roman History and Historiography*. Cambridge: Cambridge University Press, 1985.

Walbank, *Speeches*. Walbank, F. W. *Speeches in Greek Historians*. J. L. Myres Memorial Lecture 3. Oxford: Blackwell, 1965.

Walbank, "Tragedy." Walbank, Frank W. "History and Tragedy." *Historia* 9 (1960): 216–34.

Walbank and Stewart, "Antigonus." Walbank, Frank W., and Andrew F. Stewart. "Antigonus." *OCD*³ 106.

Walde, "Mnemonics." Walde, Christine. "Mnemonics." *BNP* 9:96–97.

Walker, "Why People Rehearse." Walker, W. Richard, et al. "Why People Rehearse Their Memories: Frequency of Use and Relations to the Intensity of Emotions Associated with Autobiographical Memories." *Memory* 17 (7, October 2009): 760–73.

Wallace-Hadrill, *Suetonius*. Wallace-Hadrill, Andrew. *Suetonius: The Scholar and the Caesars*. New Haven: Yale University Press, 1984.

Walton, "Burridge's Impact." Walton, Steve. "What Are the Gospels? Richard Burridge's Impact on Scholarly Understanding of the Genre of the Gospels." *CurBR* 14 (1, 2015): 81–93.

Walton, "Gospels." Walton, Steve. "What Are the Gospels? Richard Burridge's Impact on Scholarly Understanding of the Genre of the Gospels." Pages 47–57 in Keener and Wright, *Biographies and Jesus*.

Wandrey, "Literature." Wandrey, Irina. "Literature: Jewish-Hellenistic." *BNP* 7:694–99.

Wansbrough, "Introduction." Wansbrough, John. "Introduction." Pages 9–15 in *Jesus and the Oral Gospel Tradition*. Edited by Henry Wansbrough. JSNTSup 64. Sheffield: Sheffield Academic Press, 1991.

Wansbrough, *Quranic Studies*. Wansbrough, John. *Quranic Studies: Sources and Methods of Scriptural Interpretation*. London Oriental Studies 31. Oxford: Oxford University Press, 1977.

Ward, "Believing." Ward, Keith. "Believing in Miracles." *Zyg* 37 (3, 2002): 741–50.

Ward, "Possession." Ward, Colleen A. "Possession and Exorcism: Psychopathology and Psychotherapy in a Magico-Religious Context." Pages 125–44 in *Altered States of Consciousness and Mental Health: A Cross-Cultural Perspective*. Edited by Colleen A. Ward. CCRMS 12. Newbury Park, CA: Sage, 1989.

Ward et al. "Recognition." Ward, Jamie, Alan J. Parkin, Georgia Powell, Ellen J. Squires, Julia Townshend, and Veronica Bradley. "False Recognition of Unfamiliar People: 'Seeing Film Stars Everywhere.'" *Cognitive Neuropsychology* 16 (3–5, 1999): 293–315.

Wardle, "Augustus." Wardle, David. "Suetonius on Augustus as God and Man." *CQ* 62 (1, 2012): 307–26.

Wardle, "Send-off." Wardle, David. "A Perfect Send-off: Suetonius and the Dying Art of Augustus (Suetonius, Aug. 99)." *Mnemosyne* 60 (3, 2007): 443–63.

Wardle, *Valerius Maximus*. Wardle, David, ed. and trans. *Valerius Maximus: Memorable Deeds and Sayings*. Oxford: Clarendon, 1998.

Watson, "Boasting." Watson, Duane F. "Paul and Boasting." Pages 77–100 in *Paul in the Greco-Roman World: A Handbook*. Edited by J. Paul Sampley. Harrisburg, PA: Trinity Press International, 2003.

Watson, "Education." Watson, Duane F. "Education: Jewish and Greco-Roman." *DNTB* 308–13.

Watson, "Survive." Watson, Francis. "How Did Mark Survive?" Pages 1–17 in *Matthew and Mark across Perspectives: Essays in Honour of Stephen C. Barton and William R. Telford*. Edited by Kristian A. Bendoraitis and Nijay K. Gupta. LNTS 538. T&T Clark, 2016.

Weaks, "Problematizing." Weaks, Joseph Allen. "Mark without Mark: Problematizing the Reliability of a Reconstructed Text of Q." PhD dissertation, Brite Divinity School, 2010.

Weeden, "Theory." Weeden, Theodore J., Sr. "Kenneth Bailey's Theory of Oral Tradition: A Theory Contested by Its Evidence." *JSHJ* 7 (2009): 3–43.

Wehrli, "Gnome." Wehrli, Fritz. "Gnome, Anekdote und Biographie." *Museum Helveticum* 30 (1973): 193–208.

Weintraub, "Credibility." Weintraub, Ruth. "The Credibility of Miracles." *PhilSt* 82 (1996): 359–75.

Weiss, *Evangelium*. Weiss, Johannes. *Das älteste Evangelium. Ein Beitrag zum Verständnis des Markus-Evangeliums und der ältesten evangelischen Überlieferung*. Göttingen: Vandenhoeck & Ruprecht, 1903.

Welch, "Miracles." Welch, John W. "Miracles, *maleficium*, and *maiestas* in the Trial of Jesus." Pages 349–83 in *Jesus and Archaeology*. Edited by James H. Charlesworth. Grand Rapids: Eerdmans, 2006.

Welzer et al., "*Opa*." Welzer, Harald, et al. "*Opa war kein Nazi." Nationalsozialismus und Holocaust im Familiengedächtnis*. Fischer Taschenbücher. Frankfurt: Fischer-Taschenbuch Verlag, 2002.

Wenham, *Rediscovery*. Wenham, David. *The Rediscovery of Jesus' Eschatological Discourse*. Vol. 4 of *Gospel Perspectives*. Sheffield: JSOT Press, 1984.

Wenham, "Story." Wenham, David. "The Story of Jesus Known to Paul." Pages 297–311 in *Jesus of Nazareth, Lord and Christ: Essays on the Historical Jesus and New Testament Christology*. Edited by Joel B. Green and Max Turner. Grand Rapids: Eerdmans, 1994.

Werner, "Studies." Werner, Shirley. "Literacy Studies in Classics: The Last Twenty Years." Pages 333–82 in *Ancient Literacies: The Culture of Reading in Greece and Rome*. Edited by William A. Johnson and Holt N. Parker. New York: Oxford University Press, 2009.

West, "*Joseph and Asenath*." West, Stephanie. "*Joseph and Asenath*: A Neglected Greek Romance." *ClQ* 24 (1, 1974): 70–81.

West, "Rhampsinitos." West, Stephanie. "Rhampsinitos and the Clever Thief (Herodotus 2.121)." Pages 322–27 in *A Companion to Greek and Roman Historiography*. Edited by John Marincola. 2 vols. Oxford: Blackwell, 2007.

West, "Rhapsodes." West, Martin Litchfield. "Rhapsodes." *OCD*[3] 1311–12.

Whealey, "Josephus." Whealey, Alice. "Josephus on Jesus: Evidence from the First Millennium." *TZ* 51 (4, 1995): 285–304.

Whealey, "Testimonium." Whealey, Alice. "The Testimonium Flavianum in Syriac and Arabic." *NTS* 54 (4, 2008): 573–90.

White, *Content*. White, Hayden. *The Content of the Form: Narrative Discourse and Historical Representation*. Baltimore: Johns Hopkins University Press, 1987.

White, *Tropics*. White, Hayden. *Tropics of Discourse: Essays in Cultural Criticism*. Baltimore: Johns Hopkins University Press, 1978.

Whitmarsh, "Book." Whitmarsh, Tim. "'This In-between Book': Language, Politics, and Genre in the *Agricola*." Pages 305–33 in *The Limits of Ancient Biography*. Edited by Brian McGing and Judith Mossman. Swansea, Wales: Classical Press of Wales, 2006.

Whittaker, "Introduction." Whittaker, C. R. "Introduction." Pages ix–lxxxvii in vol. 1 of *Herodian "History."* Translated by C. R. Whittaker. 2 vols. LCL. Cambridge, MA: Harvard University Press, 1969.

Wiersma, "Novel." Wiersma, S. "The Ancient Greek Novel and Its Heroines: A Female Paradox." *Mnemosyne* 43 (1–2, 1990): 109–23.

Wigger, *Saint*. Wigger, John. *American Saint: Francis Asbury and the Methodists*. Oxford: Oxford University Press, 2009.

Wiles, *Gospel*. Wiles, Maurice F. *The Spiritual Gospel: The Interpretation of the Fourth Gospel in the Early Church*. Cambridge: Cambridge University Press, 1960.

Wilken, "Christians." Wilken, Robert L. "The Christians as the Romans (and Greeks) Saw Them." Pages 100–125 in *The Shaping of Christianity in the Second and Third Centuries*. Vol. 1 of *Jewish and Christian Self-Definition*. Edited by E. P. Sanders. Philadelphia: Fortress, 1980.

Wilken, "Collegia." Wilken, Robert. "Collegia, Philosophical Schools, and Theology." Pages 268–91 in *The Catacombs and the Colosseum: The Roman Empire as the Setting of Primitive Christianity*. Edited by Stephen Benko and John J. O'Rourke. Valley Forge, PA: Judson, 1971.

Wilken, "Interpretation." Wilken, Robert. "Toward a Social Interpretation of Early Christian Apologetics." *CH* 39 (4, 1970): 437–58.

Wilkins, *Discipleship*. Wilkins, Michael J. *Discipleship in the Ancient World and Matthew's Gospel*. 2nd ed. Grand Rapids: Baker, 1995. 1st ed. Leiden: Brill, 1988.

Williams, *Acts*. Williams, C. S. C. *A Commentary on the Acts of the Apostles*. New York: Harper & Row, 1957.

Williams, "Depression." Williams, J. M. G. "Depression and the Specificity of Autobiographical Memory." Pages 244–67 in *Remembering Our Past: Studies in Autobiographical Memory*. Edited by David C. Rubin. Cambridge: Cambridge University Press, 1996.

Williams, "Embassies." Williams, Kathryn F. "Tacitus' Senatorial Embassies of 69 CE." Pages 212–36 in *A Companion to Tacitus*. Edited by Victoria Emma Pagán. Blackwell Companions to the Ancient World. Malden, MA: Wiley-Blackwell, 2012.

Williams, "Germanicus." Williams, Kathryn F. "Tacitus' Germanicus and the Principate." *Latomus* 68 (1, 2009): 117–30.

Williams, "Josephus on Pharisees." Williams, David S. "Josephus or Nicolaus on the Pharisees?" *REJ* 156 (1–2, 1997): 43–58.

Williams, *Miracle Stories.* Williams, Benjamin E. *Miracle Stories in the Biblical Book* Acts of the Apostles. MBPS 59. Lewiston, NY: Edwin Mellen, 2001.

Williams, "Names." Williams, Margaret H. "Palestinian Jewish Personal Names in Acts." Pages 79–114 in *The Book of Acts in Its Palestinian Setting.* Edited by Richard Bauckham. Vol. 4 of *The Book of Acts in Its First Century Setting.* Edited by Bruce W. Winter. Grand Rapids: Eerdmans, 1995.

Williams, *Shame.* Williams, Bernard. *Shame and Necessity.* Berkeley: University of California Press, 1993.

Williams, *Trust.* Williams, Peter J. *Can We Trust the Gospels?* Wheaton: Crossway, 2018.

Williams, Conway, and Cohen, "Autobiographical Memory." Williams, Helen, Martin Conway, and Gillian Cohen. "Autobiographical Memory." Pages 21–90 in *Memory in the Real World.* Edited by Gillian Cohen and Martin A. Conway. Hove, East Sussex: Psychology Press, 2007.

Williamson, *Chronicles.* Williamson, H. G. M. *1 and 2 Chronicles.* NCBC. Grand Rapids: Eerdmans, 1982.

Willis, "Networking." Willis, Wendell. "The Networking of the Pauline Churches: An Exploratory Essay." *ResQ* 50 (2, 2008): 69–78.

Wills, "Aesop Tradition." Wills, Lawrence M. "The Aesop Tradition." Pages 222–37 in *The Historical Jesus in Context.* Edited by Amy-Jill Levine, Dale C. Allison Jr., and John Dominic Crossan. PrRR. Princeton: Princeton University Press, 2006.

Wills, *Quest.* Wills, Lawrence M. *The Quest of the Historical Gospel: Mark, John, and the Origins of the Gospel Genre.* London: Routledge, 1997.

Winger, "Word and Deed." Winger, Michael. "Word and Deed." *CBQ* 62 (2000): 679–92.

Winslow and Smith, "Challenges." Winslow, Michelle, and Graham Smith, "Ethical Challenges in the Oral History of Medicine." Pages 372–92 in *The Oxford Handbook of Oral History.* Edited by Donald A. Ritchie. Oxford: Oxford University Press, 2012.

Winter, "Burden of Proof." Winter, Dagmar. "The Burden of Proof in Jesus Research." Pages 843–51 in *How to Study the Historical Jesus.* Vol. 1 of *Handbook for the Study of the Historical Jesus.* 4 vols. Edited by Tom Holmén and Stanley E. Porter. Leiden: Brill, 2011.

Winter, *Trial.* Winter, Paul. *On the Trial of Jesus.* SJFWJ 1. Berlin: de Gruyter, 1961.

Winterbottom, "*Recitatio.*" Winterbottom, Michael. "*Recitatio.*" *OCD*³ 1295–96.

Winterbottom, "Rhetoric." Winterbottom, Michael. "Rhetoric, Latin." *OCD*³ 1314.

Wintermute, "Introduction." Wintermute, Orval S. "Jubilees: A New Translation and Introduction." *OTP* 2:35–50.

Wire, "Mark." Wire, Antoinette Clark. "Mark: News as Tradition." Pages 52–70 in *The Interface of Orality and Writing: Speaking, Seeing, Writing in the Shaping of New Genres.* Edited by Annette Weissenrieder and Robert B. Coote. WUNT 260. Tübingen: Mohr Siebeck, 2010. Repr., BPC 11. Eugene, OR: Wipf & Stock, 2015.

Witherington, *Acts.*   Witherington, Ben, III. *The Acts of the Apostles: A Socio-rhetorical Commentary.* Grand Rapids: Eerdmans, 1998.

Witherington, *Christology.*   Witherington, Ben, III. *The Christology of Jesus.* Minneapolis: Augsburg Fortress, 1990.

Witherington, "Editing."   Witherington, Ben, III. "Editing the Good News: Some Synoptic Lessons for the Study of Acts." Pages 324–47 in *History, Literature, and Society in the Book of Acts.* Edited by Ben Witherington III. Cambridge: Cambridge University Press, 1996.

Witherington, *Mark.*   Witherington, Ben, III. *The Gospel of Mark: A Socio-rhetorical Commentary.* Grand Rapids: Eerdmans, 2001.

Witherington, *Sage.*   Witherington, Ben, III. *Jesus the Sage: The Pilgrimage of Wisdom.* Minneapolis: Fortress, 1994.

Witmer, *Galilean Exorcist.*   Witmer, Amanda. *Jesus, the Galilean Exorcist: His Exorcisms in Social and Political Context.* LNTS 459. New York: Bloomsbury T&T Clark, 2012.

Wiyono, "Timor Revival."   Wiyono, Gani. "Timor Revival: A Historical Study of the Great Twentieth-Century Revival in Indonesia." *AJPS* 4 (2, 2001): 269–93.

Wojciechowski, "Boasting."   Wojciechowski, Michal. "Paul and Plutarch on Boasting." *JGRCJ* 3 (2006): 99–109.

Wojciechowski, "Tradition."   Wojciechowski, Michael. "Aesopic Tradition in the New Testament." *JGRCJ* 5 (2008): 99–109.

Woldemariam, "Comparison."   Woldemariam, Fasil. "A Targeted Comparison of Plutarch's, Xenophon's, and Nepos's Biographies of Agesilaus, with Implications for the Historical Reliability of the Synoptics." Pages 217–34 in Keener and Wright, *Biographies and Jesus.*

Wolter, *Luke.*   Wolter, Michael. *The Gospel according to Luke.* Translated by Wayne Coppins and Christoph Heilig. 2 vols. Baylor-Mohr Siebeck Studies in Early Christianity 4. Waco, TX: Baylor University Press, 2016–17.

Woodman, *Rhetoric.*   Woodman, A. J. *Rhetoric in Classical Historiography: Four Studies.* London: Croom Helm, 1988.

Woods, "Robe."   Woods, David. "Caligula, Asprenas, and the Bloodied Robe." *Mnemosyne* 71 (2018): 1–8.

Woodward, "Miracles."   Woodward, Kenneth L. "What Miracles Mean." *Newsweek* 135 (May 1, 2000): 54–60.

Woolf, "Literacy."   Woolf, Greg. "Literacy or Literacies in Rome?" Pages 46–68 in *Ancient Literacies: The Culture of Reading in Greece and Rome.* Edited by William A. Johnson and Holt N. Parker. New York: Oxford University Press, 2009.

Woolley, *Exorcism.*   Woolley, Reginald Maxwell. *Exorcism and the Healing of the Sick.* London: SPCK, 1932.

Wrede, *Messianic Secret.*   Wrede, William. *The Messianic Secret.* Translated by J. C. G. Greig. Cambridge: James Clarke, 1971.

Wright, "Apologetic."   Wright, David F. "Apologetic and Apocalyptic: The Miraculous in the *Gospel of Peter.*" Pages 401–18 in *The Miracles of Jesus.* Vol. 6 of *Gospel Perspectives.* Edited by David Wenham and Craig Blomberg. Sheffield: JSOT Press, 1986.

Wright, "Exploration."   Wright, Edward T. "An Initial Exploration of the Historical Reliability of Ancient Biographies." Pages 235–59 in Keener and Wright, *Biographies and Jesus*.

Wright, *Faithfulness*.   Wright, N. T. *Paul and the Faithfulness of God*. Vol. 4 of *Christian Origins and the Question of God*. Book 2 (parts 3 and 4). Minneapolis: Fortress, 2013.

Wright, "Inscription."   Wright, Brian J. "The First-Century Inscription of Quintus Sulpicius Maximus: An Initial Catalog of Lexical Parallels with the New Testament." *BBR* 27 (1, 2017): 53–63.

Wright, "Midrash."   Wright, Addison G. "The Literary Genre Midrash." *CBQ* 28 (2, 1966): 105–38; (4, 1966): 417–57.

Wright, *People*.   Wright, N. T. *The New Testament and the People of God*. Vol. 1 of *Christian Origins and the Question of God*. Minneapolis: Fortress Press, 1992.

Wright, *Reading*.   Wright, Brian J. *Communal Reading in the Time of Jesus: A Window into Early Christian Reading Practices*. Minneapolis: Fortress, 2017.

Wright, "Reliability."   Wright, Edward T. "On the Historical Reliability of Ancient Biographies: A Thorough Examination of Xenophon's *Agesilaus*, Cornelius Nepos's *Atticus*, Tacitus's *Agricola*, and *The Gospel according to John*." PhD diss., Asbury Theological Seminary, 2019.

Wright, "Response."   Wright, N. T. "In Grateful Dialogue: A Response." Pages 244–77 in *Jesus and the Restoration of Israel: A Critical Assessment of N. T. Wright's* Jesus and the Victory of God. Edited by Carey C. Newman. Downers Grove, IL: InterVarsity, 1999.

Wright, *Victory*.   Wright, N. T. *Jesus and the Victory of God*. Vol. 2 of *Christian Origins and the Question of God*. Minneapolis: Fortress, 1996.

Wright and Loftus, "Eyewitness Memory."   Wright, Daniel, and Elizabeth Loftus. "Eyewitness Memory." Pages 91–106 in *Memory in the Real World*. Edited by Gillian Cohen and Martin A. Conway. Hove, East Sussex: Psychology Press, 2007.

Wuellner, "Arrangement."   Wuellner, Wilhelm. "Arrangement." Pages 51–87 in *Handbook of Classical Rhetoric in the Hellenistic Period, 330 B.C.–A.D. 400*. Edited by Stanley E. Porter. Leiden: Brill, 1997.

Wuthnow et al., *Analysis*.   Wuthnow, Robert, James Davison Hunter, Albert J. Bergesen, and Edith Kurzweil. *Cultural Analysis: The Work of Peter L. Berger, Mary Douglas, Michel Foucault, and Jürgen Habermas*. London: Routledge, 2013.

Xenophontos, "Comedy."   Xenophontos, Sophia A. "Comedy in Plutarch's Parallel Lives." *GRBS* 52 (4, 2012): 603–31.

Yamamori and Chan, *Witnesses*.   Yamamori, Tetsunao, and Kim-kwong Chan. *Witnesses to Power: Stories of God's Quiet Work in a Changing China*. Waynesboro, GA: Paternoster, 2000.

Yamauchi, "Archives."   Yamauchi, Edwin M. "Archives." Pages 75–81 in vol. 1 of *Dictionary of Daily Life in Biblical and Post-biblical Antiquity*. Edited by Edwin M. Yamauchi and Marvin R. Wilson. 3 vols. Peabody, MA: Hendrickson, 2014.

Yamauchi, "Historic Homer."   Yamauchi, Edwin M. "Historic Homer: Did It Happen?" *BAR* 33 (2, 2007): 28–37, 76.

Yamauchi, *Persia*.   Yamauchi, Edwin M. *Persia and the Bible*. Grand Rapids: Baker, 1990.

Yates, *Expansion.* Yates, Timothy. *The Expansion of Christianity.* Downers Grove, IL: InterVarsity, 2004.

Yieh, *One Teacher.* Yieh, John Yueh-Han. *One Teacher: Jesus' Teaching Role in Matthew's Gospel Report.* BZNW 124. New York: de Gruyter, 2004.

Young, "Miracles in History." Young, William. "Miracles in Church History." *Chm* 102 (2, 1988): 102–21.

Young, *Parables.* Young, Brad H. *Jesus and His Jewish Parables: Rediscovering the Roots of Jesus' Teaching.* New York: Paulist, 1989.

Yuille and Cutshall, "Case Study." Yuille, John C., and Judith L. Cutshall, "A Case Study of Eyewitness Memory of a Crime." *Journal of Applied Psychology* 71 (1986): 291–301.

Yung, "Integrity." Yung, Hwa. "The Integrity of Mission in the Light of the Gospel: Bearing the Witness of the Spirit." *MissSt* 24 (2007): 169–88.

Yung, *Quest.* Yung, Hwa. *Mangoes or Bananas? The Quest for an Authentic Asian Christian Theology; Biblical Theology in an Asian Context.* Oxford: Regnum, 1997.

Ytterbrink, *Gospel.* Ytterbrink, Maria. *The Third Gospel for the First Time: Luke within the Context of Ancient Biography.* Lund, Sweden: Lund University, Centrum för teologi och religionsvetenskap, 2004.

Zadorojnyi, "Ethico-Politics." Zadorojnyi, Alexei V. "The Ethico-Politics of Writing in Plutarch's Life of Dion." *JHS* 131 (2011): 147–63.

Zadorojnyi, "Lords." Zadorojnyi, Alexei V. "Lords of the Flies: Literacy and Tyranny in Imperial Biography." Pages 351–94 in *The Limits of Ancient Biography.* Edited by Brian McGing and Judith Mossman. Swansea, Wales: Classical Press of Wales, 2006.

Zahn, "Geschichtsschreiber." Zahn, Theodor. "Der Geschichtsschreiber und sein Stoff im Neuen Testament." *ZKW* 9 (1888): 581–96.

Zambrini, "Historians." Zambrini, Andrea. "The Historians of Alexander the Great." Pages 210–20 in *A Companion to Greek and Roman Historiography.* Edited by John Marincola. 2 vols. Oxford: Blackwell, 2007.

Zaretsky, *Bibliography.* Zaretsky, I. I. *Bibliography on Spirit Possession and Spirit Mediumship.* Evanston, IL: Northwestern University Press, 1967.

Zdanowicz, Zielinski, and Germani, "Eruption." Zdanowicz, C. M., G. Zielinski, and M. Germani. "Mount Mazama Eruption: Calendrical Age Verified and Atmospheric Impact Assessed." *Geology* 27 (7, 1999): 621–24.

Zimmermann, "Formen." Zimmermann, Ruben. "Formen und Gattungen als Medien der Jesus-Erinnerung. Zur Rückgewinnung der Diachronie in der Formgeschichte des Neuen Testaments." Pages 131–67 in *Die Macht der Erinnerung.* Edited by O. Fuchs and B. Janowski. Neukirchen-Vluyn: Neukirchener Verlag, 2008.

Zimmermann, "Gleichnisse." Zimmermann, Ruben. "Gleichnisse als Medien der Jesuserinnerung. Die Historizität der Jesusparabeln im Horizont der Gedächtnisforschung." Pages 87–121 in *Hermeneutik der Gleichnisse Jesu. Methodische Neuansätze zum Verstehen urchristlicher Parabeltexte.* Edited by Ruben Zimmermann, with Gabi Kern. WUNT 231. Tübingen: Mohr-Siebeck, 2008.

Zimmermann, *Lehrer.* Zimmermann, Alfred F. *Die urchristlichen Lehrer. Studien zum*

Tradentenkreis der διδάσκαλοι im frühen Urchristentum. 2nd ed. WUNT 2.12. Tübingen: Mohr Siebeck, 1988.

Zimmermann, "Memory." Zimmermann, Ruben. "Memory and Form Criticism: The Typicality of Memory as a Bridge between Orality and Literality in the Early Christian Remembering Process." Pages 130–43 in *The Interface of Orality and Writing: Speaking, Seeing, Writing in the Shaping of New Genres*. Edited by Annette Weissenrieder and Robert B. Coote. WUNT 260. Tübingen: Mohr Siebeck, 2010. Repr., BPC 11. Eugene, OR: Wipf & Stock, 2015.

Zlotnick, "Memory." Zlotnick, Dov. "Memory and the Integrity of the Oral Tradition." *JANESCU* 16–17 (1984–85): 229–41.

Zubaida, *Law and Power*. Zubaida, Sami. *Law and Power in the Islamic World*. New York: I. B. Tauris, 2005.

Zuntz, "Heide." Zuntz, Günther. "Ein Heide las da Markusevangelium." Pages 205–22 in *Markus-Philologie*. Edited by Hubert Cancik. WUNT 33. Tübingen: Mohr, 1984.

Zurawski, "Paideia." Zurawski, Jason M. "Paideia: A Multifarious and Unifying Concept in the Wisdom of Solomon." Pages 195–214 in *Pedagogy in Ancient Judaism and Early Christianity*. Edited by Karina Martin Hogan, Matthew Goff, and Emma Wasserman. EJL 41. Atlanta: SBL Press, 2017.

Zwiep, *Ascension*. Zwiep, Arie W. *The Ascension of the Messiah in Lukan Christology*. NovTSup 87. Leiden: Brill, 1997.

Zwiep, "Orality." Zwiep, Arie. "Orality and Memory in the Story of Jairus and the Haemorrhaging Woman (Mark 5:21–43 parr.): An Attempt (Not) to Go beyond What Is Written." Paper presented in the "Memory, Narrative, and Christology in the Synoptic Gospels" Seminar at the Annual Meeting of the Society for New Testament Studies. Montreal, Canada, August 4, 2016.

Zwiep, "Review of Derico." Zwiep, Arie W. Review of *Oral Tradition and Synoptic Verbal Agreement*, by T. M. Derico. *RBL*, August 30, 2018, 5 pages.

Index of Authors

Index of Subjects

abridgement, 82, 121, 265, 274n50, 285, 289, 297, 307, 313, 313n82, 318, 319–22, 350, 359n72, 362, 366, 375, 386n100, 397, 414n78, 450n7, 458, 466n128, 480n225, 484

ad hominem argumentation, 9n30, 303n2, 416

Aesop, Life of, 49–50, 52

Africa, 452n19, 460, 463, 469, 474n185. *See also* Congo; Nigeria; Rwanda; South Africa

Agesilaus, 71–74, 265

Alexander Romance (Ps.-Callisthenes), 48–49. *See also ancient sources index*

allegorization, 80–82, 296, 347

anachronism, ancient, 112n56; in evaluating ancient works, 48, 59, 60, 62, 98, 104, 141n184, 183, 214n305, 261, 284, 293–94, 316n113, 341, 460, 484

anecdotes, 26, 30, 40n84, 44, 75–76, 91, 93–96, 101, 105–6, 109, 112, 117, 119, 120, 135–36, 138–48, 166–68, 173n195, 175, 177n234, 181, 188, 197, 250, 259, 316, 373, 383, 417, 428, 446, 447, 473

anonymity, 49, 54n191, 115, 182, 437; of gospel traditions, 406; of Gospels, alleged, 407n28

anthropology, 244n41, 249n79, 336, 344, 470

Antigonus of Carystus, 113

aphorisms, 19, 74, 112, 144n219, 348n14, 370, 389–90, 400, 426–27, 437, 448. *See also* maxims

apocryphal gospels, 22, 41, 48, 51n166, 58–59, 364, 492

Apollonius, Life of (Philostratus), 46–48. *See also ancient sources index*

apologetic, 30, 74, 75, 80n126, 82–83, 85, 88n205, 108, 124n17, 126, 127n43, 127n45, 176n222, 193, 195, 202, 230n79, 238–39, 248, 298–99, 301, 308–9, 350n28, 351n30, 447, 478

apologetic historiography, 124n17, 202, 238–39

appearance of biographees, 168–69

Arabic sources, 4, 389, 443, 470, 471–72

Aramaic, 12, 367, 385, 490–91, 492n317

archives, 17, 119, 180, 181n269, 207n239, 293, 353

aretalogies, 57–59

Argentina, 462

arguments from silence, 268–69, 402n4, 436–37, 461n90

Aristoxenus, 68n2, 75–76, 107n19, 248n73

arrangement, rhetorical, 61, 78, 81, 91, 140n181, 141, 146, 155, 230, 234, 235, 239, 306n19, 320, 353, 383, 390n138, 405–6

Artapanus, 100, 296n148, 298–99, 309n44

Aryan supremacists, 5n17, 7, 30n19, 255, 488

asides, 81n133, 133, 166, 196n141, 197

audience, adaptations for, 50

Augustine and autobiography, 85n170

Index of Scripture References

Index of Ancient Sources